JAVA HOW TO PROGRAM

SECOND EDITION

Deitel & Deitel
Books and Cyber Classrooms
published by
Prentice Hall

***How to Program* Series**
C How to Program, 2/E
C++ How to Program
Java How to Program 2/E

***Multimedia Cyber Classroom* Series**
C & C++ Multimedia Cyber Classroom
Java Multimedia Cyber Classroom

For continuing updates on Prentice Hall and Deitel & Associates, Inc. publications visit the Prentice Hall web site

`http//www.prenhall.com/deitel`

To communicate with the authors, send email to:

`deitel@deitel.com`

For information on corporate on-site seminars and public seminars offered by Deitel & Associates, Inc. worldwide, visit:

`http://www.deitel.com`

JAVA HOW TO PROGRAM

SECOND EDITION

H. M. Deitel
Deitel & Associates, Inc.

P. J. Deitel
Deitel & Associates, Inc.

PRENTICE HALL, Upper Saddle River, New Jersey 07458

Library of Congress Cataloging in Publication Data

```
Deitel, Harvey M.
   Java : how to program / H. M. Deitel, P. J. Deitel -- 2nd ed.
     p. cm. -- (How to program series)
   Includes bibliographical references and index.
   ISBN 0-13-899394-7
   1. Java (Computer program language) 2. Internet programming
  I. Deitel, Paul J.   II. Title.  III. Series
  QA76.73.J38D45  1998
  005.13'3--dc21                                        97-26424
                                                             CIP
```

Editor: ***Laura C. Steele***
Production Editor: ***Camille Trentacoste***
Editor-in-Chief: ***Marcia Horton***
Director of Production and Manufacturing: ***David W. Riccardi***
Copy Editor: ***Lawrence J. Clark***
Chapter Opener and Cover Designer: ***Tamara Newnam Cavallo***
Manufacturing Manager: ***Alexis R. Heydt***
Development Editor: ***Sondra Chavez***

Printed in the United States of America

10 9 8 7 6 5

ISBN 0-13-899394-7

Prentice-Hall International (UK) Limited, *London*
Prentice-Hall of Australia Pty. Limited, *Sydney*
Prentice-Hall Canada Inc., *Toronto*
Prentice-Hall Hispanoamericana, S.A., *Mexico*
Prentice-Hall of India Private Limited, *New Delhi*
Prentice-Hall of Japan, Inc., *Tokyo*
Simon & Schuster of Asia Pte. Ltd., *Singapore*
Editora Prentice-Hall do Brasil, Ltda., *Rio de Janeiro*

TO

Thelma Zigman (alias “Aunt Toby”)

and

Barnet Zigman (alias “Uncle Beb”)

On the occasions of your 55th wedding anniversary, Uncle Beb’s 80th birthday, and Aunt Toby’s 78th birthday:

Thank you for being the special people that you are.

May you have many more years of happiness together.

Love,

Barbara, Harvey, Paul and Abbey Deitel

Contents

Illustrations

Preface

Live in fragments no longer. Only connect.
Edward Morgan Forster

Welcome to Java and the exciting world of Internet and World Wide Web programming! This book is by an old guy and a young guy. The old guy (HMD; Massachusetts Institute of Technology 1967) has been programming and/or teaching programming for 36 years. The young guy (PJD; MIT 1991) has been programming for 14 years and has caught the teaching and writing "bug." The old guy programs and teaches from experience; the young guy does so from an inexhaustible reserve of energy. The old guy wants clarity; the young guy wants performance. The old guy seeks elegance and beauty; the young guy wants results. We got together to produce a book we hope you will find informative, interesting, challenging and entertaining.

In November 1995 we attended an Internet/World Wide Web conference in Boston to hear about Java. A Sun Microsystems representative spoke on Java in a packed convention ballroom. We were lucky to get seats. During that presentation, we saw the future of programming unfold. *Java How to Program* was born at that moment. We worked very hard to publish this book as the world's first computer science Java textbook.

We have written many textbooks over the years with second editions on our books coming as much as eight years and as little as two years after the first editions. The world of Java is evolving so rapidly that *Java How to Program: Second Edition* is being published only eleven months after the first edition. This creates tremendous challenges for us as authors, for our publisher—Prentice Hall, for instructors teaching from the book, and for students and professional people learning from the book.

Before Java appeared, we were convinced that C++ would replace C as the dominant application development language and systems programming language for the next decade. But the combination of the World Wide Web and Java now increases the prominence of the Internet in information systems strategic planning. Organizations want to integrate the Internet "seamlessly" into their information systems. Java is much more appropriate than C++ for this purpose.

Why We Wrote Java How to Program

Dr. Harvey M. Deitel taught introductory programming courses in universities for 20 years with an emphasis on developing clearly written, well-structured programs. Much of what is taught in these courses is the basic principles of programming with an emphasis on the effective use of control structures and functionalization. We present these topics in *Java How to Program* exactly the way HMD has done in his university courses. Our experience has been that students handle the material in the early chapters on control structures and methods (Java's term for functions) in about the same manner as they handle introductory Pascal or C courses. There is one noticeable difference though: students are highly motivated by the fact that they are learning a leading-edge language (Java) and a leading-edge programming paradigm (object-oriented programming) that will be immediately useful to them as they leave the university environment and head into a world in which the Internet has a massive new prominence. This increases their enthusiasm for the material—a big help when you consider that there is much more to learn in a Java course given that students must now master both the base language and substantial class libraries as well. But students quickly discover that they can do great things with Java, so they are willing to put in the extra effort.

Our goal was clear: produce a Java textbook for introductory university-level courses in computer programming for students with little or no programming experience, yet offer the depth and the rigorous treatment of theory and practice demanded by traditional, upper-level C and C++ courses and that satisfies professionals' needs. To meet these goals, we produced a comprehensive book because our text also patiently teaches the principles of control structures, object-oriented programming, the Java language and Java class libraries.

Java How to Program (first edition) was the world's first university computer science textbook on Java. We wrote it fresh on the heels of *C How to Program: Second Edition* and *C++ How to Program*, each of which has become the world's leading introductory textbook in its respective field. Approximately 250,000 university students and professional people worldwide have learned C, C++ and Java from these texts. Upon publication in August, 1997 *Java How to Program: Second Edition* will be used in more than 200 universities and hundreds of corporate training programs worldwide. Deitel & Associates, Inc. has taught more than 100 Java courses internationally to thousands of students as we were writing *Java How to Program: Second Edition.* We carefully monitored student reaction to Java and to our materials and tuned these materials accordingly.

We have prepared an interactive multimedia CD-ROM edition of this book, the *Java Multimedia Cyber Classroom.* [Prentice Hall offers a "value pack" edition of both *Java How to Program: Second Edition* and the *Java Multimedia Cyber Classroom: Second Edition* at a discount for people who want to use both the book and the multimedia CD. Please see the last few pages of this book for ordering instructions.]

We believe in Java. Its conceptualization by Sun Microsystems, the creators of Java, is brilliant: base a new language on two of the world's most widely used implementation languages, C and C++. This immediately gives Java a huge pool of highly skilled programmers who are currently responsible for implementing most of the world's new operating systems, communications systems, database systems and personal computer applications and systems software. Remove the messier, more complex and error-prone C/C++ features (such as pointers, templates, operator overloading and multiple inheritance, among others). Keep the language concise by removing special-purpose features that are used by only small segments of the programming community. Make the language truly portable so it is appropriate for implementing Internet-based and World-Wide-Web-based applications, and build in the features people really need such as strings, graphics, graphical user interface components, exception handling, multithreading, multimedia (audio, images, animation—and eventually video), file processing, Internet-based client/server networking and prepackaged data structures. Then make the language available *at no charge* to tens of millions of potential programmers worldwide.

Java was promoted in 1995 as a means of adding "dynamic content" to World-Wide-Web pages. Instead of Web pages with only text and static graphics, people's Web pages "come alive" with audios, animations, interactivity—and soon, video and three-dimensional imaging. But we saw much more than this. These features are precisely what businesses and organizations really need to meet today's information processing requirements. So we immediately viewed Java as having the potential to become one of the world's key general-purpose programming languages.

There are a number of for-sale Java products available. However, you do not need them to get started with Java. We intentionally wrote *Java How to Program: Second Edition* using only the free Java software available from Sun Microsystems over the Internet. We have seen many excellent Java for-sale products that will certainly be attractive to businesses and individuals programming in Java.

Java is empowering people and organizations to unleash their creativity. We have seen this in the 100 Java courses Deitel & Associates, Inc. taught prior to publishing *Java How to Program: Second Edition.* Once our students enter lab, we can't hold them back. They are eager to experiment and to explore portions of the Java class libraries that we haven't as yet covered in class. They produce applications that go well beyond anything we've ever tried in our introductory C and C++ courses. And they tell us about projects they "can't wait" to try after the course.

Java has weaknesses that we discuss frankly. But we should not lose sight of the fact that Java is "just a baby"—it needs time to mature. Interest in Java is huge. People really want the "Java model" to work. The apparent weaknesses are being addressed and solutions are forthcoming. For example, organizations and individuals want to transact business over the Internet. The Internet is a fundamentally insecure communications channel. But techniques exist and are being refined for performing secure transmission over insecure channels—a contradiction in terms, perhaps, but nevertheless already reality.

The computer field has never seen anything like the Internet/World Wide Web/Java "explosion" occurring today. People want to communicate. People need to communicate. Sure they have been doing that since the dawn of civilization, but computer communications have been mostly limited to digits, alphabetic characters and special characters passing back and forth. The next major wave is surely multimedia. People want to transmit pictures and they want those pictures to be in color. They want to transmit voices, sounds and audio clips. They want to transmit full motion color video. And at some point, they will insist on three-dimensional, moving-image transmission. Our current flat, two-dimensional televisions will eventually be replaced with three-dimensional versions that turn our living rooms into "theaters-in-the-round." Actors will perform their roles as if we were watching live theater. Our living rooms will be turned into miniature sports stadiums. Our business offices will enable video conferencing among colleagues half a world apart as if they were sitting around one conference table. The possibilities are intriguing and Java is sure to play a key role in making many of these possibilities become reality.

There have been predictions that the Internet will eventually replace the telephone system. Well, why stop there? It could also replace radio and television as we know them today. It's not hard to imagine the Internet replacing the newspaper with completely electronic news media. This textbook you are reading may someday appear in a museum alongside radios, TVs and newspapers in an "early media of ancient civilization" exhibit.

Teaching Approach

Java How to Program: Second Edition contains a rich collection of examples, exercises, and projects drawn from many fields to provide the student with a chance to solve interesting real-world problems. The book concentrates on the principles of good software engineering and stresses program clarity. We avoid arcane terminology and syntax specifications in favor of teaching by example. Each of our code examples has been carefully tested on several Java platforms including those for Sun's Solaris and Microsoft's Windows 95 and Windows NT.

This book is written by two educators who spend most of their time teaching edge-of-the-practice topics in industry classrooms worldwide. The text emphasizes pedagogy.

Introducing Object Orientation and Applets from Chapter One!

Java How to Program: Second Edition "jumps right in" with object-oriented programming, applets and even basic graphical user interface design from Chapter 1! People tell us this is a "gutsy" move. But Java students really want to "cut to the chase." There is great stuff to be done in Java so let's get right to it! Java is not trivial by any means, but it's fun and students can see immediate results. Students can get graphical, animated, multimedia-based, audio-intensive, multithreaded, network-based programs running quickly through Java's extensive class libraries of "reusable components." They can implement impressive projects. They can be much more creative and productive in a one- or two-semester course than is possible in C and C++ introductory courses.

Live-Code Teaching Approach

The book is loaded with live-code examples. This is the focus of the way we teach and write about programming, and the focus of each of our multimedia *Cyber Classrooms* as well. Virtually every new concept is presented in the context of a complete, working Java program (applet or application) immediately followed by one or more windows showing the program's output. We call this style of teaching and writing our **live-code approach**. *We use the language to teach the language.* Reading these programs is much like entering and running them on a computer.

World Wide Web Access

All of the code for *Java How to Program* is on the Internet at the Prentice Hall Web site **`http://www.prenhall.com/deitel`** and at the Deitel & Associates, Inc. Web site **`http://www.deitel.com`**. Please download all the code then run each program as you read the text. Make changes to the code examples and see what happens. See how the Java compiler "complains" when you make various kinds of errors. Immediately see the effects of making changes to the code. It's a great way to learn programming by doing programming. [You must respect the fact that this is copyrighted material. Feel free to use it as you study Java, but you may not republish any portion of it without explicit permission from the authors and Prentice Hall.]

Objectives

Each chapter begins with a statement of *Objectives*. This tells the student what to expect and gives the student an opportunity, after reading the chapter, to determine if he or she has met these objectives. It is a confidence builder and a source of positive reinforcement.

Quotations

The learning objectives are followed by quotations. Some are humorous, some are philosophical, and some offer interesting insights. Our students enjoy relating the quotations to the chapter material. The quotations are worth a "second look" after you read each chapter.

Outline

The chapter *Outline* helps the student approach the material in top-down fashion. This, too, helps students anticipate what is to come and set a comfortable and effective learning pace.

Approximately 12,000 lines of code in 200 Example Programs (with Program Outputs)

We present Java features in the context of complete, working Java programs. This is the focus of our teaching and our writing. We call it our "live-code" approach. Each program is followed by a window with the output produced when the program runs. This enables the student to confirm that the programs run as expected. Reading the book carefully is much like entering and running these programs on a computer. The programs range from just a few lines of code to substantial examples with several hundred lines of code. Students should download all the code for the book from our Web sites and run each program while studying that program in the text. The programs are available at both **`http://www.deitel.com`** and **`http://www.prenhall.com/deitel`**.

143 Illustrations/Figures

An abundance of charts, line drawings and program outputs is included. The discussion of control structures, for example, features carefully drawn flowcharts. [Note: We do not teach the use of flowcharting as a program development tool, but we do use a brief, flowchart-oriented presentation to specify the precise operation of Java's control structures.]

411 Programming Tips

We have included programming tips to help students focus on important aspects of program development. We highlight hundreds of these tips in the form of *Good Programming Practices, Common Programming Errors, Testing and Debugging Tips, Performance Tips,*

Portability Tips, and *Software Engineering Observations.* These tips and practices represent the best we have been able to glean from a combined five decades of programming and teaching experience. One of our students—a mathematics major—told us recently that she feels this approach is like the highlighting of axioms, theorems, and corollaries in mathematics books; it provides a basis on which to build good software.

77 Good Programming Practices
When we teach introductory courses, we state that the "buzzword" of each course is "clarity," and we highlight as *Good Programming Practices* techniques for writing programs that are clearer, more understandable, more debuggable, and more maintainable.

136 Common Programming Errors
Students learning a language tend to make certain errors frequently. Focusing the students' attention on these *Common Programming Errors* helps students avoid making the same errors. It also helps reduce the long lines outside instructors' offices during office hours!

38 Testing and Debugging Tips
When we first designed this "tip type," we thought we would use it strictly to tell people how to test and debug Java programs. In fact, many of the tips describe aspects of Java that reduce the likelihood of "bugs" and thus simplify the testing and debugging process for Java programs compared to that required for C and C++ programs.

59 Performance Tips
In our experience, teaching students to write clear and understandable programs is by far the most important goal for a first programming course. But students want to write the programs that run the fastest, use the least memory, require the smallest number of keystrokes, or dazzle in other nifty ways. Students really care about performance. They want to know what they can do to "turbo charge" their programs. So we have included 59 *Performance Tips* that highlight opportunities for improving program performance.

12 Portability Tips
Some programmers assume that if they implement an application in Java, the application will automatically be "perfectly" portable across all Java platforms. Unfortunately, this is not always the case. We include *Portability Tips* to help students write portable code and also to provide insights on how Java achieves its high degree of portability. We had many more portability tips in *C How to Program* and *C++ How to Program.* We needed fewer *Portability Tips* in *Java How to Program* because Java is designed to be portable top-to-bottom (for the most part), so much less conspicuous effort is required on the Java programmer's part to achieve portability than with either C or C++.

89 Software Engineering Observations
The object-oriented programming paradigm requires a complete rethinking about the way we build software systems. Java is an effective language for performing good software engineering. The *Software Engineering Observations* highlight architectural and design issues that affect the construction of software systems, especially large-scale systems. Much of what the student learns here will be useful in upper-level courses and in industry as the student begins to work with large, complex real-world systems.

Summary
Each chapter ends with additional pedagogical devices. We present a thorough, bullet-list-style *Summary* of the chapter. On average, there are 36 summary bullets per chapter. This helps the students review and reinforce key concepts.

Terminology
We include in a *Terminology* section an alphabetized list of the important terms defined in the chapter—again, further reinforcement. On average, there are 85 terms per chapter.

Summary of Tips, Practices, and Errors
For ease of reference, we collect and reiterate the *Good Programming Practices*, *Common Programming Errors*, *Testing and Debugging Tips, Performance Tips*, *Portability Tips*, and *Software Engineering Observations*.

341 Self-Review Exercises and Answers (Count Includes Separate Parts)
Extensive self-review exercises and answers are included for self-study. This gives the student a chance to build confidence with the material and prepare for the regular exercises. Students should be encouraged to do all the self-review exercises and check their answers.

815 Exercises (Solutions in Instructor's Manual; Count Includes Separate Parts)
Each chapter concludes with a substantial set of exercises including simple recall of important terminology and concepts; writing individual Java statements; writing small portions of Java methods and classes; writing complete Java methods, classes, applets and applications; and writing major term projects. The large number of exercises across a wide variety of areas enables instructors to tailor their courses to the unique needs of their audiences and to vary course assignments each semester. Instructors can use these exercises to form homework assignments, short quizzes, and major examinations. The solutions for the exercises are included in the *Instructor's Manual* and on the disks *available only to instructors* through their Prentice-Hall representatives. **[NOTE: Please do not write to us requesting the instructor's manual. Distribution of this publication is strictly limited to college professors teaching from the book. Instructors may obtain the solutions manual only from their regular Prentice Hall representatives.]** Solutions to approximately half of the exercises are included on the *Java Multimedia Cyber Classroom* CD (available September 1997 in bookstores and computer stores; please see the last few pages of this book for ordering instructions).

Approximately 4500 Index Entries (with approximately 7500 Page References)
We have included an extensive *Index* at the back of the book. This helps the student find any term or concept by keyword. The *Index* is useful to people reading the book for the first time and is especially useful to practicing programmers who use the book as a reference. Each of the 1537 terms in the *Terminology* sections appears in the *Index* (along with many more index items from each chapter). Students can use the *Index* in conjunction with the *Terminology* sections to be sure they have covered the key material of each chapter.

"Double Indexing" of All Java Live-Code Examples and Exercises
Java How to Program has 180 live-code examples and 1156 exercises (including parts). Many of the exercises are challenging problems or projects requiring substantial effort. We

have "double indexed" all of the live-code examples and most of the more challenging projects. For every Java source-code program in the book, we took the file name with the **`.java`** extension, such as **`LoadAudioAndPlay.java`** and indexed it both alphabetically (in this case under "L") and as a subindex item under "Examples." This makes it easier to find examples using particular features. The more substantial exercises, such as "Maze Generator and Walker," are indexed both alphabetically (in this case under "M") and as subindex items under "Exercises."

Bibliography
An extensive bibliography is included to encourage further reading.

A Tour of the Book

Chapter 1—Introduction to Computers and Java Applets—discusses what computers are, how they work and how they are programmed. The chapter gives a brief history of the development of programming languages from machine languages, to assembly languages, to high-level languages. The origin of the Java programming language is discussed. The chapter includes an introduction to a typical Java programming environment and gives a concise introduction to writing Java programs. A detailed treatment of decision making and arithmetic operations in Java is presented. After studying this chapter, the student will understand how to write simple, but complete, Java programs. A distinguishing feature of Chapter 1 is that we "jump right in" with object-oriented programming in Java; our first program uses inheritance to create a Java applet, then displays the applet window. We introduce some basics of HTML programming and discuss the relationship among HTML, the World Wide Web and the Internet. We waste no time in getting to **`Label`**s and **`TextField`**s to prompt for inputs and read them from the keyboard. With Java you can write two kinds of programs, namely, *applets* designed to be transported over the Internet and executed in World Wide Web browsers (like Netscape Navigator, Sun HotJava, and Microsoft Internet Explorer) and stand-alone *applications* designed to execute on your own computer. Because of the intense interest in Java applets and the World Wide Web, we present Java programs as applets whenever possible. As you will see in Chapter 11, it is normally straightforward to convert an applet to an application. Because of certain stringent security restrictions related to file processing and networking, the examples in those chapters (15 and 16) are presented as Java applications.

Chapter 2—Developing Java Applications—focuses on the program development process. The chapter discusses how to take a *problem statement* (i.e., a *requirements document*) and from it develop a working Java program, including performing intermediate steps in pseudocode. The chapter introduces some fundamental data types and simple control structures used for decision making (**`if`** and **`if/else`**) and repetition (**`while`**). We examine counter-controlled repetition, sentinel-controlled repetition, and introduce Java's increment, decrement and assignment operators. We have had a positive experience assigning problems 2.11 through 2.14 in our introductory courses. Since these four problems have similar structure, doing all four is a nice way for students to "get the hang" of the program development process. Students will enjoy the challenges of the "mystery programs." The more mathematically inclined students will enjoy problems on palindromes, binary-to-decimal conversion, encryption and decryption, and calculating factorials.

Chapter 3—Control Structures—discusses much of the C portion of Java, especially the sequence, selection (**`if`**, **`if/else`** and **`switch`**) and repetition (**`while`**, **`for`** and **`do/while`**) control structures. The chapter uses simple flowcharts to show the flow of control through each of the control structures. The techniques discussed in Chapter 2 and Chapter 3 constitute a large part of what has been traditionally taught in the universities under the topic of structured programming. With Java we do object-oriented programming. In doing so, we discover that the insides of the objects we build make abundant use of control structures. Chapter 3 examines repetition in detail and compares the alternatives of counter-controlled loops and sentinel-controlled loops. This chapter helps the student develop good programming habits in preparation for dealing with the more substantial programming tasks in the remainder of the text. The chapter clearly explains the labeled **`break`** and **`continue`** statements with live-code examples. The chapter concludes with a discussion of logical operators—**`&&`** (logical AND), **`&`** (boolean logical AND), `||` (logical OR), `|` (boolean logical inclusive OR), **`^`** (boolean logical exclusive OR) and **`!`** (NOT). There is a substantial exercise set including mathematical, graphical and business applications. Students will enjoy Exercise 3.26 that asks them to write a program with repetition and decision structures that prints the iterative song, "The Twelve Days of Christmas." The more mathematically inclined students will enjoy problems on binary, octal, decimal and hexadecimal number systems, calculating the mathematical constant π with an infinite series, Pythagorean triples and De Morgan's Laws. Our students particularly enjoy the challenges of triangle-printing and diamond-printing in Exercises 3.10 and 3.21; these problems really help students learn to deal with nested repetition structures—a complex topic to master in introductory courses.

Chapter 4—Methods—takes a deeper look inside objects. Objects contain data which we will generally refer to as *instance variables* and executable units called *methods* (these are often called *functions* in non-object-oriented procedural programming languages like C). We explore methods in depth and include a discussion of methods that "call themselves," so-called *recursive* methods. We discuss class library methods, programmer-defined methods and recursion. The techniques presented in Chapter 4 are essential to the production of properly structured programs, especially the kinds of larger programs and software that system programmers and application programmers are likely to develop in real-world applications. The "divide and conquer" strategy is presented as an effective means for solving complex problems by dividing them into simpler interacting components. Students enjoy the treatment of random numbers and simulation, and they appreciate the discussion of the dice game of craps that makes elegant use of control structures (this is one of our most successful lectures in our introductory courses). The chapter offers a solid introduction to recursion and includes a table summarizing the dozens of recursion examples and exercises distributed throughout the remainder of the book. Some texts leave recursion for a chapter late in the book; we feel this topic is best covered gradually throughout the text. The topic of method overloading (i.e., allowing multiple methods to have the same name as long as they have different "signatures") is motivated and explained clearly. The extensive collection of exercises at the end of the chapter includes several classical recursion problems such as the Towers of Hanoi; we revisit this problem later in the text where we employ graphics, animation and sound to make the problem "come alive." There are many mathematical and graphical examples. Our students particularly enjoy the development of a "Computer-Assisted Instruction" system in exercises 4.31 and 4.32; we ask students to develop a multimedia version of this system later in the book.

Chapter 5—Arrays—explores the processing of data in lists and tables of values. Arrays in Java are processed as objects, further evidence of Java's commitment to almost 100% object-orientation. We discuss the structuring of data into arrays, or groups, of related data items of the same type. The chapter presents numerous examples of both single-subscripted arrays and double-subscripted arrays. It is widely recognized that structuring data properly is just as important as using control structures effectively in the development of properly structured programs. Examples in the chapter investigate various common array manipulations, printing histograms, sorting data, passing arrays to functions and an introduction to the field of survey data analysis (with simple statistics). A feature of this chapter is the discussion of elementary sorting and searching techniques and the presentation of binary searching as a dramatic improvement over linear searching. The 44 end-of-chapter exercises include a variety of interesting and challenging problems such as improved sorting techniques, the design of an airline reservations system, an introduction to the concept of turtle graphics (made famous in the LOGO programming language) and the Knight's Tour and Eight Queens problems that introduce the notions of heuristic programming so widely employed in the field of artificial intelligence. The exercises conclude with a series of recursion problems including the selection sort, palindromes, linear search, binary search, the eight queens, printing an array, printing a string backwards and finding the minimum value in an array. The chapter exercises include a delightful simulation of the classic race between the tortoise and the hare, card shuffling and dealing algorithms, recursive quicksort and recursive maze traversals. A special section entitled "Building Your Own Computer" explains machine language programming and proceeds with the design and implementation of a computer simulator that allows the reader to write and run machine-language programs. This unique feature of the text will be especially useful to the reader who wants to understand how computers really work. Our students enjoy this project and often implement substantial enhancements; many enhancements are suggested in the exercises. In Chapter 17, another special section guides the reader through building a compiler; the machine language produced by the compiler is then executed on the machine-language simulator produced in Chapter 5. Information is communicated from the compiler to the simulator in sequential files (which the students will master in Chapter 15).

Chapter 6—Object-Based Programming—begins our deeper discussion of classes. The chapter represents a wonderful opportunity for teaching data abstraction the "right way"—through a language (Java) expressly devoted to implementing abstract data types (ADTs). The chapter focuses on the essence and terminology of classes and objects. What is an object? What is a class of objects? What does the inside of an object look like? How are objects created? How are they destroyed? How do objects communicate with one another? Why are classes such a natural mechanism for packaging software as reusable componentry? The chapter discusses implementing ADTs as Java-style classes, accessing class members, enforcing information hiding with `private` instance variables, separating interface from implementation, using access methods and utility methods, and initializing objects with constructors (and using overloaded constructors). The chapter discusses declaring and using constant objects, composition—the process of building classes that have references to objects as members, the **`this`** reference that enables an object to "know itself," dynamic memory allocation, static class members for containing and manipulating class-wide data, and examples of popular abstract data types such as stacks and queues. The chapter also introduces the **`package`** statement and discusses how to create reusable packages. The chapter exercises challenge the student to develop classes for complex numbers, rational numbers, times, dates, rectangles, huge integers, a class for playing Tic-Tac-Toe, a savings account class and a class for holding sets of integers.

Chapter 7—Object-Oriented Programming—discusses the relationships among classes of objects and programming with related classes. How can we exploit commonality between classes of objects to minimize the amount of work it takes to build large software systems? What is polymorphism? What does it mean to "program in the general" rather than "programming in the specific?" How does programming in the general make it easy to modify systems and add new features with minimal effort? How can we program for a whole category of objects rather than programming individually for each type of object? The chapter deals with one of the most fundamental capabilities of object-oriented programming languages, inheritance, which is a form of software reusability in which new classes are developed quickly and easily by absorbing the capabilities of existing classes and adding appropriate new capabilities. The chapter discusses the notions of superclasses and subclasses, **`protected`** members, direct superclasses, indirect superclasses, use of constructors in superclasses and subclasses, and software engineering with inheritance. The chapter compares inheritance ("is a" relationships) with composition ("has a" relationships). A feature of the chapter is its several substantial case studies. In particular, a lengthy case study implements a point, circle and cylinder class hierarchy. The exercises ask the student to compare the creation of new classes by inheritance vs. composition; to extend the inheritance hierarchies discussed in the chapter; to write an inheritance hierarchy for quadrilaterals, trapezoids, parallelograms, rectangles and squares; and to create a more general shape hierarchy with two-dimensional shapes and three-dimensional shapes. The chapter explains polymorphic behavior. When many classes are related through inheritance to a common superclass, each subclass object may be treated as a superclass object. This enables programs to be written in a general manner independent of the specific types of the subclass objects. New kinds of objects can be handled by the same program, thus making systems more extensible. Polymorphism enables programs to eliminate complex **`switch`** logic in favor of simpler "straight-line" logic. A screen manager of a video game, for example, can simply send a "draw" message to every object in a linked list of objects to be drawn. Each object knows how to draw itself. A new type of object can be added to the program without modifying that program as long as that new object also knows how to draw itself. This style of programming is typically used to implement today's popular graphical user interfaces. The chapter distinguishes between abstract classes (from which objects cannot be instantiated) and concrete classes (from which objects can be instantiated). The chapter also introduces interfaces—sets of methods that must be defined by any class that **`implements`** the interface. Abstract classes are useful for providing a basic set of methods and default implementation to classes throughout the hierarchy. Interfaces are useful in many situations similar to abstract classes, however, interfaces do not include any implementation—no method bodies and no instance variables. A feature of the chapter is its three major polymorphism case studies—a payroll system, a shape hierarchy headed up by an abstract class and a shape hierarchy headed up by an interface. The chapter exercises ask the student to discuss a number of conceptual issues and approaches, work with abstract classes, develop a basic graphics package, modify the chapter's employee class—and pursue all these projects with polymorphic programming.

Chapter 8—Strings and Characters—deals with processing words, sentences, characters and groups of characters. The key difference between Java and C here is that Java strings are objects. This makes string manipulation more convenient and much safer than in C where string and array manipulations are based on dangerous pointers. We present classes **`String`**, **`StringBuffer`**, **`Character`** and **`StringTokenizer`**. For each we provide extensive live-code examples demonstrating most of their methods "in action." In all cases we show output windows so the reader can see the precise effects of each of the string and character manipulations we discuss. Students will enjoy the card shuffling and dealing example (which they will enhance in the exercises to the later chapters on graphics and multimedia). A key feature of the chapter is an extensive collection of challenging string manipulation exercises related to limericks, pig Latin, text analysis, word processing, printing dates in various formats, check protection, writing the word equivalent of a check amount, Morse code and metric-to-English conversions. Students will enjoy the challenges of developing their own spell checker and crossword puzzle generator.

Advanced Topics

Chapters 9, 10 and 11 were co-authored with our colleague, Mr. Tem Nieto of Deitel & Associates, Inc. Tem's infinite patience, attention to detail, illustration skills and creativity are apparent throughout these chapters. [Take a fast peek at Figure 10.21 to see what happens when we turn Tem loose!] **Chapter 9—Graphics**—begins a run of chapters that present the multimedia "sizzle" of Java. We consider Chapters 9 through 18 to be the book's advanced material. Professors who have been teaching C and/or C++ at the introductory level will find that the Java topics open all kinds of opportunities to explore new areas. This is "fun stuff." Traditional C and C++ programming are pretty much confined to character-mode input/output. Some versions of C++ are supported by platform-dependent class libraries that can do graphics, but using these libraries makes your applications nonportable. Java's graphics capabilities are platform independent and hence, portable—and we mean portable in a worldwide sense. You can develop graphics-intensive Java applets and distribute them over the World Wide Web to colleagues everywhere and they will run nicely on the local Java platforms. We discuss graphics contexts and graphics objects; drawing strings, characters and bytes; color and font control; screen manipulation and paint modes; and drawing lines, rectangles, rounded rectangles, 3-dimensional rectangles, ovals, arcs and polygons. The chapter has 39 figures that painstakingly illustrate each of these graphics capabilities with live-code examples, appealing screen outputs, detailed features tables and detailed line art. Some of the 36 exercises challenge students to develop graphical versions of their solutions to previous exercises on Turtle Graphics, the Knight's Tour, the Tortoise and the Hare simulation, Maze Traversal and the Bucket Sort.

Chapter 10—Basic Graphical User Interface Components—introduces the creation of applets and applications with user-friendly graphical user interfaces (GUIs). Once again, the key to Java's treatment of these subjects is that Java is platform independent. A GUI-based applet or application developed once will run on all Java platforms. Actually, the user interface components will appear a bit different on each platform, because Java "ties into" the local GUI system, be it Microsoft's Windows, Apple's Macintosh, Motif, Sun's OpenWindows, OS/2's Warp or any other system. So Java applications running on a platform with which you are familiar will take on the appearance of GUI applications running on that platform. GUI development is a huge topic, so we divided into two chapters. These chapters truly cover the material in depth to enable you to build "industrial-strength" GUI interfaces. Through its 32 programs, tables and line drawings, the chapter illustrates GUI design principles, the **`java.awt`** (Abstract Windowing Toolkit) hierarchy, labels, push buttons, lists, text fields, choice buttons, check boxes, radio buttons, panels, handling mouse events, handling keyboard events and using three of Java's simpler GUI layout managers, namely **`FlowLayout`**, **`BorderLayout`** and **`GridLayout`**. The chapter concentrates on the delegation event model for GUI processing that was first introduced in Java 1.1. The 36 exercises challenge the student to create specific GUIs, exercise various GUI features, develop drawing programs that let the user draw with the mouse and control fonts.

Chapter 11—Advanced Graphical User Interface Components—continues the discussion started in Chapter 10. Here, we continue the detailed walkthrough of Java's GUI capabilities. The 21 figures walk the reader through the creation and manipulation of more advanced GUI components including text areas, canvases, scrollbars, frames, menus, dialog boxes, scrolling panels and popup menus. The chapter concludes with discussions of Java's more sophisticated layout managers, namely **`CardLayout`** and **`GridBagLayout`**, and shows how to develop custom layout mangers. The exercises encourage the reader to develop more substantial GUIs with the advanced components presented in the chapter.

Chapter 12—Exception Handling—is one of the most important chapters in the book from the standpoint of building so-called "mission-critical" or "business-critical" applications that require high degrees of robustness and fault tolerance. Things do go wrong, and at today's computer speeds—commonly 100 million operations per second—if they can go wrong they will, and rather quickly at that. Programmers are often a bit naive about using components. They ask, "How do I request that a component do something for me?" They also ask "What value(s) does that component return to me to indicate it has performed the job I asked it to do?" But programmers also need to be concerned with, "What happens when the component I call on to do a job experiences difficulty? How will that component signal that it had a problem?" In Java, when a component (i.e., a class object) encounters difficulty, it can "throw an exception." The environment of that component is programmed to "catch" that exception and deal with it. Java's exception handling capabilities are geared to an object-oriented world in which programmers construct systems largely from reusable, prefabricated components built by other programmers. To use a Java component, you need to know not only how that component behaves when "things go well," but also what exceptions that component throws when "things go poorly." The chapter distinguishes between rather serious system **`Error`**s (normally beyond the control of most programs) and **`Exception`**s that programs generally want to deal with to ensure robust operation. The chapter discusses the vocabulary of exception handling. The **`try`** block executes program code that may execute properly or may **`throw`** an exception if something goes wrong. Associated with each **`try`** block are one or more **`catch`** blocks that handle thrown exceptions attempting to restore order and keep systems "up and running" rather than letting them "crash." Even if order can not be fully restored, the **`catch`** blocks may perform operations that enable a system to continue executing, albeit at reduced levels of performance—such activity is often referred to as "graceful degradation." Regardless of whether exceptions are thrown or not, a **`finally`** block accompanying a **`try`** block will always execute; the **`finally`** block normally performs cleanup operations like closing files and releasing resources acquired in the **`try`** block. The chapter does contain several nice live-code examples, but its material is more crucial to many of the live-code examples in Chapters 13 through 18. The chapter enumerates many of the **`Errors`** and **`Exceptions`** of the Java packages. The chapter has some of the most appropriate quotes in the book thanks to the painstaking research performed by Barbara Deitel. You recall that we added *Testing and Debugging Tips* as a new feature to *Java How to Program* over the set of tips we had used in our C and C++ books. The vast majority of these *Testing and Debugging Tips* fell naturally out of the material in Chapter 12. Please take exception handling seriously. The mechanism chosen by Java's designers is similar to that used by C++. It is certain to be widely employed in the object-oriented programming community.

Chapter 13—Multithreading—deals with how to program applets and applications that can perform multiple activities in parallel. Although our bodies are quite good at this (breathing, eating, blood circulation, vision, hearing, etc. can all occur in parallel), our conscious minds have trouble with this. Computers used to be built with a single rather expensive processor. Today processors are becoming so inexpensive that it is possible to build computers with many processors that work in parallel—such computers are called multiprocessors. The trend is clearly towards computers that can perform many tasks in parallel. Most of today's programming languages, including C and C++, do not include features for expressing parallel operations. These languages are often referred to as "sequential" programming languages or "single-thread-of-control" languages. Java includes capabilities to enable multithreaded applications, i.e., applications that can specify that multiple activities are to occur in parallel. This makes Java better prepared to deal with the more sophisticated multimedia, network-based multiprocessor-based applications programmers will be introducing in the mid-to-late 1990s. As we will see, multithreading is even effective on single-processor systems. This is one of the key capabilities of Java that convinced us to invest in this language and write *Java How to Program.* For years, the "old guy" taught operating systems courses and wrote operating systems textbooks, but he never had a multithreaded language like Java available to demonstrate the concepts. In this chapter, we really enjoyed presenting multithreaded programs that demonstrate clearly the kinds of problems that can occur in parallel programming. There are all kinds of subtleties that develop in parallel programs that you simply never think about when writing sequential programs. A feature of the chapter is the extensive set of examples that show these problems and how to solve them. Another feature is the implementation of the "circular buffer," a popular means of coordinating control between asynchronous, concurrent "producer" and "consumer" processes that, if left to run without synchronization, would cause data to be lost and/or duplicated incorrectly, most likely with devastating results. We discuss the monitor construct developed by C. A. R. Hoare and implemented in Java; this is a standard topic in operating systems courses. The chapter discusses threads and thread methods. It walks through the various thread states and state transitions with a detailed line drawing showing the life-cycle of a thread. We discuss thread priorities and thread scheduling and use a line drawing to show Java's fixed-priority scheduling mechanism. We examine a producer/consumer relationship without synchronization, observe the trouble it causes and then solve the problem with thread synchronization. We implement a producer/consumer relationship with a circular buffer and proper synchronization with a monitor. We discuss daemon threads that kind of "hang around" and do useful work (like "garbage collection" of discarded memory) when excess processor time is available. We discuss the **`Runnable`** interface that enables you to run objects as threads without having to subclass them from class **`Thread`** and we indicate that the notion of "interface" is Java's replacement for the dangerous (albeit powerful) feature of C++ called multiple inheritance. We close with a discussion of thread groups which, for example, enable separation to be enforced between system threads like the garbage collector and user threads. The chapter has a nice complement of 26 exercises. The featured exercise is the classic readers and writers problem, a favorite in upper-level computer science courses in operating systems; citations appear in the exercises for students who wish to research this topic. This is an important problem in database-oriented transaction-processing systems. It raises subtle issues of solving problems in concurrency control while ensuring that every separate activity that needs to receive service does indeed do so without the possibility of "indefinite postponement" which could cause some activities never to receive service—a condition also referred to as "starvation." Operating systems professors will enjoy having Java-literate students. We can expect all kinds of progress in the field of parallel programming as Java's multithreading capabilities enable large numbers of computing students to pursue parallel-programming class projects. When these students enter industry over the next several years, we expect a surge in parallel systems programming and parallel applications programming. We have been predicting this for decades—Java will make it a reality.

If this is your first Java book and you are an experienced computing professional, you may well be thinking, "Hey, this just keeps getting better and better. I can't wait to get started programming in this language. It will let me do all kinds of stuff I'd like to do, but that was never easy for me to do with the other languages I've used." You've got it right. Java is an enabler. So if you liked the multithreading discussion, hold onto your hat, because Java will let you program multimedia applications and make them available instantaneously over the World Wide Web. **Chapter 14—Multimedia: Images, Animation and Audio**—deals with Java's capabilities for making computer applications come alive. It is remarkable that students in first programming courses will be writing applications with all these capabilities. The possibilities are intriguing. Imagine having access (over the Internet and through CD-ROM technology) to vast libraries of graphics images, audios and videos and being able to weave your own together with those in the libraries to form creative applications. Already more than half the new computers sold come "multimedia equipped." Within just a few years, new machines equipped for multimedia will be as common as machines with floppy disks today. We can't wait to see the kinds of term papers and classroom presentations students will be making when they have access to vast public domain libraries of images, drawings, voices, pictures, videos, animations and the like. A "paper" when most of us were in the earlier grades was a collection of characters, possibly handwritten, possibly typewritten. A "paper" in just a few short years will become a multimedia "extravaganza" that makes the subject matter come alive. It will hold your interest, pique your curiosity, make you feel what the subjects of the paper felt when they were making history. Multimedia will make your science labs much more exciting. Textbooks will come alive. Instead of looking at a static picture of some phenomenon, you will watch that phenomenon occur in a colorful, animated, presentation with sounds, videos and various other effects. It will leverage the learning process. People will be able to learn more, learn it in more depth and experience more viewpoints. The chapter discusses images and image manipulation, audios, animation, flicker elimination and the monitoring of "media clips" with **`MediaTracker`** objects. When we first learned Java, we decided to put a spinning Deitel & Associates, Inc. logo up on our Web site. We enjoyed using Java's features to do this and rapidly ran into the kinds of flicker problems than can hurt the effectiveness of animations. We evolved a sequence of programs that incrementally applied Java's flicker-elimination techniques. So the programs in this chapter are genuine hands-on, real-world solutions by real programmers solving a common problem (flicker elimination) in multimedia applications. A feature of the chapter is the discussion of image maps that enable a program to sense the presence of the mouse cursor over a region of an image, even without clicking the mouse. We present a live-code image map application with the icons Prentice Hall artists created for our *Java Multimedia Cyber Classroom* programming tips. As the user moves the mouse cursor across the six icon images of our bug character, the type of tip is displayed, either "Good Programming Practice" for the thumbs-up icon, "Portability Tip" for the bug with the suitcase icon, and so on. Once you have read the chapter, you will be eager to try out all these techniques, so we have included 67 (!) problems to challenge and entertain you. Here are the exercises that you may want to turn into term projects:

Analog Clock
Animation
Arithmetic Tutor
Artist
Automated Teller Machine
Background Audio
Bubble Help
Calendar/Tickler File
Calling Attention to an Image
Coloring B/W Photographs
Craps
Crossword
Digital Clock
Dynamic Kaleidoscope
Dynamic Customized Newsletter
Dynamic Stock Evaluator
Fashion Designer
15 Puzzle
Fireworks Designer
Flight Simulator
Floor Planner
Game of Pool
Horse Race
Image Flasher
Image Zooming
Jigsaw Puzzle Generator
Juggling Teacher
Karaoke
Knight's Tour Walker
Limericks
Maze Generator and Walker
Multimedia Aerobics
Multimedia Authoring System
Multimedia Simpletron Simulator
Music Teacher
One-Armed Bandit
Pendulum,
Pinball Machine
Physics Demo: Bouncing Ball
Physics Demo: Kinetics
Player Piano
Random Inter-Image Transition
Randomly Erasing an Image
Reaction Time Tester
Rotating Image
Roulette
Screensaver
Scrolling Image Marquee
Scrolling Test Marquee
Sheet Music Generator/Player
Shuffleboard
Story Teller
Synthesizer
Text Flasher
Tortoise and the Hare
Towers of Hanoi
Video Games

You are going to have a great time attacking some of these problems! Some will take a few hours, some are great term projects and some will probably seem unconquerable. We see all kinds of opportunities for multimedia electives starting to appear in the university computing curriculum. We really hope that you will have contests with your classmates to develop the best solutions to several of these problems.

Chapter 15—Files and Streams—deals with input/output that is accomplished through streams of data directed to and from files. This is one of the most important chapters for programmers who will be developing commercial applications. The chapter begins with an introduction to the data hierarchy from bits, to bytes, to fields, to records, to files. Next, Java's simple view of files and streams is presented. We then present a walkthrough of the dozens of classes in Java's extensive input/output files and streams class hierarchy. We put many of these classes to work in live-code examples in this chapter and in Chapter 16, "Networking." We show how programs pass data to secondary storage devices like disks and how programs retrieve data already stored on those devices. Sequential-access files are discussed using a series of three programs that show how to open and close files, how to store data sequentially in a file and how to read data sequentially from a file. Random-access files are discussed using a series of four programs that show how to sequentially create a file for random access, how to read and write data to a file with random access, and how to read data sequentially from a randomly accessed file. The fourth random-access program combines many of the techniques of accessing files both sequentially and randomly into a complete transaction-processing program. We discuss buffering and how it helps programs that do significant amounts of input/output perform better. We discuss class `File` that programs use to obtain a variety of information about files and directories. We explain how objects can be output to, and input from, secondary storage devices. Students in our industry seminars have told us that after studying the material on file processing, they were able to produce substantial file-processing programs that were immediately useful to their organizations. The exercises ask the student to implement a variety of programs that build and process both sequential-access files and random-access files.

Chapter 16—Networking—deals with applets and applications that can communicate over computer networks. What is a client? What is a server? How do clients ask servers to perform their services? How do servers give results back to clients? What is a URL (uniform resource locator)? How can a Java program load other World Wide Web pages? How can I use Java to develop collaborative applications? This chapter gives you what you need to begin implementing client/server networked Java programs immediately. We show how to write programs that "walk the Web." We discuss manipulating URLs, using a URL stream connection to read a file on a server, establishing simple clients and servers using stream sockets, client/server interaction with stream sockets, connectionless client/server interaction with datagrams, and security and the network. A key feature of the chapter is the live-code implementation of a collaborative client/server Tic-Tac-Toe game in which two clients play Tic-Tac-Toe with one another arbitrated by multithreaded server—great stuff! The multithreaded server architecture is exactly what is used today in popular UNIX, OS/2 and Windows NT network servers. The chapter has a nice collection of exercises including several suggested modifications to the multithreaded server example.

Chapter 17—Data Structures—is particularly valuable in second- and third-level university courses. The chapter discusses the techniques used to create and manipulate dynamic data structures such as linked lists, stacks, queues (i.e., waiting lines) and trees. The chapter begins with discussions of self-referential classes and dynamic memory allocation. We proceed with a discussion of how to create and maintain various dynamic data structures. For each type of data structure, we present live-code programs and show sample outputs. Although it is valuable to know how these classes are implemented, Java programmers will quickly discover that many of the data structures they need are already available in class libraries such as Java's own **`java.util`** that we discuss in Chapter 18. The chapter helps the student master Java-style references (i.e., Java's replacement for the more dangerous pointers of C and C++). One problem when working with references is that students may have trouble visualizing the data structures and how their nodes are linked together. So we have included illustrations that show the links and the sequence in which they are created. The binary tree example is a nice capstone for the study of references and dynamic data structures. This example creates a binary tree; enforces duplicate elimination; and introduces recursive preorder, inorder and postorder tree traversals. Students have a genuine sense of accomplishment when they study and implement this example. They particularly appreciate seeing that the inorder traversal prints the node values in sorted order. The chapter includes a substantial collection of exercises. A highlight of the exercises is the special section "Building Your Own Compiler." This exercise is based on earlier exercises that walk the student through the development of an infix-to-postfix-conversion program and a postfix-expression-evaluation program. We then modify the postfix evaluation algorithm to generate machine-language code. The compiler places this code in a file (using techniques the student mastered in Chapter 15). Students then run the machine language produced by their compilers on the software simulators they built in the exercises of Chapter 5! The 34 exercises include a supermarket simulation using queueing, recursively searching a list, recursively printing a list backwards, binary tree node deletion, level-order traversal of a binary tree, printing trees, writing a portion of an optimizing compiler, writing an interpreter, inserting/deleting anywhere in a linked list, analyzing the performance of binary tree searching and sorting and implementing an indexed list class.

Chapter 18—Java Utilities Package and Bit Manipulation—walks through the classes of the **`java.util`** package and discusses each of Java's bitwise operators. This is a nice chapter for reinforcing the notion of reuse. When classes already exist, it is much faster to develop software by simply reusing these classes than by "reinventing the wheel." Classes are included in class libraries because the classes are generally useful, correct, performance tuned, portability certified and/or for a variety of other reasons. Someone has invested considerable work in preparing these classes so why should you write your own? We believe the world's class libraries will grow at a phenomenal rate. If this is the case, then your skill and value as a programmer will depend on your familiarity with what classes exist and how you can reuse them cleverly to develop high-quality software rapidly. University data structures courses will be changing drastically over the next several years because most important data structures are already implemented in widely available class libraries. This chapter discusses many classes. Two of the most useful are **`Vector`** (a dynamic array that can grow and shrink as necessary) and **`Stack`** (a dynamic data structure that allows insertions and deletions from only one end—called the top—thus ensuring last-in-first-out behavior). The beauty of studying these two classes is that they are related through inheritance as discussed in Chapter 7, so the **java.util** package itself implements some classes in terms of others thus avoiding reinventing that wheel and taking advantage of reuse. We also discuss classes **Dictionary**, **Hashtable**, **Properties** (for creating and manipulating persistent **Hashtable**s), **Random** and **BitSet**. The discussion of **BitSet** includes live code for one of the classic applications of **BitSet**s, namely the *Sieve of Eratosthenes* used for determining prime numbers. The chapter discusses in detail Java's powerful bit manipulation capabilities that enable programmers to exercise lower-level hardware capabilities. This helps programs process bit strings, set individual bits on or off and store information more compactly. Such capabilities—inherited from C—are characteristic of low-level assembly languages and are valued by programmers writing system software such as operating systems and networking software. The chapter concludes with 19 exercises.

Appendix A—Java Demos—presents a huge collection of the best Java demos Abbey Deitel was able to track down on the Web. Many of these sites make their source code available to you, so you can download the code and add your own features—a truly great way to learn Java! We encourage our students to do this and we're amazed at the results! Abbey has requested that you send her the URLs of your favorite sites that you would like to share with others. Please write to Abbey c/o **deitel@deitel.com**. She will put links to them in our "Best Java Demos" list on our Web sites. You should start your search by checking out Gamelan's treasure trove at **http://www.gamelan.com**. You can save time finding the best demos by checking out the Java Applet Rating Service at **http://www.jars.com**. Here's a list of Abbey's current recommendations (the URLs and descriptions of each are in Appendix A):

Angry Fish	*Cool Beans Java Programming*	*Mazda Miata Animation*
Animated Netscape Logo	*Crazy Counter*	*Missile Commando*
Animated SDSU Logo	*Dethtris Game by Ultramaster*	*Mr. Potato Head*
Animation	*Featured Games of the Week*	*Pong*
ASTERNOID!	*15 Puzzle*	*Rubik's Cube*
Ataxx Game	*Froggie*	*San Francisco Subway Map*
Audio Files	*Graffitti*	*Slot Machine*
Black Jack	*Iceblox Game*	*Starbase*
Celebrity Painter	*Java Slider*	*Stereoscopic 3D Hypercube*
Centipedo	*Jigsaw Puzzle*	*3D Tetris*
Chat	*Marble Solitaire Game*	*Visible Human Body Sections*
Chess		

Appendix B—Java Resources—presents the best resources Abbey was able to track down on the Web. This is a great way for you to get into the "world of Java." The appendix lists various Java resources (such as consortia, journals and companies that make various key Java-related products).

animated applets	books	consultants
applets	Café Del Sol Java resource	contests
applications	class hierarchy diagrams	current information
arts and entertainment	class libraries	databases
audio sites	conferences	demos (many with source code)

developer's kit
development tools
Digital Espresso (resources)
discussion groups
documentation
downloadable applets
examples
events
exercises
FAQs (frequently asked ?s)
Gamelan (3000 java resources)
games
graphics
hottest new Java sites
Hot Java documentation
HotJava newsgroup
information
Java Applet Rating Service
java@java.sun.com (get help)
JavaSoft
Java tools
Java Users Group (JUGs)
Java World magazine
learning Java
links to Java sites
lists of resources
lists of what is new and cool
live chat sessions on Java
mailing lists
message exchange center
news
`news:comp.lang.java`
newsgroups
newsletters
products
projects
publications
puzzles
reference materials
resources
search for applets by keywords
seminars
sites
software
Sun Microsystems
SunWorld magazine online
"The Java Developer"
trade shows
training (please call us!)
tutorial called "Brewing Java"
tutorials for learning java
URLs for Java applets
user interface
utility classes
video sites
Yahoo (Web search engine)
VRML (Virtual Reality)
VRML browsers
VRML sites
VRML 3D graphics animations.
`www.gamelan.com`
`www.javasoft.com`
`www.javaworld.com`

Appendix C—Operator Precedence Chart—lists each of the Java operators and indicates their relative precedence and associativity. We list each operator on a separate line and include the full name of the operator.

Appendix D—ASCII Character Set—lists the characters of the ASCII (American Standard Code for Information Interchange) character set and indicates the character code value for each. Java uses the Unicode character set with 16-bit characters for representing all of the characters in the world's "commercially significant" languages. Unicode includes ASCII as a subset. Currently, most English-speaking countries are using ASCII and just beginning to experiment with Unicode.

Appendix E—Number Systems—discusses the binary (base 2), decimal (base 10), octal (base 8) and hexadecimal (base 16) number systems. This material is valuable for introductory courses in computer science and computer engineering. The appendix is presented with the same pedagogic learning aids as the chapters of the book. A nice feature of the appendix is its 32 exercises, 19 of which are self-review exercises with answers.

Appendix F—Object-Oriented Elevator Simulator—walks the student through a carefully paced and substantial term project. The appendix begins with a simple introduction to object-oriented thinking so the instructor can assign the elevator case study in parallel with the early chapters of the book. These sections introduce the concepts and terminology of object orientation to help students become familiar with what objects are and how they behave. Next we present a requirements specification for a substantial object-oriented system project, namely building the elevator simulator, and we carefully guide the student through the typical phases of the object-oriented design process. By the time the student has finished the early assignments, he or she has completed a precise object-oriented design of the elevator simulator and is ready—if not eager—to begin programming the elevator in Java.

This appendix forms the basis of a carefully paced term project that many instructors will choose to assign. A complete, multimedia-based implementation of the elevator with graphics, animation and audios is in the *Instructor's Manual (*that even has the elevator play "elevator music" when it's moving between floors!). [Again, please do not write to us requesting the Instructor's Manual. It is available to instructors only through their regular Prentice Hall representatives.]

This appendix is one of the most important components of the *Java How to Program* learning experience. It is intended as a term project for intense first programming courses and for most second-level programming courses. We have divided the appendix into 12 carefully paced assignments that enable the student to develop the elevator in parallel with reading the appropriate chapters of the textbook. Section F.1 begins with an introduction to object orientation. We will see that object orientation is a natural way of thinking about the world and writing computer programs. Section F.2 presents the elevator "requirements document" that describes the elevator in sufficient detail for the student to begin the design process. In **Elevator Assignment 1** (Prerequisites: Chapters 1–3) the student begins the object-oriented design process by identifying the classes in the requirements document.

Classes have attributes and behaviors. Class attributes are represented in Java programs by data. In **Elevator Assignment 2** (Prerequisite: Chapter 4) the student concentrates on determining the attributes of the classes needed to implement the elevator simulator. In **Elevator Assignment 3** (Prerequisite: Chapter 6) we concentrate on determining the behaviors of the classes needed to implement the elevator simulator. Behaviors are implemented in Java as methods—Java's term for the member functions with which C++ programmers are familiar. **Elevator Assignment 4** (Prerequisite: Chapter 6) concentrates on the interactions between class objects.

In **Elevator Assignment 5** (Prerequisite: Chapter 6) you begin programming the elevator simulator. For each of the classes you identified in the previous assignments, you write an appropriate class definition. Each class definition is written in a separate file with the `.java` extension. You then write a "driver" applet that tests each of these classes and attempts to run the complete elevator simulation. For this first version of the simulator, you design only a simple, text-oriented output that displays a message for each significant event that occurs. **Elevator Assignment 6** (Prerequisite: Chapter 6) discusses composition, a capability that allows you to create classes that have as members references to objects. Composition enables you to create a building class that contains references to the elevator and to the floors, and, in turn, create an elevator class that contains references to buttons.

Elevator Assignment 7 (Prerequisites: Chapters 9–11) focuses on enhancing the elevator's graphical user interface. **Elevator Assignment 8** (Prerequisites: Chapters 9–11) builds on the GUI you developed in Assignment 7; you will add to the GUI and begin graphically representing the events occurring in your simulation. **Elevator Assignment 9** (Prerequisite: Chapter 13) covers the steps necessary to provide interaction between the GUI and events generated by your simulator. The interaction in many cases will be done with multithreading. **Elevator Assignment 10** (Prerequisite: Chapter 13) covers the steps necessary to provide animation for your simulator. **Elevator Assignment 11** (Prerequisite: Chapter 14) covers the steps necessary to provide additional animation as well some audio for your simulator. **Elevator Assignment 12** (Prerequisite: Chapter 14) enhances the animation of the previous assignment. In **Section F.15** we list several design review questions that address some of the problems that could be encountered in a more elaborate elevator simulator. In **Section F.16** we list nine significant modifications that can be made to your elevator simulator; some of these require the data structures techniques of Chapters 17 and 18.

The Java Multimedia Cyber Classroom

We have implemented an interactive, CD-ROM-based, software version of *Java How to Program: Second Edition* called the *Java Multimedia Cyber Classroom: Second Edition.* It is loaded with features for learning and reference. The *Cyber Classroom* is normally wrapped with the textbook at a discount. If you have already purchased the textbook, you can get a copy of the Cyber Classroom CD directly from Prentice Hall. Please see the ordering instructions on the last few pages of this book.

There is an introductory video with the authors overviewing the Cyber Classroom's features. The 180 live-code example Java programs in the textbook truly "come alive" in the Cyber Classroom. We have placed executables for all these examples "under the hood" of the Cyber Classroom, so if you are viewing a program and want to execute it, you simply click on the lightning bolt icon and the program will run. You will immediately see—and hear for the audio-based multimedia programs—the program's outputs. If you want to modify a program and see and hear the effects of your changes, simply click on the floppy-disk icon that causes the source code to be "lifted off" the CD and "dropped into" one of your own directories so you can edit the text, recompile the program and try out your new version. Click on the audio icon and Paul Deitel will talk about the program and "walk you through" the code. [You will not hear Harvey Deitel's voice in these audios—our friends at Prentice Hall like Paul's voice better!]

The Cyber Classroom also provides all kinds of navigational aids including extensive hyperlinking. The Cyber Classroom remembers in a "history list" recent sections you have visited and allows you to move forward or backward in that history list. The thousands of index entries are hyperlinked to their text occurrences. You can key in a term and the Cyber Classroom will locate its occurrences throughout the text. The Table of Contents entries are "hot," so clicking on a chapter name immediately takes you to that chapter. Using the *Java Multimedia Cyber Classroom* is a bit like having a personal tutor to help you learn how to program in the Java programming language.

Students and professional users of our *Cyber Classrooms* tell us they like the interactivity and that the *Cyber Classroom* is an effective reference because of the extensive hyperlinking and other navigational features. We recently had an email from a person who said that he lives "in the boonies" and can not take a live course at a university, so the *Cyber Classroom* was the solution to his educational needs.

Professors have sent us emails indicating their students enjoy using the *Cyber Classroom*, spend more time on the course and master more of the material than in textbook-only courses. Also, the *Cyber Classroom* helps shrink lines outside professors' offices during office hours. We have also published the *C & C++ Multimedia Cyber Classroom* and hope to publish *Cyber Classroom* editions of our forthcoming *Visual Basic How to Program* and *Visual C++ How to Program* textbooks.

Acknowledgments

One of the great pleasures of writing a textbook is acknowledging the efforts of many people whose names may not appear on the cover, but whose hard work, cooperation, friendship, and understanding were crucial to the production of the book.

Three other people at Deitel & Associates, Inc. devoted long hours to this project. We would like to acknowledge the efforts of Tem Nieto, Barbara Deitel and Abbey Deitel.

Tem Nieto, a graduate of the Massachusetts Institute of Technology, is one of our full-time colleagues at Deitel & Associates, Inc. Tem teaches C, C++ and Java seminars and works with us on textbook writing, course development and multimedia authoring efforts. He is co-authoring our next book, *Visual Basic How to Program.* Tem co-authored Chapters 9, 10 and 11; Appendix F on the object-oriented, multimedia-based elevator simulator project and the Special Section entitled "Building Your Own Compiler" in Chapter 17.

Barbara Deitel managed the preparation of the manuscript and coordinated with Prentice Hall all the efforts related to production of the book. Barbara's efforts are by far the most painstaking of what we do to develop books. She has infinite patience. She handled the endless details involved in publishing an 1100-page, two-color book; a 500-page instructor's manual and the 650 megabyte CD *Cyber Classroom.* She used FrameMaker page-layout software to prepare the book. Barbara mastered this complex software package and did a marvelous job giving the book its clean style. She spent long hours researching the quotes at the beginning of each chapter. Barbara prepared every one of the 7800 page references in the 38-page index. She did all this in parallel with handling her additional extensive financial and administrative responsibilities at Deitel & Associates, Inc.

Abbey Deitel, a graduate of Carnegie Mellon University's industrial management program, and now pursuing a management career with Deitel & Associates, Inc., wrote Appendix A, "Java Demos," and Appendix B, "Java Resources" and suggested the title for the book. We asked Abbey to surf the World Wide Web and track down the best Java sites. She didn't have to go far. She immediately discovered Gamelan, a wonderful site listing thousands of significant Java resources including many nice demos. She used every major Web search engine and collected this information for you in Appendices A and B. For each resource and demo, Abbey has provided a brief explanation. She rejected hundreds of sites and has listed for you the best she could find. Abbey will be maintaining current versions of these resources and demo listings on our Web sites **`http://www.prenhall.com/deitel`** and **`http://www.deitel.com`** She asks that you send URLs for your favorite sites to her by email at **`deitel@deitel.com`** and she will post links to these on our sites.

We are fortunate to have been able to work on this project with a talented and dedicated team of publishing professionals at Prentice Hall. This book happened because of the encouragement, enthusiasm, and persistence of our computer science editor, Laura Steele, and her boss—one of the best friends we've ever had in publishing—Marcia Horton, Editor-in-Chief of Prentice Hall's Engineering and Computer Science Division. Camille Trentacoste did a marvelous job as production manager.

The *Java Multimedia Cyber Classroom: Second Edition* was developed in parallel with *Java How to Program: Second Edition.* We sincerely appreciate the "new media" insight, savvy and technical expertise of our editor Mark Taub. He did a remarkable job bringing the *Java Multimedia Cyber Classroom: Second Edition,* to publication under a tight schedule. We also want to thank Logan Campbell, President of the Prentice Hall Professional and Technical Reference Division, for making impressive resources available to our projects.

We owe special thanks to the creativity of Tamara Newnam Cavallo who did the art work for our programming tips icons and the cover. She created the delightful creature who shares with you the book's programming tips. Please help us name this endearing little bug. Some early suggestions: D. Bug, InterGnat, DeetleBug (an unfortunate moniker that was attached to the old guy in high school), Feature and the "drunk bug on the cover."

We sincerely appreciate the efforts of our reviewers (some first edition, some second edition, and some both):

Peter Jones (JavaSoft)
Ian Smith (Georgia Institute of Technology)
Jim Roberts (Carnegie-Mellon University)
Andrew M. Brown (Bell Laboratories)
Gordon Bradley (Naval Postgraduate School)
Richard Enbody (Michigan State University)
Ken Merson (Borland)
Mark Ellis (Reuters)
Robert Herrmann (JavaSoft)
Jerry Gulla (JavaSoft)
Kate Baumgartner Lowrie (Kronos)

Under an impossibly tight time schedule, they scrutinized every aspect of the text and made countless suggestions for improving the accuracy and completeness of the presentation.

We would sincerely appreciate your comments, criticisms, corrections, and suggestions for improving the text. Please send your suggestions for improving and adding to our list of *Good Programming Practices, Common Programming Errors, Testing and Debugging Tips, Performance Tips, Portability Tips,* and *Software Engineering Observations.* We will acknowledge all contributors in the next edition of our book. Please address all correspondence to our email address:

deitel@deitel.com

or write to us as follows:

Harvey M. Deitel (author)
Paul J. Deitel (author)
c/o Computer Science Editor
College Book Editorial
Prentice Hall
1 Lake Street
Upper Saddle River, New Jersey 07458

We will respond immediately. Well, that's it for now. Welcome to the new and exciting world of Java programming. We hope you enjoy this look at contemporary computer applications development using multimedia, multithreading, the Internet and the World Wide Web. Good luck!

Dr. Harvey M. Deitel
Paul J. Deitel

About the Authors

Dr. Harvey M. Deitel, CEO of Deitel & Associates, Inc., has 36 years experience in the computing field including extensive industry and academic experience. He is one of the world's leading computer science instructors and seminar presenters. Dr. Deitel earned B.S. and M.S. degrees from the Massachusetts Institute of Technology and a Ph.D. from Boston University. He worked on the pioneering virtual memory operating systems projects at IBM and MIT that developed techniques widely implemented today in systems like UNIX, OS/2, and Windows NT. He has 20 years of college teaching experience including earning tenure and serving as the Chairman of the Computer Science Department at Boston College before founding Deitel & Associates, Inc. with Paul J. Deitel. He is author or co-author of several dozen books and multimedia packages and is currently writing five more. With translations published in Japanese, Russian, Spanish, Chinese, Korean, and French, Dr. Deitel's texts have earned international recognition.

Paul J. Deitel, Executive Vice President of Deitel & Associates, Inc., is a graduate of the Massachusetts Institute of Technology's Sloan School of Management where he studied Information Technology. Through Deitel & Associates, Inc. he has delivered Java, C and C++ courses for industry clients including Digital Equipment Corporation, Sun Microsystems, Rogue Wave Software, Software 2000, Computervision, Stratus, Fidelity, Cambridge Technology Partners, Open Environment Corporation, One Wave, Hyperion Software, Lucent Technologies, Adra Systems, Entergy, CableData Systems, NASA at the Kennedy Space Center, the National Severe Storm Center and IBM. He has lectured on C++ and Java for the Boston Chapter of the Association for Computing Machinery and will be delivering intermediate and advanced Java courses at the C++ World conference presented by SIGS Publications. He teaches satellite-based Java courses through a cooperative venture of Deitel & Associates, Inc., Prentice Hall and the Technology Education Network. He is the co-author of ten books and multimedia packages with Harvey Deitel and is currently writing five more.

The Deitels are co-authors of the world's best-selling introductory college computer science textbooks, *C How to Program*, *C++ How to Program* and *Java How to Program*. The Deitels are also co-authors of the *C & C++ Multimedia Cyber Classroom*—Prentice Hall's first multimedia-based textbook—and the *Java Multimedia Cyber Classroom.*

About Deitel & Associates, Inc.

Deitel & Associates, Inc. is an internationally recognized corporate training and publishing organization specializing in programming languages and object technology education. The company provides courses on Java, C++, C, Visual Basic, and Object-Oriented Analysis and Design. The principals of Deitel & Associates, Inc. are Dr. Harvey M. Deitel and Paul

J. Deitel. The company's clients include some of the world's largest computer companies, government agencies and business organizations. Through its publishing partnership with Prentice Hall, Deitel & Associates, Inc. publishes leading-edge programming textbooks, professional books, interactive, CD-ROM based multimedia *Cyber Classrooms* and satellite courses. They will soon begin publishing videotape courses and World-Wide-Web-based courses. Deitel & Associates, Inc. and the authors can be reached via email at

`deitel@deitel.com`

To learn more about Deitel & Associates, Inc. and its on-site course curriculum, visit:

`http://www.deitel.com`

To learn more about Deitel & Deitel Prentice Hall publications, visit:

`http://www.prenhall.com/deitel`

For a current list of Deitel/Prentice Hall publications including textbooks and multimedia packages, and for complete worldwide ordering information, please see the last few pages of this book.

1

Introduction to Computers and Java Applets

Objectives

- To understand basic computer science concepts.
- To become familiar with different types of programming languages.
- To understand the Java program development environment.
- To be able to write simple Java programs.
- To be able to use simple input and output statements.
- To become familiar with fundamental data types.
- To be able to use arithmetic operators.
- To understand the precedence of arithmetic operators.
- To be able to write simple decision-making statements.

Our life is frittered away by detail ... Simplify, simplify.
Henry Thoreau

High thoughts must have high language.
Aristophanes

My object all sublime
I shall achieve in time.
W. S. Gilbert

Get hold of portable property.
Charles Dickens, *Great Expectations*

Outline

1.1 Introduction

Welcome to Java! We have worked hard to create what we hope will be an informative, entertaining and challenging learning experience for you. Java is a powerful computer programming language that is fun to use for novices while simultaneously being appropriate for experienced programmers building substantial information systems. *Java How to Program* is designed to be an effective learning tool for each of these audiences.

How can one book appeal to both groups? The answer is that the common core of the book emphasizes achieving program *clarity* through the proven techniques of *structured programming* and *object-oriented programming*. Nonprogrammers will learn programming the right way from the beginning. We have attempted to write in a clear and straightforward manner. The book is abundantly illustrated. Perhaps most importantly, the book presents hundreds of working Java programs and shows the outputs produced when those programs are run on a computer.

The early chapters introduce the fundamentals of computers, computer programming, and the Java computer programming language. Novices who have taken our courses tell us that the material in those chapters presents a solid foundation for the deeper treatment of Java in the later chapters. Experienced programmers typically read the early chapters quickly and find that the treatment of Java in the later chapters is rigorous and challenging.

Many experienced programmers have told us that they appreciate our treatment of structured programming. Often they have been programming in structured languages like C or Pascal, but because they were never formally introduced to structured programming, they are not writing the best possible code in these languages. As they review structured programming in the chapter, "Control Structures," they are able to improve their C and Pascal programming styles as well. So whether you are a novice or an experienced programmer, there is much here to inform, entertain, and challenge you.

Most people are familiar with the exciting things computers do. Using this textbook, you will learn how to command computers to do those things. It is *software* (i.e., the instructions you write to command the computer to perform *actions* and make *decisions*) that controls computers (often referred to as *hardware*), and Java is one of today's most popular software development languages. Java was developed by Sun Microsystems and is available free over the Internet from the Sun site **`http://www.javasoft.com`**

The use of computers is increasing in almost every field of endeavor. In an era of steadily rising costs, computing costs have been decreasing dramatically because of the rapid developments in both hardware and software technology. Computers that might have filled large rooms and cost millions of dollars two decades ago can now be inscribed on the surfaces of silicon chips smaller than a fingernail, and costing perhaps a few dollars each. Ironically, silicon is one of the most abundant materials on earth—it is an ingredient in common sand. Silicon chip technology has made computing so economical that approximately 200 million general-purpose computers are in use worldwide helping people in business, industry, government, and their personal lives. That number could easily double in a few years.

This book will challenge you for several reasons. Your peers over the last few years probably learned C or Pascal as their first programming language. They probably learned the programming methodology called *structured programming.* You will learn both structured programming and the exciting newer methodology, *object-oriented programming.* Why do we teach both? We certainly anticipate that object-orientation will be the key programming methodology for the mid-to-late 1990s. So you will build and work with many *objects* in this course. But you will discover that the internal structure of those objects is often best built using structured programming techniques. Also, the logic of manipulating objects is occasionally best expressed with structured programming.

Another reason we present both methodologies is that over the next decade there will be a massive migration from C-based systems (built primarily with structured programming techniques) to C++ and Java-based systems (built primarily with object-oriented programming techniques). There is a huge amount of so-called "legacy C code" in place because C has been in use for a quarter of a century and its use in recent years has been increasing dramatically. Once people learn C++ and/or Java, they find these languages to be more powerful than C, and these people often choose to move their programming projects to C++ and/or Java. They begin converting their legacy systems, a process that is relatively straightforward. Then they begin employing the object-oriented programming capabilities of C++ and/or Java to realize the full benefits of these languages.

Java is certain to become the implementation language of choice in the 1990s for implementing Internet-based applications. Why is Java an attractive first programming language? There are many reasons. Each of them individually may seem attractive, but perhaps not attractive enough to justify switching from "main-line," industry-proven languages like C and C++. But taken as a whole, Java provides an attractive package for advancing the state of programming language education, especially at the introductory and intermediate levels. Over the near term C, and especially C++, are secure as the "heavy-duty" implementation languages programmers need to build the complex, large-scale systems to support their day-to-day operations. For the near term, Java will seem to many people a nice language for making World Wide Web pages "come alive." But as Java evolves, people will start to see it as a perfectly viable, if not preferred language, for meeting most of an organization's programming needs.

For many years languages like C and C++ appealed to universities because of their portability. Introductory courses could be offered in these languages on any hardware/operating system combination as long as a C/C++ compiler was available.

But the programming world has become more complex and more demanding. Today users want applications with graphical user interfaces (GUIs). They want applications that use the multimedia capabilities of graphics, images, animation, audio, and even video. They want applications that can run on computer networks like the Internet and communicate with other applications. They want applications that can take advantage of the flexibility and performance improvements of multithreading (multithreading enables programmers to specify that many activities should occur in parallel). They want applications with richer file processing than C or C++. They want applications that are not limited to the desktop or even to some local computer network, but that can integrate Internet components as well. They want applications that can be written quickly and correctly in a manner that takes advantage of a world of "reuse, reuse, reuse of prebuilt software components." They want easy access to a growing universe of reusable software components. And programmers want all these benefits in a truly portable manner so that applications written on one platform will run without modification on any other. Java offers all these benefits to the programming community.

Another reason Java is attractive for university courses is that it is fully object oriented. One reason that C++ use has grown so quickly is that it extends C programming into the arena of object orientation. For the huge community of C programmers this has been a powerful advantage. C++ includes ANSI/ISO C and offers the ability to do object-oriented programming as well (ANSI is the American National Standards Institute and ISO is the International Standards Organization). C has been around since 1969. During that time, an enormous amount of C code has been written. Because C++ includes C, many organizations find it to be an ideal next step. Programmers can take their C code, compile it, often with nominal changes, in a C++ compiler and continue writing C-like code while mastering the object paradigm. Then the programmers can gradually migrate portions of the legacy C code into C++ as time permits. New systems can be entirely written in object-oriented C++. Such strategies have been appealing to many organizations. The downside is that even after adopting this strategy, companies tend to continue producing C-like code for many years. This, of course, means that they do not quickly realize the full benefits of object-oriented programming and they produce programs that are confusing and hard to maintain due to their hybrid design. Many organizations wish they could plunge 100% into object-oriented development, but the realities of mountains of legacy code and the temptation to take a C-programming approach often prevent this.

Java is a fully object-oriented language. You cannot write C-like, so called procedural programs in Java. You must create and manipulate objects. For universities this is powerfully appealing. Students will learn object-oriented programming from the start. They will simply think in an object-oriented manner.

Here, too, there is a trade-off. Organizations turning to Java for new applications development do not want to convert all their legacy code to Java. So Java allows for so-called *native code*. This means that existing C code and C++ code can be integrated with Java code. Although this may seem a bit awkward (and it certainly is), it presents a pragmatic solution to a problem most organizations face.

Java is currently available from Sun Microsystems at no charge. Anyone can download over the Internet the complete Java Developer's Kit (JDK) from the Sun Microsystems World Wide Web site **`http://www.javasoft.com`** (don't wait until the last minute to do so however, because this is a busy site). This site provides versions of the JDK for Windows 95, Windows NT, Solaris and Macintosh, and provides links to sites with JDKs for other platforms. The fact that Java is free is appealing to universities facing tight budgets and lengthy budget planning cycles. Also, as bug fixes and new versions of Java become available, these become available immediately over the Internet, so universities can keep their Java software literally up to the minute.

Can Java be taught in a first programming course—the intended audience for this book? We think so. Prior to writing this book, Deitel & Associates, Inc. instructors taught 100 Java courses to over 1500 people at all levels of expertise including many nonprogrammers. We found that nonprogrammers become productive faster with Java than with the C or C++ programming languages. They were anxious to experiment with Java's powerful features for graphics, graphical user interfaces, multimedia, animation, multithreading, networking and the like—and they were successful building substantial Java programs even in their first courses.

For many years, the Pascal programming language was the preferred vehicle for use in introductory and intermediate programming courses. Many people said that C was too difficult a language for these courses. In 1992, we published the first edition of *C How to Program,* to encourage universities to try C instead of Pascal in these courses. We used the same pedagogic approach we had used in our university courses for a dozen years, but wrapped the concepts in C rather than Pascal. We found that students were able to handle the C at about the same level as the Pascal. But there was one noticeable difference. Students expressed their appreciation that they were learning a language (C) likely to be valuable to them in industry.

Our industry clients appreciated the availability of C-literate graduates who could work immediately on substantial projects rather than having to first go through costly and time-consuming training programs.

The first edition of *C How to Program* included a 60-page introduction to C++ and object-oriented programming. We saw C++ coming on strong, but we felt it would be at least a few more years before the universities would be ready to teach C++ and object-oriented programming (OOP) in introductory courses.

During 1993 we saw a surge in interest in C++ and OOP among our industry clients. But we still did not sense that the universities were ready to switch to C++ and OOP en masse. So in January 1994 we published the Second Edition of C *How to Program* with a 300-page section on C++ and OOP. In May 1994 we published the first edition of *C++ How to Program,* a 950-page book devoted to the premise that C++ and OOP were now ready for prime time in introductory university courses for many schools that wanted to be at the leading edge of programming languages education.

In 1995, we were following the introduction of Java carefully. In November 1995 we attended an Internet conference in Boston. A representative from Sun Microsystems gave a presentation on Java that filled one of the large ballrooms at the Hynes Convention Center in Boston. As the presentation proceeded, it became very clear to us that Java would play a significant part in the development of interactive, multimedia web pages. But we immediately saw a much greater potential for the language. We saw Java as the proper language for universities to teach first-year programming language students in this modern world of graphics, images, animation, audio, video, networking, multithreading, and collaborative computing. At the time, we were busy writing the second edition of *C++ How to Program.* We discussed with our publisher, Prentice Hall, our vision of Java making a strong impact in the university curriculum. We all agreed to delay the second edition of *C++ How to Program* a bit so that we could get the first edition of *Java How to Program* to the market in time for fall 1996 courses. As the second edition of *Java How to Program* appears, it is being used in approximately 200 universities and hundreds of corporate training programs worldwide.

This first chapter has two parts. The first part introduces the basics of computers and computer programming. The second part gets you started immediately writing some simple Java programs.

So there you have it! You are about to start on a challenging and rewarding path. As you proceed, please share your thoughts on Java and *Java How to Program* with us via email over the Internet at **deitel@deitel.com**. We will make every effort to respond to you quickly.

Prentice Hall maintains **http://www.prenhall.com/deitel**—a World Wide Web site dedicated to our Prentice Hall textbooks and multimedia products *Java How to Program, Java Multimedia Cyber Classroom, C How to Program, C++ How to Program* and *C & C++ Multimedia Cyber Classroom.* The site contains frequently asked questions (FAQs), errata, updates, additional text and examples, and new developments in programming languages and object-oriented programming technologies. If you would like to learn more about the authors or Deitel & Associates, Inc. please visit our World Wide Web site at **http://www.deitel.com**. Thank you and good luck!

1.2 What Is a Computer?

A *computer* is a device capable of performing computations and making logical decisions at speeds millions, and even billions, of times faster than human beings can. For example, many of today's personal computers can perform tens of millions of additions per second. A person operating a desk calculator might require decades to complete the same number of calculations a powerful personal computer can perform in one second. (Points to ponder: How would you know whether the person added the numbers correctly? How would you know whether the computer added the numbers correctly?) Today's fastest *supercomputers* can perform hundreds of billions of additions per second—about as many calculations as hundreds of thousands of people could perform in one year! And trillion-instruction-per-second computers are already functioning in research laboratories.

Computers process *data* under the control of sets of instructions called *computer programs*. These computer programs guide the computer through orderly sets of actions specified by people called *computer programmers*.

The various devices (such as the keyboard, screen, disks, memory, and processing units) that comprise a computer system are referred to as *hardware*. The computer programs that run on a computer are referred to as *software*. Hardware costs have been declining dramatically in recent years, to the point that personal computers have become a commodity. Unfortunately, software development costs have been rising steadily as programmers develop ever more powerful and complex applications, without being able to improve the technology of software development. In this book you will learn proven software development methods that can reduce software development costs—top-down stepwise refinement, functionalization and object-oriented programming.

1.3 Computer Organization

Regardless of differences in physical appearance, virtually every computer may be envisioned as being divided into six *logical units* or sections. These are:

1. *Input unit.* This is the "receiving" section of the computer. It obtains information (data and computer programs) from various *input devices* and places this information at the disposal of the other units so that the information may be processed. Most information is entered into computers today through typewriter-like keyboards, "mouse" devices, disks and tapes. In the future, perhaps most information will be entered by speaking to computers, by electronically scanning images, and by video recording.
2. *Output unit.* This is the "shipping" section of the computer. It takes information processed by the computer and places it on various *output devices* to make the information available for use outside the computer. Information output from computers is displayed on screens, printed on paper, magnetically recorded on disks and tapes, or used to control other devices.
3. *Memory unit.* This is the rapid access, relatively low-capacity "warehouse" section of the computer. It retains information that has been entered through the input unit so that the information may be made immediately available for processing

when it is needed. The memory unit also retains information that has already been processed until that information can be placed on output devices by the output unit. The memory unit is often called either *memory, primary memory* or *random access memory (RAM).*

4. *Arithmetic and logic unit (ALU).* This is the "manufacturing" section of the computer. It is responsible for performing calculations such as addition, subtraction, multiplication, and division. It contains the decision mechanisms that allow the computer, for example, to compare two items from the memory unit to determine whether or not they are equal.
5. *Central processing unit (CPU).* This is the "administrative" section of the computer. It is the computer's coordinator and is responsible for supervising the operation of the other sections. The CPU tells the input unit when information should be read into the memory unit, tells the ALU when information from the memory unit should be utilized in calculations, and tells the output unit when to send information from the memory unit to certain output devices.
6. *Secondary storage unit.* This is the long-term, high-capacity "warehousing" section of the computer. Programs or data not being used by the other units are normally placed on secondary storage devices (such as disks) until they are needed, possibly hours, days, months, or even years later. Information in secondary storage takes longer to access than information in primary memory. The cost per unit of secondary storage is much less than the cost per unit of primary memory.

1.4 Evolution of Operating Systems

Early computers were capable of performing only one *job* or *task* at a time. This form of computer operation is often called single-user *batch processing.* The computer runs a single program at a time while processing data in groups or *batches.* In these early systems, users generally submitted their jobs to the computer center on decks of punched cards. Users often had to wait hours or even days before printouts were returned to their desks.

Software systems called *operating systems* were developed to help make it more convenient to use computers. Early operating systems managed the smooth transition between jobs. This minimized the time it took for computer operators to switch between jobs, and hence increased the amount of work, or *throughput,* computers could process.

As computers became more powerful, it became evident that single-user batch processing rarely utilized the computer's resources efficiently. Instead, it was thought that many jobs or tasks could be made to *share* the resources of the computer to achieve better utilization. This is called *multiprogramming.* Multiprogramming involves the "simultaneous" operation of many jobs on the computer—the computer shares its resources among the jobs competing for its attention. With early multiprogramming operating systems, users still submitted jobs on decks of punched cards and waited hours or days for results.

In the 1960s, several groups in industry and the universities pioneered *timesharing* operating systems. Timesharing is a special case of multiprogramming in which users access the computer through *terminals*, typically devices with keyboards and screens. In a typical timesharing computer system, there may be dozens or even hundreds of users sharing the computer at once. The computer does not actually run all the users' jobs simultaneously. Rather, it runs a small portion of one user's job and then moves on to service the next user. The computer does this so quickly that it may provide service to each user several times per second. Thus the users' programs *appear* to be running simultaneously. An advantage of timesharing is that the user receives almost immediate responses to requests rather than having to wait long periods for results as with previous modes of computing. Also, if a particular user is currently idle, the computer can continue to process other users rather than wait for one user.

1.5 Personal, Distributed, and Client/Server Computing

In 1977, Apple Computer popularized the phenomenon of *personal computing*. Initially, it was a hobbyist's dream. Computers became economical enough for people to buy them for their own personal use. In 1981, IBM, the world's largest computer vendor, introduced the IBM Personal Computer. Almost overnight, personal computing became legitimate in business, industry, and government organizations.

But these computers were "stand-alone" units—people did their work on their own machines and then transported disks back and forth to share information. Although early personal computers were not powerful enough to timeshare several users, these machines could be linked together in computer networks, sometimes over telephone lines and sometimes in *local area networks (LANs)* within an organization. This led to the phenomenon of *distributed computing* in which an organization's computing, instead of being performed strictly at some central computer installation, is distributed over networks to the sites at which the real work of the organization is performed. Personal computers were powerful enough to handle the computing requirements of individual users, and to handle the basic communications tasks of passing information back and forth electronically.

Today's most powerful personal computers are as powerful as the million dollar machines of just a decade ago. The most powerful desktop machines—called *workstations*—provide individual users with enormous capabilities. Information is easily shared across computer networks where some computers called *file servers* offer a common store of programs and data that may be used by *client* computers distributed throughout the network, hence the term *client/server computing.* C and C++ have become the programming languages of choice for writing software for operating systems, for computer networking and for distributed client/server applications. Java is rapidly becoming the language of choice for developing Internet-based applications. Today's popular operating systems such as UNIX, OS/2, Windows 95 and Windows NT provide the kinds of capabilities discussed in this section.

1.6 Machine Languages, Assembly Languages, and High-Level Languages

Programmers write instructions in various programming languages, some directly understandable by the computer and others that require intermediate *translation* steps. Hundreds of computer languages are in use today. These may be divided into three general types:

1. Machine languages

2. Assembly languages
3. High-level languages

Any computer can directly understand only its own *machine language.* Machine language is the "natural language" of a particular computer. It is defined by the hardware design of that computer. Machine languages generally consist of strings of numbers (ultimately reduced to 1s and 0s) that instruct computers to perform their most elementary operations one at a time. Machine languages are *machine dependent,* i.e., a particular machine language can be used on only one type of computer. Machine languages are cumbersome for humans, as can be seen by the following section of a machine-language program that adds overtime pay to base pay and stores the result in gross pay.

```
+1300042774
+1400593419
+1200274027
```

As computers became more popular, it became apparent that machine-language programming was simply too slow and tedious for most programmers. Instead of using the strings of numbers that computers could directly understand, programmers began using English-like abbreviations to represent the elementary operations of the computer. These English-like abbreviations formed the basis of *assembly languages. Translator programs* called *assemblers* were developed to convert assembly-language programs to machine language at computer speeds. The following section of an assembly-language program also adds overtime pay to base pay and stores the result in gross pay, but more clearly than its machine-language equivalent.

```
LOAD BASEPAY
ADD OVERPAY
STORE GROSSPAY
```

Although such code is clearer to humans, it is incomprehensible to computers until translated to machine language.

Computer usage increased rapidly with the advent of assembly languages, but these still required many instructions to accomplish even the simplest tasks. To speed the programming process, *high-level languages* were developed in which single statements could be written to accomplish substantial tasks. The translator programs that convert high-level language programs into machine language are called *compilers.* High-level languages allow programmers to write instructions that look almost like everyday English and contain commonly used mathematical notations. A payroll program written in a high-level language might contain a statement such as:

```
grossPay = basePay + overTimePay
```

Obviously, high-level languages are much more desirable from the programmer's standpoint than either machine languages or assembly languages. The programming languages C, C++, and Java are among the most powerful and most widely used high-level languages.

The process of compiling a high-level language program into machine language can take a considerable amount of computer time. *Interpreter* programs were developed to directly execute high-level language programs without the need for compiling those programs into machine language. Although compiled programs execute much faster than interpreted programs, interpreters are popular in program development environments in which programs are recompiled frequently as new features are added and errors are corrected. Once a program is developed, a compiled version can be produced to run most efficiently.

1.7 History of C++

C++ evolved from C which evolved from two previous languages, BCPL and B. BCPL was developed in 1967 by Martin Richards as a language for writing operating systems software and compilers. Ken Thompson modeled many features in his language B after their counterparts in BCPL and used B to create early versions of the UNIX operating system at Bell Laboratories in 1970 on a DEC PDP-7 computer. Both BCPL and B were "typeless" languages—every data item occupied one "word" in memory. For example, it was the programmer's responsibility to treat a data item as a whole number or a real number.

The C language was evolved from B by Dennis Ritchie at Bell Laboratories and was originally implemented on a DEC PDP-11 computer in 1972. C uses many important concepts of BCPL and B while adding data typing and other features. C initially became widely known as the development language of the UNIX operating system. Today, virtually all new major operating systems are written in C and/or C++. Over the past two decades, C has become available for most computers. C is hardware independent. With careful design, it is possible to write C programs that are *portable* to most computers.

By the late 1970s, C had evolved into what is now referred to as "traditional C," or "Kernighan and Ritchie C." The publication by Prentice Hall in 1978 of Kernighan and Ritchie's book, *The C Programming Language,* brought wide attention to the language (Ke78). This publication became one of the most successful computer science books ever.

The widespread use of C with various types of computers (sometimes called *hardware platforms*) led to many variations. These were similar, but often incompatible. This was a serious problem for programmers who needed to write portable programs that would run on several platforms. It became clear that a standard version of C was needed. In 1983, the X3J11 technical committee was created under the American National Standards Committee on Computers and Information Processing (X3) to "provide an unambiguous and machine-independent definition of the language." In 1989, the standard was approved. ANSI cooperated with the International Standards Organization (ISO) to standardize C worldwide; the joint standard document was published in 1990 and is referred to as ANSI/ISO 9899: 1990. The second edition of Kernighan and Ritchie, published in 1988, reflects this version called ANSI C, a version of the language now used worldwide (Ke88).

C++, an extension of C, was developed by Bjarne Stroustrup in the early 1980s at Bell Laboratories. C++ provides a number of features that "spruce up" the C language, but more importantly, it provides capabilities for *object-oriented programming.*

There is a revolution brewing in the software community. Building software quickly, correctly, and economically remains an elusive goal, and this at a time when demands for new and more powerful software are soaring. *Objects* are essentially reusable software *components* that model items in the real world. Software developers are discovering that using a modular, object-oriented design and implementation approach can make software development groups much more productive than is possible with previous popular programming techniques such as structured programming. Object-oriented programs are easier to understand, correct and modify.

Many other object-oriented languages have been developed, including Smalltalk, developed at Xerox's Palo Alto Research Center (PARC). Smalltalk is a pure object-oriented language—literally everything is an object. C++ is a hybrid language—it is possible to program in either a C-like style, an object-oriented style, or both.

1.8 History of Java

Perhaps the microprocessor revolution's most important contribution to date is that it made possible the development of personal computers which may soon number 300 million worldwide. Personal computers have had a profound impact on people and the way organizations conduct and manage their business.

Many people believe that the next major area in which microprocessors will have a profound impact is in intelligent consumer electronic devices. Recognizing this, Sun Microsystems funded an internal corporate research project code-named Green in 1991. The project resulted in the development of a C and C++ based language which its creator, James Gosling, called Oak after an oak tree outside his window at Sun. It was later discovered that there already was a computer language called Oak. When a group of Sun people visited a local coffee place, the name Java was suggested and it stuck.

But the Green project ran into some difficulties. The marketplace for intelligent consumer electronic devices was not developing as quickly as Sun had anticipated. Worse yet, a major contract for which Sun competed was awarded to another company. So the project was in danger of being cancelled. By sheer good fortune, the World Wide Web exploded in popularity in 1993 and Sun people saw the immediate potential of using Java to create Web pages with so-called dynamic content. This breathed new life into the project.

Sun formally announced Java at a major conference in May 1995. Ordinarily, an event like this would not have generated that much attention. However, Java generated immediate interest in the business community because of the phenomenal commercial interest in the World Wide Web. Java was not an academic language like Pascal or a language designed by one person or a small group for their own local use like C or C++. Rather, Java was designed for commercial reasons and it generated mammoth interest in the business community because of another Internet related development, the World Wide Web.

1.9 Java Class Libraries

Java programs consist of pieces called *classes*. You can program each piece you may need to form a Java program. But most Java programmers take advantage of rich collections of existing classes in Java class libraries. Thus, there are really two pieces to learning the Java "world." The first is learning the Java language itself so that you can program your own classes, and the second is learning how to use the classes in the extensive Java class libraries. Throughout the book, we discuss many library classes. Class libraries are provided primarily by compiler vendors, but many class libraries are supplied by independent software vendors.

Software Engineering Observation 1.1

Use a building block approach to creating programs. Avoid reinventing the wheel. Use existing pieces—this is called software reuse and it is central to object-oriented programming.

Software Engineering Observation 1.2

When programming in Java you will typically use the following building blocks: classes from class libraries, classes and create yourself, and classes other people create and make available to you.

The advantage of creating your own classes is that you will know exactly how they work. You will be able to examine the Java code. The disadvantage is the time-consuming and complex effort that goes into designing and developing new classes and methods.

Performance Tip 1.1

Using library classes instead of writing your own versions can improve program performance because these classes are carefully written to perform efficiently.

Portability Tip 1.1

Using library classes instead of writing your own versions can improve program portability because these classes are included in virtually all Java implementations.

Software Engineering Observation 1.3

Extensive class libraries of reusable software components are available over the Internet in general and the World Wide Web in particular. Many of these libraries are available at no charge.

1.10 Other High-Level Languages

Hundreds of high-level languages have been developed, but only a few have achieved broad acceptance. *FORTRAN* (FORmula TRANslator) was developed by IBM Corporation between 1954 and 1957 to be used for scientific and engineering applications that require complex mathematical computations. FORTRAN is still widely used, especially in engineering applications.

COBOL (COmmon Business Oriented Language) was developed in 1959 by a group of computer manufacturers and government and industrial computer users. COBOL is used primarily for commercial applications that require precise and efficient manipulation of large amounts of data. Today, about half of all business software is still programmed in COBOL. Approximately one million people are actively writing COBOL programs.

Pascal was designed at about the same time as C. It was created by Professor Nicklaus Wirth and was intended for academic use. We say more about Pascal in the next section.

1.11 Structured Programming

During the 1960s, many large software development efforts encountered severe difficulties. Software schedules were typically late, costs greatly exceeded budgets, and the finished products were unreliable. People began to realize that software development was a far more complex activity than they had imagined. Research activity in the 1960s resulted in the evolution of *structured programming*—a disciplined approach to writing programs that are clearer than unstructured programs, easier to test and debug, and easier to modify. Chapter 3, "Control Structures," discusses the principles of structured programming.

One of the more tangible results of this research was the development of the Pascal programming language by Nicklaus Wirth in 1971. Pascal, named after the seventeenth-century mathematician and philosopher Blaise Pascal, was designed for teaching structured programming in academic environments and rapidly became the preferred programming language in most universities. Unfortunately, the language lacks many features needed to make it useful in commercial, industrial, and government applications, so it has not been widely accepted in these environments.

The Ada programming language was developed under the sponsorship of the United States Department of Defense (DOD) during the 1970s and early 1980s. Hundreds of separate languages were being used to produce DOD's massive command-and-control software systems. DOD wanted a single language that would fulfill most of its needs. Pascal was chosen as a base, but the final Ada language is quite different from Pascal. The language was named after Lady Ada Lovelace, daughter of the poet Lord Byron. Lady Lovelace is generally credited with writing the world's first computer program in the early 1800s (for the Analytical Engine mechanical computing device designed by Charles Babbage). One important capability of Ada is called *multitasking;* this allows programmers to specify that many activities are to occur in parallel. The other widely used high-level languages we have discussed—including C and C++—generally allow the programmer to write programs that perform only one activity at a time. Java, again, supports multithreading.

1.12 Basics of a Typical Java Environment

Java systems generally consist of several parts: an environment, the language, the Java Applications Programming Interface (API), and various class libraries. The following discussion explains a typical Java program development environment as shown in Fig. 1.1.

Java programs normally go through five phases to be executed (Fig. 1.1). These are: *edit, compile, load, verify* and *execute.* If you are not using UNIX, Windows 95 or Windows NT, refer to the manuals for your system's Java environment, or ask your instructor how to accomplish these tasks in your environment, although your environment will probably be quite similar to that in Fig. 1.1.

Phase 1 consists of editing a file. This is accomplished with an *editor program.* The programmer types a Java program using the editor and makes corrections if necessary. When the programmer specifies that the file in the editor should be saved, the program is stored on a secondary storage device such as a disk. Java program file names end with the **`.java`** extension. Two editors widely used on UNIX systems are **`vi`** and **`emacs`**. On Windows 95 and Windows NT simple edit programs like the DOS Edit command and the Windows Notepad will suffice. Java integrated development environments (IDEs) such as Microsoft's Visual J++ and Symantec's Visual Cafe have built-in editors that are smoothly integrated into the programming environment. We assume the reader knows how to edit a program.

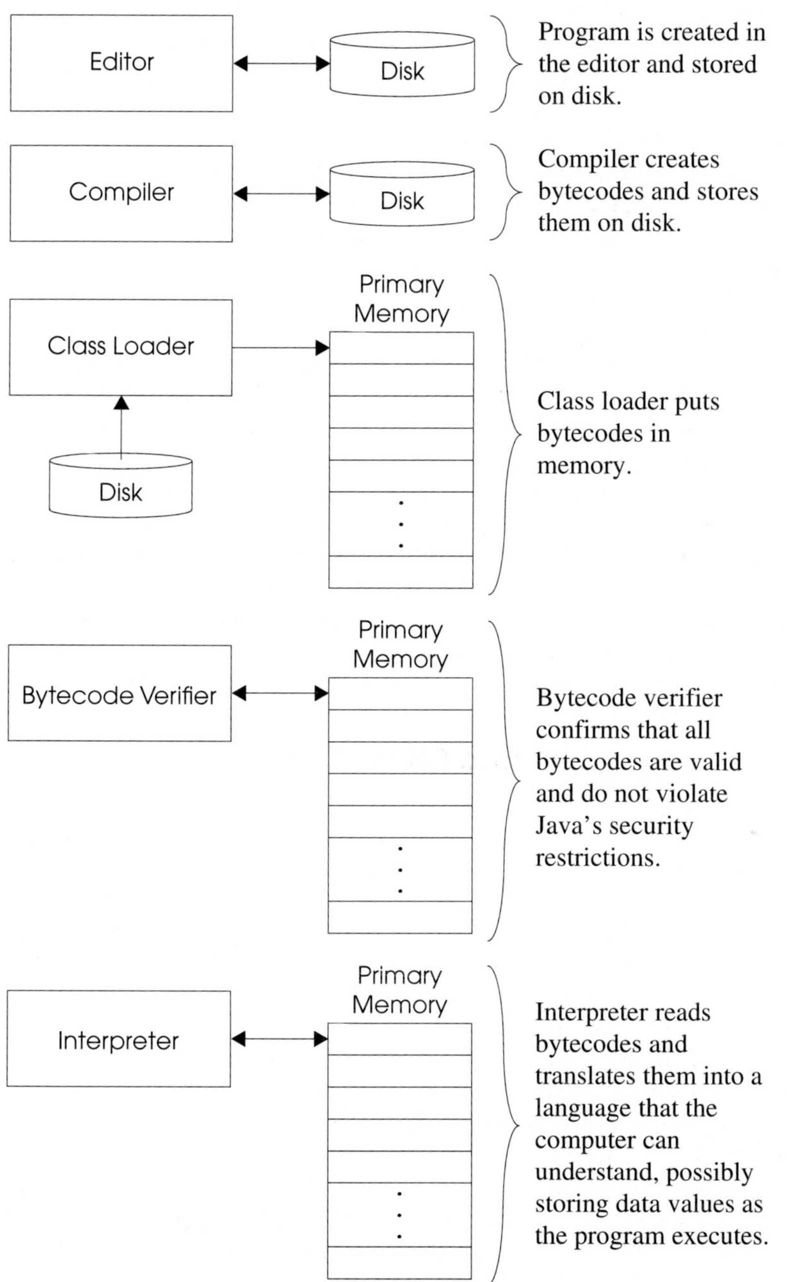

Fig. 1.1 A typical Java environment.

In Phase 2, the programmer gives the command ***javac*** to *compile* the program. The Java compiler translates the Java program into *bytecodes*—the language understood by the Java interpreter. To compile a program called **Welcome.java**, type

```
javac Welcome.java
```

at the command-line of your system (i.e., the MS-DOS prompt in Windows 95 and Windows NT or the shell prompt in UNIX). If the program compiles correctly, a file called **Welcome.class** is produced. This is the file containing the bytecodes that will be interpreted during the execution phase.

Phase 3 is called *loading*. The program must first be placed in memory before it can be executed. This is done by the *class loader* which takes the **.class** file (or files) containing the bytecodes and transfers it to memory. The **.class** file can be loaded from a disk on your system or over a network (such as your local university or company network or even the Internet). There are two types of programs for which the class loader loads **.class** files—*applications* and *applets*. An application is a program such as a word processor program, a spreadsheet program, a drawing program, an email program, etc. that is normally stored and executed from the user's local computer. An applet is a small program that is normally stored on a remote computer that users connect to via a World Wide Web browser. Applets are loaded from a remote computer into the browser, executed in the browser and discarded when execution completes. To execute an applet again, the user must point their browser at the appropriate location on the World Wide Web and reload the program into the browser.

Applications are loaded into memory and executed using the ***java*** *interpreter*. When executing a Java application called **Welcome**, the command

```
java Welcome
```

invokes the **java** interpreter for the **Welcome** application and causes the class loader to load information used in the **Welcome** program.

The class loader is also executed when a Java applet is loaded into a World Wide Web browser such as Netscape's Navigator, Microsoft's Internet Explorer or Sun's HotJava. Browsers are used to view documents on the World Wide Web called *HTML* (*Hypertext Markup Language*) documents. HTML is used to format a document in a manner that is easily understood by the browser application (we will introduce you to HTML in Section 1.16). An HTML document may refer to a Java applet. When the browser sees an applet in an HTML document, the browser launches the Java class loader to load the applet. The browsers that support Java have the Java interpreter built into the browser. Once the applet is loaded, the Java interpreter in the browser begins executing the applet. Applets can also be executed from the command-line using the ***appletviewer*** *command* provided with the *Java Developer's Kit* (*JDK*)—a set of tools including the compiler (**javac**), interpreter (**java**), **appletviewer** and other tools used by Java programmers. Like Netscape Navigator, Internet Explorer and HotJava, the **appletviewer** requires an HTML document to invoke an applet. For example, if the **Welcome.html** file refers to the **Welcome** applet, the **appletviewer** command is used as follows:

```
appletviewer Welcome.html
```

This causes the class loader to load the information used in the **Welcome** applet. The **appletviewer** is commonly referred to as the minimum browser—it only knows how to interpret applets.

Before the bytecodes in an applet are executed by the Java interpreter built into a browser or the **appletviewer**, they are verified by the *bytecode verifier* in Phase 4 (this also happens in applications that download bytecodes from a network). This ensures that the bytecodes for classes that are loaded from the Internet (referred to as *downloaded classes*) are valid and that they do not violate Java's security restrictions. Java must enforce strong security because Java programs arriving over the network should not be able to cause damage to your files and your system.

Finally, in Phase 5, the computer, under the control of its CPU, interprets the program one bytecode at a time, thus performing the actions specified by the program.

Programs may not work on the first try. Each of the preceding phases can fail because of various types of errors that we will discuss in this text. For example, an executing program might attempt to divide by zero (an illegal operation in Java just as it is in arithmetic). This would cause the Java program to print an error message. The programmer would return to the edit phase, make the necessary corrections, and proceed through the remaining phases again to determine that the corrections work properly.

Common Programming Error 1.1

Errors like division-by-zero errors occur as a program runs, so these errors are called run-time errors or execution-time errors. Fatal run-time errors cause programs to terminate immediately without having successfully performed their jobs. Nonfatal run-time errors allow programs to run to completion, often producing incorrect results.

Most programs in Java input and/or output data. When we say that a program prints a result, we normally mean that the result is displayed on a screen. Data may be output to other devices such as disks and hardcopy printers.

1.13 A Tour of the Book

In Chapter 1, "Introduction to Computers and Java Applets," we present some historical information and we introduce some simple Java applets. The book uses a technique we call the *live-code approach.* Every concept is presented in the context of a complete working Java program which is immediately followed by the screen output produced when that program is executed on a computer. With Java you can write two kinds of programs namely, *applets* designed to be transported over the Internet and executed in World Wide Web browsers like Netscape Navigator, Microsoft's Internet Explorer and Sun's HotJava, and stand-alone *applications* that are stored on your own computer and are designed to execute independent of a World Wide Web browser. Because of the intense interest in Java applets and graphical user interfaces, we work almost exclusively with applets in the early chapters. Throughout the book, we introduce various graphical user interface components. These components are discussed in detail in Chapters 10 and 11.

In Chapter 2, "Developing Java Applications," we focus on the program development process. The chapter discusses how to take a *problem statement* (i.e., a *requirements document*) and from it develop a working Java program. The chapter introduces some fundamental data types and some simple control structures used for decision making.

Chapter 3, "Control Structures," discusses much of the C portion of Java, especially the sequence, selection, and repetition control structures. The chapter uses simple flowcharts to show the flow of control through each of the control structures. The chapter concludes with a structured programming summary that enumerates each of the control structures. The techniques discussed in Chapter 2 and Chapter 3 constitute a large part of what has been traditionally taught in the universities under the topic of structured programming. With Java we seek to do object-oriented programming. We will discover that the insides of objects can make abundant use of control structures.

In Chapter 4, "Methods," we take a deeper look inside objects. Objects contain data that we will generally refer to as instance variables, and executable units called methods (these are often called *functions* in non-object-oriented, procedural programming languages like C). We explore methods in depth and include a discussion of methods that call themselves, so-called *recursive methods*.

Chapter 5, "Arrays," explores the processing of data in lists and tables of values. Arrays in Java are processed as objects, further evidence of Java's commitment to almost 100% object orientation.

Chapter 6, "Object-Based Programming," focuses on the essence and terminology of objects. What is an object? What is a class of objects? What does the inside of an object look like? How are objects created? How are they destroyed? How do objects communicate with one another? Why are classes such a natural mechanism for packaging software as reusable componentry?

Chapter 7, "Object-Oriented Programming," discusses the relationships among classes of objects and programming with related classes. How can we exploit commonality between classes of objects to minimize the amount of work it takes to build large software systems? What does it mean to "program in the general" rather than "programming in the specific?" How does programming in the general make it easy to modify software systems and add new features with minimal effort? How can we program for a whole category of objects rather than programming individually for each type of object?

Chapter 8 "Strings and Characters," deals with the processing of words, sentences, characters and groups of characters. The key difference between Java and C here is that Java strings are objects thus making string manipulation more convenient than in C, but more importantly, safer than in C where string manipulation, like array manipulation, is based on dangerous pointers.

Chapter 9, "Graphics," begins to introduce the multimedia "sizzle" of Java. Traditional C and C++ programming are pretty much confined to character mode input/output. Some versions of C++ are supported by platform-dependent class libraries that can do graphics, but using one of these libraries makes your applications nonportable. The beauty of Java's graphics capabilities is that they are platform independent and hence, portable.

Chapter 10, "Basic Graphical User Interface Components," introduces the creation of applets and applications with user-friendly graphical user interfaces (GUIs). Chapter 11,

"Advanced Graphical User Interface Components," continues the discussion started in Chapter 10. Once again, the key to Java's treatment of these subjects is platform independence. A GUI-based applet or application developed once will run on all Java platforms. Actually, although no rewriting is required to run Java GUI applications on different platforms, the user interface components will appear a bit different on different platforms. The reason for this is that Java actually "ties into" the local GUI system, be it Microsoft's Windows, Apple's Macintosh OS, Motif, Sun's OpenWindows, OS/2's Warp, or any other system. So Java applications running on a platform with which you are familiar will take on the appearance of GUI applications running on that platform.

Chapter 12, "Exception Handling," is one of the most important chapters in the book from the standpoint of building so-called mission-critical or business-critical applications. Things do go wrong, and in fact at today's computer speeds—commonly 100 million operations per second—if something can go wrong it probably will, and rather quickly at that. Programmers are often a bit naive about using prebuilt components. They ask, "How do I ask a component to do something for me?" They also ask "What value(s) does that component return to me to indicate it has performed the job I asked it to do?" But programmers also need to be concerned with, "What happens when the component I call upon to do a job for me experiences difficulty? How will that component signal to me that it had a problem?" In Java, when a component (i.e., a class object) encounters difficulty, it can "throw" an exception. The environment of that component is programmed to "catch" that exception and deal with it. Java's exception handling capabilities are especially geared to an object-oriented world in which programmers construct software systems largely from reusable components built by other programmers. To use a Java component, you need to know not only how that component behaves when "things go well," but what exceptions that component throws when "things go poorly."

Chapter 13, "Multithreading," deals with how to program applets and applications that can perform multiple activities in parallel. Although our bodies are quite good at this (breathing, eating, blood circulation, vision, hearing, etc. can all occur in parallel), our conscious minds have trouble with this. Computers used to be built with a single rather expensive processor. Today processors are becoming so inexpensive that it is possible to build computers with many processors that work in parallel—such computers are called multiprocessors. The trend is clearly toward computers that can perform many tasks in parallel. Most of today's programming languages, including C and C++, do not include features for expressing parallel operations. These languages are often referred to as sequential programming languages or single-thread-of-control languages. Java includes capabilities to enable multithreaded applications, i.e., applications that can specify that multiple activities are to occur in parallel. This makes Java better prepared to deal with the more sophisticated multimedia, network-based multiprocessor-based applications programmers will be introducing in the mid-to-late 1990s. As we will see, multithreading is even effective on single-processor systems.

Chapter 14, "Multimedia: Images, Animation and Audio," deals with Java's capabilities for images, animation, audio, and eventually video. It is remarkable that students in first programming courses will be writing applications with all these capabilities. The possibilities are intriguing and endless. Imagine having access (over the Internet and through

CD-ROM technology) to vast libraries of graphics images, audios and videos and being able to weave your own together with those in the libraries to form creative applications. Already more than half the new computers sold come multimedia equipped with CD readers and sound cards. Within just a few years, new machines equipped for multimedia will be as common as machines with floppy disks today.

Chapter 15, "Files and Streams," deals with input/output that is accomplished through streams of data directed from and to files. This is one of the most important chapters for programmers who will be developing commercial applications. How does a program pass data to a secondary storage device like a disk? How does a program retrieve data already stored on disk? What are sequential files? What are random access files? What is buffering and how does it help programs that do significant amounts of input/output perform better?

Chapter 16, "Networking," deals with applets and applications that can communicate over computer networks. What is a client? What is a server? How do clients ask servers to perform their services? How do servers give results back to clients? What is a URL (uniform resource locator)? How can a Java program load other World Wide Web pages? How can I use Java to develop collaborative applications? Chapter 16 makes abundant use of the streams technology in Chapter 15.

Chapter 17, "Data Structures," deals with arranging elements of data into useful aggregations such as linked lists, stacks, queues and trees. Each data structure has certain important properties that are useful in a wide variety of applications. We walk through the details of building each of these popular data structures. This is a particularly valuable experience in crafting useful classes, certainly a crucial skill for Java programmers. Much of the value of this chapter is in general principles that are useful to the Java programmers in implementing a very wide variety of classes. Although it is useful to know how these classes work on the inside, Java programmers will quickly discover that most of the data structures they need are already available in class libraries such as Java's own **`java.util`** that we discuss in Chapter 18. Chapter 17 reinforces much of the class crafting discussed in Chapters 6 and 7 on object-based programming and object-oriented programming.

Chapter 18, "Java Utilities Package and Bit Manipulation," walks through the classes of the **`java.util`** package. This is a nice chapter for reinforcing the notion of reuse, reuse, reuse. When classes already exist, it is much faster to develop software by reusing these classes than by "reinventing the wheel." Classes are included in class libraries because the classes are generally useful, correct, performance tuned, portability certified and/or for a variety of other reasons. Someone has invested considerable work in preparing these classes so why reinvent the wheel? Our belief is that the world's class libraries will grow exponentially over the next many years. If this is the case, then your skill and value as a programmer will depend in large measure on your familiarity with what classes already exist and how to reuse them cleverly to develop high-quality software rapidly. This chapter discusses many classes. Two of the most useful are **`Vector`** (a dynamic array that can grow and shrink as necessary) and **`Stack`** (a dynamic data structure that allows insertions and deletions from only one end—the "top"—thus ensuring last-in-first-out behavior). The beauty of studying these two classes is that they are related through inheritance as discussed in Chapter 7, so the **`java.util`** package itself implements some classes in terms of others thus avoiding reinventing the wheel and taking advantage of reuse, reuse, reuse.

Welcome to the new and exciting world of Java programming. We hope you enjoy this look at contemporary applications development using the Internet, the World Wide Web, multimedia and multithreading.

1.14 General Notes about Java and This Book

Java is a powerful language. Experienced programmers sometimes take pride in being able to create some weird, contorted, convoluted usage of a language. This is a poor programming practice. It makes programs more difficult to read, more likely to behave strangely, more difficult to test and debug, and more difficult to adapt to changing requirements. This book is also geared for novice programmers, so we stress *clarity*. The following is our first "good programming practice."

Good Programming Practice 1.1

Write your Java programs in a simple and straightforward manner. This is sometimes referred to as KIS ("keep it simple"). Do not "stretch" the language by trying bizarre usages.

We will include many of these tips throughout the text to highlight those practices that can help you write programs that are clearer, more understandable, more maintainable, and easier to test and debug. These practices are only guidelines; you will, no doubt, develop your own preferred programming style. We will also highlight Common Programming Errors (problems to watch out for so you do not make these errors in your programs), Performance Tips (techniques that will help you write programs that run faster and use less memory), Portability Tips (techniques that will help you write programs that can run, with little or no modifications, on a variety of computers; these tips also include general observations about how Java achieves its high degree of portability), and Software Engineering Observations (thoughts and concepts that affect and improve the overall architecture of a software system, and particularly, of large software systems).

You have heard that Java is a portable language, and that programs written in Java can run on many different computers. *Portability is an elusive goal.* The ANSI C standard document (An90) contains a lengthy list of portability issues, and complete books have been written that discuss portability (Ja89) (Ra90).

Portability Tip 1.2

Although it is easier to write portable programs in Java than in most other programming languages, there are differences among compilers, interpreters and computers that can make portability difficult to achieve. Simply writing programs in Java does not guarantee portability in all cases. The programmer will occasionally need to deal directly with compiler and computer variations.

We have done a careful walkthrough of Sun's Java documentation and audited our presentation against it for completeness and accuracy. However, Java is a rich language, and there are some subtleties in the language and some topics we have not covered. If you need additional technical details on Java, we suggest that you read the most current Java documentation available over the Internet at **`http://www.javasoft.com`**. Our book contains an extensive bibliography of books and papers on the Java language in particular and on object-oriented programming in general.

Good Programming Practice 1.2

Read the documentation for the version of Java you are using. Refer to this documentation frequently to be sure you are aware of the rich collection of Java features and that you are using these features correctly.

Good Programming Practice 1.3

Your computer and compiler are good teachers. If after carefully reading your Java documentation manual you are not sure how a feature of Java works, experiment and see what happens. Study each error or warning message you get when you compile your programs and correct the programs to eliminate these messages.

In this book we explain how Java works in its current implementations. Perhaps the most striking problem with the early versions of Java is that Java programs execute interpretively on the client's machine. Interpreters execute slowly compared to fully compiled machine code.

Performance Tip 1.2

Actually, interpreters have one huge advantage over compilers for the Java world, namely that an interpreted program can begin execution immediately as soon as it is downloaded to the client's machine, whereas a source program to be compiled must first suffer a potentially long delay as the program is compiled before it can be executed.

Although only Java interpreters were available at the client's site on early Java systems, Java compilers have been written for most popular platforms. These compilers take the Java bytecodes and compile them into the native machine code of the client's machine. These compiled programs run comparably to compiled C or C++ code. Thus, there will be some trade-offs in various Java applets and applications. Java applications designed to run locally will be prime candidates for these new compilers.

Applets present some more interesting issues. Remember, an applet could be coming from virtually any Web server in the world. So the applet will have to be able to run on any possible Java platform. Short, fast executing Java applets can certainly still be interpreted. But what about more substantial, compute-intensive applets. Here the user may be willing to suffer the compilation delay in favor of getting better execution performance. For some especially performance-intensive applets the user may have no choice; interpreted code would run too slowly for the applet to perform properly, so the applet would have to be compiled.

An intermediate step between interpreters and compilers is a *just-in-time (JIT)* compiler that, as the interpreter runs, produces compiled code for the programs and executes the programs in machine language rather than reinterpreting them. JIT compilers do not produce machine language that is as efficient as a full compiler. However, full compilers for Java are under development now.

For organizations wanting to do heavy-duty information systems development, Integrated Development Environments (IDEs) are beginning to appear from the major software suppliers. The IDEs provide many tools for supporting the software development process. Several Java IDEs on the market today are just as powerful as those available for C and C++ systems development. This is a strong signal that Java has been accepted as a viable language for developing substantial software systems.

Sun has announced its Java Database Connectivity (JDBC) standard. This is intended for people developing industrial strength database applications. It signals Sun's intention to make Java effective for developing enterprise information systems. This is a more comprehensive mission for Java than simply developing Web pages with active content.

Another indication from Sun Microsystems about its commitment to Java was the announcement of several microprocessors designed to run Java bytecode programs directly. This would offer a huge performance increase over interpreting Java bytecode programs. Initially, three different Java microprocessors were announced varying in price from only a few dollars to as much as $100 each. Sun envisions substantial markets for these microprocessors including the originally intended Java market—intelligent consumer electronic devices such as television set-top boxes, VCRs, security systems, and the like.

1.15 Introduction to Java Programming

Java facilitates a disciplined approach to computer program design. We now introduce Java programming and present several examples that illustrate many important features of Java. Each example is analyzed one statement at a time. In Chapter 2 and Chapter 3 we present a detailed treatment of *program development* and *program control* in Java.

1.16 A Simple Java Applet: Printing a Line of Text

Java uses notations that may appear strange to nonprogrammers. We begin by considering a simple Java *applet* that displays a line of text. An applet is a program that runs in a World Wide Web browser when an HTML document containing the applet is loaded into the browser. The program and its screen output are shown in Fig. 1.2.

```
// A first program in Java
import java.applet.Applet;   // import Applet class
import java.awt.Graphics;    // import Graphics class

public class Welcome extends Applet {
   public void paint( Graphics g )
   {
      g.drawString( "Welcome to Java Programming!", 25, 25 );
   }
}
```

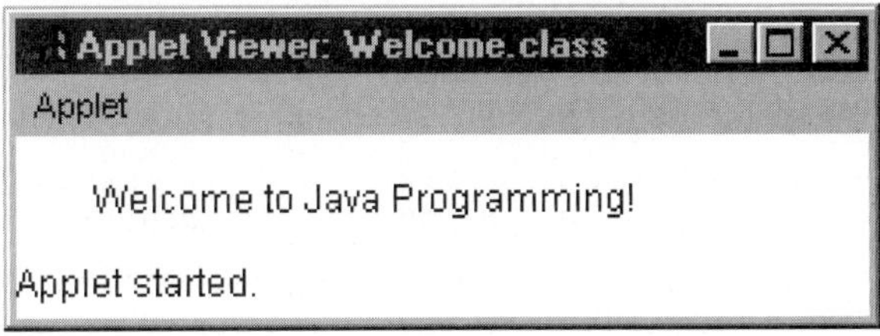

Fig. 1.2 A first program in Java and the program's screen output.

This program illustrates several important Java features. We consider each line of the program in detail. We have inserted line numbers for the reader's convenience; these line numbers are not part of Java programs. Line 8 does the "real work" of the program, namely displaying the phrase **`Welcome to Java Programming!`** on the screen. But let us consider each line of the program in order. Line 1

```
// A first program in Java
```

begins with **`//`** indicating that the remainder of the line is a *comment.* Programmers insert comments to *document* programs and improve program readability. Comments also help other people read and understand your program. Comments do not cause the computer to perform any action when the program is run. Comments are ignored by the Java compiler and do not cause any bytecodes to be generated. The comment **`A first program in Java`** simply describes the purpose of the program. A comment that begins with **`//`** is called a *single-line comment* because the comment terminates at the end of the current line. Note that a **`//`** comment can begin in the middle of a line and continue until the end of that line (as in lines 2 and 3).

Good Programming Practice 1.4

Every program should begin with a comment describing the purpose of the program.

Java contains many predefined pieces called *classes* (or *data types*) that are grouped by directories or folders on your computer's disk drive into categories of related classes called *packages.* The packages are referred to collectively as the *Java class library* or the *Java applications programming interface (Java API).* Lines 2 and 3

```
import java.applet.Applet;   // import Applet class
import java.awt.Graphics;    // import Graphics class
```

are ***`import`*** *statements* that tell the compiler where to search for the classes required to compile a Java program. These specific lines tell the compiler that class ***`Applet`*** is located in package ***`java.applet`*** and class ***`Graphics`*** is located in package ***`java.awt`***.

Each piece of the package name is a directory or folder on disk. All the packages in the Java API are stored in the directory **`java`** that contains many subdirectories including **`applet`** and **`awt`**. When you create an applet in Java, you normally import the **`Applet`** class. You import the **`Graphics`** class so the program can draw graphics (such as lines, rectangles, ovals and strings of characters) on the screen.

One of the great strengths of Java is the large number of classes in the packages of the Java API that programmers can simply *reuse* rather than building new classes (and thus "reinventing the wheel"). We discuss the classes and packages of the Java API in detail throughout the book. We demonstrate how to create your own packages of classes in Chapter 6.

Every Java program is composed of at least one *class definition.* When you create a class definition, you always use pieces of an existing class definition. You never really create a class definition "from scratch." Java provides a mechanism called *inheritance* for creating new classes from existing class definitions. Line 5

```
public class Welcome extends Applet {
```

begins a ***class** definition* for the **Welcome** class. The **class** keyword introduces a class definition in Java and is immediately followed by the *class name* (**Welcome** in this class). The ***extends** keyword* followed by a class name indicates the class (in this case **Applet**) from which our new class inherits. In this inheritance relationship, **Applet** is called the *superclass* or *base class* and **Welcome** is called the *subclass* or *derived class*. We discuss inheritance in detail in Chapter 7, "Object-Oriented Programming." In this example, using inheritance results in a new class definition that has the capabilities defined in the Java API's **Applet** class as well as the new features we are adding in our **Welcome** class definition (specifically, the ability to display **Welcome to Java Programming!** on the screen).

The benefit of extending class **Applet** is that a World Wide Web browser expects every Java applet to have certain capabilities and class **Applet** already provides all those capabilities—programmers do not need to define all these capabilities on their own (again programmers do not need to "reinvent the wheel"). The inheritance mechanism is easy to use; the programmer does not need to know the details of class **Applet** or any other class from which new classes are inherited. The programmer needs to know only that class **Applet** has already defined these capabilities. To make the best use of any class, however, the programmer should study all the capabilities of the class that is extended.

Good Programming Practice 1.5

Investigate the capabilities of any class in the Java API documentation carefully before inheriting a subclass from it. This helps ensure that the programmer does not redefine a capability that is already provided.

Classes are used as "templates" or "blueprints" to *instantiate* (or *create*) *objects* in memory for use in a program. An object is a region in the computer's memory in which information is stored for use by the program. Our **Welcome** class is used to create an object that executes the applet. The browser in which the applet executes is responsible for creating an instance of class **Welcome**. The keyword ***public*** on line 5 is required to enable the browser to create an instance of the applet and execute it. The class that inherits from **Applet** to create an applet is always a **public** class. The **public** keyword and related keywords (such as **private** and **protected**) are discussed in detail in Chapter 6, "Object-Based Programming."

When you save your applet in a file, the applet's class name is used as part of the file name. For our applet, the file name must be **Welcome.java**. Please note that the file name must be spelled exactly the same as the class name and have the **.java** file name extension added to the end.

Common Programming Error 1.2

It is an error if the file name is not identical in both spelling and capitalization to the class name with the **.java** *file name extension.*

Common Programming Error 1.3

It is an error not to end a Java file name with the **.java** *extension.*

At the end of line 5, the *left brace,* **{**, begins the *body* of the class definition. The corresponding *right brace*, **}**, on line 10 ends the class definition. Line 6

```
public void paint( Graphics g )
```

introduces a program building block called a *method.* Methods are explained in detail in Chapter 4. Every Java program contains at least one method that defines a set of *instructions* or *tasks* or *actions* to be performed during the program's execution. These instructions are performed when the method is *called* during the program's execution.

The applet in Fig. 1.2 contains the definition for method **paint** (lines 6 through 9). Method **paint** is one of several applet methods that are called automatically for you (by the browser in which the applet executes) during an applet's execution. The task of method **paint** is to draw graphics (such as lines, rectangles, ovals, and strings of characters) on the screen. Methods are able to return results to the program when they complete their tasks. The **void** keyword indicates that this method does not return any results when it completes its task. The set of parentheses after **paint** defines the method's *parameter list.* The parameter list is where methods receive data required to complete their tasks. Normally this data is supplied by the programmer in the program. However, method **paint** receives the information it needs automatically when the method is called. The **paint** method's parameter list indicates that it requires a **Graphics** object (that is named **g**) to perform its task. The **Graphics** object is used by **paint** to draw graphics on the screen. The **public** keyword at the beginning of line 6 is required so the browser can automatically call your **paint** method. For now, all method definitions will begin with the **public** keyword. Other alternatives are introduced in Chapter 6.

The left brace, **{**, on line 7 begins the method definition's body. The corresponding right brace, **}**, on line 9 ends the method definition's body. Line 8

```
g.drawString( "Welcome to Java Programming!", 25, 25 );
```

instructs the computer to perform an *action* (or task), namely to display the characters of the character string **Welcome to Java Programming!** on the screen. This action is accomplished using method **drawString** defined by class **Graphics** (this class defines all the graphical drawing capabilities of a Java program such as drawing strings of characters and drawing shapes such as rectangles, ovals, and lines). Unlike method **paint**, method **drawString** is not called automatically for you. Method **drawString** is called using the **Graphics** object **g** (in **paint**'s parameter list) followed by a dot operator (**.**) followed by the method name **drawString**. The method name is followed by a set of parentheses containing the data **drawString** needs to perform its task. The data is provided in a comma-separated list known as the *argument list.*

The first argument in this argument list is a *string* of characters contained between the quotation marks. A string is sometimes called a *character string*, a *message*, or a *literal.* The last two arguments in the list—25 and 25—are the *coordinates* (or position) at which the string should be drawn in the applet's area on the screen. Coordinates are measured from the upper-left corner of the applet in *pixels* (the upper-left corner of the white area in the screen capture of Fig. 1.2). A pixel ("picture element") is the unit of display for your computer's screen. On a color screen a pixel appears as one colored dot on the screen. Many personal computers have 640 pixels for the width of the screen and 480 pixels for the height of the screen for a total of 640 times 480 or 307,200 displayable picture elements. Many computer screens have higher screen resolutions, i.e., they have more pixels per row and more pixels per column of the screen. The higher the screen resolution, the smaller the applet appears on the screen. Most drawing methods from class **`Graphics`** require a set of coordinates to specify where to draw on the applet. The first coordinate is the *x coordinate* representing the number of pixels from the left side of the applet and the second coordinate is the *y coordinate* representing the number of pixels from the top of the applet.

The entire line 8, including **`g.drawString`**, its arguments in parentheses, and the *semicolon* (**`;`**), is called a *statement*. Every statement must end with a semicolon (also known as the *statement terminator*). When the preceding statement is executed, it draws the message **`Welcome to Java Programming!`** on the screen at the coordinates 25 and 25. Note that the quotation marks enclosing the character string are *not* displayed on the screen.

Common Programming Error 1.4

Omitting the semicolon at the end of a statement is a syntax error. A syntax error *is caused when the compiler cannot recognize a statement. The compiler normally issues an error message to help the programmer locate and fix the incorrect statement. Syntax errors are violations of the language. Syntax errors are also called* compile *errors,* compile-time errors*, or* compilation errors *because they appear during the compilation phase.*

Good Programming Practice 1.6

Place a space after each comma (`,`) in a statement to make programs more readable.

Good Programming Practice 1.7

Indent the entire body of each method one level of indentation within the braces that define the body of the method. This makes the structure of a program stand out and helps make programs easier to read.

Good Programming Practice 1.8

Set a convention for the size of indent you prefer and then uniformly apply that convention. The tab key may be used to create indents, but tab stops may vary among users' computers. We recommend using either 1/4-inch tab stops or (preferably) three spaces to form a level of indent.

Once the Welcome class is complete, the class must be compiled using **`javac`** (the Java compiler from the Java Developer's Kit discussed in Section 1.12). The command

```
javac Welcome.java
```

compiles class **`Welcome`** and stores the resulting bytecodes in the file **`Welcome.class`**.

After compiling the program of Fig. 1.2, it is necessary to create an *HTML (Hypertext Markup Language)* file to load the applet into a browser to execute. Browsers display the contents of documents that contain text (also know as *text files*). To execute a Java applet in a browser, you must provide an HTML text file that indicates which applet the browser should load and execute. Figure 1.3 contains a simple HTML file—**`Welcome.html`**— that can be used to load into a browser the applet defined in Fig. 1.2.

```
1  <html>
2  <applet code="Welcome.class" width=275 height=55>
3  </applet>
4  </html>
```

Fig. 1.3 The **Welcome.html** file that loads the **Welcome** applet class of Fig. 1.2 into a browser.

Many HTML codes (referred to as *tags*) come in pairs. For example, lines 1 and 4 of Fig. 1.3 indicate the beginning and the end, respectively, of the HTML tags in the file. All HTML tags begin with a *left angle bracket* **<** and end with a *right angle bracket* **>**. Lines 2 and 3 are special HTML tags for Java applets. They tell the browser to load a specific applet and define the size of the applet's display area (its width and height in pixels) in the browser. Normally, the applet and its corresponding HTML file are stored in the same directory on disk. Typically, an HTML file is loaded into your browser from a computer other than your own that is connected to the Internet. However, HTML files also can reside on your computer. When an HTML file that specifies an applet to execute is loaded into a browser, the browser automatically loads the applet's **.class** file (or files) from the same directory on the computer from which the HTML file was loaded.

The ***<applet>*** *tag* is composed of several pieces. The first piece of the **<applet>** tag on line 2 (**code="Welcome.class"**) indicates that the file **Welcome.class** contains the compiled applet class. When you compile your Java programs, every class is compiled into a separate file that has the same name as the class and ends with the **.class** extension. The second and third pieces of the **applet** tag indicate the ***width*** and the ***height*** of the applet in pixels. The upper-left corner of the applet's display area is always at x-coordinate 0 and y-coordinate 0. The width of this applet is 275 pixels and its height is 55 pixels. Generally, each applet should be less than 640 pixels wide and 480 pixels tall (most computer screens support these dimensions as the minimum width and height). On line 3, the **</applet>** tag terminates the **<applet>** tag that began on line 2. On line 4, the **</html>** tag specifies the end of the HTML tags that began on line 1 with **<html>**.

To demonstrate our applet, we use the **appletviewer** command from Sun's Java Developer's Kit (JDK). Consult the Deitel & Associates, Inc. website

http://www.deitel.com

for more information on how to obtain the JDK from Sun's **www.javasoft.com** site, and how to use each of the pieces of software in the JDK. The **appletviewer** is a program that executes Java applets. It only understands the **<applet>** and **</applet>** HTML tags so it is sometimes referred to as the "minimal browser" (it ignores all other HTML tags). The appletviewer is an ideal place to test an applet's execution before adding it to an HTML file that will be viewed by people using World Wide Web browsers to view documents on the Internet. The **appletviewer** is invoked for the **Welcome** applet from your computer's command line as follows:

```
appletviewer Welcome.html
```

Note that the **appletviewer** requires an HTML file to load an applet.

Common Programming Error 1.5

Running the **`appletviewer`** *with a file name that does not end with* **`.html`** *is an error that prevents the* **`appletviewer`** *from loading your applet for execution.*

Portability Tip 1.3

Attempt to execute your applets in every browser that people who view your applet use. This will help ensure that people who view your applet experience the functionality you expect.

From this point in the text, we do not display the HTML files used to load each applet into a browser. However, you can download the examples in *Java How to Program* by pointing your World Wide Web browser at the Deitel & Associates, Inc. web site

`http://www.deitel.com`

With each applet, we have provided a sample HTML file that can be used to test the applet.

`Welcome to Java Programming!` can be printed several ways. Two **`drawString`** statements in the **`paint`** method can print multiple lines as in Fig. 1.4. Note that each **`drawString`** can draw at any pixel location on the applet. The reason the two output lines appear as shown in the output window is that we specified the same *x* coordinate (25) for each **`drawString`** so the strings appear aligned at their left sides and we specified different *y* coordinates (25 on line 8 and 40 on line 9) so the strings appear at different vertical locations on the applet. If we reverse lines 8 and 9 in the program, the output window will still appear as shown because the pixel coordinates in each **`drawString`** statement are completely independent of the coordinates in all other **`drawString`** statements.

```
1  // Displaying multiple strings
2  import java.applet.Applet;  // import Applet class
3  import java.awt.Graphics;   // import Graphics class
4
5  public class Welcome extends Applet {
6     public void paint( Graphics g )
7     {
8        g.drawString( "Welcome to", 25, 25 );
9        g.drawString( "Java Programming", 25, 40 );
10    }
11 }
```

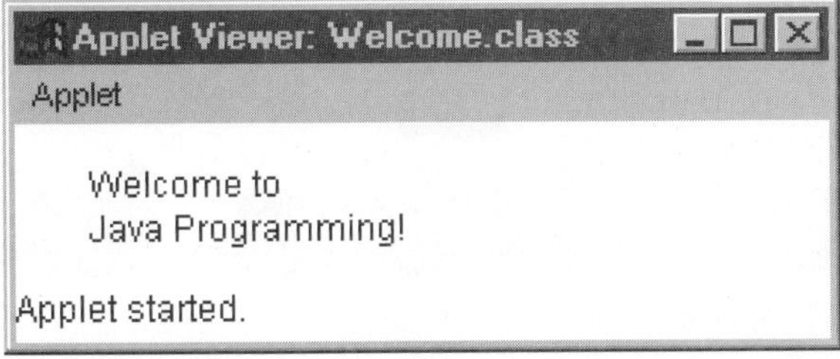

Fig. 1.4 Displaying multiple strings.

1.17 Another Java Applet: Adding Integers

Our next applet inputs integers typed by a user at the keyboard, computes the sum of these values and displays the result. As the user types each integer and presses the *Enter* key, the integer is read into the program and added to the total.

This program uses some *Graphical User Interface (GUI) components* of the Java API. GUI components are program pieces that facilitate data entry by the user of your program and data outputs by your program. For example, Fig. 1.5 contains a Netscape Navigator window. In the window, there is a bar containing *menus* (*File*, *Edit*, *View*, etc.). Below the menu bar there is a set of *buttons* that each have a defined task in Netscape Navigator. Below the buttons there is a *text field* in which the user can type the name of the World Wide Web site to visit. To the left of the text field is a *label* that indicates the purpose of the text field. The menus, buttons, text fields and labels are part of Netscape Navigator's GUI. They enable you to interact with the Navigator program.

Java contains classes that implement the GUI components described here and others that will be described in the Basic Graphical User Interface Components and Advanced Graphical User Interface Components chapters (Chapters 10 and 11). Our next applet (Fig. 1.6) uses a label and a text field to enable you to interact with the applet.

Fig. 1.5 A sample Netscape Navigator window with GUI components.

```
1  // Addition program
2  import java.applet.Applet;
3  import java.awt.*;     // import the java.awt package
4  import java.awt.event.*;  // import the java.awt.event package
5
6  public class Addition extends Applet implements ActionListener {
7     Label prompt;       // message that prompts user to input
8     TextField input;    // input values are entered here
9     int number;         // variable that stores input value
10    int sum;            // variable that stores sum of integers
11
12    // setup the graphical user interface components
13    // and initialize variables
14    public void init()
15    {
16       prompt = new Label( "Enter integer and press Enter:" );
17       add( prompt );  // put prompt on applet
18
19       input = new TextField( 10 );
20       add( input );   // put input TextField on applet
21
22       sum = 0;        // set sum to 0
23
24      // "this" applet handles action events for TextField input
25       input.addActionListener( this );
26    }
27
28    // process user's action in TextField input
29    public void actionPerformed( ActionEvent e )
30    {
31       // get the number and convert it to an integer
32       number = Integer.parseInt( e.getActionCommand() );
33
34       sum = sum + number;    // add number to sum
35       input.setText( "" );   // clear data entry field
36       showStatus( Integer.toString( sum ) );  // display sum
37    }
38 }
```

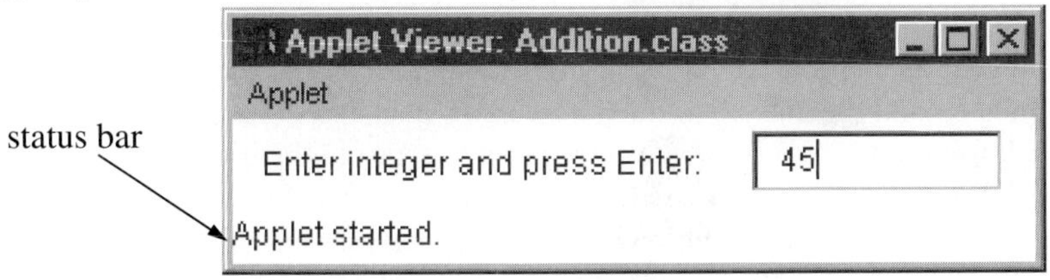

Fig. 1.6 An addition program "in action" (part 1 of 2).

Line 1

```
// Addition program
```

states the purpose of the program.

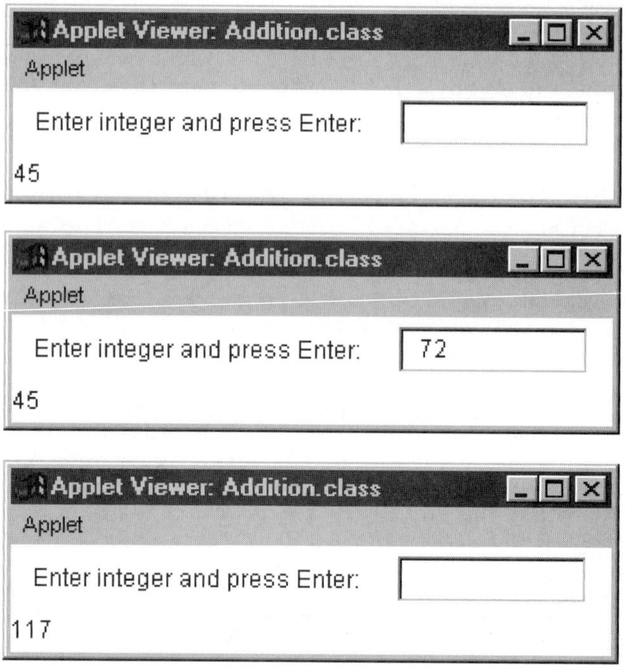

Fig. 1.6 An addition program "in action" (part 2 of 2).

Lines 2 through 4

```
import java.applet.Applet;
import java.awt.*;
import java.awt.event.*;
```

specify to the compiler where to locate the classes used in this applet. The first **import** statement specifies the location of class **Applet** and allows the programmer to use the shorthand name **Applet** in the program. Actually, the **import** statement at line 2 is not required if we always use the complete name of class **Applet**—**java.applet.Applet**. The second **import** specifies the location of the entire **java.awt** package. The asterisk (*****) indicates that all the classes in the **java.awt** package should be available to the compiler for compilation. This allows the programmer to use in the program the shorthand name of any class from the **java.awt** package. Remember that our last two programs only imported from the **java.awt** package the **Graphics** class. In this program, we use the **TextField** and **Label** classes of the **java.awt** package. Importing an entire package into a program is also a shorthand notation so the programmer does not have to list a separate **import** statement for every class used from that package. Remember that you can always use the complete name of every class—i.e., **java.awt.Label** and **java.awt.TextField**—instead of **import** statements. The last **import** specifies the location of the entire **java.awt.event** package. This package contains data types that enable a program to process a user's interactions with a program's GUI.

As stated earlier, every Java program is based on at least one class definition that extends and enhances an existing class definition via inheritance. Remember that applets must inherit from the **Applet** class. Line 6

```
public class Addition extends Applet
             implements ActionListener {
```

says that class **Addition** inherits from **Applet** and *implements* ***ActionListener***. When you create a class definition, you must extend another class that provides you with a default set of capabilities. In addition, you can implement one or more *interfaces*. An interface specifies one or more capabilities (i.e., methods) *that you must define* in your class definition. The interface **ActionListener** specifies that this class *must define a method* with the first line

```
public void actionPerformed( ActionEvent e )
```

This method's task is to process a user's interaction with the **TextField** in this example. We discuss the details of this interaction and method **actionPerformed** shortly.

Remember that all class definitions start with an opening left brace, **{**, and end with a closing right brace, **}**.

Common Programming Error 1.6

If braces do not occur in matching pairs it is a syntax error.

Good Programming Practice 1.9

*Whenever you type an opening left brace, **{**, in your program, immediately type the closing right brace, **}**. This helps prevent missing braces.*

Lines 7 through 10

```
Label prompt;      // message that prompts user to input
TextField input;   // input values are entered here
int number;        // variable that stores input value
int sum;           // variable that stores sum of integers
```

are *declarations*. The words **prompt** and **input** are *references*—names that are used to refer to our ***Label*** and ***TextField*** *objects* in the program. An object contains information for use by a program. We will define the term "object" more precisely later when we study object-based programming and object-oriented programming in Chapters 6 and 7, respectively. The words **number** and **sum** are the names of *variables*. A variable is similar to an object. The main difference between a variable and an object is that an object is defined by a class definition that can contain both information and methods whereas a variable is defined by a *primitive (or built-in) data type* such as ***int*** (integer values, i.e., whole numbers such as 7, –11, 0, 31914). Every piece of data in a Java program is an object except for variables of the primitive types. We discuss the other primitive data types in Chapter 2.

Each declaration declares one or more references or variables and ends with a semicolon. The reference **input** is of type **TextField** (in the screen captures for Fig. 1.6, the **TextField** is the box to the right of the words "**Enter an Integer and press**

Enter:"). **TextField**s are used to get information from the user at the keyboard or display information on the screen. The reference **prompt** is of type **Label**. A **Label** contains a string of characters to display on the screen. Normally, a **Label** is associated with another graphical user interface element on the screen (such as the label

```
Enter an Integer and press Enter:
```

associated with the **TextField** in this program). The variables **number** and **sum** are of primitive data type **int**. All variables and references must be declared with a name and a type before they can be used in a program.

A variable or reference name is any valid *identifier.* An identifier is a series of characters consisting of letters, digits, underscores (_), and dollar signs (**$**) that does not begin with a digit and does not contain any spaces. Java allows identifiers of any length. Some valid identifiers are **$value**, **m_inputField1** and **button7**. Two invalid identifiers are **7button** (because it begins with a digit) and **input field** (because it contains a space). Java is *case sensitive*—uppercase and lowercase letters are different, so **a1** and **A1** are different identifiers.

Good Programming Practice 1.10

Choosing meaningful variable names and reference names helps a program to be "self-documenting," i.e., it becomes easier to understand a program simply by reading it rather than having to read manuals or use excessive comments.

The declarations on lines 6 through 9 are for names that can be used throughout the class definition (i.e., in all methods of the class). Such references and variables are collectively known as instance variables—every instance of the class contains one of each instance variable.

This applet contains two methods—**init** (definition begins on line 14) and **actionPerformed** (definition begins on line 29). Method **init** is normally provided in an applet to *initialize* variables and references that are used in the applet. Method **init** is a special method that is normally the first method defined by the programmer to be called in every applet. In fact, applets always begin with a series of three method calls—**init**, **start** (discussed in a later example), and **paint**. These methods are called from the browser in which the applet is executing. Your applet class gets a "free" version of each of these methods from the **Applet** class when you specify **extends Applet** in the first line of your applet's class definition. The free version of each of these methods is defined with an empty body (i.e., by default each of these methods does not perform a task). One of the reasons we inherit all applets from class **Applet** is to get our free copies of the methods that get called automatically during the execution of an applet.

Why would you want a free copy of a method that does nothing? The predefined start-up sequence of method calls made by the browser for every applet is always **init**, **start** and **paint**—this guarantees an applet programmer a level of consistency for every applet as the applet begins executing. Every applet does not need all three of these methods. However, the browser expects each of these methods to be defined. Inheriting the default version of these methods guarantees the browser that it can treat each applet uniformly as applet execution begins. Also, the programmer can concentrate on defining only the methods required for a particular applet.

The first line of the **init** method always appears as

```
public void init()
```

indicating that **init** is a **public** method that returns no information (**void**) when it completes and receives no arguments (empty parentheses after **init**) to perform its task.

Line 16

```
prompt = new Label( "Enter integer and press Enter:" );
```

creates a **Label** object that is initialized with the string literal **"Enter integer and press Enter:"**. This indicates to the user what to do in **TextField input**. This message is called a *prompt* because it directs the user to take a specific action. The ***new** operator* creates an object as the program executes by obtaining enough memory to store an object of the type specified to the right of **new**. The value in parentheses after the type is used to *initialize* (give an initial value to) the object being created. Reference **prompt** is given the result of the **new** operation with *assignment operator* **=**. The statement is read as, "**prompt** *gets* the value of **new Label("Enter integer and press Enter:")**." The **=** operator is called a *binary operator* because it has two *operands*—**prompt** and the value of the expression **new Label("Enter integer and press Enter:")**.

Line 17

```
add( prompt );   // put prompt on applet
```

places the **Label** GUI component **prompt** on the applet so it can be displayed when the applet is executed. Method **add** is one of the many methods inherited from class **Applet** by class **Addition**.

Line 19

```
input = new TextField( 10 );
```

creates a **TextField** object using the **new** operator and assigns the result to reference **input**. The value **10** specifies the number of characters that can be displayed in the **TextField**. This determines the actual width of the **TextField** on the screen.

Line 20

```
add( input );    // put input TextField on applet
```

places the **TextField** GUI component **input** on the applet so it can be displayed when the applet is executed. Once a **TextField** is displayed, the user can position the mouse pointer in the **TextField** and click the mouse button to make the **TextField** active. This enables the user to type in the **TextField**.

Line 22

```
sum = 0;            // set sum to 0
```

is an *assignment statement* that sets **sum** to **0**. Note that the variables **number** and **sum** are not created with the **new** operator. Only class objects may be created with **new**. Primitive variables are created automatically by Java.

Line 25

```
input.addActionListener( this );
```

specifies that ***this*** applet should *listen* for events from the **TextField input**. The **this** keyword enables the applet to refer to itself (we discuss **this** in detail in Chapter 6). When the user interacts with a GUI component an *event* is sent to the applet. GUI events are messages indicating that the user of the program interacted with one of the program's GUI components. For example, when you type a number from the keyboard into **TextField input** in this program and press the *Enter* key (or *Return* key), an event is sent to the applet indicating that the user pressed the *Enter* key while typing in the **TextField**. This indicates to the applet that *an action was performed* by the user in the **TextField** and automatically calls method **actionPerformed** to process the user's interaction. This style of programming is known as *event-driven programming*—the user interacts with a GUI component, the program is notified of the event and the program processes the event. The user's interaction with the GUI "drives" the program. The methods that are called when an event occurs are also known as *event handling methods*. When a GUI event occurs in a program, Java creates an object containing information about the event that occurred and *automatically calls* an appropriate event handling method. Before any event can be processed, each GUI component must know where the event handling method that will be called when an event occurs is defined. In line 25, method ***addActionListener*** is used to tell **input** that the applet (**this**) contains a method that *listens* for *action events* (i.e., method **actionPerformed**).

Method **actionPerformed** (line 29) is one of several methods we discuss that process interactions between the user and GUI components. The first line of method **actionPerformed**

```
public void actionPerformed( ActionEvent e )
```

indicates that **actionPerformed** is a **public** method that returns nothing (**void**) when it completes its task. Method **actionPerformed** receives one argument—an **ActionEvent**—when it is called automatically in response to an action performed on a GUI component (in this case pressing the *Enter* key in a **TextField**) by the user. The **ActionEvent** argument contains information about the action that occurred. Line 32

```
number = Integer.parseInt( e.getActionCommand() );
```

uses **ActionEvent** method ***getActionCommand*** to get an event-specific piece of information. For example, when the user presses the *Enter* key while typing in a **TextField**, method **getActionCommand** returns the characters the user typed in the **TextField** as a ***String***. A **String** object is an object that can store a string of characters (**String**s are discussed in detail in Chapter 8). Method **Integer.parseInt** converts its **String** argument to an integer. Finally, the integer returned by **Integer.parseInt** is assigned to variable **number**. Any subsequent references to **number** in the program use this same integer value.

Method **Integer.parseInt** is a special method of class **Integer** called a ***static*** *method*. Such methods are always called using their class name followed by a dot

(**.**) and the method name. We discuss **static** methods in Chapter 6, Object-Based Programming. Class **Integer** is part of the package **java.lang**. Notice that class **Integer** is not imported with an **import** statement at the beginning of the program. Package **java.lang** is automatically imported in every Java program.

The assignment statement at line 34

```
sum = sum + number;     // add number to sum
```

calculates the sum of the variables **sum** and **number**, and assigns the result to variable **sum** using the assignment operator **=**. The statement is read as, "**sum** *gets* the value of **sum + number**." Most calculations are performed in assignment statements.

Good Programming Practice 1.11

Place spaces on either side of a binary operator. This makes the operator stand out and makes the program more readable.

Line 35

```
input.setText( "" );    // clear data entry field
```

uses method **setText** of class **TextField** to set the **input TextField** to the empty string—i.e., the string with no characters in it. This clears (or erases) the text that the user typed in the **TextField**.

After performing the calculation and clearing the **TextField**, we display the result in the *status bar* at the bottom of the **appletviewer** window (or your browser). In the four outputs of Fig. 1.6, the **appletviewer** status bar is at the bottom of the window where "applet started," "45," "45," and "117" are displayed, respectively. [In Fig. 1.5, the Netscape Navigator status bar is at the bottom of the screen where "Document: Done" is displayed.] Line 36

```
showStatus( Integer.toString( sum ) );    // display sum
```

uses class **Applet**'s **showStatus** method to put a **String** in the status bar. Method **showStatus** only knows how to display **String**s. Therefore, the integer value of **sum** must be converted to a **String** before it can be placed in the status bar. The **String** displayed is the result of the method call **Integer.toString(sum)** that takes the integer **sum** and converts it to a **String**. Method **Integer.toString** is another **static** method of class **Integer**. Many classes provide **static** methods. Such methods can always be called by specifying their class name followed by a dot (**.**) and the method name.

1.18 Memory Concepts

Variable names such as **sum** and **number** actually correspond to *locations* in the computer's memory. Every variable has a *name,* a *type,* a *size* and a *value.*

In the addition program of Fig. 1.6, when the statement

```
number = Integer.parseInt( e.getActionCommand() );
```

is executed, the value typed by the user in the **TextField** is placed into a memory location to which the name **number** has been assigned by the compiler. Suppose the user enters

45 as the value for **number**. The computer places that **45** into location **number** as shown in Fig. 1.7. The value 0 was placed in **sum** in the applet's **init** method with the statement

```
sum = 0;
```

Whenever a value is placed in a memory location, this value replaces the previous value in that location. The previous value is destroyed.

Once the program has obtained a value, it adds that value and **sum** and places the result into variable **sum**. The statement

```
sum = sum + number;
```

that performs the addition also involves destroying a value. This occurs when the calculated sum of **sum** and **number** is placed into location **sum** (without regard to what value may already be in **sum**). After **sum** is calculated, memory appears as in Fig. 1.8. Note that the value of variable **number** appears exactly as it did before it was used in the calculation of **sum**. The value was used, but not destroyed, as the computer performed the calculation. Thus, when a value is read out of a memory location, the process is nondestructive.

1.19 Arithmetic

Most programs perform arithmetic calculations. The *arithmetic operators* are summarized in Fig. 1.9. Note the use of various special symbols not used in algebra. The *asterisk (*)* indicates multiplication and the *percent sign (%)* is the *modulus operator* which is discussed shortly. The arithmetic operators in Fig. 1.9 are binary operators because they each operate on two operands. For example, the expression **sum + value** contains the binary operator **+** and the two operands **sum** and **value**.

number	**45**
sum	**0**

Fig. 1.7 Memory locations showing the name and value of a variable.

number	**45**
sum	**45**

Fig. 1.8 Memory locations after a calculation.

Java operation	Arithmetic operator	Algebraic expression	Java expression
Addition	`+`	f + 7	`f + 7`
Subtraction	`-`	p – c	`p - c`
Multiplication	`*`	bm	`b * m`
Division	`/`	x / y *or* $\frac{x}{y}$ *or* x ÷ y	`x / y`
Modulus	`%`	r mod s	`r % s`

Fig. 1.9 Arithmetic operators.

Integer division yields an integer quotient; for example, the expression **`7 / 4`** evaluates to **`1`**, and the expression **`17 / 5`** evaluates to **`3`**. Note that any fractional part in integer division is simply discarded (i.e., truncated)—no rounding occurs. Java provides the modulus operator, **`%`**, that yields the remainder after integer division. The modulus operator is an integer operator that can be used only with integer operands. The expression **`x % y`** yields the remainder after **`x`** is divided by **`y`**. Thus, **`7 % 4`** yields **`3`**, and **`17 % 5`** yields **`2`**. In later chapters, we consider many interesting applications of the modulus operator such as determining if one number is a multiple of another.

Common Programming Error 1.7

Attempting to use the modulus operator, `%`, with noninteger operands is a syntax error.

Arithmetic expressions in Java must be written in *straight-line form* to facilitate entering programs into the computer. Thus, expressions such as "**`a`** divided by **`b`**" must be written as **`a / b`** so that all constants, variables, and operators appear in a straight line. The algebraic notation

$$\frac{a}{b}$$

is generally not acceptable to compilers, although some special-purpose software packages do exist that support more natural notation for complex mathematical expressions.

Parentheses are used in Java expressions in the same manner as in algebraic expressions. For example, to multiply **`a`** times the quantity **`b + c`** we write:

```
a * (b + c)
```

Java applies the operators in arithmetic expressions in a precise sequence determined by the following *rules of operator precedence,* which are generally the same as those followed in algebra:

1. Operators in expressions contained within pairs of parentheses are evaluated first. Thus, *parentheses may be used to force the order of evaluation to occur in any sequence desired by the programmer.* Parentheses are said to be at the "highest level

of precedence." In cases of *nested* or *embedded* parentheses, the operators in the innermost pair of parentheses are applied first.

2. Multiplication, division, and modulus operations are applied next. If an expression contains several multiplication, division, and modulus operations, operators are applied from left to right. Multiplication, division, and modulus are said to be on the same level of precedence.
3. Addition and subtraction operations are applied last. If an expression contains several addition and subtraction operations, operators are applied from left to right. Addition and subtraction also have the same level of precedence.

The rules of operator precedence enable Java to apply operators in the correct order. When we say operators are applied from left to right, we are referring to the *associativity* of the operators. We will see that some operators associate from right to left. Fig. 1.10 summarizes these rules of operator precedence. This table will be expanded as additional Java operators are introduced. A complete precedence chart is included in the appendices.

Now let us consider several expressions in light of the rules of operator precedence. Each example lists an algebraic expression and its Java equivalent.

The following is an example of an arithmetic mean (average) of five terms:

Algebra: $m = \dfrac{a + b + c + d + e}{5}$

Java: **`m = (a + b + c + d + e) / 5;`**

The parentheses are required because division has higher precedence than addition. The entire quantity **`(a + b + c + d + e)`** is to be divided by **`5`**. If the parentheses are erroneously omitted, we obtain **`a + b + c + d + e / 5`** which evaluates as

$$a + b + c + d + \frac{e}{5}$$

Operator(s)	Operation(s)	Order of evaluation (precedence)
`( )`	Parentheses	Evaluated first. If the parentheses are nested, the expression in the innermost pair is evaluated first. If there are several pairs of parentheses "on the same level" (i.e., not nested), they are evaluated left to right.
`*, /, or %`	Multiplication Division Modulus	Evaluated second. If there are several, they are evaluated left to right.
`+ or -`	Addition Subtraction	Evaluated last. If there are several, they are evaluated left to right.

Fig. 1.10 Precedence of arithmetic operators.

The following is an example of the equation of a straight line:

Algebra: $y = mx + b$

Java: `y = m * x + b;`

No parentheses are required. The multiplication is applied first because multiplication has a higher precedence than addition. The assignment occurs last because it has a lower precedence that multiplication and division.

The following example contains modulus (%), multiplication, division, addition, and subtraction operations:

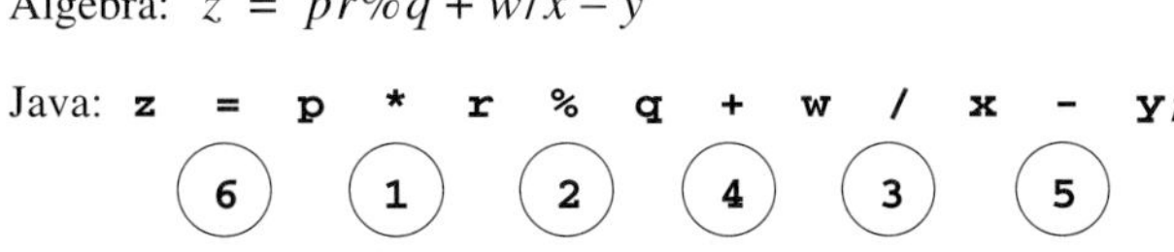

The circled numbers under the statement indicate the order in which Java applies the operators. The multiplication, modulus, and division are evaluated first in left-to-right order (i.e., they associate from left to right) since they have higher precedence than addition and subtraction. The addition and subtraction are applied next. These are also applied left to right.

Not all expressions with several pairs of parentheses contain nested parentheses. For example, the expression

```
a * (b + c) + c * (d + e)
```

does not contain nested parentheses. Rather, the parentheses are said to be "on the same level."

To develop a better understanding of the rules of operator precedence, consider how a second-degree polynomial is evaluated.

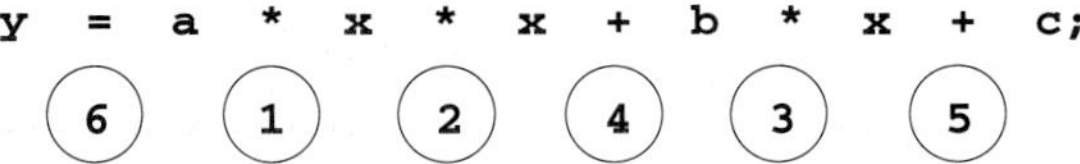

The circled numbers under the statement indicate the order in which Java applies the operators. There is no arithmetic operator for exponentiation in Java, so we have represented x^2 as **x * x**.

Suppose **a**, **b**, **c**, and **x** are initialized as follows: **a = 2**, **b = 3**, **c = 7**, and **x = 5**. Figure 1.11 illustrates the order in which the operators are applied in the preceding second-degree polynomial.

As in algebra, it is acceptable to place unnecessary parentheses in an expression to make the expression clearer. These unnecessary parentheses are also called *redundant parentheses*. For example, the preceding assignment statement might be parenthesized as

```
y = (a * x * x) + (b * x) + c;
```

Step 1. **`y = 2 * 5 * 5 + 3 * 5 + 7;`**

`2 * 5 is 10` (Leftmost multiplication)

Step 2. **`y = 10 * 5 + 3 * 5 + 7;`**

`10 * 5 is 50` (Leftmost multiplication)

Step 3. **`y = 50 + 3 * 5 + 7;`**

`3 * 5 is 15` (Multiplication before addition)

Step 4. **`y = 50 + 15 + 7;`**

`50 + 15 is 65` (Leftmost addition)

Step 5. **`y = 65 + 7;`**

`65 + 7 is 72` (Last addition)

Step 6. **`y = 72;`** (Last operation—assignment)

Fig. 1.11 Order in which a second-degree polynomial is evaluated.

1.20 Decision Making: Equality and Relational Operators

This section introduces a simple version of Java's **`if`** *structure* that allows a program to make a decision based on the truth or falsity of some *condition.* If the condition is met, i.e., the condition is *true,* the statement in the body of the **`if`** structure is executed. If the condition is not met, i.e., the condition is *false,* the body statement is not executed. We will see an example shortly.

Conditions in **`if`** structures can be formed by using the *equality operators* and *relational operators* summarized in Fig. 1.12. The relational operators all have the same level of precedence and associate left to right. The equality operators both have the same level of precedence, which is lower than the precedence of the relational operators. The equality operators also associate left to right.

Common Programming Error 1.8

It is a syntax error if the operators **`==`**, **`!=`**, **`>=`**, *and* **`<=`** *contain spaces between their symbols as in* **`= =`**, **`! =`**, **`> =`** *and* **`< =`**, *respectively.*

Standard algebraic equality operator or relational operator	Java equality or relational operator	Example of Java condition	Meaning of Java condition
Equality operators			
=	`==`	`x == y`	`x` is equal to `y`
≠	`!=`	`x != y`	`x` is not equal to `y`
Relational operators			
>	`>`	`x > y`	`x` is greater than `y`
<	`<`	`x < y`	`x` is less than `y`
≥	`>=`	`x >= y`	`x` is greater than or equal to `y`
≤	`<=`	`x <= y`	`x` is less than or equal to `y`

Fig. 1.12 Equality and relational operators.

Common Programming Error 1.9

Reversing the operators **!=**, **>=**, *and* **<=** *as in* **=!**, **=>**, *and* **=<**, *are each syntax errors.*

Common Programming Error 1.10

Confusing the equality operator **==** *with the assignment operator* **=**. *The equality operator should be read "is equal to" and the assignment operator should be read "gets" or "gets the value of." Some people prefer to read the equality operator as "double equals" or "equals equals."*

The following example uses six **if** statements to compare two numbers input into text fields by the user. If the condition in any of these **if** statements is satisfied, the **drawString** statement associated with that **if** is executed. When the user presses the *Enter* key (or *Return* key) in the second **TextField**, the numbers are read into variables **number1** and **number2**. The comparisons are performed in the **paint** method. The program consists of three methods—**init** to create the graphical user interface, **paint** to display the results of the comparisons, and **actionPerformed** to read the values from the **TextField**s when the user presses *Enter* while typing in the second **TextField**. The program and four sample outputs are shown in Fig. 1.13.

The definition of applet class **Comparison** begins at lines 7 and 8

```
public class Comparison extends Applet
                  implements ActionListener {
```

indicating that the class **extends Applet** and **implements ActionListener**. As we discussed in the program of Fig. 1.6, **implements ActionListener** specifies that this class must provide a definition of method **actionPerformed** to process action events. Lines 9 through 13

```
// Using if statements, relational
// operators, and equality operators
import java.applet.Applet;
import java.awt.*;
import java.awt.event.*;

public class Comparison extends Applet
             implements ActionListener {
   Label prompt1;      // prompt user to input first value
   TextField input1;   // input first value here
   Label prompt2;      // prompt user to input second value
   TextField input2;   // input second value here
   int number1, number2;  // store input values

   // setup the graphical user interface components
   // and initialize variables
   public void init()
   {
      prompt1 = new Label( "Enter an integer" );
      add( prompt1 );  // put prompt1 on applet

      input1 = new TextField( 10 );
      add( input1 );   // put input1 on applet

      prompt2 =
         new Label( "Enter an integer and press Enter" );
      add( prompt2 );  // put prompt2 on applet

      input2 = new TextField( 10 );
      input2.addActionListener( this );
      add( input2 );   // put input2 on applet
   }

   // display the results
   public void paint( Graphics g )
   {
      g.drawString( "The comparison results are:", 70, 75 );

      if ( number1 == number2 )
         g.drawString( number1 + " == " + number2, 100, 90 );

      if ( number1 != number2 )
         g.drawString( number1 + " != " + number2, 100, 105 );

      if ( number1 < number2 )
         g.drawString( number1 + " < " + number2, 100, 120 );

      if ( number1 > number2 )
         g.drawString( number1 + " > " + number2, 100, 135 );

```

Fig. 1.13 Using equality and relational operators (part 1 of 4).

```
51         if ( number1 <= number2 )
52            g.drawString( number1 + " <= " + number2, 100, 150 );
53
54         if ( number1 >= number2 )
55            g.drawString( number1 + " >= " + number2, 100, 165 );
56      }
57
58      // process user's action on the input2 text field
59      public void actionPerformed( ActionEvent e )
60      {
61         number1 = Integer.parseInt( input1.getText() );
62         number2 = Integer.parseInt( input2.getText() );
63         repaint();
64      }
65   }
```

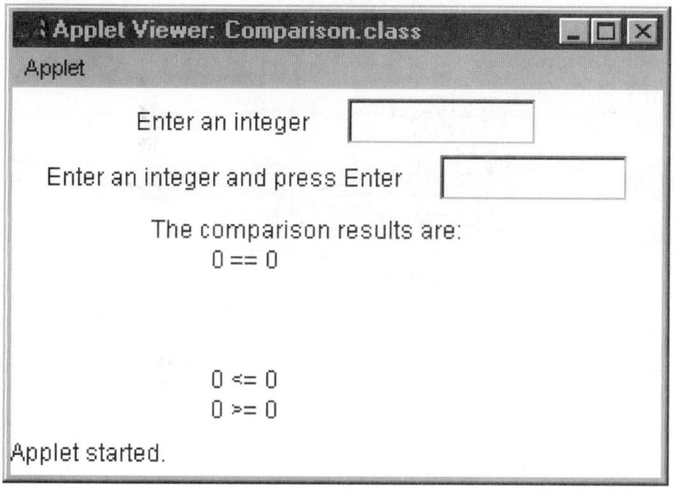

Applet Viewer: Comparison.class
Applet
Enter an integer
Enter an integer and press Enter
The comparison results are:
0 == 0
0 <= 0
0 >= 0
Applet started.

Fig. 1.13 Using equality and relational operators (part 2 of 4).

```
Label prompt1;       // prompt user to input first value
TextField input1;    // input first value here
Label prompt2;       // prompt user to input second value
TextField input2;    // input second value here
int number1, number2;  // store input values
```

declare the instance variables for this class. Note that there are two separate declarations for **Label**s and two separate declarations for **TextField**s. Variables or references of the same type may be declared in one declaration or in multiple declarations. If more than one name is declared in a declaration, the names are separated by *commas* (**,**). This is referred to as a *comma-separated list* (as shown in the **int** declaration above).

Method **init** creates each of the **Label** and **TextField** objects and uses method **add** to attach the GUI components to the applet. Line 30

```
input2.addActionListener( this );
```

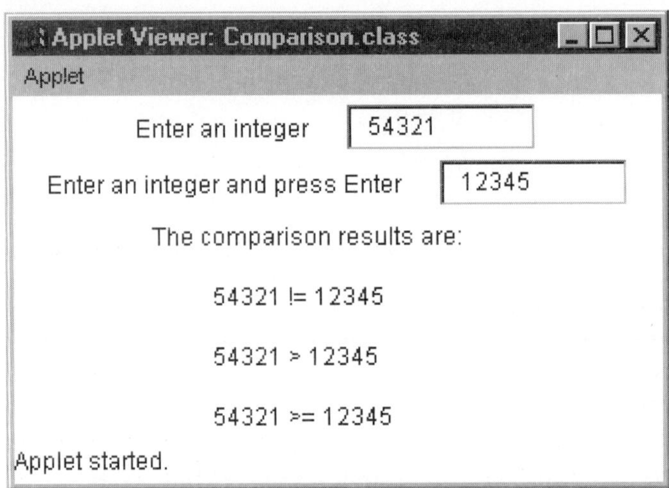

Fig. 1.13 Using equality and relational operators (part 3 of 4).

specifies that **`this`** applet should *listen* for events from **`TextField input2`**. When you type a number from the keyboard into **`TextField input2`** in this program and press the *Enter* key (or *Return* key), an event is sent to the applet indicating that the user pressed the *Enter* key while typing in **`TextField input2`**. This indicates to the applet that *an action was performed* by you in **`TextField input`** and automatically calls method **`actionPerformed`** (line 59) to process the user's interaction. Note that the program in Fig. 1.13 uses two separate **`TextField`** objects to input two integers. When the user presses the *Enter* key in the *second* **`TextField`**, method **`actionPerformed`** is called.

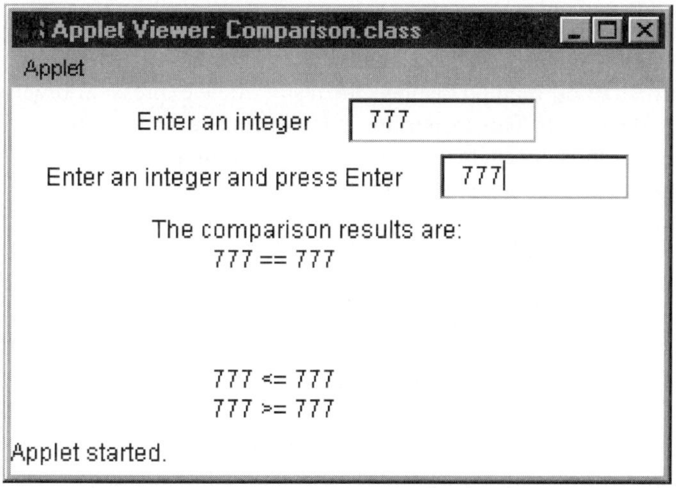

Applet Viewer: Comparison.class
Applet
Enter an integer 777
Enter an integer and press Enter 777
The comparison results are:
777 == 777
777 <= 777
777 >= 777
Applet started.

Fig. 1.13 Using equality and relational operators (part 4 of 4).

Lines 61 and 62

```
number1 = Integer.parseInt( input1.getText() );
number2 = Integer.parseInt( input2.getText() );
```

read the text entered by the user in the **TextField**s **input1** and **input2**, convert the text into integers and store the values in variables **number1** and **number2**. Method **getText** of class **TextField** is used to read the text from each **TextField**. When **input1.getText()** is executed, the text from **TextField input1** is retrieved. Similarly, when **input2.getText()** is executed, the text from the **TextField input2** is retrieved.

In the first two programs, we used method **paint** to display information on the screen. Remember that the **paint** method is special in that it is automatically called at least once for you when the applet executes (**paint** can be called again if the applet is covered with another window then uncovered). However, in this example we want to display different information on the screen each time the user enters new values into the **TextFields** and presses the *Enter* key in **TextField input2**. Line 63

```
repaint();
```

results in a call to the **paint** method. The **repaint** method is one of the many methods inherited when we define our **Comparison** class to extend class **Applet**. When called, **repaint** first invokes (calls) another inherited method called **update**. Method **update** erases any information on the applet that was displayed previously with **paint**, then calls **paint** again for you.

The **if** structure from line 39 in **paint**

```
if ( number1 == number2 )
   g.drawString( number1 + " == " + number2, 100, 90 );
```

compares the values of the variables **number1** and **number2** for equality. If they are equal, the **drawString** method displays the result of the expression **number1 + " == " + number2** on the screen. This expression is interesting because it concatenates an integer with a string literal, then concatenates another integer with the result of the first concatenation. Java has a version of the **+** operator that enables a string and a value of another data type (including another string) to be concatenated—the result of this operation is always a new string. If we assume **number1** and **number2** both have the value 1000, the expression evaluates as follows: First **number1** is converted to a string and concatenated with the string **" == "** which results in the string **"1000 == "**. Next, **number2** is converted to a string and concatenated with **"1000 == "** which results in the string **"1000 == 1000"**. This string is displayed on the screen. Note that the automatic conversion of integers **number1** and **number2** only occurs because they are concatenated with the string literal **" == "**. String concatenation is discussed in detail in Chapter 8, "Strings and Characters."

Common Programming Error 1.11

*Confusing the **+** operator used for string concatenation with the **+** operator used for addition can lead to strange results. For example, assuming **y** has the value **5**, the Java statement **g.drawString("y + 2 = " + y + 2, 30, 30);** displays **y + 2 = 52** not **y + 2 = 7** because the value of **y** gets concatenated with the **2** instead of added to it.*

Common Programming Error 1.12

*Adding values with the **+** operator for display on the screen with the **drawString** method when none of the values is a string results in a syntax error. To automatically convert values of other types to strings, at least one operand of the **+** operator must be a string.*

Common Programming Error 1.13

*Replacing **==** in the condition of an **if** structure such as **if (x == 1)** with **=** as in **if (x = 1)** is a syntax error.*

Notice the indentation in the **if** statements throughout the program. Such indentation enhances program readability.

Good Programming Practice 1.12

*Indent the statement in the body of an **if** structure to make the body of the structure stand out and to enhance program readability.*

Good Programming Practice 1.13

There should be no more than one statement per line in a program.

Common Programming Error 1.14

*Placing a semicolon immediately after the right parenthesis after the condition in an **if** structure is normally a logic error. The semicolon would cause the body of the **if** structure to be empty, so the **if** structure itself would perform no action regardless of whether or not its condition is true. Worse yet, the intended body statement of the **if** structure would now become a statement in sequence with the **if** structure and would always be executed.*

Notice the use of spacing in Fig. 1.13. In Java statements, *white space* characters such as tabs, newlines, and spaces are normally ignored by the compiler. So, statements may be split over several lines and may be spaced according to the programmer's preferences without affecting the meaning of a program. It is incorrect to split identifiers and string literals. Ideally, statements should be kept small, but it is not always possible to do so.

Good Programming Practice 1.14

A lengthy statement may be spread over several lines. If a single statement must be split across lines, choose breaking points that make sense such as after a comma in a comma-separated list, or after an operator in a lengthy expression. If a statement is split across two or more lines, indent all subsequent lines.

The chart in Fig. 1.14 shows the precedence of the operators introduced in this chapter. The operators are shown top to bottom in decreasing order of precedence. Notice that all these operators, with the exception of the assignment operator **=**, associate from left to right. Addition is left associative, so an expression like **x + y + z** is evaluated as if it had been written **(x + y) + z**. The assignment operator **=** associates from right to left, so an expression like **x = y = 0** is evaluated as if it had been written **x = (y = 0)** which, as we will soon see, first assigns the value **0** to variable **y** and then assigns the result of that assignment—**0**—to **x**.

Good Programming Practice 1.15

Refer to the operator precedence chart when writing expressions containing many operators. Confirm that the operators in the expression are performed in the order you expect. If you are uncertain about the order of evaluation in a complex expression, use parentheses to force the order, exactly as you would do in algebraic expressions. Be sure to observe that some operators such as assignment (=) associate right to left rather than left to right.

We have introduced many important features of Java including printing data on the screen, inputting data from the keyboard, performing calculations, and making decisions. In Chapter 2, we build on these techniques as we introduce *structured programming.* You will become more familiar with indentation techniques. We will study how to specify and vary the order in which statements are executed—this order is called *flow of control.*

Operators	Associativity	Type
()	left to right	parentheses
*** / %**	left to right	multiplicative
+ -	left to right	additive
< <= > >=	left to right	relationals
== !=	left to right	equalities
=	right to left	assignment

Fig. 1.14 Precedence and associativity of the operators discussed so far.

Summary

- The various devices (such as the keyboard, screen, disks, memory, and processing units) that comprise a computer system are referred to as hardware.
- The computer programs that run on a computer are referred to as software.
- Operating systems are software systems that make it more convenient to use computers and to get the best performance from computers.
- With distributed computing, an organization's computing is distributed via networking to the sites where the real work of the organization is performed.
- File servers store programs and data that may be shared by client computers distributed throughout the network, hence the term client/server computing.
- Any computer can directly understand only its own machine language.
- Machine languages generally consist of strings of numbers (ultimately reduced to 1s and 0s) that instruct computers to perform their most elementary operations one at a time. Machine languages are machine dependent.
- English-like abbreviations form the basis of assembly languages. Assemblers translate assembly-language programs into machine language.
- Compilers translate high-level language programs into machine-language programs. High-level languages contain English words and conventional mathematical notations.
- Interpreter programs directly execute high-level language programs without the need for compiling those programs into machine language. An advantage of interpreted programs is that they can begin executing without the delay associated with compilation.
- Although compiled programs execute faster than interpreted programs, interpreters are popular in program-development environments in which programs are recompiled frequently as new features are added and errors are corrected. Once a program is developed, a compiled version can then be produced to run most efficiently.
- Structured programming is a disciplined approach to writing programs that are clearer than unstructured programs, easier to test and debug, and easier to modify.
- Java systems consist of the environment, the language, and the class libraries.
- Errors like division-by-zero errors occur as a program runs, so these errors are called run-time errors or execution-time errors.
- Fatal errors cause programs to terminate immediately without successful completion. Nonfatal errors allow programs to run to completion, often producing incorrect results.
- Objects are essentially reusable software components that model items in the real world.
- An applet is a program that runs in a World Wide Web browser like Netscape's Navigator, Microsoft's Internet Explorer or Sun's HotJava.
- Comments are used to *document* programs and improve program readability. Comments do not cause the computer to perform any action when the program is run. Comments are ignored by the Java compiler.

- A comment that begins with `//` is called a single-line comment because the comment terminates at the end of the current line.
- Java contains predefined pieces called classes that are grouped into categories of related classes called packages. The packages together are referred to as the Java class library or the Java applications programming interface (Java API).
- The **`import`** statement specifies where to locate classes required to compile a Java program and enables the programmer to use the shorthand name of each class imported.
- The **`Graphics`** class enables the program to draw graphics such as lines, rectangles, ovals and strings of characters on the screen.
- All Java applets must inherit from the **`Applet`** class.
- Classes are used to instantiate objects in memory for use in a program. An object is a region in the computer's memory in which information is stored for use by the program.
- The applet's class name is used as part of the file name (which must end with **`.java`**).
- The left brace, **`{`**, begins the body of every class definition. A corresponding right brace, **`}`**, must end each class definition.
- The **`paint`** method is called automatically and is used to display information.
- Return type **`void`** indicates that a method returns nothing when it completes its task.
- The parameter list is where a method receives information required to complete its task.
- The left brace, **`{`**, begins every method definition's body. A corresponding right brace, **`}`**, must end each method definition's body.
- A string is sometimes called a character string, a message, or a literal.
- Every statement must end with a semicolon (the statement terminator).
- Coordinates are measured from the upper-left corner (x-coordinate 0 and y-coordinate 0) of the applet in pixels. Most drawing methods from the **`Graphics`** class require at least one set of coordinates to specify where to draw on the applet.
- It is necessary to create an HTML (Hypertext Markup Language) file to load an applet into a browser to execute.
- Every class is compiled into a separate file that has the same name as the class and ends with the **`.class`** extension.
- The HTML **`applet`** tag invokes a Java applet. The applet tag must specify the **`.class`** file for the applet and the **`width`** and the **`height`** of the applet in pixels.
- The **`appletviewer`** is a program that tests Java applets. The **`appletviewer`** requires an HTML file to load an applet.
- Graphical User Interface (GUI) components can be added to your programs to facilitate data entry and data output.
- A variable is defined by a primitive (or built-in) data type such as **`int`**. Every piece of data in a Java program is an object except for variables of the primitive types.

- An interface specifies one or more capabilities that you must define in your class definition. The interface **ActionListener** specifies that a class must define a method with the first line

```
public void actionPerformed( ActionEvent e )
```

- When the user interacts with a GUI component, the program is notified of the event and the program processes the event. The user's interaction with the GUI "drives" the program. This is known as event-driven programming.
- The methods that are called when an event occurs are also known as event-handling methods. Before any event can be processed, each GUI component knows where the event-handling method is defined that will be called when an event occurs.
- **TextField**s are used to get information from the user at the keyboard or display information on the screen.
- A **Label** contains a string literal to display on the screen. Normally, a label is associated with another graphical user interface component.
- All variables and references must be declared with a name and a type before they can be used in a program.
- An identifier is a series of characters consisting of letters, digits, underscores (_), and dollar signs (**$**) that does not begin with a digit. Java allows identifiers of any length. Java is case sensitive—uppercase and lowercase letters are different.
- The declaration of a variable in a method definition must appear before the variable is used in the method.
- The **init** method is supplied in an applet to initialize variables and references in the applet. The **init** method is automatically called for you when the applet begins executing.
- Applets always begin with a series of three method calls—**init**, **start**, and **paint**. If you do not define any one (or more) of these three methods, you get a "free" version of that method from the **Applet** class that does nothing.
- A prompt tells the user to take a specific action.
- The assignment **=** operator is called a binary operator because it has two operands.
- The **add** method is used to place GUI components on an applet.
- Variables of primitive data types are not created with the **new** operator. Only class type objects must be allocated dynamically with **new**.
- An interaction between a user and a GUI component generates an event.
- Processing user interactions with GUI components is referred to as event-driven programming.
- The **actionPerformed** method is called when the user presses the *Enter* key while typing in a **TextField**. Note that the **TextField** must be told where **actionPerformed** is defined using method **addActionListener** first.

- The **ActionEvent** argument of method **actionPerformed** contains information about the action event that occurred.
- For a **TextField** action event, **ActionEvent** method **getActionCommand** returns a string containing the text the user typed in the **TextField**.
- A **String** is an object that can store a string literal.
- The **Integer.parseInt** method converts its **String** argument to an integer.
- The **setText** method of the **TextField** class places text in the specified text field.
- Most calculations are performed in assignment statements.
- The status bar is located at the bottom of the **appletviewer** or browser window.
- The **Applet** class's **showStatus** method puts a **String** in the status bar.
- Every variable has a name, a type, a size and a value.
- Whenever a value is placed in a memory location, this new value replaces the previous value in that location. The previous value is destroyed.
- When a value is read out of a memory location, the process is nondestructive.
- The arithmetic operators presented in this chapter are all binary operators.
- Integer division yields an integer result.
- The modulus operator, **%**, yields the remainder after integer division.
- Java applies the operators in arithmetic expressions in a precise sequence determined by the rules of operator precedence. Parentheses may be used to force the order of evaluation to occur in any sequence.
- The **if** structure allows a program to make a decision based on the truth or falsity of some condition. If the condition is true, the statement in the body of the **if** structure is executed. If the condition is false, the body statement is not executed.
- Conditions in **if** structures can be formed by using the equality and relational operators.
- The **getText** method of the **TextField** class reads the text from a text field.
- The **repaint** method calls the **update** method which erases any information on the applet, then calls **paint**.
- Java has a special version of the **+** operator that enables a string and a value of another data type (including another string) to be added together to produce a new string. The process of adding strings to other strings is called string concatenation.
- White space characters such as tabs, newlines, and spaces are normally ignored by the compiler. Statements may be split over several lines and may be spaced according to the programmer's preferences. It is incorrect to split identifiers and string literals.

Terminology

action event
ActionEvent class
actionPerformed method
add method

addActionListener method
ANSI C
applet
Applet class
appletviewer
application
arithmetic and logic unit (ALU)
arithmetic operators
assembly language
assignment operator (**=**)
associativity of operators
base class
binary operators
body of a method
bytecodes
C
C standard library
C++
C++ class libraries
case sensitive
central processing unit (CPU)
character string
class
.class file extension
class keyword
client/server computing
comment (**//**)
compile error
compiler
computer
computer program
condition
CPU
decision
declaration
derived class
distributed computing
drawString method
editor
equality operators
  == "is equal to"
  != "is not equal to"
execution-time error
extends keyword
fatal error
file server
flow of control
getText method
Graphics class
hardware
high-level language
HTML (Hypertext Markup Language)
identifier
if structure
import statement
inheritance
input device
input/output (I/O)
int primitive type
integer (**int**)
Integer class
integer division
interface
interpreter
Java
Java Developer's Kit (JDK)
.java file extension
Java Virtual Machine
Label class
logic error
machine dependent
machine independent
machine language
memory
memory location
message
method
Microsoft Internet Explorer browser
modulus operator (**%**)
multiplication operator (*****)
multiprocessor
multiprogramming
multitasking
multithreading
Netscape Navigator browser
nested parentheses
nonfatal error
object
object-oriented design (OOD)
object-oriented programming (OOP)
operand
operator
output device
paint method
parentheses **()**
parseInt method

precedence
primary memory
procedural programming
programming language
public keyword
reference
relational operators
> "is greater than"
< "is less than"
>= "is greater than or equal to"
<= "is less than or equal to"
repaint method
reserved words
right-to-left associativity
rules of operator precedence
run-time error
semicolon (**;**) statement terminator
software
statement
statement terminator (**;**)
string
structured programming
Sun Hotjava browser
syntax error
Textfield class
update method
variable
variable name
variable value
void keyword
white-space characters
World Wide Web

Common Programming Errors

1.1 Errors like division-by-zero errors occur as a program runs, so these errors are called run-time errors or execution-time errors. Fatal run-time errors cause programs to terminate immediately without having successfully performed their jobs. Nonfatal run-time errors allow programs to run to completion, often producing incorrect results.

1.2 It is an error if the file name is not identical in both spelling and capitalization to the class name with the **.java** file name extension.

1.3 It is an error not to end a Java file name with the **.java** extension.

1.4 Omitting the semicolon at the end of a statement is a syntax error. A syntax error is caused when the compiler cannot recognize a statement. The compiler normally issues an error message to help the programmer locate and fix the incorrect statement. Syntax errors are violations of the language. Syntax errors are also called compile errors, compile-time errors, or compilation errors because they appear during the compilation phase.

1.5 Running the **appletviewer** with a file name that does not end with **.html** is an error that prevents the **appletviewer** from loading your applet for execution.

1.6 If braces do not occur in matching pairs it is a syntax error.

1.7 Attempting to use the modulus operator, **%**, with noninteger operands is a syntax error.

1.8 It is a syntax error if the operators **==**, **!=**, **>=**, and **<=** contain spaces between their symbols as in **= =**, **! =**, **> =** and **< =**, respectively.

1.9 Reversing the operators **!=**, **>=**, and **<=** as in **=!**, **=>**, and **=<**, are each syntax errors.

1.10 Confusing the equality operator **==** with the assignment operator **=**. The equality operator should be read "is equal to" and the assignment operator should be read "gets" or "gets the value of." Some people prefer to read the equality operator as "double equals" or "equals equals."

1.11 Confusing the **+** operator used for string concatenation with the **+** operator used for addition can lead to strange results. For example, assuming **y** has the value **5**, the Java statement **g.drawString("y + 2 = " + y + 2, 30, 30);** displays **y + 2 = 52** not **y + 2 = 7** because the value of **y** gets concatenated with the **2** instead of added to it.

1.12 Adding values with the **+** operator for display on the screen with the **drawString** method when none of the values is a string results in a syntax error. To automatically convert values of other types to strings, at least one operand of the **+** operator must be a string.

1.13 Replacing **==** in the condition of an **if** structure such as **if (x == 1)** with **=** as in **if (x = 1)** is a syntax error.

1.14 Placing a semicolon immediately after the right parenthesis after the condition in an **if** structure is normally a logic error. The semicolon would cause the body of the **if** structure to be empty, so the **if** structure itself would perform no action regardless of whether or not its condition is true. Worse yet, the intended body statement of the **if** structure would now become a statement in sequence with the **if** structure and would always be executed.

Good Programming Practices

1.1 Write your Java programs in a simple and straightforward manner. This is sometimes referred to as KIS ("keep it simple"). Do not "stretch" the language by trying bizarre usages.

1.2 Read the documentation for the version of Java you are using. Refer to this documentation frequently to be sure you are aware of the rich collection of Java features and that you are using these features correctly.

1.3 Your computer and compiler are good teachers. If after carefully reading your Java documentation manual you are not sure how a feature of Java works, experiment and see what happens. Study each error or warning message you get when you compile your programs and correct the programs to eliminate these messages.

1.4 Every program should begin with a comment describing the purpose of the program.

1.5 Investigate the capabilities of any class in the Java API documentation carefully before inheriting a subclass from it. This helps ensure that the programmer does not redefine a capability that is already provided.

1.6 Place a space after each comma (**,**) in a statement to make programs more readable.

1.7 Indent the entire body of each method one level of indentation within the braces that define the body of the method. This makes the structure of a program stand out and helps make programs easier to read.

1.8 Set a convention for the size of indent you prefer and then uniformly apply that convention. The tab key may be used to create indents, but tab stops may vary among users' computers. We recommend using either 1/4-inch tab stops or (preferably) three spaces to form a level of indent.

1.9 Whenever you type an opening left brace, **{**, in your program, immediately type the closing right brace, **}**. This helps prevent missing braces.

1.10 Choosing meaningful variable names helps a program to be "self-documenting," i.e., it becomes easier to understand a program simply by reading it rather than having to read manuals or use excessive comments.

1.11 Place spaces on either side of a binary operator. This makes the operator stand out and makes the program more readable.

1.12 Indent the statement in the body of an `if` structure to make the body of the structure stand out and to enhance program readability.

1.13 There should be no more than one statement per line in a program.

1.14 A lengthy statement may be spread over several lines. If a single statement must be split across lines, choose breaking points that make sense such as after a comma in a comma-separated list, or after an operator in a lengthy expression. If a statement is split across two or more lines, indent all subsequent lines.

1.15 Refer to the operator precedence chart when writing expressions containing many operators. Confirm that the operators in the expression are performed in the order you expect. If you are uncertain about the order of evaluation in a complex expression, use parentheses to force the order, exactly as you would do in algebraic expressions. Be sure to observe that some operators such as assignment (`=`) associate right to left rather than left to right.

Performance Tips

1.1 Using library classes instead of writing your own versions can improve program performance because these classes are carefully written to perform efficiently.

1.2 Actually, interpreters have one huge advantage over compilers for the Java world, namely that an interpreted program can begin execution immediately as soon as it is downloaded to the client's machine, whereas a source program to be compiled must first suffer a potentially long delay as the program is compiled before it can be executed.

Portability Tips

1.1 Using library classes instead of writing your own versions can improve program portability because these classes are included in virtually all Java implementations.

1.2 Although it is easier to write portable programs in Java than in most other programming languages, there are differences among compilers, interpreters and computers that can make portability difficult to achieve. Simply writing programs in Java does not guarantee portability in all cases. The programmer will occasionally need to deal directly with compiler and computer variations.

1.3 Always execute your applets in every browser that people who view your applet use. This will help ensure people who view your applet experience the functionality you expect.

Software Engineering Observations

1.1 Use a building block approach to creating programs. Avoid reinventing the wheel. Use existing pieces—this is called software reuse and it is central to object-oriented programming.

1.2 When programming in Java you will typically use the following building blocks: classes from class libraries, classes you create yourself, and classes other people create and make available to you.

1.3 Extensive class libraries of reusable software components are available over the Internet in general and the World Wide Web in particular. Many of these libraries are available at no charge.

Self-Review Exercises

1.1 Fill in the blanks in each of the following:

a) The company that popularized personal computing was ________.
b) The computer that made personal computing legitimate in business and industry was the ________.
c) Computers process data under the control of sets of instructions called ________.
d) The six key logical units of the computer are the ________, ________, ________, ________, ________, and the ________.
e) The three classes of languages discussed in the chapter are ________, ________, and ________.
f) The programs that translate high-level language programs into machine language are called ________.
g) The ________ language was developed by Wirth for teaching structured programming in universities.
h) The Department of Defense developed the Ada language with a capability called ________ which allows programmers to specify that many activities can proceed in parallel.

1.2 Fill in the blanks in each of the following sentences about the Java environment.

a) The ________ command from the Java Developer's Kit executes a Java applet.
b) The ________ command from the Java Developer's Kit executes a Java application
c) The ________ command from the Java Developer's Kit compiles a Java program.
d) An ________ file is required to invoke a Java applet.
e) A Java program file must end with the ________ file extension.
f) When a Java program is compiled, the file produced by the compiler ends with the ________ file extension.
g) The file produced by the Java compiler contains ________ that are interpreted to execute a Java applet or application.

1.3 Fill in the blanks in each of the following.

a) The ________ begins the body of every method and the ________ ends the body of every method.
b) Every statement ends with a ________.
c) The ________ structure is used to make decisions.

1.4 State whether each of the following is true or false. If false, explain why.

a) Comments cause the computer to print the text after the **//** on the screen when the program is executed.
b) All variables must be given a type when they are declared.
c) Java considers the variables **number** and **NuMbEr** to be identical.

d) The modulus operator (**%**) can be used only with integer operands.
e) The arithmetic operators *****, **/**, **%**, **+**, and **-** all have the same level of precedence.

1.5 Write Java statements to accomplish each of the following:
a) Declare the variables **c**, **thisIsAVariable**, **q76354**, and **number** to be of type **int**.
b) Prompt the user to enter an integer. Hint: Declare a **Label** reference, create a **Label object**, and specify how to place the **Label** on the applet.
c) Read an integer from the keyboard and store the value entered in integer variable **age**. Assume that the **TextField** called **input** exists and that the **ActionEvent** argument **e** in method **actionPerformed** contains the information about the event that occurred.
d) If the variable **number** is not equal to **7**, display **"The variable number is not equal to 7"** at x-coordinate 10 and y-coordinate 10 from the **paint** method. Assume **Graphics** object **g** as the argument to the **paint** method.
e) Print the message **"This is a Java program"** on one line from the **paint** method. Assume **Graphics** object **g** as the argument to the **paint** method and choose your own coordinates.
f) Print the message **"This is a Java program"** on two lines where the first line ends with **Java**. Assume **Graphics** object **g** as the argument to the **paint** method and choose your own coordinates.

1.6 Identify and correct the errors in each of the following statements:
a)
```
if ( c < 7 );
   g.drawString( "c is less than 7", 25, 25 );
```
b)
```
if ( c => 7 )
   g.drawString( "c is equal to or greater than 7", 25, 25 );
```

Answers to Self-Review Exercises

1.1 a) Apple. b) IBM Personal Computer. c) programs. d) input unit, output unit, memory unit, arithmetic and logic unit, central processing unit, secondary storage unit. e) machine languages, assembly languages, high-level languages. f) compilers. g) Pascal. h) multitasking.

1.2 a) **appletviewer**. b) **java**. c) **javac**. d) HTML. e) **.java**. f) **.class**. g) bytecodes.

1.3 a) Left brace (**{**), right brace (**}**). b) Semicolon. c) **if**.

1.4 a) False. Comments do not cause any action to be performed when the program is executed. They are used to document programs and improve their readability.
b) True.
c) False. Java is case sensitive, so these variables are distinct.
d) True.
e) False. The operators *****, **/**, and **%** are on the same level of precedence, and the operators **+** and **-** are on a lower level of precedence.

1.5 a)
```
int c, thisIsAVariable, q76354, number;
```
b)
```
Label prompt;
prompt = new Label( "Enter an integer" );
add( prompt );
```

c) `age = Integer.parseInt( e.getActionCommand() );`

d)
```
if ( number != 7 )
   g.drawString( "The variable number is not equal to 7.",
                 10, 10 );
```
e) `g.drawString( "This is a Java program", 10, 10 );`

f)
```
g.drawString( "This is a Java", 10, 10 );
g.drawString( "program", 10, 25 );
```

1.6 a) Error: Semicolon after the right parenthesis of the condition in the **`if`** statement. Correction: Remove the semicolon after the right parenthesis. Note: The result of this error is that the output statement will be executed whether or not the condition in the **`if`** statement is true. The semicolon after the right parenthesis is considered an empty statement—a statement that does nothing. We will learn more about the empty statement in the next chapter.

b) Error: The relational operator **=>**. Correction: Change **=>** to **>=**.

Exercises

1.7 Categorize each of the following items as either hardware or software:

a) CPU
b) Java compiler
c) ALU
d) Java interpreter
e) input unit
f) an editor program

1.8 Why might you want to write a program in a machine-independent language instead of a machine-dependent language? Why might a machine-dependent language be more appropriate for writing certain types of programs?

1.9 Fill in the blanks in each of the following statements:

a) Which logical unit of the computer receives information from outside the computer for use by the computer? __________.
b) The process of instructing the computer to solve specific problems is called __________.
c) What type of computer language uses English-like abbreviations for machine-language instructions? __________.
d) Which logical unit of the computer sends information that has already been processed by the computer to various devices so that the information may be used outside the computer? __________.
e) Which logical unit of the computer retains information? __________.
f) Which logical unit of the computer performs calculations? __________.
g) Which logical unit of the computer makes logical decisions? __________.
h) The level of computer language most convenient to the programmer for writing programs quickly and easily is __________.
i) The only language that a computer can directly understand is called that computer's __________.
j) Which logical unit of the computer coordinates the activities of all the other logical units? __________.

1.10 Fill in the blanks in each of the following:

a) __________ are used to document a program and improve its readability.

b) An object of the __________ class is capable of receiving input from the user at the keyboard or displaying information on an applet.
c) A Java statement that makes a decision is __________.
d) Calculations are normally performed by __________ statements.
e) An object of the __________ class is used to display text that is normally associated with another GUI component on an applet.

1.11 Write Java statements that accomplish each of the following:
a) Display the message **"Enter two numbers"** using a **Label**.
b) Assign the product of variables **b** and **c** to variable **a**.
c) State that a program performs a sample payroll calculation (i.e., use text that helps to document a program).

1.12 State which of the following are true and which are false. Explain your answers.
a) Java operators are evaluated from left to right.
b) The following are all valid variable names: **_under_bar_**, **m928134**, **t5**, **j7**, **her_sales$**, **his_$account_total**, **a**, **b$**, **c**, **z**, **z2**.
c) A valid Java arithmetic expression with no parentheses is evaluated from left to right.
d) The following are all invalid variable names: **3g, 87, 67h2, h22, 2h.**

1.13 Fill in the blanks in each of the following:
a) What arithmetic operations are on the same level of precedence as multiplication? __________.
b) When parentheses are nested, which set of parentheses is evaluated first in an arithmetic expression? __________.
c) A location in the computer's memory that may contain different values at various times throughout the execution of a program is called a __________.

1.14 What, if anything, prints when each of the following Java statements is performed? If nothing prints, then answer "nothing." Assume **x = 2** and **y = 3**.
a) `g.drawString( Integer.toString( x ), 25, 25 );`
b) `g.drawString( Integer.toString( x + x ), 25, 25 );`
c) `g.drawString( "x =", 25, 25 );`
d) `g.drawString( "x =" + x, 25, 25 );`
e) `g.drawString( ( x + y ) + " = " + ( y + x ), 25, 25 );`
f) `z = x + y;`

1.15 Which of the following Java statements contain variables whose values are destroyed?
a) `p = i + j + k + 7;`
b)
```
g.drawString( "variables whose values are destroyed",
              25, 25 );
```
c) `g.drawString( "a = 5", 25, 25 );`

1.16 Given $y = ax^3 + 7$, which of the following are correct statements for this equation?
a) `y = a * x * x * x + 7;`
b) `y = a * x * x * (x + 7);`
c) `y = (a * x) * x * (x + 7);`
d) `y = (a * x) * x * x + 7;`
e) `y = a * (x * x * x) + 7;`
f) `y = a * x * (x * x + 7);`

1.17 State the order of evaluation of the operators in each of the following Java statements, and show the value of **x** after each statement is performed.

a) `x = 7 + 3 * 6 / 2 - 1;`

b) `x = 2 % 2 + 2 * 2 - 2 / 2;`

c) `x = (3 * 9 * (3 + (9 * 3/ (3))));`

1.18 Write a Java applet that asks the user to enter two numbers, obtains the two numbers from the user, and prints the sum, product, difference, and quotient of the two numbers. Use the graphical user interface techniques shown in Fig. 1.13.

1.19 Write a Java applet that asks the user to enter two integers, obtains the numbers from the user, and displays the larger number followed by the words "**is larger**" in the status bar of the applet. If the numbers are equal, print the message "**These numbers are equal**." Use the graphical user interface techniques shown in Fig. 1.13.

1.20 Write a Java applet that inputs three integers from the user at the keyboard, and prints the sum, average, product, smallest, and largest of these numbers. Use the GUI techniques shown in Fig. 1.13.

1.21 Write a Java applet that inputs from the user at the keyword the radius of a circle and prints the circle's diameter, circumference, and area. Use the constant value 3.14159 for π. Use the GUI techniques shown in Fig. 1.6.

1.22 Write a Java applet that prints a box, an oval, an arrow, and a diamond using asterisks (*****) as follows:

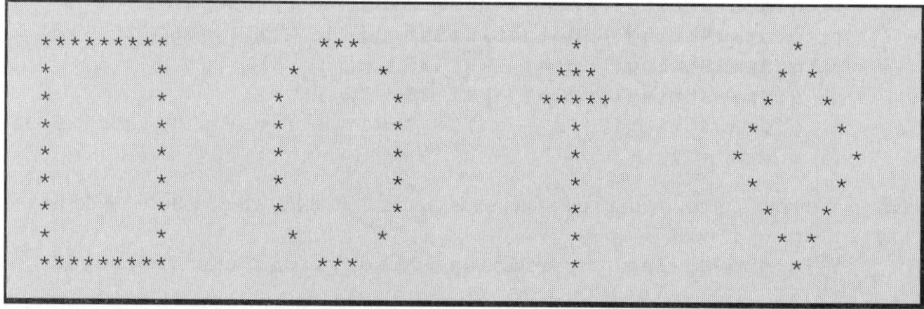

1.23 Here's a peek ahead. Java's **Graphics** class provides many drawing capabilities that will be discussed in detail in Chapter 9, "Graphics." Write a Java applet that uses the following statement to draw a rectangle from the applet's **paint** method.

```
g.drawRect( 10, 10, 50, 50 );
```

The **drawRect** method of the **Graphics** class requires four arguments. The first two are the coordinates of the upper-left corner of the rectangle. The third argument is the width of the rectangle in pixels. The fourth argument is the height of the rectangle in pixels.

1.24 Modify the applet you created in Exercise 1.23 to output a variety of rectangles of different sizes and locations.

1.25 The **Graphics** class contains a **drawOval** method that takes the exact same four arguments as the **drawRect** method. However, the arguments for the **drawOval** method specify the "bounding box" for the oval. The sides of the bounding box are the boundaries of the oval. Write a Java applet that draws an oval and a rectangle with the same four arguments. You will see that the oval touches the rectangle at the center of each side.

1.26 Modify the solution to Exercise 1.25 to output a variety of ovals of different shapes and sizes.

1.27 What does the following code print?

```
g.drawString( "*", 25, 25 );
g.drawString( "***", 25, 55 );
g.drawString( "*****", 25, 85 );
g.drawString( "****", 25, 70 );
g.drawString( "**", 25, 40 );
```

1.28 Write a Java applet that reads integers and determines and prints the largest and the smallest integers in the group. Use only the programming techniques you learned in this chapter.

1.29 Write a Java applet that reads an integer and determines and prints whether it is odd or even. (Hint: Use the modulus operator. An even number is a multiple of two. Any multiple of two leaves a remainder of zero when divided by 2.)

1.30 Write a Java applet that reads in two integers and determines and prints if the first is a multiple of the second. (Hint: Use the modulus operator.)

1.31 Write a Java applet that displays a checkerboard pattern as follows:

1.32 Distinguish between the terms fatal error and nonfatal error. Why might you prefer to experience a fatal error rather than a nonfatal error?

1.33 Here's another peek ahead. In this chapter you learned about integers and the data type **int**. Java can also represent uppercase letters, lowercase letters, and a considerable variety of special symbols. Every character has a corresponding integer representation. The set of characters a computer uses and the corresponding integer representations for those characters is called that computer's character set. You can indicate a character value in a program by simply enclosing that character in single quotes as with **'A'**.

You can determine the integer equivalent of a character by preceding that character with **(int)**—this is called a cast (we will say more about casts in Chapter 2).

```
(int) 'A'
```

The following statement would output a character and its integer equivalent from an applet's **paint** method

```
g.drawString( "The character " + 'A' +
              " has the value " + (int) 'A', 25, 25 );
```

When the preceding statement executes, it displays the character **A** and the value 65 (on systems that use the so-called Unicode character set) as part of the string.

Write a Java applet that prints the integer equivalents of some uppercase letters, lowercase letters, digits and special symbols. At a minimum, determine the integer equivalents of the following: **A B C a b c 0 1 2 $ * + /** and the blank character.

1.34 Write a Java applet that inputs a five-digit number from the user at the keyboard using a **TextField** object, separates the number into its individual digits and prints the digits separated from one another by three spaces each. For example, if the user types in the number **42339**, the program should print

```
4   2   3   3   9
```

1.35 Using only the programming techniques you learned in this chapter, write a Java applet that calculates the squares and cubes of the numbers from 0 to 10 and prints the resulting values in table format as follows:

```
number  square  cube
0       0       0
1       1       1
2       4       8
3       9       27
4       16      64
5       25      125
6       36      216
7       49      343
8       64      512
9       81      729
10      100     1000
```

1.36 Write a Java applet that enables the user to enter four integers representing the upper-left corner coordinates, the width and the height of a rectangle. Use **`Graphics`** method **`drawRect`** (introduced in Exercise 1.23) to draw a rectangle using the values entered by the user. Each time the user enters a new set of values, your applet should redraw the rectangle with the new dimensions. Use the GUI techniques shown in Fig. 1.13.

1.37 Modify your solution to exercise 1.36 to enable the user to choose a rectangle or an oval as the shape to draw. See exercise 1.25 for more information on drawing ovals.

2

Developing Java Applications

Objectives

- To understand basic problem solving techniques.
- To be able to develop algorithms through the process of top-down, stepwise refinement.
- To be able to use the `if` and `if/else` selection structures to choose among alternative actions.
- To be able to use the `while` repetition structure to execute statements in a program repeatedly.
- To understand counter-controlled repetition and sentinel-controlled repetition.
- To be able to use the increment, decrement, and assignment operators.

Let's all move one place on.
Lewis Carroll

The wheel is come full circle.
William Shakespeare, King Lear

How many apples fell on Newton's head before he took the hint!
Robert Frost, Comment

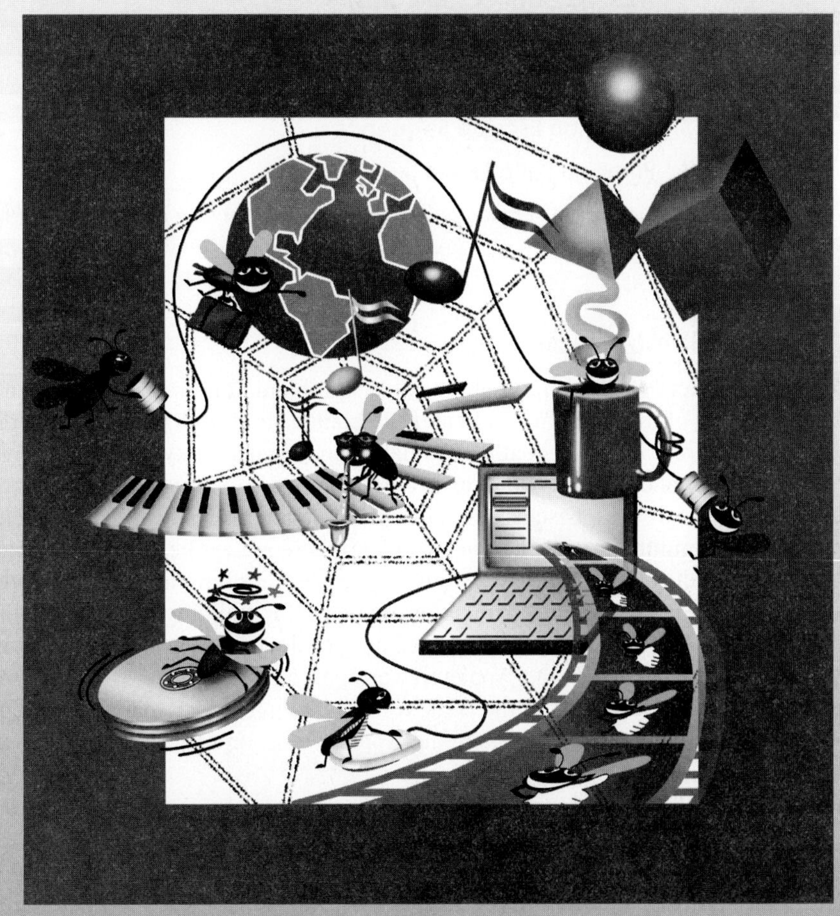

Outline

2.1 Introduction

Before writing a program to solve a problem, it is essential to have a thorough understanding of the problem and a carefully planned approach to solving the problem. When writing a program, it is equally essential to understand the types of building blocks that are available and to employ proven program construction principles. In this chapter and in Chapter 3 we discuss these issues in our presentation of the theory and principles of structured programming. The techniques you learn here are applicable to most high-level languages including Java. When we study object-based programming in more depth in Chapter 6, we will see that control structures are helpful in building and manipulating objects.

In Chapter 1, we presented an introduction to Java programming using applets which are executed in the Appletviewer or in a World Wide Web browser. In this chapter, we present concepts in the context of Java applications. An application is a stand-alone program that does not require the Appletviewer or a World Wide Web browser to execute.

2.2 Algorithms

Any computing problem can be solved by executing a series of actions in a specific order. A *procedure* for solving a problem in terms of

1. the *actions* to be executed, and
2. the *order* in which these actions are to be executed

is called an *algorithm*. The following example demonstrates that correctly specifying the order in which the actions are to be executed is important.

Consider the "rise-and-shine algorithm" followed by one junior executive for getting out of bed and going to work: (1) get out of bed, (2) take off pajamas, (3) take a shower, (4) get dressed, (5) eat breakfast, (6) carpool to work.

This routine gets the executive to work well-prepared to make critical decisions. Suppose, however, that the same steps are performed in a slightly different order: (1) get out of bed, (2) take off pajamas, (3) get dressed, (4) take a shower, (5) eat breakfast, (6) carpool to work.

In this case, our junior executive shows up for work soaking wet. Specifying the order in which statements are to be executed in a computer program is called *program control*. In this chapter and Chapter 3, we investigate the program control capabilities of Java.

2.3 Pseudocode

Pseudocode is an artificial and informal language that helps programmers develop algorithms. The pseudocode we present here is particularly useful for developing algorithms that will be converted to structured portions of Java programs. Pseudocode is similar to everyday English; it is convenient and user-friendly although it is not an actual computer programming language.

Pseudocode programs are not actually executed on computers. Rather, they help the programmer "think out" a program before attempting to write it in a programming language such as Java. In this chapter, we give several examples of pseudocode programs.

The style of pseudocode we present consists purely of characters, so programmers may conveniently type pseudocode programs using an editor program. The computer can produce a fresh printed copy of a pseudocode program on demand. A carefully prepared pseudocode program may be converted easily to a corresponding Java program. This is done in many cases simply by replacing pseudocode statements with their Java equivalents.

Pseudocode consists only of executable statements—those that are executed when the program has been converted from pseudocode to Java and is run. Declarations are not executable statements. For exampie, the declaration

```
int i;
```

tells the compiler the type of variable **i** and instructs the compiler to reserve space in memory for the variable. This declaration does not cause any action—such as input, output, or a calculation—to occur when the program is executed. Some programmers choose to list variables and mention the purpose of each at the beginning of a pseudocode program.

2.4 Control Structures

Normally, statements in a program are executed one after the other in the order in which they are written. This is called *sequential execution*. Various Java statements we will soon discuss enable the programmer to specify that the next statement to be executed may be other than the next one in sequence. This is called *transfer of control.*

During the 1960s, it became clear that the indiscriminate use of transfers of control was the root of much difficulty experienced by software development groups. The finger of blame was pointed at the **`goto`** *statement* that allows the programmer to specify a transfer of control to one of a very wide range of possible destinations in a program. The notion of so-called *structured programming* became almost synonymous with *"**`goto`** elimination."* Java does not have a **`goto`** statement.

The research of Bohm and Jacopini[1] had demonstrated that programs could be written without any **`goto`** statements. The challenge of the era became for programmers to shift their styles to "**`goto`**-less programming." It was not until the 1970s that programmers started taking structured programming seriously. The results have been impressive as software development groups have reported reduced development times, more frequent on-time delivery of systems, and more frequent within-budget completion of software projects. The key to these successes is that structured programs are clearer, easier to debug and modify, and more likely to be bug-free in the first place.

Bohm and Jacopini's work demonstrated that all programs could be written in terms of only three *control structures*, namely the *sequence structure*, the *selection structure*, and the *repetition structure*. The sequence structure is built into Java. Unless directed otherwise, the computer executes Java statements one after the other in the order in which they are written. The *flowchart* segment of Fig. 2.1 illustrates a typical sequence structure in which two calculations are performed in order.

A flowchart is a graphical representation of an algorithm or of a portion of an algorithm. Flowcharts are drawn using certain special-purpose symbols such as rectangles, diamonds, ovals, and small circles; these symbols are connected by arrows called *flowlines* that indicate the order in which the actions of the algorithm execute.

Like pseudocode, flowcharts are often useful for developing and representing algorithms, although pseudocode is strongly preferred by most programmers. Flowcharts show

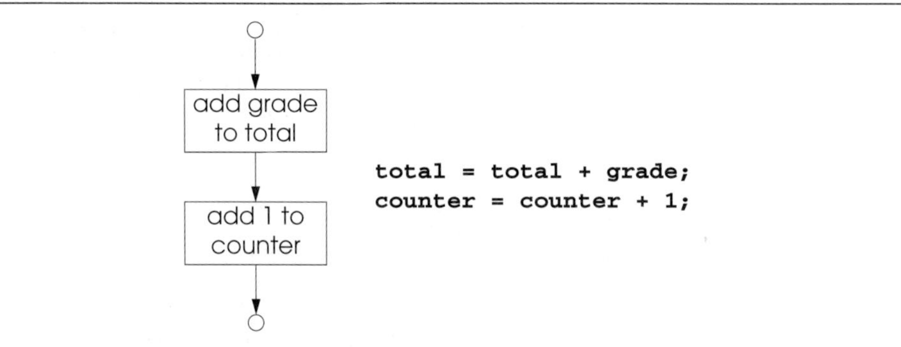

Fig. 2.1 Flowcharting Java's sequence structure.

1. Bohm, C., and G. Jacopini, "Flow Diagrams, Turing Machines, and Languages with Only Two Formation Rules," Communications of the ACM, Vol. 9, No. 5, May 1966, pp. 336–371.

clearly how control structures operate; that is all we use them for in this text. The reader should carefully compare the pseudocode and flowchart representations of each control structure.

Consider the flowchart segment for the sequence structure in Fig. 2.1. We use the *rectangle symbol*, also called the *action symbol,* to indicate any type of action including a calculation or an input/output operation. The flowlines in the figure indicate the order in which the actions are to be performed—first, **grade** is to be added to **total** then **1** is to be added to **counter**. Java allows us to have as many actions as we want in a sequence structure. As we will soon see, anywhere a single action may be placed, we may place several actions in sequence.

When drawing a flowchart that represents a *complete* algorithm, an *oval symbol* containing the word "Begin" is the first symbol used in the flowchart; an oval symbol containing the word "End" indicates where the algorithm ends. When drawing only a portion of an algorithm as in Fig. 2.1, the oval symbols are omitted in favor of using *small circle symbols* also called *connector symbols.*

Perhaps the most important flowcharting symbol is the *diamond symbol*, also called the *decision symbol,* which indicates that a decision is to be made. We will discuss the diamond symbol in the next section.

Java provides three types of selection structures; we discuss each of these in this chapter and Chapter 3. The **if** selection structure either performs (selects) an action if a condition is true or skips the action if the condition is false. The **if/else** selection structure performs an action if a condition is true and performs a different action if the condition is false. The **switch** selection structure (Chapter 3) performs one of many different actions depending on the value of an expression.

The **if** structure is called a *single-selection structure* because it selects or ignores a single action (or as we will soon see, a single group of actions). The **if/else** structure is called a *double-selection structure* because it selects between two different actions (or groups of actions). The **switch** structure is called a *multiple-selection structure* because it selects among many different actions (or groups of actions).

Java provides three types of repetition structures, namely **while**, **do/while** and **for** (**do/while** and **for** are covered in Chapter 3) Each of the words **if**, **else**, **switch**, **while**, **do**, and **for** are Java *keywords*. These words are reserved by the language to implement various features such as Java's control structures. Keywords may not be used as identifiers such as for variable names. A complete list of Java keywords is shown in Fig. 2.2.

Common Programming Error 2.1

Using a keyword as an identifier is a syntax error.

Well, that is all there is. Java has only seven control structures: sequence, three types of selection and three types of repetition. Each program is formed by combining as many of each type of control structure as is appropriate for the algorithm the program implements. As with the sequence structure of Fig. 2.1, we will see that each control structure is flowcharted with two small circle symbols, one at the entry point to the control structure and one at the exit point.

Java Keywords

`abstract`	`boolean`	`break`	`byte`	`case`
`catch`	`char`	`class`	`continue`	`default`
`do`	`double`	`else`	`extends`	`false`
`final`	`finally`	`float`	`for`	`if`
`implements`	`import`	`instanceof`	`int`	`interface`
`long`	`native`	`new`	`null`	`package`
`private`	`protected`	`public`	`return`	`short`
`static`	`super`	`switch`	`synchronized`	`this`
`throw`	`throws`	`transient`	`true`	`try`
`void`	`volatile`	`while`		

Keywords that are reserved but not used by Java

`const`	`goto`

Fig. 2.2 Java keywords.

Single-entry/single-exit control structures make it easy to build programs—the control structures are attached to one another by connecting the exit point of one control structure to the entry point of the next. This is similar to the way a child stacks building blocks, so we call this *control-structure stacking*. We will learn that there is only one other way control structures may be connected—a method called *control-structure nesting*. Thus, algorithms in Java programs are constructed from only seven different types of control structures combined in only two ways.

2.5 The `if` Selection Structure

A selection structure is used to choose among alternative courses of action in a program. For example, suppose that the passing grade on an examination is 60 (out of 100). Then the pseudocode statement

If student's grade is greater than or equal to 60
    Print "Passed"

determines if the condition "student's grade is greater than or equal to 60" is true or false. If the condition is true, then "Passed" is printed, and the next pseudocode statement in order is "performed" (remember that pseudocode is not a real programming language). If the condition is false, the print statement is ignored, and the next pseudocode statement in order is performed. Note that the second line of this selection structure is indented. Such indentation is optional, but it is highly recommended because it emphasizes the inherent structure of structured programs. The Java compiler ignores *whitespace characters* like blanks, tabs and newlines used for indentation and vertical spacing. Programmers insert these whitespace characters to enhance program clarity.

Good Programming Practice 2.1

Consistently applying reasonable indentation conventions throughout your programs greatly improves program readability. We suggest a fixed-size tab of about 1/4 inch or three spaces per indent.

The preceding pseudocode *If* statement may be written in Java as

```
if ( grade >= 60 )
   System.out.println( "Passed" );
```

Notice that the Java code corresponds closely to the pseudocode. This is one of the properties of pseudocode that makes it such a useful program development tool. The statement in the body of the **if** structure outputs the character string **"Passed"** to your computer's screen. **System.out.println** will be discussed in more detail in the program of Fig. 2.7.

Good Programming Practice 2.2

Pseudocode is often used to "think out" a program during the program design process. Then the pseudocode program is converted to Java.

The flowchart of Fig. 2.3 illustrates the single-selection **if** structure. This flowchart contains what is perhaps the most important flowcharting symbol—the *diamond symbol,* also called the *decision symbol,* which indicates that a decision is to be made. The decision symbol contains an expression, such as a condition, that can be either true or false. The decision symbol has two flowlines emerging from it. One indicates the direction to be taken when the expression in the symbol is true; the other indicates the direction to be taken when the expression is false. A decision can be made on any expression that evaluates to a value of Java's **boolean** type, i.e., any expression that evaluates to true of false.

Note that the **if** structure, too, is a single-entry/single-exit structure. We will soon learn that the flowcharts for the remaining control structures also contain (besides small circle symbols and flowlines) only rectangle symbols to indicate the actions to be performed, and diamond symbols to indicate decisions to be made. This is the *action/decision model of programming* we have been emphasizing.

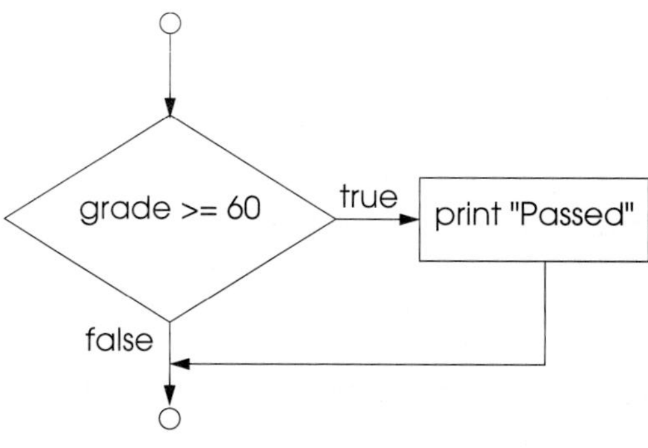

Fig. 2.3 Flowcharting the single-selection **if** structure.

We can envision seven bins, each containing only control structures of one of the seven types. These control structures are empty. Nothing is written in the rectangles or in the diamonds. The programmer's task, then, is assembling a program from as many of each type of control structure as the algorithm demands, combining those control structures in only two possible ways (stacking or nesting), and then filling in the actions and decisions in a manner appropriate for the algorithm. We will discuss the variety of ways in which actions and decisions may be written.

2.6 The `if/else` Selection Structure

The **`if`** selection structure performs an indicated action only when the condition is true; otherwise the action is skipped. The **`if/else`** selection structure allows the programmer to specify that a different action is to be performed when the condition is true than when the condition is false. For example, the pseudocode statement

If student's grade is greater than or equal to 60
    Print "Passed"
else
    Print "Failed"

prints *Passed* if the student's grade is greater than or equal to 60 and prints *Failed* if the student's grade is less than 60. In either case, after printing occurs, the next pseudocode statement in sequence is "performed." Note that the body of the *else* is also indented.

Good Programming Practice 2.3

Indent both body statements of an **`if/else`** *structure.*

The indentation convention you choose should be carefully applied throughout your programs. It is difficult to read programs that do not obey uniform spacing conventions.

Good Programming Practice 2.4

If there are several levels of indentation, each level should be indented the same additional amount of space.

The preceding pseudocode *if/else* structure may be written in Java as

```
if ( grade >= 60 )
   System.out.println( "Passed" );
else
   System.out.println( "Failed" );
```

The flowchart of Fig. 2.4 nicely illustrates the flow of control in the **`if/else`** structure. Once again, note that (besides small circles and arrows) the only symbols in the flowchart are rectangles (for actions) and a diamond (for a decision). We continue to emphasize this action/decision model of computing. Imagine again a deep bin containing as many empty double-selection structures as might be needed to build a Java algorithm. The programmer's job is to assemble the selection structures (by stacking and nesting) with other control structures required by the algorithm, and to fill in the empty rectangles and empty diamonds with actions and decisions appropriate to the algorithm being implemented.

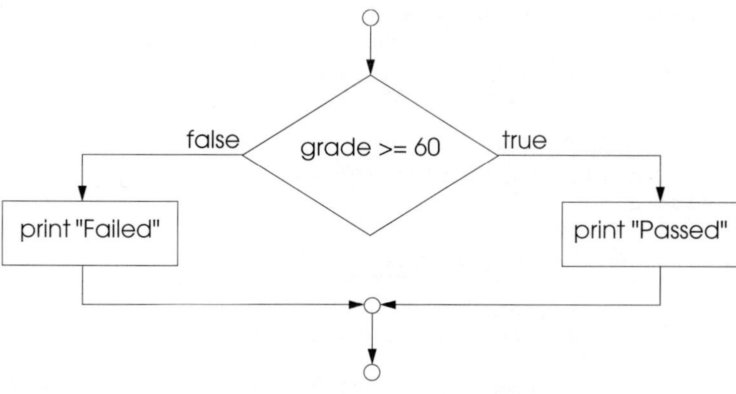

Fig. 2.4 Flowcharting the double-selection **`if/else`** structure.

The *conditional operator* (**`?:`**) is closely related to the **`if/else`** structure. The **`?:`** is Java's only *ternary operator*—it takes three operands. The operands together with the **`?:`** form a *conditional expression.* The first operand is a **`boolean`** expression, the second is the value for the conditional expression if the condition is true, and the third is the value for the conditional expression if the condition is false. For example, the output statement

```
System.out.println( grade >= 60 ? "Passed" : "Failed" );
```

contains a conditional expression that evaluates to the string **`"Passed"`** if the condition **`grade >= 60`** is true and evaluates to the string **`"Failed"`** if the condition is false. Thus, this statement with the conditional operator performs essentially the same as the preceding **`if/else`** statement. The precedence of the conditional operator is low, so the entire conditional expression is normally placed in parentheses. We will see that conditional operators can be used in some situations where **`if/else`** statements cannot.

Nested **`if/else`** *structures* test for multiple cases by placing **`if/else`** structures inside **`if/else`** structures. For example, the following pseudocode statement will print **`A`** for exam grades greater than or equal to 90, **`B`** for grades in the range 80 to 89, **`C`** for grades in the range 70 to 79, **`D`** for grades in the range 60 to 69, and **`F`** for all other grades.

```
If student's grade is greater than or equal to 90
    Print "A"
else
    If student's grade is greater than or equal to 80
        Print "B"
    else
        If student's grade is greater than or equal to 70
            Print "C"
        else
            If student's grade is greater than or equal to 60
                Print "D"
            else
                Print "F"
```

This pseudocode may be written in Java as

```
if ( grade >= 90 )
   System.out.println( "A" );
else
   if ( grade >= 80 )
      System.out.println( "B" );
   else
      if ( grade >= 70 )
         System.out.println( "C" );
      else
         if ( grade >= 60 )
            System.out.println( "D" );
         else
            System.out.println( "F" );
```

If **grade** is greater than or equal to 90, the first four conditions will be true, but only the **System.out.println** statement after the first test will be executed. After that particular **System.out.println** is executed, the **else**-part of the "outer" **if/else** statement is skipped. Most Java programmers prefer to write the preceding **if** structure as

```
if ( grade >= 90 )
   System.out.println( "A" );
else if ( grade >= 80 )
   System.out.println( "B" );
else if ( grade >= 70 )
   System.out.println( "C" );
else if ( grade >= 60 )
   System.out.println( "D" );
else
   System.out.println( "F" );
```

Both forms are equivalent. The latter form is popular because it avoids the deep indentation of the code to the right. Such deep indentation often leaves little room on a line, forcing lines to be split and decreasing program readability.

It is important to note that the Java compiler always associates an **else** with the previous **if** unless told to do otherwise by the placement of braces (**{}**). This is referred to as the *dangling-else problem.* For example,

```
if ( x > 5 )
   if ( y > 5 )
      System.out.println( "x and y are > 5" );
else
   System.out.println( "x is <= 5" );
```

appears to indicate that if **x** is greater than **5**, the **if** structure in its body determines if **y** is also greater than **5**. If so, the string **"x and y are > 5"** is output. Otherwise, it *appears* that if **x** is not greater than **5**, the **else** part of the **if/else** structure outputs the string **"x is <= 5"**.

Beware! The preceding nested **if** structure does not execute as it appears. The compiler actually interprets the preceding structure as

```
if ( x > 5 )
   if ( y > 5 )
      System.out.println( "x and y are > 5" );
   else
      System.out.println( "x is <= 5" );
```

in which the body of the first **if** structure is an **if/else** structure. This structure tests if **x** is greater than **5**. If so, execution continues by testing if **y** is also greater than **5**. If the second condition is true, the proper string—**"x and y are > 5"**—is displayed. However, if the second condition is false, the string **"x is <= 5"** is displayed even though we know **x** is greater than **5**.

To force the preceding nested **if** structure to execute as it was originally intended, the structure must be written as follows:

```
if ( x > 5 ) {
   if ( y > 5 )
      System.out.println( "x and y are > 5" );
}
else
   System.out.println( "x is <= 5" );
```

The braces (**{}**) indicate to the compiler that the second **if** structure is in the body of the first **if** structure and that the **else** is matched with the first **if** structure. In exercises 2.21 and 2.22 you will investigate the dangling-else problem further.

The **if** selection structure normally expects only one statement in its body. To include several statements in the body of an **if**, enclose the statements in braces (**{** and **}**). A set of statements contained within a pair of braces is called a *compound statement*.

Software Engineering Observation 2.1

A compound statement can be placed anywhere in a program that a single statement can be placed.

The following example includes a compound statement in the **else** part of an **if/else** structure.

```
if (grade >= 60)
   System.out.println( "Passed" );
else {
   System.out.println( "Failed" );
   System.out.println( "You must take this course again." );
}
```

In this case, if **grade** is less than 60, the program executes both statements in the body of the **else** and prints

```
Failed.
You must take this course again.
```

Notice the braces surrounding the two statements in the **else** clause. These braces are important. Without the braces, the statement

```
System.out.println( "You must take this course again." );
```

would be outside the body of the **else**-part of the **if**, and would execute regardless of whether the grade is less than 60.

Common Programming Error 2.2

Forgetting one or both of the braces that delimit a compound statement can lead to syntax errors or logic errors.

Syntax errors (such as when one brace in a compound statement is left out of the program) are caught by the compiler. A *logic error* (such as the one caused when both braces in a compound statement are left out of the program) has its effect at execution time. A *fatal logic error* causes a program to fail and terminate prematurely. A *nonfatal logic error* allows a program to continue executing but the program produces incorrect results.

Software Engineering Observation 2.2

*Just as a compound statement can be placed anywhere a single statement can be placed, it is also possible to have no statement at all, i.e., the empty statement. The empty statement is represented by placing a semicolon (**;**) where a statement would normally be.*

Common Programming Error 2.3

*Placing a semicolon after the condition in an **if** structure leads to a logic error in single-selection **if** structures and a syntax error in double-selection **if** structures (if the **if** part contains a non-empty body statement).*

Good Programming Practice 2.5

Some programmers prefer to type the beginning and ending braces of compound statements before typing the individual statements within the braces. This helps avoid omitting one or both of the braces.

In this section, we introduced the notion of a compound statement. A compound statement may contain declarations (as does the body of **main**, for example). If so, the compound statement is called a *block*. The declarations in a block are commonly placed first in the block before any action statements, but declarations may be intermixed with action statements. We will discuss the use of blocks in Chapter 4. The reader should avoid using blocks until that time.

2.7 The `while` Repetition Structure

A *repetition structure* allows the programmer to specify that an action is to be repeated while some condition remains true. The pseudocode statement

While there are more items on my shopping list
Purchase next item and cross it off my list

describes the repetition that occurs during a shopping trip. The condition, "there are more items on my shopping list" may be true or false. If it is true, then the action, "Purchase next item and cross it off my list" is performed. This action will be performed repeatedly while the condition remains true. The statement(s) contained in the *while* repetition structure constitute the body of the *while*. The *while* structure body may be a single statement or a compound statement. Eventually, the condition will become false (when the last item on the shopping list has been purchased and crossed off the list). At this point, the repetition terminates, and the first pseudocode statement after the repetition structure is executed.

Common Programming Error 2.4

Not providing in the body of a **`while`** *structure an action that eventually causes the condition in the* **`while`** *to become false. Normally, such a repetition structure will never terminate—an error called an "infinite loop."*

Common Programming Error 2.5

Spelling the keyword **`while`** *with an uppercase* **`W`** *as in* **`While`** *(remember that Java is a case-sensitive language). All of Java's reserved keywords such as* **`while`**, **`if`**, *and* **`else`** *contain only lowercase letters.*

As an example of a **`while`** structure, consider a program segment designed to find the first power of 2 larger than 1000. Suppose integer variable **`product`** has been initialized to 2. When the following **`while`** structure finishes executing, **`product`** contains the result:

```
int product = 2;

while ( product <= 1000 )
   product = 2 * product;
```

The flowchart of Fig. 2.5 nicely illustrates the flow of control in the **`while`** repetition structure that corresponds to the preceding **`while`** structure. Once again, note that (besides small circles and arrows) the flowchart contains only a rectangle symbol and a diamond symbol. Imagine, again, a deep bin of empty **`while`** structures that may be stacked and nested with other control structures to form a structured implementation of an algorithm's flow of control. The empty rectangles and diamonds are then filled in with appropriate actions and decisions. The flowchart clearly shows the repetition. The flowline emerging from the rectangle wraps back to the decision which is tested each time through the loop until the decision eventually becomes false. At this point, the **`while`** structure is exited and control passes to the next statement in the program.

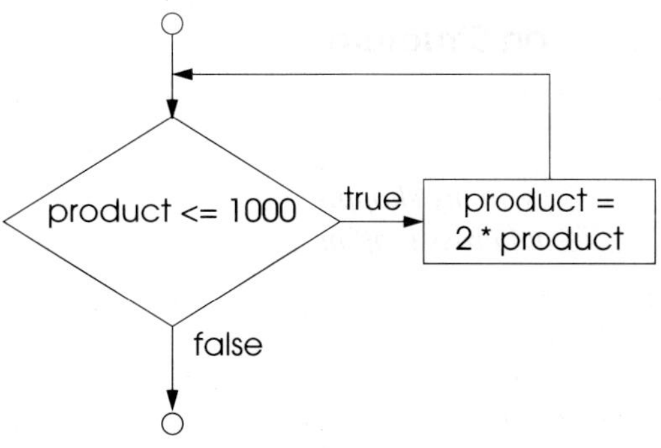

Fig. 2.5 Flowcharting the **`while`** repetition structure.

When the **while** structure is entered, **product** is 2. Variable **product** is repeatedly multiplied by 2, taking on the values 4, 8, 16, 32, 64, 128, 256, 512, and 1024 successively. When **product** becomes 1024, the condition in the **while** structure, **product <= 1000**, becomes false. This terminates the repetition with 1024 as the final value of **product**. Execution continues with the next statement after the **while**. Note: If a **while** structure's condition is initially false the body statement(s) will never be performed.

2.8 Formulating Algorithms: Case Study 1 (Counter-Controlled Repetition)

To illustrate how algorithms are developed, we solve several variations of a class-averaging problem. Consider the following problem statement:

A class of ten students took a quiz. The grades (one of the letters A, B, C, D, or F) for this quiz are available to you. Determine the class average on the quiz.

The average is calculated by first associating a grade point value with each letter grade. The letter grade A has the grade point value 4, B has the value 3, C has the value 2, D has the value 1 and F has the value 0. The class average is equal to the sum of the grade point values divided by the number of students. The algorithm for solving this problem on a computer must input each of the grades, perform the averaging calculation, and print the result.

Let us use pseudocode to list the actions to be executed and specify the order in which these actions should be executed. We use *counter-controlled repetition* to input the grades one at a time. This technique uses a variable called a *counter* to specify the number of times a set of statements should execute. In this example, repetition terminates when the counter exceeds 10. In this section, we present a pseudocode algorithm (Fig. 2.6) and the corresponding program (Fig. 2.7). In the next section, we show how pseudocode algorithms are developed. Counter-controlled repetition is often called *definite repetition* because the number of repetitions is known before the loop begins executing.

Note the references in the algorithm to a total and a counter. A *total* is a variable used to accumulate the sum of a series of values. A *counter* is a variable used to count—in this case, to count the number of grades entered. Variables used to store totals are normally initialized to zero before being used in a program; otherwise the sum would include the previous value stored in the total's memory location. Counter variables are normally initialized to zero or one, depending on their use (we present examples showing each of these uses).

In the program of Fig. 2.7, the Java compiler ensures that variables **counter** and **total** are initialized before they are used in a calculation. Uninitialized variables used in calculations results in error messages from the compiler stating that the variables may not have been initialized.

Common Programming Error 2.6

Not initializing a counter or total results in an error message from the compiler stating that the variable may not have been initialized. You must initialize the variable to allow the compiler to complete compilation of your program.

Good Programming Practice 2.6

Initialize counters and totals.

Set total to zero
Set grade counter to one

While grade counter is less than or equal to ten
    Input the next grade

    If the letter grade is equal to A
        Add grade point value 4 to the total
    else if the letter grade is equal to B
        Add grade point value 3 to the total
    else if the letter grade is equal to C
        Add grade point value 2 to the total
    else if the letter grade is equal to D
        Add grade point value 1 to the total
    else if the letter grade is equal to F
        Add grade point value 0 to the total

    Add one to the grade counter

Set the class average to the total divided by ten
Print the class average

Fig. 2.6 Pseudocode algorithm that uses counter-controlled repetition to solve the class average problem.

```
// Fig. 2.7: Average.java
// Class average program with
// counter-controlled repetition
import java.io.*;

public class Average {
   public static void main( String args[] ) throws IOException
   {
      int counter, grade, total, average;

      // initialization phase
      total = 0;
      counter = 1;

      // processing phase
      while ( counter <= 10 ) {
         System.out.print( "Enter letter grade: " );
         grade = System.in.read();

```

Fig. 2.7 Java program for the class-average problem with counter-controlled repetition (part 1 of 2).

```
20          if ( grade == 'A' )
21             total = total + 4;
22          else if ( grade == 'B' )
23             total = total + 3;
24          else if ( grade == 'C' )
25             total = total + 2;
26          else if ( grade == 'D' )
27             total = total + 1;
28
29          System.in.skip( 2 );    // skip the newline character
30          counter = counter + 1;
31       }
32
33       // termination phase
34       average = total / 10;       // integer division
35       System.out.println( "Class average is " + average );
36    }
37 }
```

```
Enter letter grade: A
Enter letter grade: A
Enter letter grade: A
Enter letter grade: A
Enter letter grade: A
Enter letter grade: B
Enter letter grade: B
Enter letter grade: C
Enter letter grade: D
Enter letter grade: F
Class average is 2
```

Fig. 2.7 Java program for the class-average problem with counter-controlled repetition (part 2 of 2).

This is our first application in Java, so there are some additional features that must be explained before we can continue. An application begins execution at the **main** method (line 7). Applications are executed using the Java interpreter (**java**) rather than using the Appletviewer or a World Wide Web browser.

The statement

```
import java.io.*;
```

in line 4 imports the Java input/output package to enable the program to read data from the keyboard and output data to the screen.

When creating an application you must still define a class as we did in Chapter 1. However, the class you define does not extend class **Applet** because we are not creating an applet. Method **main** is defined inside class **Average** in this application. Method **main** must have the following first line:

```
public static void main( String args[] )
```

If **main** does not begin with this line, the Java interpreter will not be able to execute your program. We will explain the key pieces of this line in later chapters. For now, if you are creating an application, simply copy this line when you define your **main** method.

In Fig. 2.7, method **main** actually begins with line 7

```
public static void main( String args[] ) throws IOException
```

which contains some optional information. The user will be typing letter grades at the keyboard that we will read into the program to calculate the average of the grades for the class. When information is read from the keyboard, Java tests for problems during the input (e.g., there is no more data to input). If a problem occurs, Java generates an *exception* that tells the programmer what went wrong (we cover exceptions in detail in Chapter 12). Exceptions, as their name implies, are exceptional cases during a program's execution—they do not happen frequently, but they can happen. The programmer can process the exception and allow the program to continue, or the programmer can ignore the exception, in which case the program may terminate.

Java is extremely strict about exception processing. If you compile a program that does input from the keyboard, Java *expects* you to write your program to handle any input problems that may occur. If you want to ignore the exceptions, you must indicate to the compiler that you are aware of the problems that might occur. At the end of line 7, the words **throws IOException** are our indication to the compiler that we are aware of the fact that an input/output exception can occur when the program attempts to read from the keyboard and that we are consciously ignoring these input/output exceptions in our program. This is referred to as *declaring the exception*. The words **throws IOException** are referred to as the ***throws*** *clause of method* **main**.

We have chosen to ignore exceptions at this point in the text so we can focus on the discussion of algorithms and control structures. In Chapter 12, we show how to process exceptions.

Software Engineering Observation 2.3

A program should be written to process exceptional cases that can occur during the execution of the program. This results in programs that are more robust and more likely to execute properly.

Testing and Debugging Tip 2.1

Java is strict about processing exceptional cases in a program. Java has better security and error handling requirements than C or C++. This leads to programs that are easier to debug and maintain.

If we do not declare the exception and we do not process the exception, the compiler issues the error message, "Exception **java.io.IOException** must be caught, or it must be declared in the throws clause of this method."

Line 9

```
int counter, grade, total, average;
```

declares variables **counter**, **grade**, **total** and **average** to be of type **int**. Notice that the declaration appears in the body of method **main**. In Chapter 1, all variables were declared as instance variables outside the methods of the class. It is also possible to place declarations in a method definition. The declaration of a variable in a method definition must appear before the variable is used in the method. A variable declared in one method of a class cannot be accessed directly by other methods of a class. Such variables are known as *local variables*. Also, local variables must be initialized before they are used in a program. We will consider methods in depth in Chapter 4.

Good Programming Practice 2.7

Always place a blank line before a declaration that appears between executable statements. This makes the declarations stand out in the program and contributes to program clarity.

Good Programming Practice 2.8

If you prefer to place declarations at the beginning of a method, separate those declarations from the executable statements in that method with one blank line to highlight where the declarations end and the executable statements begin.

Common Programming Error 2.7

Using a local variable before it is initialized (normally with an assignment statement) results in a compile error.

Lines 12 and 13

```
total = 0;
counter = 1;
```

are assignment statements that initialize variable **total** to **0** and variable **counter** to **1**.

Line 16

```
while ( counter <= 10 ) {
```

indicates that the **while** structure should continue as long as the value of **counter** is less than or equal to 10.

Lines 17 and 18

```
System.out.print( "Enter letter grade: " );
grade = System.in.read();
```

correspond to the pseudocode statement, *"Input the next grade."* The first line displays the prompt **Enter letter grade:** on the screen. Output to the screen and input from the keyboard in Java is often accomplished with *streams*. Thus, the first line above sends the stream of characters **Enter letter grade:** to the *standard output stream object*—***System.out***—which is normally "connected" to the screen. We discuss **System.out** in detail in Chapter 15, "Files and Streams." The method **System.out.print** takes its argument—the character string "**Enter letter grade:**"—and sends it to the screen to be displayed.

The second line above uses the *standard input stream object*—***System.in***—to obtain one letter grade from the user. The **System.in** object takes input from the standard input stream which is usually the keyboard. The **System.in.read** method reads one character from the keyboard and stores that character in integer variable **grade**. Characters are normally stored in variables of type **char**. However, a feature of Java is that characters can be stored in most integer data types because they are represented as 2-byte integers in Java. Thus, we can treat a character as either an integer or a character depending on its use. For example, the statement

```
System.out.println( "The character (" + 'a' +
                    ") has the value " + ( (int) 'a' ) );
```

prints the character **a** and its integer value as follows

```
The character (a) has the value 97
```

The integer 97 is the character's numerical representation in the computer. Java uses the *ISO (International Standards Organization) Unicode character set* in which 97 represents the lowercase letter **'a'**. Many computers today use the *ASCII (American Standard Code for Information Interchange) character set*. The ASCII character set is a subset of the Unicode character set. ASCII characters and their decimal values are shown in the Appendices.

Note the use of the single quotes around the character **a** in the preceding statement. When writing a program that contains a literal character value, the character must be placed in single quotes (**'**). If you place the character in double quotes (**"**), it is interpreted by Java as a string literal. String literals cannot be assigned directly to **char** or **int** variables.

After the grade is entered by the user, it is processed in the nested **if/else** structure (lines 20–27). Notice that each **if** condition tests the variable **grade** for equality with a literal character in single quotes that represents the letter grade.

The program is now ready to increment the variable counter to indicate that a grade has been processed, and read the next grade from the user. However, when the user types a character at the keyboard and presses the *Enter* (or *Return*) key, two characters are actually sent to the program through the input stream—the letter grade (such as "A") and the *newline* character. A newline character is automatically sent to the program when the user presses the *Enter* key (this also results in a newline character being output to the screen which causes the next characters output to appear at the beginning of the next line on the screen). Line 29

```
System.in.skip( 2 );     // skip the newline character
```

indicates that the program should skip **2** bytes (the newline character—remember a character is 2 bytes) in the input stream. This enables the user at the keyboard to enter the next grade when the program returns to line 19 to read the next grade. Without this **skip** line, the program will attempt to process the newline character as a valid letter grade. Line 30

```
counter = counter + 1;
```

adds **1** to **counter** so the condition in the **while** structure will eventually become false and terminate the loop.

Finally, lines 34 and 35

```
average = total / 10;       // integer division
System.out.println( "Class average is " + average );
```

calculate the result and display the string literal "**Class average is**" followed by the value of variable **average**. Method **System.out.println** outputs its argument followed by a newline character (thus leaving the screen cursor positioned at the left margin of the next line).

To execute this Java application (after it has been compiled), type the command

```
java Average
```

at your computer's command line (the DOS prompt on a Windows 95 or Windows NT system or at the shell prompt on a UNIX system) and press the *Enter* key. This executes the Java interpreter and tells it that the **main** method that begins the execution of this application is defined in class **Average**. See your instructor if you have questions about executing commands from the command line of your computer.

Note that the averaging calculation in the program produced an integer result. Actually, the sum of the grade point values in this example is 29 which when divided by 10 should yield 2.9, i.e., a number with a decimal point. We will see how to deal with such numbers (called floating-point numbers) in the next section.

In the programs of Fig. 2.7, Fig. 2.9 and Fig. 2.11, we input individual characters from the user at the keyboard using the **System.in.read** method. This is actually due to Java's limited capabilities for reading information from the standard input stream using object **System.in**—it is only capable of reading one keystroke of information at a time (or a group of keystrokes as we will see in Chapter 15). Often it is necessary to read information such as integers and other data types into a program. For example, grades could be input as integers from 0 to 100. Chapter 1 demonstrated how to read integers from the user via **TextField**s in an applet. Java mechanisms that enable input of miscellaneous data types are demonstrated throughout the text. Chapter 15 discusses how to read various data types using input streams that are connected to files on disk rather than the standard input stream.

2.9 Formulating Algorithms with Top-Down, Stepwise Refinement: Case Study 2 (Sentinel-Controlled Repetition)

Let us generalize the class-average problem. Consider the following problem:

> *Develop a class-averaging program that will process an arbitrary number of letter grades each time the program is run.*

In the first class-average example, the number of grades (10) was known in advance. In this example, no indication is given of how many grades are to be entered. The program must process an arbitrary number of grades. How can the program determine when to stop the input of grades? How will it know when to calculate and print the class average?

One way to solve this problem is to use a special value called a *sentinel value* (also called a *signal value*, a *dummy value*, or a *flag value*) to indicate "end of data entry." The user types grades in until all legitimate grades have been entered. The user then types the sentinel value to indicate that the last grade has been entered. Sentinel-controlled repetition is often called *indefinite repetition* because the number of repetitions is not known before the loop begins executing.

Clearly, the sentinel value must be chosen so that it cannot be confused with an acceptable input value. Because grades on a quiz are the letters A, B, C, D and F, Z is an acceptable sentinel value for this problem. Thus, a run of the class-average program might process a stream of inputs such as A, A, C, C, B, and Z. The program would then compute and print the class average for the grades A, A, C, C, and B (Z is the sentinel value, so it should not enter into the averaging calculation).

Common Programming Error 2.8

Choosing a sentinel value that is also a legitimate data value results in a logic error and may prevent a sentinel-controlled loop from terminating properly.

We approach the class-average program with a technique called *top-down, stepwise refinement*, a technique that is essential to the development of well-structured algorithms. We begin with a pseudocode representation of the *top:*

Determine the class average for the quiz

The top is a single statement that conveys the overall function of the program. As such, the top is, in effect, a complete representation of a program. Unfortunately, the top rarely conveys a sufficient amount of detail from which to write the Java algorithm. So we now begin the refinement process. We divide the top into a series of smaller tasks and list these in the order in which they need to be performed. This results in the following *first refinement*.

Initialize variables
Input, sum up, and count the quiz grades
Calculate and print the class average

Here, only the sequence structure has been used—the steps listed are to be executed in order, one after the other.

Software Engineering Observation 2.4

Each refinement, as well as the top itself, is a complete specification of the algorithm; only the level of detail varies.

To proceed to the next level of refinement, i.e., the *second refinement*, we commit to specific variables. We need a running total of the numbers, a count of how many numbers have been processed, a variable to receive the value of each grade as it is input, and a variable to hold the calculated average. The pseudocode statement

Initialize variables

may be refined as follows:

Initialize total to zero
Initialize counter to zero

Notice that only the variables *total* and *counter* are initialized before they are used; the variables *average* and *grade* (for the calculated average and the user input, respectively) need not be initialized because their values are written over as they are calculated or input.

The pseudocode statement

Input, sum up, and count the quiz grades

requires a repetition structure (i.e., a loop) that successively inputs each grade. Because we do not know in advance how many grades are to be processed, we will use sentinel-controlled repetition. The user at the keyboard will type legitimate grades in one at a time. After the last legitimate grade is typed, the user will type the sentinel value. The program will test for the sentinel value after each grade is input and will terminate the loop when the sentinel value is entered by the user. The second refinement of the preceding pseudocode statement is then

Input the first grade (possibly the sentinel)
While the user has not as yet entered the sentinel value
    If the letter grade is equal to A
        Add grade point value 4 to the total
    else if the letter grade is equal to B
        Add grade point value 3 to the total
    else if the letter grade is equal to C
        Add grade point value 2 to the total
    else if the letter grade is equal to D
        Add grade point value 1 to the total
    else if the letter grade is equal to F
        Add grade point value 0 to the total

    Add one to the grade counter
    Input the next grade (possibly the sentinel)

Notice that in pseudocode, we do not use braces around the set of statements that form the body of the *while* structure. We simply indent all these statements under the *while* to show that they all belong to the *while*. Again, pseudocode is only an informal program development aid.

The pseudocode statement

Calculate and print the class average

may be refined as follows:

If the counter is not equal to zero
    Set the average to the total divided by the counter
    Print the average
else
    Print "No grades were entered"

Notice that we are being careful here to test for the possibility of division by zero—a *logic error* that if undetected would cause the program to produce invalid output. The complete second refinement of the pseudocode algorithm for the class average problem is shown in Fig. 2.8.

Testing and Debugging Tip 2.2

When performing division by an expression whose value could be zero, explicitly test for this case and handle it appropriately in your program (such as printing an error message) rather than allowing the division by zero to occur.

Initialize total to zero
Initialize counter to zero

Input the first grade (possibly the sentinel)
While the user has not as yet entered the sentinel value
    If the letter grade is equal to A
        Add grade point value 4 to the total
    else if the letter grade is equal to B
        Add grade point value 3 to the total
    else if the letter grade is equal to C
        Add grade point value 2 to the total
    else if the letter grade is equal to D
        Add grade point value 1 to the total
    else if the letter grade is equal to F
        Add grade point value 0 to the total

    Add one to the grade counter
    Input the next grade (possibly the sentinel)

If the counter is not equal to zero
    Set the average to the total divided by the counter
    Print the average
else
    Print "No grades were entered"

Fig. 2.8 Pseudocode algorithm that uses sentinel-controlled repetition to solve the class-average problem.

Good Programming Practice 2.9

Include completely blank lines in pseudocode programs to make the pseudocode more readable. The blank lines separate pseudocode control structures and separate the phases of the programs.

Software Engineering Observation 2.5

Many algorithms can be divided logically into three phases: an initialization phase that initializes the program variables; a processing phase that inputs data values and adjusts program variables accordingly; and a termination phase that calculates and prints the final results.

The pseudocode algorithm in Fig. 2.8 solves the more general class averaging problem. This algorithm was developed after only two levels of refinement. Sometimes more levels are necessary.

Software Engineering Observation 2.6

The programmer terminates the top-down, stepwise refinement process when the pseudocode algorithm is specified in sufficient detail for the programmer to be able to convert the pseudocode to a Java applet or application. Implementing the Java applet or application is then normally straightforward.

The Java application and a sample execution are shown in Fig. 2.9. Although the grade point value for each letter grade is an integer, the averaging calculation is likely to produce a number with a decimal point (i.e., a real number). The type **int** cannot represent real numbers. The program introduces the data type ***double*** to handle numbers with decimal points (also called *floating-point numbers*) and introduces a special operator called a *cast operator* to handle the type conversion we will need for the averaging calculation. These features are explained in detail after the application is presented.

```
// Fig. 2.9: Average.java
// Class average application with
// sentinel-controlled repetition.
import java.io.*;

public class Average {
   public static void main( String args[] ) throws IOException
   {
      double average;  // number with decimal point
      int counter, grade, total;

      // initialization phase
      total = 0;
      counter = 0;

      // processing phase
      System.out.print( "Enter letter grade, Z to end: " );
      grade = System.in.read();

      while ( grade != 'Z' ) {
         if ( grade == 'A' )
            total = total + 4;
         else if ( grade == 'B' )
            total = total + 3;
         else if ( grade == 'C' )
            total = total + 2;
         else if ( grade == 'D' )
            total = total + 1;

         System.in.skip( 2 );
         counter = counter + 1;
         System.out.print( "Enter letter grade, Z to end: " );
         grade = System.in.read();
      }
```

Fig. 2.9 Class-average problem with sentinel-controlled repetition (part 1 of 2).

```

      // termination phase
      if ( counter != 0 ) {
         average = (double) total / counter;
         System.out.println( "Class average is " + average );
      }
      else
         System.out.println( "No grades were entered" );
   }
}
```

```
Enter letter grade, Z to end: A
Enter letter grade, Z to end: A
Enter letter grade, Z to end: A
Enter letter grade, Z to end: A
Enter letter grade, Z to end: A
Enter letter grade, Z to end: B
Enter letter grade, Z to end: B
Enter letter grade, Z to end: B
Enter letter grade, Z to end: B
Enter letter grade, Z to end: B
Enter letter grade, Z to end: Z
Class average is 3.5
```

Fig. 2.9 Class-average problem with sentinel-controlled repetition (part 2 of 2).

In this example, we see that control structures may be stacked on top of one another (in sequence) just as a child stacks building blocks. The **`while`** structure is immediately followed by an **`if/else`** structure in sequence. We also see the only other structured way control structures may be connected in Java, namely through nesting of one control structure inside another as shown by the nested **`if/else`** structure inside the **`while`** structure.

Notice the compound statement in the **`while`** loop in Fig 2.9. Without the braces, the last four statements in the body of the loop would fall outside the loop, causing the computer to interpret this code incorrectly as follows

```
while ( grade != 'Z' )
   if ( grade == 'A' )
      total = total + 4;
   else if ( grade == 'B' )
      total = total + 3;
   else if ( grade == 'C' )
      total = total + 2;
   else if ( grade == 'D' )
      total = total + 1;

System.in.skip( 2 );
counter = counter + 1;
System.out.print( "Enter letter grade, Z to end: " );
grade = System.in.read();
```

This would cause an infinite loop in the program if the user does not input the character "**Z**" for the first grade.

Common Programming Error 2.9

Omitting the curly braces that are needed to delineate a compound statement can lead to logic errors such as infinite loops.

Good Programming Practice 2.10

In a sentinel-controlled loop, the prompts requesting data entry should explicitly remind the user what the sentinel value is.

Averages do not always evaluate to integer values. Often, an average is a value such as 3.333 or 2.7 that contains a fractional part. These values are referred to as floating-point numbers and are represented by the data type **double**. The variable **average** is declared to be of type **double** to capture the fractional result of our calculation. However, the result of the calculation **total / counter** is an integer because **total** and **counter** are both integer variables. Dividing two integers results in *integer division* in which any fractional part of the calculation is lost (i.e., *truncated*). Because the calculation is performed first, the fractional part is lost before the result is assigned to **average**. To produce a floating-point calculation with integer values, we must create temporary values that are floating-point numbers for the calculation. Java provides the *unary cast operator* to accomplish this task. Line 38

```
average = (double) total / counter;
```

includes the cast operator **(double)** which creates a temporary floating-point copy of its operand, **total**. Using a cast operator in this manner is called *explicit conversion*. The value stored in **total** is still an integer. The calculation now consists of a floating-point value (the temporary **double** version of **total**) divided by the integer **counter**.

The Java compiler only knows how to evaluate expressions in which the data types of the operands are identical. To ensure that the operands are of the same type, the compiler performs an operation called *promotion* (also called *implicit conversion*) on selected operands. For example, in an expression containing the data types **int** and **double**, **int** operands are *promoted* to **double**. In our example, after **counter** is promoted to **double**, the calculation is performed and the result of the floating-point division is assigned to **average**. Later in this chapter we discuss all the standard data types and their order of promotion.

Cast operators are available for any data type. The cast operator is formed by placing parentheses around a data type name. The cast operator is a *unary operator*, i.e., an operator that takes only one operand. In Chapter 1, we studied the binary arithmetic operators. Java also supports unary versions of the plus (**+**) and minus (**-**) operators, so the programmer can write expressions like **-7** or **+5**. Cast operators associate from right to left and have the same precedence as other unary operators such as unary **+** and unary **-**. This precedence is one level higher than that of the *multiplicative operators* *****, **/**, and **%**, and one level lower than that of parentheses (see the operator precedence chart in Appendix C). We indicate the cast operator with the notation ***(type)*** in our precedence charts.

Common Programming Error 2.10

Using floating-point numbers in a manner that assumes they are represented precisely can lead to incorrect results. Floating-point numbers are represented only approximately by most computers.

Good Programming Practice 2.11

Do not compare floating-point values for equality or inequality. Rather, test that the difference is less than a specified small value.

Despite the fact that floating-point numbers are not always "100% precise," they have numerous applications. For example, when we speak of a "normal" body temperature of 98.6 we do not need to be precise to a large number of digits. When we view the temperature on a thermometer and read it as 98.6, it may actually be 98.5999473210643. The point here is that calling this number simply 98.6 is fine for most applications.

Another way floating-point numbers develop is through division. When we divide 10 by 3, the result is 3.3333333... with the sequence of 3s repeating infinitely. The computer allocates only a fixed amount of space to hold such a value, so clearly the stored floating-point value can only be an approximation.

2.10 Formulating Algorithms with Top-Down, Stepwise Refinement: Case Study 3 (Nested Control Structures)

Let us work through another complete problem. We will once again formulate the algorithm using pseudocode and top-down, stepwise refinement, and we will write a corresponding Java program.

Consider the following problem statement:

A college offers a course that prepares students for the state licensing exam for real estate brokers. Last year, several of the students who completed this course took the licensing examination. Naturally, the college wants to know how well its students did on the exam. You have been asked to write a program to summarize the results. You have been given a list of these 10 students. Next to each name is written a 1 if the student passed the exam and a 2 if the student failed.

Your program should analyze the results of the exam as follows:

1. Input each test result (i.e., a 1 or a 2). Display the message "Enter result" on the screen each time the program requests another test result.
2. Count the number of test results of each type.
3. Display a summary of the test results indicating the number of students who passed and the number of students who failed.
4. If more than 8 students passed the exam, print the message "Raise tuition."

After reading the problem statement carefully, we make the following observations about the problem:

1. The program must process test results for 10 students. A counter-controlled loop will be used.

2. Each test result is a number—either a 1 or a 2. Each time the program reads a test result, the program must determine if the number is a 1 or a 2. We test for a 1 in our algorithm. If the number is not a 1, we assume that it is a 2. (An exercise at the end of the chapter considers the consequences of this assumption.)
3. Two counters are used to keep track of the exam results—one to count the number of students who passed the exam and one to count the number of students who failed the exam.
4. After the program has processed all the results, it must decide if more than 8 students passed the exam.

Let us proceed with top-down, stepwise refinement. We begin with a pseudocode representation of the top:

Analyze exam results and decide if tuition should be raised

Once again, it is important to emphasize that the top is a complete representation of the program, but several refinements are likely to be needed before the pseudocode can be naturally evolved into a Java program. Our first refinement is

Initialize variables
Input the ten exam grades and count passes and failures
Print a summary of the exam results and decide if tuition should be raised

Here, too, even though we have a complete representation of the entire program, further refinement is necessary. We now commit to specific variables. Counters are needed to record the passes and failures, a counter will be used to control the looping process, and a variable is needed to store the user input. The pseudocode statement

Initialize variables

may be refined as follows:

Initialize passes to zero
Initialize failures to zero
Initialize student to one

Notice only the counters for the number of passes, number of failures and number of students are initialized. The pseudocode statement

Input the ten quiz grades and count passes and failures

requires a loop that successively inputs the result of each exam. Here it is known in advance that there are precisely ten exam results, so counter-controlled looping is appropriate. Inside the loop (i.e., *nested* within the loop) a double-selection structure will determine whether each exam result is a pass or a failure, and will increment the appropriate counter accordingly. The refinement of the preceding pseudocode statement is then

```
While student counter is less than or equal to ten
    Input the next exam result

    If the student passed
       Add one to passes
```

else
Add one to failures

Add one to student counter

Notice the use of blank lines to set off the *if/else* control structure to improve program readability. The pseudocode statement

Print a summary of the exam results and decide if tuition should be raised

may be refined as follows:

Print the number of passes
Print the number of failures
If more than eight students passed
Print "Raise tuition"

The complete second refinement appears in Fig. 2.10. Notice that blank lines are also used to set off the *while* structure for program readability.

This pseudocode is now sufficiently refined for conversion to Java. The Java program and two sample executions are shown in Fig. 2.11.

Note that we have taken advantage of a feature of Java that allows variable initialization to be incorporated into declarations. Looping programs may require initialization at the beginning of each repetition; such initialization would normally occur in assignment statements.

```
Initialize passes to zero
Initialize failures to zero
Initialize student to one

While student counter is less than or equal to ten
    Input the next exam result

    If the student passed
        Add one to passes
    else
        Add one to failures

    Add one to student counter

Print the number of passes
Print the number of failures
If more than eight students passed
    Print "Raise tuition"
```

Fig. 2.10 Pseudocode for examination-results problem.

```
// Fig. 2.11: Analysis.java
// Analysis of examination results
import java.io.*;

public class Analysis {
   public static void main( String args[] ) throws IOException
   {
      // initializing variables in declarations
      int passes = 0, failures = 0, student = 1, result;

      // process 10 students; counter-controlled loop
      while ( student <= 10 ) {
         System.out.print( "Enter result (1=pass,2=fail): " );
         result = System.in.read();

         if ( result == '1' )      // if/else nested in while
            passes = passes + 1;
         else
            failures = failures + 1;

         student = student + 1;
         System.in.skip( 2 );
      }

      System.out.println( "Passed " + passes );
      System.out.println( "Failed " + failures );

      if ( passes > 8 )
         System.out.println( "Raise tuition " );
   }
}
```

```
Enter result (1=pass,2=fail): 1
Enter result (1=pass,2=fail): 2
Enter result (1=pass,2=fail): 2
Enter result (1=pass,2=fail): 1
Enter result (1=pass,2=fail): 1
Enter result (1=pass,2=fail): 1
Enter result (1=pass,2=fail): 2
Enter result (1=pass,2=fail): 1
Enter result (1=pass,2=fail): 1
Enter result (1=pass,2=fail): 2
Passed 6
Failed 4
```

Fig. 2.11 Java program and sample execution for examination-results problem (part 1 of 2).

```
Enter result (1=pass,2=fail): 1
Enter result (1=pass,2=fail): 1
Enter result (1=pass,2=fail): 1
Enter result (1=pass,2=fail): 2
Enter result (1=pass,2=fail): 1
Enter result (1=pass,2=fail): 1
Enter result (1=pass,2=fail): 1
Enter result (1=pass,2=fail): 1
Enter result (1=pass,2=fail): 1
Enter result (1=pass,2=fail): 1
Passed 9
Failed 1
Raise tuition
```

Fig. 2.11 Java program and sample execution for examination-results problem (part 2 of 2).

Good Programming Practice 2.12

Initializing variables when they are declared in methods helps the programmer avoid compiler messages warning of uninitialized data. Instance variables of primitive data type **`int`** *are automatically initialized to zero and instance variables of primitive data types* **`boolean`** *are automatically initialized to* **`false`**.

Software Engineering Observation 2.7

Experience has shown that the most difficult part of solving a problem on a computer is developing the algorithm for the solution. Once a correct algorithm has been specified, the process of producing a working Java program from the algorithm is normally straightforward.

Software Engineering Observation 2.8

Many experienced programmers write programs without ever using program development tools like pseudocode. These programmers feel that their ultimate goal is to solve the problem on a computer, and that writing pseudocode merely delays the production of final outputs. Although this may work for simple and familiar problems, it can lead to serious errors on large, complex projects.

2.11 Assignment Operators

Java provides several assignment operators for abbreviating assignment expressions. For example the statement

```
c = c + 3;
```

can be abbreviated with the *addition assignment operator* **`+=`** as

```
c += 3;
```

The **+=** operator adds the value of the expression on the right of the operator to the value of the variable on the left of the operator and stores the result in the variable on the left of the operator. Any statement of the form

variable **=** *variable operator expression***;**

where *operator* is one of the binary operators **+**, **-**, *****, **/**, or **%** (or others we will discuss later in the text), can be written in the form

*variable operator***=** *expression***;**

Thus the assignment **c += 3** adds **3** to **c**. Figure 2.12 shows the arithmetic assignment operators, sample expressions using these operators, and explanations.

Performance Tip 2.1

Programmers can write programs a bit faster and compilers can compile programs a bit faster when the "abbreviated" assignment operators are used. Some compilers generate code that runs faster when "abbreviated" assignment operators are used.

Performance Tip 2.2

Many of the performance tips we mention in this text result in nominal improvements, so the reader may be tempted to ignore them. Significant performance improvement is often realized when a supposedly nominal improvement is placed in a loop that may repeat a large number of times.

2.12 Increment and Decrement Operators

Java provides the unary *increment operator*, **++**, and the unary *decrement operator*, **--**, which are summarized in Fig. 2.13. If a variable **c** is incremented by 1, the increment operator **++** can be used rather than the expressions **c = c + 1** or **c += 1**. If an increment or decrement operator is placed before a variable, it is referred to as the *preincrement* or *predecrement operator,* respectively. If an increment or decrement operator is placed after a variable, it is referred to as the *postincrement* or *postdecrement operator,* respectively.

Assignment operator	Sample expression	Explanation	Assigns
Assume: **int c = 3, d = 5, e = 4, f = 6, g = 12;**			
+=	c += 7	c = c + 7	10 to c
-=	d -= 4	d = d - 4	1 to d
*=	e *= 5	e = e * 5	20 to e
/=	f /= 3	f = f / 3	2 to f
%=	g %= 9	g = g % 9	3 to g

Fig. 2.12 Arithmetic assignment operators.

Operator	Called	Sample expression	Explanation
`++`	preincrement	`++a`	Increment **a** by 1 then use the new value of **a** in the expression in which **a** resides.
`++`	postincrement	`a++`	Use the current value of **a** in the expression in which **a** resides, then increment **a** by 1.
`--`	predecrement	`--b`	Decrement **b** by 1 then use the new value of **b** in the expression in which **b** resides.
`--`	postdecrement	`b--`	Use the current value of **b** in the expression in which **b** resides, then decrement **b** by 1.

Fig. 2.13 The increment and decrement operators.

Preincrementing (predecrementing) a variable causes the variable to be incremented (decremented) by 1, then the new value of the variable is used in the expression in which it appears. Postincrementing (postdecrementing) the variable causes the current value of the variable to be used in the expression in which it appears, then the variable value is incremented (decremented) by 1.

The applet of Fig. 2.14 demonstrates the difference between the preincrementing version and the postincrementing version of the **++** increment operator. Postincrementing the variable **c** causes it to be incremented after it is used in the **g.drawString** method call (line 13). Preincrementing the variable **c** causes it to be incremented before it is used in the **g.drawString** method call (line 19).

```
1  // Fig. 2.14: Increment.java
2  // Preincrementing and postincrementing
3  import java.awt.Graphics;
4  import java.applet.Applet;
5
6  public class Increment extends Applet {
7     public void paint( Graphics g )
8     {
9        int c;
10
11       c = 5;
12       g.drawString( Integer.toString( c ), 25, 25 );
13       g.drawString( Integer.toString( c++ ),   // postincrement
14                     25, 40 );
15       g.drawString( Integer.toString( c ), 25, 55 );
16
```

Fig. 2.14 The difference between preincrementing and postincrementing (part 1 of 2).

```
      c = 5;
      g.drawString( Integer.toString( c ), 25, 85 );
      g.drawString( Integer.toString( ++c ),   // preincrement
                    25, 100 );
      g.drawString( Integer.toString( c ), 25, 115 );
   }
}
```

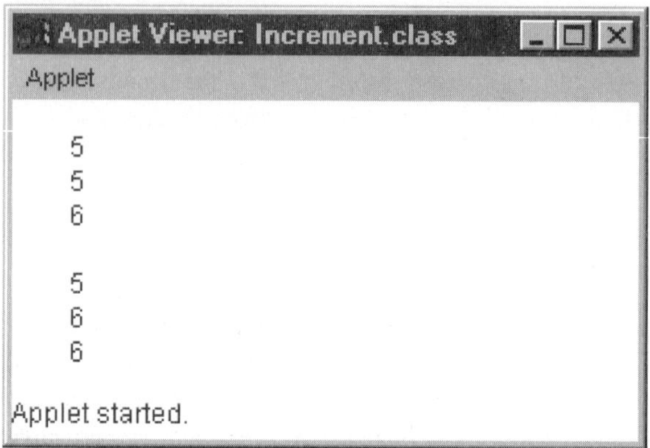

Fig. 2.14 The difference between preincrementing and postincrementing (part 1 of 2).

The program displays the value of **c** before and after the **++** operator is used. The decrement operator (**--**) works similarly.

Good Programming Practice 2.13

Unary operators should be placed next to their operands with no intervening spaces.

The three assignment statements in Fig 2.11

```
passes = passes + 1;
failures = failures + 1;
student = student + 1;
```

can be written more concisely with assignment operators as

```
passes += 1;
failures += 1;
student += 1;
```

with preincrement operators as

```
++passes;
++failures;
++student;
```

or with postincrement operators as

```
passes++;
failures++;
student++;
```

It is important to note here that when incrementing or decrementing a variable in a statement by itself, the preincrement and postincrement forms have the same effect, and the predecrement and postdecrement forms have the same effect. It is only when a variable appears in the context of a larger expression that preincrementing the variable and postincrementing the variable have different effects (and similarly for predecrementing and postdecrementing).

Common Programming Error 2.11

Attempting to use the increment or decrement operator on an expression other than a simple variable name, e.g., writing `++(x + 1)` *is a syntax error.*

The chart in Fig. 2.15 shows the precedence and associativity of the operators introduced to this point. The operators are shown top-to-bottom in decreasing order of precedence. The second column describes the associativity of the operators at each level of precedence. Notice that the conditional operator (`?:`), the unary operators increment (`++`), decrement (`--`), plus (`+`), minus (`-`) and casts, and the assignment operators `=`, `+=`, `-=`, `*=`, `/=` and `%=` associate from right to left. All other operators in the operator precedence chart of Fig. 2.15 associate from left to right. The third column names the groups of operators.

2.13 Common Escape Sequences

When outputting information, it is sometimes helpful to add some formatting with special characters called *escape sequences*. Some common escape sequences are listed in Fig. 2.16.

Operators						Associativity	Type
`()`						left to right	parentheses
`++`	`--`	`+`	`-`	`(`*type*`)`		right to left	unary
`*`	`/`	`%`				left to right	multiplicative
`+`	`-`					left to right	additive
`<`	`<=`	`>`	`>=`			left to right	relational
`==`	`!=`					left to right	equality
`?:`						right to left	conditional
`=`	`+=`	`-=`	`*=`	`/=`	`%=`	right to left	assignment

Fig. 2.15 Precedence of the operators encountered so far in the text.

Escape Sequence	Description
`\n`	Newline. Position the cursor to the beginning of the next line.
`\t`	Horizontal tab. Move the cursor to the next tab stop.
`\r`	Carriage return. Position the cursor to the beginning of the current line; do not advance to the next line.
`\\`	Backslash. Used to print a backslash character.
`\'`	Single quote. Used to print a single-quote character.
`\"`	Double quote. Used to print a double-quote character.
`\u####`	Unicode character. Used to place any Unicode-character constant in a Java program. The **####** is a hexadecimal representation of the Unicode value (see Appendix E for information on hexadecimal numbers).

Fig. 2.16 Some common escape sequences.

In Fig. 2.16, the backslash (****) that starts each escape sequence is called an *escape character*. It indicates that a "special" character is to be output. When a backslash is encountered in a string of characters, the next character is combined with the backslash to form an escape sequence.

Escape sequences can be used as individual characters in single quotes or as characters in a string. The application of Fig. 2.17 demonstrates some common escape sequences. The first output statement (lines 7 and 8) uses **\'** twice to wrap a character in single quotes. The second output statement (lines 9 and 10) uses **\"** twice to wrap a string in double quotes. The third output statement (line 11) uses **** to output a backslash character. The fourth output statement (line 12) uses **\t** twice to output a line of text with two tabs in the middle. Tab characters can be used to output information in columns. The fifth output statement (line 13) uses **\n** twice to output text double-spaced—i.e., with a blank line between lines of text. Note that the **System.out.println** method actually performs the same task as the **System.out.print** method, but it adds a **\n** character to the output automatically. Finally, the last output statement uses a **\r** character to demonstrate repositioning the cursor at the start of the current line. Notice that the **#** characters overwrite some of the ***** characters that were output before the **\r** character.

```
1  // Fig. 2.17: EscapeSequences.java
2  // Demonstrating common escape sequences
3
4  public class EscapeSequences {
5     public static void main( String args[] )
6     {
7        System.out.println( "Displaying single quotes: " +
8                            "\'A\'" );
```

Fig. 2.17 Demonstrating common escape sequences (part 1 of 2).

```
        System.out.println( "Displaying double quotes: " +
                            "\"string\"" );
        System.out.println( "Displaying a backslash: \\" );
        System.out.println( "Text separated\t\tby two tabs" );
        System.out.println( "Here is double\n\nspaced text" );
        System.out.println( "**********\r#####" );
    }
}
```

```
Displaying single quotes: 'A'
Displaying double quotes: "string"
Displaying a backslash: \
Text separated          by two tabs
Here is double

spaced text
#####*****
```

Fig. 2.17 Demonstrating common escape sequences (part 2 of 2).

2.14 Primitive Data Types

The table in Fig. 2.18 lists the primitive data types in Java. The primitive types are the building blocks for more complicated types. Like its predecessor languages C and C++, Java requires all variables to have a type before they can be used in a program. For this reason, Java is referred to as a *strongly-typed language*.

Type	Size in bits	Values	Standard
boolean	1	**true** or **false**	
char	16	**'\u0000'** to **'\uFFFF'**	(ISO Unicode character set)
byte	8	–128 to +127	
short	16	–32,768 to +32,767	
int	32	–2,147,483,648 to +2,147,483,647	
long	64	–9,223,372,036,854,775,808 to +9,223,372,036,854,775,807	
float	32	–3.40292347E+38 to +3.40292347E+38	(IEEE 754 floating point)
double	64	–1.79769313486231570E+308 to +1.79769313486231570E+308	(IEEE 754 floating point)

Fig. 2.18 The Java primitive data types.

Unlike C and C++, the primitive types in Java are portable across all computer platforms that support Java. This and many other portability features of Java enable programmers to write programs once without knowing which computer platform will execute the program. This is sometimes referred to as "WORA" (Write Once Run Anywhere).

In C and C++ programs, programmers frequently had to write separate versions of programs to support different computer platforms because the primitive data types were not guaranteed to be identical from computer to computer. For example, an **`int`** value on one machine might be represented by 16 bits (or 2 bytes) of memory and an **`int`** value on another machine might be represented by 32 bits (or 4 bytes) of memory. In Java, **`int`** values are always 32 bits (or 4 bytes).

Portability Tip 2.1

All primitive data types in Java are portable across all platforms that support Java.

Each data type in the table is listed with its size in bits (there are 8 bits to a byte) and its range of values. Because the designers of Java want it to be portable, they chose to use internationally recognized standards for both character formats (Unicode) and for floating-point numbers (IEEE 754).

Summary

- A procedure for solving a problem in terms of the actions to be executed and the order in which these actions should be executed is called an algorithm.
- Specifying the order in which statements are to be executed in a computer program is called program control.
- Pseudocode helps the programmer “think out” a program before attempting to write it in a programming language such as Java.
- Declarations are messages to the compiler telling it the names and attributes of variables and telling it to reserve space for variables.
- A selection structure is used to choose among alternative courses of action.
- The **`if`** selection structure executes an indicated action only when the condition is true.
- The **`if/else`** selection structure specifies separate actions to be executed when the condition is true and when the condition is false.
- Whenever more than one statement is to be executed where normally only a single statement is expected, these statements must be enclosed in braces forming a compound statement. A compound statement can be placed anywhere a single statement can be placed.
- An empty statement indicating that no action is to be taken is indicated by placing a semicolon (**`;`**) where a statement would normally be.
- A repetition structure specifies that an action is to be repeated while some condition remains true.

- The format for the **while** repetition structure is

```
while ( condition )
    statement
```

- A Java application begins execution at the **main** method. Applications are executed using the Java interpreter (**java**).
- Method **main** must have the following first line:

```
public static void main( String args[] )
```

- If **main** does not begin with this line, the Java interpreter will not be able to execute your program.
- Exceptions are exceptional cases during a program's execution—they do not happen frequently, but they can happen. Exceptions can be processed to allow the program to continue or can be ignored, in which case the program may terminate.
- Java is extremely strict about exception processing. If you compile a program that does input from the keyboard, Java expects you to write your program so it handles any input problems that may occur. If you want to ignore the exceptions, you must indicate to the compiler that you are aware of the problems that might occur by declaring the exception in the **throws** clause of the method.
- The standard output stream object—**System.out**—outputs information to the standard output stream which is normally "connected" to the screen.
- Method **System.out.print** sends its argument to the screen to be displayed. When using this method, the characters to be output are sometimes placed in a buffer (a temporary holding area in the computer's memory) and not actually displayed on the screen.
- Method **System.out.println** sends its argument followed by a newline character to the screen to be displayed.
- The standard input stream object—**System.in**—obtains input from the standard input stream which is usually the keyboard. The **System.in.read** method reads one character from the keyboard and returns it as its integer value which is the character's numerical representation in the computer. Java uses the *ISO (International Standards Organization) Unicode character set* to represent characters in memory. Method **System.in.skip** enables the program to skip characters in the input stream.
- The Java interpreter executes applications written in Java. To run the Java interpreter for an application, at the command line, type **java** followed by the name of the class in which method **main** is defined and press *Enter*.
- A value that contains a fractional part is referred to as a floating-point number and is represented by the data type **float** or **double**.
- Unary cast operator **(double)** creates a temporary floating-point copy of its operand.
- Java provides the arithmetic assignment operators **+=**, **-=**, ***=**, **/=**, and **%=** that help abbreviate certain common types of expressions.

- The increment operator, **++**, and the decrement operator, **--**, increment or decrement a variable by 1. If the operator is prefixed to the variable, the variable is incremented or decremented by 1 first, then used in its expression. If the operator is postfixed to the variable, the variable is used in its expression, then incremented or decremented by 1.
- The primitive types (**boolean**, **char**, **byte**, **short**, **int**, **long**, **float**, and **double**) are the building blocks for more complicated types in Java.
- Java requires all variables to have a type before they can be used in a program. For this reason, Java is referred to as a strongly-typed language.
- Primitive types in Java are portable across all computer platforms that support Java.
- Java uses internationally recognized standards for both character formats (Unicode) and for floating-point numbers (IEEE 754).

Terminology

-- operator
++ operator
?: operator
action
action/decision model
algorithm
application
arithmetic assignment operators:
  +=, **-=**, ***=**, **/=**, and **%=**
block
body of a loop
cast operator
compound statement
conditional operator (**?:**)
control structure
counter-controlled repetition
decision
decrement operator (**--**)
definite repetition
double
double-selection structure
empty statement (**;**)
exception
if selection structure
if/else selection structure
implicit conversion
increment operator (**++**)
indefinite repetition
infinite loop
initialization
integer division
IOException
ISO Unicode character set
keyword
logic error
loop counter
loop-continuation condition
main method
nested control structures
newline character
nonfatal error
postdecrement operator
postincrement operator
predecrement operator
preincrement operator
promotion
pseudocode
repetition
repetition structures
selection
sentinel value
sequential execution
single-entry/single-exit control structures
single-selection structure
stacked control structures
standard input stream
standard output stream
structured programming
syntax error
System.in
System.in.read
System.in.skip
System.out
System.out.print

`System.out.println`
top-down, stepwise refinement
unary operator
`while` repetition structure
whitespace characters

Common Programming Errors

2.1 Using a keyword as an identifier is a syntax error.

2.2 Forgetting one or both of the braces that delimit a compound statement can lead to syntax errors or logic errors.

2.3 Placing a semicolon after the condition in an `if` structure leads to a logic error in single-selection `if` structures and a syntax error in double-selection `if` structures (if the `if` part contains a non-empty body statement).

2.4 Not providing in the body of a `while` structure an action that eventually causes the condition in the `while` to become false. Normally, such a repetition structure will never terminate—an error called an "infinite loop."

2.5 Spelling the keyword `while` with an uppercase `W` as in `While` (remember that Java is a case-sensitive language). All of Java's reserved keywords such as `while`, `if`, and `else` contain only lowercase letters.

2.6 Not initializing a counter or total results in an error message from the compiler stating that the variable may not have been initialized. You must initialize the variable to allow the compiler to complete compilation of your program.

2.7 Using a local variable before it is initialized (normally with an assignment statement) results in a compile error.

2.8 Choosing a sentinel value that is also a legitimate data value results in a logic error and may prevent a sentinel-controlled loop from terminating properly.

2.9 Omitting the curly braces that are needed to delineate a compound statement can lead to logic errors such as infinite loops.

2.10 Using floating-point numbers in a manner that assumes they are represented precisely can lead to incorrect results. Floating-point numbers are represented only approximately by most computers.

2.11 Attempting to use the increment or decrement operator on an expression other than a simple variable name, e.g., writing `++(x + 1)` is a syntax error.

Good Programming Practices

2.1 Consistently applying reasonable indentation conventions throughout your programs greatly improves program readability. We suggest a fixed-size tab of about 1/4 inch or three spaces per indent.

2.2 Pseudocode is often used to "think out" a program during the program design process. Then the pseudocode program is converted to Java.

2.3 Indent both body statements of an **if/else** structure.

2.4 If there are several levels of indentation, each level should be indented the same additional amount of space.

2.5 Some programmers prefer to type the beginning and ending braces of compound statements before typing the individual statements within the braces. This helps avoid omitting one or both of the braces.

2.6 Initialize counters and totals.

2.7 Always place a blank line before a declaration that appears between executable statements. This makes the declarations stand out in the program and contributes to program clarity.

2.8 If you prefer to place declarations at the beginning of a method, separate those declarations from the executable statements in that method with one blank line to highlight where the declarations end and the executable statements begin.

2.9 Include completely blank lines in pseudocode programs to make the pseudocode more readable. The blank lines separate pseudocode control structures and separate the phases of the programs.

2.10 In a sentinel-controlled loop, the prompts requesting data entry should explicitly remind the user what the sentinel value is.

2.11 Do not compare floating-point values for equality or inequality. Rather, test that the difference is less than a specified small value.

2.12 Initializing variables when they are declared in methods helps the programmer avoid compiler messages warning of uninitialized data. Instance variables of primitive data type **int** are automatically initialized to zero and instance variables of primitive data types **boolean** are automatically initialized to **false**.

2.13 Unary operators should be placed next to their operands with no intervening spaces.

Performance Tips

2.1 Programmers can write programs a bit faster and compilers can compile programs a bit faster when the "abbreviated" assignment operators are used. Some compilers generate code that runs faster when "abbreviated" assignment operators are used.

2.2 Many of the performance tips we mention in this text result in nominal improvements, so the reader may be tempted to ignore them. Significant performance improvement is often realized when a supposedly nominal improvement is placed in a loop that may repeat a large number of times.

Portability Tip

2.1 All primitive data types in Java are portable across all platforms that support Java.

Software Engineering Observations

2.1 A compound statement can be placed anywhere in a program that a single statement can be placed.

2.2 Just as a compound statement can be placed anywhere a single statement can be placed, it is also possible to have no statement at all, i.e., the empty statement. The empty statement is represented by placing a semicolon (`;`) where a statement would normally be.

2.3 A program should be written to process exceptional cases that can occur during the execution of the program. This results in programs that are more robust and more likely to execute properly.

2.4 Each refinement, as well as the top itself, is a complete specification of the algorithm; only the level of detail varies.

2.5 Many algorithms can be divided logically into three phases: an initialization phase that initializes the program variables; a processing phase that inputs data values and adjusts program variables accordingly; and a termination phase that calculates and prints the final results.

2.6 The programmer terminates the top-down, stepwise refinement process when the pseudocode algorithm is specified in sufficient detail for the programmer to be able to convert the pseudocode to a Java applet or applications. Implementing the Java applet or application is then normally straightforward.

2.7 Experience has shown that the most difficult part of solving a problem on a computer is developing the algorithm for the solution. Once a correct algorithm has been specified, the process of producing a working Java program from the algorithm is normally straightforward.

2.8 Many experienced programmers write programs without ever using program development tools like pseudocode. These programmers feel that their ultimate goal is to solve the problem on a computer, and that writing pseudocode merely delays the production of final outputs. Although this may work for simple and familiar problems, it can lead to serious errors on large, complex projects.

Testing and Debugging Tips

2.1 Java is strict about processing exceptional cases in a program. Java has better security and error handling requirements than C or C++. This leads to programs that are easier to debug and maintain.

2.2 When performing division by an expression whose value could be zero, explicitly test for this case and handle it appropriately in your program (such as printing an error message) rather than allowing the division by zero to occur.

Self-Review Exercises

2.1 Answer each of the following questions.

a) All programs can be written in terms of three types of control structures: ________, __________, and __________.

b) The _________ selection structure is used to execute one action when a condition is true and another action when that condition is false.
c) Repetition of a set of instructions a specific number of times is called _______ repetition.
d) When it is not known in advance how many times a set of statements will be repeated, a __________ value can be used to terminate the repetition.

2.2 Write four different Java statements that each add 1 to integer variable `x`.

2.3 Write Java statements to accomplish each of the following:
a) Assign the sum of `x` and `y` to `z` and increment the value of `x` by 1 after the calculation.
b) Test if the value of the variable `count` is greater than 10. If it is, print "`Count is greater than 10`"
c) Decrement the variable `x` by 1 then subtract it from the variable `total`.
d) Calculate the remainder after `q` is divided by `divisor` and assign the result to `q`. Write this statement two different ways.

2.4 Write a Java statement to accomplish each of the following tasks.
a) Declare variables `sum` and `x` to be of type `int`.
b) Assign `1` to variable `x`.
c) Assign `0` to variable `sum`.
d) Add variable `x` to variable `sum` and assign the result to variable `sum`.
e) Print `"The sum is: "` followed by the value of variable `sum`.

2.5 Combine the statements that you wrote in Exercise 2.4 into a Java application that calculates and prints the sum of the integers from 1 to 10. Use the `while` structure to loop through the calculation and increment statements. The loop should terminate when the value of `x` becomes 11.

2.6 Determine the values of each variable after the calculation is performed. Assume that when each statement begins executing all variables have the integer value 5.
a) `product *= x++;`
b) `quotient /= ++x;`

2.7 Identify and correct the errors in each of the following:
a)
```
while ( c <= 5 ) {
    product *= c;
    ++c;
```
b)
```
if ( gender == 1 )
    System.out.println( "Woman" );
else;
    System.out.println( "Man" );
```

2.8 What is wrong with the following `while` repetition structure:
```
while ( z >= 0 )
    sum += z;
```

Answers to Self-Review Exercises

2.1 a) Sequence, selection, and repetition. b) `if/else`. c) Counter-controlled or definite. d) Sentinel, signal, flag, or dummy.

2.2
```
x = x + 1;
x += 1;
```

```
++x;
x++;
```

2.3 a) `z = x++ + y;`
b)
```
if ( count > 10 )
   System.out.println( "Count is greater than 10" );
```
c) `total -= --x;`
d) `q %= divisor;`
`q = q % divisor;`

2.4 a) `int sum, x;`
b) `x = 1;`
c) `sum = 0;`
d) `sum += x;` or `sum = sum + x;`
e) `System.out.println( "The sum is: " + sum );`

2.5
```
// Calculate the sum of the integers from 1 to 10
public class Calculate {
   public static void main( String args[] )
   {
      int sum, x;
      x = 1;
      sum = 0;
      while ( x <= 10 ) {
         sum += x;
         ++x;
      }
      System.out.println( "The sum is: " + sum );
   }
}
```

2.6 a) `product = 25, x = 6;`
b) `quotient = 0, x = 6;`

2.7 a) Error: Missing the closing right brace of the **while** body.
Correction: Add closing right brace after the statement **++c;**.
b) Error: Semicolon after **else** results in a logic error. The second output statement will always be executed.
Correction: Remove the semicolon after **else**.

2.8 The value of the variable **z** is never changed in the **while** structure. Therefore, if the loop-continuation condition **(z >= 0)** is true, an infinite loop is created. To prevent the infinite loop, **z** must be decremented so that it eventually becomes less than 0.

Exercises

2.9 Identify and correct the errors in each of the following (Note: There may be more than one error in each piece of code):

a)
```
if ( age >= 65 );
   System.out.println( "Age greater than or equal to 65" );
else
   System.out.println( "Age is less than 65 )";
```

b)
```
int x = 1, total;
while ( x <= 10 ) {
   total += x;
   ++x;
}
```
c)
```
While ( x <= 100 )
   total += x;
   ++x;
```
d)
```
while ( y > 0 ) {
   System.out.println( y );
   ++y;
```

2.10 What does the following program print?

```
public class Mystery {
   public static void main( String args[] )
   {
      int y, x = 1, total = 0;
      while ( x <= 10 ) {
         y = x * x;
         System.out.println( y );
         total += y;
         ++x;
      }
      System.out.println( "Total is " + total );
   }
}
```

For Exercise 2.11 through 2.14 perform each of these steps:

a) Read the problem statement.
b) Formulate the algorithm using pseudocode and top-down, stepwise refinement.
c) Write a Java program.
d) Test, debug, and execute the Java program.

2.11 Because of energy conservation, ecology and the high price of gasoline, drivers are concerned with the mileage obtained by their automobiles. One driver has kept track of several tankfuls of gasoline by recording miles driven and gallons used for each tankful. Develop a Java applet that will input the miles driven and gallons used (both as integers) for each tankful. The program should calculate and display the miles per gallon obtained for each tankful and print the combined miles per gallon obtained for all tankfuls up to this point. All average calculations should produce floating-point results. Use two **TextField**s to input the data (see Fig. 1.13 for hints).

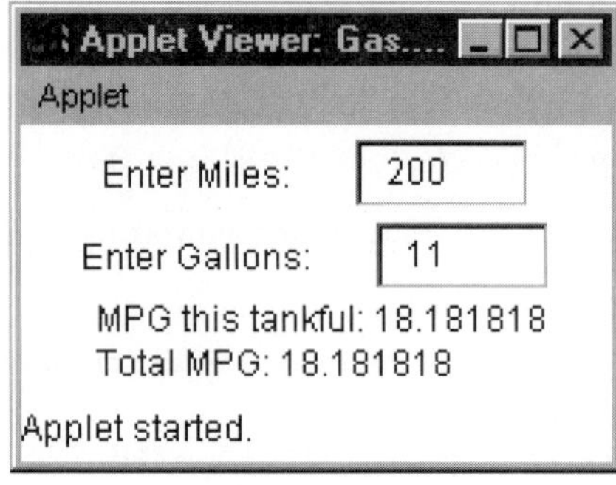

Applet Viewer: Gas....
Applet
Enter Miles: 333
Enter Gallons: 13
MPG this tankful: 25.615385
Total MPG: 22.208334
Applet started.

2.12 Develop a Java applet that will determine if a department store customer has exceeded the credit limit on a charge account. For each customer, the following facts are available:

a) Account number
b) Balance at the beginning of the month
c) Total of all items charged by this customer this month
d) Total of all credits applied to this customer's account this month
e) Allowed credit limit

The program should input each of these facts from **`TextField`**s as integers, calculate the new balance (= beginning balance + charges – credits), display the new balance and determine if the new balance exceeds the customer's credit limit. For those customers whose credit limit is exceeded, the program should display the message, "Credit limit exceeded."

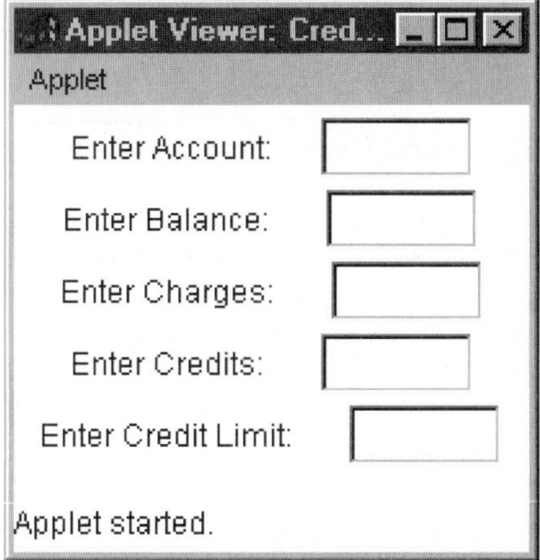

2.13 A large company pays its salespeople on a commission basis. The salespeople receive $200 per week plus 9 percent of their gross sales for that week. For example, a salesperson who sells $5000 worth of merchandise in a week receives $200 plus 9 percent of $5000, or a total of $650. You have been supplied with a list of items sold by each salesperson. The values of these items are as follows:

Item	Value
A	239.99
B	129.75
C	99.95
D	350.89

Develop a Java application that inputs one salesperson's items sold for last week and calculates and displays that salesperson's earnings. There is no limit to the number of items sold by a salesperson.

```
Enter the product sold ( A-D ). X to quit
A
Enter the product sold ( A-D ). X to quit
B
Enter the product sold ( A-D ). X to quit
C
Enter the product sold ( A-D ). X to quit
X
Total sales is $242.272
```

2.14 Develop a Java applet that will determine the gross pay for each of several employees. The company pays "straight-time" for the first 40 hours worked by each employee and pays "time-and-a-half" for all hours worked in excess of 40 hours. You are given a list of the employees of the company, the number of hours each employee worked last week, and the hourly rate of each employee. Your program should input this information for each employee, and should determine and display the employee's gross pay. Use **TextField**s to input the data.

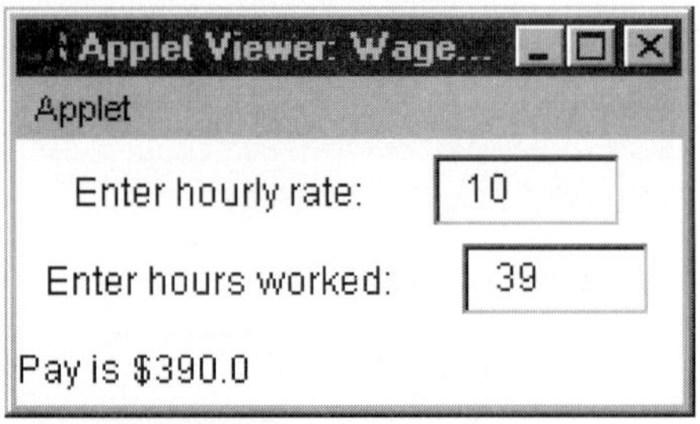

```
Applet Viewer: Wage...
Applet
Enter hourly rate:   10
Enter hours worked:  39
Pay is $390.0
```

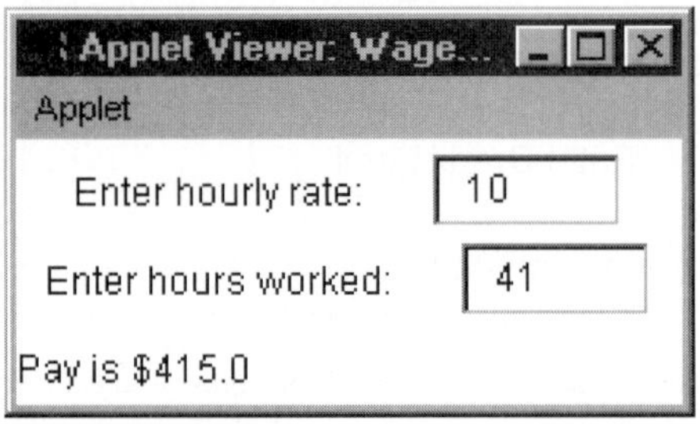

```
Applet Viewer: Wage...
Applet
Enter hourly rate:   10
Enter hours worked:  41
Pay is $415.0
```

2.15 The process of finding the largest value (i.e., the maximum of a group of values) is used frequently in computer applications. For example, a program that determines the winner of a sales contest would input the number of units sold by each salesperson. The salesperson who sells the most units wins the contest. Write a pseudocode program and then a Java application that inputs a series of 10 single-digit numbers as characters, and determines and prints the largest of the numbers. Hint: Your program should use three variables as follows:

`counter:` A counter to count to 10 (i.e., to keep track of how many numbers have been input, and to determine when all 10 numbers have been processed)

`number:` The current digit input to the program

`largest:` The largest number found so far.

2.16 Write a Java application that utilizes looping to print the following table of values:

```
N        10*N     100*N    1000*N

1        10       100      1000
2        20       200      2000
3        30       300      3000
4        40       400      4000
5        50       500      5000
```

2.17 Using an approach similar to Exercise 2.15, find the *two* largest values of the 10 digits entered. Note: You may input each number only once.

2.18 Modify the program in Fig. 2.11 to validate its inputs. On any input, if the value entered is other than 1 or 2, keep looping until the user enters a correct value.

2.19 What does the following program print?

```
public class Mystery2 {
   public static void main( String args[] )
   {
      int count = 1;
      while ( count <= 10 ) {
         System.out.println( count % 2 == 1 ?
                             "*****" : "++++++++" );
         ++count;
      }
   }
}
```

2.20 What does the following program print?

```
public class Mystery3 {
   public static void main( String args[] )
   {
      int row = 10, column;
      while ( row >= 1 ) {
         column = 1;
         while ( column <= 10 ) {
            System.out.print( row % 2 == 1 ? "<" : ">" );
            ++column;
         }
         --row;
         System.out.println();
      }
   }
}
```

2.21 *(Dangling-Else Problem)* Determine the output for each of the following when **x** is **9** and **y** is **11** and when **x** is **11** and **y** is **9**. Note that the compiler ignores the indentation in a Java program. Also, the Java compiler always associates an **else** with the previous **if** unless told to do otherwise by the placement of braces (**{}**). Because, on first glance, the programmer may not be sure which **if** an **else** matches, this is referred to as the "dangling-else" problem. We have eliminated the indentation from the following code to make the problem more challenging. (Hint: Apply indentation conventions you have learned.)

a)
```
if ( x < 10 )
if ( y > 10 )
System.out.println( "*****" );
else
System.out.println( "#####" );
System.out.println( "$$$$$" );
```
b)
```
if ( x < 10 ) {
if ( y > 10 )
System.out.println( "*****" );
}
else {
System.out.println( "#####" );
System.out.println( "$$$$$" );
}
```

2.22 *(Another Dangling-Else Problem)* Modify the following code to produce the output shown. Use proper indentation techniques. You may not make any changes other than inserting braces. The compiler ignores indentation in a Java program. We have eliminated the indentation from the following code to make the problem more challenging. Note: It is possible that no modification is necessary.

```
if ( y == 8 )
if ( x == 5 )
System.out.println( "@@@@@" );
else
System.out.println( "#####" );
System.out.println( "$$$$$" );
System.out.println( "&&&&&" );
```

a) Assuming **x = 5** and **y = 8**, the following output is produced.

```
@@@@@
$$$$$
&&&&&
```

b) Assuming **x = 5** and **y = 8**, the following output is produced.

```
@@@@@
```

c) Assuming **x = 5** and **y = 8**, the following output is produced.

```
@@@@@
&&&&&
```

d) Assuming **x = 5** and **y = 7**, the following output is produced. Note: The last three output statements after the **else** are all part of a compound statement.

```
#####
$$$$$
&&&&&
```

2.23 Write an applet that reads in the size of the side of a square and prints a hollow square of that size out of asterisks using the **drawString** method inside your applet's **paint** method. Use a **TextField** to read the size from the user. Your program should work for squares of all side sizes between 1 and 20. For example, if your program reads a size of 5, the output should look as follows

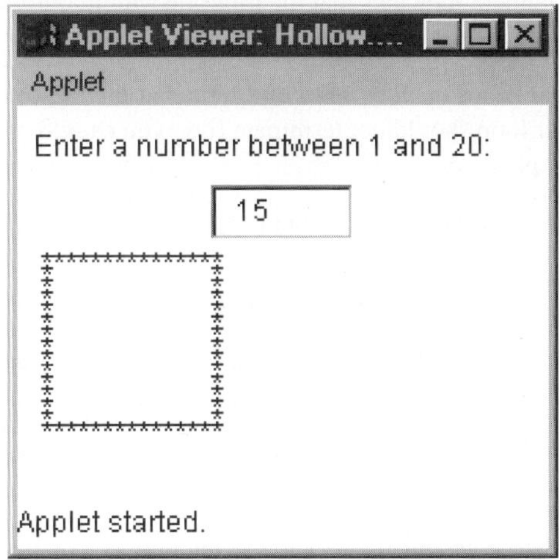

2.24 A palindrome is a number or a text phrase that reads the same backwards as forwards. For example, each of the following five-digit integers are palindromes: 12321, 55555, 45554 and 11611. Write an applet that reads in a five-digit integer and determines whether or not it is a palindrome.

2.25 Write an applet that inputs an integer containing only 0s and 1s (i.e., a "binary" integer) and print its decimal equivalent. (Hint: Use the modulus and division operators to pick off the "binary" number's digits one at a time from right to left. Just as in the decimal number system where the rightmost digit has a positional value of 1, and the next digit left has a positional value of 10, then 100, then 1000, etc., in the binary number system the rightmost digit has a positional value of 1, the next digit left has a positional value of 2, then 4, then 8, etc. Thus the decimal number 234 can be interpreted as 4 * 1 + 3 * 10 + 2 * 100. The decimal equivalent of binary 1101 is 1 * 1 + 0 * 2 + 1 * 4 + 1 * 8 or 1 + 0 + 4 + 8 or 13.)

2.26 Write an application that displays the following checkerboard pattern

Your program may use only three output statements, one of the form

```
System.out.print( "* " );
```

one of the form

```
System.out.print( " " );
```

and one of the form

```
System.out.println();
```

Note that the preceding statement indicates that the program should output a single newline character to drop to the next line on the output.

2.27 Write an applet that keeps displaying in the status bar the multiples of the integer 2, namely 2, 4, 8, 16, 32, 64, etc. Your loop should not terminate (i.e., you should create an infinite loop). What happens when you run this program?

2.28 What's wrong with the following statement? Provide the correct statement to add one to the sum of **x** and **y**.

```
System.out.println( ++(x + y) );
```

2.29 Write an applet that reads three non-zero values entered by the user in **TextField**s and determines and prints if they could represent the sides of a triangle.

2.30 Write an applet that reads three non-zero integers and determines and prints if they could be the sides of a right triangle.

2.31 A company wants to transmit data over the telephone, but they are concerned that their phones may be tapped. All of their data is transmitted as four-digit integers. They have asked you to write a program that will encrypt their data so that it may be transmitted more securely. Your applet should read a four-digit integer entered by the user in a **TextField** and encrypt it as follows: Replace each digit by *(the sum of that digit plus 7) modulus 10*. Then, swap the first digit with the third, and swap the second digit with the fourth. Then print the encrypted integer. Write a separate applet that inputs an encrypted four-digit integer, and decrypts it to form the original number.

2.32 The factorial of a non-negative integer n is written $n!$ (pronounced "n factorial") and is defined as follows:

$n! = n \cdot (n - 1) \cdot (n - 2) \cdot \ldots \cdot 1$ (for values of n greater than or equal to 1)

and

$n! = 1$ (for $n = 0$).

For example, $5! = 5 \cdot 4 \cdot 3 \cdot 2 \cdot 1$ which is 120.

a) Write an applet that reads a non-negative integer from a **TextField** and computes and prints its factorial.

b) Write an applet that estimates the value of the mathematical constant *e* by using the formula:

$$e = 1 + \frac{1}{1!} + \frac{1}{2!} + \frac{1}{3!} + \ldots$$

c) Write an applet that computes the value of e^x by using the formula:

$$e^x = 1 + \frac{x}{1!} + \frac{x^2}{2!} + \frac{x^3}{3!} + \ldots$$

3

Control Structures

Objectives

- To be able to use the **`for`** and **`do/while`** repetition structures to execute statements in a program repeatedly.
- To understand multiple selection using the **`switch`** selection structure.
- To be able to use the **`break`** and **`continue`** program control statements.
- To be able to use the logical operators.

Who can control his fate?
William Shakespeare, Othello

The used key is always bright.
Benjamin Franklin

Man is a tool-making animal.
Benjamin Franklin

Intelligence . . . is the faculty of making artificial objects, especially tools to make tools.
Henry Bergson

Outline

3.1 Introduction

Before writing a program to solve a particular problem, it is essential to have a thorough understanding of the problem and a carefully planned approach to solving the problem. When writing a program, it is equally essential to understand the types of building blocks that are available and to employ proven program construction principles. In this chapter we discuss all of these issues in our presentation of the theory and principles of structured programming. The techniques that you will learn here are applicable to most high-level languages including Java. When we begin our formal treatment of object-based programming in Java in Chapter 6, we will see that the control structures we study here in Chapter 3 are helpful in building and manipulating objects.

3.2 Essentials of Counter-Controlled Repetition

Counter-controlled repetition requires:

1. The *name* of a control variable (or loop counter).
2. The *initial value* of the control variable.
3. The *increment* (or *decrement*) by which the control variable is modified each time through the loop.
4. The condition that tests for the *final value* of the control variable (i.e., whether looping should continue).

Consider the simple program shown in Fig. 3.1, which prints the numbers from 1 to 10. The declaration

```
int counter = 1;
```

```
// Fig. 3.1: WhileCounter.java
// Counter-controlled repetition
import java.awt.Graphics;
import java.applet.Applet;

public class WhileCounter extends Applet {
   public void paint( Graphics g )
   {
      int counter = 1;              // initialization
      int yPos = 25;

      while ( counter <= 10 ) {     // repetition condition
         g.drawString( Integer.toString( counter ),
                       25, yPos );
         ++counter;                 // increment
         yPos += 15;
      }
   }
}
```

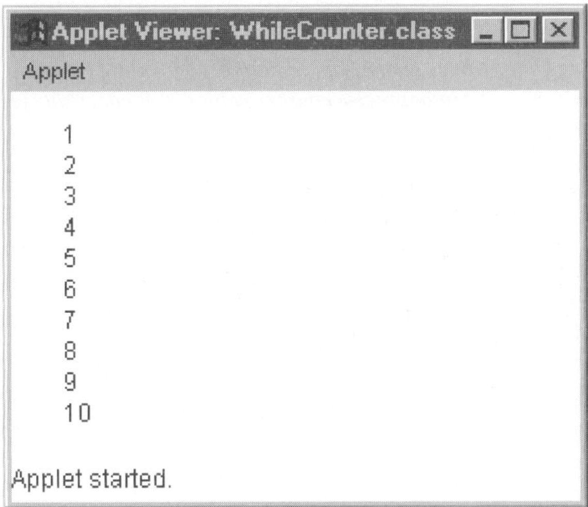

Fig. 3.1 Counter-controlled repetition.

names the control variable (**counter**), declares it to be an integer, reserves space for it in memory, and sets it to an *initial value* of **1**. Declarations that require initialization are, in effect, executable statements.

The declaration and initialization of **counter** could also have been accomplished with the statements

```
int counter;
counter = 1;
```

The declaration is not executable, but the assignment is. We use both methods of initializing variables.

The statement

```
++counter;
```

increments the loop counter by 1 each time the loop is performed. The loop-continuation condition in the **while** structure tests if the value of the control variable is less than or equal to **10** (the last value for which the condition is true). Note that the body of this **while** is performed even when the control variable is **10**. The loop terminates when the control variable exceeds **10** (i.e., **counter** becomes **11**).

The program in Fig. 3.1 can be made more concise by initializing **counter** to **0** and by replacing the **while** structure with

```
while ( ++counter <= 10 ) {     // repetition condition
   g.drawString( Integer.toString( counter ), 25, yPos );
   yPos += 15;
}
```

This code saves a statement because the incrementing is done directly in the **while** condition before the condition is tested. Coding in such a condensed fashion takes practice.

Common Programming Error 3.1

Because floating-point values may be approximate, controlling counting loops with floating-point variables may result in imprecise counter values and inaccurate tests for termination.

Good Programming Practice 3.1

Control counting loops with integer values.

Good Programming Practice 3.2

Indent the statements in the body of each control structure.

Good Programming Practice 3.3

Put a blank line before and after each major control structure to make it stand out in the program.

Good Programming Practice 3.4

Too many levels of nesting can make a program difficult to understand. As a general rule, try to avoid using more than three levels of indentation.

Good Programming Practice 3.5

Vertical spacing above and below control structures, and indentation of the bodies of control structures within the control structure headers gives programs a two-dimensional appearance that enhances readability.

3.3 The `for` Repetition Structure

The **for** repetition structure handles all the details of counter-controlled repetition. To illustrate the power of **for**, let us rewrite the program of Fig. 3.1. The result is shown in Fig. 3.2. The program operates as follows.

```
// Fig. 3.2: ForCounter.java
// Counter-controlled repetition with the for structure
import java.awt.Graphics;
import java.applet.Applet;

public class ForCounter extends Applet {
   public void paint( Graphics g )
   {
      int yPos = 25;

      // Initialization, repetition condition, and incrementing
      // are all included in the for structure header.
      for ( int counter = 1; counter <= 10; counter++ ) {
         g.drawString( Integer.toString( counter ), 25, yPos );
         yPos += 15;
      }
   }
}
```

Fig. 3.2 Counter-controlled repetition with the **for** structure.

When the **for** structure begins executing, the control variable **counter** is initialized to 1. Note that **counter** is declared inside the **for** and thus is known only within the **for** structure's body. Then, the loop-continuation condition **counter <= 10** is checked. Because the initial value of **counter** is 1, the condition is satisfied, so the body statement prints the value of **counter**, namely 1. Variable **counter** is then incremented in the expression **counter++**, and the loop begins again with the loop-continuation test. Because the control variable is now equal to 2, the final value is not exceeded, so the program performs the body statement again. This process continues until the control variable **counter** is incremented to 11—this causes the loop-continuation test to fail and repetition terminates. The program continues by performing the first statement after the **for** structure (in this case, the implied **return** statement at the end of the program).

Figure 3.3 takes a closer look at the **for** structure of Fig. 3.2. Notice that the **for** structure "does it all"—it specifies each of the items needed for counter-controlled repeti-

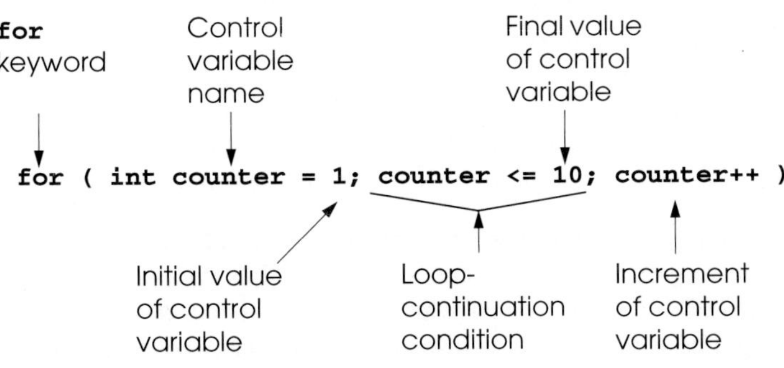

Fig. 3.3 Components of a typical **for** header.

tion with a control variable. If there is more than one statement in the body of the **for** (as in Fig. 3.2), braces are required to define the body of the loop.

Notice that Fig. 3.2 uses the loop-continuation condition **counter <= 10**. If the programmer incorrectly wrote **counter < 10**, then the loop would only be executed 9 times. This is a common logic error called an *off-by-one error.*

Common Programming Error 3.2

Using an incorrect relational operator or using an incorrect final value of a loop counter in the condition of a **while***,* **for** *or* **do/while** *structure can cause off-by-one errors.*

Good Programming Practice 3.6

Using the final value in the condition of a **while** *or* **for** *structure and using the* **<=** *relational operator will help avoid off-by-one errors. For a loop used to print the values 1 to 10, for example, the loop-continuation condition should be* **counter <= 10** *rather than* **counter < 10** *(which is an off-by-one error) or* **counter < 11** *(which is also correct).*

The general format of the **for** structure is

```
for ( expression1; expression2; expression3 )
    statement
```

where *expression1* initializes the loop's control variable, *expression2* is the loop-continuation condition, and *expression3* increments the control variable. In most cases the **for** structure can be represented with an equivalent **while** structure as follows:

```
expression1;

while ( expression2 ) {
    statement
    expression3;
}
```

There is an exception to this rule which we will discuss in Section 3.7.

Sometimes, *expression1* and *expression3* in a **for** structure are comma-separated lists of expressions that enable the programmer to use multiple initialization expressions and/or multiple increment expressions. For example, there may be several control variables in a single **for** structure that must be initialized and incremented.

Good Programming Practice 3.7

Place only expressions involving the control variables in the initialization and increment sections of a **for** *structure. Manipulations of other variables should appear either before the loop (if they execute only once like initialization statements) or in the loop body (if they execute once per repetition like incrementing or decrementing statements).*

The three expressions in the **for** structure are optional. If *expression2* is omitted, Java assumes that the loop-continuation condition is true, thus creating an infinite loop. One might omit *expression1* if the control variable is initialized elsewhere in the program. *expression3* might be omitted if the increment is calculated by statements in the body of the **for** or if no increment is needed. The increment expression in the **for** structure acts like a stand-alone statement at the end of the body of the **for**. Therefore, the expressions

```
counter = counter + 1
counter += 1
++counter
counter++
```

are all equivalent in the incrementing portion of the **for** structure. Many programmers prefer the form **counter++** because the incrementing occurs after the loop body is executed. The postincrementing form therefore seems more natural. Because the variable being incremented here does not appear in an expression, preincrementing and postincrementing both have the same effect. The two semicolons in the **for** structure are required.

Common Programming Error 3.3

*Using commas instead of the two required semicolons in a **for** header is a syntax error.*

Common Programming Error 3.4

*Placing a semicolon immediately to the right of the right parenthesis of a **for** header makes the body of that **for** structure an empty statement. This is normally a logic error.*

The initialization, loop-continuation condition, and increment portions of a **for** structure can contain arithmetic expressions. For example, assume that **x = 2** and **y = 10**. If **x** and **y** are not modified in the loop body, the statement

```
for ( int j = x; j <= 4 * x * y; j += y / x )
```

is equivalent to the statement

```
for ( int j = 2; j <= 80; j += 5 )
```

The "increment" of a **for** structure may be negative in which case it is really a decrement and the loop actually counts downwards.

If the loop-continuation condition is initially false, the body of the **for** structure is not performed. Instead, execution proceeds with the statement following the **for**.

The control variable is frequently printed or used in calculations in the body of a **for** structure, but it does not have to be. It is common to use the control variable for controlling repetition while never mentioning it in the body of the **for** structure.

Testing and Debugging Tip 3.1

*Although the value of the control variable can be changed in the body of a **for** loop, avoid doing so because this practice can lead to subtle errors.*

The **for** structure is flowcharted much like the **while** structure. For example, the flowchart of the **for** statement

```
for ( int counter = 1; counter <= 10; counter++ ) {
   g.drawString( Integer.toString( counter ), 25, yPos );
   yPos += 15;
}
```

is shown in Fig. 3.4. This flowchart makes it clear that the initialization occurs only once and that incrementing occurs each time *after* the body statement is performed. Note that

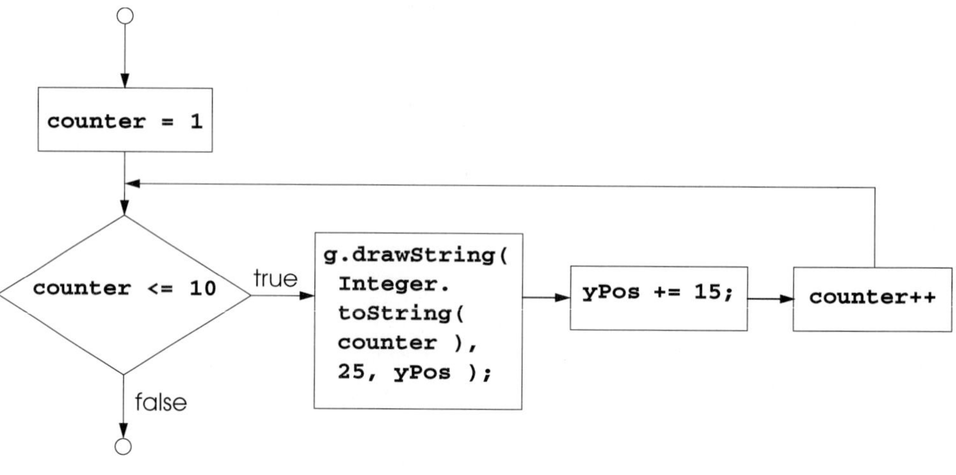

Fig. 3.4 Flowcharting a typical **`for`** repetition structure.

(besides small circles and arrows) the flowchart contains only rectangle symbols and a diamond symbol. Imagine, again, that the programmer has access to a deep bin of empty **`for`** structures—as many as the programmer might need to stack and nest with other control structures to form a structured implementation of an algorithm's flow of control. The rectangles and diamonds are then filled with actions and decisions appropriate to the algorithm.

3.4 Examples Using the `for` Structure

The following examples show methods of varying the control variable in a **`for`** structure. In each case, we write the appropriate **`for`** header. Note the change in the relational operator for loops that decrement the control variable.

a) Vary the control variable from **`1`** to **`100`** in increments of **`1`**.

```
for ( int i = 1; i <= 100; i++ )
```

b) Vary the control variable from **`100`** to **`1`** in increments of **`-1`** (decrements of **`1`**).

```
for ( int i = 100; i >= 1; i-- )
```

Common Programming Error 3.5

Not using the proper relational operator in the loop-continuation condition of a loop that counts downwards (such as using **`i <= 1`** *in a loop counting down to 1) can cause an infinite loop.*

c) Vary the control variable from **`7`** to **`77`** in steps of **`7`**.

```
for ( int i = 7; i <= 77; i += 7 )
```

d) Vary the control variable from **`20`** to **`2`** in steps of **`-2`**.

```
for ( int i = 20; i >= 2; i -= 2 )
```

e) Vary the control variable over the following sequence of values: **2**, **5**, **8**, **11**, **14**, **17**, **20**.

```
for ( int j = 2; j <= 20; j += 3 )
```

f) Vary the control variable over the following sequence of values: **99**, **88**, **77**, **66**, **55**, **44**, **33**, **22**, **11**, **0**.

```
for ( int j = 99; j >= 0; j -= 11 )
```

The next two sample programs demonstrate simple applications of the **for** repetition structure. The program of Fig. 3.5 uses the **for** structure to sum all the even integers from **2** to **100**.

Note that the body of the **for** structure in Fig. 3.5 could actually be merged into the rightmost portion of the **for** header by using a *comma* as follows:

```
for ( int number = 2; number <= 100;
      sum += number, number += 2)
   ;
```

Similarly, the initialization **sum = 0** could be merged into the initialization section of the **for** structure.

```
// Fig. 3.5: Sum.java
// Counter-controlled repetition with the for structure
import java.awt.Graphics;
import java.applet.Applet;

public class Sum extends Applet {
   public void paint( Graphics g )
   {
      int sum = 0;

      for ( int number = 2; number <= 100; number += 2 )
         sum += number;

      g.drawString( "Sum is " + sum, 25, 25 );
   }
}
```

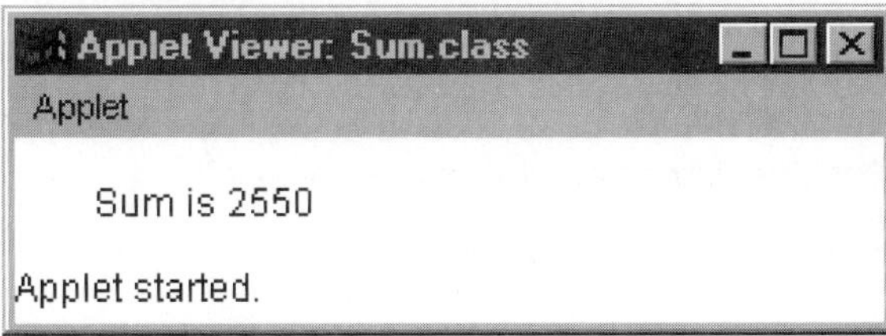

Fig. 3.5 Summation with **for**.

Good Programming Practice 3.8

Although statements preceding a **for** *and statements in the body of a* **for** *can often be merged into the* **for** *header, avoid doing so because it makes the program more difficult to read.*

Good Programming Practice 3.9

Limit the size of control structure headers to a single line if possible.

The next example computes compound interest using the **for** structure. Consider the following problem statement:

A person invests $1000.00 in a savings account yielding 5 percent interest. Assuming that all interest is left on deposit, calculate and print the amount of money in the account at the end of each year for 10 years. Use the following formula for determining these amounts:

$$a = p\,(1 + r)^{n}$$

where

p is the original amount invested (i.e., the principal)
r is the annual interest rate
n is the number of years
a is the amount on deposit at the end of the nth year.

This problem involves a loop that performs the indicated calculation for each of the 10 years the money remains on deposit. The solution is shown in Fig. 3.6.

```
// Fig. 3.6: Interest.java
// Calculating compound interest
import java.awt.Graphics;
import java.applet.Applet;

public class Interest extends Applet {
   public void paint( Graphics g )
   {
      double amount, principal = 1000.0, rate = .05;
      int yPos = 40;

      g.drawString( "Year", 25, 25 );
      g.drawString( "Amount on deposit", 100, 25 );

      for ( int year = 1; year <= 10; year++ ) {
         amount = principal * Math.pow( 1.0 + rate, year );
         g.drawString( Integer.toString( year ), 25, yPos );
        g.drawString( Double.toString( amount ), 100, yPos );
         yPos += 15;
      }
   }
}
```

Fig. 3.6 Calculating compound interest with **for** (part 1 of 2).

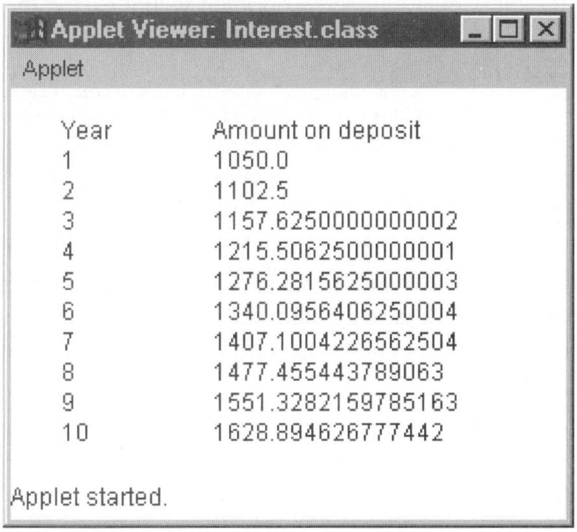

```
Applet Viewer: Interest.class
Applet

Year    Amount on deposit
1       1050.0
2       1102.5
3       1157.6250000000002
4       1215.5062500000001
5       1276.2815625000003
6       1340.0956406250004
7       1407.1004226562504
8       1477.455443789063
9       1551.3282159785163
10      1628.894626777442

Applet started.
```

Fig. 3.6 Calculating compound interest with **for** (part 2 of 2).

The **for** structure executes its body 10 times, varying a control variable from 1 to 10 in increments of 1. Java does not include an exponentiation operator. Instead, we use **Math** class method **Math.pow** for this purpose. **Math.pow(x, y)** calculates the value of **x** raised to the **y**th power. Method **Math.pow** takes two arguments of type **double** and returns a **double** value. Type **double** is a floating-point type much like **float**, but a variable of type **double** can store a value of greater magnitude with greater precision than **float**. Constants (like **1000.0** and **.05** in Fig. 3.6) are treated as type **double** by Java.

Line 18 uses method **Double.toString** to convert the value of **amount** to a string of characters that can be displayed by **drawString**. Class **Double** is located in package **java.lang**. Notice the number of decimal places to the right of the decimal point in each of the output window's rows. In Chapter 6 we introduce number formatting techniques.

Notice that the variables **amount**, **principal**, and **rate** are of type **double**. We did this for simplicity because we are dealing with fractional parts of dollars and we need a type that allows decimal points in its values. Unfortunately, this can cause trouble. Here is a simple explanation of what can go wrong when using **float** or **double** to represent dollar amounts (assuming that dollar amounts are displayed with two digits to the right of the decimal point): Two **double** dollar amounts stored in the machine could be 14.234 (which would normally be rounded to 14.23 for display purposes) and 18.673 (which would normally be rounded to 18.67 for display purposes). When these amounts are added, they produce the internal sum 32.907 which would normally be rounded to 32.91 for display purposes. Thus your printout could appear as

```
  14.23
+ 18.67
-------
  32.91
```

but a person adding the individual numbers as printed would expect the sum 32.90! You have been warned!

Good Programming Practice 3.10

Do not use variables of type **`float`** *or* **`double`** *to perform precise monetary calculations. The imprecision of floating-point numbers can cause errors that will result in incorrect monetary values. In the exercises, we explore the use of integers to perform monetary calculations. Note: Class libraries are becoming available for properly performing monetary calculations.*

Note that the calculation **`1.0 + rate`** that appears as an argument to the **`Math.pow`** method is contained in the body of the **`for`** statement. In fact, this calculation produces the same result each time through the loop, so repeating the calculation is wasteful.

Performance Tip 3.1

Avoid placing expressions whose values do not change inside loops. But even if you do, many of today's sophisticated optimizing compilers will automatically place such expressions outside loops in the generated machine-language code.

3.5 The `switch` Multiple-Selection Structure

We have discussed the **`if`** single-selection structure and the **`if/else`** double-selection structure. Occasionally, an algorithm will contain a series of decisions in which a variable or expression is tested separately for each of the constant integral values it may assume, and different actions are taken. Java provides the **`switch`** multiple-selection structure (as shown in Fig. 3.7) to handle such decision making.

```java
// Fig. 3.7: SwitchTest.java
// Counting letter grades
import java.awt.*;
import java.applet.Applet;
import java.awt.event.*;

public class SwitchTest extends Applet
             implements ActionListener {
   Label prompt;       // label for TextField
   TextField input;    // TextField to enter grades

   int aCount = 0, bCount = 0, cCount = 0,
       dCount = 0, fCount = 0;

   public void init()
   {
      prompt = new Label( "Enter grade" );
      input = new TextField( 2 );
      input.addActionListener( this );
      add( prompt );
```

Fig. 3.7 An example using **`switch`** (part 1 of 3).

```
      add( input );
   }

   public void paint( Graphics g )
   {
      g.drawString( "Totals for each letter grade:", 25, 40 );
      g.drawString( "A: " + aCount, 25, 55 );
      g.drawString( "B: " + bCount, 25, 70 );
      g.drawString( "C: " + cCount, 25, 85 );
      g.drawString( "D: " + dCount, 25, 100 );
      g.drawString( "F: " + fCount, 25, 115 );
   }

   public void actionPerformed( ActionEvent e )
   {
      String val = e.getActionCommand();
      char grade = val.charAt( 0 );

      showStatus( "" );       // clear status bar area
      input.setText( "" );    // clear input TextField

      switch ( grade ) {

         case 'A': case 'a':  // Grade was uppercase A
            ++aCount;         // or lowercase a.
            break;

         case 'B': case 'b':  // Grade was uppercase B
            ++bCount;         // or lowercase b.
            break;

         case 'C': case 'c':  // Grade was uppercase C
            ++cCount;         // or lowercase c.
            break;

         case 'D': case 'd':  // Grade was uppercase D
            ++dCount;         // or lowercase d.
            break;

         case 'F': case 'f':  // Grade was uppercase F
            ++fCount;         // or lowercase f.
            break;

         default:             // catch all other characters
            showStatus( "Incorrect grade. Enter new grade." );
            break;
      }

      repaint();  // display summary of results
   }
}
```

Fig. 3.7 An example using **`switch`** (part 2 of 3).

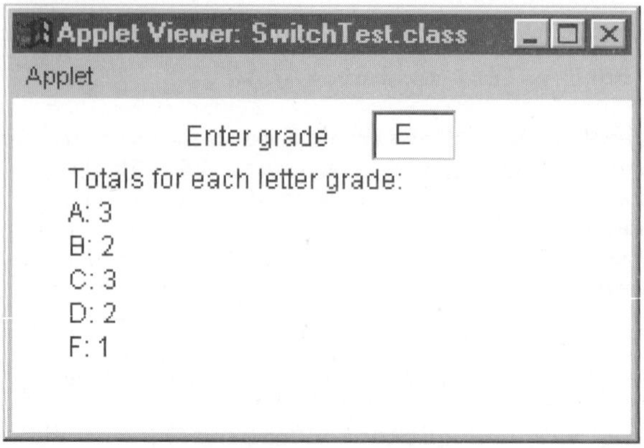

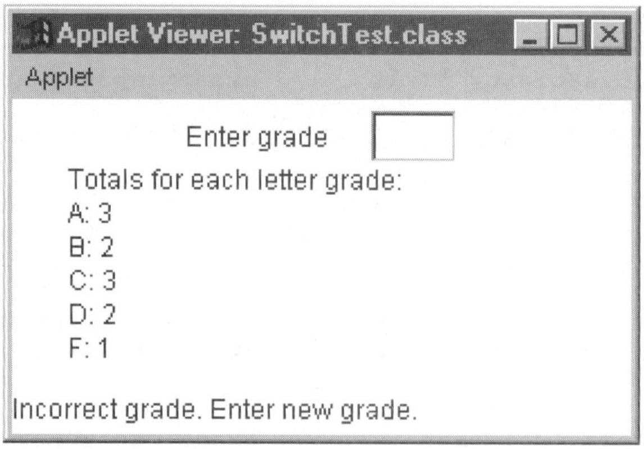

Fig. 3.7 An example using **`switch`** (part 3 of 3).

The **`switch`** structure consists of a series of **`case`** labels, and an optional **`default`** case. The program in Fig. 3.7 uses **`switch`** to count the number of each different letter grade that students earned on an exam.

In the program, the user enters letter grades for a class into a **`TextField`**. When the *Enter* key is pressed, method **`actionPerformed`** (line 34) is called to read the letter grade and process it. The line

```
String val = e.getActionCommand();
```

takes the **`String`** entered by the user in the **`TextField`** and assigns it to **`val`**. Remember that method **`actionPerformed`** automatically receives the data in the **`TextField`** (as a **`String`**) when the user presses the *Enter* key and that **`e.getActionCommand()`** allows us to obtain the value as a **`String`** in our program. However, we actually want to process an individual character typed by the user. The line

```
char grade = val.charAt( 0 );
```

uses the **charAt** method to select the character at position 0 (zero) of the string and assign it to the variable **grade**. Java considers the first character in a string to be at position 0. The **charAt** method can be used to select a character at any position in a string. For example, if the string **s** contains "**hello**," the statement

```
char letter = s.charAt( 4 );
```

selects the fifth character ("**o**") and assigns it to variable **letter**. If the position number specified is outside of the characters in the string (i.e., less than zero, or greater than or equal to the length of the string), an exception is generated. Exceptions are discussed in detail in Chapter 12.

After clearing the **TextField** and status bar, the **switch** structure is entered. The keyword **switch** is followed by the variable name **grade** in parentheses. This is called the *controlling expression.* The value of this expression is compared with each of the ***case*** *labels.* Assume the user has entered the letter **C** as a grade. **C** is automatically compared to each **case** in the **switch**. If a match occurs (**case 'C':**), the statements for that **case** are executed. For the letter **C**, **cCount** is incremented by **1**, and the **switch** structure is exited immediately with the **break** statement.

The **break** statement causes program control to proceed with the first statement after the **switch** structure. The **break** statement is used because the **case**s in a **switch** statement would otherwise run together. If **break** is not used anywhere in a **switch** structure, then each time a match occurs in the structure, the statements for all the remaining **case**s will be executed. (This feature is perfect for programming the iterative song "The Twelve Days of Christmas!") If no match occurs, the **default** case is executed and an error message is printed.

Each **case** can have multiple actions. The **switch** structure is different from other structures in that braces are not required around multiple actions in a **case** of a **switch**. The general **switch** structure (using a **break** in each **case**) is flowcharted in Fig. 3.8. (Note: As an exercise flowchart the general **switch** structure without **break** statements.)

The flowchart makes it clear that each **break** statement at the end of a **case** causes control to immediately exit the **switch** structure. Again, note that (besides small circles and arrows) the flowchart contains only rectangle symbols and diamond symbols. Imagine, again, that the programmer has access to a deep bin of empty **switch** structures—as many as the programmer might need to stack and nest with other control structures to form a structured implementation of an algorithm's flow of control. Again, the rectangles and diamonds are filled with actions and decisions appropriate to the algorithm. Although nested control structures are common, it is rare to find nested **switch** structures in a program.

Common Programming Error 3.6

Forgetting a ***break*** *statement when one is needed in a* ***switch*** *structure.*

Good Programming Practice 3.11

Provide a ***default*** *case in* ***switch*** *statements. Cases not explicitly tested in a* ***switch*** *statement without a* ***default*** *case are ignored. Including a* ***default*** *case focuses the programmer on the need to process exceptional conditions. There are situations in which no* ***default*** *processing is needed.*

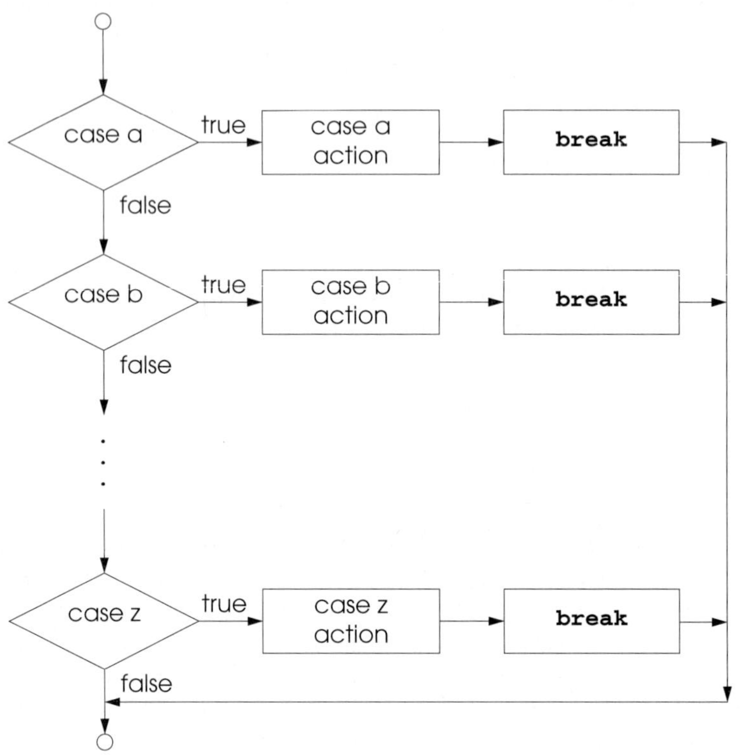

Fig. 3.8 The **`switch`** multiple-selection structure.

Good Programming Practice 3.12

*Although the **`case`** clauses and the **`default`** case clause in a **`switch`** structure can occur in any order, it is considered a good programming practice to place the **`default`** clause last.*

Good Programming Practice 3.13

*In a **`switch`** structure when the **`default`** clause is listed last, the **`break`** for that **`case`** statement is not required. Some programmers include this **`break`** for clarity and symmetry with other cases.*

Note that several **`case`** labels listed together (such as **`case 'D': case 'd':`** in Fig. 3.7) simply means that the same set of actions is to occur for each of the cases.

When using the **`switch`** structure, remember that the expression after each **`case`** can only be a *constant integral expression,* i.e., any combination of character constants and integer constants that evaluates to a constant integer value. A character constant is represented as the specific character in single quotes such as **'A'**. An integer constant is simply an integer value.

Common Programming Error 3.7

Omitting the space between the word **case** *and the integral value being tested in a* **switch** *structure can cause a logic error. For example, writing* **case3:** *instead of writing* **case 3:** *simply creates an unused label (we will say more about labels later). The problem is that the* **switch** *structure will not perform the appropriate actions when the* **switch***'s controlling expression has a value of 3.*

When we discuss object-oriented programming in Chapter 7, we will present a more elegant way to implement **switch** logic. We will use a technique called polymorphism to create programs that are often clearer, easier to maintain, and easier to extend than programs using **switch** logic.

3.6 The do/while Repetition Structure

The **do/while** repetition structure is similar to the **while** structure. In the **while** structure, the loop-continuation condition is tested at the beginning of the loop before the body of the loop is performed. The **do/while** structure tests the loop-continuation condition *after* the loop body is performed, therefore *the loop body is executed at least once.* When a **do/while** terminates, execution continues with the statement after the **while** clause. Note that it is not necessary to use braces in the **do/while** structure if there is only one statement in the body. However, the braces are usually included to avoid confusion between the **while** and **do/while** structures. For example,

```
while ( condition )
```

is normally regarded as the header to a **while** structure. A **do/while** with no braces around the single statement body appears as

```
do
    statement
while ( condition );
```

which can be confusing. The last line—**while(** *condition* **);**—may be misinterpreted by the reader as a **while** structure containing an empty statement. Thus, the **do/while** with one statement is often written as follows to avoid confusion:

```
do {
    statement
} while (condition);
```

Good Programming Practice 3.14

Some programmers always include braces in a **do/while** *structure even if the braces are not necessary. This helps eliminate ambiguity between the* **while** *structure and the* **do/ while** *structure containing one statement.*

Common Programming Error 3.8

Infinite loops are caused when the loop-continuation condition in a **while**, **for**, *or* **do/while** *structure never becomes false. To prevent this, make sure there is not a semicolon immediately after the header of a* **while** *structure. In a counter-controlled loop, make sure the control variable is incremented (or decremented) in the body of the loop. In a sentinel-controlled loop, make sure the sentinel value is eventually input.*

The program in Fig. 3.9 uses a **do/while** structure to print the numbers from 1 to 10. Note that the control variable **counter** is preincremented in the loop-continuation test.

The **do/while** flowchart (Fig. 3.10) makes it clear that the loop-continuation condition is not executed until the action is performed at least once. The flowchart contains only a rectangle and a diamond. Imagine, also, that the programmer has access to a bin of empty **do/while** structures—as many as the programmer might need to stack and nest with other control structures to form a structured implementation of an algorithm. The rectangles and diamonds are filled with actions and decisions appropriate to the algorithm.

```
// Fig. 3.9: DoWhileTest.java
// Using the do/while repetition structure
import java.awt.Graphics;
import java.applet.Applet;

public class DoWhileTest extends Applet {
   public void paint( Graphics g )
   {
      int counter = 1;
      int xPos = 25;

      do {
         g.drawString( Integer.toString( counter ), xPos, 25 );
         xPos += 15;
      } while ( ++counter <= 10 );
   }
}
```

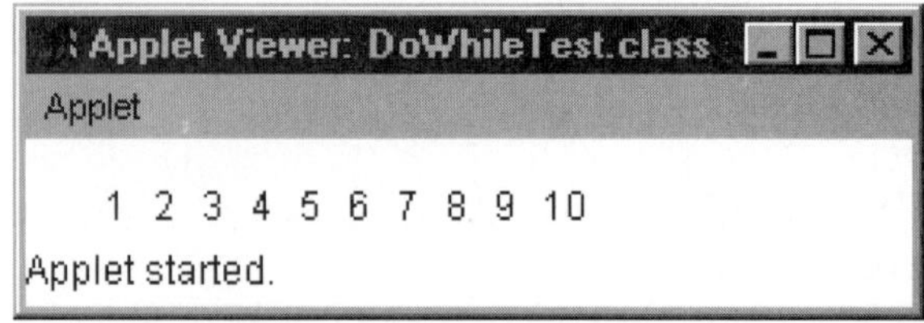

Fig. 3.9 Using the **do/while** repetition structure.

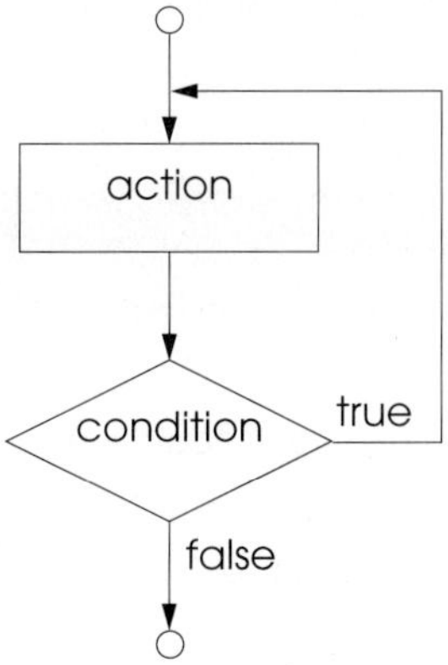

action
condition
true
false

Fig. 3.10 Flowcharting the **`do/while`** repetition structure.

3.7 The `break` and `continue` Statements

The **`break`** and **`continue`** statements alter the flow of control. The **`break`** statement, when executed in a **`while`**, **`for`**, **`do/while`**, or **`switch`** structure, causes immediate exit from that structure. Execution continues with the first statement after the structure. Common uses of the **`break`** statement are to escape early from a loop, or to skip the remainder of a **`switch`** structure (as in Fig. 3.7). Figure 3.11 demonstrates the **`break`** statement in a **`for`** repetition structure. When the **`if`** structure detects that **`count`** has become **`5`**, **`break`** is executed. This terminates the **`for`** statement and the program proceeds to the second **`drawString`**, i.e., the one after the **`for`**. The loop fully executes only four times.

```
// Fig. 3.11: BreakTest.java
// Using the break statement in a for structure
import java.awt.Graphics;
import java.applet.Applet;

public class BreakTest extends Applet {
   public void paint( Graphics g )
   {
      int count, xPos = 25;

      for ( count = 1; count <= 10; count++ ) {
         if ( count == 5 )
            break;  // break loop only if count == 5

         g.drawString( Integer.toString( count ), xPos, 25 );
         xPos += 10;
      }

```

Fig. 3.11 Using the **`break`** statement in a **`for`** structure (part 1 of 2).

```
      g.drawString( "Broke out of loop at count = " + count,
                    25, 40 );
   }
}
```

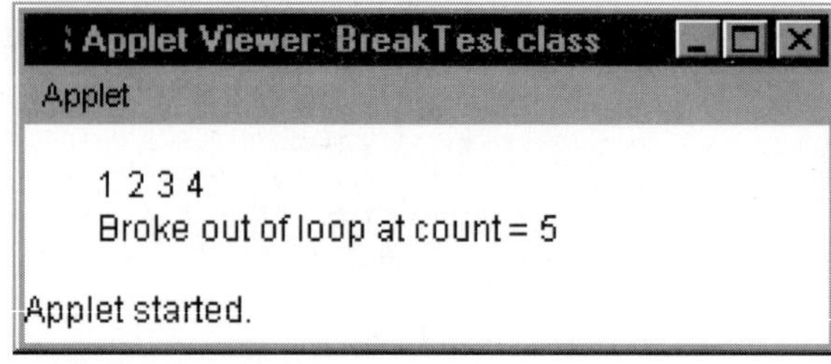

Fig. 3.11 Using the **break** statement in a **for** structure (part 2 of 2).

The **continue** statement, when executed in a **while**, **for**, or **do/while** structure, skips the remaining statements in the body of that structure, and proceeds with the next iteration of the loop. In **while** and **do/while** structures, the loop-continuation test is evaluated immediately after the **continue** statement is executed. In the **for** structure, the increment expression is executed, then the loop-continuation test is evaluated. Earlier, we stated that the **while** structure could be used in most cases to represent the **for** structure. The one exception occurs when the increment expression in the **while** structure follows the **continue** statement. In this case, the increment is not executed before the repetition-continuation condition is tested, and the **while** does not execute in the same manner as the **for**. Figure 3.12 uses the **continue** statement in a **for** structure to skip the output statement in the structure when **count** is **5** and begin the next iteration of the loop.

```
// Fig. 3.12: ContinueTest.java
// Using the continue statement in a for structure
import java.awt.Graphics;
import java.applet.Applet;

public class ContinueTest extends Applet {
   public void paint( Graphics g )
   {
      int xPos = 25;

      for ( int count = 1; count <= 10; count++ ) {
         if ( count == 5 )
            continue;   // skip remaining code in loop
                        // only if count == 5

         g.drawString( Integer.toString( count ), xPos, 25 );
         xPos += 10;
      }

```

Fig. 3.12 Using the **continue** statement in a **for** structure (part 1 of 2).

```
        g.drawString( "Used continue to skip printing 5",
                      25, 40 );
    }
}
```

Fig. 3.12 Using the **continue** statement in a **for** structure (part 2 of 2).

Good Programming Practice 3.15

Some programmers feel that **break** *and* **continue** *violate structured programming. Because the effects of these statements can be achieved by structured programming techniques we will soon learn, these programmers do not use* **break** *and* **continue**.

Software Engineering Observation 3.1

There is a tension between achieving quality software engineering and achieving the best performing software. Often, one of these goals is achieved at the expense of the other.

3.8 The Labeled break and continue Statements

The **break** statement can only break out of an immediately enclosing **while**, **for**, **do/while** or **switch** structure. To break out of a nested set of structures, you can use the *labeled* **break** *statement*. This statement, when executed in a **while**, **for**, **do/while** or **switch**, causes immediate exit from that structure and any number of enclosing structures; program execution resumes with the first statement after the enclosing *labeled compound statement* (i.e., a set of statements enclosed in curly braces and preceded by a label). Labeled **break** statements are commonly used to terminate nested looping structures containing **while**, **for**, **do/while** or **switch** structures. Figure 3.13 demonstrates the labeled **break** statement in a nested **for** structure. The labeled compound statement (lines 11–28) begins with a label (an identifier followed by a colon); here we use the label **stop**. When the **if** structure at line 18 detects that **row** is equal to **5**, the statement

```
break stop;
```

is executed. This terminates both the **for** structure at line 16 and its enclosing **for** structure at line 12, and the program proceeds to the statement at line 30, i.e., the first statement after the labeled compound statement. The inner **for** structure fully executes only four times. Notice that the **drawString** at line 27 never executes because it is included in the labeled compound statement and the outer **for** structure never completes.

```
// Fig. 3.13: BreakLabelTest.java
// Using the break statement with a label
import java.awt.Graphics;
import java.applet.Applet;

public class BreakLabelTest extends Applet {
   public void paint( Graphics g )
   {
      int xPos, yPos = 0;

      stop: {  // labeled compound statement
         for ( int row = 1; row <= 10; row++ ) {
            xPos = 25;
            yPos += 15;

            for ( int column = 1; column <= 5 ; column++ ) {

               if ( row == 5 )
                  break stop; // jump to end of stop block

               g.drawString( "#", xPos, yPos );
               xPos += 7;
            }
         }

         yPos += 15;
         g.drawString( "Loops terminated normally", 25, yPos );
      }

      yPos += 15;
      g.drawString( "End of paint method", 25, yPos );
   }
}
```

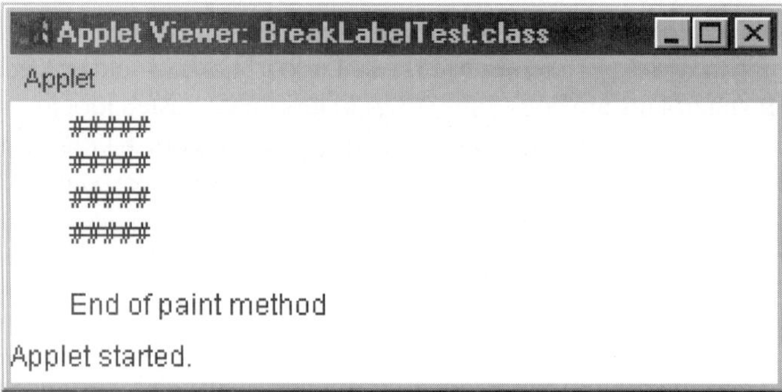

Fig. 3.13 Using a labeled **`break`** statement in a nested **`for`** structure.

The **continue** statement proceeds with the next iteration (repetition) of the immediately enclosing **while**, **for** or **do/while** structure. The *labeled* ***continue*** *statement*, when executed in a repetition structure (**while**, **for** or **do/while**), skips the remaining statements in that structure's body and any number of enclosing repetition structures, and proceeds with the next iteration of the enclosing *labeled repetition structure* (i.e., a repetition structure preceded by a label). In labeled **while** and **do/while** structures, the loop-continuation test is evaluated immediately after the **continue** statement is executed. In a labeled **for** structure, the increment expression is executed, then the loop-continuation test is evaluated. Figure 3.14 uses the labeled **continue** statement in a nested **for** structure to cause execution to continue with the next iteration of the outer **for** structure. The labeled **for** structure (lines 11–24) starts at the **nextRow** label. When the **if** structure at line 18 in the inner **for** structure detects that **column** is greater than **row**, the statement

```
continue nextRow;
```

is executed and execution continues with the next iteration of the outer **for** loop. Even though the inner **for** structure counts from 1 to 10, the number of **#** characters output on a row never exceeds the value of **row**.

```
1  // Fig. 3.14: ContinueLabelTest.java
2  // Using the continue statement with a label
3  import java.awt.Graphics;
4  import java.applet.Applet;
5
6  public class ContinueLabelTest extends Applet {
7     public void paint( Graphics g )
8     {
9        int xPos, yPos = 0;
10
11       nextRow:   // target label of continue statement
12          for ( int row = 1; row <= 5; row++ ) {
13             xPos = 25;
14             yPos += 15;
15
16             for ( int column = 1; column <= 10; column++ ) {
17
18                if ( column > row )
19                   continue nextRow; // next iteration of
20                                     // labeled loop
21
22                g.drawString( "#", xPos, yPos );
23                xPos += 7;
24             }
25          }
26    }
27 }
```

Fig. 3.14 Using a labeled **continue** statement in a nested **for** structure (part 1 of 2).

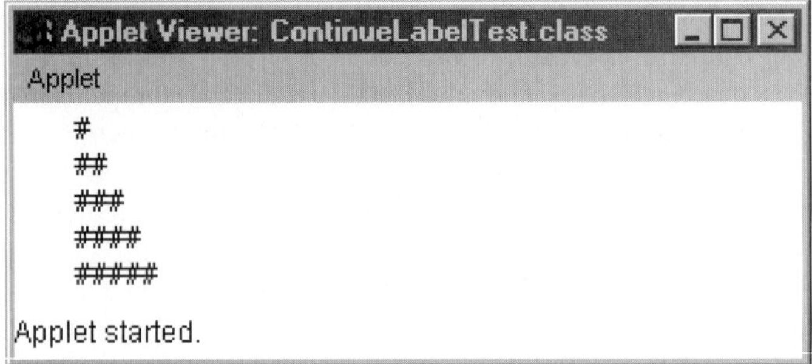

Fig. 3.14 Using a labeled **continue** statement in a nested **for** structure (part 2 of 2).

3.9 Logical Operators

So far we have studied only *simple conditions* such as **count <= 10**, **total > 1000**, and **number != sentinelValue**. These conditions were expressed in terms of the relational operators **>**, **<**, **>=**, and **<=**, and the equality operators **==** and **!=**. Each decision tested one condition. To test multiple conditions in the process of making a decision, we had to perform these tests in separate statements or in nested **if** or **if/else** structures.

Java provides *logical operators* that may be used to form more complex conditions by combining simple conditions. The logical operators are **&&** *(logical AND)*, **&** *(boolean logical AND)*, **||** *(logical OR)*, **|** *(boolean logical inclusive OR)*, **^** *(boolean logical exclusive OR)* and **!** *(logical NOT also called logical negation)*. We will consider examples of each of these.

Suppose we wish to ensure at some point in a program that two conditions are *both* **true** before we choose a certain path of execution. In this case we can use the logical **&&** operator as follows:

```
if ( gender == 1 && age >= 65 )
   ++seniorFemales;
```

This **if** statement contains two simple conditions. The condition **gender == 1** might be evaluated, for example, to determine if a person is a female. The condition **age >= 65** is evaluated to determine if a person is a senior citizen. The two simple conditions are evaluated first because the precedences of **==** and **>=** are both higher than the precedence of **&&**. The **if** statement then considers the combined condition

```
gender == 1 && age >= 65
```

This condition is **true** if and only if both of the simple conditions are **true**. Finally, if this combined condition is indeed **true**, then the count of **seniorFemales** is incremented by **1**. If either or both of the simple conditions are **false**, then the program skips the incrementing and proceeds to the statement following the **if**. The preceding combined condition can be made more readable by adding redundant parentheses

```
( gender == 1 ) && ( age >= 65 )
```

The table of Fig. 3.15 summarizes the **&&** operator. The table shows all four possible combinations of **false** and **true** values for expression1 and expression2. Such tables are often called *truth tables.* Java evaluates to **false** or **true** all expressions that include relational operators, equality operators, and/or logical operators.

Now let us consider the || (logical OR) operator. Suppose we wish to ensure that either *or* both of two conditions are **true** before we choose a certain path of execution. In this case we use the || operator as in the following program segment:

```
if ( semesterAverage >= 90 || finalExam >= 90 )
   System.out.println ( "Student grade is A" );
```

This statement also contains two simple conditions. The condition **semesterAverage >= 90** is evaluated to determine if the student deserves an "A" in the course because of a solid performance throughout the semester. The condition **finalExam >= 90** is evaluated to determine if the student deserves an "A" in the course because of an outstanding performance on the final exam. The **if** statement then considers the combined condition

```
semesterAverage >= 90 || finalExam >= 90
```

and awards the student an "A" if either or both of the simple conditions are **true**. Note that the message "**Student grade is A**" is not printed only when both of the simple conditions are **false**. Figure 3.16 is a truth table for the logical OR operator (||).

expression1	expression2	expression1 && expression2
false	false	false
false	true	false
true	false	false
true	true	true

Fig. 3.15 Truth table for the **&&** (logical AND) operator.

expression1	expression2	expression1 || expression2
false	false	false
false	true	true
true	false	true
true	true	true

Fig. 3.16 Truth table for the logical OR (||) operator.

The `&&` operator has a higher precedence than the `||` operator. Both operators associate from left to right. An expression containing `&&` or `||` operators is evaluated only until truth or falsity is known. Thus, evaluation of the expression

```
gender == 1 && age >= 65
```

will stop immediately if `gender` is not equal to `1` (i.e., the entire expression is `false`), and continue if `gender` is equal to `1` (i.e., the entire expression could still be `true` if the condition `age >= 65` is `true`). This performance feature for evaluation of logical AND and logical OR expressions is called *short-circuit evaluation.*

Common Programming Error 3.9

In expressions using operator `&&`, it is possible that a condition—we will call this the dependent condition—may require another condition to be true for it to be meaningful to evaluate the dependent condition. In this case, the dependent condition should be placed after the other condition or an error might occur.

Performance Tip 3.2

In expressions using operator `&&`, if the separate conditions are independent of one another make the condition that is most likely to be `false` the leftmost condition. In expressions using operator `||`, make the condition that is most likely to be `true` the leftmost condition. This can reduce a program's execution time.

The *boolean logical AND (`&`)* and *boolean logical inclusive OR (`|`)* operators, work identically to the regular logical AND and logical OR operators with one exception—the boolean logical operators always evaluate both of their operands (i.e., there is no short-circuit evaluation). Therefore, the expression

```
gender == 1 & age >= 65
```

evaluates `age >= 65` regardless of whether `gender` is equal to `1`. This is useful if the right operand of the boolean logical AND or boolean logical inclusive OR operator has a needed *side effect*—a modification of a variable's value. For example, the expression

```
birthday == true | ++age >= 65
```

guarantees that the condition `++age >= 65` will be evaluated. Thus, the variable `age` will be incremented in the preceding expression regardless of whether the overall expression is `true` or `false`.

A condition containing the *boolean logical exclusive OR (`^`)* operator is `true` *if and only if* one of its operands results in a `true` value and one results in a `false` value. If both operands are `true` or both operands are `false`, the result of the entire condition is `false`. Figure 3.17 is a truth table for the boolean logical exclusive OR operator (`^`). This operator is also guaranteed to evaluate both of its operands (i.e., there is no short-circuit evaluation).

expression1	expression2	expression1 ^ expression2
false	**false**	**false**
false	**true**	**true**
true	**false**	**true**
true	**true**	**false**

Fig. 3.17 Truth table for the boolean logical exclusive OR (**^**) operator.

Java provides the **!** (logical negation) operator to enable a programmer to "reverse" the meaning of a condition. Unlike the logical operators **&&**, **&**, **||** and **|**, which combine two conditions (binary operators), the logical negation operator has only a single condition as an operand (unary operator). The logical negation operator is placed before a condition to choose a path of execution if the original condition (without the logical negation operator) is **false**, such as in the following program segment:

```
if ( ! ( grade == sentinelValue ) )
   System.out.println( "The next grade is " + grade );
```

The parentheses around the condition **grade == sentinelValue** are needed because the logical negation operator has a higher precedence than the equality operator. Figure 3.18 is a truth table for the logical negation operator.

In most cases, the programmer can avoid using logical negation by expressing the condition differently with an appropriate relational or equality operator. For example, the preceding statement may also be written as follows:

```
if ( grade != sentinelValue )
   System.out.println( "The next grade is " + grade );
```

This flexibility can help a programmer express a condition in a more convenient manner.

The program of Fig. 3.19 demonstrates all the logical operators and boolean logical operators by producing their truth tables.

In the output of Fig. 3.19, the letters **F** and **T** indicate **false** and **true** for the operands in each condition. The result of the condition is shown as **true** or **false**.

The chart in Fig. 3.20 shows the precedence and associativity of the Java operators introduced to this point. The operators are shown from top to bottom in decreasing order of precedence.

expression	!expression
false	**true**
true	**false**

Fig. 3.18 Truth table for operator **!** (logical NOT).

```
// Fig. 3.19: LogicalOperators.java
// Demonstrating the logical operators
import java.awt.Graphics;
import java.applet.Applet;

public class LogicalOperators extends Applet {
   public void paint( Graphics g )
   {
      g.drawString( "Logical AND (&&)", 10, 25 );
      g.drawString( "F && F: " + ( false && false ), 10, 40 );
      g.drawString( "F && T: " + ( false && true ), 10, 55 );
      g.drawString( "T && F: " + ( true && false ), 10, 70 );
      g.drawString( "T && T: " + ( true && true ), 10, 85 );

      g.drawString( "Logical OR (||)", 215, 25 );
      g.drawString( "F || F: " + ( false || false ), 215, 40 );
      g.drawString( "F || T: " + ( false || true ), 215, 55 );
      g.drawString( "T || F: " + ( true || false ), 215, 70 );
      g.drawString( "T || T: " + ( true || true ), 215, 85 );

      g.drawString( "Boolean logical AND (&)", 10, 115 );
      g.drawString( "F & F: " + ( false & false ), 10, 130 );
      g.drawString( "F & T: " + ( false & true ), 10, 145 );
      g.drawString( "T & F: " + ( true & false ), 10, 160 );
      g.drawString( "T & T: " + ( true & true ), 10, 175 );

      g.drawString( "Boolean logical inclusive OR (|)",
                    215, 115 );
      g.drawString( "F | F: " + ( false | false ), 215, 130 );
      g.drawString( "F | T: " + ( false | true ), 215, 145 );
      g.drawString( "T | F: " + ( true | false ), 215, 160 );
      g.drawString( "T | T: " + ( true | true ), 215, 175 );

      g.drawString( "Boolean logical exclusive OR (^)",
                    10, 205 );
      g.drawString( "F ^ F: " + ( false ^ false ), 10, 220 );
      g.drawString( "F ^ T: " + ( false ^ true ), 10, 235 );
      g.drawString( "T ^ F: " + ( true ^ false ), 10, 250 );
      g.drawString( "T ^ T: " + ( true ^ true ), 10, 265 );

      g.drawString( "Logical NOT (!)",
                    215, 205 );
      g.drawString( "!F: " + ( !false ), 215, 220 );
      g.drawString( "!T: " + ( !true ), 215, 235 );
   }
}
```

Fig. 3.19 Demonstrating the logical operators (part 1 of 2).

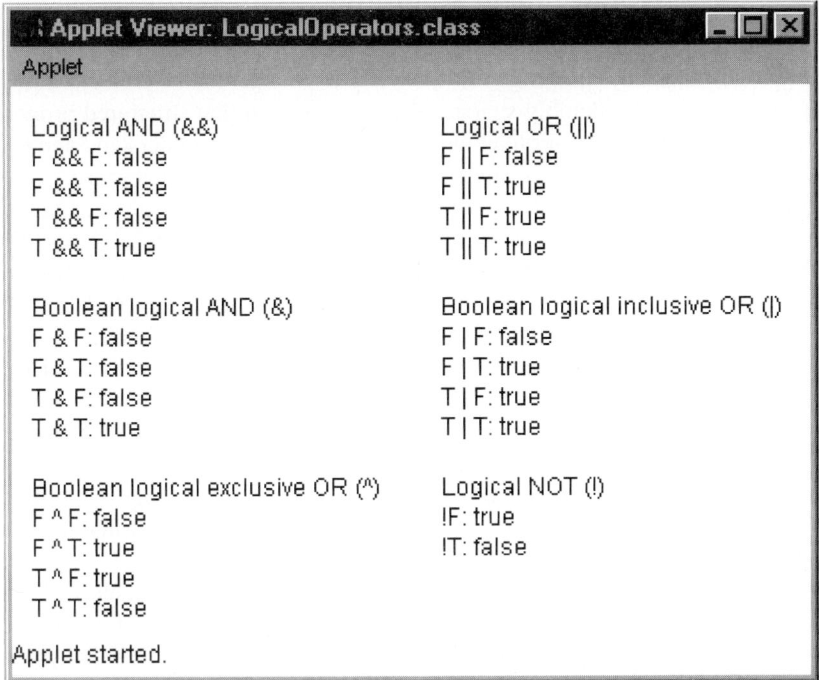

Fig. 3.19 Demonstrating the logical operators (part 2 of 2).

Operators						Associativity	Type
`()`						left to right	parentheses
`++`	`--`	`+`	`-`	`!`	`(`*type*`)`	right to left	unary
`*`	`/`	`%`				left to right	multiplicative
`+`	`-`					left to right	additive
`<`	`<=`	`>`	`>=`			left to right	relational
`==`	`!=`					left to right	equality
`&`						left to right	boolean logical AND
`^`						left to right	boolean logical exclusive OR
`|`						left to right	boolean logical inclusive OR
`&&`						left to right	logical AND
`||`						left to right	logical OR
`?:`						right to left	conditional
`=`	`+=`	`-=`	`*=`	`/=`	`%=`	right to left	assignment

Fig. 3.20 Operator precedence and associativity.

3.10 Structured Programming Summary

Just as architects design buildings by employing the collective wisdom of their profession, so should programmers design programs. Our field is younger than architecture is, and our collective wisdom is considerably sparser. We have learned that structured programming produces programs that are easier than unstructured programs to understand and hence are easier to test, debug, modify, and even prove correct in a mathematical sense.

Figure 3.21 summarizes Java's control structures. Small circles are used in the figure to indicate the single entry point and the single exit point of each structure. Connecting individual flowchart symbols arbitrarily can lead to unstructured programs. Therefore, the programming profession has chosen to combine flowchart symbols to form a limited set of control structures, and to build structured programs by properly combining control structures in two simple ways. For simplicity, only single-entry/single-exit control structures are used—there is only one way to enter and only one way to exit each control structure.

Connecting control structures in sequence to form structured programs is simple—the exit point of one control structure is connected directly to the entry point of the next control structure, i.e., the control structures are simply placed one after another in a program; we have called this "control structure stacking." The rules for forming structured programs also allow for control structures to be nested.

Figure 3.22 shows the rules for forming properly structured programs which assume the rectangle flowchart symbol may be used to indicate any action including input/output.

Applying the rules of Fig. 3.22 to the simplest flowchart (Fig. 3.23) always results in a structured flowchart with a neat, building-block appearance. For example, repeatedly applying rule 2 to the simplest flowchart results in a structured flowchart containing many rectangles in sequence (Fig. 3.24). Notice that rule 2 generates a stack of control structures; so let us call rule 2 the *stacking rule*.

Rule 3 is called the *nesting rule*. Repeatedly applying rule 3 to the simplest flowchart results in a flowchart with neatly nested control structures. For example, in Fig. 3.25, the rectangle in the simplest flowchart is first replaced with a double-selection (**`if/else`**) structure. Then rule 3 is applied again to both of the rectangles in the double-selection structure, replacing each of these rectangles with double-selection structures. The dashed boxes around each of the double-selection structures represent the rectangle that was replaced.

Rule 4 generates larger, more involved, and more deeply nested structures. The flowcharts that emerge from applying the rules in Fig. 3.22 constitute the set of all possible structured flowcharts and hence the set of all possible structured programs.

The beauty of the structured approach is that we use only seven single-entry/single-exit pieces and assemble them in only two ways. Figure 3.26 shows the same stacked building blocks that emerge from applying rule 2 and the kinds of nested building blocks that emerge from applying rule 3. The figure also shows the kind of overlapped building blocks that cannot appear in structured flowcharts (because of the elimination of the **`goto`** statement).

If the rules in Fig. 3.22 are followed, an unstructured flowchart (such as that in Fig. 3.27) cannot be created. If you are uncertain if a particular flowchart is structured, apply the rules of Fig. 3.22 in reverse to try to reduce the flowchart to the simplest flowchart. If the flowchart is reducible to the simplest flowchart, the original flowchart is structured; otherwise, it is not.

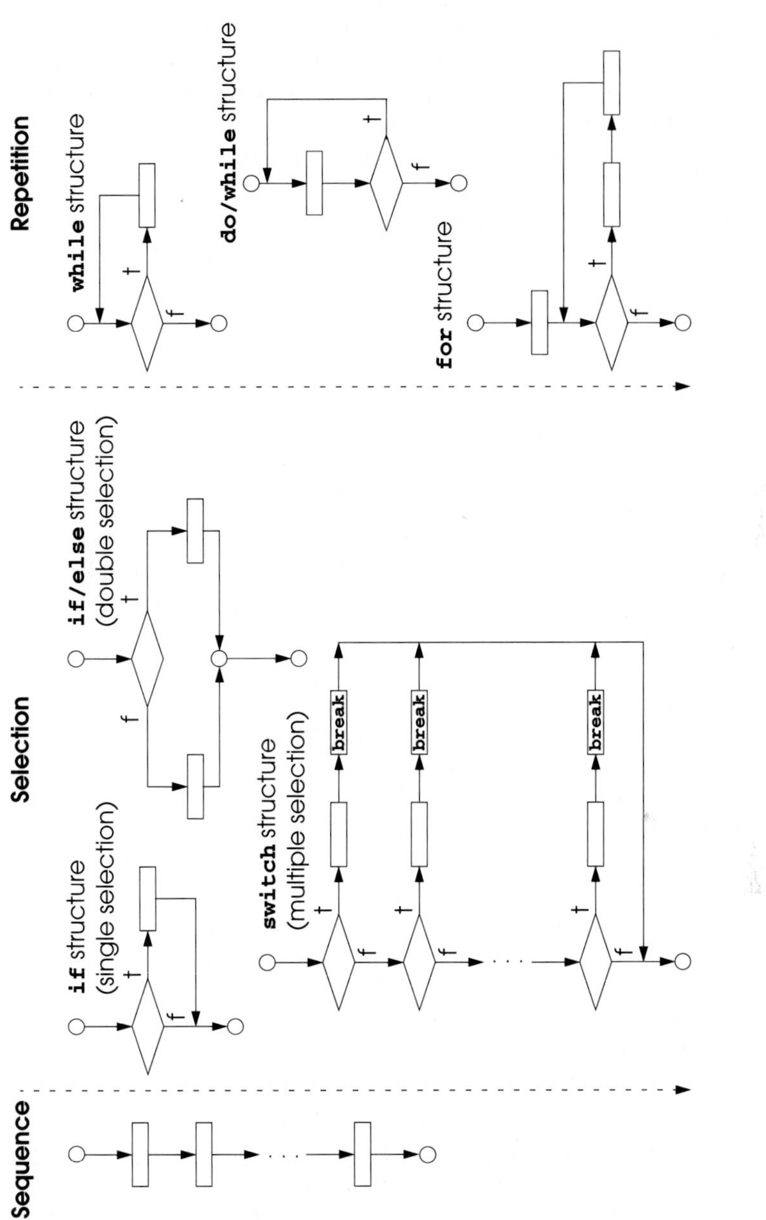

Fig. 3.21 Java's single-entry/single-exit sequence, selection, and repetition structures.

Rules for Forming Structured Programs

1) Begin with the "simplest flowchart" (Fig. 3.23).
2) Any rectangle (action) can be replaced by two rectangles (actions) in sequence.
3) Any rectangle (action) can be replaced by any control structure (sequence, **`if`**, **`if/else`**, **`switch`**, **`while`**, **`do/while`**, or **`for`**).
4) Rules 2 and 3 may be applied as often as you like and in any order.

Fig. 3.22 Rules for forming structured programs.

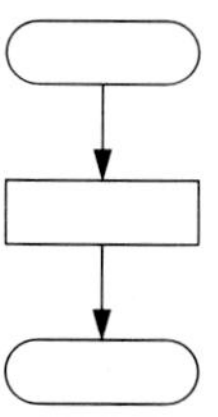

Fig. 3.23 The simplest flowchart.

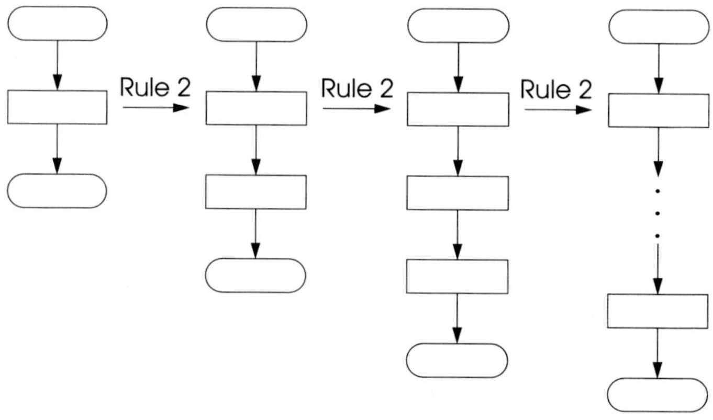

Fig. 3.24 Repeatedly applying rule 2 of Fig. 3.22 to the simplest flowchart.

Structured programming promotes simplicity. Bohm and Jacopini have given us the result that only three forms of control are needed:

- Sequence
- Selection
- Repetition

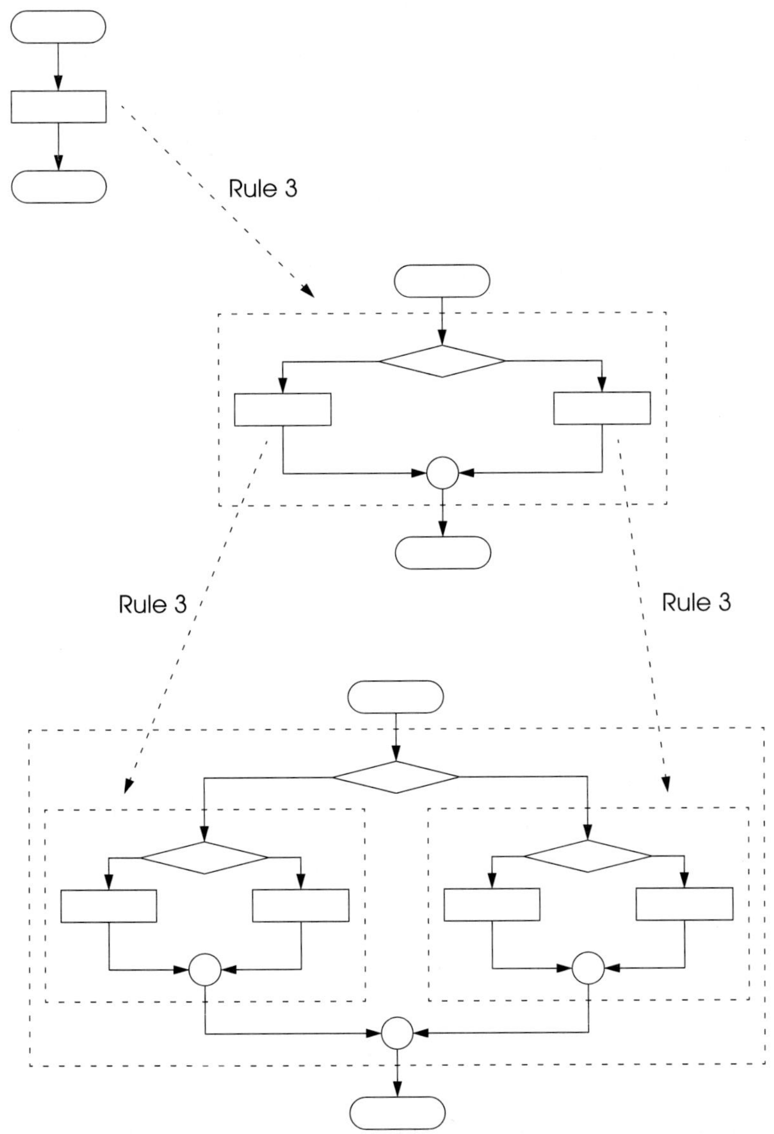

Fig. 3.25 Applying rule 3 of Fig. 3.22 to the simplest flowchart.

Sequence is trivial. Selection is implemented in one of three ways:

- **`if`** structure (single selection)
- **`if/else`** structure (double selection)
- **`switch`** structure (multiple selection)

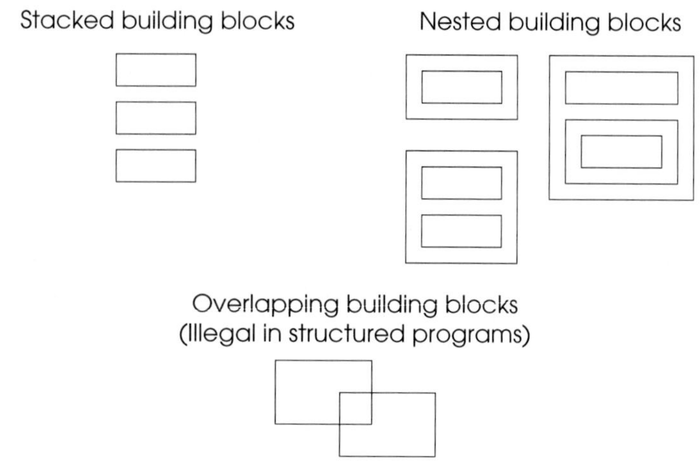

Fig. 3.26 Stacked, nested, and overlapped building blocks.

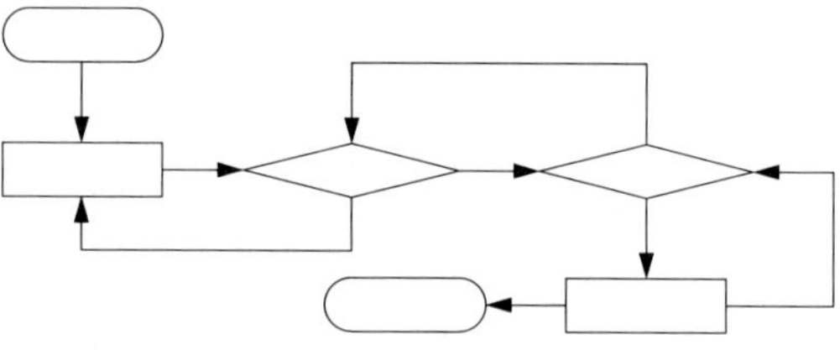

Fig. 3.27 An unstructured flowchart.

In fact, it is straightforward to prove that the simple **`if`** structure is sufficient to provide any form of selection—everything that can be done with the **`if/else`** structure and the **`switch`** structure can be implemented by combining **`if`** structures (although perhaps not as conveniently).

Repetition is implemented in one of three ways:

- **`while`** structure
- **`do/while`** structure
- **`for`** structure

The **`while`** structure is sufficient to provide any form of repetition; everything that can be done with the **`do/while`** structure and the **`for`** structure can be done with the **`while`** structure (although perhaps not as conveniently).

Combining these results illustrates that any form of control ever needed in a Java program can be expressed in terms of:

- sequence
- **`if`** structure (selection)
- **`while`** structure (repetition)

And these control structures can be combined in only two ways—stacking and nesting. Indeed, structured programming promotes simplicity.

In this chapter, we discussed how to compose programs from control structures containing only actions and decisions. In Chapter 4, Methods, we discuss in detail another program structuring unit called the *method* (methods are often called functions or procedures in other programming languages). We will learn to compose large programs by combining methods that, in turn, are composed of control structures. We will also discuss how using methods promotes software reusability. Then we discuss the details of Java's other program structuring unit called the *class*. We will then proceed with our treatment of object-oriented programming.

Summary

- The **for** repetition structure handles all the details of counter-controlled repetition. The general format of the **for** structure is

  for *(expression1***;** *expression2***;** *expression3)*
      statement

  where *expression1* initializes the loop's control variable, *expression2* is the loop-continuation condition, and *expression3* increments the control variable.

- The **do/while** repetition structure tests the loop-continuation condition at the end of the loop, so the body of the loop will be executed at least once. The format for the **do/while** structure is

  do
      statement
  while (*condition***);**

- The **break** statement, when executed in one of the repetition structures (**for**, **while**, and **do/while**), causes immediate exit from the structure.

- The **continue** statement, when executed in one of the repetition structures (**for**, **while**, and **do/while**), skips any remaining statements in the body of the structure, and proceeds with the next iteration of the loop.

- The **switch** statement handles a series of decisions in which a particular variable or expression is tested for values it may assume, and different actions are taken. In most programs, it is necessary to include a **break** statement after the statements for each **case**. Several **case**s can execute the same statements by listing the **case** labels together before the statements. The **switch** structure can only test for constant integral expressions.

- Logical operators may be used to form complex conditions by combining conditions. The logical operators are **&&**, **&**, **||**, **|**, **^**, and **!**, meaning logical AND, boolean logical AND, logical OR, boolean logical inclusive OR, boolean logical exclusive OR and logical NOT (negation), respectively.

Terminology

&& operator
|| operator
! operator
boolean logical AND (**&**)
boolean logical exclusive OR (**^**)
boolean logical inclusive OR (**|**)
break
case label
continue
counter-controlled repetition
default case in **switch**
definite repetition
do/while repetition structure
for repetition structure
infinite loop
labeled **break** statement
labeled compound statement
labeled **continue** statement
labeled repetition structure
logical AND (**&&**)
logical negation (**!**)
logical operators
logical OR (**||**)
long
loop-continuation condition
multiple selection
nested control structures
off-by-one error
repetition structures
short-circuit evaluation
single-entry/single-exit control structures
stacked control structures
switch selection structure
while repetition structure

Common Programming Errors

3.1 Because floating-point values may be approximate, controlling counting loops with floating-point variables may result in imprecise counter values and inaccurate tests for termination.

3.2 Using an incorrect relational operator or using an incorrect final value of a loop counter in the condition of a **while** or **for** structure can cause off-by-one errors.

3.3 Using commas instead of the two required semicolons in a **for** header is a syntax error.

3.4 Placing a semicolon immediately to the right of the right parenthesis of a **for** header makes the body of that **for** structure an empty statement. This is normally a logic error.

3.5 Not using the proper relational operator in the loop-continuation condition of a loop that counts downwards (such as using **i <= 1** in a loop counting down to 1) can cause an infinite loop.

3.6 Forgetting a **break** statement when one is needed in a **switch** structure.

3.7 Omitting the space between the word **case** and the integral value being tested in a **switch** structure can cause a logic error. For example, writing **case3:** instead of writing **case 3:** simply creates an unused label (we will say more about labels later). The problem is that the **switch** structure will not perform the appropriate actions when the **switch**'s controlling expression has a value of 3.

3.8 Infinite loops are caused when the loop-continuation condition in a **while**, **for**, or **do/while** structure never becomes false. To prevent this, make sure there is not a semicolon immediately after the header of a **while** structure. In a counter-controlled loop, make sure the control variable is incremented (or decremented) in the body of the loop. In a sentinel-controlled loop, make sure the sentinel value is eventually input.

3.9 In expressions using operator `&&`, it is possible that a condition—we will call this the dependent condition—may require another condition to be true for it to be meaningful to evaluate the dependent condition. In this case, the dependent condition should be placed after the other condition or an error might occur.

Good Programming Practices

3.1 Control counting loops with integer values.

3.2 Indent the statements in the body of each control structure.

3.3 Put a blank line before and after each major control structure to make it stand out in the program.

3.4 Too many levels of nesting can make a program difficult to understand. As a general rule, try to avoid using more than three levels of indentation.

3.5 Vertical spacing above and below control structures, and indentation of the bodies of control structures within the control structure headers gives programs a two-dimensional appearance that enhances readability.

3.6 Using the final value in the condition of a `while` or `for` structure and using the `<=` relational operator will help avoid off-by-one errors. For a loop used to print the values 1 to 10, for example, the loop-continuation condition should be `counter <= 10` rather than `counter < 10` (which is an off-by-one error) or `counter < 11` (which is also correct).

3.7 Place only expressions involving the control variables in the initialization and increment sections of a `for` structure. Manipulations of other variables should appear either before the loop (if they execute only once like initialization statements) or in the loop body (if they execute once per repetition like incrementing or decrementing statements).

3.8 Although statements preceding a `for` and statements in the body of a `for` can often be merged into the `for` header, avoid doing so because it makes the program more difficult to read.

3.9 Limit the size of control structure headers to a single line if possible.

3.10 Do not use variables of type `float` or `double` to perform precise monetary calculations. The imprecision of floating-point numbers can cause errors that will result in incorrect monetary values. In the exercises, we explore the use of integers to perform monetary calculations. Note: Class libraries are becoming available for properly performing monetary calculations.

3.11 Provide a `default` case in `switch` statements. Cases not explicitly tested in a `switch` statement without a `default` case are ignored. Including a `default` case focuses the programmer on the need to process exceptional conditions. There are situations in which no `default` processing is needed.

3.12 Although the `case` clauses and the `default` case clause in a `switch` structure can occur in any order, it is considered a good programming practice to place the `default` clause last.

3.13 In a `switch` structure when the `default` clause is listed last, the `break` statement for that `case` is not required. Some programmers include this `break` for clarity and symmetry with other cases.

3.14 Some programmers always include braces in a `do/while` structure even if the braces are not necessary. This helps eliminate ambiguity between the `while` structure and the `do/while` structure containing one statement.

3.15 Some programmers feel that `break` and `continue` violate structured programming. Because the effects of these statements can be achieved by structured programming techniques we will soon learn, these programmers do not use `break` and `continue`.

Performance Tips

3.1 Avoid placing expressions whose values do not change inside loops. But even if you do, many of today's sophisticated optimizing compilers will automatically place such expressions outside loops in the generated machine-language code.

3.2 In expressions using operator `&&`, if the separate conditions are independent of one another make the condition that is most likely to be false the leftmost condition. In expressions using operator `||`, make the condition that is most likely to be true the leftmost condition. This can reduce a program's execution time.

Software Engineering Observation

3.1 There is a tension between achieving quality software engineering and achieving the best performing software. Often, one of these goals is achieved at the expense of the other.

Testing and Debugging Tip

3.1 Although the value of the control variable can be changed in the body of a `for` loop, avoid doing so because this practice can lead to subtle errors.

Self-Review Exercises

3.1 State whether the following are true or false. If the answer is false, explain why.

a) The `default` case is required in the `switch` selection structure.

b) The `break` statement is required in the default case of a `switch` selection structure.

c) The expression `( x > y && a < b )` is true if either `x > y` is true or `a < b` is true.

d) An expression containing the `||` operator is true if either or both of its operands is true.

3.2 Write a Java statement or a set of Java statements to accomplish each of the following:

a) Sum the odd integers between 1 and 99 using a `for` structure. Assume the integer variables `sum` and `count` have been declared.

b) Calculate the value of `2.5` raised to the power of `3` using the `pow` method.

c) Print the integers from 1 to 20 using a **while** loop and the counter variable **x**. Assume that the variable **x** has been declared, but not initialized. Print only 5 integers per line. Hint: Use the calculation **x % 5**. When the value of this is 0, print a newline character, otherwise print a tab character. Assume this is an application—use the **System.out.println()** method to output the newline character and use the **System.out.print('\t')** method to output the tab character.

d) Repeat Exercise 3.2 (c) using a **for** structure.

3.3 Find the error in each of the following code segments and explain how to correct it.

a)
```
x = 1;

while ( x <= 10 );
   x++;
}
```
b)
```
for ( y = .1; y != 1.0; y += .1 )
   System.out.println( y );
```
c)
```
switch ( n ) {

   case 1:
      System.out.println( "The number is 1" );

   case 2:
      System.out.println( "The number is 2" );
      break;

   default:
      System.out.println( "The number is not 1 or 2" );
      break;
}
```
d) The following code should print the values 1 to 10.
```
n = 1;

while ( n < 10 )
   System.out.println( n++ );
```

Answers to Self-Review Exercises

3.1 a) False. The **default** case is optional. If no default action is needed, then there is no need for a **default** case.

b) False. The **break** statement is used to exit the **switch** structure. The **break** statement is not required when the **default** case is the last case.

c) False. Both of the relational expressions must be true in order for the entire expression to be true when using the **&&** operator.

d) True.

3.2 a)
```
sum = 0;
for ( count = 1; count <= 99; count += 2 )
   sum += count;
```
b)
```
Math.pow( 2.5, 3 )
```

c)
```
x = 1;

while ( x <= 20 ) {
   System.out.print( x );

   if ( x % 5 == 0 )
      System.out.println();
   else
      System.out.print( '\t' );

   x++;
}
```
d)
```
for ( x = 1; x <= 20; x++ ) {
   System.out.print( x );

   if ( x % 5 == 0 )
      System.out.println();
   else
      System.out.print( '\t' );
}
```

or

```
for ( x = 1; x <= 20; x++ )

   if ( x % 5 == 0 )
      System.out.println( x );
   else
      System.out.print( x + "\t" );
```

3.3 a) Error: The semicolon after the **`while`** header causes an infinite loop.
Correction: Replace the semicolon by a **`{`** or remove both the **`;`** and the **`}`**.

b) Error: Using a floating-point number to control a **`for`** repetition structure.
Correction: Use an integer, and perform the proper calculation in order to get the values you desire.

```
for ( y = 1; y != 10; y++ )
   System.out.println( (float) y / 10 );
```

c) Error: Missing **`break`** statement in the statements for the first **`case`**.
Correction: Add a **`break`** statement at the end of the statements for the first **`case`**. Note that this is not necessarily an error if the programmer wants the statement of **`case 2:`** to execute every time the **`case 1:`** statement executes.

d) Error: Improper relational operator used in the **`while`** repetition-continuation condition.
Correction: Use **`<=`** rather than **`<`** or change **`10`** to **`11`**.

Exercises

3.4 Find the error in each of the following (Note: there may be more than one error):

a)
```
For ( x = 100, x >= 1, x++ )
   System.out.println( x );
```

b) The following code should print whether integer **value** is odd or even:

```
switch ( value % 2 ) {

   case 0:
      System.out.println( "Even integer" );

   case 1:
      System.out.println( "Odd integer" );
}
```

c) The following code should output the odd integers from 19 to 1:

```
for ( x = 19; x >= 1; x += 2 )
   System.out.println( x );
```

d) The following code should output the even integers from 2 to 100:

```
counter = 2;
do {
   System.out.println( counter );
   counter += 2;
} While ( counter < 100 );
```

3.5 What does the following program do?

```
public class Printing {
   public static void main( String args[] )
   {
      for ( int i = 1; i <= 10; i++ ) {

         for ( int j = 1; j <= 5; j++ )
            System.out.print( '@' );

         System.out.println();
      }
   }
}
```

3.6 Write an application that finds the smallest of several letters. Assume that the first value read is a digit (read as a character) that specifies the number of letters remaining.

3.7 Write an applet that calculates the product of the odd integers from 1 to 15 then prints the results on the applet.

3.8 The *factorial* method is used frequently in probability problems. The factorial of a positive integer *n* (written *n!* and pronounced "n factorial") is equal to the product of the positive integers from 1 to *n*. Write an applet that evaluates the factorials of the integers from 1 to 5. Display the results in tabular format. What difficulty might prevent you from calculating the factorial of 20?

3.9 Modify the compound interest program of Fig. 3.6 to repeat its steps for interest rates of 5 percent, 6 percent, 7 percent, 8 percent, 9 percent, and 10 percent. Use a **for** loop to vary the interest rate.

3.10 Write an application that prints the following patterns separately one below the other. Use **`for`** loops to generate the patterns. All asterisks (**`*`**) should be printed by a single statement of the form **`System.out.print( '*' );`** (this causes the asterisks to print side by side). Hint: The last two patterns require that each line begin with an appropriate number of blanks.

```
(A)          (B)          (C)          (D)
*            **********   **********            *
**           *********     *********           **
***          ********       ********          ***
****         *******         *******         ****
*****        ******           ******        *****
******       *****             *****       ******
*******      ****               ****      *******
********     ***                 ***     ********
*********    **                   **    *********
**********   *                     *   **********
```

3.11 One interesting application of computers is drawing graphs and bar charts (sometimes called "histograms"). Write an applet that reads five numbers (each between 1 and 30). For each number read, your program should print a line containing that number of adjacent asterisks. For example, if your program reads the number seven, it should print **`*******`**.

3.12 A mail order house sells five different products whose retail prices are product 1 — \$2.98, product 2—\$4.50, product 3—\$9.98, product 4—\$4.49, and product 5—\$6.87. Write an applet that reads a series of pairs of numbers as follows:

1) Product number
2) Quantity sold for one day

Your program should use a **`switch`** structure to help determine the retail price for each product. Your program should calculate and display the total retail value of all products sold last week. Use a **`TextField`** to obtain the product number from the user.

3.13 Modify the program of Fig. 3.7 so that it calculates the grade point average for the class. A grade of 'A' is worth 4 points, 'B' is worth 3 points, etc.

3.14 Modify the program in Fig. 3.6 so that it uses only integers to calculate the compound interest. (Hint: Treat all monetary amounts as integral numbers of pennies. Then "break" the result into its dollar portion and cents portion by using the division and modulus operations respectively. Insert a period.)

3.15 Assume **`i = 1`**, **`j = 2`**, **`k = 3`**, and **`m = 2`**. What does each of the following statements print? Are the parentheses necessary in each case?

a) `System.out.println( i == 1 );`
b) `System.out.println( j == 3 );`
c) `System.out.println( i >= 1 && j < 4 );`
d) `System.out.println( m <= 99 & k < m );`
e) `System.out.println( j >= i || k == m );`

f) `System.out.println( k + m < j | 3 - j >= k );`
g) `System.out.println( !( k > m ) );`

3.16 Write an application that prints a table of the binary, octal, and hexadecimal equivalents of the decimal numbers in the range 1 through 256. If you are not familiar with these number systems, read the appendix, "Number Systems," first.

3.17 Calculate the value of π from the infinite series

$$\pi = 4 - \frac{4}{3} + \frac{4}{5} - \frac{4}{7} + \frac{4}{9} - \frac{4}{11} + \cdots$$

Print a table that shows the value of π approximated by 1 term of this series, by two terms, by three terms, etc. How many terms of this series do you have to use before you first get 3.14? 3.141? 3.1415? 3.14159?

3.18 *(Pythagorean Triples)* A right triangle can have sides that are all integers. The set of three integer values for the sides of a right triangle is called a Pythagorean triple. These three sides must satisfy the relationship that the sum of the squares of two of the sides is equal to the square of the hypotenuse. Write an application to find all Pythagorean triples for **side1**, **side2**, and the **hypotenuse** all no larger than 500. Use a triple-nested **for** loop that tries all possibilities. This is an example of "brute force" computing. You will learn in more advanced computer science courses that there are large numbers of interesting problems for which there is no known algorithmic approach other than using sheer brute force.

3.19 Modify Exercise 3.10 to combine your code from the four separate triangles of asterisks into a single application that prints all four patterns side by side making clever use of nested **for** loops.

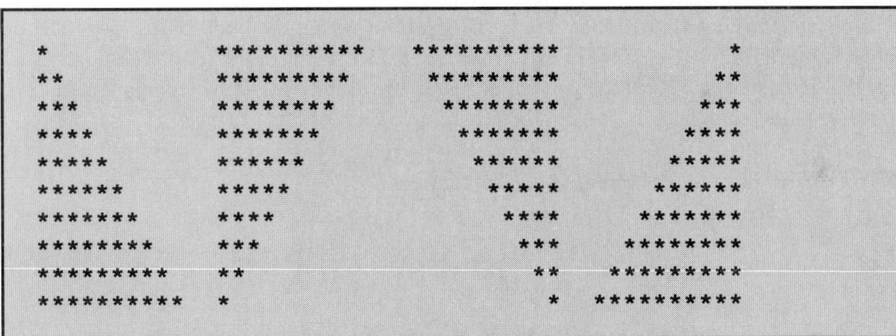
```
*           **********  **********           *
**          *********    *********          **
***         ********      ********         ***
****        *******        *******        ****
*****       ******          ******       *****
******      *****            *****      ******
*******     ****              ****     *******
********    ***                ***    ********
*********   **                  **   *********
**********  *                    *  **********
```

3.20 *(De Morgan's Laws)* In this chapter, we discussed the logical operators **&&**, **&**, **||**, **|**, and **!**. De Morgan's Laws can sometimes make it more convenient for us to express a logical expression. These laws state that the expression **!(***condition1* **&&** *condition2***)** is logically equivalent to the expression **(!***condition1* **||** **!***condition2***)**. Also, the expression **!(***condition1* **||** *condition2***)** is logically equivalent to the expression **(!***condition1* **&&** **!***condition2***)**. Use De Morgan's Laws to write equivalent expressions for each of the following, and then write a program to show that both the original expression and the new expression in each case are equivalent:

a) `!( x < 5 ) && !( y >= 7 )`
b) `!( a == b ) || !( g != 5 )`
c) `!( ( x <= 8 ) && ( y > 4 ) )`
d) `!( ( i > 4 ) || ( j <= 6 ) )`

3.21 Write an applet that prints the following diamond shape. You may use an output statement in your **`paint`** method that prints a single asterisk (*). Maximize your use of repetition (with nested **`for`** structures) and minimize the number of output statements.

```
    *
   ***
  *****
 *******
*********
 *******
  *****
   ***
    *
```

3.22 Modify the program you wrote in Exercise 3.21 to read an odd number in the range 1 to 19 to specify the number of rows in the diamond. Your program should then display a diamond of the appropriate size.

3.23 A criticism of the **`break`** statement and the **`continue`** statement is that each is unstructured. Actually **`break`** statements and **`continue`** statements can always be replaced by structured statements, although doing so can be awkward. Describe in general how you would remove any **`break`** statement from a loop in a program and replace that statement with some structured equivalent. (Hint: The **`break`** statement leaves a loop from within the body of the loop. The other way to leave is by failing the loop-continuation test. Consider using in the loop-continuation test a second test that indicates "early exit because of a 'break' condition.") Use the technique you developed here to remove the break statement from the program of Fig. 3.11.

3.24 What does the following program segment do?

```
for ( i = 1; i <= 5; i++ ) {

   for ( j = 1; j <= 3; j++ ) {

      for ( k = 1; k <= 4; k++ )
         System.out.print( '*' );
      System.out.println();
   }
   System.out.println();
}
```

3.25 Describe in general how you would remove any **`continue`** statement from a loop in a program and replace that statement with some structured equivalent. Use the technique you developed here to remove the **`continue`** statement from the program of Fig. 3.12.

3.26 *("The Twelve Days of Christmas" Song)* Write an application that uses repetition and **switch** structures to print the song "The Twelve Days of Christmas." One **switch** structure should be used to print the day (i.e., "First," "Second," etc.). A separate **switch** structure should be used to print the remainder of each verse.

4
Methods

Objectives

- To understand how to construct programs. modularly from small pieces called methods.
- To introduce the common math methods available in the Java API.
- To be able to create new methods.
- To understand the mechanisms used to pass information between methods.
- To introduce simulation techniques using random number generation.
- To understand how the visibility of identifiers is limited to specific regions of programs.
- To understand how to write and use methods that call themselves.

Form ever follows function.
Louis Henri Sullivan

E pluribus unum.
(One composed of many.)
Virgil

O! call back yesterday, bid time return.
William Shakespeare, *Richard II*

Call me Ishmael.
Herman Melville, *Moby Dick*

When you call me that, smile.
Owen Wister

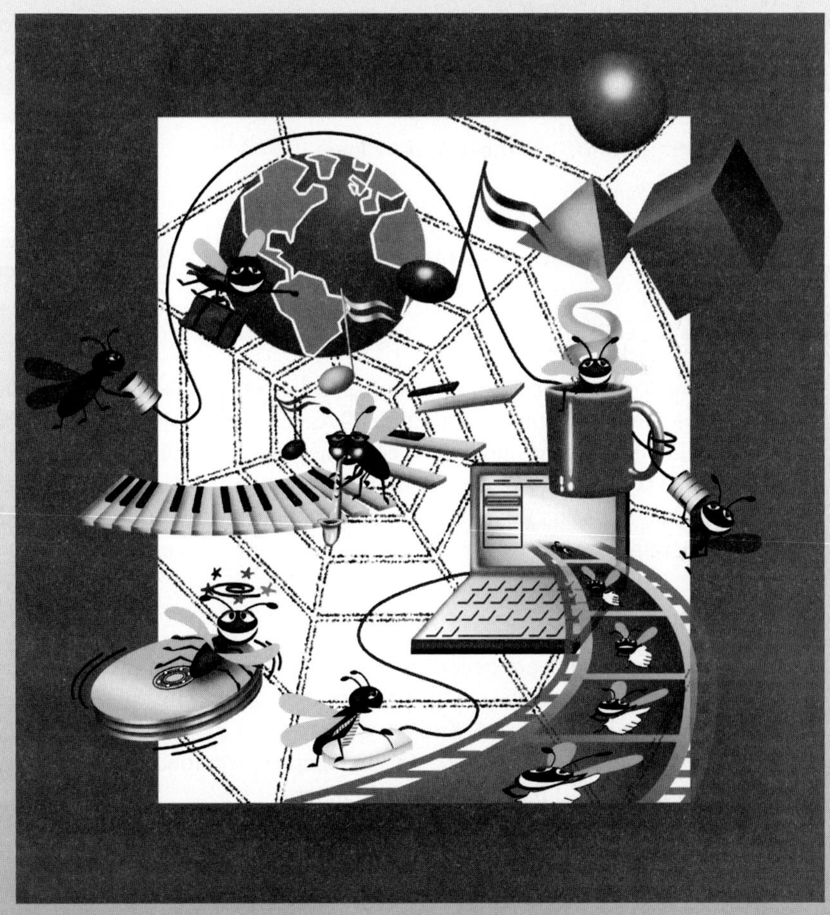

Outline

4.1 Introduction

Most computer programs that solve real-world problems are much larger than the programs presented in the first few chapters. Experience has shown that the best way to develop and maintain a large program is to construct it from small, simple pieces or *modules*. This technique is called *divide and conquer.* This chapter describes many key features of the Java language that facilitate the design, implementation, operation, and maintenance of large programs.

4.2 Program Modules in Java

Modules in Java are called *methods* and *classes.* Java programs are written by combining new methods and classes the programmer writes with "pre-packaged" methods and classes available in the *Java API* (also referred to as the *Java class library*) and in various other method and class libraries. In this chapter, we concentrate on methods; we will discuss classes in detail beginning with Chapter 6.

The Java API provides a rich collection of classes and methods for performing common mathematical calculations, string manipulations, character manipulations, input/output, error checking, and many other useful operations. This makes the programmer's job easier because these methods provide many of the capabilities programmers need. The Java API methods are provided as part of the Java Developer's Kit (JDK).

Good Programming Practice 4.1

Familiarize yourself with the rich collection of classes and methods in the Java API and with the rich collections of classes available in various class libraries.

Software Engineering Observation 4.1

Avoid reinventing the wheel. When possible, use Java API classes and methods instead of writing new classes and methods. This reduces program development time.

The programmer can write methods to define specific tasks that may be used at many points in a program. These are sometimes referred to as *programmer-defined methods.* The actual statements defining the method are written only once and these statements are hidden from other methods.

A method is *invoked* (i.e., made to perform its designated task) by a *method call.* The method call specifies the method name and provides information (as *arguments*) that the called method needs to do its job. A common analogy for this is the hierarchical form of management. A boss (the *calling method* or *caller*) asks a worker (the *called method*) to perform a task and *return* (i.e., report back) the results when the task is done. The boss method does not know *how* the worker method performs its designated tasks. The worker may call other worker methods, and the boss will be unaware of this. We will soon see how this "hiding" of implementation details promotes good software engineering. Figure 4.1 shows the **main** method communicating with several worker methods in a hierarchical manner. Note that **worker1** acts as a boss method to **worker4** and **worker5**. Relationships among methods may be other than the hierarchical structure shown in this figure.

4.3 Math Class Methods

Math class methods allow the programmer to perform certain common mathematical calculations. We use various **Math** class methods here to introduce the concept of methods. Later in the book, we will discuss many of the other methods in the Java API.

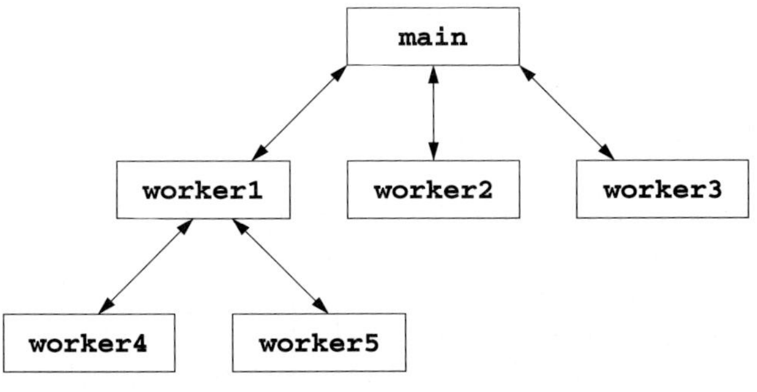

Fig. 4.1 Hierarchical boss method/worker method relationship.

Methods are normally called by writing the name of the method followed by a left parenthesis followed by the *argument* (or a comma-separated list of arguments) of the method followed by a right parenthesis. For example, a programmer desiring to calculate and print the square root of **900.0** might write

```
System.out.println( Math.sqrt( 900.0 ) );
```

When this statement is executed, the method **Math.sqrt** is called to calculate the square root of the number contained in the parentheses (**900.0**). The number **900.0** is the *argument* of the **Math.sqrt** method. The preceding statement would print **30.0**. The **Math.sqrt** method takes an argument of type **double** and returns a result of type **double**. Note that all **Math** class methods must be invoked by preceding the method name with the class name **Math** and a dot (**.**) operator. Normally we invoke methods through an object or directly as in the following two lines of code from an applet

```
g.drawString( "Welcome to Java programming!", 25, 25 );
showStatus( "hello" );
```

The first statement might appear in your applet's **paint** method. The statement invokes the **drawString** method of the **Graphics** object **g** (also referred to as *sending the* ***drawString*** *message to object* ***g***). The second statement could appear in any method of your applet. The statement invokes the **showStatus** method directly and displays a string in the status bar of your browser or the Appletviewer. In Chapter 6, we discuss in detail the different types of methods associated with classes and how they are invoked.

Software Engineering Observation 4.2

It is not necessary to import the ***Math*** *class into a program to use* ***Math*** *class methods. The* ***Math*** *class is part of the* ***java.lang*** *package which is automatically imported by the compiler.*

Common Programming Error 4.1

Forgetting to invoke a ***Math*** *class method by preceding the method name with the class name* ***Math*** *and a dot operator (***.***) results in a syntax error.*

Method arguments may be constants, variables, or expressions. If **c1 = 13.0**, **d = 3.0**, and **f = 4.0**, then the statement

```
System.out.println( Math.sqrt( c1 + d * f ) );
```

calculates and prints the square root of **13.0 + 3.0 * 4.0 = 25.0**, namely **5.0**.

Some **Math** class methods are summarized in Fig. 4.2. In the figure, the variables **x** and **y** are of type **double**. The **Math** class also defines two commonly used mathematical constants—**Math.PI** and **Math.E**. The constant **Math.PI** (3.14159265358979323846) of class **Math** is the ratio of a circle's circumference to its diameter. The constant **Math.E** (2.7182818284590452354) is the base value for natural logarithms (calculated with the **Math.log** method).

Method	Description	Example
`abs( x )`	absolute value of *x* (this method also has versions for **float**, **int**, and **long** values)	if **x** > 0 then **abs(x)** is **x** if **x** = 0 then **abs(x)** is 0 if **x** < 0 then **abs(x)** is **-x**
`ceil( x )`	rounds *x* to the smallest integer not less than *x*	**ceil(9.2)** is **10** **ceil(-9.8)** is -9
`cos( x )`	trigonometric cosine of *x* (*x* in radians)	**cos(0.0)** is **1**
`exp( x )`	exponential method e^x	**exp(1.0)** is **2.71828** **exp(2.0)** is **7.38906**
`floor( x )`	rounds *x* to the largest integer not greater than *x*	**floor(9.2)** is **9** **floor(-9.8)** is **-10**
`log( x )`	natural logarithm of *x* (base *e*)	**log(2.718282)** is **1** **log(7.389056)** is **2**
`max( x, y )`	larger value of *x* and *y* (this method also has versions for **float**, **int**, and **long** values)	**max(2.3, 12.7)** is **12.7** **max(-2.3, -12.7)** is **-2.3**
`min( x, y )`	smaller value of *x* and *y* (this method also has versions for **float**, **int**, and **long** values)	**min(2.3, 12.7)** is **2.3** **min(-2.3, -12.7)** is **-12.7**
`pow( x, y )`	*x* raised to power *y* (x^y)	**pow(2, 7)** is **128** **pow(9, .5)** is **3**
`sin( x )`	trigonometric sine of *x* (*x* in radians)	**sin(0.0)** is **0**
`sqrt( x )`	square root of *x*	**sqrt(900.0)** is **30** **sqrt(9.0)** is **3**
`tan( x )`	trigonometric tangent of *x* (*x* in radians)	**tan(0.0)** is **0**

Fig. 4.2 Commonly used **Math** class methods.

4.4 Methods

Methods allow the programmer to modularize a program. All variables declared in method definitions are *local variables*—they are known only in the method in which they are defined. Most methods have a list of *parameters* that provide the means for communicating information between methods. A method's parameters are also local variables.

There are several motivations for modularizing a program with methods. The divide-and-conquer approach makes program development more manageable. Another motivation is *software reusability*—using existing methods as building blocks to create new programs. With good method naming and definition, programs can be created from standardized methods, rather than being built by using customized code. A third motivation is to avoid repeating code in a program. Packaging code as a method allows that code to be executed from several locations in a program simply by calling the method.

Software Engineering Observation 4.3

Each method should be limited to performing a single, well-defined task, and the method name should effectively express that task. This promotes software reusability.

Software Engineering Observation 4.4

If you cannot choose a concise name that expresses what the method does, it is possible that your method is attempting to perform too many diverse tasks. It is usually best to break such a method into several smaller methods.

4.5 Method Definitions

Each program we have presented has consisted of a class definition that contained at least one method definition that called Java API methods to accomplish its tasks. We now consider how programmers write their own customized methods.

Consider an applet that uses a method **square** (invoked from the applet's **paint** method) to calculate the squares of the integers from 1 to 10.

In Fig. 4.3, method **square** is *invoked* or *called* in **paint** on line 14 with the call

```
square( x )
```

The **square** method receives a copy of the value of **x** in the *parameter* **y**. Then **square** calculates **y * y**. The result is passed back to the point in **paint** where **square** was invoked, and the result is displayed. This process is repeated ten times using the **for** repetition structure.

```
1  // Fig. 4.3: SquareInt.java
2  // A programmer-defined square method
3  import java.awt.Graphics;
4  import java.applet.Applet;
5
6  public class SquareInt extends Applet {
7
8     // output the squared values of 1 through 10
9     public void paint( Graphics g )
10    {
11       int xPosition = 25;
12
13       for ( int x = 1; x <= 10; x++ ) {
14          g.drawString( String.valueOf( square( x ) ),
15                        xPosition, 25);
16          xPosition += 20;
17       }
18    }
```

Fig. 4.3 Using a programmer-defined method (part 1 of 2).

```
19
20      // square method definition
21      public int square(int y)
22      {
23         return y * y;
24      }
25   }
```

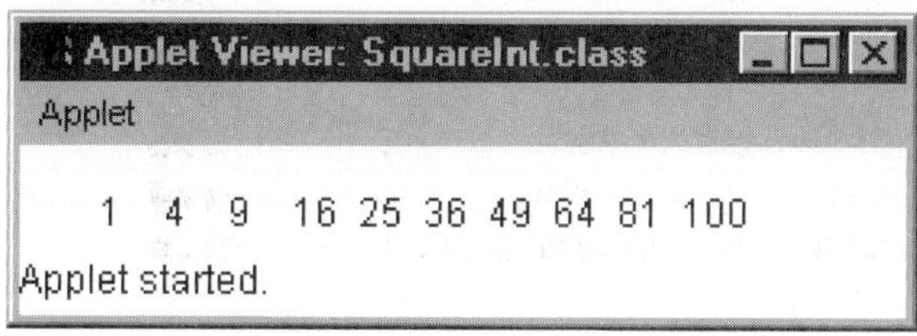

Fig. 4.3 Using a programmer-defined method (part 2 of 2).

The definition of method **square** (line 21) shows that **square** expects an integer parameter **y**. The keyword **int** preceding the method name indicates that **square** returns an integer result. The **return** statement in **square** passes the result of the calculation back to the calling method. Note that the entire method definition is contained between the braces of the class **SquareInt**. All methods must be defined inside a class definition.

Good Programming Practice 4.2

Place a blank line between method definitions to separate the methods and enhance program readability.

Common Programming Error 4.2

Defining a method outside the braces of a class definition is a syntax error.

The format of a method definition is

```
return-value-type method-name( parameter-list )
{
    declarations and statements
}
```

The *method-name* is any valid identifier. The *return-value-type* is the data type of the result returned from the method to the caller. The return-value-type **void** indicates that a method does not return a value.

Common Programming Error 4.3

Omitting the return-value-type in a method definition is a syntax error.

Common Programming Error 4.4

Forgetting to return a value from a method that is supposed to return a value is a syntax error. If a return-value-type other than **void** *is specified, the method must contain a* **return** *statement.*

Common Programming Error 4.5

Returning a value from a method whose return type has been declared **`void`** *is a syntax error.*

The *parameter-list* is a comma-separated list containing the declarations of the parameters received by the method when it is called. If a method does not receive any values, the *parameter-list* is empty (i.e., the method name is followed by an empty set of parentheses). A type must be listed explicitly for each parameter in the parameter list of a method or a syntax error occurs.

Common Programming Error 4.6

Declaring method parameters of the same type as **`float x, y`** *instead of* **`float x, float y`**. *The parameter declaration* **`float x, y`** *is a syntax error because types are required for each parameter in the parameter list.*

Common Programming Error 4.7

Placing a semicolon after the right parenthesis enclosing the parameter list of a method definition is a syntax error.

Common Programming Error 4.8

Redefining a method parameter as a local variable in the method is a syntax error.

Good Programming Practice 4.3

Although it is not incorrect to do so, do not use the same names for the arguments passed to a method and the corresponding parameters in the method definition. This helps avoid ambiguity.

The *declarations* and *statements* within braces form the *method body*. The method body is also referred to as a *block*. A block is simply a compound statement that includes declarations. Variables can be declared in any block, and blocks can be nested. *A method cannot be defined inside another method.*

Common Programming Error 4.9

Defining a method inside another method is a syntax error.

Good Programming Practice 4.4

Choosing meaningful method names and meaningful parameter names makes programs more readable and helps avoid excessive use of comments.

Software Engineering Observation 4.5

A method should usually be no longer than one page. Better yet, a method should usually be no longer than half a page. Regardless of how long a method is, it should perform one task well. Small methods promote software reusability.

Testing and Debugging Tip 4.1

Small methods are easier to test and debug than large ones.

Software Engineering Observation 4.6

Programs should be written as collections of small methods. This makes programs easier to write, debug, maintain and modify.

Software Engineering Observation 4.7

A method requiring a large number of parameters may be performing too many tasks. Consider dividing the method into smaller methods that perform the separate tasks. The method header should fit on one line if possible.

Software Engineering Observation 4.8

The method header and method calls should all agree in the number, type, and order of arguments and parameters.

There are three ways to return control to the point at which a method was invoked. If the method does not return a result, control is returned simply when the method-ending right brace is reached, or by executing the statement

```
return;
```

If the method does return a result, the statement

```
return expression;
```

returns the value of *expression* to the caller. When a return statement is executed, control returns immediately to the point at which a method was invoked.

Note that the example of Fig. 4.3 actually contains two method definitions—**`paint`** (line 9) and **`square`** (line 21). Remember that the **`paint`** method is automatically called to enable the applet to display information. In this example, the **`paint`** method repeatedly invokes the **`square`** method to perform a calculation, then **`paint`** outputs the result. Methods in a class definition are allowed to invoke all other methods in the same class definition (there is an exception to this discussed in Chapter 6).

Our second example uses a programmer-defined method called **`maximum`** to determine and return the largest of three integers (Fig. 4.4). The three integers are input by the user into **`TextField`**s. When the user presses the *Enter* key in one of the **`TextField`**s, the **`actionPerformed`** method is invoked, the strings in the **`TextField`**s are read and converted to integers, and the integers are passed to the **`maximum`** method which determines the largest integer. This value is returned to the **`actionPerformed`** method by the **`return`** statement in the **`maximum`** method. The value returned is assigned to the variable **`max`** which is then displayed in the **`result TextField`**.

```
// Fig. 4.4: Maximum.java
// Finding the maximum of three integers
import java.awt.*;
import java.applet.Applet;
import java.awt.event.*;
```

Fig. 4.4 Programmer-defined **`maximum`** method (part 1 of 3).

```

public class Maximum extends Applet implements ActionListener {
   Label label1, label2, label3, resultLabel;
   TextField number1, number2, number3, result;
   int num1, num2, num3, max;

   // set up labels and text fields
   public void init()
   {
      label1 = new Label( "Enter first integer:" );
      number1 = new TextField( "0", 10 );
      label2 = new Label( "Enter second integer:" );
      number2 = new TextField( "0", 10 );
      label3 = new Label( "Enter third integer:" );
      number3 = new TextField( "0", 10 );
      resultLabel = new Label( "Maximum value is:" );
      result = new TextField( "0", 10 );
      result.setEditable( false );

      number1.addActionListener( this );
      number2.addActionListener( this );
      number3.addActionListener( this );

      add( label1 );
      add( number1 );
      add( label2 );
      add( number2 );
      add( label3 );
      add( number3 );
      add( resultLabel );
      add( result );
   }

   // maximum method definition
   public int maximum( int x, int y, int z )
   {
      return Math.max( x, Math.max( y, z ) );
   }

   // get the integers and call the maximum method
   public void actionPerformed( ActionEvent e )
   {
      num1 = Integer.parseInt( number1.getText() );
      num2 = Integer.parseInt( number2.getText() );
      num3 = Integer.parseInt( number3.getText() );
      max = maximum( num1, num2, num3 );
      result.setText( Integer.toString( max ) );
   }
}
```

Fig. 4.4 Programmer-defined **maximum** method (part 2 of 3).

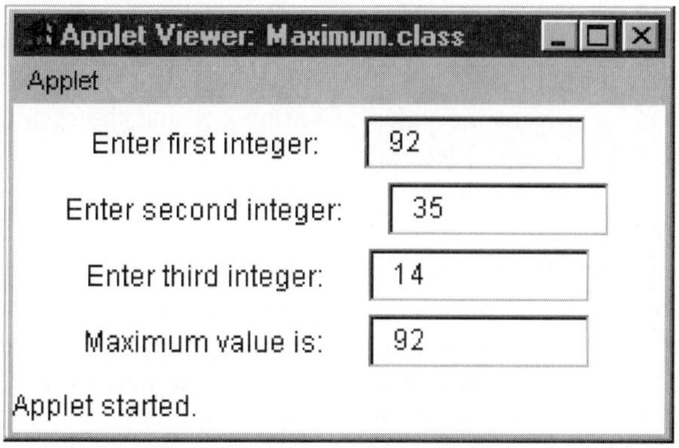

Applet Viewer: Maximum.class
Applet
Enter first integer: 92
Enter second integer: 35
Enter third integer: 14
Maximum value is: 92
Applet started.

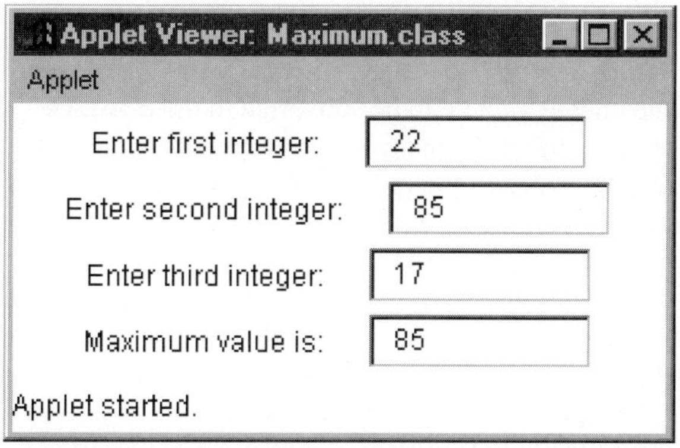

Applet Viewer: Maximum.class
Applet
Enter first integer: 22
Enter second integer: 85
Enter third integer: 17
Maximum value is: 85
Applet started.

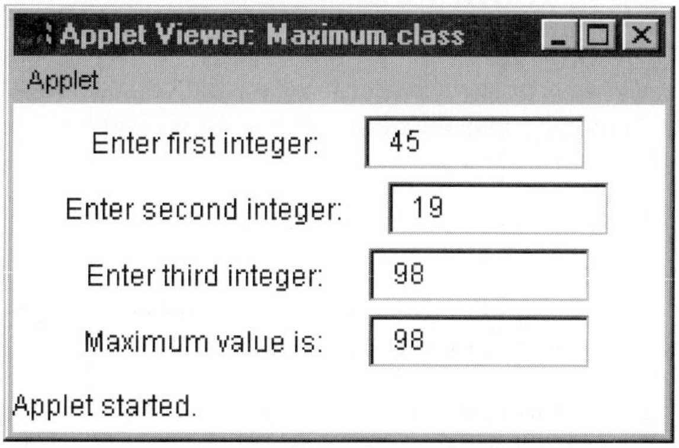

Applet Viewer: Maximum.class
Applet
Enter first integer: 45
Enter second integer: 19
Enter third integer: 98
Maximum value is: 98
Applet started.

Fig. 4.4 Programmer-defined **`maximum`** method (part 3 of 3).

Notice the implementation of the method **`maximum`** (line 40). The first line indicates that the method returns an integer, that the method's name is **`maximum`** and that the method takes three integer parameters (**`x`**, **`y`**, and **`z`**) to accomplish its task. Also, the body of the method contains the statement

```
return Math.max( x, Math.max( y, z ) );
```

which returns the largest of the three integers using two calls to the **Math.max** method. First, method **Math.max** is invoked with the values of variables **y** and **z** to determine the larger of these two values. Next the value of variable **x** and the result of the first call to **Math.max** are passed to method **Math.max**. Finally, the result of the second call to **Math.max** is returned to the point at which **maximum** was invoked (i.e., the **action** method in this program).

Another important feature of method definitions is the *coercion of arguments,* i.e., the forcing of arguments to the appropriate type to pass to a method. For example, the **Math** class method **sqrt** can be called with an integer argument even though the method is defined in the **Math** class to receive a **double** argument, and the method will still work correctly. The statement

```
System.out.println( Math.sqrt( 4 ) );
```

correctly evaluates **Math.sqrt(4)**, and prints the value **2**. The method definition's parameter list causes the integer value **4** to be converted to the **double** value **4.0** before the value is passed to **Math.sqrt**. In many cases, argument values that do not correspond precisely to the parameter types in the method definition are converted to the proper type before the method is called. In some cases, these conversions can lead to compiler errors if Java's *promotion rules* are not followed. The promotion rules specify how types can be converted to other types without losing data. In our **Math.sqrt** example above, an **int** is automatically converted to a **double** without changing its value. However, a **double** converted to an **int** truncates the fractional part of the **double** value. Converting large integer types to small integer types (e.g., **long** to **int**) may also result in changed values.

The promotion rules apply to expressions containing values of two or more data types; such expressions are also referred to as *mixed-type expressions*. The type of each value in a mixed-type expression is promoted to the "highest" type in the expression (actually a temporary version of each value is created and used for the expression—the original values remain unchanged). Figure 4.5 lists the primitive data types and the types to which each is allowed to be promoted automatically.

Type	Allowed promotions
double	None (there are no primitive types larger than **double**)
float	**double**
long	**float** or **double**
int	**long**, **float** or **double**
char	**int**, **long**, **float** or **double**
short	**int**, **long**, **float** or **double**
byte	**short**, **int**, **long**, **float** or **double**
boolean	None (**boolean** values are not considered to be numbers in Java)

Fig. 4.5 Allowed promotions for primitive data types.

Converting values to lower types can result in incorrect values. Therefore, in cases where information may be lost due to conversion, the Java compiler requires the programmer to use a cast operator to force the conversion to occur. To invoke our **square** method that uses an integer parameter (Fig. 4.3) with the **double** variable **y**, the method call is written as **square((int) y)**. This explicitly converts the value of **y** to an integer for use in method **square**. Thus, if **y**'s value is **4.5**, method **square** returns **16** not **20.25**.

Common Programming Error 4.10

Converting a primitive-data-type value to another primitive data type may change the value if the new data type is not an allowed promotion (e.g. **double** *to* **int***).*

4.6 Java API Packages

As we have seen, Java contains many predefined classes that are grouped by directories on disk into categories of related classes called packages. Together, these packages are referred to as the Java applications programming interface (Java API).

Throughout the text, **import** statements are used to specify the location of classes required to compile a Java program. For example, to tell the compiler to load the **Applet** class from the **java.applet** package, the statement

```
import java.applet.Applet;
```

is used. One of the great strengths of Java is the large number of classes in the packages of the Java API that programmers can reuse rather than "reinventing the wheel." We exercise a large number of these classes in this book. Fig. 4.6 lists alphabetically the packages of the Java API and a description of each package.

Java API package	Explanation
java.applet	*The Java Applet Package.* This package contains the Applet class and several interfaces that enable the creation of applets, interaction of applets with the browser, and playing audio clips.
java.awt	*The Java Abstract Windowing Toolkit Package.* This package contains all the classes and interfaces required to create and manipulate graphical user interfaces (these classes are discussed in detail in Chapter 10, Basic Graphical User Interface Components and Chapter 11, Advanced Graphical User Interface Components).
java.awt.datatransfer	*The Java Data Transfer Package.* This package contains classes and interfaces that enable transfer of data between a Java program and the computer's clipboard (a temporary storage area for data).

Fig. 4.6 The Java API packages (part 1 of 3).

Java API package	Explanation
`java.awt.event`	*The Java Abstract Windowing Toolkit Event Package.* This package contains classes and interfaces that enable event handling for GUI components.
`java.awt.image`	*The Java Abstract Windowing Toolkit Image Package.* This package contains classes and interfaces that enable storing and manipulation of images in a program.
`java.awt.peer`	*The Java Abstract Windowing Toolkit Peer Package.* This package contains interfaces that enable Java's graphical user interface components to interact with their platform-specific versions (i.e., a button is implemented differently on each computer platform so its peer is used to actually display and manipulate the button in a platform-specific manner). Programmers should not use this package directly.
`java.beans`	*The Java Beans Package.* This package contains classes and interfaces that enable the programmer to create reusable software components. Java beans can interact with non-Java and Java software components.
`java.io`	*The Java Input/Output Package.* This package contains classes that enable programs to input and output data (see Chapter 15, Files and Streams).
`java.lang`	*The Java Language Package.* This package is automatically imported by the compiler into all programs. The package contains basic classes and interfaces required by many Java programs (these classes are discussed throughout the text).
`java.lang.reflect`	*The Java Core Reflection Package.* This package contains classes and interfaces that enable a program to discover the accessible variables and methods of a class dynamically during the execution of a program.
`java.net`	*The Java Networking Package.* This package contains classes that enable programs to communicate via the Internet or corporate intranets (see Chapter 16, Networking)

`java.rmi`
`java.rmi.dgc`
`java.rmi.registry`
`java.rmi.server`
	The Java Remote Method Invocation Packages. These packages contain classes and interfaces that enable the programmer to create distributed Java programs. Using remote method invocation, a program can call a method of a separate program on the same computer or on a computer anywhere on the Internet.

Fig. 4.6 The Java API packages (part 2 of 3).

Java API package	Explanation

`java.security`
`java.security.acl`
`java.security.interfaces`
	The Java Security Packages.
	These packages contains classes and interfaces that enable a Java program to encrypt data and control the access privileges provided to a Java program for security purposes.

`java.sql`	*The Java Database Connectivity Package.* This package contain classes and interfaces that enable a Java program to interact with a database.
`java.text`	*The Java Text Package.* This package contains classes and interfaces that enable a Java program to manipulate numbers, dates, characters and strings. This package provides many of Java's internationalization capabilities. Internationalization enables a Java program to be customized to a specific locale. For example, an applet may display strings in different languages based on the World Wide Web browser in which the applet is executing.
`java.util`	*The Java Utilities Package.* This package contains utility classes and interfaces such as: date and time manipulations, random number processing capabilities (**`Random`**), storing and processing large amounts of data, breaking strings into smaller pieces called tokens (**`StringTokenizer`**), and other capabilities (see Chapter 18, Java Utilities Package and Bit Manipulation).
`java.util.zip`	*The Java Utilities Zip Package.* This package contains utility classes and interfaces that enable a Java program to combine Java **`.class`** files and other resource files (such as images and audio) into a single compressed file called a *Java archive (JAR) file*. This package also enables a Java program to read JAR files.

Fig. 4.6 The Java API packages (part 3 of 3).

4.7 Random Number Generation

We now take a brief and, it is hoped, entertaining diversion into a popular programming application, namely simulation and game playing. In this section and the next section, we will develop a nicely structured game-playing program that includes multiple methods. The program uses most of the control structures we have studied.

There is something in the air of a gambling casino that invigorates people from the high-rollers at the plush mahogany-and-felt craps tables to the quarter-poppers at the one-armed bandits. It is the *element of chance,* the possibility that luck will convert a pocketful of money into a mountain of wealth. The element of chance can be introduced through the ***`random`*** method from the **`Math`** class.

Consider the following statement:

```
double randomValue = Math.random();
```

The **random** method generates a **double** value from 0.0 up to (but not including) 1.0. If **random** truly produces values at random, every value from 0.0 up to (but not including) 1.0 has an equal *chance* (or *probability*) of being chosen each time **random** is called.

The range of values produced directly by **random** is often different than what is needed in a specific application. For example, a program that simulates coin tossing might require only 0 for "heads" and 1 for "tails." A program that simulates rolling a six-sided die would require random integers in range 1 to 6. A program that randomly predicts the next type of spaceship (out of four possibilities) that will fly across the horizon in a video game would require random integers in the range 1 through 4.

To demonstrate **random**, let us develop a program to simulate 20 rolls of a six-sided die and print the value of each roll. We use the multiplication operator (*) in conjunction with **random** as follows

```
(int) ( Math.random() * 6 )
```

to produce integers in the range 0 to 5. This is called *scaling*. The number 6 is called the *scaling factor*. We then *shift* the range of numbers produced by adding 1 to our previous result. Figure 4.7 confirms that the results are in the range 1 to 6. The integer cast operator is used to truncate the floating-point part (the part after the decimal point) of each value produced by the preceding expression.

```
// Fig. 4.7: RandomInt.java
// Shifted, scaled random integers
import java.awt.Graphics;
import java.applet.Applet;

public class RandomInt extends Applet {
   public void paint( Graphics g )
   {
      int xPosition = 25;
      int yPosition = 25;
      int value;

      for ( int i = 1; i <= 20; i++ ) {
         value = 1 + (int) ( Math.random() * 6 );
         g.drawString( Integer.toString( value ),
                       xPosition, yPosition );

         if ( i % 5 != 0 )
            xPosition += 40;
         else {
            xPosition = 25;
            yPosition += 15;
         }
      }
   }
}
```

Fig. 4.7 Shifted, scaled random integers (part 1 of 2).

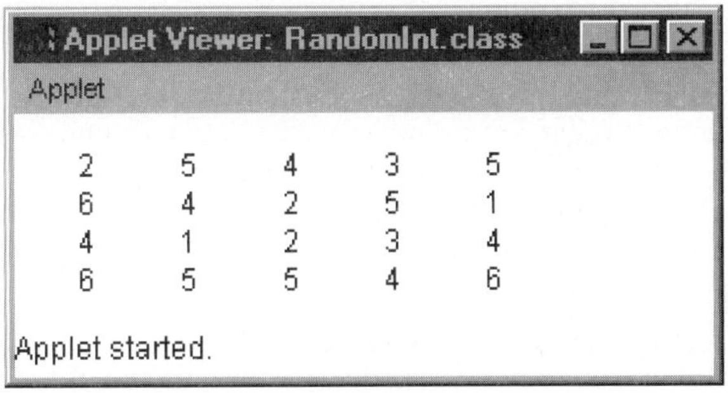

Applet Viewer: RandomInt.class

Applet

```
2    5    4    3    5
6    4    2    5    1
4    1    2    3    4
6    5    5    4    6
```

Applet started.

Fig. 4.7 Shifted, scaled random integers (part 2 of 2).

To show that these numbers occur approximately with equal likelihood, let us simulate 6000 rolls of a die with the program of Fig. 4.8. Each integer from 1 to 6 should appear approximately 1000 times.

```
// Fig. 4.8: RollDie.java
// Roll a six-sided die 6000 times
import java.awt.Graphics;
import java.applet.Applet;

public class RollDie extends Applet {
   int frequency1 = 0, frequency2 = 0,
       frequency3 = 0, frequency4 = 0,
       frequency5 = 0, frequency6 = 0;

   // summarize results
   public void start()
   {
      for ( int roll = 1; roll <= 6000; roll++ ) {
         int face = 1 + (int) ( Math.random() * 6 );

         switch ( face ) {
            case 1:
               ++frequency1;
               break;
            case 2:
               ++frequency2;
               break;
            case 3:
               ++frequency3;
               break;
            case 4:
               ++frequency4;
               break;
```

Fig. 4.8 Rolling a six-sided die 6000 times (part 1 of 2).

```
            case 5:
               ++frequency5;
               break;
            case 6:
               ++frequency6;
               break;
         }
      }
   }

   // display results
   public void paint( Graphics g )
   {
      g.drawString( "Face", 25, 25 );
      g.drawString( "Frequency", 100, 25 );
      g.drawString( "1", 25, 40 );
      g.drawString( Integer.toString( frequency1 ), 100, 40 );
      g.drawString( "2", 25, 55 );
      g.drawString( Integer.toString( frequency2 ), 100, 55 );
      g.drawString( "3", 25, 70 );
      g.drawString( Integer.toString( frequency3 ), 100, 70 );
      g.drawString( "4", 25, 85 );
      g.drawString( Integer.toString( frequency4 ), 100, 85 );
      g.drawString( "5", 25, 100 );
      g.drawString( Integer.toString( frequency5 ),
                    100, 100 );
      g.drawString( "6", 25, 115 );
      g.drawString( Integer.toString( frequency6 ),
                    100, 115 );
   }
}
```

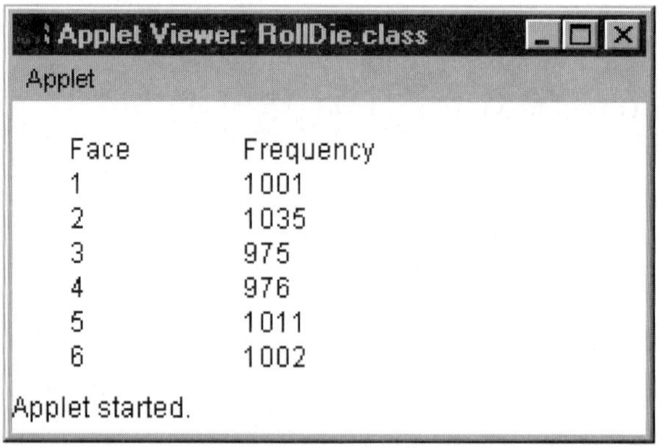

Applet Viewer: RollDie.class

Applet

Face	Frequency
1	1001
2	1035
3	975
4	976
5	1011
6	1002

Applet started.

Fig. 4.8 Rolling a six-sided die 6000 times (part 2 of 2).

As the program output shows, by scaling and shifting we have utilized the **random** method to realistically simulate the rolling of a six-sided die. Note that *no* **default** case is provided in the **switch** structure. After we study arrays in Chapter 5, we will show how to replace the entire **switch** structure elegantly with a single-line statement. Run the program several times and observe the results. Notice that a *different* sequence of random numbers is obtained each time the program is executed.

The values produced directly by **random** are always in the range:

```
0.0 ≤ Math.random() < 1.0
```

Previously we demonstrated how to write a single statement to simulate the rolling of a six-sided die with the statement:

```
int face = 1 + (int) ( Math.random() * 6 );
```

which always assigns an integer (at random) to variable **face** in the range 1 ≤ **face** ≤ 6. Note that the width of this range (i.e., the number of consecutive integers in the range) is 6 and the starting number in the range is 1. Referring to the preceding statement, we see that the width of the range is determined by the number used to scale **random** with the multiplication operator (i.e., 6), and the starting number of the range is equal to the number (i.e., 1) added to **(int) (Math.random() * 6)**. We can generalize this result as follows

```
n = a + (int) ( Math.random() * b );
```

where **a** is the *shifting value* (which is equal to the first number in the desired range of consecutive integers), and **b** is the scaling factor (which is equal to the width of the desired range of consecutive integers). In the exercises, we will see that it is possible to choose integers at random from sets of values other than ranges of consecutive integers.

4.8 Example: A Game of Chance

One of the most popular games of chance is a dice game known as "craps," which is played in casinos and back alleys throughout the world. The rules of the game are straightforward:

> *A player rolls two dice. Each die has six faces. These faces contain 1, 2, 3, 4, 5, and 6 spots. After the dice have come to rest, the sum of the spots on the two upward faces is calculated. If the sum is 7 or 11 on the first throw, the player wins. If the sum is 2, 3, or 12 on the first throw (called "craps"), the player loses (i.e., the "house" wins). If the sum is 4, 5, 6, 8, 9, or 10 on the first throw, then that sum becomes the player's "point." To win, you must continue rolling the dice until you "make your point," (i.e., roll your point value). The player loses by rolling a 7 before making the point.*

The program in Fig. 4.9 simulates the game of craps.

Notice that the player must roll two dice on the first roll, and must do so later on all subsequent rolls. We define a method **rollDice** (line 108) to roll the dice and compute and display their sum. Method **rollDice** is defined once, but it is called from two places in the program (lines 58 and 78). Interestingly, **rollDice** takes no arguments, so we have indicated an empty parameter list. The method **rollDice** does return the sum of the two dice, so a return type of **int** is indicated in the method header.

The game is reasonably involved. The player may win or lose on the first roll, or may win or lose on any subsequent roll. The variable **gameStatus** is used to keep track of this. Variable **gameStatus** is declared to be of type **int**. Line 9 of the program

```
// Fig. 4.9: Craps.java
// Craps
import java.awt.*;
import java.applet.Applet;
import java.awt.event.*;

public class Craps extends Applet implements ActionListener {
   // constant variables for status of game
   final int WON = 0, LOST = 1, CONTINUE = 2;

   // other variables used in program
   boolean firstRoll = true;   // true if first roll
   int sumOfDice = 0;          // sum of the dice
   int myPoint = 0;   // point if no win/loss on first roll
   int gameStatus = CONTINUE;  // game not over yet

   // graphical user interface components
   Label die1Label, die2Label, sumLabel, pointLabel;
   TextField firstDie, secondDie, sum, point;
   Button roll;

   // setup graphical user interface components
   public void init()
   {
      die1Label = new Label( "Die 1" );
      add( die1Label );
      firstDie = new TextField( 10 );
      firstDie.setEditable( false );
      add( firstDie );

      die2Label = new Label( "Die 2" );
      add( die2Label );
      secondDie = new TextField( 10 );
      secondDie.setEditable( false );
      add( secondDie );

      sumLabel = new Label( "Sum is" );
      add( sumLabel );
      sum = new TextField( 10 );
      sum.setEditable( false );
      add( sum );

      pointLabel = new Label( "Point is" );
      add( pointLabel );
      point = new TextField( 10 );
      point.setEditable( false );
      add( point );

```

Fig. 4.9 Program to simulate the game of craps (part 1 of 4).

```
      roll = new Button( "Roll Dice" );
      roll.addActionListener( this );
      add( roll );
   }

   // process one roll of the dice
   public void play()
   {
      if ( firstRoll ) {                 // first roll of the dice
         sumOfDice = rollDice();

         switch ( sumOfDice ) {
            case 7: case 11:             // win on first roll
               gameStatus = WON;
               point.setText( "" );  // clear point text field
               break;
            case 2: case 3: case 12: // lose on first roll
               gameStatus = LOST;
               point.setText( "" );  // clear point text field
               break;
            default:                     // remember point
               gameStatus = CONTINUE;
               myPoint = sumOfDice;
               point.setText( Integer.toString( myPoint ) );
               firstRoll = false;
               break;
         }
      }
      else {
         sumOfDice = rollDice();

         if ( sumOfDice == myPoint )     // win by making point
            gameStatus = WON;
         else
            if ( sumOfDice == 7 )        // lose by rolling 7
               gameStatus = LOST;
      }

      if ( gameStatus == CONTINUE )
         showStatus( "Roll again." );
      else {
         if ( gameStatus == WON )
            showStatus( "Player wins. " +
               "Click Roll Dice to play again." );
         else
            showStatus( "Player loses. " +
               "Click Roll Dice to play again." );

         firstRoll = true;
      }
   }
```

Fig. 4.9 Program to simulate the game of craps (part 2 of 4).

```

   // call method play when button is clicked
   public void actionPerformed( ActionEvent e )
   {
      play();
   }

   // roll the dice
   int rollDice()
   {
      int die1, die2, workSum;

      die1 = 1 + ( int ) ( Math.random() * 6 );
      die2 = 1 + ( int ) ( Math.random() * 6 );
      workSum = die1 + die2;

      firstDie.setText( Integer.toString( die1 ) );
      secondDie.setText( Integer.toString( die2 ) );
      sum.setText( Integer.toString( workSum ) );

      return workSum;
   }
}
```

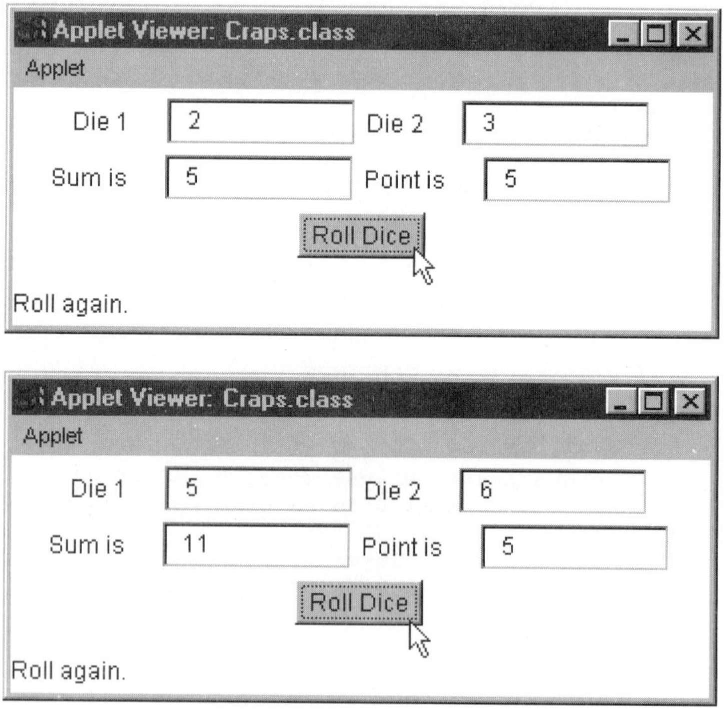

Fig. 4.9 Program to simulate the game of craps (part 3 of 4).

Fig. 4.9 Program to simulate the game of craps (part 4 of 4).

```
final int WON = 0, LOST = 1, CONTINUE = 2;
```

creates variables that define the three states of a game of craps—game won, game lost, or continue rolling the dice. Keyword **`final`** at the beginning of the declaration indicates that these are *constant variables*. Constant variables must be initialized when they are declared, and cannot be modified thereafter. Constant variables are often called *named constants* or *read-only variables*. Keyword **`final`** is discussed in detail in Chapters 5 and 6.

Common Programming Error 4.11

*After a **`final`** variable has been defined, attempting to assign another value to the variable is a syntax error.*

Good Programming Practice 4.5

*Use only uppercase letters in the names of **`final`** variables. This makes these constants stand out in a program.*

Good Programming Practice 4.6

*Using meaningfully named **`final`** variables rather than integer constants (such as 2) makes programs more readable.*

The user clicks the "**`Roll Dice`**" button to roll the dice. This invokes the **`actionPerformed`** method (line 102) of the applet which then invokes the **`play`** method (line 55). The **`play`** method checks the **`boolean`** variable **`firstRoll`** to determine if it is **`true`** or **`false`** (if it is **`true`**, this is the first roll of the game). After the first roll, if the game is won or lost, the program proceeds to the **`if/else`** structure at line 90 which displays in the status bar

```
Player wins. Click Roll Dice to play again.
```

if **`gameStatus`** is equal to **`WON`** and

```
Player loses. Click Roll Dice to play again.
```

if **`gameStatus`** is equal to **`LOST`**.

After the first roll, if the game is not over, **sum** is saved in **myPoint** and displayed in **TextField point**. The program then waits for the user to click button "**Roll Dice**" again. Each time the "**Roll Dice**" button is clicked, method **play** is invoked and method **rollDice** is called to produce a new **sum**. If **sum** matches **myPoint**, **gameStatus** is set to **WON**, the **if/else** structure at line 90 is executed, and the game is complete. If **sum** is equal to **7**, **gameStatus** is set to **LOST**, **if/else** structure at line 90 is executed, and the game is complete. Clicking the "**Roll Dice**" button starts a new game. Throughout the program, the four **TextField**s are updated with the new values of the dice and the sum on each roll and the **point TextField** is updated each time a new game is started.

Note the interesting use of the various program control mechanisms we have discussed. The craps program uses four methods—**init**, **actionPerformed**, **play** and **rollDice**—and the **switch**, **if/else**, and nested **if** structures. In the exercises, we investigate various interesting characteristics of the game of craps.

4.9 Automatic Variables

Chapters 1 through 3 used identifiers for variable names. The attributes of variables include name, type, size, and value. We also use identifiers as names for user-defined methods. Actually, each identifier in a program has other attributes including *duration* and *scope*.

An identifier's *duration* (also called its *lifetime*) determines the period during which that identifier exists in memory. Some identifiers exist briefly, some are repeatedly created and destroyed, and others exist for the entire execution of a program.

An identifier's *scope* is where the identifier can be referenced in a program. Some identifiers can be referenced throughout a program, while others can be referenced from only limited portions of a program. This section discusses duration of identifiers. Section 4.10 discusses the scope of identifiers.

Identifiers that represent local variables in a method—i.e., parameters and variables declared in the method body—have *automatic duration*. Automatic duration variables are created when program control enters the block in which they are declared, they exist while the block is active, and they are destroyed when the block is exited. For the remainder of the text, we will refer to variables of automatic duration simply as automatic variables.

Performance Tip 4.1

Automatic duration is a means of conserving memory because automatic duration variables are created when the block in which they are declared is entered and are destroyed when the block is exited.

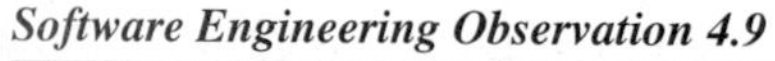

Software Engineering Observation 4.9

Automatic duration is an example of the principle of least privilege. *This principle states that each component of a system should have sufficient rights and privileges to accomplish its designated task, but no additional rights or privileges. This helps prevent accidental and/or malicious errors from occurring in systems. Why have variables stored in memory and accessible when they are not needed?*

The instance variables of a class are automatically initialized by the compiler if the programmer does not provide initial values. Variables of the primitive data types are initialized to zero except boolean variables which are initialized to **false**. References are initialized to **null**. Unlike instance variables of a class, automatic variables must be initialized by the programmer before they can be used in an expression.

Testing and Debugging Tip 4.2

Automatic variables must be initialized before they are used in a method; otherwise, the compiler issues an error message

Java also has identifiers of *static duration*. Variables and methods of static duration exist from the point at which the class that defines them is loaded into memory for execution until the program terminates. For static duration variables, storage is allocated and initialized once when their classes are loaded into memory. For static duration methods, the names of the methods exist when their classes are loaded into memory. Even though the static duration variable and method names exist when their classes are loaded into memory, this does not mean that these identifiers can be used throughout the program. Duration and scope (where a name can be used) are separate issues as shown in Section 4.10.

4.10 Scope Rules

The *scope* of an identifier is the portion of the program in which the identifier can be referenced. A local variable declared in a block can be referenced only in that block or in blocks nested within that block. The scopes for an identifier are *class scope* and *block scope*.

Methods and instance variables of a class have *class scope*. Class scope begins at the opening left brace, **{**, of the class definition and terminates at the closing right brace, **}**, of the class definition. Class scope enables methods of a class to directly invoke all methods defined in the same class or inherited into the class (such as the methods inherited into our applets from the Applet class) and to directly access all instance variables defined in the class. (In Chapter 6, we will see that **static** methods are an exception to this rule.) In a sense, all instance variables and methods of a class are *global* to the methods of the class in which they are defined—i.e., the methods can modify the instance variables directly and invoke other methods of the class.

Identifiers declared inside a block have *block scope.* Block scope begins at the identifier's declaration and ends at the terminating right brace (**}**) of the block. Local variables declared at the beginning of a method have block scope as do method parameters, which are also local variables of the method. Any block may contain variable declarations. When blocks are nested, and an identifier in an outer block has the same name as an identifier in an inner block, the compiler generates a syntax error stating that the variable is already defined. If a local variable in a method has the same name as an instance variable, the instance variable is "hidden" until the block terminates execution. In Chapter 6, we discuss how to access such "hidden" instance variables.

Common Programming Error 4.12

Accidentally using the same name for an identifier in an inner block of a method as is used for an identifier in an outer block of the same method results in a syntax error from the compiler.

Good Programming Practice 4.7

Avoid local variable names that hide instance variable names. This can be accomplished by avoiding the use of duplicate identifiers in a program.

The program of Fig. 4.10 demonstrates scoping issues with instance variables and automatic local variables. Note that the main output for the program is sent to the command line (or to the Java console if you are using a browser such as Netscape Navigator).

```java
// Fig. 4.10: Scoping.java
// A scoping example
import java.awt.Graphics;
import java.applet.Applet;

public class Scoping extends Applet {
   int x = 1;       // instance variable

   public void paint( Graphics g )
   {
      g.drawString( "See command line for output", 25, 25 );

      int x = 5;    // local variable to paint

      System.out.println( "local x in paint is " + x );

      a();          // a has automatic local x
      b();          // b uses instance variable x
      a();          // a reinitializes automatic local x
      b();          // instance variable x retains its value

      System.out.println( "\nlocal x in paint is " + x );
   }

   void a()
   {
      int x = 25;   // initialized each time a is called

      System.out.println( "\nlocal x in a is " + x +
                          " after entering a" );
      ++x;
      System.out.println( "local x in a is " + x +
                          " before exiting a" );
   }

   void b()
   {
      System.out.println( "\ninstance variable x is " + x +
                          " on entering b" );
      x *= 10;
      System.out.println( "instance variable x is " + x +
                          " on exiting b" );
   }
}
```

Fig. 4.10 A scoping example (part 1 of 2).

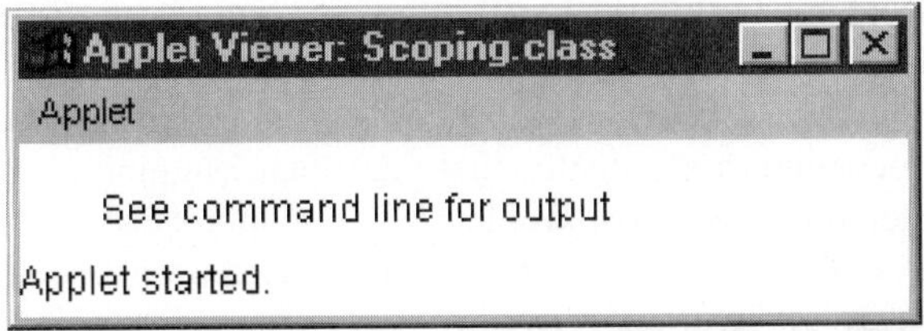


```
local x in paint is 5

local x in a is 25 after entering a
local x in a is 26 before exiting a

instance variable x is 1 on entering b
instance variable x is 10 on exiting b

local x in a is 25 after entering a
local x in a is 26 before exiting a

instance variable x is 10 on entering b
instance variable x is 100 on exiting b

local x in paint is 5
```

Fig. 4.10 A scoping example (part 2 of 2).

An instance variable **x** (line 7) is declared and initialized to 1. This instance variable is hidden in any block (or method) in which a variable named **x** is declared. In **paint**, a local variable **x** is declared and initialized to **5**. This variable is printed to show that the instance variable **x** is hidden in **paint**. The program defines two other methods—each takes no arguments and returns nothing. Method **a** defines automatic variable **x** and initializes it to **25**. When **a** is called, the variable is printed, incremented, and printed again before exiting the method. Each time this method is called, automatic variable **x** is recreated and initialized to **25**. Method **b** does not declare any variables. Therefore, when it refers to variable **x**, the instance variable **x** is used. When **b** is called, the instance variable is printed, multiplied by **10**, and printed again before exiting the method. The next time method **b** is called, the instance variable has its modified value, **10**. Finally, the program prints the local variable **x** in **paint** again to show that none of the method calls modified the value of **x** because the methods all referred to variables in other scopes.

4.11 Recursion

The programs we have discussed are generally structured as methods that call one another in a disciplined, hierarchical manner. For some problems, it is useful to have methods call themselves. A *recursive method* is a method that calls itself either directly or indirectly through another method. Recursion is an important topic discussed at length in upper-level computer science courses. In this section and the next, simple examples of recursion are presented. This book contains an extensive treatment of recursion. Figure 4.15 (at the end of Section 4.13) summarizes the recursion examples and exercises in the book.

We consider recursion conceptually first, and then examine several programs containing recursive methods. Recursive problem-solving approaches have a number of elements in common. A recursive method is called to solve a problem. The method actually knows how to solve only the simplest case(s), or so-called *base case(s)*. If the method is called with a base case, the method simply returns a result. If the method is called with a more complex problem, the method divides the problem into two conceptual pieces: a piece that the method knows how to do and a piece that the method does not know how to do. To make recursion feasible, the latter piece must resemble the original problem, but be a slightly simpler or slightly smaller version of the original problem. Because this new problem looks like the original problem, the method launches (calls) a fresh copy of itself to go to work on the smaller problem—this is referred to as a *recursive call* and is also called the *recursion step*. The recursion step also includes the keyword **`return`** because its result will be combined with the portion of the problem the method knew how to solve to form a result that will be passed back to the original caller.

The recursion step executes while the original call to the method is still open, i.e., it has not finished executing. The recursion step can result in many more recursive calls, as the method divides each new subproblem into two conceptual pieces. For the recursion to eventually terminate, each time the method calls itself with a slightly simpler version of the original problem, the sequence of smaller and smaller problems must converge on the base case. At that point, the method recognizes the base case, returns a result to the previous copy of the method, and a sequence of returns ensues up the line until the original method call eventually returns the final result to the caller. This sounds exotic compared to the conventional problem solving we performed to this point. As an example of these concepts at work, let us write a recursive program to perform a popular mathematical calculation.

The factorial of a non-negative integer *n,* written *n!* (and pronounced "*n* factorial"), is the product

$$n \cdot (n - 1) \cdot (n - 2) \cdot \ldots \cdot 1$$

with 1! equal to 1, and 0! defined to be 1. For example, 5! is the product $5 \cdot 4 \cdot 3 \cdot 2 \cdot 1$, which is equal to 120.

The factorial of an integer, **`number`**, greater than or equal to 0, can be calculated *iteratively* (nonrecursively) using **`for`** as follows:

```
factorial = 1;
for ( int counter = number; counter >= 1; counter-- )
   factorial *= counter;
```

A recursive definition of the factorial method is arrived at by observing the following relationship:

$$n! = n \cdot (n - 1)!$$

For example, 5! is clearly equal to 5 * 4! as is shown by the following:

$$5! = 5 \cdot 4 \cdot 3 \cdot 2 \cdot 1$$
$$5! = 5 \cdot (4 \cdot 3 \cdot 2 \cdot 1)$$
$$5! = 5 \cdot (4!)$$

The evaluation of 5! would proceed as shown in Fig. 4.11. Figure 4.11a shows how the succession of recursive calls proceeds until 1! is evaluated to be 1, which terminates the recursion. Figure 4.11b shows the values returned from each recursive call to its caller until the final value is calculated and returned.

The program of Fig. 4.12 uses recursion to calculate and print the factorials of the integers 0 to 10 (the choice of the data type **`long`** will be explained momentarily). The recursive method **`factorial`** first tests to see if a terminating condition is true, i.e., is **`number`** less than or equal to 1. If **`number`** is indeed less than or equal to 1, **`factorial`** returns 1, no further recursion is necessary, and the program terminates. If **`number`** is greater than 1, the statement

```
return number * factorial( number - 1 );
```

expresses the problem as the product of **`number`** and a recursive call to **`factorial`** evaluating the factorial of **`number - 1`**. Note that **`factorial( number - 1 )`** is a slightly simpler problem than the original calculation **`factorial( number )`**.

Method **`factorial`** has been declared to receive a parameter of type **`long`** and return a result of type **`long`**. As can be seen in Fig. 4.12, factorial values become large quickly. We have chosen the data type **`long`** so the program can calculate factorials greater than 20!. Unfortunately, the **`factorial`** method produces large values so quickly that even **`long`** does not help us print many factorial values before the size of a **`long`** variable is exceeded.

As we explore in the exercises, **`float`** and **`double`** may ultimately be needed by the user desiring to calculate factorials of larger numbers. This points to a weakness in most programming languages, namely that the languages are not easily extended to handle the

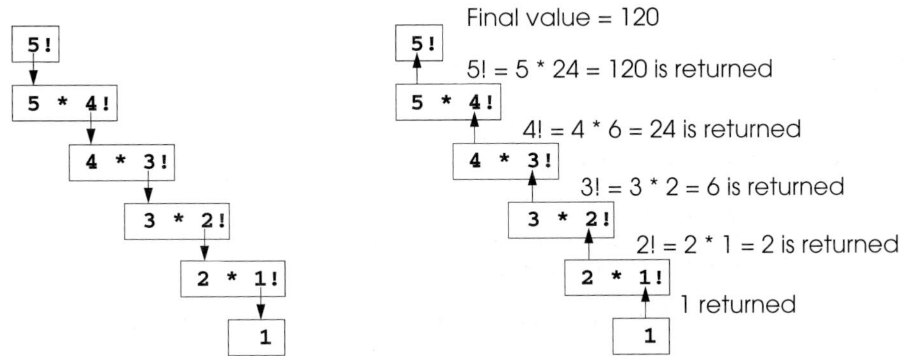

Fig. 4.11 Recursive evaluation of 5!.

unique requirements of various applications. As we will see in the section of the book on object-oriented programming, Java is an extensible language that allows us to create arbitrarily large integers if we wish.

```
// Fig. 4.12: FactorialTest.java
// Recursive factorial method
import java.awt.Graphics;
import java.applet.Applet;

public class FactorialTest extends Applet {
   public void paint( Graphics g )
   {
      int yPosition = 25;

      for ( long i = 0; i <= 10; i++ )  {
         g.drawString( i + "! = " + factorial( i ),
                          25, yPosition );
         yPosition += 15;
      }
   }

   // Recursive definition of method factorial
   public long factorial( long number )
   {
      if ( number <= 1 )  // base case
         return 1;
      else
         return number * factorial( number - 1 );
   }
}
```

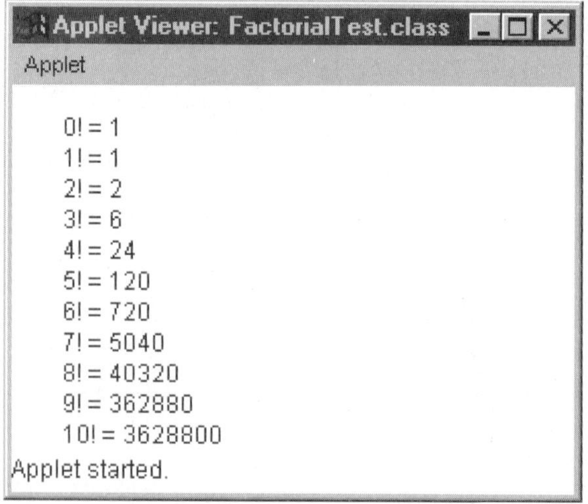

Fig. 4.12 Calculating factorials with a recursive method.

Common Programming Error 4.13

Forgetting to return a value from a recursive method when one is needed results in a syntax error.

Common Programming Error 4.14

Either omitting the base case, or writing the recursion step incorrectly so that it does not converge on the base case, will cause infinite recursion, eventually exhausting memory. This is analogous to the problem of an infinite loop in an iterative (nonrecursive) solution.

4.12 Example Using Recursion: The Fibonacci Series

The Fibonacci series

0, 1, 1, 2, 3, 5, 8, 13, 21, …

begins with 0 and 1 and has the property that each subsequent Fibonacci number is the sum of the previous two Fibonacci numbers.

The series occurs in nature and, in particular, describes a form of spiral. The ratio of successive Fibonacci numbers converges on a constant value of 1.618…. This number, too, repeatedly occurs in nature and has been called the *golden ratio* or the *golden mean*. Humans tend to find the golden mean aesthetically pleasing. Architects often design windows, rooms, and buildings whose length and width are in the ratio of the golden mean. Postcards are often designed with a golden mean length/width ratio.

The Fibonacci series may be defined recursively as follows:

$$fibonacci(0) = 0$$
$$fibonacci(1) = 1$$
$$fibonacci(n) = fibonacci(n-1) + fibonacci(n-2)$$

Figure 4.13 calculates the ith Fibonacci number recursively using method **`fibonacci`**. Notice that Fibonacci numbers tend to become large quickly. Therefore, we have chosen the data type **`long`** for the parameter type and the return type in method **`fibonacci`**. In Fig. 4.13, each pair of output lines shows a separate run of the program.

```
// Fig. 4.13: FibonacciTest.java
// Recursive fibonacci method
import java.awt.*;
import java.applet.Applet;
import java.awt.event.*;

public class FibonacciTest extends Applet
             implements ActionListener {
   Label numLabel, resultLabel;
   TextField num, result;

```

Fig. 4.13 Recursively generating Fibonacci numbers (part 1 of 4).

```
   public void init()
   {
     numLabel = new Label( "Enter an integer and press return" );
      num = new TextField( 10 );
      num.addActionListener( this );
      resultLabel = new Label( "Fibonacci value is" );
      result = new TextField( 15 );
      result.setEditable( false );

      add( numLabel );
      add( num );
      add( resultLabel );
      add( result );
   }

   public void actionPerformed( ActionEvent e )
   {
      long number, fibonacciValue;

      number = Long.parseLong( num.getText() );
      showStatus( "Calculating ..." );
      fibonacciValue = fibonacci( number );
      showStatus( "Done." );
      result.setText( Long.toString( fibonacciValue ) );
   }

   // Recursive definition of method fibonacci
   long fibonacci( long n )
   {
      if ( n == 0 || n == 1 )  // base case
         return n;
      else
         return fibonacci( n - 1 ) + fibonacci( n - 2 );
   }
}
```

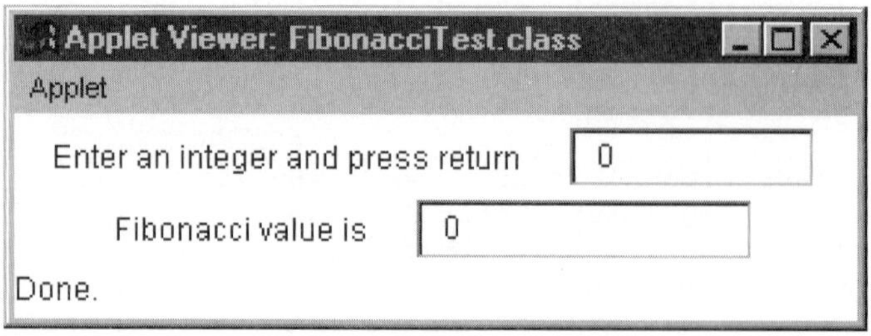

Applet Viewer: FibonacciTest.class
Applet
Enter an integer and press return 0
Fibonacci value is 0
Done.

Fig. 4.13 Recursively generating Fibonacci numbers (part 2 of 4).

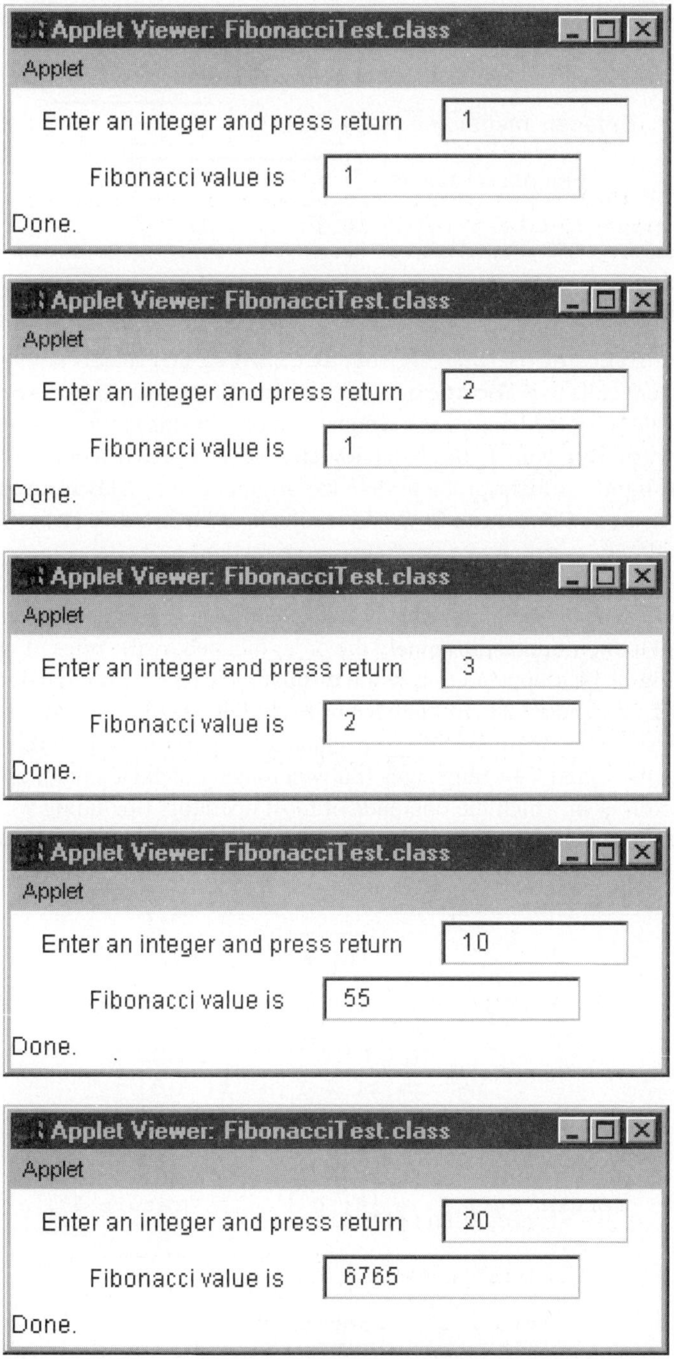

Applet Viewer: FibonacciTest.class
Applet
Enter an integer and press return 1
Fibonacci value is 1
Done.

Applet Viewer: FibonacciTest.class
Applet
Enter an integer and press return 2
Fibonacci value is 1
Done.

Applet Viewer: FibonacciTest.class
Applet
Enter an integer and press return 3
Fibonacci value is 2
Done.

Applet Viewer: FibonacciTest.class
Applet
Enter an integer and press return 10
Fibonacci value is 55
Done.

Applet Viewer: FibonacciTest.class
Applet
Enter an integer and press return 20
Fibonacci value is 6765
Done.

Fig. 4.13 Recursively generating Fibonacci numbers (part 3 of 4).

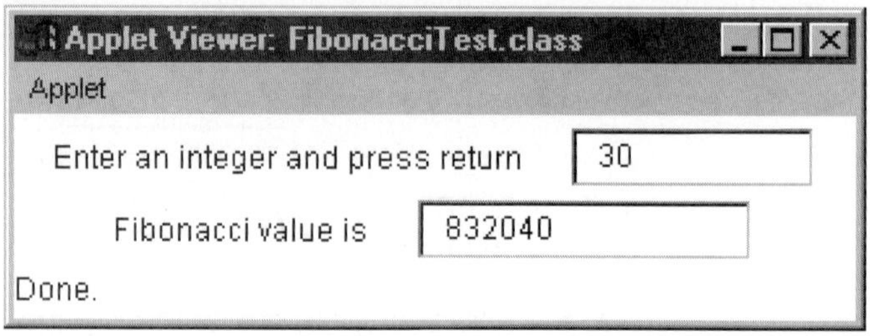

Applet Viewer: FibonacciTest.class
Applet
Enter an integer and press return 30
Fibonacci value is 832040
Done.

Fig. 4.13 Recursively generating Fibonacci numbers (part 4 of 4).

The call to **`fibonacci`** (line 33) from **`actionPerformed`** is not a recursive call, but all subsequent calls to **`fibonacci`** are recursive. Each time **`fibonacci`** is invoked, it immediately tests for the base case—**`n`** equal to 0 or 1. If this is true, **`n`** is returned. Interestingly, if **`n`** is greater than 1, the recursion step generates *two* recursive calls, each of which is for a slightly simpler problem than the original call to **`fibonacci`**. Figure 4.14 shows how method **`fibonacci`** would evaluate **`fibonacci(3)`**—we abbreviate **`fibonacci`** simply as **`f`** to make the figure more readable.

This figure raises some interesting issues about the order in which Java compilers will evaluate the operands of operators. This is a different issue from the order in which operators are applied to their operands, namely the order dictated by the rules of operator precedence. From Fig. 4.14 it appears that while evaluating **`f(3)`**, two recursive calls will be made, namely **`f(2)`** and **`f(1)`**. But in what order will these calls be made? Most programmers simply assume the operands will be evaluated left to right. In Java this is true.

Strangely, the C and C++ languages (on which many of Java's features are based) do not specify the order in which the operands of most operators (including **`+`**) are evaluated. Therefore, the programmer may make no assumption in those languages about the order in

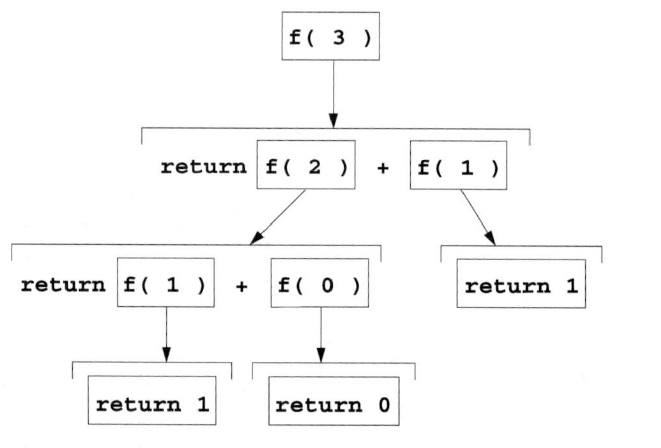

Fig. 4.14 Set of recursive calls to method **`fibonacci`**.

which these calls execute. The calls could in fact execute `f(2)` first and then `f(1)`, or the calls could execute in the reverse order, `f(1)` then `f(2)`. In this program and in most other programs, it turns out the final result would be the same. But in some programs the evaluation of an operand may have *side effects* that could affect the final result of the expression.

The Java language specifies the order of evaluation of the operands is left-to-right. Thus, the method calls are in fact `f(2)` first, then `f(1)`.

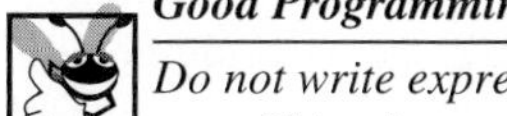

Good Programming Practice 4.8

Do not write expressions that depend on the order of evaluation of the operands of an operator. This often results in programs that are difficult to read, debug, modify, and maintain.

A word of caution is in order about recursive programs like the one we use here to generate Fibonacci numbers. Each invocation of the **`fibonacci`** method that does not match one of the base cases (i.e., 0 or 1) results in two more recursive calls to the **`fibonacci`** method. This rapidly gets out of hand. Calculating the fibonacci value of 20 using the program in Fig. 4.13 requires 21,891 calls to the **`fibonacci`** method, calculating the fibonacci value of 30 requires 2,692,537 calls to the **`fibonacci`** method.

As you try larger values, you will notice that each consecutive fibonacci number you ask the applet to calculate results in a substantial increase in calculation time and number of calls to the **`fibonacci`** method. For example, the fibonacci value of 31 requires 4,356,617 calls and the fibonacci value of 32 requires 7,049,155 calls. As you can see, the number of calls to fibonacci is increasing quickly—1,664,080 additional calls between fibonacci of 30 and 31, and 2,692,538 additional calls between fibonacci of 31 and 32. This difference in number of calls made between fibonacci of 31 and 32 is more than 1.5 times the difference for fibonacci of 30 and 31. Problems of this nature humble even the world's most powerful computers! Computer scientists study in the field of complexity theory how hard algorithms have to work to do their jobs. Complexity issues are discussed in detail in the upper-level computer science curriculum course generally called "Algorithms."

Performance Tip 4.2

Avoid fibonacci-style recursive programs which result in an exponential "explosion" of calls.

4.13 Recursion vs. Iteration

In the previous sections, we studied two methods that can easily be implemented either recursively or iteratively. In this section we compare the two approaches and discuss why the programmer might choose one approach over the other in a particular situation.

Both iteration and recursion are based on a control structure: Iteration uses a repetition structure (such as **`for`**, **`while`** or **`do/while`**); recursion uses a selection structure (such as **`if`**, **`if/else`** or **`switch`**). Both iteration and recursion involve repetition: Iteration explicitly uses a repetition structure; recursion achieves repetition through repeated method calls. Iteration and recursion each involve a termination test: Iteration terminates when the loop-continuation condition fails; recursion terminates when a base case is recognized. Iteration with counter-controlled repetition and recursion each gradually approach termination: Iteration keeps modifying a counter until the counter assumes a value that makes the loop-continuation condition fail; recursion keeps producing simpler versions of the original problem until the base case is reached. Both iteration and recursion can occur infinitely: An infinite loop occurs with iteration if the loop-continuation test never becomes false; infinite recursion occurs if the recursion step does not reduce the problem each time in a manner that converges on the base case.

Recursion has many negatives. It repeatedly invokes the mechanism, and consequently the overhead, of method calls. This can be expensive in both processor time and memory space. Each recursive call causes another copy of the method (actually only the method's variables) to be created; this can consume considerable memory. Iteration normally occurs within a method so the overhead of repeated method calls and extra memory assignment is omitted. So why choose recursion?

Software Engineering Observation 4.10

Any problem that can be solved recursively can also be solved iteratively (nonrecursively). A recursive approach is normally chosen in preference to an iterative approach when the recursive approach more naturally mirrors the problem and results in a program that is easier to understand and debug. Another reason to choose a recursive solution is that an iterative solution may not be apparent.

Performance Tip 4.3

Avoid using recursion in performance situations. Recursive calls take time and consume additional memory.

Common Programming Error 4.15

Accidentally having a nonrecursive method call itself either directly, or indirectly through another method can cause infinite recursion.

Most programming textbooks introduce recursion much later than we have done here. We feel that recursion is a sufficiently rich and complex topic that it is better to introduce it earlier and spread the examples over the remainder of the text. Figure 4.15 summarizes the recursion examples and exercises in the text.

Let us reconsider some observations we make repeatedly throughout the book. Good software engineering is important. High performance is often important. Unfortunately, these goals are often at odds with one another. Good software engineering is key to making more manageable the task of developing larger and more complex software systems. High performance in these systems is key to realizing the systems of the future that will place ever greater computing demands on hardware. Where do methods fit in here?

Software Engineering Observation 4.11

Modularizing programs in a neat, hierarchical manner promotes good software engineering. But it has a price.

Performance Tip 4.4

A heavily modularized program—as compared to a monolithic (i.e., one-piece) program without methods—makes potentially large numbers of method calls and these consume execution time and space on a computer's processor(s). But monolithic programs are difficult to program, test, debug, maintain, and evolve.

So modularize your programs judiciously, always keeping in mind the delicate balance between performance and good software engineering.

Chapter	Recursion Examples and Exercises
Chapter 4	Factorial method
	Fibonacci method
	Greatest common divisor
	Sum of two integers
	Multiply two integers
	Raising an integer to an integer power
	Towers of Hanoi
	Visualizing recursion
Chapter 5	Sum the elements of an array
	Print an array
	Print an array backwards
	Check if a string is a palindrome
	Minimum value in an array
	Selection sort
	Eight Queens
	Linear search
	Binary search
	Quicksort
	Maze traversal
Chapter 8	Printing a string input at the keyboard backwards
Chapter 17	Linked list insert
	Linked list delete
	Search a linked list
	Print a linked list backwards
	Binary tree insert
	Preorder traversal of a binary tree
	Inorder traversal of a binary tree
	Postorder traversal of a binary tree

Fig. 4.15 Summary of recursion examples and exercises in the text.

4.14 Method Overloading

Java enables several methods of the same name to be defined as long as these methods have different sets of parameters (based on the number of parameters, the types of the parameters and the order of the parameters). This is called *method overloading*. When an overloaded method is called, the Java compiler selects the proper method by examining the number, types, and order of the arguments in the call. Method overloading is commonly used to create several methods of the same name that perform similar tasks, but on different data types.

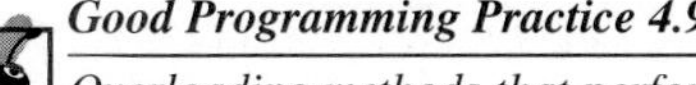

Good Programming Practice 4.9

Overloading methods that perform closely related tasks can make programs more readable and understandable.

Figure 4.16 uses overloaded method **square** to calculate the square of an **int** and the square of a **double**.

Overloaded methods are distinguished by their *signature*—a combination of the method's name and its parameter types. If the Java compiler only looked at method names during compilation, the code in Fig. 4.16 would be ambiguous—the compiler would not know how to distinguish the two **square** methods. Logically, the compiler uses longer "mangled" or "decorated" names that include the original method name, the types of each parameter and the exact order of the parameters to determine if the methods in a class are unique in that class.

For example in Fig. 4.16, the compiler might use the logical name "*square of int*" for the **square** method that specifies an **int** parameter and "*square of double*" for the **square** method that specifies a **double** parameter. If a method **foo**'s definition begins as follows

```
// Fig. 4.16: MethodOverload.java
// Using overloaded methods
import java.awt.Graphics;
import java.applet.Applet;

public class MethodOverload extends Applet {
   public void paint( Graphics g )
   {
      g.drawString( "The square of integer 7 is " + square( 7 ),
                    25, 25 );
      g.drawString( "The square of double 7.5 is " +
                    square( 7.5 ), 25, 40 );
   }

   int square( int x )
   {
      return x * x;
   }

   double square( double y )
   {
      return y * y;
   }
}
```

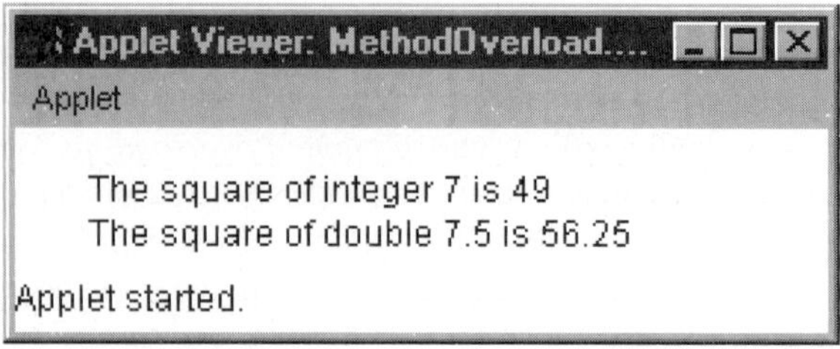

Fig. 4.16 Using overloaded methods.

```
void foo( int a, float b )
```

the compiler might use the logical name "*foo of int and float*." If the parameters are specified as follows

```
void foo( float a, int b )
```

the compiler might use the logical name "*foo of float and int*." Note that the order of the parameters is important to the compiler. The preceding two **foo** methods are considered to be unique by the compiler.

So far, the logical names of methods used by the compiler did not mention the return types of the methods. This is because methods cannot be distinguished by return type. The program of Fig. 4.17 illustrates the compiler errors generated when two methods have the same signature and different return types. Overloaded methods can have different return types, but must have different parameter lists. Also, overloaded methods need not have the same number of parameters.

Common Programming Error 4.16

Creating overloaded methods with identical parameter lists and different return types is a syntax error.

```
// Fig. 4.17: MethodOverload.java
// Overloaded methods with identical signatures and
// different return types.
import java.awt.Graphics;
import java.applet.Applet;

public class MethodOverload extends Applet {
   int square( double x )
   {
      return x * x;
   }

   double square( double y )
   {
      return y * y;
   }
}
```

```
MethodOverload.java:13: Methods can't be redefined with a
      different return type: double square(double) was
      int square(double)
   double square( double y )
          ^
1 error
```

Fig. 4.17 Compiler error messages generated from overloaded methods with identical parameter lists and different return types.

4.15 Methods of the Applet Class

We have written many applets to this point in the text, but we have not yet discussed the key methods of the Applet class that are called automatically during the execution of an applet. Figure 4.18 lists the key methods of the **Applet** class, when they get called, and the purpose of each method.

Method	When the method is called and its purpose
public void init()	This method is called once by the Appletviewer or browser when an applet is loaded for execution. It performs initialization of an applet. Typical actions performed here are initialization of instance variables and GUI components of the Applet, loading of sounds to play or images to display (Chapter 14, Multimedia), and creation of threads (Chapter 13, Multithreading).
public void start()	This method is called after the **init** method completes execution and every time the user of the browser returns to the HTML page on which the applet resides (after browsing another HTML page). This method performs any tasks that must be completed when the applet is loaded for the first time into the browser and that must be performed every time the HTML page on which the applet resides is revisited. Typical actions performed here include starting an animation (Chapter 14, Multimedia) and starting other threads of execution (Chapter 13, Multithreading).
public void paint(Graphics g)	This method is called after the **init** method completes execution and the **start** method has started executing to draw on the applet. It is also called automatically every time the applet needs to be repainted. For example, if the user of the browser covers the applet with another open window on the screen then uncovers the applet, the **paint** method is called. Typical actions performed here involve drawing with the **Graphics** object **g** that is automatically passed to the **paint** method for you.
public void stop()	This method is called when the applet should stop executing—normally when the user of the browser leaves the HTML page on which the applet resides. This method performs any tasks that are required to suspend the applet's execution. Typical actions performed here are to stop execution of animations and threads.
public void destroy()	This method is called when the applet is being removed from memory—normally when the user of the browser exits the browsing session. This method performs any tasks that are required to destroy resources allocated to the applet. Typical actions performed here include terminating threads (Chapter 13, Multithreading).

Fig. 4.18 Applet methods called automatically during an applet's execution.

These **Applet** methods are defined by the Java API to do nothing unless you provide a definition in your applet's class definition. If you would like to use one of these methods in an applet you are defining, you *must* define the first line of the method as shown in Fig. 4.18. Otherwise, the method will not get called automatically during the applet's execution.

Common Programming Error 4.17

Providing a definition for one of the **Applet** *methods* **init**, **start**, **paint**, **stop**, *or* **destroy** *that does not match the method headers shown in Fig. 4.18 results in a method that will not be called automatically during the execution of the applet.*

The ***setSize*** and ***repaint*** methods are also of interest to many applet programmers. As you know, when an applet is invoked via an HTML page, the applet's width and height in pixels are specified in the HTML code (see Fig. 1.3). The applet's size can be changed during the applet's execution by invoking method **setSize**. For example, the statement

```
setSize( 200, 400 );
```

makes the applet's width 200 pixels and its height 400 pixels. This statement is normally placed in the applet's **init** method.

The applet's **paint** method is normally called automatically. What if you would like to change the appearance of the applet in response to the user's interactions with the applet? In such situations, you may want to call **paint** directly. However, to call **paint**, we must pass it the **Graphics** parameter it expects. This poses a problem for us. We do not have a **Graphics** object at our disposal to pass to **paint** (we discuss this issue in Chapter 14, Multimedia). For this reason, the **repaint** method is provided for you. The statement

```
repaint();
```

invokes another method called ***update*** and passes it the **Graphics** object for you. The **update** method erases any drawing that was previously done on the applet then invokes the **paint** method and passes it the **Graphics** object for you. The **repaint** and **update** methods are discussed in detail in Chapter 14, Multimedia.

Summary

- The best way to develop and maintain a large program is to divide it into several smaller program modules each of which is more manageable than the original program. Modules are written in Java as classes and methods.
- A method is invoked by a method call. The method call mentions the method by name and provides information (as arguments) that the called method needs to perform its task.
- Methods are invoked in a program by writing the name of the method followed by the arguments of the method in parentheses.
- Each argument of a method may be a constant, a variable, or an expression.
- A local variable is known only in a method definition. Methods are not allowed to know the implementation details of any other method (including local variables).

- The general format for a method definition is

  return-value-type method-name **(** *parameter-list* **)**
  {
  declarations and statements
  }

  The return-value-type states the type of the value returned to the calling method. If a method does not return a value, the return-value-type is **void**. The method-name is any valid identifier. The parameter-list is a comma-separated list containing the declarations of the variables that will be passed to the method. If a method does not receive any values, parameter-list is empty. The method-body is the set of declarations and statements that constitute the method.
- An empty parameter list is specified with empty parentheses.
- The arguments passed to a method should match in number, type, and order with the parameters in the method definition.
- When a program encounters a method, control is transferred from the point of invocation to the called method, the method is executed, and control returns to the caller.
- A called method can return control to the caller in one of three ways. If the method does not return a value, control is returned when the method-ending right brace is reached, or by executing the statement

  return;

  If the method does return a value, the statement

  return *expression***;**

  returns the value of *expression*.
- Method **Math.random** generates a double value from 0.0 up to (but not including) 1.0.
- Values produced by **Math.random** can be scaled and shifted to produce values in a specific range.
- The general equation for scaling and shifting a random number is

  ```
  n = a + (int) ( Math.random() * b );
  ```

  where **a** is the shifting value (which is equal to the first number in the desired range of consecutive integers), and **b** is the scaling factor (which is equal to the width of the desired range of consecutive integers).
- Each variable identifier has the attributes duration (lifetime) and scope. An identifier's duration determines when that identifier exists in memory. An identifier's scope is where the identifier can be referenced in a program.
- Identifiers that represent local variables in a method—i.e., parameters and variables declared in the method body—have automatic duration. Automatic duration variables are created when program control enters the block in which they are declared, they exist while the block is active, and they are destroyed when the block is exited.

- Java also has identifiers of *static duration*. Variables and methods of static duration exist from the point at which the class in which they are defined is loaded into memory for execution until the program terminates. For static duration variables, storage is allocated and initialized once when their class is loaded into memory. For static duration methods, the name of the method exists when their class is loaded into memory.
- The scopes for an identifier are class scope and block scope. An instance variable declared outside any method has class scope. Such an identifier is "known" in all methods of the class. Identifiers declared inside a block have block scope. Block scope ends at the terminating right brace (`}`) of the block.
- Local variables declared at the beginning of a method have block scope as do method parameters, which are considered local variables of the method.
- Any block may contain variable declarations.
- A recursive method is a method that calls itself either directly or indirectly.
- If a recursive method is called with a base case, the method simply returns a result. If the method is called with a more complex problem, the method divides the problem into two or more conceptual pieces: a piece that the method knows how to do and a slightly smaller version of the original problem. Because this new problem looks like the original problem, the method launches a recursive call to work on the smaller problem.
- For recursion to terminate, each time the recursive method calls itself with a slightly simpler version of the original problem, the sequence of smaller and smaller problems must converge on the base case. When the method recognizes the base case, the result is returned to the previous method call, and a sequence of returns ensues all the way up the line until the original call of the method eventually returns the final result.
- Both iteration and recursion are based on a control structure: Iteration uses a repetition structure; recursion uses a selection structure.
- Both iteration and recursion involve repetition: Iteration explicitly uses a repetition structure; recursion achieves repetition through repeated method calls.
- Iteration and recursion each involve a termination test: Iteration terminates when the loop-continuation condition fails; recursion terminates when a base case is recognized.
- Iteration and recursion can occur infinitely: An infinite loop occurs with iteration if the loop-continuation test never becomes false; infinite recursion occurs if the recursion step does not reduce the problem in a manner that converges on the base case.
- Recursion repeatedly invokes the mechanism, and consequently the overhead, of method calls. This can be expensive in both processor time and memory space.
- A method that does not return a value is declared with a **`void`** return type. If an attempt is made either to return a value from the method or to use the result of the method invocation in the calling method, the compiler reports a syntax error.
- The **`final`** qualifier creates "constant variables." A constant variable must be initialized when the variable is declared, and cannot be modified thereafter. Constant variables are often called named constants or read-only variables.

- It is possible to define methods with the same name but with different parameter lists (based on the types of the parameters, the number of parameters and the order of the parameters). This is called method overloading. When an overloaded method is called, the compiler selects the proper method by examining the arguments in the call.
- Overloaded methods can have different return values, and must have different parameter lists. Two methods differing only by return type will result in a syntax error.
- The applet's **init** method is called once by the Appletviewer or browser when an applet is loaded for execution. It performs initialization of an applet. The applet's **start** method is called after the **init** method completes execution and every time the user of the browser returns to the HTML page on which the applet resides (after browsing another HTML page).
- The applet's **paint** method is called after the **init** method completes execution and the **start** method has started executing to draw on the applet. It is also called automatically every time the applet needs to be repainted.
- The applet's **stop** method is called when the applet should suspend execution—normally when the user of the browser leaves the HTML page on which the applet resides.
- The applet's **destroy** method is called when the applet is being removed from memory—normally when the user of the browser exits the browsing session.

Terminology

argument in a method call
automatic duration
automatic variable
base case in recursion
block
block scope
call a method
called method
caller
calling method
class
class scope
coercion of arguments
constant variable
copy of a value
destroy method
divide and conquer
duration
element of chance
factorial method
file scope
final
init method
invoke a method
iteration
Java API (Java class library)
local variable
Math class methods
Math.E
Math.PI
Math.random method
method
method call
method declaration
method definition
method overloading
mixed-type expression
modular program
named constant
overloading
paint method
parameter in a method definition
programmer-defined method
promotion rules
random number generation
read-only variable
recursion
recursion step

recursive call
recursive method
reference parameter
reference types
repaint method
return
return-value-type
scaling
scope
setSize method
shifting
side effects
signature
simulation
software engineering
software reusability
start method
static storage duration
stop method
update method
void

Common Programming Errors

4.1 Forgetting to invoke a **Math** class method by preceding the method name with the class name **Math** and a dot operator (**.**) results in a syntax error.

4.2 Defining a method outside the braces of a class definition is a syntax error.

4.3 Omitting the return-value-type in a method definition is a syntax error.

4.4 Forgetting to return a value from a method that is supposed to return a value is a syntax error. If a return-value-type other than **void** is specified, the method must contain a **return** statement.

4.5 Returning a value from a method whose return type has been declared **void** is a syntax error.

4.6 Declaring method parameters of the same type as **float x, y** instead of **float x, float y**. The parameter declaration **float x, y** is a syntax error because types are required for each parameter in the parameter list.

4.7 Placing a semicolon after the right parenthesis enclosing the parameter list of a method definition is a syntax error.

4.8 Redefining a method parameter as a local variable in the method is a syntax error.

4.9 Defining a method inside another method is a syntax error.

4.10 Converting a primitive-data-type value to another primitive data type may change the value if the new data type is not an allowed promotion (e.g. **double** to **int**).

4.11 After a **final** variable has been defined, attempting to assign another value to the variable is a syntax error.

4.12 Accidentally using the same name for an identifier in an inner block of a method as is used for an identifier in an outer block of the same method results in a syntax error from the compiler.

4.13 Forgetting to return a value from a recursive method when one is needed results in a syntax error.

4.14 Either omitting the base case, or writing the recursion step incorrectly so that it does not converge on the base case, will cause infinite recursion, eventually exhausting memory. This is analogous to the problem of an infinite loop in an iterative (nonrecursive) solution. Infinite recursion can also be caused by providing an unexpected input.

4.15 Accidentally having a nonrecursive method call itself either directly, or indirectly through another method can cause infinite recursion.

4.16 Creating overloaded methods with identical parameter lists and different return types is a syntax error.

4.17 Providing a definition for one of the **`Applet`** methods **`init`**, **`start`**, **`paint`**, **`stop`**, or **`destroy`** that does not match the method headers shown in Fig. 4.18 results in a method that will not be called automatically during the execution of the applet.

Good Programming Practices

4.1 Familiarize yourself with the rich collection of classes and methods in the Java API and with the rich collections of classes available in various class libraries.

4.2 Place a blank line between method definitions to separate the methods and enhance program readability.

4.3 Although it is not incorrect to do so, do not use the same names for the arguments passed to a method and the corresponding parameters in the method definition. This helps avoid ambiguity.

4.4 Choosing meaningful method names and meaningful parameter names makes programs more readable and helps avoid excessive use of comments.

4.5 Use only uppercase letters in the names of **`final`** variables. This makes these constants stand out in a program.

4.6 Using meaningfully named **`final`** variables rather than integer constants (such as 2) makes programs more readable.

4.7 Avoid local variable names that hide instance variable names. This can be accomplished by avoiding the use of duplicate identifiers in a program.

4.8 Do not write expressions that depend on the order of evaluation of the operands of an operator. This often results in programs that are difficult to read, debug, modify, and maintain.

4.9 Overloading methods that perform closely related tasks can make programs more readable and understandable.

Performance Tips

4.1 Automatic duration is a means of conserving memory because automatic duration variables are created when the block in which they are declared is entered and are destroyed when the block is exited.

4.2 Avoid fibonacci-style recursive programs which result in an exponential "explosion" of calls.

4.3 Avoid using recursion in performance situations. Recursive calls take time and consume additional memory.

4.4 A heavily modularized program—as compared to a monolithic (i.e., one-piece) program without methods—makes potentially large numbers of method calls and these consume execution time and space on a computer's processor(s). But monolithic programs are difficult to program, test, debug, maintain, and evolve.

Software Engineering Observations

4.1 Avoid reinventing the wheel. When possible, use Java API classes and methods instead of writing new classes and methods. This reduces program development time.

4.2 It is not necessary to import the **`Math`** class into a program to use **`Math`** class methods. The **`Math`** class is part of the **`java.lang`** package which is automatically imported by the compiler.

4.3 Each method should be limited to performing a single, well-defined task, and the method name should effectively express that task. This promotes software reusability.

4.4 If you cannot choose a concise name that expresses what the method does, it is possible that your method is attempting to perform too many diverse tasks. It is usually best to break such a method into several smaller methods.

4.5 A method should usually be no longer than one page. Better yet, a method should usually be no longer than half a page. Regardless of how long a method is, it should perform one task well. Small methods promote software reusability.

4.6 Programs should be written as collections of small methods. This makes programs easier to write, debug, maintain and modify.

4.7 A method requiring a large number of parameters may be performing too many tasks. Consider dividing the method into smaller methods that perform the separate tasks. The method header should fit on one line if possible.

4.8 The method header and method calls should all agree in the number, type, and order of arguments and parameters.

4.9 Automatic duration is an example of the principle of least privilege. This principle states that each component of a system should have sufficient rights and privileges to accomplish its designated task, but no additional rights or privileges. This helps prevent accidental and/or malicious errors from occurring in systems. Why have variables stored in memory and accessible when they are not needed?

4.10 Any problem that can be solved recursively can also be solved iteratively (nonrecursively). A recursive approach is normally chosen in preference to an iterative approach when the recursive approach more naturally mirrors the problem and results in a program that is easier to understand and debug. Another reason to choose a recursive solution is that an iterative solution may not be apparent.

4.11 Modularizing programs in a neat, hierarchical manner promotes good software engineering. But it has a price.

Testing and Debugging Tips

4.1 Small methods are easier to test and debug than large ones.

4.2 Automatic variables must be initialized before they are used in a method; otherwise, the compiler issues an error message.

Self-Review Exercises

4.1 Answer each of the following:

a) Program modules in Java are called __________ and__________.
b) A method is invoked with a __________.
c) A variable known only within the method in which it is defined is called a__________.
d) The ________ statement in a called method can be used to pass the value of an expression back to the calling method.
e) The keyword __________ is used in a method header to indicate that a method does not return a value.
f) The __________ of an identifier is the portion of the program in which the identifier can be used.
g) The three ways to return control from a called method to a caller are________, ________, and __________.
h) The __________ method is invoked once when an applet begins execution.
i) The __________ method is used to produce random numbers.
j) The __________ method is invoked each time the user of a browser revisits the HTML page on which an applet resides.
k) The __________ method is invoked to draw on an applet.
l) Variables declared in a block or in the parameter list of a method are assumed to be of __________ duration.
m) The __________ method is invoked to change the width and height of an applet during the applet's execution.
n) The _________ method invokes the applet's **`update`** method which in turn invokes the applet's **`paint`** method.
o) The __________ method is invoked for an applet each time the user of a browser leaves an HTML page on which the applet resides.
p) A method that calls itself either directly or indirectly is a__________ method.
q) A recursive method typically has two components: one that provides a means for the recursion to terminate by testing for a _________ case, and one that expresses the problem as a recursive call for a slightly simpler problem than the original call.
r) In Java, it is possible to have various methods with the same name that each operate on different types and/or numbers of arguments. This is called method__________.
s) The __________ qualifier is used to declare read-only variables.

4.2 For the following program, state the scope (either class scope or block scope) of each of the following elements.

a) The variable **`x`**.
b) The variable **`y`**.

c) The method **cube**.

d) The method **paint**.

e) The variable **yPos**.

```
public class CubeTest extends Applet {
   int x;
   public void paint( Graphics g )
   {
      int yPos = 25;

      for ( x = 1; x <= 10; x++ ) {
         g.drawString( cube( x ), 25, yPos );
         yPos += 15;
      }
   }
   public int cube( int y )
   {
      return y * y * y;
   }
}
```

4.3 Write an application that tests if the examples of the math library method calls shown in Fig. 4.2 actually produce the indicated results.

4.4 Give the method header for each of the following methods.

a) Method **hypotenuse** that takes two double-precision, floating-point arguments, **side1** and **side2**, and returns a double-precision, floating-point result.

b) Method **smallest** that takes three integers, **x**, **y**, **z**, and returns an integer.

c) Method **instructions** that does not receive any arguments and does not return a value. (Note: Such methods are commonly used to display instructions to a user.)

d) Method **intToFloat** that takes an integer argument, **number**, and returns a floating-point result.

4.5 Find the error in each of the following program segments and explain how the error can be corrected:

a)
```
int g() {
   System.out.println( "Inside method g" );
   int h() {
      System.out.println( "Inside method h" );
   }
}
```

b)
```
int sum(int x, int y) {
   int result;
   result = x + y;
}
```

c)
```
int sum( int n ) {
   if ( n == 0 )
      return 0;
   else
      n + sum( n - 1 );
}
```

d)
```
void f( float a ); {
    float a;

    System.out.println( a );
}
```
e)
```
void product() {
    int a = 6, b = 5, c = 4, result;
    result = a * b * c;
    System.out.println( "Result is " + result );
    return result;
}
```

4.6 Write a complete Java applet to prompt the user for the **double** radius of a sphere and call method **sphereVolume** to calculate and display the volume of that sphere using the assignment

```
volume = ( 4 / 3 ) * Math.PI * Math.pow( radius, 3 )
```

The user should input the radius through a **TextField**. A string can be converted to a **double** value as follows (assume **e** is the **ActionEvent** object passed to the **actionPerformed** method when the user presses the *Enter* key in the **TextField**):

```
// Create a Double object using the text field value.
Double val = new Double( e.getActionCommand() );

// Pull the primitive data type double value out of
// the Double object.
double radius = val.doubleValue();  //
```

The result can be converted to a **String** with method **Double.toString**.

Answers to Self-Review Exercises

4.1 a) Methods and classes. b) Method call. c) Local variable. d) **return**. e) **void**. f) Scope. g) **return;** or **return** *expression***;** or encountering the closing right brace of a method. h) **init**. i) **Math.random**. j) **start**. k) **paint**. l) Automatic. m) **resize**. n) **repaint**. o) **stop**. p) Recursive. q) Base. r) Overloading. s) **final**.

4.2 a) Class scope. b) Block Scope. c) Class scope. d) Class scope. f) Block scope.

4.3 The following solution demonstrates the **Math** class methods in Fig. 4.2.

```
// Exercise 4.3: MathTest.java
// Testing the Math class methods

public class MathTest {
   public static void main( String args[] )
   {
      System.out.println( "Math.abs( 23.7 ) = " +
                          Math.abs( 23.7 ) );
      System.out.println( "Math.abs( 0.0 ) = " +
                          Math.abs( 0.0 ) );
      System.out.println( "Math.abs( -23.7 ) = " +
                          Math.abs( -23.7 ) );
```

```
        System.out.println( "Math.ceil( 9.2 ) = " +
                            Math.ceil( 9.2 ) );
        System.out.println( "Math.ceil( -9.8 ) = " +
                            Math.ceil( -9.8 ) );
        System.out.println( "Math.cos( 0.0 ) = " +
                            Math.cos( 0.0 ) );
        System.out.println( "Math.exp( 1.0 ) = " +
                            Math.exp( 1.0 ) );
        System.out.println( "Math.exp( 2.0 ) = " +
                            Math.exp( 2.0 ) );
        System.out.println( "Math.floor( 9.2 ) = " +
                            Math.floor( 9.2 ) );
        System.out.println( "Math.floor( -9.8 ) = " +
                            Math.floor( -9.8 ) );
        System.out.println( "Math.log( 2.718282 ) = " +
                            Math.log( 2.718282 ) );
        System.out.println( "Math.log( 7.389056 ) = " +
                            Math.log( 7.389056 ) );
        System.out.println( "Math.max( 2.3, 12.7 ) = v +
                            Math.max( 2.3, 12.7 ) );
        System.out.println( "Math.max( -2.3, -12.7 ) = " +
                            Math.max( -2.3, -12.7 ) );
        System.out.println( "Math.min( 2.3, 12.7 ) = " +
                            Math.min( 2.3, 12.7 ) );
        System.out.println( "Math.min( -2.3, -12.7 ) = " +
                            Math.min( -2.3, -12.7 ) );
        System.out.println( "Math.pow( 2, 7 ) = " +
                            Math.pow( 2, 7 ) );
        System.out.println( "Math.pow( 9, .5 ) = " +
                            Math.pow( 9, .5 ) );
        System.out.println( "Math.sin( 0.0 ) = " +
                            Math.sin( 0.0 ) );
        System.out.println( "Math.sqrt( 25.0 ) = " +
                            Math.sqrt( 25.0 ) );
        System.out.println( "Math.tan( 0.0 ) = " +
                            Math.tan( 0.0 ) );
    }
}
```

```
Math.abs( 23.7 ) = 23.7
Math.abs( 0.0 ) = 0
Math.abs( -23.7 ) = 23.7
Math.ceil( 9.2 ) = 10
Math.ceil( -9.8 ) = -9
Math.cos( 0.0 ) = 1
Math.exp( 1.0 ) = 2.71828
Math.exp( 2.0 ) = 7.38906
Math.floor( 9.2 ) = 9
Math.floor( -9.8 ) = -10
Math.log( 2.718282 ) = 1
Math.log( 7.389056 ) = 2
Math.max( 2.3, 12.7 ) = 12.7
```

```
Math.max( -2.3, -12.7 ) = -2.3
Math.min( 2.3, 12.7 ) = 2.3
Math.min( -2.3, -12.7 ) = -12.7
Math.pow( 2, 7 ) = 128
Math.pow( 9, .5 ) = 3
Math.sin( 0.0 ) = 0
Math.sqrt( 25.0 ) = 5
Math.tan( 0.0 ) = 0
```

4.4
a) **`double hypotenuse( double side1, double side2 )`**
b) **`int smallest( int x, int y, int z )`**
c) **`void instructions()`**
d) **`float intToFloat( int number )`**

4.5
a) Error: Method **`h`** is defined in method **`g`**.
Correction: Move the definition of **`h`** out of the definition of **`g`**.
b) Error: The method is supposed to return an integer, but does not.
Correction: Delete variable **`result`** and place the following statement in the method:

```
return x + y;
```

c) Error: The result of **`n + sum(n - 1)`** is not returned by this recursive method; **`sum`** returns an improper result.
Correction: Rewrite the statement in the **`else`** clause as

```
return n + sum(n - 1);
```

d) Error: The semicolon after the right parenthesis that encloses the parameter list, and redefining the parameter **`a`** in the method definition are each incorrect.
Correction: Delete the semicolon after the right parenthesis of the parameter list, and delete the declaration **`float a;`**.
e) Error: The method returns a value when it is not supposed to.
Correction: Change the return type to **`int`**.

4.6 The following solution calculates the volume of a sphere using the radius entered by the user.

```
// Ex. 4.6: SphereTest.java
import java.applet.Applet;
import java.awt.*;
import java.awt.event.*;

public class SphereTest extends Applet
             implements ActionListener {
   Label prompt;
   TextField input;

   public void init()
   {
      prompt = new Label( "Enter sphere radius: " );
      input = new TextField( 10 );
      input.addActionListener( this );
```

```
        add( prompt );
        add( input );
    }

    public void actionPerformed( ActionEvent e )
    {
        Double val = new Double( e.getActionCommand() );
        double radius = val.doubleValue();
        showStatus( "Volume is " + sphereVolume( radius ) );
    }

    public double sphereVolume( double radius )
    {
        double volume;
        volume = ( 4 / 3 ) * Math.PI * Math.pow( radius, 3 );
        return volume;
    }
}
```

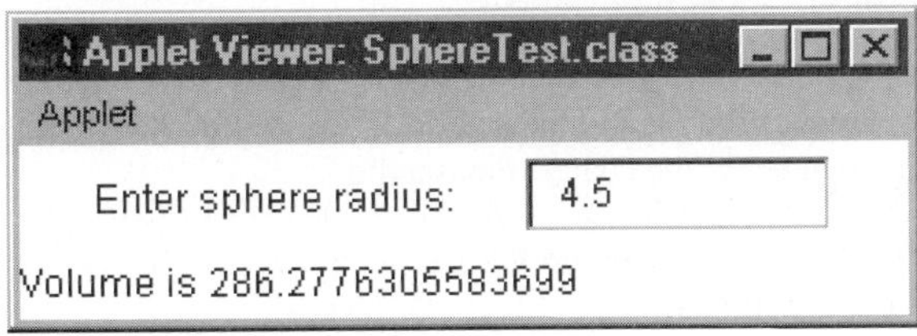

Exercises

4.7 Show the value of x after each of the following statements is performed:

a) **`x = Math.abs( 7.5 );`**
b) **`x = Math.floor( 7.5 );`**
c) **`x = Math.abs( 0.0 );`**
d) **`x = Math.ceil( 0.0 );`**
e) **`x = Math.abs( -6.4 );`**
f) **`x = Math.ceil( -6.4 );`**
g) **`x = Math.ceil( -Math.abs( -8 + Math.floor( -5.5 ) ) );`**

4.8 A parking garage charges a $2.00 minimum fee to park for up to three hours. The garage charges an additional $0.50 per hour for each hour *or part thereof* in excess of three hours. The maximum charge for any given 24-hour period is $10.00. Assume that no car parks for longer than 24 hours at a time. Write an applet that calculates and displays the parking charges for each customer who parked their car in this garage yesterday. You should enter in a **`TextField`** the hours parked for each customer. The program should display the charge for the current customer and should calculate and display the running total of yesterday's receipts. The program should use the method **`calculateCharges`** to determine the charge for each customer. Use the techniques described in Self-Review Exercise 4.6 to read the double value from a **`TextField`**.

4.9 An application of method **`Math.floor`** is rounding a value to the nearest integer. The statement

```
y = Math.floor( x + .5 );
```

will round the number **x** to the nearest integer and assign the result to **y**. Write an applet that reads double values and uses the preceding statement to round each of these numbers to the nearest integer. For each number processed, display both the original number and the rounded number. Use the techniques described in Self-Review Exercise 4.6 to read the double value from a **TextField**.

4.10 **Math.floor** may be used to round a number to a specific decimal place. The statement

```
y =Math.floor( x * 10 + .5 ) / 10;
```

rounds **x** to the tenths position (the first position to the right of the decimal point). The statement

```
y = Math.floor( x * 100 + .5 ) / 100;
```

rounds **x** to the hundredths position (i.e., the second position to the right of the decimal point). Write an applet that defines four methods to round a number **x** in various ways:

a) **roundToInteger(number)**
b) **roundToTenths(number)**
c) **roundToHundredths(number)**
d) **roundToThousandths(number)**

For each value read, your program should display the original value, the number rounded to the nearest integer, the number rounded to the nearest tenth, the number rounded to the nearest hundredth, and the number rounded to the nearest thousandth.

4.11 Answer each of the following questions.

a) What does it mean to choose numbers "at random?"
b) Why is the **Math.random** method useful for simulating games of chance?
c) Why is it often necessary to scale and/or shift the values produced by **Math.random**?
d) Why is computerized simulation of real-world situations a useful technique?

4.12 Write statements that assign random integers to the variable n in the following ranges:

a) $1 \le n \le 2$
b) $1 \le n \le 100$
c) $0 \le n \le 9$
d) $1000 \le n \le 1112$
e) $-1 \le n \le 1$
f) $-3 \le n \le 11$

4.13 For each of the following sets of integers, write a single statement that will print a number at random from the set.

a) 2, 4, 6, 8, 10.
b) 3, 5, 7, 9, 11.
c) 6, 10, 14, 18, 22.

4.14 Write a method **integerPower(base, exponent)** that returns the value of

$$base^{exponent}$$

For example, **integerPower(3, 4) = 3 * 3 * 3 * 3**. Assume that **exponent** is a positive, non-zero integer, and **base** is an integer. Method **integerPower** should use **for** or **while** to control the calculation. Do not use any math library methods. Incorporate this method into an applet that reads integer values from **TextFields** for **base** and **exponent** from the user and performs the calculation with the **integerPower** method.

4.15 Define a method **hypotenuse** that calculates the length of the hypotenuse of a right triangle when the other two sides are given. The method should take two arguments of type **double** and return the hypotenuse as a **double**. Incorporate this method into an applet that reads integer values for **side1** and **side2** from the user at the keyboard and performs the calculation with the **hypotenuse** method. Determine the length of the hypotenuse for each of the following triangles.

Triangle	Side 1	Side 2
1	3.0	4.0
2	5.0	12.0
3	8.0	15.0

4.16 Write a method **multiple** that determines for a pair of integers whether the second integer is a multiple of the first. The method should take two integer arguments and return **true** if the second is a multiple of the first, and **false** otherwise. Incorporate this method into an applet that inputs a series of pairs of integers (one pair at a time using **TextField**s).

4.17 Write an applet that inputs integers (one at a time) and passes them one at a time to method **isEven** which uses the modulus operator to determine if an integer is even. The method should take an integer argument and return **true** if the integer is even and **false** otherwise.

4.18 Write a method **squareOfAsterisks** that displays a solid square of asterisks whose side is specified in integer parameter **side**. For example, if **side** is **4**, the method displays

```
****
****
****
****
```

Incorporate this method into an applet that reads an integer value for **side** from the user at the keyboard and performs the drawing with the **squareOfAsterisks** method. Note that this method should be called from the applet's **paint** method and should be passed the **Graphics** object from **paint**.

4.19 Modify the method created in Exercise 4.18 to form the square out of whatever character is contained in character parameter **fillCharacter**. Thus if **side** is **5** and **fillCharacter** is "**#**" then this method should print

```
#####
#####
#####
#####
#####
```

4.20 Use techniques similar to those developed in Exercises 4.18 and 4.19 to produce a program that graphs a wide range of shapes.

4.21 Modify the program of Exercise 4.18 to draw a solid square with the **fillRect** method of the **Graphics** class. Method **fillRect** receives four arguments—x coordinate, y coordinate, width and height. Allow the user to enter the coordinates at which the square should appear. (See Exercises 1.25–1.28 for more information on **Graphics** class methods.)

4.22 Write program segments that accomplish each of the following:

a) Calculate the integer part of the quotient when integer **a** is divided by integer **b**.

b) Calculate the integer remainder when integer **a** is divided by integer **b**.

c) Use the program pieces developed in a) and b) to write a method **displayDigits** that receives an integer between **1** and **99999** and prints it as a series of digits, each pair of which is separated by two spaces. For example, the integer **4562** should be printed as

4 5 6 2.

d) Incorporate the method developed in c) into an applet that inputs an integer from the user at the keyboard and invokes **displayDigits** from the applet's **paint** method by passing the method both the integer entered and the **Graphics** object.

4.23 Implement the following integer methods:

a) Method **celsius** returns the Celsius equivalent of a Fahrenheit temperature using the calculation

```
C = 5 / 9 * ( F - 32 );
```

b) Method **fahrenheit** returns the Fahrenheit equivalent of a Celsius temperature.

```
F = 9 / 5 * C + 32;
```

c) Use these methods to write an applet that enables the user to enter either a Fahrenheit temperature and display the Celsius equivalent or enter a Celsius temperature and display the Fahrenheit equivalent.

4.24 Write a method **minimum3** that returns the smallest of three floating-point numbers. Use the **Math.min** method to implement **minimum3**. Incorporate the method into an applet that reads three values from the user and determines the smallest value. Display the result in the status bar.

4.25 An integer number is said to be a *perfect number* if its factors, including 1 (but not the number itself), sum to the number. For example, 6 is a perfect number because 6 = 1 + 2 + 3. Write a method **perfect** that determines if parameter **number** is a perfect number. Use this method in an applet that determines and prints all the perfect numbers between 1 and 1000. Print the factors of each perfect number to confirm that the number is indeed perfect. Challenge the computing power of your computer by testing numbers much larger than 1000.

4.26 An integer is said to be *prime* if it is divisible only by 1 and itself. For example, 2, 3, 5, and 7 are prime, but 4, 6, 8, and 9 are not.

a) Write a method that determines if a number is prime.

b) Use this method in an applet that determines and prints all the prime numbers between 1 and 10000. How many of these 10000 numbers do you really have to test before being sure that you have found all the primes?

c) Initially you might think that $n/2$ is the upper limit for which you must test to see if a number is prime, but you need only go as high as the square root of n. Why? Rewrite the program, and run it both ways. Estimate the performance improvement.

4.27 Write a method that takes an integer value and returns the number with its digits reversed. For example, given the number 7631, the method should return 1367. Incorporate the method into an applet that reads a value from the user. Display the result of the method in the status bar.

4.28 The *greatest common divisor (GCD)* of two integers is the largest integer that evenly divides each of the two numbers. Write a method **gcd** that returns the greatest common divisor of two integers. Incorporate the method into an applet that reads two values from the user. Display the result of the method in the status bar.

4.29 Write a method **qualityPoints** that inputs a student's average and returns 4 if a student's average is 90–100, 3 if the average is 80–89, 2 if the average is 70–79, 1 if the average is 60–69, and 0 if the average is lower than 60. Incorporate the method into an applet that reads a value from the user. Display the result of the method in the status bar.

4.30 Write an applet that simulates coin tossing. Let the program toss the coin each time the user presses the "**Toss**" button. Count the number of times each side of the coin appears. Display the results. The program should call a separate method **flip** that takes no arguments and returns **false** for tails and **true** for heads. *Note:* If the program realistically simulates the coin tossing, then each side of the coin should appear approximately half the time.

4.31 Computers are playing an increasing role in education. Write a program that will help an elementary school student learn multiplication. Use **Math.random** to produce two positive one-digit integers. It should then display a question in the status bar such as:

```
How much is 6 times 7?
```

The student then types the answer into a **TextField**. Your program checks the student's answer. If it is correct, draw the string **"Very good!"** on the applet then ask another multiplication question. If the answer is wrong, draw the string **"No. Please try again."** on the applet; then, let the student try the same question again repeatedly until the student finally gets it right. A separate method should be used to generate each new question. This method should be called once when the applet begins execution and each time the user answers the question correctly. All drawing on the applet should be performed by the **paint** method.

4.32 The use of computers in education is referred to as *computer-assisted instruction* (CAI). One problem that develops in CAI environments is student fatigue. This can be eliminated by varying the computer's dialogue to hold the student's attention. Modify the program of Exercise 4.31 so the various comments are printed for each correct answer and each incorrect answer as follows:

Responses to a correct answer

```
Very good!
Excellent!
Nice work!
Keep up the good work!
```

Responses to an incorrect answer

```
No. Please try again.
Wrong. Try once more.
Don't give up!
No. Keep trying.
```

Use random number generation to choose a number from 1 to 4 that will be used to select an appropriate response to each answer. Use a **switch** structure in the **paint** method to issue the responses.

4.33 More sophisticated computer-aided instructions systems monitor the student's performance over a period of time. The decision to begin a new topic is often based on the student's success with previous topics. Modify the program of Exercise 4.32 to count the number of correct and incorrect responses typed by the student. After the student types 10 answers, your program should calculate the percentage of correct responses. If the percentage is lower than 75 percent, print **Please ask your instructor for extra help** and reset the program so another student can try the program.

4.34 Write an applet that plays the "guess the number" game as follows: Your program chooses the number to be guessed by selecting a random integer in the range 1 to 1000. The applet displays the prompt **Guess a number between 1 and 1000** next to a **TextField**. The player types a first guess into the **TextField** and presses the *Enter* key. If the player's guess is incorrect, your program should display **Too high. Try again.** or **Too low. Try again.** in the status bar to help the player "zero in" on the correct answer and should clear the **TextField** so the user can enter the next guess. When the user enters the correct answer, display **Congratulations. You guessed the number!** in the status bar and clear the **TextField** so the user can play again. Note: The guessing technique employed in this problem is similar to a *binary search*.

4.35 Modify the program of Exercise 4.34 to count the number of guesses the player makes. If the number is 10 or fewer, print **Either you know the secret or you got lucky!** If the player guesses the number in 10 tries, then print **Ahah! You know the secret!** If the player makes more than 10 guesses, then print **You should be able to do better!** Why should it take no more than 10 guesses? Well with each "good guess" the player should be able to eliminate half of the numbers. Now show why any number 1 to 1000 can be guessed in 10 or fewer tries.

4.36 Write a recursive method **power (base, exponent)** that when invoked returns

$$base^{exponent}$$

For example, **power(3, 4) = 3 * 3 * 3 * 3**. Assume that **exponent** is an integer greater than or equal to 1. *Hint:* The recursion step would use the relationship

$$base^{exponent} = base \cdot base^{exponent - 1}$$

and the terminating condition occurs when **exponent** is equal to **1** because

$$base^{1} = base$$

Incorporate this method into an applet that enables the user to enter the **base** and **exponent**.

4.37 The Fibonacci series

0, 1, 1, 2, 3, 5, 8, 13, 21, ...

begins with the terms 0 and 1 and has the property that each succeeding term is the sum of the two preceding terms. a) Write a *nonrecursive* method **fibonacci(n)** that calculates the *n*th Fibonacci number. Incorporate this method into an applet that enables the user to enter the value of **n**. b) Determine the largest Fibonacci number that can be printed on your system. Modify the program of part a) to use **double** instead of **int** to calculate and return Fibonacci numbers, and use this modified program to repeat part b).

4.38 *(Towers of Hanoi)* Every budding computer scientist must grapple with certain classic problems, and the Towers of Hanoi (see Fig. 4.19) is one of the most famous of these. Legend has it that in a temple in the Far East, priests are attempting to move a stack of disks from one peg to another. The initial stack had 64 disks threaded onto one peg and arranged from bottom to top by decreasing size. The priests are attempting to move the stack from this peg to a second peg under the constraints that exactly one disk is moved at a time, and at no time may a larger disk be placed above a smaller disk. A third peg is available for temporarily holding disks. Supposedly the world will end when the priests complete their task, so there is little incentive for us to facilitate their efforts.

Fig. 4.19 The Towers of Hanoi for the case with four disks.

Let us assume that the priests are attempting to move the disks from peg 1 to peg 3. We wish to develop an algorithm that will print the precise sequence of peg-to-peg disk transfers.

If we were to approach this problem with conventional methods, we would rapidly find ourselves hopelessly knotted up in managing the disks. Instead, if we attack the problem with recursion in mind, it immediately becomes tractable. Moving n disks can be viewed in terms of moving only $n - 1$ disks (and hence the recursion) as follows:

a) Move $n - 1$ disks from peg 1 to peg 2, using peg 3 as a temporary holding area.
b) Move the last disk (the largest) from peg 1 to peg 3.
c) Move the $n - 1$ disks from peg 2 to peg 3, using peg 1 as a temporary holding area.

The process ends when the last task involves moving $n = 1$ disk, i.e., the base case. This is accomplished by trivially moving the disk without the need for a temporary holding area.

Write an applet to solve the Towers of Hanoi problem. Allow the user to enter the number of disks in a **`TextField`**. Use a recursive **`tower`** method with four parameters:

a) The number of disks to be moved
b) The peg on which these disks are initially threaded
c) The peg to which this stack of disks is to be moved
d) The peg to be used as a temporary holding area

Your program should print at the command line (using **`System.out.println`**) the precise instructions it will take to move the disks from the starting peg to the destination peg. For example, to move a stack of three disks from peg 1 to peg 3, your program should print the following series of moves:

1 → 3 (This means move one disk from peg 1 to peg 3.)
1 → 2
3 → 2
1 → 3
2 → 1
2→ 3
1→ 3

4.39 Any program that can be implemented recursively can be implemented iteratively, although sometimes with more difficulty and less clarity. Try writing an iterative version of the Towers of Hanoi. If you succeed, compare your iterative version with the recursive version you developed in

Exercise 4.38. Investigate issues of performance, clarity, and your ability to demonstrate the correctness of the programs.

4.40 *(Visualizing Recursion)* It is interesting to watch recursion "in action." Modify the factorial method of Fig. 4.12 to print its local variable and recursive call parameter. For each recursive call, display the outputs on a separate line and add a level of indentation. Do your utmost to make the outputs clear, interesting, and meaningful. Your goal here is to design and implement an output format that helps a person understand recursion better. You may want to add such display capabilities to the many other recursion examples and exercises throughout the text.

4.41 The greatest common divisor of integers **x** and **y** is the largest integer that evenly divides both **x** and **y**. Write a recursive method **gcd** that returns the greatest common divisor of **x** and **y**. The **gcd** of **x** and **y** is defined recursively as follows: If **y** is equal to **0**, then **gcd(x, y)** is **x**; otherwise **gcd(x, y)** is **gcd(y, x % y)** where **%** is the modulus operator. Use this method to replace the one you wrote in the applet of Exercise 4.28.

4.42 Exercises 4.31 through 4.33 developed a computer-assisted instruction program to teach an elementary school student multiplication. This exercise suggests enhancements to that program.

a) Modify the program to allow the user to enter a grade-level capability. A grade level of 1 means to use only single-digit numbers in the problems, a grade level of two means to use numbers as large as two-digits, etc.
b) Modify the program to allow the user to pick the type of arithmetic problems he or she wishes to study. An option of 1 means addition problems only, 2 means subtraction problems only, 3 means multiplication problems only, 4 means division problems only, and 5 means to randomly intermix problems of all these types.

4.43 Write method **distance** that calculates the distance between two points (x1, y1) and (x2, y2). All numbers and return values should be of type **double**. Incorporate this method into an applet that enables the user to enter the coordinates of the points.

4.44 What does the following method do?

```
// Parameter b must be a positive
// integer to prevent infinite recursion
int mystery( int a, int b )
{
   if ( b == 1 )
      return a;
   else
      return a + mystery( a, b - 1 );
}
```

4.45 After you determine what the program of Exercise 4.44 does, modify the method to operate properly after removing the restriction of the second argument being non-negative. Also, incorporate the method into an applet that enables the user to enter two integers and test the method.

4.46 Write an application that tests as many of the math library methods in Fig. 4.2 as you can. Exercise each of these methods by having your program print out tables of return values for a diversity of argument values.

4.47 Find the error in the following recursive method and explain how to correct it:

```
int sum( int n )
{
   if ( n == 0 )
      return 0;
   else
      return n + sum(n);
}
```

4.48 Modify the craps program of Fig. 4.9 to allow wagering. Initialize variable **`bankBalance`** to 1000 dollars. Prompt the player to enter a **`wager`**. Check that **`wager`** is less than or equal to **`bankBalance`** and if not have the user to reenter **`wager`** until a valid **`wager`** is entered. After a correct **`wager`** is entered, run one game of craps. If the player wins, increase **`bankBalance`** by **`wager`** and print the new **`bankBalance`**. If the player loses, decrease **`bankBalance`** by **`wager`**, print the new **`bankBalance`**, check if **`bankBalance`** has become zero, and if so print the message **`"Sorry. You busted!"`** As the game progresses, print various messages to create some "chatter" such as **`"Oh, you're going for broke, huh?"`**, or **`"Aw cmon, take a chance!"`**, or **`"You're up big. Now's the time to cash in your chips!"`**. Implement the "chatter" as a separate method that randomly chooses the string to display.

4.49 Write an applet that uses a method **`circleArea`** to prompt the user for the radius of a circle, and to calculate and print the area of that circle.

5

Arrays

Objectives

- To introduce the array data structure.
- To understand the use of arrays to store, sort, and search lists and tables of values.
- To understand how to declare an array, initialize an array, and refer to individual elements of an array.
- To be able to pass arrays to methods.
- To understand basic sorting techniques.
- To be able to declare and manipulate multiple-subscript arrays.

With sobs and tears he sorted out
Those of the largest size …
Lewis Carroll

Attempt the end, and never stand to doubt;
Nothing's so hard, but search will find it out.
Robert Herrick

Now go, write it before them in a table,
and note it in a book.
Isaiah 30:8

'Tis in my memory lock'd,
And you yourself shall keep the key of it.
William Shakespeare

Outline

5.1 Introduction

This chapter serves as an introduction to the important topic of data structures. *Arrays* are data structures consisting of related data items of the same type. Arrays are "static" entities in that they remain the same size once they are created, although an array reference may be reassigned to a new array of a different size. In Chapter 17, "Data Structures," we introduce dynamic data structures such as lists, queues, stacks, and trees that may grow and shrink as programs execute. In Chapter 18, "Java Utilities Package and Bit Manipulation," we discuss class **`Vector`** which is an array-like class whose objects can grow and shrink in response to a Java program's changing storage requirements.

5.2 Arrays

An array is a group of contiguous memory locations that all have the same name and the same type. To refer to a particular location or element in the array, we specify the name of the array and the *position number* of the particular element in the array.

Figure 5.1 shows an integer array called **`c`**. This array contains twelve *elements.* Any one of these elements may be referred to by giving the name of the array followed by the position number of the particular element in square brackets (**`[]`**). The first element in every array is the *zeroth element.* Thus, the first element of array **`c`** is referred to as **`c[0]`**, the second element of array **`c`** is referred to as **`c[1]`**, the seventh element of array **`c`** is referred to as **`c[6]`**, and, in general, the *i*th element of array **`c`** is referred to as **`c[i-1]`**. Array names follow the same conventions as other variable names.

The position number in square brackets is more formally called a *subscript.* A subscript must be an integer or an integer expression. If a program uses an expression as a subscript, then the expression is evaluated to determine the subscript. For example, if we assume that variable **`a`** is equal to **`5`** and that variable **`b`** is equal to **`6`**, then the statement

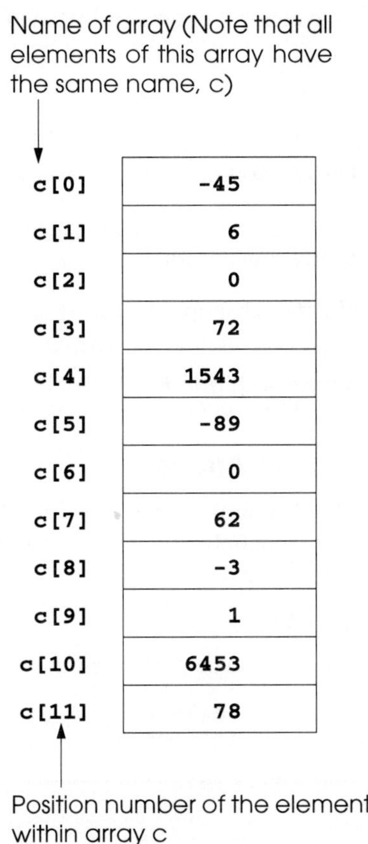

Fig. 5.1 A 12-element array.

```
c[ a + b ] += 2;
```

adds 2 to array element **c[11]**. Note that a subscripted array name is an *lvalue*—it can be used on the left side of an assignment to place a new value into an array element.

Let us examine array **c** in Fig. 5.1 more closely. The *name* of the array is **c**. The *length* of the array is determined by the following expression:

```
c.length
```

Every array in Java "knows" its own length. The array's twelve elements are referred to as **c[0]**, **c[1]**, **c[2]**, …, **c[11]**. The *value* of **c[0]** is **-45**, the value of **c[1]** is **6**, the value of **c[2]** is **0**, the value of **c[7]** is **62**, and the value of **c[11]** is **78**. To calculate the sum of the values contained in the first three elements of array **c** and store the result in variable **sum**, we would write

```
sum = c[ 0 ] + c[ 1 ] + c[ 2 ];
```

To divide the value of the seventh element of array **c** by **2** and assign the result to the variable **x**, we would write

```
x = c[ 6 ] / 2;
```

Common Programming Error 5.1

It is important to note the difference between the "seventh element of the array" and "array element seven." Because array subscripts begin at 0, the "seventh element of the array" has a subscript of 6, while "array element seven" has a subscript of 7 and is actually the eighth element of the array. This confusion is a source of "off-by-one" errors.

The brackets used to enclose the subscript of an array are an operator in Java. Brackets have the same level of precedence as parentheses. The chart in Fig. 5.2 shows the precedence and associativity of the operators introduced to this point in the text. They are shown top to bottom in decreasing order of precedence with their associativity and type.

5.3 Declaring and Allocating Arrays

Arrays occupy space in memory. The programmer specifies the type of the elements and uses the **new** operator to allocate the number of elements required by each array. To allocate 12 elements for integer array **c**, the declaration

```
int c[] = new int[ 12 ];
```

is used. The preceding statement can also be performed in two steps as follows:

```
int c[];              // declares the array
c = new int[ 12 ];    // allocates the array
```

Operators						Associativity	Type
`()`	`[]`	`.`				left to right	parentheses
`++`	`--`	`+`	`-`	`!`	*(type)*	right to left	unary
`*`	`/`	`%`				left to right	multiplicative
`+`	`-`					left to right	additive
`<`	`<=`	`>`	`>=`			left to right	relational
`==`	`!=`					left to right	equality
`&`						left to right	boolean logical AND
`^`						left to right	boolean logical exclusive OR
`|`						left to right	boolean logical inclusive OR
`&&`						left to right	logical AND
`||`						left to right	logical OR
`?:`						right to left	conditional
`=`	`+=`	`-=`	`*=`	`/=`	`%=`	right to left	assignment

Fig. 5.2 Operator precedence and associativity.

When arrays are allocated, the elements are automatically initialized to zero for the numeric primitive-data-type variables, to **false** for **boolean** variables or to **null** for references (any nonprimitive type).

Common Programming Error 5.2

Unlike C or C++ the number of elements in the array is never specified in the square brackets after the array name in a declaration. The declaration **int c[12];** *causes a syntax error.*

Memory may be reserved for several arrays with a single declaration. The following declaration reserves 100 elements for integer array **b** and 27 elements for integer array **x**.

```
int b[] = new int[ 100 ], x[] = new int[ 27 ];
```

Arrays may be declared to contain other data types. For example, an array of type **String** can store a set of character strings (**String**s will be discussed in Chapter 8).

5.4 Examples Using Arrays

The program in Fig. 5.3 uses the **new** operator to dynamically allocate an array of ten elements which are initially zero, then it prints the array in tabular format.

The first two statements in the **paint** method of Fig. 5.3 display the column headings for the columns printed in the **for** structure. Variable **yPosition** is used to determine the vertical position at which the **drawString** method outputs on the applet. The **String.valueOf** method is used to convert each integer to a string that can be displayed on the applet. Note the expression **n.length** in the **for** structure (line 23) to determine the length of the array.

```
1  // Fig. 5.3: InitArray.java
2  // initializing an array
3  import java.awt.Graphics;
4  import java.applet.Applet;
5
6  public class InitArray extends Applet {
7     int n[];         // declare an array of integers
8
9     // initialize instance variables
10    public void init()
11    {
12       n = new int[ 10 ];  // dynamically allocate array
13    }
14
15    // paint the applet
16    public void paint( Graphics g )
17    {
18       int yPosition = 25;  // starting y position on applet
19
```

Fig. 5.3 Initializing the elements of an array to zeros (part 1 of 2).

```
        g.drawString( "Element", 25, yPosition );
        g.drawString( "Value", 100, yPosition );

        for ( int i = 0; i < n.length; i++ ) {
           yPosition += 15;
           g.drawString( String.valueOf( i ), 25, yPosition );
           g.drawString( String.valueOf( n[ i ] ),
                         100, yPosition );
        }
     }
  }
```

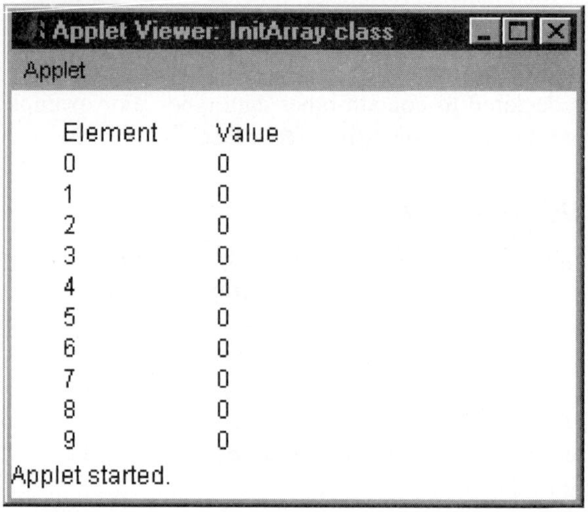

Applet Viewer: InitArray.class
Applet

Element	Value
0	0
1	0
2	0
3	0
4	0
5	0
6	0
7	0
8	0
9	0

Applet started.

Fig. 5.3 Initializing the elements of an array to zeros (part 2 of 2).

The elements of an array can be initialized in the array declaration by following the declaration with an equal sign and a comma-separated list (enclosed in braces) of *initializers.* In this case, the array size is determined by the number of elements in the initializer list. For example, the statement

```
int n[] = { 1, 2, 3, 4, 5 };
```

creates a five-element array with subscripts of **0**, **1**, **2**, **3**, and **4**.

The program in Fig. 5.4 initializes an integer array with ten values (line 7) and prints the array in tabular format.

```
1  // Fig. 5.4: InitArray.java
2  // initializing an array with a declaration
3  import java.awt.Graphics;
4  import java.applet.Applet;
5
```

Fig. 5.4 Initializing the elements of an array with a declaration (part 1 of 2).

```
public class InitArray extends Applet {
   int n[] = { 32, 27, 64, 18, 95, 14, 90, 70, 60, 37 };

   // paint the applet
   public void paint( Graphics g )
   {
      int yPosition = 25;    // starting y position on applet

      g.drawString( "Element", 25, yPosition );
      g.drawString( "Value", 100, yPosition );

      for ( int i = 0; i < n.length; i++ ) {
         yPosition += 15;
         g.drawString( String.valueOf( i ), 25, yPosition );
         g.drawString( String.valueOf( n[ i ] ),
                       100, yPosition );
      }
   }
}
```

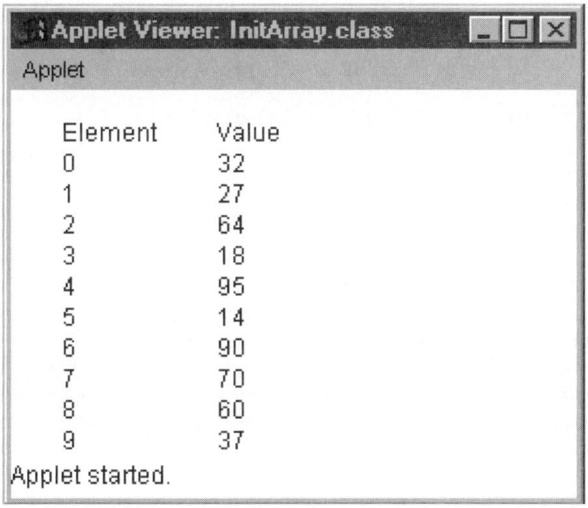

Applet Viewer: InitArray.class

Applet

Element	Value
0	32
1	27
2	64
3	18
4	95
5	14
6	90
7	70
8	60
9	37

Applet started.

Fig. 5.4 Initializing the elements of an array with a declaration (part 2 of 2).

The program in Fig. 5.5 initializes the elements of a ten-element array **s** to the even integers **2**, **4**, **6**, …, **20**, and prints the array in tabular format. These numbers are generated by multiplying each successive value of the loop counter by **2** and adding **2**.

```
// Fig. 5.5: InitArray.java
// initialize array s to the even integers from 2 to 20
import java.awt.Graphics;
import java.applet.Applet;
```

Fig. 5.5 Generating values to be placed into elements of an array (part 1 of 2).

```java

public class InitArray extends Applet {
   final int ARRAY_SIZE = 10;
   int s[];

   // initialize instance variables
   public void init()
   {
      s = new int[ ARRAY_SIZE ];

      // Set the values in the array
      for ( int i = 0; i < s.length; i++ )
         s[ i ] = 2 + 2 * i;
   }

   // paint the applet
   public void paint( Graphics g )
   {
      int yPosition = 25;   // starting y position on applet

      g.drawString( "Element", 25, yPosition );
      g.drawString( "Value", 100, yPosition );

      for ( int i = 0; i < s.length; i++ ) {
         yPosition += 15;
         g.drawString( String.valueOf( i ), 25, yPosition );
         g.drawString( String.valueOf( s[ i ] ),
                       100, yPosition );
      }
   }
}
```

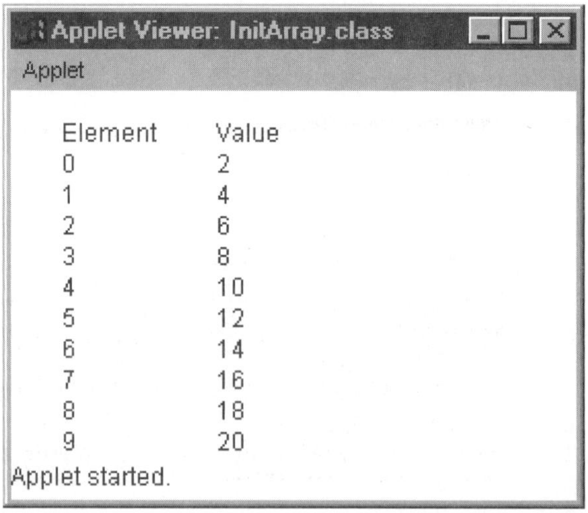

Applet Viewer: InitArray.class

Applet

Element	Value
0	2
1	4
2	6
3	8
4	10
5	12
6	14
7	16
8	18
9	20

Applet started.

Fig. 5.5 Generating values to be placed into elements of an array (part 2 of 2).

Line 7

```
final int ARRAY_SIZE = 10;
```

uses the **final** qualifier to declare a so-called *constant variable* **ARRAY_SIZE** whose value is **10**. Constant variables must be initialized with a constant expression when they are declared and cannot be modified thereafter (Fig. 5.6 and Fig. 5.7). If an attempt is made to modify a **final** variable after it is declared, the compiler issues the error message:

```
Can't assign a value to a final variable
```

Constant variables are also called *named constants* or *read-only variables.* They are often used to make a program more readable. Note that the term "constant variable" is an oxymoron—a contradiction in terms—like "jumbo shrimp" or "freezer burn."

Common Programming Error 5.3

Assigning a value to a constant variable in an executable statement is a syntax error.

```
// Fig. 5.6: FinalTest.java
// a final object must be initialized
import java.applet.Applet;

public class FinalTest extends Applet {
   final int x;  // Error: Final variables must be initialized
}
```

```
FinalTest.java:5: Blank final variable 'x' may not have
   been initialized. It must be assigned a value in an
   initializer, or in every constructor.
public class FinalTest extends Applet {
             ^
1 error
```

Fig. 5.6 A **final** object must be initialized.

```
// Fig. 5.7: FinalTest.java
// using a properly initialized constant variable
import java.awt.Graphics;
import java.applet.Applet;

public class FinalTest extends Applet {
   final int x = 7;  // initialize constant variable

```

Fig. 5.7 Correctly initializing and using a constant variable (part 1 of 2).

```
    public void paint( Graphics g )
    {
       g.drawString( "The value of x is: " + x, 25, 25 );
    }
}

```

Applet Viewer: FinalTest.class
Applet
The value of x is: 7
Applet started.

Fig. 5.7 Correctly initializing and using a constant variable (part 2 of 2).

The program of Fig. 5.8 sums the values contained in the ten-element integer array **a**. The statement in the body of the **for** loop does the totaling. It is important to remember that the values being supplied as initializers for array **a** normally would be read into the program. For example, the user could enter the values through a **TextField** in the applet.

```
// Fig. 5.8: SumArray.java
// Compute the sum of the elements of the array
import java.awt.Graphics;
import java.applet.Applet;

public class SumArray extends Applet {
   int a[] = { 1, 2, 3, 4, 5, 6, 7, 8, 9, 10 };
   int total;

   // initialize instance variables
   public void init()
   {
      total = 0;

      for ( int i = 0; i < a.length; i++ )
         total += a[ i ];
   }

   // paint the applet
   public void paint( Graphics g )
   {
      g.drawString( "Total of array elements: " + total,
                    25, 25 );
   }
}
```

Fig. 5.8 Computing the sum of the elements of an array (part 1 of 2).

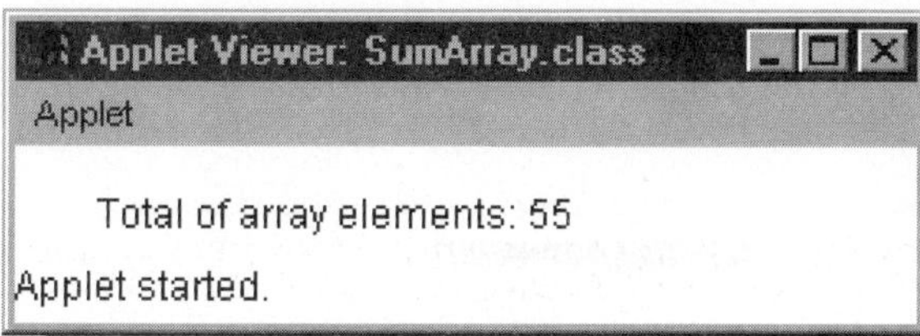

Fig. 5.8 Computing the sum of the elements of an array (part 2 of 2).

Our next example uses arrays to summarize the results of data collected in a survey. Consider the problem statement:

Forty students were asked to rate the quality of the food in the student cafeteria on a scale of 1 to 10 (1 means awful and 10 means excellent). Place the forty responses in an integer array and summarize the results of the poll.

This is a typical array processing application (see Fig. 5.9). We wish to summarize the number of responses of each type (i.e., 1 through 10). The array **`responses`** is a 40-element integer array of the students' responses to the survey. We use an eleven-element array **`frequency`** to count the number of occurrences of each response. We ignore the first element, **`frequency[ 0 ]`**, because it is more logical to have the response 1 increment **`frequency[ 1 ]`** than **`frequency[ 0 ]`**. This allows us to use each response directly as a subscript on the **`frequency`** array.

```
// Fig. 5.9: StudentPoll.java
// Student poll program
import java.awt.Graphics;
import java.applet.Applet;

public class StudentPoll extends Applet {
   int responses[] = { 1, 2, 6, 4, 8, 5, 9, 7, 8, 10,
                       1, 6, 3, 8, 6, 10, 3, 8, 2, 7,
                       6, 5, 7, 6, 8, 6, 7, 5, 6, 6,
                       5, 6, 7, 5, 6, 4, 8, 6, 8, 10 };
   int frequency[];

   // initialize instance variables
   public void init()
   {
      frequency = new int[ 11 ];

     for ( int answer = 0; answer < responses.length; answer++ )
         ++frequency[ responses[ answer ] ];
   }

```

Fig. 5.9 A simple student-poll analysis program (part 1 of 2).

```
22     // paint the applet
23     public void paint( Graphics g )
24     {
25        int yPosition = 25;    // starting y position on applet
26
27        g.drawString( "Rating", 25, yPosition );
28        g.drawString( "Frequency", 100, yPosition );
29
30        for ( int rating = 1;
31              rating < frequency.length; rating++ ) {
32           yPosition += 15;
33           g.drawString( String.valueOf( rating ),
34                         25, yPosition );
35           g.drawString( String.valueOf( frequency[ rating ] ),
36                         100, yPosition );
37        }
38     }
39  }
```

Applet Viewer: StudentPoll.class

Applet

Rating	Frequency
1	2
2	2
3	2
4	2
5	5
6	11
7	5
8	7
9	1
10	3

Applet started.

Fig. 5.9 A simple student-poll analysis program (part 2 of 2).

Good Programming Practice 5.1

Strive for program clarity. It is sometimes worthwhile to trade off the most efficient use of memory or processor time in favor of writing clearer programs.

Performance Tip 5.1

Sometimes performance considerations far outweigh clarity considerations.

The **`for`** loop on line 18 takes the responses one at a time from the array **`response`** and increments one of the ten counters (**`frequency[ 1 ]`** to **`frequency[ 10 ]`**) in the **`frequency`** array. The key statement in the loop is

```
++frequency[ responses[ answer ] ];
```

This statement increments the appropriate **`frequency`** counter depending on the value of **`responses[ answer ]`**.

Let's consider several iterations of the **`for`** loop. When counter **`answer`** is **`0`**, **`responses[ answer ]`** is **`1`**, so **`++frequency[ responses[ answer ] ];`** is actually interpreted as

```
++frequency[ 1 ];
```

which increments array element one.

When **`answer`** is **`1`**, **`responses[ answer ]`** is **`2`**, so the statement **`++frequency[ responses[ answer ] ];`** is actually interpreted as

```
++frequency[ 2 ];
```

which increments array element two.

When **`answer`** is **`2`**, **`responses[ answer ]`** is **`6`**, so the statement **`++frequency[ responses[ answer ] ];`** is actually interpreted as

```
++frequency[ 6 ];
```

which increments array element six, and so on. Note that regardless of the number of responses processed in the survey, only an eleven-element array is required (ignoring element zero) to summarize the results. Also note that the results of this program are correct because the elements of the **`frequency`** array were automatically initialized to zero when the array was allocated with **`new`**. If the elements were not initialized to zero, the frequency counts for each response in the survey would be incorrect.

If the data contained invalid values such as 13, the program would attempt to add **`1`** to **`frequency[ 13 ]`**. This is outside the bounds of the array. In the C and C++ programming languages, such a reference would be allowed by the compiler and at execution time. The program would "walk" past the end of the array to where it thought element number 13 was located and add 1 to whatever happened to be at that location in memory. This could potentially modify another variable in the program or even result in the program terminating prematurely. Java provides mechanisms to prevent accessing elements outside the bounds of the array.

Testing and Debugging Tip 5.1

When a Java program is executed, the Java interpreter checks array element references to be sure they are valid (i.e., all subscripts must be greater than or equal to 0 and less than the length of the array). If there is an invalid reference, Java generates an exception.

Testing and Debugging Tip 5.2

Exceptions are used to indicate that an error occurred in a program. They enable the programmer to recover from an error and continue the execution of the program instead of abnormally terminating the program. When an invalid array reference is made, an **`ArrayIndexOutOfBoundsException`** *is generated. Chapter 12 covers "Exception Handling" in detail.*

Common Programming Error 5.4

Referring to an element outside the array bounds.

Testing and Debugging Tip 5.3

When looping through an array, the array subscript should never go below 0 and should always be less than the total number of elements in the array (one less than the size of the array). Make sure the loop terminating condition prevents accessing elements outside this range.

Testing and Debugging Tip 5.4

Programs should validate the correctness of all input values to prevent erroneous information from affecting a program's calculations.

Our next example (Fig. 5.10) reads numbers from an array and graphs the information in the form of a bar chart or histogram—each number is printed, and then a bar consisting of that many asterisks is printed beside the number. The nested **for** loop (line 26) actually draws the bars.

```
1  // Fig. 5.10: Histogram.java
2  // Histogram printing program
3  import java.awt.Graphics;
4  import java.applet.Applet;
5
6  public class Histogram extends Applet {
7     int n[] = { 19, 3, 15, 7, 11, 9, 13, 5, 17, 1 };
8
9     // paint the applet
10    public void paint( Graphics g )
11    {
12       int xPosition;        // position of * in histogram
13       int yPosition = 25;   // vertical position in applet
14
15       g.drawString( "Element", 25, yPosition );
16       g.drawString( "Value", 100, yPosition );
17       g.drawString( "Histogram", 175, yPosition );
18
19       for ( int i = 0; i < n.length; i++ ) {
20          yPosition += 15;
21          g.drawString( String.valueOf( i ), 25, yPosition );
22          g.drawString( String.valueOf( n[ i ] ),
23                        100, yPosition );
24          xPosition = 175;
25
26          for ( int j = 1; j <= n[ i ]; j++ ) { // print one bar
27             g.drawString( "*", xPosition, yPosition );
28             xPosition += 7;
29          }
30       }
31    }
32 }
```

Fig. 5.10 A program that prints histograms (part 1 of 2).

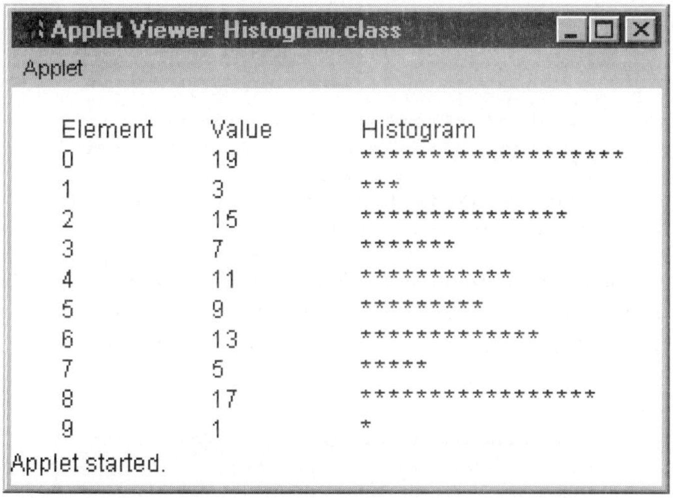

```
Applet Viewer: Histogram.class
Applet

Element   Value   Histogram
0         19      *******************
1         3       ***
2         15      ***************
3         7       *******
4         11      ***********
5         9       *********
6         13      *************
7         5       *****
8         17      *****************
9         1       *
Applet started.
```

Fig. 5.10 A program that prints histograms (part 2 of 2).

In Chapter 4 we stated that we would show a more elegant method of writing the dice-rolling program of Fig. 4.8. The problem was to roll a single six-sided die 6000 times to test whether the random number generator produces random numbers. An array version of this program is shown in Fig. 5.11.

```java
// Fig. 5.11: RollDie.java
// Roll a six-sided die 6000 times
import java.awt.Graphics;
import java.applet.Applet;

public class RollDie extends Applet {
   int face;
   int frequency[];

   // initialize instance variables
   public void init()
   {
      frequency = new int[ 7 ];

      for ( int roll = 1; roll <= 6000; roll++ ) {
         face = 1 + (int) ( Math.random() * 6 );
         ++frequency[ face ];
      }
   }

```

Fig. 5.11 Dice-rolling program using arrays instead of **switch** (part 1 of 2).

```java
    // paint the applet
    public void paint( Graphics g )
    {
       int yPosition = 25;

       g.drawString( "Face", 25, yPosition );
       g.drawString( "Frequency", 100, yPosition );

       for ( face = 1; face < frequency.length; face++ ) {
          yPosition += 15;
          g.drawString( String.valueOf( face ), 25, yPosition );
          g.drawString( String.valueOf( frequency[ face ] ),
                        100, yPosition );
       }
    }
}
```

```
Applet Viewer: RollDie.class
Applet
Face    Frequency
1       971
2       1008
3       1003
4       1020
5       998
6       1000
Applet started.
```

Fig. 5.11 Dice-rolling program using arrays instead of **`switch`** (part 2 of 2).

5.5 References and Reference Parameters

Two ways to pass arguments to methods (or functions) in many programming languages (like C and C++) are *call-by-value* and *call-by-reference.* Normally the programmer specifies the particular way each argument will be passed. When an argument is passed call-by-value, a *copy* of the argument's value is made and passed to the called method.

Testing and Debugging Tip 5.5

With call-by-value, changes to the called method's copy do not affect the original variable's value in the calling method. This prevents the accidental side effects that so greatly hinder the development of correct and reliable software systems.

With call-by-reference, the caller gives the called method the ability to directly access the caller's data and to modify that data if the called method so chooses. Call-by-reference can improve performance because it can eliminate the overhead of copying large amounts of data, but call-by-reference can weaken security because the called method can access the caller's data.

Software Engineering Observation 5.1

Java, unlike other languages, does not allow the programmer to choose whether to pass each argument call-by-value or call-by-reference. Primitive data type variables are always passed call-by-value and objects are always passed call-by-reference.

To pass an object call-by-reference, simply specify in the method call the reference to the object by name. Mentioning the object by its parameter name in the body of the called method actually refers to the original object in memory, and the original object can be accessed directly by the called method.

Because arrays are treated as objects by Java, arrays are passed to methods call-by-reference—a called method can access the element values in the caller's original arrays. The name of an array is actually a reference to an object that contains the array elements and the **length** instance variable that indicates the number of elements in the array. In the next section, we demonstrate call-by-value and call-by-reference using arrays.

Performance Tip 5.2

Passing arrays by reference makes sense for performance reasons. If arrays were passed by value, a copy of each element would be passed. For large, frequently passed arrays, this would waste time and would consume considerable storage for the copies of the arrays.

Software Engineering Observation 5.2

When returning information from a method via a **return** *statement, primitive data type variables are always returned by value and objects are always returned by reference.*

5.6 Passing Arrays to Methods

To pass an array argument to a method, specify the name of the array without any brackets. For example, if array **hourlyTemperatures** has been declared as

```
int hourlyTemperatures[] = new int[ 24 ];
```

the method call

```
modifyArray( hourlyTemperatures );
```

passes array **hourlyTemperatures** to method **modifyArray**. In Java every array object "knows" its own size (via the **length** instance variable). Thus, when we pass an array object into a method we do not separately pass the size of the array as an argument.

Although entire arrays are passed call-by-reference, *individual array elements of primitive data types are passed call-by-value exactly as simple variables are* (individual array elements that are not of primitive types are still passed call-by-reference). Such simple single pieces of data are called *scalars* or *scalar quantities.* To pass an array element to a method, use the subscripted name of the array element as an argument in the method call.

For a method to receive an array through a method call, the method's parameter list must specify that an array will be received. For example, the method header for method **modifyArray** might be written as

```
void modifyArray( int b[] )
```

indicating that **modifyArray** expects to receive an integer array in parameter **b**. Because arrays are passed by reference, when the called method uses the array name **b**, it refers to the actual array in the caller (array **hourlyTemperatures** in the preceding call).

Figure 5.12 demonstrates the difference between passing an entire array and passing an array element. The program prints the five elements of integer array **a**. Next, **a** is passed to method **modifyArray** where each element is multiplied by 2. Then **a** is reprinted in **main**. As the output shows, the elements of **a** are indeed modified by **modifyArray**.

```
// Fig. 5.12: PassArray.java
// Passing arrays and individual array elements to methods
import java.awt.Graphics;
import java.applet.Applet;

public class PassArray extends Applet {
   int a[] = {0, 1, 2, 3, 4};

   public void paint( Graphics g )
   {
      int xPosition = 25, yPosition = 25;

      g.drawString(
         "Effects of passing entire array call-by-reference:",
         xPosition, yPosition );
      yPosition += 15;
      g.drawString( "The values of the original array are:",
                    xPosition, yPosition );
      xPosition += 15;
      yPosition += 15;

      for ( int i = 0; i < a.length; i++ ) {
         g.drawString( String.valueOf( a[ i ] ),
                       xPosition, yPosition );
         xPosition += 15;
      }

      xPosition = 25;
      yPosition += 30;

      modifyArray( a );  // array a passed call-by-reference

      g.drawString( "The values of the modified array are:",
                    xPosition, yPosition );
      xPosition += 15;
      yPosition += 15;

      for ( int i = 0; i < a.length; i++ ) {
         g.drawString( String.valueOf( a[ i ] ),
                       xPosition, yPosition );
```

Fig. 5.12 Passing arrays and individual array elements to methods (part 1 of 2).

```
            xPosition += 15;
         }

         xPosition = 25;
         yPosition += 30;

         g.drawString(
            "Effects of passing array element call-by-value:",
            xPosition, yPosition );
         yPosition += 15;
         g.drawString( "a[3] before modifyElement: " + a[ 3 ],
                       xPosition, yPosition );
         yPosition += 15;

         modifyElement( a[ 3 ] );

         g.drawString( "a[3] after modifyElement: " + a[ 3 ],
                       xPosition, yPosition );
      }

      public void modifyArray( int b[] )
      {
         for ( int j = 0; j < b.length; j++ )
            b[ j ] *= 2;
      }

      public void modifyElement( int e )
      {
         e *= 2;
      }
   }
```

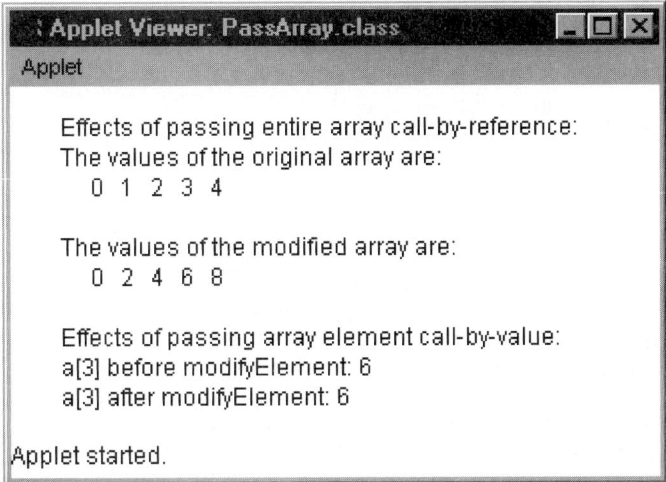

Fig. 5.12 Passing arrays and individual array elements to methods (part 2 of 2).

Next, the program prints the value of **a[3]** and passes it to method **modifyElement**. Method **modifyElement** multiplies its argument by 2. Note that when **a[3]** is reprinted in **main**, it has not been modified because individual primitive-data-type array elements are passed call-by-value.

5.7 Sorting Arrays

Sorting data (i.e., placing the data into some particular order such as ascending or descending) is one of the most important computing applications. A bank sorts all checks by account number so that it can prepare individual bank statements at the end of each month. Telephone companies sort their lists of accounts by last name and, within that, by first name to make it easy to find phone numbers. Virtually every organization must sort some data and in many cases massive amounts of data. Sorting data is an intriguing problem that has attracted some of the most intense research efforts in the field of computer science. In this chapter we discuss the simplest sorting scheme. In the exercises and in Chapter 17, we investigate more complex schemes that yield superior performance.

Performance Tip 5.3

Sometimes, the simplest algorithms perform poorly. Their virtue is that they are easy to write, test and debug. More complex algorithms are sometimes needed to realize maximum performance.

The program in Fig. 5.13 sorts the values of the ten-element array **a** into ascending order. The technique we use is called the *bubble sort* or the *sinking sort* because the smaller values gradually "bubble" their way to the top of the array like air bubbles rising in water, while the larger values sink to the bottom of the array. The technique is to make several passes through the array. On each pass, successive pairs of elements are compared. If a pair is in increasing order (or the values are identical), we leave the values as they are. If a pair is in decreasing order, their values are swapped in the array. Note the use in this program of method **print** (line 32) to output the contents of the array preceded by a string.

```
1   // Fig. 5.13: BubbleSort.java
2   // This program sorts an array's values into
3   // ascending order
4   import java.awt.Graphics;
5   import java.applet.Applet;
6
7   public class BubbleSort extends Applet {
8      int a[] = { 2, 6, 4, 8, 10, 12, 89, 68, 45, 37 };
9
10     public void paint( Graphics g )
11     {
12        print( g, "Data items in original order", a, 25, 25 );
13
14        sort();
15
```

Fig. 5.13 Sorting an array with bubble sort (part 1 of 2).

```
      print( g, "Data items in ascending order", a, 25, 55 );
   }

   public void sort()
   {
      int hold;  // temporary holding area for swap

      for ( int pass = 1; pass < a.length; pass++ ) // passes
         for ( int i = 0; i < a.length - 1; i++ ) // one pass
            if ( a[ i ] > a[ i + 1 ] ) {       // one comparison
               hold = a[i];                    // one swap
               a[ i ] = a[ i + 1 ];
               a[ i + 1 ] = hold;
            }
   }

   public void print( Graphics g, String head, int b[],
                      int x, int y )
   {
      g.drawString( head, x, y );
      x += 15;
      y += 15;

      for ( int i = 0; i < b.length; i++ ) {
         g.drawString( String.valueOf( b[ i ] ), x, y );
         x += 20;
      }
   }
}
```

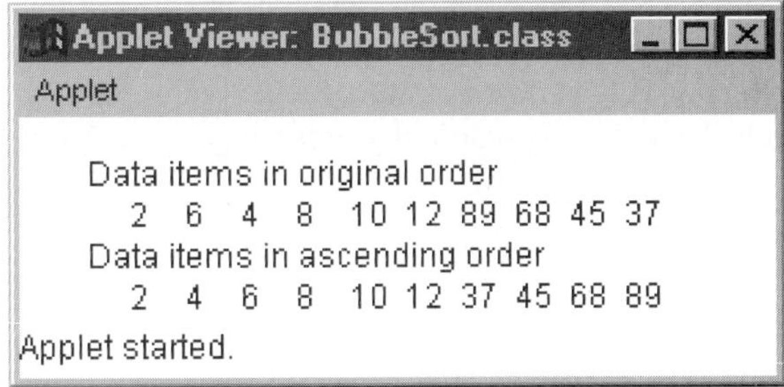

Fig. 5.13 Sorting an array with bubble sort (part 2 of 2).

First the program compares **a[0]** to **a[1]**, then **a[1]** to **a[2]**, then **a[2]** to **a[3]**, and so on until it completes the pass by comparing **a[8]** to **a[9]**. Although there are ten elements, only nine comparisons are performed. Because of the way the successive comparisons are made, a large value may move down the array many positions on a single pass, but a small value may move up only one position. On the first pass, the largest value is guaranteed to sink to the bottom element of the array, **a[9]**. On the second pass, the second largest value is guaranteed to sink to **a[8]**. On the ninth pass, the ninth largest value sinks to **a[1]**. This leaves the smallest value in **a[0]**, so only nine passes are needed to sort a ten-element array.

The sorting is performed by the nested **for** loop (line 23) in the **sort** method. If a swap is necessary, it is performed by the three assignments

```
hold = a[ i ];
a[ i ] = a[ i + 1 ];
a[ i + 1 ] = hold;
```

where the extra variable **hold** temporarily stores one of the two values being swapped. The swap cannot be performed with only the two assignments

```
a[ i ] = a[ i + 1 ];
a[ i + 1 ] = a[ i ];
```

If, for example, **a[i]** is **7** and **a[i + 1]** is **5**, after the first assignment both values will be **5** and the value **7** will be lost. Hence the need for the extra variable **hold**.

The chief virtue of the bubble sort is that it is easy to program. However, the bubble sort runs slowly. This becomes apparent when sorting large arrays. In the exercises, we will develop more efficient versions of the bubble sort and investigate some far more efficient sorts than the bubble sort. More advanced courses (often titled "Data Structures" or "Algorithms" or "Computational Complexity") investigate sorting and searching in greater depth.

5.8 Searching Arrays: Linear Search and Binary Search

Often, a programmer will be working with large amounts of data stored in arrays. It may be necessary to determine whether an array contains a value that matches a certain *key value.* The process of locating a particular element value in an array is called *searching.* In this section we discuss two searching techniques—the simple *linear search* technique and the more efficient *binary search* technique. Exercises 5.31 and 5.32 at the end of this chapter ask you to implement recursive versions of the linear search and the binary search.

The linear search (Fig. 5.14) compares each element of an array with a *search key*. If the array being searched is not in any particular order, it is just as likely that the value will be found in the first element as the last. On average, therefore, the program will have to compare the search key with half the elements of the array.

```
// Fig. 5.14: LinearSearch.java
// Linear search of an array
import java.awt.*;
import java.awt.event.*;
import java.applet.Applet;

public class LinearSearch extends Applet
             implements ActionListener {
   int a[];
   int element;
   String searchKey;
   Label enterLabel, resultLabel;
   TextField enter, result;
```

Fig. 5.14 Linear search of an array (part 1 of 3).

```

    public void init()
    {
       a = new int[ 100 ];

       for ( int i = 0; i < a.length; i++ ) // create data
          a[ i ] = 2 * i;

       enterLabel = new Label( "Enter integer search key" );
       add( enterLabel );

       enter = new TextField( 10 );
       enter.addActionListener( this );
       add( enter );

       resultLabel = new Label( "Result" );
       add( resultLabel );

       result = new TextField( 25 );
       result.setEditable( false );
       add( result );
    }

    public int linearSearch( int key )
    {
       for ( int n = 0; n < a.length; n++ )
          if ( a[ n ] == key )
             return n;

       return -1;
    }

    public void actionPerformed( ActionEvent e )
    {
       searchKey = e.getActionCommand();
       element =
          linearSearch( Integer.parseInt( searchKey ) );

       if ( element != -1 )
          result.setText( "Found value in element " +
                          element );
       else
          result.setText( "Value not found" );
    }
 }
```

Fig. 5.14 Linear search of an array (part 2 of 3).

The linear search method works well for small arrays or for unsorted arrays. However, for large arrays linear searching is inefficient. If the array is sorted, the high-speed binary search technique can be used.

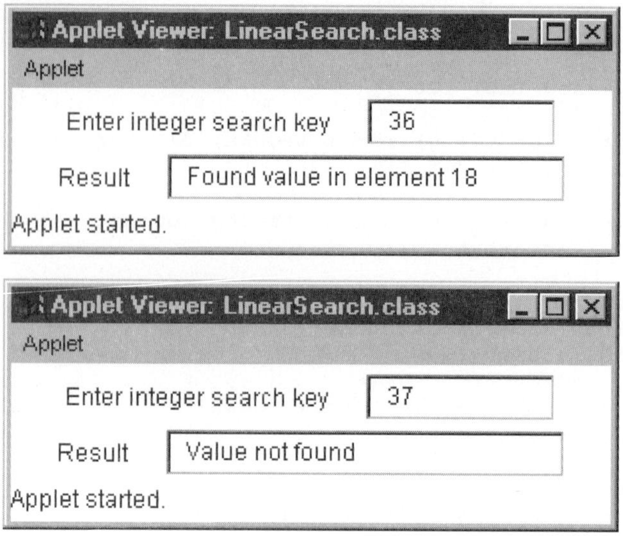

Applet Viewer: LinearSearch.class
Applet
Enter integer search key 36
Result Found value in element 18
Applet started.

Applet Viewer: LinearSearch.class
Applet
Enter integer search key 37
Result Value not found
Applet started.

Fig. 5.14 Linear search of an array (part 3 of 3).

The binary search algorithm eliminates half of the elements in the array being searched after each comparison. The algorithm locates the middle array element and compares it to the search key. If they are equal, the search key has been found and the subscript of that element is returned. Otherwise, the problem is reduced to searching half of the array. If the search key is less than the middle array element, the first half of the array is searched, otherwise the second half of the array is searched. If the search key is not the middle element in the specified subarray (piece of the original array), the algorithm is repeated on one quarter of the original array. The search continues until the search key is equal to the middle element of a subarray or until the subarray consists of one element that is not equal to the search key (i.e., the search key is not found).

In a worst case scenario, searching an array of 1024 elements will take only 10 comparisons using a binary search. Repeatedly dividing 1024 by 2 (because after each comparison we are able to eliminate half of the array) yields the values 512, 256, 128, 64, 32, 16, 8, 4, 2, and 1. The number 1024 (2^{10}) is divided by 2 only ten times to get the value 1. Dividing by 2 is equivalent to one comparison in the binary search algorithm. An array of 1,048,576 (2^{20}) elements takes a maximum of 20 comparisons to find the key. An array of one billion elements takes a maximum of 30 comparisons to find the key. This is a tremendous increase in performance over the linear search that required comparing the search key to an average of half the elements in the array. For a one billion element array, this is a difference between an average of 500 million comparisons and a maximum of 30 comparisons! The maximum number of comparisons needed for the binary search of any sorted array is the exponent of the first power of 2 greater than the number of elements in the array.

Figure 5.15 presents the iterative version of method **`binarySearch`** (line 64). The method receives two arguments—an integer **`key`** (the search key) and the **`Graphics`** object **`gg`** (used for output). If **`key`** does not match the middle element of a subarray, the

low subscript or **high** subscript (both declared in the method) is adjusted so a smaller subarray can be searched. If **key** is less than the middle element, the **high** subscript is set to **middle - 1**, and the search is continued on the elements from **low** to **middle - 1**. If **key** is greater than the middle element, the **low** subscript is set to **middle + 1**, and the search is continued on the elements from **middle + 1** to **high**. The program uses a 15-element array. The first power of 2 greater than the number of array elements is 16 (2^4), so a maximum of 4 comparisons are required to find the **key**. Method **printRow** outputs each subarray during the binary search process. The middle element in each subarray is marked with an asterisk (*****) to indicate the element to which the **key** is compared.

```
// Fig. 5.15: BinarySearch.java
// Binary search of an array
import java.awt.*;
import java.applet.Applet;
import java.awt.event.*;

public class BinarySearch extends Applet
             implements ActionListener {
   int a[];
   int element;
   String searchKey;
   int xPosition;   // applet horizontal drawing position
   int yPosition;   // applet vertical drawing position
   Label enterLabel, resultLabel;
   TextField enter, result;
   boolean timeToSearch = false;

   public void init()
   {
      a = new int[ 15 ];

      for ( int i = 0; i < a.length; i++ ) // create data
         a[ i ] = 2 * i;

      enterLabel = new Label( "Enter key" );
      add( enterLabel );

      enter = new TextField( 5 );
      enter.addActionListener( this );
      add( enter );

      resultLabel = new Label( "Result" );
      add( resultLabel );

      result = new TextField( 22 );
      result.setEditable( false );
      add( result );
   }
```

Fig. 5.15 Binary search of a sorted array (part 1 of 4).

```java

   public void paint( Graphics g )
   {
      if ( timeToSearch ) { // prevents search 1st time called
         element = binarySearch(
            Integer.parseInt( searchKey ), g );

         if ( element != -1 )
            result.setText(
               "Found value in element " + element );
         else
            result.setText( "Value not found" );
      }
   }

   public void actionPerformed( ActionEvent event )
   {
      timeToSearch = true;
      xPosition = 25;
      yPosition = 75;
      searchKey = event.getActionCommand().toString();
      repaint();  // call paint to start search and output
   }

   // Binary search
   public int binarySearch( int key, Graphics gg )
   {
      gg.drawString( "Portions of array searched",
                     xPosition, yPosition );
      yPosition += 15;

      int low = 0;                   // low subscript
      int high = a.length - 1;       // high subscript
      int middle;                    // middle subscript

      while ( low <= high ) {
         middle = ( low + high ) / 2;

         printRow( low, middle, high, gg );

         if ( key == a[ middle ] )  // match
            return middle;
         else if ( key < a[ middle ] )
            high = middle - 1;  // search low end of array
         else
            low = middle + 1;   // search high end of array
      }

      return -1;   // searchKey not found
   }

```

Fig. 5.15 Binary search of a sorted array (part 2 of 4).

```
   // Print one row of output showing the current
   // part of the array being processed.
   void printRow( int low, int mid, int high, Graphics gg )
   {
      xPosition = 25;

      for ( int i = 0; i < a.length; i++ ) {
         if ( i < low || i > high )
            gg.drawString( "", xPosition, yPosition );
         else if ( i == mid )    // mark middle value
            gg.drawString( String.valueOf( a[ i ] ) + "*",
                           xPosition, yPosition );
         else
            gg.drawString( String.valueOf( a[ i ] ),
                           xPosition, yPosition );

         xPosition += 20;
      }

      yPosition += 15;
   }
}
```

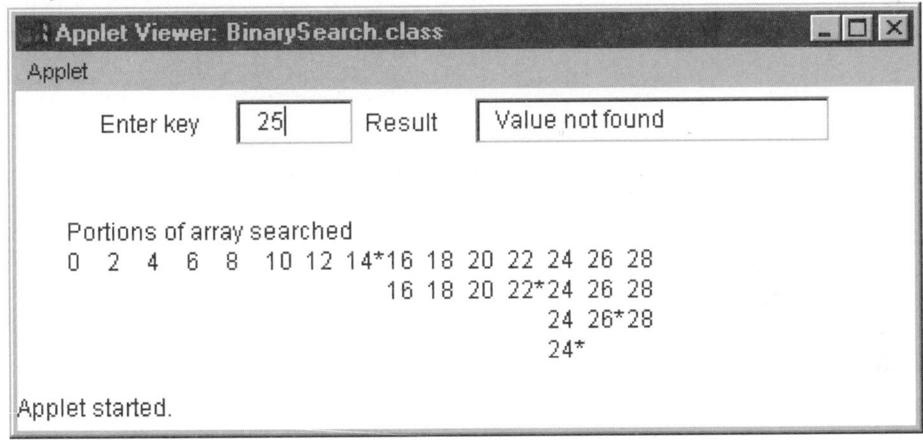

Fig. 5.15 Binary search of a sorted array (part 3 of 4).

5.9 Multiple-Subscripted Arrays

Multiple-subscripted arrays with two subscripts are often used to represent *tables* of values consisting of information arranged in *rows* and *columns*. To identify a particular table element, we must specify the two subscripts: By convention, the first identifies the element's row, and the second identifies the element's column. Tables or arrays that require two subscripts to identify a particular element are called *double-subscripted arrays*. Note that multiple-subscripted arrays can have more than two subscripts. Java does not support multiple-subscripted arrays directly, but does allow the programmer to specify single-subscripted arrays whose elements are also single-subscripted arrays, thus achieving the same effect.

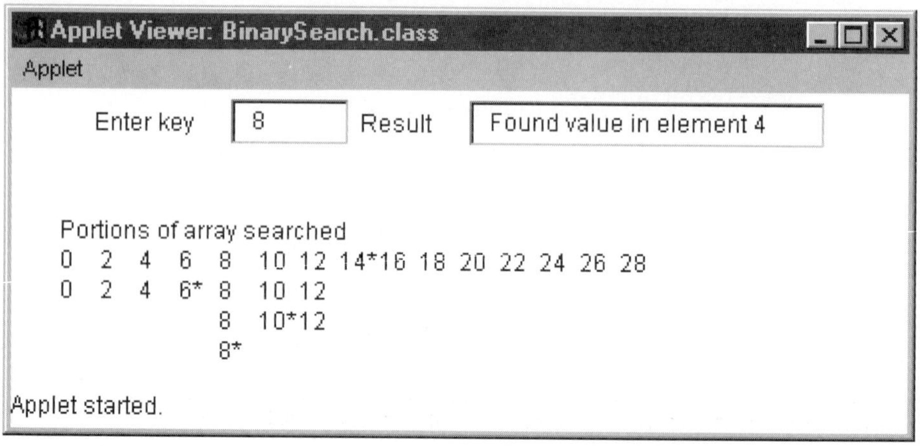

```
Applet Viewer: BinarySearch.class
Applet
Enter key  8      Result  Found value in element 4

Portions of array searched
0  2  4  6  8  10 12 14*16 18 20 22 24 26 28
0  2  4  6* 8  10 12
            8  10*12
            8*
Applet started.
```

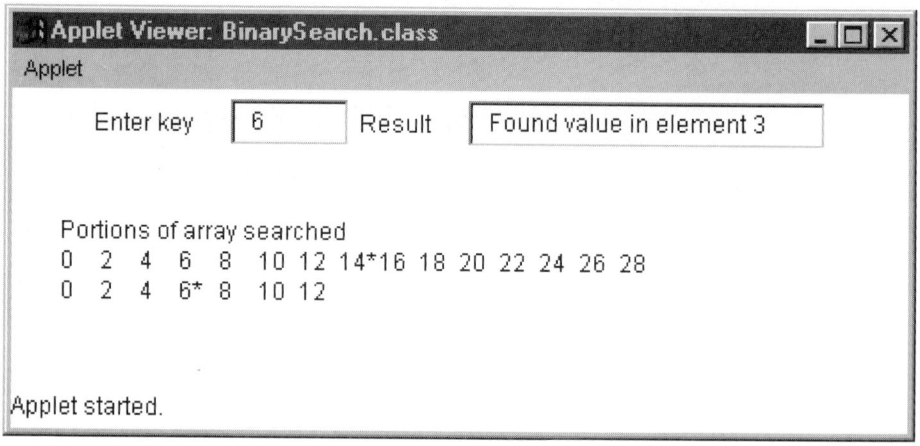

```
Applet Viewer: BinarySearch.class
Applet
Enter key  6      Result  Found value in element 3

Portions of array searched
0  2  4  6  8  10 12 14*16 18 20 22 24 26 28
0  2  4  6* 8  10 12
Applet started.
```

Fig. 5.15 Binary search of a sorted array (part 4 of 4).

Figure 5.16 illustrates a double-subscripted array, **a**, that contains three rows and four columns, so it is said to be a 3-by-4 array. In general, an array with *m* rows and *n* columns is called an *m-by-n array.*

Every element in array **a** is identified in Fig. 5.16 by an element name of the form **a[i][j]**; **a** is the name of the array, and **i** and **j** are the subscripts that uniquely identify each element in **a**. Notice that the names of the elements in the first row all have a first subscript of **0**; the names of the elements in the fourth column all have a second subscript of **3**.

Multiple-subscripted arrays can be initialized in declarations like a single-subscripted array. A double-subscripted array **b[2][2]** could be declared and initialized with

```
int b[][] = { { 1, 2 }, { 3, 4 } };
```

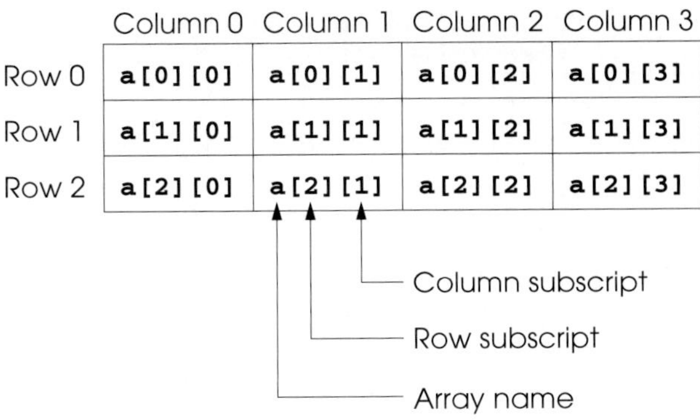

Fig. 5.16 A double-subscripted array with three rows and four columns.

The values are grouped by row in braces. So, **1** and **2** initialize **b[0][0]** and **b[0][1]**, and **3** and **4** initialize **b[1][0]** and **b[1][1]**.

Multiple-subscripted arrays are maintained as arrays of arrays. The declaration

```
int b[][] = { { 1, 2 }, { 3, 4, 5 } };
```

creates integer array **b** with row **0** containing two elements (**1** and **2**) and row **1** containing three elements (**3**, **4** and **5**).

A multiple-subscripted array with the same number of columns in every row can be allocated dynamically. For example, a 3-by-3 array is allocated as follows:

```
int b[][];
b = new int[ 3 ][ 3 ];
```

A multiple-subscripted array in which each row has a different number of columns can be allocated dynamically as follows:

```
int b[][];
b = new int[ 2 ][ ];    // allocate rows
b[ 0 ] = new int[ 5 ]; // allocate columns for row 0
b[ 1 ] = new int[ 3 ]; // allocate columns for row 1
```

The preceding code creates a two-dimensional array with two rows. The row **0** has five columns and the row **1** has three columns.

Figure 5.17 demonstrates initializing double-subscripted arrays in declarations. The program declares two arrays in method **paint** (line 9).

The declaration of **array1** provides six initializers in two sublists. The first sublist initializes the first row of the array to the values 1, 2, and 3; and the second sublist initializes the second row of the array to the values 4, 5, and 6. The declaration of **array2** provides three initializers in two sublists. The sublist for the first row explicitly initializes the first row to have two elements with values 1 and 2, respectively. The sublist for the second row initializes the second row to have one element with value 4.

```java
// Fig. 5.17: InitArray.java
// Initializing multidimensional arrays
import java.awt.Graphics;
import java.applet.Applet;

public class InitArray extends Applet {

   // paint the applet
   public void paint( Graphics g )
   {
      int array1[][] = { { 1, 2, 3 }, { 4, 5, 6 } };
      int array2[][] = { { 1, 2 }, { 4 } };

      g.drawString( "Values in array1 by row are", 25, 25 );
      printArray( array1, g, 40 );

      g.drawString( "Values in array2 by row are", 25, 70 );
      printArray( array2, g, 85 );
   }

   public void printArray( int a[][], Graphics g, int y )
   {
      int x = 25;

      for ( int i = 0; i < a.length; i++ ) {

         for ( int j = 0; j < a[ i ].length; j++ )  {
           g.drawString( String.valueOf( a[ i ][ j ] ), x, y );
            x += 15;
         }

         x = 25;
         y += 15;
      }
   }
}
```

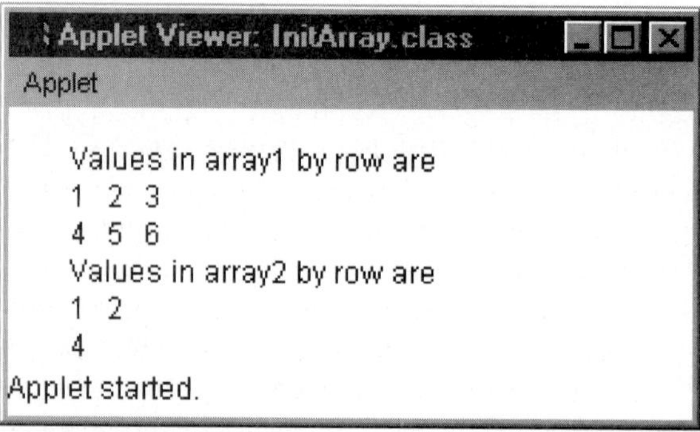

Fig. 5.17 Initializing multidimensional arrays.

The program calls method **printArray** (lines 15 and 18) to output each array's elements. Notice that the method definition specifies the array parameter as **int a[][]** to indicate that a double-subscripted array will be received as an argument. Also, a **Graphics** reference is passed as an argument to enable the **printArray** method to output the contents of each array on the applet. Note the use of a nested **for** structure to output the rows of each double-subscripted array. In the outer **for** structure, the expression **a.length** determines the number of rows in the array. In the inner **for** structure, the expression **a[i].length** determines the number of columns in each row of the array.

Many common array manipulations use **for** repetition structures. For example, the following **for** structure sets all the elements in the third row of array **a** in Fig. 5.16 to zero:

```
for ( int col = 0; col < a[ 2 ].length; col++)
   a[ 2 ][ col ] = 0;
```

We specified the *third* row, therefore we know that the first subscript is always **2** (**0** is the first row, and **1** is the second row). The **for** loop varies only the second subscript (i.e., the column subscript). The preceding **for** structure is equivalent to the assignment statements:

```
a[ 2 ][ 0 ] = 0;
a[ 2 ][ 1 ] = 0;
a[ 2 ][ 2 ] = 0;
a[ 2 ][ 3 ] = 0;
```

The following nested **for** structure determines the total of all the elements in array **a**.

```
total = 0;

for ( int row = 0; row < a.length; row++ )
   for ( int col = 0; col < a[ row ].length; col++ )
      total += a[ row ][ col ];
```

The **for** structure totals the elements of the array one row at a time. The outer **for** structure begins by setting the **row** subscript to **0** so the elements of the first row may be totaled by the inner **for** structure. The outer **for** structure then increments **row** to **1**, so the second row can be totaled. Then, the outer **for** structure increments **row** to **2**, so the third row can be totaled. The result can be displayed when the nested **for** structure terminates.

The program of Fig. 5.18 performs several other common array manipulations on 3-by-4 array **grades**. Each row of the array represents a student and each column represents a grade on one of the four exams the students took during the semester. The array manipulations are performed by four methods. Method **minimum** determines the lowest grade of any student for the semester. Method **maximum** determines the highest grade of any student for the semester. Method **average** determines a particular student's semester average. Method **printArray** outputs the double-subscripted array in a tabular format.

Methods **minimum**, **maximum**, and **printArray** each use the **grades** array and the variables **students** (number of rows in the array) and **exams** (number of columns in the array). Each method loops through array **grades** using nested **for** structures. The following nested **for** structure is from the method **minimum** definition:

```
// Fig. 5.18: DoubleArray.java
// Double-subscripted array example
import java.awt.Graphics;
import java.applet.Applet;

public class DoubleArray extends Applet {
   int grades[][] = { { 77, 68, 86, 73 },
                      { 96, 87, 89, 81 },
                      { 70, 90, 86, 81 } };
   int students, exams;
   int xPosition, yPosition;

   // initialize instance variables
   public void init()
   {
      students = grades.length;
      exams = grades[ 0 ].length;
   }

   // paint the applet
   public void paint( Graphics g )
   {
      xPosition = 25;
      yPosition = 25;

      g.drawString( "The array is:", xPosition, yPosition );
      yPosition += 15;
      printArray( g );
      xPosition = 25;
      yPosition += 30;
      g.drawString( "Lowest grade:", xPosition, yPosition );
      int min = minimum();
      g.drawString( String.valueOf( min ),
                    xPosition + 85, yPosition );
      yPosition += 15;
      g.drawString( "Highest grade:", xPosition, yPosition );
      int max = maximum();
      g.drawString( String.valueOf( max ),
                    xPosition + 85, yPosition );
      yPosition += 15;

      for ( int i = 0; i < students; i++ ) {
         g.drawString( "Average for student " + i + " is ",
                       25, yPosition );
         double ave = average( grades[ i ] );
         g.drawString( String.valueOf( ave ), 165, yPosition );
         yPosition += 15;
      }
   }

```

Fig. 5.18 Example of using double-subscripted arrays (part 1 of 3).

```
      // find the minimum grade
      public int minimum()
      {
         int lowGrade = 100;

         for ( int i = 0; i < students; i++ )
            for ( int j = 0; j < exams; j++ )
               if ( grades[ i ][ j ] < lowGrade )
                  lowGrade = grades[ i ][ j ];

         return lowGrade;
      }

      // find the maximum grade
      public int maximum()
      {
         int highGrade = 0;

         for ( int i = 0; i < students; i++ )
            for ( int j = 0; j < exams; j++ )
               if ( grades[ i ][ j ] > highGrade )
                  highGrade = grades[ i ][ j ];

         return highGrade;
      }

      // determine the average grade for a particular
      // student (or set of grades)
      public double average( int setOfGrades[] )
      {
         int total = 0;

         for ( int i = 0; i < setOfGrades.length; i++ )
            total += setOfGrades[ i ];

         return (double) total / setOfGrades.length;
      }

      // print the array
      public void printArray( Graphics g )
      {
         xPosition = 80;

         for ( int i = 0; i < exams; i++ ) {
            g.drawString( "[" + i + "]", xPosition, yPosition );
            xPosition += 30;
         }

         for ( int i = 0; i < students; i++ ) {
            xPosition = 25;
            yPosition += 15;
```

Fig. 5.18 Example of using double-subscripted arrays (part 2 of 3).

```
            g.drawString( "grades[" + i + "]",
                          xPosition, yPosition );
            xPosition = 80;

            for ( int j = 0; j < exams; j++ )  {
               g.drawString( String.valueOf( grades[ i ][ j ] ),
                             xPosition, yPosition );
               xPosition += 30;
            }
         }
      }
}
```

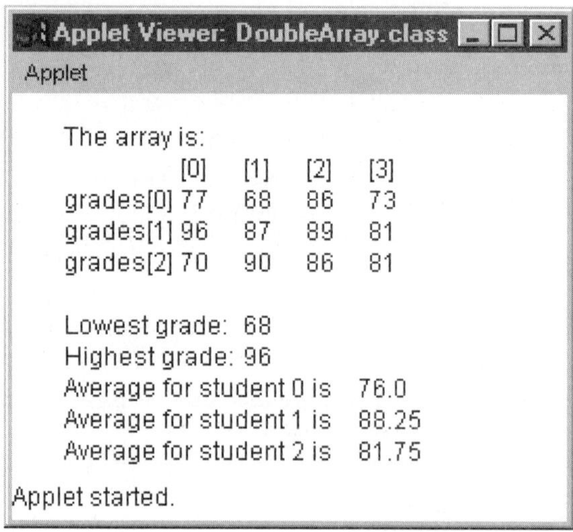

Fig. 5.18 Example of using double-subscripted arrays (part 3 of 3).

```
int lowGrade = 100;

for ( int i = 0; i < students; i++ )
   for ( int j = 0; j < exams; j++ )
      if ( grades[ i ][ j ] < lowGrade )
         lowGrade = grades[ i ][ j ];
```

The outer **`for`** structure begins by setting **`i`** (i.e., the row subscript) to **`0`** so the elements of the first row can be compared to variable **`lowGrade`** in the body of the inner **`for`** structure. The inner **`for`** structure loops through the four grades of a particular row and compares each grade to **`lowGrade`**. If a grade is less than **`lowGrade`**, **`lowGrade`** is set to that grade. The outer **`for`** structure then increments the row subscript by **`1`**. The elements of the second row are compared to variable **`lowGrade`**. The outer **`for`** structure then increments the row subscript to **`2`**. The elements of the third row are compared to variable **`lowGrade`**. When execution of the nested structure is complete, **`lowGrade`** contains the smallest grade in the double-subscripted array. Method **`maximum`** works similarly to method **`minimum`**.

Method **average** takes one argument—a single-subscripted array of test results for a particular student. When **average** is called, the argument is **grades[i]** which specifies that a particular row of the double-subscripted array **grades** is to be passed to **average**. For example, the argument **grades[1]** represents the four values (a single-subscripted array of grades) stored in the second row of the double-subscripted array **grades**. Remember that in Java a double-subscripted array is an array with elements that are single-subscripted arrays. Method **average** calculates the sum of the array elements, divides the total by the number of test results, and returns the floating-point result as a **double** value.

Summary

- Java stores lists of values in arrays. An array is a contiguous group of related memory locations. These locations are related by the fact that they all have the same name and the same type. To refer to a particular location or element within the array, we specify the name of the array and the subscript of the element.
- A subscript may be an integer or an integer expression. If a program uses an expression as a subscript, then the expression is evaluated to determine the particular element of the array.
- Java arrays always begin with element 0, thus it is important to note the difference when referring to the seventh element of the array as opposed to array element seven. The seventh element has a subscript of **6**, while array element seven has a subscript of **7** (actually the eighth element of the array). This is a source of "off-by-one" errors.
- Arrays occupy space in memory. To reserve 100 elements for integer array **b** and 27 elements for integer array **x**, the programmer writes

```
int b[] = new int[ 100 ], x[] = new int[ 27 ];
```

- The elements of an array can be initialized by declaration, by assignment, and by input.
- Java prevents referencing elements beyond the bounds of an array.
- To pass an array to a method, the name of the array is passed. To pass a single element of an array to a method, simply pass the name of the array followed by the subscript (contained in square brackets) of the particular element.
- Arrays are passed to methods call-by-reference—therefore the called methods can modify the element values in the caller's original arrays. Single elements of primitive-data-type arrays are passed to methods call-by-value.
- To receive an array argument, the method's parameter list must specify that an array will be received.
- An array can be sorted using the bubble-sort technique. Several passes of the array are made. On each pass, successive pairs of elements are compared. If a pair is in order (or the values are identical), it is left as is. If a pair is out of order, the values are swapped. For small arrays, the bubble sort is acceptable, but for larger arrays it is inefficient compared to more sophisticated sorting algorithms.

- The linear search compares each element of the array with the search key. If the array is not in any particular order, it is just as likely that the value will be found in the first element as the last. On average, therefore, the program will have to compare the search key with half the elements of the array. Linear search works well for small arrays and is acceptable even for large unsorted arrays.
- For sorted arrays the binary search eliminates from consideration one half of the elements in the array after each comparison. The algorithm locates the middle element of the array and compares it to the search key. If they are equal, the search key is found and the array subscript of that element is returned. Otherwise, the problem is reduced to searching one half of the array that is still under consideration.
- In a worst case scenario, searching a sorted array of 1024 elements will take only 10 comparisons using a binary search.
- Arrays may be used to represent tables of values consisting of information arranged in rows and columns. To identify a particular element of a table, two subscripts are specified: The first identifies the row in which the element is contained, and the second identifies the column in which the element is contained. Tables or arrays that require two subscripts to identify a particular element are called double-subscripted arrays.
- To pass one row of a double-subscripted array to a method that receives a single-subscripted array, simply pass the name of the array followed by the row subscript.

Terminology

`a[i]`
`a[i][j]`
array
array initializer list
binary search of an array
bounds checking
bubble sort
column subscript
constant variable
declare an array
double-subscripted array
element of an array
`final`
initialize an array
initializer
linear search of an array
lvalue
m-by-n array
multiple-subscripted array
name of an array
named constant
off-by-one error
pass-by-reference
pass-by-value
pass of a bubble sort
passing arrays to methods
position number
row subscript
search key
searching an array
single-subscripted array
sinking sort
sorting
sorting an array
square brackets **`[]`**
subscript
table of values
tabular format
temporary area for exchange of values
value of an element
zeroth element

Common Programming Errors

5.1 It is important to note the difference between the "seventh element of the array" and "array element seven." Because array subscripts begin at 0, the "seventh element of the array" has a subscript of 6, while "array element seven" has a subscript of 7 and is actually the eighth element of the array. This confusion is a source of "off-by-one" errors.

5.2 Unlike C or C++ the number of elements in the array is never specified in the square brackets after the array name in a declaration. The declaration **`int c[ 12 ];`** causes a syntax error.

5.3 Assigning a value to a constant variable in an executable statement is a syntax error.

5.4 Referring to an element outside the array bounds.

Good Programming Practice

5.1 Strive for program clarity. It is sometimes worthwhile to trade off the most efficient use of memory or processor time in favor of writing clearer programs.

Performance Tips

5.1 Sometimes performance considerations far outweigh clarity considerations.

5.2 Passing arrays by reference makes sense for performance reasons. If arrays were passed by value, a copy of each element would be passed. For large, frequently passed arrays, this would waste time and would consume considerable storage for the copies of the arrays.

5.3 Sometimes, the simplest algorithms perform poorly. Their virtue is that they are easy to write, test and debug. More complex algorithms are sometimes needed to realize maximum performance.

Software Engineering Observations

5.1 Java, unlike other languages, does not allow the programmer to choose whether to pass each argument call-by-value or call-by-reference. Primitive-data-type variables are always passed call-by-value and objects are always passed call-by-reference.

5.2 When returning information from a method via a **`return`** statement, primitive-data-type variables are always returned by value and objects are always returned by reference.

Testing and Debugging Tips

5.1 When a Java program is executed, the Java interpreter checks array element references to be sure they are valid (i.e., all subscripts must be greater than or equal to 0 and less than the length of the array). If there is an invalid reference, Java generates an exception.

5.2 Exceptions are used to indicate that an error occurred in a program. They enable the programmer to recover from an error and continue the execution of the program instead of abnormally terminating the program. When an invalid array reference is made, an **`ArrayIndex-`**

OutOfBoundsException is generated. Chapter 12 covers "Exception Handling" in detail.

5.3 When looping through an array, the array subscript should never go below 0 and should always be less than the total number of elements in the array (one less than the size of the array). Make sure the loop terminating condition prevents accessing elements outside this range.

5.4 Programs should validate the correctness of all input values to prevent erroneous information from affecting a program's calculations.

5.5 With call-by-value, changes to the called method's copy do not affect the original variable's value in the calling method. This prevents the accidental side effects that so greatly hinder the development of correct and reliable software systems.

Self-Review Exercises

5.1 Answer each of the following:

a) Lists and tables of values are stored in __________.
b) The elements of an array are related by the fact that they have the same __________ and __________.
c) The number used to refer to a particular element of an array is called its __________.
d) The process of placing the elements of an array in order is called __________ the array.
e) The process of determining if an array contains a certain key value is called________ the array.
f) An array that uses two subscripts is referred to as a __________ array.

5.2 State whether the following are true or false. If the answer is false, explain why.

a) An array can store many different types of values.
b) An array subscript should normally be of data type **float**.
c) An individual array element that is passed to a method and modified in that method will contain the modified value when the called method completes execution.

5.3 Answer the following questions regarding an array called **fractions**.

a) Define a constant variable **ARRAY_SIZE** initialized to 10.
b) Declare an array with **ARRAY_SIZE** elements of type **float** and initialize the elements to **0**.
c) Name the fourth element from the beginning of the array.
d) Refer to array element 4.
e) Assign the value **1.667** to array element 9.
f) Assign the value **3.333** to the seventh element of the array.
g) Sum all the elements of the array using a **for** repetition structure. Define the integer variable **x** as a control variable for the loop.

5.4 Answer the following questions regarding an array called **table**.

a) Declare the array to be an integer array and to have 3 rows and 3 columns. Assume the constant variable **ARRAY_SIZE** has been defined to be 3.
b) How many elements does the array contain?
c) Use a **for** repetition structure to initialize each element of the array to the sum of its subscripts. Assume the integer variables **x** and **y** are declared as control variables.

5.5 Find the error in each of the following program segments and correct the error.

a) `ARRAY_SIZE = 10;   // ARRAY_SIZE was declared final`

b) Assume `int b[] = new int[ 10 ];`
```
for ( int i = 0; i <= b.length; i++ )
   b[ i ] = 1;
```

c) Assume `int a[][] = { { 1, 2 }, { 3, 4 } };`
```
   a[ 1, 1 ] = 5;
```

Answers to Self-Review Exercises

5.1 a) Arrays. b) Name, type. c) Subscript. d) Sorting. e) Searching. f) Double-subscripted.

5.2 a) False. An array can store only values of the same type.

b) False. An array subscript should normally be an integer or an integer expression.

c) False for individual primitive-data-type elements of an array because they are passed call-by-value. If an entire array is passed to a method, then any modifications to the array elements will be reflected in the original. Also, an individual element of a class type passed to a method is passed call-by-reference and changes to the object will be reflected in the original array element.

5.3 a) `final int ARRAY_SIZE = 10;`

b) `float fractions[] = new float[ ARRAY_SIZE ];`

c) `fractions[ 3 ]`

d) `fractions[ 4 ]`

e) `fractions[ 9 ] = 1.667;`

f) `fractions[ 6 ] = 3.333;`

g)
```
float total = 0;
for ( int x = 0; x < fractions.length; x++ )
   total += fractions[ x ];
```

5.4 a) `int table[][] = new int[ ARRAY_SIZE ][ ARRAY_SIZE ];`

b) Nine.

c)
```
for ( int x = 0; x < table.length; x++ )
   for ( int y = 0; y < table[ x ].length; y++ )
      table[ x ][ y ] = x + y;
```

5.5 a) Error: Assigning a value to a constant variable using an assignment statement.
Correction: Assign a value to the constant variable in a **`final int ARRAY_SIZE`** declaration.

b) Error: Referencing an array element outside the bounds of the array (`b[10]`).
Correction: Change the `<=` operator to `<`.

c) Error: Array subscripting done incorrectly.
Correction: Change the statement to `a[1][1] = 5;`

Exercises

5.6 Fill in the blanks in each of the following:

a) Java stores lists of values in __________.

b) The elements of an array are related by the fact that they __________.

c) When referring to an array element, the position number contained within brackets is called a __________.
d) The names of the four elements of array **p** are _______, _______, _______, and _______.
e) Naming an array, stating its type, and specifying the number of elements in the array is called __________ the array.
f) The process of placing the elements of an array into either ascending or descending order is called __________.
g) In a double-subscripted array, the first subscript identifies the __________ of an element, and the second subscript identifies the __________ of an element.
h) An m-by-n array contains _________ rows, _________ columns, and ________ elements.
i) The name of the element in row 3 and column 5 of array **d** is __________.

5.7 State which of the following are true and which are false; for those that are false, explain why they are false.
a) To refer to a particular location or element within an array, we specify the name of the array and the value of the particular element.
b) An array declaration reserves space for the array.
c) To indicate that 100 locations should be reserved for integer array **p**, the programmer writes the declaration
p[100];
d) A Java program that initializes the elements of a 15-element array to zero must contain at least one **for** statement.
e) A Java program that totals the elements of a double-subscripted array must contain nested **for** statements.

5.8 Write Java statements to accomplish each of the following:
a) Display the value of the seventh element of character array **f**.
b) Initialize each of the 5 elements of single-subscripted integer array **g** to **8**.
c) Total the elements of floating-point array **c** of 100 elements.
d) Copy 11- element array **a** into the first portion of array **b** containing 34 elements.
e) Determine and print the smallest and largest values contained in 99-element floating-point array **w**.

5.9 Consider a 2-by-3 integer array **t**.
a) Write a declaration for **t**.
b) How many rows does **t** have?
c) How many columns does **t** have?
d) How many elements does **t** have?
e) Write the names of all the elements in the second row of **t**.
f) Write the names of all the elements in the third column of **t**.
g) Write a single statement that sets the element of **t** in row 1 and column 2 to zero.
h) Write a series of statements that initializes each element of **t** to zero. Do not use a repetition structure.
i) Write a nested **for** structure that initializes each element of **t** to zero.
j) Write a statement that inputs the values for the elements of **t** from the terminal.
k) Write a series of statements that determines and prints the smallest value in array **t**.
l) Write a statement that displays the elements of the first row of **t**.
m) Write a statement that totals the elements of the fourth column of **t**.
n) Write a series of statements that prints the array **t** in neat, tabular format. List the column subscripts as headings across the top and list the row subscripts at the left of each row.

5.10 Use a single-subscripted array to solve the following problem. A company pays its salespeople on a commission basis. The salespeople receive $200 per week plus 9 percent of their gross sales for that week. For example, a salesperson who grosses $5000 in sales in a week receives $200 plus 9 percent of $5000, or a total of $650. Write a program (using an array of counters) that determines how many of the salespeople earned salaries in each of the following ranges (assume that each salesperson's salary is truncated to an integer amount):

a) $200-$299
b) $300-$399
c) $400-$499
d) $500-$599
e) $600-$699
f) $700-$799
g) $800-$899
h) $900-$999
i) $1000 and over

5.11 The bubble sort presented in Fig. 5.13 is inefficient for large arrays. Make the following simple modifications to improve the performance of the bubble sort.

a) After the first pass, the largest number is guaranteed to be in the highest-numbered element of the array; after the second pass, the two highest numbers are "in place," and so on. Instead of making nine comparisons on every pass, modify the bubble sort to make eight comparisons on the second pass, seven on the third pass, and so on.
b) The data in the array may already be in the proper order or near-proper order, so why make nine passes if fewer will suffice? Modify the sort to check at the end of each pass if any swaps have been made. If none has been made, then the data must already be in the proper order, so the program should terminate. If swaps have been made, then at least one more pass is needed.

5.12 Write statements that perform the following single-subscripted array operations:

a) Set the 10 elements of integer array **`counts`** to zeros.
b) Add 1 to each of the 15 elements of integer array **`bonus`**.
c) Print the 5 values of integer array **`bestScores`** in column format.

5.13 Use a single-subscripted array to solve the following problem. Read in 20 numbers, each of which is between 10 and 100, inclusive. As each number is read, print it only if it is not a duplicate of a number already read. Provide for the "worst case" in which all 20 numbers are different. Use the smallest possible array to solve this problem.

5.14 Label the elements of 3-by-5 double-subscripted array **`sales`** to indicate the order in which they are set to zero by the following program segment:

```
for ( int row = 0; row < sales.length; row++ )
   for ( int col = 0; col < sales[ row ].length; col++ )
      sales[ row ][ col ] = 0;
```

5.15 Write a program to simulate the rolling of two dice. The program should use **`Math.random`** to roll the first die, and should use **`Math.random`** again to roll the second die. The sum of the two values should then be calculated. *Note:* Since each die can show an integer value from 1 to 6, the sum of the values will vary from 2 to 12 with 7 being the most frequent sum and 2 and 12 being the least frequent sums. Figure 5.19 shows the 36 possible combinations of the two dice. Your program should roll the dice 36,000 times. Use a single-subscripted array to tally the numbers of times each possible sum appears. Print the results in a tabular format. Also, determine if the totals are reasonable, i.e., there are six ways to roll a 7, so approximately one sixth of all the rolls should be 7.

	1	2	3	4	5	6
1	2	3	4	5	6	7
2	3	4	5	6	7	8
3	4	5	6	7	8	9
4	5	6	7	8	9	10
5	6	7	8	9	10	11
6	7	8	9	10	11	12

Fig. 5.19 The 36 possible outcomes of rolling two dice.

5.16 What does the following program do?

```
// Exercise 5.16
// What does this program do?
import java.awt.*;
import java.applet.Applet;

public class MysteryClass extends Applet {
   int result;

   public void start()
   {
      int a[] = { 1, 2, 3, 4, 5, 6, 7, 8, 9, 10 };

      result = whatIsThis( a, a.length );
   }

   public void paint( Graphics g )
   {
      g.drawString( "Result is " + result, 25, 25 );
   }

   public int whatIsThis( int b[], int size )
   {
      if ( size == 1 )
         return b[0];
      else
         return b[ size - 1 ] + whatIsThis( b, size - 1 );
   }
}
```

5.17 Write a program that runs 1000 games of craps and answers the following questions:

a) How many games are won on the first roll, second roll, …, twentieth roll, and after the twentieth roll?
b) How many games are lost on the first roll, second roll, …, twentieth roll, and after the twentieth roll?
c) What are the chances of winning at craps? (*Note:* You should discover that craps is one of the fairest casino games. What do you suppose this means?)

d) What is the average length of a game of craps?
e) Do the chances of winning improve with the length of the game?

5.18 (*Airline Reservations System*) A small airline has just purchased a computer for its new automated reservations system. You have been asked to program the new system. You are to write a program to assign seats on each flight of the airline's only plane (capacity: 10 seats).

Your program should display the following menu of alternatives:

```
Please type 1 for "smoking"
Please type 2 for "nonsmoking"
```

If the person types 1, then your program should assign a seat in the smoking section (seats 1-5). If the person types 2, then your program should assign a seat in the nonsmoking section (seats 6-10). Your program should then print a boarding pass indicating the person's seat number and whether it is in the smoking or nonsmoking section of the plane.

Use a single-subscripted array to represent the seating chart of the plane. Initialize all the elements of the array to 0 to indicate that all seats are empty. As each seat is assigned, set the corresponding elements of the array to 1 to indicate that the seat is no longer available.

Your program should, of course, never assign a seat that has already been assigned. When the smoking section is full, your program should ask the person if it is acceptable to be placed in the nonsmoking section (and vice versa). If yes, then make the appropriate seat assignment. If no, then print the message **"Next flight leaves in 3 hours."**

5.19 What does the following program do?

```
// Exercise 5.19
// What does this program do?
import java.awt.*;
import java.applet.Applet;

public class MysteryClass extends Applet {
   int yPosition;
   int a[] = { 1, 2, 3, 4, 5, 6, 7, 8, 9, 10 };

   public void paint( Graphics g )
   {
      yPosition = 25;
      someMethod( a, 0, g );
   }

   public void someMethod( int b[], int x, Graphics g )
   {
      if ( x < b.length ) {
         someMethod( b, x + 1, g );
         g.drawString( String.valueOf( b[ x ] ),
                       25, yPosition );
         yPosition += 15;
      }
   }
}
```

5.20 Use a double-subscripted array to solve the following problem. A company has four salespeople (1 to 4) who sell five different products (1 to 5). Once a day, each salesperson passes in a slip for each different type of product sold. Each slip contains:

1. The salesperson number
2. The product number
3. The total dollar value of that product sold that day

Thus, each salesperson passes in between 0 and 5 sales slips per day. Assume that the information from all of the slips for last month is available. Write a program that will read all this information for last month's sales, and summarize the total sales by salesperson by product. All totals should be stored in the double-subscripted array **`sales`**. After processing all the information for last month, print the results in tabular format with each of the columns representing a particular salesperson and each of the rows representing a particular product. Cross total each row to get the total sales of each product for last month; cross total each column to get the total sales by salesperson for last month. Your tabular printout should include these cross totals to the right of the totaled rows and to the bottom of the totaled columns.

5.21 (*Turtle Graphics*) The Logo language, which is popular among young computer users, made the concept of *turtle graphics* famous. Imagine a mechanical turtle that walks around the room under the control of a Java program. The turtle holds a pen in one of two positions, up or down. While the pen is down, the turtle traces out shapes as it moves; while the pen is up, the turtle moves about freely without writing anything. In this problem you will simulate the operation of the turtle and create a computerized sketchpad as well.

Use a 20-by-20 array **`floor`** which is initialized to zeros. Read commands from an array that contains them. Keep track of the current position of the turtle at all times and whether the pen is currently up or down. Assume that the turtle always starts at position 0,0 of the floor with its pen up. The set of turtle commands your program must process are as follows:

Command	Meaning
1	Pen up
2	Pen down
3	Turn right
4	Turn left
5,10	Move forward 10 spaces (or a number other than 10)
6	Print the 20-by-20 array
9	End of data (sentinel)

Suppose that the turtle is somewhere near the center of the floor. The following "program" would draw and print a 12-by-12 square leaving the pen in the up position:

```
2
5,12
3
5,12
3
5,12
3
5,12
1
6
9
```

As the turtle moves with the pen down, set the appropriate elements of array **floor** to **1**s. When the **6** command (print) is given, wherever there is a **1** in the array, display an asterisk, or some other character you choose. Wherever there is a zero, display a blank. Write a program to implement the turtle graphics capabilities discussed here. Write several turtle graphics programs to draw interesting shapes. Add other commands to increase the power of your turtle graphics language.

5.22 (*Knight's Tour*) One of the more interesting puzzlers for chess buffs is the Knight's Tour problem, originally proposed by the mathematician Euler. The question is this: Can the chess piece called the knight move around an empty chessboard and touch each of the 64 squares once and only once? We study this intriguing problem in depth here.

The knight makes L-shaped moves (over two in one direction and then over one in a perpendicular direction). Thus, from a square in the middle of an empty chessboard, the knight can make eight different moves (numbered 0 through 7) as shown in Fig. 5.20.

a) Draw an 8-by-8 chessboard on a sheet of paper and attempt a Knight's Tour by hand. Put a **1** in the first square you move to, a **2** in the second square, a **3** in the third, etc. Before starting the tour, estimate how far you think you will get, remembering that a full tour consists of 64 moves. How far did you get? Was this close to your estimate?

b) Now let us develop a program that will move the knight around a chessboard. The board is represented by an 8-by-8 double-subscripted array **board**. Each of the squares is initialized to zero. We describe each of the eight possible moves in terms of both their horizontal and vertical components. For example, a move of type 0 as shown in Fig. 5.20 consists of moving two squares horizontally to the right and one square vertically upward. Move 2 consists of moving one square horizontally to the left and two squares vertically upward. Horizontal moves to the left and vertical moves upward are indicated with negative numbers. The eight moves may be described by two single-subscripted arrays, **horizontal** and **vertical**, as follows:

	0	1	2	3	4	5	6	7
0								
1				2		1		
2			3				0	
3					K			
4			4				7	
5				5		6		
6								
7								

Fig. 5.20 The eight possible moves of the knight.

```
horizontal[ 0 ] = 2
horizontal[ 1 ] = 1
horizontal[ 2 ] = -1
horizontal[ 3 ] = -2
horizontal[ 4 ] = -2
horizontal[ 5 ] = -1
horizontal[ 6 ] = 1
horizontal[ 7 ] = 2

vertical[ 0 ] = -1
vertical[ 1 ] = -2
vertical[ 2 ] = -2
vertical[ 3 ] = -1
vertical[ 4 ] = 1
vertical[ 5 ] = 2
vertical[ 6 ] = 2
vertical[ 7 ] = 1
```

c) Let the variables **currentRow** and **currentColumn** indicate the row and column of the knight's current position. To make a move of type **moveNumber**, where **moveNumber** is between 0 and 7, your program uses the statements

```
currentRow += vertical[ moveNumber ];
currentColumn += horizontal[ moveNumber ];
```

d) Keep a counter that varies from **1** to **64**. Record the latest count in each square the knight moves to. Test each potential move to see if the knight already visited that square. Test every potential move to ensure that the knight does not land off the chessboard. Write a program to move the knight around the chessboard. Run the program. How many moves did the knight make?

e) After attempting to write and run a Knight's Tour program, you have probably developed some valuable insights. We will use these to develop a *heuristic* (or strategy) for moving the knight. Heuristics do not guarantee success, but a carefully developed heuristic greatly improves the chance of success. You may have observed that the outer squares are more troublesome than the squares nearer the center of the board. In fact, the most troublesome, or inaccessible, squares are the four corners.

f) Intuition may suggest that you should attempt to move the knight to the most troublesome squares first and leave open those that are easiest to get to so when the board gets congested near the end of the tour there will be a greater chance of success.

g) We may develop an "accessibility heuristic" by classifying each of the squares according to how accessible they are, then always moving the knight (using the knight's L-shaped moves) to the most inaccessible square. We label a double-subscripted array **accessibility** with numbers indicating from how many squares each particular square is accessible. On a blank chessboard, each center square is rated as **8**, each corner square is rated as **2**, and the other squares have accessibility numbers of **3**, **4**, or **6** as follows:

```
2 3 4 4 4 4 3 2
3 4 6 6 6 6 4 3
4 6 8 8 8 8 6 4
4 6 8 8 8 8 6 4
4 6 8 8 8 8 6 4
4 6 8 8 8 8 6 4
3 4 6 6 6 6 4 3
2 3 4 4 4 4 3 2
```

h) Write a version of the Knight's Tour using the accessibility heuristic. The knight should always move to the square with the lowest accessibility number. In case of a tie, the knight may move to any of the tied squares. Therefore, the tour may begin in any of the four corners. (*Note:* As the knight moves around the chessboard, your program should reduce the accessibility numbers as more squares become occupied. In this way, at any given time during the tour, each available square's accessibility number will remain equal to precisely the number of squares from which that square may be reached.) Run this version of your program. Did you get a full tour? Modify the program to run 64 tours, one starting from each square of the chessboard. How many full tours did you get?

i) Write a version of the Knight's Tour program which, when encountering a tie between two or more squares, decides what square to choose by looking ahead to those squares reachable from the "tied" squares. Your program should move to the square for which the next move would arrive at a square with the lowest accessibility number.

5.23 (*Knight's Tour: Brute Force Approaches*) In Exercise 5.22 we developed a solution to the Knight's Tour problem. The approach used, called the "accessibility heuristic," generates many solutions and executes efficiently.

As computers continue increasing in power, we will be able to solve more problems with sheer computer power and relatively unsophisticated algorithms. Let us call this approach "brute force" problem solving.

a) Use random number generation to enable the knight to walk around the chess board (in its legitimate L-shaped moves, of course) at random. Your program should run one tour and print the final chessboard. How far did the knight get?

b) Most likely, the preceding program produced a relatively short tour. Now modify your program to attempt 1000 tours. Use a single-subscripted array to keep track of the number of tours of each length. When your program finishes attempting the 1000 tours, it should print this information in neat tabular format. What was the best result?

c) Most likely, the preceding program gave you some "respectable" tours but no full tours. Now "pull all the stops out" and simply let your program run until it produces a full tour. (*Caution:* This version of the program could run for hours on a powerful computer.) Once again, keep a table of the number of tours of each length, and print this table when the first full tour is found. How many tours did your program attempt before producing a full tour? How much time did it take?

d) Compare the brute force version of the Knight's Tour with the accessibility-heuristic version. Which required a more careful study of the problem? Which algorithm was more difficult to develop? Which required more computer power? Could we be certain (in advance) of obtaining a full tour with the accessibility-heuristic approach? Could we be certain (in advance) of obtaining a full tour with the brute force approach? Argue the pros and cons of brute force problem solving in general.

5.24 (*Eight Queens*) Another puzzler for chess buffs is the Eight Queens problem. Simply stated: Is it possible to place eight queens on an empty chessboard so that no queen is "attacking" any other, i.e., no two queens are in the same row, the same column, or along the same diagonal? Use the thinking developed in Exercise 5.22 to formulate a heuristic for solving the Eight Queens problem. Run your program. (*Hint:* It is possible to assign a value to each square of the chessboard indicating how many squares of an empty chessboard are "eliminated" if a queen is placed in that square. Each of the corners would be assigned the value 22, as in Fig. 5.21.) Once these "elimination numbers" are placed in all 64 squares, an appropriate heuristic might be: Place the next queen in the square with the smallest elimination number. Why is this strategy intuitively appealing?

Fig. 5.21 The 22 squares eliminated by placing a queen in the upper left corner.

5.25 (*Eight Queens: Brute Force Approaches*) In this exercise you will develop several brute force approaches to solving the Eight Queens problem introduced in Exercise 5.24.

a) Solve the Eight Queens exercise, using the random brute force technique developed in Exercise 5.23.
b) Use an exhaustive technique, i.e., try all possible combinations of eight queens on the chessboard.
c) Why do you suppose the exhaustive brute force approach may not be appropriate for solving the Knight's Tour problem?
d) Compare and contrast the random brute force and exhaustive brute force approaches.

5.26 (*Knight's Tour: Closed Tour Test*) In the Knight's Tour, a full tour occurs when the knight makes 64 moves touching each square of the chess board once and only once. A closed tour occurs when the 64th move is one move away from the square in which the knight started the tour. Modify the program you wrote in Exercise 5.22 to test for a closed tour if a full tour has occurred.

5.27 (*The Sieve of Eratosthenes*) A prime integer is any integer that is evenly divisible only by itself and 1. The Sieve of Eratosthenes is a method of finding prime numbers. It operates as follows:

a) Create an array with all elements initialized to 1 (true). Array elements with prime subscripts will remain 1. All other array elements will eventually be set to zero.
b) Starting with array subscript 2 (subscript 1 must be prime), every time an array element is found whose value is 1, loop through the remainder of the array and set to zero every element whose subscript is a multiple of the subscript for the element with value 1. For array subscript 2, all elements beyond 2 in the array that are multiples of 2 will be set to zero (subscripts 4, 6, 8, 10, etc.); for array subscript 3, all elements beyond 3 in the array that are multiples of 3 will be set to zero (subscripts 6, 9, 12, 15, etc.); and so on.

When this process is complete, the array elements that are still set to one indicate that the subscript is a prime number. These subscripts can then be printed. Write a program that uses an array of 1000 elements to determine and print the prime numbers between 1 and 999. Ignore element 0 of the array.

5.28 (*Bucket Sort*) A bucket sort begins with a single-subscripted array of positive integers to be sorted, and a double-subscripted array of integers with rows subscripted from 0 to 9 and columns subscripted from 0 to n - 1 where n is the number of values in the array to be sorted. Each row of the double-subscripted array is referred to as a bucket. Write a method **`bucketSort`** that takes an integer array as an argument and performs as follows:

a) Place each value of the single-subscripted array into a row of the bucket array based on the value's ones digit. For example, 97 is placed in row 7, 3 is placed in row 3, and 100 is placed in row 0. This is called a "distribution pass."
b) Loop through the bucket array row-by-row and copy the values back to the original array. This is called a "gathering pass." The new order of the preceding values in the single-subscripted array is 100, 3, and 97.

c) Repeat this process for each subsequent digit position (tens, hundreds, thousands, etc.).

On the second pass, 100 is placed in row 0, 3 is placed in row 0 (because 3 has no tens digit), and 97 is placed in row 9. After the gathering pass, the order of the values in the single-subscripted array is 100, 3, and 97. On the third pass, 100 is placed in row 1, 3 is placed in row 0 and 97 is placed in row 0 (after the 3). After the last gathering pass, the original array is now in sorted order.

Note that the double-subscripted array of buckets is ten times the size of the integer array being sorted. This sorting technique provides better performance than a bubble sort, but requires much more memory. The bubble sort requires space for only one additional element of data. This is an example of the space-time trade-off: The bucket sort uses more memory than the bubble sort, but performs better. This version of the bucket sort requires copying all the data back to the original array on each pass. Another possibility is to create a second double-subscripted bucket array and repeatedly swap the data between the two bucket arrays.

Recursion Exercises

5.29 (*Selection Sort*) A selection sort searches an array looking for the smallest element in the array. Then, the smallest element is swapped with the first element of the array. The process is repeated for the subarray beginning with the second element of the array. Each pass of the array results in one element being placed in its proper location. This sort performs comparably to the bubble sort—for an array of n elements, n - 1 passes must be made, and for each subarray, n - 1 comparisons must be made to find the smallest value. When the subarray being processed contains one element, the array is sorted. Write recursive method **`selectionSort`** to perform this algorithm.

5.30 (*Palindromes*) A palindrome is a string that is spelled the same way forwards and backwards. Some examples of palindromes are: "radar," "able was i ere i saw elba," and (if blanks are ignored) "a man a plan a canal panama." Write a recursive method **`testPalindrome`** that returns 1 if the string stored in the array is a palindrome, and 0 otherwise. The method should ignore spaces and punctuation in the string.

5.31 (*Linear Search*) Modify Fig. 5.14 to use recursive method **`linearSearch`** to perform a linear search of the array. The method should receive an integer array and the size of the array as arguments. If the search key is found, return the array subscript; otherwise, return –1.

5.32 (*Binary Search*) Modify the program of Fig. 5.15 to use a recursive method **`binarySearch`** to perform the binary search of the array. The method should receive an integer array and the starting subscript and ending subscript as arguments. If the search key is found, return the array subscript; otherwise, return –1.

5.33 (*Eight Queens*) Modify the Eight Queens program you created in Exercise 5.24 to solve the problem recursively.

5.34 (*Print an array*) Write a recursive method **`printArray`** that takes an array and the size of the array as arguments and returns nothing. The method should stop processing and return when it receives an array of size zero.

5.35 (*Print a string backwards*) Write a recursive method **`stringReverse`** that takes a character array containing a string as an argument, prints the string backwards, and returns nothing. The method should stop processing and return when the terminating null character is encountered.

5.36 (*Find the minimum value in an array*) Write a recursive method **`recursiveMinimum`** that takes an integer array and the array size as arguments and returns the smallest element of the array. The method should stop processing and return when it receives an array of 1 element.

5.37 (*Quicksort*) In the examples and exercises of this chapter, we discussed the sorting techniques of bubble sort, bucket sort, and selection sort. We now present the recursive sorting technique called Quicksort. The basic algorithm for a single-subscripted array of values is as follows:

a) *Partitioning Step:* Take the first element of the unsorted array and determine its final location in the sorted array, i.e., all values to the left of the element in the array are less than the element, and all values to the right of the element in the array are greater than the element. We now have one element in its proper location and two unsorted subarrays.
b) *Recursive Step:* Perform step 1 on each unsorted subarray.

Each time step 1 is performed on a subarray, another element is placed in its final location of the sorted array, and two unsorted subarrays are created. When a subarray consists of one element, it must be sorted, therefore that element is in its final location.

The basic algorithm seems simple enough, but how do we determine the final position of the first element of each subarray. As an example, consider the following set of values (the element in bold is the partitioning element—it will be placed in its final location in the sorted array):

37 2 6 4 89 8 10 12 68 45

a) Starting from the rightmost element of the array, compare each element to **37** until an element less than **37** is found, then swap **37** and that element. The first element less than **37** is 12, so **37** and 12 are swapped. The new array is:

   12 2 6 4 89 8 10 **37** 68 45

   Element 12 is in italic to indicate that it was just swapped with **37**.
b) Starting from the left of the array, but beginning with the element after 12, compare each element to **37** until an element greater than **37** is found, then swap **37** and that element. The first element greater than **37** is 89, so **37** and 89 are swapped. The new array is:

   12 2 6 4 **37** 8 10 *89* 68 45

c) Starting from the right, but beginning with the element before 89, compare each element to **37** until an element less than **37** is found, then swap **37** and that element. The first element less than **37** is 10, so **37** and 10 are swapped. The new array is:

   12 2 6 4 *10* 8 **37** 89 68 45

d) Starting from the left, but beginning with the element after 10, compare each element to **37** until an element greater than **37** is found, then swap **37** and that element. There are no more elements greater than **37**, so when we compare **37** to itself we know that **37** has been placed in its final location of the sorted array.

Once the partition has been applied on the above array, there are two unsorted subarrays. The subarray with values less than 37 contains 12, 2, 6, 4, 10, and 8. The subarray with values greater than 37 contains 89, 68, and 45. The sort continues with both subarrays being partitioned in the same manner as the original array.

Based on the preceding discussion, write recursive method **`quickSort`** to sort a single-subscripted integer array. The method should receive as arguments an integer array, a starting subscript, and an ending subscript. Method **`partition`** should be called by **`quickSort`** to perform the partitioning step.

5.38 (*Maze Traversal*) The following grid of **#**s and dots (**.**) is a double-subscripted array representation of a maze.

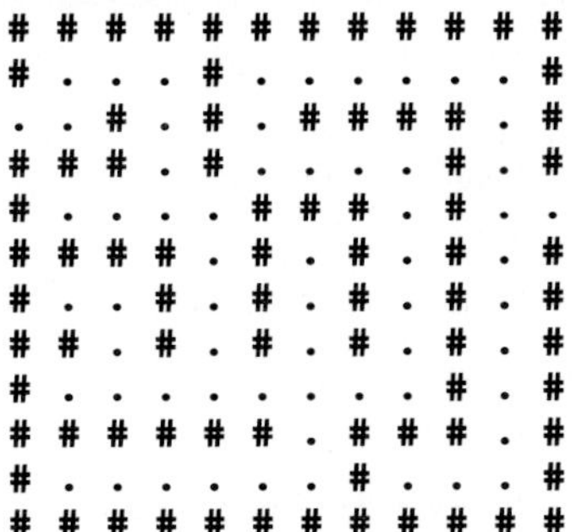

```
# # # # # # # # # # # #
# . . . # . . . . . . #
. . # . # . # # # # . #
# # # . # . . . . # . #
# . . . . # # # . # . .
# # # # . # . # . # . #
# . . # . # . # . # . #
# # . # . # . # . # . #
# . . . . . . . . # . #
# # # # # # . # # # . #
# . . . . . . # . . . #
# # # # # # # # # # # #
```

In the preceding double-subscripted array, the **#**s represent the walls of the maze and the dots represent squares in the possible paths through the maze. Moves can only be made to a location in the array that contains a dot.

There is a simple algorithm for walking through a maze that guarantees finding the exit (assuming there is an exit). If there is not an exit, you will arrive at the starting location again. Place your right hand on the wall to your right and begin walking forward. Never remove your hand from the wall. If the maze turns to the right, you follow the wall to the right. As long as you do not remove your hand from the wall, eventually you will arrive at the exit of the maze. There may be a shorter path than the one you have taken, but you are guaranteed to get out of the maze if you follow the algorithm.

Write recursive method **mazeTraverse** to walk through the maze. The method should receive as arguments a 12-by-12 character array representing the maze, and the starting location of the maze. As **mazeTraverse** attempts to locate the exit from the maze, it should place the character **X** in each square in the path. The method should display the maze after each move so the user can watch as the maze is solved.

5.39 (*Generating Mazes Randomly*) Write a method **mazeGenerator** that takes as an argument a double-subscripted 12-by-12 character array and randomly produces a maze. The method should also provide the starting and ending locations of the maze. Try your method **mazeTraverse** from Exercise 5.38 using several randomly generated mazes.

5.40 (*Mazes of Any Size*) Generalize methods **mazeTraverse** and **mazeGenerator** of Exercises 5.38 and 5.39 to process mazes of any width and height.

5.41 (*Simulation: The Tortoise and the Hare*) In this problem you will recreate one of the truly great moments in history, namely the classic race of the tortoise and the hare. You will use random number generation to develop a simulation of this memorable event.

Our contenders begin the race at "square 1" of 70 squares. Each square represents a possible position along the race course. The finish line is at square 70. The first contender to reach or pass square 70 is rewarded with a pail of fresh carrots and lettuce. The course weaves its way up the side of a slippery mountain, so occasionally the contenders lose ground.

There is a clock that ticks once per second. With each tick of the clock, your program should adjust the position of the animals according to the following rules:

Animal	Move type	Percentage of the time	Actual move
Tortoise	Fast plod	50%	3 squares to the right
	Slip	20%	6 squares to the left
	Slow plod	30%	1 square to the right
Hare	Sleep	20%	No move at all
	Big hop	20%	9 squares to the right
	Big slip	10%	12 squares to the left
	Small hop	30%	1 square to the right
	Small slip	20%	2 squares to the left

Use variables to keep track of the positions of the animals (i.e., position numbers are 1–70). Start each animal at position 1 (i.e., the "starting gate"). If an animal slips left before square 1, move the animal back to square 1.

Generate the percentages in the preceding table by producing a random integer, i, in the range $1 \leq i \leq 10$. For the tortoise, perform a "fast plod" when $1 \leq i \leq 5$, a "slip" when $6 \leq i \leq 7$, or a "slow plod" when $8 \leq i \leq 10$. Use a similar technique to move the hare.

Begin the race by printing

```
BANG !!!!!
AND THEY'RE OFF !!!!!
```

Then, for each tick of the clock (i.e., each repetition of a loop), print a 70-position line showing the letter **T** in the position of the tortoise and the letter **H** in the position of the hare. Occasionally, the contenders will land on the same square. In this case, the tortoise bites the hare and your program should print **OUCH!!!** beginning at that position. All print positions other than the **T**, the **H**, or the **OUCH!!!** (in case of a tie) should be blank.

After each line is printed, test if either animal has reached or passed square 70. If so, then print the winner and terminate the simulation. If the tortoise wins, print **TORTOISE WINS!!! YAY!!!** If the hare wins, print **Hare wins. Yuch.** If both animals win on the same tick of the clock, you may want to favor the turtle (the "underdog"), or you may want to print **It's a tie**. If neither animal wins, perform the loop again to simulate the next tick of the clock. When you are ready to run your program, assemble a group of fans to watch the race. You'll be amazed at how involved your audience gets!

Later in the book we introduce a number of Java capabilities such as graphics, images, animation, sound and multithreading. As you study those features, you might enjoy enhancing your tortoise and hare contest simulation.

Special Section: Building Your Own Computer

In the next several problems, we take a temporary diversion away from the world of high-level language programming. We "peel open" a computer and look at its internal structure. We introduce machine language programming and write several machine language programs. To make this an especially valuable experience, we then build a computer (through the technique of software-based *simulation)* on which you can execute your machine language programs!

5.42 (*Machine-Language Programming*) Let us create a computer we will call the Simpletron. As its name implies, it is a simple machine, but, as we will soon see, a powerful one as well. The Simpletron runs programs written in the only language it directly understands, that is, Simpletron Machine Language, or SML for short.

The Simpletron contains an *accumulator*—a "special register" in which information is put before the Simpletron uses that information in calculations or examines it in various ways. All information in the Simpletron is handled in terms of *words.* A word is a signed four-digit decimal number such as `+3364`, `-1293`, `+0007`, `-0001`, etc. The Simpletron is equipped with a 100-word memory, and these words are referenced by their location numbers `00`, `01`, ..., `99`.

Before running an SML program, we must *load* or place the program into memory. The first instruction (or statement) of every SML program is always placed in location `00`. The simulator will start executing at this location.

Each instruction written in SML occupies one word of the Simpletron's memory (and hence instructions are signed four-digit decimal numbers). We shall assume that the sign of an SML instruction is always plus, but the sign of a data word may be either plus or minus. Each location in the Simpletron's memory may contain either an instruction, a data value used by a program, or an unused (and hence undefined) area of memory. The first two digits of each SML instruction are the*operation code* specifying the operation to be performed. SML operation codes are summarized in Fig. 5.22.

Operation code	Meaning
Input/output operations:	
`static final int READ = 10;`	Read a word from the keyword into a specific location in memory.
`static final int WRITE = 11;`	Write a word from a specific location in memory to the screen.
Load/store operations:	
`static final int LOAD = 20;`	Load a word from a specific location in memory into the accumulator.
`static final int STORE = 21;`	Store a word from the accumulator into a specific location in memory.
Arithmetic operations:	
`static final int ADD = 30;`	Add a word from a specific location in memory to the word in the accumulator (leave result in accumulator).
`static final int SUBTRACT = 31;`	Subtract a word from a specific location in memory from the word in the accumulator (leave result in accumulator).

Fig. 5.22 Simpletron Machine Language (SML) operation codes (part 1 of 2).

Operation code	Meaning
`static final int DIVIDE = 32;`	Divide a word from a specific location in memory into the word in the accumulator (leave result in accumulator).
`static final int MULTIPLY = 33;`	Multiply a word from a specific location in memory by the word in the accumulator (leave result in accumulator).
Transfer of control operations:	
`static final int BRANCH = 40;`	Branch to a specific location in memory.
`static final int BRANCHNEG = 41;`	Branch to a specific location in memory if the accumulator is negative.
`static final int BRANCHZERO = 42;`	Branch to a specific location in memory if the accumulator is zero.
`static final int HALT = 43;`	Halt—the program has completed its task.

Fig. 5.22 Simpletron Machine Language (SML) operation codes (part 2 of 2).

The last two digits of an SML instruction are the *operand*—the address of the memory location containing the word to which the operation applies. Let's consider several simple SML programs.

The first SML program (Example 1) reads two numbers from the keyboard and computes and prints their sum. The instruction **+1007** reads the first number from the keyboard and places it into location **07** (which has been initialized to zero). Then instruction **+1008** reads the next number into location **08**. The *load* instruction, **+2007**, puts the first number into the accumulator, and the *add* instruction, **+3008**, adds the second number to the number in the accumulator. *All SML arithmetic instructions leave their results in the accumulator.* The *store* instruction, **+2109**, places the result back into memory location **09** from which the *write* instruction, **+1109**, takes the number and prints it (as a signed four-digit decimal number). The *halt* instruction, **+4300**, terminates execution.

Example 1 Location	Number	Instruction
00	+1007	(Read A)
01	+1008	(Read B)
02	+2007	(Load A)
03	+3008	(Add B)
04	+2109	(Store C)
05	+1109	(Write C)
06	+4300	(Halt)
07	+0000	(Variable A)
08	+0000	(Variable B)
09	+0000	(Result C)

Example 2 Location	Number	Instruction
`00`	`+1009`	`(Read A)`
`01`	`+1010`	`(Read B)`
`02`	`+2009`	`(Load A)`
`03`	`+3110`	`(Subtract B)`
`04`	`+4107`	`(Branch negative to 07)`
`05`	`+1109`	`(Write A)`
`06`	`+4300`	`(Halt)`
`07`	`+1110`	`(Write B)`
`08`	`+4300`	`(Halt)`
`09`	`+0000`	`(Variable A)`
`10`	`+0000`	`(Variable B)`

This SML program reads two numbers from the keyboard and determines and prints the larger value. Note the use of the instruction **`+4107`** as a conditional transfer of control, much the same as Java's **`if`** statement. Now write SML programs to accomplish each of the following tasks.

a) Use a sentinel-controlled loop to read ten positive numbers and compute and print their sum.
b) Use a counter-controlled loop to read seven numbers, some positive and some negative, and compute and print their average.
c) Read a series of numbers and determine and print the largest number. The first number read indicates how many numbers should be processed.

5.43 (*A Computer Simulator*) It may at first seem outrageous, but in this problem you are going to build your own computer. No, you will not be soldering components together. Rather, you will use the powerful technique of *software-based simulation* to create an object-oriented *software model* of the Simpletron. You will not be disappointed. Your Simpletron simulator will turn the computer you are using into a Simpletron, and you will actually be able to run, test, and debug the SML programs you wrote in Exercise 5.42. Your Simpletron will be an event-driven applet—you will click a button to execute each SML instruction and you will be able to see the instruction "in action."

When you run your Simpletron simulator, it should begin by displaying:

```
*** Welcome to Simpletron! ***
*** Please enter your program one instruction   ***
*** (or data word) at a time into the input     ***
*** text field. I will display the location     ***
*** number and a question mark (?). You then    ***
*** type the word for that location. Press the ***
*** Done button to stop entering your program. ***
```

The program should display an **`input TextField`** in which the user will type each instruction one at a time and a **`Done`** button for the user to click when the complete SML program has been entered. Simulate the memory of the Simpletron with a single-subscripted array **`memory`** that has 100 elements. Now assume that the simulator is running, and let us examine the dialog as we enter the program of Example 2 of Exercise 5.42:

```
00 ? +1009
01 ? +1010
02 ? +2009
03 ? +3110
04 ? +4107
05 ? +1109
06 ? +4300
07 ? +1110
08 ? +4300
09 ? +0000
10 ? +0000
```

Your program should use a **TextField** to display the memory location followed by a question mark. Each of the values to the right of a question mark is typed by the user into the **input TextField**. When the **Done** button is clicked, the program should display:

```
*** Program loading completed ***
*** Program execution begins  ***
```

The SML program has now been placed (or loaded) in array **memory**. The Simpletron should provide an "**Execute next instruction**" button the user can click to execute each instruction in your SML program. Execution begins with the instruction in location **00** and, like Java, continues sequentially, unless directed to some other part of the program by a transfer of control.

Use the variable **accumulator** to represent the accumulator register. Use the variable **instructionCounter** to keep track of the location in memory that contains the instruction being performed. Use the variable **operationCode** to indicate the operation currently being performed, i.e., the left two digits of the instruction word. Use the variable **operand** to indicate the memory location on which the current instruction operates. Thus, **operand** is the rightmost two digits of the instruction currently being performed. Do not execute instructions directly from memory. Rather, transfer the next instruction to be performed from memory to a variable called **instructionRegister**. Then "pick off" the left two digits and place them in **operationCode**, and "pick off" the right two digits and place them in **operand**. Each of the preceding registers should have a corresponding **TextField** in which its current value can be displayed at all times. When Simpletron begins execution, the special registers are all initialized to 0.

Now let us "walk through" the execution of the first SML instruction, **+1009** in memory location **00**. This is called an *instruction execution cycle.*

The **instructionCounter** tells us the location of the next instruction to be performed. We *fetch* the contents of that location from **memory** by using the Java statement

```
instructionRegister = memory[ instructionCounter ];
```

The operation code and the operand are extracted from the instruction register by the statements

```
operationCode = instructionRegister / 100;
operand = instructionRegister % 100;
```

Now the Simpletron must determine that the operation code is actually a *read* (versus a *write*, a *load*, etc.). A **switch** differentiates among the twelve operations of SML.

In the **switch** structure, the behavior of various SML instructions is simulated as follows (we leave the others to the reader):

read: Display the prompt "**Enter an integer**." Enable the **input TextField** so a value can be entered by the user. Read the value entered, convert it to an integer, and store it in location **memory[operand]**.

load: **accumulator = memory[operand];**

add: **accumulator += memory[operand];**

branch: We will discuss the branch instructions shortly.

halt: This instruction prints the message
***** Simpletron execution terminated *****

When the SML program completes execution, the name and contents of each register as well as the complete contents of memory should be displayed. Such a printout is often called a *computer dump* (and, no, a computer dump is not a place where old computers go). To help you program your dump method, a sample dump format is shown in Fig. 5.23. Note that a dump after executing a Simpletron program would show the actual values of instructions and data values at the moment execution terminated. The sample dump assumes the output will be sent to the display screen with a series of **System.out.print** and **System.out.println** method calls. However, we encourage you to experiment with a version that can be displayed on the applet using the **Graphics** method **drawString** or an array of **TextField** objects.

Let us proceed with the execution of our program's first instruction, namely the **+1009** in location **00**. As we have indicated, the **switch** statement simulates this by prompting the user to enter a value into the **input TextField**, reading the value, converting the value to an integer and storing it in memory location **memory[operand]**. Because your Simpletron is event driven, it waits for the user to type a value into the **input TextField** and press the *Enter key*. The value is then read into location **09**.

```
REGISTERS:
accumulator            +0000
instructionCounter        00
instructionRegister    +0000
operationCode             00
operand                   00

MEMORY:
       0     1     2     3     4     5     6     7     8     9
 0 +0000 +0000 +0000 +0000 +0000 +0000 +0000 +0000 +0000 +0000
10 +0000 +0000 +0000 +0000 +0000 +0000 +0000 +0000 +0000 +0000
20 +0000 +0000 +0000 +0000 +0000 +0000 +0000 +0000 +0000 +0000
30 +0000 +0000 +0000 +0000 +0000 +0000 +0000 +0000 +0000 +0000
40 +0000 +0000 +0000 +0000 +0000 +0000 +0000 +0000 +0000 +0000
50 +0000 +0000 +0000 +0000 +0000 +0000 +0000 +0000 +0000 +0000
60 +0000 +0000 +0000 +0000 +0000 +0000 +0000 +0000 +0000 +0000
70 +0000 +0000 +0000 +0000 +0000 +0000 +0000 +0000 +0000 +0000
80 +0000 +0000 +0000 +0000 +0000 +0000 +0000 +0000 +0000 +0000
90 +0000 +0000 +0000 +0000 +0000 +0000 +0000 +0000 +0000 +0000
```

Fig. 5.23 A sample dump.

At this point, simulation of the first instruction is completed. All that remains is to prepare the Simpletron to execute the next instruction. Since the instruction just performed was not a transfer of control, we need merely increment the instruction counter register as follows:

```
++instructionCounter;
```

This completes the simulated execution of the first instruction. When the user clicks the **Execute next instruction** button, the entire process (i.e., the instruction execution cycle) begins again with the fetch of the next instruction to be executed.

Now let us consider how the branching instructions—the transfers of control—are simulated. All we need to do is adjust the value in the instruction counter appropriately. Therefore, the unconditional branch instruction (**40**) is simulated within the **switch** as

```
instructionCounter = operand;
```

The conditional "branch if accumulator is zero" instruction is simulated as

```
if ( accumulator == 0 )
   instructionCounter = operand;
```

At this point you should implement your Simpletron simulator and run each of the SML programs you wrote in Exercise 5.42. You may embellish SML with additional features and provide for these in your simulator.

Your simulator should check for various types of errors. During the program loading phase, for example, each number the user types into the Simpletron's **memory** must be in the range **-9999** to **+9999**. Your simulator should test that each number entered is in this range, and, if not, keep prompting the user to reenter the number until the user enters a correct number.

During the execution phase, your simulator should check for various serious errors, such as attempts to divide by zero, attempts to execute invalid operation codes, accumulator overflows (i.e., arithmetic operations resulting in values larger than **+9999** or smaller than **-9999**), and the like. Such serious errors are called *fatal errors.* When a fatal error is detected, your simulator should print an error message such as:

```
*** Attempt to divide by zero ***
*** Simpletron execution abnormally terminated ***
```

and should print a full computer dump in the format we have discussed previously. This will help the user locate the error in the program.

5.44 (*Modifications to the Simpletron Simulator*) In Exercise 5.43, you wrote a software simulation of a computer that executes programs written in Simpletron Machine Language (SML). In this exercise, we propose several modifications and enhancements to the Simpletron Simulator. In Exercises 17.26 and 17.27, we propose building a compiler that converts programs written in a high-level programming language (a variation of Basic) to Simpletron Machine Language. Some of the following modifications and enhancements may be required to execute the programs produced by the compiler.

a) Extend the Simpletron Simulator's memory to contain 1000 memory locations to enable the Simpletron to handle larger programs.
b) Allow the simulator to perform modulus calculations. This requires an additional Simpletron Machine Language instruction.

c) Allow the simulator to perform exponentiation calculations. This requires an additional Simpletron Machine Language instruction.
d) Modify the simulator to use hexadecimal values rather than integer values to represent Simpletron Machine Language instructions.
e) Modify the simulator to allow output of a newline. This requires an additional Simpletron Machine Language instruction.
f) Modify the simulator to process floating-point values in addition to integer values.
g) Modify the simulator to handle string input. *Hint:* Each Simpletron word can be divided into two groups, each holding a two-digit integer. Each two-digit integer represents the ASCII decimal equivalent of a character. Add a machine-language instruction that will input a string and store the string beginning at a specific Simpletron memory location. The first half of the word at that location will be a count of the number of characters in the string (i.e., the length of the string). Each succeeding half-word contains one ASCII character expressed as two decimal digits. The machine-language instruction converts each character into its ASCII equivalent and assigns it to a "half-word."
h) Modify the simulator to handle output of strings stored in the format of part (g). *Hint:* Add a machine-language instruction that will print a string beginning at a certain Simpletron memory location. The first half of the word at that location is a count of the number of characters in the string (i.e., the length of the string). Each succeeding half-word contains one ASCII character expressed as two decimal digits. The machine-language instruction checks the length and prints the string by translating each two-digit number into its equivalent character.

6

Object-Based Programming

Objectives

- To understand encapsulation and data hiding.
- To understand the notions of data abstraction and abstract data types (ADTs).
- To create Java ADTs, namely classes.
- To be able to create, use and destroy objects.
- To be able to control access to object instance variables and methods.
- To appreciate the value of object orientation.
- To understand class variables and class methods.
- To understand the use of the **`this`** reference.

My object all sublime
I shall achieve in time.
W. S. Gilbert

Is it a world to hide virtues in?
William Shakespeare, Twelfth Night

Your public servants serve you right.
Adlai Stevenson

But what, to serve our private ends,
Forbids the cheating of our friends?
Charles Churchill

This above all: to thine own self be true.
William Shakespeare, Hamlet

Have no friends not equal to yourself.
Confucius

Outline

6.1 Introduction

Now we investigate object orientation in Java in greater depth. Why have we deferred this until now? First, the objects we will build will be composed in part of structured program pieces, so we needed to establish a basis in structured programming with control structures. Second, we wanted to study methods in depth. Third, we wanted to familiarize the reader with arrays which are Java objects.

Through our discussions of object-oriented Java programs in Chapters 1 through 5, we have introduced many of the basic concepts (i.e., "object think") and terminology (i.e., "object speak") of object-oriented programming in Java. In these chapters, we also discussed our program-development methodology: We analyzed many typical problems that required a program—either a Java applet or a Java application—to be built, determined what classes from the Java API were needed to implement the program, determined what instance variables our applet or application needed to have, determined what methods our applet or application needed to have and specified how an object of our class needed to collaborate with objects of Java API classes to accomplish the overall goals of the program.

Let us briefly review some key concepts and terminology of object orientation. OOP *encapsulates* data (*attributes*) and methods (*behaviors*) into *objects;* the data and methods of an object are intimately tied together. Objects have the property of *information hiding.* This means that although objects may know how to communicate with one another across well-defined *interfaces,* objects normally are not allowed to know how other objects are implemented—implementation details are hidden within the objects themselves. Surely it is possible to drive a car effectively without knowing the details of how engines, transmissions and exhaust systems work internally. We will see why information hiding is so crucial to good software engineering.

In C and other *procedural programming languages,* programming tends to be *action-oriented,* whereas in Java programming is *object-oriented.* In C, the unit of programming is the *function* (functions are called *methods* in Java). In Java, the unit of programming is the *class* from which objects are eventually *instantiated* (i.e., created). Functions do not disappear in Java; rather they are encapsulated as methods with the data they process within the "walls" of classes.

C programmers concentrate on writing functions. Groups of actions that perform some task are formed into functions and functions are grouped to form programs. Data is certainly important in C, but the view is that data exists primarily in support of the actions that functions perform. The *verbs* in a system-requirements document help the C programmer determine the set of functions that will work together to implement the system.

Java programmers concentrate on creating their own *user-defined types* called *classes.* Classes are also referred to as *programmer-defined types*. Each class contains data as well as the set of methods that manipulate the data. The data components of a class are called *instance variables* (these are called *data members* in C++). Just as an instance of a built-in type such as **int** is called a *variable,* an instance of a user-defined type (i.e., a class) is called an *object.* The focus of attention in Java is on objects rather than methods. The *nouns* in a system-requirements document help the Java programmer determine an initial set of classes with which to begin the design process. These classes are then used to instantiate objects that will work together to implement the system.

This chapter explains how to create and use objects, a subject we like to call *object-based programming (OBP).* Chapter 7 introduces *inheritance* and *polymorphism*—the two key technologies that enable true *object-oriented programming (OOP).*

Performance Tip 6.1

All Java objects are passed by reference. Only a memory address is passed, not a copy of a possibly large object (as would be the case in a pass by value).

Software Engineering Observation 6.1

It is important to write programs that are understandable and easy to maintain. Change is the rule rather than the exception. Programmers should anticipate that their code will be modified. As we will see, classes facilitate program modifiability.

6.2 Implementing a Time Abstract Data Type with a Class

The applet of Fig. 6.1 consists of two classes—**Time1** and **TimeTest**. Class **Time1** is defined in file **Time1.java** (specified in the comment at line 1). Class **TimeTest** is defined in file **TimeTest.java** (specified in the comment at line 45). Note that although these two classes are defined in separate files, we number the lines in the program consecutively across both files for discussion purposes in the text.

Figure 6.1 (part 1) contains a simple definition for class **Time1**. Our **Time1** class definition begins on line 5. The *body* of the class definition is delineated with left and right braces (**{** and **}**). Class **Time1** contains three integer instance variables—**hour**, **minute** and **second**.

```
1  // Fig. 6.1: Time1.java
2  // Time1 class definition
3  import java.text.DecimalFormat;  // used for number formatting
4
5  public class Time1 {
6     private int hour;     // 0 - 23
7     private int minute;   // 0 - 59
8     private int second;   // 0 - 59
9
10    // Time1 constructor initializes each instance variable
11    // to zero. Ensures that each Time1 object starts in a
12    // consistent state.
13    public Time1() { setTime( 0, 0, 0 ); }
14
15    // Set a new time value using military time. Perform
16    // validity checks on the data. Set invalid values
17    // to zero.
18    public void setTime( int h, int m, int s )
19    {
20       hour = ( ( h >= 0 && h < 24 ) ? h : 0 );
21       minute = ( ( m >= 0 && m < 60 ) ? m : 0 );
22       second = ( ( s >= 0 && s < 60 ) ? s : 0 );
23    }
24
25    // Convert time to String in military-time format
26    public String toMilitaryString()
27    {
28       DecimalFormat twoDigits = new DecimalFormat( "00" );
29
30       return twoDigits.format( hour ) +
31              twoDigits.format( minute );
32    }
33
34    // Convert time to String in standard-time format
35    public String toString()
36    {
37       DecimalFormat twoDigits = new DecimalFormat( "00" );
38
39       return ( ( hour == 12 || hour == 0 ) ? 12 : hour % 12 ) +
40              ":" + twoDigits.format( minute ) +
41              ":" + twoDigits.format( second ) +
42              ( hour < 12 ? " AM" : " PM" );
43    }
44 }
```

Fig. 6.1 Abstract data type **Time1** implementation as a class (part 1 of 3).

```
45 // Fig. 6.1: TimeTest.java
46 // Class TimeTest to exercise class Time1
47 import java.awt.Graphics;
48 import java.applet.Applet;
49
50 public class TimeTest extends Applet {
51    private Time1 t;
52
53    public void init()
54    {
55       t = new Time1();
56    }
57
58    public void paint( Graphics g )
59    {
60       g.drawString( "The initial military time is: " +
61                     t.toMilitaryString(), 25, 25 );
62       g.drawString( "The initial standard time is: " +
63                     t.toString(), 25, 40 );
64
65       t.setTime( 13, 27, 6 );
66       g.drawString( "Military time after setTime is: " +
67                     t.toMilitaryString(), 25, 70 );
68       g.drawString( "Standard time after setTime is: " +
69                     t.toString(), 25, 85 );
70
71       t.setTime( 99, 99, 99 );
72       g.drawString( "After attempting invalid settings:",
73                     25, 115 );
74       g.drawString( "Military time: " +
75                     t.toMilitaryString(), 25, 130 );
76       g.drawString( "Standard time: " + t.toString(),
77                     25, 145 );
78    }
79 }
```

Fig. 6.1 Abstract data type **Time1** implementation as a class (part 2 of 3).

The **public** and **private** keywords are called *member access modifiers.* Any instance variable or method declared with the member access modifier **public** is accessible wherever the program has access to an object of class **Time**. Any instance variable or method declared with member access modifier **private** is accessible only to methods of the class. Every instance variable or method definition should be explicitly preceded by a member access modifier. Member access modifiers can appear multiple times and in any order in a class definition.

Good Programming Practice 6.1

Group members by member access modifier in a class definition for clarity and readability.

The three integer instance variables **hour**, **minute** and **second** are each declared (lines 6–8) with the **private** member access modifier. This indicates that these instance

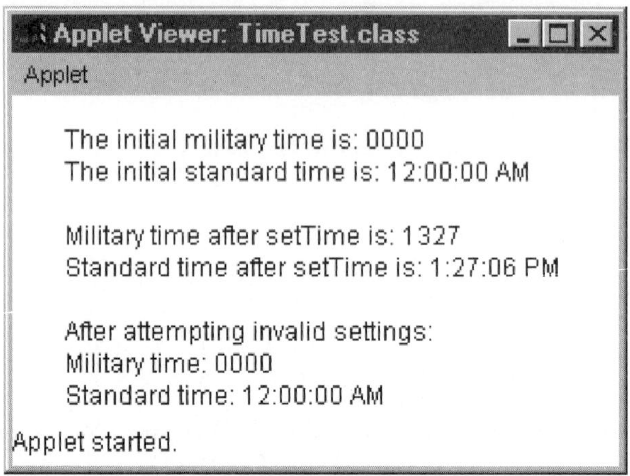

Fig. 6.1 Abstract data type **`Time1`** implementation as a class (part 3 of 3).

variables of the class are only accessible to methods of the class. Instance variables are normally declared **`private`** and methods are normally declared **`public`**. It is possible to have **`private`** methods and **`public`** data as we will see later. The **`private`** methods are often called *utility methods* or *helper methods* because they can only be called by other methods of that class and are used to support the operation of those methods. Using **`public`** data is uncommon and is a dangerous programming practice.

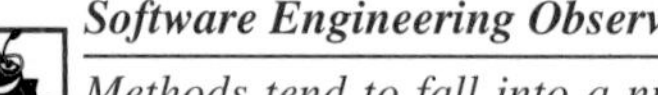

Software Engineering Observation 6.2

Methods tend to fall into a number of different categories: methods that get the values of **`private`** *instance variables; methods that set the values of* **`private`** *instance variables; methods that implement the features of the class; and methods that perform various mechanical chores for the class such as initializing class objects, assigning class objects, converting between classes and built-in types or between classes and other classes.*

Access methods can read or display data. Another common use for access methods is to test the truth or falsity of conditions—such methods are often called *predicate methods.* An example of a predicate method would be an **`isEmpty`** method for any container class—a class capable of holding many objects—such as a linked list, a stack or a queue (these data structures are discussed in depth in Chapters 17 and 18). A program might test **`isEmpty`** before attempting to read another item from the container object. A program might test **`isFull`** before attempting to insert another item into a container object.

Class **`Time`** contains the following **`public`** methods—**`Time`** (line 13), **`setTime`** (line 18), **`toMilitaryString`** (line 26) and **`toString`** (line 35). These are the *public methods,* or *public services* or *public interface* of the class. These methods are used by *clients* (i.e., portions of a program that are users) of the class to manipulate the data stored in objects of the class.

Notice the method with the same name as the class (line 13); it is the *constructor* method of that class. A constructor is a special method that initializes the instance variables of a class object. A class's constructor method is called automatically when an object of that class is created (instantiated). It is common to have several constructors for a class; this is accomplished through method overloading (as we will see in a later example). Constructors can take arguments but cannot return a value.

Common Programming Error 6.1

Attempting to declare a return type for a constructor and/or attempting to return a value from a constructor is a syntax error.

Method **setTime** (line 18) takes three integer arguments and uses them to set the time. Each argument is used in a conditional expression that determines if the value is in range. For example, the **hour** value must be greater than or equal to 0 and less than 24 because we represent the time in military time format. Any value outside this range is an invalid value and is set to zero. In such a case, the program may want to indicate that an invalid time setting occurred. We explore this possibility in the exercises.

Method **toMilitaryString** (line 26) takes no arguments and returns a **String** (from package **java.lang** that is imported automatically). This method produces a military-time-format string consisting of four digits—two for the hour and two for the minute. For example 0830 represents 8:30 AM. Line 28

```
DecimalFormat twoDigits = new DecimalFormat( "00" );
```

creates an instance of class **DecimalFormat** (from package **java.text** imported at line 3) to help format the military time. Object **twoDigits** is initialized with the string **"00"** that indicates the number format should consist of two digits—each **0** is a placeholder for a digit. If the number being formatted is a single digit, it is automatically preceded by a leading **0** (i.e., **8** is formatted as **08**). The return statement at lines 30 and 31

```
return twoDigits.format( hour ) +
       twoDigits.format( minute );
```

uses method **format** (that returns a formatted string) from object **twoDigits** to format the **hour** and **minute** values into two-digit strings. Those strings are concatenated with the **+** operator and returned from method **toMilitaryString**.

Method **toString** (line 35) takes no arguments and returns a **String**. This method produces a standard-time-format string consisting of the **hour**, **minute** and **second** values separated by colons and an AM or PM indicator as in **1:27:06 PM**. This method uses the same **DecimalFormat** techniques as method **toMilitaryString** to guarantee that the **minute** and **second** values each appear with two digits.

Once the class has been defined, it can be used as a type in declarations such as:

```
Time1 sunset,          // reference to object of type Time1
      TimeArray[];     // reference to array of Time1 objects
```

The class name is a new type specifier. There may be many objects of a class, just as there may be many variables of a primitive data type such as **int**. The programmer can create new class types as needed; this is one of the reasons why Java is an *extensible language.*

Figure 6.1 (part 2) uses the **Time1** class. Applet **TimeTest** declares an instance variable of class **Time1** called **t** (line 51). Note that class **Time1** was not imported into the

TimeTest.java file. This is because both classes in this program are defined in the same directory on disk and the compiled **.class** files for each class are placed in that same directory. If the **.class** files for the classes used in a program are in the same directory as the class that uses them, **import** statements are not required. We import classes from the Java API because their **.class** files are not stored in the same directory with each program we write.

Object **t** is instantiated in the **init** method with line 55

```
t = new Time1();
```

When the object is instantiated, the **Time1** constructor is called automatically and invokes method **setTime** to explicitly initialize each private instance variable to **0**. Next, the applet's **paint** method is automatically invoked and the time is printed in military format (using method **toMilitaryString**) and standard format (using method **toString**) to confirm that the data were initialized properly. The time is then set to another correct value using the **setTime** method and the time is printed again in both formats. Method **setTime** then attempts to set the instance variables to invalid values and the time is again printed in both formats.

Again, note that the instance variables **hour**, **minute** and **second** are each declared **private**. Private instance variables of a class are not accessible outside the class. The philosophy here is that the actual data representation used within the class is of no concern to the class's clients. For example, it would be perfectly reasonable for the class to represent the time internally as the number of seconds since midnight. Clients could use the same public methods and get the same results without being aware of this. In this sense, the implementation of a class is said to be *hidden* from its clients. Exercise 6.18 asks you to make precisely this modification to the **Time1** class of Fig. 6.1 and show that there is no visible change to the clients of the class.

Software Engineering Observation 6.3

Information hiding promotes program modifiability and simplifies the client's perception of a class.

Software Engineering Observation 6.4

Clients of a class can (and should) use the class without knowing the internal details of how the class is implemented. If the class implementation is changed (to improve performance, for example), provided the class's interface remains constant, the class clients' source code need not change. This makes it much easier to modify systems.

In this program, the **Time1** constructor simply initializes the instance variables to 0 (i.e., the military time equivalent of 12 AM). This ensures that the object is created in a *consistent state*—i.e., all instance variable values are valid. Invalid values cannot be stored in the instance variables of a **Time1** object because the constructor is automatically called when the **Time1** object is created and subsequent attempts by a client to modify the instance variables are scrutinized by the method **setTime**.

Instance variables can be initialized where they are declared in the class body, by the class's constructor, or they can be assigned values by "set" methods.

Good Programming Practice 6.2

Initialize instance variables of a class in that class's constructor.

Every class may include a *finalizer* method called **finalize** that does "termination housekeeping" on each class object before the memory for the object is garbage collected by the system. We will discuss garbage collection and finalizers in detail later.

It is interesting that the **toMilitaryString** and **toString** methods take no arguments. This is because these methods implicitly know that they are to manipulate the instance variables of the particular **Time1** object for which they are invoked. This makes method calls more concise than conventional function calls in procedural programming. It also reduces the likelihood of passing the wrong arguments, the wrong types of arguments and/or the wrong number of arguments as often happens in C function calls.

Software Engineering Observation 6.5

Using an object-oriented programming approach can often simplify method calls by reducing the number of parameters to be passed. This benefit of object-oriented programming derives from the fact that encapsulation of instance variables and methods within an object gives the methods the right to access the instance variables.

Classes simplify programming because the client (or user of the class object) need only be concerned with the operations encapsulated in the object. Such operations are usually designed to be client oriented rather than implementation oriented. Clients need not be concerned with a class's implementation. Interfaces do change, but less frequently than implementations. When an implementation changes, implementation-dependent code must change accordingly. By hiding the implementation we eliminate the possibility of other program parts becoming dependent on the details of the class implementation.

Often, classes do not have to be created "from scratch." Rather, they may be *derived* from other classes that provide operations the new classes can use, or classes can include objects of other classes as members. Such *software reuse* can greatly enhance programmer productivity. Deriving new classes from existing classes is called *inheritance* and is discussed in detail in Chapter 7. Including class objects as members of other classes is called *composition* or *aggregation* and is discussed later in this chapter.

6.3 Class Scope

A class's instance variables and methods belong to that *class's scope.* Within a class's scope, class members are immediately accessible by all of that class's methods and can be referenced simply by name. Outside a class's scope, class members cannot be referenced directly by name. Those class members (such as **public** members) that are visible can only be accessed off a "handle," i.e., primitive data type members can be referred to by **objectReferenceName.primitiveVariableName** and object members can be referenced by **objectReferenceName.objectMemberName**.

Variables defined in a method are known only to that method, i.e., they are local variables to that method. Such variables may be said to have block scope. If a method defines a variable with the same name as a variable with class scope (i.e., an instance variable), the class-scope variable is hidden by the method-scope variable in the method scope. A hidden instance variable can be accessed in the method by preceding its name with the keyword **this** and the dot operator as in **this.x**.

6.4 Controlling Access to Members

The member access modifiers **public** and **private** are used to control access to a class's instance variables and methods. (In Chapter 7, we will introduce the additional access specifier **protected**.)

As we stated previously, the primary purpose of **public** methods is to present to the class's clients a view of the *services* the class provides—i.e., the public interface of the class. Clients of the class need not be concerned with how the class accomplishes its tasks. For this reason, the **private** members of a class as well as the definitions of its **public** methods (i.e., the class's implementation) are not accessible to the clients of a class.

Common Programming Error 6.2

An attempt by a method which is not a member of a particular class to access a **private** *member of that class is a syntax error.*

Figure 6.2 demonstrates that **private** class members are not accessible by name outside the class. Lines 17 and 19 attempt to directly access the **private** instance variables **hour** and **minute** of **Time1** object **t**. When this program is compiled, the compiler generates two errors stating that the **private** member specified in each statement is not accessible. (Note: This program assumes the **Time1** class from Fig. 6.1 is used.)

```
1  // Fig. 6.2: TimeTest.java
2  // Demonstrate errors resulting from attempts
3  // to access private class members.
4  import java.awt.Graphics;
5  import java.applet.Applet;
6
7  public class TimeTest extends Applet {
8     private Time1 t;
9
10    public void init()
11    {
12       t = new Time1();
13    }
14
15    public void paint( Graphics g )
16    {
17       t.hour = 7;
18
19       g.drawString( "minute = " + t.minute, 25, 25 );
20    }
21 }
```

Fig. 6.2 Erroneous attempt to access private members of a class (part 1 of 2).

```
TimeTest.java:17: Variable hour in class Time1 not
                  accessible from class TimeTest.
      t.hour = 7;
       ^
TimeTest.java:19: Variable minute in class Time1 not
                  accessible from class TimeTest.
      g.drawString( "minute = " + t.minute, 25, 25 );
                                   ^
2 errors
```

Fig. 6.2 Erroneous attempt to access private members of a class (part 2 of 2).

Good Programming Practice 6.3

Our preference is to list the **`private`** *members of a class first.*

Good Programming Practice 6.4

Despite the fact that **`private`** *and* **`public`** *members may be repeated and intermixed, list all the* **`private`** *members of a class first in one group and then list all the* **`public`** *members in another group.*

Software Engineering Observation 6.6

Keep all the instance variables of a class **`private`**. *When necessary provide* **`public`** *methods to set the values of* **`private`** *instance variables and to get the values of* **`private`** *instance variables. This architecture helps hide the implementation of a class from its clients, which reduces bugs and improves program modifiability.*

Software Engineering Observation 6.7

Class designers use **`private`** *and* **`public`** *members to enforce the notion of information hiding and the principle of least privilege.*

Access to **`private`** data should be carefully controlled by the class's methods. For example, to allow clients to read the value of **`private`** data, the class can provide a *"get" method* (also called an *accessor method*). To enable clients to modify **`private`** data, the class can provide a *"set" method* (also called a *mutator method*). Such modification would seem to violate the notion of **`private`** data. But a *set* method can provide data validation capabilities (such as range checking) to ensure that the value is set properly. A *set* method can also translate between the form of the data used in the interface and the form used in the implementation. A *get* method need not expose the data in "raw" format; rather, the *get* method can edit the data and limit the view of the data the client will see.

Software Engineering Observation 6.8

The class designer need not provide set and/or get methods for each **`private`** *data* member; *these capabilities should be provided only when it makes sense and after careful thought by the class designer.*

Testing and Debugging Tip 6.1

Making the instance variables of a class **`private`** *and the methods of the class* **`public`** *facilitates debugging because problems with data manipulations are localized to the class's methods.*

6.5 Creating Packages

As we have seen in almost every example in the text, classes and interfaces from preexisting libraries such as the Java API can be imported into a Java program. Each class and interface in the Java API belongs to a specific package that contains a group of related classes and interfaces. Packages provide a mechanism for software reuse. One of our goals as programmers is to create reusable software components so we are not required to repeatedly redefine code in separate programs. The program of Fig. 6.3 illustrates how to create your own package and use a class from that package in a program.

Line 3

```
package com.deitel.jhtp2.ch06;    // place Time1 in a package
```

uses a ***`package`*** *statement* to define a **`package`** named **`com.deitel.jhtp2.ch06`**. Placing a **`package`** statement at the beginning of a Java source file indicates that the class defined in the file is part of the specified package. The only two statements in Java that can appear outside the braces of a class definition are **`package`** statements and **`import`** statements.

When a Java source file containing a **`package`** statement is compiled, the resulting **`.class`** file is placed in the directory specified by the **`package`** statement. The preceding **`package`** statement, indicates that the class in this file—**`Time1`**—should be placed in the directory **`ch06`**. The other names—**`com`**, **`deitel`**, and **`jhtp2`**—are also directories. The directory names in the **`package`** statement specify the exact location of the classes in the package. To locate the classes in this package, the compiler first looks in the directory **`com`**. Directory **`com`** contains the subdirectory **`deitel`**. Directory **`deitel`** contains the subdirectory **`jhtp2`**. Finally, directory **`jhtp2`** contains subdirectory **`ch06`**.

In an effort to provide unique names for every package, Sun Microsystems (the creator of Java) has defined a convention for package naming. Every package name should start with your Internet domain name in reverse order. For example, our Internet domain name is **`deitel.com`** so we began our package name with **`com.deitel`**. After the domain name is reversed, you can choose the names you want for your package. If you are part of a company with many divisions or a university with many schools, you may want to use the name of your division or school as the next name in the package. We chose to use **`jhtp2`** as the next name in our package name to indicate that this class is from *Java How to Program: Second Edition*. The last name in our package name specifies that this package is for Chapter 6.

Like all other classes, a class in a package must be compiled. However, there is an extra option that must be passed to the compiler that specifies where to create all the directories in the **`package`** statement. For example, we used the compilation command

```
javac -d c:\packages Time1.java
```

```java
// Fig. 6.3: Time1.java
// Time1 class definition
package com.deitel.jhtp2.ch06;    // place Time1 in a package
import java.text.DecimalFormat;  // used for number formatting

public class Time1 {
   private int hour;     // 0 - 23
   private int minute;   // 0 - 59
   private int second;   // 0 - 59

   // Time1 constructor initializes each instance variable
   // to zero. Ensures that each Time1 object starts in a
   // consistent state.
   public Time1() { setTime( 0, 0, 0 ); }

   // Set a new time value using military time. Perform
   // validity checks on the data. Set invalid values
   // to zero.
   public void setTime( int h, int m, int s )
   {
      hour = ( ( h >= 0 && h < 24 ) ? h : 0 );
      minute = ( ( m >= 0 && m < 60 ) ? m : 0 );
      second = ( ( s >= 0 && s < 60 ) ? s : 0 );
   }

   // Convert time to String in military-time format
   public String toMilitaryString()
   {
      DecimalFormat twoDigits = new DecimalFormat( "00" );

      return twoDigits.format( hour ) +
             twoDigits.format( minute );
   }

   // Convert time to String in standard-time format
   public String toString()
   {
      DecimalFormat twoDigits = new DecimalFormat( "00" );

      return ( ( hour == 12 || hour == 0 ) ? 12 : hour % 12 ) +
             ":" + twoDigits.format( minute ) +
             ":" + twoDigits.format( second ) +
             ( hour < 12 ? " AM" : " PM" );
   }
}
```

Fig. 6.3 Creating a package for software reuse (part 1 of 2).

```
// Fig. 6.3: TimeTest.java
// Class TimeTest to use imported class Time1
import java.awt.Graphics;
import java.applet.Applet;
import com.deitel.jhtp2.ch06.Time1;  // import our Time1 class

public class TimeTest extends Applet {
   private Time1 t;

   public void init()
   {
      t = new Time1();
      t.setTime( 13, 27, 06 );
   }

   public void paint( Graphics g )
   {
      g.drawString( "Military time is: " +
                    t.toMilitaryString(), 25, 25 );
      g.drawString( "Standard time is: " +
                    t.toString(), 25, 40 );
   }
}
```

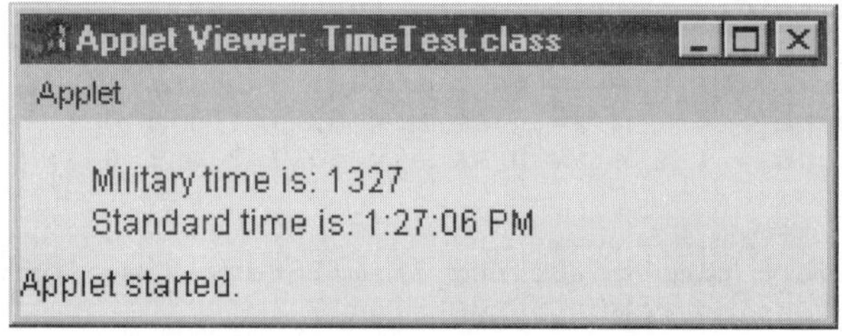

Fig. 6.3 Creating a package for software reuse (part 2 of 2).

to specify that the first directory specified in our package name should be placed in the directory **c:\packages** (on our Windows 95 computer). After executing the compilation command, the directory **c:\packages** contains a directory called **com**, **com** contains a directory called **deitel**, **deitel** contains a directory called **jhtp2**, and **jhtp2** contains a directory called **ch06**. In the **ch06** directory, you can find the file **Time1.class**. If you are operating on a UNIX computer, a typical compilation command would be

```
javac -d $HOME/packages Time1.java
```

This results in the same directory structure discussed above with the **packages** directory appearing in the home directory for your UNIX account.

There is one final step that is required to enable your programs to use the new package—the package must be inserted into your *class path*. The class path indicates to the compiler where to search on your computer for your packages. The class path is specified with an *environment variable* called **CLASSPATH**. Environment variables are often used to indicate the locations on your computer of certain types of information (such as class libraries).

On Windows 95, **CLASSPATH** is defined in a start-up file called **autoexec.bat** that executes when you turn on your computer. To use the new package on a Windows 95 computer, open the **autoexec.bat** file in a text editor and add the line:

```
set CLASSPATH=c:\packages
```

If a **CLASSPATH** environment variable already exists in this file, add a semicolon (**;**) followed by **c:\packages** to the end of the existing path. You will need to restart your computer for these changes to take effect. On Windows NT, the **CLASSPATH** can be set through the *System* option in the *Control Panel* (see your instructor for help if necessary).

On UNIX computers, your class path is also defined in a start-up file. However, the name of this file and how you define the environment variable depend on the UNIX shell used on your computer. For the C shell, open the file **.login** in a text editor and add the line:

```
setenv CLASSPATH $HOME/packages
```

If a **CLASSPATH** environment variable already exists in this file, add a colon (**:**) followed by **$HOME/packages** to the end of the existing path. From your command line, execute the command

```
source .login
```

for these environment variable changes to take effect.

For Bourne and Korn shells, open the file **.profile** in a text editor and add the lines:

```
CLASSPATH=$HOME/packages
export CLASSPATH
```

If a **CLASSPATH** environment variable already exists in this file, add a colon (**:**) followed by **$HOME/packages** to the end of the existing path. From your command line, execute the command

```
. .profile
```

for these environment variable changes to take effect.

6.6 Initializing Class Objects: Constructors

When an object is created, its members can be initialized by a *constructor* method. A constructor is a method with the same name as the class. The programmer provides the constructor which is then invoked automatically each time an object of that class is instantiated. Instance variables can be initialized implicitly to their default values (0 for primitive numeric types, **false** for **boolean**s and **null** for references), can be initialized in a constructor of the class, or their values may be set later after the object is created. Constructors cannot specify return types or return values. Constructors may be overloaded to provide a variety of means for initializing objects of a class.

Good Programming Practice 6.5

When appropriate (almost always), provide a constructor to ensure that every object is properly initialized with meaningful values.

When an object of a class is created, *initializers* can be provided in parentheses to the right of the class name. These initializers are passed as arguments to the class's constructor. This technique is demonstrated in the next example.

If no constructors are defined for a class, the compiler creates a *default constructor* that takes no arguments. The default constructor for a class calls the constructor for the class that this class extends then proceeds to initialize the instance variables in the manner we discussed previously (i.e., primitive numeric data type variables to **0**, ***boolean***s to ***false*** and references to ***null***). It is also possible for the programmer to provide a *no-argument constructor* as we will see in the next example. If any constructors are defined for a class by the programmer, Java will not create a default constructor for the class.

Common Programming Error 6.3

If constructors are provided for a class, but none are no-argument constructors, and an attempt is made to call a no-argument constructor to initialize an object of the class, a syntax error occurs. A constructor may be called with no arguments only if there are no constructors for the class (the default constructor is called) or if there is a no-argument constructor.

6.7 Using Overloaded Constructors

Methods of a class can be overloaded, but only by other methods of the same class. To overload a method of a class, simply provide a separate method definition with the same name for each version of the method. Remember that overloaded methods must have different parameter lists.

Common Programming Error 6.4

Attempting to overload a method of a class with a method not in that class's scope.

The constructor from Fig. 6.1 initialized **hour**, **minute** and **second** to **0** (i.e., 12 midnight in military time). Figure 6.4 overloads the constructor method to provide a convenient variety of ways to initialize **Time2** objects. The constructors guarantee that every object begins its existence in a consistent state. In this program, each constructor calls method **setTime** with the values passed to the constructor to ensure that the value supplied for **hour** is in the range 0 to 23 and that the values for **minute** and **second** are each in the range 0 to 59. If a value is out of range, it is set to zero by **setTime** (this is an example of ensuring that an instance variable remains in a consistent state). Line 68 shows that the no-argument constructor is invoked by placing an empty set of parentheses after the class name when allocating a **Time2** object with **new**. Lines 69 through 72 of the program demonstrate passing arguments to the **Time2** constructors. The appropriate constructor is invoked by matching the number, types and order of the arguments specified in the constructor call with the number, types and order of the parameters specified in each method definition. The matching constructor is called automatically.

```
// Fig. 6.4: Time2.java
// Time2 class definition
package com.deitel.jhtp2.ch06;    // place Time2 in a package
import java.text.DecimalFormat;   // used for number formatting

public class Time2 {
   private int hour;      // 0 - 23
   private int minute;    // 0 - 59
   private int second;    // 0 - 59

   // Time2 constructor initializes each instance variable
   // to zero. Ensures that Time object starts in a
   // consistent state.
   public Time2() { setTime( 0, 0, 0 ); }

   // Time2 constructor: hour supplied, minute and second
   // defaulted to 0.
   public Time2( int h ) { setTime( h, 0, 0 ); }

   // Time2 constructor: hour and minute supplied, second
   // defaulted to 0.
   public Time2( int h, int m ) { setTime( h, m, 0 ); }

   // Time2 constructor: hour, minute and second supplied.
   public Time2( int h, int m, int s ) { setTime( h, m, s ); }

   // Set a new Time value using military time. Perform
   // validity checks on the data. Set invalid values
   // to zero.
   public void setTime( int h, int m, int s )
   {
      hour = ( ( h >= 0 && h < 24 ) ? h : 0 );
      minute = ( ( m >= 0 && m < 60 ) ? m : 0 );
      second = ( ( s >= 0 && s < 60 ) ? s : 0 );
   }

   // Convert time to String in military-time format
   public String toMilitaryString()
   {
      DecimalFormat twoDigits = new DecimalFormat( "00" );

      return twoDigits.format( hour ) +
             twoDigits.format( minute );
   }

```

Fig. 6.4 Using overloaded constructors (part 1 of 4).

```
   // Convert time to String in standard-time format
   public String toString()
   {
      DecimalFormat twoDigits = new DecimalFormat( "00" );

      return ( ( hour == 12 || hour == 0 ) ? 12 : hour % 12 ) +
             ":" + twoDigits.format( minute ) +
             ":" + twoDigits.format( second ) +
             ( hour < 12 ? " AM" : " PM" );
   }
}
```

Fig. 6.4 Using overloaded constructors (part 2 of 4).

```
// Fig. 6.4: TimeTest.java
// Using overloaded constructors
import java.awt.Graphics;
import java.applet.Applet;
import com.deitel.jhtp2.ch06.Time2;

public class TimeTest extends Applet {
   private Time2 t1, t2, t3, t4, t5;

   public void init()
   {
      t1 = new Time2();
      t2 = new Time2( 2 );
      t3 = new Time2( 21, 34 );
      t4 = new Time2( 12, 25, 42 );
      t5 = new Time2( 27, 74, 99 );
   }

   public void paint( Graphics g )
   {
      g.drawString( "Constructed with:", 25, 25 );
      g.drawString( "all arguments defaulted:", 25, 40 );
      g.drawString( "    " + t1.toMilitaryString(),
                    25, 55 );
      g.drawString( "    " + t1.toString(), 25, 70 );

      g.drawString( "hour specified; minute " +
                    "and second defaulted:", 25, 85 );
      g.drawString( "    " + t2.toMilitaryString(),
                    25, 100 );
      g.drawString( "    " + t2.toString(), 25, 115 );

```

Fig. 6.4 Using overloaded constructors (part 3 of 4).

```
        g.drawString( "hour and minute specified; " +
                      "second defaulted:", 25, 130 );
        g.drawString( "    " + t3.toMilitaryString(),
                      25, 145 );
        g.drawString( "    " + t3.toString(), 25, 160 );

        g.drawString( "hour, minute, and second specified:",
                      25, 175 );
        g.drawString( "    " + t4.toMilitaryString(),
                      25, 190 );
        g.drawString( "    " + t4.toString(), 25, 205 );

        g.drawString( "all invalid values specified:",
                      25, 220 );
        g.drawString( "    " + t5.toMilitaryString(),
                      25, 235 );
        g.drawString( "    " + t5.toString(), 25, 250 );
    }
}
```

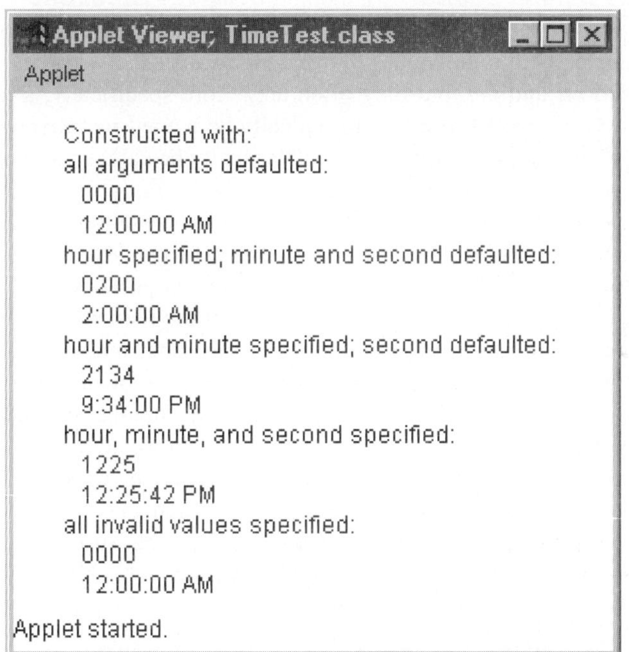

Fig. 6.4 Using overloaded constructors (part 4 of 4).

Notice that the constructors that do not explicitly receive three values for **hour**, **minute** and **second** call **setTime** with zeros for the missing values to satisfy **set-Time**'s requirement of three arguments.

Note that each **Time2** constructor could be written to include a copy of the appropriate statements from method **setTime**. This may be slightly more efficient because the extra call to **setTime** is eliminated. However, coding the **Time2** constructors and method **setTime** identically makes maintenance of this program more difficult. If the implementation of method **setTime** changes, the implementation of the **Time2** constructors would need to change accordingly. Having the **Time2** constructors call **setTime** directly requires any changes to the implementation of **setTime** to be made only once. This reduces the likelihood of a programming error when altering the implementation.

Software Engineering Observation 6.9

If a method of a class already provides all or part of the functionality required by a constructor (or other method) of the class, call that method from the constructor (or other method). This simplifies the maintenance of the code and reduces the likelihood of an error if the implementation of the code is modified. It is also an effective example of reuse.

6.8 Using *Set* and *Get* Methods

Private instance variables can be manipulated only by methods of the class. A typical manipulation might be the adjustment of a customer's bank balance (e.g., a private instance variable of a class **BankAccount**) by a method **computeInterest**.

Classes often provide **public** methods to allow clients of the class to *set* (i.e., assign values to) or *get* (i.e., obtain the values of) **private** instance variables. These methods need not be called *set* and *get*, but they often are. More specifically, a method that sets instance variable **interestRate** would typically be named **setInterestRate** and a method that gets the **interestRate** would typically be called **getInterestRate**. *Get* methods are also commonly called *accessor methods* or *query methods.*

It would seem that providing *set* and *get* capabilities is essentially the same as making the instance variables **public**. This is another subtlety of Java that makes the language so desirable for software engineering. If an instance variable is **public**, the instance variable may be read or written at will by any method in the program. If an instance variable is **private**, a **public** *get* method certainly seems to allow other methods to read the data at will but the *get* method controls the formatting and display of the data. A **public** *set* method can—and most likely will—carefully scrutinize attempts to modify the instance variable's value. This ensures that the new value is appropriate for that data item. For example, an attempt to *set* the day of the month to 37 would be rejected, an attempt to *set* a person's weight to a negative value would be rejected, and so on.

The benefits of data integrity are not automatic simply because instance variables are made **private**—the programmer must provide validity checking. Java provides the framework in which programmers can design better programs in a convenient manner.

Software Engineering Observation 6.10

Methods that set the values of **private** *data should verify that the intended new values are proper; if they are not, the* set *methods should place the* **private** *instance variables into an appropriate consistent state.*

A class's *set* methods can return values indicating that attempts were made to assign invalid data to objects of the class. This enables clients of the class to test the return values of *set* methods to determine if the objects they are manipulating are valid and to take appropriate action if the objects are not valid.

Good Programming Practice 6.6

Every method that modifies the private instance variables of an object should ensure that the data remains in a consistent state.

Figure 6.5 extends our **Time** class to include *get* and *set* methods for the **hour**, **minute** and **second private** instance variables. The *set* methods strictly control the setting of the instance variables. Attempts to set any instance variable to an incorrect value cause the instance variable to be set to zero (thus leaving the instance variable in a consistent state). Each *get* method simply returns the appropriate instance variable's value.

```
// Fig. 6.5: Time3.java
// Time3 class definition
package com.deitel.jhtp2.ch06;     // place Time3 in a package
import java.text.DecimalFormat;    // used for number formatting

public class Time3 {
   private int hour;       // 0 - 23
   private int minute;     // 0 - 59
   private int second;     // 0 - 59

   // Time3 constructor initializes each instance variable
   // to zero. Ensures that Time object starts in a
   // consistent state.
   public Time3() { setTime( 0, 0, 0 ); }

   // Time3 constructor: hour supplied, minute and second
   // defaulted to 0.
   public Time3( int h ) { setTime( h, 0, 0 ); }

   // Time3 constructor: hour and minute supplied, second
   // defaulted to 0.
   public Time3( int h, int m ) { setTime( h, m, 0 ); }

   // Time3 constructor: hour, minute and second supplied.
   public Time3( int h, int m, int s ) { setTime( h, m, s ); }

   // Set Methods
   // Set a new Time3 value using military time. Perform
   // validity checks on the data. Set invalid values
   // to zero.
   public void setTime( int h, int m, int s )
   {
      setHour( h );     // set the hour
      setMinute( m );   // set the minute
      setSecond( s );   // set the second
   }

```

Fig. 6.5 Using set and get methods (part 1 of 7).

```
38       // set the hour
39       public void setHour( int h )
40          { hour = ( ( h >= 0 && h < 24 ) ? h : 0 ); }
41
42       // set the minute
43       public void setMinute( int m )
44          { minute = ( ( m >= 0 && m < 60 ) ? m : 0 ); }
45
46       // set the second
47       public void setSecond( int s )
48          { second = ( ( s >= 0 && s < 60 ) ? s : 0 ); }
49
50       // Get Methods
51       // get the hour
52       public int getHour() { return hour; }
53
54       // get the minute
55       public int getMinute() { return minute; }
56
57       // get the second
58       public int getSecond() { return second; }
59
60       // Convert time to String in military-time format
61       public String toMilitaryString()
62       {
63          DecimalFormat twoDigits = new DecimalFormat( "00" );
64
65          return twoDigits.format( hour ) +
66                 twoDigits.format( minute );
67       }
68
69       // Convert time to String in standard-time format
70       public String toString()
71       {
72          DecimalFormat twoDigits = new DecimalFormat( "00" );
73
74          return ( ( hour == 12 || hour == 0 ) ? 12 : hour % 12 ) +
75                 ":" + twoDigits.format( minute ) +
76                 ":" + twoDigits.format( second ) +
77                 ( hour < 12 ? " AM" : " PM" );
78       }
79    }
```

Fig. 6.5 Using set and get methods (part 2 of 7).

The **TimeTest** applet provides a graphical user interface that enables the user to exercise the methods of class **Time3**. The user can set the hour, minute or second value by typing a value in the appropriate text field and pressing the *Enter* key. The user can also click the "**Add 1 to second**" button to increment the time by one second. The **TextField** and **Button** events in this applet are all processed in method **actionPerformed** (line 127). Notice the use of **e.getSource()** to determine which GUI component generated the event. For example, line 129

```
80  // Fig. 6.5: TimeTest.java
81  // Demonstrating the Time3 class set and get methods
82  import java.awt.*;
83  import java.awt.event.*;
84  import java.applet.Applet;
85  import com.deitel.jhtp2.ch06.Time3;
86
87  public class TimeTest extends Applet implements ActionListener {
88     private Time3 t;
89     private Label hourLabel, minuteLabel, secondLabel;
90     private TextField hourField, minuteField,
91                       secondField, display;
92     private Button tickButton;
93
94     public void init()
95     {
96        t = new Time3();
97
98        hourLabel = new Label( "Set Hour" );
99        hourField = new TextField( 10 );
100       hourField.addActionListener( this );
101       add( hourLabel );
102       add( hourField );
103
104       minuteLabel = new Label( "Set minute" );
105       minuteField = new TextField( 10 );
106       minuteField.addActionListener( this );
107       add( minuteLabel );
108       add( minuteField );
109
110       secondLabel = new Label( "Set Second" );
111       secondField = new TextField( 10 );
112       secondField.addActionListener( this );
113       add( secondLabel );
114       add( secondField );
115
116       display = new TextField( 30 );
117       display.setEditable( false );
118       add( display );
119
120       tickButton = new Button( "Add 1 to Second" );
121       tickButton.addActionListener( this );
122       add( tickButton );
123
124       updateDisplay();
125    }
```

Fig. 6.5 Using set and get methods (part 3 of 7).

```
if ( e.getSource() == tickButton )
```

determines if **`tickButton`** was clicked by the user. If so, the body of the **`if`** structure is executed. Otherwise, the condition in the **`if`** structure at line 131 is tested, etc.

```

   public void actionPerformed( ActionEvent e )
   {
      if ( e.getSource() == tickButton )
         tick();
      else if ( e.getSource() == hourField ) {
         t.setHour(
            Integer.parseInt( e.getActionCommand() ) );
         hourField.setText( "" );
      }
      else if ( e.getSource() == minuteField ) {
         t.setMinute(
            Integer.parseInt( e.getActionCommand() ) );
         minuteField.setText( "" );
      }
      else if ( e.getSource() == secondField ) {
         t.setSecond(
            Integer.parseInt( e.getActionCommand() ) );
         secondField.setText( "" );
      }

      updateDisplay();
   }

   public void updateDisplay()
   {
      display.setText( "Hour: " + t.getHour() +
         "; Minute: " + t.getMinute() +
         "; Second: " + t.getSecond() );
      showStatus( "Standard time is: " + t.toString() +
         "; Military time is: " + t.toMilitaryString() );
   }

   public void tick()
   {
      t.setSecond( ( t.getSecond() + 1 ) % 60 );

      if ( t.getSecond() == 0 ) {
         t.setMinute( ( t.getMinute() + 1 ) % 60 );

         if ( t.getMinute() == 0 )
            t.setHour( ( t.getHour() + 1 ) % 24 );
      }
   }
}
```

Fig. 6.5 Using set and get methods (part 4 of 7).

After each operation, the resulting time is displayed as a string in the status bar of the applet. The output windows illustrate the applet before and after the following operations: setting the hour to 23, setting the minute to 59, setting the second to 58 and incrementing the minute twice with the "**Add 1 to second**" button.

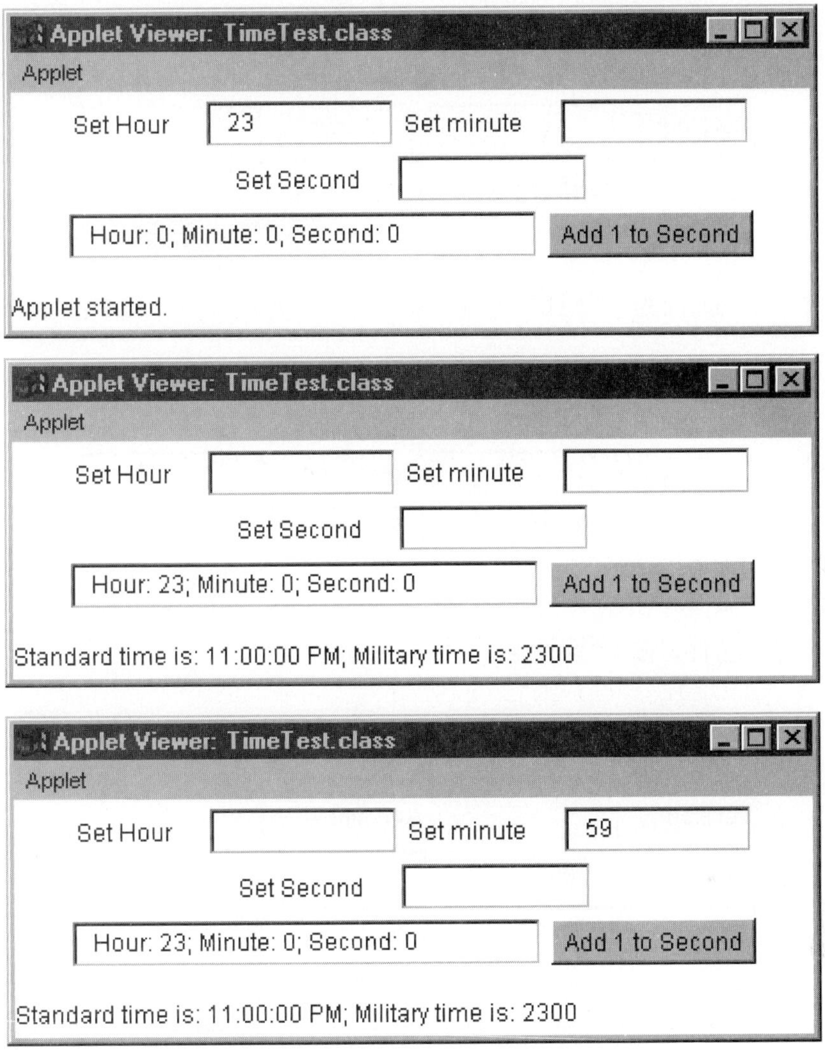

Applet Viewer: TimeTest.class
Applet
Set Hour 23 Set minute
Set Second
Hour: 0; Minute: 0; Second: 0 Add 1 to Second
Applet started.

Applet Viewer: TimeTest.class
Applet
Set Hour Set minute
Set Second
Hour: 23; Minute: 0; Second: 0 Add 1 to Second
Standard time is: 11:00:00 PM; Military time is: 2300

Applet Viewer: TimeTest.class
Applet
Set Hour Set minute 59
Set Second
Hour: 23; Minute: 0; Second: 0 Add 1 to Second
Standard time is: 11:00:00 PM; Military time is: 2300

Fig. 6.5 Using set and get methods (part 5 of 7).

Note that when the "**`Add 1 to second`**" button is clicked, the applet's **`tick`** method is called. Method **`tick`** uses the *set* and *get* methods to increment the second properly. Although this works, it incurs the performance burden of issuing multiple method calls. In the Section 6.12, we discuss the notion of package access as a means of eliminating this performance burden.

Common Programming Error 6.5

A constructor can call other methods of the class, such as set *or* get *methods, but because the constructor is initializing the object, the instance variables may not yet be in a consistent state. Using instance variables before they have been properly initialized is an error.*

Applet Viewer: TimeTest.class
Applet
Set Hour Set minute
Set Second
Hour: 23; Minute: 59; Second: 0 Add 1 to Second
Standard time is: 11:59:00 PM; Military time is: 2359

Applet Viewer: TimeTest.class
Applet
Set Hour Set minute
Set Second 58
Hour: 23; Minute: 59; Second: 0 Add 1 to Second
Standard time is: 11:59:00 PM; Military time is: 2359

Applet Viewer: TimeTest.class
Applet
Set Hour Set minute
Set Second
Hour: 23; Minute: 59; Second: 58 Add 1 to Second
Standard time is: 11:59:58 PM; Military time is: 2359

Fig. 6.5 Using set and get methods (part 6 of 7).

Set methods are certainly important from a software engineering standpoint because they can perform validity checking. *Set* and *get* methods have another important software engineering advantage as discussed in the following *Software Engineering Observation.*

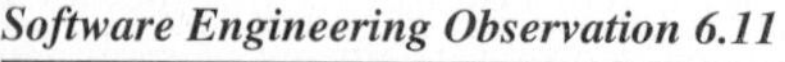

Software Engineering Observation 6.11

Accessing private data through set *and* get *methods not only protects the instance variables from receiving invalid values, but it also insulates clients of the class from the representation of the instance variables. Thus, if the representation of the data changes (typically to reduce the amount of storage required or to improve performance), only the method implementations need to change—the clients need not change as long as the interface provided by the methods remains the same.*

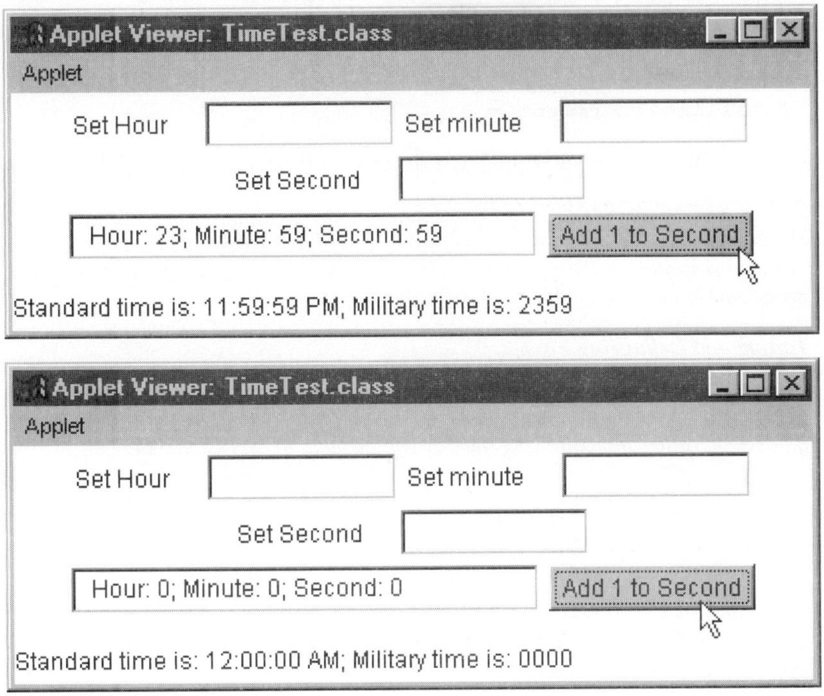

Fig. 6.5 Using set and get methods (part 7 of 7).

6.9 Software Reusability

Java programmers concentrate on crafting new classes and reusing existing classes. Many *class libraries* exist and others are being developed worldwide. Software is then constructed from existing, well-defined, carefully tested, well-documented, portable, widely available components. This kind of software reusability speeds the development of powerful, high-quality software. *Rapid applications development (RAD)* is of great interest today.

To realize the full potential of software reusability we need to improve cataloging schemes, licensing schemes, protection mechanisms that ensure master copies of classes are not corrupted, description schemes that system designers use to determine if existing objects meet their needs, browsing mechanisms that determine what classes are available and how closely they meet software developer requirements, and the like. Many interesting research and development problems have been solved and many more need to be solved; these problems will be solved because the potential value of software reuse is enormous.

6.10 Final Instance Variables

We have repeatedly emphasized the *principle of least privilege* as one of the most fundamental principles of good software engineering. Let us see one way in which this principle applies to instance variables.

Some instance variables need to be modifiable and some do not. The programmer may use the keyword **final** to specify that a variable is not modifiable and that any attempt to modify the variable is an error. For example,

```
final int increment = 5;
```

declares a constant instance variable **increment** of type **int** and initializes it to 5.

Software Engineering Observation 6.12

Declaring an instance variable as **final** *helps enforce the principle of least privilege. If an instance variable should not be modified, then declare it to be* **final** *to expressly forbid modification.*

Testing and Debugging Tip 6.2

Accidental attempts to modify a **final** *instance variable are caught at compile time rather than causing execution-time errors. It is always preferable to get bugs out at compile time, if possible, rather than allowing them to slip through to execution time.*

Common Programming Error 6.6

Attempting to modify a **final** *instance variable.*

The program of Fig. 6.6 creates a **final** instance variable **increment** of type **int** and initializes it to 5 in its declaration (line 10). A **final** variable cannot be modified by assignment so it *must* be initialized.

```
1   // Fig. 6.6: Increment.java
2   // Initializing a final variable
3   import java.awt.*;
4   import java.awt.event.*;
5   import java.applet.Applet;
6
7   public class Increment extends Applet
8               implements ActionListener {
9      private int count, total;
10     private final int increment = 5; // constant variable
11     private Button incr;
12
13     public void init()
14     {
15        count = 0;
16        total = 0;
17        incr = new Button( "Click to increment" );
18        incr.addActionListener( this );
19        add( incr );
20     }
21
```

Fig. 6.6 Initializing a **final** variable (part 1 of 2).

```
   public void actionPerformed( ActionEvent e )
   {
      total += increment;
      count++;
      showStatus( "After increment " + count +
                  ": total = " + total );
   }
}

```

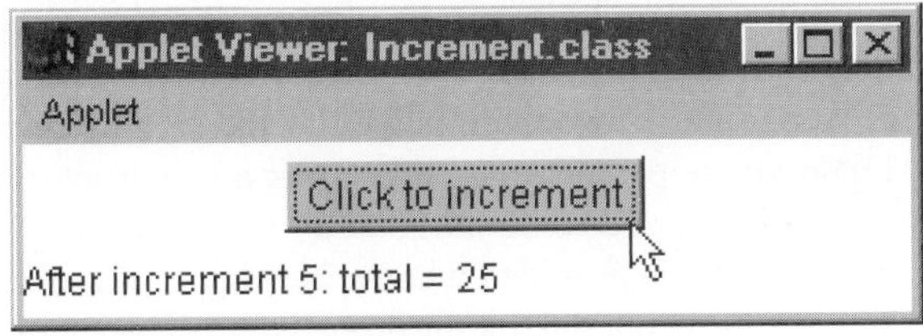

Fig. 6.6 Initializing a **`final`** variable (part 2 of 2).

Figure 6.7 illustrates compiler errors produced for the program of Fig. 6.6 if instance variable **`increment`** is declared **`final`**, but is not initialized in the declaration.

```
Increment.java:7: Blank final variable 'increment' may
                  not have been initialized. It must be
                  assigned a value in an initializer, or
                  in every constructor.
public class Increment extends Applet
             ^
1 error
```

Fig. 6.7 Compiler error message as a result of not initializing **`increment`**.

Common Programming Error 6.7

*Not initializing a **`final`** instance variable.*

Software Engineering Observation 6.13

*Constant class members (**`final`** objects and **`final`** "variables") must be initialized. Assignments are not allowed.*

6.11 Composition: Objects as Instance Variables of Other Classes

An **`AlarmClock`** class object needs to know when it is supposed to sound its alarm, so why not include a **`Time`** object as a member of the **`AlarmClock`** object? Such a capability is called *composition.* A class can have objects of other classes as members.

Software Engineering Observation 6.14

One form of software reuse is composition in which a class has objects of other classes as members.

Figure 6.8 uses classes **Employee** and **Date** to demonstrate objects as members of other objects. Class **Employee** contains instance variables **firstName**, **lastName**, **birthDate** and **hireDate**. Members **birthDate** and **hireDate** are **Date** objects that contains instance variables **month**, **day** and **year**. The program instantiates an **Employee** object and initializes and displays its instance variables. The constructor takes eight arguments (**fName**, **lName**, **bMonth**, **bDay**, **bYear**, **hMonth**, **hDay** and **hYear**). Arguments **bMonth**, **bDay** and **bYear** are passed to the **birthDate** constructor and **hMonth**, **hDay** and **hYear** are passed to the **hireDate** constructor.

A member object does not need to be initialized immediately with constructor arguments. If an empty argument list is provided when a member object is created, the object's default constructor (or no-argument constructor if one is available) will be called automatically. Values, if any, established by the default constructor (or no-argument constructor) can then be overridden by *set* methods.

```
// Fig. 6.8: Date.java
// Declaration of the Date class.
package com.deitel.jhtp2.ch06;

public class Date {
   private int month;  // 1-12
   private int day;    // 1-31 based on month
   private int year;   // any year

   // Constructor: Confirm proper value for month;
   // call method function checkDay to confirm proper
   // value for day.
   public Date( int mn, int dy, int yr )
   {
      if ( mn > 0 && mn <= 12 )       // validate the month
         month = mn;
      else {
         month = 1;
         System.out.println( "Month " + mn +
                             " invalid. Set to month 1." );
      }

      year = yr;                      // could also check
      day = checkDay( dy );           // validate the day

      System.out.println(
         "Date object constructor for date " + toString() );
   }
```

Fig. 6.8 Demonstrating an object with a member object (part 1 of 5).

```

   // Utility method to confirm proper day value
   // based on month and year.
   private int checkDay( int testDay )
   {
      int daysPerMonth[] = { 0, 31, 28, 31, 30,
                             31, 30, 31, 31, 30,
                             31, 30, 31 };

      if ( testDay > 0 && testDay <= daysPerMonth[ month ] )
         return testDay;

      if ( month == 2 &&   // February: Check for leap year
           testDay == 29 &&
           ( year % 400 == 0 ||
             ( year % 4 == 0 && year % 100 != 0 ) ) )
         return testDay;

      System.out.println( "Day " + testDay +
                          " invalid. Set to day 1." );

      return 1;  // leave object in consistent state
   }

   // Create a String of the form month/day/year
   public String toString()
      { return month + "/" + day + "/" + year; }
}
```

Fig. 6.8 Demonstrating an object with a member object (part 2 of 5).

```
// Fig. 6.8: Employee.java
// Declaration of the Employee class.
package com.deitel.jhtp2.ch06;

public class Employee {
   private String firstName;
   private String lastName;
   private Date birthDate;
   private Date hireDate;

   public Employee( String fName, String lName,
                    int bMonth, int bDay, int bYear,
                    int hMonth, int hDay, int hYear)
   {
      firstName = fName;
      lastName = lName;
      birthDate = new Date( bMonth, bDay, bYear );
      hireDate = new Date( hMonth, hDay, hYear );
   }
```

Fig. 6.8 Demonstrating an object with a member object (part 3 of 5).

```java

   public String toString()
   {
      return lastName + ", " + firstName +
             "  Hired: " + hireDate.toString() +
             "  Birthday: " + birthDate.toString();
   }
}
```

Fig. 6.8 Demonstrating an object with a member object (part 4 of 5).

```java
// Fig. 6.8: EmployeeTest.java
// Demonstrating an object with a member object.
import java.awt.Graphics;
import java.applet.Applet;
import com.deitel.jhtp2.ch06.Employee;

public class EmployeeTest extends Applet {
   private Employee e;

   public void init()
   {
      e = new Employee( "Bob", "Jones", 7, 24, 49,
                        3, 12, 88 );
   }

   public void paint( Graphics g )
   {
      g.drawString( e.toString(), 25, 25 );
   }
}
```

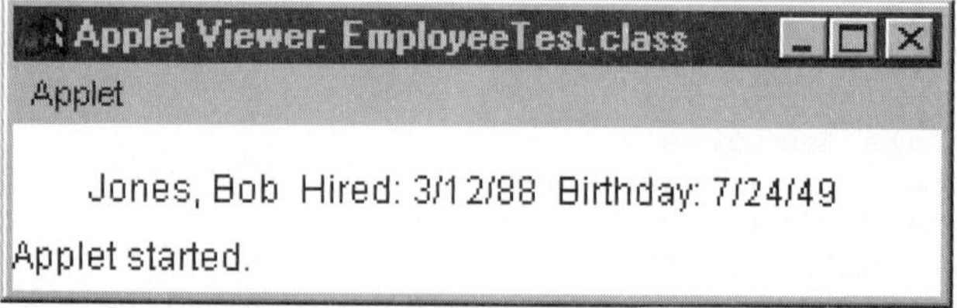


```
Date object constructor for date 7/24/49
Date object constructor for date 3/12/88
```

Fig. 6.8 Demonstrating an object with a member object (part 5 of 5).

Performance Tip 6.2

Initialize member objects explicitly at constructor time. This eliminates the overhead of doubly initializing member objects—once when the member object's default constructor is called and again when set *methods are used to provide initial values for the member object.*

Note that both class **Date** and class **Employee** in Fig. 6.8 are defined as part of the package **com.deitel.jhtp2.ch06** as specified on lines 3 and 59, respectively. Because they are in the same package, class **Employee** does not need to import class **Date** to use it. When the compiler searches for the file **Date.class**, the compiler knows to search the directory where **Employee.class** is located. Classes in a package never need to import other classes from the same package.

6.12 Package Access

When no access modifier is provided for a method or variable when it is defined in a class, the method or variable is considered to have *package access* (sometimes known as *friendly* access) If your program consists of one class definition, this has no specific effects on the program. However, if your program uses multiple classes from the same package (i.e., a group of related classes), these classes can access each other's package-access methods and data directly through a reference to an object. Package access enables objects of different classes to interact without the need for *set* and *get* methods that provide access to data, thus eliminating some of the method call overhead.

Let us consider a mechanical example of package access. The program of Fig. 6.9 contains two classes—the **PackageDataTest** applet class and the **PackageData** class. In the **PackageData** class definition, the lines

```
int x;      // package access instance variable
String s;   // package access instance variable
```

declare the instance variables **x** and **s** with no member access modifiers; therefore, these are package access instance variables. The **PackageDataTest** applet creates an instance of the **PackageData** class to demonstrate the ability to modify the **PackageData** instance variables directly (as shown on lines 21 and 22). The results of the modification can be seen in the output window.

```
1  // Fig. 6.9: PackageDataTest.java
2  // Classes in the same package (i.e., the same directory)
3  // can use package access data of other classes in the
4  // same package.
5  import java.awt.Graphics;
6  import java.applet.Applet;
7
8  public class PackageDataTest extends Applet {
9     private PackageData d;
10
11    public void init()
12    {
13       d = new PackageData();
14    }
15
```

Fig. 6.9 Package access to members of a class (part 1 of 2).

```
   public void paint( Graphics g )
   {
      g.drawString( "After instantiation: ", 25, 25 );
      g.drawString( d.toString(), 40, 40 );

      d.x = 77;
      d.s = "Good bye";
      g.drawString( "After changing values: ", 25, 55 );
      g.drawString( d.toString(), 40, 70 );
   }
}

class PackageData {
   int x;      // Package access instance variable
   String s;   // Package access instance variable

   // constructor
   public PackageData()
   {
      x = 0;
      s = "Hello";
   }

   public String toString()
   {
      return "x: " + x + "    s: " + s;
   }
}
```

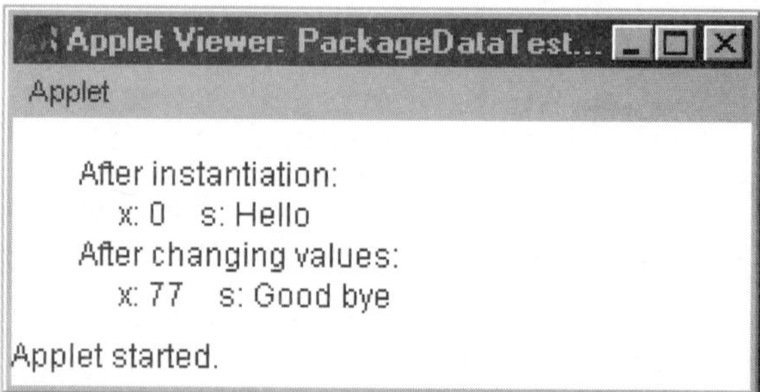

Fig. 6.9 Package access to members of a class (part 2 of 2).

Note that when this program is compiled, two separate files are produced—a **`.class`** file for class **`PackageData`** and a **`.class`** file for class **`PackageDataTest`**. These two files are placed in the same directory automatically and are considered to be part of the same package (they are certainly related by the fact that they are in the same program). Because they are part of the same package, class **`PackageDataTest`** is allowed to modify the package access data of objects of class **`PackageData`**.

Software Engineering Observation 6.15

Some people in the OOP community feel that package access corrupts information hiding and weakens the value of the object-oriented design approach.

6.13 Using the `this` Reference

When a method of a class references another member of that class for a specific object of that class, how does Java ensure that the proper object is referenced? The answer is that each object has access to a reference to itself—called the ***this*** *reference*.

The **this** reference is implicitly used to refer to both the instance variables and methods of an object. For now, we show a simple example of using the **this** reference explicitly; later, we show some substantial and subtle examples of using **this**.

Performance Tip 6.3

Java conserves storage by maintaining only one copy of each method per class; this method is invoked by every object of that class. Each object, on the other hand, has its own copy of the class's instance variables.

Figure 6.10 demonstrates the explicit use of the **this** reference to enable a method of class **ThisTest** to print the private data **x** of a **ThisTest** object.

```
// Fig. 6.10: ThisTest.java
// Using the this reference to refer to
// instance variables and methods.
import java.awt.Graphics;
import java.applet.Applet;

public class ThisTest extends Applet {
   private int x = 12;

   public void paint( Graphics g )
   {
      g.drawString( this.toString(), 25, 25 );
   }

   public String toString()
   {
      return "x = " + x + "   this.x = " + this.x;
   }
}
```

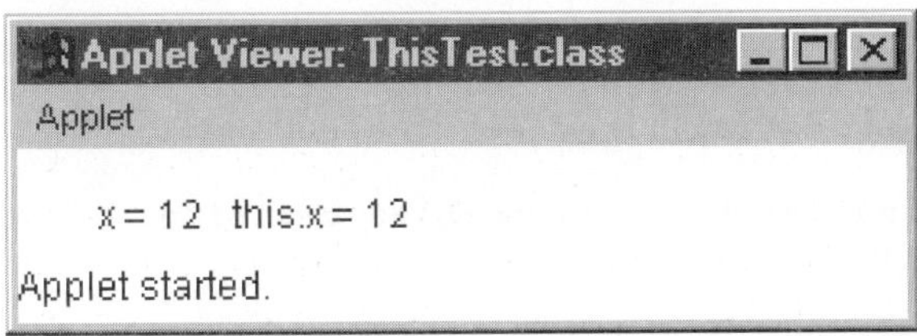

Fig. 6.10 Using the **this** reference.

The **toString** method in Fig. 6.10 forms a string containing the value of **x**. First **toString** accesses the value of **x** directly, then **toString** refers to **x** through the **this** reference and the dot operator (**.**).

Another use of the **this** reference is in enabling *concatenated method calls* (also called *cascaded method calls*). Figure 6.11 illustrates returning a reference to a **Time4** object to enable method calls of class **Time4** to be concatenated. Methods **setTime**, **setHour**, **setMinute** and **setSecond** each return **this** with a return type of **Time4**.

```
// Fig. 6.11: Time4.java
// Time4 class definition
package com.deitel.jhtp2.ch06;     // place Time4 in a package
import java.text.DecimalFormat;    // used for number formatting

public class Time4 {
   private int hour;      // 0 - 23
   private int minute;    // 0 - 59
   private int second;    // 0 - 59

   // Time4 constructor initializes each instance variable
   // to zero. Ensures that Time object starts in a
   // consistent state.
   public Time4() { setTime( 0, 0, 0 ); }

   // Time4 constructor: hour supplied, minute and second
   // defaulted to 0.
   public Time4( int h ) { setTime( h, 0, 0 ); }

   // Time4 constructor: hour and minute supplied, second
   // defaulted to 0.
   public Time4( int h, int m ) { setTime( h, m, 0 ); }

   // Time4 constructor: hour, minute and second supplied.
   public Time4( int h, int m, int s ) { setTime( h, m, s ); }

   // Set Methods
   // Set a new Time value using military time. Perform
   // validity checks on the data. Set invalid values
   // to zero.
   public Time4 setTime( int h, int m, int s )
   {
      setHour( h );      // set the hour
      setMinute( m );    // set the minute
      setSecond( s );    // set the second

      return this;       // enables chaining
   }

```

Fig. 6.11 Chaining method calls (part 1 of 5).

```
   // set the hour
   public Time4 setHour( int h )
   {
      hour = ( ( h >= 0 && h < 24 ) ? h : 0 );

      return this;     // enables chaining
   }

   // set the minute
   public Time4 setMinute( int m )
   {
      minute = ( ( m >= 0 && m < 60 ) ? m : 0 );

      return this;     // enables chaining
   }

   // set the second
   public Time4 setSecond( int s )
   {
      second = ( ( s >= 0 && s < 60 ) ? s : 0 );

      return this;     // enables chaining
   }

   // Get Methods
   // get the hour
   public int getHour() { return hour; }

   // get the minute
   public int getMinute() { return minute; }

   // get the second
   public int getSecond() { return second; }

   // Convert time to String in military-time format
   public String toMilitaryString()
   {
      DecimalFormat twoDigits = new DecimalFormat( "00" );

      return twoDigits.format( hour ) +
             twoDigits.format( minute );
   }

```

Fig. 6.11 Chaining method calls (part 2 of 5).

Why does the technique of returning the **this** reference work? The dot operator (**.**) associates from left to right, so the expression

```
t.setHour( 18 ).setMinute( 30 ).setSecond( 22 );
```

first evaluates **t.setHour(18)** then returns a reference to object **t** as the value of this method call. The remaining expression is then interpreted as

```
   // Convert time to String in standard-time format
   public String toString()
   {
      DecimalFormat twoDigits = new DecimalFormat( "00" );

      return ( ( hour == 12 || hour == 0 ) ? 12 : hour % 12 ) +
             ":" + twoDigits.format( minute ) +
             ":" + twoDigits.format( second ) +
             ( hour < 12 ? " AM" : " PM" );
   }
}
```

Fig. 6.11 Chaining method calls (part 3 of 5).

```
// Fig. 6.11: TimeTest.java
// Chaining method calls together with the this reference
import java.awt.Graphics;
import java.applet.Applet;
import com.deitel.jhtp2.ch06.Time4;

public class TimeTest extends Applet {
   private Time4 t;

   public void init()
   {
      t = new Time4();
   }

   public void paint( Graphics g )
   {
      t.setHour( 18 ).setMinute( 30 ).setSecond( 22 );
      g.drawString( "Military time: " +
                    t.toMilitaryString(), 25, 25 );
      g.drawString( "Standard time: " + t.toString(),
                    25, 40 );

      g.drawString( "New standard time: " +
         t.setTime( 20, 20, 20 ).toString(), 25, 70 );
   }
}
```

Fig. 6.11 Chaining method calls (part 4 of 5).

```
t.setMinute( 30 ).setSecond( 22 );
```

The **`t.setMinute( 30 )`** call executes and returns a reference to **`t`**. The remaining expression is interpreted as

```
t.setSecond( 22 );
```

Note the calls

```
t.setTime( 20, 20, 20 ).toString();
```

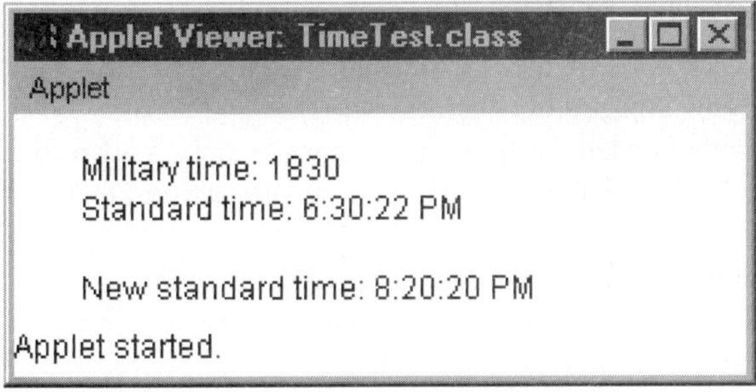

Fig. 6.11 Chaining method calls (part 5 of 5).

also use the concatenation feature. These method calls must appear in this order in this expression because **`toString`** as defined in the class does not return a reference to **`t`**. Placing the call to **`toString`** before the call to **`setTime`** causes a syntax error.

Common Programming Error 6.8

In a method in which a method parameter has the same name as one of the class members, use **`this`** *explicitly if you want to access the class member; otherwise, you will incorrectly reference the method parameter.*

Good Programming Practice 6.7

Avoid using method parameter names that conflict with class member names.

Good Programming Practice 6.8

Explicitly using **`this`** *can increase program clarity in some contexts in which* **`this`** *is optional.*

6.14 Finalizers

We have seen that constructor methods are capable of initializing data in an object of a class when the class is created. Often, constructors acquire various system resources such as memory (when the **`new`** operator is used). We need a disciplined way to give resources back to the system when they are no longer needed to avoid resource leaks. The most common resource acquired by constructors is memory. But, in Java we do not have to worry about returning memory to the system because Java performs automatic "garbage collection" of memory. Therefore, memory leaks that are common in other languages like C and C++ cannot happen in Java. However, other resource leaks can occur.

Each class in Java can have a *finalizer method* that returns resources to the system. The finalizer method for an object is guaranteed to be called to perform *termination housekeeping* on the object just before Java garbage collects the object. A class's finalizer method always has the name **`finalize`**. A finalizer receives no parameters and returns no value (i.e., its return type is **`void`**). A class may have only one **`finalize`** method—finalizer overloading is not allowed.

Finalizers have not been provided for the classes presented so far. Actually, finalizers are rarely used with simple classes. We will see a sample **`finalize`** method in Fig. 6.12.

6.15 Static Class Members

Each object of a class has its own copy of all the instance variables of the class. In certain cases only one copy of a particular variable should be shared by all objects of a class. A **static** class variable is used for these and other reasons. A **static** class variable represents "class-wide" information. The declaration of a **static** member begins with the keyword **static**.

Let us motivate the need for **static** classwide data with a video game example. Suppose we have a video game in which we have **Martian**s and other space creatures. Each **Martian** tends to be brave and willing to attack other space creatures when the **Martian** is aware that there are at least 5 **Martian**s present. If there are fewer than five **Martian**s present, each **Martian** becomes cowardly. So each **Martian** needs to know the **martianCount**. We could endow class **Martian** with **martianCount** as instance data. If we do this, then every **Martian** will have a separate copy of the instance data and every time we create a new **Martian** we will have to update the instance variable **martianCount** in every **Martian**. This wastes space with the redundant copies and wastes time in updating the separate copies. Instead, we declare **martianCount** to be **static**. This makes **martianCount** classwide data. Every **Martian** can see the **martianCount** as if it were instance data of the **Martian**, but only one copy of the static **martianCount** is maintained by Java. This saves space. We save time by having the **Martian** constructor increment the static **martianCount**. Because there is only one copy, we do not have to increment separate copies of **martianCount** for each **Martian** object.

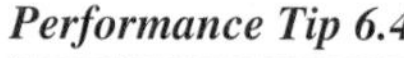

Performance Tip 6.4

Use **static** *class variables to save storage when a single copy of the data will suffice.*

Although **static** class variables may seem like global variables, **static** class variables have class scope. A class's **public static** class members can be accessed through any object of that class, or they can be accessed through the class name using the dot operator. A class's **private static** class members can be accessed through methods of the class. Actually, **static** class members exist even when no objects of that class exist. To access a **public** or package **static** class member when no objects of the class exist, simply prefix the class name and the dot operator to the class member. To access a **private static** class member when no objects of the class exist, a **public** or friendly **static** method must be provided and the method must be called by prefixing its name with the class name and dot operator.

The program of Fig. 6.12 demonstrates the use of a **private static** instance variable and a **public static** method. The instance variable **count** is initialized to zero by default. Instance variable **count** maintains a count of the number of objects of class **Employee** that have been instantiated. When objects of class **Employee** exist, member **count** can be referenced through any method of an **Employee** object—in this example, **count** is referenced by the constructor. When no objects of class **Employee** exist, member **count** can still be referenced, but only through a call to **static** method **getCount** as follows:

```
Employee.getCount()
```

```
1  // Fig. 6.12: Employee.java
2  // Declaration of the Employee class.
3  public class Employee {
4     private String firstName;
5     private String lastName;
6     private static int count;  // # of objects instantiated
7
8     public Employee( String fName, String lName )
9     {
10       firstName = fName;
11       lastName = lName;
12
13       ++count;  // increment static count of employees
14       System.out.println( "Employee object constructor: " +
15                           firstName + " " + lastName );
16    }
17
18    protected void finalize()
19    {
20       --count;  // decrement static count of employees
21       System.out.println( "Employee object finalizer: " +
22                           firstName + " " + lastName );
23    }
24
25    public String getFirstName() { return firstName; }
26
27    public String getLastName() { return lastName; }
28
29    public static int getCount() { return count; }
30 }
```

Fig. 6.12 Using a **static** class variable to maintain a count of the number of objects of a class (part 1 of 3).

In this example, method **getCount** is used to determine the number of **Employee** objects currently instantiated. Note that when there are no objects instantiated in the program, the **Employee.getCount()** method call is issued. However, when there are objects instantiated, method **getCount** can also be called through one of the objects as in

```
e1.getCount()
```

Notice that the **Employee** class has a **finalize** method (line 18). This method is included to show when it is called in a program. Note that the method is declared **protected**. Method **finalize** is normally declared **protected** so it is not part of the **public** services of a class. We will discuss the protected access modifier in Chapter 7.

Method **paint** of the applet **EmployeeTest** declares, instantiates and uses two **Employee** objects. When **paint** is done with these objects, the references **e1** and **e2** are set to **null**—i.e., they no longer refer to the objects that were instantiated on lines 42 and 43. This "marks the objects for garbage collection" because there are no more references to the objects in the program.

```java
// Fig. 6.12: EmployeeTest.java
// Test Employee class with static class variable,
// static class method, and dynamic memory.
import java.awt.Graphics;
import java.applet.Applet;

public class EmployeeTest extends Applet {
   public void paint( Graphics g )
   {
      g.drawString( "Employees before instantiation: " +
                    Employee.getCount(), 25, 25 );
      Employee e1 = new Employee( "Susan", "Baker" );
      Employee e2 = new Employee( "Bob", "Jones" );

      g.drawString( "Employees after instantiation: " +
                    e1.getCount(), 25, 40 );

      g.drawString( "Employee 1: " + e1.getFirstName() +
                    " " + e1.getLastName(), 25, 70 );
      g.drawString( "Employee 2: " + e2.getFirstName() +
                    " " + e2.getLastName(), 25, 85 );

      // mark objects referred to by e1 and e2
      // for garbage collection
      e1 = null;
      e2 = null;

      System.gc();  // explicit call to garbage collector

      g.drawString( "Employees after garbage collection: " +
                    Employee.getCount(), 25, 115 );
   }
}
```

Fig. 6.12 Using a **static** class variable to maintain a count of the number of objects of a class (part 2 of 3).

Eventually, the garbage collector reclaims the memory for these objects (or the memory is reclaimed by the operating system when the program terminates). Because we cannot be sure when the garbage collector will execute, we make an explicit call to the garbage collector with the statement

```java
System.gc();  // explicit call to garbage collector
```

A method declared **static** cannot access nonstatic class members. Unlike nonstatic methods, a **static** method has no **this** reference because **static** class variables and **static** class methods exist independent of any objects of a class.

Common Programming Error 6.9

Referring to the **this** *reference within a* **static** *method is a syntax error.*

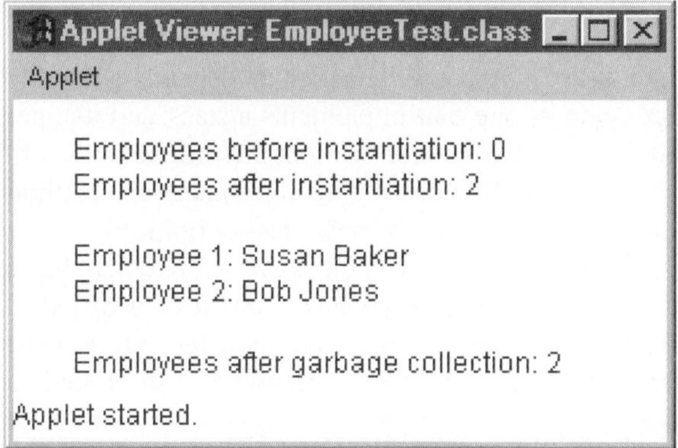


```
Employee object constructor: Susan Baker
Employee object constructor: Bob Jones
Employee object finalizer: Susan Baker
Employee object finalizer: Bob Jones
```

Fig. 6.12 Using a **`static`** class variable to maintain a count of the number of objects of a class (part 3 of 3).

Common Programming Error 6.10

It is a syntax error for a **`static`** *method to call an instance method or to access an instance variable.*

Software Engineering Observation 6.16

Any **`static`** *class variables and* **`static`** *class methods exist and can be used even if no objects of that class have been instantiated.*

6.16 Data Abstraction and Information Hiding

Classes normally hide their implementation details from the clients of the classes. This is called *information hiding*. As an example of information hiding, let us consider a data structure called a *stack*.

Think of a stack in terms of a pile of dishes. When a dish is placed on the pile, it is always placed at the top (referred to as *pushing* the dish onto the stack), and when a dish is removed from the pile, it is always removed from the top (referred to as *popping* the dish off the stack). Stacks are known as *last-in, first-out (LIFO) data structures*—the last item pushed (inserted) on the stack is the first item popped (removed) from the stack.

The programmer may create a stack class and hide from its clients the implementation of the stack. Stacks can easily be implemented with arrays and other methods (such as linked lists; see Chapter 17, "Data Structures" and Chapter 18, "Java Utilities Packages and Bit Manipulation"). A client of a stack class need not know how the stack is implemented. The client simply requires that when data items are placed in the stack, they will be recalled in last-in, first-out order. This concept is referred to as *data abstraction,* and Java classes define abstract data types (ADTs). Although users may happen to know the details of how a class is implemented, users may not write code that depends on these details. This means that a particular class (such as one that implements a stack and its operations of *push* and *pop*) can be replaced with another version without affecting the rest of the system, as long as the public services of that class does not change (i.e. every method still has the same name, return type and parameter list in the new class definition).

The job of a high-level language is to create a view convenient for programmers to use. There is no single accepted standard view—that is one reason why there are so many programming languages. Object-oriented programming in Java presents yet another view.

Most programming languages emphasize actions. In these languages, data exists in support of the actions programs need to take. Data is "less interesting" than actions, anyway. Data is "crude." There are only a few built-in data types, and it is difficult for programmers to create their own new data types.

This view changes with Java and the object-oriented style of programming. Java elevates the importance of data. The primary activity in Java is creating new data types (i.e., classes) and expressing the interactions among objects of those data types.

To move in this direction, the programming-languages community needed to formalize some notions about data. The formalization we consider is the notion of *abstract data types (ADTs).* ADTs receive as much attention today as structured programming did over the last two decades. ADTs do not replace structured programming. Rather, they provide an additional formalization to further improve the program development process.

What is an abstract data type? Consider the built-in type **int**. What comes to mind is the notion of an integer in mathematics, but **int** on a computer is not precisely what an integer is in mathematics. In particular, computer **int**s are normally quite limited in size. For example, **int** on a 32-bit machine is limited approximately to the range –2 billion to +2 billion. If the result of a calculation falls outside this range, an error occurs and the machine responds in some machine-dependent manner, including the possibility of "quietly" producing an incorrect result. Mathematical integers do not have this problem. So the notion of a computer **int** is really only an approximation to the notion of a real-world integer. The same is true with **float**.

The point is that even the built-in data types provided with programming languages like Java are really only approximations or models of real-world concepts and behaviors. We have taken **int** for granted until this point, but now you have a new perspective to consider. Types like **int**, **float**, **char** and others are all examples of abstract data types. They are essentially ways of representing real-world notions to some satisfactory level of precision within a computer system.

An abstract data type actually captures two notions, namely a *data representation* and the *operations* that are allowed on that data. For example, the notion of **int** defines addition, subtraction, multiplication, division and modulus operations in Java, but division by zero is undefined. Another example is the notion of negative integers whose operations and data representation are clear, but the operation of taking the square root of a negative integer is undefined. In Java, the programmer uses classes to implement abstract data types.

Java has a small set of primitive types. ADTs extend the base programming language.

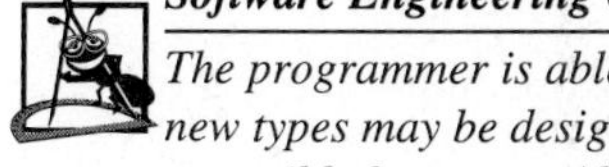

Software Engineering Observation 6.17

The programmer is able to create new types through the use of the class mechanism. These new types may be designed to be used as conveniently as the built-in types. Thus, Java is an extensible language. Although the language is easy to extend with these new types, the base language itself is not changeable.

New Java classes can be proprietary to an individual, to small groups, to companies, and so on. Many classes are placed in standard *class libraries* intended for wide distribution. This does not necessarily promote standards although de facto standards are emerging. The full value of Java will be realized only when substantial, standardized class libraries become more widely available than they are today. In the United States, such standardization often happens through *ANSI*, the *American National Standards Institute*. Worldwide standardization often happens through *ISO, the International Standards Organization*. Regardless of how these libraries ultimately appear, the reader who learns Java and object-oriented programming will be ready to take advantage of the new kinds of rapid, component-oriented software development made possible with class libraries.

6.16.1 Example: Queue Abstract Data Type

Each of us stands in line from time to time. A waiting line is also called a *queue*. We wait in line at the supermarket checkout counter, we wait in line to get gasoline, we wait in line to board a bus, we wait in line to pay a toll on the highway, and students know all too well about waiting in line during registration to get the courses they want. Computer systems use many waiting lines internally, so we write programs that simulate what queues are and do.

A queue is a good example of an abstract data type. A queue offers well-understood behavior to its clients. Clients put things in a queue one at a time—using an *enqueue* operation, and the clients get those things back one at a time on demand—using a *dequeue* operation. Conceptually, a queue can become infinitely long. A real queue, of course, is finite. Items are returned from a queue in *first-in, first-out (FIFO)* order—the first item inserted in the queue is the first item removed from the queue.

The queue hides an internal data representation that keeps track of the items currently waiting in line, and it offers a set of operations to its clients, namely *enqueue* and *dequeue*. The clients are not concerned about the implementation of the queue. Clients merely want the queue to operate "as advertised." When a client enqueues a new item, the queue should accept that item and place it internally in some kind of first-in, first-out data structure. When the client wants the next item from the front of the queue, the queue should remove the item from its internal representation and should deliver the item to the outside world in FIFO order, i.e., the item that has been in the queue the longest should be the next one returned by the next *dequeue* operation.

The queue ADT guarantees the integrity of its internal data structure. Clients may not manipulate this data structure directly. Only the queue ADT has access to its internal data. Clients may cause only allowable operations to be performed on the data representation; operations not provided in the ADT's public interface are rejected by the ADT in some appropriate manner. This could mean issuing an error message, terminating execution, or simply ignoring the operation request.

Summary

- Members of a class are accessed using the member access operator—the dot operator (**.**).
- Classes enable the programmer to model objects with attributes and behaviors. Class types are defined in Java using the keyword **class**.
- Class definitions begin with the keyword **class**. The body of the class definition is delineated with braces (**{** and **}**). Class definitions terminate with a semicolon.
- Any instance variable or method declared **public** in a class is visible to any method with access to an object of the class.
- Any instance variable or method declared **private** is visible only to other members of the class.
- Member access modifiers can appear multiple times and in any order in a class definition.
- A constructor is a special method with the same name as the class that is used to initialize the members of a class object. Constructors are called when objects of their classes are instantiated.
- The set of **public** methods of a class is called the class's public services or interface.
- Calling methods is more concise than calling functions in procedural programming because most data used by the method is already in the object.
- Within a class's scope, class members may be referenced simply by their names. Outside a class's scope, accessible class members are referenced through a reference to an object.
- The member selection operator **.** is used to access class members.
- Public methods of a class present a view of the services the class provides to the clients of the class.
- Class **DecimalFormat** (from package **java.text**) is used to format numbers for output purposes.
- Packages provide a mechanism for software reuse.
- Placing a **package** statement at the beginning of a Java source file indicates that the class defined in the file is part of the specified package.
- The only two statements in Java that can appear outside the braces of a class definition are **package** statements and **import** statements.
- In an effort to provide unique names for every package, Sun Microsystems (the creator of Java) has defined a convention for package naming. Every package name should start with your Internet domain name in reverse order.
- The compilation command

  ```
  javac -d base_directory ClassName.java
  ```

  uses the **-d** compiler option to specify that the package defined in **ClassName.java** should be stored in **base_directory**.

A package must be inserted into your class path before the classes in the package can be used in a program. The class path indicates to the compiler where to search on your computer for your packages. The class path is specified with an environment variable called **CLASSPATH**.

- To enable clients to read **private** data, the class can provide *get* methods. To enable clients to modify **private** data, the class can provide *set* methods.
- Instance variables of a class are normally made **private** and methods of a class are normally made **public**. Some methods may be **private** and serve as utility methods to the other methods of the class.
- Constructors can be overloaded.
- Once a class object is properly initialized, all methods that manipulate the object should ensure that the object remains in a consistent state.
- When an object of a class is declared, initializers can be provided. These initializers are passed to the class's constructor.
- Constructors may not specify return types, nor may they attempt to return values.
- A finalizer performs termination housekeeping before the system garbage collects an object's storage.
- The keyword **final** specifies that an object is not modifiable.
- A **final** object must be initialized in its declaration.
- Classes can be composed of objects of other classes.
- The **this** reference is implicitly used to reference both methods and instance variables from within an object.
- The **new** operator automatically creates an object of the proper size, and returns a reference of the correct type.
- A static class variable represents "classwide" information. The declaration of a static member begins with the keyword **static**.
- Static class variables have class scope.
- A method declared **static** cannot access nonstatic class members. A **static** method has no **this** reference because **static** class variables and **static** methods exist independent of any objects of a class.

Terminology

-d compiler option
abstract data type (ADT)
access method
aggregation
attribute
behavior
cascaded method calls
class
class definition
class library
class method (**static**)
CLASSPATH environment variable
class scope
class variable
client of a class
composition

concatenated method calls
consistent state for an instance variable
constructor
container class
data type
default constructor
dot operator (`.`)
encapsulation
extends
extensibility
finalizer
get method
helper method
implementation of a class
information hiding
initialize a class object
instance method
instance of a class
instance variable
instantiate an object of a class
interface to a class
member access control
member access operator (`.`)
member access modifiers
message
method
method calls
mutator method
`new` operator
no-argument constructor
object
object-based programming (OBP)
object-oriented programming (OOP)
package access
`package` statement
predicate method
principle of least privilege
`private`
programmer-defined type
`public`
public interface of a class
query method
rapid applications development (RAD)
reusable code
services of a class
set method
software reusability
static class variable
static method
`this` reference
user-defined type
utility method

Common Programming Errors

6.1 Attempting to declare a return type for a constructor and/or attempting to return a value from a constructor is a syntax error.

6.2 An attempt by a method which is not a member of a particular class to access a **`private`** member of that class is a syntax error.

6.3 If constructors are provided for a class, but none are no-argument constructors, and an attempt is made to call a no-argument constructor to initialize an object of the class, a syntax error occurs. A constructor may be called with no arguments only if there are no constructors for the class (the default constructor is called) or if there is a no-argument constructor.

6.4 Attempting to overload a method of a class with a method not in that class's scope.

6.5 A constructor can call other methods of the class, such as set or get methods, but because the constructor is initializing the object, the instance variables may not yet be in a consistent state. Using instance variables before they have been properly initialized is an error.

6.6 Attempting to modify a **`final`** instance variable.

6.7 Not initializing a **`final`** instance variable.

6.8 In a method in which a method parameter has the same name as one of the class members, use **`this`** explicitly if you want to access the class member; otherwise, you will incorrectly reference the method parameter.

6.9 Referring to the **`this`** reference within a **`static`** method is a syntax error.

6.10 It is a syntax error for a ***`static`*** method to call an instance method or to access an instance variable.

Good Programming Practices

6.1 Group members by member access modifier in a class definition for clarity and readability.

6.2 Initialize instance variables of a class in that class's constructor.

6.3 Our preference is to list the **`private`** members of a class first.

6.4 Despite the fact that **`private`** and **`public`** members may be repeated and intermixed, list all the **`private`** members of a class first in one group and then list all the **`public`** members in another group.

6.5 When appropriate (almost always), provide a constructor to ensure that every object is properly initialized with meaningful values.

6.6 Every method that modifies the private instance variables of an object should ensure that the data remains in a consistent state.

6.7 Avoid using method parameter names that conflict with class member names.

6.8 Explicitly using ***`this`*** can increase program clarity in some contexts in which ***`this`*** is optional.

Performance Tips

6.1 All Java objects are passed by reference. Only a memory address is passed, not a copy of a possibly large object (as would be the case in a pass by value).

6.2 Initialize member objects explicitly at constructor time. This eliminates the overhead of doubly initializing member objects—once when the member object's default constructor is called and again when set methods are used to provide initial values for the member object.

6.3 Java conserves storage by maintaining only one copy of each method per class; this method is invoked by every object of that class. Each object, on the other hand, has its own copy of the class's instance variables.

6.4 Use **`static`** class variables to save storage when a single copy of the data will suffice.

Software Engineering Observations

6.1 It is important to write programs that are understandable and easy to maintain. Change is the rule rather than the exception. Programmers should anticipate that their code will be modified. As we will see, classes facilitate program modifiability.

6.2 Methods tend to fall into a number of different categories: methods that get the values of **`private`** instance variables; methods that set the values of **`private`** instance variables; methods that implement the features of the class; and methods that perform various mechanical chores for the class such as initializing class objects, assigning class objects, converting between classes and built-in types or between classes and other classes.

6.3 Information hiding promotes program modifiability and simplifies the client's perception of a class.

6.4 Clients of a class can (and should) use the class without knowing the internal details of how the class is implemented. If the class implementation is changed (to improve performance, for example), provided the class's interface remains constant, the class clients' source code need not change. This makes it much easier to modify systems.

6.5 Using an object-oriented programming approach can often simplify method calls by reducing the number of parameters to be passed. This benefit of object-oriented programming derives from the fact that encapsulation of instance variables and methods within an object gives the methods the right to access the instance variables.

6.6 Keep all the instance variables of a class **`private`**. When necessary provide **`public`** methods to set the values of **`private`** instance variables and to get the values of **`private`** instance variables. This architecture helps hide the implementation of a class from its clients, which reduces bugs and improves program modifiability.

6.7 Class designers use **`private`** and **`public members`** to enforce the notion of information hiding and the principle of least privilege.

6.8 The class designer need not provide set and/or get methods for each **`private`** data *member*; these capabilities should be provided only when it makes sense and after careful thought by the class designer.

6.9 If a method of a class already provides all or part of the functionality required by a constructor (or other method) of the class, call that method from the constructor (or other method). This simplifies the maintenance of the code and reduces the likelihood of an error if the implementation of the code is modified. It is also an effective example of reuse.

6.10 Methods that set the values of **`private`** data should verify that the intended new values are proper; if they are not, the set methods should place the **`private`** instance variables into an appropriate consistent state.

6.11 Accessing private data through set and get methods not only protects the instance variables from receiving invalid values, but it also insulates clients of the class from the representation of the instance variables. Thus, if the representation of the data changes (typically to reduce the amount of storage required or to improve performance), only the method implementations need to change—the clients need not change as long as the interface provided by the methods remains the same.

6.12 Declaring an instance variable as **`final`** helps enforce the principle of least privilege. If an instance variable should not be modified, then declare it **`final`** to expressly forbid modification.

6.13 Constant class members (**final** objects and **final** "variables") must be initialized. Assignments are not allowed.

6.14 One form of software reuse is composition in which a class has objects of other classes as members.

6.15 Some people in the OOP community feel that package access corrupts information hiding and weakens the value of the object-oriented design approach.

6.16 Any **static** class variables and **static** class methods exist and can be used even if no objects of that class have been instantiated.

6.17 The programmer is able to create new types through the use of the class mechanism. These new types may be designed to be used as conveniently as the built-in types. Thus, Java is an extensible language. Although the language is easy to extend with these new types, the base language itself is not changeable.

Testing and Debugging Tips

6.1 Making the instance variables of a class **private** and the methods of the class **public** facilitates debugging because problems with data manipulations are localized to the class's methods.

6.2 Accidental attempts to modify a **final** instance variable are caught at compile time rather than causing execution-time errors. It is always preferable to get bugs out at compile time, if possible, rather than allowing them to slip through to execution time.

Self-Review Exercises

6.1 Fill in the blanks in each of the following:

a) Class members are accessed via the ________ operator in conjunction with an object of the class.
b) Members of a class specified as ________ are accessible only to methods of the class.
c) A ________ is a special method used to initialize the instance variables of a class.
d) A ________ method is used to assign values to **private** instance variables of a class.
e) Methods of a class are normally made ________ and instance variables of a class are normally made ________.
f) A ________ method is used to retrieve values of **private** data of a class.
g) The keyword ________ introduces a class definition.
h) Members of a class specified as ________ are accessible anywhere an object of the class is in scope.
i) The ________ operator dynamically allocates memory for an object of a specified type and returns a ________ to that type.
j) A constant object must be ________; it cannot be modified after it is created.
k) A ________ instance variable represents classwide information.
l) The keyword ________ specifies that an object or variable is not modifiable after it is initialized.
m) A method declared **static** cannot access ________ class members.

Answers to Self-Review Exercises

6.1 a) dot (**.**). b) **private**. c) constructor. d) set. e) **public**, **private**. f) get. g) **class**. h) **public**. i) **new**, reference. j) initialized. k) **static**. m) **final**. n) non-**static**.

Exercises

6.2 Create a class called **Complex** for performing arithmetic with complex numbers. Write a driver program to test your class.

Complex numbers have the form

realPart + imaginaryPart * *i*

where *i* is

$\sqrt{-1}$

Use floating-point variables to represent the private data of the class. Provide a constructor method that enables an object of this class to be initialized when it is declared. Provide a no-argument constructor with default values in case no initializers are provided. Provide **public** methods for each of the following:

a) Addition of two **Complex** numbers: The real parts are added together and the imaginary parts are added together.
b) Subtraction of two **Complex** numbers: The real part of the right operand is subtracted from the real part of the left operand and the imaginary part of the right operand is subtracted from the imaginary part of the left operand.
c) Printing **Complex** numbers in the form **(a, b)** where **a** is the real part and **b** is the imaginary part.

6.3 Create a class called **Rational** for performing arithmetic with fractions. Write a driver program to test your class.

Use integer variables to represent the **private** instance variables of the class—the **numerator** and the **denominator**. Provide a constructor method that enables an object of this class to be initialized when it is declared. The constructor should store the fraction in reduced form (i.e., the fraction

2/4

would be stored in the object as 1 in the **numerator** and 2 in the **denominator**). Provide a no-argument constructor with default values in case no initializers are provided. Provide **public** methods for each of the following:

a) Addition of two **Rational** numbers. The result of the addition should be stored in reduced form.
b) Subtraction of two **Rational** numbers. The result of the subtraction should be stored in reduced form.
c) Multiplication of two **Rational** numbers. The result of the multiplication should be stored in reduced form.
d) Division of two **Rational** numbers. The result of the division should be stored in reduced form.

e) Printing **Rational** numbers in the form **a/b** where **a** is the **numerator** and **b** is the **denominator**.
f) Printing **Rational** numbers in floating-point format. (Consider providing formatting capabilities that enable the user of the class to specify the number of digits of precision to the right of the decimal point.)

6.4 Modify the **Time3** class of Fig. 6.5 to include the **tick** method that increments the time stored in a **Time3** object by one second. Also provide method **incrementMinute** to increment the minute and method **incrementHour** to increment the hour. The **Time3** object should always remain in a consistent state. Write a driver program that tests the **tick** method, the **incrementMinute** method and the **incrementHour** method to ensure that they work correctly. Be sure to test the following cases:
a) Incrementing into the next minute.
b) Incrementing into the next hour.
c) Incrementing into the next day (i.e., 11:59:59 PM to 12:00:00 AM).

6.5 Modify the **Date** class of Fig. 6.8 to perform error checking on the initializer values for instance variables **month**, **day** and **year**. Also, provide a method **nextDay** to increment the day by one. The **Date** object should always remain in a consistent state. Write a driver program that tests the **nextDay** method in a loop that prints the date during each iteration of the loop to illustrate that the **nextDay** method works correctly. Be sure to test the following cases:
a) Incrementing into the next month.
b) Incrementing into the next year.

6.6 Combine the modified **Time3** class of Exercise 6.4 and the modified **Date** class of Exercise 6.5 into one class called **DateAndTime** (in Chapter 7 we will discuss inheritance which will enable us to accomplish this task quickly without modifying the existing class definitions). Modify the **tick** method to call the **nextDay** method if the time is incremented into the next day. Modify methods **toString** and **PrintMilitary** to output the date in addition to the time. Write a driver program to test the new class **DateAndTime**. Specifically test incrementing the time to the next day.

6.7 Modify the set methods in the program of Fig. 6.5 to return appropriate error values if an attempt is made to set one of the instance variables **hour**, **minute** or **second** of an object of class **Time** to an invalid value.

6.8 Create a class **Rectangle**. The class has attributes **length** and **width**, each of which defaults to 1. It has methods that calculate the **perimeter** and the **area** of the rectangle. It has *set* and *get* methods for both **length** and **width**. The *set* methods should verify that **length** and **width** are each floating-point numbers larger than 0.0 and less than 20.0.

6.9 Create a more sophisticated **Rectangle** class than the one you created in Exercise 6.8. This class stores only the Cartesian coordinates of the four corners of the rectangle. The constructor calls a *set* method that accepts four sets of coordinates and verifies that each of these is in the first quadrant with no single *x* or *y* coordinate larger than 20.0. The *set* method also verifies that the supplied coordinates do, in fact, specify a rectangle. Methods calculate the **length**, **width**, **perimeter** and **area**. The length is the larger of the two dimensions. Include a predicate method **square** which determines if the rectangle is a square.

6.10 Modify the **Rectangle** class of Exercise 6.9 to include a **draw** method that displays the rectangle inside a 25-by-25 box enclosing the portion of the first quadrant in which the rectangle resides. Use the methods of the **Graphics** class to help output the **Rectangle**. If you feel ambitious you might include methods to scale the size of the rectangle, rotate it and move it around within the designated portion of the first quadrant.

6.11 Create a class **HugeInteger** which uses a 40-element array of digits to store integers as large as 40-digits each. Provide methods **inputHugeInteger**, **outputHugeInteger**, **addHugeIntegers** and **substractHugeIntegers**. For comparing **HugeInteger** objects provide methods **isEqualTo**, **isNotEqualTo**, **isGreaterThan**, **isLessThan**, **IsGreaterThanOrEqualTo** and **isLessThanOrEqualTo**—each of these is a "predicate" method that simply returns **true** if the relationship holds between the two **HugeInteger**s and returns **false** if the relationship does not hold. Provide a predicate method **isZero**. If you feel ambitious, also provide the method **multiplyHugeIntegers**, the method **divideHugeIntegers** and the method **modulusHugeIntegers**.

6.12 Create a class **TicTacToe** that will enable you to write a complete program to play the game of tic-tac-toe. The class contains as private data a 3-by-3 double array of integers. The constructor should initialize the empty board to all zeros. Allow two human players. Wherever the first player moves, place a 1 in the specified square; place a 2 wherever the second player moves. Each move must be to an empty square. After each move determine if the game has been won, or if the game is a draw. If you feel ambitious, modify your program so that the computer makes the moves for one of the players automatically. Also, allow the player to specify whether he or she wants to go first or second. If you feel exceptionally ambitious, develop a program that will play three-dimensional tic-tac-toe on a 4-by-4-by-4 board (Note: This is a challenging project that could take many weeks of effort!).

6.13 Explain the notion of package access in Java. Explain the negative aspects of package access as described in the text.

6.14 What happens when a return type, even **void**, is specified for a constructor?

6.15 Create a **Date** class with the following capabilities:

a) Output the date in multiple formats such as

```
MM/DD/YY
June 14, 1992
DDD YYYY
```

b) Use overloaded constructors to create **Date** objects initialized with dates of the formats in part (a).

6.16 Create class **SavingsAccount**. Use a **static** class variable to store the **annualInterestRate** for each of the savers. Each object of the class contains a **private** instance variable **savingsBalance** indicating the amount the saver currently has on deposit. Provide method **calculateMonthlyInterest** to calculate the monthly interest by multiplying the **balance** by **annualInterestRate** divided by 12; this interest should be added to **savingsBalance**. Provide a **static** method **modifyInterestRate** that sets the **annualInterestRate** to a new value. Write a driver program to test class **SavingsAccount**. Instantiate two different **savingsAccount** objects, **saver1** and **saver2**, with balances of $2000.00 and $3000.00, respectively. Set **annualInterestRate** to 4%, then calculate the monthly interest and print the new balances for each of the savers. Then set the **annualInterestRate** to 5% and calculate the next month's interest and print the new balances for each of the savers.

6.17 Create class **IntegerSet**. Each object of the class can hold integers in the range 0 through 100. A set is represented internally as an array of ones and zeros. Array element **a[i]** is 1 if integer *i* is in the set. Array element **a[j]** is 0 if integer *j* is not in the set. The no-argument constructor initializes a set to the so-called "empty set," i.e., a set whose array representation contains all zeros.

Provide the following methods: Method **unionOfIntegerSets** creates a third set which is the set-theoretic union of two existing sets (i.e., an element of the third set's array is set to 1 if that element is 1 in either or both of the existing sets, otherwise the element of the third set is set to 0. Method **intersectionOfIntegerSets** creates a third set which is the set-theoretic intersection of two existing sets, i.e., an element of the third set's array is set to 0 if that element is 0 in either or both of the existing sets, otherwise the element of the third set is set to 1. Method **insertElement** inserts a new integer *k* into a set (by setting **a[k]** to 1). Method **deleteElement** deletes integer *m* (by setting **a[m]** to 0). Method **setPrint** prints a set as a list of numbers separated by spaces. Print only those elements that are present in the set. Print **---** for an empty set. Method **isEqualTo** determines if two sets are equal. Write a program to test your **IntegerSet** class. Instantiate several **IntegerSet** objects. Test that all your methods work properly.

6.18 It would be perfectly reasonable for the **Time1** class of Fig. 6.1 to represent the time internally as the number of seconds since midnight rather than the three integer values **hour**, **minute** and **second**. Clients could use the same public methods and get the same Modify the **Time1** class of Fig. 6.1 to implement the **Time1** as the number of seconds since midnight and show that there is no visible change to the clients of the class.

7

Object-Oriented Programming

Objectives

- To understand inheritance and software reusability.
- To understand superclasses and subclasses.
- To appreciate how polymorphism makes systems extensible and maintainable.
- To understand the distinction between abstract classes and concrete classes.
- To learn how to create abstract classes and interfaces.

Say not you know another entirely, till you have divided an inheritance with him.
Johann Kasper Lavater

This method is to define as the number of a class the class of all classes similar to the given class.
Bertrand Russell

Good as it is to inherit a library, it is better to collect one.
Augustine Birrell

General propositions do not decide concrete cases.
Oliver Wendell Holmes

A philosopher of imposing stature doesn't think in a vacuum. Even his most abstract ideas are, to some extent, conditioned by what is or is not known in the time when he lives.
Alfred North Whitehead

Outline

7.1 Introduction

In this chapter we discuss *object-oriented programming (OOP)* and its key component technologies—*inheritance* and *polymorphism.* Inheritance is a form of software reusability in which new classes are created from existing classes by absorbing their attributes and behaviors and embellishing these with capabilities the new classes require. Software reusability saves time in program development. It encourages the reuse of proven and debugged high-quality software, thus reducing problems after a system becomes operational. These are exciting possibilities. Polymorphism enables us to write programs in a general fashion to handle a wide variety of existing and yet-to-be-specified related classes. Polymorphism makes it easy to add new capabilities to a system. Inheritance and polymorphism are effective techniques for dealing with software complexity.

When creating a new class, instead of writing completely new instance variables and instance methods, the programmer can designate that the new class is to *inherit* the instance variables and instance methods of a previously defined *superclass.* The new class is referred to as a *subclass.* Each subclass itself becomes a candidate to be a superclass for some future subclass.

The *direct superclass* of a subclass is the superclass from which the subclass explicitly inherits. An indirect superclass is inherited from two or more levels up the class hierarchy.

With *single inheritance,* a class is derived from one superclass. Java does not support *multiple inheritance* (as C++ does) but it does support the notion of *interfaces.* Interfaces help Java achieve many of the advantages of multiple inheritance without the associated problems. We will discuss the details of interfaces in this chapter where we consider both general principles as well as a detailed specific example of creating and using interfaces.

A subclass normally adds instance variables and instance methods of its own, so a subclass is generally larger than its superclass. A subclass is more specific than its superclass and represents a smaller group of objects. With single inheritance, the subclass starts out essentially the same as the superclass. The real strength of inheritance comes from the ability to define in the subclass additions to, or replacements for, the features inherited from the superclass.

Every object of a subclass is also an object of that subclass's superclass. However, the converse is not true—superclass objects are not objects of that superclass's subclasses. We will take advantage of this "subclass-object-is-a-superclass-object" relationship to perform some powerful manipulations. For example, we can link a wide variety of different objects related to a common superclass through inheritance into a linked list of superclass objects. This allows a variety of objects to be processed in a general way. As we will see in this and the next chapter, this is a key thrust of object-oriented programming.

We add a new form of member access control in this chapter, namely **`protected`** access. Subclass methods and methods of other classes in the same package as the superclass can access **`protected`** superclass members.

Experience in building software systems indicates that significant portions of the code deal with closely related special cases. It becomes difficult in such systems to see the "big picture" because the designer and the programmer become preoccupied with the special cases. Object-oriented programming provides several ways of "seeing the forest through the trees"—a process called *abstraction.*

If a procedural program has many closely related special cases, then it is common to see **`switch`** statements that distinguish among the special cases and provide the processing logic to deal with each case individually. We will show how to use inheritance and polymorphism to replace such **`switch`** logic with much simpler logic.

We distinguish between the *"is a" relationship* and the *"has a" relationship.* "Is a" is inheritance. In an "is a" relationship, an object of a subclass type may also be treated as an object of the superclass type. "Has a" is composition (as we discussed in Chapter 6). In a "has a" relationship, a class object has one or more objects of other classes as members.

A subclass's methods may need to access certain of its superclass's instance variables and methods.

Software Engineering Observation 7.1

A subclass cannot directly access **`private`** *members of its superclass.*

This is a crucial aspect of software engineering in Java. If a subclass could access the superclass's **`private`** members, this would violate information hiding in the superclass.

Testing and Debugging Tip 7.1

Hiding **`private`** *members is a huge help in testing, debugging and correctly modifying systems. If a subclass could access its superclass's* **`private`** *members, it would then be possible for classes derived from that subclass to access that data as well, and so on. This would propagate access to what is supposed to be* **`private`** *data, and the benefits of information hiding would be lost throughout the class hierarchy.*

A subclass can, however, access the **`public`**, **`protected`** and package access members of its superclass. Superclass members that should not be accessible to a subclass via inheritance are declared **`private`** in the superclass. A subclass can effect state changes in superclass **`private`** members only through **`public`**, **`protected`** and package access methods provided in the superclass.

One problem with inheritance is that a subclass can inherit methods that it does not need or should expressly not have. When a superclass member is inappropriate for a subclass, that member can be *overridden* in the subclass with an appropriate implementation.

Perhaps most exciting is the notion that new classes can inherit from abundant *class libraries*. Organizations develop their own class libraries and can take advantage of other libraries available worldwide. Someday, most software may be constructed from *standardized reusable components* just as hardware is often constructed today. This will help meet the challenges of developing the ever more powerful software we will need in the future.

7.2 Superclasses and Subclasses

Often an object of one class "is an" object of another class as well. A rectangle certainly *is a* quadrilateral (as are squares, parallelograms and trapezoids). Thus, class **`Rectangle`** can be said to *inherit* from class **`Quadrilateral`**. In this context, class **`Quadrilateral`** is a superclass and class **`Rectangle`** is a subclass. A rectangle *is a* specific type of quadrilateral, but it is incorrect to claim that a quadrilateral *is a* rectangle (the quadrilateral could be a parallelogram). Figure 7.1 shows several simple inheritance examples.

Because inheritance normally produces subclasses with *more* features than their superclasses, the terms superclass and subclass can be confusing. There is another way, however, to view these terms that makes perfectly good sense. Because every subclass object "is an" object of its superclass, and because one superclass can have many subclasses, the set of objects represented by a superclass is normally larger than the set of objects represented by any of that superclass's subclasses.

Inheritance relationships form tree-like hierarchical structures. A superclass exists in a hierarchical relationship with its subclasses. A class can certainly exist by itself, but it is when a class is used with the mechanism of inheritance that the class becomes either a superclass that supplies attributes and behaviors to other classes, or the class becomes a subclass that inherits those attributes and behaviors.

Superclass	Subclasses
`Student`	`GraduateStudent` `UndergraduateStudent`

`Shape`	`Circle`
	`Triangle`
	`Rectangle`

`Loan`	`CarLoan`
	`HomeImprovementLoan`
	`MortgageLoan`

`Employee`	`FacultyMember` `StaffMember`
`Account`	`CheckingAccount` `SavingsAccount`

Fig. 7.1 Some simple inheritance examples.

Let us develop a simple inheritance hierarchy. A typical university community has thousands of people who are community members. These people consist of employees, students and alumni. Employees are either faculty members or staff members. Faculty members are either administrators (such as deans and department chairpersons) or teaching faculty. This yields the inheritance hierarchy shown in Fig. 7.2. Note that the inheritance hierarchy could contain many other classes. For example, students can be graduate students or undergraduate students. Undergraduate students can be freshman, sophomores, juniors, and seniors. And so on.

Another substantial inheritance hierarchy is the **`Shape`** hierarchy of Fig. 7.3. There are abundant examples of hierarchies in the real world but students are not accustomed to categorizing the real world in this manner, so it takes some adjustment in their thinking. Actually, biology students have had some practice with hierarchies. Everything we study in biology is grouped into a hierarchy headed by living things and these can be plants or animals and so on.

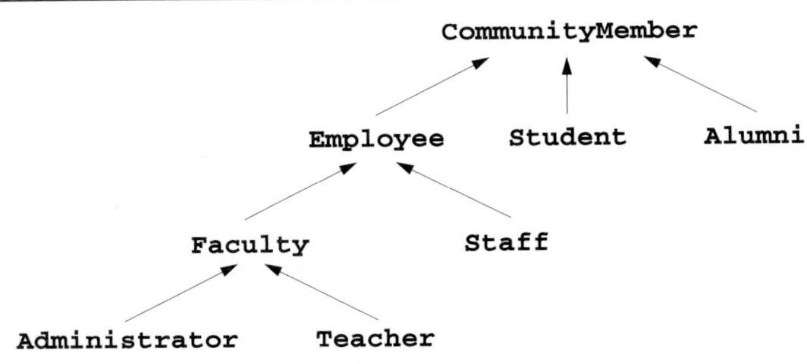

Fig. 7.2 An inheritance hierarchy for university community members.

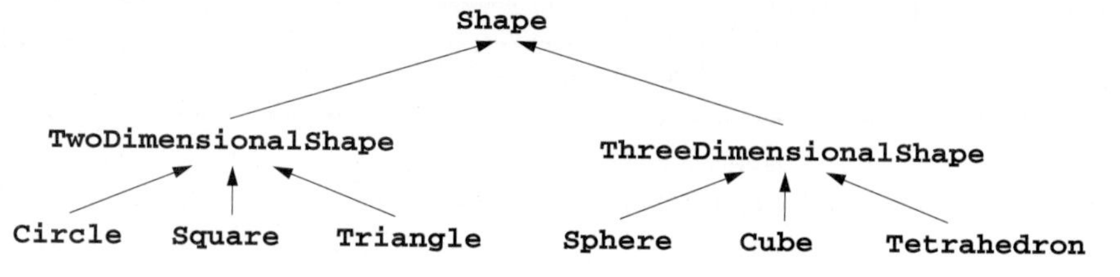

Fig. 7.3 A portion of a **Shape** class hierarchy.

To specify that class **CommissionWorker** is derived from (or inherits from) class **Employee**, class **CommissionWorker** could be defined in Java as follows

```
class CommissionWorker extends Employee { ... }
```

With inheritance **private** members of a superclass are not directly accessible from that class's subclasses. Package access members of the superclass are only accessible in a subclass if both the superclass and its subclass are in the same package. All other superclass members become members of the subclass.

It is possible to treat superclass objects and subclass objects similarly; that commonality is expressed in the attributes and behaviors of the superclass. Objects of all classes derived from a common superclass can all be treated as objects of that superclass.

We will consider many examples in which we can take advantage of this relationship with an ease of programming not available in non-object-oriented languages such as C.

7.3 `protected` Members

Public members of a superclass are accessible by all methods in the program. **Private** members of a superclass are accessible only by methods of the superclass.

Protected access serves as an intermediate level of protection between **public** access and **private** access. **Protected** members of a superclass may be accessed only by methods of the superclass, by methods of subclasses and by methods of other classes in the same package.

Subclass methods can normally refer to **public** and **protected** members of the superclass simply by using the member names (package access members can also be accessed if the superclass and subclass are in the same package). When a subclass method overrides a superclass method, the superclass method may be accessed from the subclass by preceding the superclass method name with **super** followed by the dot character (**.**).

7.4 Relationship between Superclass Objects and Subclass Objects

An object of a subclass can be treated as an object of its corresponding superclass. This makes possible some interesting manipulations. For example, despite the fact that objects of a variety of classes derived from a particular superclass may be quite different from one another, we can create an array of them—as long as we treat them as superclass objects. But the reverse is not true: A superclass object is not also automatically a subclass object.

Common Programming Error 7.1

Treating a superclass object as a subclass object can cause errors.

The programmer may, however, use an explicit cast to convert a superclass reference to a subclass reference. This can only be done when the superclass reference is actually referencing a subclass object, otherwise Java will throw a **ClassCastException**.

Common Programming Error 7.2

Assigning an object of a superclass to a subclass reference (without a cast) is a syntax error.

Software Engineering Observation 7.2

If an object has been assigned to a reference of one of its superclasses, it is acceptable to cast that object back to its own type. In fact, this must be done in order to send that object any of its messages that do not appear in that superclass.

Our first example of inheritance is shown in Fig. 7.4.

```
// Fig. 7.4: Point.java
// Definition of class Point

public class Point {
   protected int x, y; // coordinates of the Point

   // No-argument constructor
   public Point() { setPoint( 0, 0 ); }

   // Constructor
   public Point( int a, int b ) { setPoint( a, b ); }

   // Set x and y coordinates of Point
   public void setPoint( int a, int b )
   {
      x = a;
      y = b;
   }

   // get x coordinate
   public int getX() { return x; }

   // get y coordinate
   public int getY() { return y; }

   // convert the point into a String representation
   public String toString()
      { return "[" + x + ", " + y + "]"; }
}
```

Fig. 7.4 Assigning subclass references to superclass references (part 1 of 4).

```
30 // Fig. 7.4: Circle.java
31 // Definition of class Circle
32
33 public class Circle extends Point {   // inherits from Point
34    protected double radius;
35
36    // No-argument constructor
37    public Circle()
38    {
39       // implicit call to superclass constructor occurs here
40       setRadius( 0 );
41    }
42
43    // Constructor
44    public Circle( double r, int a, int b )
45    {
46       super( a, b );  // explicit call to superclass constructor
47       setRadius( r );
48    }
49
50    // Set radius of Circle
51    public void setRadius( double r )
52       { radius = ( r >= 0.0 ? r : 0.0 ); }
53
54    // Get radius of Circle
55    public double getRadius() { return radius; }
56
57    // Calculate area of Circle
58    public double area() { return Math.PI * radius * radius; }
59
60    // convert the Circle to a String
61    public String toString()
62    {
63       return "Center = " + "[" + x + ", " + y + "]" +
64              "; Radius = " + radius;
65    }
66 }
```

Fig. 7.4 Assigning subclass references to superclass references (part 2 of 4).

Lines 1–29 show a **Point** class definition. Lines 30–66 show a **Circle** class definition; we will see that class **Circle** inherits from class **Point**. Lines 67–107 show an applet that demonstrates assigning subclass references to superclass references and casting superclass references to subclass references.

Let us first examine the **Point** class definition in lines 1–29. The **public** interface to **Point** contains methods **setPoint**, **getX**, **getY**, **toString** and two **Point** constructors. The instance variables **x** and **y** of **Point** are specified as **protected**. This prevents clients of **Point** objects from directly accessing the data (unless they are in the same package), but enables classes derived from **Point** to access the inherited instance variables directly. If the data were specified as **private**, the non-**private** methods of **Point** would have to be used to access the data, even by subclasses.

```
67  // Fig. 7.4: Test.java
68  // Casting superclass references to subclass references
69  import java.awt.Graphics;
70  import java.applet.Applet;
71  import java.text.DecimalFormat;
72
73  public class Test extends Applet {
74     private Point pointRef, p;
75     private Circle circleRef, c;
76
77     public void init()
78     {
79        p = new Point( 30, 50 );
80        c = new Circle( 2.7, 120, 89 );
81     }
82
83     public void paint( Graphics g )
84     {
85        DecimalFormat precision2 = new DecimalFormat( "#.00" );
86
87        g.drawString( "Point p: " + p.toString(), 25, 25 );
88        g.drawString( "Circle c: " + c.toString(), 25, 40 );
89
90        // Attempt to treat a Circle as a Point
91        pointRef = c;   // assign Circle to pointRef
92        g.drawString( "Circle c (via pointRef): " +
93                      pointRef.toString(), 25, 70 );
94
95        // Treat a Circle as a Circle (with some casting)
96        circleRef = (Circle) pointRef;  // cast super to sub
97        g.drawString( "Circle c (via circleRef): " +
98                       circleRef.toString(), 25, 100);
99        g.drawString( "Area of c (via circleRef): " +
100                     precision2.format( circleRef.area() ),
101                     25, 115 );
102
103       // Attempt to refer to Point object
104       // with Circle reference
105       circleRef = (Circle) p;     // line 39 in Test.java
106    }
107 }
```

Fig. 7.4 Assigning subclass references to superclass references (part 3 of 4).

In Chapter 1, we stated that every class definition in Java must extend another class. However, notice that class **Point** (line 4) does not explicitly use the **extends** keyword. If a new class definition does not explicitly extend an existing class definition, Java implicitly uses class **Object** (package **java.lang**) as the superclass for the new class definition. Class **Object** provides a set of methods that can be used with any object of any class.

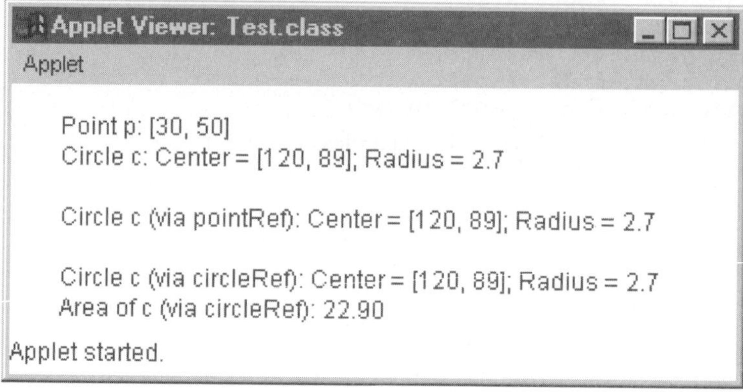


```
Exception occurred during event dispatching:
java.lang.ClassCastException:
        at Test.paint(Test.java:39)
        at java.awt.Component.dispatchEventImpl
            (Component.java:1401)
        at java.awt.Container.dispatchEventImpl
            (Container.java:833)
        at java.awt.Component.dispatchEvent
            (Component.java:1382)
        at java.awt.EventDispatchThread.run
            (EventDispatchThread.java:63)
```

Fig. 7.4 Assigning subclass references to superclass references (part 4 of 4).

Software Engineering Observation 7.3

Every class in Java extends **`Object`** *unless specified otherwise in the first line of the class definition. Thus, class* **`Object`** *is the superclass of the entire Java class hierarchy.*

Class **`Circle`** (lines 30–66) inherits from class **`Point`**. This is specified in the first line of the class definition

```
public class Circle extends Point {  // inherits from Point
```

Keyword **`extends`** in the class definition indicates inheritance. All the (non–**`private`**) members of class **`Point`** are inherited into class **`Circle`**. Thus, the **`public`** interface to **`Circle`** includes the **`Point`** **`public`** methods as well as the two overloaded **`Circle`** constructors and **`Circle`** methods **`setRadius`**, **`getRadius`**, **`area`** and **`toString`**. Notice that method area (line 58) uses predefined constant **`Math.PI`** from class **`Math`** (package **`java.lang`**) to calculate the area of a circle.

The **`Circle`** constructors (lines 37 and 44) must invoke the **`Point`** constructor to initialize the superclass portion (variables **`x`** and **`y`** inherited from **`Point`**) of a **`Circle`** object. The first line of the body of the constructor at line 44

```
super( a, b );  // explicit call to superclass constructor
```

explicitly invokes the **Point** constructor (defined at line 11) using the superclass constructor call syntax—i.e., **super** followed by a set of parentheses containing the arguments to the superclass constructor (in this case the values **a** and **b** are passed to initialize the superclass members **x** and **y**). The call to the superclass constructor must be the first line in the body of the subclass constructor.

Common Programming Error 7.3

It is a syntax error if a **super** *call by a subclass to its superclass constructor is not the first statement in the subclass constructor.*

The no-argument constructor at line 37 does not explicitly call a superclass constructor. Therefore, an implicit call is automatically made to the Point class no-argument constructor (defined at line 8) that initializes superclass members **x** and **y** to zeros. If the **Point** class did not provide a no-argument constructor, a compiler error would occur.

A subclass can redefine a superclass method using the same signature; this is called *overriding* a superclass method. When that method is mentioned by name in the subclass, the subclass version is automatically selected. We have actually been overriding methods in every applet in the book. When we extend **Applet** to create a new applet class, the new class inherits versions of **init** and **paint** (and many other methods). Each time we defined **init** or **paint**, we were overriding the original version that was inherited. Also, when we provided method **toString** for many of the classes in Chapter 6, we were overriding the original version of **toString** provided by class **Object**. As we will soon see, the **super** reference followed by the dot operator may be used to access the superclass version of that method from the subclass.

Note that class **Circle**'s **toString** method (line 61) overrides the **Point** class **toString** method (line 27). Class **Point**'s **toString** method overrides the original **toString** method provided by class **Object**. Because class **Object** provides the original **toString** method, every class inherits a **toString** method. This method is used to convert any object of any class into a **String** representation and is sometimes called implicitly by the program (e.g., when an object is added to a **String**). **Circle** method **toString** directly accesses the **protected** instance variables **x** and **y** that were inherited from the **Point** class.

Software Engineering Observation 7.4

A redefinition of a superclass method in a subclass need not have the same signature as the superclass method. Such a redefinition is not method overriding but is simply an example of method overloading.

Software Engineering Observation 7.5

Any object can be converted to a **String** *with an explicit or implicit call to the object's* **toString** *method.*

Software Engineering Observation 7.6

Each class should override method **toString** *to return useful information about objects of that class.*

Common Programming Error 7.4

It is a syntax error if a method in a superclass and a method in its subclass have the same signature but a different return type.

The applet (lines 67–107) instantiates **Point** object **p** and **Circle** object **c** (lines 79–80). These objects are output from method **paint** to show that they were initialized correctly (lines 87–88).

Next, **Circle c**, a subclass object, is assigned to **pointRef** (line 91). It is always acceptable in Java to assign a subclass reference to a superclass reference (because of the "is a" relationship of inheritance). The converse of this is dangerous, as we will see. Interestingly, when this **pointRef** is sent the **toString** message, Java knows that the object really is a **Circle**, so it chooses the **Circle toString** method instead of using the **Point toString** method as you might have expected. This is an example of polymorphism and dynamic binding, concepts we treat in depth later in this chapter.

In line 96, we cast **pointRef** (which admittedly is referencing a **Circle**) to a **Circle** and assign the result to **circleRef** (this cast would be dangerous if **pointRef** were really referencing a **Point** as we will soon see). Then, we use **circleRef** to print successfully the various facts about **Circle circleRef**. The **drawString** statement at line 99 that outputs the area of the circle uses an instance of class **DecimalFormat** (package **java.text**) called **precision2** to output the area of the circle with two digits to the right of the decimal point. The format **"#.00"** (specified at line 85) uses **0** twice to indicate the proper number of digits after the decimal point. Each **0** is a required decimal place. The **#** to the left of the decimal point indicates any number of digits.

Next, we attempt a dangerous cast in line 105. We cast **Point p** to **circleRef**. At execution time when this is attempted, Java determines that **p** really references a **Point**, recognizes the cast to **Circle** as being dangerous, and throws a **ClassCastException**. Because we made no provision to deal with this exception here, the program ignores the exception. We will discuss exception handling in depth in Chapter 12. The second output window shows the error messages displayed when the **ClassCastException** occurs. Such error messages normally include the file name and line number at which the error occurred so you can go to that specific line in the program for debugging. Note that the first line number specified—**Test.java:39**—is different from the line numbers for file **Test.java** shown in the text. This is because the examples in the text are numbered with consecutive line numbers for all files in the same program for discussion purposes. If you open the file **Test.java** in an editor, you will find that the error did indeed occur at line 39 (which is line 105 in the whole program).

7.5 Using Constructors and Finalizers in Subclasses

When an object of a subclass is instantiated, the superclass's constructor should be called to do any necessary initialization of the superclass instance variables of the subclass object. An explicit call to the superclass constructor (via the **super** reference) can be provided as the first statement in the subclass constructor. Otherwise the subclass constructor will call the superclass default constructor (or no-argument constructor) implicitly.

Common Programming Error 7.5

If a subclass constructor invokes a superclass default constructor (or no-argument constructor) and if the superclass does not have a default constructor (or no-argument constructor), a syntax error occurs.

Superclass constructors are not inherited by subclasses. Subclass constructors, however, can call superclass constructors via the **super** reference. Figure 7.5 shows the order in which superclass and subclass constructors and finalizers are called.

Software Engineering Observation 7.7

When an object of a subclass is created, first the superclass constructor executes, then the subclass constructor executes.

```
// Fig. 7.5: Point.java
// Definition of class Point
public class Point {
   protected int x, y; // coordinates of the Point

   // no-argument constructor
   public Point()
   {
      setPoint( 0, 0 );
      System.out.println( "Point constructor: " +
                          toString() );
   }

   // constructor
   public Point( int a, int b )
   {
      setPoint( a, b );
      System.out.println( "Point constructor: " +
                          toString() );
   }

   // finalizer
   protected void finalize() throws Throwable
   {
      System.out.println( "Point finalizer: " +
                          toString() );
      super.finalize();  // call superclass finalize method
   }

   // Set x and y coordinates of Point
   public void setPoint( int a, int b )
   {
      x = a;
      y = b;
   }
```

Fig. 7.5 Order in which constructors and finalizers are called (part 1 of 6).

```

    // get x coordinate
    public int getX() { return x; }

    // get y coordinate
    public int getY() { return y; }

    // convert the point into a String representation
    public String toString()
       { return "[" + x + ", " + y + "]"; }
}
```

Fig. 7.5 Order in which constructors and finalizers are called (part 2 of 6).

```
// Fig. 7.5: Circle.java
// Definition of class Circle
public class Circle extends Point {  // inherits from Point
   protected double radius;

   // no-argument constructor
   public Circle()
   {
      // implicit call to superclass constructor here
      setRadius( 0 );
      System.out.println( "Circle constructor: " +
                          toString() );
   }

   // Constructor
   public Circle( double r, int a, int b )
   {
      super( a, b );  // call the superclass constructor
      setRadius( r );
      System.out.println( "Circle constructor: " +
                          toString() );
   }

   // finalizer
   protected void finalize() throws Throwable
   {
      System.out.println( "Circle finalizer: " +
                          toString() );
      super.finalize();  // call superclass finalize method
   }

   // Set radius of Circle
   public void setRadius( double r )
      { radius = ( r >= 0 ? r : 0 ); }

```

Fig. 7.5 Order in which constructors and finalizers are called (part 3 of 6).

```
   // Get radius of Circle
   public double getRadius() { return radius; }

   // Calculate area of Circle
   public double area()
      { return Math.PI * radius * radius; }

   // convert the Circle to a String
   public String toString()
   {
      return "Center = " + super.toString() +
             "; Radius = " + radius;
   }
}
```

Fig. 7.5 Order in which constructors and finalizers are called (part 4 of 6).

```
// Fig. 7.5: Test.java
// Demonstrate when superclass and subclass
// constructors and finalizers are called.
import java.awt.Graphics;
import java.applet.Applet;

public class Test extends Applet {
   private Circle circle1, circle2;

   public void init()
   {
      circle1 = new Circle( 4.5, 72, 29 );
      circle2 = new Circle( 10, 5, 5 );
   }

   public void start()
   {
      circle2 = null; // Circle can now be garbage collected
      circle1 = null; // Circle can now be garbage collected

      System.gc();    // call the garbage collector
   }

   public void paint( Graphics g )
   {
      g.drawString(
         "See command line or Java Console for output",
         25, 25 );
   }
}
```

Fig. 7.5 Order in which constructors and finalizers are called (part 5 of 6).

```
Point constructor: Center = [72, 29]; Radius = 0.0
Circle constructor: Center = [72, 29]; Radius = 4.5
Point constructor: Center = [5, 5]; Radius = 0.0
Circle constructor: Center = [5, 5]; Radius = 10.0
Circle finalizer: Center = [72, 29]; Radius = 4.5
Point finalizer: Center = [72, 29]; Radius = 4.5
Circle finalizer: Center = [5, 5]; Radius = 10.0
Point finalizer: Center = [5, 5]; Radius = 10.0
```

Fig. 7.5 Order in which constructors and finalizers are called (part 6 of 6).

Class **Point** (lines 1–46) contains two constructors, a finalizer, other public methods and **protected** instance variables **x** and **y**. The constructor and finalizer each print that they are executing then display the **Point** for which they are invoked. Notice the first line of the **finalize** method (line 23)

```
protected void finalize() throws Throwable
```

Method **finalize** should always be defined as **protected** so subclasses have access to the method, but classes that simply use **Point** objects do not. The **throws Throwable** (part of the exception handling mechanism described in Chapter 12) is provided because it is part of the original definition of **finalize** in class **Object**. This is required to complete the proper overriding of method **finalize**.

Class **Circle** (lines 47–95) derives from **Point** and contains two constructors, a finalizer, other public methods and protected instance variable **radius**. The constructor and finalizer each print that they are executing then display the **Circle** for which they are invoked. Note that the **Circle** method **toString** invokes **Point**'s **toString** via **super** (line 83).

Common Programming Error 7.6

*When a superclass method is overridden in a subclass, it is common to have the subclass version call the superclass version and do some additional work. Not using the **super** reference to reference the superclass's method causes infinite recursion because the subclass method actually calls itself.*

Common Programming Error 7.7

*Cascading **super** references to refer to a member (method or variable) several levels up the hierarchy (as in **super.super.x**) is a syntax error.*

Good Programming Practice 7.1

The last statement in a **finalize** *method should always be* **super.finalize();** *to ensure that the superclass's* **finalize** *method is called.*

Lines 96–125 show an applet for testing this **Point/Circle** inheritance hierarchy. The applet begins in method **init** by instantiating **Circle** object **circle1** (line 107). This invokes the **Circle** constructor at line 62 which immediately invokes the **Point** constructor at line 15. The **Point** constructor outputs the values received from the **Circle** constructor by calling method **toString** and returns program control to the **Circle** constructor. Then, the **Circle** constructor outputs the complete **Circle** by calling method **toString**. **Circle** object **circle2** is instantiated next. Again, the **Point** and **Circle** constructors both execute. Notice in the command-line output window that the body of the **Point** constructor is performed before the body of the **Circle** constructor showing that objects are constructed "inside out."

In the **start** method, we set **circle2** to **null** then set **circle1** to **null**. Since each of these objects is no longer needed, Java marks the memory occupied by **circle2** and **circle1** for *garbage collection.* Java guarantees that before the garbage collector runs to reclaim the space for each of these objects, the **finalize** methods for each object will be called. The garbage collector is a low-priority thread that runs automatically whenever processor time is available. We choose here to force the garbage collector to run with the call **System.gc()** in line 116. Java does not guarantee the order in which objects will be garbage collected nor the order in which finalizers will be run. Notice in the command-line output window that both the **Circle** and **Point finalize** methods are called when each **Circle** object is garbage collected.

7.6 Implicit Subclass-Object-to-Superclass-Object Conversion

Despite the fact that a subclass object also "is a" superclass object, the subclass type and the superclass type are different. Subclass objects can be treated as superclass objects. This makes sense because the subclass has members corresponding to each of the superclass members—remember that the subclass normally has more members than the superclass has. Assignment in the other direction is not allowed because assigning a superclass object to a subclass reference would leave the additional subclass members undefined.

Common Programming Error 7.8

Assigning a subclass object to a reference to a corresponding superclass, then attempting to reference subclass-only members with that superclass reference is a syntax error.

A reference to a subclass object may be implicitly converted into a reference to a superclass object because a subclass object *is a* superclass object through inheritance.

There are four possible ways to mix and match superclass references and subclass references with superclass objects and subclass objects:

1. Referring to a superclass object with a superclass reference is straightforward.
2. Referring to a subclass object with a subclass reference is straightforward.
3. Referring to a subclass object with a superclass reference is safe because the subclass object *is an* object of its superclass as well. Such code can only refer to su-

perclass members. If this code refers to subclass-only members through the superclass reference, the compiler will report a syntax error.

4. Referring to a superclass object with a subclass reference is a syntax error. The subclass reference must first be cast to a superclass reference.

Common Programming Error 7.9

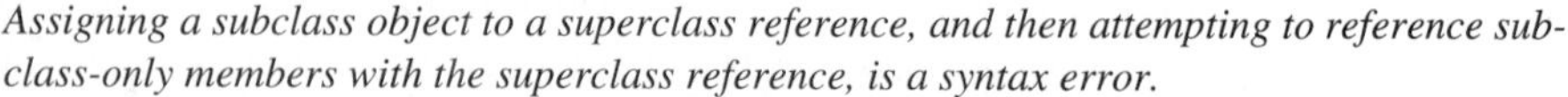

Assigning a subclass object to a superclass reference, and then attempting to reference subclass-only members with the superclass reference, is a syntax error.

As convenient as it may be to treat subclass objects as superclass objects, and to do this by manipulating all these objects with superclass references, there appears to be a problem. In a payroll system, for example, we would like to be able to walk through an array of employees and calculate the weekly pay for each person. But intuition suggests that using superclass references would enable the program to call only the superclass payroll calculation routine (if indeed there is such a routine in the superclass). We need a way to invoke the proper payroll calculation routine for each object, whether it is a superclass object or a subclass object, and to do this simply by using the superclass reference. Actually, this is precisely how Java behaves and is discussed later in this chapter when we consider polymorphism and dynamic binding.

7.7 Software Engineering with Inheritance

We can use inheritance to customize existing software. When we use inheritance to create a new class from an existing class, the new class inherits the attributes and behaviors of an existing class, then we can add attributes and behaviors or override superclass behaviors to customize the class to meet our needs.

It can be difficult for students to appreciate the problems faced by designers and implementors on large-scale software projects in industry. People experienced on such projects will invariably state that a key to improving the software development process is encouraging software reuse. Object-oriented programming in general, and Java in particular, certainly does this.

It is the availability of substantial and useful class libraries that delivers the maximum benefits of software reuse through inheritance. As interest in Java grows, interest in Java class libraries will increase. Just as shrink-wrapped software produced by independent software vendors became an explosive growth industry with the arrival of the personal computer, so, too, will the creation and sale of Java class libraries. Application designers will build their applications with these libraries, and library designers will be rewarded by having their libraries wrapped with the applications. What we see coming is a massive worldwide commitment to the development of Java class libraries for a huge variety of applications arenas.

Software Engineering Observation 7.8

Creating a subclass does not affect its superclass's source code or the superclass's Java bytecodes; the integrity of a superclass is preserved by inheritance.

A superclass specifies commonality. All classes derived from a superclass inherit the capabilities of that superclass. In the object-oriented design process, the designer looks for commonality among a set of classes and factors it out to form desirable superclasses. Subclasses are then customized beyond the capabilities inherited from the superclass.

Software Engineering Observation 7.9

Just as the designer of non-object-oriented systems should avoid unnecessary proliferation of functions, the designer of object-oriented systems should avoid unnecessary proliferation of classes. Proliferating classes creates management problems and can hinder software reusability simply because it is more difficult for a potential reuser of a class to locate that class in a huge collection. The trade-off is to create fewer classes, each providing substantial additional functionality, but such classes might be too rich for certain reusers.

Performance Tip 7.1

If classes produced through inheritance are larger than they need to be, memory and processing resources may be wasted. Inherit from the class "closest" to what you need.

Note that reading a set of subclass declarations can be confusing because inherited members are not shown, but inherited members are nevertheless present in the subclasses. A similar problem can exist in the documentation of subclasses.

Software Engineering Observation 7.10

In an object-oriented system, classes are often closely related. "Factor out" common attributes and behaviors and place these in a superclass. Then use inheritance to form subclasses without having to repeat common attributes and behaviors.

Software Engineering Observation 7.11

Modifications to a superclass do not require subclasses to change as long as the public interface to the superclass remains unchanged.

7.8 Composition vs. Inheritance

We have discussed *is a* relationships which are implemented by inheritance. We have also discussed *has a* relationships (and seen examples in preceding chapters) in which a class may have objects of other classes as members—such relationships create new classes by *composition* of existing classes. For example, given the classes **`Employee`**, **`BirthDate`**, and **`TelephoneNumber`**, it is improper to say that an **`Employee`** *is a* **`BirthDate`** or that an **`Employee`** *is a* **`TelephoneNumber`**. But it is certainly appropriate to say that an **`Employee`** *has a* **`BirthDate`** and that an **`Employee`** *has a* **`TelephoneNumber`**.

7.9 Case Study: Point, Circle, Cylinder

Now let us consider a substantial inheritance example. We consider a point, circle, cylinder hierarchy. First we develop and use class **`Point`** (Fig. 7.6). Then we present an example in which we derive class **`Circle`** from class **`Point`** (Fig. 7.7). Finally, we present an example in which we derive class **`Cylinder`** from class **`Circle`** (Fig. 7.8).

Figure 7.6 shows class **`Point`**. Part 1 is the class **`Point`** definition. Class **`Point`** is defined as part of package **`com.deitel.jhtp2.ch07`** (line 3). Note that **`Point`**'s instance variables are **`protected`**. Thus, when class **`Circle`** is derived from class **`Point`**, the methods of class **`Circle`** will be able to directly reference coordinates **`x`** and **`y`** rather than using access methods. This may result in better performance.

```java
// Fig. 7.6: Point.java
// Definition of class Point
package com.deitel.jhtp2.ch07;

public class Point {
   protected int x, y; // coordinates of the Point

   // no-argument constructor
   public Point() { setPoint( 0, 0 ); }

   // constructor
   public Point( int a, int b ) { setPoint( a, b ); }

   // Set x and y coordinates of Point
   public void setPoint( int a, int b )
   {
      x = a;
      y = b;
   }

   // get x coordinate
   public int getX() { return x; }

   // get y coordinate
   public int getY() { return y; }

   // convert the point into a String representation
   public String toString()
      { return "[" + x + ", " + y + "]"; }
}
```

Fig. 7.6 Testing class **Point** (part 1 of 3).

```java
// Fig. 7.6: Test.java
// Applet to test class Point
import java.awt.Graphics;
import java.applet.Applet;
import com.deitel.jhtp2.ch07.Point;

public class Test extends Applet {
   private Point p;

   public void init()
   {
      p = new Point( 72, 115 );
   }

```

Fig. 7.6 Testing class **Point** (part 2 of 3).

```
   public void paint( Graphics g )
   {
      g.drawString( "X coordinate is " + p.getX(), 25, 25 );
      g.drawString( "Y coordinate is " + p.getY(), 25, 40 );

      p.setPoint( 10, 10 );
      g.drawString( "The new location of p is " +
                    p.toString(), 25, 70 );
   }
}
```

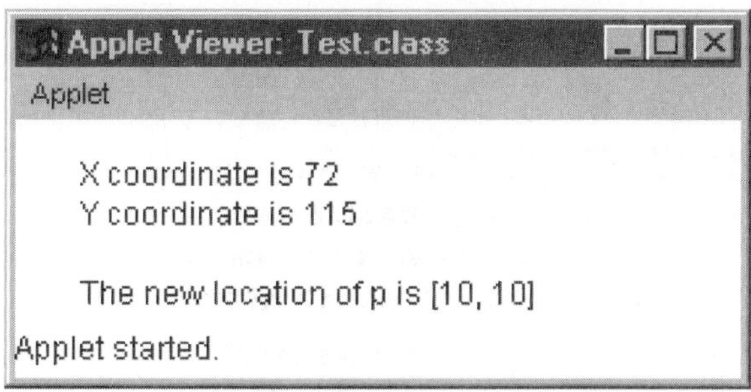

Fig. 7.6 Testing class **Point** (part 3 of 3).

Figure 7.6, parts 2 and 3, shows a **Test** applet for testing class **Point**. The **paint** method must use methods **getX** and **getY** to read the values of **protected** instance variables **x** and **y**. Remember that **protected** instance variables are accessible only to methods of their class, their subclasses and other classes in the same package.

Our next example is shown in Fig. 7.7. The **Point** class definition and the method definitions from Fig. 7.6 are imported here, so the class definition is not shown again. Parts 1 and 2 of Fig. 7.7 show the **Circle** class definition with the **Circle** method definitions. Parts 3 and 4 show a **Test** applet.

```
// Fig. 7.7: Circle.java
// Definition of class Circle
package com.deitel.jhtp2.ch07;

public class Circle extends Point {  // inherits from Point
   protected double radius;

   // no-argument constructor
   public Circle()
   {
      // implicit call to super class constructor
      setRadius( 0 );
   }

```

Fig. 7.7 Testing class **Circle** (part 1 of 4).

```
   // Constructor
   public Circle( double r, int a, int b )
   {
      super( a, b );  // call the superclass constructor
      setRadius( r );
   }

   // Set radius of Circle
   public void setRadius( double r )
      { radius = ( r >= 0.0 ? r : 0.0 ); }

   // Get radius of Circle
   public double getRadius() { return radius; }

   // Calculate area of Circle
   public double area()
      { return Math.PI * radius * radius; }

   // convert the Circle to a String
   public String toString()
   {
      return "Center = " + super.toString() +
             "; Radius = " + radius;
   }
}
```

Fig. 7.7 Testing class **Circle** (part 2 of 4).

```
// Fig. 7.7: Test.java
// Applet to test class Circle
import java.awt.Graphics;
import java.applet.Applet;
import java.text.DecimalFormat;
import com.deitel.jhtp2.ch07.Circle;

public class Test extends Applet {
   private Circle c;

   public void init()
   {
      c = new Circle( 2.5, 37, 43 );
   }

   public void paint( Graphics g )
   {
      DecimalFormat precision2 = new DecimalFormat( "#.00" );

      g.drawString( "X coordinate is " + c.getX(), 25, 25 );
      g.drawString( "Y coordinate is " + c.getY(), 25, 40 );
      g.drawString( "Radius is " + c.getRadius(), 25, 55 );
```

Fig. 7.7 Testing class **Circle** (part 3 of 4).

```
62
63         c.setRadius( 4.25 );
64         c.setPoint( 2, 2 );
65         g.drawString( "The new location and radius of c are ",
66                       25, 85 );
67         g.drawString( c.toString(), 40, 100 );
68         g.drawString( "Area is " +
69                       precision2.format( c.area() ), 25, 115 );
70     }
71  }
```

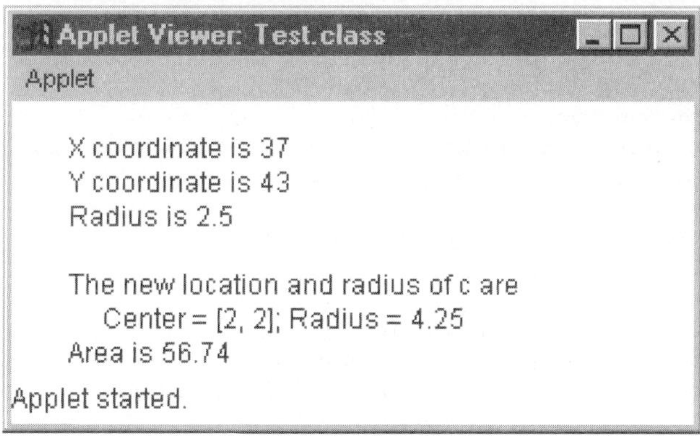

Fig. 7.7 Testing class **Circle** (part 4 of 4).

Note that class **Circle extends** class **Point**. This means that the **public** interface to **Circle** includes the **Point** methods as well as the **Circle** methods **setRadius**, **getRadius**, **area**, **toString** and the **Circle** constructors. Applet **Test** instantiates an object of class **Circle** (line 52) then uses *get* methods to obtain the information about the **Circle** object. Applet **Test**'s **paint** method indirectly references the **protected** data of class **Circle** through method calls. Applet **Test** then uses *set* methods **setRadius** and **setPoint** to reset the radius and coordinates of the center of the circle. Finally, **paint** displays the **Circle** object **c** and calculates and prints its area.

Our last example is shown in Fig. 7.8. The **Circle** class definitions of Fig. 7.7 is imported here. Part 1 shows the **Cylinder** class definition with the **Cylinder** method definitions. Part 2 is a **Test** applet to test the **Cylinder** class.

Note that class **Cylinder extends** class **Circle**. This means that the **public** interface to **Cylinder** includes the **Circle** methods and **Point** methods as well as the **Cylinder** constructor and **Cylinder** methods **setHeight**, **getHeight**, **area** (which overrides the **Circle area** method), **volume** and **toString**. The **Test** applet instantiates an object of class **Cylinder** (line 57) then uses *get* methods (lines 64–67) to obtain the information about the **Cylinder** object. Again, the **Test** applet's **paint** method cannot directly reference the **protected** data of class **Cylinder**. The **Test** applet uses *set* methods **setHeight**, **setRadius**, and **setPoint** to reset the **height**, **radius**, and coordinates of the **cylinder**. Then, the **Test** applet uses **toString**, **area**, and **volume** to print the attributes and some facts about the **Cylinder**.

```
// Fig. 7.8: Cylinder.java
// Definition of class Cylinder
package com.deitel.jhtp2.ch07;

public class Cylinder extends Circle {
   protected double height;  // height of Cylinder

   // No-argument constructor
   public Cylinder()
   {
      // implicit call to superclass constructor here
      setHeight( 0 );
   }

   // constructor
   public Cylinder( double h, double r, int a, int b )
   {
      super( r, a, b );
      setHeight( h );
   }

   // Set height of Cylinder
   public void setHeight( double h )
      { height = ( h >= 0 ? h : 0 ); }

   // Get height of Cylinder
   public double getHeight() { return height; }

   // Calculate area of Cylinder (i.e., surface area)
   public double area()
   {
      return 2 * super.area() +
             2 * Math.PI * radius * height;
   }

   // Calculate volume of Cylinder
   public double volume() { return super.area() * height; }

   // Convert the Cylinder to a String
   public String toString()
   {
      return super.toString() + "; Height = " + height;
   }
}
```

Fig. 7.8 Testing class **Cylinder** (part 1 of 3).

This example nicely demonstrates inheritance and defining and referencing **protected** instance variables. The reader should now be confident with the basics of inheritance. In the next several sections, we show how to program with inheritance hierarchies in a general manner using polymorphism. Data abstraction, inheritance, and polymorphism are the crux of object-oriented programming.

```
// Fig. 7.8: Test.java
// Applet to test class Cylinder
import java.awt.Graphics;
import java.applet.Applet;
import java.text.*;
import com.deitel.jhtp2.ch07.Cylinder;

public class Test extends Applet {
   private Cylinder c;

   public void init()
   {
      c = new Cylinder( 5.7, 2.5, 12, 23 );
   }

   public void paint( Graphics g )
   {
      DecimalFormat precision2 = new DecimalFormat( "#.00" );

      g.drawString( "X coordinate is " + c.getX(), 25, 25 );
      g.drawString( "Y coordinate is " + c.getY(), 25, 40 );
      g.drawString( "Radius is " + c.getRadius(), 25, 55 );
      g.drawString( "Height is " + c.getHeight(), 25, 70 );

      c.setHeight( 10 );
      c.setRadius( 4.25 );
      c.setPoint( 2, 2 );

      g.drawString( "The new location, radius and height" +
                    " of c are ", 25, 100 );
      g.drawString( c.toString(), 40, 115 );
      g.drawString( "Area is " +
                    precision2.format( c.area() ), 25, 130 );
      g.drawString( "Volume is " +
                   precision2.format( c.volume() ), 25, 145 );
   }
}
```

Fig. 7.8 Testing class **Cylinder** (part 2 of 3).

7.10 Introduction to Polymorphism

With *polymorphism,* it is possible to design and implement systems that are more easily *extensible.* Programs can be written to process generically—as superclass objects—objects of all existing classes in a hierarchy. Classes that do not exist during program development can be added with little or no modifications to the generic part of the program—as long as those classes are part of the hierarchy that is being processed generically. The only parts of a program that need modification are those parts that require direct knowledge of the particular class that is added to the hierarchy. We will study two substantial class hierarchies and will show how objects throughout those hierarchies are manipulated polymorphically.

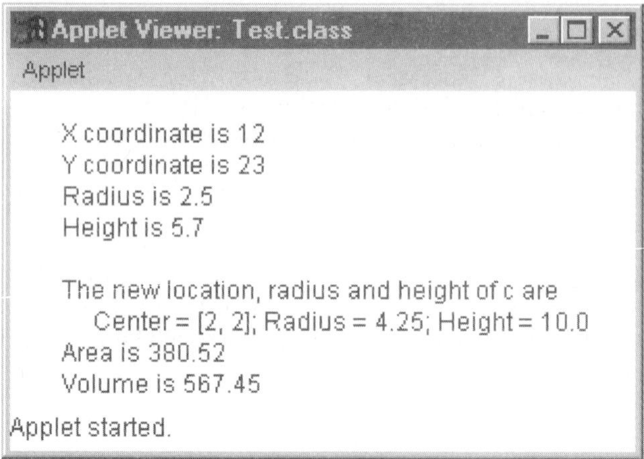

Fig. 7.8 Testing class **`Cylinder`** (part 3 of 3).

7.11 Type Fields and `switch` Statements

One means of dealing with objects of many different types is to use a **`switch`** statement to take an appropriate action on each object based on that object's type. For example, in a hierarchy of shapes in which each shape has a **`shapeType`** instance variable, a **`switch`** structure could determine which **`print`** method to call based on the object's **`shapeType`**.

There are many problems with using **`switch`** logic. The programmer might forget to make such a type test when one is warranted. The programmer may forget to test all possible cases in a **`switch`**. If a **`switch`**-based system is modified by adding new types, the programmer might forget to insert the new cases in existing **`switch`** statements. Every addition or deletion of a class demands that every **`switch`** statement in the system be modified; tracking these down can be time consuming and error prone.

As we will see, polymorphic programming can eliminate the need for **`switch`** logic. The programmer can use Java's polymorphism mechanism to perform the equivalent logic automatically, thus avoiding the kinds of errors typically associated with **`switch`** logic.

Testing and Debugging Tip 7.2

An interesting consequence of using polymorphism is that programs take on a simplified appearance. They contain less branching logic in favor of simpler sequential code. This simplification facilitates testing, debugging, and program maintenance.

7.12 Dynamic Method Binding

Suppose a set of shape classes such as **`Circle`**, **`Triangle`**, **`Rectangle`**, **`Square`**, etc. are all derived from superclass **`Shape`**. In object-oriented programming, each of these classes might be endowed with the ability to draw itself. Although each class has its own **`draw`** method, the **`draw`** method for each shape is quite different. When drawing a shape, whatever that shape may be, it would be nice to be able to treat all these shapes generically as objects of the superclass **`Shape`**. Then to draw any shape, we could simply call method

draw of superclass **Shape** and let the program determine dynamically (i.e., at execution time) which subclass **draw** method to use.

To enable this kind of behavior, we declare **draw** in the superclass, and then we override **draw** in each of the subclasses to draw the appropriate shape.

Software Engineering Observation 7.12

When a subclass chooses not to redefine a method, the subclass simply inherits its immediate superclass's method definition.

If we use a superclass reference to refer to a subclass object and invoke the **draw** method, the program will choose the correct subclass's **draw** method dynamically (i.e., at execution time). This is called *dynamic method binding* which will be illustrated in the case studies later in this chapter.

7.13 final Methods and Classes

We saw in Chapter 4 that variables can be declared **final** to indicate that they cannot be modified after they are declared and that they must be initialized when they are declared. It is also possible to define methods and classes with the **final** modifier.

A method that is declared **final** cannot be overridden in a subclass. Methods that are declared **static** and methods that are declared **private** are implicitly **final**. Because a **final** method's definition can never change, the compiler can optimize the program by removing calls to **final** methods and replacing them with the expanded code of their definitions at each method call location—a technique known as *inlining the code.*

A class that is declared **final** cannot be a superclass—i.e., **final** classes cannot be inherited. All methods in a **final** class are implicitly **final**.

Performance Tip 7.2

The compiler can decide to inline a **final** *method call and will do so for small, simple* **final** *methods. Inlining does not violate encapsulation or information hiding (but does improve performance because it eliminates the overhead of making a method call).*

Performance Tip 7.3

Pipelined processors are able to improve performance by executing portions of the next several instructions simultaneously, but not if those instructions follow a method call. Thus, inlining (which the compiler can perform on a **final** *method) can improve performance in pipelined processors because it eliminates the out-of-line transfer of control associated with a method call.*

Software Engineering Observation 7.13

A class declared **final** *cannot be subclassed. Every method of a* **final** *class is implicitly* **final**.

7.14 Abstract Superclasses and Concrete Classes

When we think of a class as a type, we assume that objects of that type will be instantiated. However, there are cases in which it is useful to define classes for which the programmer never intends to instantiate any objects. Such classes are called *abstract classes.* Because these are used as superclasses in inheritance situations, we will normally refer to them as *abstract superclasses*. No objects of abstract superclasses can be instantiated.

The sole purpose of an abstract class is to provide an appropriate superclass from which other classes may inherit interface and/or implementation (we will see examples of each shortly). Classes from which objects can be instantiated are called *concrete classes*.

We could have an abstract superclass **TwoDimensionalObject** and derive concrete classes such as **Square**, **Circle**, **Triangle**, etc. We could also have an abstract superclass **ThreeDimensionalObject** and derive concrete classes such as **Cube**, **Sphere**, **Cylinder**, etc. Abstract superclasses are too generic to define real objects; we need to be more specific before we can think of instantiating objects. That is what concrete classes do; they provide the specifics that make it reasonable to instantiate objects.

A class is made abstract by declaring it with the keyword **abstract**.

A hierarchy does not need to contain any **abstract** classes, but as we will see, many good object-oriented systems have class hierarchies headed by **abstract** superclasses. In some cases, **abstract** classes constitute the top few levels of the hierarchy. A good example of this is a shape hierarchy. The hierarchy could begin with **abstract** superclass **Shape**. On the next level down we can have two more **abstract** superclasses, namely **TwoDimensionalShape** and **ThreeDimensionalShape**. The next level down would start defining concrete classes for two-dimensional shapes such as **Circle** and **Square**, and concrete classes for three-dimensional shapes such as **Sphere** and **Cube**.

7.15 Polymorphism Examples

Here is an example of polymorphism. If class **Rectangle** is derived from class **Quadrilateral**, then a **Rectangle** object *is a* more specific version of a **Quadrilateral** object. An operation (such as calculating the perimeter or the area) that can be performed on an object of class **Quadrilateral** can also be performed on an object of class **Rectangle**. Such operations can also be performed on other "kinds of" **Quadrilateral**s such as **Square**s, **Parallelogram**s and **Trapezoid**s. When a request is made through a superclass reference to use a method, Java chooses the correct overridden method polymorphically in the appropriate subclass associated with the object.

Here is another example of polymorphism. Suppose we have a video game that manipulates objects of many varieties including objects of class **Martian**, **Venutian**, **Plutonian**, **SpaceShip**, **LaserBeam**, and the like. Each of these classes extends a common superclass like **GamePiece** that contains a method called **drawYourself**. This method is defined by each subclass. A Java screen manager program would simply maintain some kind of container (such as a **GamePiece** array) of objects of these various classes. To refresh the screen periodically the screen manager would simply send each object the same message, namely **drawYourself**. Each object would respond in its own unique way. A **Martian** object would draw itself with the appropriate number of antennae. A **SpaceShip** object would draw itself bright and silvery. A **LaserBeam** object would draw itself as a bright red beam across the screen. Thus, the same message sent to a variety of objects would take on "many forms"—hence the term *polymorphism*.

Such a polymorphic screen manager makes it especially easy to add new types of objects to a system with minimal impact. Suppose we want to add **Mercurian**s to our video game. We certainly have to build a new class **Mercurian** that extends **GamePiece** and provides its own definition of the **drawYourself** method. Then when objects of class **Mercurian** appear in the container, the screen manager need not be modified. It simply sends the message **drawYourself** to every object in the container regardless of the object's type, so the new **Mercurian** objects just "fit right in." Thus, with polymorphism, new types of objects not even envisioned when a system is created may be added without modifications to the system (other than the new class itself, of course).

Through the use of polymorphism, one method call can cause different actions to occur depending on the type of the object receiving the call. This gives the programmer tremendous expressive capability. We will see examples of the power of polymorphism in the next several sections.

Software Engineering Observation 7.14

With polymorphism, the programmer can deal in generalities and let the execution-time environment concern itself with the specifics. The programmer can command a wide variety of objects to behave in manners appropriate to those objects without even knowing the types of those objects.

Software Engineering Observation 7.15

Polymorphism promotes extensibility: Software written to invoke polymorphic behavior is written independent of the types of the objects to which messages (i.e., method calls) are sent. Thus, new types of objects that can respond to existing messages can be added into such a system without modifying the base system.

Software Engineering Observation 7.16

*If a method is declared **final** it cannot be overridden in subclasses, so that method calls may not be sent polymorphically to objects of those subclasses. The method call may still be sent to subclasses but they will all respond identically rather than polymorphically.*

Software Engineering Observation 7.17

*An **abstract** class defines a common interface for the various members of a class hierarchy. The **abstract** class contains methods that will be defined in the subclasses. All classes in the hierarchy can use this same interface through polymorphism.*

Although we cannot instantiate objects of **abstract** superclasses, we *can* declare references to **abstract** superclasses. Such references can be used to enable polymorphic manipulations of subclass objects when such objects are instantiated from concrete classes.

Let us consider more applications of polymorphism. A screen manager needs to display a variety of objects, including new types of objects that will be added to the system even after the screen manager is written. The system may need to display various shapes (i.e., the superclass is **Shape**) such as **Square**, **Circle**, **Triangle**, **Rectangle**, and the like (each of these shape classes is derived from the superclass **Shape**). The screen manager uses superclass references (to **Shape**) to manage all the objects to be displayed. To draw any object (regardless of the level at which that object appears in the inheritance hierarchy), the screen manager uses a superclass reference to the object and simply sends a **draw** message to the object. Method **draw** has been declared **abstract** in superclass **Shape** and has been overridden in each of the subclasses. Each **Shape** object knows how to draw itself. The screen manager does not have to worry about what type each object is or whether the screen manager has seen objects of that type before—the screen manager simply tells each object to **draw** itself.

Polymorphism is particularly effective for implementing layered software systems. In operating systems, for example, each type of physical device may operate quite differently from the others. Even so, commands to *read* or *write* data from and to devices can have a certain uniformity. The *write* message sent to a device-driver object needs to be interpreted specifically in the context of that device driver and how that device driver manipulates devices of a specific type. However, the *write* call itself is really no different from the *write* to any other device in the system—simply place some number of bytes from memory onto that device. An object-oriented operating system might use an **abstract** superclass to provide an interface appropriate for all device drivers. Then, through inheritance from that **abstract** superclass, subclasses are formed that all operate similarly. The capabilities (i.e., the **public** interface) offered by the device drivers are provided as **abstract** methods in the **abstract** superclass. The implementations of these **abstract** methods are provided in the subclasses that correspond to the specific types of device drivers.

It is common in object-oriented programming to define an *iterator class* that can walk through all the objects in a container (such as an array). If you want to print a list of objects in a linked list, for example, an iterator object can be instantiated that will return the next element of the linked list each time the iterator is called. Iterators are commonly used in polymorphic programming to walk through an array or a linked list of objects from various levels of a hierarchy. The references in such a list would all be superclass references (see Chapter 17, "Data Structures," for more on linked lists). A list of objects of superclass class **TwoDimensionalShape** could contain objects from the classes **Square**, **Circle**, **Triangle**, etc. Sending a **draw** message to each object in the list would, using polymorphism, draw the correct picture on the screen.

7.16 Case Study: A Payroll System Using Polymorphism

Let us use **abstract** methods and polymorphism to perform payroll calculations based on the type of an employee (Fig. 7.9). We use an **abstract** superclass **Employee**. The subclasses of **Employee** are **Boss**, who gets paid a fixed weekly salary regardless of the number of hours worked, **CommissionWorker**, who gets a flat base salary plus a percentage of sales, **PieceWorker**, who gets paid by the number of items produced, and **HourlyWorker**, who gets paid by the hour and receives overtime pay. Each of the subclasses of **Employee** in this example have been declared **final** because we do not intend to inherit from them again.

An **earnings** method call certainly applies generically to all employees. But the way each person's earnings are calculated depends on the class of the employee, and these classes are all derived from the superclass **Employee**. So **earnings** is declared **abstract** in superclass **Employee** and appropriate implementations of **earnings** are provided for each of the subclasses. Then, to calculate any employee's earnings, the program simply uses a superclass reference to that employee's object and invokes the **earnings** method. In a real payroll system, the various **Employee** objects might be referenced by individual elements in an array of **Employee** references. The program would simply walk through the array one element at a time using the **Employee** references to invoke the **earnings** method of each object.

Software Engineering Observation 7.18

If a subclass is derived from a superclass with an **abstract** *method, and if no definition is supplied in the subclass for that* **abstract** *method (i.e., if that method is not overridden in the subclass), then that method remains* **abstract** *in the subclass. Consequently, the subclass is also an* **abstract** *class and must be explicitly declared as an* **abstract** *class.*

Software Engineering Observation 7.19

The ability to declare an **abstract** *method gives the class designer considerable power over how subclasses will be implemented in a class hierarchy. Any new class that wants to inherit from this class is forced to override the* **abstract** *method (either directly or by inheriting from a class that has overridden the method). Otherwise that new class will contain an* **abstract** *method and thus be an* **abstract** *class unable to instantiate objects.*

Software Engineering Observation 7.20

Even if a class is **abstract** *it can still have instance data and non-***abstract** *methods subject to the normal rules of inheritance by subclasses.*

Common Programming Error 7.10

Attempting to instantiate an object of an **abstract** *class (i.e., a class that contains one or more* **abstract** *methods) is a syntax error.*

Common Programming Error 7.11

It is a syntax error if a class with one or more **abstract** *methods is not explicitly declared* **abstract**.

Let us consider the **Employee** class (Fig. 7.9, lines 1–28). The **public** methods include a constructor that takes the first name and last name as arguments; a **getFirstName** method that returns the first name; a **getLastName** method that returns the last name; a toString method that returns the first name and last name separated by a space; and an **abstract** method—**earnings**. Why is this method **abstract**? The answer is that it does not make sense to provide an implementation of this method in the **Employee** class. We cannot calculate the earnings for a generic employee—we must first know *what kind of* employee it is. By making this method **abstract** we are indicating that we will provide an implementation in each subclass, but not in the superclass itself.

```
1  // Fig. 7.9: Employee.java
2  // Abstract superclass Employee
3
4  public abstract class Employee {
5     private String firstName;
6     private String lastName;
7
```

Fig. 7.9 **Employee** class hierarchy using an **abstract** superclass (part 1 of 8).

```
    // Constructor
    public Employee( String first, String last )
    {
       firstName = first;
       lastName = last;
    }

    // Return the first name
    public String getFirstName() { return firstName; }

    // Return the last name
    public String getLastName() { return lastName; }

    public String toString()
       { return firstName + ' ' + lastName; }

    // Abstract method that must be implemented for each
    // derived class of Employee from which objects
    // are instantiated.
    abstract double earnings();
}
```

Fig. 7.9 `Employee` class hierarchy using an `abstract` superclass (part 2 of 8).

```
// Fig. 7.9: Boss.java
// Boss class derived from Employee

public final class Boss extends Employee {
   private double weeklySalary;

   // Constructor for class Boss
   public Boss( String first, String last, double s)
   {
      super( first, last );  // call superclass constructor
      setWeeklySalary( s );
   }

   // Set the Boss's salary
   public void setWeeklySalary( double s )
      { weeklySalary = ( s > 0 ? s : 0 ); }

   // Get the Boss's pay
   public double earnings() { return weeklySalary; }

   // Print the Boss's name
   public String toString()
   {
      return "Boss: " + super.toString();
   }
}
```

Fig. 7.9 `Employee` class hierarchy using an `abstract` superclass (part 3 of 8).

```
55 // Fig. 7.9: CommissionWorker.java
56 // CommissionWorker class derived from Employee
57
58 public final class CommissionWorker extends Employee {
59    private double salary;      // base salary per week
60    private double commission;  // amount per item sold
61    private int quantity;       // total items sold for week
62
63    // Constructor for class CommissionWorker
64    public CommissionWorker( String first, String last,
65                             double s, double c, int q)
66    {
67       super( first, last );  // call superclass constructor
68       setSalary( s );
69       setCommission( c );
70       setQuantity( q );
71    }
72
73    // Set CommissionWorker's weekly base salary
74    public void setSalary( double s )
75       { salary = ( s > 0 ? s : 0 ); }
76
77    // Set CommissionWorker's commission
78    public void setCommission( double c )
79       { commission = ( c > 0 ? c : 0 ); }
80
81    // Set CommissionWorker's quantity sold
82    public void setQuantity( int q )
83       { quantity = ( q > 0 ? q : 0 ); }
84
85    // Determine CommissionWorker's earnings
86    public double earnings()
87       { return salary + commission * quantity; }
88
89    // Print the CommissionWorker's name
90    public String toString()
91    {
92       return "Commission worker: " + super.toString();
93    }
94 }
```

Fig. 7.9 **Employee** class hierarchy using an **abstract** superclass (part 4 of 8).

Class **Boss** (Fig. 7.9, lines 29–54) is derived from **Employee**. The **public** methods include a constructor that takes a first name, a last name, and a weekly salary as arguments and passes the first name and last name to the **Employee** constructor to initialize the **firstName** and **lastName** members of the superclass part of the subclass object; a **setWeeklySalary** method to assign a new value to **private** instance variable **weeklySalary**; an **earnings** method defining how to calculate a **Boss**'s earnings; and a **toString** method that forms a **String** containing the type of the employee (i.e., **"Boss: "**) followed by the boss's name.

```
95  // Fig. 7.9: PieceWorker.java
96  // PieceWorker class derived from Employee
97
98  public final class PieceWorker extends Employee {
99     private double wagePerPiece; // wage per piece output
100    private int quantity;         // output for week
101
102    // Constructor for class PieceWorker
103    public PieceWorker( String first, String last,
104                        double w, int q )
105    {
106       super( first, last );  // call superclass constructor
107       setWage( w );
108       setQuantity( q );
109    }
110
111    // Set the wage
112    public void setWage( double w )
113       { wagePerPiece = ( w > 0 ? w : 0 ); }
114
115    // Set the number of items output
116    public void setQuantity( int q )
117       { quantity = ( q > 0 ? q : 0 ); }
118
119    // Determine the PieceWorker's earnings
120    public double earnings()
121       { return quantity * wagePerPiece; }
122
123    public String toString()
124    {
125       return "Piece worker: " + super.toString();
126    }
127 }
```

Fig. 7.9 **`Employee`** class hierarchy using an **`abstract`** superclass (part 5 of 8).

Class **`CommissionWorker`** (Fig. 7.9, lines 55–94) is derived from **`Employee`**. The **`public`** methods include a constructor that takes a first name, a last name, a salary, a commission, and a quantity of items sold as arguments and passes the first name and last name to the **`Employee`** constructor; *set* methods to assign new values to instance variables **`salary`**, **`commission`**, and **`quantity`**; an **`earnings`** method to calculate a **`CommissionWorker`**'s earnings; and a **`toString`** method that forms a **`String`** containing the employee type (i.e., **`"Commission worker: "`**) followed by the worker's name.

Class **`PieceWorker`** (Fig. 7.9, lines 95–127) is derived from **`Employee`**. The **`public`** methods include a constructor that takes a first name, a last name, a wage per piece, and a quantity of items produced as arguments and passes the first name and last name to the **`Employee`** constructor; *set* methods to assign new values to private methods **`wagePerPiece`** and **`quantity`**; an **`earnings`** method defining how to calculate a **`PieceWorker`**'s earnings; and a **`toString`** method that forms a **`String`** containing the type of the employee (i.e., **`"Piece worker: "`**) followed by the pieceworker's name.

```
128 // Fig. 7.9: HourlyWorker.java
129 // Definition of class HourlyWorker
130
131 public final class HourlyWorker extends Employee {
132    private double wage;    // wage per hour
133    private double hours;   // hours worked for week
134
135    // Constructor for class HourlyWorker
136    public HourlyWorker( String first, String last,
137                         double w, double h )
138    {
139       super( first, last );   // call superclass constructor
140       setWage( w );
141       setHours( h );
142    }
143
144    // Set the wage
145    public void setWage( double w )
146       { wage = ( w > 0 ? w : 0 ); }
147
148    // Set the hours worked
149    public void setHours( double h )
150       { hours = ( h >= 0 && h < 168 ? h : 0 ); }
151
152    // Get the HourlyWorker's pay
153    public double earnings() { return wage * hours; }
154
155    public String toString()
156    {
157       return "Hourly worker: " + super.toString();
158    }
159 }
```

Fig. 7.9 **`Employee`** class hierarchy using an **`abstract`** superclass (part 6 of 8).

Class **`HourlyWorker`** (Fig. 7.9, lines 128–159) is derived from **`Employee`**. The **`public`** methods include a constructor that takes a first name, a last name, a wage, and the number of hours worked as arguments and passes the first name and last name to the **`Employee`** constructor to initialize the **`firstName`** and **`lastName`** members of the superclass part of the subclass object; *set* methods to assign new values to private methods **`wage`** and **`hours`**; an **`earnings`** method defining how to calculate an **`HourlyWorker`**'s earnings; and a **`toString`** method that forms a **`String`** containing the type of the employee (i.e., **`"Hourly worker: "`**) followed by the hourly worker's name.

The **`Test`** applet (Fig. 7.9, lines 160–218) begins by declaring **`Employee`** reference, **`ref`**. Each of the types of **`Employee`**s is handled similarly in **`Test`**, so we will discuss only the case in which **`Test`** deals with a **`Boss`** object.

Line 175

```
Boss b = new Boss ("John", "Smith", 800.00);
```

```
// Fig. 7.9: Test.java
// Driver for Employee hierarchy
import java.awt.Graphics;
import java.applet.Applet;
import java.text.DecimalFormat;

public class Test extends Applet {
   private Employee ref;  // superclass reference
   private Boss b;
   private CommissionWorker c;
   private PieceWorker p;
   private HourlyWorker h;

   public void init()
   {
      b = new Boss( "John", "Smith", 800.00 );
      c = new CommissionWorker( "Sue", "Jones",
                                400.0, 3.0, 150);
      p = new PieceWorker( "Bob", "Lewis", 2.5, 200 );
      h = new HourlyWorker( "Karen", "Price", 13.75, 40 );
   }

   public void paint( Graphics g )
   {
      DecimalFormat precision2 = new DecimalFormat( "#.00" );

      ref = b;  // superclass reference to subclass object
      g.drawString( ref.toString() + " earned $" +
                    precision2.format( ref.earnings() ),
                    25, 25 );
      g.drawString( b.toString() + " earned $" +
                    precision2.format( b.earnings() ),
                    25, 40 );

      ref = c;  // superclass reference to subclass object
      g.drawString( ref.toString() + " earned $" +
                    precision2.format( ref.earnings() ),
                    25, 55 );
      g.drawString( c.toString() + " earned $" +
                    precision2.format( c.earnings() ),
                    25, 70 );

      ref = p;  // superclass reference to subclass object
      g.drawString( ref.toString() + " earned $" +
                    precision2.format( ref.earnings() ),
                    25, 85 );
      g.drawString( p.toString() + " earned $" +
                    precision2.format( p.earnings() ),
                    25, 100 );

```

Fig. 7.9 **Employee** class hierarchy using an **abstract** superclass (part 7 of 8).

```
210         ref = h;  // superclass reference to subclass object
211         g.drawString( ref.toString() + " earned $" +
212                       precision2.format( ref.earnings() ),
213                       25, 115 );
214         g.drawString( h.toString() + " earned $" +
215                       precision2.format( h.earnings() ),
216                       25, 130 );
217     }
218 }
```

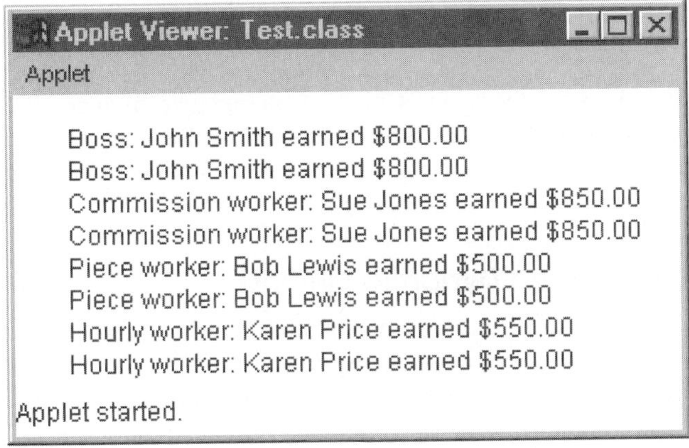

Fig. 7.9 **`Employee`** class hierarchy using an **`abstract`** superclass (part 8 of 8).

instantiates subclass object **`b`** of class **`Boss`** and provides various constructor arguments including a first name, a last name, and a fixed weekly salary.

Line 186

```
ref = b;  // superclass reference to subclass object
```

places in superclass reference **`ref`** a reference to subclass **`Boss`** object **`b`**. This is precisely what we must do to effect polymorphic behavior.

The expression in line 187

```
ref.toString()
```

invokes the **`toString`** method of the object referenced by **`ref`**. The system invokes the subclass object's **`toString`** method—precisely what we call polymorphic behavior. This method call is an example of dynamic method binding—the decision as to what method to invoke is deferred until execution time.

The method call in line 188

```
ref.earnings()
```

invokes the **`earnings`** method of the object referred to by **`ref`**. The system invokes the subclass object's **`earnings`** method rather than the superclass's **`earnings`** method. This is also an example of dynamic method binding.

The call

```
b.toString()
```

at line 190 explicitly invokes the **Boss** version of method **toString** by using the dot member selection operator off the specific **Boss** reference **b**. This call is included for comparison purposes to ensure that the dynamically bound method invoked with **ref.toString()** was indeed the proper method.

The line

```
b.earnings();
```

explicitly invokes the **Boss** version of method **earnings** by using the dot member selection operator off the specific **Boss** object **b**. This call is also included for comparison purposes to ensure that the dynamically bound method invoked with **ref.earnings()** was indeed the proper method.

7.17 New Classes and Dynamic Binding

Polymorphism certainly works nicely when all possible classes are known in advance. But it also works when new kinds of classes are added to systems.

New classes are accommodated by dynamic method binding (also called *late binding*). An object's type need not be known at compile time for a polymorphic call to be compiled. At execution time, the call is matched with the method of the called object.

A screen manager program can now handle (without recompilation) new types of display objects as they are added to the system. The **draw** method call remains the same. The new objects themselves each contain a **draw** method implementing the actual drawing capabilities. This makes it easy to add new capabilities to systems with minimal impact. It also promotes software reuse.

Performance Tip 7.4

Polymorphism as implemented with dynamic method binding is efficient.

Performance Tip 7.5

The kinds of polymorphic manipulations made possible with dynamic binding can also be accomplished by using hand-coded **switch** *logic based on type fields in objects. The polymorphic code generated by the Java compiler runs with comparable performance to efficiently coded* **switch** *logic.*

7.18 Case Study: Inheriting Interface and Implementation

Our next example (Fig. 7.10) reexamines the **Point**, **Circle**, **Cylinder** hierarchy except that we now head the hierarchy with **abstract** superclass **Shape**. **Shape** has an **abstract** method—**getName**—so **Shape** is an **abstract** superclass. **Shape** contains two other methods, **area** and **volume**, each of which has an implementation that returns a value of zero. **Point** inherits these implementations from **Shape**. This makes sense because both the area and volume of a point are zero. **Circle** inherits the **volume** method from **Point**, but **Circle** provides its own implementation for the **area** method. **Cylinder** provides its own implementations for both the **area** (which we interpret as the surface area of the cylinder) and **volume** methods.

```
// Fig. 7.10: Shape.java
// Definition of abstract superclass Shape

public abstract class Shape {
   public double area() { return 0.0; }
   public double volume() { return 0.0; }
   public abstract String getName();
}
```

Fig. 7.10 Shape, point, circle, cylinder hierarchy (part 1 of 6).

```
// Fig. 7.10: Point.java
// Definition of class Point

public class Point extends Shape {
   protected int x, y; // coordinates of the Point

   // no-argument constructor
   public Point() { setPoint( 0, 0 ); }

   // constructor
   public Point( int a, int b ) { setPoint( a, b ); }

   // Set x and y coordinates of Point
   public void setPoint( int a, int b )
   {
      x = a;
      y = b;
   }

   // get x coordinate
   public int getX() { return x; }

   // get y coordinate
   public int getY() { return y; }

   // convert the point into a String representation
   public String toString()
      { return "[" + x + ", " + y + "]"; }

   // return the class name
   public String getName() { return "Point"; }
}
```

Fig. 7.10 Shape, point, circle, cylinder hierarchy (part 2 of 6).

```
// Fig. 7.10: Circle.java
// Definition of class Circle

public class Circle extends Point {  // inherits from Point
   protected double radius;

   // no-argument constructor
   public Circle()
   {
      // implicit call to superclass constructor here
      setRadius( 0 );
   }

   // Constructor
   public Circle( double r, int a, int b )
   {
      super( a, b );  // call the superclass constructor
      setRadius( r );
   }

   // Set radius of Circle
   public void setRadius( double r )
      { radius = ( r >= 0 ? r : 0 ); }

   // Get radius of Circle
   public double getRadius() { return radius; }

   // Calculate area of Circle
   public double area() { return Math.PI * radius * radius; }

   // convert the Circle to a String
   public String toString()
      { return "Center = " + super.toString() +
               "; Radius = " + radius; }

   // return the class name
   public String getName() { return "Circle"; }
}
```

Fig. 7.10 Shape, point, circle, cylinder hierarchy (part 3 of 6).

Note that although **Shape** is an **abstract** superclass, it still contains implementations of methods **area** and **volume**, and these implementations are inheritable. The **Shape** class provides an inheritable interface in the form of three methods that all classes of the hierarchy will contain. The **Shape** class also provides some implementations that subclasses in the first few levels of the hierarchy will use.

This case study emphasizes that a subclass can inherit interface and/or implementation from a superclass.

```
// Fig. 7.10: Cylinder.java
// Definition of class Cylinder

public class Cylinder extends Circle {
   protected double height;  // height of Cylinder

   // no-argument constructor
   public Cylinder()
   {
      // implicit call to superclass constructor here
      setHeight( 0 );
   }

   // constructor
   public Cylinder( double h, double r, int a, int b )
   {
      super( r, a, b );   // call superclass constructor
      setHeight( h );
   }

   // Set height of Cylinder
   public void setHeight( double h )
      { height = ( h >= 0 ? h : 0 ); }

   // Get height of Cylinder
   public double getHeight() { return height; }

   // Calculate area of Cylinder (i.e., surface area)
   public double area()
   {
      return 2 * super.area() +
             2 * Math.PI * radius * height;
   }

   // Calculate volume of Cylinder
   public double volume() { return super.area() * height; }

   // Convert a Cylinder to a String
   public String toString()
      { return super.toString() + "; Height = " + height; }

   // Return the class name
   public String getName() { return "Cylinder"; }
}
```

Fig. 7.10 Shape, point, circle, cylinder hierarchy (part 4 of 6).

Software Engineering Observation 7.21

Hierarchies designed for implementation inheritance tend to have their functionality high in the hierarchy—each new subclass inherits one or more methods that were defined in a superclass and uses the superclass definitions.

```
// Fig. 7.10: Test.java
// Driver for point, circle, cylinder hierarchy
import java.awt.Graphics;
import java.applet.Applet;
import java.text.DecimalFormat;

public class Test extends Applet {
   private Point point;
   private Circle circle;
   private Cylinder cylinder;
   private Shape arrayOfShapes[];

   public void init()
   {
      point = new Point( 7, 11 );
      circle = new Circle( 3.5, 22, 8 );
      cylinder = new Cylinder( 10, 3.3, 10, 10 );

      arrayOfShapes = new Shape[ 3 ];

      // aim arrayOfShapes[0] at subclass Point object
      // aim arrayOfShapes[1] at subclass Circle object
      // aim arrayOfShapes[2] at subclass Cylinder object
      arrayOfShapes[ 0 ] = point;
      arrayOfShapes[ 1 ] = circle;
      arrayOfShapes[ 2 ] = cylinder;
   }

   public void paint( Graphics g )
   {
      g.drawString( point.getName() + ": " +
                    point.toString(), 25, 25 );

      g.drawString( circle.getName() + ": " +
                    circle.toString(), 25, 40 );

      g.drawString( cylinder.getName() + ": " +
                    cylinder.toString(), 25, 55 );

      DecimalFormat precision2 = new DecimalFormat( "#0.00" );
      int yPos = 85;

      // Loop through arrayOfShapes and print the name,
      // area, and volume of each object.
      for ( int i = 0; i < arrayOfShapes.length; i++ ) {
         g.drawString( arrayOfShapes[ i ].getName() + ": " +
                       arrayOfShapes[ i ].toString(),
                       25, yPos );
         yPos += 15;
```

Fig. 7.10 Shape, point, circle, cylinder hierarchy (part 5 of 6).

```
172            g.drawString( "Area = " + precision2.format(
173                          arrayOfShapes[ i ].area() ),
174                          25, yPos );
175            yPos += 15;
176            g.drawString( "Volume = " + precision2.format(
177                          arrayOfShapes[ i ].volume() ),
178                          25, yPos );
179            yPos += 30;
180         }
181      }
182   }
```

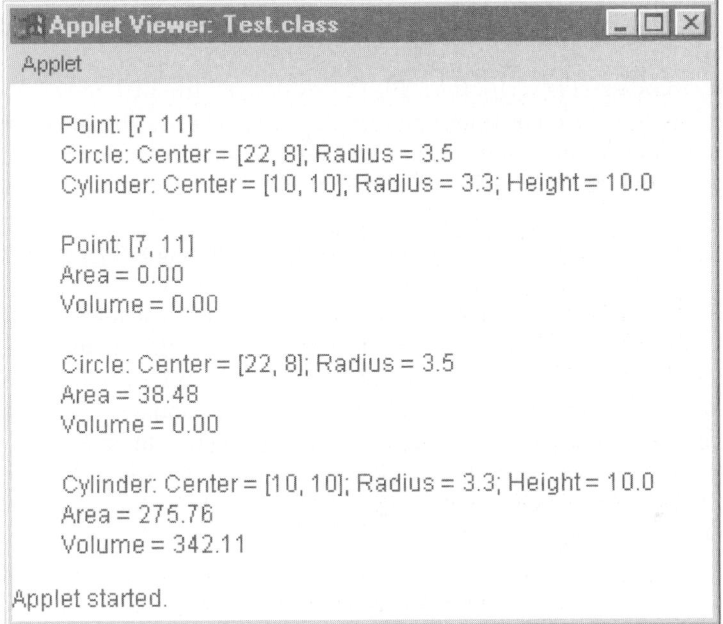

Fig. 7.10 Shape, point, circle, cylinder hierarchy (part 6 of 6).

Software Engineering Observation 7.22

Hierarchies designed for interface inheritance tend to have their functionality lower in the hierarchy—a superclass specifies one or more methods that should be called identically for each object in the hierarchy (i.e., they have the same signature), but the individual subclasses provide their own implementations of the method(s).

Superclass **`Shape`** (Fig. 7.10, lines 1–8) consists of three **`public`** methods and does not contain any data. Method **`getName`** is **`abstract`**, so it is overridden in each of the subclasses. Methods **`area`** and **`volume`** are defined to return **`0.0`**. These methods are overridden in subclasses when it is appropriate for those classes to have a different **`area`** calculation and/or a different **`volume`** calculation.

Class **Point** (Fig. 7.10, lines 9–40) is derived from **Shape**. A **Point** has an area of 0.0 and a volume of 0.0, so the superclass methods **area** and **volume** are not overridden here—they are inherited as defined in **Shape**. Method **getName** is an implementation of the **abstract** method in the superclass. Other methods include **setPoint** to assign new **x** and **y** coordinates to a **Point** and **getX** and **getY** to return the **x** and **y** coordinates of a **Point**.

Class **Circle** (Fig. 7.10, lines 41–78) is derived from **Point**. A **Circle** has a volume of 0.0, so superclass method **volume** is not overridden here—it is inherited from class **Point** which inherited it from **Shape**. A **Circle** has an area different from that of a **Point**, so the **area** method is overridden in this class. Method **getName** is an implementation of the **abstract** method in the superclass. If this method is not overridden here, the **Point** version of **getName** would be inherited. Other methods include **setRadius** to assign a new **radius** to a **Circle** and **getRadius** to return the **radius** of a **Circle**.

Class **Cylinder** (Fig. 7.10, lines 79–122) is derived from **Circle**. A **Cylinder** has area and volume different from those of class **Circle**, so the **area** and **volume** methods are both overridden in this class. Method **getName** is an implementation of the **abstract** method in the superclass. If this method had not been overridden here, the **Circle** version of **getName** would be inherited. Other methods include **setHeight** to assign a new **height** to a **Cylinder** and **getHeight** to return the **height** of a **Cylinder**.

The **Test** applet (Fig. 7.10, lines 123–182) begins by instantiating **Point** object **point**, **Circle** object **circle**, and **Cylinder** object **cylinder** (lines 137–139). Next, array **arrayOfShapes** is instantiated (line 141). This array of superclass references is used to refer to each of the subclass objects instantiated. Next, the reference **point** is assigned to array element **arrayOfShapes[0]**, the reference **circle** is assigned to array element **arrayOfShapes[1]**, and the reference **cylinder** is assigned to array element **arrayOfShapes[2]** (lines 146–148). Methods **getName** and **toString** are invoked as each object is output to illustrate that the objects are initialized correctly (lines 141–149). Next, a **for** structure walks through **arrayOfShapes** and the following calls are made during each iteration of the loop

```
arrayOfShapes[ i ].getName()
arrayOfShapes[ i ].toString()
arrayOfShapes[ i ].area()
arrayOfShapes[ i ].volume()
```

Each of these method calls is invoked on the object to which **arrayOfShapes[i]** currently refers. The output illustrates that the methods are invoked properly. First, the string **"Point: "** and the coordinates of the object **point** are output; the area and volume are both **0**. Next, the string **"Circle: "**, the coordinates of object **circle**, and the radius of object **circle** are output; the area of **circle** is calculated and the volume is **0**. Finally, the string **"Cylinder: "**, the coordinates of object **cylinder**, the radius of object **cylinder** and the height of object **cylinder** are output; the area of **cylinder** is calculated and the volume of **cylinder** is calculated. All the method calls to **getName**, **toString**, **area**, and **volume** are resolved at runtime with dynamic binding.

7.19 Case Study: Creating and Using Interfaces

Our next example (Fig. 7.11) reexamines the **Point**, **Circle**, **Cylinder** hierarchy one last time replacing **abstract** superclass **Shape** with the interface **Shape**. An interface definition begins with the keyword ***interface*** and contains a set of **public abstract** methods. Interfaces may also contain **public final static** data. To use an interface, a class must specify that it **implements** the interface and that class must define every method in the interface with the number of arguments and the return type specified in the interface definition. If the class leaves one method in the interface undefined, the class becomes an **abstract** class and must be declared **abstract** in the first line of its class definition.

Common Programming Error 7.12

Leaving a method of an **interface** *undefined in a class that* **implements** *the interface results in a compile error indicating that the class must be declared* **abstract**.

An interface is typically used in place of an abstract class when there is no default implementation to inherit—i.e., no instance variables and no default method implementations. Like a **public abstract** class, an **interface** is normally defined in a file by itself with the same name as the interface and the **.java** extension. The definition of interface **Shape** begins at line 4. Interface **Shape** has **abstract** methods **area**, **volume**, and **getName**. Line 12

```
public class Point implements Shape {
```

indicates that class **Point** implements the **Shape** interface. Class **Point** has been modified in this example to include definitions of all three methods in the interface. Method **area** is defined at line 39. Method **volume** is defined at line 42. Method **getName** is defined at line 45. These three methods satisfy the implementation requirement for the three methods defined in the interface.

When a class implements an interface, the same "is a" relationship provided by inheritance applies. In our example, class **Point** implements **Shape**. Therefore, a **Point** object "is a" **Shape**. In face, objects of any class that extends **Point** are also **Shape** objects. Using this relationship, we have maintained the original definitions of class **Circle**, class **Cylinder** and applet class **Test** from Fig. 7.10 to illustrate that an interface can be used instead of an abstract class to polymorphically process **Shape**s. Notice that the output for the program is identical to Fig. 7.10.

```
1  // Fig. 7.11: Shape.java
2  // Definition of interface Shape
3
4  interface Shape {
5     double area();
6     double volume();
7     String getName();
8  }
```

Fig. 7.11 Point, circle, cylinder hierarchy with a **Shape** interface (part 1 of 6).

```
// Fig. 7.11: Point.java
// Definition of class Point

public class Point implements Shape {
   protected int x, y; // coordinates of the Point

   // no-argument constructor
   public Point() { setPoint( 0, 0 ); }

   // constructor
   public Point( int a, int b ) { setPoint( a, b ); }

   // Set x and y coordinates of Point
   public void setPoint( int a, int b )
   {
      x = a;
      y = b;
   }

   // get x coordinate
   public int getX() { return x; }

   // get y coordinate
   public int getY() { return y; }

   // convert the point into a String representation
   public String toString()
      { return "[" + x + ", " + y + "]"; }

   // return the area
   public double area() { return 0.0; }

   // return the volume
   public double volume() { return 0.0; }

   // return the class name
   public String getName() { return "Point"; }
}
```

Fig. 7.11 Point, circle, cylinder hierarchy with a **Shape** interface (part 2 of 6).

One benefit of using interfaces is that a class can implement as many interfaces as it needs in addition to extending a class. To implement more than one interface, simply provide a comma-separated list of interface names after keyword **implements** in the class definition. This is particularly useful in the GUI event-handling mechanism. A class that implements more than one event-listener interface (such as **ActionListener** in earlier examples) can process different types of GUI events as we will see in Chapters 10 and 11.

Another use of interfaces is to define a set of constants that can be used in many class definitions. Consider interface **Constants**

```
// Fig. 7.11: Circle.java
// Definition of class Circle

public class Circle extends Point {  // inherits from Point
   protected double radius;

   // no-argument constructor
   public Circle()
   {
      // implicit call to superclass constructor here
      setRadius( 0 );
   }

   // Constructor
   public Circle( double r, int a, int b )
   {
      super( a, b );  // call the superclass constructor
      setRadius( r );
   }

   // Set radius of Circle
   public void setRadius( double r )
      { radius = ( r >= 0 ? r : 0 ); }

   // Get radius of Circle
   public double getRadius() { return radius; }

   // Calculate area of Circle
   public double area() { return Math.PI * radius * radius; }

   // convert the Circle to a String
   public String toString()
      { return "Center = " + super.toString() +
               "; Radius = " + radius; }

   // return the class name
   public String getName() { return "Circle"; }
}
```

Fig. 7.11 Point, circle, cylinder hierarchy with a **Shape** interface (part 3 of 6).

```
interface Constants {
   public static final int ONE = 1;
   public static final int TWO = 2;
   public static final int THREE = 3;
}
```

Any class that implements the **Constants** interface, can use the constant integers **ONE**, **TWO** and **THREE** anywhere in the class definition. Because there are no methods declared in this interface, a class that implements the interface is not required to provide any implementation.

```java
// Fig. 7.11: Cylinder.java
// Definition of class Cylinder

public class Cylinder extends Circle {
   protected double height;  // height of Cylinder

   // no-argument constructor
   public Cylinder()
   {
      // implicit call to superclass constructor here
      setHeight( 0 );
   }

   // constructor
   public Cylinder( double h, double r, int a, int b )
   {
      super( r, a, b );   // call superclass constructor
      setHeight( h );
   }

   // Set height of Cylinder
   public void setHeight( double h )
      { height = ( h >= 0 ? h : 0 ); }

   // Get height of Cylinder
   public double getHeight() { return height; }

   // Calculate area of Cylinder (i.e., surface area)
   public double area()
   {
      return 2 * super.area() +
             2 * Math.PI * radius * height;
   }

   // Calculate volume of Cylinder
   public double volume() { return super.area() * height; }

   // Convert a Cylinder to a String
   public String toString()
      { return super.toString() + "; Height = " + height; }

   // Return the class name
   public String getName() { return "Cylinder"; }
}
```

Fig. 7.11 Point, circle, cylinder hierarchy with a **Shape** interface (part 4 of 6).

```
// Fig. 7.11: Test.java
// Driver for point, circle, cylinder hierarchy
import java.awt.Graphics;
import java.applet.Applet;
import java.text.DecimalFormat;

public class Test extends Applet {
   private Point point;
   private Circle circle;
   private Cylinder cylinder;
   private Shape arrayOfShapes[];

   public void init()
   {
      point = new Point( 7, 11 );
      circle = new Circle( 3.5, 22, 8 );
      cylinder = new Cylinder( 10, 3.3, 10, 10 );

      arrayOfShapes = new Shape[ 3 ];

      // aim arrayOfShapes[0] at subclass Point object
      // aim arrayOfShapes[1] at subclass Circle object
      // aim arrayOfShapes[2] at subclass Cylinder object
      arrayOfShapes[ 0 ] = point;
      arrayOfShapes[ 1 ] = circle;
      arrayOfShapes[ 2 ] = cylinder;
   }

   public void paint( Graphics g )
   {
      g.drawString( point.getName() + ": " +
                    point.toString(), 25, 25 );

      g.drawString( circle.getName() + ": " +
                    circle.toString(), 25, 40 );

      g.drawString( cylinder.getName() + ": " +
                    cylinder.toString(), 25, 55 );

      DecimalFormat precision2 = new DecimalFormat( "#0.00" );
      int yPos = 85;

      // Loop through arrayOfShapes and print the name,
      // area, and volume of each object.
      for ( int i = 0; i < arrayOfShapes.length; i++ ) {
         g.drawString( arrayOfShapes[ i ].getName() + ": " +
                       arrayOfShapes[ i ].toString(),
                       25, yPos );
         yPos += 15;
```

Fig. 7.11 Point, circle, cylinder hierarchy with a **Shape** interface (part 5 of 6).

```
         g.drawString( "Area = " + precision2.format(
                       arrayOfShapes[ i ].area() ),
                       25, yPos );
         yPos += 15;
         g.drawString( "Volume = " + precision2.format(
                       arrayOfShapes[ i ].volume() ),
                       25, yPos );
         yPos += 30;
      }
   }
}
```

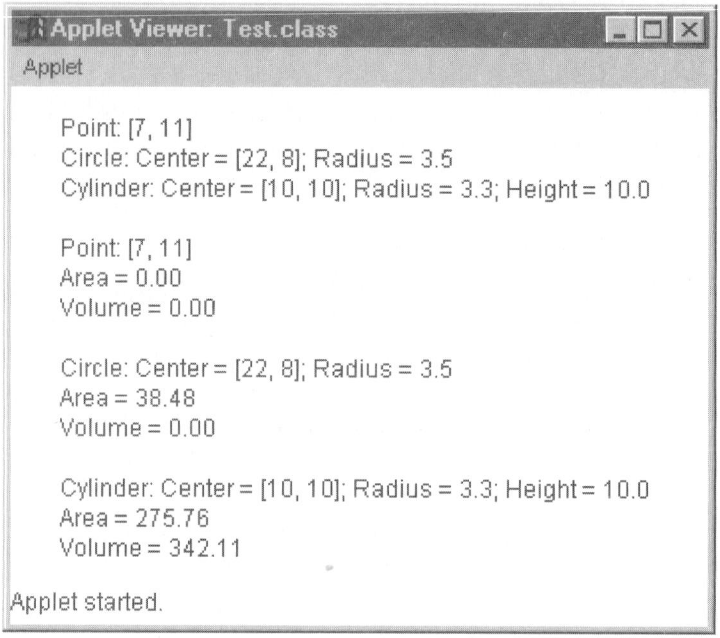

```
Applet Viewer: Test.class
Applet

Point: [7, 11]
Circle: Center = [22, 8]; Radius = 3.5
Cylinder: Center = [10, 10]; Radius = 3.3; Height = 10.0

Point: [7, 11]
Area = 0.00
Volume = 0.00

Circle: Center = [22, 8]; Radius = 3.5
Area = 38.48
Volume = 0.00

Cylinder: Center = [10, 10]; Radius = 3.3; Height = 10.0
Area = 275.76
Volume = 342.11

Applet started.
```

Fig. 7.11 Point, circle, cylinder hierarchy with a **Shape** interface (part 6 of 6).

7.20 Type-Wrapper Classes for Primitive Types

Each of the primitive types has a *type-wrapper class*. These classes are called **Character**, **Byte**, **Short**, **Integer**, **Long**, **Float**, **Double** and **Boolean**. Each type-wrapper class enables you to manipulate primitive types as objects of class **Object**. Therefore, values of the primitive data types can be processed polymorphically if they are maintained as objects of the type-wrapper classes. Many of the classes we will develop or reuse manipulate and share **Object**s. These classes cannot polymorphically manipulate variables of primitive types, but they can polymorphically manipulate objects of the type-wrapper classes, because every class ultimately is derived from class **Object**.

Each of the numeric classes—**Byte**, **Short**, **Integer**, **Long**, **Float** and **Double**—inherits from class **Number**. Each of the type wrappers is declared **final**, so their methods are implicitly **final** and may not be overridden. Note that many of the methods that process the primitive data types are defined as **static** methods of the type-wrapper classes. If you need to manipulate a primitive value in your program, first refer to the documentation for the type-wrapper classes—the method you need may already be defined. We will use the type-wrapper classes polymorphically in our study of data structures in chapters 17 and 18.

Summary

- One of the keys to the power of object-oriented programming is achieving software reusability through inheritance.
- Through inheritance, a new class inherits the instance variables and methods of a previously defined superclass. In this case, the new class is referred to as a subclass.
- With single inheritance, a class is derived from one superclass. With multiple inheritance, a subclass inherits from multiple (possibly unrelated) superclasses. Java does not support multiple inheritance, but Java does provide the notion of interfaces (discussed in Chapter 13, "Multithreading") that offer many of the benefits of multiple inheritance without the associated problems.
- A subclass normally adds instance variables and methods of its own, so a subclass generally is larger than its superclass. A subclass is more specific than its superclass and normally represents fewer objects.
- A subclass cannot access the **private** members of its superclass. A subclass can, however, access the **public**, **protected** and package access members of its superclass; the subclass must be in the superclass's package to use superclass members with package access.
- A subclass constructor always calls the constructor for its superclass first (either explicitly or implicitly) to create and initialize the subclass's superclass members.
- Inheritance enables software reusability which saves time in development and encourages the use of previously proven and debugged high-quality software.
- Someday most software will be constructed from standardized reusable components exactly as hardware often is today.
- An object of a subclass can be treated as an object of its corresponding superclass but the reverse is not true.
- A superclass exists in a hierarchical relationship with its subclasses.
- When a class is used with the mechanism of inheritance, it becomes either a superclass that supplies attributes and behaviors to other classes, or the class becomes a subclass that inherits those attributes and behaviors.
- An inheritance hierarchy can be arbitrarily deep within the physical limitations of a particular system, but most inheritance hierarchies have only a few levels.
- Hierarchies are useful for understanding and managing complexity. With software becoming increasingly complex, Java provides mechanisms for supporting hierarchical structures through inheritance and polymorphism.

- **Protected** access serves as an intermediate level of protection between **public** access and **private** access. **Protected** members of a superclass may be accessed by methods of the superclass, by methods of subclasses and by methods of classes in the same package; no other methods can access the **protected** members of a superclass.
- A superclass may be either a direct superclass of a subclass or an indirect superclass of a subclass. A direct superclass is the class that a subclass explicitly **extends**. An indirect superclass is inherited from several levels up the class hierarchy tree.
- When a superclass member is inappropriate for a subclass, the programmer may override that member in the subclass.
- It is important to distinguish between "is a" relationships and "has a" relationships. In a "has a" relationship, a class object has a reference to an object of another class as a member. In an "is a" relationship, an object of a subclass type may also be treated as an object of the superclass type. "Is a" is inheritance. "Has a" is composition.
- A subclass object can be assigned to a superclass reference. This kind of assignment makes sense because the subclass has members corresponding to each of the superclass members.
- A reference to a subclass object may be implicitly converted into a reference for a superclass object.
- It is possible to convert a superclass reference to a subclass reference by using an explicit cast. If the target is not a subclass object a **classCastException** is thrown.
- A superclass specifies commonality. All classes derived from a superclass inherit the capabilities of that superclass. In the object-oriented design process, the designer looks for commonality among classes and factors it out to form superclasses. Subclasses are then customized beyond the capabilities inherited from the superclass.
- Reading a set of subclass declarations can be confusing because inherited superclass members are not listed in the subclass declarations, but these members are indeed present in the subclasses.
- For a subclass object, first a superclass constructor is called either explicitly or implicitly, then the subclass constructor is called.
- With polymorphism, it becomes possible to design and implement systems that are more easily extensible. Programs can be written to process objects of types that may not exist when the program is under development.
- Polymorphic programming can eliminate the need for **switch** logic thus avoiding the kinds of errors associated with **switch** logic.
- An abstract method is declared by preceding the method's definition with the keyword **abstract** in the superclass.
- Subclasses can provide their own implementations of a superclass method if necessary, but if they do not, the superclass's implementation is used.

- There are many situations in which it is useful to define classes for which the programmer never intends to instantiate any objects. Such classes are called **abstract** classes. Because these are used only as superclasses, we will normally refer to them as **abstract** superclasses. No objects of an **abstract** class may be instantiated.
- Classes from which objects can be instantiated are called concrete classes.
- A class is made abstract by declaring one or more of its methods to be **abstract**. Such a class must be explicitly declared abstract.
- If a subclass is derived from a superclass with an **abstract** method without supplying a definition for that **abstract** method in the subclass, then that method remains **abstract** in the subclass. Consequently, the subclass is also an **abstract** class (and cannot instantiate any objects).
- When a request is made through a superclass reference to use a method, Java chooses the correct overridden method in the subclass associated with the object.
- Through the use of polymorphism, one method call can cause different actions to occur depending on the type of the object receiving the call.
- Although we cannot instantiate objects of **abstract** superclasses, we can declare references to **abstract** superclasses. Such references can then be used to enable polymorphic manipulations of subclass objects when such objects are instantiated from concrete classes.
- New kinds of classes are regularly added to systems. New classes are accommodated by dynamic method binding (also called late binding). The type of an object need not be known at compile time for a method call to be compiled. At execution time, the appropriate method of the receiving object is selected.
- With dynamic method binding, at execution time the call to a method is routed to the method version appropriate for the class of the object receiving the call.
- When a superclass provides a method, subclasses can override the method, but they do not have to override it. Thus a subclass can use a superclass's version of a method.
- An interface definition begins with the keyword ***interface*** and contains a set of **public abstract** methods. Interfaces may also contain **public final static** data.
- To use an interface, a class must specify that it **implements** the interface and that class must define every method in the interface with the number of arguments and the return type specified in the interface definition.
- An interface is typically used in place of an abstract class when there is no default implementation to inherit.
- When a class implements an interface, the same "is a" relationship provided by inheritance applies.
- To implement more than one interface, simply provide a comma-separated list of interface names after keyword **implements** in the class definition.

Terminology

abstract class
abstract method
abstract superclass
abstraction
base class
Boolean class
Char class
class hierarchy
client of a class
composition
direct superclass
Double class
dynamic method binding
extends
extensibility
final class
final instance variable
final method
garbage collection
"has a" relationship
hierarchical relationship
implementation inheritance
implicit reference conversion
indirect superclass
infinite recursion error
inheritance
inheritance hierarchy
Integer class
interface
interface inheritance
"is a" relationship
late binding
Long class
member access control
member object
method overriding
multiple inheritance
Number class
Object class
object-oriented programming (OOP)
override a method
override an **abstract** method
polymorphism
overriding vs. overloading
protected member of a class
reference to an **abstract** class
single inheritance
software reusability
standardized software components
subclass
subclass constructor
subclass reference
super
superclass
superclass constructor
superclass reference
switch logic
this
type-wrapper class
"uses a" relationship

Common Programming Errors

7.1 Treating a superclass object as a subclass object can cause errors.

7.2 Assigning an object of a superclass to a subclass reference (without a cast) is a syntax error.

7.3 It is a syntax error if a **super** call by a subclass to its superclass constructor is not the first statement in the subclass constructor.

7.4 It is a syntax error if a method in a superclass and a method in its subclass have the same signature but a different return type.

7.5 If a subclass constructor invokes a superclass default constructor (or no-argument constructor) and if the superclass does not have a default constructor (or no-argument constructor), a syntax error occurs.

7.6 When a superclass method is overridden in a subclass, it is common to have the subclass version call the superclass version and do some additional work. Not using the **super** reference to reference the superclass's method causes infinite recursion because the subclass method actually calls itself.

7.7 Cascading **super** references to refer to a member (method or variable) several levels up the hierarchy (as in **super.super.x**) is a syntax error.

7.8 Assigning a subclass object to a reference to a corresponding superclass, then attempting to reference subclass-only members with that superclass reference is a syntax error.

7.9 Assigning a subclass object to a superclass reference, and then attempting to reference subclass-only members with the superclass reference, is a syntax error.

7.10 Attempting to instantiate an object of an **abstract** class (i.e., a class that contains one or more **abstract** methods) is a syntax error.

7.11 It is a syntax error if a class with one or more **abstract** methods is not explicitly declared **abstract**.

7.12 Leaving a method of an **interface** undefined in a class that **implements** the interface results in a compile error indicating that the class must be declared **abstract**.

Good Programming Practice

7.1 The last statement in a **finalize** method should always be **super.finalize();** to ensure that the superclass's **finalize** method is called.

Performance Tips

7.1 The compiler can decide to inline a **final** method call and will do so for small, simple **final** methods. Inlining does not violate encapsulation or information hiding (but does improve performance because it eliminates the overhead of making a method call).

7.2 Pipelined processors are able to improve performance by executing portions of the next several instructions simultaneously, but not if those instructions follow a method call. Thus, inlining (which the compiler can perform on a **final** method) can improve performance in pipelined processors because it eliminates the out-of-line transfer of control associated with a method call.

7.3 If classes produced through inheritance are larger than they need to be, memory and processing resources may be wasted. Inherit from the class "closest" to what you need.

7.4 Polymorphism as implemented with dynamic method binding is efficient.

7.5 The kinds of polymorphic manipulations made possible with dynamic binding can also be accomplished by using hand-coded **switch** logic based on type fields in objects. The polymorphic code generated by the Java compiler runs with comparable performance to efficiently coded **switch** logic.

Software Engineering Observations

7.1 A subclass cannot directly access **private** members of its superclass.

7.2 If an object has been assigned to a reference of one of its superclasses, it is acceptable to cast that object back to its own type. In fact, this must be done in order to send that object any of its messages that do not appear in that superclass.

7.3 Every class in Java extends Object unless specified otherwise in the first line of the class definition. Thus, class **Object** is the superclass of the entire Java class hierarchy.

7.4 A redefinition of a superclass method in a subclass need not have the same signature as the superclass method. Such a redefinition is not method overriding but is simply an example of method overloading.

7.5 Any object can be converted to a **String** with an explicit or implicit call to the object's **toString** method.

7.6 Each class should override method **toString** to return useful information about objects of that class.

7.7 When an object of a subclass is created, first the superclass constructor executes, then the subclass constructor executes.

7.8 Creating a subclass does not affect its superclass's source code or the superclass's Java bytecodes; the integrity of a superclass is preserved by inheritance.

7.9 Just as the designer of non-object-oriented systems should avoid unnecessary proliferation of functions, the designer of object-oriented systems should avoid unnecessary proliferation of classes. Proliferating classes creates management problems and can hinder software reusability simply because it is more difficult for a potential reuser of a class to locate that class in a huge collection. The trade-off is to create fewer classes, each providing substantial additional functionality, but such classes might be too rich for certain reusers.

7.10 In an object-oriented system, classes are often closely related. "Factor out" common attributes and behaviors and place these in a superclass. Then use inheritance to form subclasses without having to repeat common attributes and behaviors.

7.11 Modifications to a superclass do not require subclasses to change as long as the public interface to the superclass remains unchanged.

7.12 When a subclass chooses not to redefine a method, the subclass simply inherits its immediate superclass's method definition.

7.13 A class declared **final** cannot be subclassed. Every method of a **final** class is implicitly **final**.

7.14 With polymorphism, the programmer can deal in generalities and let the execution-time environment concern itself with the specifics. The programmer can command a wide variety of objects to behave in manners appropriate to those objects without even knowing the types of those objects.

7.15 Polymorphism promotes extensibility: Software written to invoke polymorphic behavior is written independent of the types of the objects to which messages (i.e., method calls) are sent. Thus, new types of objects that can respond to existing messages can be added into such a system without modifying the base system.

7.16 If a method is declared **final** it cannot be overridden in subclasses, so that method calls may not be sent polymorphically to objects of those subclasses. The method call may still be sent to subclasses but they will all respond identically rather than polymorphically.

7.17 An **abstract** class defines a common interface for the various members of a class hierarchy. The **abstract** class contains methods that will be defined in the subclasses. All classes in the hierarchy can use this same interface through polymorphism.

7.18 If a subclass is derived from a superclass with an **abstract** method, and if no definition is supplied in the subclass for that **abstract** method (i.e., if that method is not overridden in the subclass), then that method remains **abstract** in the subclass. Consequently, the subclass is also an **abstract** class and must be explicitly declared as an **abstract** class.

7.19 The ability to declare an **abstract** method gives the class designer considerable power over how subclasses will be implemented in a class hierarchy. Any new class that wants to inherit from this class is forced to override the **abstract** method (either directly or by inheriting from a class that has overridden the method). Otherwise that new class will contain an **abstract** method and thus be an **abstract** class unable to instantiate objects.

7.20 Even if a class is **abstract** it can still have instance data and non-**abstract** methods subject to the normal rules of inheritance by subclasses.

7.21 Hierarchies designed for implementation inheritance tend to have their functionality high in the hierarchy—each new subclass inherits one or more methods that were defined in a superclass and uses the superclass definitions.

7.22 Hierarchies designed for interface inheritance tend to have their functionality lower in the hierarchy—a superclass specifies one or more methods that should be called identically for each object in the hierarchy (i.e., they have the same signature), but the individual subclasses provide their own implementations of the method(s).

Testing and Debugging Tips

7.1 An interesting consequence of using polymorphism is that programs take on a simplified appearance. They contain less branching logic in favor of simpler sequential code. This simplification facilitates testing, debugging, and program maintenance.

7.2 Hiding **private** members is a huge help in testing, debugging and correctly modifying systems. If a subclass could access its superclass's **private** members, it would then be possible for classes derived from that subclass to access that data as well, and so on. This would propagate access to what is supposed to be **private** data, and the benefits of information hiding would be lost throughout the class hierarchy.

Self-Review Exercises

7.1 Fill in the blanks in each of the following:

a) If the class **Alpha** inherits from the class **Beta**, class **Alpha** is called the _________ class and class **Beta** is called the _________ class.
b) Inheritance enables _________ which saves time in development, and encourages using previously proven and high-quality software components.
c) An object of a _________ class can be treated as an object of its corresponding _________ class.
d) The four member access specifiers are ________, ________, ________, and ________.
e) A "has a" relationship between classes represents _________ and an "is a" relationship between classes represents _________ .
f) Using polymorphism helps eliminate _________ logic.
g) If a class contains one or more **abstract** methods, it is an _________ class.
h) A method call resolved at runtime is referred to as _________ binding.

7.2 a) A subclass may call any method of its superclass by prepending __________ to the method call.
b) A superclass typically represents a larger number of objects than its subclass represents (T/F).
c) A subclass typically encapsulates less functionality than does its superclass. (T/F).

Answers to Self-Review Exercises

7.1 a) sub, super. b) software reusability. c) sub, super. d) **public**, **protected**, **private** and package access. e) composition, inheritance. f) **switch**. g) **abstract**. i) dynamic.

7.2 a) super
b) T
c) F

Exercises

7.3 Consider the class **Bicycle**. Given your knowledge of some common components of bicycles, show a class hierarchy in which the class **Bicycle** inherits from other classes, which, in turn, inherit from yet other classes. Discuss the instantiation of various objects of class **Bicycle**. Discuss inheritance from class **Bicycle** for other closely related subclasses.

7.4 Define each of the following terms: single inheritance, multiple inheritance, interface, superclass and subclass.

7.5 Discuss why casting a superclass reference to a subclass reference is potentially dangerous.

7.6 Distinguish between single inheritance and multiple inheritance. Why does Java not support multiple inheritance? What feature of Java helps realize the benefits of multiple inheritance?

7.7 (True/False) A subclass is generally smaller than its superclass.

7.8 (True/False) A subclass object is also an object of that subclass's superclass.

7.9 Some programmers prefer not to use **protected** access because it breaks information hiding in the superclass. Discuss the relative merits of using **protected** access vs. **private** access in superclasses.

7.10 Many programs written with inheritance could be solved with composition instead, and vice versa. Discuss the relative merits of these approaches in the context of the **Point**, **Circle**, **Cylinder** class hierarchy in this chapter. Rewrite the program of Fig. 7.10 (and the supporting classes) to use composition rather than inheritance. After you do this, reassess the relative merits of the two approaches both for the **Point**, **Circle**, **Cylinder** problem and for object-oriented programs in general.

7.11 Rewrite the **Point**, **Circle**, **Cylinder** program of Fig. 7.10 as a **Point**, **Square**, **Cube** program. Do this two ways—once with inheritance and once with composition.

7.12 In the chapter, we stated, "When a superclass member is inappropriate for a subclass, that member can be overridden in the subclass with an appropriate implementation." If this is done, does the subclass-is-a-superclass-object relationship still hold? Explain your answer.

7.13 Study the inheritance hierarchy of Fig. 7.2. For each class, indicate some common attributes and behaviors consistent with the hierarchy. Add some other classes (i.e., **UndergraduateStudent**, **GraduateStudent**, **Freshman**, **Sophomore**, **Junior**, **Senior**, etc., to enrich the hierarchy.

7.14 Write an inheritance hierarchy for classes **Quadrilateral**, **Trapezoid**, **Parallelogram**, **Rectangle**, and **Square**. Use **Quadrilateral** as the superclass of the hierarchy. Make the hierarchy as deep (i.e., as many levels) as possible. The **private** data of **Quadrilateral** should include the *(x, y)* coordinate pairs for the four endpoints of the **Quadrilateral**. Write a driver program that instantiates and displays objects of each of these classes. [In Chapter 9, "Graphics" you will learn how to use Java's drawing capabilities.]

7.15 Write down all the shapes you can think of—both two-dimensional and three-dimensional—and form those shapes into a shape hierarchy. Your hierarchy should have superclass `Shape` from which class `TwoDimensionalShape` and class `ThreeDimensionalShape` are derived. Once you have developed the hierarchy, define each of the classes in the hierarchy. We will use this hierarchy in the exercises to process all shapes as objects of superclass `Shape`.

7.16 How is it that polymorphism enables you to program "in the general" rather than "in the specific." Discuss the key advantages of programming "in the general."

7.17 Discuss the problems of programming with `switch` logic. Explain why polymorphism is an effective alternative to using `switch` logic.

7.18 Distinguish between inheriting interface and inheriting implementation. How do inheritance hierarchies designed for inheriting interface differ from those designed for inheriting implementation?

7.19 Distinguish between non-`abstract` methods and `abstract` methods.

7.20 (True/False) All methods in an `abstract` superclass must be declared `abstract`.

7.21 Suggest one or more levels of `abstract` superclasses for the `Shape` hierarchy discussed in the beginning of this chapter (the first level is `Shape` and the second level consists of the classes `TwoDimensionalShape` and `ThreeDimensionalShape`).

7.22 How does polymorphism promote extensibility?

7.23 You have been asked to develop a flight simulator that will have elaborate graphical outputs. Explain why polymorphic programming would be especially effective for a problem of this nature.

7.24 Develop a basic graphics package. Use the `Shape` class inheritance hierarchy from Fig. 7.3. Limit yourself to two-dimensional shapes such as squares, rectangles, triangles, and circles. Interact with the user. Let the user specify the position, size, shape, and fill characters to be used in drawing each shape. The user can specify many items of the same shape. As you create each shape, place a `Shape` reference to each new `Shape` object into an array. Each class has its own `draw` method. Write a polymorphic screen manager that walks through the array sending `draw` messages to each object in the array to form a screen image. Redraw the screen image each time the user specifies an additional shape. Investigate the methods of class `Graphics` to help draw each shape.

7.25 Modify the payroll system of Fig. 7.9 to add `private` instance variables `birthDate` (use class `Date` from Fig. 6.8) and `departmentCode` (an `int`) to class `Employee`. Assume this payroll is processed once per month. Then, as your program calculates the payroll for each `Employee` (polymorphically), add a $100.00 bonus to the person's payroll amount if this is the month in which the `Employee`'s birthday occurs.

7.26 In Exercise 7.15, you developed a `Shape` class hierarchy and defined the classes in the hierarchy. Modify the hierarchy so that class `Shape` is an `abstract` superclass containing the interface to the hierarchy. Derive `TwoDimensionalShape` and `ThreeDimensionalShape` from class `Shape`—these classes should also be `abstract`. Use an `abstract print` method to output the type and dimensions of each class. Also include `area` and `volume` methods so these calculations can be performed for objects of each concrete class in the hierarchy. Write a driver program that tests the `Shape` class hierarchy.

7.27 Rewrite your solution to exercise 7.26 to use a `Shape` interface instead of an abstract `Shape` class.

8

Strings

Objectives

- To be able to create and manipulate nonmodifiable character string objects of class **`String`**.
- To be able to create and manipulate modifiable character string objects of class **`StringBuffer`**.
- To be able to create and manipulate objects of class **`Character`**.
- To be able to use a **`StringTokenizer`** object to break a **`String`** object into individual components called tokens.

The chief defect of Henry King
Was chewing little bits of string.
Hilaire Belloc

Vigorous writing is concise. A sentence should contain no unnecessary words, a paragraph no unnecessary sentences.
William Strunk, Jr.

I have made this letter longer than usual, because I lack the time to make it short.
Blaise Pascal

The difference between the almost-right word & the right word is really a large matter—it's the difference between the lightning bug and the lightning.
Mark Twain

Mum's the word.
Miguel de Cervantes, *Don Quixote de la Mancha*

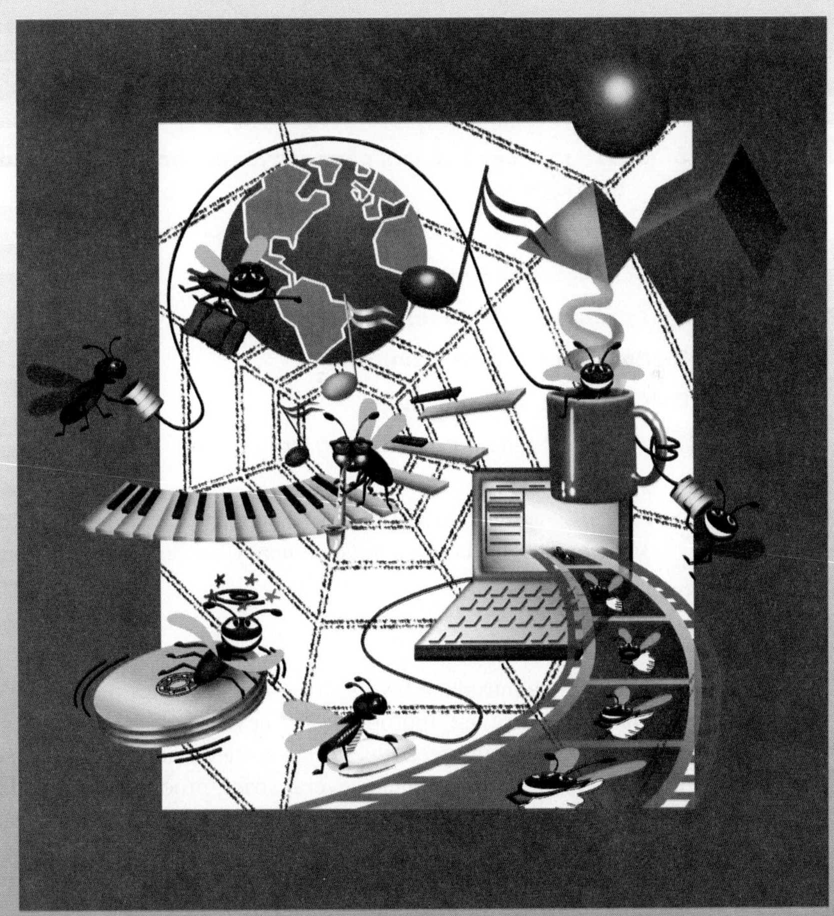

Outline

8.1 Introduction

In this chapter, we introduce Java's string and character processing capabilities. The techniques discussed here are appropriate for developing text editors, word processors, page layout software, computerized typesetting systems, and other kinds of text-processing software. We have already presented several string processing capabilities in the text. In this chapter we discuss in detail the capabilities of class **`String`**, class **`StringBuffer`** and class **`Character`** from the **`java.lang`** package and class **`StringTokenizer`** from the **`java.util`** package.

8.2 Fundamentals of Characters and Strings

Characters are the fundamental building blocks of Java source programs. Every program is composed of a sequence of characters that—when grouped together meaningfully—is interpreted by the computer as a series of instructions used to accomplish a task. A program may contain *character constants.* A character constant is an integer value represented as a character in single quotes. As we stated previously, the value of a character constant is the integer value of the character in the Unicode character set. For example, **'z'** represents the integer value of **z**, and **'\n'** represents the integer value of newline. See Appendix D for the integer equivalents of these characters.

A string is a series of characters treated as a single unit. A string may include letters, digits, and various *special characters* such as **+**, **-**, *****, **/**, **$**, and others. A string in Java is an object of class **String**. *String literals* or *string constants* (which are often referred to as *anonymous* ***String*** *objects*) in Java are written as a sequence of characters in double quotation marks as follows:

"John Q. Doe"(a name)
"9999 Main Street"(a street address)
"Waltham, Massachusetts"(a city and state)
"(201) 555-1212"(a telephone number)

Performance Tip 8.1

Java treats all anonymous ***Strings*** *with the same contents as one anonymous* ***String*** *object that has many references. This conserves memory.*

A **String** may be assigned in a declaration to a **String** reference. The declarations

```
String color = "blue";
```

initializes a **String** reference **color** to refer to the anonymous **String** object **"blue"**.

8.3 String Constructors

Class **String** provides nine constructors for initializing **String** objects in a variety of ways. Seven of the constructors are demonstrated in Fig. 8.1. All the constructors are used in the **StringConstructors** applet's **init** method. The statement

```
// Fig. 8.1: StringConstructors.java
// This program demonstrates the String class constructors.
import java.awt.Graphics;
import java.applet.Applet;

public class StringConstructors extends Applet {
   char charArray[] = { 'b', 'i', 'r', 't', 'h', ' ',
                        'd', 'a', 'y' };
```

Fig. 8.1 Demonstrating the **String** class constructors (part 1 of 2).

```
      byte byteArray[] = { 'n', 'e', 'w', ' ',
                           'y', 'e', 'a', 'r' };
      StringBuffer buffer;
      String s, s1, s2, s3, s4, s5, s6, s7;

      public void init()
      {
         s = new String( "hello" );
         buffer = new StringBuffer();
         buffer.append( "Welcome to Java Programming!" );

         // use the String constructors
         s1 = new String();
         s2 = new String( s );
         s3 = new String( charArray );
         s4 = new String( charArray, 6, 3 );
         s5 = new String( byteArray, 4, 4 );
         s6 = new String( byteArray );
         s7 = new String( buffer );
      }

      public void paint( Graphics g )
      {
         g.drawString( "s1 = " + s1, 25, 25 );
         g.drawString( "s2 = " + s2, 25, 40 );
         g.drawString( "s3 = " + s3, 25, 55 );
         g.drawString( "s4 = " + s4, 25, 70 );
         g.drawString( "s5 = " + s5, 25, 85 );
         g.drawString( "s6 = " + s6, 25, 100 );
         g.drawString( "s7 = " + s7, 25, 115 );
      }
   }
```

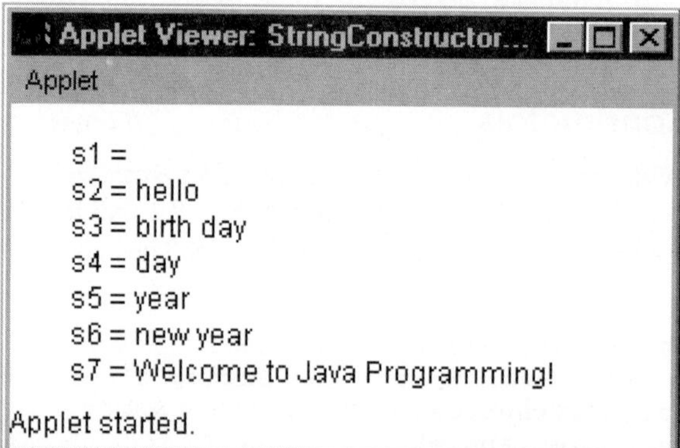

Fig. 8.1 Demonstrating the **String** class constructors (part 2 of 2).

```
s1 = new String();
```

instantiates a new **String** object and assigns it to reference **s1** using the **String** class's default constructor. The new **String** object contains no characters and has a length of 0.

The statement

```
s2 = new String( s );
```

instantiates a new **String** object and assigns it to reference **s2** using the **String** class's copy constructor. The new **String** object contains a copy of the characters in the **String** object **s** that is passed as an argument to the constructor.

The statement

```
s3 = new String( charArray );
```

instantiates a new **String** object and assigns it to reference **s3** using the **String** class constructor that takes a character array as an argument. The new **String** object contains a copy of the characters in the array.

The statement

```
s4 = new String( charArray, 6, 3 );
```

instantiates a new **String** object and assigns it to reference **s4** using the **String** class constructor that takes a character array and two integers as arguments. The second argument specifies the starting position (the ***offset***) from which characters in the array are copied. The third argument specifies the number of characters (the ***count***) to be copied from the array. The new **String** object contains a copy of the specified characters in the array. If the **offset** or the **count** specified as arguments result in accessing an element outside the bounds of the character array, a **StringIndexOutOfBoundsException** is thrown. We discuss exceptions in detail in Chapter 12.

The statement

```
s5 = new String( byteArray, 4, 4 );
```

instantiates a new **String** object and assigns it to reference **s5** using the **String** class constructor that receives a byte array and two integers as arguments. The second and third arguments specify the **offset** and **count**, respectively. The new **String** object contains a copy of the specified bytes in the array. If the **offset** or the **count** specified as arguments result in accessing an element outside the bounds of the character array, a **StringIndexOutOfBoundsException** is thrown.

The statement

```
s6 = new String( byteArray );
```

instantiates a new **String** object and assigns it to reference **s6** using the **String** class constructor that takes a **byte** array as an argument. The new **String** object contains a copy of the bytes in the array.

The statement

```
s7 = new String( buffer );
```

instantiates a new **String** object and assigns it to reference **s7** using the **String** class constructor that receives a **StringBuffer** as an argument. The new **String** object contains a copy of the characters in the **StringBuffer**. A **StringBuffer** is a dynamically resizable string. The lines

```
buffer = new StringBuffer();
buffer.append( "Welcome to Java Programming!" );
```

create a new object of class **StringBuffer**, assign it to **StringBuffer** reference **buffer** and use the **StringBuffer** method **append** to add the string "**Welcome to Java Programming**" to object **buffer**. We discuss **StringBuffer**s in detail later in this chapter.

8.4 String Methods length, charAt, and getChars

This section presents **String** methods **length**, **charAt** and **getChars**. The methods are used in applet **StringMisc**'s **paint** method (Fig. 8.2). The statement

```
g.drawString( "Length of s1: " + s1.length(), 25, 40 );
```

uses the **String** method **length** to determine the number of characters in **String s1**. Like arrays, **String**s always know their own size. However, unlike arrays, **String**s do not have a **length** instance variable that specifies the number of elements in a **String**.

```
// Fig. 8.2: StringMisc.java
// This program demonstrates the length, charAt and getChars
// methods of the String class.
//
// Note: Method getChars requires a starting point
// and ending point in the String. The starting point is the
// actual subscript from which copying starts. The ending point
// is one past the subscript at which the copying ends.
import java.awt.Graphics;
import java.applet.Applet;

public class StringMisc extends Applet {
   String s1;
   char charArray[];

   public void init()
   {
      s1 = new String( "hello there" );
      charArray = new char[ 5 ];
   }

   public void paint( Graphics g )
   {
      // output the string
      g.drawString( "s1: " + s1, 25, 25 );

```

Fig. 8.2 The **String** class character manipulation methods (part 1 of 2).

```
27        // test the length method
28        g.drawString( "Length of s1: " + s1.length(), 25, 40 );
29
30        // loop through the characters in s1 and display reversed
31        g.drawString( "The string reversed is: ", 25, 55 );
32        int xPosition = 155;
33
34        for ( int i = s1.length() - 1; i >= 0; i-- ) {
35           g.drawString( String.valueOf( s1.charAt( i ) ),
36                         xPosition, 55 );
37           xPosition += 10;
38        }
39
40        // copy characters from string into char array
41        s1.getChars( 0, 5, charArray, 0 );
42        g.drawString( "The character array is: ", 25, 70 );
43        g.drawChars( charArray, 0, charArray.length, 158, 70 );
44     }
45  }
```

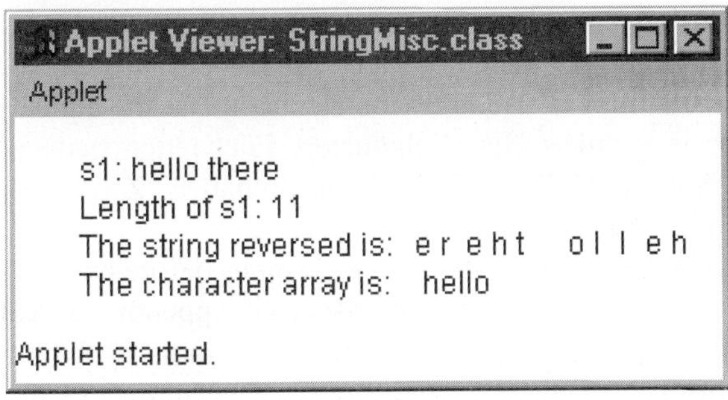

Fig. 8.2 The **String** class character manipulation methods (part 2 of 2).

Common Programming Error 8.1

Attempting to determine the length of a **String** *via an instance variable called* **length** *(e.g.,* **s1.length***) is a syntax error. The* **String** *method* **length** *must be used. (e.g.* **s1.length()***).*

The **for** structure at line 34 displays the characters of the **String s1** in reverse order. The **String** method **charAt** is used to select the character at a specific position in the **String**. Method **charAt** receives an integer argument that is used as the *position number* (or *index*) and returns the character at that position. Like arrays, the first element of a **String** is considered to be at position 0 of the **String**.

Common Programming Error 8.2

Attempting to access a character that is outside the bounds of a **String** *(i.e., an index less than 0 or an index greater than or equal to the* **String***'s length) results in a* **StringIndexOutOfBoundsException**

The statement

```
s1.getChars( 0, 5, charArray, 0 );
```

uses the **String** method **getChars** to copy the characters of a **String** into a character array. The first argument is the starting index from which characters are copied in the **String**. The second argument is the index that is one past the last character to be copied from the **String**. The third argument is the character array into which the characters are copied. The last argument is the starting index where the copied characters are placed in the character array. The result of the preceding statement is displayed with the statement

```
g.drawChars( charArray, 0, charArray.length, 158, 70 );
```

which uses **Graphics** method **drawChars** to output the character array. The second argument specifies the index of the first character to be output. The third argument specifies the index one beyond the last character to be output.

8.5 Comparing Strings

Java provides a variety of methods for comparing **String** objects demonstrated in the next two examples. To understand just what it means for one string to be "greater than" or "less than" another string, consider the process of alphabetizing a series of last names. The reader would, no doubt, place "Jones" before "Smith" because the first letter of "Jones" comes before the first letter of "Smith" in the alphabet. But the alphabet is more than just a list of 26 letters—it is an ordered list of characters. Each letter occurs in a specific position within the list. "Z" is more than just a letter of the alphabet; "Z" is specifically the twenty-sixth letter of the alphabet.

How does the computer know that one letter comes before another? All characters are represented inside the computer as numeric codes (see Appendix D: ASCII Character Set); when the computer compares two strings, it actually compares the numeric codes of the characters in the strings.

Figure 8.3 demonstrates the **String** methods **equals**, **equalsIgnoreCase**, **compareTo** and **regionMatches**, and demonstrates using the equality operator **==** to compare **String** objects.

```
// Fig. 8.3: StringCompare
// This program demonstrates the methods equals,
// equalsIgnoreCase, compareTo, and regionMatches
// of the String class.
import java.awt.Graphics;
import java.applet.Applet;

public class StringCompare extends Applet {
   String s1, s2, s3, s4;

   public void init()
   {
      s1 = new String( "hello" );
      s2 = new String( "good bye" );
```

Fig. 8.3 Demonstrating **String** comparisons (part 1 of 3).

```
      s3 = new String( "Happy Birthday" );
      s4 = new String( "happy birthday" );
   }

   public void paint( Graphics g )
   {
      g.drawString( "s1 = " + s1, 25, 25 );
      g.drawString( "s2 = " + s2, 25, 40 );
      g.drawString( "s3 = " + s3, 25, 55 );
      g.drawString( "s4 = " + s4, 25, 70 );

      // test for equality
      if ( s1.equals( "hello" ) )
         g.drawString( "s1 equals \"hello\"", 25, 100 );
      else
         g.drawString( "s1 does not equal \"hello\"",
                       25, 100 );

      // test for equality with ==
      if ( s1 == "hello" )
         g.drawString( "s1 equals \"hello\"", 25, 115 );
      else
         g.drawString( "s1 does not equal \"hello\"",
                       25, 115 );

      // test for equality--ignore case
      if ( s3.equalsIgnoreCase( s4 ) )
         g.drawString( "s3 equals s4", 25, 130 );
      else
         g.drawString( "s3 does not equal s4", 25, 130 );

      // test compareTo
      g.drawString( "s1.compareTo( s2 ) is " +
                    s1.compareTo( s2 ), 25, 160 );
      g.drawString( "s2.compareTo( s1 ) is " +
                    s2.compareTo( s1 ), 25, 175 );
      g.drawString( "s1.compareTo( s1 ) is " +
                    s1.compareTo( s1 ), 25, 190 );
      g.drawString( "s3.compareTo( s4 ) is " +
                    s3.compareTo( s4 ), 25, 205 );
      g.drawString( "s4.compareTo( s3 ) is " +
                    s4.compareTo( s3 ), 25, 220 );

      // test regionMatches (case sensitive)
      if ( s3.regionMatches( 0, s4, 0, 5 ) )
         g.drawString(
            "First 5 characters of s3 and s4 match",
            25, 250 );
```

Fig. 8.3 Demonstrating **String** comparisons (part 2 of 3).

```
63          else
64             g.drawString(
65                "First 5 characters of s3 and s4 do not match",
66                25, 250 );
67
68          // test regionMatches (ignore case)
69          if ( s3.regionMatches( true, 0, s4, 0, 5 ) )
70             g.drawString(
71                "First 5 characters of s3 and s4 match",
72                25, 265 );
73          else
74             g.drawString(
75                "First 5 characters of s3 and s4 do not match",
76                25, 265 );
77       }
78    }
```

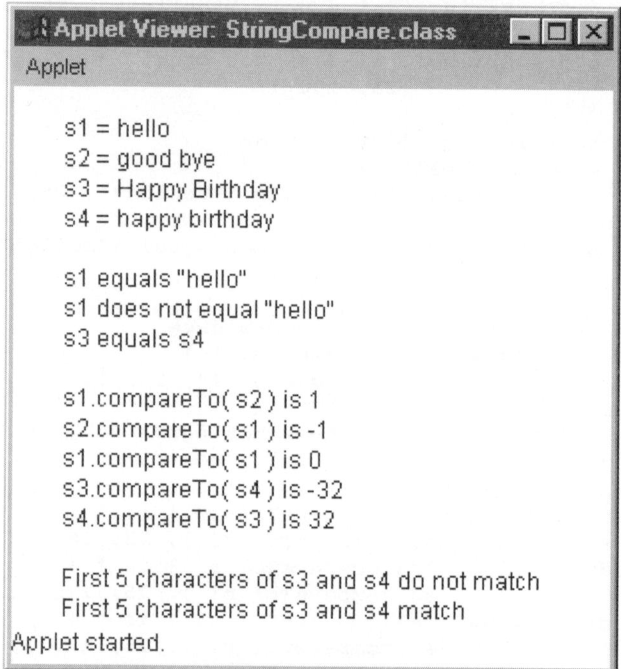

Fig. 8.3 Demonstrating **`String`** comparisons (part 3 of 3).

The condition in the **`if`** structure at line 27

```
s1.equals( "hello" )
```

uses the **`equals`** method to compare **`String s1`** for equality with the anonymous **`String "hello"`**. Method **`equals`** (which is inherited by class **`String`** from its superclass **`Object`**) is used to test any two objects for equality (i.e., the contents of the two objects are identical). The method returns **`true`** if the objects are equal and **`false`** otherwise. The result of the preceding call to **equals** is **true** because **String s1** was initialized with a copy of the anonymous **String "hello"**. Method **equals** uses a *lexicographical comparison*—the integer Unicode values that represent each character in each **String** are compared. Thus, if the **String "hello"** is compared to the **String "HELLO"** the result is **false** because the integer representation of a lowercase letter is different from that of the corresponding uppercase letter.

The condition in the **if** structure at line 34

```
s1 == "hello"
```

uses the equality operator **==** to compare **String s1** for equality with the anonymous **String "hello"**. *Operator == actually has different functionality when it is used to compare references and when it is used to compare values of primitive data types.* When primitive data type values are compared with **==**, the result is **true** if both values are identical. When references are compared with **==**, the result is **true** if both references *refer to the same object in memory.* To compare the actual contents (or state information) of objects for equality, methods (such as **equals**) must be invoked. The preceding condition evaluates to **false** in this program because the reference **s1** was initialized with the statement

```
s1 = new String( "hello" );
```

which creates a new **String** object with a copy of anonymous **String "hello"** and assigns the new object to reference **s1**. If **s1** had been initialized with the statement

```
s1 = "hello";
```

which directly assigns the anonymous **String "hello"** to the reference **s1**, the condition would produce a **true** result. This is because Java treats all anonymous **String**s with the same contents as one anonymous **String** object that has many references. Thus, lines 13, 27 and 34 all refer to the same anonymous **String** object **"hello"** in memory.

If you are sorting **String**s, you may compare them for equality with method **equalsIgnoreCase** which ignores the case of the letters in each **String** when performing the comparison. Thus, the **String "hello"** and the **String "HELLO"** compare as equal. The **if** structure at line 41 uses the condition

```
s3.equalsIgnoreCase( s4 )
```

to compare **String s3**—**Happy Birthday**—for equality with **String s4**—**happy birthday**. The result of this comparison is **true**.

Lines 47 through 56 use the **String** method **compareTo** to compare **String** objects. For example, the expression

```
s1.compareTo( s2 )
```

on line 48 compares **String s1** to **String s2**. Method **compareTo** returns 0 if the **Strings** are equal, a negative number if the **String** that invokes **compareTo** is less than the **String** that is passed as an argument, and a positive number if the **String** that invokes **compareTo** is greater than the **String** that is passed as an argument. Method

compareTo uses a lexicographical comparison. The value returned is the difference between the integer representations of the first character that is different in each **String**. When comparing **s4** and **s3**, the first character in each **String** is different and the value returned is 32 because the integer representation of **h** is 104 and the integer representation of **H** is 72.

The condition in the **if** structure at line 59

```
s3.regionMatches( 0, s4, 0, 5 )
```

uses **String** method **regionMatches** to compare portions of two **String** objects for equality. The first argument is the starting index in the **String** that invokes the method. The second argument is a **String** for comparison. The third argument is the starting index in the **String** for comparison. The last argument is the number of characters to compare between the two **String**s. The method returns **true** only if the specified number of characters are lexicographically equal.

Finally, the condition in the **if** structure at line 69

```
s3.regionMatches( true, 0, s4, 0, 5 )
```

uses the second version of **String** method **regionMatches** to compare portions of two **String** objects for equality. If the first argument is **true**, the method ignores the case of the characters being compared. The remaining arguments are identical to those described for the **regionMatches** method with four arguments.

The second example of this section (Fig. 8.4) demonstrates the **startsWith** and **endsWith** methods of class **String**. Applet **StringStartEnd** contains an array of **String**s called **strings** containing **"started"**, **"starting"**, **"ended"** and **"ending"**. The **paint** method consists of three **for** structures that test the elements of the array to determine if they start with or end with a particular set of characters.

The first **for** structure (line 16) uses the version of method **startsWith** that takes a **String** argument. The condition in the **if** structure (line 17)

```
strings[ i ].startsWith( "st" )
```

```
1  // Fig. 8.4: StringStartEnd.java
2  // This program demonstrates the methods startsWith and
3  // endsWith of the String class.
4  import java.awt.Graphics;
5  import java.applet.Applet;
6
7  public class StringStartEnd extends Applet{
8     String strings[] = { "started", "starting",
9                          "ended", "ending" };
10
```

Fig. 8.4 The **String** class **startsWith** and **endsWith** methods (part 1 of 2).

```
    public void paint( Graphics g )
    {
       int yPosition = 25;

       // Test method startsWith
       for ( int i = 0; i < strings.length; i++ )
          if ( strings[ i ].startsWith( "st" ) ) {
             g.drawString( "\"" + strings[ i ] +
                "\" starts with \"st\"", 25, yPosition );
             yPosition += 15;
          }

       yPosition += 15;

       // Test method startsWith starting from position
       // 2 of the string
       for ( int i = 0; i < strings.length; i++ )
          if ( strings[ i ].startsWith( "art", 2 ) ) {
             g.drawString( "\"" + strings[ i ] +
                "\" starts with \"art\" at position 2",
                25, yPosition );
             yPosition += 15;
          }

       yPosition += 15;

       // Test method endsWith
       for ( int i = 0; i < strings.length; i++ )
          if ( strings[ i ].endsWith( "ed" ) ) {
             g.drawString( "\"" + strings[ i ] +
                "\" ends with \"ed\"", 25, yPosition );
             yPosition += 15;
          }
    }
 }
```

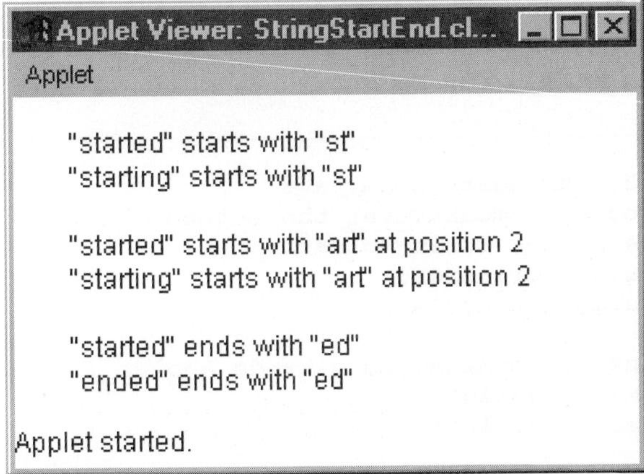

Fig. 8.4 The **`String`** class **`startsWith`** and **`endsWith`** methods (part 2 of 2).

determines if the **String** at location **i** of array **strings** starts with the characters **"st"**. If so, the method returns **true** and the **String** is displayed on the applet.

The second **for** structure (line 27) uses the version of method **startsWith** that takes a **String** and an integer as arguments. The integer argument specifies the index at which the comparison should begin in the **String**. The condition in the **if** structure

```
strings[ i ].startsWith( "art", 2 )
```

determines if the **String** at location **i** of array **strings** starts with the characters **"art"** beginning with the character at index **2** in each **String**. If so, the method returns **true** and the **String** is displayed on the applet.

The third **for** structure (line 38) uses method **endsWith** that takes a **String** argument. The condition in the **if** structure

```
strings[ i ].endsWith( "ed" )
```

determines if the **String** at location **i** of array **strings** ends with the characters **"ed"**. If so, the method returns **true** and the **String** is displayed on the applet.

8.6 String Method hashCode

Often, it is necessary to store **String**s and other data types in a manner that allows the information to be found quickly. One of the best ways to store information for fast lookup is a hash table. A *hash table* stores information using a special calculation on the object to be stored that produces a *hash code*. The hash code is used to choose the location in the table at which to store the object. When the information needs to be retrieved, the same calculation is performed, the hash code is determined and a lookup of that location in the table results in the value that was stored there previously. Every object has the ability to be stored in a hash table. Class **Object** defines method **hashCode** to perform the hash code calculation. This method is inherited into all subclasses of **Object**. Method **hashCode** is overridden by **String** to provide a good hash code distribution based on the contents of the **String**. We will say more about hashing in Chapter 18.

The example in Fig. 8.5 demonstrates the **hashCode** method for two **String**s containing **"hello"** and **"Hello"**.

```
// Fig. 8.5: StringHashCode.java
// This program demonstrates the method
// hashCode of the String class.
import java.awt.Graphics;
import java.applet.Applet;

public class StringHashCode extends Applet {
   String s1 = "hello",
          s2 = "Hello";

```

Fig. 8.5 The **String** class **hashCode** method (part 1 of 2).

```
    public void paint( Graphics g )
    {
       g.drawString( "The hash code for \"" +
          s1 + "\" is " + s1.hashCode(), 25, 25 );
       g.drawString( "The hash code for \"" +
          s2 + "\" is " + s2.hashCode(), 25, 40 );
    }
}
```

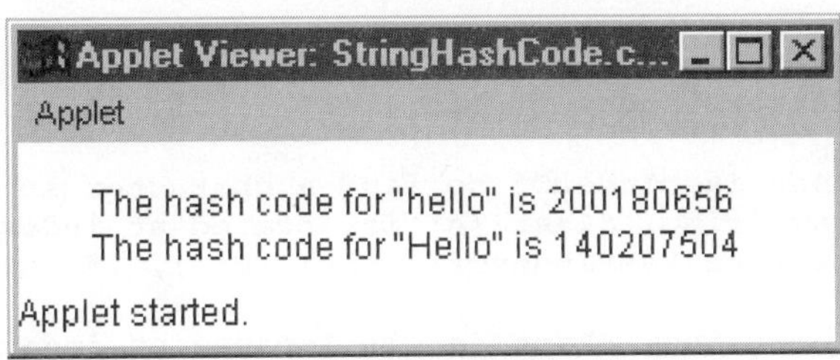

Fig. 8.5 The **String** class **hashCode** method (part 2 of 2).

Note that the hash code values for each of the **String**s is different. That is because the **String**s themselves are lexicographically different. We will discuss hash tables in more detail in Chapter 18.

8.7 Locating Characters and Substrings in Strings

Often it is useful to search for a character or set of characters in a **String**. For example, if you are creating your own word processor, you may want to provide a capability for searching through the document. The program of Fig. 8.6 demonstrates the many versions of **String** methods **indexOf** and **lastIndexOf** that search for a specified character in a **String**. All the searches in this example are performed on the **String** letters (initialized with **"abcdefghijklmabcdefghijklm"**) in the **paint** method of applet class **StringIndexMethods**.

The output statements at lines 13 through 20 use method **indexOf** to locate the first occurrence of a character in a **String**. If the character is found, the index of that character in the **String** is returned; otherwise –1 is returned. There are two versions of **indexOf** that search for characters in a **String**. The expression

```
1  // Fig. 8.6: StringIndexMethods.java
2  // This program demonstrates the String
3  // class index methods.
4  import java.awt.Graphics;
5  import java.applet.Applet;
6
7  public class StringIndexMethods extends Applet {
8     String letters = "abcdefghijklmabcdefghijklm";
9
```

Fig. 8.6 The **String** class searching methods (part 1 of 3).

```
   public void paint( Graphics g )
   {
      // test indexOf to locate a character in a string
      g.drawString( "'c' is located at index " +
         letters.indexOf( (int) 'c' ), 25, 25 );

      g.drawString( "'a' is located at index " +
         letters.indexOf( (int) 'a', 1 ), 25, 40 );

      g.drawString( "'$' is located at index " +
         letters.indexOf( (int) '$' ), 25, 55 );

      // test lastIndexOf to find a character in a string
      g.drawString( "Last 'c' is located at index " +
         letters.lastIndexOf( (int) 'c' ), 25, 85 );

      g.drawString( "Last 'a' is located at index " +
         letters.lastIndexOf( (int) 'a', 25 ), 25, 100 );

      g.drawString( "Last '$' is located at index " +
         letters.lastIndexOf( (int) '$' ), 25, 115 );

      // test indexOf to locate a substring in a string
      g.drawString( "\"def\" is located at index " +
         letters.indexOf( "def" ), 25, 145 );

      g.drawString( "\"def\" is located at index " +
         letters.indexOf( "def", 7 ), 25, 160 );

      g.drawString( "\"hello\" is located at index " +
         letters.indexOf( "hello" ), 25, 175 );

      // test lastIndexOf to find a substring in a string
      g.drawString( "Last \"def\" is located at index " +
         letters.lastIndexOf( "def" ), 25, 205 );

      g.drawString( "Last \"def\" is located at index " +
         letters.lastIndexOf( "def", 25 ), 25, 220 );

      g.drawString( "Last \"hello\" is located at index " +
         letters.lastIndexOf( "hello" ), 25, 235 );
   }
}
```

Fig. 8.6 The **String** class searching methods (part 2 of 3).

```
letters.indexOf( (int) 'c' )
```

uses the version of method **indexOf** that takes one integer argument that is the integer representation of a character—the reason for the integer cast operation in the preceding expression. The expression

```
letters.indexOf( (int) 'a', 1 )
```

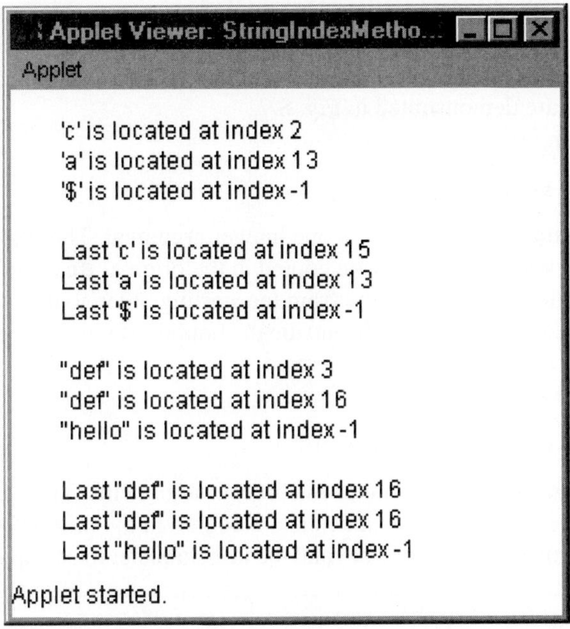

Fig. 8.6 The **String** class searching methods (part 3 of 3).

uses the second version of method **indexOf** that takes two integer arguments—the integer representation of a character and the starting index at which the search of the **String** should begin.

The output statements at lines 23 through 30 use method **lastIndexOf** to locate the last occurrence of a character in a **String**. The search is performed from the end of the **String** toward the beginning of the **String**. If the character is found, the index of that character in the **String** is returned; otherwise –1 is returned. There are two versions of **lastIndexOf** that search for characters in a **String**. The expression

```
letters.lastIndexOf( (int) 'c' )
```

uses the version of method **lastIndexOf** that takes one integer argument that is the integer representation of a character. The expression

```
letters.lastIndexOf( (int) 'a', 25 )
```

uses the version of method **lastIndexOf** that takes two integer arguments—the integer representation of a character and the highest index at which to begin searching for the character.

Lines 33 through 50 of the program demonstrate the **indexOf** and **lastIndexOf** methods—each of which takes a **String** as its first argument. These versions of the methods perform identically to those described above except that they search for sets of characters (or substrings) that are specified by their **String** arguments.

8.8 Extracting Substrings from **Strings**

Class **String** provides two **substring** methods to enable a new **String** object to be created by copying part of an existing **String** object. Each method returns a **String** object. Both methods are demonstrated in Fig. 8.7.

The expression

```
letters.substring( 20 )
```

uses the **substring** method that takes one integer argument. The argument specifies the starting index from which characters are copied in the original **String**. The substring returned contains copies of the characters from the starting index to the end of the **String**. If the index specified as an argument is outside the bounds of the **String**, a **StringIndexOutOfBoundsException** is generated.

The expression

```
letters.substring( 0, 6 )
```

uses the **substring** method that takes two integer arguments. The first argument specifies the starting index from which characters are copied in the original **String**. The second argument specifies the index one beyond the last character to be copied (i.e., copy up to

```
// Fig. 8.7: SubString.java
// This program demonstrates the String class substring methods.
import java.awt.Graphics;
import java.applet.Applet;

public class SubString extends Applet {
   String letters = "abcdefghijklmabcdefghijklm";

   public void paint( Graphics g )
   {
      // test substring methods
      g.drawString( "Substring from index 20 to end is " +
         "\"" + letters.substring( 20 ) + "\"", 25, 25 );

      g.drawString( "Substring from index 0 upto 6 is " +
         "\"" + letters.substring( 0, 6 ) + "\"", 25, 40 );
   }
}
```

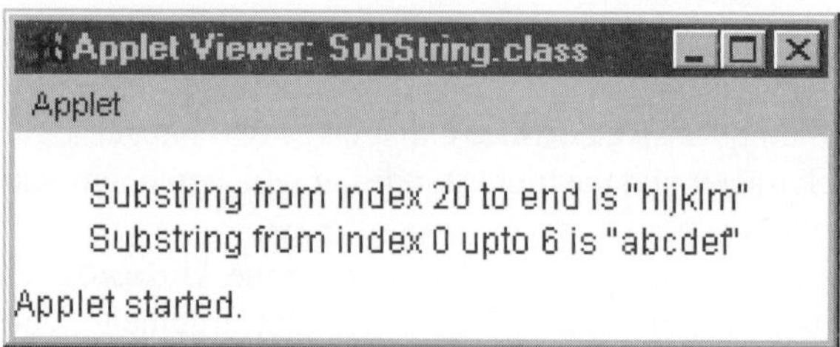

Fig. 8.7 The **String** class **substring** methods.

but not including that index in the **String**). The substring returned contains copies of the specified characters from the original **String**. If the arguments are outside the bounds of the **String**, a **StringIndexOutOfBoundsException** is generated.

8.9 Concatenating Strings

The **String** method **concat** (Fig. 8.8) concatenates two **String** objects and returns a new **String** object containing the characters from both original **String**s. If the argument **String** has no characters in it, the original **String** is returned. The expression

```
s1.concat( s2 )
```

appends the characters from the **String s2** to the end of the **String s1**. The original **String**s **s1** and **s2** are not modified.

```
// Fig. 8.8: StringConcat.java
// This program demonstrates the String class concat method.
// Note that the concat method returns a new String object. It
// does not modify the object that invoked the concat method.
import java.awt.Graphics;
import java.applet.Applet;

public class StringConcat extends Applet {
   String s1 = new String( "Happy " ),
          s2 = new String( "Birthday" );

   public void paint( Graphics g )
   {
      g.drawString( "s1 = " + s1, 25, 25 );
      g.drawString( "s2 = " + s2, 25, 40 );
      g.drawString( "Result of s1.concat( s2 ) = " +
                    s1.concat( s2 ), 25, 55 );
      g.drawString( "s1 after concatenation = " + s1,
                    25, 70 );
   }
}
```

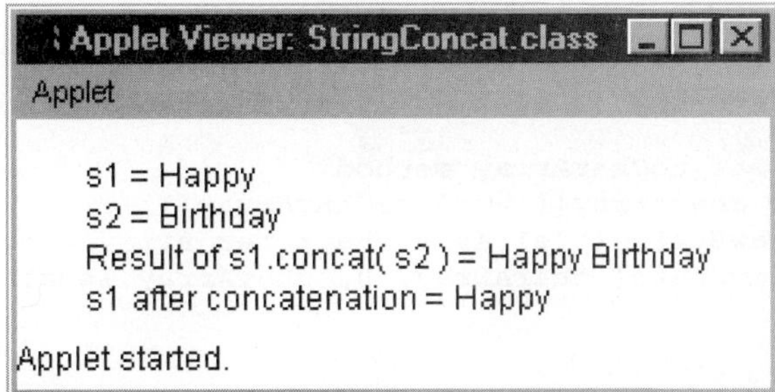

Fig. 8.8 The **String** method **concat**.

8.10 Miscellaneous **String** Methods

Class **String** provides several methods that return modified copies of **String**s or that return a character array. These methods are demonstrated in the **paint** method of applet class **StringMisc2** in Fig. 8.9.

```
// Fig. 8.9: StringMisc2.java
// This program demonstrates the String class replace,
// toLowerCase, toUpperCase, trim, toString, and toCharArray
// methods.
import java.awt.Graphics;
import java.applet.Applet;

public class StringMisc2 extends Applet {
   String s1 = new String( "hello" ),
          s2 = new String( "GOOD BYE" ),
          s3 = new String( "   spaces   " );

   public void paint( Graphics g )
   {
      g.drawString( "s1 = " + s1, 25, 25 );
      g.drawString( "s2 = " + s2, 25, 40 );
      g.drawString( "s3 = " + s3, 25, 55 );

      // test method replace
      g.drawString( "Replace 'l' with 'L' in s1: " +
                    s1.replace( 'l', 'L' ), 25, 85 );

      // test toLowerCase and toUpperCase
      g.drawString( "s1 after toUpperCase = " +
                    s1.toUpperCase(), 25, 115 );
      g.drawString( "s2 after toLowerCase = " +
                    s2.toLowerCase(), 25, 130 );

      // test trim method
      g.drawString( "s3 after trim = \"" + s3.trim() + "\"",
                    25, 160 );

      // test toString method
      g.drawString( "s1 = " + s1.toString(), 25, 190 );

      // test toCharArray method
      char charArray[] = s1.toCharArray();
      g.drawString( "s1 as a character array = ", 25, 220 );
      g.drawChars( charArray, 0, charArray.length, 172, 220 );
   }
}
```

Fig. 8.9 Miscellaneous **String** methods (part 1 of 2).

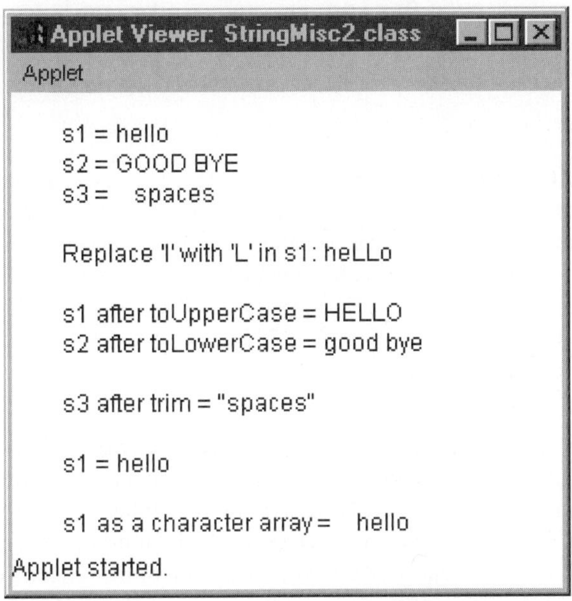

Fig. 8.9 Miscellaneous **String** methods (part 2 of 2).

The expression

```
s1.replace( 'l', 'L' )
```

from line 21 uses **String** method **replace** to generate a new **String** object in which every occurrence in **String s1** of character **'l'** is replaced with character **'L'**. The method returns a new **String** object containing the converted **String**, or if there were no occurrences of the first argument in the **String**, the original **String** is returned. The **String** object is unchanged.

The expression

```
s1.toUpperCase()
```

from line 25 uses **String** method **toUpperCase** to generate a new **String** object with uppercase letters where corresponding lowercase letters reside in **s1**. The method returns a new **String** object containing the converted **String**, or if there are no characters that have uppercase versions in the **String**, the original **String** is returned. The original **String** is unchanged.

The expression

```
s2.toLowerCase()
```

from line 27 uses **String** method **toLowerCase** to generate a new **String** object with lowercase letters where corresponding uppercase letters reside in **s1**. The method returns a new **String** object containing the converted **String**, or if there are no characters that have lowercase versions in the **String**, the original **String** is returned. The original **String** is unchanged.

The expression

```
s3.trim()
```

from line 30 uses **String** method **trim** to generate a new **String** object that removes all whitespace characters (such as spaces, newlines and tabs) that appear at the beginning or end of the **String** to which the **trim** call is sent. The method returns a new **String** object containing the **String** without leading or trailing whitespace characters. The original **String** is unchanged.

The expression

```
s1.toString()
```

from line 34 returns the **String s1**. Why is the **toString** method provided for class **String**? All objects can be converted to **String**s in Java by using method **toString** which originates in the **Object** class. If a class that inherits from **Object** (such as **String**) does not override method **toString**, the default version from class **Object** is used. The default version creates a **String** consisting of the object's class name and the hash code for the object. The **toString** method is normally used to express the contents of an object as text. Method **toString** is provided in class **String** to ensure that the proper **String** value is returned.

The statement

```
char charArray[] = s1.toCharArray();
```

from line 37 creates a new character array containing a copy of the characters in **String s1** and assigns it to **charArray**.

8.11 Using String Method valueOf

Class **String** provides a set of **static** class methods that take arguments of various types, convert those arguments to strings and return them as **String** objects. Applet class **StringValueOf** (Fig. 8.10) demonstrates the **String** class **valueOf** methods.

```
// Fig. 8.10: StringValueOf.java
// This program demonstrates the String class valueOf methods.
import java.awt.Graphics;
import java.applet.Applet;

public class StringValueOf extends Applet {
   char charArray[] = { 'a', 'b', 'c', 'd', 'e', 'f' };
   boolean b = true;
   char c = 'Z';
   int i = 7;
```

Fig. 8.10 The **String** class **valueOf** methods (part 1 of 2).

```
    long l = 10000000;
    float f = 2.5f;
    double d = 33.333;
    Object o = "hello";  // Assign String to Object reference

    public void paint( Graphics g )
    {
       g.drawString( "char array = " +
                     String.valueOf( charArray ), 25, 25 );
       g.drawString( "part of char array = " +
                     String.valueOf( charArray, 3, 3 ),
                     25, 40 );

       g.drawString( "boolean = " + String.valueOf( b ),
                     25, 70 );
       g.drawString( "char = " + String.valueOf( c ),
                     25, 85 );
       g.drawString( "int = " + String.valueOf( i ),
                     25, 100 );
       g.drawString( "long = " + String.valueOf( l ),
                     25, 115 );
       g.drawString( "float = " + String.valueOf( f ),
                     25, 130 );
       g.drawString( "double = " + String.valueOf( d ),
                     25, 145 );
       g.drawString( "Object = " + String.valueOf( o ),
                     25, 160 );
    }
}
```

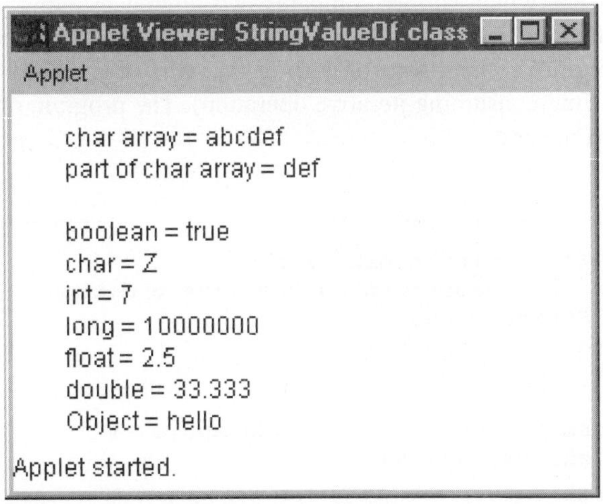

Applet Viewer: StringValueOf.class

Applet

char array = abcdef
part of char array = def

boolean = true
char = Z
int = 7
long = 10000000
float = 2.5
double = 33.333
Object = hello

Applet started.

Fig. 8.10 The **`String`** class **`valueOf`** methods (part 2 of 2).

The expression

```
String.valueOf( charArray )
```

from line 19 copies the contents of the character array **charArray** into a new **String** object and returns the new **String**.

The expression

```
String.valueOf( charArray, 3, 3 )
```

from line 21 copies a portion of the contents of the character array **charArray** into a new **String** object and returns the new **String**. The second argument specifies the starting index from which the characters are copied. The third argument specifies the number of characters to copy.

There are seven other versions of method **valueOf** that take arguments of type **boolean**, **char**, **int**, **long**, **float**, **double** and **Object**, respectively. These are demonstrated in lines 24 through 37 of the program. Note that the version of **valueOf** that takes an **Object** as an argument can do so because all **Object**s can be converted to **String**s with the **toString** method.

8.12 String Method intern

Comparing large **String** objects is a relatively slow operation. **String** method **intern** can improve **String** comparison performance. When **String** method **intern** is invoked on a **String** object it returns a reference to a **String** object in memory that is guaranteed to have the same contents. Subsequent invocations of **intern** on different **String** objects that have the same contents as the original **String** object result in multiple references to the same **String** object. This is useful for efficient **String** comparisons of large **String**s. Once **intern** has been performed, the **String** references can be compared with **==** (which simply compares two references—this is a fast operation) rather than using the **String** comparison methods such as **equals** and **equalsIgnoreCase** (which require comparisons of each of the pairs of corresponding characters in each **String**—a time-consuming iterative operation). The program of Fig. 8.11 demonstrates the **intern** method.

```
// Fig. 8.11: StringIntern.java
// This program demonstrates the intern method
// of the String class.
import java.awt.Graphics;
import java.applet.Applet;

public class StringIntern extends Applet {
   String s1, s2, s3, s4;

```

Fig. 8.11 The **String** class **intern** method (part 1 of 3).

```
    public void init()
    {
       s1 = new String( "hello" );
       s2 = new String( "hello" );
    }

    public void paint( Graphics g )
    {
       // Test strings to determine if they are the same
       // String object in memory.
       if ( s1 == s2 )
          g.drawString( "s1 and s2 are the " +
                        "same object in memory", 25, 25 );
       else
          g.drawString( "s1 and s2 are not the " +
                        "same object in memory", 25, 25 );

       // Test strings for equality of contents
       if ( s1.equals( s2 ) )
          g.drawString( "s1 and s2 are equal", 25, 45 );
       else
          g.drawString( "s1 and s2 are not equal", 55, 45 );

       // Use String intern method to get a unique copy of
       // "hello" referred to by both s3 and s4.
       s3 = s1.intern();
       s4 = s2.intern();

       // Test strings to determine if they are the same
       // String object in memory.
       if ( s3 == s4 )
          g.drawString( "s3 and s4 are the " +
                        "same object in memory", 25, 65 );
       else
          g.drawString( "s3 and s4 are not the " +
                        "same object in memory", 25, 65 );

       // Determine if s1 and s3 refer to the same object
       if ( s1 == s3 )
          g.drawString( "s1 and s3 are the " +
                        "same object in memory", 25, 85 );
       else
          g.drawString( "s1 and s3 are not the " +
                        "same object in memory", 25, 85 );

       // Determine if s2 and s4 refer to the same object
       if ( s2 == s4 )
          g.drawString( "s2 and s4 are the " +
                        "same object in memory", 25, 105 );
```

Fig. 8.11 The **String** class **intern** method (part 2 of 3).

```
        else
           g.drawString( "s2 and s4 are not the " +
                         "same object in memory", 25, 105 );

        // Determine if s1 and s4 refer to the same object
        if ( s1 == s4 )
           g.drawString( "s1 and s4 are the " +
                         "same object in memory", 25, 125 );
        else
           g.drawString( "s1 and s4 are not the " +
                         "same object in memory", 25, 125 );
     }
  }
```

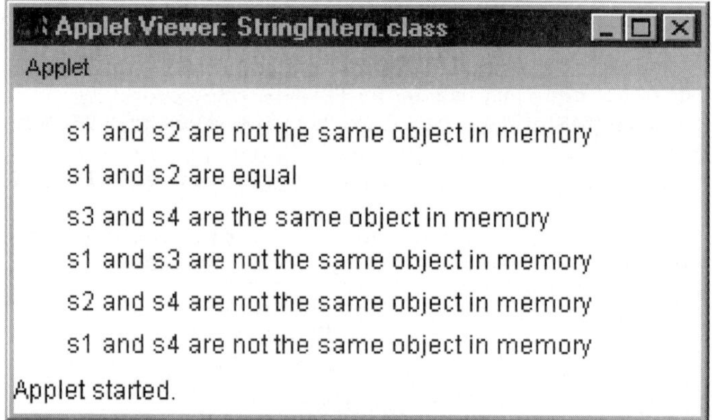

Fig. 8.11 The **String** class **intern** method (part 3 of 3).

Applet class **StringIntern** declares four **String**s—**s1**, **s2**, **s3** and **s4**. **String**s **s1** and **s2** are initialized with copies of **"hello"**. The first **if** structure uses operator **==** to determine that **String**s **s1** and **s2** are the same object in memory. The second **if** structure uses method **equals** to determine that the contents of **String**s **s1** and **s2** are equal. The statement

```
s3 = s1.intern();
```

uses method **intern** to get a reference to a **String** with the same contents as object **s1** and assigns the reference to **s3**. The statement

```
s4 = s2.intern();
```

also uses method **intern** to get a reference to a **String** object. However, because **String s1** and **String s2** have the same contents, the reference returned by this call to **intern** is a reference to the same **String** returned by **s1.intern()** in memory.

The third **if** structure uses operator **==** to determine that **String**s **s3** and **s4** are the same object in memory. The fourth **if** structure uses operator **==** to determine that **String**s **s1** and **s3** are *not* the same object in memory. Technically, they could refer to the same object, but they are not guaranteed to refer to the same object unless the objects they refer to were returned by calls to **intern** on **String**s with the same contents. In this case, **s1** refers to the **String** it was assigned in method **init**. The fifth **if** structure uses operator **==** to determine that **String**s **s2** and **s4** are *not* the same object in memory (this is because the second **intern** call results in a reference to the same object returned by **s1.intern()** not **String s2**). The sixth **if** structure uses operator **==** to determine that **String**s **s1** and **s4** are not the same object in memory.

8.13 StringBuffer Class

The **String** class provides many capabilities for processing **String**s. However, once a **String** object is created, its contents never change. The next several sections discuss the features of class **StringBuffer** for creating and manipulating dynamic string information—i.e., modifiable **String**s. Every **StringBuffer** is capable of storing a number of characters as specified by its capacity. If the capacity of a **StringBuffer** is exceeded, the capacity is automatically expanded to accommodate the additional characters. As we will see, class **StringBuffer** is also used to implement operators **+** and **+=** for **String** concatenation.

Performance Tip 8.2

String *objects are constant strings and* ***StringBuffer*** *objects are modifiable strings. Java distinguishes constant strings and modifiable strings for optimization purposes; in particular, Java can perform certain optimizations involving* ***String*** *objects (such as sharing one* ***String*** *object among multiple references) because it knows these objects will not change.*

Performance Tip 8.3

When given the choice between using a ***String*** *object to represent a string versus a* ***StringBuffer*** *object to represent that string, always use a* ***String*** *object if indeed the object will not change; this improves performance.*

Common Programming Error 8.3

Invoking ***StringBuffer*** *methods that are not methods of class* ***String*** *on* ***String*** *objects is a syntax error.*

8.14 StringBuffer Constructors

Class **StringBuffer** provides three constructors that are demonstrated in Fig. 8.12. The statement

```
buf1 = new StringBuffer();
```

uses the default **StringBuffer** constructor to create a **StringBuffer** with no characters in it and an initial capacity of 16 characters.

```
// Fig. 8.12: StringBufferConstructors.java
// This program demonstrates the StringBuffer constructors.
import java.awt.Graphics;
import java.applet.Applet;

public class StringBufferConstructors extends Applet {
   StringBuffer buf1, buf2, buf3;

   public void init()
   {
      buf1 = new StringBuffer();
      buf2 = new StringBuffer( 10 );
      buf3 = new StringBuffer( "hello" );
   }

   public void paint( Graphics g )
   {
      g.drawString( "buf1 = " + "\"" + buf1.toString() + "\"",
                    25, 25 );
      g.drawString( "buf2 = " + "\"" + buf2.toString() + "\"",
                    25, 40 );
      g.drawString( "buf3 = " + "\"" + buf3.toString() + "\"",
                    25, 55 );
   }
}
```

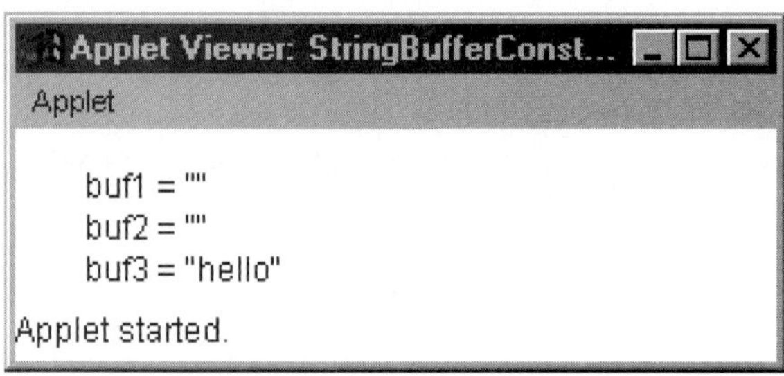

Fig. 8.12 The **StringBuffer** class constructors.

The statement

```
buf2 = new StringBuffer( 10 );
```

uses the **StringBuffer** constructor that takes an integer argument to create a **StringBuffer** with no characters in it and the initial capacity specified in the integer argument.

The statement

```
buf3 = new StringBuffer( "hello" );
```

uses the **StringBuffer** constructor that takes a **String** argument to create a **StringBuffer** containing the characters of the **String** argument and with an initial capacity which is the number of characters in the **String** argument plus 16.

The statements on lines 18 through 23 use **StringBuffer** method **toString** to convert the **StringBuffer**s into **String** objects that can be displayed with **drawString**. Note the use of operator **+** to concatenate **String**s for output. In Section 8.17 we discuss how the **StringBuffer** is used to implement the **+** operator and **+=** operator.

8.15 StringBuffer length, capacity, setLength and ensureCapacity Methods

Class **StringBuffer** provides the **length** and **capacity** methods to return the number of characters currently in a **StringBuffer** and the number of characters that can be stored in a **StringBuffer** without allocating more memory, respectively. Method **ensureCapacity** is provided to allow the programmer to guarantee that a **StringBuffer** has a minimum capacity. Method **setLength** is provided to enable the programmer to increase or decrease the length of a **StringBuffer**. The program of Fig. 8.13 demonstrates these methods.

```java
// Fig. 8.13: StringBufferCapLen.java
// This program demonstrates the length and
// capacity methods of the StringBuffer class.
import java.awt.Graphics;
import java.applet.Applet;

public class StringBufferCapLen extends Applet {
   StringBuffer buf;

   public void init()
   {
      buf = new StringBuffer( "Hello, how are you?" );
   }

   public void paint ( Graphics g )
   {
      g.drawString( "buf = " + buf.toString(), 25, 25  );
      g.drawString( "length = " + buf.length(), 25, 40 );
      g.drawString( "capacity = " + buf.capacity(),
                    25, 55 );

      buf.ensureCapacity( 75 );
      g.drawString( "New capacity = " + buf.capacity(),
                    25, 85 );

      buf.setLength( 10 );
      g.drawString( "New length = " + buf.length(),
                    25, 115 );
      g.drawString( "buf = " + buf.toString(), 25, 130 );
   }
}
```

Fig. 8.13 The **StringBuffer** class **length** and **capacity** methods (part 1 of 2).

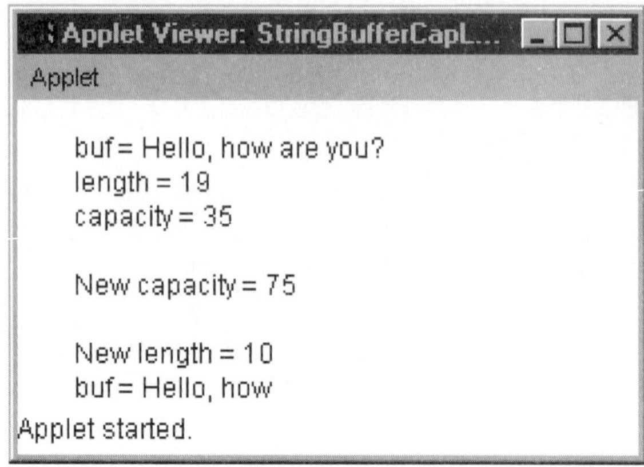

Fig. 8.13 The `StringBuffer` class `length` and `capacity` methods (part 2 of 2).

Applet class **`StringBufferCapLen`** contains one instance variable—**`StringBuffer`** object **`buf`**. Line 12 of the program uses the **`StringBuffer`** constructor that takes a **`String`** argument to instantiate and initialize the **`StringBuffer`** with **`"Hello, how are you?"`**. Notice in the output window that the capacity of the **`StringBuffer`** is initially 35. Remember that the **`StringBuffer`** constructor that takes a **`String`** argument creates a **`StringBuffer`** object with an initial capacity that is the length of the **`String`** passed as an argument plus 16.

The statement

```
buf.ensureCapacity( 75 );
```

expands the capacity of the **`StringBuffer`** to a minimum of 75 characters. Actually, if the original capacity is less than the argument, the method ensures a capacity that is the greater of the number specified as an argument or twice the original capacity plus 2. If the **`StringBuffer`**'s current capacity is more than the specified capacity, the **`StringBuffer`**'s capacity remains unchanged.

The statement

```
buf.setLength( 10 );
```

uses method **`setLength`** to set the length of the **`StringBuffer`** to 10. If the specified length is less than the current number of characters in the **`StringBuffer`**, the characters are truncated to the specified length—i.e., the characters in the **`StringBuffer`** after the specified length are discarded. If the specified length is greater than the number of characters currently in the **`StringBuffer`**, null characters (characters with the numeric representation 0) are appended to the **`StringBuffer`** until the total number of characters in the **`StringBuffer`** is equal to the specified length.

8.16 **StringBuffer charAt**, **setCharAt**, **getChars** and **reverse** Methods

Class **StringBuffer** provides the **charAt**, **setCharAt**, **getChars** and **reverse** methods to manipulate the characters in a **StringBuffer**. Method **charAt** takes an integer argument and returns the character in the **StringBuffer** at that index. Method **setCharAt** takes an integer and a character argument and sets the character at the specified position to the character argument. The index specified in the **charAt** and **setCharAt** methods must be greater than 0 and less than the **StringBuffer** length, otherwise a **StringIndexOutOfBoundsException** is generated.

Common Programming Error 8.4

Attempting to access a character that is outside the bounds of a ***StringBuffer*** *(i.e., an index less than 0 or an index greater than or equal to the* ***StringBuffer****'s length) results in a* ***StringIndexOutOfBoundsException***

Method **getChars** returns a character array containing a copy of the characters in the **StringBuffer**. This method takes four arguments—the starting index from which characters should be copied in the **StringBuffer**, the index one past the last character to be copied from the **StringBuffer**, the character array into which the characters are to be copied and the starting location in the character array where the first character should be placed. Method **reverse** reverses the contents of the **StringBuffer**. Each of these methods is demonstrated in Fig. 8.14.

```
// Fig. 8.14: StringBufferChars.java
// The charAt, setCharAt, getChars, and reverse methods
// of class StringBuffer.
import java.awt.Graphics;
import java.applet.Applet;

public class StringBufferChars extends Applet {
   StringBuffer buf;

   public void init()
   {
      buf = new StringBuffer( "hello there" );
   }

   public void paint ( Graphics g )
   {
      g.drawString( "buf = " + buf.toString(), 25, 25 );
      g.drawString( "Character at 0: " + buf.charAt( 0 ),
                    25, 40 );
      g.drawString( "Character at 4: " + buf.charAt( 4 ),
                    25, 55 );

```

Fig. 8.14 **StringBuffer** class character manipulation methods (part 1 of 2).

```
        char charArray[] = new char[ buf.length() ];
        buf.getChars( 0, buf.length(), charArray, 0 );
        g.drawString( "The characters are: ", 25, 85 );
        g.drawChars( charArray, 0, charArray.length, 142, 85 );

        buf.setCharAt( 0, 'H' );
        buf.setCharAt( 6, 'T' );
        g.drawString( "buf = " + buf.toString(), 25, 115 );

        buf.reverse();
        g.drawString( "buf = " + buf.toString(), 25, 145 );
    }
}
```

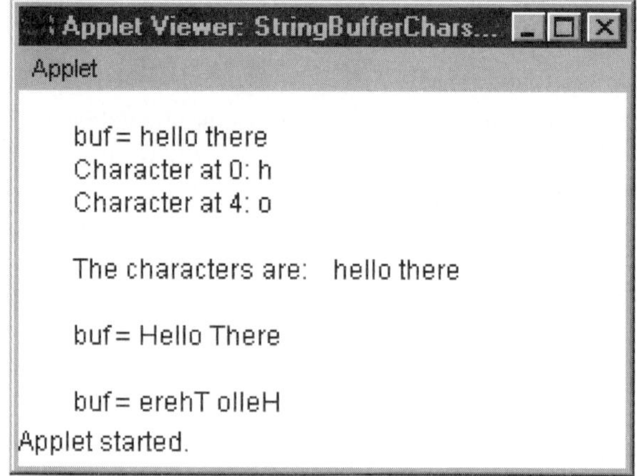

Fig. 8.14 **`StringBuffer`** class character manipulation methods (part 2 of 2).

8.17 `StringBuffer` append Methods

Class **`StringBuffer`** provides 10 overloaded **`append`** methods to allow various data type values to be added to the end of a **`StringBuffer`**. Versions are provided for each of the primitive data types and for character arrays, **`String`**s and **`Object`**s (remember that method **`toString`** produces a **`String`** representation of any **`Object`**). Each of the methods takes its argument, converts it to a **`String`** and appends it to the **`StringBuffer`**. The **`append`** methods are demonstrated in Fig. 8.15.

Actually, **`StringBuffer`**s and the **`append`** methods are used by the compiler to implement the **`+`** and **`+=`** operators for concatenating **`String`**s. For example, the statement

```
String s = "BC" + 22;
```

concatenates **`String "BC"`** and integer **`22`**. The concatenation is performed as follows:

```
new StringBuffer( "BC" ).append( 22 ).toString();
```

```
// Fig. 8.15: StringBufferAppend.java
// This program demonstrates the append
// methods of the StringBuffer class.
import java.awt.Graphics;
import java.applet.Applet;

public class StringBufferAppend extends Applet {
   Object o = "hello";  // Assign String to Object reference
   String s = "good bye";
   char charArray[] = { 'a', 'b', 'c', 'd', 'e', 'f' };
   boolean b = true;
   char c = 'Z';
   int i = 7;
   long l = 10000000;
   float f = 2.5f;
   double d = 33.333;
   StringBuffer buf;

   public void init()
   {
      buf = new StringBuffer();
   }

   public void start()
   {
      buf.append( o );
      buf.append( ' ' );
      buf.append( s );
      buf.append( ' ' );
      buf.append( charArray );
      buf.append( ' ' );
      buf.append( charArray, 0, 3 );
      buf.append( ' ' );
      buf.append( b );
      buf.append( ' ' );
      buf.append( c );
      buf.append( ' ' );
      buf.append( i );
      buf.append( ' ' );
      buf.append( l );
      buf.append( ' ' );
      buf.append( f );
      buf.append( ' ' );
      buf.append( d );
   }

   public void paint( Graphics g )
   {
      g.drawString( "buf = " + buf.toString(), 25, 25 );
   }
}
```

Fig. 8.15 The **StringBuffer** class **append** methods (part 1 of 2).

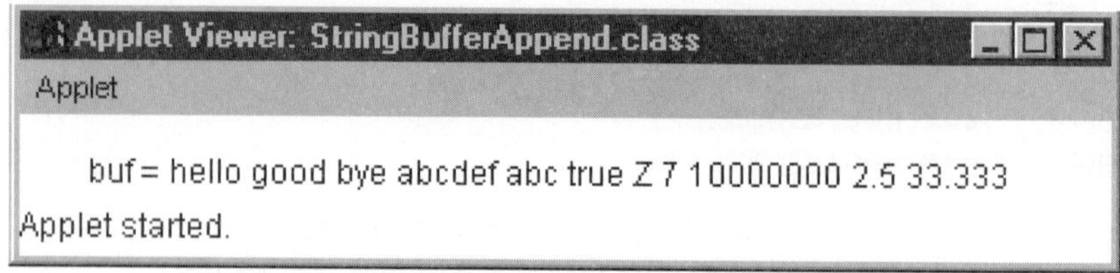

Fig. 8.15 The **StringBuffer** class **append** methods (part 2 of 2).

First, a **StringBuffer** is created with the default **String "BC"** as its contents. Next integer **22** is appended to the end of the **StringBuffer**. Finally, the **StringBuffer** is converted to a **String** with method **toString** and the result is assigned to **String s**. The statement

```
s += "!";
```

is actually performed as follows:

```
s = new StringBuffer( s ).append( "!" ).toString()
```

First, a **StringBuffer** is created with the default **String s** as its contents. Next the **String "!"** is appended to the end of the **StringBuffer**. Finally, the **StringBuffer** is converted to a **String** with method **toString** and the result is assigned to **String s**.

8.18 StringBuffer insert Methods

Class **StringBuffer** provides nine overloaded **insert** methods to allow various data type values to be inserted at any position in a **StringBuffer**. Versions are provided for each of the primitive data types and for character arrays, **String**s and **Object**s (remember that method **toString** produces a **String** representation of any **Object**). Each of the methods takes its second argument, converts it to a **String** and inserts it at the index specified by the first argument. The index specified by the second argument must be greater than or equal to **0** and less than or equal to the length of the **StringBuffer**, otherwise a **StringIndexOutOfBoundsException** is generated. The **insert** methods are demonstrated in Fig. 8.16.

```
 // Fig. 8.16: StringBufferInsert.java
// This program demonstrates the insert
// methods of the StringBuffer class.
import java.awt.Graphics;
import java.applet.Applet;

public class StringBufferInsert extends Applet {
   Object o = "hello";  // Assign String to Object reference
```

Fig. 8.16 The **StringBuffer** class **insert** methods (part 1 of 2).

```
   String s = "good bye";
   char charArray[] = { 'a', 'b', 'c', 'd', 'e', 'f' };
   boolean b = true;
   char c = 'Z';
   int i = 7;
   long l = 10000000;
   float f = 2.5f;
   double d = 33.333;
   StringBuffer buf;

   public void init()
   {
      buf = new StringBuffer();
   }

   public void start()
   {
      buf.insert( 0, o );
      buf.insert( 0, ' ' );
      buf.insert( 0, s );
      buf.insert( 0, ' ' );
      buf.insert( 0, charArray );
      buf.insert( 0, ' ' );
      buf.insert( 0, b );
      buf.insert( 0, ' ' );
      buf.insert( 0, c );
      buf.insert( 0, ' ' );
      buf.insert( 0, i );
      buf.insert( 0, ' ' );
      buf.insert( 0, l );
      buf.insert( 0, ' ' );
      buf.insert( 0, f );
      buf.insert( 0, ' ' );
      buf.insert( 0, d );
   }

   public void paint( Graphics g )
   {
      g.drawString( "buf = " + buf.toString(), 25, 25 );
   }
}
```

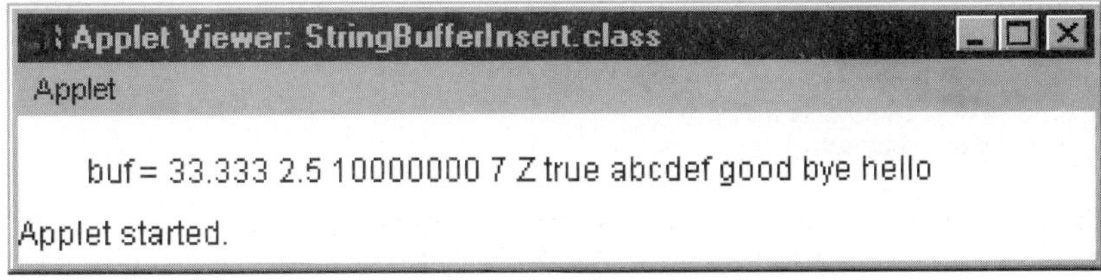

Fig. 8.16 The **StringBuffer** class **insert** methods (part 2 of 2).

8.19 Character Class Examples

Java provides a number of classes that enable the primitive data types to be treated as objects. The classes are **Boolean**, **Character**, **Double**, **Float**, **Byte**, **Short**, **Integer** and **Long**. These classes—all derived from **Number**—are known as *type wrappers* and they are part of the **java.lang** package. Objects of these classes can be used anywhere in a program that an **Object** or a **Number** is expected. In this section, we present class **Character**—the type-wrapper class for characters.

Most **Character** class methods are **static** methods that take at least a character argument and perform either a test or a manipulation of the character. The class also contains a constructor that receives a **char** argument to initialize a **Character** object and several non-**static** methods. Most of the methods of class **Character** are presented in the next three examples. For more information on class **Character** (and all the wrappers classes), see the **java.lang** package in the Java API documentation.

The program of Fig. 8.17 demonstrates some **static** methods that test characters to determine if they are a specific character type and the **static** methods that perform case conversions on characters. Each of the methods is used in the **paint** method of applet class **StaticCharMethods**. The program allows you to enter any character and apply the preceding methods to the character. Several sample outputs are shown.

```
// Fig. 8.17: StaticCharMethods.java
// Demonstrates the static character testing methods
// and case conversion methods of class Character
// from the java.lang package.
import java.applet.Applet;
import java.awt.*;
import java.awt.event.*;

public class StaticCharMethods extends Applet
             implements ActionListener {
   char c;
   Label prompt;
   TextField input;

   public void init()
   {
      c = 'A';

      prompt = new Label( "Enter a character and press Enter" );
      input = new TextField( "A", 5 );
      input.addActionListener( this );
      add( prompt );
      add( input );
   }

```

Fig. 8.17 **static** character testing methods and case conversion methods of class **Character** (part 1 of 3).

```
   public void paint( Graphics g )
   {
      g.drawString( "is defined: " +
         Character.isDefined( c ), 25, 40 );
      g.drawString( "is digit: " +
         Character.isDigit( c ), 25, 55 );
      g.drawString( "is Java letter: " +
         Character.isJavaIdentifierStart( c ), 25, 70 );
      g.drawString( "is Java letter or digit: " +
         Character.isJavaIdentifierPart( c ), 25, 85 );
      g.drawString( "is letter: " +
         Character.isLetter( c ), 25, 100 );
      g.drawString( "is letter or digit: " +
         Character.isLetterOrDigit( c ), 25, 115 );
      g.drawString( "is lower case: " +
         Character.isLowerCase( c ), 25, 130 );
      g.drawString( "is upper case: " +
         Character.isUpperCase( c ), 25, 145 );
      g.drawString( "to upper case: " +
         Character.toUpperCase( c ), 25, 160 );
      g.drawString( "to lower case: " +
         Character.toLowerCase( c ), 25, 175 );
   }

   public void actionPerformed( ActionEvent e )
   {
      String s = e.getActionCommand();
      c = s.charAt( 0 );
      repaint();
   }
}
```

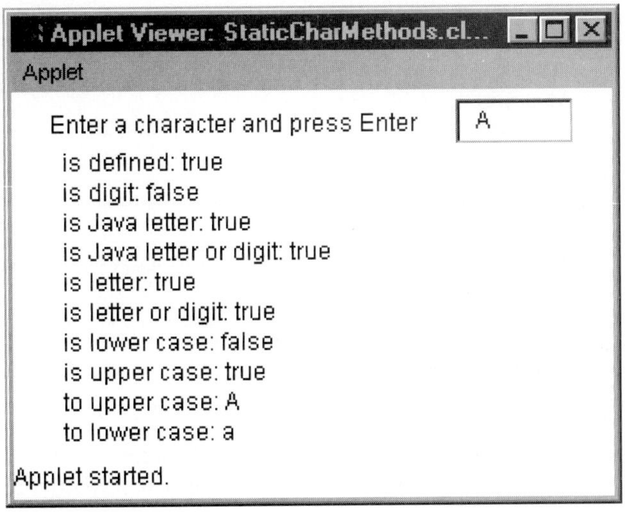

Applet Viewer: StaticCharMethods.cl...
Applet
Enter a character and press Enter A
is defined: true
is digit: false
is Java letter: true
is Java letter or digit: true
is letter: true
is letter or digit: true
is lower case: false
is upper case: true
to upper case: A
to lower case: a
Applet started.

Fig. 8.17 **`static`** character testing methods and case conversion methods of class **`Character`** (part 2 of 3).

Applet Viewer: StaticCharMethods.cl...
Applet
Enter a character and press Enter 8
is defined: true
is digit: true
is Java letter: false
is Java letter or digit: true
is letter: false
is letter or digit: true
is lower case: false
is upper case: false
to upper case: 8
to lower case: 8
Applet started.

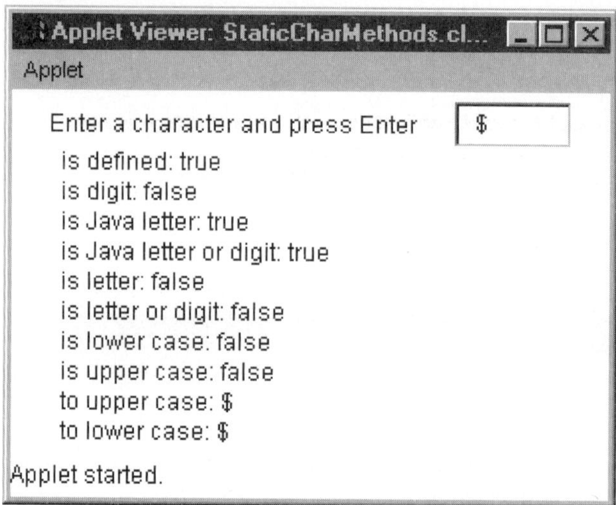

Fig. 8.17 **`static`** character testing methods and case conversion methods of class **`Character`** (part 3 of 3).

The expression

```
Character.isDefined( c )
```

uses method **`Character.isDefined`** to determine if character **`c`** is defined in the Unicode character set. If so, the method returns **`true`**; otherwise, it returns **`false`**.

The expression

```
Character.isDigit( c )
```

uses method **Character.isDigit** to determine if character **c** is a defined Unicode digit. If so, the method returns **true**; otherwise, it returns **false**.

The expression

```
Character.isJavaIdentifierStart( c )
```

uses method **Character.isJavaIdentifierStart** to determine if character **c** is a character that can be used as the first character of an identifier in Java—i.e., a letter, an underscore (_) or a dollar sign (**$**). If so, the method returns **true**; otherwise, it returns **false**.

The expression

```
Character.isJavaIdentifierPart( c )
```

uses method **Character.isJavaIdentifierStart** to determine if character **c** is a character that can be used in an identifier in Java—i.e., a digit, a letter, an underscore (_) or a dollar sign (**$**). If so, the method returns **true**; otherwise, it returns **false**.

The expression

```
Character.isLetter( c )
```

uses method **Character.isLetter** to determine if character **c** is a letter. If so, the method returns **true**; otherwise, it returns **false**.

The expression

```
Character.isLetterOrDigit( c )
```

uses method **Character.isLetterOrDigit** to determine if character **c** is a letter or a digit. If so, the method returns **true**; otherwise, it returns **false**.

The expression

```
Character.isLowerCase( c )
```

uses method **Character.isLowerCase** to determine if character **c** is a lowercase letter. If so, the method returns **true**; otherwise, it returns **false**.

The expression

```
Character.isUpperCase( c )
```

uses method **Character.isUpperCase** to determine if character **c** is an uppercase letter. If so, the method returns **true**; otherwise, it returns **false**.

The expression

```
Character.toUpperCase( c )
```

uses method **Character.toUpperCase** to convert the character **c** to its uppercase equivalent. The method returns the converted character if the character has an uppercase equivalent; otherwise, the method returns its original argument.

The expression

```
Character.toLowerCase( c )
```

uses method **Character.toLowerCase** to convert the character **c** to its lowercase equivalent. The method returns the converted character if the character has a lowercase equivalent; otherwise, the method returns its original argument.

Figure 8.18 demonstrates the **static Character** methods **digit** and **forDigit** to perform conversions between characters and digits in different number systems. Common number systems include decimal (base 10), octal (base 8), hexadecimal (base 16) and binary (base 2). The base of a number is also known as its *radix*. For more information on conversions between number systems, see Appendix E—Number Systems.

```
// Fig. 8.18: StaticCharMethods2.java
// Demonstrates the static character conversion methods
// of class Character from the java.lang package.
import java.applet.Applet;
import java.awt.*;
import java.awt.event.*;

public class StaticCharMethods2 extends Applet
             implements ActionListener {
   char c;
   int digit, radix;
   boolean charToDigit;
   Label prompt1, prompt2;
   TextField input, radixField;
   Button toChar, toInt;

   public void init()
   {
      c = 'A';
      radix = 16;
      charToDigit = true;

      prompt1 = new Label( "Enter a digit or character " );
      input = new TextField( "A", 5 );
      prompt2 = new Label( "Enter a radix " );
      radixField = new TextField( "16", 5 );
      toChar = new Button( "Convert digit to character" );
      toChar.addActionListener( this );
      toInt = new Button( "Convert character to digit" );
      toInt.addActionListener( this );
      add( prompt1 );
      add( input );
      add( prompt2 );
      add( radixField );
```

Fig. 8.18 **Character** class **static** conversion methods (part 1 of 3).

```
      add( toChar );
      add( toInt );
   }

   public void paint( Graphics g )
   {
      if ( charToDigit )
         g.drawString( "Convert character to digit: " +
            Character.digit( c, radix ), 25, 125 );
      else
         g.drawString( "Convert digit to character: " +
            Character.forDigit( digit, radix ), 25, 125 );
   }

   public void actionPerformed( ActionEvent e )
   {
      if ( e.getSource() == toChar ) {
         charToDigit = false;
         digit = Integer.parseInt( input.getText() );
         radix = Integer.parseInt( radixField.getText() );
         repaint();
      }
      else if ( e.getSource() == toInt ) {
         charToDigit = true;
         String s = input.getText();
         c = s.charAt( 0 );
         radix = Integer.parseInt( radixField.getText() );
         repaint();
      }
   }
}
```

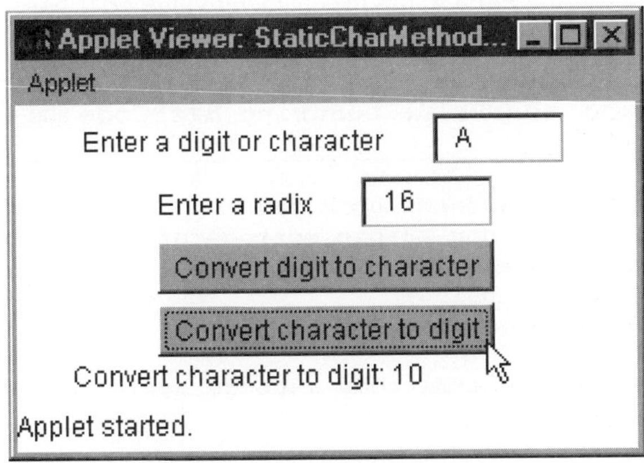

Fig. 8.18 `Character` class `static` conversion methods (part 2 of 3).

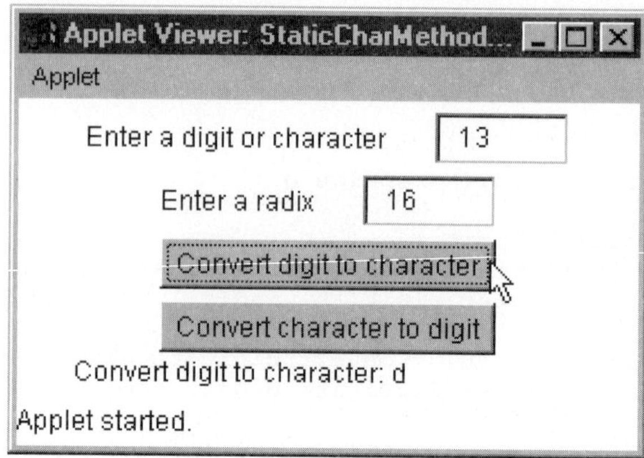

Fig. 8.18 `Character` class `static` conversion methods (part 3 of 3).

The expression

```
Character.digit( c, radix )
```

uses method **`digit`** to convert the character **`c`** into an integer in the number system specified by the integer **`radix`** (i.e., the base of the number). For example, the character **`'A'`** in base 16 (the **`radix`**) has the integer value 10.

The expression

```
Character.forDigit( digit, radix )
```

uses method **`forDigit`** to convert the integer **`digit`** into a character in the number system specified by the integer **`radix`** (also known as the base of the number). For example, the integer **`13`** in base 16 (the **`radix`**) has the character value **`'d'`**. Note that the lowercase and uppercase letters are equivalent in number systems.

The program of Fig. 8.19 demonstrates the non-**`static`** methods of class **`Character`**—the constructor, **`charValue`**, **`toString`**, **`hashCode`** and **`equals`**.

```
// Fig. 8.19: OtherCharMethods.java
// Demonstrate the non-static methods of class
// Character from the java.lang package.
import java.awt.Graphics;
import java.applet.Applet;

public class OtherCharMethods extends Applet {
   Character c1, c2;

```

Fig. 8.19 Non-`static` methods of class `Character` (part 1 of 2).

```
    public void init()
    {
       c1 = new Character( 'A' );
       c2 = new Character( 'a' );
    }

    public void paint( Graphics g )
    {
       g.drawString( "c1 = " + c1.charValue(), 25, 25 );
       g.drawString( "c2 = " + c2.toString(), 25, 40 );
       g.drawString( "hash code for c1 = " +
                     c1.hashCode(), 25, 70 );
       g.drawString( "hash code for c2 = " +
                     c2.hashCode(), 25, 85 );

       if (  c1.equals( c2 ) )
          g.drawString( "c1 and c2 are equal", 25, 115 );
       else
          g.drawString( "c1 and c2 are not equal", 25, 115 );
    }
}
```

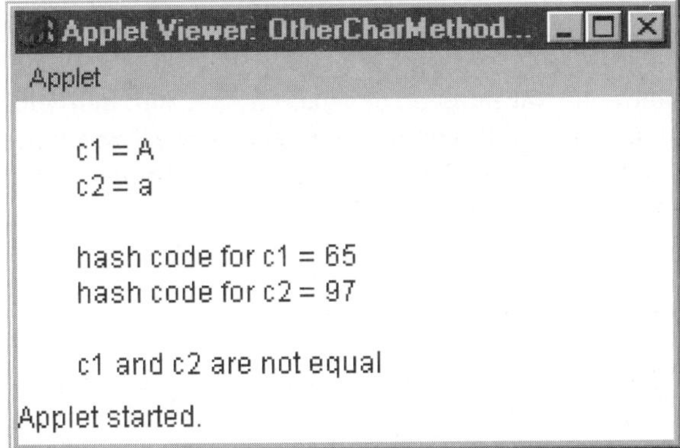

Fig. 8.19 Non-**static** methods of class **Character** (part 2 of 2).

The statements

```
c1 = new Character( 'A' );
c2 = new Character( 'a' );
```

from the **init** method of class **OtherCharMethods** instantiate two **Character** objects and pass constants of type **char** to the constructor to initialize the **Character** objects.

The expression

```
c1.charValue()
```

uses **Character** method **charValue** (which returns a **char**) to get the value of primitive data type **char** from the **Character** object **c1**.

The expression

```
c2.toString()
```

returns a **String** representation of the **Character** object **c2** using method **toString**.

The expressions

```
c1.hashCode()
c2.hashCode()
```

perform **hashCode** calculations on the **Character** objects **c1** and **c2** respectively. Remember that hash code values are used to store objects in hash tables for fast lookup capabilities (see Chapter 18).

The condition

```
c1.equals( c2 )
```

from the **if** structure at line 25 uses the **equals** method to determine if the object **c1** has the same contents as the object **c2** (i.e., the characters inside each object are equal).

8.20 Class StringTokenizer

When you read a sentence, your mind breaks the sentence into individual words, or *tokens,* each of which conveys meaning to you. Compilers also perform tokenization. They break up statements into individual pieces like keywords, identifiers, operators and other elements of a programming language. In this section we study Java's **StringTokenizer** class (from package **java.util**) that breaks a string into its component tokens.

Tokens are separated from one another by delimiters, typically *whitespace characters* such as blank, tab, newline and carriage return. Other characters may also be used as delimiters to separate tokens.

The program of Fig. 8.20 demonstrates class **StringTokenizer**. Applet class **TokenTest** displays a **TextField** where the user types a sentence to tokenize. Output in this program is sent to a **TextArea**. **TextArea**s are similar to **TextField**s—they can be used to display or enter text. The **TextArea** in this program is instantiated with the statement

```
output = new TextArea( 10, 30 );
```

specifying that the **TextArea** has **10** rows and **30** columns. We discuss **TextArea**s in detail in Chapter 11, "Advanced Graphical User Interface Components."

When return is pressed in the **TextField**, the **actionPerformed** method is invoked. The statement

```
String stringToTokenize = e.getActionCommand();
```

creates **String** reference **stringToTokenize** and assigns it **e.getActionCommand()**—the text in the **TextField**. Next, a **StringTokenizer** object is created in the statement

```
// Fig. 8.20: TokenTest.java
// Testing the StringTokenizer class of the java.util package
import java.applet.Applet;
import java.util.*;
import java.awt.*;
import java.awt.event.*;

public class TokenTest extends Applet
            implements ActionListener {
   // GUI components
   Label prompt;
   TextField input;
   TextArea output;

   public void init()
   {
      prompt = new Label( "Enter a sentence and press Enter" );
      input = new TextField( 50 );
      input.addActionListener( this );
      output = new TextArea( 10, 30 );
      output.setEditable( false );
      add( prompt );
      add( input );
      add( output );
   }

   public void actionPerformed( ActionEvent e )
   {
      String stringToTokenize = e.getActionCommand();
      StringTokenizer tokens =
         new StringTokenizer( stringToTokenize );

      output.setText( "" );

      output.append( "Number of elements: " +
         tokens.countTokens() + "\nThe tokens are:\n" );

      while ( tokens.hasMoreTokens() )
         output.append( tokens.nextToken() + "\n" );
   }
}
```

Fig. 8.20 Tokenizing strings with a **StringTokenizer** object (part 1 of 2).

```
StringTokenizer tokens =
   new StringTokenizer( stringToTokenize );
```

This statement uses the **StringTokenizer** constructor that takes a **String** argument to create a **StringTokenizer** for **stringToTokenize** that will use the default delimiter string **" \n\t\r"** consisting of a space, a newline, a tab and a carriage return for tokenization. There are two other constructors for **StringTokenizer**. In the version that takes two **String** arguments, the second **String** is the delimiter **String**. In the

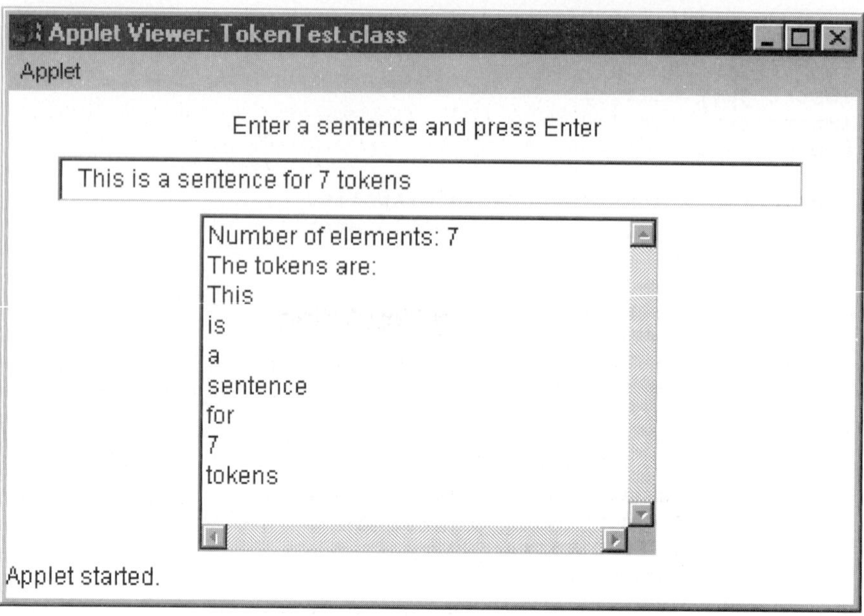

Fig. 8.20 Tokenizing strings with a **StringTokenizer** object (part 2 of 2).

version that takes three arguments, the second **String** is the delimiter **String** and the third argument (a **boolean**) determines if the delimiters are also returned as tokens (only if the argument is **true**). This is useful if you need to know what the delimiters are.

The statement

```
output.setText( "" );
```

sets the text in the text area to the null **String** **""** to clear the text area.

The statement

```
output.append( "Number of elements: " +
   tokens.countTokens() + "\nThe tokens are:\n" );
```

uses the **TextArea** method **append** to append the concatenated **String** specified as its argument to text already in the **TextArea**. In the preceding statement, the expression

```
tokens.countTokens()
```

uses the **StringTokenizer** method **countTokens** to determine the number of tokens in the **String** to be tokenized.

The **while** structure at line 38

```
while ( tokens.hasMoreTokens() )
   output.append( tokens.nextToken() + "\n" );
```

uses condition **tokens.hasMoreTokens()** to determine if there are more tokens in the **String** being tokenized. If so, the **append** method is invoked for the text area **out-**

put to append the next token to the **String** in the text area. The next token is determined with a call to **tokens.nextToken()** which returns a **String**. The token is output followed by a newline character so subsequent tokens output appear on separate lines.

If you would like to change the delimiter **String** while tokenizing a **String**, you may do so by specifying a new delimiter string in a **nextToken** call as follows:

```
tokens.nextToken( newDelimiterString );
```

This feature is not demonstrated in the program.

8.21 A Card Shuffling and Dealing Simulation

In this section, we use random number generation to develop a card shuffling and dealing simulation program. This program can then be used to implement programs that play specific card games.

We develop applet **DeckOfCards** (Fig. 8.21) that creates a deck of 52 playing cards using **Card** objects, then enables the user to deal each card by clicking on a "**Deal card**" button. Each card dealt is displayed in a **TextField**. The user can also shuffle the deck at any time by clicking on a "**Shuffle cards**" button.

```
// Fig. 8.21: DeckOfCards.java
// Card shuffling and dealing program
import java.applet.Applet;
import java.awt.*;
import java.awt.event.*;

public class DeckOfCards extends Applet
             implements ActionListener {
   private Card deck[];
   private int currentCard;

   // GUI components
   private Button dealButton, shuffleButton;
   private TextField displayCard;

   public void init()
   {
      String faces[] = { "Ace", "Deuce", "Three", "Four",
                         "Five", "Six", "Seven", "Eight",
                         "Nine", "Ten", "Jack", "Queen",
                         "King" };
      String suits[] = { "Hearts", "Diamonds",
                         "Clubs", "Spades" };

      deck = new Card[ 52 ];
      currentCard = -1;

```

Fig. 8.21 Card dealing program (part 1 of 4).

```
      for ( int i = 0; i < deck.length; i++ )
         deck[ i ] = new Card( faces[ i % 13 ],
                               suits[ i / 13 ] );

      dealButton = new Button( "Deal card" );
      dealButton.addActionListener( this );
      shuffleButton = new Button( "Shuffle cards" );
      shuffleButton.addActionListener( this );
      displayCard = new TextField( 30 );
      displayCard.setEditable( false );
      add( dealButton );
      add( shuffleButton);
      add( displayCard );
   }

   public void actionPerformed( ActionEvent e )
   {
      if ( e.getSource() == dealButton ) {
         Card dealt = dealCard();

         if ( dealt != null ) {
            displayCard.setText( dealt.toString() );
            showStatus( "Card #: " + currentCard );
         }
         else {
            displayCard.setText( "NO MORE CARDS TO DEAL" );
            showStatus( "Shuffle cards to continue" );
         }
      }
      else if ( e.getSource() == shuffleButton ) {
         displayCard.setText( "SHUFFLING ..." );
         showStatus( "" );
         shuffle();
         displayCard.setText( "DECK IS SHUFFLED" );
      }
   }

   public void shuffle()
   {
      currentCard = -1;

      for ( int i = 0; i < deck.length; i++ ) {
         int j =  (int) ( Math.random() * 52 );
         Card temp = deck[ i ];   // swap
         deck[ i ] = deck[ j ];   // the
         deck[ j ] = temp;        // cards
      }

      dealButton.setEnabled( true );
   }

```

Fig. 8.21 Card dealing program (part 2 of 4).

```
   public Card dealCard()
   {
      if ( ++currentCard < deck.length )
         return deck[ currentCard ];
      else {
         dealButton.setEnabled( false );
         return null;
      }
   }
}

class Card {
   private String face;
   private String suit;

   public Card( String f, String s )
   {
      face = f;
      suit = s;
   }

   public String toString() { return face + " of " + suit; }
}
```

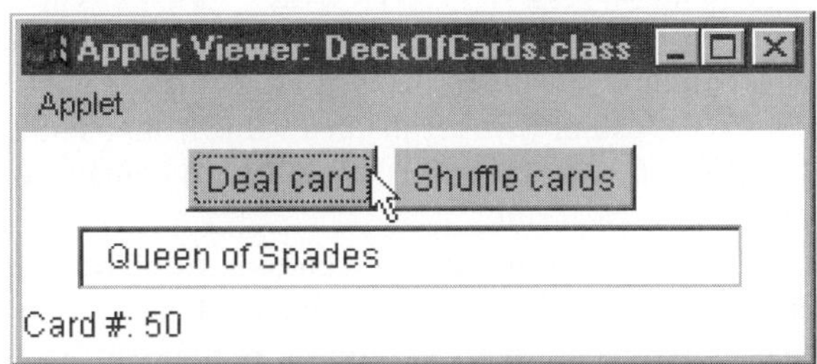

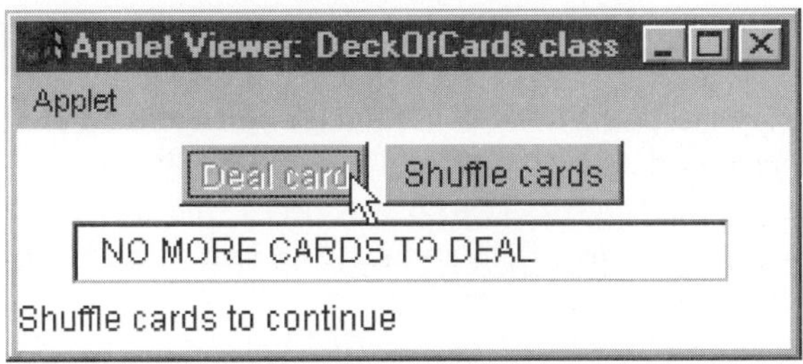

Fig. 8.21 Card dealing program (part 3 of 4).

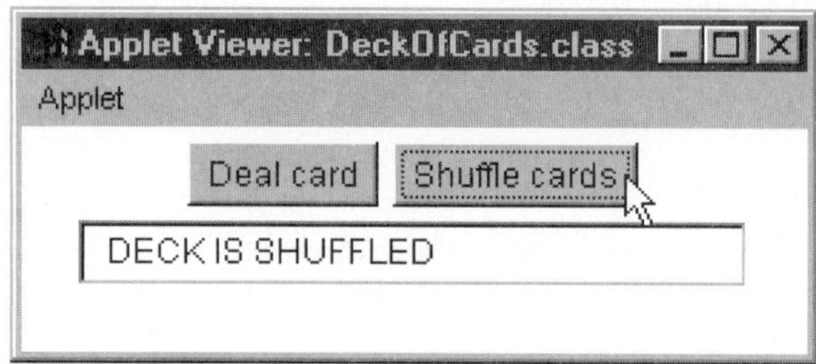

Fig. 8.21 Card dealing program (part 4 of 4).

Class **Card** contains two **String** instance variables—**face** and **suit**—that are used to store references to the face name and suit name for a specific **Card**. The constructor for the class receives two **String**s that it uses to initialize **face** and **suit**. Method **tostring** is provided to create a **String** consisting of the **face** of the card, the **String " of "** and the **suit** of the card.

Class **DeckOfCards** consists of an array **deck** of 52 **Card**s, an integer **current-Card** representing the most recently dealt card in the deck array (–1 if no cards have been dealt yet) and the GUI components used to manipulate the deck of cards. The **init** method of the applet instantiates the **deck** array (line 25) and uses the following **for** structure

```
for ( int i = 0; i < deck.length; i++ )
   deck[ i ] = new Card( faces[ i % 13 ], suits[ i / 13 ] );
```

to fill the **deck** array with **Card**s. Note that each **Card** is instantiated and initialized with two **String**s—one from the **faces** array (**String**s **"Ace"** through **"King"**) and one from the **suits** array (**"Hearts"**, **"Diamonds"**, **"Clubs"** and **"Spades"**). The calculation **i % 13** always results in a value from 0 to 12 (the thirteen subscripts of the **faces** array) and the calculation **i / 13** always results in a value from 0 to 3 (the four subscripts in the **suits** array). When the **deck** array is initialized, it contains the cards with faces Ace through King in order for each suit.

When the user clicks the "**Deal card**" button, **actionPerformed** invokes method **dealCard** (defined at line 79) to get the next card in the array. If the **deck** is not empty, a **Card** object is returned; otherwise, **null** is returned. If the reference is not **null**, the statements

```
displayCard.setText( dealt.toString() );
showStatus( "Card #:  " + currentCard );
```

are executed to display the **Card** in the text field **displayCard** and to display the card number in the status bar of the applet.

If the reference returned by **dealCard** was **null**, the **String** "**NO MORE CARDS TO DEAL**" is displayed in the text field and the **String** "**Shuffle cards to continue**" is displayed in the applet's status bar.

When the user clicks the "**Shuffle cards**" button, the **action** method invokes method **shuffle()** (defined on line 65) to shuffle the cards. The method loops through all 52 cards (array subscripts 0 to 51). For each card, a number between 0 and 51 is picked randomly. Next, the current **Card** object and the randomly selected **Card** object are swapped in the array. A total of only 52 swaps are made in a single pass of the entire array, and the array of **Card** objects is shuffled! When the shuffling is complete, the **String** "**DECK IS SHUFFLED**" is displayed in the text field.

Notice the use of method **setEnabled** at lines 76 and 84 to activate and deactivate the **dealButton**. Method **setEnabled** can be used on many GUI components. When it is called with a **false** argument, the GUI component for which it is called is disabled so the user cannot interact with it. To reactivate the button, method **setEnabled** is called with a **true** argument.

Summary

- A character constant's value is its integer value in the Unicode character set. Strings may include letters, digits and special characters such as **+**, **-**, *****, **/**, and **$**. A string in Java is an object of class **String**. String literals or string constants are often referred to as *anonymous **String** objects* and are written in double quotes in a program.
- Class **String** provides nine constructors that provide the flexibility to initialize a **String** in various ways.
- **String** method **length** returns the number of characters in a **String**.
- **String** method **charAt** selects the character at a specific position.
- Method **equals** (which is inherited by class **String** from its superclass **Object**) is used to test any two objects for equality (i.e., the contents of the two objects are identical). The method returns **true** if the objects are equal and **false** otherwise. Method **equals** uses a *lexicographical comparison.*
- Operator **==** has different functionality when used to compare references and when used to compare values of primitive data types. When primitive data type values are compared with **==**, the result is **true** if both values are identical. When references are compared with **==**, the result is **true** if both references refer to *the same object in memory.*
- Java treats all anonymous **String**s with the same contents as one anonymous **String** object that has many references.
- **String** method **equalsIgnoreCase** ignores the case of the letters in each **String** when performing a comparison.
- **String** method **compareTo** returns 0 if the **Strings** it is comparing are equal, a negative number if the **String** that invokes **compareTo** is less than the **String** that is passed as an argument, and a positive number if the **String** that invokes **compareTo** is greater than the **String** that is passed as an argument. Method **compareTo** uses a lexicographical comparison.
- **String** method **regionMatches** compares portions of two **String**s for equality.
- **String** method **startsWith** determines if the **String** for which it is called starts with the characters specified as an argument.
- **String** method **endsWith** determines if the **String** for which it is called ends with the characters specified as an argument.

- Method **hashCode** performs a hash code calculation that enables a **String** object to be stored in a hash table. This method is inherited into all subclasses of **Object** and overridden by **String**.
- **String** method **indexOf** locates the first occurrence of a character in a **String**. There is a version of this method that searches for substrings in a **String**. Method **lastIndexOf** locates the last occurrence of a character in a **String**. There is a version of this method that searches for substrings in a **String**.
- **String** method **substring** creates a new **String** by copying part of an existing **String** object.
- **String** method **concat** concatenates two **String** objects and returns a new **String** object containing the characters from both original **Strings**.
- **String** method **replace** returns a new **String** object that replaces every occurrence in a **String** of its first character argument with its second character argument. The original **String** is unchanged.
- **String** method **toUpperCase** returns a new **String** object with uppercase letters in the positions where the original **String** had lowercase letters. Method **toLowerCase** returns a new **String** object with lowercase letters in the positions where the original **String** had uppercase letters. The original **String**s are unchanged.
- **String** method **trim** returns a new **String** object in which all whitespace characters (such as spaces, newlines and tabs) have been removed from the beginning or end of a **String**. The original **String** is unchanged.
- **String** method **toCharArray** creates a new character array containing a copy of the characters in a **String** and returns the new array.
- **String** class method **valueOf** is overloaded to take arguments of various types (**boolean**, **char**, **char** arrays, **int**, **long**, **float**, **double** and **Object**), convert those arguments to strings and return them as **String** objects.
- The first time **String** method **intern** is invoked on a **String** object it returns a reference to that **String** object in memory. Subsequent invocations of **intern** on different **String** objects that have the same contents as the original **String** object result in multiple references to the original **String** object.
- Class **StringBuffer** provides three constructors that enable **StringBuffer**s to be initialized with no characters and an initial capacity of 16 characters; with no characters and an initial capacity specified in the integer argument; or with a copy of the characters of the **String** argument and an initial capacity which is the number of characters in the **String** argument plus 16.
- **StringBuffer** method **length** returns the number of characters currently stored in a **StringBuffer**. Method **capacity** returns the number of characters that can be stored in a **StringBuffer** without allocating more memory.
- Method **ensureCapacity** ensures that a **StringBuffer** has a minimum capacity. Method **setLength** increases or decreases the length of a **StringBuffer**.

- **StringBuffer** method **charAt** returns the character at the specified index. Method **setCharAt** sets the character at the specified position. Method **getChars** returns a character array containing a copy of the characters in the **StringBuffer**.
- Class **StringBuffer** provides overloaded **append** methods to allow various data type values to be added to the end of a **StringBuffer**. Versions are provided for each of the primitive data types and for character arrays, **String**s and **Object**s.
- **StringBuffer**s and the **append** methods are used by the Java compiler to implement the **+** and **+=** operators for concatenating **String**s.
- Class **StringBuffer** provides overloaded **insert** methods to allow various data type values to be inserted at any position in a **StringBuffer**. Versions are provided for each of the primitive data types and for character arrays, **String**s and **Object**s.
- Class **Character** provides a constructor that takes a character argument.
- **Character** method **isDefined** determines if a character is defined in the Unicode character set. If so, the method returns **true**; otherwise, it returns **false**.
- **Character** method **isDigit** determines if a character is a defined Unicode digit. If so, the method returns **true**; otherwise, it returns **false**.
- **Character** method **isJavaIdentifierStart** determines if a character is a character that can be used as the first character of an identifier in Java—i.e., a letter, an underscore (_) or a dollar sign (**$**). If so, the method returns **true**; otherwise, it returns **false**.
- **Character** method **isJavaIdentifierPart** determines if a character is a character that can be used in an identifier in Java—i.e., a digit, a letter, an underscore (_) or a dollar sign (**$**). If so, the method returns **true**; otherwise, it returns **false**. Method **isLetter** determines if character **c** is a letter. If so, the method returns **true**; otherwise, it returns **false**. Method **isLetterOrDigit** determines if a character is a letter or a digit. If so, the method returns **true**; otherwise, it returns **false**.
- **Character** method **isLowerCase** determines if a character is a lowercase letter. If so, the method returns **true**; otherwise, it returns **false**.
- **Character** method **isUpperCase** determines if character is an uppercase letter. If so, the method returns **true**; otherwise, it returns **false**.
- **Character** method **toUpperCase** converts a character to its uppercase equivalent. Method **toLowerCase** converts a character to its lowercase equivalent.
- **Character** method **digit** converts its character argument into an integer in the number system specified by its integer argument **radix** (i.e., the base of the number to be converted). Method **forDigit** converts its integer argument **digit** into a character in the number system specified by its integer argument **radix**.
- **Character** method **charValue** returns the **char** stored in a **Character** object. Method **toString** returns a **String** representation of a **Character**.
- **Character** method **hashCode** performs a hash code calculation on a **Character**.

- **StringTokenizer**'s default constructor creates a **StringTokenizer** for its **String** argument that will use the default delimiter string **" \n\t\r"** consisting of a space, a newline, a tab and a carriage return for tokenization.
- In the **StringTokenizer** constructor that takes two **String** arguments, the second **String** is the delimiter **String**. In the **StringTokenizer** constructor that takes three arguments, the second **String** is the delimiter **String** and the third argument (a **boolean**) determines if the delimiters are also returned as tokens.
- **StringTokenizer** method **countTokens** returns the number of tokens in the **String** to be tokenized.
- **StringTokenizer** method **hasMoreTokens()** determines if there are more tokens in the **String** being tokenized.
- **StringTokenizer** method **nextToken()** returns a **String** with the next token.

Terminology

append method of class **StringBuffer**
appending strings to other strings
array of strings
capacity method of class **StringBuffer**
Character class
character code
character constant
character set
charAt method of class **String**
charAt method of class **StringBuffer**
charValue method of class **Character**
compareTo method of class **String**
comparing strings
concat method of class **String**
concatenation
copying strings
countTokens method (**StringTokenizer**)
delimiter
digit method of class **Character**
endsWith method of class **String**
equals method of class **String**
equalsIgnoreCase method of class **String**
forDigit method of class **Character**
getChars method of class **String**
getChars method of class **StringBuffer**
hashCode method of class **Character**
hashCode method of class **String**
hash table
hasMoreTokens method
hexadecimal digits
high-order byte
indexOf method of class **String**
insert method of class **StringBuffer**
intern method of class **String**
isDefined method of class **Character**
isDigit method of class **Character**
isJavaIdentifierPart method
isJavaIdentifierStart method
isLetter method of class **Character**
isLetterOrDigit method of **Character**
isLowerCase method of class **Character**
isUpperCase method of class **Character**
lastIndexOf method of class **String**
length method of class **String**
length method of class **StringBuffer**
length of a string
literal
low-order byte
nextTokens method of **StringTokenizer**
numeric code representation of a character
printing character
regionMatches method of class **String**
replace method of class **String**
search string
setCharAt method of class **StringBuffer**
startsWith method of class **String**
string
String class
string concatenation
string constant
string literal
string processing

StringBuffer class
StringIndexOutOfBoundsException
StringTokenizer class
substring method of **String** class
toCharArray method of class **String**
token
tokenizing strings
toLowerCase method of class **Character**
toLowerCase method of class **String**
toString method of class **Character**
toString method of class **String**
toString method of class **StringBuffer**
toUpperCase method of class **Character**
toUpperCase method of class **String**
trim method of class **String**
Unicode
valueOf method of class **String**
white space characters
word processing

Common Programming Errors

8.1 Attempting to determine the length of a **String** via an instance variable called **length** (e.g., **s1.length**) is a syntax error. The **String** method **length** must be used. (e.g. **s1.length()**).

8.2 Attempting to access a character that is outside the bounds of a **String** (i.e., an index less than 0 or an index greater than or equal to the **String**'s length) results in a **StringIndexOutOfBoundsException**.

8.3 Invoking **StringBuffer** methods that are not methods of class **String** on **String** objects is a syntax error.

8.4 Attempting to access a character that is outside the bounds of a **StringBuffer** (i.e., an index less than 0 or an index greater than or equal to the **StringBuffer**'s length) results in a **StringIndexOutOfBoundsException**.

Performance Tips

8.1 Java treats all anonymous **String**s with the same contents as one anonymous **String** object that has many references. This conserves memory.

8.2 **String** objects are constant strings and **StringBuffer** objects are modifiable strings. Java distinguishes constant strings and modifiable strings for optimization purposes; in particular, Java can perform certain optimizations involving **String** objects (such as sharing one **String** object between multiple references) because it knows these objects will not change.

8.3 When given the choice between using a **String** object to represent a string versus a **StringBuffer** object to represent that string, always use a **String** object if indeed the object will not change; this improves performance.

Self-Review Exercises

8.1 State whether the following are true or false. If the answer is false, explain why.

a) When **String** objects are compared with **==**, the result is **true** if the **String**s contain the same values.

b) A **String** can be modified after it is created.

8.2 For each of the following, write a single statement that performs the indicated task.

a) Compare the string in **s1** to the string in **s2** for equality of contents.
b) Append the string **s2** to the string **s1** using **+=**.
c) Determine the length of the string in **s1**.

Answers to Self-Review Exercises

8.1 a) False. **String** objects that are compared with operator **==** are actually compared to determine if they are the same object in memory.

b) False. **String** objects are constant and cannot be modified after they are created. **StringBuffer** objects can be modified after they are created.

8.2 a) **s1.equals(s2)**
b) **s1 += s2;**
c) **s1.length()**

Exercises

Note: ***Exercises 8.3 through 8.6 are reasonably challenging. Once you have done these problems, you ought to be able to implement most popular card games easily.***

8.3 Modify the program in Fig. 8.21 so that the card dealing method deals a five-card poker hand. Then write the following additional methods:

a) Determine if the hand contains a pair.
b) Determine if the hand contains two pairs.
c) Determine if the hand contains three of a kind (e.g., three jacks).
d) Determine if the hand contains four of a kind (e.g., four aces).
e) Determine if the hand contains a flush (i.e., all five cards of the same suit).
f) Determine if the hand contains a straight (i.e., five cards of consecutive face values).
g) Determine if the hand contains a full house (i.e., two cards of one face value and three cards of another face value).

8.4 Use the methods developed in Exercise 8.3 to write a program that deals two five-card poker hands, evaluates each hand, and determines which is the better hand.

8.5 Modify the program developed in Exercise 8.4 so that it can simulate the dealer. The dealer's five-card hand is dealt "face down" so the player cannot see it. The program should then evaluate the dealer's hand and, based on the quality of the hand, the dealer should draw one, two, or three more cards to replace the corresponding number of unneeded cards in the original hand. The program should then reevaluate the dealer's hand. (*Caution:* This is a difficult problem!)

8.6 Modify the program developed in Exercise 8.5 so that it can handle the dealer's hand automatically, but the player is allowed to decide which cards of the player's hand to replace. The program should then evaluate both hands and determine who wins. Now use this new program to play 20 games against the computer. Who wins more games, you or the computer? Have one of your friends play 20 games against the computer. Who wins more games? Based on the results of these games, make appropriate modifications to refine your poker playing program (this, too, is a difficult problem). Play 20 more games. Does your modified program play a better game?

8.7 Write an applet that uses **String** method **compareTo** to compare two strings input by the user. The program should state whether the first string is less than, equal to, or greater than the second.

8.8 Write an applet that uses **String** method **regionMatches** to compare two strings input by the user. The program should input the number of characters to be compared and the starting index of the comparison. The program should state whether the first string is less than, equal to, or greater than the second string. Ignore the case of the characters when performing the comparison.

8.9 Write an applet that uses random number generation to create sentences. Use four arrays of strings called **article**, **noun**, **verb**, and **preposition**. Create a sentence by selecting a word at random from each array in the following order: **article**, **noun**, **verb**, **preposition**, **article**, and **noun**. As each word is picked, concatenate it to the previous words in the sentence. The words should be separated by spaces. When the final sentence is output, it should start with a capital letter and end with a period. The program should generate 20 sentences and output them to a text area.

The arrays should be filled as follows: the **article** array should contain the articles **"the"**, **"a"**, **"one"**, **"some"**, and **"any"**; the **noun** array should contain the nouns **"boy"**, **"girl"**, **"dog"**, **"town"**, and **"car"**; the **verb** array should contain the verbs **"drove"**, **"jumped"**, **"ran"**, **"walked"**, and **"skipped"**; the **preposition** array should contain the prepositions **"to"**, **"from"**, **"over"**, **"under"**, and **"on"**.

After the preceding program is written, modify the program to produce a short story consisting of several of these sentences. (How about the possibility of a random term paper writer!)

8.10 *(Limericks)* A limerick is a humorous five-line verse in which the first and second lines rhyme with the fifth, and the third line rhymes with the fourth. Using techniques similar to those developed in Exercise 8.9, write a Java program that produces random limericks. Polishing this program to produce good limericks is a challenging problem, but the result will be worth the effort!

8.11 Write an applet that encodes English language phrases into pig Latin. Pig Latin is a form of coded language often used for amusement. Many variations exist in the methods used to form pig Latin phrases. For simplicity, use the following algorithm:

To form a pig Latin phrase from an English language phrase, tokenize the phrase into words with an object of class **StringTokenizer**. To translate each English word into a pig Latin word, place the first letter of the English word at the end of the word and add the letters "**ay**." Thus the word "**jump**" becomes "**umpjay**," the word "**the**" becomes "**hetay**," and the word "**computer**" becomes "**omputercay**." Blanks between words remain as blanks. Assume the following: The English phrase consists of words separated by blanks, there are no punctuation marks, and all words have two or more letters. Method **printLatinWord** should display each word. Each token returned from **nextToken** is passed to method **printLatinWord** to print the pig Latin word. Enable the user to input the sentence. Keep a running display of all the converted sentences in a text area.

8.12 Write an applet that inputs a telephone number as a string in the form **(555) 555-5555**. The program should use an object of class **StringTokenizer** to extract the area code as a token, the first three digits of the phone number as a token, and the last four digits of the phone number as a token. The seven digits of the phone number should be concatenated into one string. The program should convert the area code string to **int** (remember **parseInt**!) and convert the phone number string to **long**. Both the area code and the phone number should be printed. Remember that you will have to change delimiter characters during the tokenization process.

8.13 Write an applet that inputs a line of text, tokenizes the line with an object of class **`StringTokenizer`**, and outputs the tokens in reverse order.

8.14 Use the string comparison methods discussed and the techniques for sorting arrays developed in Chapter 5 to write a program that alphabetizes a list of strings. Allow the user to enter the strings in a text field. Display the results in a text area.

8.15 Write an applet that inputs text and outputs the text in uppercase and lowercase letters.

8.16 Write an applet that inputs several lines of text and a search character, and uses method **`String`** method **`indexOf`** to determine the number of occurrences of the character in the text.

8.17 Write an applet based on the program of Exercise 8.16 that inputs several lines of text and uses **`String`** method **`indexOf`** to determine the total number of occurrences of each letter of the alphabet in the text. Uppercase and lowercase letters should be counted together. Store the totals for each letter in an array, and print the values in tabular format after the totals have been determined.

8.18 Write an applet that reads a series of strings and outputs only those strings beginning with the letter "**`b`**." The results should be output to a text area.

8.19 Write an applet that reads a series of strings and prints only those strings ending with the letters "**`ED`**." The results should be output to a text area.

8.20 Write an applet that inputs an integer code for a character and displays the corresponding character. Modify this program so that it generates all possible three-digit codes in the range 000 to 255 and attempts to print the corresponding characters. Display the results in a text area.

8.21 Write your own versions of the **`String`** methods for searching strings.

Special Section: Advanced String Manipulation Exercises

The preceding exercises are keyed to the text and designed to test the reader's understanding of fundamental string manipulation concepts. This section includes a collection of intermediate and advanced string manipulation exercises. The reader should find these problems challenging yet entertaining. The problems vary considerably in difficulty. Some require an hour or two of program writing and implementation. Others are useful for lab assignments that might require two or three weeks of study and implementation. Some are challenging term projects.

8.22 *(Text Analysis)* The availability of computers with string manipulation capabilities has resulted in some rather interesting approaches to analyzing the writings of great authors. Much attention has been focused on whether William Shakespeare ever lived. Some scholars believe there is substantial evidence indicating that Christopher Marlowe or other authors actually penned the masterpieces attributed to Shakespeare. Researchers have used computers to find similarities in the writings of these two authors. This exercise examines three methods for analyzing texts with a computer.

a) Write an applet that reads several lines of text from the keyboard and prints a table indicating the number of occurrences of each letter of the alphabet in the text. For example, the phrase

```
To be, or not to be: that is the question:
```

contains one "a," two "b's," no "c's," etc.

b) Write an applet that reads several lines of text and prints a table indicating the number of one-letter words, two-letter words, three-letter words, etc. appearing in the text. For example, the phrase

```
Whether 'tis nobler in the mind to suffer
```

contains

Word length	Occurrences
1	0
2	2
3	2
4	2 (including 'tis)
5	0
6	2
7	1

c) Write an applet that reads several lines of text and prints a table indicating the number of occurrences of each different word in the text. The first version of your program should include the words in the table in the same order in which they appear in the text. For example, the lines

```
To be, or not to be: that is the question:
Whether 'tis nobler in the mind to suffer
```

d) contain the words "to" three times, the word "be" two times, the word "or" once, etc. A more interesting (and useful) printout should then be attempted in which the words are sorted alphabetically.

8.23 *(Printing Dates in Various Formats)* Dates are printed in several common formats. Two of the more common formats are:

```
07/21/55 and July 21, 1955
```

Write an applet that reads a date in the first format and prints that date in the second format.

8.24 *(Check Protection)* Computers are frequently employed in check-writing systems such as payroll applications and accounts payable applications. Many strange stories circulate regarding weekly paychecks being printed (by mistake) for amounts in excess of $1 million. Incorrect amounts are printed by computerized check-writing systems because of human error and/or machine failure. Systems designers build controls into their systems to prevent such erroneous checks from being issued.

Another serious problem is the intentional alteration of a check amount by someone who intends to cash a check fraudulently. To prevent a dollar amount from being altered, most computerized check-writing systems employ a technique called *check protection.*

Checks designed for imprinting by computer contain a fixed number of spaces in which the computer may print an amount. Suppose a paycheck contains eight blank spaces in which the computer is supposed to print the amount of a weekly paycheck. If the amount is large, then all eight of those spaces will be filled, for example:

```
1,230.60 (check amount)
--------
12345678 (position numbers)
```

On the other hand, if the amount is less than $1000, then several of the spaces would ordinarily be left blank. For example,

```
   99.87
--------
12345678
```

contains three blank spaces. If a check is printed with blank spaces, it is easier for someone to alter the amount of the check. To prevent a check from being altered, many check-writing systems insert *leading asterisks* to protect the amount as follows:

```
***99.87
--------
12345678
```

Write an applet that inputs a dollar amount to be printed on a check, and then prints the amount in check-protected format with leading asterisks if necessary. Assume that nine spaces are available for printing the amount.

8.25 *(Writing the Word Equivalent of a Check Amount)* Continuing the discussion of the previous exercise, we reiterate the importance of designing check-writing systems to prevent alteration of check amounts. One common security method requires that the check amount be written both in numbers, and "spelled out" in words as well. Even if someone is able to alter the numerical amount of the check, it is extremely difficult to change the amount in words.

Many computerized check-writing systems do not print the amount of the check in words. Perhaps the main reason for this omission is the fact that most high-level languages used in commercial applications do not contain adequate string manipulation features. Another reason is that the logic for writing word equivalents of check amounts is somewhat involved.

Write an applet that inputs a numeric check amount and writes the word equivalent of the amount. For example, the amount 112.43 should be written as

```
ONE HUNDRED TWELVE and 43/100
```

8.26 *(Morse Code)* Perhaps the most famous of all coding schemes is the Morse code, developed by Samuel Morse in 1832 for use with the telegraph system. The Morse code assigns a series of dots and dashes to each letter of the alphabet, each digit, and a few special characters (such as period, comma, colon, and semicolon). In sound-oriented systems, the dot represents a short sound and the dash represents a long sound. Other representations of dots and dashes are used with light-oriented systems and signal-flag systems.

Separation between words is indicated by a space, or, quite simply, the absence of a dot or dash. In a sound-oriented system, a space is indicated by a short period of time during which no sound is transmitted. The international version of the Morse code appears in Fig. 8.22.

Write an applet that reads an English language phrase and encodes the phrase into Morse code. Also write a program that reads a phrase in Morse code and converts the phrase into the English language equivalent. Use one blank between each Morse-coded letter and three blanks between each Morse-coded word.

8.27 *(A Metric Conversion Program)* Write an applet that will assist the user with metric conversions. Your program should allow the user to specify the names of the units as strings (i.e., centimeters, liters, grams, etc. for the metric system and inches, quarts, pounds, etc. for the English system) and should respond to simple questions such as

Character	Code	Character	Code
A	.-	T	-
B	-...	U	..-
C	-.-.	V	...-
D	-..	W	.--
E	.	X	-..-
F	..-.	Y	-.--
G	--.	Z	--..
H	....		
I	..	Digits	
J	.---	1	.----
K	-.-	2	..---
L	.-..	3	...--
M	--	4	....-
N	-.	5	.....
O	---	6	-....
P	.--.	7	--...
Q	--.-	8	---..
R	.-.	9	----.
S	...	0	-----

Fig. 8.22 The letters of the alphabet as expressed in international Morse code.

```
"How many inches are in 2 meters?"
"How many liters are in 10 quarts?"
```

Your program should recognize invalid conversions. For example, the question

```
"How many feet in 5 kilograms?"
```

is not a meaningful question because **"feet"** are units of length while **"kilograms"** are units of mass.

Challenging string manipulation projects

8.28 *(Project: A Spelling Checker)* Many popular word processing software packages have built-in spell checkers.

In this project, you are asked to develop your own spell-checker utility. We make suggestions to help get you started. You should then consider adding more capabilities. Use a computerized dictionary (if you have access to one) as a source of words.

Why do we type so many words with incorrect spellings? In some cases, it is because we simply do not know the correct spelling, so we make a "best guess." In some cases, it is because we transpose two letters (e.g., "defualt" instead of "default"). Sometimes we double-type a letter accidentally (e.g., "hanndy" instead of "handy"). Sometimes we type a nearby key instead of the one we intended (e.g., "biryhday" instead of "birthday"). And so on.

Design and implement a spell-checker applet in Java. Your program should maintain an array **wordList** of strings. Enable the user to enter these strings. Note: In Chapters 15 and 16 we introduce file processing and networking. Once you have these capabilities, you can obtain the words for the spell checker from a computerized dictionary stored in a file.

Your program should ask a user to enter a word. The program should then look up that word in the **wordList** array. If the word is present in the array, your program should print "**Word is spelled correctly**."

If the word is not present in the array, your program should print "**word is not spelled correctly**." Then your program should try to locate other words in **wordList** that might be the word the user intended to type. For example, you can try all possible single transpositions of adjacent letters to discover that the word "default" is a direct match to a word in **wordList**. Of course, this implies that your program will check all other single transpositions such as "edfault," "dfeault," "deafult," "defalut," and "defautl." When you find a new word that matches one in **wordList**, print that word in a message such as, "**Did you mean "default?"**."

Implement other tests such as replacing each double letter with a single letter and any other tests you can develop to improve the value of your spell checker.

8.29 *(Project: A Crossword Puzzle Generator)* Most people have worked a crossword puzzle, but few have ever attempted to generate one. Generating a crossword puzzle is suggested here as a string manipulation project requiring substantial sophistication and effort.

There are many issues the programmer must resolve to get even the simplest crossword puzzle generator program working. For example, how does one represent the grid of a crossword puzzle inside the computer? Should one use a series of strings, or should double-subscripted arrays be used?

The programmer needs a source of words (i.e., a computerized dictionary) that can be directly referenced by the program. In what form should these words be stored to facilitate the complex manipulations required by the program?

The really ambitious reader will want to generate the "clues" portion of the puzzle in which the brief hints for each "across" word and each "down" word are printed for the puzzle worker. Merely printing a version of the blank puzzle itself is not a simple problem.

9

Graphics

Objectives

- To understand graphics contexts and graphics objects.
- To understand and be able to use methods for drawing strings, characters, and bytes.
- To understand and be able to manipulate colors.
- To understand and be able to manipulate fonts.
- To understand and be able to use methods for drawing lines, rectangles, rectangles with rounded corners, three-dimensional rectangles, ovals, arcs and polygons.
- To be able to copy areas of the screen.
- To understand paint modes.

One picture is worth ten thousand words.
Chinese proverb

Treat nature in terms of the cylinder, the sphere, the cone, all in perspective.
Paul Cezanne

Nothing ever becomes real till it is experienced—even a proverb is no proverb to you till your life has illustrated it.
John Keats

A picture shows me at a glance what it takes dozens of pages of a book to expound.
Ivan Sergeyevich

Outline

9.1 Introduction

We now begin our in-depth treatment of *Java's Abstract Windowing Toolkit (AWT)*—the classes that comprise the **java.awt** *package.* We present the graphics capabilities for drawing on the screen. Figure 9.1 shows a portion of the **java.awt** *class hierarchy* that includes the classes covered in this chapter. Each class in the figure inherits directly from class **Object**. Class **Color** contains methods and constants for manipulating colors. Class **Font** contains methods and constants for manipulating fonts. Class **FontMetrics** contains methods for obtaining font information. Class **Polygon** contains methods for creating polygons. Class **Graphics** contains methods for drawing strings, lines, rectangles and other shapes. Class **Toolkit** provides methods for getting graphical information from a system such as the set of displayable fonts and the display screen resolution.

To begin drawing in Java, we must first understand Java's *coordinate system* (Fig. 9.2) which is a scheme for identifying every possible point on the screen. By default, the upper-left corner of the screen has the coordinates (0, 0). A coordinate pair is composed of an *x coordinate* (the *horizontal coordinate*) and a *y coordinate* (the *vertical coordinate*). The *x* coordinate is the horizontal distance moving right from the upper-left corner. The *y* coordinate is the vertical distance moving down from the upper-left corner. The *x axis* describes every horizontal coordinate and the *y axis* describes every vertical coordinate.

This chapter was coauthored with Mr. Tem Nieto of Deitel & Associates, Inc.

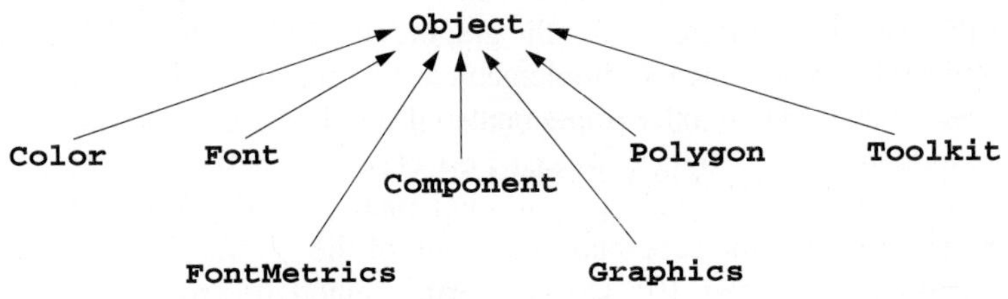

Fig. 9.1 A portion of the **java.awt** hierarchy.

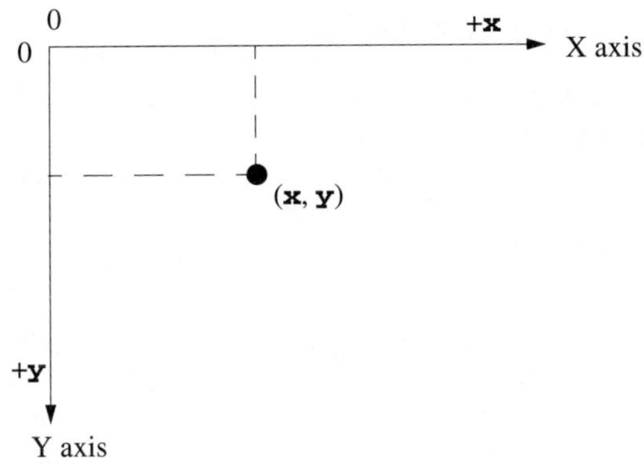

Fig. 9.2 Java coordinate system. Units are measured in pixels.

Text and shapes are displayed on the screen by specifying coordinates. Coordinate units are measured in *pixels*. A pixel is a display monitor's smallest unit of resolution.

Portability Tip 9.1

Different display monitors have different levels of resolution (i.e., the density of pixels vary).

9.2 Graphics Contexts and Graphics Objects

A *graphics context* enables drawing on the screen in Java. A **Graphics** object manages a graphics context by controlling how information is drawn. **Graphics** objects contain methods for drawing, font manipulation, color manipulation, etc. Every applet we have seen in the text that performs drawing on the screen has used the **Graphics** object **g** (the argument to the applet's **paint** method) to manage the applet's graphics context.

A **Graphics** object must be used to draw. The **Graphics** class is an **abstract** class—i.e., **Graphics** objects cannot be instantiated. The reason for this is found in Java's portability. Because drawing is performed differently on each platform that supports Java, there cannot be one class that implements drawing capabilities on all systems. For example, the graphics capabilities that enable a PC running Windows to draw a rectangle are different from the graphics capabilities that enable a UNIX workstation to draw a rectangle—and those are both different from the graphics capabilities that enable a Macintosh to draw a rectangle. When Java is implemented on each platform, a derived class of **Graphics** is created that actually implements all the drawing capabilities. This implementation is hidden from us by the **Graphics** class which supplies the interface that enables us to write programs that use graphics in a platform-independent manner.

Class **Component** is the superclass for many of the classes in the AWT (we study class **Component** in Chapter 10). **Component** method **paint** takes a **Graphics** object as an argument. This object is passed to the **paint** method by the system when a paint operation occurs for a **Component**. The header for the **paint** method is

```
public void paint( Graphics g )
```

The **Graphics** object **g** receives a reference to an object of the system's derived **Graphics** class. The preceding method header should look familiar to you—it is the same one we have been using in our applet classes. Actually, the **Component** class is an indirect base class of class **Applet** from which every applet inherits. Many capabilities of class **Applet** are inherited from class **Component**. The **paint** method defined in class **Component** does nothing by default—it must be overridden by the programmer.

The **paint** method is seldom called directly by the programmer because drawing graphics is an *event-driven process*. When an applet is initially executed, the **paint** method is automatically called (after calls to the **Applet**'s **init** and **start** methods). For **paint** to be called again, an *event*, such as the user resizing the applet, must occur.

If the programmer needs to call **paint**, a call is made to the **Component** class **repaint** method. The **repaint** method requests a call to the **Component** class **update** method as soon as possible to clear the **Component**'s background of any previous drawing, then **update** calls **paint** directly. The **repaint** method is frequently called by the programmer to force a **paint** operation. Method **repaint** should not be overridden because it performs some system-dependent tasks. The **update** method is seldom called directly and sometimes overridden. Overriding the **update** method is useful for "smoothing" animations (i.e., reducing "flicker") as we will see in Chapter 14, "Multimedia: Images, Animation, Audio." The headers for **repaint** and **update** are

```
public void repaint()
public void update( Graphics g )
```

Both methods are **public** and have a **void** return type. The **update** method takes a **Graphics** object as an argument which is supplied automatically by method **repaint**.

In this chapter we focus on the **paint** method. In the next chapter we concentrate more on the event-driven nature of graphics and discuss the **repaint** and **update** methods in more detail.

9.3 Drawing Strings, Characters, and Bytes

This section presents the **Graphics** methods for drawing strings, characters, and bytes. The methods and their parameters are summarized in Fig. 9.3.

Graphics methods for drawing strings, characters and bytes

```
public abstract void drawString(
    String string,      // string to be drawn
    int x,              // x coordinate
    int y )             // y coordinate
```

Draws a string in the current font and color at the coordinate (**x**, **y**).

```
public void drawChars(
    char chars[],       // array to be drawn
    int offset,         // starting subscript (index)
    int number,         // number of elements to draw
    int x,              // x coordinate
    int y )             // y coordinate
```

Draws a series of characters in the current font and color at the coordinate (**x**, **y**).

```
public void drawBytes(
    byte bytes[],       // array of bytes
    int offset,         // starting subscript (index)
    int number,         // number of elements to draw
    int x,              // x coordinate
    int y )             // y coordinate
```

Draws a series of bytes in the current font and color at the coordinate (**x**, **y**).

Fig. 9.3 **Graphics** methods for drawing strings, characters and bytes.

Method **drawString** draws a **String**. The method takes three arguments—the **String** to be drawn, an *x* coordinate, and a *y* coordinate. The **String** is drawn in the current color and font. The *current color* is the color in which text or shapes are drawn. The *current font* is the font in which text is drawn (the next two sections discuss how to set the current color and font). *The point (**x**, **y**) corresponds to the lower-left corner of the string*—i.e., the first character in the **String** is drawn above and to the right of the specified pixel coordinate. Therefore, if you draw a **String** at coordinate (0, 0), it will not be visible.

Method **drawChars** draws a series of characters. The method takes five arguments. The first argument is an array of characters. The second argument specifies the subscript in the array of the first character to be drawn. The third argument specifies the number of characters to be drawn. The last two arguments specify the coordinates where drawing is to begin. The point (**x**, **y**) corresponds to the lower-left corner of the first character drawn.

Method **drawBytes** draws a series of bytes. Like the **drawChars** method, the **drawBytes** method takes five arguments. The first argument is an array of bytes. The second argument specifies the subscript in the array of the first byte to be drawn. The third argument specifies the number of elements to be drawn. The last two arguments specify the coordinates where drawing is to begin. The point (**x**, **y**) corresponds to the lower-left corner of the bytes drawn.

The program of Fig. 9.4 uses the **drawString**, **drawChars**, and **drawBytes** methods to draw information on the applet.

```
// Fig. 9.4: DrawSCB.java
// Demonstrating drawString, drawChars and drawBytes
import java.applet.Applet;
import java.awt.Graphics;

public class DrawSCB extends Applet {
   private String s = "Using drawString!";
   private char c[] = { 'c', 'h', 'a', 'r', 's', ' ', '8' };
   private byte b[] = { 'b', 'y', 't', 'e', 1, 2, 3 };

   public void paint( Graphics g )
   {
      // draw a string at location (100, 25) on the applet
      g.drawString( s, 100, 25 );

      // draw a series of characters at location (100, 50)
      g.drawChars( c, 2, 3,  100, 50 );

      // draw a series of bytes at location (100, 75)
      g.drawBytes( b, 0, 5, 100, 75 );
   }
}
```

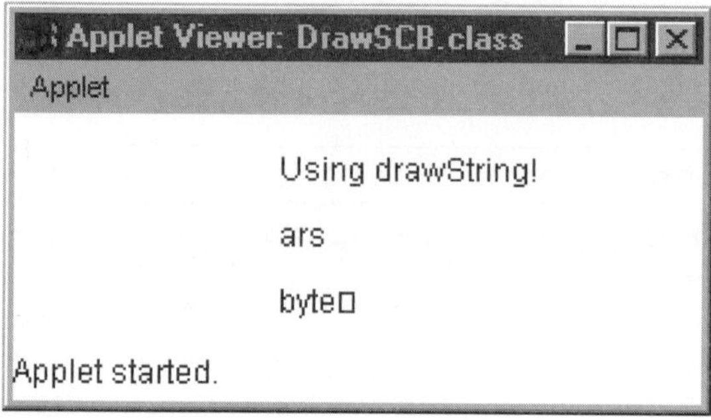

Fig. 9.4 Demonstrating **drawString**, **drawChars**, and **drawBytes**.

In the program, the **drawString** method displays "**Using drawString!**" at location (100, 25). The statement

```
g.drawChars(c, 2, 3, 100, 50);
```

displays "**ars**" at location (100, 50). The second argument, **2**, specifies that drawing is to begin with subscript **2** (the third element) of character array **c**. The third argument, **3**, specifies that three elements will be drawn. Method **drawBytes** displays a set of bytes at location (100, 75). Notice that the characters in the first four elements of array **b** are displayed as characters, but the numeric value 1 in the fifth element is displayed as a small box. This is because method **drawBytes** takes the numeric value in each element and interprets it as a character for display purposes. On this particular system, the character with the numeric value 1 was not a displayable character so the black bar was printed instead.

Common Programming Error 9.1

Passing an invalid array subscript to the **drawChars** *or* **drawBytes** *method throws an* **ArraySubscriptOutOfBoundsException**

9.4 Color Control

This section presents the constants and methods for color control. Colors enhance the appearance of a program and convey meaning. For example, a traffic light has three different color lights—red indicates stop, yellow indicates caution and green indicates go.

Color constants and color methods are defined in the **Color** *class* which inherits from the **Object** class. The predefined color constants are summarized in Fig. 9.5 and the color methods and constructors are summarized in Fig. 9.6. Note that two of the methods in Fig. 9.6 are **Graphics** methods that are specific to colors.

Every color is created from an *RGB value* (Red/Green/Blue). An RGB value is created from three parts. All three RGB parts can be integers in the range 0 to 255 or all three RGB parts can be floating point values in the range 0.0 to 1.0. The first RGB part defines the amount of red, the second defines the amount of green and the third defines the amount of blue. The larger the RGB value, the greater the amount of that particular color. Java enables the programmer to choose from $256 \times 256 \times 256$ (or approximately 16 million) colors. However, not all computers are capable of displaying all these colors. If this is the case, the computer will display the closest color it can.

Common Programming Error 9.2

Spelling any **static Color** *class constant with an initial capital letter is a syntax error.*

Color constant	Color	RGB value
public final static Color orange	orange	255, 200, 0
public final static Color pink	pink	255, 175, 175
public final static Color cyan	cyan	0, 255, 255
public final static Color magenta	magenta	255, 0, 255
public final static Color yellow	yellow	255, 255, 0
public final static Color black	black	0, 0, 0
public final static Color white	white	255, 255, 255
public final static Color gray	gray	128, 128, 128
public final static Color lightGray	light gray	192, 192, 192
public final static Color darkGray	dark gray	64, 64, 64
public final static Color red	red	255, 0, 0
public final static Color green	green	0, 255, 0
public final static Color blue	blue	0, 0, 255

Fig. 9.5 **Color** class **static** constants and RGB values.

Color methods and color related Graphics methods

```
public Color(
   int r,    // 0 - 255 red content
   int g,    // 0 - 255 green content
   int b )   // 0 - 255 blue content
```

Creates a color based on red, green, and blue contents expressed as integers

```
public Color(
   float r,  // 0.0 - 1.0 red content
   float g,  // 0.0 - 1.0 green content
   float b ) // 0.0 - 1.0 blue content
```

Creates a color based on red, green, and blue contents expressed as floats.

```
public int getRed()          // Color class
```

Returns a value between 0 and 255 representing the red content.

```
public int getBlue()         // Color class
```

Returns a value between 0 and 255 representing the blue content.

```
public int getGreen()        // Color class
```

Returns a value between 0 and 255 representing the green content.

```
public abstract Color getColor()        // Graphics class
```

Returns a **Color** object representing the current color for the graphics context.

```
public abstract void setColor(Color c) // Graphics class
```

Sets the current color for drawing with the graphics context.

Fig. 9.6 **Color** methods and color related **Graphics** methods.

Two **Color** constructors are shown in Fig 9.6—one that takes three **int** arguments and one that takes three **float** arguments with each argument specifying the amount of red, green, and blue respectively. The **int** values must be between 0 and 255 and the float values must be between 0.0 and 1.0. The **Color** object has the specified amounts of red, green, and blue. **Color** methods **getRed**, **getGreen** and **getBlue** return integer values from 0 to 255 representing the amount of red, green, and blue respectively. **Graphics** method **getColor** returns a **Color** object representing the current drawing color. **Graphics** method **setColor** sets the current drawing color.

The program of Fig. 9.7 changes the current color and draws a **String**. The program uses the version of the **Color** constructor that takes three **int** arguments

The instance variables **red**, **green**, and **blue** are declared and initialized. In the **paint** method, the current color is changed with the statement

```
g.setColor( new Color( red, green, blue ) );
```

The **setColor** method sets the current color to the **Color** object constructed with the **red**, **green**, and **blue** values. Then, the **drawString** method draws the **String** in the new current color. The statement

```
// Fig. 9.7: ShowColors.java
// Demonstrating setting and getting a Color.
import java.applet.Applet;
import java.awt.Graphics;
import java.awt.Color;

public class ShowColors extends Applet {
   private int red, green, blue;

   public void init()
   {
      // set some values
      red = 100;
      blue = 255;
      green = 125;
   }

   public void paint ( Graphics g )
   {
      g.setColor( new Color( red, green, blue ) );
      g.drawString( "ABCDEFGHIJKLMNOPQRSTUVWXYZ", 50, 33 );
      showStatus( "Current RGB: " + g.getColor() );
   }
}
```

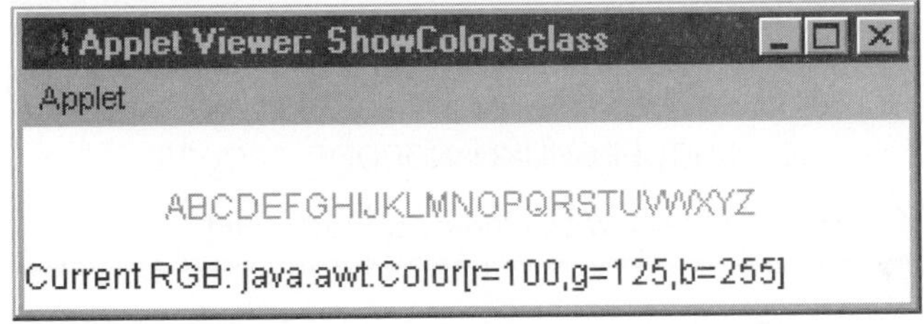

Fig. 9.7 Demonstrating setting and getting a **Color**.

```
showStatus( "Current RGB: : + g.getColor() );
```

outputs the **Color** object returned by **getColor** as a **String** and displays the information in the status bar. Notice that the **String** representation of the **Color** object contains the class name and package (**java.awt.Color**), and the red, green and blue values.

The program of Fig. 9.8 uses the **Color** constructor that takes three **float** arguments to create a new **Color** object, changes the current color and draws a **String** in the new current color.

The instance variables **red**, **green**, and **blue** are declared and initialized. Notice that each floating-point value is followed by the letter **f**. This indicates that each constant should be of type **float** rather than the default type for floating-point constants—**double**. The current color is changed in the **paint** method with the statement

```
g.setColor( new Color( red, green, blue ) );
```

```
// Fig. 9.8: ShowColors2.java
// Demonstrating the Color constructor with float arguments
import java.applet.Applet;
import java.awt.Graphics;
import java.awt.Color;

public class ShowColors2 extends Applet {
   private float red, green, blue;

   public void init()
   {
      red = 0.1f;
      green = 0.21f;
      blue = 0.33f;
   }

   public void paint( Graphics g )
   {
      g.setColor( new Color( red, green, blue ) );
      g.drawString( "ABCDEFGHIJKLMNOPQRSTUVWXYZ", 60, 33 );
      showStatus( "Current RGB: " + g.getColor() );
   }
}
```

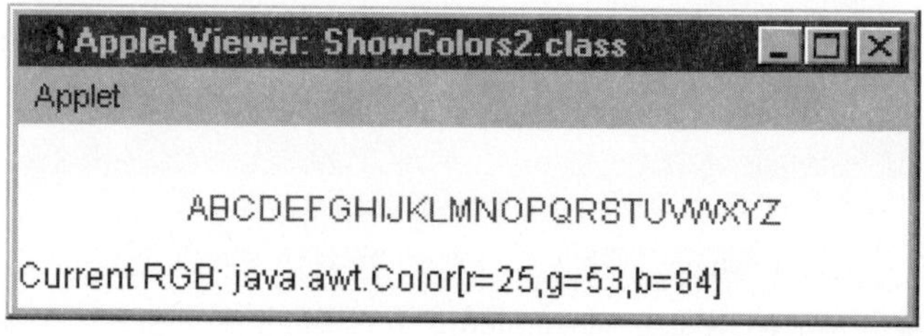

Fig. 9.8 Demonstrating the **Color** constructor with **float** arguments.

The **setColor** method sets the current color to the color constructed from **red**, **green**, and **blue**. The **drawString** method draws the string in the color set by **setColor**. The statement

```
showStatus( "Current RGB: " + g.getColor() );
```

converts the **Color** object returned by **getColor** to a **String** and displays the resulting information in the status bar. Note that integer values (not floating-point values) are displayed in the status bar for each of the values of the **red**, **green** and **blue** components.

The program of Fig. 9.9 changes the current color to **blue**. In the program, a reference to a **Color** object (instance variable **c**) is created with the line

```
private Color c;
```

The value of **c** is set to the constant **Color.blue** in the **init** method. The current color is changed to **blue** with the statement

```
// Fig. 9.9: ShowColors3.java
// Using a predefined static Color object to set the color
import java.applet.Applet;
import java.awt.Graphics;
import java.awt.Color;

public class ShowColors3 extends Applet {
   private Color c;

   public void init()
   {
      c = Color.blue;
   }

   public void paint( Graphics g )
   {
      g.setColor( c );
      g.drawString( "ABCDEFGHIJKLMNOPQRSTUVWXYZ", 50, 33 );
      showStatus( "Current RGB: " + c.getRed() + " " +
                  c.getGreen() + " " + c.getBlue() );
   }
}
```

Fig. 9.9 Using a predefined **static Color** object to set the color to **blue**.

```
g.setColor( c );
```

The **getRed**, **getGreen**, and **getBlue** methods are used to get the RGB values of the current color. The RGB value is displayed in the status bar.

9.5 Font Control

This section introduces the methods and constants for font control. Most font methods and font constants are part of class **Font**. The methods are summarized in Fig. 9.10, Fig. 9.12, and Fig. 9.14.

In Fig. 9.10, **static** constants **PLAIN**, **BOLD**, and **ITALIC** of class **Font** are used to specify the *font style*. The **Font** constructor takes three arguments—the *font name,* the font style and the *font size*. The font name is any font currently supported by the system where the program is running, such as **Monospaced**, **SansSerif** and **Serif**. The font style is **Font.PLAIN**, **Font.ITALIC**, or **Font.BOLD** (**static** constants of class **Font**). Font styles can be used in combination (e.g., **Font.ITALIC + Font.BOLD**).

Font constants, Font constructor and Graphics method setFont

```
public final static int PLAIN      // Font class
```

A constant representing a plain font style.

```
public final static int BOLD       // Font class
```

A constant representing a bold font style.

```
public final static int ITALIC     // Font class
```

A constant representing an italic font style.

```
public Font(
   String s,          // font name
   int style,         // font style
   int size)          // font point size
```

Creates a **Font** object with the specified font, style, and size.

```
public abstract void setFont(Font f)   // Graphics class
```

Sets the current font to the font, style, and size specified by the **Font** object **f**.

Fig. 9.10 **Font** constants, **Font** constructor and **Graphics** method **setFont**.

The font size is measured in points. A *point* is 1/72 of an inch. The **setFont** method sets the current font—the font in which text will be displayed. The **setFont** method takes a **Font** object as an argument.

Portability Tip 9.2

The number of fonts varies greatly across systems. The JDK guarantees that the fonts **Serif**, **Monospaced**, **SansSerif**, **Dialog** *and* **DialogInput** *will be available.*

Software Engineering Observation 9.1

If a font is not available on a system, Java will substitute that system's default font.

The program of Fig. 9.11 displays text in three different fonts with each font in a different size. The program uses the **Font** constructor to create **Font** objects **font1**, **font2** and **font3**. Each call to the **Font** constructor passes a font name (**Serif**, **Monospaced**, or **SansSerif**) as a **String**, a font style (**Font.PLAIN**, **Font.ITALIC**, or **Font.BOLD**) and a font size. The current font is changed using the **setFont** method. Once the **setFont** method is invoked, all text displayed following the call will appear in the new font.

Often it is necessary to get information about the current font such as the font name, the font style and the font size. The **Font** methods used to get font information are summarized in Fig. 9.12. The **getStyle** method returns an integer value representing the current style. The integer value returned is either **Font.PLAIN**, **Font.ITALIC**, **Font.BOLD** or any combination of **Font.PLAIN**, **Font.ITALIC** and **Font.BOLD**.

```java
// Fig. 9.11: DemoFont.java
// Demonstrating the Font constants, the Font constructor
// and the setFont method
import java.applet.Applet;
import java.awt.Graphics;
import java.awt.Font;

public class DemoFont extends Applet {
   private Font font1, font2, font3;

   public void init()
   {
      // create a font object: 12-point bold Serif
      font1 = new Font( "Serif", Font.BOLD, 12 );

      // create a font object: 24-point italic Monospaced
      font2 = new Font( "Monospaced", Font.ITALIC, 24 );

      // create a font object: 14-point plain SansSerif
      font3 = new Font( "SansSerif", Font.PLAIN, 14 );
   }

   public void paint( Graphics g )
   {
      // set the current font to font1
      g.setFont( font1 );

      // draw a string in font font1
      g.drawString( "Serif 12 point bold.", 20, 20 );

      // change the current font to font2
      g.setFont( font2 );

      // draw a string in font font2
      g.drawString( "Monospaced 24 point italic.", 20, 40 );

      // change the current font to font3
      g.setFont( font3 );

      // draw a string in font font3
      g.drawString( "SansSerif 14 point plain.", 20, 60 );
   }
}
```

Fig. 9.11 Setting fonts with **Font** objects and the **Graphics setFont** method (part 1 of 2).

Method **getSize** returns the font size in points. Method **getName** returns the current font name as a **String**. Method **getFamily** returns the name of the font family to which the current font belongs. The name of the font family is platform specific.

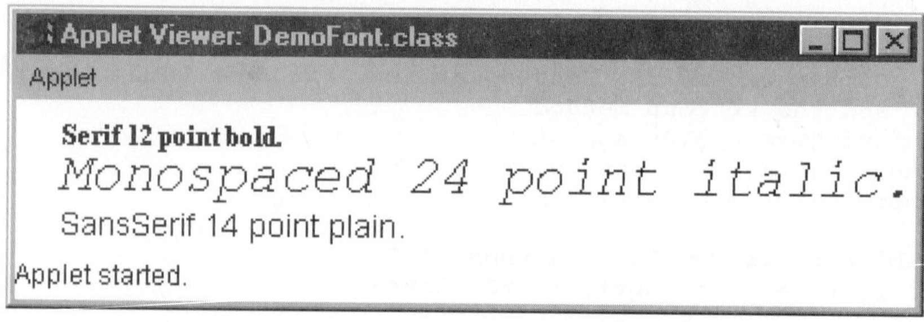

Fig. 9.11 Setting fonts with **Font** objects and the **Graphics setFont** method (part 2 of 2).

Font methods for retrieving font information

```
public int getStyle()       // Font class
```

Returns an integer value indicating the current font style.

```
public int getSize()        // Font class
```

Returns an integer value indicating the current font size.

```
public String getName()     // Font class
```

Returns the current font name as a string.

```
public String getFamily() // Font class
```

Returns the font's family name as a string.

Fig. 9.12 **Font** methods for retrieving font information.

Portability Tip 9.3

Java uses standardized font names and maps these into system-specific font names for portability. This is transparent to the programmer.

The program of Fig. 9.13 creates a **Font** object **f** that is 24-point **Monospaced** bold italic. The current font is changed to **f** with the **setFont** method. The statement

```
style = f.getStyle();
```

uses **getStyle** to determine the current font style. The integer returned is compared with the **Font** constants to display a **String** with the font's style. The statement

```
size = f.getSize();
```

determines the current font size. The font name (**Monospaced**) is determined with a call to method **getName**. The font family (**Monospaced**) is displayed with the statement

```
g.drawString( "Font family is " + f.getFamily(), 20, 60 );
```

Method **drawString** displays the text at location (20, 60). Note again that the **getStyle**, **getName**, **getSize**, and **getFamily** methods belong to the **Font** class.

```
// Fig. 9.13: DemoFont2.java
// Demonstrating the Font methods for
// retrieving font information
import java.applet.Applet;
import java.awt.Graphics;
import java.awt.Font;

public class DemoFont2 extends Applet {
   private Font f;

   public void init()
   {
      // create a font object: 24-point bold italic Monospaced
      f = new Font( "Monospaced", Font.ITALIC + Font.BOLD, 24 );
   }

   public void paint( Graphics g )
   {
      int style, size;
      String s, name;

      g.setFont( f );              // set the current font to f
      style = f.getStyle();        // determine current font style

      if ( style == Font.PLAIN )
         s = "Plain ";
      else if ( style == Font.BOLD )
         s = "Bold ";
      else if ( style == Font.ITALIC )
         s = "Italic ";
      else    // bold + italic
         s = "Bold italic ";

      size = f.getSize();      // determine current font size
      s += size + " point ";
      name = f.getName();      // determine current font name
      s += name;
      g.drawString( s, 20, 40 );

      // display font family
      g.drawString( "Font family is " + f.getFamily(), 20, 60 );
   }
}
```

Fig. 9.13 Demonstrating **getName**, **getStyle**, **getSize**, and **getFamily** (part 1 of 2).

Font methods are also available for testing the style of the current font and are summarized in Fig. 9.14. The **isPlain** method returns **true** if the current font style is plain. The **isBold** method returns **true** if the current font style is bold. The **isItalic** method returns **true** if the current font style is italic.

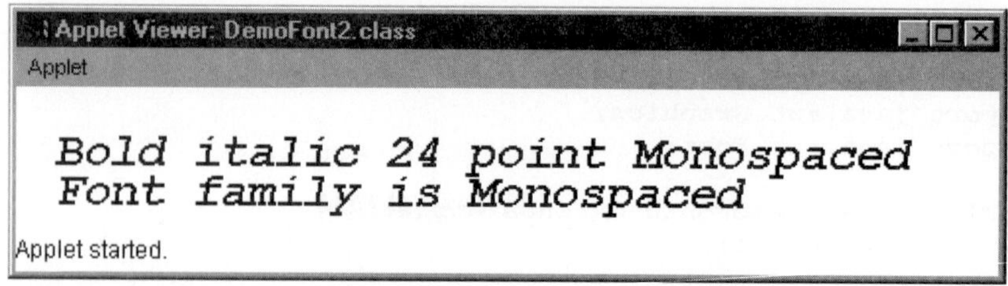

Fig. 9.13 Demonstrating **getName**, **getStyle**, **getSize**, and **getFamily** (part 2 of 2).

Font methods for testing font styles

public boolean isPlain()   // Font class

Tests a font for a plain font style. Returns **true** if the font is plain.

public boolean isBold()   // Font class

Tests a font for a bold font style. Returns **true** if the font is bold.

public boolean isItalic()   // Font class

Tests a font for an italic font style. Returns **true** if the font is italic.

Fig. 9.14 **Font** methods for testing font styles.

The program of Fig. 9.15 demonstrates the use of methods **isPlain**, **isBold**, and **isItalic**. The **Font** object **f** is created with the statement

```
f = new Font( "Monospaced", Font.ITALIC + Font.BOLD, 24 );
```

and is set as the current font with the **setFont** method. The **isBold**, **isItalic**, and **isPlain** methods are used in an **if/else** to test the font style of **f**. A **String** is drawn on the applet describing the font style.

```
// Fig. 9.15: DemoFont3.java
// Demonstrating isPlain, isBold and isItalic
import java.applet.Applet;
import java.awt.Graphics;
import java.awt.Font;

public class DemoFont3 extends Applet {
   private Font f;

```

Fig. 9.15 Demonstrating **isPlain**, **isBold**, and **isItalic** (part 1 of 2).

```
    public void init()
    {
       // create a font object: 24-point bold italic Monospaced
       f = new Font( "Monospaced", Font.ITALIC + Font.BOLD, 24 );
    }

    public void paint( Graphics g )
    {
       String s;

       g.setFont( f );          // set the current font to f

       if ( f.isPlain() == true )
          s = "Font is plain.";
       else if ( f.isBold() == true && f.isItalic() == false )
          s = "Font is bold.";
       else if ( f.isItalic() == true && f.isBold() == false )
          s = "Font is italic.";
       else    // bold + italic
          s = "Font is bold italic.";

       g.drawString( s, 20, 40 );
    }
 }
```

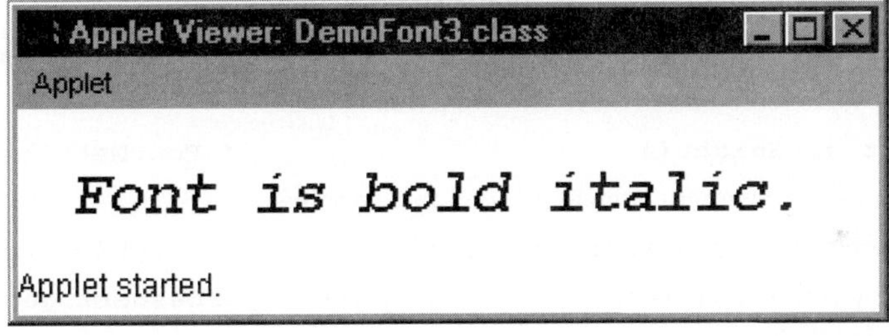

Fig. 9.15 Demonstrating **`isPlain`**, **`isBold`**, and **`isItalic`** (part 2 of 2).

Sometimes precise information about a font's metrics must be known—such as *height*, *descent* (the amount a character dips below the baseline), *ascent* (the amount a character rises above the baseline), *leading* (the difference between the height and the ascent), etc. Figure 9.16 illustrates some of the common *font metrics*. Note that the coordinate passed to **`drawString`** corresponds to the lower-left corner.

Some methods for obtaining font metrics are defined in the **`FontMetrics`** class—that inherits from the **`Object`** class. The **`FontMetrics`** methods as well as other useful methods from the **`Graphics`** class and the **`Toolkit`** class are summarized in Fig. 9.17.

The program of Fig. 9.18 uses the methods of Fig. 9.17 to obtain font metric information. The program creates two fonts—one that is **`Monospaced`** bold 14-point and one that is **`Serif`** 10-point. The object **`font1`** is set as the current font. The statement

```
showStatus( g.getFont().toString() );
```

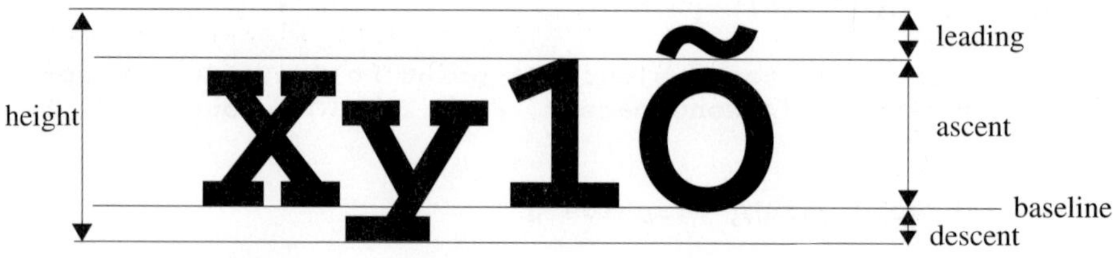

Fig. 9.16 Font metrics.

Methods useful for obtaining font metrics

```
public abstract Font getFont()                   // Graphics class
```
Returns a **Font** object representing the current font.

```
public abstract String[] getFontList()           // Toolkit class
```
Creates a list of the available fonts for a system.

```
public int getAscent()                           // FontMetrics class
```
Returns a value representing the ascent of a font in points.

```
public int getDescent()                          // FontMetrics class
```
Returns a value representing the descent of a font in points.

```
public int getLeading()                          // FontMetrics class
```
Returns a value representing the leading of a font in points.

```
public int getHeight()                           // FontMetrics class
```
Returns a value representing the height of a font in points.

```
public FontMetrics getFontMetrics()              // Graphics class
```
Returns the current font metrics. Used with **getAscent**, **getDescent**, **getLeading**, and **getHeight**.

Fig. 9.17 Methods from class **Graphics**, class **Toolkit** and class **FontMetrics** useful for obtaining font metrics.

uses the **toString** method to convert the **Font** object returned by **getFont** to a **String**. The converted **String** is then displayed in the status bar. The ascent, height, leading and descent for **font1** are determined with the four lines

```
int ascent = g.getFontMetrics().getAscent();
int descent = g.getFontMetrics().getDescent();int height =
g.getFontMetrics().getHeight();
int leading = g.getFontMetrics().getLeading();
```

The font metric information from the above lines is drawn on the applet. The ascent, height, leading, and descent information for **font2** is gathered in a similar manner and drawn on the applet. The statement

```
// Fig. 9.18: Metrics.java
// Demonstrating methods of the FontMetrics class, Graphics
// class and Toolkit class useful for obtaining font metrics
import java.applet.Applet;
import java.awt.Graphics;
import java.awt.Font;
import java.awt.Toolkit;

public class Metrics extends Applet {
   private Font font1, font2;

   public void init()
   {
      font1 = new Font( "Monospaced", Font.BOLD, 14 );
      font2 = new Font( "Serif", Font.PLAIN, 10 );
   }

   public void paint( Graphics g )
   {
      g.setFont( font1 );   // set the current font

      // display the current font in the status bar
      showStatus( g.getFont().toString() );

      // get information about the current font font1
      int ascent = g.getFontMetrics().getAscent();
      int descent = g.getFontMetrics().getDescent();
      int height = g.getFontMetrics().getHeight();
      int leading = g.getFontMetrics().getLeading();

      String s1 = "Ascent of Font font1 is   " + ascent;
      String s2 = "Descent of Font font1 is  " + descent;
      String s3 = "Height of Font font1 is   " + height;
      String s4 = "Leading of Font font1 is  " + leading;

      g.drawString( s1, 10, 10 );
      g.drawString( s2, 10, 20 );
      g.drawString( s3, 10, 30 );
      g.drawString( s4, 10, 40 );

      // get information about the font font2
      ascent = g.getFontMetrics( font2 ).getAscent();
      descent = g.getFontMetrics( font2 ).getDescent();
      height = g.getFontMetrics( font2 ).getHeight();
      leading = g.getFontMetrics( font2 ).getLeading();

      s1 = "Ascent of Font font2 is   " + ascent;
      s2 = "Descent of Font font2 is  " + descent;
      s3 = "Height of Font font2 is   " + height;
      s4 = "Leading of Font font2 is  " + leading;
```

Fig. 9.18 Program that demonstrates obtaining font metric information and obtaining a list of the system's available fonts (part 1 of 2).

```

      g.drawString( s1, 10, 60 );
      g.drawString( s2, 10, 70 );
      g.drawString( s3, 10, 80 );
      g.drawString( s4, 10, 90 );

      g.drawString( "   Font list:", 10, 110 );

      // get the list of fonts
      String fonts[] =
         Toolkit.getDefaultToolkit().getFontList();

      for ( int i = 0; i < fonts.length; i++ )
         g.drawString( fonts[ i ], 10, i * 10 + 120 );
   }
}
```

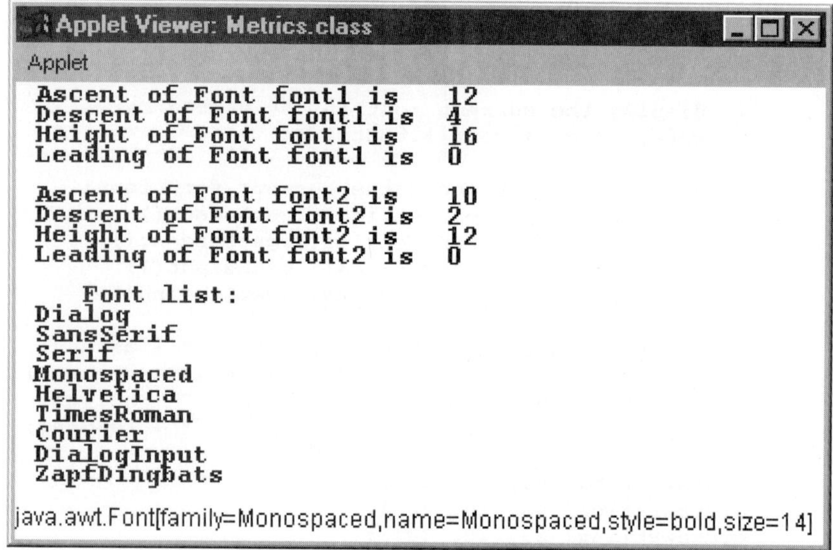

Fig. 9.18 Program that demonstrates obtaining font metric information and obtaining a list of the system's available fonts (part 2 of 2).

```
String fonts[] = Toolkit.getDefaultToolkit().getFontList();
```

gets the fonts on the system from the toolkit and stores them in an array. The *toolkit* interacts between Java and the system to get information about the system. The **getDefaultToolkit** method is a **static** method of the **Toolkit** class (**Toolkit** inherits from the **Object** class). The **getDefaultToolkit** method gets the default toolkit for the current system (i.e., returns a **Toolkit** object). The **getFontList** method of class **Toolkit** returns the names of the system's available fonts as an array of **String**s. A **for** loop is used to display the available fonts for the system.

9.6 Drawing Lines

This section presents the **Graphics** method **drawLine** for drawing lines. The **drawLine** method's parameters are summarized in Fig. 9.19. The **drawLine** method takes four integer arguments. The first two arguments specify the coordinates of one point and the last two arguments specify the coordinates of a second point. The line is drawn between the two points in the current color.The program of Fig. 9.20 uses the **drawLine** method to draw a line on the applet. The line is drawn between the points (10, 10) and (230, 95).

Graphics method **drawLine**

```
public abstract void drawLine(     // Graphics class
   int x1,     // x coordinate first point
   int y1,     // y coordinate first point
   int x2,     // x coordinate second point
   int y2 )    // y coordinate second point
```

Draws a line between the point (**x1**, **y1**) and the point (**x2**, **y2**) in the current color.

Fig. 9.19 **Graphics** method **drawLine**.

```
// Fig. 9.20: Line.java
// Demonstrating drawLine
import java.applet.Applet;
import java.awt.Graphics;

public class Line extends Applet {

   public void paint( Graphics g )
   {
      // draw a line from (10, 10) to (230, 95)
      g.drawLine( 10, 10, 230, 95 );
   }
}
```

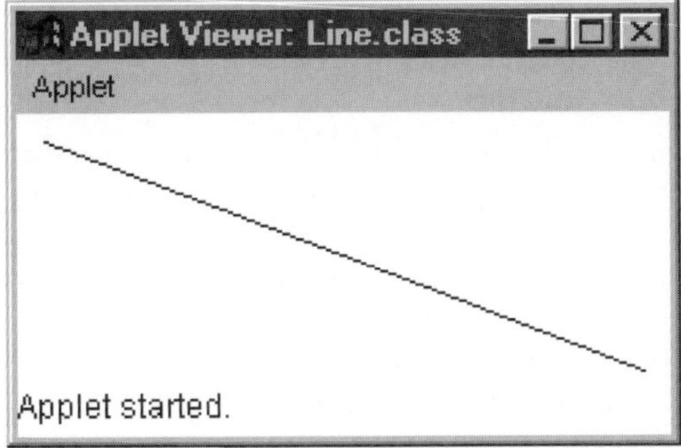

Fig. 9.20 Demonstrating **Graphics** method **drawLine**.

9.7 Drawing Rectangles

This section presents the **Graphics** methods for drawing rectangles. The methods are summarized in Fig. 9.21.

The **drawRect** method draws a rectangle. The first two arguments specify the coordinates of the upper-left corner of the rectangle. The third and fourth arguments specify the **width** and **height** of the rectangle.

The **fillRect** method draws a filled rectangle. The current color is used to fill the rectangle. The **fillRect** method takes four arguments: an **x** coordinate, a **y** coordinate, a **width** and a **height**. The point (**x**, **y**) specifies the upper-left corner of the filled rectangle.

The **clearRect** method draws a rectangle in the current *background color* over the specified rectangle. The method takes the upper-left coordinates, the **width** and **height** of the rectangle to erase.

The program of Fig. 9.22 draws a rectangle and a filled rectangle using the **drawRect** and **fillRect** methods. The **drawRect** method is used to draw a rectangle at the coordinates (10, 15). The rectangle has a width of 100 pixels and a height of 100 pixels. The **fillRect** method is used to draw a filled rectangle at the coordinates (150, 15). The filled rectangle has a width of 100 pixels and a height of 100 pixels.

Graphics methods for drawing rectangles

```
public void drawRect(            // Graphics class
   int x,          // top-left x coordinate
   int y,          // top-left y coordinate
   int width,      // width
   int height )    // height
```

Draws a rectangle of the specified **width** and **height**. The top-left corner of the rectangle has the coordinates (**x**, **y**). The rectangle is drawn in the current color.

```
public abstract void fillRect(    // Graphics class
   int x,          // top-left x coordinate
   int y,          // top-left y coordinate
   int width,      // width
   int height )    // height
```

Draws a solid rectangle in the current color with the specified **width** and **height**. The top-left corner of the rectangle has the coordinate (**x**, **y**).

```
public abstract void clearRect(  // Graphics class
   int x,          // top-left x coordinate
   int y,          // top-left y coordinate
   int width,      // width
   int height )    // height
```

Draws a rectangle in the current background color.

Fig. 9.21 **Graphics** methods for drawing rectangles.

```
// Fig. 9.22: RectangleTest.java
// Demonstrating drawRect and fillRect
import java.applet.Applet;
import java.awt.Graphics;

public class RectangleTest extends Applet {

   public void paint( Graphics g )
   {
      // draw a rectangle at location ( 10, 15 )
      g.drawRect( 10, 15, 100, 100 );

      // draw a filled rectangle at location ( 150, 15 )
      g.fillRect( 150, 15, 100, 100 );
   }
}
```

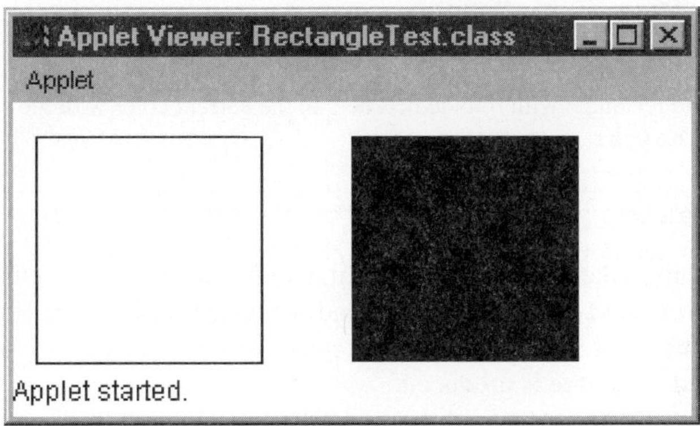

Fig. 9.22 Drawing rectangles with **Graphics** methods **drawRect** and **fillRect**.

9.8 Drawing Rounded Rectangles

This section presents the **Graphics** methods for drawing rectangles with rounded corners. The methods and their parameters are summarized in Fig. 9.23.

The **drawRoundRect** method draws a rectangle with rounded corners. The first two arguments specify the coordinates of the upper-left corner of the *bounding rectangle*—the area in which the rounded rectangle will be drawn. Note that the upper-left corner coordinates are not the edge of the rounded rectangle, but the coordinates of where the edge would be if the rectangle were not rounded. The next two arguments specify the **width** and **height**. The last two arguments specify how round the rectangle corners are. The **arcWidth** argument specifies the horizontal component and the **arcHeight** argument specifies the vertical component. Using the same value for **arcWidth** and **arcHeight** produces a quarter circle at the corner.

Graphics methods for drawing rounded rectangles

```
public abstract void drawRoundRect(      // Graphics class
   int x,              // x coordinate
   int y,              // y coordinate
   int width,          // width
   int height,         // height
   int arcWidth,       // arc width
   int arcHeight )     // arc height
```

Draws a rectangle with rounded corners in the current color with the specified **width** and **height**.

```
public abstract void fillRoundRect(      // Graphics class
   int x,              // x coordinate
   int y,              // y coordinate
   int width,          // width
   int height,         // height
   int arcWidth,       // arc width
   int arcHeight )     // arc height
```

Draws a solid rectangle with rounded corners in the current color with the specified **width** and **height**.

Fig. 9.23 **Graphics** methods for drawing rounded rectangles.

Figure 9.24 labels the arc width, arc height, width, and height. Note that a circle is produced when **width**, **height**, **arcWidth** and **arcHeight** have the same values. If the values for **width** and **height** are the same and the values of **arcWidth** and **arcHeight** are 0, a square is produced.

The **fillRoundRect** method draws a filled rectangle with rounded corners. The current color is used to fill the rectangle. The **fillRoundRect** method takes the same six arguments as the **drawRoundRect** method: an **x** coordinate, a **y** coordinate, a **width**, a **height**, an arc width and an arc height. The point (**x**, **y**) specifies the upper-left corner of the bounding rectangle.

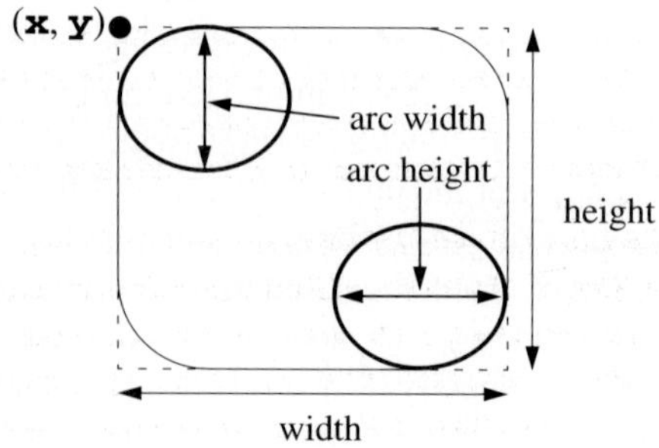

Fig. 9.24 Rounded rectangles.

Figure 9.25 draws three rounded rectangles and two filled rounded rectangles using the **drawRoundRect** and **fillRoundRect** methods. The first rounded rectangle is drawn at (10, 35) with a width of 50 and a height of 50. The arc width and arc height are 10 and 20, respectively. The second rounded rectangle is drawn at (80, 15) and is filled. The width and height of the filled rounded rectangle are 60 and 80, respectively. The third rounded rectangle forms an ellipse. The ellipse is drawn at (150, 55) and has a height of 80 and a width of 20. The arc width and arc height are both 70. The fourth rounded rectangle forms a filled square. The square is drawn at (240, 15) and has a width of 80 and a height of 80. The arc width and arc height are both 0. The last rounded rectangle drawn forms a circle. The circle is drawn at (330, 15) and has a width, height, arc width, and arc height of 80.

9.9 Drawing Three-Dimensional Rectangles

This section presents the **Graphics** methods for drawing three-dimensional rectangles. The methods are summarized in Fig. 9.26. Both **draw3DRect** and **fill3DRect** take the same arguments. The first two arguments specify the top-left corner coordinates of the rectangle. The next two arguments specify the **width** and **height** of the rectangle, respectively. The last argument determines whether or not the rectangle is raised or lowered. A **true** value specifies that the rectangle is to be raised and a **false** value specifies that the rectangle is to be lowered. Three-dimensional rectangles are drawn in the current color. The three-dimensional effect is difficult to see in certain colors.

```
// Fig. 9.25: Rectangle2.java
// Drawing rounded rectangles
import java.applet.Applet;
import java.awt.Graphics;

public class Rectangle2 extends Applet {

   public void paint( Graphics g )
   {
      // draw a rounded rectangle at (10, 35)
      g.drawRoundRect( 10, 35, 50, 50, 10, 20 );

      // draw a filled rounded rectangle at (80, 15)
      g.fillRoundRect( 80, 15, 60, 80, 50, 10 );

      // draw a rounded rectangle at (150, 55)
      g.drawRoundRect( 150, 55, 80, 20, 70, 70 );

      // draw a filled square at (240, 15)
      g.fillRoundRect( 240, 15, 80, 80, 0, 0 );

      // draw a circle at (330, 15)
      g.drawRoundRect( 330, 15, 80, 80, 80, 80 );
   }
}
```

Fig. 9.25 Demonstrating **drawRoundRect** and **fillRoundRect** (part 1 of 2).

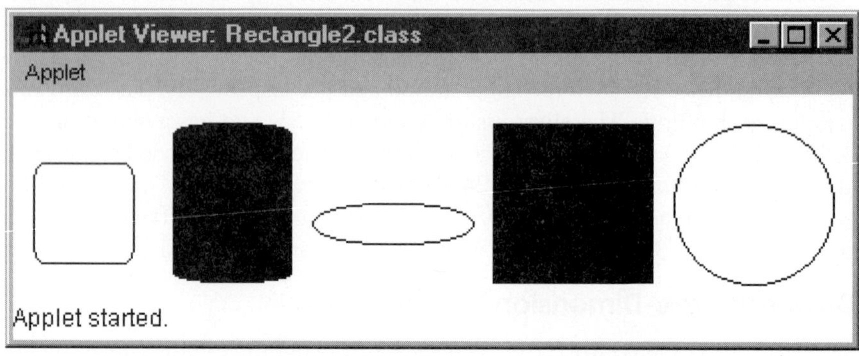

Fig. 9.25 Demonstrating **drawRoundRect** and **fillRoundRect** (part 2 of 2).

Graphics methods for drawing 3-D rectangles

```
public void draw3DRect(        // Graphics class
   int x,          // x coordinate top-left corner
   int y,          // y coordinate top-left corner
   int width,      // width of rectangle
   int height,     // height of rectangle
   Boolean b )     // raised when true
```

Draws a three-dimensional rectangle in the current color with the specified **width** and **height**. The top-left corner of the rectangle has the coordinates (**x**, **y**). The rectangle is raised when **b** is **true** and is lowered when **b** is **false**.

```
public void fill3DRect(        // Graphics class
   int x,          // x coordinate top-left corner
   int y,          // y coordinate top-left corner
   int width,      // width of rectangle
   int height,     // height of rectangle
   Boolean b )     // raised when true
```

Draws a filled three-dimensional rectangle in the current color with the specified **width** and **height**. The top-left corner of the rectangle has the coordinates (**x**, **y**). The rectangle is raised when **b** is **true** and is lowered when **b** is **false**.

Fig. 9.26 Graphics methods for drawing 3-D rectangles.

The program of Fig. 9.27 demonstrates the **draw3DRect** and **fill3DRect** methods. The three-dimensional rectangles are drawn in yellow to enhance the three dimensional effect. Both raised and lowered rectangles are demonstrated.

```
// Fig. 9.27: Draw3D.java
// Drawing 3-D rectangles
import java.applet.Applet;
import java.awt.Graphics;
import java.awt.Color;

public class Draw3D extends Applet {

   public void paint( Graphics g )
   {
      g.setColor( Color.yellow );

      // draw a raised 3D rectangle at location (10, 10)
      g.draw3DRect( 10, 10, 100, 100, true );

      // draw a sunk 3D at location (130, 10)
      g.draw3DRect( 130, 10, 100, 100, false );

      // draw a filled raised 3D rectangle at (10, 120)
      g.fill3DRect( 10, 120, 100, 100, true );

      // draw a filled sunk 3D rectangle at (130, 120)
      g.fill3DRect( 130, 120, 100, 100, false );
   }
}
```

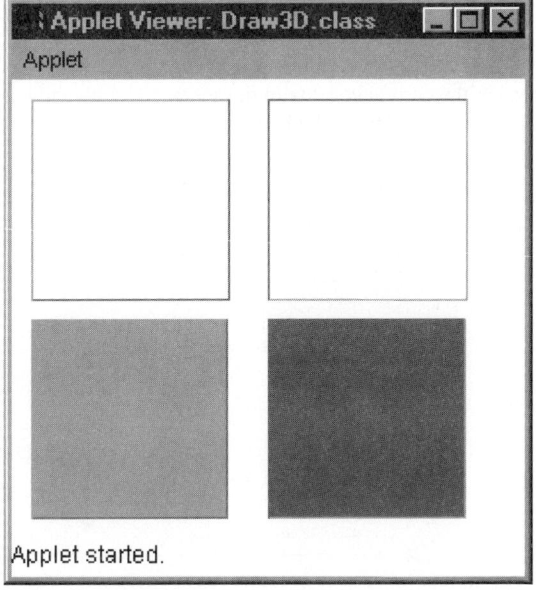

Fig. 9.27 Demonstrating **`draw3DRect`** and **`fill3DRect`**.

9.10 Drawing Ovals

This section presents the **Graphics** methods for drawing ovals. The methods are summarized in Fig. 9.28.

Both the **drawOval** and **fillOval** methods take the same two arguments. The first two arguments specify the top-left coordinate of the bounding rectangle that contains the oval. The last two arguments specify the **width** and **height**, respectively. Figure 9.29 shows an oval bounded by a rectangle.

The program of Fig. 9.30 demonstrates the **drawOval** and **fillOval** methods. The program draws two ovals on the applet—one of which is filled.

Graphics methods for drawing ovals

```
public abstract void drawOval(          // Graphics class
   int x,         // x coordinate
   int y,         // y coordinate
   int width,     // width
   int height )  // height
```

Draws an oval in the current color with the specified width and height. The bounding rectangle's top-left corner is at the coordinates (**x**, **y**).

```
public abstract void fillOval(          // Graphics class
   int x,         // x coordinate
   int y,         // y coordinate
   int width,     // width
   int height )  // height
```

Draws a filled oval in the current color with the specified width and height. The bounding rectangle's top-left corner is at the coordinates (**x**, **y**).

Fig. 9.28 **Graphics** methods for drawing ovals.

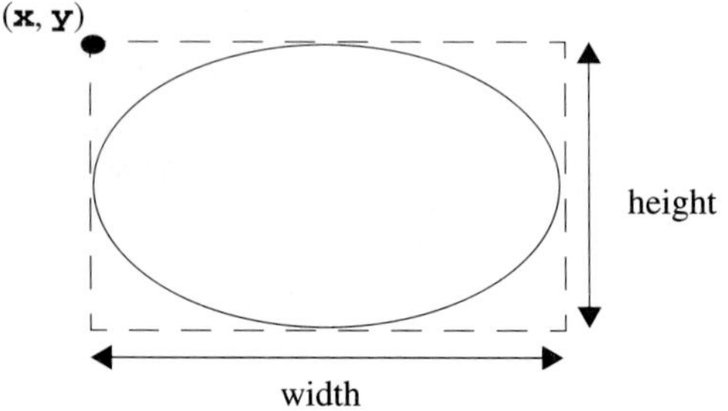

Fig. 9.29 An oval bounded by a rectangle.

```
// Fig. 9.30: DrawOval.java
// Drawing ovals
import java.applet.Applet;
import java.awt.Graphics;

public class DrawOval extends Applet {
   public void paint( Graphics g )
   {
      // draw an oval at location (10, 15)
      g.drawOval( 10, 15, 100, 70 );

      // draw an oval at location (160, 15)
      g.fillOval( 160, 15, 70, 130 );
   }
}
```

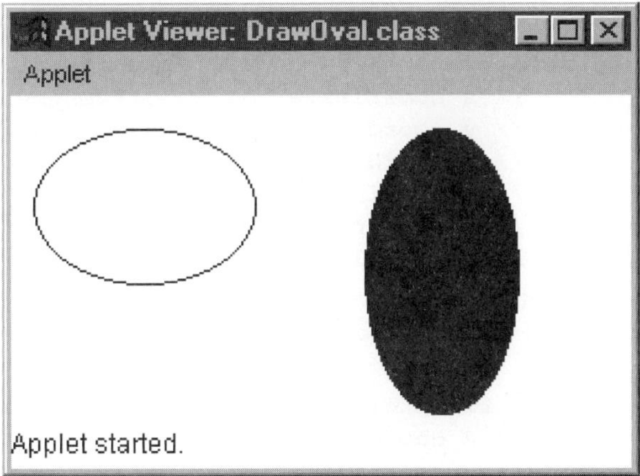

Fig. 9.30 Demonstrating **`drawOval`** and **`fillOval`**.

9.11 Drawing Arcs

This section presents **`Graphics`** methods for drawing arcs. An *arc* is a portion of a circle. Arc angles are measured in degrees. An arc is drawn between two angles—a *starting angle* and an *arc angle*. The starting angle is the degree where the arc begins. The arc angle is the last degree of the arc. Arcs *sweep* between their starting angle and their arc angle.

Figure 9.31 illustrates two arcs. The left set of axes shows an arc sweeping from zero degrees to approximately 110 degrees. Arcs that sweep in a counter-clockwise direction are measured in *positive degrees*. The right set of axes shows an arc sweeping from zero degrees to approximately –110 degrees. Arcs that sweep in a clockwise direction are measured in *negative degrees*. The **`Graphics`** methods for drawing arcs are summarized in Fig. 9.32.

Fig. 9.31 Positive and negative arc angles.

`Graphics` methods for drawing arcs

```
public abstract void drawArc(        // Graphics class
   int x,             // x coordinate
   int y,             // y coordinate
   int width,         // arc width
   int height,        // arc height
   int startAngle,    // beginning angle
   int arcAngle )     // arc angle
```

Draws an arc in the current color relative to the bounding rectangle's top-left coordinates (**`x`**, **`y`**) with the specified **`width`** and **`height`**. The arc segment is drawn from the starting angle to the arc angle.

```
public abstract void fillArc(        // Graphics class
   int x,             // x coordinate
   int y,             // y coordinate
   int width,         // arc width
   int height,        // arc height
   int startAngle,    // beginning angle
   int arcAngle )     // arc angle
```

Draws a solid arc in the current color relative to the bounding rectangle's top-left coordinates (**`x`**, **`y`**) with the specified width and height. The arc segment is drawn from the starting angle to the arc angle.

Fig. 9.32 `Graphics` methods for drawing arcs.

Both the **`drawArc`** and **`fillArc`** methods take six arguments. The first two arguments specify the top-left corner coordinates for the bounding rectangle that encloses the arc. The third and fourth arguments specify the arc width and arc height. The fifth argument specifies the starting angle. The last argument specifies the arc angle. The arc is drawn in the current color. Figure 9.33 shows an arc bounded by a rectangle. The arc angle starts at approximately 20° and sweeps to approximately –110°.

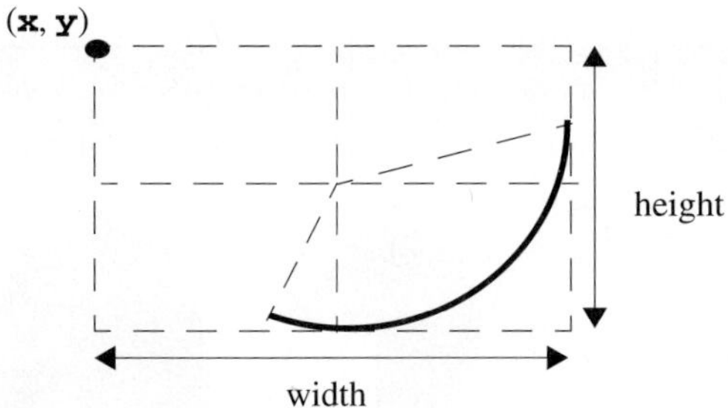

Fig. 9.33 An arc bounded by a rectangle.

The program of Fig. 9.34 demonstrates the arc methods of Fig. 9.32. Five different arcs are drawn, three of which are filled.

9.12 Drawing Polygons

Polygons are multisided shapes. Polygons are drawn with the **Graphics** methods described in Fig. 9.35. Note that some methods require a **Polygon** object—which is created with the **Polygon** class. The **Polygon** class constructors are also described in Fig. 9.35.

```
// Fig. 9.34: DrawArcs.java
// Drawing arcs
import java.applet.Applet;
import java.awt.Graphics;

public class DrawArcs extends Applet {

   public void paint( Graphics g )
   {
      // draw an arc
      g.drawArc( 15, 15, 80, 80, 0, 180 );

      // draw an arc
      g.drawArc( 100, 100, 80, 80, 0, 110 );

      // draw a solid arc
      g.fillArc( 100, 15, 70, 80, 0, 270 );

      // draw a solid arc
      g.fillArc( 15, 70, 70, 80, 0, -110 );

      // draw a solid arc
      g.fillArc( 190, 15, 80, 140, 0, -360 );
   }
}
```

Fig. 9.34 Demonstrating **drawArc** and **fillArc** (part 1 of 2).

Fig. 9.34 Demonstrating **drawArc** and **fillArc** (part 2 of 2).

The first **drawPolygon** method of Fig. 9.35 takes three arguments: an array of integers containing *x* coordinates, an array of integers containing *y* coordinates, and the number of points in the polygon. Specifying a last point different than the first point results in an *open polygon*—the last point is not connected to the first point.

The **drawPolyline** method of Fig. 9.35 takes three arguments: an array of integers containing *x* coordinates, an array of integers containing *y* coordinates, and the number of points in the set of connected lines. If the last point is different from the first point, the last point is not connected to the first point.

The second **drawPolygon** method of Fig. 9.35 requires a **Polygon** object as an argument. The **Polygon** class inherits from class **Object**.

Solid polygons or *filled polygons* are drawn with the **fillPolygon** method. The first **fillPolygon** method of Fig. 9.35 takes three arguments: an array of integers containing *x* coordinates, an array of integers containing *y* coordinates, and the number of points in the polygon. The current color is used to fill the polygon.

The second **fillPolygon** method of Fig. 9.35 requires a **Polygon** object. Filled polygons are always *closed polygons*—the last point does not have to match the first (i. e., the last point is automatically connected to the first point).

Common Programming Error 9.3

It is a logic error if the number of points specified in the third argument to method **drawPolygon** *or method* **fillPolygon** *is less than the number of elements in the arrays of coordinates that define the polygon to display.*

Common Programming Error 9.4

An **ArrayIndexOutOfBoundsException** *is thrown if the number of points specified in the third argument to method* **drawPolygon** *or method* **fillPolygon** *is greater than the number of elements in the arrays of coordinates that define the polygon to display.*

Graphics methods for drawing polygons and the Polygon constructors

```
public abstract void drawPolygon(    // Graphics class
   int xPoints[],      // x coordinates
   int yPoints[],      // y coordinates
   int points )        // number of points
```

Draws a polygon of **points** in the current color. The *x* coordinate of each point is specified in the **xPoints** array and the *y* coordinate of each point is specified in the **yPoints** array.

```
public abstract void drawPolyline(   // Graphics class
   int xPoints[],      // x coordinates
   int yPoints[],      // y coordinates
   int points )        // number of points
```

Draws a series of connected lines in the current color. The *x* coordinate of each point is specified in the **xPoints** array and the *y* coordinate of each point is specified in the **yPoints** array. The last argument specifies the number of **points**.

```
public void drawPolygon( Polygon p ) // Graphics class
```

Draws a polygon in the current color.

```
public abstract void fillPolygon(    // Graphics class
   int xPoints[],      // x coordinates
   int yPoints[],      // y coordinates
   int points )        // number of points
```

Draws a solid polygon of **points** in the current color. The *x* coordinate of each point is specified in the **xPoints** array and the *y* coordinate of each point is specified in the **yPoints** array.

```
public void fillPolygon( Polygon p ) // Graphics class
```

Draws a filled polygon in the current color.

```
public Polygon()              // Polygon class
```

Constructs a new polygon object. The polygon does not contain any points.

```
public Polygon(               // Polygon class
   int xValues[],             // x coordinates
   int yValues[],             // y coordinates
   int numberOfPoints )       // number of points
```

Constructs a new polygon object. The polygon has **numberOfPoints** sides with each point consisting of an *x* coordinate from **xValues** and a *y* coordinate from **yValues**.

Fig. 9.35 **Graphics** methods for drawing polygons and the **Polygon** constructors.

The program of Fig. 9.36 draws four polygons, two of which are filled. Each of the four methods and each of the constructors of Fig. 9.35 is used.

```
// Fig. 9.36: DrawPoly.java
// Drawing polygons
import java.applet.Applet;
import java.awt.Graphics;
import java.awt.Polygon;

public class DrawPoly extends Applet {
   // coordinates for first polygon
   private int xValues[] = { 20, 40, 50, 30, 20, 15, 20 };
   private int yValues[] = { 20, 20, 30, 50, 50, 30, 20 };

   // coordinates for second polygon
   private int xValues2[] = { 70, 90, 100, 80, 70, 65,
                              60, 70 };

   private int yValues2[] = { 70, 70, 80, 100, 100, 80,
                              60, 70 };

   // coordinates for third polygon
   private int xValues3[] = { 120, 140, 150, 190 };
   private int yValues3[] = { 10, 40, 50, 30 };

   // create references to polygons
   private Polygon p4, p5, p6;

   public void init()
   {
      // instantiate polygon objects
      p4 = new Polygon( xValues, yValues, 7 );
      p5 = new Polygon();
      p6 = new Polygon();

      // add points to p5
      p5.addPoint( 165, 105 );
      p5.addPoint( 175, 120 );
      p5.addPoint( 270, 170 );
      p5.addPoint( 200, 190 );
      p5.addPoint( 130, 150 );
      p5.addPoint( 165, 105 );

      // add points to p6
      p6.addPoint( 240, 50 );
      p6.addPoint( 260, 70 );
      p6.addPoint( 250, 90 );
   }

   public void paint( Graphics g )
   {
      // draw a polygon of 8 points
      g.drawPolygon( xValues2, yValues2, 8 );

```

Fig. 9.36 Demonstrating **drawPolygon** and **fillPolygon** (part 1 of 2).

```
        // draw a polygon object
        g.drawPolygon( p4 );

        // draw a filled polygon object
        g.fillPolygon( p5 );

        // draw a filled polygon object
        g.fillPolygon( p6 );

        // draw a filled polygon of 4 points
        g.fillPolygon( xValues3, yValues3, 4 );
    }
}
```

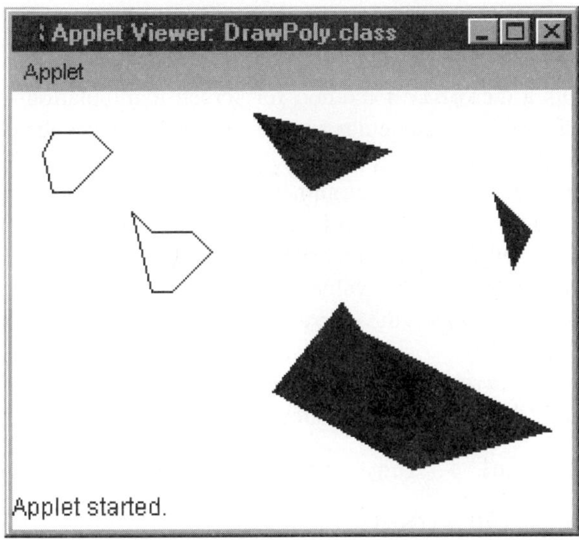

Fig. 9.36 Demonstrating **drawPolygon** and **fillPolygon** (part 2 of 2).

Six integer arrays are declared and initialized. The arrays **xValues**, **xValues2**, and **xValues3** represent the *x* coordinates for three of the polygons. The *y* coordinates are represented with the arrays **yValues**, **yValues2**, and **yValues3**.

The **Polygon** class is used to create three objects. The line

```
private Polygon p4, p5, p6;
```

creates **Polygon** references **p4**, **p5**, and **p6**. The statements

```
p4 = new Polygon( xValues, yValues, 7 );
p5 = new Polygon();
p6 = new Polygon();
```

construct **Polygon** objects and assign them to the references **p4**, **p5** and **p6**. Points are added to **p5** and **p6** with the **Polygon** method **addPoint**. The **addPoint** method takes two arguments an *x* coordinate and a *y* coordinate. The statement

```
g.drawPolygon( xValues2, yValues2, 8 );
```

draws the first polygon. The second polygon is drawn with the statement

```
g.drawPolygon( p4 );
```

The third, fourth, and fifth polygons are drawn with the statements

```
g.fillPolygon( p5 );
g.fillPolygon( p6 );
g.fillPolygon( xValues3, yValues3, 4 );
```

9.13 Screen Manipulation

This section presents a **Graphics** method for screen manipulation—**copyArea**. The **copyArea** method copies a rectangular area of the screen places the copy in another location on the screen. The **copyArea** method is summarized in Fig. 9.37.

The **copyArea** method takes six arguments. The first two arguments specify the top-left corner of the area to copy. The third and fourth arguments specify the **width** and **height** of the area to copy. The fifth and six arguments specify the offset where the copy will be placed relative to the first two values.

The program of Fig. 9.38 uses the **copyArea** method to copy a rectangular area (100 by 100) to the point (140,10).

The program draws two polygons. A rectangular area 100 by 100 starting at (0, 0) is copied to the location (140, 10) with the statement

```
g.copyArea( 0, 0, 100, 100, 140, 10 );
```

The horizontal offset of **140** is added to the *x* coordinate of **0** and the vertical offset of **10** is added to the *y* coordinate of **0**.

Graphics method copyArea

```
public abstract void copyArea(      // Graphics class
   int x,          // top-left x coordinate
   int y,          // top-left y coordinate
   int width,      // width of area to copy
   int height,     // height of area to copy
   int dx,         // horizontal distance
   int dy )        // vertical distance
```

Copies a screen area of the specified **width** and **height**. The coordinate (**x**, **y**) is the upper-left corner of the area to be copied. The values of **dx** and **dy** specify the horizontal and vertical offset from (**x**, **y**). The copy is placed relative to (**x**, **y**).

Fig. 9.37 **Graphics** method for copying an area of the screen.

```
// Fig. 9.38: DemoCopyArea.java
// Demonstrate copying one area of the screen to another
// area of the screen
import java.applet.Applet;
import java.awt.Graphics;

public class DemoCopyArea extends Applet {

   // coordinates for first polygon
   int xValues[] = { 20, 40, 50, 30, 20, 15, 20 };
   int yValues[] = { 20, 20, 30, 50, 50, 30, 20 };

   // coordinates for second polygon
   int xValues2[] = { 70, 90, 100, 80, 70, 65, 60, 70 };
   int yValues2[] = { 70, 70, 80, 100, 100, 80, 60, 70 };

   public void paint( Graphics g )
   {
      // draw a polygon of 7 points
      g.drawPolygon( xValues, yValues, 7 );

      // draw a filled polygon of 8 points
      g.fillPolygon( xValues2, yValues2, 8 );

      // copy 100 x 100 area of applet to (140, 10)
      g.copyArea( 0, 0, 100, 100, 140, 10 );
   }
}
```

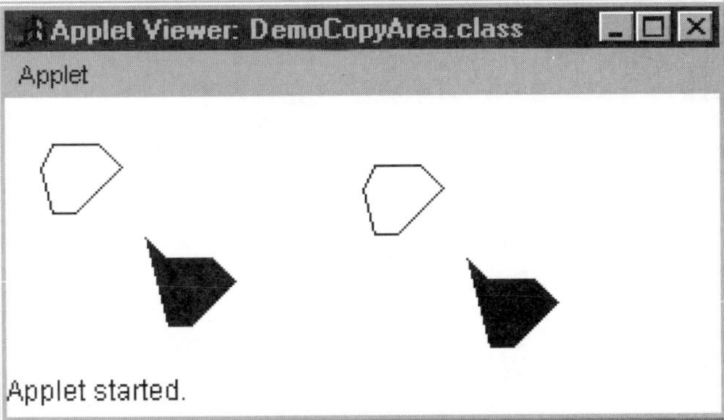

Fig. 9.38 Demonstrating **copyArea**.

9.14 Paint Modes

A *paint mode* describes how graphics are drawn. The default paint mode is *overwrite paint mode*—shapes are drawn on top of each other. When a shape is drawn, the shape overwrites anything beneath it. The other paint mode is *XOR paint mode* which allows all shapes that overlap to be seen. XOR paint mode is set with the **Graphics** method **setXORMode**. The header for method **setXORMode** is

```
public abstract void setXORMode( Color c )
```

The **setXORMode** method takes a **Color** object as an argument. This color is referred to as the *XORMode color*. When overlapping objects are drawn in the same color, the overlapping part will be drawn in the XORMode color.

The program of Fig. 9.39 demonstrates both paint modes by drawing six shapes. Each shape overlaps with at least one other shape. A pink oval is the first shape drawn. A yellow rectangle is drawn next. The yellow rectangle is drawn in overwrite paint mode and covers part of the pink oval. The next shape drawn is an orange rectangle. The orange rectangle is drawn in overwrite paint mode and covers part of the yellow rectangle. The XOR mode is then set with the statement

```
g.setXORMode( Color.yellow );
```

The XORMode color is yellow. The next shape drawn is an oval in XOR mode. The current color is orange. Drawing an orange oval on the orange rectangle results in the XOR mode color being used. The oval is drawn in yellow. The portion of the oval that overlaps with the yellow rectangle is drawn in orange. A blue circle (a 360° arc) and a red square are also drawn on the yellow rectangle.

```
// Fig. 9.39: PaintMode.java
// Demonstrating the XOR paint mode
import java.applet.Applet;
import java.awt.Graphics;
import java.awt.Color;

public class PaintMode extends Applet {

   public void paint( Graphics g )
   {
      // draw pink oval
      g.setColor( Color.pink );
      g.fillOval( 20, 10, 100, 50 );

      // draw a yellow rectangle over part of the oval
      g.setColor( Color.yellow );
      g.fillRect( 100, 10, 100, 50 );

      // draw an orange rectangle
      g.setColor( Color.orange );
      g.fillRect( 190, 10, 80, 50 );

      // set XOR mode to yellow
      g.setXORMode( Color.yellow );
      g.fillOval( 180, 25, 60, 20 );

```

Fig. 9.39 Program that demonstrates the **setXORMode** method (part 1 of 2).

```
      // draw a blue arc
      g.setColor( Color.blue );
      g.fillArc( 150, 20, 20, 20, 0, 360 );

      // draw a red square
      g.setColor( Color.red );
      g.fillRect( 120, 25, 20, 20 );
   }
}
```

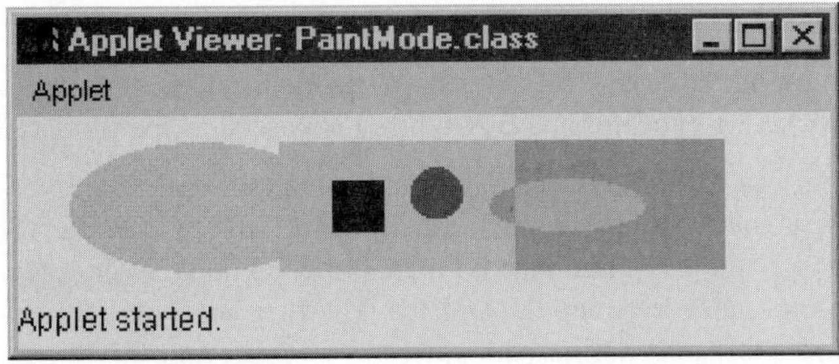

Fig. 9.39 Program that demonstrates the **setXORMode** method (part 2 of 2).

Summary

- The **java.awt** package contains the classes necessary to work with graphics.
- Class **Color** contains methods and constants for manipulating colors.
- Class **Font** contains methods and constants for manipulating fonts.
- Class **FontMetrics** contains methods for getting information about a font.
- Class **Polygon** contains methods for creating polygons.
- Class **Graphics** contains methods for drawing various shapes.
- The **Toolkit** class contains tools used by the AWT.
- A coordinate system describes every point on the screen. The upper-left corner of the screen has the coordinates (0, 0). Coordinates are composed an *x* coordinate (the horizontal distance from the upper-left corner) and a *y* coordinate (the vertical distance from the upper-left corner).
- Text and shapes are precisely drawn using coordinates. Units are measured in pixels. A pixel is a monitor's smallest unit of resolution.
- A graphics context enables drawing. A **Graphics** object manages a graphics context by controlling how information is drawn. **Graphics** objects contain methods for drawing, font manipulation, color manipulation, etc.
- Class **Graphics** is an **abstract** class—**Graphics** objects cannot be instantiated.

- The **repaint** method requests a call to the **Component** class **update** method as soon as possible which in turn calls **paint**. The **repaint** method is frequently called by the programmer to force a call to **paint**. The **update** method is sometimes overridden for "smoothing" animations (i.e., reducing "flicker").
- **Graphics** method **drawString** takes three arguments—the string to be drawn, an *x* coordinate and a *y* coordinate. The **String** is drawn in the current color and font. The point (**x**, **y**) corresponds to the lower-left corner of the **String**.
- **Graphics** method **drawChars** takes five arguments—an array of characters, the starting subscript in the array, the number of characters to be drawn and the coordinates at which the characters should be displayed. The point (**x**, **y**) corresponds to the lower-left corner of the characters drawn.
- **Graphics** method **drawBytes** takes five arguments. The arguments are the same as method **drawChars** except that a **byte** array is passed as the first argument.
- Color constants and color methods are defined in the **Color** class. Every color is created from an RGB value (Red/Green/Blue). An RGB value is created from three integer or three floating-point parts. Each RGB part is either an integer value between 0 and 255 or a floating point value between 0.0 and 1.0. The first RGB part defines the amount of red; the second RGB part defines the amount of green; and the third part defines the amount of blue. The larger the RGB value; the greater the amount of that particular color.
- The **Color** methods **getRed**, **getGreen**, **getBlue** return integer values between 0 and 255 representing the amount of red, green, and blue respectively. The **Graphics** method **getColor** returns a **Color** object representing the current color. The **Graphics** method **setColor** sets the current color.
- Most font methods and font constants are part of the **Font** class. The **static** constants **PLAIN**, **BOLD**, and **ITALIC** are used to specify the font style and are defined in the **Font** class.
- The **Font** constructor takes three arguments—the font name, the font style and the font size in points.
- The **Graphics** method **setFont** sets the current font.
- The **Font** method **getStyle** returns an integer value representing the current style. The integer value returned is either **Font.PLAIN**, **Font.ITALIC**, **Font.BOLD**, or any combination of **Font.PLAIN**, **Font.ITALIC**, and **Font.BOLD**.
- The **Font** method **getSize** returns the font size. The integer value returned represents the size of the font in points. The **Font** method **getName** returns the current font name as a **String**.
- The **Font** method **getFamily** returns the name of the font family to which the current font belongs. The name of the font family is platform specific.

- The **Font** method **isPlain** returns **true** if the current font style is plain. The **isBold** method returns **true** if the current font style is bold. The **isItalic** method returns **true** if the current font style is italic.
- Font metrics include height, descent (the amount a character dips below the baseline), ascent (the amount a character rises above the baseline) and leading (the difference between the height and the ascent).
- Methods for getting font metrics are defined in the **FontMetric** class.
- The toolkit interacts between Java and the system to get information about the system. The **getDefaultToolkit** method is a **static** method of the **Toolkit** class. The **getDefaultToolkit** method gets the default toolkit for the current system (i.e., returns a **Toolkit** object). The **Toolkit** method **getFontList** returns the names of the system's available fonts.
- The **Graphics** method **drawLine** draws a line between the two specified points in the current color.
- The **Graphics** method **drawRect** draws a rectangle with the specified upper-left corner, width and height.
- The **Graphics** method **fillRect** draws a filled rectangle with the specified upper-left corner, width and height. The current color is used to fill the rectangle.
- The **Graphics** method **clearRect** draws a rectangle in the current background color over the specified rectangle.
- The **Graphics** method **drawRoundRect** draws a rectangle with rounded corners with the specified upper-left corner, width, height, arc width and arc height.
- The **Graphics** method **fillRoundRect** draws a filled rectangle with rounded corners with the specified upper-left corner, width, height, arc width and arc height. The current color is used to fill the rectangle.
- The **Graphics** method **draw3DRect** draws a three-dimensional rectangle and the **fill3DRect** method draws a filled three-dimensional rectangle. Both **draw3DRect** and **fill3DRect** take the same arguments. The last argument determines whether or not the rectangle is raised or lowered. A **true** value specifies that the rectangle is to be raised and a **false** value specifies that the rectangle is to be lowered.
- An arc is a portion of a circle. Arc angles in Java are measured in degrees. An arc is drawn between two angles—a starting angle and an arc angle. The starting angle is the degree where the arc begins. The arc angle is the last degree of the arc. The arc sweeps between the starting angle and the arc angle.
- Arcs that sweep in a counter-clockwise direction are measured in positive degrees. Arcs that sweep in a clockwise direction are measured in negative degrees.
- **Graphics** method **drawArc** draws an arc and the **fillArc** method draws a filled arc. Both the **drawArc** and **fillArc** methods take six arguments—the top-left corner *x* and *y* coordinates, the arc width, the arc height, the starting angle and the arc angle.

- *Polygons* are multi-sided shapes. A **Polygon** object is created with the **Polygon** class. One version of the **Graphics** method **drawPolygon** takes three arguments: an array of integers containing *x* coordinates, an array of integers containing *y* coordinates, and the number of points in the polygon. Specifying a last point different than the first point results in an *open polygon*—the last point is not connected to the first point. The other version of the **drawPolygon** method takes one **Polygon** object.
- Solid polygons or filled polygons are drawn with the **Graphics** method **fillPolygon** method. Filled polygons are always closed polygons—the last point does not have to match the first (i. e., the last point is always connected to the first point).
- The **Polygon** method **addPoint** adds a point to a polygon and takes two arguments—an *x* coordinate and a *y* coordinate.
- The **Graphics** method **copyArea** copies a rectangular area of the screen and draws the copied area on another area of the screen.
- A paint mode describes how graphics are drawn. The default paint mode is overwrite paint mode—when a shape is drawn, the shape overwrites anything beneath it. The other paint mode is XOR paint mode—which allows all shapes that overlap to be seen. XOR paint mode is set with the **Graphics** method **setXORMode**. The **setXORMode** method takes a **Color** object as an argument.

Terminology

addPoint method
angle
arc bounded by a rectangle
arc height
arc sweeping through an angle
arc width
ascent
awt hierarchy
awt package
background color
baseline
bounding rectangle
clearRect method
closed polygon
Color.black
Color.blue
Color.cyan
Color.darkGray
Color.gray
Color.green
Color.lightGray
Color.magenta
Color.orange
Color.pink
Color object
Component class
coordinate
coordinate system
copyArea method
current color
current font
degree
descent
draw3DRect method
drawArc method
drawBytes method
drawChars method
drawing arc
drawing bytes
drawing strings
drawLine method
drawOval method
drawRect method
drawPolygon method
drawPolyline method
drawRoundRect method
drawString method
event

`Color.red`
`Color.white`
`Color.yellow`
`Color` class
`Color` constructor
`fillPolygon` method
`fillRect` method
`fillRoundRect` method
`Font.BOLD`
`Font.ITALIC`
`Font.PLAIN`
font
`Font` class
`Font` constructor
font metrics
font name
font style
`FontMetrics` class
`getAscent` method
`getBlue` method
`getDescent` method
`getGreen` method
`getFamily` method
`getFont` method
`getFontList` method
`getFontMetrics` method
`getHeight` method
`getLeading` method
`getName` method
`getRed` method
`getSize` method
`getStyle` method
`Graphics` class
graphics context
graphics object
horizontal component
`isBold` method
event-driven process
`fill3DRect` method
`fillArc` method
filled polygon
`fillOval` method
`isItalic` method
`isPlain` method
leading
`Monospaced` font
negative degrees
open polygon
overwrite paint mode
`paint` method
paint mode
pixel
point
polygon
`Polygon` class
`Polygon` constructor
positive degrees
`repaint` method
RGB value
`SansSerif` font
`Serif` font
`setColor` method
`setFont` method
`setXORMode` method
solid polygons
toolkit
`Toolkit` class
`update` method
vertical component
x axis
x coordinate
XOR paint mode
y axis
y coordinate

Common Programming Errors

9.1 Passing an invalid array subscript to the **`drawChars`** or **`drawBytes`** method throws an **`ArraySubscriptOutOfBoundsException`**.

9.2 Spelling any **`static Color`** class constant with an initial capital letter is a syntax error.

9.3 It is a logic error if the number of points specified in the third argument to method **`drawPolygon`** or method **`fillPolygon`** is less than the number of elements in the arrays of coordinates that define the polygon to display.

9.4 An **`ArrayIndexOutOfBoundsException`** is thrown if the number of points specified in the third argument to method **`drawPolygon`** or method **`fillPolygon`** is greater than the number of elements in the arrays of coordinates that define the polygon to display.

Portability Tips

9.1 Different display monitors have different levels of resolution (i.e., the density of pixels vary).

9.2 The number of fonts varies greatly across systems. The JDK guarantees that the fonts **`Serif`**, **`Monospaced`**, **`SansSerif`**, **`Dialog`** and **`DialogInput`** will be available.

9.3 Java uses standardized font names and maps these into system-specific font names for portability. This is transparent to the programmer.

Software Engineering Observation

9.1 If a font is not available on a system, Java will substitute that system's default font.

Self-Review Exercises

9.1 Fill in the blanks in each of the following:

a) The return type of **`getName`** is __________.
b) A rectangular area of the screen can be copied with the __________ method.
c) The __________ method draws a line between two points.
d) RGB is short for __________, __________, and __________.
e) Font sizes are measured in units called __________.
f) The __________ method draws a series of bytes.

9.2 State which of the following statements are true and which are false. If a statement is false, explain why.

a) The first two arguments of **`drawOval( x, y, 50, 100 )`** specify the center coordinate of the oval.
b) In the Java coordinate system, *x* values increase from left to right.
c) The **`fillPolygon`** method draws a solid polygon in the current color.
d) The **`drawArc`** method allows negative angles.
e) The **`drawRoundRect`** method can be used to draw a circle.
f) The **`getSize`** method returns the size of the current font in centimeters.
g) The pixel coordinate (0, 0) is located at the exact center of the monitor.

9.3 Find the error(s) in each of the following and explain how to correct the error(s). Assume **g** is a **Graphics** object.

a)
```
char x[] = { '1', '2', '0', '2', '*', '*', 'P', 'C', 'M' };
g.drawChars( x, 6, 8, 435, 80 );   // draw chars PCM
```
b)
```
g.setFont( "SansSerif" );
```
c)
```
g.erase( x, y, w, h );    // clear rectangle at (x, y)
```
d)
```
Font fish = new Font( "Carp", Font.BOLDITALIC, 12 );
```
e)
```
g.setColor( Color.Yellow );   // change color to yellow
```

Answers to Self-Review Exercises

9.1 a) **String** b) **copyArea** c) **drawLine** d) red, green, blue e) points f) **drawBytes**

9.2
a) False. The first two arguments specify the upper-left corner of the rectangle.
b) True.
c) True.
d) True.
e) True.
f) False. Font sizes are measured in points.
g) False. The coordinate (0,0) corresponds to the upper-left corner of the monitor.

9.3
a) The last valid subscript is exceeded. The **drawChars** method attempts to draw eight characters—from the sixth subscript. The **8** should be changed to a **3**.
b) The **setFont** method takes a **Font** object as an argument—not a **String**.
c) The **Graphics** class does not have an **erase** method. The **clearRect** method should be used.
d) **Carp** is not a valid font. A font such as **Monospaced**, **Serif**, etc. should be used.
e) **Yellow** should begin with a lowercase letter: **g.setColor(Color.yellow);**.

Exercises

9.4 Fill in the blanks in each of the following:
a) The **getSize** method belongs to the __________ class.
b) The return type of **isBold** is __________.
c) The three constants that specify font style are __________, __________, and __________.
d) The __________ method returns an integer representing a color's RGB green value.

9.5 State which of the following statements are true and which are false. If a statement is false, explain why.
a) The **drawPolygon** method automatically connects the endpoints of the polygon.
b) The **drawLine** method draws a line between two points.
c) The **fillArc** method uses degrees to specify the angle.
d) In the Java coordinate system, *y* values increase from top to bottom.
e) The **Graphics** class inherits directly from class **Object**.
f) The **Graphics** class is an **abstract** class.
g) The **Font** class inherits directly from class **Graphics**.

9.6 Find the error(s) in each of the following. Explain how to correct the error(s).

a) `String listOfFonts[] = Toolkit.getFontList();`

b) `Toolkit.setXORMode( green );`

c) `String x = graphicsObject.getAscent();`

d) `Graphics myGraphics = new Graphics();`

9.7 Write a program that draws a series of eight concentric circles. The circles should be separated by 10 pixels. Use the **`drawRoundRect`** method.

9.8 Write a program that draws a series of eight concentric circles. The circles should be separated by 10 pixels. Use the **`drawArc`** method.

9.9 Write a program that uses the **`drawArc`** method to draw a spiral. Note: You will need multiple calls to **`drawArc`**.

9.10 Write a program that uses the **`drawPolygon`** method to draw a spiral.

9.11 Write a program that draws lines of random lengths.

9.12 Write a program that draws lines in random colors.

9.13 Write a program that combines the capabilities of the programs you wrote for Exercise 9.11 and Exercise 9.12.

9.14 Write a program that gets a list of fonts from your system and draws a 12-point bold string in each font.

9.15 Write a program that displays five triangles of different sizes. Each triangle should be filled with a different color.

9.16 Write a program that randomly draws characters in different font sizes.

9.17 Write a program that randomly draws characters in different colors.

9.18 Write a program that draws an 8-by-8 grid. Use the **`drawLine`** method.

9.19 Write a program that draws a 10-by-10 grid. Use the **`drawRect`** method.

9.20 Write a program that draws a tetrahedron (a pyramid) on the applet.

9.21 Write a program that draws a cube on the applet.

9.22 Modify the program of Fig. 9.18 to display each font name in that font. The program should also print the metrics for each font.

9.23 In Exercise 1.21, you wrote an applet that input the radius of a circle from the user and displayed the circle's diameter, circumference and area. Modify your solution to Exercise 1.21 to read a set of coordinates in addition to the radius. Then, draw the circle and display the circle's diameter, circumference and area.

9.24 Write an applet that simulates a screen saver. The applet should randomly draw lines. After drawing 100 lines, the applet should clear itself and start drawing lines again.

9.25 Modify your solution to Exercise 9.24 to enable the user to enter the number of random lines that should be drawn before the applet clears itself and starts drawing lines again. Use a text field to obtain the value. The user should be able to type a new number into the text field at any time during the program's execution.

9.26 Modify your solution to Exercise 9.25 to randomly choose different shapes to display.

9.27 Write a graphical version of your solution to Exercise 4.38—the *Towers of Hanoi.* After studying Chapter 14, you will be able to implement a version of this exercise using Java's image, animation and audio capabilities.

9.28 Modify the die-rolling program of Fig. 5.11 so that it updates the counts for each side of the die after each roll. Use `Graphics` method `drawString` to output the totals.

9.29 Modify your solution to Exercise 5.21—*Turtle Graphics*—to add a graphical user interface using text fields and buttons. Also, draw lines rather than drawing asterisks (`*`). When the turtle graphics program specifies a move, translate the number of positions into a number of pixels on the screen by multiplying the number of positions by 10 (or any value you choose).

9.30 Produce a graphical version of the Knight's Tour problem (Exercise 5.22, 5.23, 5.26). As each move is made, the appropriate cell of the chessboard should be updated with the proper move number. If the result of the program is a *full tour* or a *closed tour*, the program should display an appropriate message.

9.31 Produce a graphical version of the *Tortoise and the Hare* simulation (Exercise 5.41). Simulate the mountain by drawing an arc that extends from the bottom-left of the applet to the top-right of the applet. The tortoise and the hare should race up the mountain. Implement the graphical output so the tortoise and the hare are actually printed on the arc every move. Note: Extend the length of the race from 70 to 300 to allow yourself a larger graphics area.

9.32 Produce a graphical version of the Maze Traversal problem (Exercises 5.38-5.40). Use the mazes you produced as guides for creating the graphical versions. While the maze is being solved, a small circle should be displayed in the maze indicating the current position.

9.33 Produce a graphical version of the Bucket Sort (Exercise 5.28) that shows each value being placed into the appropriate bucket and eventually being copied back to the original array.

9.34 Write an applet that uses method `drawPolyline` to draw a spiral.

9.35 Write an applet that inputs four numbers and graphs the numbers as a pie chart. Use method `fillArc` to draw the pieces of the pie.

9.36 Write an applet that inputs four numbers and graphs the numbers as a bar graph. Use method `fillRect` to draw the bars in the chart.

10

Basic Graphical User Interface Components

Objectives

- To understand the design principles of graphical user interfaces.
- To be able to build graphical user interfaces.
- To understand the packages **`java.awt`** and **`java.awt.event`**.
- To be able to create and manipulate buttons, labels, lists, text fields and panels.
- To understand mouse events and keyboard events.
- To understand and be able to use layout managers.

… the wisest prophets make sure of the event first.
Horace Walpole

Do you think I can listen all day to such stuff?
Lewis Carroll

Speak the affirmative; emphasize your choice by utter ignoring of all that you reject.
Ralph Waldo Emerson

You pays your money and you takes your choice.
Punch

Guess if you can, choose if you dare.
Pierre Corneille

All hope abandon, ye who enter here!
Dante Alighieri

Exit, pursued by a bear.
William Shakespeare

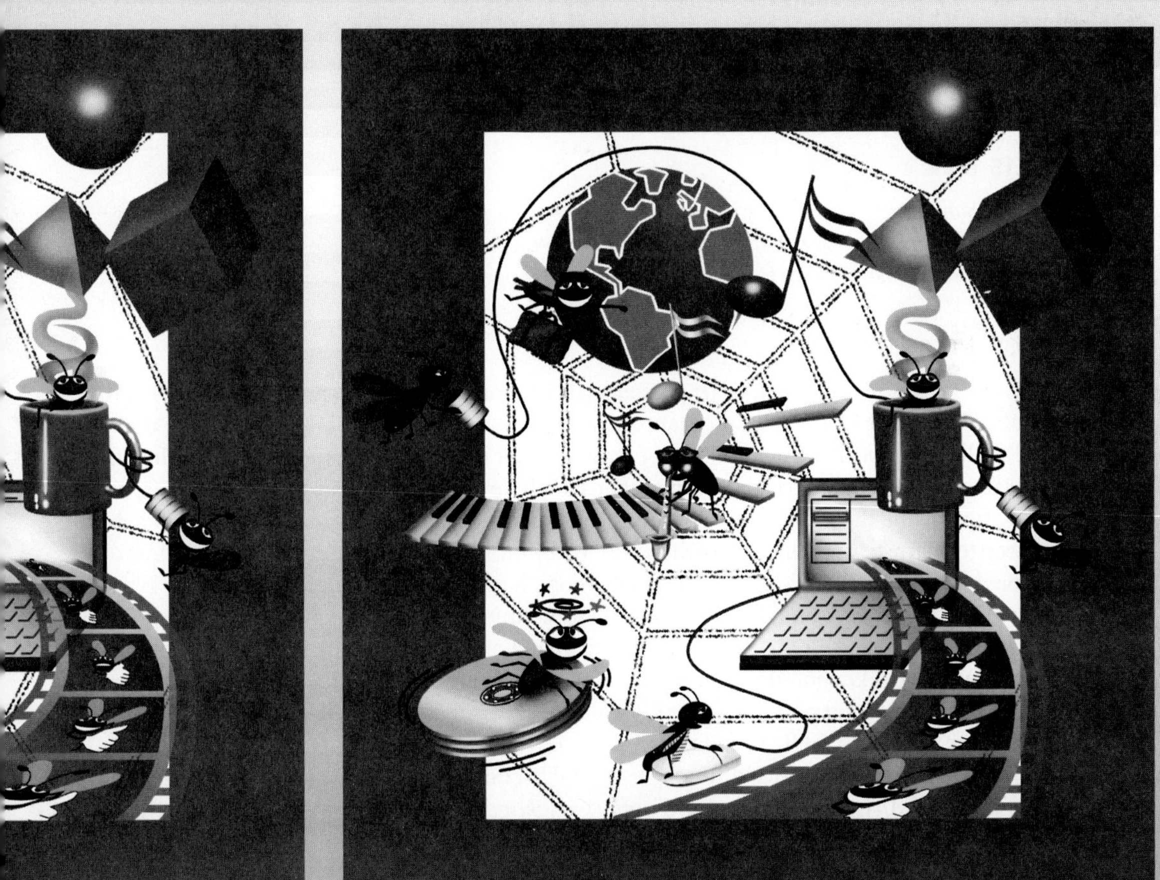

Outline

10.1 Introduction
10.2 Labels
10.3 Push Buttons
10.4 Text Fields
10.5 Choice Buttons
10.6 Checkboxes and Radio Buttons
10.7 Single-Selection Lists
10.8 Multiple-Selection Lists
10.9 Mouse Events
10.10 Mouse Event Adapter Classes
10.11 Keyboard Events
10.12 `FlowLayout` Layout Manager
10.13 `BorderLayout` Layout Manager
10.14 `GridLayout` Layout Manager
10.15 Panels

Summary • Terminology • Common Programming Errors • Good Programming Practices • Performance Tip • Portability Tip • Software Engineering Observation • Self-Review Exercises • Answers to Self-Review Exercises • Exercises

10.1 Introduction[1]

A *graphical user interface* (*GUI*) presents a pictorial interface to a program. A GUI (pronounced "GOO-EE") gives a program a distinctive "look" and "feel." By providing different applications with a consistent set of intuitive user interface components, GUIs allow the user to spend less time trying to remember which keystroke sequences do what and spend more time using the program in a productive manner. Consistent user interfaces also enable a user to learn new applications faster. Interaction between the user and the program is through the GUI. A GUI resembling a telephone keypad is shown in Fig. 10.1.

GUIs are built from *GUI components* (sometimes called *widgets*—shorthand notation for *window gadgets*). A GUI component is a visual object with which the user interacts via the mouse or the keyboard. Several GUI components are listed in Fig 10.2. In the sections that follow, we discuss each of these GUI components in detail. In the next chapter, we discuss more advanced GUI components.

The classes that are used to create the GUI components of Fig. 10.2 are part of the ***`java.awt`*** *(Abstract Windowing Toolkit) package*. Figure 10.3 shows the inheritance hierarchy for the components in Fig. 10.2 and additional classes from **`java.awt`** that are

1. This chapter was coauthored with Tem Nieto of Deitel & Associates, Inc.

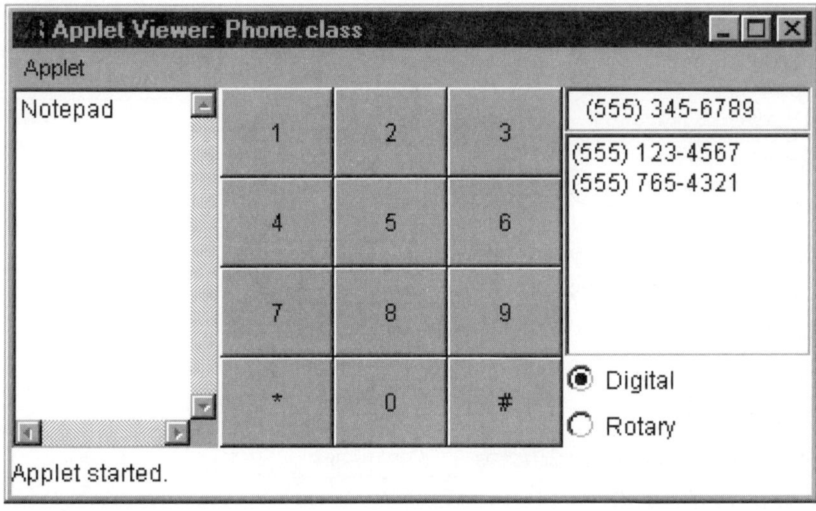

Fig. 10.1 A GUI resembling a telephone keypad.

covered in this chapter. The arrows indicate that the class "pointed from" **`extend`**s the class "pointed to." To effectively use GUI components, the ***`java.awt`*** inheritance hierarchy must be understood—especially class **`Component`** and class **`Container`**. Much of each GUI component's functionality is derived from one or both of these classes. A class that inherits from the **`Component`** class *is a component*. Class **`Label`** inherits from class **`Component`** and class **`Component`** inherits from **`Object`**. Thus, a **`Label`** is a **`Component`** and an **`Object`** but a **`Component`** is only an **`Object`**. A class that inherits from class **`Container`** *is a container*. A container is an area where components can be placed.

Component	Description
`Label`	An area where uneditable text can be displayed.
`Button`	An area that triggers an event when clicked.
`TextField`	An area in which the user inputs data from the keyboard. The area can also display information.
`Choice`	A drop-down list of items from which the user can make a selection by clicking on an item in the list.
`Checkbox`	A boolean GUI component that is either selected or not selected.
`List`	An area where a list of items is displayed from which the user can make a selection by clicking once on any element in the list. Double-clicking an element in the list generates an action event.
`Panel`	A container in which components can be placed.

Fig. 10.2 Basic GUI components.

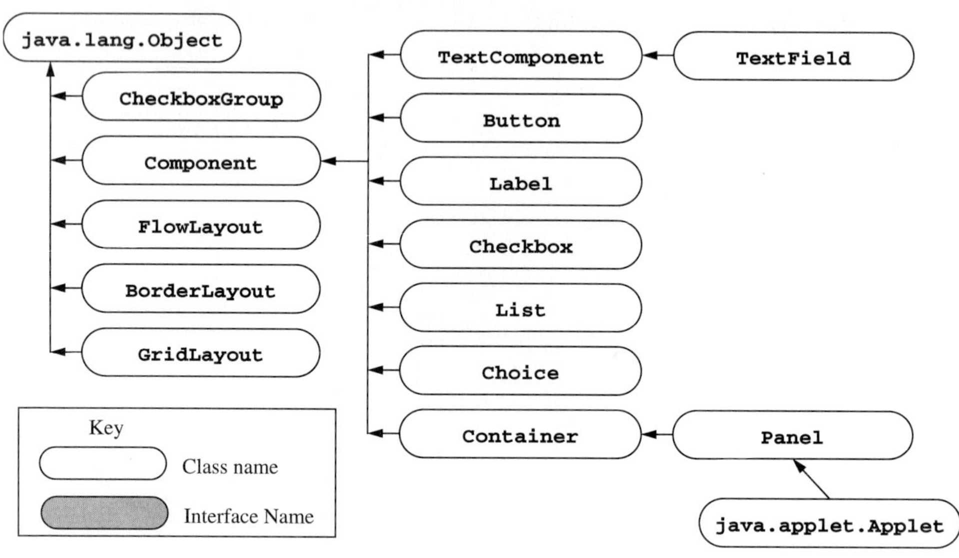

Fig. 10.3 A portion of the **`java.awt`** inheritance hierarchy.

Portability Tip 10.1

The look of a particular GUI component may vary across platforms. Java "ties" into the "local" GUI which varies from platform to platform.

Class **`Component`** defines the set of methods that can be applied to an object of any subclass of **`Component`**. Two of the methods that originate in class **`Component`** have been used frequently to this point in the text—**`paint`** and **`repaint`**. It is important to understand the methods of class **`Component`** because most of the functionality inherited by every subclass of **`Component`** is defined by the **`Component`** class originally. Operations common to all GUI components are found in class **`Component`**.

Good Programming Practice 10.1

Study the methods of class **`Component`** *in the Java Developer's Kit on-line documentation to learn the capabilities common to every GUI component.*

Class **`Container`** defines the set of methods that can be applied to an object of any subclass of **`Container`**. One method that originates in class **`Container`** that has been used frequently to this point in the text is **`add`** for adding components to an applet. Recall from Fig. 10.3 that **`Applet`** derives from class **`Panel`** and **`Panel`** derives from **`Container`**. Therefore, an **`Applet`** is a **`Container`**.

Good Programming Practice 10.2

Study the methods of class **`Container`** *in the Java Developer's Kit on-line documentation to learn the capabilities common to every container for GUI components.*

10.2 Labels

***Label*s** are used to provide text instructions or information on a GUI. A **Label** displays a single line of *read-only text*. Once **Label**s are created, programs rarely change a **Label**'s contents. Like other objects, a **Label** must be instantiated with a call to a constructor. Several **Label** constructors and methods are shown in Fig. 10.4.

The program of Fig. 10.5 creates two **Label**s and adds them to the applet. The first two **Label** constructors of Fig. 10.4 are used. The program also demonstrates methods ***setText*** and ***getText*** for setting and getting the text on a **Label**.

Class Label constructors and methods

```
public Label()
```

Constructs an empty **Label**—text is not displayed.

```
public Label( String s )            // label text
```

Constructs a **Label** that displays the text **s** with default left-justified alignment.

```
public Label( String s,             // label text
              int alignment )       // alignment
```

Constructs a **Label** that displays the text **s** with the specified **alignment**. Possible alignments are **Label.LEFT**, **Label.CENTER** and **Label.RIGHT**

```
public String getText()
```

Returns the **Label** text.

```
public void setText( String s )   // read-only string to display
```

Sets the **Label** text.

```
public void setAlignment( int alignment )   // alignment
```

Sets the **Label** alignment to **Label.LEFT**, **Label.CENTER** or **Label.RIGHT**

Fig. 10.4 Class **Label** constructors and methods.

```
// Fig. 10.5: MyLabel.java
// Demonstrating the Label class.
import java.applet.Applet;
import java.awt.*;

public class MyLabel extends Applet {
   private Label label1, label2;

   public void init()
   {
      // call label constructor with no text
      label1 = new Label();

```

Fig. 10.5 Demonstrating the **Label** class (part 1 of 2).

```
14         // set the label's text
15         label1.setText( "Started with no text" );
16 
17         // call label constructor with a string argument
18         label2 = new Label( "This is read-only text" );
19 
20         // add label components to applet container
21         add( label1 );
22         add( label2 );
23      }
24 
25      public void paint( Graphics g )
26      {
27         g.drawString( "label1's text is: " + label1.getText(),
28            25, 40 );
29         g.drawString( "label2's text is: " + label2.getText(),
30            25, 55 );
31      }
32   }
```

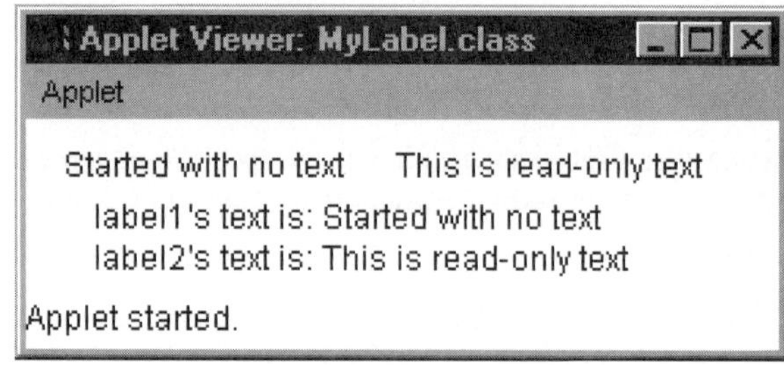

Fig. 10.5 Demonstrating the **Label** class (part 2 of 2).

The program declares two **Label** references with the line

```
private Label label1, label2;
```

Both **Label** objects are instantiated in the **init** method (line 9). The statement

```
label1 = new Label();
```

creates a **Label** object with no initial text. **Label** method **setText** can be used at a later point in the program to place text on the **Label** as shown in the statement

```
label1.setText( "Started with no text" );
```

The object **label2** is created with the statement

```
label2 = new Label( "This is read-only text" );
```

By default, all **Label** objects contain left-aligned text. A **Label**'s alignment can also be specified using the third constructor in Fig. 10.4 or using the **setAlignment** method after the **Label** is instantiated.

GUI components are only displayed when they have been added to a container using method **add** and the container is displayed on the screen. So far, all GUI components have been added directly to applets. Remember from Fig. 10.3 that class **Applet** is a **Container** and inherits all the public interface methods of class **Container** including method **add** for attaching GUI components to a **Container**. Thus, lines 21 and 22

```
add( label1 );
add( label2 );
```

add **label1** and **label2** to the applet.

Common Programming Error 10.1

Forgetting to add a component to a container is a run-time logic error.

Common Programming Error 10.2

*Adding to a container a component that has not been instantiated throws a **NullPointerException**.*

In method **paint** (line 25), the statements

```
g.drawString( "label1's text is: " + label1.getText(),
   25, 40 );
g.drawString( "label2's text is: " + label2.getText(),
   25, 55 );
```

use **Label** method **getText** to read the text from each **Label** and output the text.

10.3 Push Buttons

A *button* is a component the user clicks to trigger a specific action. A Java program can use three types of buttons: *push buttons*, *choice buttons* and *checkboxes*. We discuss choice buttons and checkboxes in later sections.

A push button generates a *button event* when the user clicks the button with the mouse. Push buttons are created with class **Button** that inherits from class **Component**. The text on the face of a **Button** is called a *button label*. A GUI can have many **Button**s, but each button label should be unique. **Button**s with the same labels are ambiguous to the user.

Common Programming Error 10.3

*Having more than one **Button** with the same label makes the **Button**s ambiguous to the user.*

Good Programming Practice 10.3

Provide a unique name for each button label.

In the previous section, we did not discuss event handling because there are no specific events for **Label** objects. GUIs are *event driven*, i.e., they generate events when the user interacts with the GUI. An *event* is an action initiated by the user of the program interacting with the GUI such as the user moving the mouse, clicking the mouse, clicking a button, etc.

Events are sent to a Java program by the underlying windowing system. Information about a GUI event is stored in an object of a class that extends **AWTEvent**. Figure 10.6 illustrates the hierarchy of event classes in package **java.awt.event**. Many of these event classes are discussed throughout this chapter and Chapter 11.

To process an event, the programmer must perform two key tasks—register an *event listener* and implement an *event handler*. An event listener is an object of a class that implements one or more of several event-listener interfaces from package **java.awt.event** shown in Fig. 10.7 (Note: A shaded background indicates an interface in the diagram). An event-listener object "listens" for specific types of events generated by other objects (normally GUI components) in a program. An event handler is a method that is automatically called in response to a particular type of event. Each event-listener interface provides one or more event-handling methods. If a class implements one or more of the event-listener interfaces, that class must provide a definition for every method of each implemented interface. The use of event listeners in event handling is known as the *delegation event model*—the processing of an event is delegated to a particular object in the program.

Most of the components of Fig. 10.2 generate specific types of events. We discuss the event handling for each component as it is introduced.

The applet of Fig. 10.8 creates two **Button**s and adds them to the applet. Event-handling code is provided by the class **Button1Handler** and class **Button2Handler** (lines 25 and 37, respectively).

The statement

```
private Button pushButton1, pushButton2;
```

creates two **Button** references. Lines 13 and 18

```
pushButton1 = new Button( "Button 1" );
pushButton2 = new Button( "Button 2" );
```

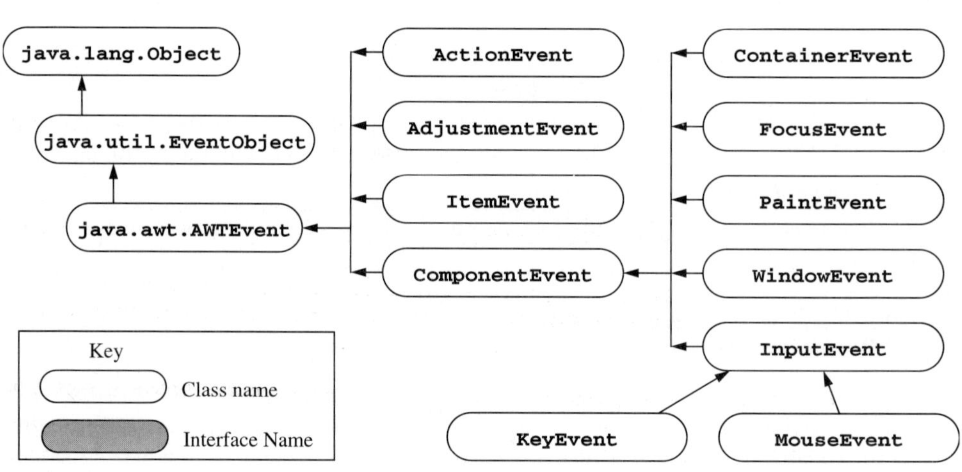

Fig. 10.6 Event classes of package **java.awt.event**.

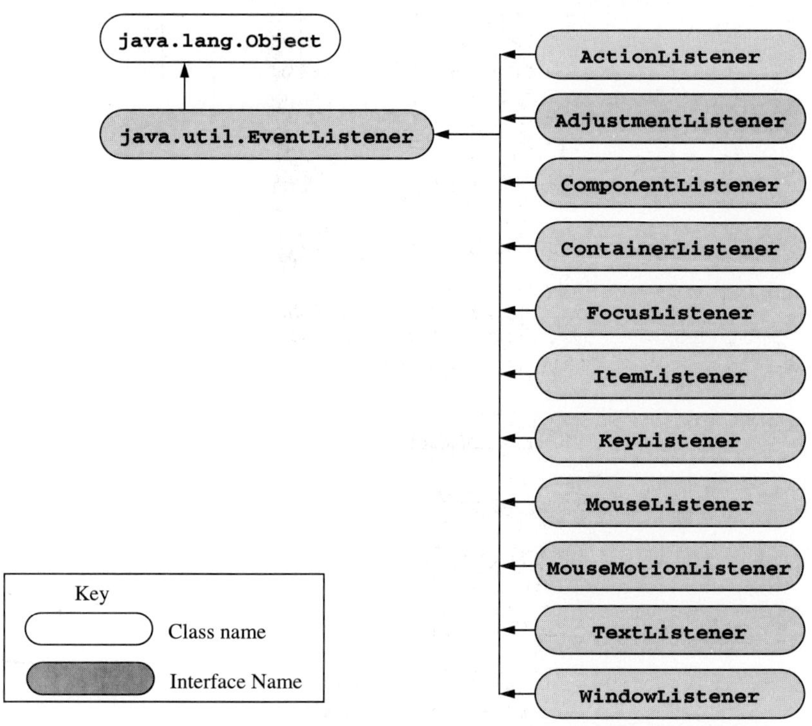

Fig. 10.7 Event-listener interfaces of package **`java.awt.event`**.

```
// Fig. 10.8: MyButtons.java
// Creating push buttons.
import java.applet.Applet;
import java.awt.*;
import java.awt.event.*;

public class MyButtons extends Applet {
   private Button pushButton1, pushButton2;

   public void init()
   {
      // create buttons
      pushButton1 = new Button( "Button 1" );
      pushButton1.addActionListener(
         new Button1Handler( this ) );
      add( pushButton1 );

      pushButton2 = new Button( "Button 2" );
      pushButton2.addActionListener(
         new Button2Handler( this ) );
```

Fig. 10.8 Demonstrating push buttons and action events (part 1 of 2).

```
      add( pushButton2 );
   }
}

class Button1Handler implements ActionListener {
   Applet applet;

   public Button1Handler( Applet a ) { applet = a; }

   public void actionPerformed( ActionEvent e )
   {
      applet.showStatus( "You pressed: " +
         e.getActionCommand() );
   }
}

class Button2Handler implements ActionListener {
   Applet applet;

   public Button2Handler( Applet a ) { applet = a; }

   public void actionPerformed( ActionEvent e )
   {
      applet.showStatus( "You pressed: " +
         e.paramString() );
   }
}
```

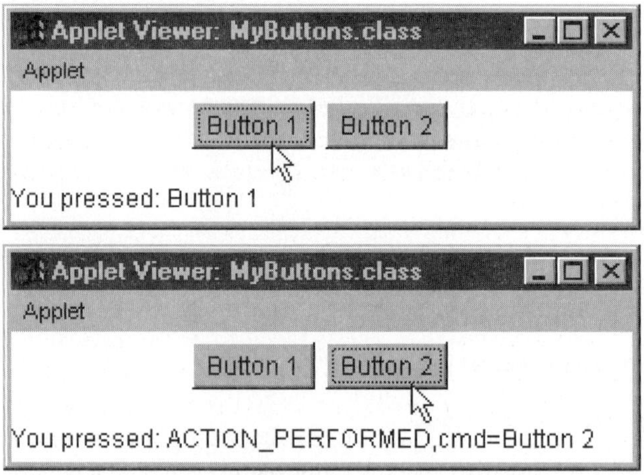

Applet Viewer: MyButtons.class
Applet
Button 1 Button 2
You pressed: Button 1

Applet Viewer: MyButtons.class
Applet
Button 1 Button 2
You pressed: ACTION_PERFORMED,cmd=Button 2

Fig. 10.8 Demonstrating push buttons and action events (part 2 of 2).

instantiate **pushButton1** and **pushButton2**. The string passed to the **Button** constructor is used as the button label.

Buttons generate "action" events. An action event can be processed by any **ActionListener** object (an object of any class that implements interface **ActionListener**). Such a class provides a definition of method **actionPerformed**. Once an

ActionListener object is registered to "handle" an action event, method **actionPerformed** is called automatically whenever an action event occurs. Lines 14 and 19

```
pushButton1.addActionListener(
   new Button1Handler( this ) );
pushButton2.addActionListener(
   new Button2Handler( this ) );
```

register an **ActionListener** object for each **Button**. If an event listener is not registered for a particular GUI component, then no events are handled for that component. Method **addActionListener** can be found in every GUI component class that generates action events. In this program, action events for **pushButton1** are handled by a **Button1Handler** object and action events for **pushButton2** are handled by a **Button2Handler** object. Each class receives a reference to the applet as an argument to its constructor. This enables each event listener to use the applet's **showStatus** method to display strings in the browser status bar.

Common Programming Error 10.4

Forgetting to register an event-handler object for a particular GUI component results in no events being handled for that component.

Performance Tip 10.1

The event-handling mechanism of Java 1.1 is much more efficient than the event-handling mechanism of Java 1.0. In Java.1.0, all events were sent into the program, even if they were not handled, resulting in many extraneous method calls to event-handling methods. In Java 1.1, only events for which an event-handler object is registered are delivered to the program.

When a **Button** is clicked, method **actionPerformed** of the registered event-listener object is called. Method **actionPerformed** receives an **ActionEvent** object as an argument. The **ActionEvent** contains specific information about the action event that occurred.

Method **actionPerformed** (line 30) in class **Button1Handler** uses method **getActionCommand** of class **ActionEvent** to obtain a **String** containing the label from the button that generated the event.

Method **actionPerformed** (line 42) in class **Button2Handler** uses method **paramString** of class **AWTEvent** (the superclass of **ActionEvent**) to obtain a **String** containing the event ID and the label from the button that generated the event. In the case of an action event, the event ID is **ACTION_PERFORMED** (a **static** integer constant from class **ActionEvent**). See the status bar in each output window in Fig. 10.8 for the results after each button is pressed.

Using a separate class to define an event listener is a common programming practice for separating the GUI interface from the implementation of its event handler. For the remainder of this chapter and Chapter 11, many programs use separate event-listener classes to process GUI events in an attempt to make the code more reusable. Any class that has potential for reuse beyond the example in which the class is introduced has been placed in a package so it can be imported into other programs for reuse.

Good Programming Practice 10.4

Use separate classes to process GUI events.

Software Engineering Observation 10.1

Using separate classes to handle common GUI events leads to more reusable software components that can be placed in packages and used in many programs.

10.4 Text Fields

TextField**s* are single-line areas in which text can be entered by the user from the keyboard or text can simply be displayed. When the user types data into a **TextField** and presses the *Enter* key, an action event is generated. If an event listener is registered for the **TextField**, the event is processed and the data in the **TextField** can be used in the program. Class **TextField** extends class ***TextComponent. Figure 10.9 summarizes the constructors and several methods of class **TextField**.

Common Programming Error 10.5

*Using a lowercase **f** in **TextField** is a syntax error.*

The program of Fig. 10.10 uses class **TextField** to create and manipulate four **TextField**s.

Class TextField constructors and methods

```
public TextField()
```

Constructs a **TextField** object.

```
public TextField( int columns )   // number of columns
```

Constructs an empty **TextField** object with the specified number of columns.

```
public TextField( String s )      // text displayed in TextField
```

Constructs a **TextField** object displaying **s**.

```
public TextField( String s,       // text displayed in TextField
                  int columns ) // number of columns
```

Constructs a **TextField** object displaying **s** in the specified number of columns.

```
public void setEchoChar( char c )  // character to echo
```

Sets the character to be displayed as the user types in the **TextField**. This is particularly useful for disguising a typed in passwords

```
public void setEditable( boolean b ) // true == editable
```

Sets the editability of the **TextField**, **true** is editable, **false** is uneditable.

Fig. 10.9 Class **TextField** constructors and methods.

```
1  // Fig. 10.10: MyTextfield.java
2  // Demonstrating the TextField class.
3  import java.applet.Applet;
4  import java.awt.*;
5  import java.awt.event.*;
6
7  public class MyTextfield extends Applet {
8     private TextField text1, text2, text3, text4;
9     private TextFieldHandler handler;
10
11    public void init()
12    {
13       setBackground( Color.lightGray );
14
15       // setup handler object
16       handler = new TextFieldHandler( this );
17
18       // construct textfield with default sizing
19       text1 = new TextField();
20       text1.addActionListener( handler );
21       add( text1 );
22
23       // construct TextField with default text
24       text2 = new TextField( "Enter text here" );
25       text2.addActionListener( handler );
26       add( text2 );
27
28       // construct textfield with default text
29       text3 = new TextField( "Hidden text" );
30       text3.setEchoChar( '*' );
31       text3.addActionListener( handler );
32       add( text3 );
33
34       // construct textfield with default text and
35       // 40 visible elements and no event handler
36       text4 = new TextField( "Uneditable text field", 40 );
37       text4.setEditable( false );
38       add( text4 );
39    }
40 }
```

Fig. 10.10 Program that demonstrates **`TextField`**s (part 1 of 2).

Line 16 in the applet's **`init`** method

```
handler = new TextFieldHandler( this );
```

creates an event-listener object for the **`TextField`**s in this example. The argument to the constructor is a reference to the applet so the event listener can use applet method **`showStatus`** to display information when an action event is generated in one of the **`TextField`**s. After the **`TextField`**s **`text1`**, **`text2`** and **`text3`** are instantiated, the event listener **`handler`** is registered (lines 20, 25 and 31) to handle the action events.

```
class TextFieldHandler implements ActionListener {
   private Applet applet;

   public TextFieldHandler( Applet a ) { applet = a; }

   public void actionPerformed( ActionEvent e )
   {
      applet.showStatus( "Text is: " +
         e.getActionCommand() );
   }
}
```

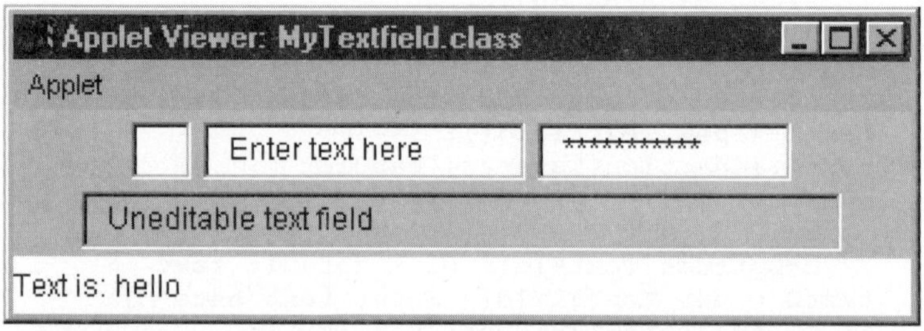

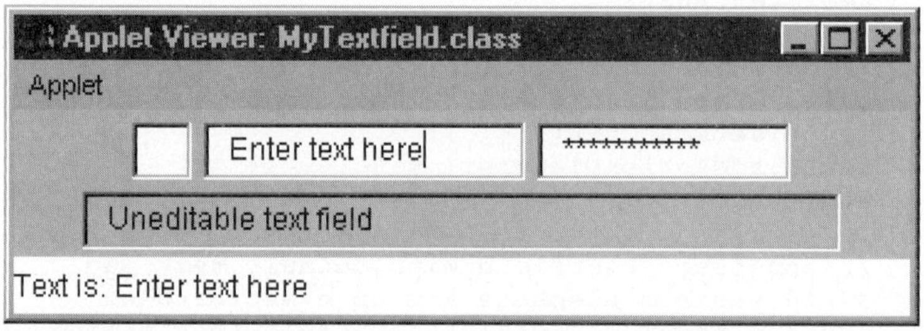

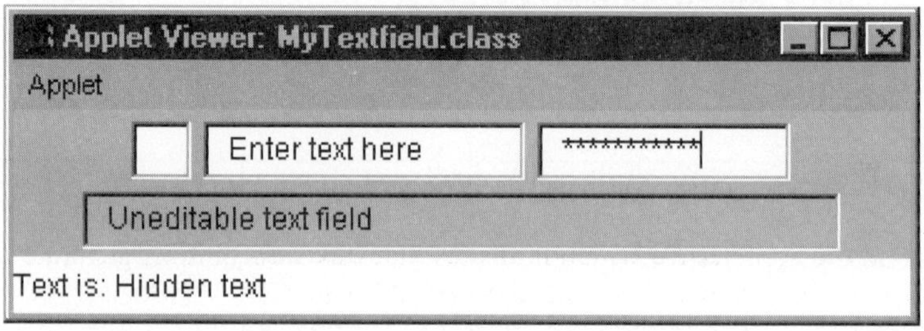

Fig. 10.10 Program that demonstrates **TextField**s (part 2 of 2).

The **TextField** object **text1** is instantiated with the statement

```
text1 = new TextField();
```

at line 19. The **TextField** created does not display any text and has a default size. It is difficult to see text in this **TextField** because it is so small. However, the user can still enter information and cause action events by pressing *Enter* in the **TextField**.

Object **text2** is instantiated with the statement

```
text2 = new TextField( "Enter text here: " );
```

at line 24. The number of visible columns is the minimum required to display the default text. The size of a column is the average width of a character in the current font. The arrow keys can be used to scroll through any **TextField** regardless of the number of columns.

Object **text3** is instantiated with the statement

```
text3 = new TextField( "Hidden text" );
```

at line 29. **TextField** method **setEchoChar** (line 30) is used to set the masking character displayed in **text3** in place of each character in the string. This is particularly useful for sensitive information such as passwords. Notice that only asterisks (*****) are displayed.

Object **text4** is instantiated (line 36) with 40 visible columns and displays the text "**Uneditable text field**." **TextField** method **setEditable** (line 37) is used with a **false** argument to prevent the user from entering text in the **TextField**. An uneditable **TextField** uses its container's background color in the **TextField** to indicate that the **TextField** is uneditable. The first line of method **init** sets the background color to light gray to illustrate this feature.

The **TextField**s are added to the applet with the **Component** method **add**. When the user presses *Return* in any of the first three **TextField**s the **handler** event listener (implemented by class **TextFieldHandler** at line 42) uses **ActionEvent** method **getActionCommand** to get the text in the **TextField** that generated the event and display the text in the browser's status bar.

The first output window illustrates the applet after the user typed "**hello**" in the first **TextField** and pressed *Enter*. Note that the **TextField** is so small that you cannot see the text the user typed. The second output window illustrates the applet after the user typed pressed *Enter* in the second **TextField**. The third output window illustrates the applet after the user typed pressed *Enter* in the third **TextField**.

10.5 Choice Buttons

A ***Choice*** *button* (sometimes called a *drop-down list*) provides a list of items from which the user can make a selection. Class **Choice** that inherits from class **Component** and implements **ItemSelectable** which indicates that **Choice** buttons generate *item events* (i.e., an item can be selected from a **Choice**). All **Choice** objects are also **ItemSelectable** objects. The **Choice** class constructor takes no arguments. Some common methods of class **Choice** are listed in Fig. 10.11.

The program of Fig. 10.12 uses a **Choice** to provide a list of three fonts. When a font is selected, the text in a **TextField** is changed to that font and a string containing the selected item's index and the font name is displayed in the **TextField**. The program uses some methods from Fig. 10.11.

Common methods of class `Choice`

`public String getItem( int index )`

Returns the **`Choice`** item at index.

`public synchronized void add( String s )`

Adds an item to a **`Choice`** button.

`public synchronized String getSelectedItem()`

Returns the selected **`Choice`** item.

`public int getSelectedIndex()`

Returns the index of the selected **`Choice`** item.

`public synchronized String insert( String s, int index )`

Inserts a new item at the specified index of the **`Choice`**.

`public synchronized void remove( String s )`

Removes the first occurrence of the specified string from the **`Choice`**.

Fig. 10.11 Common methods of class **`Choice`**.

```
// Fig. 10.12: MyChoice.java
// Using a Choice button to select a font.
import java.applet.Applet;
import java.awt.*;
import java.awt.event.*;
import com.deitel.jhtp2.ch10.FontNameHandler;

public class MyChoice extends Applet {
   private Choice fonts;
   private TextField t;

   public void init()
   {
      // Create a Choice button and add items to it
      fonts = new Choice();
      fonts.add( "Monospaced" );  // Courier
      fonts.add( "SansSerif" );   // Helvetica
      fonts.add( "Serif" );       // Times

      t = new TextField( fonts.getItem( 0 ), 30 );
      t.setEditable( false );
      t.setFont( new Font( fonts.getItem( 0 ),
         Font.PLAIN, 12 ) );

      fonts.addItemListener( new FontNameHandler( t ) );
      fonts.addItemListener( new SetTextFieldHandler( t ) );

```

Fig. 10.12 Program that uses a **`Choice`** button to select a font (part 1 of 4).

```
28         add( fonts );
29         add( t );
30      }
31   }
32
33   class SetTextFieldHandler implements ItemListener {
34      private TextField field;
35
36      public SetTextFieldHandler( TextField t ) { field = t; }
37
38      public void itemStateChanged( ItemEvent e )
39      {
40         Choice choice = (Choice) e.getItemSelectable();
41
42         field.setText( "Index: " + choice.getSelectedIndex() +
43            "; Font: " + e.getItem() );
44      }
45   }
```

Fig. 10.12 Program that uses a **Choice** button to select a font (part 2 of 4).

```
46   // Fig. 10.12: FontNameHandler.java
47   // Class capable of listening for events from a Choice
48   // or List object and setting the font on the specified
49   // Component passed to the constructor.
50   package com.deitel.jhtp2.ch10;
51   import java.awt.*;
52   import java.awt.event.*;
53
54   public class FontNameHandler implements ItemListener {
55      private Component component;
56
57      public FontNameHandler( Component c ) { component = c; }
58
59      public void itemStateChanged( ItemEvent e )
60      {
61         component.setFont( new Font( e.getItem().toString(),
62            component.getFont().getStyle(),
63            component.getFont().getSize() ) );
64      }
65   }
```

Fig. 10.12 Program that uses a **Choice** button to select a font (part 3 of 4).

Line 15

```
fonts = new Choice();
```

creates a **Choice** object. Items are added to the **Choice** with **Choice** method ***add***. that inserts a single **String** item at the end of the **Choice**. A numeric *index* keeps track of the ordering of items. The first item is added at index 0; the next item is added at index 1, and so forth. The first item added to a **Choice** appears as the currently selected item when the **Choice** is displayed. Other items are selected by clicking the **Choice**. When clicked, the **Choice** expands into a list from which the user can make a selection.

When the **TextField** is created (line 20), the call **fonts.getItem(0)** retrieves the first string in the **Choice** to initialize the text in the **TextField**. Then, the **TextField** is set as uneditable by the user. Line 22

```
t.setFont( new Font( fonts.getItem( 0 ),
   Font.PLAIN, 12 ) );
```

sets the **TextField** font by creating a new **Font** object using the item at index 0, which is **"Monospaced"**. The font is set for the **TextField** with **Component** method **setFont**.

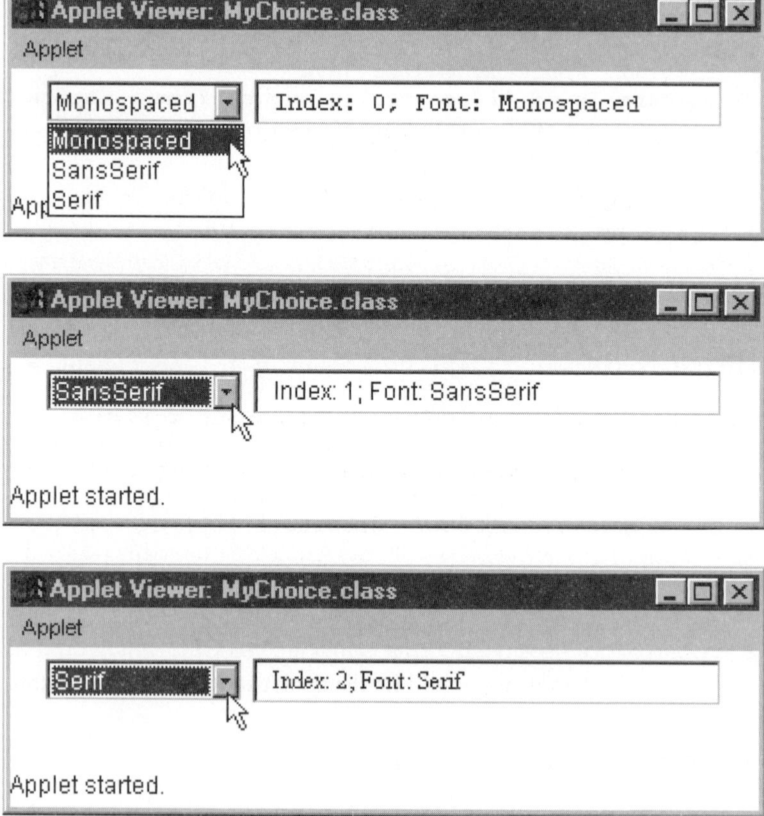

Fig. 10.12 Program that uses a **Choice** button to select a font (part 4 of 4).

Lines 25 and 26

```
fonts.addItemListener( new FontNameHandler( t ) );
fonts.addItemListener( new SetTextFieldHandler( t ) );
```

add two separate listener objects to the **fonts** object. A **Choice** generates an item event when an item is selected by the user. Item events are handled by event listeners that implement the **ItemListener** interface. Method **itemStateChanged** is the only method in this interface. The method receives an **ItemEvent** object as its argument. In this example, classes **FontNameHandler** (line 46) and **SetTextFieldHandler** (line 33) in the statements above both implement **ItemListener**. When an item event occurs on **fonts**, both registered event listeners are executed. Note that the registered event listeners can be called in any order. The **SetTextFieldHandler** object uses the reference to **TextField t** to set the text in the **TextField**. The **FontNameHandler** object uses the reference to **TextField t** to set the font in the **TextField**.

The **SetTextFieldHandler**'s **itemStateChanged** method (line 38) uses the statement

```
Choice choice = (Choice) e.getItemSelectable();
```

to get the actual **Choice** object that generated the item event. Class **ItemEvent** contains method **getItemSelectable** to get the **ItemSelectable** object that generated the item event.

Notice that class **FontNameHandler** is defined as a public class in a separate file. This class has been specifically designed for reuse. Its constructor receives a reference to any **Component**. This allows a **FontNameHandler** event listener to set the font on any **Component** in response to an item event. When a **FontNameHandler** is registered to listen for item events, the listener automatically sets the font on the specified **Component** using the statement

```
component.setFont( new Font( e.getItem().toString(),
   component.getFont().getStyle(),
   component.getFont().getSize() ) );
```

at line 61. The first argument to the **Font** constructor uses **ItemEvent** method **getItem** to get the item selected by the user. The second and third arguments both use **Component** method **getFont** to get the **component**'s current font. Then, **Font** methods **getStyle** and **getSize** are used to determine the style and size of the font, respectively. Class **FontNameHandler** is placed in package **com.deitel.jhtp2.ch10** (line 50) for reuse purposes. This class is imported into the applet so it can be used in this example.

10.6 Checkboxes and Radio Buttons

Class ***Checkbox*** is used to create *checkboxes* and *radio buttons*. These are *state buttons* (i.e., buttons that have on/off or true/false values) that generate item events. Radio buttons are sets of **Checkbox**es that are related by a **CheckboxGroup**. Only one **Checkbox** in a **CheckboxGroup** can be selected at a time. We first discuss **Checkbox**es.

Class **Checkbox** inherits from class **Component** and implements **ItemSelectable**. Two **Checkbox** class constructors and a **CheckboxGroup** constructor are summarized in Fig. 10.13.

The program of Fig. 10.14 uses two **Checkbox** objects to change the font style of the text displayed in a **TextField**. One **Checkbox** applies a bold style when selected and the other applies an italic style when selected. If both are selected, the style of the font is bold/italic. When the program is initially executed, neither **Checkbox** is checked.

Checkbox and CheckboxGroup constructors

```
public Checkbox( String s )
```

Constructs a **Checkbox** object with label **s**. The **Checkbox** object is initially unchecked.

```
public Checkbox(
   String s,           // radio button label
   CheckboxGroup c,    // CheckboxGroup owning radio button
   boolean state )     // state of radio button
```

Constructs a single radio button with the label **s** and the **boolean state**. The radio button is added to the existing **CheckboxGroup c**. If **c** is **null**, this constructor creates a normal **Checkbox** object with the specified **state**.

```
public CheckboxGroup()
```

Constructs a **CheckboxGroup** object.

Fig. 10.13 **Checkbox** and **CheckboxGroup** constructors.

```
// Fig. 10.14: MyCheckbox.java
// Creating Checkbox buttons.
import java.applet.Applet;
import java.awt.*;
import java.awt.event.*;

public class MyCheckbox extends Applet implements ItemListener {
   private TextField t;
   private Checkbox bold, italic;

   public void init()
   {
      t = new TextField( "Watch the font style change", 40 );
      t.setFont( new Font( "Serif", Font.PLAIN, 14 ) );
      add( t );

      // create checkbox objects
      bold = new Checkbox( "Bold" );
      bold.addItemListener( this );
      add( bold );
```

Fig. 10.14 Program that creates a set of two **Checkbox** buttons (part 1 of 3).

```

      italic = new Checkbox( "Italic" );
      italic.addItemListener( this );
      add( italic );
   }

   public void itemStateChanged( ItemEvent e )
   {
      // test state of each Checkbox
      int valBold =
         ( bold.getState() ? Font.BOLD : Font.PLAIN );
      int valItalic =
         ( italic.getState() ? Font.ITALIC : Font.PLAIN );

      t.setFont(
         new Font( "Serif", valBold + valItalic, 14 ) );
   }
}
```

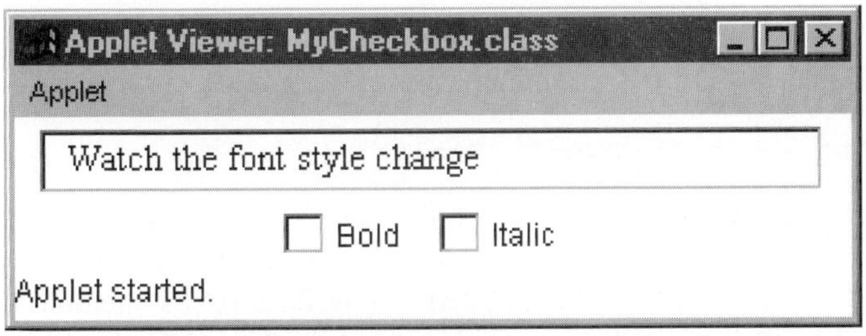

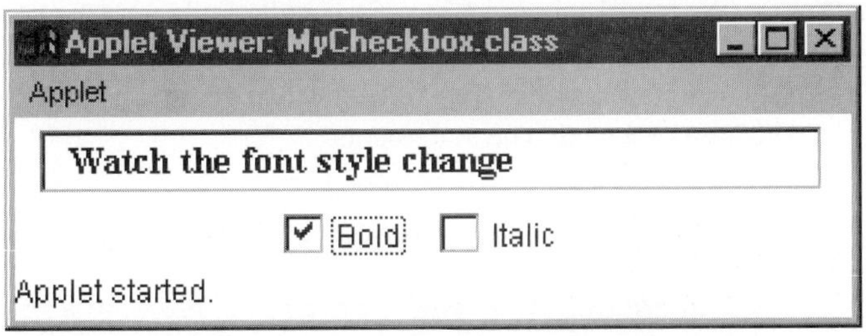

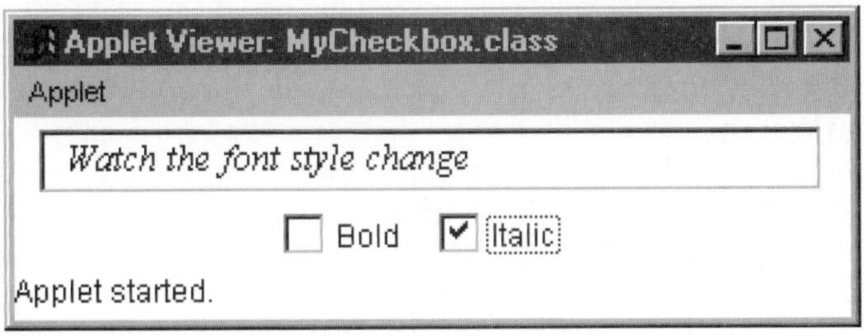

Fig. 10.14 Program that creates a set of two **Checkbox** buttons (part 2 of 3).

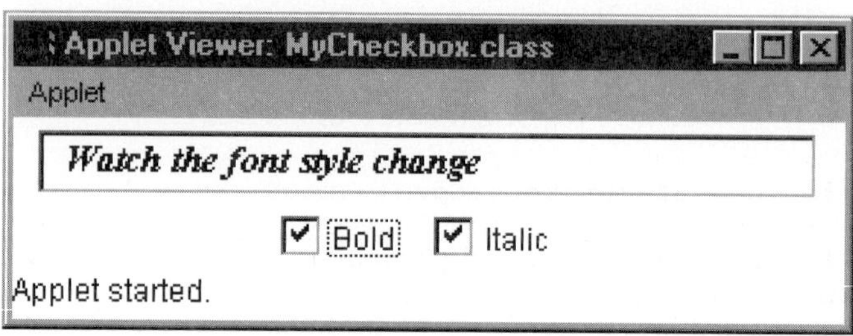

Fig. 10.14 Program that creates a set of two **Checkbox** buttons (part 3 of 3).

After the **TextField** is created and initialized, the **init** method creates two **Checkbox** objects. Object **bold** is constructed with line 18

```
bold = new Checkbox( "Bold" );
```

The **String** passed to the constructor is the *checkbox label* that appears to the right of **Checkbox**. Object **italic** is instantiated and given a label with line 22

```
italic = new Checkbox( "Italic" );
```

Before each **Checkbox** is added to the applet, the applet uses method **addItemListener** (lines 19 and 23) to register itself as the **ItemListener** for each **Checkbox**. The applet implements the **ItemListener** interface so its method **itemStateChanged** can be called when the user clicks one of the **Checkbox**es.

The **itemStateChanged** method (line 27) is called when a **Checkbox** object is clicked. In this program, we do not need to know which **ItemSelectable** generates the item event. We simply need to know the state of each **Checkbox** so we can determine the style of the font in the **TextField**. The statements

```
int valBold =
   ( bold.getState() ? Font.BOLD : Font.PLAIN );
int valItalic =
   ( italic.getState() ? Font.ITALIC : Font.PLAIN );
```

use conditional operations to determine the state of the **bold** and **italic** **Checkbox**es. **Checkbox** method **getState** returns a **boolean** representing a **Checkbox**'s state. Once the state of each **Checkbox** is determined, the sum of **valBold** and **valItalic** is used as the style of the new font used to set the **TextField**'s display font.

Checkboxes can also be grouped together to form *radio buttons*—a group of buttons where only one button in the group can be **true** and selecting that button forces all other buttons in the group to be **false** (i.e., unchecked). A set of radio buttons is created with a ***CheckboxGroup*** object and several **Checkbox** objects. Class **CheckboxGroup** inherits directly from class **Object** and is not a **Component**. Thus, **CheckboxGroup** objects *cannot be added to a container*. Remember that only objects of classes derived from **Component** can be added to a container. The three argument **Checkbox** constructor used to create radio buttons and the **CheckboxGroup** constructor were summarized in Fig. 10.13.

Common Programming Error 10.1

Using an uppercase **b** *for box in* **Checkbox** *or* **CheckboxGroup** *is a syntax error.*

Common Programming Error 10.2

Adding a **CheckboxGroup** *object (or an object of any other class that does not derive from* **Component***) to a container is a syntax error.*

The program of Fig. 10.15 is similar to the previous program. The user can alter the font style of a **TextField**'s text. The program uses radio buttons that permit only a single **Checkbox** in the group to be selected at a time.

```
// Fig. 10.15: RadioButton.java
// Creating radio buttons using CheckboxGroup and Checkbox.
import java.applet.Applet;
import java.awt.*;
import java.awt.event.*;

public class RadioButton extends Applet
             implements ItemListener {
   private TextField t;
   private Font plainFont, boldFont, italicFont,boldItalicFont;
   private CheckboxGroup fontStyle;
   private Checkbox plain, bold, italic, boldItalic;

   public void init()
   {
      t = new TextField( "Watch the font style change", 40 );
      add( t );

      // Create CheckboxGroup to maintain radio buttons
      fontStyle = new CheckboxGroup();

      plain = new Checkbox( "Plain", fontStyle, true );
      plain.addItemListener( this );
      add( plain );
      bold = new Checkbox( "Bold", fontStyle, false );
      bold.addItemListener( this );
      add( bold );
      italic = new Checkbox( "Italic", fontStyle, false );
      italic.addItemListener( this );
      add( italic );
      boldItalic = new Checkbox( "Bold/Italic",
                                 fontStyle, false );
      boldItalic.addItemListener( this );
      add( boldItalic );
```

Fig. 10.15 Creating and manipulating radio buttons (part 1 of 3).

```java

      plainFont = new Font( "Serif", Font.PLAIN, 14 );
      boldFont = new Font( "Serif", Font.BOLD, 14 );
      italicFont = new Font( "Serif", Font.ITALIC, 14 );
      boldItalicFont = new Font( "Serif",
                                 Font.BOLD + Font.ITALIC, 14 );
      t.setFont( plainFont );
   }

   public void itemStateChanged( ItemEvent e )
   {
      if ( e.getSource() == plain )
         t.setFont( plainFont );
      else if ( e.getSource() == bold )
         t.setFont( boldFont );
      else if ( e.getSource() == italic )
         t.setFont( italicFont );
      else if ( e.getSource() == boldItalic )
         t.setFont( boldItalicFont );
   }
}
```

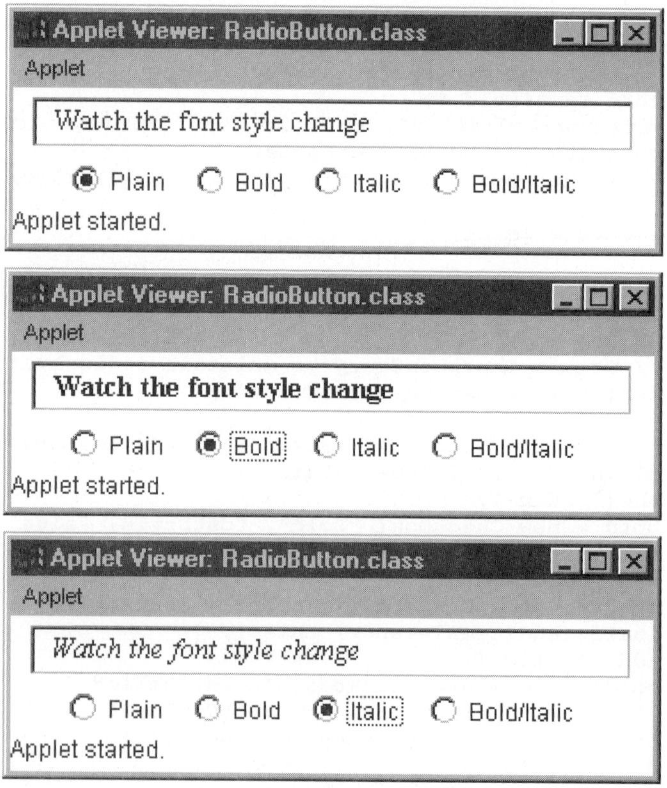

Fig. 10.15 Creating and manipulating radio buttons (part 2 of 3).

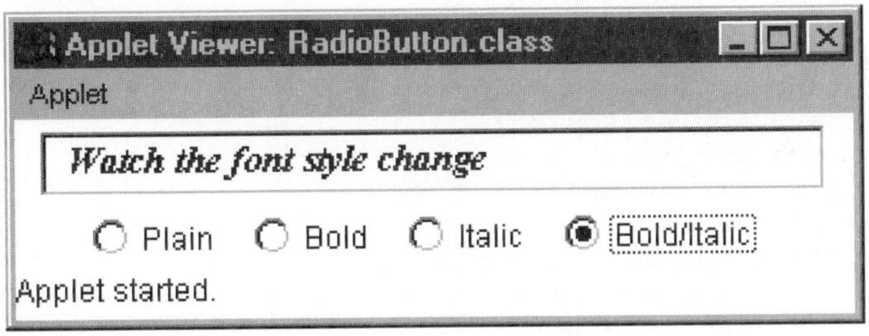

Fig. 10.15 Creating and manipulating radio buttons (part 3 of 3).

Line 11

```
private CheckboxGroup fontStyle;
```

creates a reference to a **CheckboxGroup** named **fontStyle**. The statement at line 20

```
fontStyle = new CheckboxGroup();
```

in **init** instantiates **fontStyle** that is the "glue" that binds the four **Checkbox**es together to form radio buttons. Each **Checkbox** is instantiated with a statement like line 22

```
plain = new Checkbox( "Plain", fontStyle, true );
```

that creates **Checkbox plain** and associates it with the **fontStyle** group. The third argument to this constructor call, the initial button state **true**, indicates that **plain** should be selected when it is displayed. The other three **Checkbox**es are constructed with a third argument of **false** and are not selected when they are displayed. If more than one **Checkbox** associated with a **CheckboxGroup** has **true** as the third argument to its constructor, the last selected **Checkbox** associated with the **CheckboxGroup** is the one that appears selected. Note that all radio buttons can be set to **false** initially.

The applet implements interface **ItemListener** so it can handle item events generated by the **Checkbox**es. Each **Checkbox** in the program has the applet registered as its **ItemListener** (lines 23, 26, 29 and 33). When a **Checkbox** is clicked, **CheckboxGroup fontStyle** turns off the previously selected **Checkbox** and method **itemStateChanged** (line 44) is called. This determines which **Checkbox** was clicked using method **getSource** (inherited indirectly from **EventObject** into **ItemEvent**), then sets the font in the **TextField** to one of the **Font** objects created in method **init**.

10.7 Single-Selection Lists

A ***List*** displays a series of items from which the user may select one or more items. Lists are created with the **List** class that inherits from class **Component** and implements **ItemSelectable**. **List**s generate both item events and action events.

The program of Fig. 10.16 creates a **List** of 13 colors. When a color name is clicked once in the **List**, the applet displays a string in the browser's status bar indicating the item selected and the index of that item in the **List**. When a color name is double-clicked in the **List**, the applet's background changes to that color.

```
// Fig. 10.16: MyList.java
// Creating a List.
import java.applet.Applet;
import java.awt.*;
import java.awt.event.*;

public class MyList extends Applet
             implements ActionListener, ItemListener {
   private List colorList;

   private String colorNames[] =
      { "Black", "Blue", "Cyan", "Dark Gray", "Gray", "Green",
        "Light Gray", "Magenta", "Orange", "Pink", "Red",
        "White", "Yellow" };

   private Color colors[] =
      { Color.black, Color.blue, Color.cyan, Color.darkGray,
        Color.gray, Color.green, Color.lightGray,
        Color.magenta, Color.orange, Color.pink, Color.red,
        Color.white, Color.yellow };

   public void init()
   {
      // create a list with 5 items visible
      // do not allow multiple selections
      colorList = new List( 5, false );
      colorList.addActionListener( this );
      colorList.addItemListener( this );

      // add items to the list
      for ( int i = 0; i < colorNames.length; i++ )
         colorList.add( colorNames[ i ] );

      // add list to applet
      add( colorList );
   }

   public void actionPerformed( ActionEvent e )
   {
      setBackground( colors[ colorList.getSelectedIndex() ] );
      repaint();     // update applet
   }

   public void itemStateChanged( ItemEvent e )
   {
      showStatus( colorList.getSelectedItem() + "; index " +
                  colorList.getSelectedIndex() );
   }
}
```

Fig. 10.16 Program that creates a **List** (part 1 of 2).

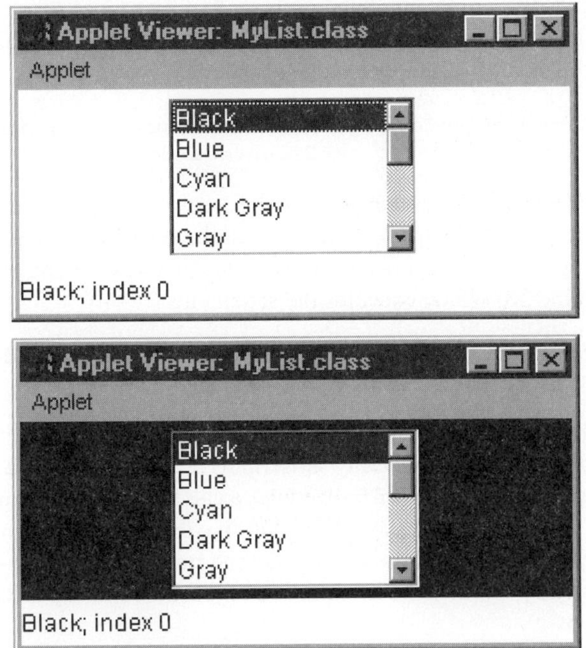

Fig. 10.16 Program that creates a **List** (part 2 of 2).

The **colorList** object is instantiated with line 26

```
colorList = new List( 5, false );
```

in method **init**. The constructor arguments indicate that object **colorList** has five lines visible and does not allow multiple selections. Items are added to the **List** with **List** method **add** and the items appear in the order that they are added. Only **String**s can be added to a **List**.

Common Programming Error 10.3

Attempting to add an item that is not a string to a **List** *is a syntax error.*

Object **colorList** has 13 items added to it with the **add** method in the **for** loop at line 31. Only five **List** items are visible at a time, so a *scrollbar* automatically appears at the **List**'s right side. The scrollbar allows all the items to be viewed by scrolling through the items using the arrows at the top and bottom of the scrollbar. Holding the mouse button down with the *mouse cursor* (the small arrow that represents the mouse location on the screen) on the up arrow causes the **List** to scroll toward the first item. Holding the mouse button down with the mouse cursor on the down arrow causes the **List** to scroll toward the last item. Holding the mouse button down with the mouse cursor on the box in the middle of the scrollbar and dragging the box, scrolls through the items. The scrollbar only appears when the number of items in the **List** exceeds the number of visible items.

In this example, the applet implements both **ActionListener** and **ItemListener**. Clicking an item once triggers an item event and calls the applet's **itemStateChanged** method (line 44) which executes the statement

```
showStatus( colorList.getSelectedItem() + "; index " +
            colorList.getSelectedIndex() );
```

List method **getSelectedItem** returns the item clicked by the user and method **getSelectedIndex** returns the integer index of the selected item in the **List**.

Double clicking an item triggers an action event and calls the applet's **actionPerformed** method (line 38) which executes the statements

```
setBackground( colors[ colorList.getSelectedIndex() ] );
repaint();     // update applet
```

Component method **setBackground** sets the background color of the applet to one of the colors in the array **colors**. The array subscript is provided by the **List** method **getSelectedIndex**. Method **repaint** schedules a call to **Component** method **update**. Method **update** redraws or refreshes the applet by filling the background of the applet with the current background color and calling method **paint**. Method **repaint** is useful because it automatically supplies the **Graphics** object that both **update** and **paint** require to do their jobs.

10.8 Multiple-Selection Lists

A *multiple-selection list* enables the user to select many items from a **List** by clicking once on each desired item. A second click on an item after a short delay de-selects the item. The program of Fig. 10.17 uses a multiple-selection **List** to copy items from one **List** to another. Several **List** items can be copied at a time by selecting the desired items and clicking the button between the **List** objects. Note that the items selected can be from anywhere in the **List**.

```
// Fig. 10.17: MyList2.java
// Copying items from one List to another.
import java.applet.Applet;
import java.awt.*;
import java.awt.event.*;

public class MyList2 extends Applet implements ActionListener {
   private List colorList, copyList;
   private Button copy;
   private String colorNames[] =
      { "Black", "Blue", "Cyan", "Dark Gray", "Gray", "Green",
        "Light Gray", "Magenta", "Orange", "Pink", "Red",
        "White", "Yellow" };

```

Fig. 10.17 Using a multiple-selection **List** (part 1 of 2).

```
15      public void init()
16      {
17         // create a list with 5 items visible
18         // allow multiple selections
19         colorList = new List( 5, true );
20
21         // add items to the list
22         for ( int i = 0; i < colorNames.length; i++ )
23            colorList.add( colorNames[ i ] );
24
25         add( colorList );
26
27         // create copy button
28         copy = new Button( "Copy >>>" );
29         copy.addActionListener( this );
30         add( copy );
31
32         // create a list with 5 items visible
33         // do not allow multiple selections
34         copyList = new List( 5, false );
35         add( copyList );
36      }
37
38      public void actionPerformed( ActionEvent e )
39      {
40         String colors[];
41
42         // get the selected states
43         colors = colorList.getSelectedItems();
44
45         // copy them to copyList
46         for ( int i = 0; i < colors.length; i++ )
47            copyList.add( colors[ i ] );
48      }
49   }
```

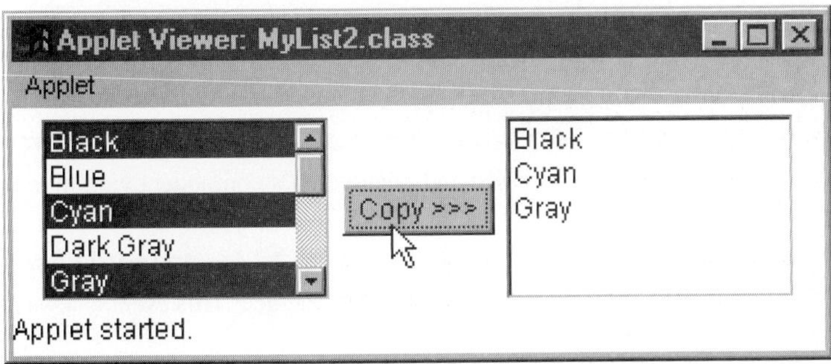

Fig. 10.17 Using a multiple-selection **List** (part 2 of 2).

The object **colorList** is instantiated in the **init** method with the line 19

```
colorList = new List( 5, true );
```

The constructor arguments indicate that five items are visible in the **List** and that multiple selections are allowed. Five items are also visible for object **copyList**. Multiple selections are not allowed for object **copyList**. **Button** object **copy** is also instantiated. When the user clicks **copy**, the selected items in **colorList** are copied to **copyList**.

To capture items from a multiple-selection **List**, an external event must be triggered (i.e., some other component should be used to indicate that multiple selections were made in a **List**). In this program, **copy** is used to trigger the event. This applet implements **ActionListener** to listen for action events from the **copy** button. Note: It is possible to generate an action event on a multiple-selection **List** by double-clicking one of the items. However, this event only occurs if an event listener is registered to listen for the action event on the **List**.

When the user clicks **copy** and **actionPerformed** (line 38) is called, the **String** array **colors** stores the selected items. Line 43

```
colors = colorList.getSelectedItems();
```

uses method ***getSelectedItems*** to get the strings representing the selected items in the **List**. The **for** loop adds each element of **colors** into **copyList**.

10.9 Mouse Events

This section presents the ***MouseListener*** and ***MouseMotionListener*** event-listener interfaces for handling *mouse events*. A mouse event occurs when the user interacts with the mouse. Mouse events can be trapped for any GUI component that derives from **Component**. The **MouseListener** and **MouseMotionListener** methods are summarized in Fig. 10.18.

MouseListener and MouseMotionListener interface methods

public void mousePressed(MouseEvent e) // MouseListener

Called when a mouse button is pressed with the mouse cursor on a component.

public void mouseClicked(MouseEvent e) // MouseListener

Called when a mouse button is pressed and released on a component without moving the mouse cursor.

public void mouseReleased(MouseEvent e) // MouseListener

Called when a mouse button is released after being dragged. This event is always preceded by a **mouseDragged** event.

public void mouseEntered(MouseEvent e) // MouseListener

Called when the mouse cursor enters the bounds of a component.

Fig. 10.18 **MouseListener** and **MouseMotionListener** interface methods (part 1 of 2).

MouseListener and **MouseMotionListener** interface methods
public void mouseExited(MouseEvent e) // MouseListener
Called when the mouse cursor leaves the bounds of a component.
public void mouseDragged(MouseEvent e) // MouseMotionListener
Called when the mouse button is pressed and the mouse is moved. This event is always preceded by a call to **mousePressed**.
public void mouseMoved(MouseEvent e) // MouseMotionListener
Called when the mouse is moved with the mouse cursor on a component.

Fig. 10.18 **MouseListener** and **MouseMotionListener** interface methods (part 2 of 2).

Each of the mouse event-handling methods takes a **MouseEvent** object as its argument. A **MouseEvent** object contains information about the mouse event that occurred including the *x* and *y* coordinates where the event occurred. **MouseListener** and **MouseMotionListener** methods are called automatically if listener objects are registered for a particular component. Method ***mousePressed*** is called when a mouse button is pressed with the mouse cursor over a component. Using methods and constants of class **InputEvent** (the superclass of **MouseEvent**), a program can determine which mouse button is clicked. Method ***mouseClicked*** is called whenever a mouse button is released without moving the mouse after a **mousePressed** operation. Method ***mouseReleased*** is called whenever a mouse button is released after a dragging operation. Method ***mouseEntered*** is called when the mouse cursor enters the physical boundaries of a component. Method ***mouseExited*** is called when the mouse cursor leaves the physical boundaries of a component. Method ***mouseDragged*** is called when the mouse button is pressed and held, and the mouse is moved (a process known as *dragging*). The **mouseDragged** event is preceded by a **mousePressed** event and followed by a **mouseReleased** event. Method ***mouseMoved*** is called when the mouse is moved with the mouse cursor over a component.

Applet **MouseTracker** of Fig. 10.19 demonstrates all the **MouseListener** and **MouseMotionListener** methods. The applet implements both interfaces so it can listen for its own mouse events. Note that all seven methods from these two interfaces must be defined by the programmer when a class implements both interfaces.

```
// Fig. 10.19: MouseTracker.java
// Demonstrating mouse events.
import java.applet.Applet;
import java.awt.*;
import java.awt.event.*;

```

Fig. 10.19 Demonstrating mouse event handling (part 1 of 3).

```
public class MouseTracker extends Applet
             implements MouseListener, MouseMotionListener {
   private int xPos, yPos = -10;  // off screen for 1st paint
   private String s = "";

   public void init()
   {
      // applet listens to its own mouse events
      addMouseListener( this );
      addMouseMotionListener( this );
   }

   public void paint( Graphics g )
   {
      g.drawString( s + " @ [" + xPos + ", " + yPos + "]",
                    xPos, yPos );
   }

   private void setValues( String event, int x, int y )
   {
      s = event;
      xPos = x;
      yPos = y;
      repaint();
   }

   // MouseListener event handlers
   public void mouseClicked( MouseEvent e )
      { setValues( "Clicked", e.getX(), e.getY() ); }

   public void mousePressed( MouseEvent e )
      { setValues( "Pressed", e.getX(), e.getY() ); }

   public void mouseReleased( MouseEvent e )
      { setValues( "Released", e.getX(), e.getY() ); }

   public void mouseEntered( MouseEvent e )
      { showStatus( "Mouse in applet area" ); }

   public void mouseExited( MouseEvent e )
      { showStatus( "Mouse outside applet area" ); }

   // MouseMotionListener event handlers
   public void mouseDragged( MouseEvent e )
      { setValues( "Dragging", e.getX(), e.getY() ); }

   public void mouseMoved( MouseEvent e )
      { setValues( "Moving", e.getX(), e.getY() ); }
}
```

Fig. 10.19 Demonstrating mouse event handling (part 2 of 3).

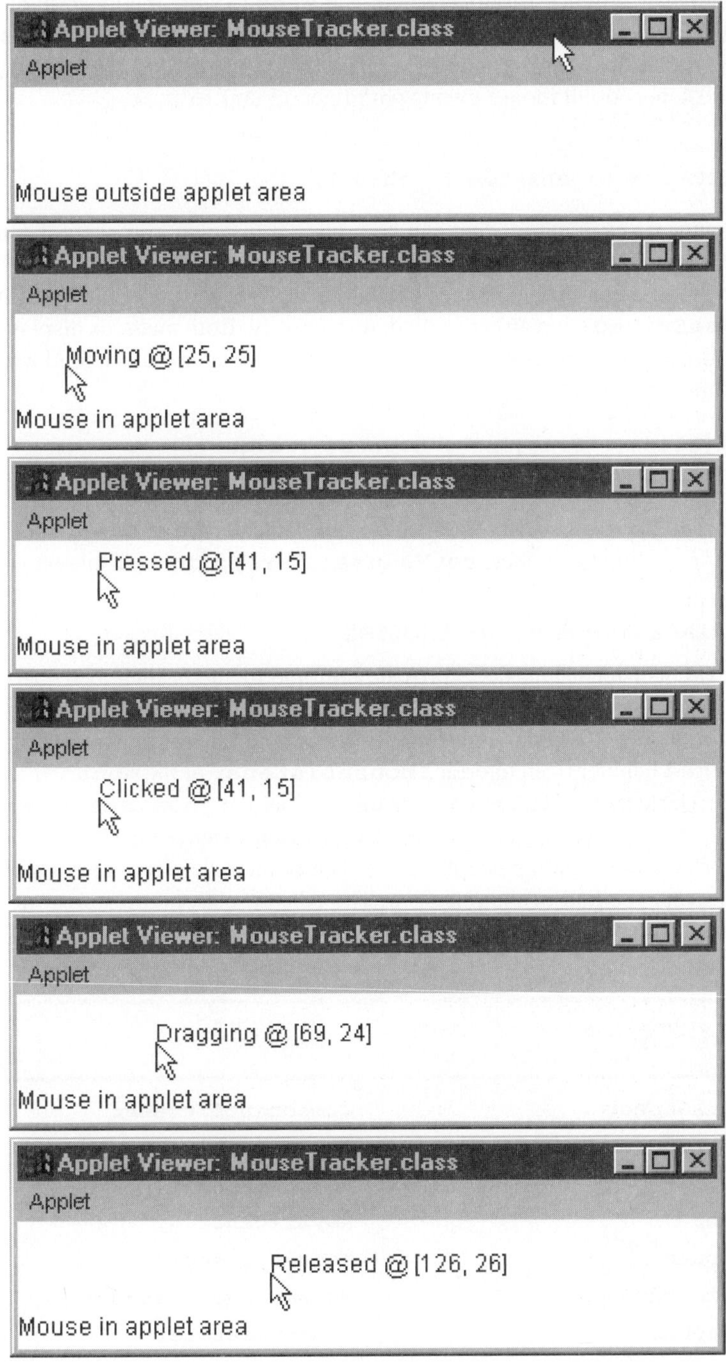

Fig. 10.19 Demonstrating mouse event handling (part 3 of 3).

The applet uses instance variables **xPos** and **yPos** to store the location of the mouse when a mouse event occurs. The strings output from the **paint** method (line 19) are always displayed at these coordinates. The applet's **init** method (line 12) registers the applet as the listener for all mouse events with lines 15 and 16

```
addMouseListener( this )
addMouseMotionListener( this );
```

These are **Component** methods that can be used to register mouse event listeners for an object of any class that extends **Component**.

When the mouse enters or exits the applet area, method **mouseEntered** (line 43) and method **mouseExited** (line 46) are called, respectively. Both methods display a message in the status bar area. When any of the other five events occur, our method **setValues** (line 25) is called as follows

```
setValues( "Dragging", e.getX(), e.getY() );
```

This sets the string to be displayed by **paint** and the coordinates at which the string is to be displayed. The **MouseEvent** reference **e** is used to call **MouseEvent** methods **getX** and **getY**. After setting the values, **setValues** calls **repaint** to display the new string.

10.10 Mouse Event Adapter Classes

Many of the event-listener interfaces provide multiple methods such as the **MouseListener** and **MouseMotionListener** interfaces. It is not always desirable to define every method in an event-listener interface. For example, a program may only need the **mouseClicked** handler from interface **MouseListener** or the **mouseDragged** handler from **MouseMotionListener**. For this reason, the **java.awt.event** package provides the event-listener *adapter classes*. Every event-listener interface with more than one method has a corresponding adapter class. The adapter class provides a default implementation of every method in the interface. The adapter classes are shown in Fig. 10.20 along with the interfaces they implement.

Event adapter class	Implements
ComponentAdapter	**ComponentListener**
ContainerAdapter	**ContainerListener**
FocusAdapter	**FocusListener**
KeyAdapter	**KeyListener**
MouseAdapter	**MouseListener**
MouseMotionAdapter	**MouseMotionListener**
WindowAdapter	**WindowListener**

Fig. 10.20 Event adapter classes and the interfaces they implement.

The programmer can extend the adapter class to inherit the default implementation of every method and simply override the method or methods needed for event handling in the program. The default implementation of each method has an empty body.

The **Drag** applet of Fig. 10.21 uses the **mouseDragged** event to create a simple drawing program. The user can draw pictures with the mouse by dragging the mouse on the applet. The program also demonstrates how to use the **MouseMotionAdapter** class.

```
// Fig. 10.21: Drag.java
// Using the MouseMotionAdapter class.
import java.applet.Applet;
import java.awt.*;
import java.awt.event.*;

public class Drag extends Applet {
   private int xValue = -10, yValue = -10;

   public void init()
   {
      addMouseMotionListener( new MotionHandler( this ) );
   }

   public void paint( Graphics g )
   {
      g.drawString( "Drag the mouse to draw", 10, 20 );
      g.fillOval( xValue, yValue, 4, 4 );
   }

   // Override Component class update method to allow all ovals
   // to remain on the screen by not clearing the background.
   public void update( Graphics g ) { paint( g ); }

   // set the drawing coordinates and repaint
   public void setCoordinates( int x, int y )
   {
      xValue = x;
      yValue = y;
      repaint();
   }
}

// Class to handle only mouse drag events for the Drag applet
class MotionHandler extends MouseMotionAdapter {
   private Drag dragger;

   public MotionHandler( Drag d ) { dragger = d; }

   public void mouseDragged( MouseEvent e )
      { dragger.setCoordinates( e.getX(), e.getY() ); }
}
```

Fig. 10.21 Program that demonstrates method **mouseDragged** (part 1 of 2).

Fig. 10.21 Program that demonstrates method **mouseDragged** (part 2 of 2).

The instance variables **xValue** and **yValue** store the coordinates of the **mouseDragged** event. Initially, the coordinates are set outside the applet area to prevent an oval from drawing on the applet area in the first call to **paint**. Line 12

```
addMouseMotionListener( new MotionHandler( this ) );
```

registers an object of class **MotionHandler** to listen for the applet's mouse motion events. The **MotionHandler** constructor receives a reference to the applet as its argument. This enables the event handler to interact with the applet when an event occurs.

The applet's **paint** method (line 15) draws a filled oval at the current coordinates. The applet's **update** method (line 23) is overridden to prevent clearing the background when **repaint** is called. Normally, **update** draws a filled rectangle the size of the applet in the current background color, then calls **paint**. The overridden version simply calls **paint** directly. This allows everything the user draws to remain on the screen. Note: This does not keep a permanent record of every oval drawn. If the applet space is covered by another window on the screen, all the ovals except the last one drawn are lost. The applet's **setCoordinates** method (line 26) is used by the event handler to set the **xValue** and **yValue** variables and call **repaint**.

Class **MotionHandler** (line 35) is defined to extend **MouseMotionAdapter**. This allows the class to define only the **mouseDragged** event-handling method because **MouseMotionAdapter** already provides a default definition of both **mouseDragged** and **mouseMoved**. Class **MotionHandler** overrides **mouseDragged** as follows:

```
public void mouseDragged( MouseEvent e )
   { dragger.setCoordinates( e.getX(), e.getY() ); }
```

Reference **dragger** is used to call the applet's **setCoordinates** method. This sets the coordinates at which the next oval should be drawn and calls **repaint**. Method **repaint** calls the overridden **update** method and **update** calls **paint** to draw the new oval.

The **MouseDetails** applet of Fig. 10.22 demonstrates how to determine the number of mouse clicks (i.e., the click count) and how to distinguish between the different mouse buttons. The event listener in this program is an object of class **DetailHandler** (line 30) that extends **MouseAdapter** so only the **mouseClicked** method needs to be defined.

```
1  // Fig. 10.22: MouseDetails.java
2  // Demonstrating mouse clicks and distinguishing mouse buttons.
3  import java.applet.Applet;
4  import java.awt.*;
5  import java.awt.event.*;
6
7  public class MouseDetails extends Applet {
8     private String s = "";
9     private int xPos, yPos;
10
11    public void init()
12    {
13       addMouseListener( new DetailHandler( this ) );
14    }
15
16    public void paint( Graphics g )
17    {
18       g.drawString( "Clicked @ [" + xPos + ", " + yPos + "]",
19                     xPos, yPos );
20    }
21
22    public void setCoordinates( int x, int y )
23    {
24       xPos = x;
25       yPos = y;
26       repaint();
27    }
28 }
29
30 class DetailHandler extends MouseAdapter {
31    private MouseDetails details;
32
33    public DetailHandler( MouseDetails m ) { details = m; }
34
35    public void mouseClicked( MouseEvent e )
36    {
37       details.setCoordinates( e.getX(), e.getY() );
38
39       String s = "Clicked " + e.getClickCount() + " time(s)";
40
41       if ( e.isMetaDown() )      // Right mouse button
42          s += " with right mouse button";
```

Fig. 10.22 Distinguishing among mouse buttons (part 1 of 2).

```
      else if ( e.isAltDown() )  // Middle mouse button
         s += " with center mouse button";
      else                        // Left mouse button
         s += " with left mouse button";

      details.showStatus( s );
   }
}
```

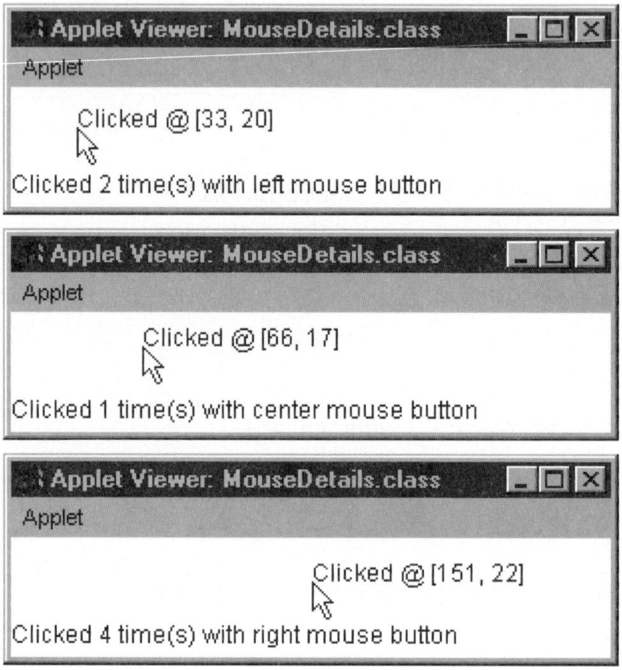

Fig. 10.22 Distinguishing among mouse buttons (part 2 of 2).

A user of a Java program may be on a system with a one-button, two-button or three-button mouse. Java provides a mechanism to distinguish among mouse buttons. Class **`MouseEvent`** inherits several methods from class **`InputEvent`** that can distinguish between mouse buttons on a multi-button mouse or can mimic a multi-button mouse with a combined keystroke and mouse-button click. Figure 10.23 shows the **`InputEvent`** methods used to distinguish between mouse-button clicks. Java assumes that every mouse contains a left mouse button. Thus, it is simple to test for a left-mouse-button click. However, users with a one- or two-button mouse must use a combination of pressing keys on the keyboard and clicking the mouse at the same time to simulate the missing buttons on the mouse. In the case of a one-button or two-button mouse, this program assumes that the center mouse button is clicked if the user holds the *Alt* key and clicks the left mouse button on a two-button mouse or the only mouse button on a one-button mouse. In the case of a one-button mouse, this program assumes that the right mouse button is clicked if the user holds the *Meta* key and clicks the mouse button.

InputEvent constant	Description
isMetaDown()	This method returns **true** when the user clicks the right mouse button on a mouse with two or three buttons. To simulate a right-mouse-button click on a one-button mouse, the user can press the *Meta* key on the keyboard and click the mouse button.
isAltDown()	This method returns **true** when the user clicks the middle mouse button on a mouse with three buttons. To simulate a middle-mouse-button click on a one-button or two-button mouse, the user can press the *Alt* key on the keyboard and click the mouse button.

Fig. 10.23 InputEvent class modifier constants.

Method **mouseClicked** (line 35) first calls the applet's **setCoordinates** method to output a string indicating where the user clicked on the applet. A string is created containing the number of mouse clicks (as returned by **e.getClickCount()** at line 39). The nested **if** structure at line 41 uses methods **isMetaDown** and **isAltDown** to determine which mouse button the user clicked and appends an appropriate string to **String s** in each case. The resulting string is displayed in the status bar.

10.11 Keyboard Events

This section presents the **KeyListener** event-listener interface for handling *key events*. Key events are generated when keys on the keyboard are pressed and released. A class that implements **KeyListener** must provide definitions for method **keyPressed**, **keyReleased** and **keyTyped** each of which receives a **KeyEvent** as its argument. As with **MouseEvent**, **KeyEvent** derives from **InputEvent**. Method **keyPressed** is called in response to pressing an *action key* (i.e., an arrow key, *Home*, *End*, *Page Up*, *Page Down*, a function key, *Num Lock*, *Print Screen*, *Scroll Lock*, *Caps Lock*, and *Pause*). Method **keyTyped** is called in response to pressing any other key on the keyboard. Method **keyReleased** is called after the key is released in any **keyPressed** or **keyTyped** event.

The program of Fig. 10.24 demonstrates the **KeyListener** methods. The applet implements the **KeyListener** interface, so all three methods are defined in the applet.

```
// Fig. 10.24: Key.java
// Demonstrating keystroke events.
import java.applet.Applet;
import java.awt.*;
import java.awt.event.*;

public class Key extends Applet implements KeyListener {
   private String line1 = "";
   private String line2 = "";
   private String line3 = "";
```

Fig. 10.24 Demonstrating key event handling (part 1 of 3).

```

    public void init()
    {
       // allow applet to process Key events
       addKeyListener( this );

       // make applet the active component for key events
       requestFocus();
    }

    public void paint( Graphics g )
    {
       g.drawString( line1, 25, 25 );
       g.drawString( line2, 25, 40 );
       g.drawString( line3, 25, 55 );
    }

    public void keyPressed( KeyEvent e )
    {
       line1 = "Key pressed: " +
                e.getKeyText( e.getKeyCode() );
       setLines2and3( e );
    }

    public void keyReleased( KeyEvent e )
    {
       line1 = "Key released: " +
                e.getKeyText( e.getKeyCode() );
       setLines2and3( e );
    }

    public void keyTyped( KeyEvent e )
    {
       line1 = "Key typed: " + e.getKeyChar();
       setLines2and3( e );
    }

    private void setLines2and3( KeyEvent e )
    {
       line2 = "This key is " +
               ( e.isActionKey() ? "" : "not " ) +
               "an action key";

       String temp =
          e.getKeyModifiersText( e.getModifiers() );

       line3 = "Modifier keys pressed: " +
               ( temp.equals( "" ) ? "none" : temp );
       repaint();
    }
}
```

Fig. 10.24 Demonstrating key event handling (part 2 of 3).

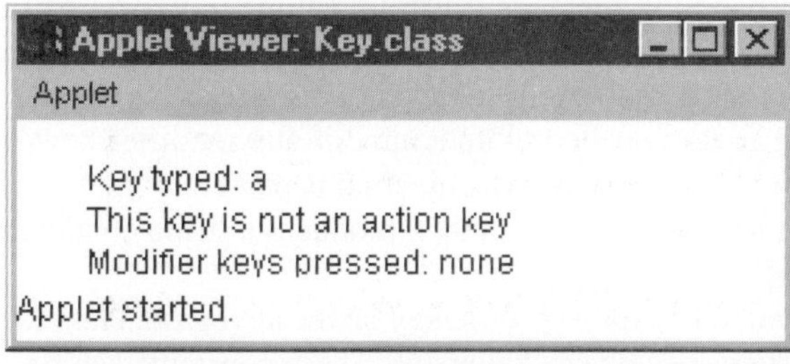

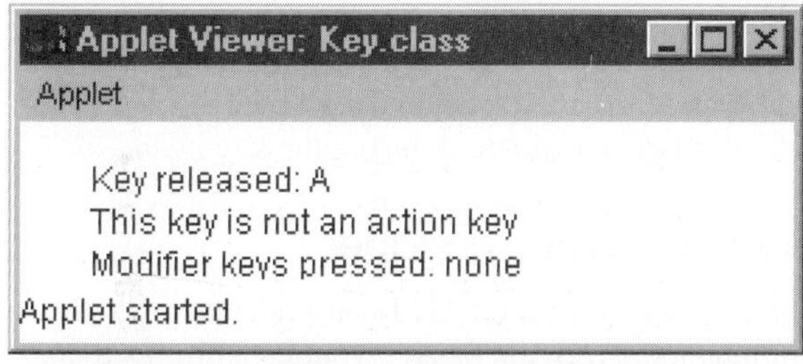

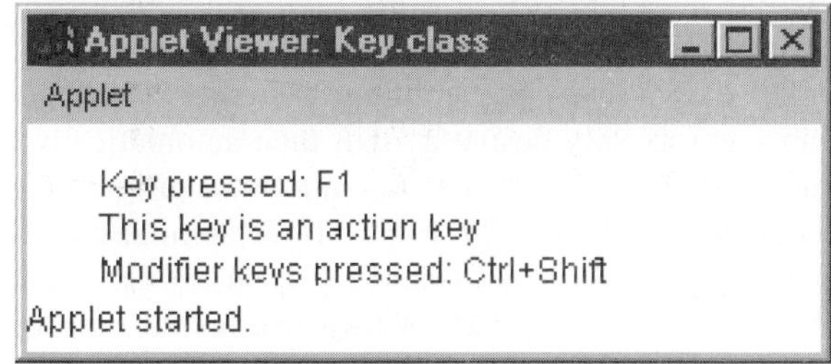

Fig. 10.24 Demonstrating key event handling (part 3 of 3).

The applet's **init** method (line 12) registers the applet to handle its own key events with method **addKeyListener**. Also, method **requestFocus** (inherited from class **Component**) is called to give the applet the *input focus*. This enables the applet to recognize when the user presses a key on the keyboard. Method **paint** (line 21) outputs the three strings **line1**, **line2** and **line3** that are created during the execution of each of the key event handlers.

Methods **keyPressed** (line 28) and **keyReleased** (line 35) use **KeyEvent** method **getKeyCode** to get the *virtual key code* of the key that was pressed. Class **KeyEvent** maintains a set of constants—the virtual key code constants—that represent every key on the keyboard. These constants can be compared with the return value of **getKeyCode** to test for individual keys on the keyboard. The value returned by **getKeyCode** is passed to **KeyEvent** method **getKeyText** that returns a **String** containing the name of the key that was pressed. For a complete list of virtual key constants, see the online documentation for class **KeyEvent** (package **java.awt.event**). Method **keyTyped** (line 42) uses **KeyEvent** method **getKeyChar** to get the actual Unicode character typed.

All three event-handling methods finish by calling method **setLines2and3** (line 48) and passing it the **KeyEvent** object. This method uses **KeyEvent** method **isActionKey** to determine if the key in the event was an action key. Also, **InputEvent** method **getModifiers** is called to determine if any modifier keys were pressed when the key event occurred. The result of this method is passed to method **getKeyModifiersText** of class **KeyEvent**. This method produces a string containing the names of the pressed modifier keys.

Note: If you need to test for a specific key on the keyboard, class **KeyEvent** provides a *key constant* for every key on the keyboard. These constants can be used from the key-event handlers to determine if a particular key was pressed. Also, to determine whether the *Alt*, *Control*, *Meta* or *Shift* keys are pressed individually, **InputEvent** methods **isAltDown**, **isControlDown**, **isMetaDown** and **isShiftDown** each return a **boolean** indicating if the particular key was pressed during the key event.

10.12 FlowLayout Layout Manager

Layout managers are provided to arrange GUI components on a container for presentation purposes. The layout managers provide basic layout capabilities that are easier to use than determining the exact position and size of every GUI component. This enables the programmer to concentrate on the basic "look and feel" and lets the layout managers process most of the layout details. Most Java programming environments provide GUI design tools that help a programmer graphically design a GUI, then automatically write Java code to create the GUI. Some of these GUI designers also allow the programmer to use the layout managers described here and in Chapter 11. Figure 10.25 summarizes the layout managers presented in this chapter. Other layout managers are discussed in Chapter 11.

All the previous examples used the ***FlowLayout*** layout manager—the default for **Panel**s and **Applet**s. Class ***FlowLayout*** inherits from class **Object** and implements the ***LayoutManger*** *interface*. Interface **LayoutManager** defines the methods that a layout manager uses to arrange components on a container.

FlowLayout is the most basic layout manager. GUI components are placed on a container from left to right in the order in which they are added to the container. When the edge of the container is reached, components are continued on the next line. The **FlowLayout** class constructors are summarized in Fig. 10.26.

Layout manager	Description
FlowLayout	Default for **Applet**s and **Panel**s. Places components sequentially (left to right) in the order they were added.
BorderLayout	Arranges the components into five areas: North, South, East, West, and Center.
GridLayout	Arranges the components into rows and columns.

Fig. 10.25 Layout managers.

`FlowLayout` constructors

```
public FlowLayout()
```

Constructs a **`FlowLayout`** in which components are center aligned by default.

```
public FlowLayout( int alignment ) // component alignment
```

Constructs a **`FlowLayout`** with a specified alignment. The value for alignment is either **`FlowLayout.RIGHT`**, **`FlowLayout.LEFT`**, or **`FlowLayout.CENTER`**.

```
public FlowLayout(
   int alignment,         // component alignment
   int horizontal_gap,    // horizontal pixels between components
   int vertical_gap )     // vertical pixels between components
```

Constructs a **`FlowLayout`** with a specified alignment. The value for alignment is either **`FlowLayout.RIGHT`**, **`FlowLayout.LEFT`**, or **`FlowLayout.CENTER`**. The distance in pixels between components is specified by the last two arguments.

Fig. 10.26 `FlowLayout` constructors.

The program of Fig. 10.27 creates three **`Button`** objects and adds them to the applet using the default **`FlowLayout`** layout manager. The components are automatically center aligned on the applet. When the user clicks **`left`**, the layout manager for the applet is changed to a left-aligned **`FlowLayout`**. When the user clicks **`right`**, the layout manager for the applet is changed to a right-aligned **`FlowLayout`**. When the user click **`center`**, the layout manager for the applet is changed to a center-aligned **`FlowLayout`**. The applet is registered as the **`ActionListener`** for each of the three **`Button`**s.

```
// Fig. 10.27: FlowLayoutDemo.java
// Demonstrating FlowLayout alignments.
import java.applet.Applet;
import java.awt.*;
import java.awt.event.*;

public class FlowLayoutDemo extends Applet
             implements ActionListener {
   private Button left, center, right;

   public void init()
   {
      left = new Button( "Left" );
      left.addActionListener( this );
      add( left );

      center = new Button( "Center" );
      center.addActionListener( this );
```

Fig. 10.27 Program that demonstrates components in **`FlowLayout`** (part 1 of 3).

```
      add( center );

      right = new Button( "Right" );
      right.addActionListener( this );
      add( right );
   }

   public void actionPerformed( ActionEvent e )
   {
      int align;

      if ( e.getSource() == left )
         align = FlowLayout.LEFT;
      else if ( e.getSource() == center )
         align = FlowLayout.CENTER;
      else
         align = FlowLayout.RIGHT;

      setLayout( new FlowLayout( align ) );
      validate();  // re-align attached components
   }
}
```

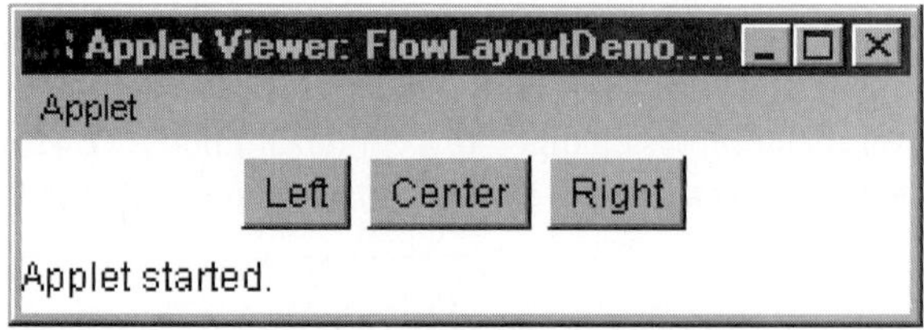

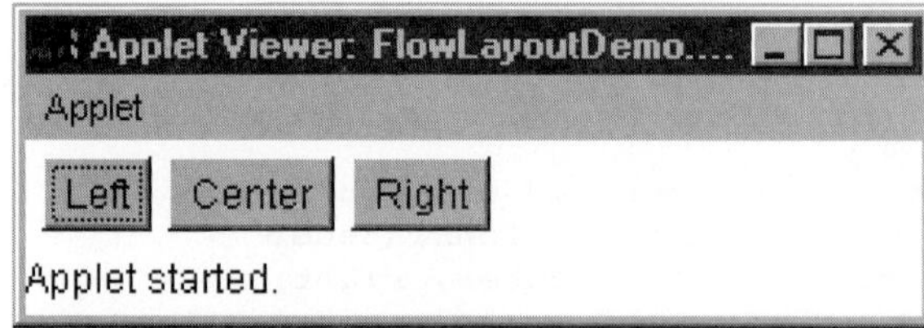

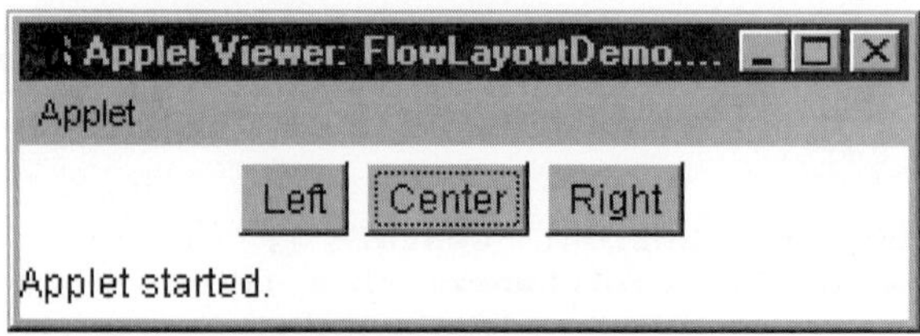

Fig. 10.27 Program that demonstrates components in **`FlowLayout`** (part 2 of 3).

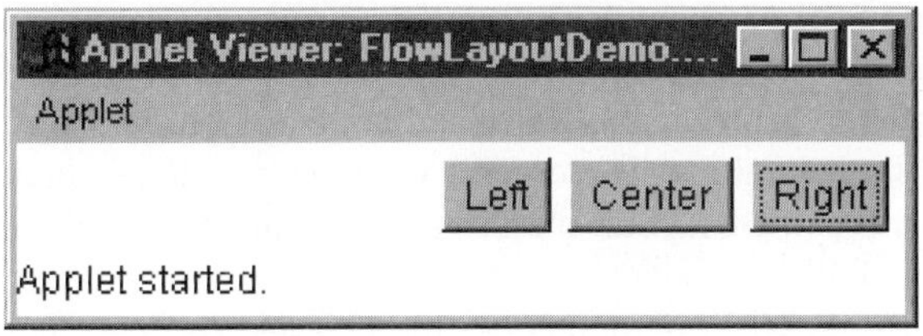

Fig. 10.27 Program that demonstrates components in **FlowLayout** (part 3 of 3).

The applet's **actionPerformed** method (line 26) uses method **getSource** (inherited from **EventObject** into **AWTEvent** and **AWTEvent** into **ActionEvent**) to determine which button generated the event. Method **getSource** returns a reference to the source of the event. According to which button was clicked the variable align is set to **FlowLayout.LEFT**, **FlowLayout.CENTER** or **FlowLayout.RIGHT**.

A container's layout is set with method ***setLayout*** of class **Container**. Line 37

```
setLayout( new FlowLayout( align ) );
```

constructs a new **FlowLayout** layout manager with the specified alignment, which is then set for the applet using method **setLayout**. Normally the layout is set before any GUI components are added to a container. In this example, the layout is reset after every button event. After the **setLayout** statement, a call is made to the **Container** method **validate** that recomputes the layout of all the GUI components in the container. Note: Each container can have only one layout manager at a time (separate containers in the same program can have different layout managers).

10.13 BorderLayout Layout Manager

The ***BorderLayout*** layout manager arranges components into five regions: *North, South, East, West, and Center* (North corresponds to the top of the container). Class **BorderLayout** inherits from **Object** and implements the **LayoutManager2** interface. The **BorderLayout** class constructors are summarized in Fig. 10.28.

BorderLayout constructors
public BorderLayout() Constructs a **BorderLayout** with no pixel gaps between components.
public BorderLayout(int horizontalGap, int verticalGap) Constructs a **BorderLayout** with horizontal components separated by **horizontalGap** pixels and vertical components separated by **verticalGap** pixels.

Fig. 10.28 **BorderLayout** constructors.

In a **BorderLayout**, up to five components can be used—one for each position. The components placed in the North and South regions extend horizontally to the sides of the container and are as tall as the components placed in those sections. The East and West regions expand vertically between the North and South regions and are as wide as the components placed in those sections. The component placed in the Center region expands to take all remaining space in the layout. If all five regions are occupied, the entire container's space is covered by GUI components.

The program of Fig. 10.29 demonstrates the **BorderLayout** layout manager using five **Button**s. In the **init** method (line 13), **setLayout** is used to specify a **BorderLayout** for the applet with five pixels of horizontal-gap space between components and five pixels of vertical-gap space between components.

```
1  // Fig. 10.29: Border.java
2  // Demonstrating BorderLayout.
3  import java.applet.Applet;
4  import java.awt.*;
5  import java.awt.event.*;
6
7  public class Border extends Applet implements ActionListener {
8     private Button b[];
9     private String names[] =
10       { "Hide North", "Hide South", "Hide East",
11         "Hide West", "Hide Center" };
12
13    public void init()
14    {
15       // set layout to border layout
16       setLayout( new BorderLayout( 5, 5 ) );
17
18       // instantiate button objects
19       b = new Button[ names.length ];
20
21       for ( int i = 0; i < names.length; i++ ) {
22          b[ i ] = new Button( names[ i ] );
23          b[ i ].addActionListener( this );
24       }
25
26       // order not important
27       add( b[ 0 ], BorderLayout.NORTH );  // North position
28       add( b[ 1 ], BorderLayout.SOUTH );  // South position
29       add( b[ 2 ], BorderLayout.EAST );     // East position
30       add( b[ 3 ], BorderLayout.WEST );    // West position
31       add( b[ 4 ], BorderLayout.CENTER );  // Center position
32    }
33
```

Fig. 10.29 Program that demonstrates components in **BorderLayout** (part 1 of 3).

```
   public void actionPerformed( ActionEvent e )
   {
      for ( int i = 0; i < b.length; i++ )
         if ( e.getSource() == b[ i ] )
            b[ i ].setVisible( false );
         else
            b[ i ].setVisible( true );

      validate();
   }
}
```

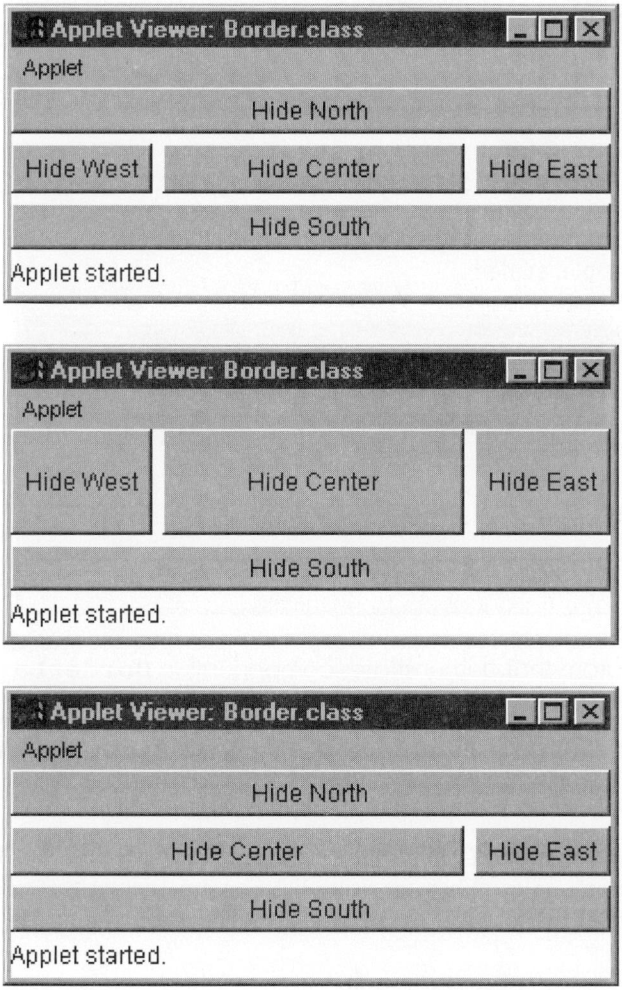

Fig. 10.29 Program that demonstrates components in **`BorderLayout`** (part 2 of 3).

Fig. 10.29 Program that demonstrates components in **`BorderLayout`** (part 3 of 3).

Notice the difference in the **`add`** method's arguments. For example, line 27

```
add( b[ 0 ], BorderLayout.NORTH );
```

specifies that the **`Button b[0]`** is to be placed in the **`NORTH`** position. The components can be added in any order. When the user clicks on a particular **`Button`** in the layout, method **`actionPerformed`** (line 34) is called. The **`for`** loop at line 36 uses the **`if`** structure

```
if ( e.getSource() == b[ i ] )
   b[ i ].setVisible( false );
else
   b[ i ].setVisible( true );
```

to hide the particular **Button** that generated the event. Method **setVisible** is called with a **false** argument to hide the **Button**. If the current **Button** in the array is not the one that generated the event, method **setVisible** is called with a **true** argument to ensure that the **Button** is displayed on the screen. Then, method **validate** is called to recalculate the layout of the container. Notice in the screen captures of Fig. 10.29, that certain regions in the **BorderLayout** change shape as **Button**s are hidden and displayed in other regions.

Common Programming Error 10.4

Forgetting to specify the region to which a GUI component should be added in a **BorderLayout** *results in that component not being displayed. There is no error message to indicate this problem.*

Common Programming Error 10.5

Adding more than one component to a particular region in a **BorderLayout** *results in only the last component added being displayed. There is no error message to indicate this problem.*

10.14 GridLayout Layout Manager

The ***GridLayout*** layout manager divides the container into a grid so components can be placed in rows and columns. Class **GridLayout** inherits directly from class **Object** and implements the **LayoutManager** interface. Each component is given the same size. Components are added to a **GridLayout** starting at the top-left cell of the grid proceeding left-to-right until the row is full. Then, the process continues left-to-right on the next row, etc. The **GridLayout** class's constructors are summarized in Fig. 10.30.

GridLayout constructors

```
public GridLayout(
   int rows,          // number of rows
   int columns)       // number of columns
```

Constructs a **GridLayout** of **rows** number of rows and **columns** number of columns.

```
public GridLayout(
   int rows,         // number of rows
   int columns,      // number of columns
   int h,            // horizontal spacing between components
   int v)            // vertical spacing between components
```

Constructs a **GridLayout** with each component separated horizontally by **h** pixels and separated vertically by **v** pixels.

Fig. 10.30 **GridLayout** constructors.

The program of Fig. 10.31 demonstrates the **GridLayout** layout manager using six **Button**s. The **Button** objects initially are arranged in a grid with two rows and three columns. In **init** (line 13), method ***setLayout*** specifies a **GridLayout**. The first component is added to the first column of the first row. The next component is added to the second column of the first row, etc. When a **Button** is pressed, the applet's **actionPerformed** method (line 28) is called. Every call to **actionPerformed** toggles the layout between a grid of three rows and two columns and a grid of two rows and three columns with five pixels of gap space horizontally and vertically. Method **validate** recomputes the container's layout on each call to **actionPerformed**.

```
1  // Fig. 10.31: Grid.java
2  // Demonstrating GridLayout.
3  import java.applet.Applet;
4  import java.awt.*;
5  import java.awt.event.*;
6
7  public class Grid extends Applet implements ActionListener {
8     private Button b[];
9     private String names[] =
10       { "one", "two", "three", "four", "five", "six" };
11    private boolean toggle = true;
12
13    public void init()
14    {
15       // set layout to grid layout
16       setLayout( new GridLayout( 2, 3, 5, 5 ) );
17
18       // create and add buttons
19       b = new Button[ names.length ];
20
21       for (int i = 0; i < names.length; i++ ) {
22          b[ i ] = new Button( names[ i ] );
23          b[ i ].addActionListener( this );
24          add( b[ i ] );
25       }
26    }
27
28    public void actionPerformed( ActionEvent e )
29    {
30       if ( toggle )
31          setLayout( new GridLayout( 3, 2 ) );
32       else
33          setLayout( new GridLayout( 2, 3, 5, 5 ) );
34
35       toggle = !toggle;
36       validate();
37    }
38 }
```

Fig. 10.31 Program that demonstrates components in **GridLayout** (part 1 of 2).

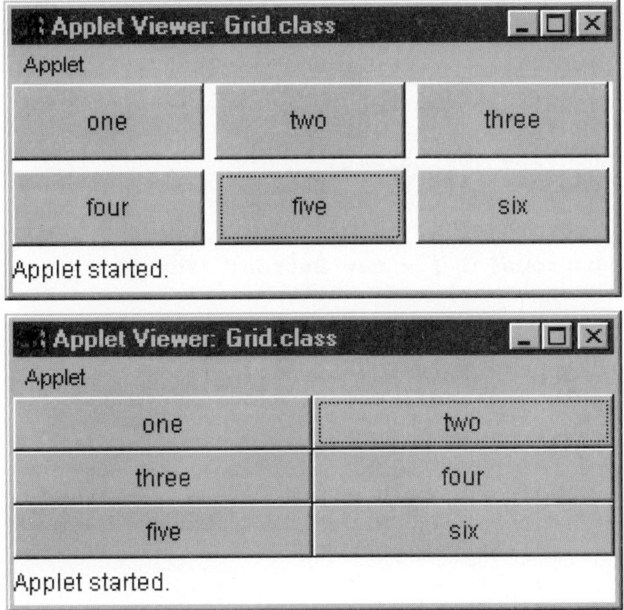

Fig. 10.31 Program that demonstrates components in **`GridLayout`** (part 2 of 2).

10.15 Panels

Complex GUIs (like Fig. 10.1) require that each component be placed in an exact location. They usually consist of multiple panels with each panel's components arranged in a specific layout. As mentioned earlier, a *panel* is a container. Class **`Panel`** inherits from class **`Container`** and class **`Applet`** inherits from **`Panel`**. Thus **`Panel`**s and **`Applet`**s are containers and may have components, including other panels, added to them. The **`Panel`** constructor takes no arguments.

The program of Fig. 10.32 demonstrates how a panel can be used to create a more complex layout for components.

```
// Fig. 10.32: PanelDemo.java
// Using a panel to help layout components.
import java.applet.Applet;
import java.awt.*;
import java.awt.event.*;

public class PanelDemo extends Applet {
   private Panel buttonPanel;
   private Button buttons[];
```

Fig. 10.32 Demonstrating a **`Panel`** with five **`Button`**s in **`GridLayout`** attached to the applet's South region in **`BorderLayout`** (part 1 of 2).

```
10
11      public void init()
12      {
13         buttonPanel = new Panel();
14         buttons = new Button[ 5 ];
15
16         buttonPanel.setLayout(
17            new GridLayout( 1, buttons.length ) );
18
19         for ( int i = 0; i < buttons.length; i++ ) {
20            buttons[ i ] = new Button( "Button " + (i + 1) );
21            buttonPanel.add( buttons[ i ] );
22         }
23
24         setLayout( new BorderLayout() );
25         add( buttonPanel, BorderLayout.SOUTH );
26      }
27   }
```

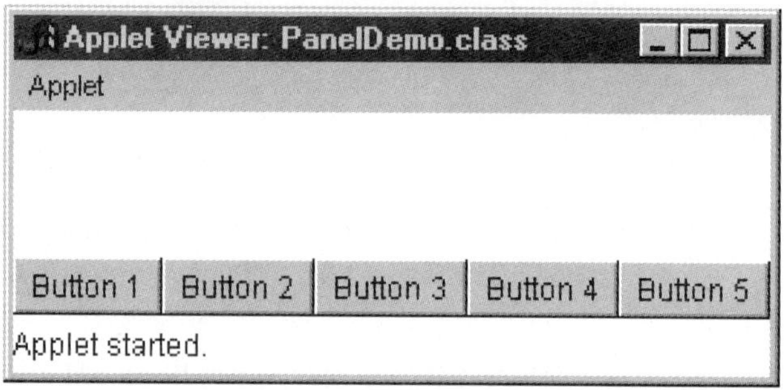

Fig. 10.32 Demonstrating a **Panel** with five **Button**s in **GridLayout** attached to the applet's South region in **BorderLayout** (part 2 of 2).

After the **Panel buttonPanel** is created, its layout is set with line 16

```
buttonPanel.setLayout(
   new GridLayout( 1, buttons.length ) );
```

This creates a grid on the panel of one row and five columns (there are five **Button**s in array **buttons**). The five **Button**s in array **buttons** are added to the panel in the loop using line 21

```
buttonPanel.add( buttons[ i ] );
```

Finally, lines 24 and 25

```
setLayout( new BorderLayout() );
add( buttonPanel, BorderLayout.SOUTH );
```

set the applet's layout to a **BorderLayout** and add **buttonPanel** to the South region of the applet. Note that the South region is as tall as the buttons on **buttonPanel**. A

Panel is sized to the components it contains. As more components are added to a **Panel**, the **Panel** grows to accommodate all the components.

Common Programming Error 10.6

*Adding a component to a container that has not been instantiated throws a **NullPointerException**.*

Summary

- A graphical user interface (GUI) presents a pictorial interface to a program. A GUI (pronounced "GOO-EE") gives a program a distinctive "look" and "feel."
- A GUI component (or widget) is a visual object with which the user may interact via the mouse or the keyboard.
- Classes used to create GUI components are part of the **java.awt** package.
- Class **Component** defines the set of methods that can be applied to an object of any subclass of **Component**. Operations common to all GUI components are found in class **Component**.
- Class **Container** defines the set of methods that can be applied to an object of any subclass of **Container**.
- Labels are used to display text on a GUI.
- An **Applet** is a **Container** and inherits all the public interface methods of class **Container** including method **add** for attaching GUI components to a **Container**.
- A button is a component the user clicks to trigger a specific action. A Java program can use three types of buttons: push buttons, choice buttons and checkboxes (created with class **Button**, **Choice** and **Checkbox**, respectively).
- GUIs are event driven, i.e., they generate events when the user interacts with the GUI. An event is an action initiated by the user of the program interacting with the GUI such as the user moving the mouse, clicking the mouse, clicking a button, etc. Events are sent to a program by the windowing system.
- Information about a GUI event is stored in an object of a class that extends **AWTEvent**. The event classes are found in package **java.awt.event**.
- To process an event, the programmer must register an event listener and implement an event handler. An event listener is an object of a class that implements one or more event-listener interfaces. An event-listener object "listens" for specific types of events generated by other objects (normally GUI components) in a program. The event-listener interfaces can be found in package **java.awt.event**. An event handler is a method that is automatically called in response to a particular type of event.
- The use of event listeners in event handling is known as the delegation event model—the processing of an event is delegated to a particular object in the program.
- An action event can be processed by any **ActionListener** object (an object of any class that implements the **ActionListener** interface). Such a class provides a definition of method **actionPerformed**. Once an **ActionListener** object is regis-

tered to "handle" an action event, method **actionPerformed** is called automatically whenever an action event occurs.

- If an event listener is not registered for a particular GUI component, then no events are handled for that component.
- Method **addActionListener** can be found in every GUI component class that generates action events.
- Using a separate class to define an event listener is a common programming practice for separating the GUI interface from the implementation of its event handler. Programs often use separate event-listener classes to process GUI events in an attempt to make the code more reusable.
- **TextField**s are single-line areas in which text can be entered by the user from the keyboard or text can simply be displayed. When the user types data into a **TextField** and presses the *Enter* key, an action event is generated.
- **TextComponent** method **setEditable**, when passed a **false** value, specifies that a **TextField** is read-only.
- **TextComponent** method **setEchoChar** takes a character argument and uses it as a masking character for the specified **TextField**. This is useful for password protection of the text typed in a **TextField**.
- A **Choice** button (sometimes called a drop-down list) provides a list of items from which the user can make a selection. **Choice** buttons implement **ItemSelectable** which indicates that **Choice** buttons generate item events. Method **addItemListener** registers a listener for an **ItemSelectable** object.
- Interface **ItemListener** method **itemStateChanged** handles item events.
- Items are added to a **Choice** button with method **add**. A numeric index keeps track of the ordering of items. The first item is added at index 0. The first item added is displayed when the **Choice** button is added to a container. Other items are selected by clicking the **Choice** which expands into a list from which the user can make a selection.
- **Choice** method **getItem** returns the item at a specified index, **getSelectedItem** returns the selected item from a **Choice**, **countItems** returns the number of items in a **Choice**, **getSelectedIndex** returns the index of a selected item.
- Class **ItemEvent** contains method **getItemSelectable** to get the **ItemSelectable** object that generated the item event.
- Class **Checkbox** is used to create checkboxes and radio buttons. These are state buttons (i.e., buttons that have **true/false** values) that generate item events. Radio buttons are sets of checkboxes that are related by a **CheckboxGroup**. Only one **Checkbox** in a **CheckboxGroup** can be selected at a time. **Checkbox** method **getState** returns a **boolean** representing a **Checkbox**'s state.
- **List**s display a series of items from which the user may select one or more items. **List**s generate both item events and action events. **String**s are added to the **List** with method **add**. Single clicking a **List** item triggers an item event. Double clicking a **List** item triggers an action event.

- Multiple-selection **Lists** can have more than one item selected at a time. Multiple selection is enabled by passing **true** as the second argument in the **List** constructor. To capture items from a multiple-selection **List**, an external event must be triggered. A **Button** is commonly used to trigger the event. Method **getSelectedItems** returns the selected items in the **List**.
- A mouse event occurs when the user interacts with the mouse. Interfaces **MouseListener** and **MouseMotionListener** are provided for handling mouse events.
- Methods in interface **MouseListener** include: **mousePressed** (called when the user presses a mouse button), **mouseClicked** (called when the user releases the mouse button after a **mousePressed** and does not move the mouse), **mouseReleased** (called after a **mouseDragged**), **mouseEntered** (called when the mouse cursor enters the area of a component) and **mouseExited** (called when the mouse cursor exits the area of a component).
- Methods in interface **MouseMotionListener** include: **mouseDragged** (called when the user presses and holds a mouse button then drags the mouse) and **mouseMoved** (called when the user moves the mouse).
- Methods **addMouseListener** and **addMouseMotionListener** of class **Component** register **MouseListener** and **MouseMotionListener** event listeners for any GUI component.
- The **java.awt.event** package provides event-listener adapter classes for every event-listener interface with more than one method. An adapter class provides a default implementation of every method in the interface. The default implementation of each method has an empty body.
- Key events are generated when keys on the keyboard are pressed and released. A class that implements **KeyListener** must provide definitions for method **keyPressed**, **keyReleased** and **keyTyped**, each of which receives a **KeyEvent** as its argument.
- Method **keyPressed** is called in response to pressing an action key (i.e., an arrow key, *Home*, *End*, *Page Up*, *Page Down*, a function key, *Num Lock*, *Print Screen*, *Scroll Lock*, *Caps Lock*, and *Pause*). Method **keyTyped** is called in response to pressing any other key on the keyboard. Method **keyReleased** is called after the key is released in any **keyPressed** or **keyTyped** event.
- **Component** method **addKeyListener** registers **KeyListeners** for components
- **KeyEvent** method **getKeyCode** gets the Unicode value of the key that was pressed. **KeyEvent** method **getKeyText** returns a **String** containing the name of the key whose key code is passed as an argument. **KeyEvent** method **getKeyChar** gets the actual character typed.
- **KeyEvent** method **isActionKey** determines if the key in an event is an action key.
- **InputEvent** method **getModifiers** determines if any modifier keys were pressed when the key event occurred. Method **getKeyModifiersText** of class **KeyEvent** produces a string containing the names of the pressed modifier keys.

- **InputEvent** methods **isAltDown**, **isControlDown**, **isMetaDown** and **isShiftDown** each return a **boolean** indicating if the particular key was pressed during the key event.
- Layout managers are used to arrange components on a container. The default for applets is the **FlowLayout** layout manager.
- Container method **setLayout** specifies a new layout for a container.
- **FlowLayout** is the most basic layout manager. GUI components are placed on a container from left to right—one after the other. A **Flowlayout** may be right, left, or center aligned. Center is the default alignment.
- **Container** method **validate** recomputes the layout of all the GUI components in a container when the layout is changed.
- The **BorderLayout** layout manager arranges components into five areas: North, South, East, West, and Center. In **BorderLayout**, up to five components can be used—one for each position.
- The **GridLayout** layout manager places components into rows and columns. Each component is given the same size. The first component added will be placed in the first column of the first row. The next component added will be placed in the second column of the first row and so forth.

Terminology

ActionEvent class
ActionListener interface
actionPerformed method
add method of class **Choice**
add method of class **Container**
add method of class **List**
addActionListener method
addItemListener method
addMouseListener method
addMouseMotionListener method
AdjustmentEvent class
AdjustmentListener interface
attach a component to a container
AWT (another/abstract windowing toolkit)
AWTEvent class
BorderLayout layout manager
button
Button class
button event
button label
Center in **BorderLayout**
checkbox
Checkbox class
CheckboxGroup class
choice button
Choice class
clicking
component
Component class
ComponentAdapter class
ComponentEvent class
ComponentListener interface
container
Container class
ContainerAdapter class
ContainerEvent class
ContainerListener interface
control key
default text in a text field
delegation event model
dragging
drop-down list
East in **BorderLayout**
event
event driven
event handler
event listener
EventListener interface

EventObject class
FlowLayout layout manger
FocusAdapter class
FocusEvent class
FocusListener interface
getActionCommand method
getClickCount method (**MouseEvent**)
getItem method of class **ItemEvent**
getItemSelectable method (**ItemEvent**)
getKeyChar method of class **KeyEvent**
getKeyCode method of class **KeyEvent**
getKeyText method of class **KeyEvent**
getKeyModifiersText method
getModifiers method of class **InputEvent**
getSelectedIndex method of class **Choice**
getSelectedIndex method of class **List**
getSelectedItem method of class **Choice**
getSelectedItem method of class **List**
getSelectedItems method of class **List**
getState method of class **Checkbox**
getText method of class **Label**
getText method of class **TextField**
graphical user interface (GUI)
GridLayout layout manager
GUI component
import java.awt.*;
import java.awt.event.*;
index
InputEvent class
insert method of class **Choice**
isActionKey method of class **KeyEvent**
isAltDown method of class **InputEvent**
isControlDown method (**InputEvent**)
isMetaDown method of class **InputEvent**
isShitfDown method of class **InputEvent**
ItemEvent class
ItemListener interface
ItemSelectable interface
itemStateChanged method
keyboard
key constants
KeyAdapter class
KeyEvent class
KeyListener interface
label
Label class
layout manager
LayoutManager interface
list
List class
look and feel
meta key
mouse
MouseAdapter class
mouseClicked method
mouseDragged method
mouseEntered method
MouseEvent class
mouseExited method
MouseListener interface
MouseMotionAdapter class
MouseMotionListener interface
mouseMoved method
mouse cursor
mousePressed method
mouseReleased method
multiple selections
North in **BorderLayout**
PaintEvent class
panel
Panel class
paramString method
push button
radio button
remove method of class **Choice**
requestFocus method of class **Component**
scrollbar
setAlignment method of class **Label**
setBackground method of class **Component**
setEchoChar method of class **TextField**
setEditable method of class **TextField**
setFont method of class **Component**
setLayout method of class **Container**
setText method of class **Label**
setVisible method of class **Component**
shift key
South in **BorderLayout**
state button
TextComponent class
text field
TextField class
TextListener interface
true/false **Checkbox** setting
update method of class **Component**
validate method of class **Container**
virtual key code

West in **BorderLayout**
widgets
WindowAdapter class
WindowEvent class
WindowListener interface

Common Programming Errors

10.1 Forgetting to add a component to a container is a run-time logic error.

10.2 Adding to a container a component that has not been instantiated throws a **NullPointer-Exception**.

10.3 Having more than one button with the same label makes the buttons ambiguous to the user.

10.4 Forgetting to register an event-handler object for a particular GUI component results in no events being handled for that component.

10.5 Using a lowercase **f** in **TextField** is a syntax error.

10.6 Using an uppercase **b** for box in **Checkbox** or **CheckboxGroup** is a syntax error.

10.7 Adding a **CheckboxGroup** object (or an object of any other class that does not derive from **Component**) to a container is a syntax error.

10.8 Attempting to add an item that is not a string to a **List** is a syntax error.

10.9 Forgetting to specify the region to which a GUI component should be added in a **Border-Layout** results in that component not being displayed. There is no error message to indicate this problem.

10.10 Adding more than one component to a particular region in a **BorderLayout** results in only the last component added being displayed. There is no error message to indicate this problem.

10.11 Adding a component to a container that has not been instantiated throws a **NullPointer-Exception**.

Good Programming Practices

10.1 Study the methods of class **Component** in the Java Developer's Kit on-line documentation to learn the capabilities common to every GUI component.

10.2 Study the methods of class **Container** in the Java Developer's Kit on-line documentation to learn the capabilities common to every container for GUI components.

10.3 Provide a unique name for each button label.

10.4 Use separate classes to process GUI events.

Performance Tip

10.1 The event-handling mechanism of Java 1.1 is much more efficient than the event-handling mechanism of Java 1.0. In Java.1.0, all events were sent into the program, even if they were not handled, resulting in many extraneous method calls to event-handling methods. In Java 1.1, only events for which an event-handler object is registered are delivered to the program.

Portability Tip

10.1 The look of a particular GUI component may vary across platforms. Java "ties" into the "local" GUI which varies from platform to platform.

Software Engineering Observation

10.1 Using separate classes to handle common GUI events leads to more reusable software components that can be placed in packages and used in many programs.

Self-Review Exercises

10.1 Fill in the blanks in each of the following:

a) A __________ event occurs when the mouse is moved and an event listener is registered to handle the event.

b) Text that cannot be modified by the user is called __________ text.

c) A __________ arranges GUI components on an applet or panel.

d) The **add** method for attaching GUI components to an applet or panel is a ________ class method.

e) GUI is an acronym for __________.

f) The __________ method is used to set the layout manager for a container.

g) A **mouseDragged** event is preceded by a __________ event and followed by a __________ event.

10.2 State which of the following statements are true and which are false. If a statement is false, explain why.

a) **BorderLayout** is the default layout manager for a panel.

b) When the mouse cursor is moved into the bounds of a GUI component, a **mouseOver** event occurs.

c) A panel cannot be added to another panel.

d) When building a GUI, one or more classes must be imported from package **java.awt**.

e) In a **BorderLayout**, two buttons added to the North region will be placed side-by-side.

f) When using **BorderLayout**, a maximum of five components may be used.

10.3 Find the error(s) in each of the following and explain how to correct it (them).

a) `buttonName = Button( "Caption" );`

b) `Label aLabel, Label;       // create references`

c) `txtField = new TextField( 50, "Default Text" );`

d)
```
public void init()
{
   setLayout( new BorderLayout() );
   button1 = new Button( "North Star" );
   button2 = new Button( "South Pole" );
   add( button1 );
   add( button2 );
}
```

10.4 Briefly answer the following.

a) Explain what the asterisk (*****) means in the following statement:

```
import java.awt.*;
```

b) Explain difference between a text field and a label.

Answers to Self-Review Exercises

10.1 a) **`mouseMoved`**. b) static (read-only). c) Layout manager. d) **`Container`**. e) graphical user interface. f) **`setLayout`**. g) **`mousePressed`**, **`mouseReleased`**.

10.2
a) False. The default is **`FlowLayout`**.
b) False. A **`mouseEnter`** event occurs.
c) False. A panel can be added to another panel because **`Panel`** derives from **`Container`** and **`Container`** derives from **`Component`**. Therefore, a **`Panel`** is a **`Component`**.
d) True.
e) False. Only the last button added will be displayed. Remember that only one component can be added to each region in a **`BorderLayout`**.
f) True

10.3
a) **`new`** is needed to instantiate the object.
b) **`Label`** is a class name and cannot be used as an identifier
c) The arguments passed to the constructor are reversed. The **`String`** must be passed first.
d) **`BorderLayout`** has been set and components are being added without specifying the region. Proper **`add`** statements might be:

```
add( button1, BorderLayout.NORTH );
add( button2, BorderLayout.SOUTH );
```

10.4
a) The asterisk is a wildcard that specifies that all classes from the **`java.awt`** package are to be imported.
b) A label is a component that displays non-modifiable text. A text field is a component with a border that displays either modifiable text or non-modifiable text. A text field can also accept user input—whereas a label cannot. Text fields also generate action events.

Exercises

10.5 Fill in the blanks in each of the following:
a) The **`TextField`** class inherits directly from ________.
b) The layout managers discussed in this chapter are ________, ________, and ________.
c) **`Container`** method ________ attaches a GUI component to a panel or to an applet.
d) A ________ event occurs when a mouse button is released.
e) The ________ class is used to create a radio button group.

10.6 State which of the following statements are true and which are false. If a statement is false, explain why.
a) Only one layout manager can be used per container.
b) GUI components can be added to a panel using **`BorderLayout`** in any order.
c) The **`add`** method adds items to a **`Choice`** button.
d) Radio buttons provide a series of mutually exclusive buttons (only one can be **`true`** at a time).
e) **`Graphics`** method **`setFont`** is used to set the font for text fields.
f) A **`List`** object always displays a scrollbar.
g) A **`Mouse`** object contains a method called **`mouseDragged`**.
h) The **`BorderLayout`** layout manager implements **`LayoutManager`**.
i) The **`GridLayout`** layout manager implements **`LayoutManager`**.
j) The **`FlowLayout`** layout manager does not implement **`LayoutManager`**.

10.7 State which of the following statements are true and which are false. If a statement is false, explain why.

a) An applet is a container.
b) A panel is a component.
c) A label is a container.
d) A list is a panel.
e) A button is a component.
f) A text field is an object.
g) **`LayoutManager`** inherits from **`Object`**.
h) **`CheckboxGroup`** inherits from **`Component`**.

10.8 Find any error(s) in each of the following and explain how to correct it (them).

a) `import java.awt.*        // include AWT package`
b) `panelObject.GridLayout( 8, 8 ); // set GridLayout`
c) `setLayout( new FlowLayout( FlowLayout.DEFAULT ) );`
d) `add( eastButton, EAST );   // BorderLayout`

10.9 Create the following GUI. You do not have to provide any functionality.

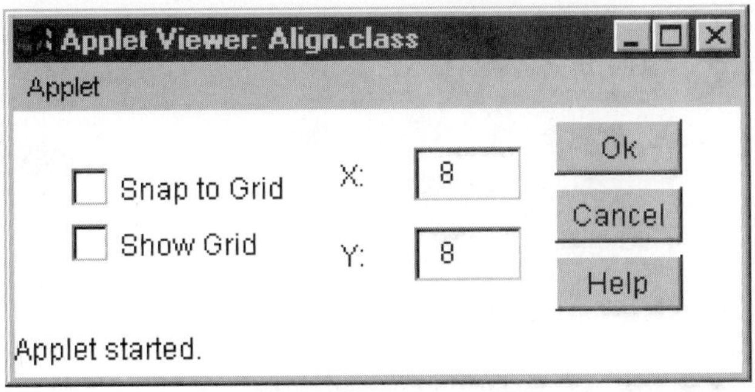

10.10 Create the following GUI. You do not have to provide any functionality.

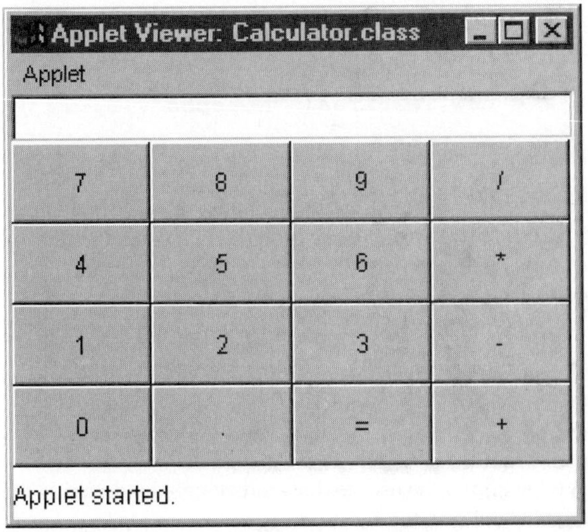

10.11 Create the following GUI. You do not have to provide any functionality.

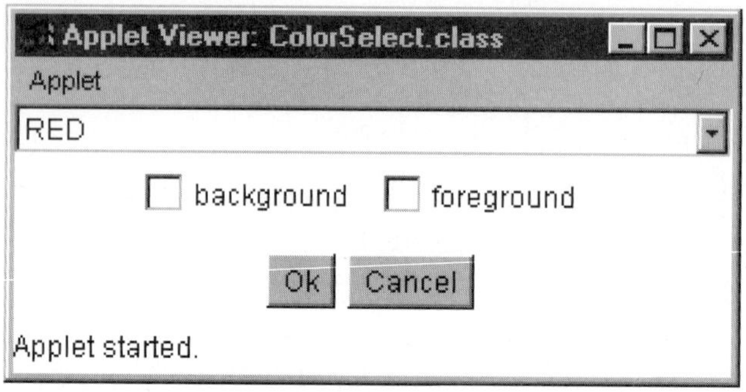

10.12 Create the following GUI. You do not have to provide any functionality.

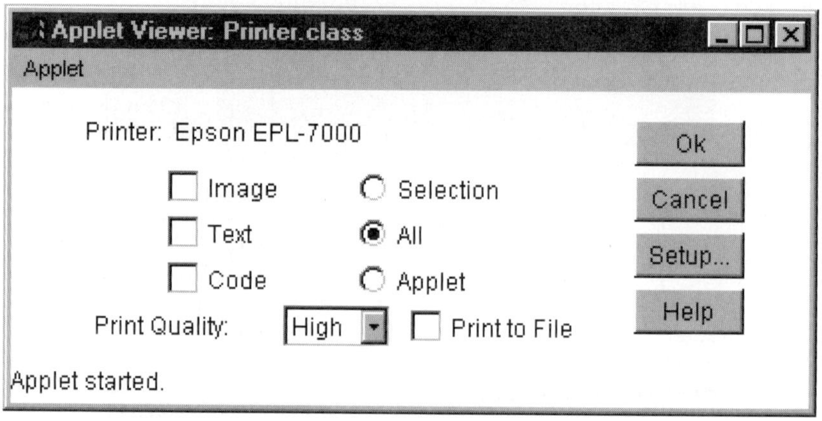

10.13 Create the GUI of Fig. 10.1. The left-most component is a **`TextArea`**. We discuss **`TextArea`**s in the next chapter. The **`TextArea`** is created with the **`TextArea`** class and a call to the **`TextArea`** constructor:

```
TextArea a = new TextArea( "Notepad", 5, 12 );
```

You do not have to provide any functionality for this GUI.

10.14 Write a temperature conversion program that converts from Fahrenheit to Celsius. The Fahrenheit temperature should be entered from the keyboard (via a **`TextField`**). A **`TextField`** should be used to display the converted temperature. Use the following formula for the conversion:

$$Celsius = 5/9 \times (Fahrenheit - 32)$$

10.15 Enhance the temperature conversion program of Exercise 10.14 by adding the Kelvin temperature scale. The program should also allow the user to make conversions between any two scales. Use the following formula (in addition to the one in Exercise 10.14): $Kelvin = Celsius + 273$.

10.16 Write an applet that allows the user to draw a rectangle by dragging the mouse on the applet. The upper-left coordinate should be the location where the user presses the mouse button and the lower-right coordinate should be the location where the user releases the mouse button. Also display the area of the rectangle in the status bar. Use the formula: $area = width \times height$.

10.17 Modify the program of Exercise. 10.16 to draw different shapes. The user should be allowed to choose from an oval, an arc, a line, a rectangle with rounded corners, and a predefined polygon. Also display the mouse coordinates in the status bar.

10.18 Write a program that will allow the user to draw a shape on an applet with the mouse. The shape drawn should be determined by the following keys: c draws a circle, o draws an oval, r draws a rectangle, and l draws a line. The size and placement of the shape should be determined by the **`mousePressed`** and **`mouseReleased`** events. Display the name of the current shape in the status bar. The initial shape should default to a circle.

10.19 Create an applet that enables the user to paint a picture. The user should be able to choose the shape to draw, the color in which the shape should appear and whether the shape should be filled with color. Use the graphical user interface components we discussed in this chapter such as **`Choice`** buttons, radio buttons and **`Checkbox`**es to allow the user to select various options. The program should override the **`update`** method so the user can draw several shapes and see all the shapes at the same time on the applet. The program should provide a **`Button`** object that allows the user to erase the applet. If you feel ambitious, try to provide a "rubber-banding" effect as the user drags the mouse to draw a shape (i.e., the user should be able to see the outline of the shape). Note: You may have to use **`Graphics`** method **`setXORMode`** to help implement this effect. Techniques from Chapter 14 will allow you to have both capabilities.

10.20 Write a program that uses **`System.out.println`** statements to print out events as they occur. Provide a **`Choice`** button with a minimum of four different items. The user should be able to choose an event to "monitor" from the **`Choice`** button. When that particular event occurs, display information about the event in the status bar. Use the **`toString`** method on the event to convert it to a string representation.

10.21 Write a program that draws a square. As the mouse is moved on the applet, the square should be repainted with the upper-left corner of the square following the exact path of the mouse cursor.

10.22 Modify the program of Fig. 10.21 to incorporate colors. Provide a "toolbar" at the bottom of the applet that lists the following six colors: red, black, magenta, blue, green, and yellow. The toolbar should consist of six buttons, each with the appropriate color name. When a button is clicked, drawing should occur in the new color. Display the current drawing color in the status bar.

10.23 Modify the program of Fig. 10.21 to allow the user to erase. Erasing is done by drawing over information in the background color. When the shift key is held while dragging the mouse, drawing should be done in the background color.

10.24 Write a program that plays "guess the number" as follows: Your program chooses the number to be guessed by selecting an integer at random in the range 1–1000. The program then displays in a label:

```
I have a number between 1 and 1000 can you guess my number?
Please enter your first guess.
```

A **`TextField`** should be used to input the guess. As each guess is input the background color should change to either red or blue. Red indicates that the user is getting "warmer" and blue indicates that the user is getting "colder." A second uneditable **TextField** should display either "**Too High**" or "**Too Low**" to help the user zero in on the correct answer. When the user gets the correct answer "**Correct!**" should be displayed and the **TextField** used for input should be changed to uneditable.

A **Button** should be provided to allow the user to play the game again. When the **Button** is clicked, a new random number should be generated and the input **TextField** changed to editable.

10.25 It is often useful to display the events that occur during the execution of a program to help understand when the events occur and how they are generated. Write an applet that enables the user to generate and process every event discussed in this chapter. The applet should provide methods from the **ActionListener**, **ItemListener**, **MouseListener**, **MouseMotionListener**, and **KeyListener** interfaces to display messages when the events occur. Use method **toString** to convert the event objects received in each event handler into a **String** that can be displayed. Method **toString** creates a **String** containing all the information in the event object.

10.26 Modify your solution to Exercise 10.19 to enable the user to select a font and a font size, then type text into a **TextField**. When the user presses *Enter,* the text should be displayed on the applet in the chosen font and size. Modify the applet further to allow the user to specify the exact position at which the text should be displayed.

10.27 Write an applet that allows the user to select a shape from a **Choice** button, then draws that shape 20 times with random locations and dimensions in the **paint** method. The first item in the **Choice** should be the default shape that is displayed the first time **paint** is called.

10.28 Modify Exercise 10.27 to draw each of the 20 randomly-sized shapes in a randomly-selected color. Use all 13 predefined **Color** objects in an array of **Colors**.

10.29 Modify Exercise 10.28 to allow the user to select the color in which shapes should be drawn from a **Choice** button.

10.30 Write an applet using methods from interfaces **MouseListener** and **MouseMotionListener** that allows the user to press the mouse button, drag the mouse and release the mouse button. When the mouse is released, draw a rectangle with the appropriate upper-left corner, width and height. Use a separate event-listener class to handle the **mousePressed** and **mouseReleased** events. Hint: The **mousePressed** method should capture the set of coordinates at which the user presses and holds the mouse button initially and the **mouseReleased** method should capture the set of coordinates at which the user releases the mouse button. Both methods should call methods in the applet to set the appropriate coordinate values. All calculations of the width, height, and upper-left corner should be performed by the applet's **paint** method before the shape is drawn.

10.31 Modify Exercise 10.30 to provided a "rubber-banding" effect. As the user drags the mouse, the user should be able to see the current size of the rectangle to know exactly what the rectangle will look like when the mouse button is released. Use a separate class that to handle the **mouseDragged** events. Hint: **mouseDragged** should perform the same tasks as **mouseReleased**.

10.32 Modify Exercise 10.31 to allow the user to select which shape to draw. A **Choice** button should provide options including at least (Rectangle, Oval, Line, and Rounded Rectangle).

10.33 Modify Exercise 10.32 to allow the user to select the drawing color.

10.34 Modify Exercise 10.33 to allow the user to specify if a shape should be filled or empty when it is drawn. The user should click a **`Checkbox`** to indicate filled or empty.

10.35 *(Painting program)* Rewrite Exercise 10.34 to allow the user to draw multiple shapes and store each shape in an array of shapes (maintained with an object of class **`Vector`**). For this applet, create your own classes from which objects will be created to store each shape the user draws. The classes should store the location, dimensions and color of each shape and should indicate if the shape is filled or unfilled. Your classes should all derive from a class called **`MyShape`** that has all the common features of every shape type. Every subclass of **`MyShape`** should have its own method draw that returns **`void`** and receives a **`Graphics`** object as its argument. When the applet's **`paint`** method is called, it should walk through the array of shapes and display each shape by calling the shape's **`draw`** method (passing the **`Graphics`** object as an argument). Each shape's **`draw`** method should know how to draw the shape. As a minimum, your program should provide the following classes: **`MyPoint`**, **`MyRectangle`**, **`MyOval`**, **`MyLine`**, **`MyArc`** and **`MyRoundedRectangle`**. Design the class hierarchy for maximum software reuse and place all your classes in the package **`shapes`**. Import this package into your applet.

10.36 Modify Exercise 10.35 to provide an "Undo" button that can be used repeatedly to undo the last painting operation. If there are no shapes in the array of shapes, the Undo button should be disabled.

11

Advanced Graphical User Interface Components

Objectives

- To be able to create and manipulate text areas, canvases, scrollbars, frames, menus, dialog boxes, popup menus, and scrolling panels.
- To be able to use different mouse pointers.
- To be able to use advanced layout managers.

I claim not to have controlled events, but confess plainly that events have controlled me.
Abraham Lincoln

A good symbol is the best argument, and is a missionary to persuade thousands.
Ralph Waldo Emerson

Capture its reality in paint!
Paul Cézanne

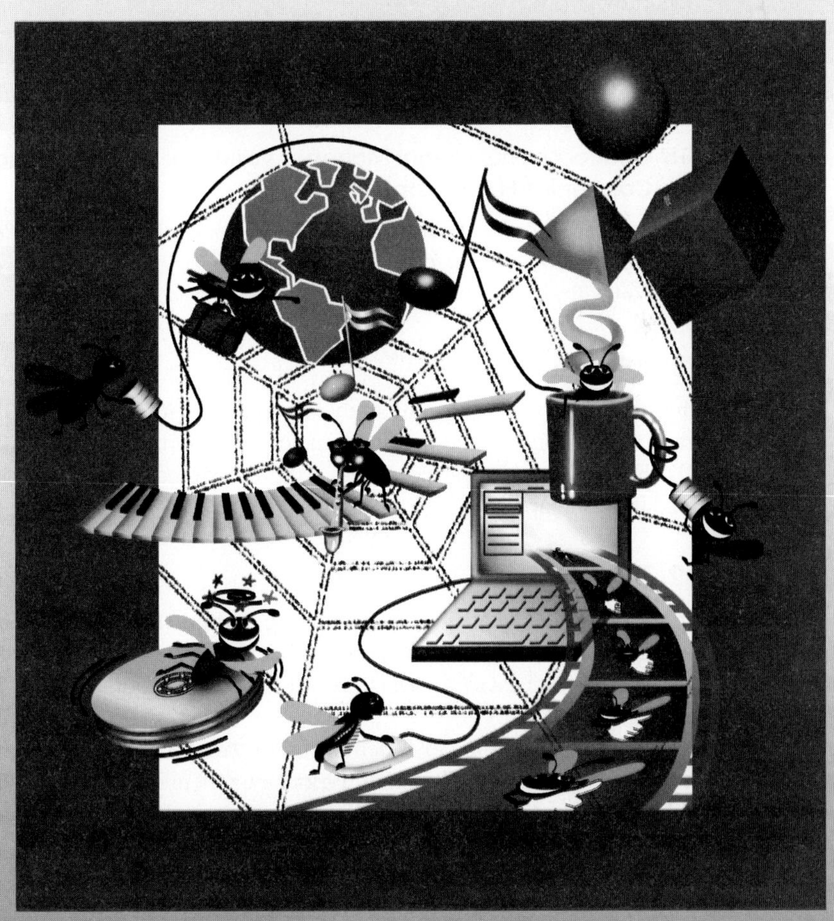

Outline

11.1 Introduction[1]

In this chapter, we continue our study of graphical user interfaces (GUIs). We discuss more advanced components and layout managers and lay the groundwork for building complex GUIs. Figure 11.1 shows the **`java.awt`** inheritance hierarchy for the components discussed in this chapter.

11.2 TextAreas

Text areas provide an area for manipulating multiple lines of text. Like class **`TextField`**, class ***`TextArea`*** inherits from **`TextComponent`** that defines some common methods for **`TextField`**s and **`TextArea`**s. Several **`TextArea`** constructors are summarized in Fig. 11.2.

The program of Fig. 11.3 demonstrates **`TextArea`**s. One **`TextArea`** displays text that the user can select. The other **`TextArea`** is uneditable. Its purpose is to display the text the user selected in the first **`TextArea`** or typed in the first **`TextArea`**. **`TextArea`**s

---

1.This chapter was coauthored with Mr. Tem Nieto of Deitel & Associates, Inc.

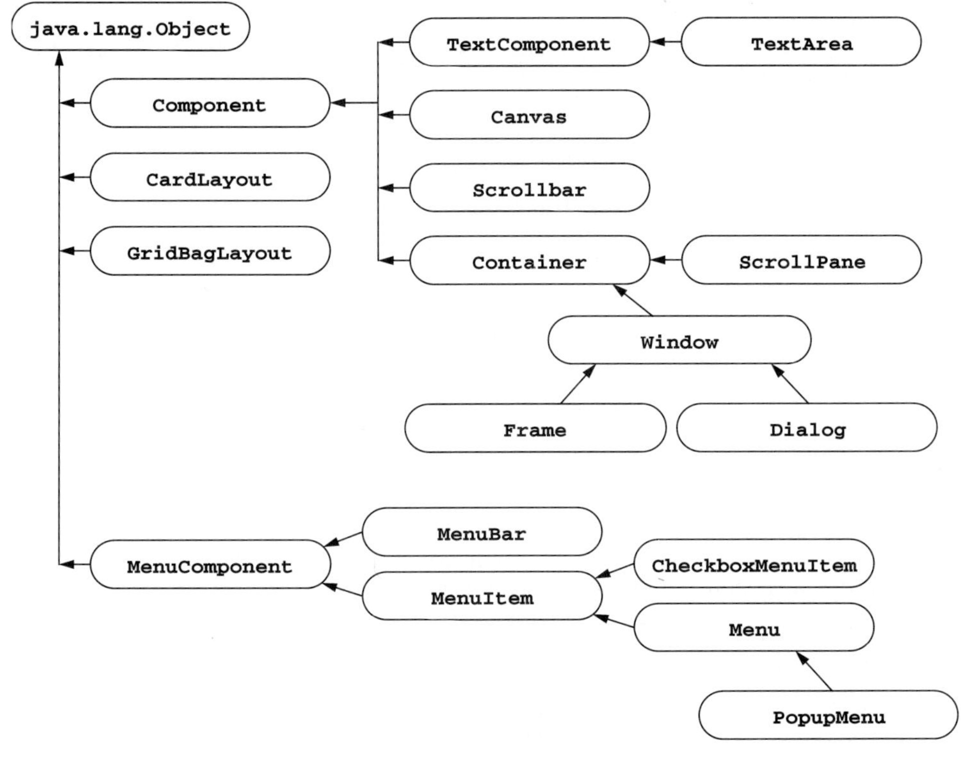

Fig. 11.1 Hierarchy of **java.awt** components discussed in this chapter.

do not have action events like **TextField**s. Therefore, an external event (clicking the button between the **TextArea**s) causes the selected text in the left **TextArea** to be copied and displayed in the right **TextArea**. Both **TextArea**s and **TextField**s can have event listeners that are notified when the user of the program alters the text. When the user types in the first **TextArea** in this program, the registered ***TextListener*** is called to handle the event and display the entire contents of the first **TextArea** in the second **TextArea**.

The applet instantiates **TextArea** objects **t1** and **t2**. Each **TextArea** has **5** visible rows and **20** visible columns. Line 18

```
t1 = new TextArea( s, 5, 20, TextArea.SCROLLBARS_NONE );
```

specifies that the default string **s** should be displayed. The last argument to this constructor indicates that the **TextArea** should be displayed without scrollbars. When text reaches the right side of this **TextArea** it automatically "wraps" to the next line. This is referred to as *automatic word wrap*. By default, **TextArea**s have horizontal and vertical scrollbars and do not provide automatic word wrap (as is the case with **t2**). The applet is registered to listen for *text events* on object **t1** with line 19

TextArea class constructors

public TextArea()

Constructs a **TextArea** with default size (normally controlled by the layout of the container to which it is attached).

public TextArea(int rows, int columns)

Constructs a **TextArea** with the specified number of **rows** and **columns**.

public TextArea(String s)

Constructs a **TextArea** containing the text **s**.

public TextArea(String s, int rows, int columns)

Constructs a **TextArea** containing the text **s** and the specified number of **rows** and **columns**.

public TextArea(String s, int rows, int columns, int scrollbars)

Constructs a **TextArea** containing text **s** and the specified number of **rows** and **columns**. The **scrollbars** argument specifies which scrollbars should be visible using one of the **TextArea** constants: **SCROLLBARS_BOTH**, **SCROLLBARS_HORIZONTAL_ONLY**, **SCROLLBARS_NONE**, or **SCROLLBARS_VERTICAL_ONLY**

Fig. 11.2 **TextArea** class constructors.

```
// Fig. 11.3: TextAreaDemo.java
// Copying selected text from one text area to another.
import java.applet.Applet;
import java.awt.*;
import java.awt.event.*;

public class TextAreaDemo extends Applet
             implements ActionListener, TextListener {
   private TextArea t1, t2;
   private Button copy;

   public void init()
   {
      String s = "This is a demo string to illustrate " +
                 "copying text from one TextArea to " +
                 "another TextArea using an external event";

      t1 = new TextArea( s, 5, 20, TextArea.SCROLLBARS_NONE );
      t1.addTextListener( this );
      add( t1 );

      copy = new Button( "Copy >>>" );
      copy.addActionListener( this );
      add( copy );
```

Fig. 11.3 Copying selected text from one text area to another. (part 1 of 2)

```
25
26          t2 = new TextArea( 5, 20 );
27          t2.setEditable( false );
28          add( t2 );
29       }
30
31       public void actionPerformed( ActionEvent e )
32       {
33          t2.setText( t1.getSelectedText() );
34       }
35
36       public void textValueChanged( TextEvent e )
37       {
38          TextComponent source = ( TextComponent ) e.getSource();
39          t2.setText( source.getText() );
40       }
41    }
```

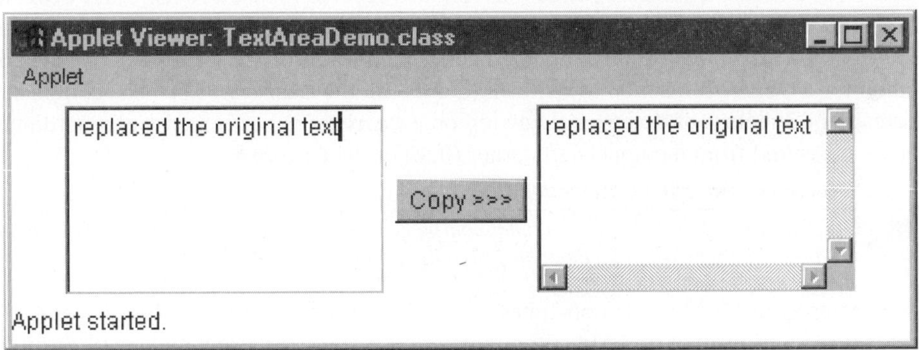

Fig. 11.3 Copying selected text from one text area to another. (part 2 of 2)

```
t1.addTextListener( this );
```

Because the applet implements **TextListener** (line 8), it must provide a definition for method ***textValueChanged*** that receives a **TextEvent** as its argument. This method is called in this program when the user alters the text in **t1**.

Lines 22 and 23 instantiate **Button** object **copy** with the label "**Copy>>>**" and register the applet as the action event handler for **copy**. This button provides the external event that determines when the selected text in **t1** should be copied to **t2**.

When the user clicks **copy**, **actionPerformed** (line 31) is invoked and the statement

```
t2.setText( t1.getSelectedText() );
```

uses **TextComponent** method ***getSelectedText*** to get the selected text in **t1**. The method returns a **String** that is placed in **t2** with **TextComponent** method **setText**. Text is selected by highlighting it with the mouse (drag the mouse over the text you would like to select).

When the user types in **t1**, a text event occurs and method **textValueChanged** (line 36) executes the statements

```
TextComponent source = ( TextComponent ) e.getSource();
t2.setText( source.getText() );
```

The first statement uses method **getSource** (inherited into **TextEvent** from **EventObject**) to get the source of the event. This result is cast to **TextComponent** because the return value of **getSource** is **Object** and we are assigning the result to a reference of type **TextComponent** called **source**. Next, **getText** gets the **String** in the event source (**t1**) and the result is passed to **setText** so it can be displayed in **t2**.

11.3 Creating a Customized Subclass of Canvas

A *canvas* is a dedicated drawing area that can also receive mouse events. Class ***Canvas*** inherits from **Component**. By default, a **Canvas** is not capable of drawing because the **Canvas**'s **paint** method only sets the background color of the **Canvas**. The **paint** method for a **Canvas** must be overridden to draw on the **Canvas**. This is accomplished by creating a subclass of **Canvas**. Drawing on a **Canvas** is performed with coordinates that are measured from the upper-left corner (0, 0) of the **Canvas**.

Software Engineering Observation 11.1

Graphics drawn directly on an applet can be covered by components. Canvases eliminate this problem by providing a dedicated area for graphics.

The applet of Fig. 11.4 demonstrates a customized subclass of **Canvas**. Class **CustomCanvas** has its own **paint** method that draws a circle or a square depending on the value passed to its **draw** method. For this purpose, **CustomCanvas** line 38

```
public final static int CIRCLE = 1, SQUARE = 2;
```

defines constants that are used to specify the shape a **CustomCanvas** draws on itself with each call to its **paint** method.

The applet consists of three classes—**MyCanvas** to run the applet, **CustomCanvas** to draw the chosen shape and **ButtonHandler** to handle button events for the applet.

```
// Fig. 11.4: MyCanvas.java
// Using a customized Canvas object.
import java.applet.Applet;
import java.awt.*;

public class MyCanvas extends Applet {
   private Panel p;
   private CustomCanvas c;
   private Button circle, square;

   public void init()
   {
      c = new CustomCanvas();    // instantiate canvas
      c.setBackground( Color.green );

      square = new Button( "Square" );
      square.addActionListener(
         new ButtonHandler( c, CustomCanvas.SQUARE ) );
      circle = new Button( "Circle" );
      circle.addActionListener(
         new ButtonHandler( c, CustomCanvas.CIRCLE ) );

      p = new Panel();
      p.setLayout( new GridLayout( 2, 1 ) );
      p.add( circle );
      p.add( square );

      setLayout( new BorderLayout() );
      add( p, BorderLayout.WEST );
      add( c, BorderLayout.CENTER );     // add canvas
   }
}
```

Fig. 11.4 Extending the **Canvas** class (part 1 of 5).

```
// Fig. 11.4: CustomCanvas.java
// A customized Canvas class.
import java.awt.*;

public class CustomCanvas extends Canvas {
   public final static int CIRCLE = 1, SQUARE = 2;
   private int shape;

   public void paint( Graphics g )
   {
      if ( shape == CIRCLE )
         g.fillOval( 50, 10, 60, 60 );
      else if ( shape == SQUARE )
         g.fillRect( 50, 10, 60, 60 );
   }
```

Fig. 11.4 Extending the **Canvas** class (part 2 of 5).

```
48
49      public void draw( int s )
50      {
51         shape = s;
52         repaint();
53      }
54   }
```

Fig. 11.4 Extending the **Canvas** class (part 3 of 5).

```
55   // Fig. 11.4: ButtonHandler.java
56   // Handle event for a button in the MyCanvas applet.
57   import java.awt.event.*;
58
59   public class ButtonHandler implements ActionListener {
60      private CustomCanvas canvas;
61      private int shape;
62
63      public ButtonHandler( CustomCanvas c, int s )
64      {
65         canvas = c;
66         shape = s;
67      }
68
69      public void actionPerformed( ActionEvent e )
70      {
71         canvas.draw( shape );
72      }
73   }
```

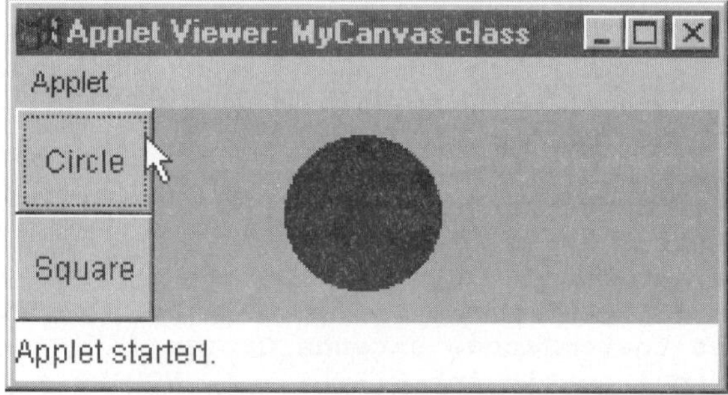

Fig. 11.4 Extending the **Canvas** class (part 4 of 5).

Method **init** (line 11) of class **MyCanvas** instantiates a **CustomCanvas** object and sets its background color to green so the **CustomCanvas** area is visible on the applet. Next, **Button** objects **circle** and **square** are instantiated. Lines 17, 18, 20 and 21

```
square.addActionListener(
   new ButtonHandler( c, CustomCanvas.SQUARE ) );
circle.addActionListener(
   new ButtonHandler( c, CustomCanvas.CIRCLE ) );
```

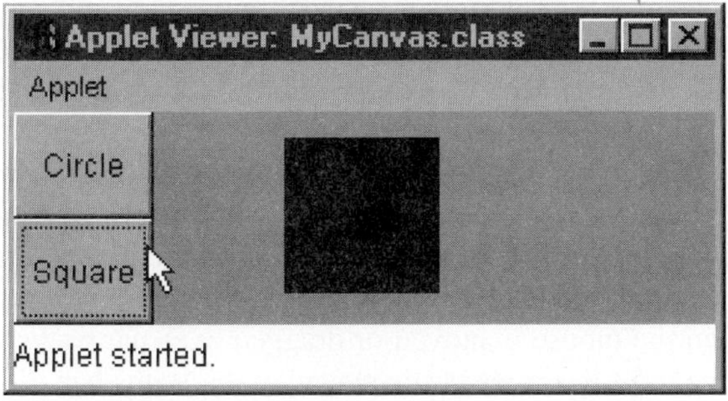

Fig. 11.4 Extending the **Canvas** class (part 5 of 5).

register action event listeners for each **Button**. Class **ButtonHandler**'s constructor requires two arguments—a reference to the **CustomCanvas** object that is used to call **CustomCanvas** method **draw** and an **int** value indicating the shape to draw. For layout of the buttons, **Panel p** is created with a **GridLayout** of two rows and one column and the buttons are added to the **Panel**. Finally, the **Panel** is added to the West region and the **CustomCanvas** is added to the Center region of the applet's **BorderLayout**. Note that the **BorderLayout** automatically expands the **CustomCanvas** to fill the Center region. Normally, **Component** method **setSize** is invoked to set the width and height of a **Canvas** because the default size of a **Canvas** is 0-by-0 pixels.

Common Programming Error 11.1

*Forgetting to call the **setSize** method on a canvas is a run-time logic error. The canvas would not be seen because its default size is 0-by-0 pixels.*

Class **CustomCanvas** (line 37) contains one instance variable **shape** that keeps track of the shape to be drawn. Method **paint** (line 41) is overridden in class **CustomCanvas** to draw a shape on the canvas. If **shape** is **CIRCLE**, **Graphics** method **fillOval** draws a solid circle. If **shape** is **SQUARE**, **Graphics** method **fillRect** draws a solid square. Method **draw** (line 49) sets the **private** instance variable **shape** and calls **repaint** to refresh the **CustomCanvas** object. Note that calling **repaint** for the **CustomCanvas** invokes the **update** and **paint** methods of class **CustomCanvas** not of the applet. When **paint** is called, the appropriate shape is drawn on the canvas.

Class **ButtonHandler** (line 59) implements **ActionListener** so **ButtonHandler** objects can listen for action events. Each instance of **ButtonHandler** in this example listens for an action event on one of the buttons (**circle** or **square**). When a button is clicked, the appropriate **ButtonHandler** object calls **CustomCanvas** method **draw** and passes the **shape** value stored in the **ButtonHandler** object when it was instantiated (lines 18 and 20).

11.4 Creating a Self-Contained Subclass of Canvas

Canvases do not generate any events but are capable of recognizing mouse events. The program of Fig. 11.5 allows the user to draw an oval on a canvas with the mouse. Class **SelfContainedCanvas** listens for its own mouse events and draws an oval on itself. The location and size of the oval are determined by the user pressing and holding the mouse button, dragging the mouse and releasing the mouse button. Class **SelfContainedCanvas** is placed in package **com.deitel.jhtp2.ch11** for future reuse. For this reason, it is imported (line 7) into the **MyCanvas2** applet.

Method **init** (line 13) of applet class **MyCanvas2** creates an instance of class **SelfContainedCanvas**, uses **Component** method ***setSize*** to resize the canvas and sets the background color of the canvas to yellow so the canvas area is visible against the background of the applet. The applet registers itself (line 20) to listen for its own mouse motion events. When the mouse is moved or dragged over the background of the applet, the coordinates of the mouse pointer are displayed in the status bar.

```
1  // Fig. 11.5: MyCanvas2.java
2  // Creating a self-contained canvas that processes
3  // its own mouse events.
4  import java.applet.Applet;
5  import java.awt.*;
6  import java.awt.event.*;
7  import com.deitel.jhtp2.ch11.SelfContainedCanvas;
8
9  public class MyCanvas2 extends Applet
10                implements MouseMotionListener {
11    private SelfContainedCanvas c;
12
13    public void init()
14    {
15       c = new SelfContainedCanvas();
16       c.setSize( 185, 70 );  // resize canvas
17       c.setBackground( Color.yellow );
18       add( c );    // add canvas to applet
19
20       addMouseMotionListener( this );
21    }
22
23    public void mouseDragged( MouseEvent e )
24    {
25       showStatus( "Applet x: " + e.getX() +
26                   "; Applet y: " + e.getY() );
27    }
28
29    public void mouseMoved( MouseEvent e )
30    {
31       showStatus( "Applet x: " + e.getX() +
32                   "; Applet y: " + e.getY() );
33    }
34 }
```

Fig. 11.5 Capturing mouse events with a **Canvas** (part 1 of 3).

```
// Fig. 11.5: SelfContainedCanvas.java
// A self-contained Canvas class that
// handles its own mouse events.
package com.deitel.jhtp2.ch11;

import java.awt.*;
import java.awt.event.*;

public class SelfContainedCanvas extends Canvas
             implements MouseListener, MouseMotionListener {
   private int x1, y1, x2, y2;

   public SelfContainedCanvas()
   {
      addMouseListener( this );
      addMouseMotionListener( this );
   }

   public void paint( Graphics g )
   {
      int x, y, width, height;

      // determine upper-left corner of bounding rectangle
      x = Math.min( x1, x2 );
      y = Math.min( y1, y2 );

      // determine width and height of bounding rectangle
      width = Math.abs( x1 - x2 );
      height = Math.abs( y1 - y2 );

      g.drawOval( x, y, width, height );
   }

   public void mousePressed( MouseEvent e )
   {
      x1 = e.getX();
      y1 = e.getY();
   }

   public void mouseReleased( MouseEvent e )
   {
      x2 = e.getX();
      y2 = e.getY();
      repaint();
   }

```

Fig. 11.5 Capturing mouse events with a **Canvas** (part 2 of 3).

```
81      public void mouseDragged( MouseEvent e )
82      {
83         x2 = e.getX();
84         y2 = e.getY();
85         repaint();
86      }
87
88      // These methods not used but must be defined because
89      // we implement MouseListener and MouseMotionListener.
90      public void mouseClicked( MouseEvent e ) { }
91      public void mouseEntered( MouseEvent e ) { }
92      public void mouseExited( MouseEvent e ) { }
93      public void mouseMoved( MouseEvent e ) { }
94   }
```

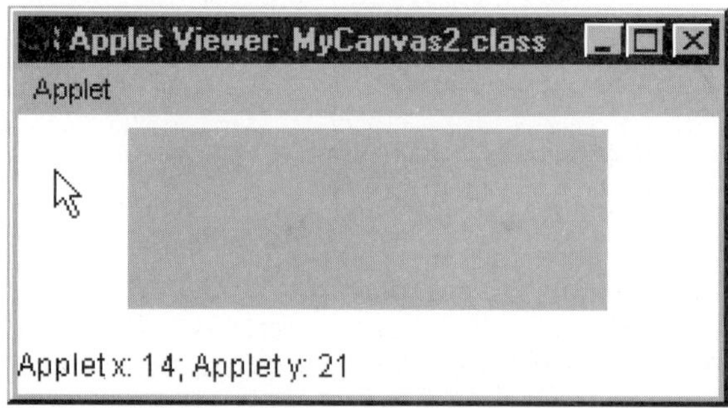

Fig. 11.5 Capturing mouse events with a **Canvas** (part 3 of 3).

Class **SelfContainedCanvas** (line 35) extends class **Canvas** and implements both the **MouseListener** and **MouseMotionListener** interfaces to handle its own mouse events. Instance variables **x1** and **y1** store the initial coordinates where the **mousePressed** event occurs on the canvas. Instance variables **x2** and **y2** store the coordinates where the user drags the mouse or releases the mouse button. All the coordinates are with respect to the upper-left corner of the canvas. The **SelfContainedCanvas** constructor (line 47) uses methods **addMouseListener** and **addMouseMotionListener** to register that **SelfContainedCanvas** objects handle their own mouse events and mouse motion events. For this purpose, the class provides definitions of all the methods in interfaces **MouseListener** and **MouseMotionListener**. However, only **mousePressed** (line 68), **mouseDragged** (line 74) and **mouseReleased** (line 81) are implemented to actually perform tasks. The remaining methods (lines 90–93) are given empty bodies. The definition of mouse event handling methods with empty bodies could have been avoided here by using the **MouseAdapter** and **MouseMotionAdapter** event adapter classes described in Chapter 10.

Method **paint** (line 53) is overridden in class **SelfContainedCanvas** to draw an oval. The width, height and upper-left corner are determined by the user pressing and holding the mouse button, dragging the mouse and releasing the mouse button on the **SelfContainedCanvas** drawing area.

The initial coordinates **x1** and **y1** on the **SelfContainedCanvas** drawing area are captured in method **mousePressed** (line 68). As the user drags the mouse after the initial **mousePressed** operation, the program generates a series of calls to **mouseDragged** (line 74) while the user continues to hold the mouse button and move the mouse. Each call captures in variables **x2** and **y2** the current location of the mouse with respect to the upper-left corner of the canvas and calls **repaint** to draw the current version of the oval. Drawing is strictly confined to the canvas even if the user drags outside the **SelfContainedCanvas** drawing area. Anything drawn off the canvas is *clipped*.

The calculations provided in method **paint** determine the proper upper-left corner using method **Math.min** twice to find the smaller *x* coordinate and *y* coordinate. The oval's width and height must be positive values or the oval is not displayed. Method **Math.abs** gets the absolute value of the subtractions **x1 - x2** and **y1 - y2** that determine the width and height of the oval's bounding rectangle, respectively. When the calculations are complete, **paint** draws the oval.

When the user releases the mouse button, method **mouseReleased** (line 81) captures in variables **x2** and **y2** the final location of the mouse and invokes repaint to draw the final version of the oval.

11.5 Scrollbars

Scrollbars enable the user to "scroll" through a range of integer values. Stand-alone scrollbars are created with class ***Scrollbar*** which inherits from **Component** and implements interface ***Adjustable***. Components that implement **Adjustable** generate adjustment events that are processed by method ***adjustmentValueChanged*** of interface ***AdjustmentListener***. Figure 11.6 shows a stand-alone horizontal scrollbar.

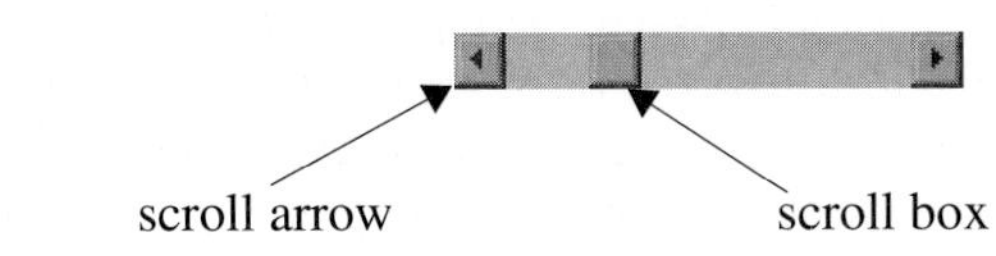

Fig. 11.6 A scrollbar component.

Scrollbars have either a *horizontal orientation* or a *vertical orientation*. The *scroll arrows* for a horizontal scrollbar point left and right with the minimum value being the extreme left and the maximum value being the extreme right. The scroll arrows for a vertical scrollbar point up and down—with the minimum value being the extreme top and the maximum value being the extreme bottom. The relative position of the *scroll box* (also called a *slider*) indicates the current value of the scrollbar.

Class **Scrollbar** has three constructors one of which is presented here. The orientation of a **Scrollbar** is specified by one of two **static** class variables. These constants and the **Scrollbar** constructor are summarized in Fig. 11.7.

The constructor takes five integer arguments. The first argument, ***Scrollbar.HORIZONTAL*** or ***Scrollbar.VERTICAL***, specifies the orientation. The second argument specifies the *initial value* of the scrollbar. The scroll box is initially at this position. The third argument specifies the *visible area* of the scroll box. When a scrollbar is used to scroll through a visible area (such as a large drawing area), the visible area argument normally represents a percentage of the total visible area that can be seen. For example, if the scrollbar represents the values from 0 to 100, the visible area argument could be 10 to indicate that 10% (10 divided by 100) of the total visible area can be seen at a time. In our example, we set the visible area argument to 1. The fourth constructor argument specifies the *minimum value* of the scrollbar. If the initial value is less than the minimum value, the initial value is changed to the minimum value. The fifth argument specifies the *maximum value* the scrollbar can have. If the initial value is larger than the maximum value, the initial value is set to the maximum value.

Common Programming Error 11.2

Passing a value to the ***Scrollbar*** *constructor of Fig. 11.7 other than* ***Scrollbar.HORIZONTAL*** *or* ***Scrollbar.VERTICAL*** *for the* ***orientation*** *argument throws an* ***IllegalArgumentException***

Scrollbar constants and a Scrollbar constructor

```
public final static int HORIZONTAL
```

Constant that specifies a horizontal orientation for a scrollbar.

```
public final static int VERTICAL
```

Constant that specifies a vertical orientation for a scrollbar.

```
public Scrollbar(
   int orientation,      // HORIZONTAL or VERTICAL
   int initialValue,     // initial value of scrollbar
   int visibleArea,      // scroll box size
   int minimumValue,     // minimum value of scrollbar
   int maximumValue )    // maximum value of scrollbar
```

Constructs a scrollbar with the specified orientation (**HORIZONTAL** or **VERTICAL**), initial value, visible area, minimum value, and maximum value.

Fig. 11.7 **Scrollbar** constants and a **Scrollbar** constructor.

The program of Fig. 11.8 allows the user to size an oval drawn on a canvas. The width and height of the oval are controlled with horizontal and a vertical scrollbars, respectively. Applet **ScrollbarDemo** creates the **Scrollbar**s that are used to draw an oval on the **OvalCanvas** attached to the applet. Class **OvalCanvas** is a subclass of **Canvas** that knows how to draw an oval on itself using its own instance variables to determine the width and height of the oval. The instance variable values are set when the user interacts with the **Scrollbar**s. Instances of class **ScrollbarHandler** invoke **OvalCanvas** methods **setOvalWidth** and **setOvalHeight** to set the width and height of the oval drawn.

```
// Fig. 11.08: ScrollbarDemo.java
// Using Scrollbars to size an oval.
import java.applet.Applet;
import java.awt.*;

public class ScrollbarDemo extends Applet {
   private Scrollbar scrollHeight, scrollWidth;
   private OvalCanvas c;

   public void init()
   {
      setSize( 215, 235 );

      c = new OvalCanvas();
      c.setSize( 200, 200 );
      c.setBackground( Color.yellow );

      scrollHeight = new Scrollbar( Scrollbar.VERTICAL, 100,
                                    1, 0, 200 );
      scrollHeight.addAdjustmentListener(
         new ScrollbarHandler( c, OvalCanvas.HEIGHT ) );

      scrollWidth = new Scrollbar( Scrollbar.HORIZONTAL, 100,
                                   1, 0, 200 );
      scrollWidth.addAdjustmentListener(
         new ScrollbarHandler( c, OvalCanvas.WIDTH ) );

      setLayout( null );   // No layout

      add( scrollHeight );
      scrollHeight.setBounds( 200, 0, 15, 200 );

      add( scrollWidth );
      scrollWidth.setBounds( 0, 200, 200, 15 );

      add( c );
      c.setLocation( 0, 0 );
   }
}
```

Fig. 11.8 Using **Scrollbar**s to size an oval (part 1 of 3).

```
40  // Fig. 11.08: OvalCanvas.java
41  // A customized Canvas class.
42  import java.awt.*;
43
44  public class OvalCanvas extends Canvas {
45     public static int WIDTH = 1, HEIGHT = 2;
46     private int ovalWidth, ovalHeight;
47
48     public OvalCanvas()
49     {
50        setOvalWidth( 100 );
51        setOvalHeight( 100 );
52     }
53
54     public void paint( Graphics g )
55     {
56        g.drawOval( 0, 0, ovalWidth, ovalHeight );
57     }
58
59     public void setOvalWidth( int w )
60     {
61        ovalWidth = w;
62        repaint();
63     }
64
65     public void setOvalHeight( int h )
66     {
67        ovalHeight = h;
68        repaint();
69     }
70  }
```

Fig. 11.8 Using **Scrollbar**s to size an oval (part 2 of 3).

Method **init** begins by setting the size of the applet (line 12). Next, **init** instantiates **OvalCanvas** object **c**, sets its size and sets its background color (lines14-16). Line 18

```
scrollHeight = new Scrollbar( Scrollbar.VERTICAL, 100,
                               1, 0, 200 );
```

instantiates **Scrollbar** object **scrollHeight** to control the height of the oval drawn on the **OvalCanvas**. The orientation of **scrollHeight** is vertical with an initial value of **100**. The scroll box visible area is set to **1**. The minimum value is **0** and the maximum value is **200**. The horizontal scrollbar object **scrollWidth** is constructed similarly with horizontal orientation (line 23).

Event listener objects must be registered for each **Scrollbar** object so the user's interactions with the **Scrollbar**s can be processed and the oval's size can be changed accordingly. Line 20

```
scrollHeight.addAdjustmentListener(
   new ScrollbarHandler( c, OvalCanvas.HEIGHT ) );
```

```
71 // Fig. 11.08: ScrollbarHandler.java
72 // Class to handle Scrollbar events.
73 import java.awt.event.*;
74
75 public class ScrollbarHandler implements AdjustmentListener {
76    private OvalCanvas canvas;
77    private int dimension;
78
79    public ScrollbarHandler( OvalCanvas c, int d )
80    {
81       canvas = c;
82       dimension = d;
83    }
84
85    public void adjustmentValueChanged( AdjustmentEvent e )
86    {
87       if ( dimension == OvalCanvas.WIDTH )
88          canvas.setOvalWidth( e.getValue() );
89       else if ( dimension == OvalCanvas.HEIGHT )
90          canvas.setOvalHeight( e.getValue() );
91    }
92 }
```

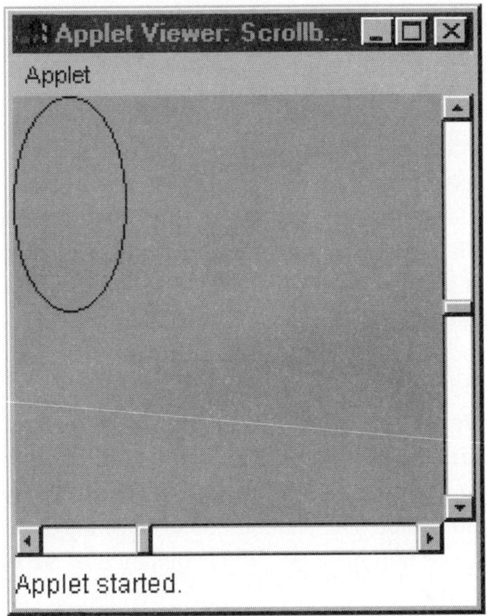

Fig. 11.8 Using **`Scrollbar`**s to size an oval (part 1 of 3).

uses method **`addAdjustmentListener`** (from interface **`Adjustable`** implemented by class **`Scrollbar`**) to register a listener for adjustment events performed on **`scroll-Height`**. These events occur when the user clicks the scroll arrows at either end of the **`Scrollbar`**, drags the scroll box, or clicks between the scroll box and the scroll arrows. An instance of class **`ScrollbarHandler`** (line 71) is registered to handle the adjustment events. Class **ScrollbarHandler**'s constructor is passed a reference to the **OvalCanvas c** so the event handler can invoke **OvalCanvas** methods and an integer value so the event handler knows which **OvalCanvas** method to invoke. In this case, the **ScrollbarHandler** invokes **OvalCanvas** method **setOvalHeight** in response to an adjustment event on **scrollHeight**. Line 25 registers an adjustment listener for **scrollWidth**. This **ScrollbarHandler** invokes **OvalCanvas** method **setOvalWidth** in response to an adjustment event on **scrollWidth**.

Finally, method **init** places the GUI components on the applet. Line 28

```
setLayout( null );   // No layout
```

turns off the layout manager for the applet. This is referred to as *setting a **null** layout*. When no layout manager is used, each GUI component must be sized and placed at specific pixel locations on the applet (or the container that has a **null** layout). After **scrollHeight** is added to the applet, line 31

```
scrollHeight.setBounds( 200, 0, 15, 200 );
```

uses **Component** method ***setBounds*** to position and size the **Scrollbar**. The first two arguments are the *x* and *y* coordinates for the upper-left corner of the **Scrollbar**. The last two arguments are the width and height of the **Scrollbar** in pixels. A similar statement is used to position and size **scrollWidth**. Line 37

```
c.setLocation( 0, 0 );
```

positions **OvalCanvas** object **c** at position (0, 0) on the applet. Previously, **c** was set to 200-by-200 pixels with a call to **Component** method **setSize**.

The **Canvas** subclass **OvalCanvas** (line 40) contains a constructor (line 48), a **paint** method (line 54), a **setOvalWidth** method (line 59) and a **setOvalHeight** method (line 65). Methods **setOvalWidth** and **setOvalHeight** set the **private** instance variables **width** and **height**, respectively. The class provides two integer constants—**WIDTH** and **HEIGHT**—that are used by instances of class **ScrollbarHandler** to determine which method to call in the **OvalCanvas** when an adjustment event occurs on a **Scrollbar**. Method **paint** draws the oval.

Class **ScrollbarHandler** (line 75) implements interface **AdjustmentListener** so instances of **ScrollbarHandler** can listen for adjustment events. The constructor receives as its first argument a reference to the **OvalCanvas** for which the width or height of the oval should be set. The second constructor argument is an integer that indicates the dimension (width or height) a particular instance of **ScrollbarHandler** will set. When an adjustment event occurs, method **adjustmentValueChanged** (line 85) for the appropriate event handler object is invoked. The argument to **adjustmentValueChanged** is an **AdjustmentEvent** object containing all the information about the adjustment event that occurred. If the **dimension** is **OvalCanvas.WIDTH**, line 88

```
canvas.setOvalWidth( e.getValue() );
```

invokes **OvalCanvas** method **setOvalWidth** and passes it the result of **e.getValue()** (the current value of **scrollWidth**—the **Scrollbar** that generated the event). If the **dimension** is **OvalCanvas.HEIGHT**, line 90

```
canvas.setOvalHeight( e.getValue() );
```

invokes **OvalCanvas** method **setOvalHeight** and passes it the result of **e.getValue()** (the current value of **scrollHeight**—the **Scrollbar** that generated the event).

11.6 Frames

A ***Frame*** is a *window* with a *title bar* and a *border*. Class **Frame** that extends class ***Window*** (that inherits from **Container**) and implements interface ***MenuContainer*** (so it can have a menu bar attached to it as shown in Section 11.8). The **Window** class contains methods for window management that are common to both **Frame**s and **Dialog**s (Section 11.9). Unlike **Frame**s, **Window** objects do not have title bars or borders. The default layout manager for **Window**s and **Frame**s is **BorderLayout**.

Common Programming Error 11.3

The default layout manager for subclasses of ***Window*** *is* ***BorderLayout****. Forgetting to specify* ***BorderLayout.NORTH****,* ***BorderLayout.SOUTH****,* ***BorderLayout.EAST****,* ***BorderLayout.WEST*** *or* ***BorderLayout.CENTER*** *when adding a component to a* ***Window*** *prevents that component from being displayed properly on the user interface.*

All windows generate *window events* when the user manipulates the window. Event listeners are registered for window events with method ***addWindowListener*** of class **Window**. The ***WindowListener*** interface (implemented by window event listeners) provides seven methods for handling window events.

Frames are typically used to build windowed applications (programs that do not require a browser to run). However, **Frame**s can also be used with applets. The program of Fig. 11.9 creates an applet with a single **Button**. When the user clicks the **Button**, an object of class **ColorFrame** (a subclass of **Frame** created for this example) is displayed.

```
// Fig. 11.09: MyFrame.java
// Creating a subclass of Frame.
import java.applet.Applet;
import java.awt.*;
import java.awt.event.*;
import com.deitel.jhtp2.ch11.ColorFrame;

public class MyFrame extends Applet implements ActionListener {
   private ColorFrame f;
   private Button showFrame;

   public void init()
   {
      showFrame = new Button( "Show frame" );
      add( showFrame );
      showFrame.addActionListener( this );

```

Fig. 11.9 Creating a subclass of **Frame** (part 1 of 4).

```
      f = new ColorFrame( "Select a color" );
   }

   public void actionPerformed( ActionEvent e )
   {
      f.setVisible( true );  // show the frame
   }
}
```

Fig. 11.9 Creating a subclass of **Frame** (part 2 of 4).

```
// Fig. 11.09: ColorFrame.java
// ColorFrame class allows user to select a color and
// changes the frame's background to that color.
package com.deitel.jhtp2.ch11;
import java.awt.*;
import java.awt.event.*;

public class ColorFrame extends Frame implements ItemListener {
   private Color colors[] = { Color.white, Color.red,
      Color.green, Color.blue, Color.magenta };
   private String colorNames[] =
      { "White", "Red", "Green", "Blue", "Magenta" };
   private Choice colorChoice;

   public ColorFrame( String s )
   {
      // call base class constructor
      super( s );
      setSize( 275, 150 );
      addWindowListener( new CloseWindow() );

      colorChoice = new Choice();

      for ( int i = 0; i < colorNames.length; i++ )
         colorChoice.add( colorNames[ i ] );

      add( colorChoice, BorderLayout.NORTH );
      colorChoice.addItemListener( this );
   }

   public void itemStateChanged( ItemEvent e )
   {
     setBackground( colors[ colorChoice.getSelectedIndex() ] );
      repaint();
   }
}
```

Fig. 11.9 Creating a subclass of **Frame** (part 3 of 4).

```
62  // Fig. 11.09: CloseWindow.java
63  // Class to close a window.
64  package com.deitel.jhtp2.ch11;
65  import java.awt.event.*;
66
67  public class CloseWindow extends WindowAdapter {
68     public void windowClosing( WindowEvent e )
69     {
70        e.getWindow().setVisible( false );
71     }
72  }
```

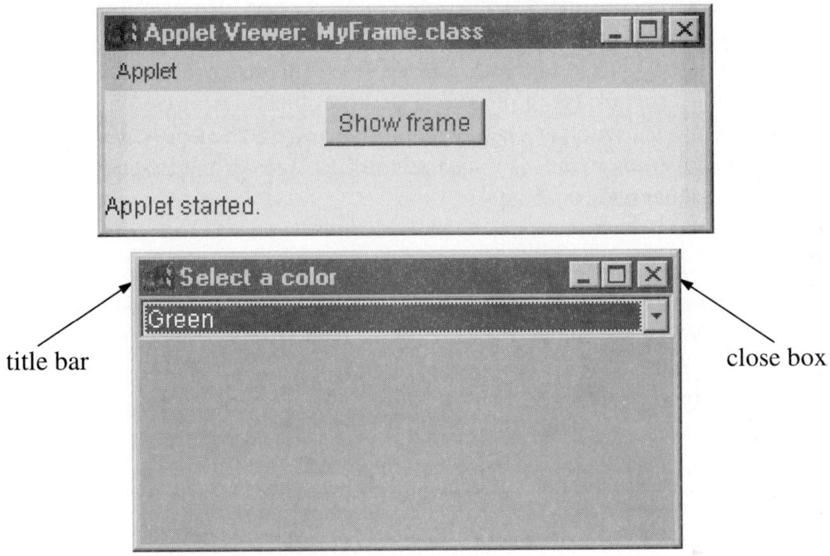

title bar

close box

Fig. 11.9 Creating a subclass of **Frame** (part 4 of 4).

The program consists of three classes—applet class **MyFrame** to illustrate instantiating and displaying a window, class **ColorFrame** to create the window to be displayed, and class **CloseWindow** to handle window event generated when the user closes the **ColorFrame** window. Class **ColorFrame** and class **CloseWindow** are placed in the package **com.deitel.jhtp2.ch11** for future reuse in other examples in this chapter.

Applet class **MyFrame** (line 8) creates a references to **ColorFrame** object **f** and a **Button** object **showFrame**. The action event generated when the user clicks **showFrame** causes **ColorFrame f** to be displayed on the screen. The applet's **init** method creates the **Button** and **ColorFrame** objects. The applet is registered as the action listener for **Button showFrame** (line 16). Thus, when the user clicks **showFrame**, the applet's **actionPerformed** method (line 21) is called. Line 23

```
f.setVisible( true );  // show the frame
```

displays the **ColorFrame** on the screen. By default (unlike most other components), windows of all types *are not shown* on the screen until **Component** method ***setVisible*** is invoked with a **true** argument. Any window can be hidden by invoking **setVisible** with a **false** argument (Note that **setVisible** can be used with any **Component** object). If **setVisible(true)** has already been called on a window and the window is not currently displayed on the screen (i.e., it is hidden by another window), **Window** method ***show*** can be invoked to display the window.

Common Programming Error 11.4

*Forgetting to call the **setVisible** method with a **true** argument on a window is a run-time logic error; the window is not displayed.*

Class **ColorFrame** (line 33) is a subclass of **Frame** that also implements **ItemListener** so it can handle the item events generated by the **colorChoice** button of type **Choice** that is attached to the **ColorFrame**. The instance variables of class **ColorFrame** include array **colors** of several **Color** objects, array **colorNames** with the **String** name of each color in **colors** and the **colorChoice Choice** button. The **ColorFrame** constructor (line 40) instantiates the pieces of the **ColorFrame** and registers its event listener objects. Line 43

```
super( s );
```

passes constructor argument **s** (a **String**) to the superclass **Frame** constructor. This **String** is used as the text in the title bar of the **Frame** (located at the top of the window).

All windows must be sized before they are displayed. A window has no default size. **Component** method **setSize** (line 44) is used to size a window to the width and height specified as arguments.

Common Programming Error 11.5

*Forgetting to call the **setSize** method on a window is a run-time logic error. If the window displayed is a **Frame** or **Dialog** object, only the title bar appears.*

Line 45

```
addWindowListener( new CloseWindow() );
```

uses **Window** method **addWindowListener** to register an instance of class **CloseWindow** to handle the window events for the **ColorFrame** object. Lines 47–53 create the **colorChoice** button, add it to the North region of the **ColorFrame** and register the **colorFrame** to listen for the item events. When an item event occurs, **ColorFrame**'s **itemStateChanged** method is invoked to set the background color of the **ColorFrame** and **repaint** the **ColorFrame**.

Most windows have an icon at the top-left or top-right corner that enable a user to close the window and terminate a program. Clicking this icon (also known as the *exit icon* or *close box*) for a Java **Frame** (or any other type of window) has no effect unless the programmer writes the code to close the **Frame**. Class **CloseWindow** (line 67) is provided to close the window when the user clicks the close box in the upper-right corner of the window (see the second screen capture in this example) or when the user selects *Close* from the menu that appears when the user clicks on the icon in the upper-left corner of the window (on the left side of the title bar).

Seven methods are provided by interface **WindowListener**—***windowActivated***, ***windowClosed***, ***windowClosing***, ***windowDeactivated***, ***windowDeiconified***, ***windowIconified*** and ***windowOpened***. In this example, we only need to close the window. Class **CloseWindow** extends class ***WindowAdapter*** (that implements interface **WindowListener**) so we can simply override the **windowClosing** method to close the window. Remember that the event adapter classes provide a default implementation of each method (with an empty body) in the corresponding event listener interface. Line 70

```
e.getWindow().setVisible( false );
```

uses ***WindowEvent*** object **e** (the argument to **windowClosing**) to invoke **WindowEvent** method ***getWindow***. This returns a reference to the window that generated the *window-closing* event. That reference is used to invoke method **setVisible** with a **false** argument to hide the window.

If a window will not be used again during the execution of the program, the **Window** method ***dispose*** should be invoked on the window. Windowing systems generally have a limit to the number of windows that can be allocated. Invoking **dispose** returns the resources used by the window back to the windowing system so these resources can be used by another window in the future.

Good Programming Practice 11.1

Invoking ***dispose*** *on a window releases windowing system resources.*

11.7 Converting an Applet into a GUI-based Application

Frames are often used to create *GUI-based applications*. The **Frame** provides the space in which the application GUI is built. When the **Frame** is closed, the application terminates. In this section, we demonstrate how to convert an applet into a GUI-based application. Remember from Chapter 2 that a Java application is executed using the **java** interpreter (not a World Wide Web browser) and specifying the name of the class that contains method **main**. The program of Fig.11.10 modifies applet class **MyFrame** of Fig. 11.9 by adding a main method so the program can be executed as an application. Class **CloseWindowAndExit** is defined to terminate the application when the user clicks the close box on the application window.

Class **MyFrame** of Fig. 11.10 is identical to class **MyFrame** of Fig. 11.9 except that it now contains a main method (line 28). Lines 31 and 32

```
Frame app = new Frame( "Application" );
app.setSize( 300, 100 );
```

create an instance of class **Frame** and set its size to 300-by-100 pixels. This is the **Frame** to which we will attach an instance of the applet class **MyFrame**. Line 35

```
app.addWindowListener( new CloseWindowAndExit() );
```

registers an instance of class **CloseWindowAndExit** to handle the closing of the application window and termination of the program.

```
// Fig. 11.10: MyFrame.java
// Creating a subclass of Frame.
import java.applet.Applet;
import java.awt.*;
import java.awt.event.*;
import com.deitel.jhtp2.ch11.ColorFrame;
import com.deitel.jhtp2.ch11.CloseWindowAndExit;

public class MyFrame extends Applet implements ActionListener {
   private ColorFrame f;
   private Button showFrame;

   public void init()
   {
      showFrame = new Button( "Show frame" );
      add( showFrame );
      showFrame.addActionListener( this );

      f = new ColorFrame( "Select a color" );
   }

   public void actionPerformed( ActionEvent e )
   {
      f.setVisible( true );  // show the frame
   }

   // Allow this applet to run as an application also
   public static void main( String args[] )
   {
      // create application Frame and resize
      Frame app = new Frame( "Application" );
      app.setSize( 300, 100 );

      // register window handler to terminate application
      app.addWindowListener( new CloseWindowAndExit() );

      // create applet instance
      MyFrame m = new MyFrame();

      // initialize and start the applet
      m.init();
      m.start();

      // add applet to center of Frame
      app.add( m, BorderLayout.CENTER );

      // display the frame (everything attached is painted)
      app.setVisible( true );
   }
}
```

Fig. 11.10 Creating a GUI-based application from an applet (part 1 of 2).

```
51 // Fig. 11.10: CloseWindowAndExit.java
52 // Frame in which an applet can execute as an application.
53 package com.deitel.jhtp2.ch11;
54 import java.awt.event.*;
55
56 public class CloseWindowAndExit extends WindowAdapter {
57    public void windowClosing( WindowEvent e )
58    {
59       System.exit( 0 );
60    }
61 }
```

Fig. 11.10 Creating a GUI-based application from an applet (part 2 of 2).

Line 38

```
MyFrame m = new MyFrame();
```

creates an instance of the applet class **MyFrame**. This statement invokes the default constructor for class **MyFrame** that is provided automatically because we did not define a constructor (as we normally do not for an applet). Class **MyFrame** extends class **Applet** that extends class **Panel**. Therefore, an instance of **MyFrame** is considered to be an instance of **Panel**. In this program, the **MyFrame** instance operates as a specialized subclass of **Panel**—not as an applet. Because it does not function as an applet, it is our responsibility to be sure that the normal start-up sequence of method calls for an applet is performed (i.e., **init**, **start** and **paint**). Lines 41 and 42 explicitly invoke methods **init** and **start** for object **m**. Method paint will be invoked implicitly as we will see shortly.

Line 45

```
app.add( m, BorderLayout.CENTER );
```

adds the applet instance **m** to the Center region of the **Frame**'s default **BorderLayout**. This allows the **Panel** on which the applet is based to expand to fill the entire **Frame**. Finally, line 48

```
app.setVisible( true );
```

displayed the **Frame**. When a **Frame** is displayed, all of the components attached to the **Frame** are automatically painted. Therefore, the **paint** method of applet instance **m** is called automatically as a result of this statement.

Class **CloseWindowAndExit** (line 56) extends **WindowAdapter** so we can implement method **windowClosing** without implementing the remaining six methods of interface **WindowListener**. This class has been placed in a package (line 53) for future reuse. When the user clicks the close box on the application window, method windowClosing (line 57) is invoked. Line 59

```
System.exit( 0 );
```

uses **static** method **exit** of class **System** (**java.lang** package) to terminate the program. The argument **0** indicates that the application terminated successfully. This value is passed to the environment that ran the program. This is useful if the program is executed from a batch file (on Window 95/Windows NT systems) or a shell script (on UNIX systems). When the program terminates, all windows associated with the application are automatically closed and the windowing resources are returned to the system. Note: Our applet does not implement methods **stop** and **destroy**. If you are creating an applet that can also execute as an application, you should explicitly call the **stop** and **destroy** methods of your applet class before terminating the application.

11.8 Using Menus with Frames

Menus are an integral part of GUIs. ***Menus*** allow the user to perform actions without unnecessarily "cluttering" a graphical user interface with extra GUI components. Menus can only be used with **Frame**s. Later in this chapter we will see that ***PopupMenus*** can be used with any GUI component. The ***MenuComponent*** portion of the **java.awt** hierarchy is illustrated in Fig. 11.1. All classes that are used to provide menu functionality to a **Frame** are derived from class **MenuComponent**. Class **MenuComponent** is the superclass for ***MenuBar*** and ***MenuItem***. Class **MenuItem** has two subclasses—***CheckboxMenuItem*** and ***Menu***. Class ***PopupMenu*** is a subclass of **Menu**.

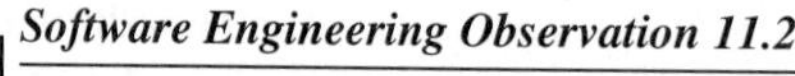

Software Engineering Observation 11.2

Menus simplify GUIs by reducing the number of components the user views.

Class **MenuItem** contains the constructor and methods necessary to manage menu items. A *menu item* is a string inside a menu that when selected causes an action to be performed. A menu item can be used to initiate an action or it can be another **Menu** called a *submenu* that provides more menu items from which the user can select. Submenus are useful for grouping related menu items in a menu.

Class **MenuBar** contains the constructor and methods necessary to manage a menu bar. A *menu bar* is a container for menus.

Class **Menu** contains the constructors and methods necessary for managing **Menu**s. **Menu**s contain menu items and are added to menu bars or to other **Menu**s as submenus. When a menu is clicked, the menu expands to show a listing of menu items. Clicking a menu item generates an action event.

Class **CheckboxMenuItem** contains the constructor and methods necessary to manage menu items that can be toggled. When a **CheckboxMenuItem** is selected, a check appears to the left of the menu item. When the **CheckboxMenuItem** is selected again, the check to the left of the menu item is removed.

The application of Fig. 11.11 creates a simple notepad application. The GUI-based application consists of application class **ScratchPadTest** to create an instance of class **ScratchPad**. Class **ScratchPad** (a subclass of **Frame**) contains a **TextArea** and a **MenuBar** with a single **Menu**. The **Menu** contains three menu items—submenu **fontMenu**, submenu **colorMenu** and **readOnly** (a **CheckboxMenuItem**). When the user selects a font or color, the text in the **TextArea** is changed to the selected font or color. When the user selects the **readOnly** menu item, the **TextComponent** method **setEditable** is invoked to toggle the users ability to type in the **TextArea**. If the **readOnly** menu item appears with a check next to it, the **TextArea** is uneditable. Class **ScratchPad** was placed in package **com.deitel.jhtp2.ch11** for future reusability.

```java
// Fig. 11.11: ScratchPad.java
// Incorporating menus into a subclass of Frame.
package com.deitel.jhtp2.ch11;
import java.awt.*;
import java.awt.event.*;

public class ScratchPad extends Frame
            implements ActionListener, ItemListener {
   private TextArea t;
   private String fontNames[] =
      { "TimesRoman", "Courier", "Helvetica" };
   private String colorNames[] =
      { "Black", "Red", "Green", "Blue" };
   private Color colorValues[] =
      { Color.black, Color.red, Color.green, Color.blue };

   private MenuBar bar;
   private Menu formatMenu, fontMenu, colorMenu;
   private MenuItem fonts[], colors[];
   private CheckboxMenuItem readOnly;

   public ScratchPad()
   {
      super( "ScratchPad Application" );
      setSize( 300, 200 );

```

Fig. 11.11 Incorporating menus into a subclass of **Frame** (part 1 of 4).

```
      t = new TextArea( "", 2, 20,
                        TextArea.SCROLLBARS_VERTICAL_ONLY);
      add( t, BorderLayout.CENTER );

      t.setFont( new Font( "TimesRoman", Font.PLAIN, 12 ) );
      t.setForeground( colorValues[ 0 ] );

      // create menubar
      bar = new MenuBar();

      // create the format menu
      formatMenu = new Menu( "Format" );

      // create font menu
      fontMenu = new Menu( "Font" );

      fonts = new MenuItem[ fontNames.length ];

      for ( int i = 0; i < fonts.length; i++ ) {
         fonts[ i ] = new MenuItem( fontNames[ i ] );
         fontMenu.add( fonts[ i ] );
         fonts[ i ].addActionListener( this );
      }

      formatMenu.add( fontMenu );
      formatMenu.addSeparator();

      // create color menu
      colorMenu = new Menu( "Color" );

      colors = new MenuItem[ colorNames.length ];

      for ( int i = 0; i < colors.length; i++ ) {
         colors[ i ] = new MenuItem( colorNames[ i ] );
         colorMenu.add( colors[ i ] );
         colors[ i ].addActionListener( this );
      }

      formatMenu.add( colorMenu );
      formatMenu.addSeparator();

      // create "read-only" menu item
      readOnly = new CheckboxMenuItem( "Read-Only" );
      readOnly.addItemListener( this );

      formatMenu.add( readOnly );

      // add menu to menu bar
      bar.add( formatMenu );
```

Fig. 11.11 Incorporating menus into a subclass of **`Frame`** (part 2 of 4).

```
77          // set the menubar for the frame
78          setMenuBar( bar );
79
80          setVisible( true );
81       }
82
83       // Handle font and color menu selections
84       public void actionPerformed( ActionEvent e )
85       {
86          for ( int i = 0; i < fonts.length; i++ )
87             if ( e.getSource() == fonts[ i ] ) {
88                t.setFont( new Font( fonts[ i ].getLabel(),
89                   Font.PLAIN, 12 ) );
90                break;
91             }
92
93          for ( int i = 0; i < colors.length; i++ )
94             if ( e.getSource() == colors[ i ] ) {
95                t.setForeground( colorValues[ i ] );
96                break;
97             }
98       }
99
100      // Handle "read-only" menu selections
101      public void itemStateChanged( ItemEvent e )
102      {
103         t.setEditable( ! t.isEditable() );
104      }
105   }
```

Fig. 11.11 Incorporating menus into a subclass of **Frame** (part 3 of 4).

Class **ScratchPad** (line 7) is a completely self-contained class—it implements **ActionListener** and **ItemListener** so it can handle all its own events generated when the user selects **MenuItem**s and **CheckboxMenuItem**s, respectively. Class **ScratchPad**'s constructor begins in lines 24–32 by passing the title of the window—"**ScratchPad Application**"—to the **Frame** class constuctor, setting the size of the **ScratchPad**, instantiating **TextArea t**, adding **t** to the Center of the **BorderLayout**, and setting the initial font and color for the text in the **TextArea**. The remainder of the constructor sets up all the menu components.

Line 35

```
bar = new MenuBar();
```

creates the **MenuBar** that will be attached to the **ScratchPad**. Line 38

```
formatMenu = new Menu( "Format" );
```

creates **formatMenu** and passes the string "**Format**" to be the name of the menu. This menu will be attached to **MenuBar** object **bar**. Line 41

```
fontMenu = new Menu( "Font" );
```

```
106 // Fig. 11.11: ScratchPadTest.java
107 // Class to test ScratchPad.
108 import com.deitel.jhtp2.ch11.ScratchPad;
109 import com.deitel.jhtp2.ch11.CloseWindowAndExit;
110
111 public class ScratchPadTest {
112    public static void main( String args[] )
113    {
114       ScratchPad e = new ScratchPad();
115       e.addWindowListener( new CloseWindowAndExit() );
116    }
117 }
```

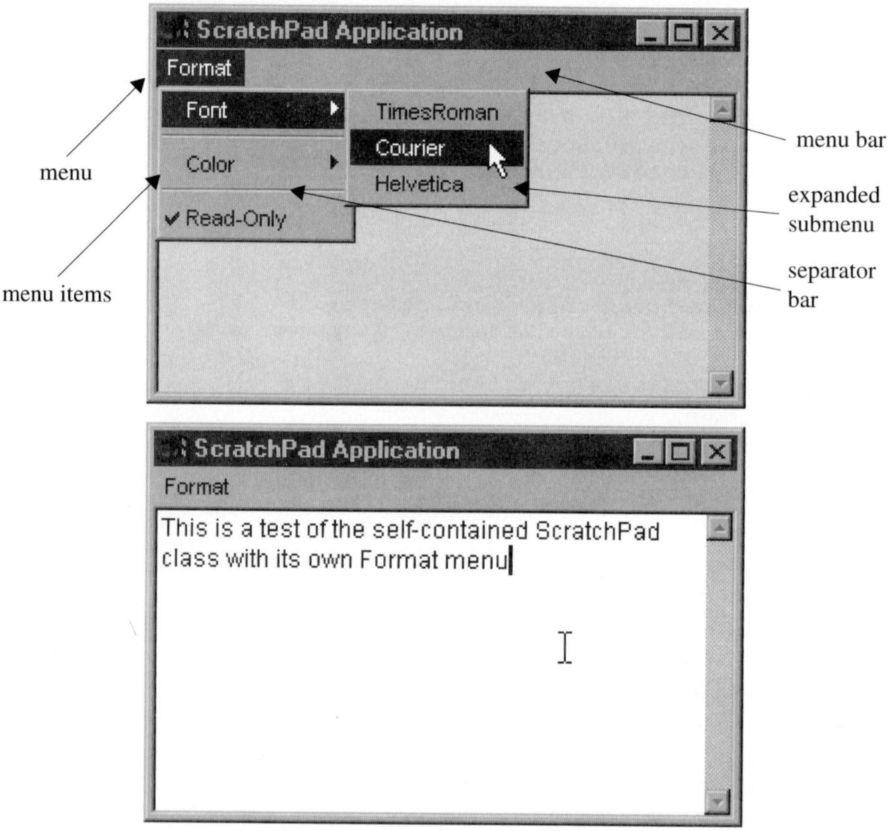

Fig. 11.11 Incorporating menus into a subclass of **Frame** (part 4 of 4).

creates **fontMenu** and passes the string "**Font**" to be the name of the menu. This menu will be added to **formatMenu** as a submenu. Line 43

```
fonts = new MenuItem[ fontNames.length ];
```

creates fonts as an array of **MenuItem**s. The array elements are created in the **for** structure at line 45 that instantiates each **MenuItem** with a string from array **fontNames** as the name of the **MenuItem**, adds each **MenuItem** to **fontMenu** and registers the **ScratchPad** as the action event listener for each **MenuItem**. Lines 51 and 52

```
formatMenu.add( fontMenu );
formatMenu.addSeparator();
```

add **fontMenu** to **formatMenu** and place a separator bar (see the screen capture) in the **formatMenu**. Lines 55–66 perform the same tasks for **colorMenu** described above for **fontMenu**.

Lines 69 and 70

```
readOnly = new CheckboxMenuItem( "Read-Only" );
readOnly.addItemListener( this );
```

create **CheckboxMenuItem** object **readOnly** and register the **ScratchPad** to listen for item events on the **readOnly** object. Line 72 adds **readOnly** to **formatMenu**.

Line 75

```
bar.add( formatMenu );
```

adds **formatMenu** to **MenuBar** object **bar**. Line 78

```
setMenuBar( bar );
```

uses **Frame** method **setMenuBar** to place the **MenuBar** object bar on the **ScratchPad**. When all the menu items are set up, the **ScratchPad** is displayed with method **setVisible** (line 80).

Common Programming Error 11.6

*Forgetting to set the menu bar with **Frame** method **setMenuBar** results in the menu bar not being displayed on the **Frame**.*

Common Programming Error 11.7

*Using a lowercase **i** in **MenuItem** or **CheckboxMenuItem** is a syntax error.*

Common Programming Error 11.8

*Using a lowercase **b** in class name **MenuBar** is a syntax error.*

Common Programming Error 11.9

*Using an uppercase **b** in class name **CheckboxMenuItem** is a syntax error.*

Common Programming Error 11.10

Forgetting to add a menu item to a menu is a run-time logic error. The menu item will not appear in the menu.

Common Programming Error 11.11

*Attempting to use a **Checkbox** component instead of a **CheckboxMenuItem** in a menu is a syntax error.*

Method **actionPerformed** (line 84) uses two **for** structures to determine which font or color menu item generated the action event and sets the font or color of the **TextArea**, respectively. **EventObject** method **getSource** (inherited into **ActionEvent**) gets a reference to the particular menu item that generated the action event.

Method **itemStateChanged** (line 101) is called if the user selects the **CheckboxMenuItem readOnly** in the **formatMenu**. Line 103

```
t.setEditable( ! t.isEditable() );
```

toggles the **TextArea**'s editability by passing **setEditable** the opposite of the value returned by **TextComponent** method **isEditable** that returns **true** if the **TextComponent** is editable and **false** otherwise.

Class **ScratchPadTest** provides method **main** to start the application. Line 114

```
ScratchPad e = new ScratchPad();
```

creates an instance of class **ScratchPad**. Line 115

```
e.addWindowListener( new CloseWindowAndExit() );
```

registers an instance of the window event listener class **CloseWindowAndExit** to handle the closing of the window and termination of the application. Note that both class **ScratchPad** and class **CloseWindowAndExit** (originally from Fig. 11.10) are imported into this application from package **com.deitel.jhtp2.ch11**.

11.9 Dialogs

A ***Dialog*** *box* is a window with a title bar. **Dialog** boxes are commonly used to gather information from the user or to show information to the user. Class **Dialog** inherits from class **Window**.

Dialog boxes can either be *modal* or *modeless*. A *modal dialog box* does not allow any other window in the application to be accessed until the dialog box is dismissed. A *modeless dialog box* allows other windows to be accessed while the dialog is displayed. **BorderLayout** is the default layout manager for **Dialog** boxes.

The program of Fig. 11.12 demonstrates a modal **Dialog** box and a modeless **Dialog** box. The application class **DialogBoxDemo** controls the application. It provides a **File** menu containing two options "**Select color ...**" and "**Exit**." The first option displays the modeless **SelectColorDialog** (a subclass of **Dialog**). The second option terminates the program. **DialogBoxDemo** also provides a **Help** menu with an "**About**" option that displays the modal **MessageBox** (a subclass of **Dialog**). Attached to the Center region of the **DialogBoxDemo** application window is an object of class **SelfContainedCanvas2** that extends our original **SelfContainedCanvas** class of Fig. 11.5. The new class enables setting the drawing color for the oval on the canvas. **MessageBox**, **SelectColorDialog** and **SelfContainedCanvas2** are all part of package **com.deitel.jhtp2.ch11** for future reuse.

```
// Fig. 11.12: DialogBoxDemo.java
// Demonstrating modal and modeless Dialog boxes.
import java.awt.*;
import java.awt.event.*;
import com.deitel.jhtp2.ch11.CloseWindowAndExit;
import com.deitel.jhtp2.ch11.SelfContainedCanvas2;
import com.deitel.jhtp2.ch11.SelectColorDialog;
import com.deitel.jhtp2.ch11.MessageBox;

public class DialogBoxDemo extends Frame
             implements ActionListener, ItemListener {
   private MessageBox information;
   private MenuItem about, colors, exit;
   private MenuBar bar;
   private Menu helpMenu, fileMenu;
   private SelfContainedCanvas2 canvas;
   private SelectColorDialog selectColor;

   public DialogBoxDemo()
   {
      super( "Dialog boxes" );
      setSize( 275, 150 );

      // create Help menu
      helpMenu = new Menu( "Help" );
      about = new MenuItem( "About" );
      about.addActionListener( this );
      helpMenu.add( about );

      // create File menu
      fileMenu = new Menu( "File" );
      colors = new MenuItem( "Select color ..." );
      colors.addActionListener( this );
      fileMenu.add( colors );
      fileMenu.addSeparator();
      exit = new MenuItem( "Exit" );
      exit.addActionListener( this );
      fileMenu.add( exit );

      // setup MenuBar
      bar = new MenuBar();
      bar.add( fileMenu );
      bar.add( helpMenu );
      bar.setHelpMenu( helpMenu );
      setMenuBar( bar );

      // create About dialog
      information = new MessageBox(
         this, "Message", "Dialog box example", 200 );

```

Fig. 11.12 Demonstrating modal and modeless **Dialog** boxes (part 1 of 8).

```
      // create SelectColorDialog
      selectColor = new SelectColorDialog(
         this, "Click once on desired color" );

      // create SelfContainedCanvas2
      canvas = new SelfContainedCanvas2();
      add( canvas, BorderLayout.CENTER );

      setVisible( true );  // show window
   }

   public void actionPerformed( ActionEvent e )
   {
      if ( e.getSource() == about )
         information.setVisible( true );
      else if ( e.getSource() == colors )
         selectColor.setVisible( true );
      else if ( e.getSource() == exit )
         System.exit( 0 );
   }

   public void itemStateChanged( ItemEvent e )
   {
      canvas.setDrawingColor( selectColor.getColor() );
   }

   public static void main( String args[] )
   {
      DialogBoxDemo d = new DialogBoxDemo();
      d.addWindowListener( new CloseWindowAndExit() );
   }
}
```

Fig. 11.12 Demonstrating modal and modeless **Dialog** boxes (part 2 of 8).

```
// Fig. 11.12: MessageBox.java
// Class that implements a modal message dialog box.
package com.deitel.jhtp2.ch11;
import java.awt.*;
import java.awt.event.*;
import com.deitel.jhtp2.ch11.CloseWindow;

public class MessageBox extends Dialog
             implements ActionListener {
   private Label message;
   private Button close;

   public MessageBox( Frame parent, String title,
      String messageString, int width )
   {
```

Fig. 11.12 Demonstrating modal and modeless **Dialog** boxes (part 3 of 8).

```
      super( parent, title, true );
      setSize( width, 100 );
      setResizable( false );

      message = new Label( messageString, Label.CENTER );
      add( message, BorderLayout.CENTER );

      close = new Button( "Close" );
      close.addActionListener( this );
      add( close, BorderLayout.SOUTH );

      addWindowListener( new CloseWindow() );
   }

   public void actionPerformed( ActionEvent e )
   {
      setVisible( false );
   }
}
```

Fig. 11.12 Demonstrating modal and modeless **Dialog** boxes (part 4 of 8).

```
// Fig. 11.12: SelectColorDialog.java
// Modeless dialog that allows user to choose drawing color.
package com.deitel.jhtp2.ch11;
import java.awt.*;
import java.awt.event.*;
import com.deitel.jhtp2.ch11.CloseWindow;

public class SelectColorDialog extends Dialog
             implements ItemListener {
   private List colorList;
   private String colorNames[] =
      { "Black", "Blue", "Cyan", "Dark Gray", "Gray", "Green",
        "Light Gray", "Magenta", "Orange", "Pink", "Red",
        "White", "Yellow" };
   private Color colors[] =
      { Color.black, Color.blue, Color.cyan, Color.darkGray,
       Color.gray, Color.green, Color.lightGray, Color.magenta,
        Color.orange, Color.pink, Color.red, Color.white,
        Color.yellow };
   private Color currentColor;

   public SelectColorDialog( Frame parent, String title )
   {
      super( parent, title, false );
      setSize( 275, 150 );
      addWindowListener( new CloseWindow() );

```

Fig. 11.12 Demonstrating modal and modeless **Dialog** boxes (part 5 of 8).

```
144         // create a list with 5 items visible
145         // do not allow multiple selections
146         colorList = new List( 5, false );
147         colorList.addItemListener( this );
148         colorList.addItemListener( ( ItemListener ) parent );
149 
150         // add items to the list
151         for ( int i = 0; i < colorNames.length; i++ )
152            colorList.add( colorNames[ i ] );
153 
154         // add list to applet
155         add( colorList, BorderLayout.CENTER );
156 
157         currentColor = colors[ 0 ];   // black
158      }
159 
160      public void itemStateChanged( ItemEvent e )
161      {
162         currentColor = colors[ colorList.getSelectedIndex() ];
163      }
164 
165      public Color getColor() { return currentColor; }
166   }
```

Fig. 11.12 Demonstrating modal and modeless **Dialog** boxes (part 6 of 8).

```
167   // Fig. 11.12: SelfContainedCanvas2.java
168   // Adds ability to set drawing color for a SelfContainedCanvas.
169   package com.deitel.jhtp2.ch11;
170   import java.awt.*;
171   import com.deitel.jhtp2.ch11.SelfContainedCanvas;
172 
173   public class SelfContainedCanvas2 extends SelfContainedCanvas {
174      private Color color = Color.black;
175 
176      public void paint( Graphics g )
177      {
178         g.setColor( color );
179         super.paint( g );
180      }
181 
182      public void setDrawingColor( Color c ) { color = c; }
183   }
```

Fig. 11.12 Demonstrating modal and modeless **Dialog** boxes (part 7 of 8).

The **DialogBoxDemo** class (line 10) creates instances of **MessageBox**, **SelectColorDialog**, **SelfContainedCanvas2** and all the menu components for the application's graphical user interface. The constructor (line 19) calls the superclass constructor, creates the GUI components and attaches them to the interface and displays the **DialogBoxDemo** frame. Also, the **DialogBoxDemo** class implements the event listener inter-

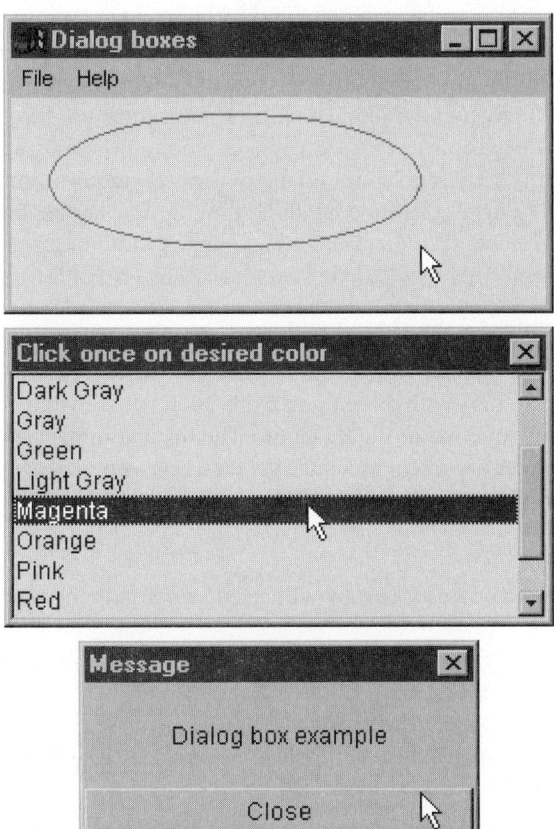

Fig. 11.12 Demonstrating modal and modeless **Dialog** boxes (part 8 of 8).

faces **ActionListener** and **ItemListener**. **DialogBoxDemo** handles its own menu item events in method **actionPerformed** (line 62) from interface **ActionListener**. **DialogBoxDemo** implements **ItemListener** so it can set the drawing color for the oval on the attached **SelfContainedCanvas2** object. The **itemStateChanged** method (line7) is executed in response to an item event on the **SelectColorDialog** object. This method uses method **getColor** from the **SelectColor** dialog to get the currently selected color and passes the color to method **setDrawingColor** of class **SelfContainedCanvas2**.

There is one new statement in the constructor. Line 44

```
bar.setHelpMenu( helpMenu );
```

sets the *help menu* for the menu bar with **MenuBar** method ***setHelpMenu***. The help menu automatically appears as the rightmost menu on the menu bar.

Normally, class **Dialog** is extended to create custom **Dialog** boxes. **MessageBox** and **SelectColorDialog** both extend **Dialog** for this purpose. Class **MessageBox** (line 90) defines a modal **Dialog** class that is used to display information to the user. The user must dismiss the **Dialog** before interacting with other windows in the application. Otherwise, the system simply beeps at the user when an attempt is made to interact with any other part of the application (Note: **Dialog**s also can be used from applets).

Class **MessageBox** consists of a **Label** containing the message to the user and a **Button** to dismiss the **Dialog**. The constructor (line 95) requires four arguments—a reference to the parent **Frame**, a string containing the title for the title bar of the **Dialog**, a string containing the message to the user and an integer width in pixels for the dialog box. The first two arguments are passed to the superclass **Dialog** constructor in line 98

```
super( parent, title, true );
```

The **parent** reference indicates the owner of the **Dialog** object. When a modal **Dialog** is displayed, all interactions with the **parent** are intercepted by the modal **Dialog**. The title is displayed in the title bar of the **Dialog**. The third argument specifies the modality of the **Dialog**. A **true** argument indicates the **Dialog** is modal and a **false** argument indicates the **Dialog** is modeless. Line 100

```
setResizable( false );
```

uses **Dialog** method **setResizable** with a **false** argument to prevent the user from resizing the **Dialog**.

Class **MessageBox** handles its own action event. When the user clicks the **close** button, **actionPerformed** (line 112) uses **Component** method **setVisible** to hide the **MessageBox**. The **MessageBox** can also be dismissed by clicking its close box. This event is handled by an instance of our class **CloseWindow** (originally defined in Fig. 11.9) registered to handle window events at line 109.

Class **SelectColorDialog** (line 124) provides a **List** of colors from which the user can make a selection. The third constructor parameter (line 138) specifies to the superclass **Dialog** constructor that **SelectColorDialog** objects are modeless **Dialog**s—the user can interact with other parts of the program when a **SelectColorDialog** is displayed. Line 142 registers an instance of class **CloseWindow** to close the **Dialog** when the user clicks the close box. The class implements **ItemListener** to process a click on an item in the **List**. Two item event listeners are registered. Lines 147 and 148

```
colorList.addItemListener( this );
colorList.addItemListener( ( ItemListener ) parent );
```

specify that the **itemStateChanged** methods of both the **SelectColorDialog** object (**this**) and the **DialogBoxDemo** object (**parent**) should be invoked in response to an item event. When the user clicks on the **List**, method **itemStateChanged** (line 160) determines the index selected in the **List** and uses the index as the subscript into the **colors** array. The selected color is stored in instance variable **currentColor** so it can be retrieved by the **DialogBoxDemo** object (in its **itemStateChanged** method) using method **getColor** (line 165) when a color selection is made.

Class **SelfContainedCanvas2** (line 173) extends the definition from Fig. 11.5 by providing instance variable **color** for the current drawing color and adding a **paint** method that sets the drawing color and calls the superclass **paint** method with line 179

```
super.paint( g );
```

Method **setDrawingColor** is invoked when the user selects a color in the **SelectColorDialog**.

11.10 ScrollPane: A Scrolling Container Class

It is sometimes desirable to provide an area that is not completely visible on the screen, but that the user can scroll through with scrollbars. For example, you may want to create a drawing program with a scrollable **Canvas** on which the user can draw shapes. The program of Fig. 11.13 uses a 1000 pixel by 1000 pixel instance of class **SelfContainedCanvas** (from Fig. 11.5) that enables the user to draw an oval that is larger than the visible area of the applet on the screen. The **SelfContainedCanvas** is attached to a 275 pixel by 275 pixel instance of class ***ScrollPane*** that provides a scrollable container to which a single GUI component can be attached. Because the instance of **ScrollPane** in this example is too small to display the entire **SelfContainedCanvas**, the **ScrollPane** automatically provides horizontal and vertical scrollbars that enable the user to scroll through the **SelfContainedCanvas**.

```
// Fig. 11.13: ScrollPaneTest.java
// Testing class ScrollPane
import java.awt.*;
import java.awt.event.*;
import java.applet.Applet;
import com.deitel.jhtp2.ch11.SelfContainedCanvas;

public class ScrollPaneTest extends Applet {
   private SelfContainedCanvas drawCanvas;
   private ScrollPane drawCanvasScroller;

   public void init()
   {
      drawCanvas = new SelfContainedCanvas();
      drawCanvas.setSize( 1000, 1000 );
      drawCanvasScroller = new ScrollPane();
      drawCanvasScroller.add( drawCanvas );
      drawCanvasScroller.setSize( 275, 275 );
      add( drawCanvasScroller );

      Adjustable horizontal =
         drawCanvasScroller.getHAdjustable();
      horizontal.setUnitIncrement( 4 );
      Adjustable vertical =
         drawCanvasScroller.getVAdjustable();
      vertical.setUnitIncrement( 4 );
   }
}
```

Fig. 11.13 Demonstrating a **ScrollPane** (part 1 of 2).

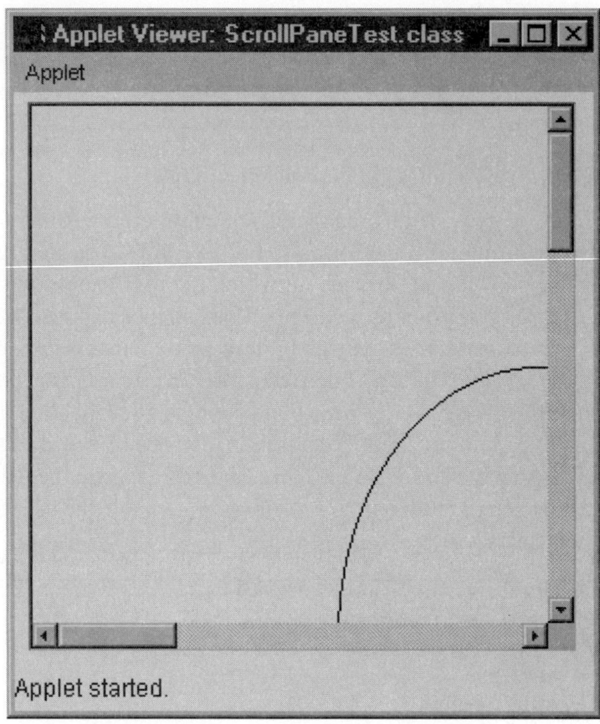

Fig. 11.13 Demonstrating a **ScrollPane** (part 2 of 2).

The applet's **init** method (line 12) creates an instance of the imported class **SelfContainedCanvas** and sets its size to 1000-by-1000 pixels with lines 14 and 15

```
drawCanvas = new SelfContainedCanvas();
drawCanvas.setSize( 1000, 1000 );
```

Next, the applet creates an instance of class **ScrollPane** called **drawCanvasScroller**, adds the **drawCanvas** object to the **drawCanvasScroller** and sets the size of the **drawCanvasScroller** to 275-by-275 pixels with lines 16–18

```
drawCanvasScroller = new ScrollPane();
drawCanvasScroller.add( drawCanvas );
drawCanvasScroller.setSize( 275, 275 );
```

After the **drawCanvasScroller** is attached to the applet, lines 21 and 22

```
Adjustable horizontal =
   drawCanvasScroller.getHAdjustable();
```

use **ScrollPane** method ***getHAdjustable*** to get the horizontal scrollbar's ***Adjustable*** object. This object enables the programmer to set the *unit increment* for the scrollbar. The unit increment is the number of pixels the **ScrollPane** scrolls when the user clicks on the scrollbar's scroll arrows. Line 23

```
horizontal.setUnitIncrement( 4 );
```

uses **Adjustable** method ***setUnitIncrement*** to set the unit increment. Lines 24–26 perform the same tasks for the vertical scrollbar. **ScrollPane** method ***getVAdjustable*** gets the **Adjustable** object for the vertical scrollbar.

11.11 Using PopupMenu Objects

Many of today's computer applications provide so called *context-sensitive popup menus*. These menus provide options that are specific to the component for which the *popup trigger event* was generated. On most systems, the popup trigger event occurs when the user presses and releases the right mouse button. Instances of class ***PopupMenu*** (a subclass of **Menu**) can be attached to any instance of a **Component** subclass.

Figure 11.14 creates a **PopupMenu** containing **MenuItem**s with the names of the 13 predefined colors in class **Color**. The **PopupMenu** is attached to an instance of class **SelfContainedCanvas3** (a subclass of class **SelfContainedCanvas2** from Fig. 11.12). When the user clicks the right mouse button on the **SelfContainedCanvas3** area (the entire area in the application window) a **PopupMenu** of colors is displayed. If the user clicks on a **MenuItem**, an action event is generated and the **actionPerformed** method of class **SelfContainedCanvas3** sets the drawing color to the selected color.

```
// Fig. 11.14: PopupTest.java
// Class to test popup menus.
import java.awt.*;
import com.deitel.jhtp2.ch11.SelfContainedCanvas3;
import com.deitel.jhtp2.ch11.CloseWindowAndExit;

public class PopupTest extends Frame {
   private SelfContainedCanvas3 canvas;

   public PopupTest()
   {
      super( "Popup Test Example" );

      canvas = new SelfContainedCanvas3();
      add( canvas, BorderLayout.CENTER );
      setSize( 300, 200 );
      setVisible( true );
   }

   public static void main( String args[] )
   {
      PopupTest p = new PopupTest();
      p.addWindowListener( new CloseWindowAndExit() );
   }
}
```

Fig. 11.14 Using a **PopupMenu** object (part 1 of 3).

```
// Fig. 11.14: SelfContainedCanvas3.java
// Class that extends SelfContainedCanvas2 and adds
// a popup menu to select drawing color.
package com.deitel.jhtp2.ch11;
import java.awt.*;
import java.awt.event.*;

public class SelfContainedCanvas3 extends SelfContainedCanvas2
      implements ActionListener {
   private String colorNames[] =
      { "Black", "Blue", "Cyan", "Dark Gray", "Gray", "Green",
        "Light Gray", "Magenta", "Orange", "Pink", "Red",
        "White", "Yellow" };
   private Color colorValues[] =
      { Color.black, Color.blue, Color.cyan, Color.darkGray,
       Color.gray, Color.green, Color.lightGray, Color.magenta,
        Color.orange, Color.pink, Color.red, Color.white,
        Color.yellow };
   private MenuItem colors[];
   private PopupMenu popup;

   public SelfContainedCanvas3()
   {
      popup = new PopupMenu( "Colors" );
      colors = new MenuItem[ colorNames.length ];

      for ( int i = 0; i < colorNames.length; i++ ) {
         colors[ i ] = new MenuItem( colorNames[ i ] );
         popup.add( colors[ i ] );
         colors[ i ].addActionListener( this );
      }

      add( popup );  // add popup to this canvas
      enableEvents( AWTEvent.MOUSE_EVENT_MASK );
   }

   public void actionPerformed( ActionEvent e )
   {
      for ( int i = 0; i < colors.length; i++ )
         if ( e.getSource() == colors[ i ] ) {
            setDrawingColor( colorValues[ i ] );
            break;
         }
   }

   public void processMouseEvent( MouseEvent e )
   {
      if ( e.isPopupTrigger() )
         popup.show( this, e.getX(), e.getY() );

```

Fig. 11.14 Using a **PopupMenu** object (part 2 of 3).

```
76          super.processMouseEvent( e );
77       }
78    }
```

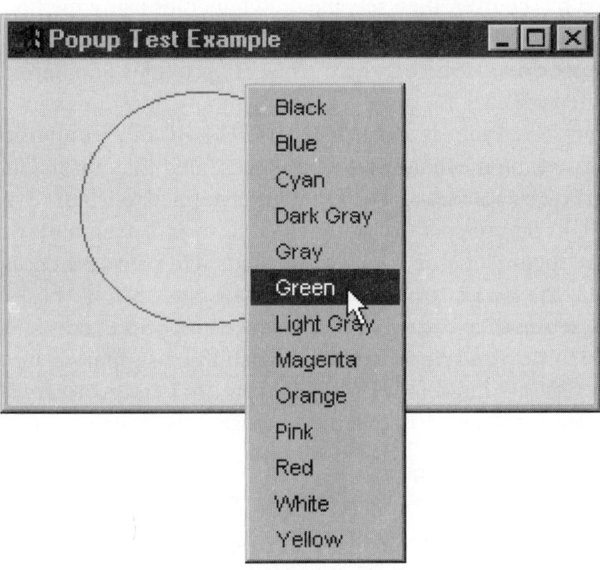

Fig. 11.14 Using a **PopupMenu** object (part 3 of 3).

The program consists of two classes—**PopupTest** to execute the program as a GUI-based application and **SelfContainedCanvas3** to allow the user to draw ovals in a color selected from a **PopupMenu**. Class **PopupTest** (line 7) is a subclass of **Frame** that creates a **SelfContainedCanvas3** object and attaches it to the Center region of the **Frame**.

Class **SelfContainedCanvas3** is a subclass of **SelfContainedCanvas2** that also implements **ActionListener** so it can process its own action events in method **actionPerformed** when the user selects an option in the **PopupMenu**. The constructor (line 47) creates an instance of class **PopupMenu** called popup and an array of **MenuItem**s called colors. The **for** structure at line 52 creates a **MenuItem** for each **String** in the array **colorNames**, adds each **MenuItem** to the **PopupMenu** with line 54

```
popup.add( colors[ i ] );
```

and registers the **SelfContainedCanvas3** object to handle the action event for each **MenuItem** object. Line 58 uses the **Component** method ***add*** to attach **popup** to the **SelfContainedCanvas3** object. Line 59

```
enableEvents( AWTEvent.MOUSE_EVENT_MASK );
```

uses **Component** method ***enableEvents*** to indicate that mouse events should be activated for the **SelfContainedCanvas3** object. Constant **MOUSE_EVENT_MASK** from the **AWTEvent** class specifies that the mouse events can be processed with **Component** method ***processMouseEvent***.

Method **actionPerformed** (line 62) determines which **MenuItem** in the **PopupMenu** was selected by the user, then sets the drawing color using method **setDrawingColor** that was inherited from class **SelfContainedCanvas2**.

The method **processMouseEvent** (line 71) provides an alternate form of mouse processing that intercepts all mouse events (not mouse motion events) before they are delivered to the registered mouse event listeners. This is an entirely different event handling mechanism from the mechanism we have presented thus far in Chapters 10 and 11. Methods such as **processMouseEvent** are often defined to handle events in classes that extend existing GUI components (as we have done in this example). See class **Component** in the online documentation for other methods like **processMouseEvent**.

Remember that the **SelfContainedCanvas** class in Fig. 11.5 processes its own **mousePressed**, **mouseDragged** and **mouseReleased** events so the user can draw an oval on the **SelfContainedCanvas** (capabilities supported in class **SelfContainedCanvas3** via its indirect inheritance from **SelfContainedCanvas**). When method **processMouseEvent** intercepts a mouse event it executes lines 73–74

```
if ( e.isPopupTrigger() )
   popup.show( this, e.getX(), e.getY() );
```

The condition uses **MouseEvent** method ***isPopupTrigger*** to determine if the mouse event is the event trigger that causes a **PopupMenu** to appear. If so, method ***show*** of class **PopupMenu** is invoked to display the **PopupMenu**. The first argument to **PopupMenu** method **show** specifies the *origin component* whose position helps determine where the **PopupMenu** will appear on the screen. The last two arguments are the *x* and *y* coordinates from the origin component's upper-left corner at which the **PopupMenu** should appear.

Finally, line 76

```
super.processMouseEvent( e );
```

invokes the original **Component** class version of method **processMouseEvent** (our version overrides the original version) to guarantee that the registered mouse event listeners are also notified of the mouse event that occurred.

11.12 Layout Managers

In the previous chapter, we introduced three layout managers—**FlowLayout**, **BorderLayout** and **GridLayout**. This section presents two additional layout managers (summarized in Fig. 11.15). We discuss these layout managers in the sections that follow.

11.13 CardLayout Layout Manager

The ***CardLayout*** *layout manager* arranges components into a "deck" of cards where only the top card is visible. Any card in the deck can be placed at the top of the deck at any time using methods of class **CardLayout**. Each card is usually a container such as a panel and each card can use any layout manager. Class **CardLayout** inherits from **Object** and implements the **LayoutManager2** interface.

Layout manager	Description
CardLayout	A layout manager that stacks components like a deck of cards. Each container in the stack can use any layout manager. Only the container at the "top" of the deck is visible.
GridBagLayout	A layout manager similar to **GridLayout**. Unlike **GridLayout** each component size can vary and components can be added in any order.

Fig. 11.15 Advanced layout managers.

The program of Fig. 11.16 creates five panels. **Panel deck** uses the **CardLayout** layout manager to control the card that is displayed. **Panel**s **card1**, **card2** and **card3** are used as individual cards in **deck**. **Panel buttons** contains four buttons that enable the user to manipulate the deck. When the user clicks **firstButton**, the first card in **deck** (i.e., **card1**) is displayed. When the user clicks **lastButton**, the last card (i.e., **card3**) in **deck** is displayed. Each time the user clicks **prevButton**, the previous card in **deck** is displayed. Each time the user clicks **nextButton**, the next card in **deck** is displayed. Clicking **prevButton** or **nextButton** repeatedly allows the user to cycle through the **deck** of cards. The applet implements **ActionListener**, so the action events generated by the **Button**s on **Panel buttons** are handled by the applet in its **actionPerformed** method.

```
// Fig. 11.16: CardDeck.java
// Demonstrating CardLayout.
import java.applet.Applet;
import java.awt.*;
import java.awt.event.*;

public class CardDeck extends Applet implements ActionListener {
   private Canvas c;
   private CardLayout cardManager;
   private Panel deck, card1, card2, card3, buttons;
   private Button b1, b2, b3, prevButton, nextButton,
                  lastButton, firstButton;

   public void init()
   {
      setLayout( new BorderLayout() );

      // create the panel with CardLayout
      deck = new Panel();
      cardManager = new CardLayout();
      deck.setLayout( cardManager );

```

Fig. 11.16 Demonstrating the **CardLayout** layout manager (part 1 of 3).

```
      // set up card1 and add it to Panel deck
      b1 = new Button( "card one" );
      card1 = new Panel();
      card1.add( b1 );         // add a button
      deck.add( card1, b1.getLabel() );  // add card to deck

      // set up card2 and add it to Panel deck
      b2 = new Button( "card two" );
      c = new Canvas();
      c.setBackground( Color.green );
      c.setSize( 80, 80 );
      card2 = new Panel();
      card2.add( b2 );         // add a button
      card2.add( c );          // add a canvas
      deck.add( card2, b2.getLabel() );  // add card to deck

      // set up card3 and add it to Panel deck
      b3 = new Button( "card three" );
      card3 = new Panel();
      card3.setLayout( new BorderLayout() );   // set layout
      card3.add( new Button( "North" ), BorderLayout.NORTH );
      card3.add( new Button( "West" ), BorderLayout.WEST );
      card3.add( new Button( "East" ), BorderLayout.EAST );
      card3.add( new Button( "Pole" ), BorderLayout.SOUTH );
      card3.add( b3, BorderLayout.CENTER );
      deck.add( card3, b3.getLabel() );  // add card to deck

      // create and layout Panel buttons that will control deck
      buttons = new Panel();
      buttons.setLayout ( new GridLayout( 2, 2 ) );
      buttons.add( firstButton = new Button( "First card" ) );
      buttons.add( nextButton = new Button( "Next card" ) );
     buttons.add( prevButton = new Button( "Previous card" ) );
      buttons.add( lastButton = new Button( "Last card" ) );
      firstButton.addActionListener( this );
      nextButton.addActionListener( this );
      prevButton.addActionListener( this );
      lastButton.addActionListener( this );

      // add Panel deck and Panel buttons to the applet
      add( buttons, BorderLayout.WEST );
      add( deck, BorderLayout.EAST );
   }

   public void actionPerformed( ActionEvent e )
   {
      if ( e.getSource() == firstButton )
         cardManager.first( deck );    // show first card
      else if ( e.getSource() == prevButton )
         cardManager.previous( deck ); // show previous card
```

Fig. 11.16 Demonstrating the **CardLayout** layout manager (part 2 of 3).

```
73          else if ( e.getSource() == nextButton )
74             cardManager.next( deck );        // show next card
75          else if ( e.getSource() == lastButton )
76            cardManager.last( deck );     // show last card
77       }
78    }
```

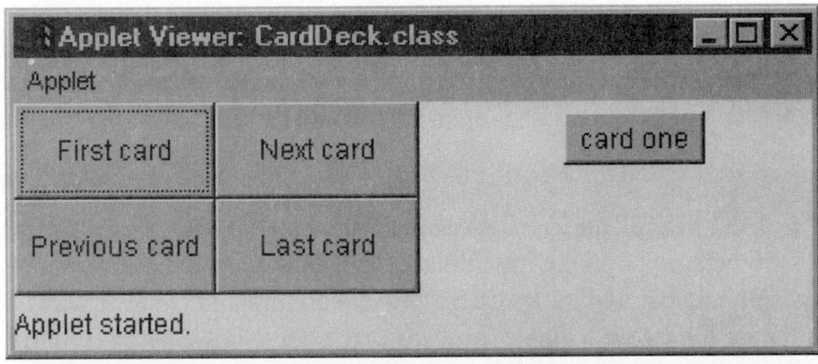

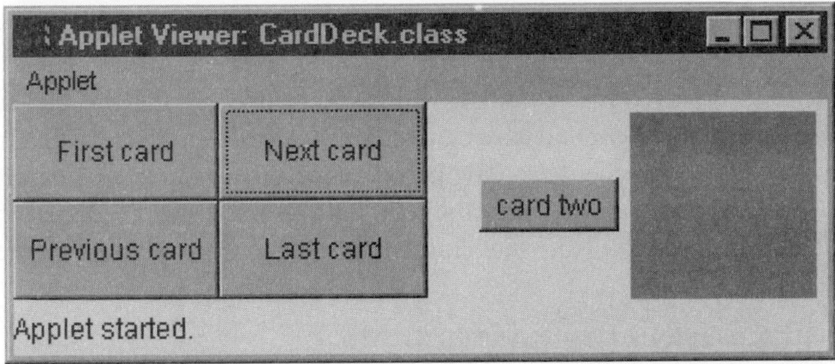

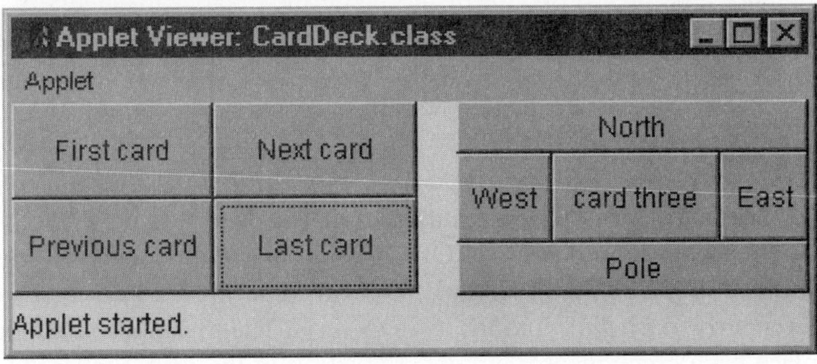

Fig. 11.16 Demonstrating the **`CardLayout`** layout manager (part 3 of 3).

Applet class **`CardDeck`** declares references to several **`Panel`**s, several **`Button`**s, and a **`Canvas`**. The applet also declares a reference of type **`CardLayout`** called **`cardManager`**. This reference is used to invoke **`CardLayout`** methods that manipulate the cards in deck.

The applet's **`init`** method (line 14) builds the GUI. The layout manager for the applet is set to **`BorderLayout`**. Lines 19–21,

```
deck = new Panel();
cardManager = new CardLayout();
deck.setLayout( cardManager );
```

create **Panel deck**, create **CardLayout** object **cardManager** and set the layout manager for deck to **cardManager**. Next, **Panel**s **card1**, **card2** and **card3** are created. As we set up each card, we add the card to **deck**. Each card has its own set of GUI components to display. Cards are added to the deck using **Container** method **add** with two arguments—a **Component** and a **String**. The **Component** is the **Panel** object that represents the card. The **String** argument identifies the card. For example, line 27

```
deck.add( card1, b1.getLabel() );   // add card to deck
```

adds **Panel card1** to deck and uses **Button b1**'s label as the **String** identifier for the card. **Panel**s **card2** and **card3** are added to **deck** at lines 37 and 48, respectively. After, the **Panel buttons** and its **Button** objects are created (lines 51–56), the applet is registered as the action event listener for each **Button** (lines 57–60). Finally, **buttons** and **deck** are added to the applet's West and East regions, respectively.

Method **actionPerformed** determines the clicked **Button** using **EventObject** method **getSource**. **CardLayout** methods ***first***, ***previous***, ***next***, and ***last*** are used to display a particular card in response to clicking the **firstButton**, **prevButton**, **nextButton** and **lastButton**, respectively. The **first** method displays the first card added to the deck. The **previous** method displays the previous card in the deck. The **next** method displays the next card in the deck. The **last** method displays the last card in the deck. Note that **deck** is passed to each of these methods.

11.14 GridBagLayout Layout Manager

The most complex and most powerful of the predefined layout managers is ***GridBagLayout***. **GridBagLayout** is similar to **GridLayout** because **GridBagLayout** also arranges components in a grid. However **GridBagLayout** is more flexible. The components can vary in size (i.e., they can occupy multiple rows and columns) and can be added in any order.

The first step in using **GridBagLayout** is determining the appearance of the GUI. This step does not involve any programming; all that is needed is a piece of paper. First, draw the GUI. Next draw a grid over the GUI dividing the components into rows and columns. The initial row and column should start with 0 so the **GridBagLayout** layout manager can properly place the components in the grid. The row and column numbers will be used to place each component in an exact position in the grid. Figure. 11.17 demonstrates drawing the lines for the rows and columns over a GUI.

To use **GridBagLayout**, a ***GridBagConstraints*** object must be constructed. This object specifies how a component is placed in a **GridBagLayout**. Several important **GridBagConstraints** instance variables are summarized in Fig. 11.18.

Variables ***gridx*** and ***gridy*** specify the row and column where the upper-left corner of the component is placed in the grid. Variable **gridx** corresponds to the column and the **gridy** variable corresponds to the row. In Fig. 11.17, the **Choice** button (displaying "**Linden**") has a **gridx** value of 1 and a **gridy** value 2.

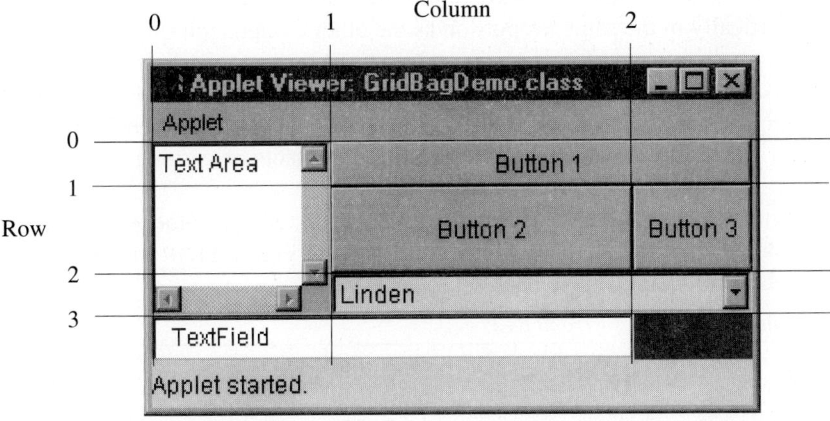

Fig. 11.17 Designing a GUI that will use **`GridBagLayout`**.

`GridBagConstraints` instance variable	**Description**
`gridx`	The column in which the component will be placed.
`gridy`	The row in which the component will be placed.
`gridwidth`	The number of columns the component occupies.
`gridheight`	The number of rows the component occupies.
`weightx`	The portion of extra space to allocate horizontally. The components can become "wider" when extra space is available.
`weighty`	The portion of extra space to allocate vertically. The components can become "taller" when extra space is available.

Fig. 11.18 `GridBagConstraints` instance variables.

Variable ***`gridwidth`*** specifies the number of columns a component occupies. In Fig. 11.17, the **`Choice`** button occupies two columns. Variable ***`gridheight`*** specifies the number of rows a component occupies. In Fig. 11.17, the **`TextArea`** occupies three rows.

Variable ***`weightx`*** specifies how to distribute extra horizontal space to components in a **`GridBagLayout`** when the container is resized. A zero value indicates that the component does not grow horizontally on its own. However, if the component spans a column containing a component with non-zero **`weightx`** value, the component with zero **`weightx`** value will grow horizontally in the same proportion as the other component(s) in the same column. This is because each component must be maintained in the same row and column in which it was originally placed.

Variable ***`weighty`*** specifies how to distribute extra vertical space to components in a **`GridBagLayout`** when the container is resized. A zero value indicates that the component does not grow vertically on its own. However, if the component spans a row containing a component with non-zero **weighty** value, the component with zero **weighty** value grows vertically in the same proportion as the other component(s) in the same row.

In Fig. 11.17, the affects of **weighty** and **weightx** cannot easily be seen until the container is resized. When it is resized additional space becomes available. Components with larger weight values will occupy more of the additional space than components with smaller weight values. In the exercises, we explore the effects of varying **weightx** and **weighty**.

Components should be given non-zero positive weight values—otherwise the components will "huddle" together in the middle of the container. Figure 11.19 shows the GUI of Fig. 11.17—where all weights have been set to zero.

Common Programming Error 11.12

*Using a negative value for either **weightx** or **weighty** is a logic error.*

GridBagConstraints instance variable ***fill*** specifies how much of the components area (the number of rows and columns the component occupies in the grid) is occupied. The variable **fill** is assigned one of the following **GridBagConstraints static** constants: ***NONE***, ***VERTICAL***, ***HORIZONTAL***, or ***BOTH***. The default value is **NONE** which indicates the component will not grow in either direction. **VERTICAL** indicates the component will grow vertically. **HORIZONTAL** indicates the component will grow horizontally. **BOTH** indicates the component will grow in both directions.

GridBagConstraints instance variable ***anchor*** specifies the location of the component in the area when the component does not fill the entire area. The variable **anchor** is assigned one of the following **GridBagConstraints static** constants: ***NORTH***, ***NORTHEAST***, ***EAST***, ***SOUTHEAST***, ***SOUTH***, ***SOUTHWEST***, ***WEST***, ***NORTHWEST***, or ***CENTER***. The default value is **CENTER**.

The program of Fig. 11.20 uses the **GridBagLayout** layout manager to arrange the components in the GUI of Fig. 11.17. The program does nothing other than demonstrate how to use **GridBagLayout**.

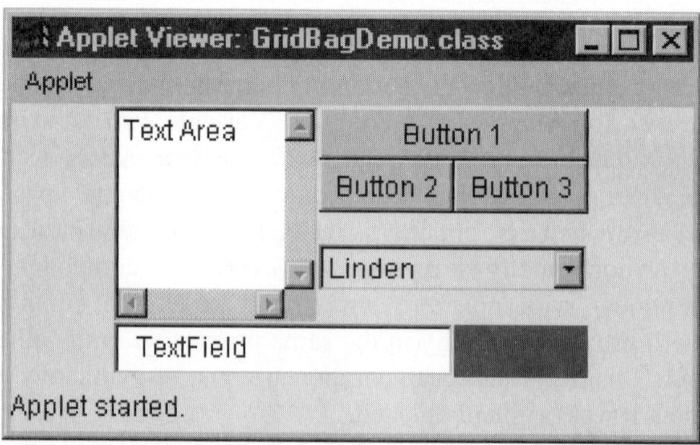

Fig. 11.19 **GridBagLayout** with the weights set to zero.

```
// Fig. 11.20: GridBagDemo.java
// Demonstrating GridBagLayout.
import java.applet.Applet;
import java.awt.*;

public class GridBagDemo extends Applet {
   private Canvas c;
   private Choice cb;
   private TextArea ta;
   private TextField tf;
   private Button b1, b2, b3;
   private GridBagLayout gbLayout;
   private GridBagConstraints gbConstraints;

   public void init()
   {
      gbLayout = new GridBagLayout();
      setLayout( gbLayout );   // applet

      // instantiate gridbag constraints
      gbConstraints = new GridBagConstraints();

      ta = new TextArea( "Text Area", 5, 10 );
      cb = new Choice( );
      cb.add( "Linden" );
      cb.add( "Birch" );
      cb.add( "Ceder" );
      tf = new TextField( "TextField" );
      b1 = new Button( "Button 1" );
      b2 = new Button( "Button 2" );
      b3 = new Button( "Button 3" );
      c = new Canvas();
      c.setBackground( Color.blue );
      c.setSize( 10, 5 );

      // text area
      // weightx and weighty are both 0: the default
      // anchor for all components is CENTER: the default
      gbConstraints.fill = GridBagConstraints.BOTH;
      addComponent( ta, 0, 0, 1, 3 );

      // button b1
      // weightx and weighty are both 0: the default
      gbConstraints.fill = GridBagConstraints.HORIZONTAL;
      addComponent( b1, 0, 1, 2, 1 );

      // choice button
      // weightx and weighty are both 0: the default
      // fill is HORIZONTAL
      addComponent( cb, 2, 1, 2, 1 );

```

Fig. 11.20 Demonstrating the `GridBagLayout` layout manager (part 1 of 3).

```
52         // button b2
53         gbConstraints.weightx = 1000;  // can grow wider
54         gbConstraints.weighty = 1;     // can grow taller
55         gbConstraints.fill = GridBagConstraints.BOTH;
56         addComponent( b2, 1, 1, 1, 1 );
57 
58         // button b3
59         // fill is BOTH
60         gbConstraints.weightx = 0;
61         gbConstraints.weighty = 0;
62         addComponent( b3, 1, 2, 1, 1 );
63 
64         // textfield
65         // weightx and weighty are both 0: fill is BOTH
66         addComponent( tf, 3, 0, 2, 1 );
67 
68         // canvas
69         // weightx and weighty are both 0: fill is BOTH
70         addComponent( c, 3, 2, 1, 1 );
71      }
72 
73      // addComponent is programmer defined
74      private void addComponent( Component c, int row, int column,
75                                 int width, int height )
76      {
77         // set gridx and gridy
78         gbConstraints.gridx = column;
79         gbConstraints.gridy = row;
80 
81         // set gridwidth and gridheight
82         gbConstraints.gridwidth = width;
83         gbConstraints.gridheight = height;
84 
85         // set constraints
86         gbLayout.setConstraints( c, gbConstraints );
87         add( c );      // add component to applet
88      }
89   }
```

Fig. 11.20 Demonstrating the **GridBagLayout** layout manager (part 2 of 3).

The GUI consists of three **Button**s, a **TextArea**, a **Choice** button, a **Canvas** and a **TextField**. The layout manager for the applet is **GridBagLayout**. Lines 17 and 18

```
gbLayout = new GridBagLayout();
setLayout( gbLayout );
```

instantiate **gbLayout** with a call to the **GridBagLayout** constructor and set the layout manager for the applet to **gbLayout**. The **GridBagConstraints** object used to determine the location and size of each component in the grid is instantiated with line 21

```
gbConstraints = new GridBagConstraints()
```

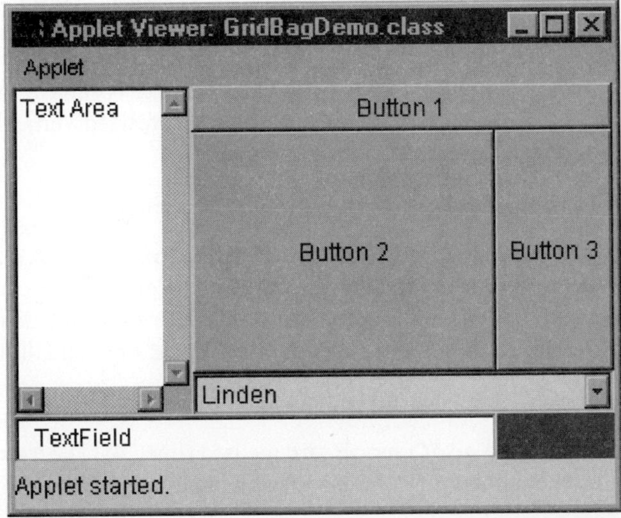

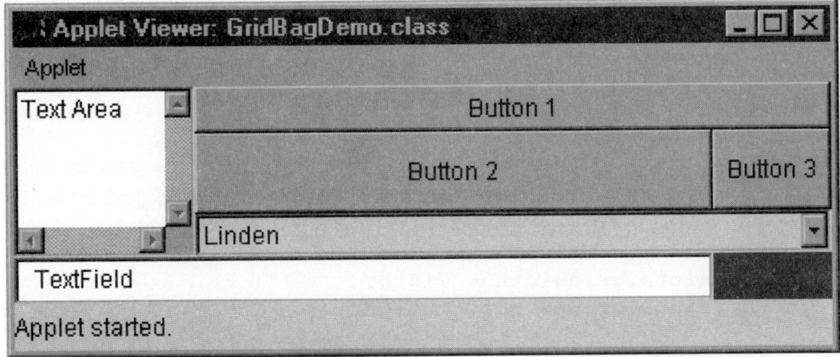

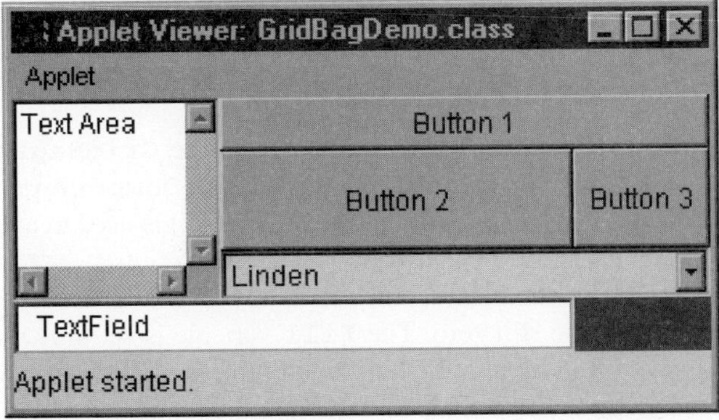

Fig. 11.20 Demonstrating the `GridBagLayout` layout manager (part 3 of 3).

Lines 23–34 instantiate each of the GUI components that will be added to the applet.

TextArea ta is the first component added to the **GridBagLayout**. The values for **weightx** and **weighty** values are not specified in **gbConstraints**, so each has the value zero by default. Thus, the **TextArea** will not resize itself if space is available. However, the **TextArea** spans multiple rows so the vertical size is subject to the **weighty** values of **Button**s **b2** and **b3**. When either **b2** or **b3** is resized vertically based on its **weighty** value, the **TextArea** is also resized. Line 39

```
gbConstraints.fill = GridBagConstraints.BOTH;
```

sets variable **fill** in **gbConstraints** to **GridBagConstraints.BOTH** causing the **TextArea** to always fill its entire allocated area in the grid. An **anchor** value is not specified in **gbConstraints**, so the default of **CENTER** is used. We do not use variable **anchor** in this program, so all components will use **CENTER** by default. Line 40

```
addComponent( ta, 0, 0, 1, 3 );
```

calls the programmer-defined ***addComponent*** method (line 74). The **TextArea** object, the row, the column, the number of columns to span, and the number of rows to span are passed as arguments.

Method **addComponent**'s parameters are a **Component** reference **c**, and integers **row**, **column**, **width** and **height**. Lines 78 and 79

```
gbContraints.gridx = column;
gbContraints.gridy = row;
```

set the **GridBagConstraints** variables **gridx** and **gridy**. The **gridx** variable is assigned the column in which the **Component** will be placed and the **gridy** value is assigned the row in which the **Component** will be placed. Lines 82 and 83

```
gbContraints.gridwidth = width;
gbContraints.gridheight = height;
```

set the **GridBagConstraints** variables **gridwidth** and **gridheight**. The **gridwidth** variable specifies the number of columns the **Component** will span and the **gridheight** variable specifies the number of rows the **Component** will span. Line 86

```
gbLayout.setConstraints( c, gbContraints );
```

sets the **GridBagConstraints** for a component in the **GridBagLayout**. Method ***setConstraints*** of class **GridBagLayout** takes a **Component** argument and a **GridBagConstraints** argument. Method **add** (line 87) is used to add the component to the applet.

Button object **b1** is the next component added (lines 44–45). The values of **weightx** and **weighty** are still zero. The **fill** variable is set to **HORIZONTAL**—the component will always fill its area in the horizontal direction. The vertical direction is not filled. Since the **weighty** value is zero, the button will only become taller if another component in the same row has a non-zero **weighty** value. Button **b1** is located at row 0, column 1. One row and two columns are occupied.

Choice button **cb** is the next component added (line 50). The **weightx** and **weighty** values are zero and the **fill** variable is set to **HORIZONTAL**. The **Choice** button will grow only in the horizontal direction. Note that the **weightx**, **weighty**, and **fill** variables remain set in **gbConstraints** until they are changed. The **Choice** button is placed at row 2, column 1. One row and two columns are occupied.

Button object **b2** is the next component added (lines 53-56). Button **b2** is given a **weightx** value of **1000** and a **weighty** value of **1**. The area occupied by the button is capable of growing in the vertical and horizontal direction. The **fill** variable is set to **BOTH** which specifies that the button will always fill the entire area. When the applet is resized, **b2** will grow. The button is placed at row 1, column 1. One row and one column are occupied.

Button **b3** is added next (lines 60–62). Both the **weightx** value and **weighty** value are set to zero and the value of **fill** is **BOTH**. Button **b3** will grow if the applet is resized; it is affected by the weight values of **b2**. Note that the **weightx** value for **b2** is much larger than **b3**. When resizing occurs, **b2** will occupy a larger percentage of the new space. The button is placed at row 1, column 2. One row and one column are occupied.

Both the **TextField** (line 66) and **Canvas** (line 70) have a **weightx** value of 0 and a **weighty** value of 0. The value of **fill** is **BOTH**. The **TextField** is placed at row 3, column 0 and the **Canvas** is placed at row 3, column 2. The **TextField** occupies one row and two columns. The **Canvas** occupies one row and one column.

11.15 GridBagLayout Layout Manager Variation: Using GridBagConstraints Constants RELATIVE and REMAINDER

Java also provides a variation of **GridBagLayout**. In this version, the **gridx** and **gridy** variables are not used. Rather, constants are used in their place. The **Gridbag-Constraints static** constants are ***RELATIVE*** and ***REMAINDER***. **RELATIVE** specifies that the next-to-last component in a particular row should be placed to the right of the previous component in that row. **REMAINDER** specifies that a component is the last component in a row. Any component that is not the second-to-last or last component on a row must specify values for **GridbagConstraints** variable **gridwidth** and **gridheight**. Class **GridBagDemo2** in Fig. 11.21 arranges components in **GridBagLayout** using these constants.

```
// Fig. 11.21: GridBagDemo2.java
// Demonstrating GridBagLayout constants.
import java.applet.Applet;
import java.awt.*;

public class GridBagDemo2 extends Applet {
   private Choice cb;
   private TextField tf;
   private List m;
```

Fig. 11.21 Demonstrating the **GridBagConstraints** constants **RELATIVE** and **REMAINDER**. (part 1 of 3)

```
   private Button b1, b2, b3, b4, b5;
   private GridBagLayout gbLayout;
   private GridBagConstraints gbConstraints;

   public void init()
   {
      gbLayout = new GridBagLayout();
      setLayout( gbLayout );   // applet

      // instantiate gridbag constraints
      gbConstraints = new GridBagConstraints();

      // create some components
      cb = new Choice( );
      cb.add( "Pine" );
      cb.add( "Ash" );
      cb.add( "Pecan" );
      tf = new TextField( "TextField" );
      m = new List( 3, false );
      m.add( "Java" );
      b1 = new Button( "null" );
      b2 = new Button( "eins" );
      b3 = new Button( "zwei" );
      b4 = new Button( "drei" );
      b5 = new Button( "vier" );

      // textfield
      gbConstraints.weightx = 1;
      gbConstraints.weighty = 1;
      gbConstraints.fill = GridBagConstraints.BOTH;
      gbConstraints.gridwidth = GridBagConstraints.REMAINDER;
      addComponent( tf );

      // button b1
      // weightx and weighty are 1: fill is BOTH
      gbConstraints.gridwidth = 1;
      addComponent( b1 );

      // button b2
      // weightx and weighty are 1: fill is BOTH
      gbConstraints.gridwidth = GridBagConstraints.RELATIVE;
      addComponent( b2 );

      // button b3
      // weightx and weighty are 1: fill is BOTH
      gbConstraints.gridwidth = GridBagConstraints.REMAINDER;
      addComponent( b3 );

      // choicebox
      // weightx is 1: fill is BOTH
```

Fig. 11.21 Demonstrating the **GridBagConstraints** constants **RELATIVE** and **REMAINDER**. (part 2 of 3)

```
60          gbConstraints.weighty = 0;
61          gbConstraints.gridwidth = GridBagConstraints.REMAINDER;
62          addComponent( cb );
63
64          // button b4
65          // weightx is 1: fill is BOTH
66          gbConstraints.weighty = 1;
67          gbConstraints.gridwidth = GridBagConstraints.REMAINDER;
68          addComponent( b4 );
69
70          // button b5
71          // weightx and weighty are 1: fill is BOTH
72          gbConstraints.gridwidth = GridBagConstraints.RELATIVE;
73          addComponent( b5 );
74
75          // list
76          // weightx and weighty are 1: fill is BOTH
77          gbConstraints.gridwidth = GridBagConstraints.REMAINDER;
78          addComponent( m );
79       }
80
81       // addComponent is programmer-defined
82       private void addComponent( Component c )
83       {
84          gbLayout.setConstraints( c, gbConstraints );
85          add( c );      // add component to applet
86       }
87    }
```

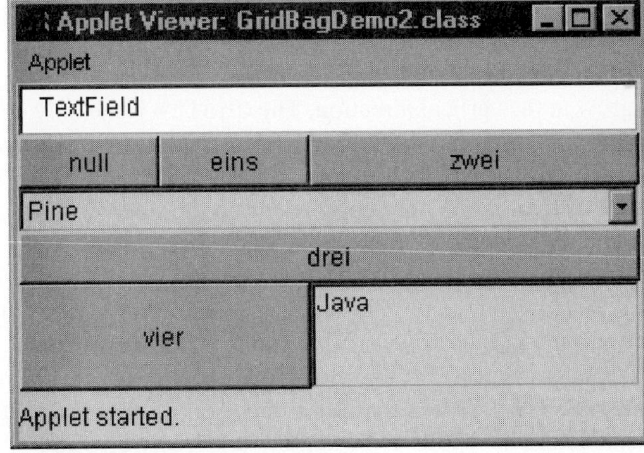

Fig. 11.21 Demonstrating the **GridBagConstraints** constants **RELATIVE** and **REMAINDER**. (part 3 of 3)

Lines 16 and 17

```
gbLayout = new GridBagLayout();
setLayout( gbLayout );
```

construct a **GridBagLayout** and set the applet's layout manager to **GridBagLayout**.

The components that are placed in **GridBagLayout** are each constructed (lines 23–34). The components are five **Button**s, one **TextField**, one **List**, and one **Choice**.

The **TextField** is added first (lines 37–41). The **weightx** and **weighty** values are set to 1. The **fill** variable is set to **BOTH**. Line 40

```
gbConstraints.gridwidth = GridBagConstraints.REMAINDER;
```

specifies that the **TextField** is the last component on the line. The **TextField** is added to the applet with a call to programmer-defined method **addComponent**.

Method **addComponent** (line 82) takes a **Component** argument. The **GridBag-Layout** method **setConstraints** sets the constraints for the component. The **add** method then adds the component to the applet.

Button b1 (lines 45–46) has **weightx** and **weighty** values of 1. The **fill** variable is **BOTH**. Because **b1** is not one of the first two components on the row, it is given a **gridwidth** of 1 so it occupies one column. The **Button** is added to the applet with a call to **addComponent**.

Button b2 (lines 50–51) has **weightx** and **weighty** values of 1. The **fill** variable is **BOTH**. The statement

```
gbConstraints.gridwidth = GridBagConstraints.RELATIVE;
```

specifies that the **Button** is to be placed relative to the previous component. The **Button** is added to the applet with a call to **addComponent**.

Button b3 (lines 55–56) has **weightx** and **weighty** values of 1. The **fill** variable is **BOTH**. This **Button** is the last component on the line, so **REMAINDER** is used. The **Button** is added to the applet with a call to **addComponent**.

The **Choice** button (lines 60–62) has a **weightx** of 1 and a **weighty** of 0. The **Choice** will not grow in the vertical direction. The **Choice** is the only component on the line, so **REMAINDER** is used. Method **addComponent** adds the **Choice** to the applet.

Button b4 (lines 64–68) has **weightx** and **weighty** values of 1. The **fill** variable is **BOTH**. This **Button** is the only component on the line, so **REMAINDER** is used. The **Button** is added to the applet with a call to **addComponent**.

Button b5 (lines 72–73) has **weightx** and **weighty** values of 1. The **fill** variable is **BOTH**. This **Button** is the next-to-last component on the line, so **RELATIVE** is used. The **Button** is added to the applet with a call to **addComponent**.

The **List** component (lines 77–78) has **weightx** and **weighty** values of 1. The **fill** variable is **BOTH**. The **List** is the last component on the line, so **REMAINDER** is used. The **List** is added to the applet with a call to **addComponent**.

Summary

- **TextArea**s provide an area for manipulating multiple lines of text. By default, **TextArea**s have horizontal and vertical scrollbars and do not provide automatic word wrap. The scrollbars are not capable of scrolling unless text extends beyond the visible rows or visible columns.

- Retrieving text from a **TextArea** is normally accomplished with an external event such as a button press or by processing the text events generated when the user types in the **TextArea**. Text events are processed by the registered **TextListener** in method **textValueChanged**. Method **addTextListener** of class **TextComponent** registers text listeners.
- **TextComponent** method **setText** places text in a **TextArea**. Method **getSelectedText** returns a **TextArea**'s selected text.
- A **Canvas** is a component where graphics can be drawn and mouse events are recognized. Class **Canvas** inherits from **Component**. A canvas has its own graphics context. **Canvas** objects have a size of 0-by-0 pixels by default.
- **Component** method **setSize** resizes a component.
- For a **Canvas** to draw on itself, its **paint** method must be overridden. The coordinates for drawing on a **Canvas** are relative to the upper-left corner of the **Canvas** (0, 0).
- A **Scrollbar** is a component that "scrolls" through a range of integer values.
- The orientation of a scrollbar is specified with constant **Scrollbar.HORIZONTAL** or constant **Scrollbar.VERTICAL**. **Scrollbar** events are generated when a scroll arrow is clicked, the scroll box is moved or the area between a scroll arrow and the scroll box is clicked. Method **adjustmentValueChanged** from interface **AdjustmentListener** handles **Scrollbar** events. Method **addAdjustmentListener** of class **Scrollbar** registers adjustment listeners.
- When no layout manager is used, each GUI component must be sized and placed at specific pixel locations on the container that has a **null** layout. **Component** methods **setBounds**, **setSize** and **setLocation** are typically used for this purpose.
- **Frame** is a window with a title bar and a border. Class **Frame** extends class **Window**. Class **Window** contains methods for window management. The default layout manager for **Window**s and **Frame**s is **BorderLayout**.
- **Frame** method **dispose** frees the resources allocated to a **Frame**. **Frame**s must be sized before being displayed. **Frame**s are not visible by default. The programmer must explicitly call **setVisible** with a **true** argument to display a **Frame**.
- **Window** method **setResizable** determines whether a **Frame** can be resized by the user. **Frame**s are resizable by default.
- A window-closing event occurs when the **Frame**'s exit icon is clicked. Window events are processed by **WindowListener** methods **windowActivated**, **windowClosed**, **windowClosing**, **windowDeactivated**, **windowDeiconified**, **windowIconified** and **windowOpened**.
- Method **addWindowListener** of class **Window** registers window event listeners. **WindowEvent** method **getWindow** returns a reference to the window that generated the event.
- **Menu**s are an integral part of GUIs. **Menu**s allow the user to perform actions without unneccessarily "cluttering" a graphical user interface with extra GUI components.

Menus can only be used with **Frame**s. Class **MenuComponent** is the base class for **MenuBar** and **MenuItem**.

- Class **MenuBar** contains the constructor and methods necessary to manage the menu bar. A menu bar is a container for menus.
- Class **Menu** contains the constructors and methods necessary for managing menus. When a menu is clicked, the menu expands to show a list of menu items. Clicking a menu item generates an action event.
- A **CheckboxMenuItem** is a menu item that toggles. When a **CheckboxMenuItem** is selected, a check appears to the left of the menu item. When the **CheckboxMenuItem** is selected again, the check to the left of the menu item is removed.
- **Menu** method **add** inserts a menu item in a menu. **MenuBar** method **add** adds a menu to the menu bar. **Frame** method **setMenuBar** attaches the menu bar on the **Frame**.
- A separator bar is a line that visually separates menu items. **Menu** method **addSeparator** adds a separator bar to a **Menu**.
- A **Dialog** box is a borderless window with a title bar. **Dialog** boxes are commonly used to gather information from the user or to show information to the user. **Dialog** inherits from **Window**. **Dialog** boxes can be modal or modeless. A modal **Dialog** box does not allow any other window in the application to be accessed until the **Dialog** box is dismissed. A modeless **Dialog** box allows other windows to be accessed while the **Dialog** is displayed.
- **MenuBar** method **setHelpMenu** sets the help menu on the menu bar.
- Class **ScrollPane** that provides a scrollable container to which a single GUI component can be attached. **ScrollPane** objects automatically provide horizontal and vertical scrollbars that enable the user to scroll through the attached GUI component.
- Context-sensitive popup menus provide options that are specific to the component for which the popup trigger event was generated. On most systems, the popup trigger event occurs when the user presses and releases the right mouse button. **PopupMenu**s can be attached to any instance of a **Component** subclass.
- The **CardLayout** layout manager arranges components into a "deck" of cards where only the top card is visible. Each card is usually a container such as a panel. The cards can use any layout manager. **CardLayout** methods **first**, **previous**, **next**, and **last** are used to show a particular card.
- The **GridBagLayout** layout manager is similar to the **GridLayout** layout manager because components are arranged in a grid. However **GridBagLayout** is more flexible. The components can vary in size and can be added in any order. **GridBagConstraints** specify how components are laid out with **GridBagLayout**.

Terminology

add method of class **Menu**
add method of class **MenuBar**
addSeparator method of class **Menu**
addTextListener method
addWindowListener method
Adjustable interface

AdjustmentEvent class
AdjustmentListener interface
adjustmentValueChanged method
automatic word wrap
border of a window
Canvas class
CardLayout layout manager
CheckboxMenuItem class
clipped
close box of a window
context-sensitive popup menu
customized subclass of **Canvas**
dedicated area for graphics
Dialog class
dispose method of class **Window**
enableEvents method of class **Component**
exit icon of a window
exit method of class **System**
external event
first method of class **CardLayout**
Frame class
getHAdjustable method (**ScrollPane**)
getSelectedText method
getVAdjustable method (**ScrollPane**)
getValue method of class **Scrollbar**
getWindow method of class **WindowEvent**
graphical user interface
GridBagConstraints class
GridBagLayout layout manager
GUI-based application
initial value of a **Scrollbar**
isPopupTrigger method (**MouseEvent**)
last method of class **CardLayout**
maximum value of a **Scrollbar**
Menu class
MenuBar class
MenuComponent class
MenuItem class
minimum value of a **Scrollbar**
modal **Dialog**
modeless **Dialog**
next method of class **CardLayout**
origin component for a **PopupMenu**
package **com.deitel.jhtp2.ch11**
PopupMenu class
popup trigger event
previous method of class **CardLayout**
processMouseEvent method (**Component**)
scroll arrow
Scrollbar class
ScrollPane class
Scrollbar.HORIZONTAL
Scrollbar.VERTICAL
scroll box
self-contained subclass of **Canvas**
separator bar in a menu
setBackground method of class **Component**
setBounds method of class **Component**
setConstraints method
setEditable method (**TextComponent**)
setFont method of class **Component**
setHelpMenu method of class **MenuBar**
setLocation method of class **Component**
setMenuBar method of class **Frame**
setResizable method of class **Window**
setSize method of class **Component**
setText method of class **TextComponent**
setUnitIncrement method (**Adjustable**)
setVisible method of class **Component**
setting a **null** layout
show method of class **PopupMenu**
slider on a **Scrollbar**
submenu
text event
TextArea class
TextEvent class
TextListener interface
textValueChanged method
title bar of a window
Window class
WindowEvent class
windowActivated method
windowClosed method
windowClosing method
windowDeactivated method
windowDeiconified method
windowIconified method
WindowListener interface
windowOpened method

Common Programming Errors

11.1 Forgetting to call the **setSize** method on a canvas is a run-time logic error. The canvas would not be seen because its default size is 0-by-0 pixels.

11.2 Passing a value to the **Scrollbar** constructor of Fig. 11.7 other than **Scrollbar.HORIZONTAL** or **Scrollbar.VERTICAL** for the **orientation** argument throws an **IllegalArgumentException**.

11.3 The default layout manager for subclasses of **Window** is **BorderLayout**. Forgetting to specify **BorderLayout.NORTH**, **BorderLayout.SOUTH**, **BorderLayout.EAST**, **BorderLayout.WEST** or **BorderLayout.CENTER** when adding a component to a **Window** prevents that component from being displayed properly on the user interface.

11.4 Forgetting to call the **setVisible** method with a **true** argument on a window is a run-time logic error; the window is not displayed.

11.5 Forgetting to call the **setSize** method on a window is a run-time logic error. If the window displayed is a **Frame** or **Dialog** object, only the title bar appears.

11.6 Forgetting to set the menu bar with **Frame** method **setMenuBar** results in the menu bar not being displayed on the **Frame**.

11.7 Using a lowercase **i** in **MenuItem** or **CheckboxMenuItem** is a syntax error.

11.8 Using a lowercase **b** in class name **MenuBar** is a syntax error.

11.9 Using an uppercase **b** in class name **CheckboxMenuItem** is a syntax error.

11.10 Forgetting to add a menu item to a menu is a run-time logic error. The menu item will not appear in the menu.

11.11 Attempting to use a **Checkbox** component instead of a **CheckboxMenuItem** in a menu is a syntax error.

11.12 Using a negative value for either **weightx** or **weighty** is a logic error.

Good Programming Practices

11.1 Invoking **dispose** on a window releases windowing system resources.

Software Engineering Observations

11.1 Graphics drawn directly on an applet can be covered by components. Canvases eliminate this problem by providing a dedicated area for graphics.

11.2 Menus simplify GUIs by reducing the number of components the user views.

Self-Review Exercises

11.1 Fill in the blanks in each of the following:

a) The __________ class is used to create a menu object.

b) The _________ method places a separator bar in a menu.
c) Passing **true** to a **TextArea**'s _______ method allows text to be modified by the user.
d) **Scrollbar** events are handled by the _________ method of interface ________.
e) The **GridBagConstraints** instance variable ________ is set to **CENTER** by default.

11.2 State which of the following statements are true and which are false. If a statement is false, explain why.

a) When the programmer creates a **Dialog** box, a minimum of one menu must be created and added to the **Dialog**.
b) When the programmer creates a **Frame**, a minimum of one menu must be created and added to the **Frame**.
c) The variable **fill** belongs to the **GridBagLayout** class.
d) **Frame**s and applets cannot be used together in the same program.
e) The top-left corner of a **Frame** or applet has a coordinate of (0, 0).
f) A **TextArea**'s text is always read-only.
g) Class **TextArea** is a direct subclass of class **Component**.

11.3 Find the error(s) in each of the following and explain how to correct the error(s).

a) `Menubar b;    // create menubar reference`
b) `myScroll = Scrollbar( 1000, 0, 222, 100, 450 );`
c) `gbc.fill = GridBagConstraints.NORTHWEST;   // set fill`
d) `m1.add( new Checkbox( "Snap to grid" ) ); // m1 is a Menu`
e)
```
// create a help Menu
help = new HelpMenu( "Help" );
```
f) `y.setBounds( x, y, w, h, c ); // size and place component`

Answers to Self-Review Exercises

11.1 a) **Menu**. b) **addSeparator**. c) **setEditable**. d) **adjustmentValueChanged**, **AdjustmentListener**. e) **anchor**.

11.2
a) False. A **Dialog** box does not have to have any menus.
b) False. A **Frame** does not have to have any menus.
c) False. The variable **fill** belongs to the **GridBagConstraints** class.
d) False. They can be used together.
e) True.
f) False. **TextArea**s are editable by default.
g) False. **TextArea** derives from class **TextComponent**.

11.3
a) **Menubar** should be **MenuBar**.
b) The first argument to the constructor should be either **Scrollbar.HORIZONTAL** or **Scrollbar.VERTICAL** and the **new** operator must be used after the = operator.
c) The constant should be either **BOTH**, **HORIZONTAL**, **VERTICAL** or **NONE**.
d) **Checkbox**es cannot be added to menus. A **CheckboxMenuItem** should be used.
e) Java does not have a **HelpMenu** class—method **setHelpMenu** of class **MenuBar** is used to set the menu that is the designated help menu.
f) The **setBounds** method should have four arguments passed—not five.

Exercises

11.4 Fill in the blanks in each of the following:

a) __________ are created by inheriting from either the **Canvas** class or the **Panel** class.
b) A **MenuItem** that is a menu is called a __________.
c) Both **TextFields** and **TextAreas** inherit directly from class __________.
d) The __________ method attaches a **MenuBar** to a **Frame**.
e) Class __________ and class __________ inherit from class **Window**.

11.5 State which of the following statements are true and which are false. If a statement is false, explain why.

a) Menus require a **MenuBar** object so they can be attached to a **Frame**.
b) A **Canvas** object is capable of receiving mouse events.
c) **CardLayout** is the default layout manager for a **Frame**.
d) Method **setEditable** is a **TextComponent** method.
e) The **GridBagLayout** layout manager implements **LayoutManager**.
f) **Canvas** objects are containers to which other GUI components can be attached.
g) Class **Frame** inherits directly from class **Container**.
h) Applets can contain menus.

11.6 Find the error(s) in each of the following. Explain how to correct the error(s).

a) `x.add( new MenuItem( "Submenu Color" ) ); // create submenu`
b) `setLayout( m = new GridbagLayout() );`
c) `String s = TextArea.getText();`
d) `Dialog d = new Dialog( a, "Dialog", true ); // a is an applet`

11.7 Write a program that displays a circle of a random size and calculates and displays the area, radius, diameter, and circumference. Use the following equations: $diameter = 2 \times radius$, $area = \pi \times radius^2$, $circumference = 2 \times \pi \times radius$. Use the constant **Math.PI** for Pi (π). All drawing should be done on a **Canvas** and the results of the calculations should be displayed in a read-only **TextArea**.

11.8 Enhance the program of Exercise 11.7 by allowing the user to alter the radius with a **Scrollbar**. The program should work for all radii in the range of 100 to 200. As the radius changes, the diameter, area, and circumference should be updated and displayed. The initial radius should be 150. Use the equations of Exercise 11.7. All drawing should be done on a **Canvas** and the results of the calculations should be displayed in a read-only **TextArea**.

11.9 Explore the effects of varying the **weightx** and **weighty** values of the program of Fig. 11.20. What happens when a component has a non-zero weight, but is not allowed to fill the whole area (i.e., the **fill** value is not **BOTH**)?

11.10 Write a program that uses the **paint** method to draw the current value of a **Scrollbar** on a **Canvas**. In addition, provide a **TextField** where a specific value can be entered. The **TextField** should display the current value of the **Scrollbar** at all times. A **Label** should be used to identify the **TextField**. The **Scrollbar** methods **setValue** and **getValue** should be used. Note: The **setValue** method is a **public** method that does not return a value and takes one integer argument—the **Scrollbar** value.

11.11 Modify the program of Fig. 11.16 to use a single **Choice** button instead of the four separate **Buttons**. Each "card" should not be modified.

11.12 Modify the program of Fig. 11.16 by adding a minimum of two new "cards" to the deck.

11.13 Write a color chooser applet that provides three **Scrollbar** objects and three **TextField** objects. Each **Scrollbar** represents the values from 0 to 255 for the red, green and blue parts of a color. Use the red, green and blue values as the arguments to the **Color** constructor to create a new **Color** object. Display the current value of each **Scrollbar** in the corresponding **TextField**. When the user changes the value of the **Scrollbar**, the **TextField** should be changed accordingly. Display the current **Color** value on the applet by drawing a filled rectangle.

11.14 Modify the applet of Exercise 11.13 to allow the user to type an integer value into a **TextField** to set the red, green or blue value. When the user presses Enter in the **TextField**, the corresponding **Scrollbar** should be set to the appropriate value.

11.15 Modify the applet of Exercise 11.14 to draw the current color as a rectangle on an instance of a subclass of **Canvas**. The subclass of **Canvas** should provide its own **paint** method to draw the rectangle and should provide set methods to set the red, green, and blue values for the current color. When any set method is invoked for the subclass of **Canvas**, the object should automatically **repaint** itself.

11.16 Modify the applet of Exercise 11.15 to allow the user to drag the mouse across the canvas to draw a shape in the current color. Enable the user to choose what shape to draw.

11.17 Modify the applet of Exercise 11.16 to enable the program to run as an application. The existing applet's code should only be modified by adding a **main** method to launch the application in its own **Frame**. Provide the user with the ability to terminate the application by clicking the close box on the window that is displayed and by selecting **Exit** from a **File** menu. Use the techniques shown in Fig. 11.10.

11.18 *(Complete drawing application)* Using the techniques developed in Exercises 10.30–10.36 and Exercises 11.13–11.17 create a complete drawing program that can execute as both an applet and an application. The program should use the GUI components of Chapters 10 and 11 to enable the user to select the shape, color and fill characteristics. Each shape should be stored in an array of **MyShape** objects where **MyShape** is the superclass in your hierarchy of shape classes. Create the user interface as a separate window containing all the GUI components that allow the user to determine the characteristics of the shape to be drawn.

11.19 A company pays its employees as managers (who receive a fixed weekly salary), hourly workers (who receive a fixed hourly wage for up to the first 40 hours they work and "time-and-a-half," i.e., 1.5 times their hourly wage, for overtime hours worked), commission workers (who receive a $250 plus 5.7% of their gross weekly sales), or pieceworkers (who receive a fixed amount of money per item for each of the items they produce—each pieceworker in this company works on only one type of item). Write an applet to compute the weekly pay for each employee. Each type of employee has its own pay code: Managers have paycode 1, hourly workers have code 2, commission workers have code 3 and pieceworkers have code 4. Use a **switch** to compute each employee's pay based on that employee's paycode. Use a **CardLayout** to display the appropriate GUI components that allow the user to enter the facts your program needs to calculate each employee's pay based on that employee's paycode.

12

Exception Handling

Objectives

- To understand exception and error handling.
- To be able to use **`try`** blocks to delineate code in which an exception may occur.
- To be able to **`throw`** exceptions.
- To use **`catch`** blocks to specify exception handlers.
- To use the **`finally`** block to release resources.
- To understand the Java exception hierarchy.
- To create programmer-defined exceptions.

It is common sense to take a method and try it. If it fails, admit it frankly and try another. But above all, try something.
Franklin Delano Roosevelt

O! throw away the worser part of it,
And live the purer with the other half.
William Shakespeare

If they're running and they don't look where they're going
I have to come out from somewhere and catch them.
Jerome David Salinger

And oftentimes excusing of a fault
Doth make the fault the worse by the excuse.
William Shakespeare

I never forget a face, but in your case I'll make an exception.
Groucho (Julius Henry) Marx

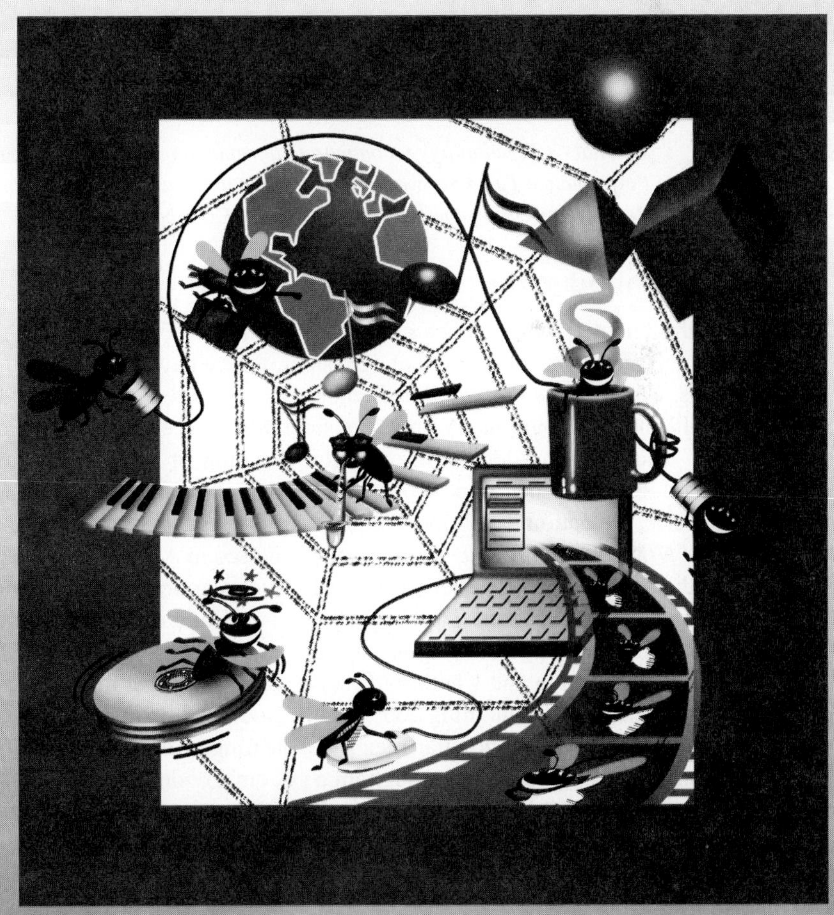

Outline

12.1 Introduction

In this chapter, we introduce *exception handling*. The extensibility of Java can increase the number and types of errors that can occur. Every new class can add its own error possibilities. The features presented here enable programmers to write clearer, more robust, more fault-tolerant programs. We also consider when exception handling should not be used.

The style and details of exception handling in Java as presented in this chapter are based in part on the work of Andrew Koenig and Bjarne Stroustrup as presented in their paper, "Exception Handling for C++ (revised)," published in the *Proceedings of the USENIX C++ Conference* held in San Francisco in April, 1990. Their work forms the basis of the ANSI (draft) standard version of C++ exception handling. Java's designers chose to implement an exception-handling mechanism similar to that used in C++.

Error-handling code varies in nature and quantity among software systems depending on the application and whether the software is a product for release. Products tend to contain far more error-handling code than "casual" software does.

There are many popular means for dealing with errors. Most commonly, error-handling code is interspersed throughout a system's code. Errors are dealt with at the places in the code where the errors can occur. The advantage to this approach is that a programmer reading code can see the error processing in the immediate vicinity of the code and determine if the proper error checking has been implemented.

The problem with this scheme is that the code in a sense becomes "polluted" with the error processing. It becomes more difficult for a programmer concerned with the application itself to read the code and determine if it is functioning correctly. This can make it difficult to understand and maintain the application.

Some common examples of exceptions are an out-of-bounds array subscript, arithmetic overflow (i.e., a value outside the representable range of values), division by zero, invalid method parameters and memory exhaustion.

Good Programming Practice 12.1

Using Java exception handling enables the programmer to remove the error-handling code from the "main line" of the program's execution. This improves program clarity and enhances modifiability.

Separating error-handling code from the main line of program code is consistent with the virtues of separability we have discussed in the contexts of both structured programming and object-oriented programming.

Java exception handling enables a program to catch all types of exceptions, or to catch all exceptions of a certain type, or to catch all exceptions of related types. This makes programs more robust by reducing the likelihood that errors will not be caught by a program.

Exception handling is provided to enable programs to catch and handle errors rather than letting them occur and suffering the consequences. Exception handling is designed for dealing with *synchronous errors* such as an attempt to divide by zero (that occurs as the program executes the divide instruction). Exception handling is not designed to deal with *asynchronous* events such as disk I/O completions, network message arrivals, mouse clicks, keystrokes and the like; these are best handled through other means, such as interrupt processing.

Exception handling is used in situations in which the system can recover from the malfunction causing the exception. The recovery procedure is called an *exception handler*.

Exception handling is typically used in situations in which a malfunction will be dealt with in a different scope from that which detected the malfunction. A program that carries on an interactive dialog with a user should not use exceptions to process keyboard input problems.

Software Engineering Observation 12.1

Use exceptions for malfunctions that must be processed in a different scope from where they occur. Use conventional error-handling techniques for local error processing in which a program is able to deal with its own errors.

Good Programming Practice 12.2

Avoid using exception handling for purposes other than error handling because this can reduce program clarity.

There is another reason to avoid using exception handling techniques for conventional program control. Exception handling is designed for error processing which is an infrequent activity that is often used because a program is about to terminate. It is not required that Java implement exception handling for the kind of optimal performance that might be expected of regular application code.

Performance Tip 12.1

Although it is possible to use exception handling for purposes other than error handling, this can reduce program performance.

Performance Tip 12.2

When an exception does not occur, little or no overhead is imposed by the presence of exception-handling code. When exceptions happen, they do incur execution-time overhead.

Testing and Debugging Tip 12.1

Exception handling helps improve a program's fault tolerance. It becomes "more pleasant" to write error-processing code, so programmers are more likely to provide it.

Good Programming Practice 12.3

Using Java's standardized exception handling rather than having programmers use a diversity of "home-grown" techniques can improve program clarity on large projects.

Most programs written today support only a single thread of execution. The techniques discussed in this chapter apply even for multithreaded programs. We discuss multithreading in Chapter 13.

We will see that exceptions are objects of classes that are derived from superclass **`Exception`**. We will show how to deal with "uncaught" exceptions. We will consider how unexpected exceptions are handled by Java. We will show how related exception types can be represented by exception subclasses that are derived from a common exception superclass.

Exception handling can be viewed as another means of returning control from a method or exiting a block of code. Normally, when an exception occurs, the exception will be handled by a caller of the method generating the exception, by a caller of that caller, or however far back in the call chain it becomes necessary to go to find a handler for that exception.

Software Engineering Observation 12.2

Exception handling is particularly well-suited to systems of separately developed components. Such systems are typical of real-world software systems and products. Exception handling makes it easier to combine the components and have them work together effectively.

Software Engineering Observation 12.3

With other programming languages that do not support exception handling, programmers often delay writing error-processing code, and sometimes programmers simply forget to include it. This often results in less-robust, and thus inferior, software products. Java forces the programmer to deal with exception handling from the inception of a project. Still, the programmer must put considerable effort into incorporating an exception-handling strategy into software projects.

Software Engineering Observation 12.4

It is best to incorporate your exception-handling strategy into a system from the inception of the design process. It is difficult to add effective exception handling after a system has been implemented.

12.2 When Exception Handling Should Be Used

Exception handling should be used

- to process only exceptional situations.
- to process exceptions from program components that are not geared to handling those exceptions directly.
- to process exceptions from software components such as methods, libraries, and classes that are likely to be widely used, and where it does not make sense for those components to handle their own exceptions.
- on large projects to handle error processing in a uniform manner project wide.

Software Engineering Observation 12.5

The client of a library class will likely have unique error processing in mind for an exception generated in the library class. It is unlikely that a library class will perform error processing that would meet the unique needs of all clients. Exceptions are an appropriate means for dealing with errors produced by library classes.

12.3 Other Error-Handling Techniques

We have presented various ways of dealing with exceptional situations prior to this chapter. A program can ignore the exceptions. This can be devastating for software products released to the general public, or for special-purpose software needed for mission-critical situations. But for software developed for your own purposes, it is common to ignore many kinds of errors. A program could be directed to abort upon encountering an exceptional situation. This prevents a program from running to completion and producing incorrect results. For many types of errors this is a good strategy. Such a strategy is inappropriate for mission-critical applications. Resource issues are also important here. If a program obtains a resource, the program should normally return that resource before program termination.

Common Programming Error 12.1

Aborting a program could leave a resource in a state in which other programs would not be able to acquire the resource, hence we would have a so-called "resource leak."

Good Programming Practice 12.4

If your method is capable of handling a given type of exception then handle it rather than passing the exception on to other regions of your program. This makes programs clearer.

Performance Tip 12.3

If an error can be processed locally instead of throwing an exception, do so. This will improve program execution speed. Exception handling is slow compared to local processing.

12.4 The Basics of Java Exception Handling

Java exception handling is geared to situations in which the method that detects an error is unable to deal with it. Such a method will *throw an exception*. There is no guarantee that there will be "anything out there" (i.e., an *exception handler*—code that executes when an exception has been detected) specifically geared to processing that kind of exception. If there is, the exception will be *caught* and *handled*. The following *Testing and Debugging Tip* describes what happens if no appropriate exception handler can be found.

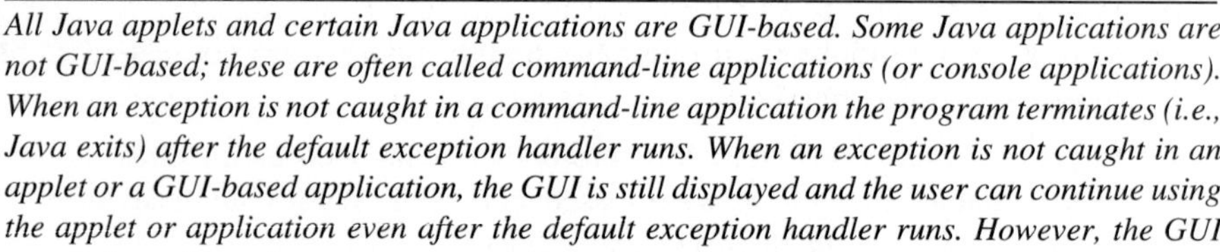

Testing and Debugging Tip 12.2

All Java applets and certain Java applications are GUI-based. Some Java applications are not GUI-based; these are often called command-line applications (or console applications). When an exception is not caught in a command-line application the program terminates (i.e., Java exits) after the default exception handler runs. When an exception is not caught in an applet or a GUI-based application, the GUI is still displayed and the user can continue using the applet or application even after the default exception handler runs. However, the GUI may be in an inconsistent state.

The programmer encloses in a **`try`** *block* the code that may generate an exception. The **`try`** block is immediately followed by zero or more **`catch`** *blocks*. Each **`catch`** block specifies the type of exception it can catch and contains an exception handler. After the last **`catch`** block, an optional **`finally`** block provides code that always executes regardless of whether or not an exception occurs; as we will see the **`finally`** block is an ideal place for code that releases resources to prevent "resource leaks." If there are no **`catch`** blocks following a **`try`** block, the **`finally`** block is required.

When an exception is thrown, program control leaves the **`try`** block and the **`catch`** blocks are searched in order for an appropriate handler (we will soon discuss what makes a handler "appropriate"). If the type of the thrown exception matches the parameter type in one of the **`catch`** blocks, the code for that **`catch`** block is executed. If no exceptions are thrown in the **`try`** block, the exception handlers for that block are skipped and the program resumes execution after the last **`catch`** block. If a **`finally`** block appears after the last **`catch`** block, it is executed regardless of whether or not an exception is thrown.

We can specify with a **`throws`** clause the exceptions a method throws. An exception can be thrown from statements in the method, or the exception can be thrown from a method called directly or indirectly from the **`try`** block. The point at which the **`throw`** is executed is called the *throw point*.

Once an exception is thrown, the block in which the exception is thrown expires and control cannot return to the throw point. Thus Java uses the *termination model of exception handling* rather than the *resumption model of exception handling*. In the resumption model, control would return to the point at which the exception was thrown and resume execution.

When an exception occurs, it is possible to communicate information to the exception handler from the vicinity in which the exception occurred. That information is the type of the thrown object itself or information can be harvested from the vicinity in which the exception occurs and placed into the thrown object.

Software Engineering Observation 12.6

A key to Java-style exception handling is that the portion of a program or system that handles the exception can be distant from the portion of the program that generates the exception.

12.5 A Simple Exception Handling Example: Divide by Zero

Now let us consider a simple example of exception handling. The applet of Fig. 12.1 uses **`try`**, **`throw`**, and **`catch`** to detect, indicate, and handle exceptions. The applet displays two **TextField**s in which the user can type integers. When the user presses the *Enter* key in the second **TextField**, method **actionPerformed** is called to read the two integers from the **TextField**s and pass the integers to method **quotient** to calculate the quotient of the two values and return a **double** result. If the user types 0 in the second **TextField**, the program uses an exception to indicate that the user is attempting a division by zero. Also, if the user types a value that is not an integer in either **TextField** a **NumberFormatException** occurs.

```
// Fig. 12.1: DivideByZeroException.java
// Definition of class DivideByZeroException.
// Used to throw an exception when a
// divide-by-zero is attempted.
public class DivideByZeroException
             extends ArithmeticException {
   public DivideByZeroException()
   {
      super( "Attempted to divide by zero" );
   }
}
```

Fig. 12.1 A simple exception handling example with divide by zero (part 1 of 4).

```
// Fig. 12.1: DivideByZeroTest.java
// A simple exception handling example.
// Checking for a divide-by-zero-error.
import java.applet.Applet;
import java.awt.*;
import java.awt.event.*;
import java.text.DecimalFormat;

public class DivideByZeroTest extends Applet
             implements ActionListener {
   private Label prompt1, prompt2;
   private TextField input1, input2;
   private int number1, number2;
   private double result;

   // Initialization
   public void init()
   {
      prompt1 = new Label( "Enter numerator" );
      add( prompt1 );

      input1 = new TextField( 10 );
      add( input1 );

      prompt2 =
         new Label( "Enter denominator and press Enter" );
```

Fig. 12.1 A simple exception handling example with divide by zero (part 2 of 4).

```
      add( prompt2 );

      input2 = new TextField( 10 );
      input2.addActionListener( this );
      add( input2 );
   }

   // Process GUI events
   public void actionPerformed( ActionEvent e )
   {
      DecimalFormat precision3 = new DecimalFormat( "#.000" );

      try {
         number1 = Integer.parseInt( input1.getText() );
         number2 = Integer.parseInt( input2.getText() );
         input1.setText( "" );
         input2.setText( "" );

         result = quotient( number1, number2 );
         showStatus( number1 + " / " + number2 + " = " +
                     precision3.format( result ) );
      }
      catch ( NumberFormatException nfe ) {
         showStatus( "You must enter two integers" );
      }
      catch ( DivideByZeroException dbze ) {
         showStatus( dbze.toString() );
      }
   }

   // Definition of method quotient. Used to demonstrate
   // throwing an exception when a divide-by-zero error
   // is encountered.
   public double quotient( int numerator, int denominator )
      throws DivideByZeroException
   {
      if ( denominator == 0 )
         throw new DivideByZeroException();

      return ( double ) numerator / denominator;
   }
}
```

Fig. 12.1 A simple exception handling example with divide by zero (part 3 of 4).

Consider the sample executions shown in the five output windows. The first two windows show a successful execution. The first window shows the two values—20 and 5—that the user typed. The second window shows the result of the division performed by method **quotient**. In the third output window, the user attempted to enter a string in the second **TextField**, but the user was notified that an integer must be entered. In the last two windows, a zero denominator is entered and the program detects the problem, throws an exception and issues an appropriate diagnostic message. Now let's discuss the program.

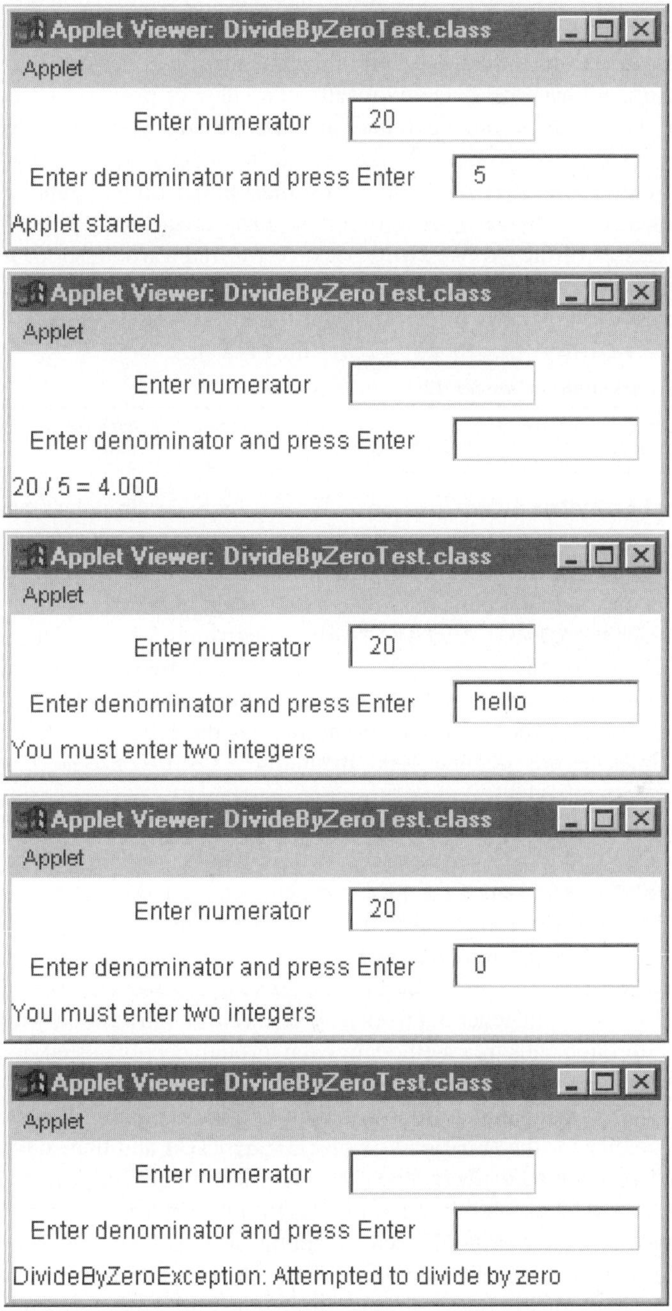

Applet Viewer: DivideByZeroTest.class
Applet
Enter numerator 20
Enter denominator and press Enter 5
Applet started.

Applet Viewer: DivideByZeroTest.class
Applet
Enter numerator
Enter denominator and press Enter
20 / 5 = 4.000

Applet Viewer: DivideByZeroTest.class
Applet
Enter numerator 20
Enter denominator and press Enter hello
You must enter two integers

Applet Viewer: DivideByZeroTest.class
Applet
Enter numerator 20
Enter denominator and press Enter 0
You must enter two integers

Applet Viewer: DivideByZeroTest.class
Applet
Enter numerator
Enter denominator and press Enter
DivideByZeroException: Attempted to divide by zero

Fig. 12.1 A simple exception handling example with divide by zero (part 4 of 4).

Java can test for a division by zero when the values in the division are both integers. However, our program is going to perform a floating-point division of two integers by casting the first integer to a **double** before the calculation is performed. Floating-point division by zero is allowed by Java and results in a value of positive or negative infinity (constants for these values can be found in class **Float** and class **Double** of the **java.lang** package). We would still like to indicate to the user of our program that they are attempting a division by zero. To do so, we must either find an appropriate **Exception** class for a divide-by-zero situation or we must create one. When we search the **Exception** classes of the **java.lang** package we find a whole set of **RuntimeException** classes. The one that most closely matches our needs is **ArithmeticException**. We could use this class directly, but instead we choose to create our own more specific class **DivideByZeroException** (lines 1–11).

Good Programming Practice 12.5

Associating each type of serious execution-time malfunction with an appropriately named **Exception** *class improves program clarity.*

Class **DivideByZeroException** is formed by extending class **ArithmeticException**. The constructor (lines 7–10) uses a **super** call to the constructor for **ArithmeticException** passing it the string **"Attempted to divide by zero"** as the exception message that indicates what went wrong.

Now consider the **DivideByZeroTest** applet (lines 12–79). The applet's **init** method (lines 28–43) builds a graphical user interface with two **Label**s and two **TextField**s and registers the applet as the **ActionListener** for **TextField input2**.

After the user enters the denominator and presses the *Enter* key, method **actionPerformed** (lines 46–66) is called. Next, method **actionPerformed** proceeds with a **try** block (lines 50–59) which encloses the code that may **throw** an exception. The statements that read the integers from the **TextField**s (lines 51 and 52) each use method **Integer.parseInt** to convert **String**s to **int** values. Method **parseInt** throws a **NumberFormatException** if the **String** being converted is not a valid integer. The division that can cause the divide-by-zero error is not explicitly listed in the **try** block. Rather, the call to method **quotient** (line 56) invokes the code that attempts the division. Method **quotient** (lines 71–79) **throw**s the **DivideByZeroException** object as we will see momentarily. In general, errors may surface through explicitly mentioned code in a **try** block, through calls to a method, or even through deeply nested method calls initiated by code in a **try** block.

The **try** block is immediately followed by two **catch** blocks—lines 60–62 contain the exception handler for the **NumberFormatException** and lines 63–65 contain the exception handler for the **DivideByZeroException**. In general, when an exception is thrown within a **try** block, the exception is caught by a **catch** block that specifies an appropriate type that matches the thrown exception. In Fig. 12.1, the first **catch** block specifies that it will catch exception objects of type **NumberFormatException** (this type matches the type of the object thrown in method **Integer.parseInt**) and the second **catch** block specifies that it will catch exception objects of type **DivideByZe-**

roException (this type matches the type of the object thrown in method **quotient**). Only the matching catch handler executes if an exception is thrown. Both our exception handlers simply display an error message in the browser's status bar, but exception handlers can be more elaborate than this. After executing, an exception-handler control proceeds to the first statement after the last **catch** block.

If, when executed, the code in the **try** block does not **throw** an exception, then the **catch** handlers are skipped and execution resumes with the first line of code after the **catch** handlers. In Fig. 12.1, method **actionPerformed** simply returns, but the program could continue executing more statements after the **catch** blocks.

Testing and Debugging Tip 12.3

With exception handling, a program can continue executing after dealing with a problem. This helps ensure robust applications that contribute to what is called mission-critical computing *or* business-critical computing.

Now let us examine method **quotient**. When the **if** statement determines that **denominator** is zero, the body of the **if** executes a **throw** statement that creates and **throw**s a new **DivideByZeroException** object. This object will be caught by the **catch** block specifying type **DivideByZeroException** after the **try** block. The thrown object is received in parameter **dbze** (line 63) specified in the second **catch** handler, and the message is printed there by converting **dbze** to a **String** via **toString** and passing this **String** to **showStatus**.

If **denominator** is not zero, no exception is thrown, the division is performed and the result of the division is returned to the point of invocation of method **quotient** in the **try** block (line 56). We then use **showStatus** to display the calculation and its result. The **catch** blocks are skipped and the **actionPerformed** method completes execution normally.

Note that when **quotient** throws the **DivideByZeroException**, **quotient**'s block expires. This would cause any of its objects to be marked for garbage collection and the finalizers for these objects would run before garbage collection takes place. If this exception is thrown, the **try** block also expires before the **showStatus** in line 57 can execute. Here, too, if there were any automatic object references created in the **try** prior to the exception being thrown, these objects would be marked for eventual garbage collection and their finalizers would be run before garbage collection occurs. Note: Finalizers are not guaranteed to be called if the program terminates unless prior to termination, the following statement is executed

```
System.runFinalizersOnExit( true );
```

This guarantees that all objects that have not been finalized, will have their **finalize** methods called before the program terminates.

If a **NumberFormatException** is generated by lines 51 or 52, the **try** block expires and execution continues with the exception handler at line 60. A message is displayed in the status bar so the user knows to enter integers, then the **actionPerformed** method continues with the next valid statement after the **catch** blocks (i.e., the method terminates in this example).

12.6 Try Blocks

An exception that occurs in a **try** block is normally caught by a handler specified by a **catch** block immediately following that **try** block.

```
try {
   ...
}
catch(   ) {
   ...
}
```

A **try** block can be followed by zero or more **catch** blocks.

Common Programming Error 12.2

*It is a syntax error to separate with other code the **catch** handlers that correspond to a particular **try** block.*

If a **try** block executes and no exceptions are thrown, all the exception handlers are skipped and control resumes with the first statement after the last exception handler. If a **finally** block follows the last **catch** block, the code in the **finally** block executes regardless of whether or not an exception is thrown.

Testing and Debugging Tip 12.4

*A **finally** block is an excellent place in which to place code that will release resources acquired in a **try** block. This strategy is an effective way to avoid resource leaks.*

12.7 Throwing an Exception

The **throw** statement is executed to indicate that an exception has occurred. This is called *throwing an exception*. A **throw** statement specifies an object to be thrown. The operand of a **throw** can be of any class derived from class **Throwable**. The two immediate subclasses of class **Throwable** are **Exception** and **Error**. **Error**s are particularly serious system problems that generally should not be caught. **Exception**s are caused by problems most Java programmers will want to deal with. If the operand is an object of class **Exception**, it is called an *exception object*.

Testing and Debugging Tip 12.5

*When **toString** is invoked on any **Throwable** object, its printout includes the descriptive **String** that was supplied to the constructor.*

Testing and Debugging Tip 12.6

*If it is necessary to pass information about the malfunction that caused an exception, such information can be placed in the thrown object. That information can then be referenced through the parameter name in the **catch** handler.*

Testing and Debugging Tip 12.7

An object can be thrown without containing information to be passed; in this case, knowledge that an exception of this type has been raised may provide sufficient information for the handler to do its job correctly.

When an exception is thrown, control exits the current **try** block and proceeds to an appropriate **catch** handler (if one exists) after that **try** block. It is possible that the **throw** point could be in a deeply nested scope within a **try** block; control will still proceed to the **catch** handler. It is also possible that the **throw** point could be in a deeply nested method call; still, control will proceed to the **catch** handler.

A **try** block may appear to contain no error checking and include no **throw** statements, but code referenced in the **try** block could certainly cause error-checking code in constructors to execute and possibly throw exceptions. Code in a **try** block may perform array subscripting on an array object. If an invalid array subscript is specified, the system throws an **ArrayIndexOutOfBoundsException**. Any method call can invoke code that might **throw** an exception or call another method that throws an exception.

Although an exception can terminate program execution, it need not do this. However, an exception does terminate at least the block in which the exception occurred.

12.8 Catching an Exception

Exception handlers are contained in **catch** blocks. Each **catch** block starts with the keyword **catch** followed by parentheses containing a class name (specifying the type of exception to be caught) and a parameter name. The object caught by the handler can be referenced through this parameter. This is followed by a block delineating the exception-handling code. When an exception is caught, the code in the **catch** block is executed.

Common Programming Error 12.3

*Assuming that after an exception is processed, control will return to the first statement after the **throw** can lead to errors.*

Common Programming Error 12.4

*Specifying a comma-separated list of **catch** arguments is a syntax error. A **catch** can have only a single argument.*

Common Programming Error 12.5

*It is a syntax error to **catch** the same type in two different **catch** blocks associated with a particular **try** block.*

A **catch** that catches an **Exception** object

```
catch( Exception e )
```

means to catch all exceptions.

Common Programming Error 12.6

*Placing **catch(Exception e)** before other **catch** blocks that catch specific types of exceptions would prevent those blocks from ever being executed; **catch(Exception e)** should always be placed last in the list of exception handlers following a **try** block, or a syntax error occurs.*

Software Engineering Observation 12.7

*If you catch all exceptions with **catch(Exception e)** you can use the **instanceof** operator to probe the type of the exception. For example, the boolean condition **x instanceof Y** evaluates to **true** if object **x** is an instance of class **Y**, and **false** otherwise.*

It is possible that no handler will match a particular thrown object. This causes the search for a match to continue in the next enclosing **try** block. As this process continues, it may eventually be determined that there is no handler in the program that matches the type of the thrown object; in this case a non-GUI-based application terminates—applets and GUI-based applications return to their regular event processing.

It is possible that several exception handlers will provide an acceptable match to the type of the exception. This can happen for several reasons. First, there can be a "catch-all" handler **catch(Exception e)** that will catch any exception. Second, because of inheritance relationships, it is possible that a subclass object can be caught either by a handler specifying the subclass type, or by handlers specifying the types of any superclasses of that subclass. The first exception handler that matches the exception type is executed.

Software Engineering Observation 12.8

If several handlers match the type of an exception, and if each of these handles the exception differently, then the order of the handlers will affect the manner in which the exception is handled.

Common Programming Error 12.7

It is a syntax error if a **catch** *that catches a superclass object is placed before a* **catch** *that catches an object of a subclass of that superclass.*

Sometimes a program may process many closely related types of exceptions. Instead of providing separate exception classes and **catch** handlers for each, a programmer can provide a single exception class and **catch** handler for a group of exceptions. As each exception occurs, the exception object can be created with different instance data such as a type code. The **catch** handler can examine this data to distinguish the type of the exception. Actually, this style of programming is discouraged in object-oriented languages like Java because inheritance takes care of this situation more elegantly.

By default, if no handler is found for an exception, a non-GUI-based application terminates. Although this may seem like the right thing to do, it is not what programmers using other languages without exception-handling features are used to doing. Rather, errors often simply happen and then program execution continues, possibly only "hobbling" along.

A **try** block followed by several exception handlers resembles a **switch** statement, but a **break** statement is not used to exit an exception handler in a manner that skips over the remaining exception handlers. Each **catch** block defines a distinct scope whereas all the cases in a **switch** statement are contained within the single scope of the **switch**.

An exception cannot access objects defined within its **try** block because the **try** block has expired when the handler begins executing.

What happens when an exception occurs in an exception handler? The **try** block that noticed the exception has expired when the exception handler begins running, so exceptions occurring in an exception handler need to be processed outside the **try** block in which the original exception was thrown. The outer **try** block watches for errors occurring in the original **try** block's **catch** handlers.

Exception handlers can be written in a variety of ways. They could simply rethrow an exception (we will see how to do this in the next section). They could convert one type of exception into another by throwing a different type of exception. They could perform any necessary recovery and resume execution after the last exception handler. They could look at the situation causing the error, remove the cause of the error, and retry by calling the original method that caused an exception. They could simply return some status value to their environment, etc.

It is not possible to return to the **throw** point by issuing a **return** statement in a **catch** handler. Such a **return** simply returns to the method that called the method containing the **catch** block. Again, the **throw** point is in a block that has expired, so returning via a **return** statement would not make sense.

Software Engineering Observation 12.9

Another reason not to use exceptions for conventional flow of control is that these "additional" exceptions can "get in the way" of genuine error-type exceptions. It becomes more difficult for the programmer to keep track of the larger number of exception cases. Exceptional situations should be rare, not commonplace.

Common Programming Error 12.8

Assuming that an exception thrown from a **catch** *handler will be processed by that handler or any other handler associated with the same* **try** *block can lead to logic errors.*

12.9 Rethrowing an Exception

It is possible that the **catch** handler that catches an exception may decide it cannot process the exception or it may want to let some other **catch** handler handle it. In this case, the handler that received **Exception e** can simply rethrow the exception with the statement

```
throw e;
```

Such a **throw** rethrows the exception to the next enclosing **try** block.

Even if a handler can process an exception, and regardless of whether it does any processing on that exception, the handler can still rethrow the exception for further processing outside the handler. A rethrown exception is detected by the next enclosing **try** block and is handled by an exception handler listed after that enclosing **try** block.

12.10 Throws Clause

A **throws** clause lists the exceptions that can be thrown by a method.

```
int g( float h ) throws a, b, c
{
   // method body
}
```

The types of exceptions that are thrown by a method are specified in the method definition with a **throws** clause. A method can **throw** objects of the indicated classes, or it can **throw** objects of subclasses.

Some exceptions can occur at any point during the execution of the program. Many of these exceptions can be avoided by coding properly. These are *run-time exceptions* and they derive from class **RuntimeException**. For example, if your program attempts to access an out-of-range array subscript, an exception of type **ArrayIndexOutOf-**

BoundsException (derived from **RuntimeException**) is thrown. Your program can clearly avoid such a problem; hence, it is a run-time exception.

Another run-time exception occurs when your program creates an object reference but has not yet created an object and attached it to the reference. Attempting to use such a **null** reference causes a **NullPointerException** to be thrown. Clearly, your program could have avoided this circumstance; hence, it is a run-time exception. Another run-time exception is an invalid cast which throws a **ClassCastException** (see Chapter 7).

There are a variety of exceptions that are not **RuntimeException**s. Two of the most common are **InterruptedException**s (see Chapter 13, "Multithreading") and **IOException**s (see Chapter 15, "Files and Streams").

Not all errors and exceptions that can be thrown from a method are listed in the **throws** clause. **Error**s do not need to be listed, nor do **RuntimeException**s (avoidable exceptions). **Error**s are serious system problems that can occur almost anywhere and most users will not have the need to deal with them. You should be dealing with **RuntimeException**s directly rather than passing them on to other regions of your program. Non-**RuntimeException**s a method explicitly throws and non-**RuntimeException**s thrown by methods the method calls must be listed in the method's **throws** clause.

Software Engineering Observation 12.10

*If a non-**RuntimeException** is thrown by a method, or if that method calls methods that throw non-**RuntimeException**s, each of those exceptions must be declared in the **throws** clause of that method or caught in a **try/catch** in that method.*

Java distinguishes *checked* **Exception**s versus *unchecked* **RuntimeException**s and **Error**s. A method's checked exceptions need to be listed in that method's **throws** clause. Because **Error**s and **RuntimeException**s can be thrown from almost any method, it would be cumbersome for programmers to be required to list them; these are not required to be listed in a method's **throws** clause, and hence are said to be "unchecked." All non-**RuntimeException**s a method can **throw** must be listed in that method's **throws** clause, and hence are said to be "checked."

Common Programming Error 12.9

*It is a syntax error if a method throws a checked exception not in that method's **throws** clause.*

Common Programming Error 12.10

*Attempting to throw a checked exception from a method that has no **throws** clause is a syntax error.*

Software Engineering Observation 12.11

*If your method calls other methods that explicitly **throw** checked exceptions, those exceptions must be listed in the **throws** clause of your method, unless your method catches those exceptions. This is Java's "**catch**-or-declare" requirement.*

Common Programming Error 12.11

*If a subclass method overrides a superclass method, it is an error for the subclass method to list more exceptions in its **throws** list than the overridden superclass method does. A subclass **throws** list can contain a subset of a superclass's **throws** list.*

Java's **catch**-or-declare requirement demands that the programmer either **catch** each checked exception or place it in the **throws** clause of a method. Of course placing a checked exception in the **throws** clause would force other methods to deal with the checked exception as well. If a programmer feels a particular checked exception is unlikely to occur, the programmer might elect to catch that checked exception and do nothing with it to avoid being forced to deal with it later. This can of course come back to haunt you because as a program evolves it may become important to deal with this checked exception.

Testing and Debugging Tip 12.8

Do not try to circumvent Java's **catch***-or-declare requirement by simply catching exceptions and doing nothing with them. Exceptions are generally of a serious enough nature that they need to be dealt with rather than suppressed.*

Testing and Debugging Tip 12.9

The Java compiler, through the **throws** *list used with exception handling, forces programmers to deal with the exceptions that can be thrown from each method a program calls. This helps avoid bugs that arise in programs when programmers ignore the fact that things can go wrong and make no provisions for these problems.*

Software Engineering Observation 12.12

Subclass methods that do not override their corresponding superclass methods exhibit the same exception-handling behavior of the inherited superclass methods. The **throws** *list of a subclass method that overrides a superclass method may not have more exceptions than the* **throws** *list of the overridden superclass method.*

Common Programming Error 12.12

The Java compiler requires that a method either catch any checked exceptions thrown in the method (either directly from the method's code itself or indirectly through called methods), or declare checked **Exception***s the method can* **throw** *to other methods; otherwise the Java compiler issues a syntax error.*

Testing and Debugging Tip 12.10

Suppose a method **throws** *all subclasses of a particular superclass. You may be tempted to list only the superclass in the* **throws** *clause. Instead, explicitly list all the subclasses. This focuses the programmer's attention on the specific* **Exception***s that must be dealt with and will often help avoid bugs caused by processing* **Exception***s in too general a manner.*

Figures 12.2 through 12.7 list Java's **Error**s and **Exception**s hierarchically for the packages **java.lang**, **java.util**, **java.io**, **java.awt**, and **java.net**. The exception and error classes for the other packages of the Java API can be found in the Java on-line documentation. The on-line documentation for each method in the API specifies if that method throws exceptions and what the exceptions are that can be thrown. We show Java's **Error** hierarchy in Fig. 12.2. Most Java programmers will simply ignore **Error**s. They are serious but rare events.

Figure 12.3 is particularly important because it lists almost all of Java's **Runtime-Exception**s. Although Java programmers will not declare these exceptions in **throws** clauses, these are the exceptions that will commonly be caught and handled in Java applications. All but two of Java's **RuntimeException**s are in the **java.lang** package.

The `java.lang` package errors

```
Error  (all in java.lang except for AWTError which is in java.awt)

    LinkageError

        ClassCircularityError
        ClassFormatError
        ExceptionInInitializerError f
        IncompatibleClassChangeError

            AbstractMethodError
            IllegalAccessError
            InstantiationError
            NoSuchFieldError
            NoSuchMethodError

        NoClassDefFoundError
        UnsatisfiedLinkError
        VerifyError

    ThreadDeath

    VirtualMachineError  (Abstract class)

        InternalError
        OutOfMemoryError
        StackOverflowError
        UnknownError

 AWTError (in java.awt)
```

Fig. 12.2 The `java.lang` package errors .

The `java.lang` package exceptions

```
Exception

    ClassNotFoundException
    CloneNotSupportedException
    IllegalAccessException
    InstantiationException
    InterruptedException
    NoSuchFieldException
    NoSuchMethodException

    RuntimeException

        ArithmeticException
        ArrayStoreException
        ClassCastException

        IllegalArgumentException

            IllegalThreadStateException
            NumberFormatException

        IllegalMonitorStateException
        IllegalStateException

        IndexOutOfBoundsException

            ArrayIndexOutOfBoundsException
            StringIndexOutOfBoundsException

        NegativeArraySizeException
        NullPointerException
        SecurityException
```

Fig. 12.3 The `java.lang` package exceptions.

Figure 12.4 lists Java's other two **RuntimeExceptions** data types. We will encounter these exceptions in Chapter 18 when we study the **Vector** class. A **Vector** is a dynamic array that can grow and shrink to accommodate a program's varying storage requirements.

Figure 12.5 lists Java's **IOExceptions**. These are all checked exceptions that can occur during input/output and file processing.

Figure 12.6 lists the **java.awt** package's only **Exception**, the **AWTException**. This is a checked exception that is thrown by various abstract windowing toolkit methods.

Figure 12.7 lists the **IOExceptions** of the **java.net** package. These are all checked **Exceptions** that indicate various networking problems.

The `java.util` package exceptions

```
Exception

    RuntimeException

        EmptyStackException
        MissingResourceException
        NoSuchElementException

    TooManyListenersException
```

Fig. 12.4 The **java.util** package exceptions.

The `java.io` package exceptions

```
Exception

    IOException

        CharConversionException
        EOFException
        FileNotFoundException
        InterruptedIOException
```

Fig. 12.5 The **java.io** package exceptions (part 1 of 2).

The `java.io` package exceptions

```
ObjectStreamException
   InvalidClassException
   InvalidObjectException
   NotActiveException
   NotSerializableException
   OptionalDataException
   StreamCorruptedException
   WriteAbortedException

SyncFailedException
UnsupportedCodingException
UTFDataFormatException
```

Fig. 12.5 The **java.io** package exceptions (part 2 of 2).

The `java.awt` package exceptions

```
Exception

      AWTException
      RuntimeException
         IllegalStateException
            IllegalComponentStateException
```

Fig. 12.6 The **java.awt** package exceptions.

12.11 Constructors, Finalizers, and Exception Handling

First, let us deal with an issue we have mentioned, but that has yet to be satisfactorily resolved. What happens when an error is detected in a constructor? The problem is that a constructor cannot return a value, so how do we let the program know that an object has not been properly constructed? One scheme is simply to return the improperly constructed object and hope that anyone using the object would make appropriate tests to determine that the object is in fact bad. Another scheme is to set some global variable outside the constructor but this is a poor-programming practice. A thrown exception passes to the outside world the information about the failed constructor and the responsibility to deal with the failure.

The `java.net` package exceptions

```
Exception

    IOException
        BindException
        MalformedURLException
        ProtocolException
        SocketException
            ConnectException
            NoRouteToHostException
        UnknownHostException
        UnknownServiceException
```

Fig. 12.7 The **`java.net`** package exceptions.

Exceptions thrown in constructors cause objects built as part of the object being constructed to be marked for eventual garbage collection. Before each object is garbage collected, its finalizer will be called. Once again, Java does not guarantee the order in which objects will be garbage collected and therefore it does not guarantee the order in which finalizers will be called.

12.12 Exceptions and Inheritance

Various exception classes can be derived from a common superclass. If a **`catch`** is written to catch exception objects of a superclass type, it can also catch all objects of subclasses of that superclass. This can allow for polymorphic processing of related errors.

Using inheritance with exceptions enables an exception handler to catch related errors with a concise notation. One could certainly catch each subclass exception object individually, but it is more concise to catch the superclass exception object instead. This only makes sense if the handling behavior would be the same for all subclasses of course. Otherwise, catch each subclass exception individually.

Testing and Debugging Tip 12.11

Catching subclass exception objects individually is subject to error if the programmer forgets to explicitly test for one or more of the subclass types; catching the superclass guarantees that objects of all subclasses will be caught.

12.13 `finally` Block

Programs that obtain certain types of resources must explicitly return those resources to the system to avoid so-called *resource leaks.* In programming languages like C and C++ the most common kind of resource leak is a memory leak. Java performs automatic garbage collection of memory no longer needed by programs, thus avoiding most memory leaks. But other kinds of resource leaks can occur in Java.

Software Engineering Observation 12.13

A **`finally`** *block typically contains code to release resources acquired in its corresponding* **`try`** *block; this is an effective way to eliminate resource leaks. For example, the* **`finally`** *block should close any files opened in the* **`try`** *block that threw the exception.*

Testing and Debugging Tip 12.12

Actually, Java does not completely eliminate memory leaks. There is a subtle issue here. Java will not garbage collect an object until there are no more references to the object. Thus, memory leaks can occur, but only if programmers erroneously keep references to unwanted objects. Most *memory leak problems are solved by Java's garbage collection.*

The **`finally`** block is optional; if it is present it is placed after the last of a **`try`** block's **`catch`** blocks as follows

```
try {
    statements;
    resource-acquire statements;
}
catch ( AKindOfException ex1 ) {
    exception-handling statements;
}
catch (AnotherKindOfException ex2) {
    exception-handling statements;
}
finally {
    statement;
    resource-release statements;
}
```

Java guarantees that a **`finally`** block (if one is present) will be executed regardless of whether or not any exception is thrown in a **`try`** block or any of its corresponding **`catch`** blocks. Java also guarantees that a **`finally`** block (if one is present) will be executed if a **`try`** block is exited via a **`return`**, **`break`** or **`continue`** statement. Resource-release code is placed in a **`finally`** block. Suppose a resource is allocated in a **`try`** block. If no exception occurs, the **`catch`** handlers are skipped and control proceeds to the **`finally`** block which frees the resource and control proceeds to the first statement after the **`finally`** block.

If an exception occurs, the rest of the **`try`** block is skipped and if the exception is caught by one of the **`catch`** handlers, the exception is handled and control still proceeds to the **`finally`** block which releases the resource and control proceeds to the first statement after the **`finally`** block.

If an exception that occurs in the **`try`** block cannot be caught by one of the **`catch`** handlers, the rest of the **`try`** block is skipped (as the **`try`** block expires) and control proceeds to the **`finally`** block which releases the resource and then the exception is passed up the call chain until some calling method chooses to **`catch`** it. If no method chooses to deal with it, a non-GUI-based application terminates.

If a **`catch`** handler throws an exception, the **`finally`** block is still executed and the exception is passed up the call chain for a calling method to **`catch`** and handle.

The Java application of Fig. 12.8 demonstrates that the **finally** block (if one is present) executes even if an exception is not thrown in the corresponding **try** block. The figure contains methods **main**, **throwException**, and **doesNotThrowException**. Method **main** begins executing, enters its **try** block and immediately calls **throwException**. Method **throwException** throws an **Exception** (line 23), catches it (line 25) and rethrows it (line 29). The rethrown exception will be handled in **main**, but first the **finally** block (lines 31–33) executes. The rethrown exception is detected in the **try** block in **main** (lines 7–9) and handled by the **catch** block (lines 10–13).

```
1  // Fig. 12.8: UsingExceptions.java
2  // Demonstration of the try-catch-finally
3  // exception handling mechanism.
4  public class UsingExceptions {
5     public static void main( String args[] )
6     {
7        try {
8           throwException();
9        }
10       catch ( Exception e )
11       {
12          System.err.println( "Exception handled in main" );
13       }
14
15       doesNotThrowException();
16    }
17
18    public static void throwException() throws Exception
19    {
20       // Throw an exception and immediately catch it.
21       try {
22          System.out.println( "Method throwException" );
23          throw new Exception();  // generate exception
24       }
25       catch( Exception e )
26       {
27          System.err.println( "Exception handled in " +
28                              "method throwException" );
29          throw e;  // rethrow exception for further processing
30       }
31       finally {
32          System.err.println( "Finally is always executed" );
33       }
34    }
35
```

Fig. 12.8 Demonstration of the **try-catch-finally** exception handling mechanism (part 1 of 2).

```
   public static void doesNotThrowException()
   {
      try {
         System.out.println( "Method doesNotThrowException" );
      }
      catch( Exception e )
      {
         System.err.println( e.toString() );
      }
      finally {
         System.err.println( "Finally is always executed." );
      }
   }
}
```

```
Method throwException
Exception handled in method throwException
Finally is always executed
Exception handled in main
Method doesNotThrowException
Finally is always executed.
```

Fig. 12.8 Demonstration of the **try-catch-finally** exception handling mechanism (part 2 of 2).

Method **doesNotThrowException** is called. No exception is thrown in its **try** block, so the **catch** block is skipped, but the **finally** block nevertheless executes. Control proceeds past the **finally** block. Because there are no statements following **finally** control returns to **main** which also terminates.

The Java application in Fig. 12.9 demonstrates that when an exception thrown in a **try** block is not caught in a corresponding **catch** block, the exception will be detected in the next outer **try** block and will be handled by an appropriate **catch** block (if one is present) associated with that outer **try** block.

```
// Fig. 12.9: UsingExceptions.java
// Demonstration of stack unwinding.
public class UsingExceptions {
   public static void main( String args[] )
   {
      try {
         throwException();
      }
      catch ( Exception e )
      {
         System.err.println( "Exception handled in main" );
      }
   }
```

Fig. 12.9 Demonstration of stack unwinding (part 1 of 2).

```
   public static void throwException() throws Exception
   {
      // Throw an exception and catch it in main.
      try {
         System.out.println( "Method throwException" );
         throw new Exception();  // generate exception
      }
      catch( OtherException e )
      {
         System.err.println( "Exception handled in " +
                             "method throwException" );
      }
      finally {
         System.err.println( "Finally is always executed" );
      }
   }
}

class OtherException extends Exception {
   public OtherException()
   {
      super( "Another exception type" );
   }
}
```

```
Method throwException
Finally is always executed
Exception handled in main
```

Fig. 12.9 Demonstration of stack unwinding (part 2 of 2).

A **finally** block as we have seen may be entered for a variety of reasons such as a **try** completing successfully, an exception being thrown and then handled by a local **catch**, an exception being thrown for which no local **catch** is available, or a program control statement like a **return**, **break** or **continue** being issued. Normally, the **finally** block will execute then behave appropriately (we will call this **finally**'s "continuation action") depending on the reason it was entered. It is possible, however, for the **finally** block to perform some action that would cause the "continuation action" to be overridden. For example, if an exception is thrown in the **finally** block, the continuation action will be for *that* exception to be dealt with in the next enclosing block. Unfortunately, the first exception is lost. This is dangerous.

Common Programming Error 12.13

If an exception is thrown for which no local **catch** *is available, when control enters the local* **finally** *block the* **finally** *block could also* **throw** *an exception. If this happens the first exception will be lost.*

Testing and Debugging Tip 12.13

Avoid placing code that can **`throw`** *an exception in a* **`finally`** *block.*

Good Programming Practice 12.6

Java's exception-handling mechanism is intended to remove error-processing code from the main line of a program's code to improve program clarity. Do not place **`try-catch-finally`** *around every statement that may throw an exception. This makes programs difficult to read. Rather, place one* **`try`** *block around a significant portion of your code, then follow that* **`try`** *block with* **`catch`** *blocks that handle each of the things that can go wrong, then follow the* **`catch`** *blocks with a single* **`finally`** *block.*

Software Engineering Observation 12.14

As a rule, resources should be released as soon as it is apparent that they are no longer needed. This makes these resources immediately available for reuse and can improve program performance.

Software Engineering Observation 12.15

If a **`try`** *block has a corresponding* **`finally`** *block, the* **`finally`** *block will be executed even if the* **`try`** *block is exited with* **`return`**, **`break`** *or* **`continue`**; *then the effect of the* **`return`**, **`break`** *or* **`continue`** *will occur.*

12.14 Using `printStackTrace` and `getMessage`

Exceptions derive from class **`Throwable`**. Class **`Throwable`** offers a **`printStackTrace`** method that prints the method call stack. By sending this method to an **`Exception`** object that has been caught, a program can print the method call stack. This is often helpful in testing and debugging. In this section, we consider an example that exercises the **`printStackTrace`** method and another useful method, **`getMessage`**.

Testing and Debugging Tip 12.14

All **`Throwable`** *objects contain a* **`printStackTrace`** *method that prints a stack trace for the object.*

Testing and Debugging Tip 12.15

An exception that is not caught eventually causes Java's default exception handler to run. This displays the name of the exception, the optional character string that was supplied when the exception was constructed, and a complete execution stack trace. The stack trace shows the complete method call stack. This lets the programmer see the path of execution that led to the exception file-by-file (and thus class-by-class) and method-by-method. This information is helpful in debugging a program.

There are two constructors for class **`Exception`**. The first constructor

```
public Exception()
```

takes no arguments. The second constructor

```
public Exception( String informationString )
```

takes an argument **informationString** which is descriptive information about this kind of **Exception** that will be carried in every object of this class. The **informationString** stored in the **Exception** may be queried with method **getMessage**.

Testing and Debugging Tip 12.16

***Exception** classes have a constructor that accepts a **String**. Using this form of the constructor is helpful in determining the source of the exception via method **getMessage()**.*

Figure 12.10 demonstrates **getMessage** and **printStackTrace**. Method **getMessage** returns the descriptive **String** stored in an exception. Method **printStackTrace** outputs to the standard error stream (normally the command line or console) an error message with the class name of the exception, the descriptive **String** stored in the exception and a list of the methods that had not completed execution when the exception was thrown (i.e., all methods currently residing on the method call stack).

```
// Fig. 12.10: UsingExceptions.java
// Demonstrating the getMessage and printStackTrace
// methods inherited into all exception classes.
public class UsingExceptions {
   public static void main( String args[] )
   {
      try {
         method1();
      }
      catch ( UserException e )
      {
         System.err.println( e.getMessage() +
                             "\nThe stack trace is:" );
         e.printStackTrace();
      }
   }

   public static void method1() throws UserException
   {
      method2();
   }

   public static void method2() throws UserException
   {
      method3();
   }

   public static void method3() throws UserException
   {
      throw new UserException();
   }
}

```

Fig. 12.10 Using **getMessage** and **printStackTrace** (part 1 of 2).

```
34 class UserException extends Exception {
35    public UserException()
36    {
37       super( "This is a user defined exception." );
38    }
39 }
```

```
This is a user defined exception.
The stack trace is:
UserException: This is a user defined exception.
     at UsingExceptions.method3(UsingExceptions.java:30)
     at UsingExceptions.method2(UsingExceptions.java:25)
     at UsingExceptions.method1(UsingExceptions.java:20)
     at UsingExceptions.main(UsingExceptions.java:8)
```

Fig. 12.10 Using **getMessage** and **printStackTrace** (part 2 of 2).

In the program, **main** invokes **method1**, **method1** invokes **method2** and **method2** invokes **method3**. At this point, the method call stack for the program is

```
method3
method2
method1
main
```

with the last method called (**method3**) at the top and the first method called (**main**) at the bottom. When **method3** throws a **UserException** (line 30), the stack unwinds to the first method in which the exception can be caught (i.e., **main** because it contains a **catch** handler for **UserException**). The **catch** handler then uses **getMessage** and **printStackTrace** on the **UserException** object **e** to produce the output. Notice that the line numbers in the output window correspond to the line numbers in the program.

Summary

- Some common examples of exceptions are memory exhaustion, an out-of-bounds array subscript, arithmetic overflow, division by zero, and invalid method parameters.
- Exception handling is designed for dealing with synchronous malfunctions, i.e., those that occur as the result of a program's execution.
- Exception handling is typically used in situations in which a malfunction will be dealt with in a different scope from that which detected the malfunction.
- Exceptions should not be used as an alternate mechanism for specifying flow of control.
- Exception handling should be used to process exceptions from software components such as methods, libraries, and classes that are likely to be widely used, and where it does not make sense for those components to handle their own exceptions.
- Exception handling should be used on large projects to handle error processing in a standardized manner for the entire project.

- Java exception handling is geared to situations in which the method that detects an error is unable to deal with it. Such a method will **`throw`** an exception. If the exception matches the type of the parameter in one of the **`catch`** blocks, the code for that **`catch`** block is executed.
- The programmer encloses in a **`try`** block the code that may generate an error that will produce an exception. The **`try`** block is immediately followed by one or more **`catch`** blocks. Each **`catch`** block specifies the type of exception it can catch and handle. Each **`catch`** block is an exception handler.
- If no exceptions are thrown in the **`try`** block, the exception handlers for that block are skipped and the program resumes execution after the last **`catch`** block, possibly executing a **`finally`** block if one is provided.
- Exceptions are thrown in a **`try`** block in a method or from a method called directly or indirectly from the **`try`** block.
- It is possible to communicate information to the exception handler from the point of the exception. That information is the type of thrown object or it is information harvested from the vicinity and placed into the thrown object.
- The operand of a **`throw`** can be of any class derived from **`Throwable`**. The immediate subclasses of **`Throwable`** are **`Error`** and **`Exception`**.
- **`RuntimeException`**s and **`Error`**s are said to be "unchecked." Non-**`RuntimeException`**s are said to be "checked." The checked exceptions thrown by a particular method must be specified in that method's **`throws`** clause.
- Exceptions are caught by the closest exception handler (for the **`try`** block from which the exception was thrown) specifying an appropriate type.
- An exception terminates the block in which the exception occurred.
- A handler may rethrow the object to an outer try block.
- **`catch( Exception e )`** catches all **`Exception`**s.
- **`catch( Error err )`** catches all **`Error`**s.
- **`catch( Throwable t )`** catches all **`Exception`**s and **`Error`**s.
- If no handler matches a particular thrown object the search for a match continues in an enclosing **`try`** block.
- Exception handlers are searched in order for an appropriate match based on type. The first handler that matches is executed. When that handler finishes executing, control resumes with the first statement after the last **`catch`** block.
- The order of the exception handlers affects how an exception is handled.
- A subclass object can be caught either by a handler specifying that subclass type or by handlers specifying the types of any direct or indirect superclasses of that subclass.
- If no handler is found for an exception, a non-GUI-based application terminates; an applet or a GUI-based application will return to its regular event handling.

- An exception handler cannot access variables in the scope of its **try** block because by the time the exception handler begins executing, the **try** block has expired. Information the handler needs is normally passed in the thrown object.
- Exception handlers can rethrow an exception. They can convert one type of exception into another by throwing a different exception. They can perform any necessary recovery and resume execution after the last exception handler. They can look at the situation causing the error, remove the cause of the error, and retry by calling the original method that caused an exception. They can simply return some status value to their environment.
- A handler that catches a subclass object should be placed before a handler that catches a superclass object. If the superclass handler were first, it would catch superclass objects and the objects of subclasses of that superclass.
- When an exception is caught, it is possible that resources may have been allocated but not yet released in the **try** block. A **finally** block should release these resources.
- It is possible that the handler that catches an exception may decide it cannot process the exception. In this case, the handler can simply rethrow the exception. A **throw** followed by the exception object name rethrows the exception.
- Even if a handler can process an exception, and regardless of whether it does any processing on that exception, the handler can rethrow the exception for further processing outside the handler. A rethrown exception is detected by the next enclosing **try** block (normally in a calling method) and is handled by an appropriate exception handler (if there is one) listed after that enclosing **try** block.
- A **throws** clause lists the checked exceptions that may be thrown from a method. A method may **throw** the indicated exceptions, or it may **throw** subclass types. If a checked exception not listed in the **throws** clause is thrown, a syntax error occurs.
- A powerful reason for using inheritance with exceptions is to **catch** a variety of related errors easily with concise notation. One could certainly **catch** each type of subclass exception object individually, but it is more concise to simply **catch** the superclass exception object.

Terminology

ArithmeticException
array exceptions
ArrayIndexOutOfBoundsException
business-critical computing
catch a group of exceptions
catch all exceptions
catch an exception
catch block
catch(Exception e)
catch-or-declare requirement
checked **Exception**s
ClassCastException
declare exceptions that can be thrown
default exception handler
EmptyStackException
Error class
Error class hierarchy
error handling
exception
Exception class
Exception class hierarchy
exception handler
exception handling
exception object

fault tolerance
FileNotFoundException
finally block
getMessage() method of **Throwable** class
handle an exception
IllegalAccessException
IncompatibleClassChangeException
instanceof operator
InstantiationException
InternalException
InterruptedException
IOException
library exception classes
memory exhaustion
mission-critical computing
NegativeArraySizeException
NoClassDefFoundException
non-runtime exception
null reference
NullPointerException
OutOfMemoryError
printStackTrace method (**Throwable**)
resource leak
resumption model of exception handling
rethrow an exception
RuntimeException
stack unwinding
synchronous error
termination model of exception handling
throw an exception
throw point
throw statement
Throwable class
throws clause
try block
unchecked **Exception**s
UnsatisfiedLinkException

Common Programming Errors

12.1 Aborting a program could leave a resource in a state in which other programs would not be able to acquire the resource, hence we would have a so-called "resource leak."

12.2 It is a syntax error to separate with other code the **catch** handlers that correspond to a particular **try** block.

12.3 Assuming that after an exception is processed, control will return to the first statement after the **throw** can lead to errors.

12.4 Specifying a comma-separated list of **catch** arguments is a syntax error. A **catch** can have only a single argument.

12.5 It is a syntax error to ***catch*** the same type in two different ***catch*** blocks associated with a particular ***try*** block.

12.6 Placing **catch(Exception e)** before other **catch** blocks that catch specific types of exceptions would prevent those blocks from ever being executed; **catch(Exception e)** should always be placed last in the list of exception handlers following a **try** block, or a syntax error occurs.

12.7 It is a syntax error if a **catch** that catches a superclass object is placed before a **catch** that catches an object of a subclass of that superclass.

12.8 Assuming that an exception thrown from a **catch** handler will be processed by that handler or any other handler associated with the same **try** block can lead to logic errors.

12.9 It is a syntax error if a method throws a checked exception not in that method's **`throws`** clause.

12.10 Attempting to throw a checked exception from a method that has no **`throws`** clause is a syntax error.

12.11 If a subclass method overrides a superclass method, it is an error for the subclass method to list more exceptions in its ***`throws`*** list than the overridden superclass method does. A subclass ***`throws`*** list can contain a subset of a superclass's ***`throws`*** list.

12.12 The Java compiler requires that a method either catch any checked exceptions thrown in the method (either directly from the method's code itself or indirectly through called methods), or declare checked ***`Exception`***s the method can ***`throw`*** to other methods; otherwise the Java compiler issues a syntax error.

12.13 If an exception is thrown for which no local ***`catch`*** is available, when control enters the local ***`finally`*** block the ***`finally`*** block could also ***`throw`*** an exception. If this happens the first exception will be lost.

Good Programming Practices

12.1 Using Java exception handling enables the programmer to remove the error-handling code from the "main line" of the program's execution. This improves program clarity and enhances modifiability.

12.2 Avoid using exception handling for purposes other than error handling because this can reduce program clarity.

12.3 Using Java's standardized exception handling rather than having programmers use a diversity of "home-grown" techniques can improve program clarity on large projects.

12.4 If your method is capable of handling a given type of exception then handle it rather than passing the exception on to other regions of your program. This makes programs clearer.

12.5 Associating each type of serious execution-time malfunction with an appropriately named **`Exception`** class improves program clarity.

12.6 Java's exception-handling mechanism is intended to remove error-processing code from the main line of a program's code to improve program clarity. Do not place **`try-catch-finally`** around every statement that may throw an exception. This makes programs difficult to read. Rather, place one **`try`** block around a significant portion of your code, then follow that **`try`** block with **`catch`** blocks that handle each of the things that can go wrong, then follow the **`catch`** blocks with a single **`finally`** block.

Performance Tips

12.1 Although it is possible to use exception handling for purposes other than error handling, this can reduce program performance.

12.2 When an exception does not occur, little or no overhead is imposed by the presence of exception-handling code. When exceptions happen, they do incur execution-time overhead.

12.3 If an error can be processed locally instead of throwing an exception, do so. This will improve program execution speed. Exception handling is slow compared to local processing.

Software Engineering Observations

12.1 Use exceptions for malfunctions that must be processed in a different scope from where they occur. Use conventional error-handling techniques for local error processing in which a program is able to deal with its own errors.

12.2 Exception handling is particularly well-suited to systems of separately developed components. Such systems are typical of real-world software systems and products. Exception handling makes it easier to combine the components and have them work together effectively.

12.3 With other programming languages that do not support exception handling, programmers often delay writing error-processing code, and sometimes programmers simply forget to include it. This often results in less-robust, and thus inferior, software products. Java forces the programmer to deal with exception handling from the inception of a project. Still, the programmer must put considerable effort into incorporating an exception-handling strategy into software projects.

12.4 It is best to incorporate your exception-handling strategy into a system from the inception of the design process. It is difficult to add effective exception handling after a system has been implemented.

12.5 The client of a library class will likely have unique error processing in mind for an exception generated in the library class. It is unlikely that a library class will perform error processing that would meet the unique needs of all clients. Exceptions are an appropriate means for dealing with errors produced by library classes.

12.6 A key to Java-style exception handling is that the portion of a program or system that handles the exception can be distant from the portion of the program that generates the exception.

12.7 If you catch all exceptions with **`catch(Exception e)`** you can use the **`instanceof`** operator to probe the type of the exception. For example, the boolean condition **`x instanceof Y`** evaluates to **`true`** if object **`x`** is an instance of class **`Y`**, and **`false`** otherwise.

12.8 If several handlers match the type of an exception, and if each of these handles the exception differently, the order of the handlers affects the manner in which the exception is handled.

12.9 Another reason not to use exceptions for conventional flow of control is that these "additional" exceptions can "get in the way" of genuine error-type exceptions. It becomes more difficult for the programmer to keep track of the larger number of exception cases. Exceptional situations should be rare, not commonplace.

12.10 If a non-**`RuntimeException`** is thrown by a method, or if that method calls methods that throw non-**`RuntimeExceptions`**, each of those exceptions must be declared in the **`throws`** clause of that method or caught in a **`try/catch`** in that method.

12.11 If your method calls other methods that explicitly **throw** checked exceptions, those exceptions must be listed in the **throws** clause of your method, unless your method catches those exceptions. This is Java's "**catch**-or-declare" requirement.

12.12 Subclass methods that do not override their corresponding superclass **methods** exhibit the same exception handling behavior of the inherited superclass methods. The **throws** list of a subclass method that overrides a superclass method may not have more exceptions than the **throws** list of the overridden superclass method.

12.13 A **finally** block typically contains code to release resources acquired in its corresponding **try** block; this is an effective way to eliminate resource leaks. For example, the **finally** block should close any files opened in the **try** block that threw the exception.

12.14 As a rule, resources should be released as soon as it is apparent that they are no longer needed. This makes these resources immediately available for reuse and can improve program performance.

12.15 If a **try** block has a corresponding **finally** block, the **finally** block will be executed even if the **try** block is exited with **return**, **break** or **continue**; then the effect of the **return**, **break** or **continue** will occur.

Testing and Debugging Tips

12.1 Exception handling helps improve a program's fault tolerance. It becomes "more pleasant" to write error-processing code, so programmers are more likely to provide it.

12.2 All Java applets and certain Java applications are GUI-based. Some Java applications are not GUI-based; these are often called command-line applications (or console applications). When an exception is not caught in a command-line application the program terminates (i.e., Java exits) after the default exception handler runs. When an exception is not caught in an applet or a GUI-based application, the GUI is still displayed and the user can continue using the applet or application even after the default exception handler runs. However, the GUI may be in an inconsistent state.

12.3 With exception handling, a program can continue executing after dealing with a problem. This helps ensure robust applications that contribute to what is called mission-critical computing *or* business-critical computing.

12.4 A **finally** block is an excellent place in which to place code that will release resources acquired in a **try** block. This strategy is an effective way to avoid resource leaks.

12.5 When **toString** is invoked on any **Throwable** object, its printout includes the descriptive **String** that was supplied to the constructor.

12.6 If it is necessary to pass information about the malfunction that caused an exception, such information can be placed in the thrown object. That information can then be referenced through the parameter name in the **catch** handler.

12.7 An object can be thrown without containing information to be passed; in this case, knowledge that an exception of this type has been raised may provide sufficient information for the handler to do its job correctly.

12.8 Do not try to circumvent Java's **`catch`**-or-declare requirement by simply catching exceptions and doing nothing with them. Exceptions are generally of a serious enough nature that they need to be dealt with rather than suppressed.

12.9 The Java compiler, through the ***`throws`*** list used with exception handling, forces programmers to deal with the exceptions that can be thrown from each method a program calls. This helps avoid bugs that arise in programs when programmers ignore the fact that things can go wrong and make no provisions for these problems.

12.10 Suppose a method ***`throws`*** all subclasses of a particular superclass. You may be tempted to list only the superclass in the ***`throws`*** clause. Instead, explicitly list all the subclasses. This focuses the programmer's attention on the specific ***`Exception`***s that must be dealt with and will often help avoid bugs caused by processing ***`Exception`***s in too general a manner.

12.11 Catching subclass exception objects individually is subject to error if the programmer forgets to explicitly test for one or more of the subclass types; catching the superclass guarantees that objects of all subclasses will be caught.

12.12 Actually, Java does not *completely* eliminate memory leaks. There is a subtle issue here. Java will not garbage collect an object until there are no more references to the object. Thus, memory leaks can occur, but only if programmers erroneously keep references to unwanted objects. Most memory leak problems are solved by Java's garbage collection.

12.13 Avoid placing code that can **`throw`** an exception in a **`finally`** block.

12.14 All ***`Throwable`*** objects contain a **`printStackTrace`** method that prints a stack trace for the object.

12.15 An exception that is not caught eventually causes Java's default exception handler to run. This displays the name of the exception, the optional character string that was supplied when the exception was constructed, and a complete execution stack trace. The stack trace shows the complete method call stack. This lets the programmer see the path of execution that led to the exception file-by-file (and thus class-by-class) and method-by-method. This information is helpful in debugging a program.

12.16 **`Exception`** classes have a constructor that accepts a **`String`** argument. Using this form of the constructor is helpful in determining the source of the exception via method **`getMessage()`**.

Self-Review Exercises

12.1 List five common examples of exceptions.

12.2 Why should exception-handling techniques not be used for conventional program control?

12.3 Why are exceptions particularly appropriate for dealing with errors produced by library classes and methods?

12.4 What is a "resource leak?"

12.5 If no exceptions are thrown in a **`try`** block, where does control proceed to when the **`try`** block completes execution?

12.6 What happens if an exception occurs and an appropriate exception handler cannot be found?

12.7 Give a key advantage of using **`catch(Exception e)`**.

12.8 Should a conventional applet or application catch **`Error`** objects?

12.9 What happens if several handlers match the type of the thrown object?

12.10 Why would a programmer specify a superclass type as the type of a **`catch`** handler and then throw objects of subclass types?

12.11 How might a **`catch`** handler be written to process related types of errors without using inheritance among exception classes?

12.12 What is the key reason for using **`finally`** blocks?

12.13 Does throwing an **`Exception`** have to cause program termination?

12.14 What happens when a **`catch`** handler throws an **`Exception`**?

12.15 What happens to the automatic objects that have been constructed in a **`try`** block when that block throws an **`Exception`**?

Answers to Self-Review Exercises

12.1 Memory exhaustion, array subscript out of bounds, arithmetic overflow, division by zero, invalid method parameters.

12.2 (a) **`Exception`** handling is designed to handle infrequently occurring situations that often result in program termination, so compiler writers are not required to implement exception handling to perform optimally. (b) Flow of control with conventional control structures is generally clearer and more efficient than with exceptions. (c) Problems can occur because the stack is unwound when an exception occurs and resources allocated prior to the exception may not be freed. (d) The "additional" exceptions can get in the way of genuine error-type exceptions. It becomes more difficult for the programmer to keep track of the larger number of exception cases.

12.3 It is unlikely that library classes and methods could perform error processing that would meet the unique needs of all users.

12.4 A resource leak occurs when an executing program does not properly release a resource when the resource is no longer needed. If the program attempts to use the resource again in the future, the program may not be able to access the resource.

12.5 The exception handlers (in the **`catch`** blocks) for that **`try`** block are skipped and the program resumes execution after the last **`catch`** block. If there is a **`finally`** block, it is executed and the program resumes execution after the **`finally`** block.

12.6 A non-GUI-based application terminates; an applet or a GUI-based application resumes regular event processing.

12.7 The form **catch(Exception e)** catches any type of exception thrown in a **try** block. An advantage is that no thrown **Exception** can slip by.

12.8 **Error**s are usually serious problems with the underlying Java system; most programs will not want to catch **Error**s.

12.9 The first matching **Exception** handler after the **try** block is executed.

12.10 This is a nice way to catch related types of exceptions, but is should be used carefully.

12.11 Provide a single **Exception** subclass and **catch** handler for a group of exceptions. As each exception occurs, the exception object can be created with different instance data. The **catch** handler can examine this data to distinguish the type of the **Exception**.

12.12 The **finally** block is the preferred means for preventing resource leaks.

12.13 No, but it does terminate the block in which the **Exception** is thrown.

12.14 The exception will be processed by a **catch** handler (if one exists) associated with the **try** block (if one exists) enclosing the **catch** handler that caused the exception.

12.15 The objects are marked for garbage collection. A finalizer is called for each object before the object is garbage collected.

Exercises

12.16 Under what circumstances would you use the following statement?

```
catch(Exception e) { throw e; }
```

12.17 List the benefits of exception handling over conventional means of error processing.

12.18 Describe an object-oriented technique for handling related exceptions.

12.19 Until this chapter, we have found that dealing with errors detected by constructors is a bit awkward. Explain why exception handling is an effective means for dealing with constructor failure.

12.20 Suppose a program throws an exception and the appropriate exception handler begins executing. Now suppose that the exception handler itself throws the same exception. Does this create an infinite recursion? Explain your answer.

12.21 Use inheritance to create an exception superclass and various exception subclasses. Write a program to demonstrate that the **catch** specifying the superclass catches subclass exceptions.

12.22 Write a Java program that shows that all finalizers for objects constructed in a block are not necessarily called after an exception is thrown from that block.

12.23 Write a Java program that demonstrates how various exceptions are caught with **catch(Exception e)**.

12.24 Write a Java program that shows that the order of exception handlers is important. If you try to catch a superclass exception type before a subclass type, the compiler should generate errors. Explain why these errors occur.

12.25 Write a Java program that shows a constructor passing information about constructor failure to an exception handler after a `try` block.

12.26 Write a Java program that illustrates rethrowing an exception.

12.27 Write a Java program which shows that a method with its own `try` block does not have to catch every possible error generated within the `try`. Some exceptions can slip through to, and be handled in, other scopes.

13

Multithreading

Objectives

- To understand the notion of multithreading.
- To appreciate how multithreading can improve performance.
- To understand how to create, manage, and destroy threads.
- To understand the life cycle of a thread.
- To study several examples of thread synchronization.
- To understand thread priorities and scheduling.
- To understand daemon threads and thread groups.

The spider's touch, how exquisitely fine!
Feels at each thread, and lives along the line.
Alexander Pope

A person with one watch knows what time it is; a person with two watches is never sure.
Proverb

Conversation is but carving!
Give no more to every guest,
Then he's able to digest.
Jonathan Swift

Learn to labor and to wait.
Henry Wadsworth Longfellow

The most general definition of beauty . . . Multeity in Unity.
Samuel Taylor Coleridge

Outline

13.1 Introduction

It would be nice if we could "do one thing at a time" and "do it well." But that is simply not how the world works. The human body performs a great variety of operations *in parallel,* or as we will say throughout this chapter, *concurrently.* Respiration, blood circulation, and digestion for example, can occur concurrently. All of the senses—seeing, touching, smelling, tasting, and hearing—can occur concurrently. An automobile can be accelerating, turning, air conditioning, and playing music concurrently. Computers, too, perform operations concurrently. It is common today for desktop personal computers to be compiling a program, printing a file, and receiving electronic mail messages over a network concurrently.

Concurrency is important in our lives. Ironically, though, most programming languages do not enable programmers to specify concurrent activities. Rather, programming languages generally provide only a simple set of control structures that enable programmers to perform one action at a time and then proceed to the next action after the previous one is finished. The kind of concurrency that computers perform today is normally implemented as operating systems "primitives" available only to highly experienced "systems programmers."

The *Ada* programming language developed by the United States Department of Defense made concurrency primitives widely available to defense contractors building command and control systems. But Ada has not been widely used in universities and commercial industry.

Java is unique among popular general-purpose programming languages in that it makes concurrency primitives available to the personal computer applications programmer. The programmer specifies that applications contain *threads of execution,* each thread designating a portion of a program that may execute concurrently with other threads. This capability, called *multithreading,* gives the Java programmer powerful capabilities not available in C and C++, the languages on which Java is based. C and C++ are called *single-threaded* languages.

Software Engineering Observation 13.1

Unlike many languages that do not have built-in multithreading (such as C and C++) and must therefore make calls to operating system multithreading primitives, Java includes multithreading primitives as a part of the language itself (actually in classes **`Thread`**, **`ThreadGroup`** *and* **`ThreadDeath`** *of the* **`java.lang`** *package). This encourages the use of multithreading among a larger part of the applications programming community.*

We will discuss many applications of concurrent programming. When programs download large files such as audio clips or video clips from the World Wide Web, we do not want to wait until an entire clip is downloaded before starting the playback. So we can put multiple threads to work, one that downloads a clip, and another that plays the clip so that these activities, or *tasks,* may proceed concurrently. To avoid choppy playback, we will coordinate the threads so that the player thread does not begin until there is a sufficient amount of the clip in memory to keep the player thread busy.

Another example of multithreading is Java's automatic garbage collection. C and C++ place with the programmer the responsibility for reclaiming dynamically allocated memory. Java provides a *garbage collector thread* that automatically reclaims dynamically allocated memory that is no longer needed.

Testing and Debugging Tip 13.1

In C and C++, programmers must explicitly provide statements for reclaiming dynamically allocated memory. When memory is not reclaimed (because a programmer forgets to do so, or because of a logic error or because an exception diverts program control), this results in an all-to-common error called a memory leak *that can eventually exhaust the supply of free memory and may cause program termination. Java's automatic garbage collection eliminates the vast majority of memory leaks, i.e., those that are due to orphaned (unreferenced) objects.*

Java's garbage collector runs as a low-priority thread. When Java determines that there are no longer any references to an object, it marks the object for eventual garbage collection. The garbage collector thread runs when processor time is available and when there are no higher-priority runnable threads. The garbage collector will, however, run immediately when the system is out of memory.

Performance Tip 13.1

Java's garbage collection is not as efficient as the dynamic memory management code the best C and C++ programmers write, but it is relatively efficient and much safer for the programmer.

Performance Tip 13.2

Setting an object reference to **`null`** *marks that object for eventual garbage collection (if there are no other references to the object). This can help conserve memory in a system in which an automatic object is not going out of scope because the method it is in will execute for a lengthy period.*

Writing multithreaded programs can be tricky. Although the human mind can perform many functions concurrently, humans find it difficult to jump between parallel "trains of thought." To see why multithreading can be difficult to program and understand, try the following experiment: Open three books to page 1. Now try reading the books concurrently. Read a few words from the first book, then read a few words from the second book, then read a few words from the third book, then loop back and read the next few words from the first book, and so on. After a brief time you will rapidly appreciate the challenges of multithreading: switching between books, reading briefly, remembering your place in each book, moving the book you are reading closer so you can see it, pushing books you are not reading aside, and amidst all this chaos, trying to comprehend the content of the books!

Performance Tip 13.3

One problem with single-threaded applications is that possibly lengthy activities must complete before other activities can begin. Users feel they already spend too much time waiting with Internet and World Wide Web applications, so multithreading is immediately appealing.

Although Java is perhaps the world's most portable programming language, certain portions of the language are nevertheless platform dependent. In particular, there are differences among the first three Java platforms implemented, namely the Solaris implementation and the Windows-based implementations for Windows 95 and Windows NT.

The early Solaris Java platform runs a thread of a given priority to completion or until a higher-priority thread becomes ready. At that point *preemption* occurs, i.e., the processor is given to the higher-priority thread while the previously running thread must wait.

In the 32-bit Java implementations for Windows 95 and Windows NT, threads are *timesliced.* This means that each thread is given a limited amount of time (called a time *quantum*) to execute on a processor, and when that time expires the thread is made to wait while all other threads of equal priority get their chances to use their quantum in *round-robin* fashion. Then the original thread resumes execution. Thus, on Windows 95 and Windows NT, a running thread can be preempted by a thread of equal priority whereas on the early Solaris implementation, a running Java thread can only be preempted by a higher-priority thread. Future Solaris Java systems are expected to perform timeslicing as well.

Portability Tip 13.1

Java multithreading is platform dependent. Thus, a multithreaded application could behave differently on different Java implementations.

13.2 Class Thread: An Overview of the Thread Methods

In this section we overview the various thread-related methods in the Java API. We use many of these methods in live-code examples throughout the chapter. The reader should refer to the Java API directly for more details on using each method, especially the exceptions thrown by each method.

Class **Thread** has several constructors. The constructor

```
public Thread( String threadName )
```

constructs a **Thread** whose name is **threadName**. The constructor

```
public Thread()
```

constructs a **Thread** whose name is **"Thread"** concatenated with a digit, like **Thread1**, **Thread2**, and so on.

The code that "does the real work" of a thread is placed in its **run** method. The **run** method can be overridden in a subclass of **Thread** or it may be overridden in a **Runnable** object; **Runnable** is an important Java *interface* that we study in Section 13.10.

A program launches a thread's execution by calling the thread's **start** method which, in turn, calls the **run** method. When **start** launches the thread, **start** returns to its caller immediately. The caller then executes concurrently with the launched thread. The **start** method throws an **IllegalThreadStateException** if the thread it is trying to start has already been started.

The **static sleep** method is called with an argument specifying how long the currently executing thread should sleep (in milliseconds); while a thread sleeps, it does not contend for the processor, so other threads can execute. This can give lower-priority threads a chance to run.

The **interrupt** method is called to interrupt a thread. The **interrupted** method (a **static** method) returns **true** if a thread has been interrupted and **false** otherwise. Method call **isInterrupted** (a non-**static** method) is sent to some other thread to determine if it has been interrupted.

Method **suspend** suspends a thread's execution. Method **resume** resumes the execution of a suspended thread. An attempt to **resume** a thread that is not suspended lets it continue to execute.

Method **stop** stops a thread by throwing a **ThreadDeath** object. Most users will call the version of **stop** that takes no arguments.

Method **isAlive** returns **true** if **start** has been called for a given thread and the thread is not dead (i.e., its stop method has not been called and its controlling run method has not completed execution).

We will discuss the **yield** method in detail after we have considered thread priorities and thread scheduling.

Method **setName** sets the name of the **Thread**. Method **getName** returns the name of the **Thread**. Method **toString** returns a **String** consisting of the name of the thread, the priority of the thread and the thread's thread group.

The **static** method **currentThread** returns a reference to the current **Thread**.

Method **join** (which takes as an argument some number of **milliSeconds**) waits for the **Thread** to which the message is sent to die before the current **Thread** can proceed; no argument or an argument of 0 milliseconds indicates that the current **Thread** will wait forever for the target **Thread** to die before the current **Thread** proceeds. Such waiting can be dangerous; it can lead to two particularly serious problems called *deadlock* and *indefinite postponement.* We will discuss these momentarily.

Testing and Debugging Tip 13.2

Methods **dumpStack** *and* **countStackFrames** *are useful for debugging multithreaded applications. A program calls static method* **dumpStack** *(with the call* **Thread.dumpStack**) *to print a method-call stack trace for the current* **Thread**. *A program calls non-***static** *method* **countStackFrames** *to determine the number of method call stack frames in a suspended* **Thread**.

13.3 Thread States: Life Cycle of a Thread

At any time, a thread is said to be in one of several *thread states* (illustrated in Fig. 13.1). Let us say that a thread that was just created is in the *born* state. The thread remains in this state until the thread's **start** method is called; this causes the thread to enter the *ready* state. The highest-priority *ready* thread enters the *running state* when the system assigns a processor to the thread (i.e., the thread begins executing). A thread enters the *dead* state when its **run** method completes, or when the **stop** method is called for it; a *dead* thread will eventually be disposed of by the system.

One common way for a *running* thread to enter the *blocked state* is when the thread issues an input/output request. In this case, a *blocked* thread becomes *ready* when the I/O it is waiting for completes. A *blocked* thread cannot use a processor even if one is available.

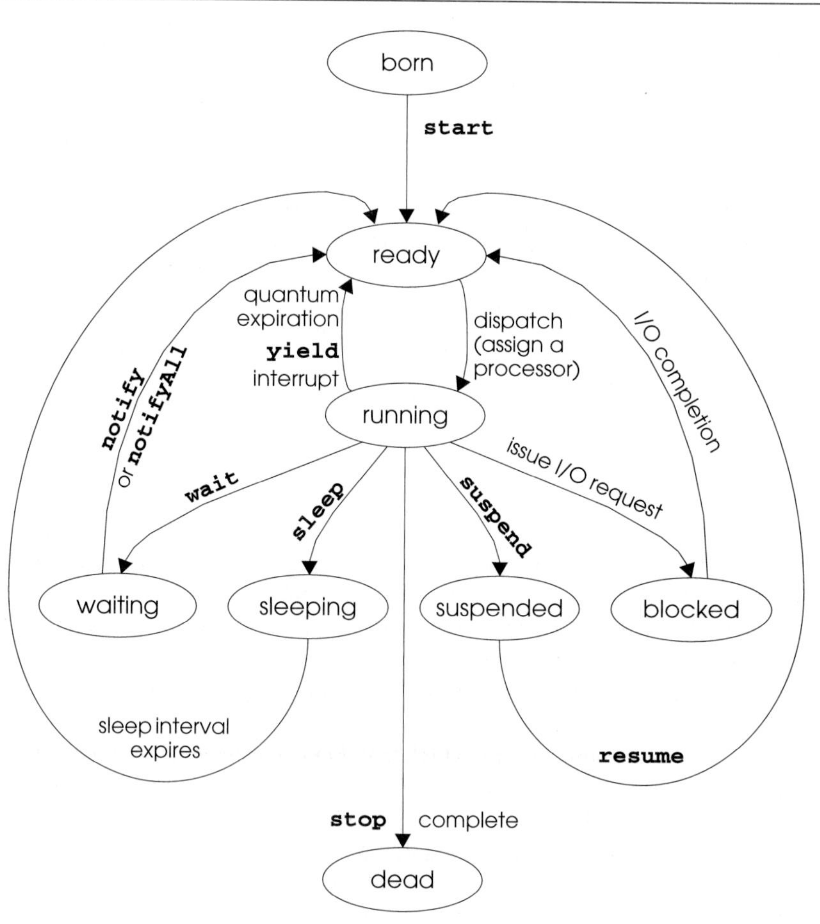

Fig. 13.1 Life cycle of a thread.

When a *running* thread's **sleep** method is called, that thread enters the *sleeping* state. A *sleeping* thread becomes *ready* after the designated sleep time expires. A *sleeping* thread cannot use a processor even if one is available.

Performance Tip 13.4

One way to delay a thread is to loop some appropriate number of times doing nothing in the body of the loop. This is called a busy wait *and leads to poor performance; while the processor is busy doing nothing for this thread, other runnable threads may be kept waiting. A better technique is to call the thread's* **sleep** *method. A sleeping thread does not use the processor.*

When a *running* thread's **suspend** method is called, that thread enters the *suspended* state. A *suspended* thread becomes ready when its **resume** method is called by another thread. A *suspended* thread cannot use a processor even if one is available.

When a *running* thread calls **wait** the thread enters a *waiting* state where it waits in a queue associated with the particular object on which **wait** was called. The first thread in the *wait* queue for a particular object becomes *ready* on a call to **notify** issued by another thread associated with that object. Every thread in the *wait* queue for a given object becomes ready on a call to **notifyAll** by another thread associated with that object. The **wait**, **notify**, and **notifyAll** methods will be discussed in more depth shortly when we consider monitors.

A thread enters the *dead state* when its **run** method completes or its **stop** method is called. The **stop** method sends a **ThreadDeath** object to the thread. **ThreadDeath** is a subclass of class **Error**.

Common Programming Error 13.1

ThreadDeath *is an* **Error**, *not an* **Exception**. *Ordinarily, user programs should not catch* **Error** *objects. If you choose to catch a* **ThreadDeath** *object, be sure to rethrow it or the thread may not die "properly."*

13.4 Thread Priorities and Thread Scheduling

Every Java applet or application is multithreaded. Every Java thread has a priority in the range **Thread.MIN_PRIORITY** (a constant of 1) and **Thread.MAX_PRIORITY** (a constant of 10). By default, each thread is given priority **Thread.NORM_PRIORITY** (a constant of 5). Each new thread inherits the priority of the thread that creates it.

Some Java platforms support a concept called *timeslicing* and some do not. Without timeslicing, each thread of a set of equal-priority threads runs to completion before that thread's peers get a chance to execute. With timeslicing, each thread receives a brief burst of processor time called a *quantum* during which that thread can execute. At the completion of the quantum, even if that thread has not finished executing, the processor is taken away from that thread and given to the next thread of equal priority if one is available.

The job of the Java *scheduler* is to keep a highest-priority thread running at all times, and if timeslicing is available, to ensure that several equally high-priority threads each execute for a quantum in *round-robin* fashion (i.e., these threads can be timesliced). Figure 13.2 illustrates Java's multilevel priority queue for threads. In the figure, threads A and B each execute for a quantum in round-robin fashion until both threads complete execution.

Next, thread C runs to completion. Then, threads D, E and F each execute for a quantum in round-robin fashion until they all complete execution. This process continues until all threads run to completion. Note that new higher-priority threads could postpone—possibly indefinitely—the execution of lower-priority threads. Such *indefinite postponement* is often referred to more colorfully as *starvation*.

A thread's priority can be adjusted with the **`setPriority`** method which takes an **`int`** argument. If the argument is not in the range 1 through 10 inclusive, then method **`setPriority`** throws an **`IllegalArgumentException`**. Method **`getPriority`** returns the thread's priority.

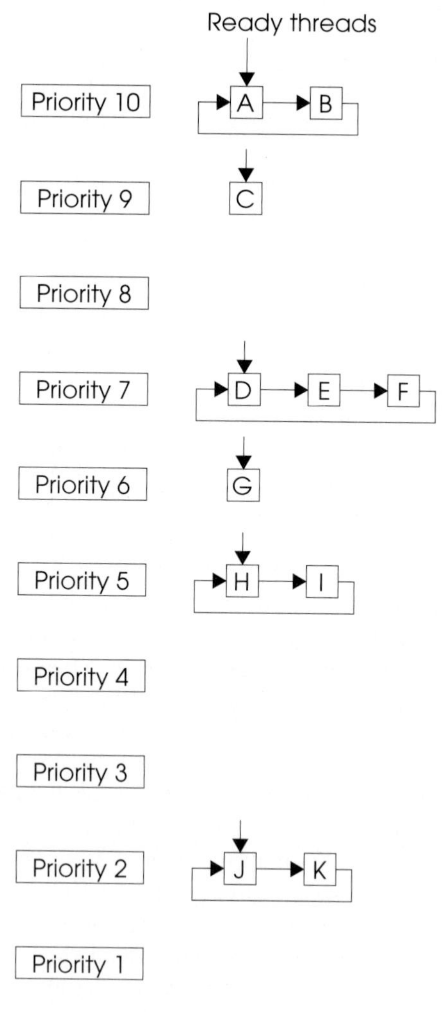

Fig. 13.2 Java thread priority scheduling.

A thread can call the **yield** method to give other threads a chance to execute. Actually, whenever a higher-priority thread becomes ready, the current thread is preempted, so a thread cannot **yield** to a higher-priority thread because the first thread will have been preempted when the higher-priority thread became ready. Similarly, **yield** always allows the highest-priority *ready* thread to run, so if only lower-priority threads are ready at the time of a **yield** call, the current thread will be the highest-priority thread and will continue executing. Therefore, a thread **yield**s to give threads of an equal priority a chance to run. On a timesliced system this is unnecessary because threads of equal priority will each execute for their quantum (or until they lose the processor for some other reason) and other threads of equal priority will execute in *round-robin* fashion. Thus **yield** is appropriate for non-timesliced systems in which a thread would ordinarily run to completion before another thread of equal priority would have an opportunity to run.

Performance Tip 13.5

On non-timesliced systems, cooperating threads of equal priority should periodically call **yield** *to enable their peers to proceed smoothly.*

Portability Tip 13.2

Applets should be programmed to work on all Java platforms to realize Java's goal of true portability.

A thread executes unless it dies, it becomes blocked for input/output (or some other reason), it calls **sleep**, it calls **wait**, it calls **yield**, it is preempted by a thread of higher priority or its quantum expires. A thread with a higher priority than the running thread can become ready (and hence preempt the running thread) if a *suspended* thread is resumed, if a *sleeping* thread finishes sleeping, if I/O completes for a thread waiting for that I/O, or if either **notify** or **notifyAll** is called on a thread that called **wait**.

The application of Fig. 13.3 demonstrates basic threading techniques including creation of a derived class from **Thread**, construction of a **Thread** and using the **Thread** class **sleep** method. Each thread of execution we create in the program displays its name after sleeping for a random amount of time between 0 and 5 seconds. The program consists of two classes—**PrintThread** and **PrintTest**.

```
// Fig. 13.3: PrintTest.java
// Show multiple threads printing at different intervals.

public class PrintTest {
   public static void main( String args[] )
   {
      PrintThread thread1, thread2, thread3, thread4;

      thread1 = new PrintThread();
      thread2 = new PrintThread();
      thread3 = new PrintThread();
      thread4 = new PrintThread();
```

Fig. 13.3 Multiple threads printing at random intervals (part 1 of 2).

```

      thread1.start();
      thread2.start();
      thread3.start();
      thread4.start();
   }
}

class PrintThread extends Thread {
   int sleepTime;

   // PrintThread constructor assigns name to thread
   // by calling Thread constructor
   public PrintThread()
   {
      // sleep between 0 and 5 seconds
      sleepTime = (int) ( Math.random() * 5000 );

      System.out.println( "Name: " + getName() +
                          ";  sleep: " + sleepTime );
   }

   // execute the thread
   public void run()
   {
      // put thread to sleep for a random interval
      try {
         Thread.sleep( sleepTime );
      }
      catch ( InterruptedException exception ) {
         System.err.println( exception.toString() );
      }

      // print thread name
     System.out.println( getName() );
   }
}
```

```
Name: Thread-1;  sleep: 843
Name: Thread-2;  sleep: 2833
Name: Thread-3;  sleep: 2354
Name: Thread-4;  sleep: 1622
Thread-1
Thread-4
Thread-3
Thread-2
```

Fig. 13.3 Multiple threads printing at random intervals (part 2 of 2).

Class **PrintThread**—which inherits from **Thread**—consists of instance variable **sleepTime**, a constructor and a **run** method. Variable **sleepTime** stores a random integer value chosen when a **PrintThread** object is constructed. Each **PrintThread** object sleeps for the amount of time specified by **sleepTime** then outputs its name.

The **PrintThread** constructor initializes **sleepTime** to a random integer between 0 and 5000 (0 to 5 seconds). Then, the name of the thread and the value of **sleepTime** are output to show the values for the particular **PrintThread** being constructed. The default constructor of class Thread automatically creates a name of the form **Thread-#** for each **PrintThread** object. The value of **#** begins at 1 for the first thread created and is incremented by one each time. Note: It is possible to create your own thread name by passing a **String** to the **Thread** class constructor.

When a **PrintThread**'s **start** method (inherited from **Thread**) is invoked, the **PrintThread** object enters the *ready* state. When the system assigns a processor to the **PrintThread** object, it enters the *running* state and its **run** method begins execution. Method **run** invokes the **sleep** method (line 40) that immediately puts the object into a *sleeping* state. When the object awakens, it is placed into a *ready* state again until it is assigned a processor. When the **PrintThread** object enters the *running* state again, it outputs its name, its **run** method terminates and the thread object enters the *dead* state. Note that the **sleep** method can throw an **InterruptedException**, therefore **sleep** must be called in a **try** block.

Class **PrintTest**'s **main** method instantiates four **PrintThread** objects and invokes the **Thread** class **start** method on each one to place all four **PrintThread** objects in a *ready* state. Note that the program terminates execution when the last **PrintThread** awakens and prints its name.

13.5 Thread Synchronization

Java uses *monitors* (as discussed by C.A.R. Hoare in his 1974 paper we cite in Exercise 13.24) to perform synchronization. Every object with **synchronized** methods is a monitor. The monitor lets only one thread at a time execute a **synchronized** method on the object. This is accomplished by *locking* the object when the **synchronized** method is invoked—also known as *obtaining the lock*. If there are several **synchronized** methods, only one **synchronized** method may be active on an object at once; all other threads attempting to invoke **synchronized** methods must wait. When a **synchronized** method finishes executing, the lock on the object is released and the monitor lets the highest-priority *ready* thread attempting to invoke a **synchronized** method proceed.

A thread executing in a **synchronized** method may determine that it cannot proceed, so the thread voluntarily calls **wait**. This removes the thread from contention for the processor and from contention for the monitor object. The thread now waits in a queue while other threads try to enter the object. When a thread executing **synchronized** method completes, the object can **notify** a waiting thread to become *ready* again so it can attempt to obtain the lock on the monitor object again and execute. The **notify** acts as a signal to the waiting thread that the condition the waiting thread has been waiting for is now satisfied, so it is acceptable for that thread to reenter the monitor. If a thread calls **notifyAll**, then all threads waiting for the object become eligible to reenter the monitor (i.e., they are all placed in a *ready* state). Remember that only one of those threads can obtain the lock on the object at a time. Methods **`wait`**, **`notify`** and **`notifyAll`** are inherited by all classes from class **`Object`**.

Common Programming Error 13.2

Threads waiting for a monitor object must eventually be awakened explicitly with a **`notify`** *or the thread will wait forever. This is a simple example of deadlock.*

Testing and Debugging Tip 13.3

Be sure that every call to **`wait`** *has a corresponding call to* **`notify`** *that will eventually end the waiting or call* **`notifyAll`** *as a safeguard.*

Performance Tip 13.6

Synchronization to achieve correctness in multithreaded programs can make programs run slower as threads wait. There is not much to say, however, for highly efficient, incorrect multithreaded programs!

Testing and Debugging Tip 13.4

The locking that occurs with the execution of **`synchronized`** *methods could lead to deadlock if the locks are never released. When exceptions occur, Java's exception mechanism coordinates with Java's synchronization mechanism to release appropriate synchronization locks to avoid these kinds of deadlocks.*

Monitor objects queue all threads waiting to enter the object to execute **`synchronized`** methods. A thread gets enqueued and waits for the object if that thread calls a **`synchronized`** method of the object while another thread is already executing in a **`synchronized`** method of that object. A thread also gets enqueued if the thread calls **`wait`** while operating inside the object. However, it is important to distinguish waiting threads that blocked because the monitor was busy vs. threads that explicitly called **`wait`** inside the monitor. Upon completion of a **`synchronized`** method, outside threads that blocked because the monitor was busy can proceed to enter the object. Threads that explicitly invoked **`wait`** can only proceed when notified via a call by another thread to **`notify`** or **`notifyAll`**. When it is acceptable for an enqueued thread to proceed, the scheduler selects the thread with the highest priority.

Common Programming Error 13.3

It is an error if a thread issues a **`wait`**, *a* **`notify`**, *or a* **`notifyAll`** *on an object without having acquired a lock for the object. This causes an* **`IllegalMonitorStateException`** *to be thrown.*

13.6 Producer/Consumer Relationship without Thread Synchronization

In a *producer/consumer relationship*, a *producer thread* calling a *produce* method may see that the consumer thread has not read the last message from a shared region of memory called a *buffer*, so the producer thread will call **`wait`**. When a *consumer thread* reads the message, it will call **`notify`** to allow a waiting producer to proceed. When a consumer thread enters the monitor and finds the buffer empty, it calls **`wait`**. A producer finding the buffer empty, writes to the buffer then calls **`notify`** so a waiting consumer can proceed.

Shared data can get corrupted if we do not synchronize access among multiple threads. Consider a producer/consumer relationship in which a producer thread deposits a sequence of numbers (we use 0, 1, 2, …) into a slot of shared memory. The consumer thread reads this data from the shared memory and prints the data. We print what the producer produces as it produces it and what the consumer consumes as it consumes it. Figure 13.4 demonstrates a producer and a consumer accessing a shared cell of memory without any synchronization. Because the threads are not synchronized, data can be lost if the producer places new data into the slot before the consumer consumes the previous data and data can be "doubled" if the consumer consumes data again before the producer produces the next item.

```
// Fig. 13.4: SharedCell.java
// Show multiple threads modifying shared object.

public class SharedCell {
   public static void main( String args[] )
   {
      HoldInteger h = new HoldInteger();
      ProduceInteger p = new ProduceInteger( h );
      ConsumeInteger c = new ConsumeInteger( h );

      p.start();
      c.start();
   }
}

class ProduceInteger extends Thread {
   private HoldInteger pHold;

   public ProduceInteger( HoldInteger h )
   {
      pHold = h;
   }

   public void run()
   {
      for ( int count = 0; count < 10; count++ ) {
         // sleep for a random interval
         try {
            Thread.sleep( (int) ( Math.random() * 3000 ) );
         }
         catch( InterruptedException e ) {
            System.err.println( e.toString() );
         }

         pHold.setSharedInt( count );
         System.out.println( "Producer set sharedInt to " +
                             count );
      }
```

Fig. 13.4 Threads modifying a shared object without synchronization (part 1 of 3).

```
39
40          pHold.setMoreData( false );
41       }
42    }
43
44    class ConsumeInteger extends Thread {
45       private HoldInteger cHold;
46
47       public ConsumeInteger( HoldInteger h )
48       {
49          cHold = h;
50       }
51
52       public void run()
53       {
54          int val;
55
56          while ( cHold.hasMoreData() ) {
57             // sleep for a random interval
58             try {
59                Thread.sleep( (int) ( Math.random() * 3000 ) );
60             }
61             catch( InterruptedException e ) {
62                System.err.println( e.toString() );
63             }
64
65             val = cHold.getSharedInt();
66             System.out.println( "Consumer retrieved " + val );
67          }
68       }
69    }
70
71    class HoldInteger {
72       private int sharedInt = -1;
73       private boolean moreData = true;
74
75       public void setSharedInt( int val ) { sharedInt = val; }
76
77       public int getSharedInt() { return sharedInt; }
78
79       public void setMoreData( boolean b ) { moreData = b; }
80
81       public boolean hasMoreData() { return moreData; }
82    }
```

Fig. 13.4 Threads modifying a shared object without synchronization (part 2 of 3).

The program consists of four classes—**SharedCell**, **ProduceInteger**, **ConsumeInteger** and **HoldInteger**. Class **SharedCell**'s **main** method (line 5) instantiates the shared **HoldInteger** object **h** and uses it as the argument to the constructors for the **ProduceInteger** object **p** and the **ConsumeInteger** object **c**. The object **h** contains the data that will be shared between the two threads.

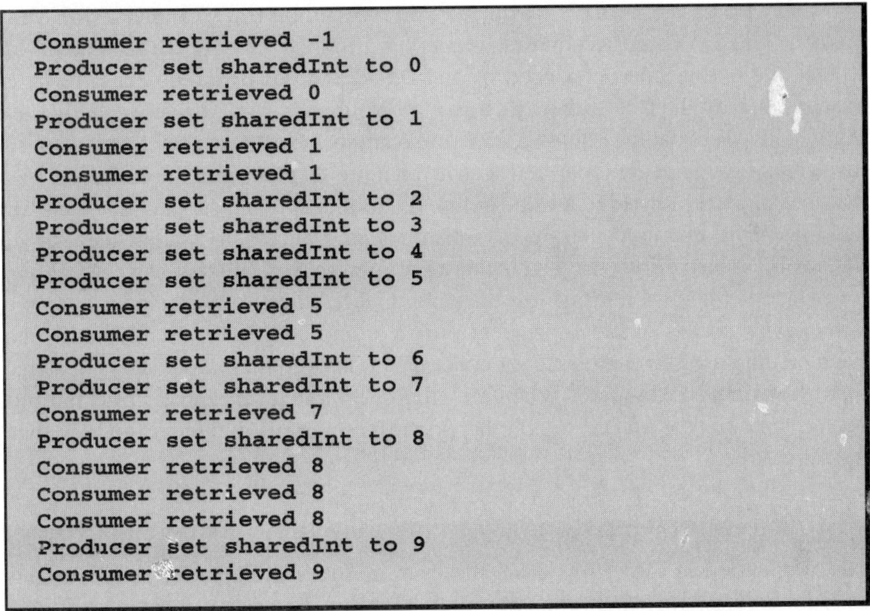

```
Consumer retrieved -1
Producer set sharedInt to 0
Consumer retrieved 0
Producer set sharedInt to 1
Consumer retrieved 1
Consumer retrieved 1
Producer set sharedInt to 2
Producer set sharedInt to 3
Producer set sharedInt to 4
Producer set sharedInt to 5
Consumer retrieved 5
Consumer retrieved 5
Producer set sharedInt to 6
Producer set sharedInt to 7
Consumer retrieved 7
Producer set sharedInt to 8
Consumer retrieved 8
Consumer retrieved 8
Consumer retrieved 8
Producer set sharedInt to 9
Consumer retrieved 9
```

Fig. 13.4 Threads modifying a shared object without synchronization (part 3 of 3).

Next, method **main** invokes the **Thread** class **start** method on the **ProduceInteger** object **p** and the **ConsumeInteger** object **c** to place them in the *ready* state. This essentially launches these threads

Class **ProduceInteger**—a subclass of **Thread**—consists of instance variable **pHold**, a constructor and a **run** method. Instance variable **pHold** is initialized in the constructor (line 21) to refer to the **HoldInteger** object **h** that was passed as an argument. Class **ProduceInteger**'s **run** method (line 24) consists of a **for** structure that loops 10 times. Each iteration of the loop first invokes method **sleep** to put the **ProduceInteger** object into the *sleeping* state for a random time interval between 0 and 3 seconds. When the thread awakens, class **HoldInteger**'s **setSharedInt** method is invoked with the value of **count** to set the shared object's instance variable **sharedInt**. Then, the value passed to **setSharedInt** is displayed with **System.out.println**. When the loop completes, the **ProduceInteger** thread invokes **HoldInteger**'s **setMoreData** method with a **false** value to indicate that it will not produce more data.

Class **ConsumeInteger**—a subclass of **Thread**—consists of instance variable **cHold**, a constructor and a **run** method. Instance variable **cHold** is initialized in the constructor (line 49) to refer to the **HoldInteger** object **h** that was passed as an argument. Class **ConsumeInteger**'s **run** method (line 52) consists of a **while** structure that executes as long as the **HoldInteger**'s **hasMoreData** method returns **true**. Each iteration of the loop invokes method **sleep** to put the **ConsumeInteger** object into the *sleeping* state for a random time interval between 0 and 3 seconds. Next, class **HoldInteger**'s **getSharedInt** method is called to get the value of the shared object's instance variable **sharedInt**. Then, the value returned by **getSharedInt** is displayed.

Class **HoldInteger**'s **setSharedInt** method (line 75) and a **getSharedInt** method (line 77) do not synchronize access to instance variable **sharedInt**. Ideally, we would like every value produced by the **ProduceInteger** object **p** to be consumed exactly once by the **ConsumeInteger** object **c**. However, when we study the output of Fig. 13.4 we see that the values 2, 3, 4, and 6 are lost (i.e., never seen by the consumer) and the values 1, 5 and 8 are incorrectly retrieved more than once by the consumer. Also, notice that the consumer retrieved a value before the producer ever assigned 0 to the **sharedInt** variable. This example clearly demonstrates that access to shared data by concurrent threads must be carefully controlled or a program may produce incorrect results.

To solve the problems of lost data and doubled data in the previous example, we will *synchronize* access of the concurrent producer and consumer threads to the shared data. Each method used by a producer or consumer to access the shared data is declared with the **synchronized** keyword. When a method declared **synchronized** is running in an object, the object is *locked* so no other **synchronized** method can run in that object at the same time.

13.7 Producer/Consumer Relationship with Thread Synchronization

The application in Fig. 13.5 demonstrates a producer and a consumer accessing a shared cell of memory with synchronization so that the consumer only consumes after the producer produces a value. Class **HoldInteger** (line 73) has been redefined for this example. It now contains three instance variables—**sharedInt**, **moreData** and **writeable**—and we have made methods **setSharedInt** and **getSharedInt** **synchronized** methods. Because **HoldInteger** now contains **synchronized** methods, objects of class **HoldInteger** are considered to be monitors. Instance variable **writeable**—known as the monitor's *condition variable*—is used by the **setSharedInt** method to determine if it can write to the shared memory location and is used by the **getSharedInt** method to determine if it can read from the shared memory location.

```
1  // Fig. 13.5: SharedCell.java
2  // Show multiple threads modifying shared object.
3  // Use synchronization to ensure that both threads
4  // access the shared cell properly.
5
6  public class SharedCell {
7     public static void main( String args[] )
8     {
9        HoldInteger h = new HoldInteger();
10       ProduceInteger p = new ProduceInteger( h );
11       ConsumeInteger c = new ConsumeInteger( h );
12
13       p.start();
14       c.start();
15    }
16 }
```

Fig. 13.5 Threads modifying a shared object with synchronization (part 1 of 4).

```

class ProduceInteger extends Thread {
   private HoldInteger pHold;

   public ProduceInteger( HoldInteger h )
   {
      pHold = h;
   }

   public void run()
   {
      for ( int count = 0; count < 10; count++ ) {
         // sleep for a random interval
         try {
            Thread.sleep( (int) ( Math.random() * 3000 ) );
         }
         catch( InterruptedException e ) {
            System.err.println( e.toString() );
         }

         pHold.setSharedInt( count );
         System.out.println( "Producer set sharedInt to " +
                             count );
      }

      pHold.setMoreData( false );
   }
}

class ConsumeInteger extends Thread {
   private HoldInteger cHold;

   public ConsumeInteger( HoldInteger h )
   {
      cHold = h;
   }

   public void run()
   {
      int val;

      while ( cHold.hasMoreData() ) {
         // sleep for a random interval
         try {
            Thread.sleep( (int) ( Math.random() * 3000 ) );
         }
         catch( InterruptedException e ) {
            System.err.println( e.toString() );
         }

```

Fig. 13.5 Threads modifying a shared object with synchronization (part 2 of 4).

```
            val = cHold.getSharedInt();
            System.out.println( "Consumer retrieved " + val );
         }
      }
}

class HoldInteger {
   private int sharedInt = -1;
   private boolean moreData = true;
   private boolean writeable = true;

   public synchronized void setSharedInt( int val )
   {
      while ( !writeable ) {
         try {
            wait();
         }
         catch ( InterruptedException e ) {
            System.err.println( "Exception: " + e.toString() );
         }
      }

      sharedInt = val;
      writeable = false;
      notify();
   }

   public synchronized int getSharedInt()
   {
      while ( writeable ) {
         try {
            wait();
         }
         catch ( InterruptedException e ) {
            System.err.println( "Exception: " + e.toString() );
         }
      }

      writeable = true;
      notify();
      return sharedInt;
   }

   public void setMoreData( boolean b ) { moreData = b; }

   public boolean hasMoreData() { return moreData; }
}
```

Fig. 13.5 Threads modifying a shared object with synchronization (part 3 of 4).

```
Producer set sharedInt to 0
Consumer retrieved 0
Producer set sharedInt to 1
Consumer retrieved 1
Producer set sharedInt to 2
Consumer retrieved 2
Producer set sharedInt to 3
Consumer retrieved 3
Producer set sharedInt to 4
Consumer retrieved 4
Producer set sharedInt to 5
Consumer retrieved 5
Producer set sharedInt to 6
Consumer retrieved 6
Producer set sharedInt to 7
Consumer retrieved 7
Producer set sharedInt to 8
Consumer retrieved 8
Producer set sharedInt to 9
Consumer retrieved 9
```

Fig. 13.5 Threads modifying a shared object with synchronization (part 4 of 4).

Instance variable **writeable** is a **boolean** used by methods **setSharedInt** and **getSharedInt** of class **HoldInteger**. If **writeable** is **true**, **setShareInt** can place a value into variable **sharedInt** because the variable currently does not contain information. However, this means **getSharedInt** currently cannot read the value of **sharedInt**. If **writeable** is **false**, **getShareInt** can read a value from variable **sharedInt** because the variable currently does contain information. However, this means **setSharedInt** currently cannot place a value into **sharedInt**.

When the **ProduceInteger** object invokes method **setSharedInt**, a lock is acquired on the **HoldInteger** object. The **while** structure at line 80 tests the **writeable** variable with the condition **!writeable**. If this condition is **true**, the **wait** method is invoked. This places the **ProduceInteger** object that called method **setSharedInt** into the *wait queue* for the **HoldInteger** object and releases the lock on it so other **synchronized** methods can be invoked on the object. The **ProduceInteger** object remains in the *wait queue* until it is *notified* that it may proceed—at which point it enters the *ready* state and waits for a processor to be assigned to it. When the **ProduceInteger** object reenters the *running* state, the lock on the **HoldInteger** object is reacquired implicitly and the **setSharedInt** method continues executing in the **while** structure with the next statement after **wait**. There are no more statements, so the **while** condition is tested again. If the condition is **false**, **sharedInt** is assigned **val** (the argument passed to **setSharedInt**), **writeable** is set to **false** to indicate that the shared memory is now full and method **notify** is invoked. If there are any *waiting* threads, the first thread in the *wait queue* is placed into the *ready* state indicating that the thread can now attempt its task again (as soon as it is assigned a processor). The **notify** method returns immediately and method **setSharedInt** returns to its caller.

Methods **getSharedInt** and **setSharedInt** are implemented similarly. When the **ConsumeInteger** object invokes method **getSharedInt**, a lock is acquired on the **HoldInteger** object. The **while** structure at line 96 tests the **writeable** variable. If **writeable** is **true** (i.e., there is nothing to consume), the **wait** method is invoked. This places the **ConsumeInteger** object that called method **getSharedInt** into the *wait queue* for the **HoldInteger** object and releases the lock on it so other **synchronized** methods can be invoked on the object. The **ConsumeInteger** object remains in the *wait queue* until it is *notified* that it may proceed—at which point it enters the *ready* state and waits for a processor to be assigned to it. When the **ConsumeInteger** object reenters the *running* state, the lock on the **HoldInteger** object is reacquired and the **setSharedInt** method continues executing in the **while** structure with the next statement after **wait**. There are no more statements, so the **while** condition is tested again. If the condition is **false**, **writeable** is set to **true** to indicate that the shared memory is now empty and method **notify** is invoked. If there are any *waiting* threads, the first thread in the *wait queue* is placed into the *ready* state indicating that the thread can now attempt its task again (as soon as it is assigned a processor). The **notify** method returns immediately and the value of **sharedInt** is returned to its caller.

When we study the output in Fig. 13.5, we observe that every integer produced is consumed once—no values are lost and no values are doubled. Also, the consumer cannot read a value until the producer produces a value.

13.8 Producer/Consumer Relationship: The Circular Buffer

The program of Fig. 13.5 does access the shared data correctly, but it may not perform optimally. Because the threads are running asynchronously, we cannot predict their relative speeds. If the producer wants to produce faster than the consumer can consume, it cannot do so. To enable the producer to continue producing we can use a *circular buffer* which has enough extra cells to handle the "extra" production. The program of Fig. 13.6 demonstrates a producer and a consumer accessing a circular buffer (in this case, a shared array of 5 cells) with synchronization so that the consumer only consumes a value when there are one or more values in the array and the producer only produces a value when there are one or more available cells in the array. This program is implemented as an applet that sends its output to a **TextArea**. Class **SharedCell**'s **start** method creates the **HoldInteger**, **ProduceInteger** and **ConsumeInteger** objects. The **HoldInteger** object **h** is passed a **TextArea** object in which the program's output will be displayed.

```
// Fig. 13.6: SharedCell.java
// Show multiple threads modifying shared object.
// Use synchronization to ensure that both threads
// access the shared cell properly.
import java.applet.Applet;
import java.awt.*;
import java.text.DecimalFormat;
```

Fig. 13.6 Threads modifying a shared array of cells (part 1 of 6).

```

public class SharedCell extends Applet {
   private TextArea output;

   public void init()
   {
      setLayout( new BorderLayout() );
      output = new TextArea();
      add( output, BorderLayout.CENTER );
   }

   public void start()
   {
      HoldInteger h = new HoldInteger( output );
      ProduceInteger p = new ProduceInteger( h );
      ConsumeInteger c = new ConsumeInteger( h );

      p.start();
      c.start();
   }
}

class ProduceInteger extends Thread {
   private HoldInteger pHold;

   public ProduceInteger( HoldInteger h )
   {
      pHold = h;
   }

   public void run()
   {
      for ( int count = 0; count < 10; count++ ) {
         // sleep for a random interval
         try {
            Thread.sleep( (int) ( Math.random() * 500 ) );
         }
         catch( InterruptedException e ) {
            System.err.println( e.toString() );
         }

         pHold.setSharedInt( count );
         System.out.println( "Produced set sharedInt to " +
                             count );
      }

      pHold.setMoreData( false );
   }
}

```

Fig. 13.6 Threads modifying a shared array of cells (part 2 of 6).

```
class ConsumeInteger extends Thread {
   private HoldInteger cHold;

   public ConsumeInteger( HoldInteger h )
   {
      cHold = h;
   }

   public void run()
   {
      int val;

      while ( cHold.hasMoreData() ) {
         // sleep for a random interval
         try {
            Thread.sleep( (int) ( Math.random() * 3000 ) );
         }
         catch( InterruptedException e ) {
            System.err.println( e.toString() );
         }

         val = cHold.getSharedInt();
         System.out.println( "Consumer retrieved " + val );
      }
   }
}

class HoldInteger {
   private int sharedInt[] = { -1, -1, -1, -1, -1 };
   private boolean moreData = true;
   private boolean writeable = true;
   private boolean readable = false;
   private int readLoc = 0, writeLoc = 0;
   private TextArea output;

   public HoldInteger( TextArea out )
   {
      output = out;
   }

   public synchronized void setSharedInt( int val )
   {
      while ( !writeable ) {
         try {
            output.append( " WAITING TO PRODUCE " + val );
            wait();
         }
         catch ( InterruptedException e ) {
            System.err.println( e.toString() );
         }
      }
```

Fig. 13.6 Threads modifying a shared array of cells (part 3 of 6).

```java

      sharedInt[ writeLoc ] = val;
      readable = true;

      output.append( "\nProduced " + val +
                     " into cell " + writeLoc );

      writeLoc = ( writeLoc + 1 ) % 5;

      output.append( "\twrite " + writeLoc +
                     "\tread " + readLoc );
      printBuffer( output, sharedInt );

      if ( writeLoc == readLoc ) {
         writeable = false;
         output.append( "\nBUFFER FULL" );
      }

      notify();
   }

   public synchronized int getSharedInt()
   {
      int val;

      while ( !readable ) {
         try {
            output.append( " WAITING TO CONSUME" );
            wait();
         }
         catch ( InterruptedException e ) {
            System.err.println( e.toString() );
         }
      }

      writeable = true;
      val = sharedInt[ readLoc ];

      output.append( "\nConsumed " + val +
                     " from cell " + readLoc );

      readLoc = ( readLoc + 1 ) % 5;

      output.append( "\twrite " + writeLoc +
                     "\tread " + readLoc );
      printBuffer( output, sharedInt );

      if ( readLoc == writeLoc ) {
         readable = false;
         output.append( "\nBUFFER EMPTY" );
      }
```

Fig. 13.6 Threads modifying a shared array of cells (part 4 of 6).

```
160
161          notify();
162          return val;
163       }
164
165       public void printBuffer( TextArea out, int buf[] )
166       {
167          DecimalFormat threeChars = new DecimalFormat( " #;-#" );
168          output.append( "\tbuffer: " );
169
170          for ( int i = 0; i < buf.length; i++ )
171             out.append( " " + threeChars.format( buf[ i ] ) );
172       }
173
174       public void setMoreData( boolean b ) { moreData = b; }
175
176       public boolean hasMoreData()
177       {
178          if ( moreData == false && readLoc == writeLoc )
179             return false;
180          else
181             return true;
182       }
183    }
```

Fig. 13.6 Threads modifying a shared array of cells (part 5 of 6).

Once again, the main changes in this example are to the definition of class **HoldInteger**. The class now contains seven instance variables—**sharedInt** is a 5-element integer array that is used as the circular buffer, **moreData** indicates if there is more data to consume from the circular buffer, **writeable** indicates if a producer can write into the circular buffer, **readable** indicates if a consumer can read from the circular buffer, **readLoc** indicates the current position from which the next value can be read by a consumer, **writeLoc** indicates the next location in which a value can be placed by a producer and **output** is the **TextArea** used for displaying output.

Method **setSharedInt** performs the same tasks as it did in Fig. 13.5 with a few modifications. When execution continues at line 110 after the **while** loop, the produced value is placed into the circular buffer at location **writeLoc**. Next, **readable** is set to **true** because there is at least one value in the buffer to be read. The value produced and the cell where the value was placed are appended to the **TextArea** with method **append**. Then, **writeLoc** is updated for the next call to **setSharedInt**. The output is continued with the current **writeLoc** and **readLoc** values and the values in the circular buffer. If the **writeLoc** is equal to the **readLoc**, the circular buffer is currently full, so **writeable** is set to **false** and the string **BUFFER FULL** is displayed. Finally, method **notify** is invoked to place the next waiting thread into the ready state.

Method **getSharedInt** also performs the same tasks in this example as it did in Fig. 13.5 with a few minor modifications. When execution continues at line 144 after the **while** loop, **writeable** is set to **true** because there is at least one open position in the

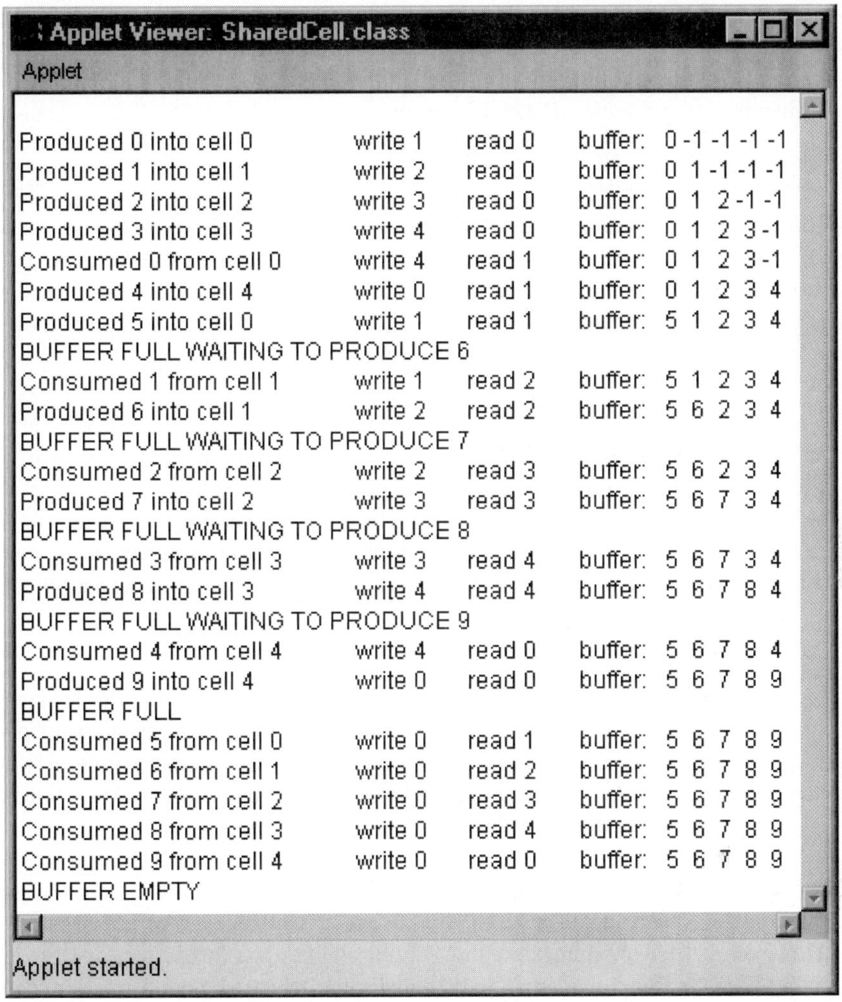

```
Applet Viewer: SharedCell.class
Applet

Produced 0 into cell 0      write 1   read 0   buffer:  0 -1 -1 -1 -1
Produced 1 into cell 1      write 2   read 0   buffer:  0  1 -1 -1 -1
Produced 2 into cell 2      write 3   read 0   buffer:  0  1  2 -1 -1
Produced 3 into cell 3      write 4   read 0   buffer:  0  1  2  3 -1
Consumed 0 from cell 0      write 4   read 1   buffer:  0  1  2  3 -1
Produced 4 into cell 4      write 0   read 1   buffer:  0  1  2  3  4
Produced 5 into cell 0      write 1   read 1   buffer:  5  1  2  3  4
BUFFER FULL WAITING TO PRODUCE 6
Consumed 1 from cell 1      write 1   read 2   buffer:  5  1  2  3  4
Produced 6 into cell 1      write 2   read 2   buffer:  5  6  2  3  4
BUFFER FULL WAITING TO PRODUCE 7
Consumed 2 from cell 2      write 2   read 3   buffer:  5  6  2  3  4
Produced 7 into cell 2      write 3   read 3   buffer:  5  6  7  3  4
BUFFER FULL WAITING TO PRODUCE 8
Consumed 3 from cell 3      write 3   read 4   buffer:  5  6  7  3  4
Produced 8 into cell 3      write 4   read 4   buffer:  5  6  7  8  4
BUFFER FULL WAITING TO PRODUCE 9
Consumed 4 from cell 4      write 4   read 0   buffer:  5  6  7  8  4
Produced 9 into cell 4      write 0   read 0   buffer:  5  6  7  8  9
BUFFER FULL
Consumed 5 from cell 0      write 0   read 1   buffer:  5  6  7  8  9
Consumed 6 from cell 1      write 0   read 2   buffer:  5  6  7  8  9
Consumed 7 from cell 2      write 0   read 3   buffer:  5  6  7  8  9
Consumed 8 from cell 3      write 0   read 4   buffer:  5  6  7  8  9
Consumed 9 from cell 4      write 0   read 0   buffer:  5  6  7  8  9
BUFFER EMPTY

Applet started.
```

Fig. 13.6 Threads modifying a shared array of cells (part 6 of 6).

buffer in which a value can be placed. Next, **`val`** is assigned the value at location **`readLoc`** in the circular buffer. The value consumed and the cell from which the value was read are appended to the **`TextArea`** with method **`append`**. Then, **`readLoc`** is updated for the next call to method **`getSharedInt`**. The output line in the **`TextArea`** is continued with the current **`writeLoc`** and **`readLoc`** values and the current values in the circular buffer. If the **`readLoc`** is equal to the **`writeLoc`**, the circular buffer is currently empty, so **`readable`** is set to **`false`** and the string **`BUFFER EMPTY`** is displayed. Finally, method **`notify`** is invoked to place the next waiting thread into the *ready* state.

In the program of Fig. 13.6, the outputs have been augmented to include the current **`writeLoc`** and **`readLoc`** values. Also, the current contents of the buffer **`sharedInt`** are displayed. The elements of the **sharedInt** array were initialized to –1 for output purposes so you can see each value inserted into the buffer. Notice that after the fifth value is placed in the fifth element of the buffer, the sixth value is inserted at the beginning of the array—thus providing the *circular buffer* effect.

13.9 Daemon Threads

A *daemon thread* is a thread that runs for the benefit of other threads. Daemon threads run in the background (i.e., when processor time is available that would otherwise go to waste). Unlike conventional user threads, daemon threads do not prevent a program from terminating. The garbage collector is a daemon thread. Non-daemon threads are conventional user threads. We designate a thread as a daemon with the method call

```
setDaemon( true );
```

An argument of **false** means that the thread is not a daemon thread. A program can include a mixture of daemon threads and non-daemon threads. When only daemon threads remain in a program, Java exits. If a thread is to be a daemon, it must be set as such before its **start** method is called or an **IllegalThreadStateException** will be thrown. Method **isDaemon** returns **true** if a thread is a daemon thread and **false** otherwise.

13.10 Runnable Interface

C++ supports multiple inheritance in which a subclass can inherit from multiple superclasses. Multiple inheritance is a powerful capability but it is complex to use and suffers from ambiguity and performance problems. Java does not support multiple inheritance. This choice is consistent with Java's omission of a number of other complex C++ topics. Java does, however, support the notion of *interfaces,* a simpler scheme that delivers some of the key advantages of multiple inheritance.

Until now we have been extending class **Thread** to create new classes that support multithreading. We overrode the **run** method to specify the tasks to be performed concurrently. However, if we want multithreading supported in a class that is already derived from a class other than **Thread**, we must **implement** the ***Runnable*** *interface* in that class. Class **Thread** itself implements the **Runnable** interface as expressed in the class header

```
public class Thread extends Object implements Runnable
```

Implementing the **Runnable** interface gives us the ability to treat our new class as a **Runnable** object (just like inheriting from a class allows us to treat our subclass as an object of its superclass). As with deriving from the **Thread** class, the code that controls the thread is placed in the **run** method.

We create a thread with the new class by passing to the **Thread** class constructor

```
public Thread( Runnable runnableObject )
```

a reference to an object of the class that implements the **Runnable** interface. The **Thread** constructor registers the **run** method of the **runnableObject** as the method to be invoked when the thread begins execution.

The constructor

```
public Thread( Runnable runnableObject, String threadName )
```

constructs a **Thread** with the name **threadName** and registers method **run** of its argument **runnableObject** as the method to be invoked when the thread begins execution.

Figure 13.7 demonstrates an applet that implements the **Runnable** interface. The applet class **RandomCharacters** displays three **TextField**s and three buttons. A separate thread of execution is associated with each **TextField** and button pair. The applet also defines the **String alphabet** that contains the letters from A to Z. This string is shared among the three threads. The applet's **start** method (line 38) instantiates three **Thread** objects and initializes each with **this**—i.e., the applet object—then invokes the **Thread** class **start** method on each **Thread** placing the threads in the *ready* state.

```
1  // Fig. 13.7: RandomCharacters.java
2  // Demonstrating the Runnableinterface
3  import java.applet.Applet;
4  import java.awt.*;
5  import java.awt.event.*;
6
7  public class RandomCharacters extends Applet
8               implements Runnable, ActionListener {
9
10    private String alphabet;
11    private TextField output1, output2, output3;
12    private Button button1, button2, button3;
13
14    private Thread thread1, thread2, thread3;
15    private boolean suspend1, suspend2, suspend3;
16
17    public void init()
18    {
19       alphabet = new String( "ABCDEFGHIJKLMNOPQRSTUVWXYZ" );
20       output1 = new TextField( 10 );
21       output1.setEditable( false );
22       output2 = new TextField( 10 );
23       output2.setEditable( false );
24       output3 = new TextField( 10 );
25       output3.setEditable( false );
26       button1 = new Button( "Suspend/Resume 1" );
27       button1.addActionListener( this );
28       button2 = new Button( "Suspend/Resume 2" );
29       button2.addActionListener( this );
30       button3 = new Button( "Suspend/Resume 3" );
31       button3.addActionListener( this );
32
33       add( output1 );
34       add( button1 );
```

Fig. 13.7 Demonstrating the **Runnable** interface (part 1 of 4).

```
      add( output2 );
      add( button2 );
      add( output3 );
      add( button3 );
   }

   public void start()
   {
      // create threads and start every time start is called
      thread1 = new Thread( this, "Thread 1" );
      thread2 = new Thread( this, "Thread 2" );
      thread3 = new Thread( this, "Thread 3" );

      thread1.start();
      thread2.start();
      thread3.start();
   }

   public void stop()
   {
      // stop threads every time stop is called
      // as the user browses another Web page
      thread1.stop();
      thread2.stop();
      thread3.stop();
   }

   public void actionPerformed( ActionEvent e )
   {
      if ( e.getSource() == button1 )
         if ( suspend1 ) {
            thread1.resume();
            suspend1 = false;
         }
         else {
            thread1.suspend();
            output1.setText( "suspended" );
            suspend1 = true;
         }
      else if ( e.getSource() == button2 )
         if ( suspend2 ) {
            thread2.resume();
            suspend2 = false;
         }
         else {
            thread2.suspend();
            output2.setText( "suspended" );
            suspend2 = true;
         }
```

Fig. 13.7 Demonstrating the **`Runnable`** interface (part 2 of 4).

```
84         else if ( e.getSource() == button3 )
85            if ( suspend3 ) {
86               thread3.resume();
87               suspend3 = false;
88            }
89            else {
90               thread3.suspend();
91               output3.setText( "suspended" );
92               suspend3 = true;
93            }
94      }
95
96      public void run()
97      {
98         int location;
99         char display;
100        Thread executingThread;
101
102        while ( true ) {
103           // sleep from 0 to 5 seconds
104           try {
105              Thread.sleep( (int) ( Math.random() * 3000 ) );
106           }
107           catch ( InterruptedException e ) {
108              e.printStackTrace();
109           }
110
111           location = (int) ( Math.random() * 26 );
112           display = alphabet.charAt( location );
113
114           executingThread = Thread.currentThread();
115
116           if ( executingThread == thread1 )
117              output1.setText( "Thread 1: " + display );
118           else if ( executingThread == thread2 )
119              output2.setText( "Thread 2: " + display );
120           else if ( executingThread == thread3 )
121              output3.setText( "Thread 3: " + display );
122        }
123     }
124 }
```

Fig. 13.7 Demonstrating the **Runnable** interface (part 3 of 4).

The **run** method (line 96) contains an infinite loop. In each iteration of the loop, the thread sleeps for a random interval from 0 to 3 seconds. Next, a random character is chosen from the **alphabet** string. The statement

```
executingThread = Thread.currentThread();
```

uses the **Thread.currentThread** method to determine the currently executing **Thread** object. The thread returned from **currentThread** is used in the nested **if/else** structure to pick the **TextField** in which the character is displayed.

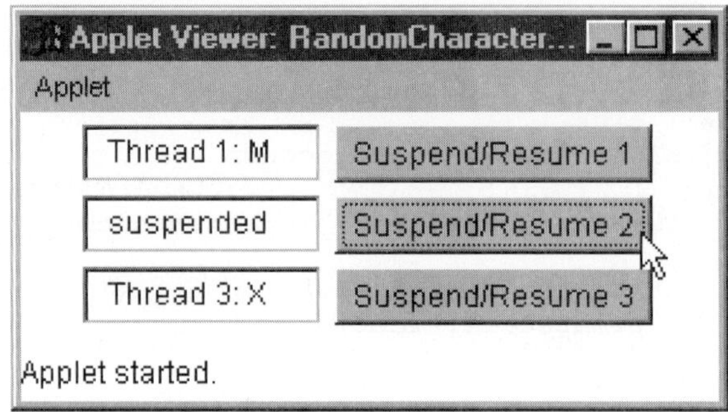

Fig. 13.7 Demonstrating the **Runnable** interface (part 4 of 4).

If the user clicks the **Suspend/Resume** button next to a particular **TextField**, the **actionPerformed** method (line 62) is invoked. The **actionPerformed** method determines which button received the event, then determines if the corresponding thread is currently suspended by testing one of the **boolean** variables **suspend1**, **suspend2** or **suspend3** (one for each thread). If the appropriate **boolean** variable is **true**, the thread's **resume** method is invoked and the **boolean** variable is set to **false**. Otherwise, the thread's **suspend** method is invoked, the string "**suspended**" is displayed in the **TextField** for the thread and the **boolean** variable is set to **true**.

The applet's **stop** method is provided to stop all three threads' execution if the user leaves the Web page on which this applet resides. If the user returns to the Web page, the three threads will be instantiated again because the applet's **start** method is invoked when the Web page is revisited.

Performance Tip 13.7

Stopping applet threads when leaving a Web page is a polite programming practice because it prevents your applet from using processor time (which can reduce performance) on the browser's machine when the applet is not being viewed. The threads can be restarted from the applet's **start** *method which is automatically invoked when the Web page is revisited by the user.*

13.11 Thread Groups

It is sometimes useful to identify various threads as belonging to a *thread group,* class **ThreadGroup** contains the methods for creating and manipulating thread groups. At constructor time the group is given a unique name via a **String** argument.

The threads in a thread group can be dealt with as a group. It may, for example, be desirable to **suspend** all the threads in a group, **resume** all the threads in a group, or even kill all the threads in a group. A thread group can be the *parent thread group* to a *child thread group.* Method calls sent to a parent thread group are also sent to all the threads in that parent's child thread groups.

Class **ThreadGroup** provides two constructors. The constructor

```
public ThreadGroup( String stringName )
```

constructs a **ThreadGroup** with name **stringName**. The constructor

```
public ThreadGroup( ThreadGroup parentThreadGroup,
                    String stringName )
```

constructs a child **ThreadGroup** of **parentThreadGroup** called **stringName**.

Class **Thread** provides three constructors that enable the programmer to instantiate a **Thread** and associate it with a **ThreadGroup**. The constructor

```
public Thread( ThreadGroup threadGroup, String stringName )
```

constructs a **Thread** that belongs to **threadGroup** and has the name **stringName**. This constructor is normally invoked for derived classes of **Thread** whose objects should be associated with a **ThreadGroup**.

The constructor

```
public Thread( ThreadGroup threadGroup,
               Runnable runnableObject )
```

constructs a **Thread** that belongs to **threadGroup** and that invokes the **run** method of **runnableObject** when the thread is assigned a processor to begin execution.

The constructor

```
public Thread( ThreadGroup threadGroup,
               Runnable runnableObject,
               String stringName )
```

constructs a **Thread** that belongs to **threadGroup** and that invokes the **run** method of **runnableObject** when the thread is assigned a processor to begin execution. The name of this **Thread** is indicated by **stringName**.

Class **ThreadGroup** contains many methods for processing groups of threads. Some of these methods are summarized here. For more information on these methods, see the Java API documentation.

1. Method **activeCount** reports the number of active threads in a thread group plus the number of active threads in all its child thread groups.

2. Method **enumerate** has four versions. Two versions copy into an array of **Thread** references the active threads in the **ThreadGroup** (one of these also allows you to recursively get copies of all the active threads in child **ThreadGroup**). Two versions copy into an array of **ThreadGroup** references the active child thread groups in the **ThreadGroup** (one of these also allows you to recursively get copies of all the active thread groups in all the child **ThreadGroups**).
3. Method **getMaxPriority** returns the maximum priority of a **ThreadGroup**. Method **setMaxPriority** sets a new maximum priority for a **ThreadGroup**.
4. Method **getName** returns as a **String** the **ThreadGroup**'s name.
5. Method **getParent** determines the parent of a thread group.
6. Method **parentOf** returns **true** if the **ThreadGroup** to which the message is sent is the parent of, or the same as, the **ThreadGroup** supplied as an argument and returns **false** otherwise.
7. Method **stop** stops every **Thread** in the **ThreadGroup** and in every subgroup of that **ThreadGroup**.
8. Method **suspend** suspends every **Thread** in the **ThreadGroup** and in every subgroup of that **ThreadGroup**.
9. Method **resume** resumes every **Thread** in the **ThreadGroup** and in every subgroup.
10. Method **destroy** destroys a **ThreadGroup** and its child **ThreadGroups**.

Testing and Debugging Tip 13.5

*Method **list** lists the **ThreadGroup**. This can help in debugging.*

Summary

- Computers perform operations concurrently such as compiling a program, printing a file, and receiving electronic mail messages over a network.
- Programming languages generally provide only a simple set of control structures that enable programmers to perform one action at a time and then proceed to the next action after the previous one is finished.
- The concurrency that computers perform today is normally implemented as operating systems "primitives" available only to highly experienced "systems programmers."
- Java makes concurrency primitives available to the programmer.
- Applications contain *threads of execution,* each thread designating a portion of a program that may execute concurrently with other threads. This capability is called multithreading.
- Java provides a low-priority *garbage collector thread* that automatically reclaims dynamically allocated memory that is no longer needed. The garbage collector runs when

processor time is available and there are no higher-priority runnable threads. The garbage collector runs immediately when the system is out of memory to try to reclaim memory.

- Method **run** contains the code that controls a thread's execution.
- A program launches a thread's execution by calling the thread's **start** method which, in turn, calls the **run** method.
- Method **interrupt** is called to interrupt a thread. The **interrupted** method returns **true** if the current thread has been interrupted and **false** otherwise. Method **isInterrupted** determines if a thread has been interrupted.
- Method **stop** stops a thread by throwing a **ThreadDeath** object into it; **ThreadDeath** is a subclass of **Error**.
- Method **isAlive** returns **true** if **start** has been called for a given thread and the thread is not dead (i.e., its stop method has not been called and its controlling run method has not completed execution).
- Method **setName** sets the name of the **Thread**. Method **getName** returns the name of the **Thread**. Method **toString** returns a **String** consisting of the name of the thread, the priority of the thread and the thread's group.
- Method **currentThread** returns a reference to the current **Thread**.
- Method **join** waits for the **Thread** to which the message is sent to die before the current **Thread** can proceed.
- Waiting can be dangerous; it can lead to two serious problems called *deadlock* and *indefinite postponement; indefinite postponement is also called starvation.*
- A thread that was just created is in the born state. The thread remains in this state until the thread's **start** method is called; this causes the thread to enter the ready state.
- A highest-priority ready thread enters the *running state* when the system assigns a processor to the thread.
- A thread enters the dead state when its **run** method completes, or when its method **stop** is called; a dead thread will eventually be disposed of by the system.
- A *running* thread enters the *blocked state* when the thread issues an input/output request. A *blocked* thread becomes *ready* when the I/O it is waiting for completes. A *blocked* thread cannot use a processor even if one is available.
- When a *running* thread's **sleep** method is called, that thread enters the *sleeping* state. A *sleeping* thread becomes *ready* after the designated sleep time expires. A *sleeping* thread cannot use a processor even if one is available.
- When a running thread's **suspend** method is called, that thread enters the *suspended* state. A suspended thread becomes ready when its **resume** method is called by another thread. A suspended thread cannot use a processor even if one is available.
- When a *running* method calls **wait** the thread enters a *waiting* state where it waits in a queue associated with the particular object in which the thread was *running*. The first

thread in the *wait* queue for a particular object becomes *ready* on a call to **notify** issued by another thread associated with that object.

- Every thread in the *wait* queue for a given object becomes ready on a call to **notifyAll** by another thread associated with that object.
- Every Java thread has a priority in the range **Thread.MIN_PRIORITY** (a constant of 1) and **Thread.MAX_PRIORITY** (a constant of 10). By default, each thread is given priority **Thread.NORM_PRIORITY** (a constant of 5).
- Some Java platforms support a concept called timeslicing and some do not. Without timeslicing, threads of equal priority run to completion before their peers get a chance to execute. With timeslicing, each thread receives a brief burst of processor time called a quantum during which that thread can execute. At the completion of the quantum, even if that thread has not finished executing, the processor is taken away from that thread and given to the next thread of equal priority if one is available.
- The job of the Java *scheduler* is to keep a highest-priority thread running at all times, and if timeslicing is available, to ensure that several equally high-priority threads each execute for a *quantum* in *round-robin* fashion.
- A thread's priority can be adjusted with the **setPriority** method. Method **getPriority** returns the thread's priority.
- A thread can call the **yield** method to give other threads a chance to execute.
- Every object that has **synchronized** methods has a monitor. The monitor lets only one thread at a time execute a **synchronized** method on the object.
- A thread executing in a **synchronized** method may determine that it cannot proceed, so the thread voluntarily calls **wait**. This removes the thread from contention for the processor and from contention for the object.
- A thread that has called **wait** is awakened by a thread that calls **notify**. The **notify** acts as a signal to the waiting thread that the condition the waiting thread has been waiting for is now satisfied, so it is acceptable for that thread to reenter the monitor.
- A *daemon thread* serves other threads. When only daemon threads remain in a program, Java will exit. If a thread is to be a daemon, it must be set as such before its **start** method is called.
- To support multithreading in a class derived from some class other than **Thread**, **implement** the **Runnable** interface in that class.
- Implementing the **Runnable** interface gives us the ability to treat the new class as a **Runnable** object (just like inheriting from a class allows us to treat our subclass as an object of its superclass). As with deriving from the **Thread** class, the code that controls the thread is placed in the **run** method.
- A thread with a **Runnable** class is created by passing to the **Thread** class constructor a reference to an object of the class that implements the **Runnable** interface. The **Thread** constructor registers the **run** method of the **runnableObject** as the method to be invoked when the thread begins execution.

- Class **ThreadGroup** contains the methods for creating and manipulating groups of related threads in a program.

Terminology

asynchronous threads
blocked on I/O
blocked (state of a thread)
busy wait
child thread group
circular buffer
concurrency
concurrent execution of threads
condition variable
consumer
consumer thread
context
countStackFrames method
currentThread method
daemon thread
dead (state of a thread)
death of a thread
deadlock
destroy method
dumpStack method
Error class **ThreadDeath** is a subclass
execution context
fixed-priority scheduling
garbage collection by a low-priority thread
getName method
getParent method of **ThreadGroup** class
getThreadGroup()
highest-priority runnable thread
IllegalArgumentException
IllegalMonitorStateException
IllegalThreadStateException
indefinite postponement
inherit thread priority
init method
InterruptedException
InterruptedException class
interrupt method
InterruptedException class
interrupted method
interthread communication
I/O completion
isAlive method
isDaemon method
isInterrupted method
join method
kill a thread
MAX_PRIORITY(10)
memory leak
MIN_PRIORITY(1)
monitor
multiple inheritance
multiprocessing
multithreaded program
multithreaded server
multithreading
new (state of a thread)
non-preemptive scheduling
NORM_PRIORITY(5)
notify method
notifyAll method
parallelism
parent thread group
parent thread
preemptive scheduling
printStackTrace method
priority of a thread
producer/consumer relationship
producer thread
programmer-defined thread
quantum
queue in a monitor
race condition
resume method
resume method of **ThreadGroup** class
ring buffer
round-robin scheduling
run method
runnable state (of a thread)
Runnable interface (in **java.lang** package)
running (thread state)
scheduler
scheduling a thread
SecurityException
set a thread to **null**
setDaemon method
setName method

setPriority method
shared objects
single-threaded language
single-threaded program
sleep method of **Thread** class
sleeping state (of a thread)
start method
starvation
stop method of **ThreadGroup** class
suspend method of **threadGroup** class
synchronization
synchronized method
thread
Thread class (in **java.lang** package)
ThreadDeath exception
thread group
ThreadGroup class
Thread.MAX_PRIORITY
Thread.MIN_PRIORITY
Thread.NORM_PRIORITY
thread priority
thread safe
Thread.sleep()
thread states
thread synchronization
timeslicing
wait method
yield method

Common Programming Errors

13.1 **ThreadDeath** is an **Error**, not an **Exception**. Ordinarily, user programs should not catch **Error** objects. If you choose to catch a **ThreadDeath** object, be sure to rethrow it or the thread may not die "properly."

13.2 Threads waiting for a monitor object must eventually be awakened explicitly with a **notify** or the thread will wait forever. This is a simple example of deadlock.

13.3 It is an error if a thread issues a **wait**, a **notify**, or a **notifyAll** on an object without having acquired a lock for the object. This causes an **IllegalMonitorStateException** to be thrown.

Performance Tips

13.1 Java's garbage collection is not as efficient as the dynamic memory management code the best C and C++ programmers write, but it is relatively efficient and much safer for the programmer.

13.2 Setting an object reference to **null** marks that object for eventual garbage collection (if there are no other references to the object). This can help conserve memory in a system in which an automatic object is not going out of scope because the method it is in will execute for a lengthy period.

13.3 One problem with single-threaded applications is that possibly lengthy activities must complete before other activities can begin. Users feel they already spend too much time waiting with Internet and World Wide Web applications, so multithreading is immediately appealing.

13.4 One way to delay a thread is to loop some appropriate number of times doing nothing in the body of the loop. This is called a busy wait and leads to poor performance; while the processor is busy doing nothing for this thread, other runnable threads may be kept waiting. A better technique is to call the thread's **sleep** method. A sleeping thread does not use the processor.

13.5 On non-timesliced systems, cooperating threads of equal priority should periodically call **yield** to enable their peers to proceed smoothly.

13.6 Synchronization to achieve correctness in multithreaded programs can make programs run slower as threads wait. There is not much to say, however, for highly efficient, incorrect multithreaded programs!

13.7 Stopping applet threads when leaving a Web page is a polite programming practice because it prevents your applet from using processor time (which can reduce performance) on the browser's machine when the applet is not being viewed. The threads can be restarted from the applet's **`start`** method which is automatically invoked when the Web page is revisited by the user.

Portability Tips

13.1 Java multithreading is platform dependent. Thus, a multithreaded application could behave differently on different Java implementations.

13.2 Applets should be programmed to work on all Java platforms to realize Java's goal of true portability.

Software Engineering Observation

13.1 Unlike many languages that do not have built-in multithreading (such as C and C++) and must therefore make calls to operating system multithreading primitives, Java includes multithreading primitives as a part of the language itself (actually in classes ***`Thread`***, ***`ThreadGroup`*** and ***`ThreadDeath`*** of the ***`java.lang`*** package). This encourages the use of multithreading among a larger part of the applications programming community.

Testing and Debugging Tips

13.1 In C and C++, programmers must explicitly provide statements for reclaiming dynamically allocated memory. When memory is not reclaimed (because a programmer forgets to do so, or because of a logic error or because an exception diverts program control), this results in an all-to-common error called a memory leak that can eventually exhaust the supply of free memory and may cause program termination. Java's automatic garbage collection eliminates the vast majority of memory leaks, i.e., those that are due to orphaned (unreferenced) objects.

13.2 Methods **`dumpStack`** and **`countStackFrames`** are useful for debugging multithreaded applications. A program calls static method **`dumpStack`** (with the call **`Thread.dumpStack`**) to print a method-call stack trace for the current **`Thread`**. A program calls non-**`static`** method **`countStackFrames`** to determine the number of method call stack frames in a suspended **`Thread`**.

13.3 Be sure that every call to **`wait`** has a corresponding call to **`notify`** that will eventually end the waiting or use **`notifyAll`** as a safeguard.

13.4 The locking that occurs with the execution of ***`synchronized`*** methods could lead to deadlock if the locks are never released. When exceptions occur, Java's exception mechanism coordinates with Java's synchronization mechanism to release appropriate synchronization locks to avoid these kinds of deadlocks.

13.5 Method **`list`** lists the **`ThreadGroup`**. This can help in debugging.

Self-Review Exercises

13.1 Fill in the blanks in each of the following:

a) C and C++ are __________-threaded languages whereas Java is a __________-threaded language.
b) Java provides a __________ thread that automatically reclaims dynamically allocated memory.
c) Java eliminates most __________ errors that occur commonly in languages like C and C++ when dynamically allocated memory is not explicitly reclaimed by the program.
d) The __________ method is used to terminate a **`Thread`**'s execution.
e) Four reasons a thread could be not runnable (i.e., blocked) are __________, __________, __________, and __________.
f) Two reasons a thread could enter the dead state are __________ and __________.
g) A thread's priority can be changed with the __________ method.
h) A thread may give up the processor to a thread of the same priority by calling the __________ method.
i) To wait for a designated number of milliseconds and then resume execution, a thread should call the __________ method.
j) A __________ thread may be made active again by calling the **`resume`** method.
k) The __________ method places the first thread in the object's wait queue into the ready state.

13.2 State whether each of the following is **`true`** or **`false`**. For those that are **`false`**, state why.

a) A thread is not runnable if it is dead.
b) In Java, a higher-priority runnable thread will preempt threads of lower priority.
c) The Windows and Windows NT Java systems use timeslicing. Therefore they can enable threads to preempt threads of the same priority.
d) Threads may **`yield`** to threads of lower priority.

Answers to Self-Review Exercises

13.1 a) single, multi. b) garbage collector. c) memory leak. d) **`stop`**. e) waiting, sleeping, suspended, blocked for I/O. f) its **`run`** method terminates, **`stop`** is called on the thread. g) **`setPriority`**. h) **`yield`**. i) **`sleep`**. j) suspended. k) **`notify`**.

13.2 a) True
b) True.
c) False. Timeslicing allows a thread to execute until its time slice (or quantum) expires. Then other threads of equal priority can execute.
d) False. Threads can only yield to threads of equal priority.

Exercises

13.3 State whether each of the following is **`true`** or **`false`**. For those that are **`false`**, state why.

a) The **`sleep`** method does not consume processor time while a thread sleeps.
b) Declaring a method **`synchronized`** guarantees that deadlock cannot occur.
c) Java provides a powerful capability called multiple inheritance.

13.4 Define each of the following terms.

a) thread
b) multithreading
c) ready state
d) blocked state
e) preemptive scheduling
f) **`Runnable`** interface
g) monitor
h) **`notify`** method
i) producer/consumer relationship

13.5 a) List each of the reasons stated in this chapter for using multithreading.
b) List additional reasons for using multithreading.

13.6 List each of the four reasons given in the text for entering the blocked state. For each of these, describe how the program will normally leave the blocked state and enter the runnable state.

13.7 Distinguish between preemptive scheduling and non-preemptive scheduling. Which does Java use?

13.8 What is timeslicing? Give a fundamental difference in how scheduling is performed on Java systems that support timeslicing vs. on Java systems that do not support timeslicing.

13.9 Why would a thread ever want to call **`yield`**?

13.10 What aspects of developing Java applets for the World Wide Web encourage applet designers to use **`yield`** and **`sleep`** abundantly?

13.11 If you choose to write your own **`start`** method, what must you be sure to do to make sure that your threads start up properly?

13.12 Distinguish among each of the following means of pausing threads:

a) busy wait.
b) sleep.
c) suspend.

13.13 Write a Java statement that tests if a thread is alive.

13.14 a) What is multiple inheritance?
b) Explain why Java does not offer multiple inheritance.
c) What feature does Java offer instead of multiple inheritance?
d) Explain the typical usage of this feature.
e) How does this feature differ from abstract classes.

13.15 Distinguish between the notions of **`extends`** and **`implements`**.

13.16 Discuss each of the following terms in the context of monitors:

a) monitor.
b) producer.
c) consumer.
d) **`wait`**.
e) **`notify`**.

f) **InterruptedException**.
g) **synchronized**.

13.17 *(Tortoise and the Hare)* In the Chapter 5 exercises you were asked to simulate the legendary race of the tortoise and the hare. Implement a new version of that simulation this time placing each of the animals in separate threads. At the start of the race call the **start** methods for each of the threads. Use **wait** and **notify**, and **notifyAll** to synchronize the animals' activities.

13.18 *(Multithreaded, Networked, Collaborative Applications)* In Chapter 16 we will cover networking in Java. A multithreaded Java application can communicate concurrently with several host computers. This creates the possibility of being able to build some interesting kinds of collaborative applications. In anticipation of studying networking in Chapter 16, develop proposals for several possible multithreaded networked applications. After studying Chapter 16, implement some of those applications.

13.19 Write a Java program to demonstrate that as a high-priority thread executes, it will delay the execution of all lower-priority threads.

13.20 If your system supports timeslicing, write a Java program that demonstrates timeslicing among several equal-priority threads. Show that a lower-priority thread's execution is deferred by the timeslicing of the higher-priority threads.

13.21 Write a Java program that demonstrates a high-priority thread using **sleep** to give lower-priority threads a chance to run.

13.22 If your system does not support timeslicing, write a Java program that demonstrates two threads using **yield** to enable one another to execute.

13.23 Two problems that can occur in systems like Java, that allow threads to wait, are deadlock, in which one or more threads will wait forever for an event that cannot occur, and indefinite postponement, in which one or more threads will be delayed for some unpredictably long time. Give an example of how each of these problems can occur in a multithreaded Java program.

13.24 *(Readers and Writers)* This exercise asks you to develop a Java monitor to solve a famous problem in concurrency control. This problem was first discussed and solved by P. J. Courtois, F. Heymans and D. L. Parnas in their research paper, "Concurrent Control with Readers and Writers," *Communications of the ACM,* Vol. 14, No. 10, October 1971, pp. 667–668. The interested student might also want to read C. A. R. Hoare's seminal research paper on monitors, "Monitors: An Operating System Structuring Concept," *Communications of the ACM,* Vol. 17, No. 10, October 1974, pp. 549–557. Corrigendum, *Communications of the ACM,* Vol. 18, No. 2, February 1975, p. 95. [The readers and writers problem is discussed at length in Chapter 5 of the author's book: Deitel, H. M., *Operating Systems*, Reading, MA: Addison Wesley, 1990.]

With multithreading, many threads can access shared data; as we have seen, access to shared data needs to be carefully synchronized to avoid corrupting the data.

Consider an airline reservation system in which may clients are attempting to book seats on particular flights between particular cities. All of the information about flights and seats is stored in a common database in memory. The database consists of many entries each representing a seat on a particular flight for a particular day between particular cities. In a typical airline reservation scenario, the client will probe around in the database looking for the "optimal" flight to meet that client's needs. So a client may probe the database many times before deciding to try and book a particular flight. A seat that was available during this probing phase could easily be booked by someone else before the client has a chance to book it after deciding on it. In that case, when the client attempts to make the reservation, the client will discover that the data has changed and the flight is no longer available.

The client probing around the database is called a *reader*. The client attempting to book the flight is called a *writer*. Clearly, any number of readers can be probing shared data at once, but each writer needs exclusive access to the shared data to prevent the data from being corrupted.

Write a multithreaded Java program that launches multiple reader threads and multiple writer threads, each attempting to access a single reservation record. A writer thread has two possible transactions, **makeReservation** and **cancelReservation**. A reader has one possible transaction, **queryReservation**.

First implement a version of your program that allows unsynchronized access to the reservation record. Show how the integrity of the database can be corrupted. Next implement a version of your program that uses Java monitor synchronization with **wait** and **notify** to enforce a disciplined protocol for readers and writers accessing the shared reservation data. In particular, your program should allow multiple readers to access the shared data simultaneously when no writer is active. But if a writer is active, then no readers should be allowed to access the shared data.

Be careful. This problem has many subtleties. For example, what happens when there are several active readers and a writer wants to write? If we allow a steady stream of readers to arrive and share the data, they could indefinitely postpone the writer (who may become tired of waiting and take his or her business elsewhere). To solve this problem, you might decide to favor writers over readers. But here, too, there is a trap, because a steady stream of writers could then indefinitely postpone the waiting readers, and they, too, might choose to take their business elsewhere! Implement your monitor with the following methods: **startReading** which is called by any reader that wants to begin accessing a reservation, **stopReading** to be called by any reader that has finished reading a reservation, **startWriting** to be called by any writer that wants to make a reservation and **stopWriting** to be called by any writer that has finished making a reservation.

13.25 Write a program that bounces a blue ball inside an applet. The ball should be initiated with a **mousePressed** event. When the ball hits the edge of the applet, the ball should bounce off the edge at a randomly selected angle between 20 and 60 degrees.

13.26 Modify the program of Exercise 13.25 to allow the user to draw up to five lines on the applet while the ball is bouncing. When the ball hits a line, it should bounce off the line at a randomly selected angle between 20 and 60 degrees.

14

Multimedia: Images, Animation, Audio

Objectives

- To understand how to get and display images.
- To be able to create animations from sequences of images; to control animation speed and flicker.
- To be able to get, play, loop and stop sounds.
- To be able to monitor the loading of images with the **MediaTracker**; to create image maps.
- To customize applets with the **param** tag.

The wheel that squeaks the loudest . . . gets the grease.
John Billings (Henry Wheeler Shaw)

Noise proves nothing. Often a hen who has merely laid an egg cackles as if she had laid an asteroid.
Mark Twain, *Following the Equator*

We'll use a signal I have tried and found far-reaching and easy to yell. Waa-hoo!
Zane Grey

A wide screen just makes a bad film twice as bad.
Samuel Goldwyn

There is a natural hootchy-kootchy motion to a goldfish.
Walt Disney

Between the motion and the act falls the shadow.
Thomas Stearns Eliot, *The Hollow Men*

What we experience of nature is in models, and all of nature's models are so beautiful.
Richard Buckminster Fuller

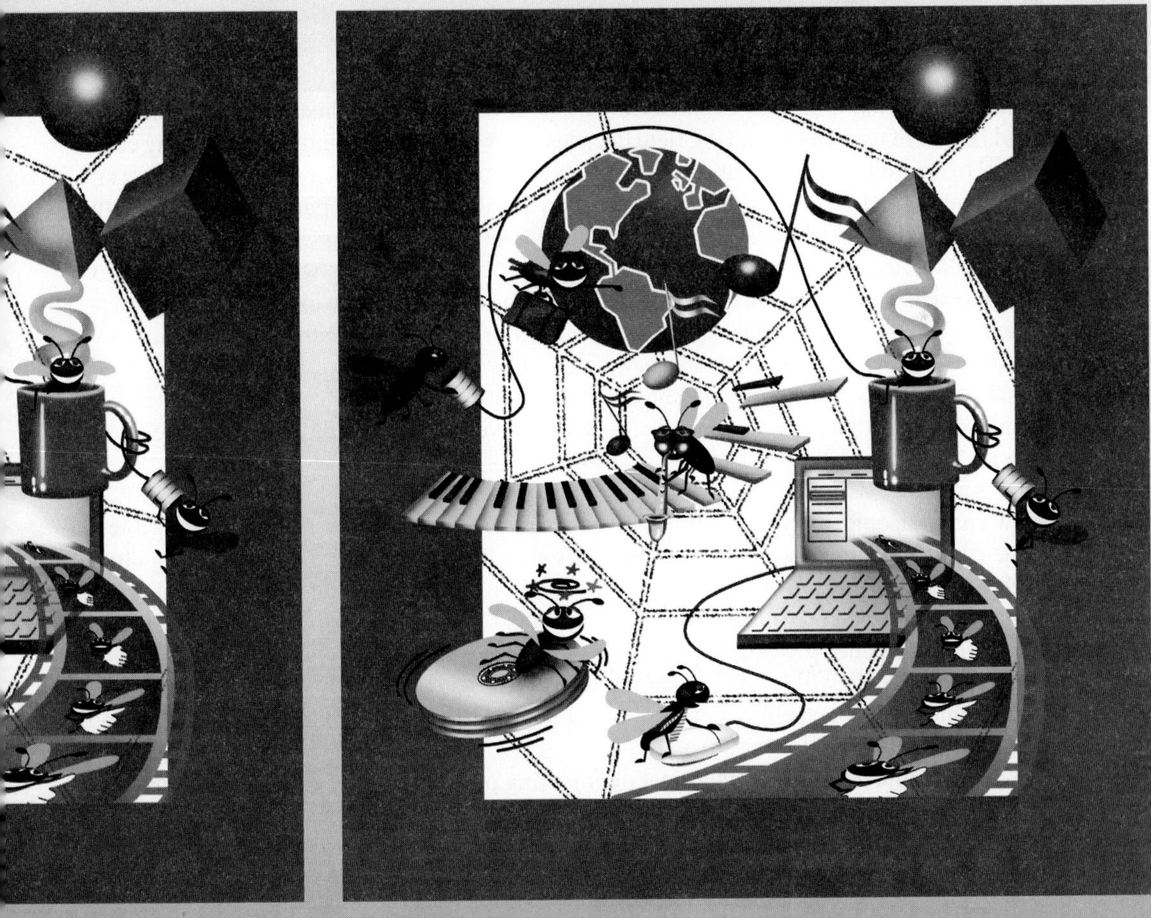

Outline

14.1 Introduction

Welcome to what may well become the largest revolution in the history of the computer field. Those of us who entered the field decades ago were primarily interested in using computers to do arithmetic calculations at high-speed. But as the computer field evolves, we are beginning to realize that the data manipulation capabilities of computers are now equally important. The "sizzle" of Java is *multimedia*, the use of *sound*, *images*, *graphics*, and *video* to make applications "come alive." Today many people consider two-dimensional color video to be the "ultimate" in multimedia. But within the decade, we expect all kinds of exciting new three-dimensional applications. Multimedia programming offers many new challenges. The field is already enormous and will grow rapidly.

People are rushing to equip their computers for multimedia. Most new computers are being sold "multimedia ready" with CD-ROM drives, audio boards and sometimes with special video capabilities.

Among those users who want graphics, two-dimensional graphics no longer suffice. Now many people want three-dimensional, high-resolution, color graphics. True three-dimensional imaging may become available within the next decade. Imagine having ultra-high-resolution, "theater-in-the-round," three-dimensional television. Sporting and entertainment events will take place on your living room floor! Medical students worldwide will see operations being performed thousands of miles away as if they were occurring in the same room. People will be able to learn how to drive with extremely realistic driving simulators in their homes before they get behind the wheel. The possibilities are exciting and endless.

Multimedia demands extraordinary computing power. Until recently, affordable computers with this kind of power were not available. But today's ultra-fast processors like the SPARC Ultra from Sun Microsystems, the Pentium from Intel, the Alpha from Digital Equipment Corporation and the R8000 from MIPS/Silicon Graphics (among others) are making effective multimedia possible. The computer and communications industries will be primary beneficiaries of the multimedia revolution. Users will be willing to pay more for the faster processors, larger memories and wider communications bandwidths that will be needed to support multimedia applications. Ironically, users may not have to pay more as fierce competition in these industries forces prices down.

We need programming languages that make creating multimedia applications easy. Most programming languages do not have built-in multimedia capabilities. But Java, through the packages of classes that are an integral part of the Java programming world, provides extensive multimedia facilities that will enable you to start developing powerful multimedia applications immediately.

In this chapter we present a series of "live-code" examples that cover many of the interesting multimedia features you will need to build useful applications. We will cover the basics of manipulating images, creating smooth animations, playing sounds, creating image maps that can sense when the cursor is over them even without a mouse click, and customizing applets via parameters supplied from the HTML file that invokes an applet. The chapter exercises suggest dozens of challenging and interesting projects and even mention some "million-dollar" ideas that may help you make your fortune! When we were creating these exercises it seemed that the ideas just kept flowing. Multimedia seems to leverage creativity in ways that we have not experienced with "conventional" computer capabilities.

14.2 Loading, Displaying and Scaling Images

Java's multimedia capabilities include graphics, images, animations, sounds and shortly video. We begin our multimedia discussion with images.

The program of Fig. 14.1 loads an image into an applet, displays the image in its original size and displays the image scaled to twice its original width and twice its original height. **Image** reference **deitel** is initialized with the statement

```
deitel = getImage( getDocumentBase(), "deitel0.gif" );
```

which uses **Applet** method **getImage** to load an image into the applet. This version of **getImage** takes two arguments—a location where the image is stored and the file name of the image. In the first argument, **Applet** method **getDocumentBase** is used to determine the location of the image on the Internet (or on your computer if that is where the applet came from). We assume that the image to be loaded is stored in the same location as the HTML file that invoked the applet. Method **getDocumentBase** returns the location of the HTML file on the Internet as an object of class **URL**. A **URL** stores a *Uniform Resource Locator*—a standard format for an address of a piece of information on the Internet. We discuss **URL**s in more depth in Chapter 16. The second argument specifies an image file name. Java currently supports two image formats—*Graphics Interchange Format (GIF)* and *Joint Photographic Experts Group (JPEG)*. File names for each of these types end with **.gif** or **.jpg**, respectively.

When method **getImage** is invoked, it launches a separate thread of execution in which the image is loaded (or downloaded from the Internet). This enables the program to continue execution while the image is loaded.

```java
// Fig. 14.1: LoadImageAndScale.java
// Load an image and display it in its original size
// and scale it to twice its original width and height.
import java.applet.Applet;
import java.awt.*;

public class LoadImageAndScale extends Applet {
   private Image deitel;

   // load the image when the applet begins executing
   public void init()
   {
      deitel = getImage( getDocumentBase(),
                         "deitel0.gif" );
   }

   // display the image
   public void paint( Graphics g )
   {
      // draw the original image
      g.drawImage( deitel, 1, 1, this );

      // draw the image with its width and height doubled
      int width = deitel.getWidth( this );
      int height = deitel.getHeight( this );
      g.drawImage( deitel, 1, 90, width * 2,
                   height * 2, this );
   }
}
```

Fig. 14.1 Loading and displaying an image in an applet (part 1 of 2).

The applet's **paint** method displays the image using **Graphics** method **drawImage**. This applet uses two versions of **drawImage**. The statement

```java
g.drawImage( deitel, 1, 1, this );
```

uses the **drawImage** method that takes four arguments. The first argument is a reference to the **Image** object in which the image is stored. The second and third arguments are the *x* and *y* coordinates where the image should be displayed on the applet (the coordinates indicate the upper-left corner of the image). The last argument is a reference to an ***ImageObserver*** object. Normally, the **ImageObserver** is the object on which the image is displayed—we used **this** to indicate the applet. An **ImageObserver** can be any object that implements the **ImageObserver** interface. Class **ImageObserver** is an interface that is implemented by class **Component** (one of class **Applet**'s indirect superclasses). This argument is important when displaying large images that require a long time to download from the Internet. It is possible that a program will display the image before it is completely downloaded. The **ImageObserver** is automatically notified to update the image that was displayed as the remainder of the image is loaded. When you run this applet, watch carefully as pieces of the image are displayed while the image loads.

Fig. 14.1 Loading and displaying an image in an applet (part 2 of 2).

The statement

```
g.drawImage( deitel, 1, 90, width * 2, height * 2, this );
```

uses another version of method **drawImage** to output a scaled version of the image. The fourth and fifth arguments specify the width and height of the image for display purposes. Java automatically scales the image to fit the specified width and height. We specified that the width and height of the scaled image should be twice the original image's width and height. These values are determined with **Image** methods **getWidth** and **getHeight**. Each method receives an **ImageObserver** as an argument. This enables the **ImageObserver** to be updated as the **Image** loads into the applet.

14.3 Introduction to Animation: An Image Loop

The applet of Fig. 14.2 demonstrates a simple animation. The applet uses the same techniques to load images and display images as used in Fig. 14.1. The next several examples demonstrate various techniques for smoothing animations. They also represent the steps that lead to the animation we currently display on the Deitel & Associates, Inc. World Wide Web site

```
http://www.deitel.com/products_and_services/training/
        java_training/JavaCurriculum.htm.
```

```java
// Fig. 14.2: DeitelLoop.java
// Load an array of images, loop through the array,
// and display each image.
import java.applet.Applet;
import java.awt.*;

public class DeitelLoop extends Applet {
   private Image deitel[];
   private int totalImages = 30,  // total number of images
               currentImage = 0,  // current image subscript
               sleepTime = 50;    // milliseconds to sleep

   // load the images when the applet begins executing
   public void init()
   {
      deitel = new Image[ totalImages ];

      for ( int i = 0; i < deitel.length; i++ )
         deitel[ i ] = getImage( getDocumentBase(),
            "images/deitel" + i + ".gif" );
   }

   // start the applet
   public void start()
   {
      currentImage = 0;  // always start with 1st image
   }

   // display the image in the Applet's Graphics context
   // then sleep and call repaint
   public void paint( Graphics g )
   {
      g.drawImage( deitel[ currentImage ], 1, 1, this );

      currentImage = ( currentImage + 1 ) % totalImages;

      try {
         Thread.sleep( sleepTime );
      }
      catch ( InterruptedException e ) {
         showStatus( e.toString() );
      }

      repaint();
   }
}
```

Fig. 14.2 Demonstrating a simple animation using an image loop (part 1 of 2).

Class **DeitelLoop** maintains an array of **Image**s that are loaded in the applet's **init** method. The **getImage** method is used to load each individual image (there are 30 in the animation) with the statement

Fig. 14.2 Demonstrating a simple animation using an image loop (part 2 of 2).

```
deitel[ i ] = getImage( getDocumentBase(),
   "images/deitel" + i + ".gif" );
```

The second argument assembles the file name from the pieces **"images/deitel"**, **i**, and **".gif"**. Each of the images in the animation is in one of the files "**deitel0.gif**" through "**deitel29.gif**." The value of the control variable in the **for** structure is used to select one of the 30 images. Remember that **getImage** launches a separate thread of execution for each image it loads.

Performance Tip 14.1

It is more efficient to load the frames of the animation as one image than to load each image separately (a painting program can be used to combine the frames of the animation into one image). Every **getImage** *method call requires a separate connection to the World Wide Web site where the images are stored.*

Performance Tip 14.2

Loading all the frames of an image as one large image may force your program to wait to begin displaying the animation.

The work of displaying the animation is this example is performed by the **Applet**'s **paint** method. Instance variable **currentImage** keeps track of the image to display. First, method **drawImage** is used to display one frame, then the applet sleeps for a fraction of a second with the statement

```
Thread.sleep( sleepTime );
```

Next, method **repaint** is invoked which, in turn, invokes the applet's **update** method to clear the background of the applet. Then, **update** invokes the **paint** method to display the next image.

When you execute this applet, notice that the images take time to load. This often results in partial images being displayed. Watch carefully as each image is displayed. You may be able to see that each image appears to display in pieces (similar to what happened in the example of Fig. 14.1). This is often the result of the image format that is used. For example, GIF images can be stored in *interlaced* and *non-interlaced* formats. The format indicates the order in which the pixels of the image are stored. The pixels of a non-interlaced image are stored in the same order that the pixels appear on the screen. As a non-interlaced image is displayed, it appears in chunks from top to bottom as the pixel information is read. The pixels of an interlaced image are stored in rows of pixels, but the rows are out of order. For example, the rows of pixels in the image may be stored in the order 1, 5, 9, 13, ..., followed by 2, 6, 10, 14, ..., and so on. When the image is displayed, it appears to fade in as the first batch of rows presents a rough outline of the picture and the subsequent batches of rows refine the displayed image until the entire image is complete.

Also, note that the animation *flickers* as each image is displayed. This is due to the applet's **`update`** method being called. When **`update`** clears the applet, it does so by drawing a filled rectangle the size of the applet in the current background color. This covers the image that was just drawn. Thus, the applet draws an image, sleeps for a fraction of a second, clears the background (causing a flicker) and draws the next image.

This applet seems to have infinite recursion in it—**`paint`** calls **`repaint`**, **`repaint`** calls **`update`**, **`update`** calls **`paint`** and **`paint`** calls **`repaint`** again. Actually, each call to **`repaint`** starts a separate thread of execution (which creates a separate method call stack) in which the repainting of the applet is performed. The "infinite recursion" is really happening as follows: **`repaint`** starts a new thread in which **`update`** is called, **`update`** calls **`paint`**, **`paint`** calls **`repaint`**, **`repaint`** starts a new thread of execution in which **`update`** is called and the previous repainting thread terminates. The method call stack for each thread never has more than three methods in the stack. Also, each stack is garbage collected automatically when its thread is garbage collected. The problem with this apparent infinite recursion is that if the user moves to another Web page, this applet will continue to use processor time on the computer and possibly degrade that computer's performance.

Performance Tip 14.3

An animation applet that uses a call to **`repaint`** *from the applet's* **`paint`** *method to implement animation occupies processor time even after the user leaves the Web page on which the animation applet resides. This may cause performance degradation.*

Software Engineering Observation 14.1

When creating an animation be sure to provide a mechanism for disabling the animation when the user browses a new Web page separate from the page on which the animation applet resides.

We will discuss several techniques over the next few examples to eliminate each of the animation deficiencies described above.

14.4 Graphics Double Buffering

If you want to develop multimedia-based applications, your users will want smooth sound and animations. Choppy presentations are unacceptable. This often happens when you write applications that draw directly to the screen. With the technique of *graphics double buffering*, while the program renders one image on the screen, it can build the next image in an *off-screen buffer*. Then, when it is time for that next image to be displayed, it can be placed on the screen smoothly. Of course, there is a *space/time trade-off*. The extra memory required can be substantial, but the improved display performance may be well worth it.

Graphics double buffering is also useful in programs that need to use drawing capabilities in methods other than **paint** (where we have done all our drawing to this point). The off-screen buffer can be passed between methods or even between objects of different classes to allow other methods or objects to draw on the off-screen buffer. The results of the drawing can then be displayed at a later time.

Performance Tip 14.4

Double buffering can reduce or eliminate flicker in an animation, but it can visibly slow the speed at which the animation runs.

When all the pixels of an image do not display at once, an animation has more flicker. When an image is drawn using graphics double buffering, by the time the image is displayed, it will have already been drawn off the screen and the fading or chunking of the image will be hidden from the user. All the pixels will be displayed for the user in one "blast" so the flicker is substantially reduced or eliminated.

The basic concept of a graphics double buffer is as follows: create a blank **Image**, draw on the blank **Image** (using methods of the **Graphics** class) and display the image.

The applet of Fig. 14.3 extends the animation of Fig. 14.2 by adding graphics double buffering. There are two key pieces to implementing a graphics double buffer—an **Image** reference (called **buffer** in this program) and a **Graphics** reference (called **gContext** in this program). The **Image** is where the actual pixels to be displayed are stored. The **Graphics** reference is used to draw the pixels. Every image has an associated graphics context—i.e., an object of class **Graphics** that enables drawing to be performed. The **Image** and **Graphics** references used for graphics double buffering are often referred to as the *off-screen image* and the *off-screen graphics context* because they are not actually manipulating screen pixels.

```
// Fig. 14.3: DeitelLoop2.java
// Load an array of images, loop through the array,
// and display each image.
import java.applet.Applet;
import java.awt.*;

public class DeitelLoop2 extends Applet {
   private Image deitel[];
   private int totalImages = 30,   // total number of images
               currentImage = 0,   // current image subscript
               sleepTime = 50;     // milliseconds to sleep

   // The next two objects are for double buffering
   private Graphics gContext; // off-screen graphics context
   private Image buffer;      // buffer in which to draw image

```

Fig. 14.3 Using graphics double buffering to reduce animation flicker (part 1 of 3).

```
    // load the images when the applet begins executing
    public void init()
    {
       deitel = new Image[ totalImages ];
       buffer = createImage( 160, 80 ); // create image buffer
       gContext = buffer.getGraphics(); // get graphics context

       // set background of buffer to white
       gContext.setColor( Color.white );
       gContext.fillRect( 0, 0, 160, 80 );

       for ( int i = 0; i < deitel.length; i++ )
          deitel[ i ] = getImage( getDocumentBase(),
             "images/deitel" + i + ".gif" );
    }

    // start the applet
    public void start()
    {
       // always start with 1st image
       gContext.drawImage( deitel[ 0 ], 0, 0, this );
       currentImage = 1;
    }

    // display the image in the Applet's Graphics context
    public void paint( Graphics g )
    {
       g.drawImage( buffer, 0, 0, this );

       // clear previous image from buffer
       gContext.fillRect( 0, 0, 160, 80 );

       // draw new image in buffer
       gContext.drawImage( deitel[ currentImage ], 0, 0, this );

       currentImage = ( currentImage + 1 ) % totalImages;

       try {
          Thread.sleep( sleepTime );
       }
       catch ( InterruptedException e ) {
          showStatus( e.toString() );
       }

       repaint();  // display buffered image
    }
 }
```

Fig. 14.3 Using graphics double buffering to reduce animation flicker (part 2 of 3).

Fig. 14.3 Using graphics double buffering to reduce animation flicker (part 3 of 3).

from the The graphics double buffer is created with the statements

```
buffer = createImage( 160, 80 ); // create image buffer
gContext = buffer.getGraphics(); // get graphics context
```

applet's **init** method. The first statement uses the applet's **createImage** method (inherited indirectly from class **Component**) to ask the system to create an image that is 160 pixels wide and 80 pixels tall (this is the size of each image we display in the animation).

Portability Tip 14.1

Class **Image** *is an abstract class, so* **Image** *objects cannot be created directly. To achieve platform independence, the Java implementation on each platform provides its own subclass of* **Image** *to store image information.*

Class **Image** provides the programmer with a uniform set of methods used to process images. Method **createImage** instantiates an object of the platform's subclass of **Image**. The second statement uses **Image** method **getGraphics** to get the graphics context (i.e., the **Graphics** object) associated with the **Image** object referenced by **buffer**. The **gContext** reference will be used to draw to the off-screen image. The statements

```
gContext.setColor( Color.white );
gContext.fillRect( 0, 0, 160, 80 );
```

set the drawing color for the off-screen graphics context to white (any shapes are drawn in the drawing color) and draw a filled rectangle in white to the off-screen image. This prepares the off-screen image to have the first animation image drawn.

The **start** method specifies that the first image in the array of images should be drawn using **gContext**. The image is stored in the **Image** object to which **buffer** refers. The **paint** method displays whatever image happens to be stored in **buffer** currently, then prepares the next image to be displayed. First, **fillRect** is used to clear the off-screen image. Then the next image is drawn to the off-screen image. After sleeping for a fraction of a second, method **repaint** is called. This causes a separate thread of execution in which **update** is invoked, **update** calls **paint**, **paint** displays the image that was just prepared and **paint** prepares the next image to be displayed.

When you execute this applet, notice that the animation is still choppy while the images load. However, once the images are completely loaded, most of the flicker from the previous animation applet has been eliminated. This version of the applet still issues a **repaint** call from **paint** which means this applet will occupy processor time on the user's computer when the user moves to another Web page. In the next example, we will eliminate all the flicker.

14.5 Using the MediaTracker to Monitor Image Loading

As you have seen in the first two animations, when the images are loading, they are frequently displayed as partial images. This makes the animation appear choppy at first. In the applet of Fig. 14.4 we extend the animation to use Java's **MediaTracker** to determine when an image is completely loaded. Once an image is completely loaded it is displayed as part of the animation.

```
// Fig. 14.4: DeitelLoop3.java
// Load an array of images, loop through the array,
// and display each image.
import java.applet.Applet;
import java.awt.*;

public class DeitelLoop3 extends Applet {
   private Image deitel[];
   private int totalImages = 30,  // total number of images
               currentImage = 0,  // current image subscript
               sleepTime = 50;    // milliseconds to sleep

   // The next two objects are for double buffering
   private Graphics gContext; // off-screen graphics context
   private Image buffer;      // buffer in which to draw image

   private MediaTracker imageTracker; // used to track images

   // load the images when the applet begins executing
   public void init()
   {
      deitel = new Image[ totalImages ];
      buffer = createImage( 160, 80 ); // create image buffer
      gContext = buffer.getGraphics(); // get graphics context

      // set background of buffer to white
      gContext.setColor( Color.white );
      gContext.fillRect( 0, 0, 160, 80 );

      imageTracker = new MediaTracker( this );

      for ( int i = 0; i < deitel.length; i++ ) {
         deitel[ i ] = getImage( getDocumentBase(),
            "images/deitel" + i + ".gif" );
```

Fig. 14.4 Using the **MediaTracker** to smooth animation startup and overriding **update** to eliminate animation flicker (part 1 of 3).

```java

         // track loading image
         imageTracker.addImage( deitel[ i ], i );
      }

      try {
         imageTracker.waitForID( 0 );
      }
      catch( InterruptedException e ) { }
   }

   // start the applet
   public void start()
   {
      // always start with 1st image
      gContext.drawImage( deitel[ 0 ], 0, 0, this );
      currentImage = 1;
   }

   // display the image in the Applet's Graphics context
   public void paint( Graphics g )
   {
      g.drawImage( buffer, 0, 0, this );

      if ( imageTracker.checkID( currentImage, true ) ) {
         // clear previous image from buffer
         gContext.fillRect( 0, 0, 160, 80 );

         // draw new image in buffer
         gContext.drawImage(
            deitel[ currentImage ], 0, 0, this );

         currentImage = ++currentImage % totalImages;
      }

      try {
         Thread.sleep( sleepTime );
      }
      catch ( InterruptedException e ) {
         showStatus( e.toString() );
      }

      repaint();  // display buffered image
   }

   // override update to eliminate flicker
   public void update( Graphics g ) { paint( g ); }
}
```

Fig. 14.4 Using the **MediaTracker** to smooth animation startup and overriding **update** to eliminate animation flicker (part 2 of 3).

Fig. 14.4 Using the **MediaTracker** to smooth animation startup and overriding **update** to eliminate animation flicker (part 3 of 3).

Performance Tip 14.5

Some people who are experienced with **MediaTracker** *objects have reported that they can have a detrimental effect on performance. Keep this in mind as an area to scrutinize if you need to tune your multimedia applications.*

When loading images into a program, the images can be registered with an object of class **MediaTracker** to enable the program to determine when an image is loaded completely. Class **MediaTracker** also provides the ability to wait for an image or several images to load before allowing a program to continue and to determine if an error occurred while loading an image.

The **MediaTracker** is instantiated with the statement

```
imageTracker = new MediaTracker( this );
```

The argument to the constructor is an **ImageObserver** (the object on which the images will be drawn). In this case, the applet (**this**) is the **ImageObserver**. After method **getImage** is invoked to load each image, the statement

```
imageTracker.addImage( deitel[ i ], i );
```

is executed to register the loading image with the **MediaTracker** object **imageTracker**. The first argument to method **addImage** is the **Image** reference to the image being loaded. The second argument is an integer ID that can be used to query the **MediaTracker** on the status of that image. The ID does not have to be unique. To track multiple images as a group, simply give them the same ID number.

Once all the images have been registered with the **imageTracker**, the statement

```
imageTracker.waitForID( 0 );
```

is executed to force the program to wait until the image identified as 0 is completely loaded. This is a blocking call—the program does not continue executing until the image is completely loaded. Class **MediaTracker** also provides a **waitForAll** method that blocks until all the images registered are completely loaded.

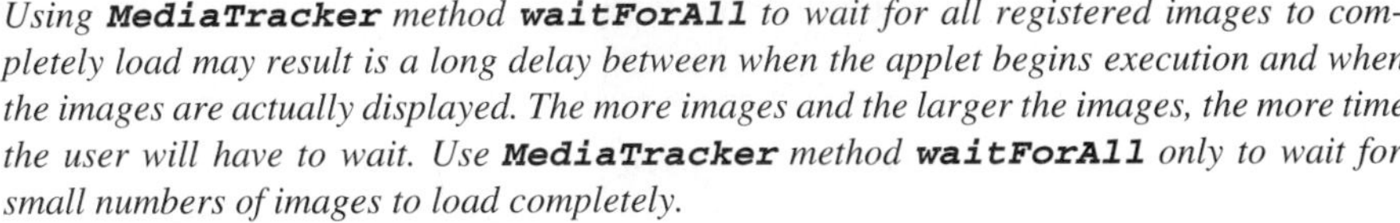

Performance Tip 14.6

Using **MediaTracker** *method* **waitForAll** *to wait for all registered images to completely load may result is a long delay between when the applet begins execution and when the images are actually displayed. The more images and the larger the images, the more time the user will have to wait. Use* **MediaTracker** *method* **waitForAll** *only to wait for small numbers of images to load completely.*

Good Programming Practice 14.1

Always display something while images load. The longer a user must wait to see information appear on the screen, the more likely they will leave the Web page before the information appears.

Once the first image has completely loaded it is prepared to display in the **start** method, then it is displayed in the **paint** method. The preparing of the next image to display is now accomplished by an **if** structure in the **paint** method. The condition

```
imageTracker.checkID( currentImage, true )
```

performs two tasks. First, method **checkID** checks the **currentImage** to determine if the image has completely loaded. If so, the method returns **true** and the **if** structure's body is executed to prepare the next image for display. If the image is not completely loaded, the method returns **false** and the **else** part of the **if/else** structure is executed to perform our browser fix. If the image has not started to load when **checkID** is invoked to check the image, the second argument indicates that the image should start loading now.

The **MediaTracker** does not eliminate flicker—it simply smooths the beginning of the animation as the images are loaded so no partial images are displayed. To eliminate all flicker, we provided our own definition of the applet's **update** method. Previously we stated that **update** clears the applet, then calls **paint**. Clearing the applet causes the flicker. Our definition of **update** overrides the one that was indirectly inherited from class **Component**. The new version simply calls **paint**—no clearing of the applet is performed. But how do we clear the image that is on the applet so the next image can be displayed? The answer is that we already do so. Every time we prepare an image to be displayed, we clear the off-screen image so the background is all white. Then, we draw the next image on the white background. When the off-screen image is displayed, the white background of the new image hides the entire image that was already on the applet.

When you execute this applet, notice that there is no more flicker! Also, notice that the first pass of the animation (when each image is displayed for the first time) is slower than the subsequent passes. This is due to our use of the **MediaTracker** to wait for each image to load. In the next example, we add a separate thread to execute the animation so we have control over when the animation executes and when it stops.

14.6 Using a Separate Thread to Run an Animation

The applet of Fig. 14.5 does not add any new multimedia or animation techniques. Rather it shows a better way to construct an animation to make it "browser friendly." As we mentioned previously, our animations will continue to execute and occupy processor time on the user's computer even after they leave the Web page. In this example, we extend the applet to implement interface **Runnable** so we can run the animation as a separate thread and have control over the execution of the thread.

```
// Fig. 14.5: DeitelLoop4.java
// Load an array of images, loop through the array,
// and display each image.
import java.applet.Applet;
import java.awt.*;

public class DeitelLoop4 extends Applet implements Runnable {
   private Image deitel[];
   private int totalImages = 30,   // total number of images
               currentImage = 0,   // current image subscript
               sleepTime = 50;     // milliseconds to sleep

   // The next two objects are for double buffering
   private Graphics gContext; // off-screen graphics context
   private Image buffer;      // buffer in which to draw image

   private MediaTracker imageTracker; // used to track images

   private Thread animate;      // animation thread

   // load the images when the applet begins executing
   public void init()
   {
      deitel = new Image[ totalImages ];
      buffer = createImage( 160, 80 ); // create image buffer
      gContext = buffer.getGraphics(); // get graphics context

      // set background of buffer to white
      gContext.setColor( Color.white );
      gContext.fillRect( 0, 0, 160, 80 );

      imageTracker = new MediaTracker( this );

      for ( int i = 0; i < deitel.length; i++ ) {
         deitel[ i ] = getImage( getDocumentBase(),
            "images/deitel" + i + ".gif" );

         // track loading image
         imageTracker.addImage( deitel[ i ], i );
      }

      try {
         imageTracker.waitForID( 0 );
      }
      catch( InterruptedException e ) { }
   }
```

Fig. 14.5 Using a separate thread to run an animation (part 1 of 3).

```

   // start the applet
   public void start()
   {
      // always start with 1st image
      gContext.drawImage( deitel[ 0 ], 0, 0, this );
      currentImage = 1;

      // create a new animation thread when user visits page
      if ( animate == null ) {
         animate = new Thread( this );
         animate.start();
      }
   }

   // terminate animation thread when user leaves page
   public void stop()
   {
      if ( animate != null ) {
         animate.stop();
         animate = null;
      }
   }

   // display the image in the Applet's Graphics context
   public void paint( Graphics g )
   {
      g.drawImage( buffer, 0, 0, this );
   }

   // override update to eliminate flicker
   public void update( Graphics g ) { paint( g ); }

   public void run()
   {
      while ( true ) {
         if ( imageTracker.checkID( currentImage, true ) ) {
            // clear previous image from buffer
            gContext.fillRect( 0, 0, 160, 80 );

            // draw new image in buffer
            gContext.drawImage(
               deitel[ currentImage ], 0, 0, this );

            currentImage = ( currentImage + 1 ) % totalImages;
         }

         try {
            Thread.sleep( sleepTime );
         }
```

Fig. 14.5 Using a separate thread to run an animation (part 2 of 3).

```
            catch ( InterruptedException e ) {
               showStatus( e.toString() );
            }

            repaint();   // display buffered image
         }
      }
   }
```

Fig. 14.5 Using a separate thread to run an animation (part 3 of 3).

`Thread` object **`animate`** is used to run the animation and **`boolean`** variable **`suspended`** indicates whether or not the applet is currently in a suspended state. When the applet's **`start`** method executes, it draws the first image on the off-screen graphics context, then creates a **`Thread`** (initialized with the applet) and invokes the thread's **`start`** method. This launches the animation thread. The applet's **`run`** method is invoked to control the animation. Everything that used to be accomplished by the **`paint`** method is now accomplished by the infinite loop in **`run`** with the exception of the actual display of the image on the applet—this is still performed by **`paint`**.

There is one other key feature—method **`stop`**. Remember that method **`stop`** is invoked automatically on an applet when the user leaves the Web page on which the applet resides. Method **`stop`** is defined to invoke the thread's **`stop`** method which terminates the thread. Thus, the applet is not executing the animation when the user moves to another Web page. Method **`start`** is invoked automatically if the user revisits the Web page containing the applet, so **`start`** can create a new thread to run the animation. If this occurs, the animation begins immediately because the images are still loaded in memory. This addition makes the animation applet more browser friendly.

14.7 Loading and Playing Audio Clips

Java programs can manipulate and play *audio clips*. It is easy for users to capture their own audio clips and there is a variety of clips available in software products and over the Internet. Your system needs to be equipped with audio hardware (speakers and a sound board).

Java provides two mechanisms for playing sounds in an applet—the **`Applet`**'s ***`play`*** method and the ***`play`*** method from the ***`AudioClip`*** *interface*. If you would like to play a sound once in a program, the **`Applet`** method **`play`** will load the sound and play it for you once; the sound is marked for garbage collection when it is done playing. The **Applet** method **play** method has two forms:

```
public void play( URL location, String soundFileName );
public void play( URL soundURL );
```

The first version loads the audio clip stored in file **soundFileName** from **location** and plays the sound. The first argument is normally a call to the applet's **getDocument-Base** or ***getCodeBase*** *method.* Method **getDocumentBase** indicates where to locate the HTML file that loaded the applet. Method **getCodeBase** indicates where the **.class** file for the applet is located. The second version of method **play** takes a **URL** that contains the location and the file name of the audio clip. The statement

```
public void play( getDocumentBase(), "hi.au" );
```

loads the audio clip in file **hi.au** and plays it once.

The program of Fig. 14.6 demonstrates loading and playing an **AudioClip**. This technique is more flexible. It allows the audio to be stored in the program so the audio can be reused throughout the program's execution. The **Applet** method **getAudioClip** has two forms that take the same arguments as the **play** method described above. Method **getAudioClip** returns a reference to an **AudioClip**. Once an **AudioClip** is loaded, three methods can be invoked for the object—**play**, **loop** and **stop**. Method **play** plays the audio once. Method **loop** continuously loops the audio clip in the background. Method **stop** terminates an audio clip that is currently playing. In the program, each of these methods is associated with a button on the applet.

```
// Fig. 14.1: LoadAudioAndPlay.java
// Load an audio clip and play it.
import java.applet.*;
import java.awt.*;
import java.awt.event.*;

public class LoadAudioAndPlay extends Applet
             implements ActionListener {
   private AudioClip sound;
   private Button playSound, loopSound, stopSound;

   // load the image when the applet begins executing
   public void init()
   {
      sound = getAudioClip( getDocumentBase(), "hi.au" );
      playSound = new Button( "Play" );
      playSound.addActionListener( this );
      add( playSound );
      loopSound = new Button( "Loop" );
      loopSound.addActionListener( this );
      add( loopSound );
```

Fig. 14.6 Loading and playing an audio clip (part 1 of 2).

```
         stopSound = new Button( "Stop" );
         stopSound.addActionListener( this );
         add( stopSound );
      }

      public void actionPerformed( ActionEvent e )
      {
         if ( e.getSource() == playSound )
            sound.play();
         else if ( e.getSource() == loopSound )
            sound.loop();
         else if ( e.getSource() == stopSound )
            sound.stop();
      }
   }

```

Fig. 14.6 Loading and playing an audio clip (part 2 of 2).

14.8 Customizing Applets via the HTML `param` Tag

When browsing the World Wide Web you will often come across applets that are in the public domain—you can use them free of charge on your own Web pages (normally in exchange for crediting the applet's creator). One common feature of such applets is the ability to customize the applet via parameters that are supplied from the HTML file that invokes the applet. For example, the following HTML file

```
<html>
<applet code="DeitelLoop5.class" width=400 height=400>
<param name="totalimages" value="30">
<param name="imagename" value="deitel">
<param name="sleeptime" value="500">
</applet>
</html>
```

invokes the applet **DeitelLoop5** (Fig. 14.7) and specifies three parameters. The **param** tag lines must appear between the starting **applet** tag and the ending **applet** tag. These values can then be used to customize the applet. Any number of **param** tags can appear between the starting and ending **applet** tags. Each parameter has a **name** and a **value**. The **Applet** method **getParameter** is used to get the **value** associated with a specific parameter and return the **value** as a **String**. The argument passed to **getParameter** is a **String** containing the name of the parameter in the **param** tag. For example, the statement

```
parameter = getParameter( "sleeptime" );
```

gets the value associated with the **sleeptime** parameter and assigns it to **String** reference **parameter**. If there is not a **param** tag containing the specified parameter, **getParameter** returns **null**.

This version of our animation applet allows users to customize the animation to use their own images. Three parameters are provided. Parameter **sleeptime** is the number of milliseconds to sleep between images being displayed. This value will be converted to an integer and used as the value for instance variable **sleepTime**. Parameter **imageName** is the base name of the images to be loaded. This **String** will be assigned to instance variable **imageName**. The applet assumes that the images are in a subdirectory named **images** that can be found in the same directory as the applet. The applet also assumes that the image file names are numbered from 0. Parameter **totalimages** represents the total number of images in the animation. Its value will be converted to an integer and assigned to instance variable **totalImages**.

The applet also provides a text field that displays the sleep time and allows the user to vary the sleep time by typing a new value in the text field. This is an extended version of our animation applet that uses a separate thread to run the animation.

```
// Fig. 14.7: DeitelLoop5.java
// Load an array of images, loop through the array,
// and display each image. This version is customizeable.
//
// HTML parameter "sleeptime" is an integer indicating the
// number of milliseconds to sleep between images.
//
// HTML parameter "imagename" is the base name of the images
// that will be displayed (i.e., "deitel" is the base name
// for images "deitel0.gif," "deitel1.gif," etc.). The applet
// assumes that images are in an "images" subdirectory of
// the directory in which the applet resides.
//
// HTML parameter "totalimages" is an integer representing the
// total number of images in the animation. The applet assumes
// images are numbered from 0 to totalimages - 1.

import java.applet.Applet;
import java.awt.*;
import java.awt.event.*;

public class DeitelLoop5 extends Applet implements Runnable {
   private Image images[];
   private int totalImages,        // total number of images
               currentImage = 0,   // current image subscript
               sleepTime;          // milliseconds to sleep
   private String imageName;   // base name of images

```

Fig. 14.7 Customizing an applet via the **param** HTML tag (part 1 of 5).

```
   // The next two objects are for double buffering
   private Graphics gContext; // off-screen graphics context
   private Image buffer;      // buffer in which to draw image

   private MediaTracker imageTracker;  // used to track images

   private Thread animate;      // animation thread

   private int width, height;

   // GUI Components to allow dynamic speed changing
   private Label sleepLabel;
   private TextField sleepDisplay;
   private Panel sleepStuff;

   // load the images when the applet begins executing
   public void init()
   {
      processHTMLParameters();

      if ( totalImages == 0 || imageName == null ) {
         showStatus( "Invalid parameters" );
         destroy();
      }

      images = new Image[ totalImages ];
      imageTracker = new MediaTracker( this );

      for ( int i = 0; i < images.length; i++ ) {
         images[ i ] = getImage( getDocumentBase(),
            "images/" + imageName + i + ".gif" );

         // track loading image
         imageTracker.addImage( images[ i ], i );
      }

      try {
         imageTracker.waitForID( 0 );
      }
      catch( InterruptedException e ) { }

      width = images[ 0 ].getWidth( this );
      height = images[ 0 ].getHeight( this );
      resize( width, height + 30 );

      buffer = createImage( width, height );
      gContext = buffer.getGraphics();

      // set background of buffer to white
      gContext.setColor( Color.white );
      gContext.fillRect( 0, 0, width, height );
```

Fig. 14.7 Customizing an applet via the **param** HTML tag (part 2 of 5).

```

      setLayout( new BorderLayout() );
      sleepLabel = new Label( "Sleep time" );
      sleepDisplay = new TextField( 5 );
      sleepDisplay.setText( String.valueOf( sleepTime ) );
      sleepStuff = new Panel();
      sleepStuff.add( sleepLabel );
      sleepStuff.add( sleepDisplay );
      add( sleepStuff, BorderLayout.SOUTH );
   }

   // start the applet
   public void start()
   {
      // always start with 1st image
      gContext.drawImage( images[ 0 ], 0, 0, this );
      currentImage = 1;

      // create a new animation thread when user visits page
      if ( animate == null ) {
         animate = new Thread( this );
         animate.start();
      }
   }

   // terminate animation thread when user leaves page
   public void stop()
   {
      if ( animate != null ) {
         animate.stop();
         animate = null;
      }
   }

   // display the image in the Applet's Graphics context
   public void paint( Graphics g )
   {
      g.drawImage( buffer, 0, 0, this );
   }

   // override update to eliminate flicker
   public void update( Graphics g ) { paint( g ); }

   public void run()
   {
      while ( true ) {
         if ( imageTracker.checkID( currentImage, true ) ) {
            // clear previous image from buffer
            gContext.fillRect( 0, 0, width, height );

```

Fig. 14.7 Customizing an applet via the **param** HTML tag (part 3 of 5).

```
            // draw new image in buffer
            gContext.drawImage(
               images[ currentImage ], 0, 0, this );

            currentImage = ( currentImage + 1 ) % totalImages;
         }

         try {
            Thread.sleep( sleepTime );
         }
         catch ( InterruptedException e ) {
            showStatus( e.toString() );
         }

         repaint();  // display buffered image
      }
   }

   public void actionPerformed( ActionEvent e )
   {
      try {
         sleepTime =  Integer.parseInt( e.getActionCommand() );
      }
      catch( NumberFormatException nfe ) {
         showStatus( "Sleep time must be an integer" );
      }
   }

   public void processHTMLParameters()
   {
      String parameter;

      parameter = getParameter( "sleeptime" );
      sleepTime = ( parameter == null ? 50 :
                    Integer.parseInt( parameter ) );

      imageName = getParameter( "imagename" );

      parameter = getParameter( "totalimages" );
      totalImages = ( parameter == null ? 0 :
                      Integer.parseInt( parameter ) );
   }
}
```

Fig. 14.7 Customizing an applet via the **param** HTML tag (part 4 of 5).

14.9 Image Maps

A common technique for creating more interesting Web pages is the use of *image maps*. An image map is an image that has *hot areas* that the user can click to accomplish a task such as loading a different Web page into a browser. When the user positions the mouse pointer over a hot area, normally a descriptive message is displayed in the status area of the

Fig. 14.7 Customizing an applet via the **param** HTML tag (part 5 of 5).

browser. This technique can be used to implement a *bubble help* system. When the user positions the mouse pointer over a particular element on the screen, a system with bubble help usually displays a message in a small window that appears automatically over the screen element. In Java, the message can be displayed in the status bar.

The program of Fig. 14.8 loads an image containing the icons from the *Java Multimedia Cyber Classroom*—the interactive-CD, multimedia version of this text. These icons may look familiar; they are designed to mimic the icons used in this book. The program allows the user to position the mouse pointer over an icon and display a descriptive message for the icon. Method **mouseMove** takes the coordinates of the mouse and passes them to method **translateLocation**. The coordinates are tested to determine in which icon the coordinates are located. Method **translateLocation** then displays a message in the status bar of the applet indicating what the icon represents.

Clicking in this applet will not cause any action. In Chapter 16, "Networking," we discuss the techniques required to load another Web page into a browser. Once we have these networking capabilities, we can modify this applet to enable each icon to be associated with a different URL.

```
// Fig. 14.8: ImageMap.java
// Demonstrating an image map.
import java.applet.Applet;
import java.awt.*;
import java.awt.event.*;

public class ImageMap extends Applet
             implements MouseListener, MouseMotionListener {
   Image mapImage;
   MediaTracker trackImage;
   int width, height;

```

Fig. 14.8 Demonstrating an image map (part 1 of 4).

```java
   public void init()
   {
      addMouseListener( this );
      addMouseMotionListener( this );
      trackImage = new MediaTracker( this );
      mapImage = getImage( getDocumentBase(), "icons2.gif" );
      trackImage.addImage( mapImage, 0 );

      try {
         trackImage.waitForAll();
      }
      catch( InterruptedException e ) { }

      width = mapImage.getWidth( this );
      height = mapImage.getHeight( this );
      resize( width, height );
   }

   public void paint( Graphics g )
   {
      g.drawImage( mapImage, 0, 0, this );
   }

   public void mouseMoved( MouseEvent e )
   {
      showStatus( translateLocation( e.getX() ) );
   }

   public void mouseExited( MouseEvent e )
   {
      showStatus( "Pointer outside ImageMap applet" );
   }

   public void mouseDragged( MouseEvent e ) {}
   public void mousePressed( MouseEvent e ) {}
   public void mouseReleased( MouseEvent e ) {}
   public void mouseEntered( MouseEvent e ) {}
   public void mouseClicked( MouseEvent e ) {}

   public String translateLocation( int x )
   {
      // determine width of each icon (there are 6)
      int iconWidth = width / 6;

      if ( x >= 0 && x <= iconWidth)
         return "Common Programming Error";
      else if ( x > iconWidth && x <= iconWidth * 2 )
         return "Good Programming Practice";
      else if ( x > iconWidth * 2 && x <= iconWidth * 3 )
         return "Performance Tip";
```

Fig. 14.8 Demonstrating an image map (part 2 of 4).

```
      else if ( x > iconWidth * 3 && x <= iconWidth * 4 )
         return "Portability Tip";
      else if ( x > iconWidth * 4 && x <= iconWidth * 5 )
         return "Software Engineering Observation";
      else if ( x > iconWidth * 5 && x <= iconWidth * 6 )
         return "Testing and Debugging Tip";

      return "";
   }
}
```

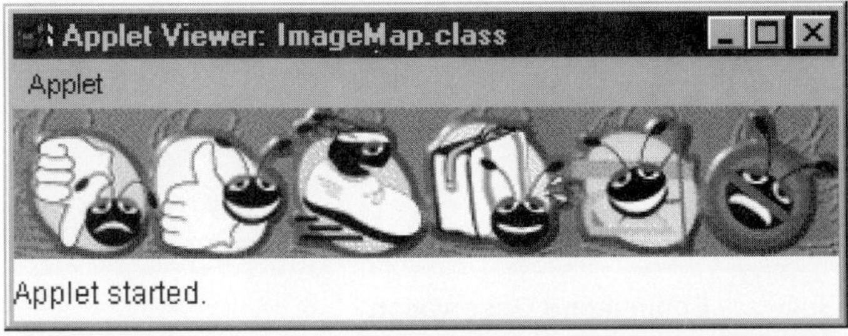

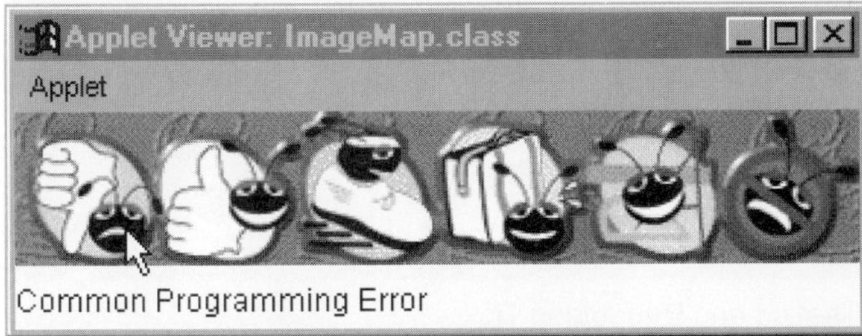

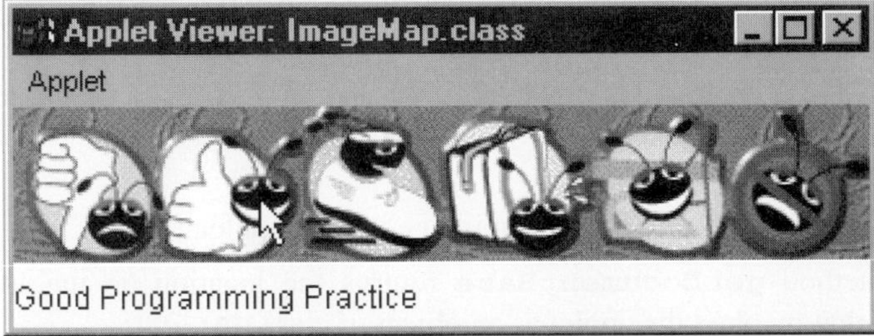

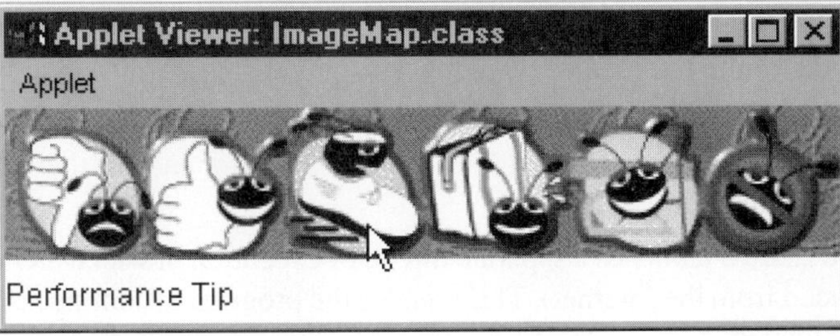

Fig. 14.8 Demonstrating an image map (part 3 of 4).

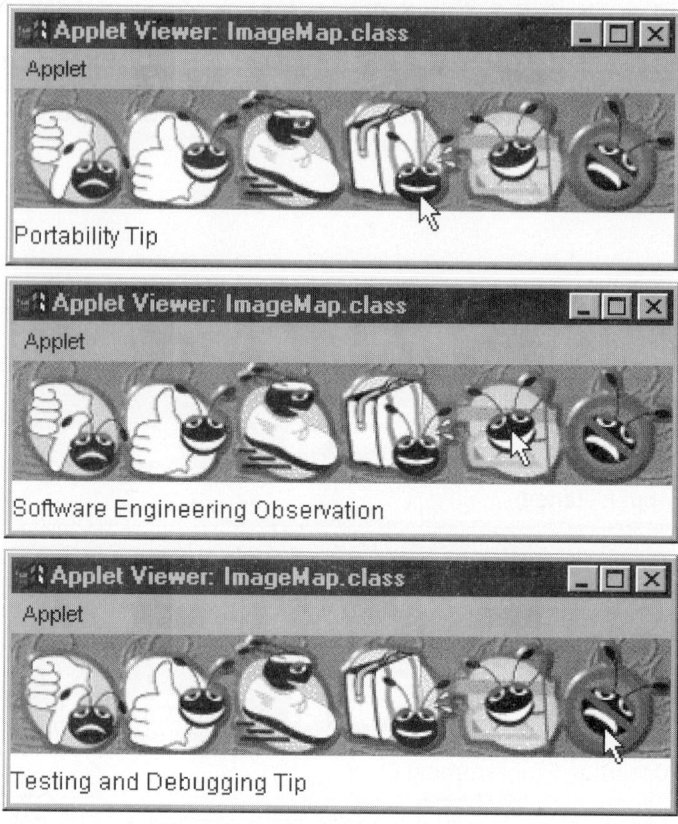

Fig. 14.8 Demonstrating an image map (part 4 of 4).

Summary

- **`Applet`** method **`getImage`** loads an image into an applet.
- **`Applet`** method **`getDocumentBase`** returns the location on the Internet of the HTML file that invoked the applet as an object of class **`URL`**.
- A **`URL`** stores a *Uniform Resource Locator*—a standard format for an address of a piece of information on the Internet.
- Java currently supports two image formats—*Graphics Interchange Format (GIF)* and *Joint Photographic Experts Group (JPEG)*. File names for each of these types end with **`.gif`** or **`.jpg`**, respectively.
- Method **`getImage`** launches a separate thread of execution in which an image is loaded (or downloaded from the Internet). This enables the program to continue execution while the image is loaded.
- **`Graphics`** method **`drawImage`** displays an image on an applet.

- **ImageObserver** is an interface that is implemented by class **Component**. The **ImageObserver** is automatically notified to update an image that was displayed as the remainder of the image is loaded.
- **Image** methods **getWidth** and **getHeight** each receive an **ImageObserver** as an argument and return the width and height of the image, respectively. The **ImageObserver** argument enables updating of the image information as the **Image** loads.
- An animation often flickers as each image is displayed. This is due to the applet's **update** method being called. When **update** clears the applet, it does so by drawing a filled rectangle the size of the applet in the current background color. This covers the image that was just drawn causing a flicker.
- Each call to **repaint** starts a separate thread of execution (which creates a separate method call stack) in which the repainting of the applet is performed.
- With the technique of *graphics double buffering*, while the program renders one image on the screen, it can be building the next image in an off-screen buffer. Then, when it is time for that next image to be displayed, it can be placed on the screen smoothly.
- Graphics double buffering is useful in programs that draw in methods other than **paint**. The off-screen buffer can be passed between methods or even between objects of different classes to allow other methods or objects to draw on the off-screen buffer.
- GIF images can be stored in interlaced and non-interlaced formats. As a non-interlaced image is displayed, it appears in chunks from top to bottom as the pixel information is read. As an interlaced image is displayed, it appears to fade in as the first batch of rows presents a rough outline of the picture and the subsequent batches of rows refine the displayed image until the entire image is complete.
- There are two key pieces to implementing a graphics double buffer—an **Image** reference and a **Graphics** reference. The **Image** is where the actual pixels to be displayed are stored. The **Graphics** reference is used to draw the pixels.
- Every image has an associated graphics context—i.e., an object of class **Graphics** that enables drawing to be performed.
- The **Image** and **Graphics** references used for graphics double buffering are often referred to as the *off-screen image* and the *off-screen graphics context* because they are not actually manipulating screen pixels.
- Applet method **createImage** asks the system to create an empty image by instantiating an object of the system-specific subclass of **Image**. The method receives two integer arguments—the width and height of the empty image.
- **Image** method **getGraphics** gets the graphics context (i.e., the **Graphics** object) associated with an **Image** object.
- Images can be registered with a **MediaTracker** object to enable the program to determine when an image is loaded completely. Class **MediaTracker** also provides the ability to wait for an image or several images to load before allowing a program to continue and to determine if an error occurred while loading an image.

- The **MediaTracker** constructor takes one argument—an **ImageObserver** (normally the object on which the images will be drawn).
- **MediaTracker** method **addImage** registers an image with a **MediaTracker** object. The first argument is an **Image** reference. The second argument is an integer ID that can be used to query the **MediaTracker** on the status of that image. To track multiple images as a group, give them the same ID number.
- **MediaTracker** method **waitForID** forces the program to wait until the image specified by the integer argument is completely loaded. **MediaTracker** method **waitForAll** blocks until all registered images are loaded completely.
- To eliminate all flicker, override the applet's **update** method to call **paint** without clearing the applet.
- To make an animation "browser friendly" run the animation as a separate thread in the applet. The applet's **start** method should instantiate a **Thread** and launch the animation. The applet's **stop** method should stop the thread to terminate the animation when the user browses a different Web page. **Thread** methods **suspend** and **resume** can also be used to let the user suspend and resume the applet.
- Java provides two mechanisms for playing sounds in an applet—the **Applet**'s ***play*** method and the ***play*** method from the ***AudioClip*** *interface*.
- To play a sound once in a program, use the **Applet** method **play** to load the sound and play it; the sound is marked for garbage collection when it is done playing.
- **Applet** method **getDocumentBase** indicates where to locate the HTML file that loaded the applet.
- **Applet** method **getCodeBase** indicates where the applet's **.class** file is located.
- The HTML **param** tag specifies a parameter for an applet. The **param** tag lines appear between the starting **applet** tag and the ending **applet** tag. Each parameter has a **name** and a **value**.
- **Applet** method **getParameter** is used to get the **value** associated with a specific parameter and return the **value** as a **String**. If there is not a **param** tag containing the specified parameter, **getParameter** returns **null**.
- An image map is an image that has *hot areas* that the user can click to accomplish a task such as loading a different Web page.

Terminology

addImage method
animation
animation loop
animation speed
.au file format for sound files
audio
AudioClip interface
audio clips
"browser-friendly" animation applet
bubble help
checkID period
display an image
double buffering to reduce flicker
drawImage method of **Graphics** class
fetch an image from a server
flicker

flicker reduction
frame of an animation
frames order
getAudioClip method
getCodeBase method
getDocumentBase method
getGraphics method
getImage method of **Applet** class
getParameter method
.gif image file
graphics
Graphics Interchange Format (GIF)
hot area
Graphics class
graphics context
graphics double buffering
image
Image class
image map
ImageObserver interface
imageUpdate method of an applet
interlaced GIF images
Joint Photographic Experts Group (JPEG)
JPEG image format
load an audio clip
load an image
loop method of **AudioClip** interface
loop on an audio clip
MediaTracker class
multimedia
non-interlaced GIF images
off-screen buffer
off-screen graphics context
off-screen image
play method of **AudioClip** interface
play method of class **Applet**
restart an animation
smooth animation
sound
sound clip
sound loop
sound track
space/time trade-off
stop an animation
stop method of **AudioClip** interface
stop an audio clip
URL of an image
waitForAll method
waitForID method

Good Programming Practice

14.1 Always display something while images load. The longer a user must wait to see information appear on the screen, the more likely they will leave the Web page before the information appears.

Performance Tips

14.1 It is more efficient to load the frames of the animation as one image than to load each image separately (a painting program can be used to combine the frames of the animation into one image). Every ***getImage*** method call requires a separate connection to the World Wide Web site where the images are stored.

14.2 Loading all the frames of an image as one large image may force your program to wait to begin displaying the animation.

14.3 An animation applet that uses a call to **repaint** from the applet's **paint** method to implement animation occupies processor time even after the user leaves the Web page on which the animation applet resides. This may cause performance degradation.

14.4 Double buffering can reduce or eliminate flicker in an animation, but it can visibly slow the speed at which the animation runs.

14.5 Some people who are experienced with **MediaTracker** objects have reported that they can have a detrimental effect on performance. Keep this in mind as an area to scrutinize if you need to tune your multimedia applications.

14.6 Using **MediaTracker** method **waitForAll** to wait for all registered images to completely load may result is a long delay between when the applet begins execution and when the images are actually displayed. The more images and the larger the images, the more time the user will have to wait. Use **MediaTracker** method **waitForAll** only to wait for small numbers of images to load completely.

Portability Tip

14.1 Class **Image** is an abstract class, so **Image** objects cannot be created directly. To achieve platform independence, the Java implementation on each platform provides its own subclass of **Image** to store image information.

Software Engineering Observation

14.1 When creating an animation be sure to provide a mechanism for disabling the animation when the user browses a new Web page separate from the page on which the animation applet resides.

Self-Review Exercises

14.1 Fill in the blanks in each of the following:

a) **Applet** method __________ loads an image into an applet.
b) **Applet** method __________ returns the location on the Internet of the HTML file that invoked the applet as an object of class **URL**.
c) A __________ is a standard format for an address of a piece of information on the Internet.
d) **Graphics** method __________ displays an image on an applet.
e) An animation often flickers as each image is displayed. This is due to the applet's __________ method being called. When this method clears the applet, it does so by drawing a filled rectangle the size of the applet in the current background color. This covers the image that was just drawn causing a flicker.
f) With the technique of __________, while the program renders one image on the screen, it can be building the next image in an off-screen buffer. Then, when it is time for that next image to be displayed, it can be placed on the screen smoothly.
g) As an __________ image is displayed, it appears to fade in as the first batch of rows presents a rough outline of the picture and the subsequent batches of rows refine the displayed image until the entire image is complete.
h) There are two key pieces to implementing a graphics double buffer—an __________ reference and a __________ reference. The first is where the actual pixels to be displayed are stored; the second is used to draw the pixels.
i) Images can be registered with a __________ object to enable the program to determine when an image is loaded completely.
j) Java provides two mechanisms for playing sounds in an applet—the **Applet**'s ***play*** method and the ***play*** method from the __________ *interface*.

k) An _________ is an image that has *hot areas* that the user can click to accomplish a task such as loading a different Web page.

14.2 State whether each of the following is true or false. If false, explain why.

a) Java currently supports two image formats. File names for each of these types end with **.jif** or **.gpg**, respectively.
b) Overriding the applet's **update** method to call **paint** without clearing the applet will significantly reduce animation flicker.
c) A sound will be garbage collected as soon as it is done playing.
d) The Java **param** tag specifies a parameter for an applet. The **param** tag lines appear between the starting **applet** tag and the ending **applet** tag. Each parameter has a **name** and a **value**.

Answers to Self-Review Exercises

14.1 a) **getImage**. b) **getDocumentBase**. c) **URL**. d) **drawImage**. e) **update**. f) graphics double buffering. g) interlaced. h) **Image**, **Graphics**. i) **MediaTracker**. j) **AudioClip**. k) image map.

14.2 a) False; should be **.gif** or **.jpg** b) True. c) False, the sound will be marked for garbage collection and will be garbage collected when the garbage collector is able to run, possibly not immediately. d) False. The **param** tag is HTML not Java.

Exercises

14.3 Describe how to make an animation "browser friendly."

14.4 Discuss the various aspects of flicker elimination in Java.

14.5 Explain the technique of graphics double buffering.

14.6 Describe the Java methods for playing and manipulating audio clips.

14.7 How can Java applets be customized with information from an HTML file?

14.8 How is a **MediaTracker** object used? What cautions should you keep in mind when using a **MediaTracker**?

14.9 Explain how image maps are used. List ten applications of image maps.

14.10 *(Animation)* Create a a general-purpose Java animation applet. Your applet should allow the user to specify the sequence of frames to be displayed, the speed at which the images are displayed, audios that should be played while the animation is running and so on.

14.11 *(Story Teller)* Record audio for a large number of nouns, verbs, articles, prepositions, etc. Then use random number generation to forms sentences and have your program speak the sentences.

14.12 *(Limericks)* Modify the limerick writing program you wrote in Exercise 8.10 to sing the limericks your program creates.

14.13 *(Screensaver)* Use animation of a series of your favorite images to create a screensaver program. Create various special effects that explode the images, spin the images, fade them in and out, move them off the edge of the screen, and the like.

14.14 *(Randomly Erasing an Image)* Suppose an image is displayed in a rectangular screen area. One way to erase the image is simply to set every pixel to the same color immediately, but this is a dull visual effect. Write a Java applet that displays an image then erases it by using random-number generation to select individual pixels to erase. After most of the image is erased, erase all of the remaining pixels at once. You can refer to individual pixels by having a line that starts and ends at the same point. You might try several variants of this problem. For example, you might display lines randomly or you might display shapes randomly to erase regions of the screen.

14.15 *(Random Inter-Image Transition)* Here is a nice visual effect. If you are displaying one image in a given area on the screen and you would like to transition to another image in the same screen area, Store the new screen image in an off-screen buffer and randomly copy pixels from the new image to the display area overlaying the previous pixels at those locations. When the vast majority of the pixels have been copied, copy the entire new image to the display area to be sure you are displaying the complete new image. To implement this program you may need to use the **`PixelGrabber`** and **`MemoryImageSource`** classes (see the Java API documentation for descriptions of these classes). You might try several variants of this problem. For example, you might select all the pixels in a randomly selected straight line or shape in the new image and overlay those pixels above the corresponding positions of the old image.

14.16 *(Background Audio)* Add background audio to one of your favorite applications by using the **`loop`** method of class **`AudioClip`** to play the sound in the background while you interact with your application in the normal way.

14.17 *(Project: Multimedia Aerobics)* Here a product idea that could help you make your fortune! Millions of people do aerobics exercises every day to help stay fit. Develop a Java aerobics applet that displays animated sequences of exercises with appropriate background music, sounds, instructions and words of encouragement. Internationalize your program by offering the instructions in several languages and by playing music appropriate for each region. Allow the users to customize their exercise programs to meet their particular exercise needs. Allow the users to customize their exercise programs for beginner, intermediate and advanced levels. Add other features as appropriate.

14.18 *(Project: Multimedia Authoring System)* Develop a general-purpose multimedia authoring system. Your program should allow the user to form multimedia presentations consisting of text, audios, images, animations and eventually, videos. Your program lets the user weave together a presentation consisting of any of these multimedia elements that are selected from a catalog your program displays. Provide controls to allow the user to customize the presentation dynamically as the presentation is delivered

14.19 *(Video Games)* Video games have become wildly popular. Develop your own Java video game program. Have a contest with your classmates to develop the best original video game.

14.20 *(Scrolling Marquee Sign)* Create a Java applet that scrolls dotted characters right-to-left (or left-to-right if that is appropriate for your language) across a Marquee-like display sign. As an option, display the text in a continuous loop so that after the text goes off the sign at one end it reappears at the other end.

14.21 *(Text Flasher)* Create a Java applet that repeatedly flashes text on the screen. Do this by interspersing the text with a plain background color image. Allow the user to control the "blink speed" and the background color or pattern.

14.22 *(Image Flasher)* Create a Java applet that repeatedly flashes an image on the screen. Do this by interspersing the image with a plain background color image.

14.23 *(Scrolling Image Marquee)* Create a Java applet that scrolls an image across a Marquee screen.

14.24 *(Physics Demo: Bouncing Ball)* Develop an animated applet that shows a bouncing ball. Give the ball a constant horizontal velocity. Allow the user to specify the coefficient of restitution, e.g., a coefficient of restitution of 75% means that after the ball bounces it returns to only 75% of its height before it was bounced. Your demo should take gravity into effect—this will cause the bouncing ball to trace a parabolic path. Track down a "boing" sound (like a spring bouncing) and play the sound every time the ball hits the ground.

14.25 *(Pendulum)* Develop an animated applet that shows a pendulum swinging. Allow the user to specify a damping factor that gradually slows the pendulum to an eventual stop.

14.26 *(Project: Flight Simulator)* Develop your own flight simulator Java applet. This is a very challenging project. It is also an excellent candidate for a contest with your classmates

14.27 *(Towers of Hanoi)* Write an animated version of the Towers of Hanoi problem we presented in Exercise 4.38. As each disk is lifted off a peg or slid onto a peg play a "whooshing" sound. As each disk lands on the pile play a "clunking" sound. Play some appropriate background music.

14.28 *(Tortoise and the Hare)* Develop a multimedia version of the Tortoise and Hare simulation we presented in Exercise 5.41. You might record an announcer's voice calling the race, "The contenders are at the starting line." "And they're off!" "The Hare pulls out in front." "The Tortoise is coming on strong." etc. As the race proceeds, play the appropriate recorded audios. Play sounds to simulate the animals' running, and don't forget the crowd cheering! Do an animation of the animals racing up the side of the slippery mountain.

14.29 *(Bubble Help)* Use an image map to implement a "bubble help" facility. When the mouse cursor passes over a given image, display some appropriate text to assist your user who may not be sure what a particular image is supposed to designate. You might build in a bit of a delay so that the help messages are only displayed when the mouse cursor lingers over an image.

14.30 *(Digital Clock)* Implement an applet that displays a digital clock on the screen. You might add options to scale the clock; display day, month and year; issue an alarm; play certain audios at designated times and the like.

14.31 *(Analog Clock)* Create a Java applet that displays an analog clock with hour, minute and second hands that move appropriately as the time changes.

14.32 *(Dynamic Stock Portfolio Evaluator)* Create a Java applet that will read a file describing an investor's stock portfolio. For each stock the investor owns, the file contains the stock ticker symbol and the number of shares of that stock the investor owns. The applet then accesses some stock quotation service available over the Internet (this requires techniques from Chapter 16, Networking) and filters out only those stock transactions for the stocks in the investor's portfolio. As the applet fetches new stock prices, it displays a spreadsheet on the screen and dynamically updates the spreadsheet. The spreadsheet shows each stock symbol, the latest price of that stock, the number of shares and the latest total value of shares of that stock. The spreadsheet also totals the latest value of the investor's entire portfolio. An investor could run your Java applet in a small portion of his or her screen while proceeding with other work.

14.33 *(Dynamic Customized Newsletter)* After you complete Chapter 16 you will understand how to develop Internet-based Java applications that access the World Wide Web. Develop a "newspaper of the future" in which your user uses a graphical user interface to design a customized dynamic newspaper which meets that user's unique information needs. Then have your application harvest information from the World Wide Web at the designated intervals, possibly continuously. You'll be amazed to see how many popular publications offer computerized versions at no charge on the Web.

14.34 *(Dynamic Audio and Graphical Kaleidoscope)* Develop a kaleidoscope applet that displays reflected graphics to simulate the popular children's toy. Incorporate audio effects that "mirror" your applet's dynamically changing graphics.

14.35 *(Automatic Jigsaw Puzzle Generator)* Create a Java jigsaw puzzle generator and manipulator. Your user specifies an image. Your applet loads and displays the image. Then your applet breaks the image into randomly selected shapes. Then it shuffles the shapes. Your user then uses the mouse to move the puzzle pieces around until the puzzle is solved. Add appropriate audio sounds as the pieces are being shuffled around and snapped back into place. You might keep tabs on each piece and where it really belongs and then use audio effects to help the user get the pieces into correct positions.

14.36 *(Teaching Juggling)* If you've ever tried juggling, you know how difficult it is. It is especially difficult to learn from a book, because books cannot possibly display the dynamics of juggling. Develop a multimedia-based Java applet that will help frustrated juggling students (like the older author) learn how to juggle. In particular, your simulation should show the detail of juggling various numbers of items. You should probably read a good book on juggling before you begin this assignment.

14.37 *(Maze Generator and Walker)* Develop a multimedia-based maze generator and traverser applet based on the maze programs you wrote in Exercises 5.38, 5.39 and 5.40. Let the user customize the maze by specifying the number of rows and columns and by indicating the level of difficulty. Have an animated mouse walk the maze. Use audio to dramatize the movement of your mouse character.

14.38 *(Knight's Tour Walker)* Develop multimedia-based versions of the Knight's Tour programs you wrote in Exercises 5.22 and 5.23.

14.39 *(Pinball Machine)* Here's another contest problem. Develop a Java applet that simulates a pinball machine of your own design. Have a contest with your classmates to develop the best original multimedia pinball machine. Use every possible multimedia trick you can think of to add "pizzazz" to your pinball game. Try to keep the game mechanisms close to those of real pinball games.

14.40 *(Roulette)* Study the rules for the game of roulette and implement a multimedia-based version of the game. Create an animated spinning roulette wheel. Use audio to simulate the sound of the ball jumping the various compartments that correspond to each of the numbers. Use an audio to simulate the sound of the ball falling into its final slot. While the roulette wheel is spinning, allow multiple players to place their bets. When the ball lands in its final slot, you should update the bank accounts of each of the players with the appropriate wins or losses.

14.41 *(Craps)* Simulate the complete game of craps. Use a graphical representation of a craps table. Allow multiple players to place their bets. Use an animation of the player who is rolling the dice and show the animated dice rolling eventually to a stop. Use audio to simulate some of the chatter around the craps table. After each roll, the system should automatically update the bank accounts of each of the players depending on the bets they have made.

14.42 *(One-Armed Bandit)* Develop a multimedia simulation of a one-armed bandit. Have three spinning wheels. Place various fruits and symbols on each wheel. Use true random-number generation to simulate the spinning of each wheel and the stopping of each wheel on a symbol.

14.43 *(Horse Race)* Create a Java simulation of a horse race. Have multiple contenders. Use audios for a race announcer. Play the appropriate audios to indicate the correct status of each of the contenders throughout the race. Use audios to announce the final results. You might try to simulate the kind of horse race games that are often played at carnivals. The players get turns at the mouse and have to perform some skill-oriented manipulation with the mouse to advance their horses.

14.44 *(Shuffleboard)* Develop a multimedia-based simulation of the game of shuffleboard. Use appropriate audio and visual effects.

14.45 *(Game of Pool)* Create a multimedia-based simulation of the game of pool. Each player takes turns using the mouse to position a pool stick and to hit the stick against the ball at the appropriate angle to try to get the pool balls to fall into the pockets. Your applet should keep score.

14.46 *(Fashion Designer)* Develop a multimedia-based fashion design tool that will help a fashion designer design high-fashion clothing. Your tool should allow the designer to choose colors, shapes, decorative accents and the like to create clothing designs.

14.47 *(Artist)* Design a Java art applet that will give an artist a great variety of capabilities to draw, use images, use animations and the like to create a dynamic multimedia art display.

14.48 *(Fireworks Designer).* Create a Java applet that someone might use to create a fireworks display. Create a variety of fireworks demonstrations. Then orchestrate the firing of the fireworks for maximum effect.

14.49 *(Floor Planner)* Develop a Java applet that will help someone arrange furniture in his or her home. Add features that help the person achieve the best possible arrangement.

14.50 *(Crossword)* Crossword puzzles are among the most popular pastimes. Develop a multimedia-based crossword puzzle program. Your program should enable the player to place and erase words easily. Tie your program to a large computerized dictionary. Your applet should be able to suggest words based on which letters have already been filled in. Provide other features that will make the crossword puzzle enthusiast's job easier.

14.51 *(15 Puzzle)* Write a multimedia-based Java applet that enables the user to play the game of 15. There is a 4-by-4 board for a total of 16 slots. One of the slots is empty. The other slots are occupied by 15 tiles numbered 1 through 15. Any tile next to the currently empty slot can be moved into the currently empty slot by clicking on the tile. Your applet should create the board with the tiles out of order. The goal is to arrange the tiles into sequential order row by row.

14.52 *(Synthesizer)* Develop a multimedia-based Java applet that simulates a synthesizer musical instrument. Your applet should display a keyboard along with a variety of sound options. The user plays music by pressing the appropriate keys in sequence and for the proper duration. The user can select from a variety of instrument sounds like piano, clarinet, drums, cymbals and the like.

14.53 *(Player Piano)* Create a Java applet that functions as a player piano. Your applet receives encoded sheet music in a file indicating what notes or combinations of notes are to be played for what durations. You can prerecord audios for each of the 88 notes on the piano.

14.54 *(Sheet Music Generator/Player)* Write a Java applet that displays sheet music for the files you created in the previous exercise.

14.55 *(Music Teacher)* Develop a Java applet that will help a student learn to play the piano. Your applet should display the keyboard and use a variety of visual and audio techniques.

14.56 *(Arithmetic Tutor)* Develop a multimedia version of the Computer-Assisted Instruction (CAI) systems you developed in Exercises 4.31, 4.32 and 4.33.

14.57 *(Karaoke)* Create a Karaoke system that plays the music for a song and displays the words for your user to sing at the appropriate time.

14.58 *(Calling Attention to an Image)* If you want to emphasize an image, you might place a row of simulated light bulbs around your image. You can let the light bulbs flash in unison or you can let them fire on and off in sequence one after the other.

14.59 *(Physics Demo: Kinetics)* If you have taken physics, implement a Java applet that will demo concepts like energy, inertia, momentum, velocity, acceleration, friction, coefficient of restitution, gravity and others. Create visual effects and use audios where appropriate for emphasis and realism.

14.60 *(On-Line Product Catalog)* Companies are rapidly realizing the potential for doing business on the Web. Develop an on-line multimedia catalog from which your customers may select products to be shipped. After reading Chapter 16, you will be able to handle the networking aspects of this problem. If you have an actual company, you should read the latest articles on secure transmission of credit card IDs over the Internet.

14.61 *(Reaction Time/Reaction Precision Tester)* Create a Java applet that moves a randomly created shape around the screen. The user moves the mouse to catch and click on the shape. The shape's speed and size can be varied. Keep statistics on how much time the user typically takes to catch a shape of a given size. The user will probably have more difficulty catching faster moving smaller shapes.

14.62 *(Image Zooming)* Create a Java applet that enables you to zoom in on, or away from, an image.

14.63 *(Calendar/Tickler File)* Create a general purpose calendar and "tickler" file. Use audio and images. For example, the applet should sing "Happy Birthday" to you when you use it on your birthday. Have the applet display images and play audios associated with important events. Have the applet remind you in advance of important events. It would be nice, for example, to have the applet give you a week's warning so you can pick up an appropriate greeting card for that special person.

14.64 *(Rotating Images)* Create a Java applet that lets you rotate an image through some number of degrees (out of a maximum of 360 degrees). As an option, the applet should let you specify that you want to spin the image continuously. The applet should let you adjust the spin speed dynamically.

14.65 *(Coloring Black and White Photographs and Images)* Create a Java applet that lets you paint a black and white photograph with color. Provide a color palette for selecting colors. Your applet should let you apply different colors to different regions of the image.

14.66 *(Project: Automated Teller Machine) [Note: This project will require that you use advanced Java techniques from Chapters 14, 15 and 16. We suggest that you do as much as you can now with the Java graphics, GUI, multithreading and multimedia technologies you studied in Chapters 9* *through 14. Then incorporate file processing after you complete Chapter 15 and incorporate client/server networking after you complete Chapter 16. This is an excellent group project.]* One of the authors had the privilege of teaching at the division of one of the largest banks in the United States that builds the hardware and software for the automated teller machines that the bank deploys worldwide. During this teaching engagement the author got a behind-the-scenes peek at the "automated teller machine of the future." Develop the framework of a Java *application* that implements an automated teller machine and simulates its interaction with a bank's accounts maintained by another computer. The first version of your applet should simulate automated teller machines pretty much as they operate today. Then let your creative juices flow and try to design your own version of the "automated teller machine of the future." Use graphics, animation, sound and any other capabilities of Java, the World Wide Web and the Internet that you wish to employ.

14.67 *(Multimedia-Based Simpletron Simulator)* Modify the Simpletron simulator that you developed in the exercises in the previous chapters to include multimedia features. Add computer-like sounds to indicate that the Simpletron is executing instructions. Add a breaking glass sound when a fatal error occurs. Use flashing lights to indicate which cells of memory and/or which registers are currently being manipulated. Use other multimedia techniques as appropriate to make your Simpletron simulator more valuable as an educational tool to its users.

15

Files and Streams

Objectives

- To be able to create, read, write and update files.
- To understand the Java streams class hierarchy.
- To be able to use the **`FileInputStream`** and **`FileOutputStream`** classes.
- To be able to use the **`DataInputStream`** and **`DataOutputStream`** classes.
- To become familiar with sequential-access and random-access file processing.
- To build a transaction-processing program with random-access files.
- To be able to use the **`File`** class.

I can only assume that a "Do Not File" document is filed in a "Do Not File" file.
Senator Frank Church
Senate Intelligence Subcommittee Hearing, 1975

Consciousness . . . does not appear to itself chopped up in bits. . . . A "river" or a "stream" are the metaphors by which it is most naturally described.
William James

I read part of it all the way through.
Samuel Goldwyn

It is quite a three-pipe problem.
Sir Athur Conan Doyle

Outline

15.1 Introduction

Storage of data in variables and arrays is temporary—the data is lost when a local variable "goes out of scope" or when the program terminates, for example. *Files* are used for long-term retention of large amounts of data, even after the program that created the data terminates. Data maintained in files is often called *persistent data*. Computers store files on *secondary storage devices* such as magnetic disks, optical disks and magnetic tapes. In this chapter, we explain how data files are created, updated, and processed by Java programs. We consider both "sequential-access" files and "random-access" files and indicate the kinds of applications for which each is best suited. Stream processing is a large subject. We have two goals in this chapter—to introduce the sequential-access and random-access file processing paradigms and to provide the reader with sufficient stream processing capabilities to support the networking features introduced in Chapter 16.

File processing is one of the most important capabilities a language must have to support commercial applications that typically process massive amounts of persistent data. In this chapter we discuss Java's powerful and abundant file-processing and stream input/output features.

Software Engineering Observation 15.1

It would be dangerous to enable applets arriving from anywhere on the World Wide Web to be able to read and write files on the client system. Most web browsers prevent applets from performing file processing on the client system. Therefore, file-processing programs are generally implemented as Java applications.

15.2 The Data Hierarchy

Ultimately, all data items processed by a computer are reduced to combinations of zeros and ones. This occurs because it is simple and economical to build electronic devices that can assume two stable states—one state represents **0** and the other state represents **1**. It is remarkable that the impressive functions performed by computers involve only the most fundamental manipulations of **0**s and **1**s.

The smallest data item in a computer can assume the value **0** or the value **1**. Such a data item is called a *bit* (short for "*b*inary dig*it*"—a digit that can assume one of two values). Computer circuitry performs various simple bit manipulations such as examining the value of a bit, setting the value of a bit, and reversing a bit (from **1** to **0** or from **0** to **1**).

It is cumbersome for programmers to work with data in the low-level form of bits. Instead, programmers prefer to work with data in forms such as *decimal digits* (i.e., 0, 1, 2, 3, 4, 5, 6, 7, 8, and 9), *letters* (i.e., A through Z, and a through z), and *special symbols* (i.e., $, @, %, &, *, (,), -, +, ", :, ?, /, and many others). Digits, letters, and special symbols are referred to as *characters*. The set of all characters used to write programs and represent data items on a particular computer is called that computer's *character set*. Since computers can process only **1**s and **0**s, every character in a computer's character set is represented as a pattern of **1**s and **0**s (characters in Java are *Unicode* characters composed of 2 *bytes*). Bytes are most commonly composed of eight bits. Programmers create programs and data items with characters; computers manipulate and process these characters as patterns of bits.

Just as characters are composed of bits, *fields* are composed of characters. A field is a group of characters that conveys meaning. For example, a field consisting solely of uppercase and lowercase letters can be used to represent a person's name.

Data items processed by computers form a *data hierarchy* in which data items become larger and more complex in structure as we progress from bits, to characters (bytes), to fields, and so on.

A *record* (i.e., a **class** in Java) is composed of several fields (called instance variables in Java). In a payroll system, for example, a record for a particular employee might consist of the following fields:

1. Employee identification number
2. Name
3. Address
4. Hourly salary rate
5. Number of exemptions claimed
6. Year-to-date earnings
7. Amount of federal taxes withheld, etc.

Thus, a record is a group of related fields. In the preceding example, each of the fields belongs to the same employee. Of course, a particular company may have many employees, and will have a payroll record for each employee. A *file* is a group of related records. A company's payroll file normally contains one record for each employee. Thus, a payroll file for a small company might contain only 22 records, whereas a payroll file for a large company might contain 100,000 records. It is not unusual for a company to have many files, some containing millions, or even billions, of characters of information. Figure 15.1 illustrates the *data hierarchy*.

To facilitate the retrieval of specific records from a file, at least one field in each record is chosen as a *record key*. A record key identifies a record as belonging to a particular person or entity that is unique from all other records in the file. In the payroll record described previously, the employee identification number would normally be chosen as the record key.

There are many ways of organizing records in a file. The most common type of organization is called a *sequential file* in which records are typically stored in order by the record-key field. In a payroll file, records are usually placed in order by employee identification number. The first employee record in the file contains the lowest employee identification number, and subsequent records contain increasingly higher employee identification numbers.

Most businesses utilize many different files to store data. For example, companies may have payroll files, accounts receivable files (listing money due from clients), accounts payable files (listing money due to suppliers), inventory files (listing facts about all the items handled by the business), and many other types of files. A group of related files is sometimes called a *database*. A collection of programs designed to create and manage databases is called a *database management system* (DBMS).

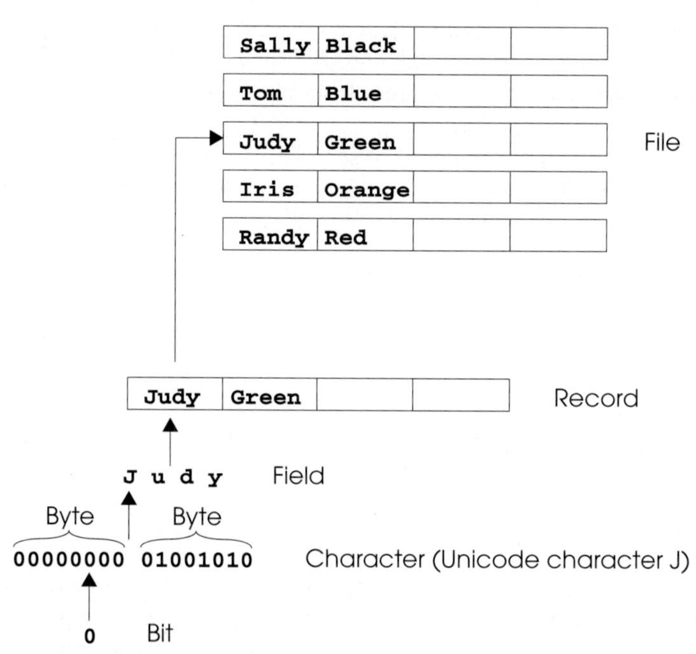

Fig. 15.1 The data hierarchy.

15.3 Files and Streams

Java views each file as a sequential stream of bytes (Fig. 15.2). Each file ends either with an *end-of-file marker* or at a specific byte number recorded in a system-maintained administrative data structure. When a file is *opened*, an object is created and a stream is associated with the object. Three stream objects are created for us automatically when we begin executing a Java program—**System.in**, **System.out** and **System.err**. The streams associated with these objects provide communication channels between a program and a particular file or device. For example, object **System.in** (*standard input stream object*) enables a program to input bytes from the keyboard, object **System.out** (*standard output stream object*) enables a program to output data to the screen, and object **System.err** (*standard error stream object*) enables a program to output error messages to the screen.

To perform file processing in Java, the package **java.io** must be imported. This package includes the definitions for the stream classes such as **FileInputStream** (for input from a file) and **FileOutputStream** (for output to a file). Files are opened by creating objects of these stream classes that are derived from (i.e., inherit the functionality of) classes **InputStream** and **OutputStream**, respectively. Thus, the methods of these stream classes can all be applied to file streams as well. To perform input and output of primitive data types, objects of class **DataInputStream** and **DataOutputStream** will be used together with the file stream classes. The inheritance relationships of many of the Java I/O classes are summarized in Fig. 15.3. The following discussion overviews the capabilities of each of the classes in Fig. 15.3.

Java offers many classes for performing input/output. In this section we give a brief overview of each and explain how they relate to one another. In the rest of the chapter, we put several key stream classes to work as we implement a variety of file-processing programs that create, manipulate and destroy sequential-access files and random-access files. We also include a detailed example on the **File** class which is useful for obtaining information about files and directories. In Chapter 16, Networking," we use stream classes extensively to implement networking applications.

InputStream (a subclass of **Object**) and ***OutputStream*** (a subclass of **Object**) are abstract classes that define methods for performing input and output respectively; their derived classes override these methods.

File input/output is done with ***FileInputStream*** (a subclass of **InputStream**) and ***FileOutputStream*** (a subclass of **OutputStream**). We use these classes extensively in the examples in this chapter.

Pipes are synchronized communication channels between threads. A pipe is established between two threads. One thread sends data to another by writing to a ***PipedOutputStream*** (a subclass of **OutputStream**). The target thread reads information from the pipe via a ***PipedInputStream*** (a subclass of **InputStream**).

0	1	2	3	4	5	6	7	8	9	...	n-1	
										...		end-of-file marker

Fig. 15.2 Java's view of a file of ***n*** bytes.

Java Streams Class Hierarchy

```
Object
    File
    FileDescriptor
    StreamTokenizer
    InputStream
        ByteArrayInputStream
        SequenceInputStream
        StringBufferInputStream
        PipedInputStream
        FileInputStream
        FilterInputStream
            DataInputStream
            BufferedInputStream
            PushBackInputStream
            LineNumberInputStream
    OutputStream
        ByteArrayOutputStream
        PipedOutputStream
        FileOutputStream
        FilterOutputStream
            DataOutputStream
            BufferedOutputStream
            PrintStream
    RandomAccessFile
```

Fig. 15.3 A portion of the class hierarchy of the **java.io** package.

A ***PrintStream*** (a subclass of **FilterOutputStream**) is used for performing output to the screen (or the "standard output" as defined by your local operating system). Actually, we have been using **PrintStream** output throughout the text to this point; **System.out** is a **PrintStream** (as is **System.err**).

A **FilterInputStream** *filters* an **InputStream** and a **FilterOutStream** *filters* an **OutputStream**; filtering simply means that the filter stream provides additional functionality such as buffering, monitoring line numbers or aggregating data bytes into meaningful primitive-data-type units.

Reading data as raw bytes is fast but crude. Usually programs want to read data as aggregates of bytes that form an **int**, a **float**, a **double**, and so on. To accomplish this we use a **DataInputStream** (a subclass of class **FilterInputStream**).

The **DataInput** interface is implemented by class **DataInputStream** and class **RandomAccessFile** (discussed below) that each need to read primitive data types from a stream. **DataInputStream**s enable a program to read binary data from an **InputStream**. We typically chain a **DataInputStream** to a **FileInputStream**; as we will explain chaining shortly. The **DataInput** interface includes methods **read** (for byte arrays), **readBoolean**, **readByte**, **readChar**, **readDouble**, **readFloat**, **readFully** (for byte arrays) **readInt**, **readLong**, **readShort**, **readUnsignedByte**, **readUnsignedShort**, **readUTF** (for Unicode format strings) and **skipBytes**.

The **DataOutput** interface is implemented by class **DataOutputStream** (a subclass of class **FilterOutputStream**) and class **RandomAccessFile** that each need to write primitive data types to an **OutputStream**. **DataOutputStream**s enable a program to write binary data to an **OutputStream**. We typically chain a **DataOutputStream** to a **FileOutputStream**. The **DataOutput** interface includes methods **flush**, **size**, **write** (for a byte), **write** (for a byte array), **writeBoolean**, **writeByte**, **writeBytes**, **writeChar**, **writeChars** (for Unicode **String**s), **writeDouble**, **writeFloat**, **writeInt**, **writeLong**, **writeShort** and **writeUTF**.

Buffering is an I/O-performance-enhancement technique. With a ***BufferedOutputStream*** (a subclass of class **FilterOutputStream**) each output statement does not necessarily result in an actual physical transfer of data to the output device. Rather, each output operation is directed to a region in memory called a *buffer* that is large enough to hold the data of many output operations. Then actual output to the output device is performed in one large *physical output operation* each time the buffer fills. The output operations directed to the output buffer in memory are often called *logical output operations*.

Performance Tip 15.1

Because typical physical output operations are extremely slow compared to typical processor speeds, buffering outputs normally yields significant performance improvements over unbuffered outputs.

With a ***BufferedInputStream*** (a subclass of class **FilterInputStream**) many "logical" chunks of data from a file are read as one large *physical input operation* into a memory buffer. As a program requests each new chunk of data, it is taken from the buffer (this is sometimes referred to as a *logical input operation*). When the buffer becomes empty, the next actual physical input operation from the input device is performed to read in the next group of "logical" chunks of data. Thus, the number of actual physical input operations is small compared with the number of read requests issued by the program.

Performance Tip 15.2

Because typical input operations are extremely slow compared to processor speeds, buffering inputs normally yields significant performance improvements over unbuffered inputs.

With a **BufferedOutputStream** a partially filled buffer can be forced out to the device at any time with an explicit **flush** as follows:

```
testBufferedOutputStream.flush();
```

A ***PushBackInputStream*** (a subclass of class **FilterInputStream**) is used for more exotic applications than most users will need. Essentially, the application reading a **PushBackInputStream** reads bytes from the stream and forms aggregates consisting of several bytes. Sometimes, to determine that one aggregate is complete, the application must read the first character the "past the end" of the first aggregate. Once the program has determined that the current aggregate is complete, the extra character is "pushed back" onto the stream. **PushBackInputStream***s* are used by programs like compilers that *parse* their inputs, i.e., break them into meaningful units (such as the keywords, identifiers and operators that the Java compiler must recognize).

A ***StreamTokenizer*** (a subclass of **Object**) is helpful for breaking up a stream of text from an input text file into meaningful pieces called *tokens*. The behavior of the **StreamTokenizer** class is similar to that of the **StringTokenizer** class we discussed in Chapter 8.

A ***RandomAccessFile*** (a subclass of **Object**) is useful for *direct-access applications* such as *transaction-processing applications* like airline-reservations systems and point-of-sale systems. With a *sequential-access file* each successive input/output request reads or writes the next consecutive set of data in the file. With a *random-access file*, each successive input/output request may be directed to any part of the file, perhaps widely separated from the part of the file referenced in the previous request. Direct-access applications provide rapid access to specific data items in large files; such applications are often used while people are waiting for answers—these answers must be made available quickly or the people may become impatient and "take their business elsewhere."

Java stream I/O includes capabilities for inputting from byte arrays in memory and outputting to byte arrays in memory. A **ByteArrayInputStream** (a subclass of abstract class **InputStream**) performs its inputs from a byte array in memory. A **ByteArrayOutputStream** (a subclass of abstract class **OutputStream**) outputs to a byte array in memory. An application of byte-array I/O is data validation. A program can input an entire line at a time from the input stream into a byte array. Then a validation routine can scrutinize the contents of the byte array and correct the data, if necessary. The program can now proceed to input from the byte array, knowing that the input data is in the proper format. Outputting to a byte array is a nice way to take advantage of the powerful output formatting capabilities of Java streams. Data can be prepared in a byte array to mimic the edited screen format. That array could then be written to a disk file to preserve the screen image.

A **StringBufferInputStream** (a subclass of abstract class **InputStream**) inputs from a **StringBuffer** object.

A **SequenceInputStream** (a subclass of abstract class **InputStream**) enables several **InputStream**s to be concatenated so that the program sees the group as one continuous **InputStream**. As the end of each input stream is reached, the stream is closed and the next stream in the sequence is opened.

A **LineNumberInputStream** (a subclass of class **FilterInputStream**) always knows what line number of the file is being read.

Class **File** enables programs to obtain information about a file or directory. We discuss class **File** extensively in Section 15.12

Many other new classes have been added to the API to facilitate internationalization and input/output of objects. We discuss these features in detail in our text *Advanced Java How to Program.*

15.4 Creating a Sequential-Access File

Java imposes no structure on a file. Thus, notions like "record" do not exist in Java files. Therefore, the programmer must structure files to meet the requirements of applications. In the following example, we see how the programmer can impose a simple record structure on a file. First we present the program, then we analyze it in detail.

Figure 15.4 creates a simple sequential-access file that might be used in an accounts receivable system to help manage the money owed by a company's credit clients. For each client, the program obtains an account number, the client's first name, the client's last name, and the client's balance (i.e., the amount the client still owes the company for goods and services received in the past). The data obtained for each client constitutes a record for that client. The account number is used as the record key in this application; that is, the file will be created and maintained in account number order. This program assumes the user enters the records in account number order. In a comprehensive accounts receivable system, a sorting capability would be provided so the user could enter the records in any order—the records would then be sorted and written to the file.

```
// Fig. 15.4: CreateSequentialFile.java
// This program uses TextFields to get information from the
// user at the keyboard and writes the information to a
// sequential file.
import java.io.*;
import java.awt.*;
import java.awt.event.*;

public class CreateSequentialFile extends Frame
             implements ActionListener {

   // TextFields where user enters account number, first name,
   // last name and balance.
   private TextField accountField, firstNameField,
                     lastNameField, balanceField;

   private Button enter,  // send record to file
                  done;   // quit program

   // Application other pieces
   private DataOutputStream output;

   public CreateSequentialFile()
   {
      super( "Create Client File" );

```

Fig. 15.4 Creating a sequential file (part 1 of 4).

```
      // Open the file
      try {
         output = new DataOutputStream(
                      new FileOutputStream( "client.dat" ) );
      }
      catch ( IOException e ) {
         System.err.println( "File not opened properly\n" +
                             e.toString() );
         System.exit( 1 );
      }

      setSize( 300, 150 );
      setLayout( new GridLayout( 5, 2 ) );

      // create the components of the Frame
      add( new Label( "Account Number" ) );
      accountField = new TextField();
      add( accountField );

      add( new Label( "First Name" ) );
      firstNameField = new TextField( 20 );
      add( firstNameField );

      add( new Label( "Last Name" ) );
      lastNameField = new TextField( 20 );
      add( lastNameField );

      add( new Label( "Balance" ) );
      balanceField = new TextField( 20 );
      add( balanceField );

      enter = new Button( "Enter" );
      enter.addActionListener( this );
      add( enter );

      done = new Button( "Done" );
      done.addActionListener( this );
      add( done );

      setVisible( true );
   }

   public void addRecord()
   {
      int accountNumber = 0;
      Double d;

      if ( ! accountField.getText().equals( "" ) ) {

```

Fig. 15.4 Creating a sequential file (part 2 of 4).

```
         // output the values to the file
         try {
            accountNumber =
               Integer.parseInt( accountField.getText() );

            if ( accountNumber > 0 ) {
               output.writeInt( accountNumber );
               output.writeUTF( firstNameField.getText() );
               output.writeUTF( lastNameField.getText() );
               d = new Double ( balanceField.getText() );
               output.writeDouble( d.doubleValue() );
            }

            // clear the TextFields
            accountField.setText( "" );
            firstNameField.setText( "" );
            lastNameField.setText( "" );
            balanceField.setText( "" );
         }
         catch ( NumberFormatException nfe ) {
            System.err.println(
               "You must enter an integer account number" );
         }
         catch ( IOException io ) {
            System.err.println(
               "Error during write to file\n" +
               io.toString() );
            System.exit( 1 );
         }
      }
   }

   public void actionPerformed( ActionEvent e )
   {
      addRecord();

      if ( e.getSource() == done ) {
         try {
            output.close();
         }
         catch ( IOException io ) {
            System.err.println( "File not closed properly\n" +
                                io.toString() );
         }

         System.exit( 0 );
      }
   }

```

Fig. 15.4 Creating a sequential file (part 3 of 4).

```
125    public static void main( String args[] )
126    {
127       new CreateSequentialFile();
128    }
129 }
```

Create Client File

Account Number	100
First Name	Bob
Last Name	Jones
Balance	24.98
Enter	Done

Fig. 15.4 Creating a sequential file (part 4 of 4).

Now let us examine this program. As stated previously, files are opened by creating objects of stream classes **`FileInputStream`** and **`FileOutputStream`**. In Fig. 15.4, the file is to be opened for output, so a **`FileOutputStream`** object is created. One argument is passed to the object's constructor—the *filename*. Existing files opened for output are *truncated*—all data in the file is discarded. If the specified file does not yet exist, then a file is created with that filename.

In this program, we output data using a **`DataOutputStream`** that is connected to a **`FileOutputStream`** via a technique called *chaining of stream objects*. For example, when the **`DataOutputStream`** object **`output`** is created, its constructor is supplied a **`FileOutputStream`** object as an argument as shown in lines 29 and 30 of Fig. 15.4:

```
output = new DataOutputStream(
            new FileOutputStream( "client.dat" ) );
```

The preceding statement creates a **`DataOutputStream`** object named **`output`** associated with the file **`client.dat`**. The argument **`"client.dat"`** is passed to the **`File-OutputStream`** constructor that opens the file. This establishes a "line of communication" with the file.

Common Programming Error 15.1

Opening an existing file for output when, in fact, the user wants to preserve the file; the contents of the file are discarded without warning.

Common Programming Error 15.2

Using an incorrect **`FileOutputStream`** *object to refer to a file.*

Common Programming Error 15.3

Not opening a file before attempting to reference it in a program.

When creating a **FileOutputStream** object and attempting to open a file, the program tests whether the open operation was successful. If the operation fails, an **IOException** is generated that must be caught by the program as shown in the following lines (28 through 36) from Fig. 15.4:

```
try {
   output = new DataOutputStream(
                new FileOutputStream( "client.dat" ) );
}
catch ( IOException e ) {
   System.err.println( "File not opened properly\n" +
                       e.toString() );
   System.exit( 1 );
}
```

If an **IOException** is generated because the open attempt was unsuccessful, the error message "**File not opened properly**" is output followed by the error message in the exception object, and the **exit** method of the **System** class is called to end the program. The argument to **exit** is returned to the environment from which the program was invoked. Argument **0** indicates that the program terminated normally; any other value indicates that the program terminated due to an error. The value returned by **exit** is used by the calling environment (most likely the operating system) to respond appropriately to the error. Some possible reasons for **IOException**s while opening files are attempting to open a nonexistent file for reading, attempting to open a file for reading without permission, and opening a file for writing when no disk space is available.

If the file is opened successfully, the program is ready to process data. The following window appears to enable the user to enter data:

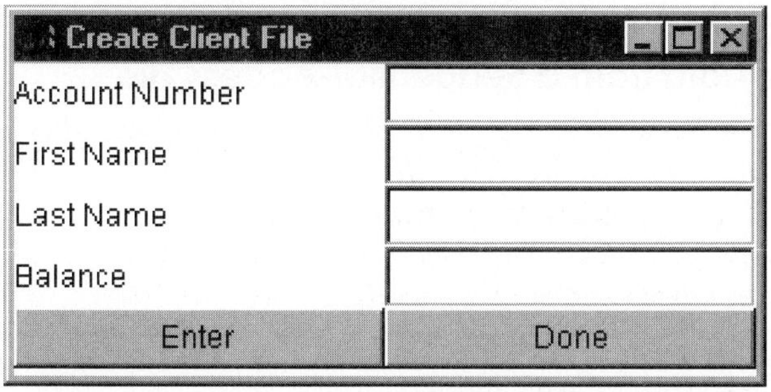

The program assumes data is input correctly and in the proper record number order. When a record is complete, the user clicks the **Enter** button to write the record to the file. This invokes the **addRecord** method of our **CreateSeqentialFile** class to perform the write operation. In this method, each field of the record is written separately with calls to the **writeInt** (write an integer value), **writeUTF** (write a string) and **writeDouble** (write a double value) methods of class **DataOutputStream**. Lines 82 through 86 of the **addRecord** method input each set of data from the user and write the data immediately to the file. The data may be retrieved by a program designed to read the file (see Section 15.5).

The user clicks the **Done** button to inform the program that there is no more data to be processed and that the program should close the file and terminate. Before terminating, the program determines if there is a record to write to disk by calling **addRecord**. A **FileOutputStream** object can be closed explicitly by the programmer using the method **close** as follows:

```
output.close();
```

or the file will be closed implicitly when Java garbage collects the object.

Performance Tip 15.3

Always release resources explicitly and at the earliest possible moment at which it is determined that the resource is no longer needed. This makes the resource immediately available to be reused by your program or by another program, thus improving resource utilization

When using chained stream objects, the outermost object (the **DataOutputStream** in this example) should be used to close the file.

Performance Tip 15.4

Explicitly close each file as soon as it is known that the program will not reference the file again. This can reduce resource usage in a program that will continue executing long after it no longer needs to be referencing a particular file. This practice also improves program clarity.

In the sample execution for the program of Fig. 15.4, we entered information for five accounts (see Fig. 15.5), and then signaled that data entry was complete by clicking the "Done" button. The program does not show how the data records actually appear in the file. To verify that the file has been created successfully, in the next section we create a program to read the file.

15.5 Reading Data from a Sequential-Access File

Data are stored in files so that they may be retrieved for processing when needed. The previous section demonstrated how to create a file for sequential access. In this section, we discuss how to read data sequentially from a file.

Sample Data			
100	**Bob**	**Jones**	**24.98**
200	**Steve**	**Doe**	**-345.67**
300	**Pam**	**White**	**0.00**
400	**Sam**	**Stone**	**-42.16**
500	**Sue**	**Rich**	**224.62**

Fig. 15.5 Sample data for the program of Fig. 15.4.

The program of Fig. 15.6 reads records from the file **"client.dat"** created by the program of Fig. 15.4 and prints the contents of the records. Files are opened for input by creating a **FileInputStream** object. The name of the file to open is passed as an argument to the **FileInputStream** constructor. In Fig. 15.4, we wrote data to the file **"client.dat"** using a **DataOutputStream** object. Data must be read from the file in the same format in which it was written to the file. Therefore, we use a **DataInputStream** chained to a **FileInputStream** in this program to read the data as shown in lines 29 and 30 of Fig. 15.6:

```
1  // Fig. 15.6: ReadSequentialFile.java
2  // This program reads a file sequentially and displays each
3  // record in text fields.
4  import java.io.*;
5  import java.awt.*;
6  import java.awt.event.*;
7
8  public class ReadSequentialFile extends Frame
9                 implements ActionListener {
10
11    // TextFields to display account number, first name,
12    // last name and balance.
13    private TextField accountField, firstNameField,
14                      lastNameField, balanceField;
15
16    private Button next,    // get next record in file
17                   done;    // quit program
18
19    // Application other pieces
20    private DataInputStream input;
21
22    // Constructor -- intialize the Frame
23    public ReadSequentialFile()
24    {
25       super( "Read Client File" );
26
27       // Open the file
28       try {
29          input = new DataInputStream(
30                      new FileInputStream( "client.dat" ) );
31       }
32       catch ( IOException e ) {
33          System.err.println( "File not opened properly\n" +
34                              e.toString() );
35          System.exit( 1 );
36       }
37
38       setSize( 300, 150 );
39       setLayout( new GridLayout( 5, 2 ) );
```

Fig. 15.6 Reading a sequential file (part 1 of 3).

```

      // create the components of the Frame
      add( new Label( "Account Number" ) );
      accountField = new TextField();
      accountField.setEditable( false );
      add( accountField );

      add( new Label( "First Name" ) );
      firstNameField = new TextField( 20 );
      firstNameField.setEditable( false );
      add( firstNameField );

      add( new Label( "Last Name" ) );
      lastNameField = new TextField( 20 );
      lastNameField.setEditable( false );
      add( lastNameField );

      add( new Label( "Balance" ) );
      balanceField = new TextField( 20 );
      balanceField.setEditable( false );
      add( balanceField );

      next = new Button( "Next" );
      next.addActionListener( this );
      add( next );

      done = new Button( "Done" );
      done.addActionListener( this );
      add( done );

      setVisible( true );
   }

   public void actionPerformed( ActionEvent e )
   {
      if ( e.getSource() == next )
         readRecord();
      else
         closeFile();
   }

   public void readRecord()
   {
      int account;
      String first, last;
      double balance;

      // input the values from the file
      try {
         account = input.readInt();
         first = input.readUTF();
```

Fig. 15.6 Reading a sequential file (part 2 of 3).

```
            last = input.readUTF();
            balance = input.readDouble();

            accountField.setText( String.valueOf( account ) );
            firstNameField.setText( first );
            lastNameField.setText( last );
            balanceField.setText( String.valueOf( balance ) );
         }
         catch ( EOFException eof ) {
            closeFile();
         }
         catch ( IOException e ) {
            System.err.println( "Error during read from file\n" +
                                e.toString() );
            System.exit( 1 );
         }
      }

      private void closeFile()
      {
         try {
            input.close();
            System.exit( 0 );
         }
         catch ( IOException e ) {
            System.err.println( "Error closing file\n" +
                                e.toString() );
            System.exit( 1 );
         }
      }

      public static void main( String args[] )
      {
         new ReadSequentialFile();
      }
   }
```

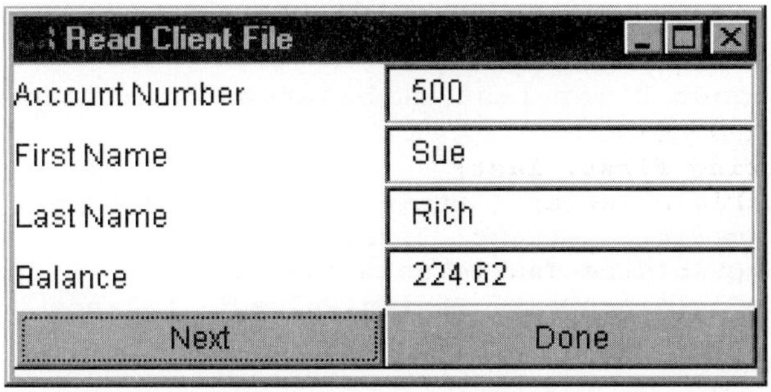

Read Client File
Account Number 500
First Name Sue
Last Name Rich
Balance 224.62
Next Done

Fig. 15.6 Reading a sequential file (part 3 of 3).

```
input = new DataInputStream(
            new FileInputStream( "client.dat" ) );
```

The preceding statement creates a **DataInputStream** object named **input** associated with the file **client.dat**. The string **"client.dat"** is passed to the **FileInputStream** constructor which opens the file and establishes a "line of communication."

When creating a **FileInputStream** object and attempting to open a file, the program tests whether the open operation was successful. If the operation fails, an **IOException** is generated that must be caught by the program as shown in the following lines (28 through 36) from Fig. 15.6:

```
try {
   input = new DataInputStream(
               new FileInputStream( "client.dat" ) );
}
catch ( IOException e ) {
   System.err.println( "File not opened properly\n" +
                       e.toString() );
   System.exit( 1 );
}
```

If an **IOException** is generated because the open attempt was unsuccessful, the error message "**File not opened properly**" is output followed by the error message in the exception object, and the **exit** method of the **System** class is called to end the program. If the file is opened successfully, the program is ready to process data.

The program reads a record each time the user clicks the "Next" button. This action causes method **readRecord** of class **ReadSequentialFile** to be invoked. The lines

```
account = input.readInt();
first = input.readUTF();
last = input.readUTF();
balance = input.readDouble();
```

read one record of information from the file. If the end-of-file marker is reached while reading, an **EndOfFileException** is thrown which causes the **closeFile** method (line 109) to be called to close the file and terminate the program.

After the preceding code is executed the first time, **account** has the value **100**, **first** has the value **"Bob"**, **last** has the value **"Jones"**, and **balance** has the value **24.98**. Each time the preceding code is executed, another record is read from the file into the variables **account**, **first**, **last**, and **balance**. The records are displayed in text fields by the following lines:

```
accountField.setText( String.valueOf( account ) );
firstNameField.setText( first );
lastNameField.setText( last );
balanceField.setText( String.valueOf( balance ) );
```

If the user clicks the "Done" button, the file is closed by invoking the **closeFile** method that calls the **close** method on the **DataInputStream** object **input**. The program terminates with a call to the **exit** method of the **System** class.

To retrieve data sequentially from a file, programs normally start reading from the beginning of the file, and read all the data consecutively until the desired data are found. It may be necessary to process the file sequentially several times (from the beginning of the file) during the execution of a program. Class **FileInputStream** does not provide the ability to reposition to the beginning of the file to read the file again. However, **RandomAccessFile** objects can reposition to the beginning of the file. Class **RandomAccessFile** provides all the capabilities of classes **FileInputStream**, **FileOutputStream**, **DataInputStream** and **DataOutputStream** and adds several other methods including **seek** that repositions the *file position pointer* (the byte number of the next byte in the file to be read or written) to any position in the file.

Performance Tip 15.5

The process of closing a file and reopening a file for the purpose of positioning the file-position pointer back to the beginning of a file is a time-consuming task for the computer. If this is done frequently, it may slow the performance of your program.

The program of Fig. 15.7 (with outputs in Fig. 15.8) enables a credit manager to display the account information for those customers with zero balances (i.e., customers who do not owe the company any money), credit balances (i.e., customers to whom the company owes money), and debit balances (i.e., customers who owe the company money for goods and services received in the past).

```
// Fig. 15.7: CreditInquiry.java
// This program reads a file sequentially and displays the
// contents in a text area based on the type of account the
// user requests (credit balance, debit balance or zero balance.
import java.io.*;
import java.awt.*;
import java.awt.event.*;
import java.text.DecimalFormat;

public class CreditInquiry extends Frame
             implements ActionListener {

   // application window components
   private TextArea recordDisplay;
   private Button done, credit, debit, zero;
   private Panel buttonPanel;

   private RandomAccessFile input;
   private String accountType;

   public CreditInquiry()
   {
      super( "Credit Inquiry Program" );

      // Open the file
```

Fig. 15.7 Credit inquiry program (part 1 of 4).

```
      try {
         input = new RandomAccessFile( "client.dat", "r" );
      }
      catch ( IOException e ) {
         System.err.println( e.toString() );
         System.exit( 1 );
      }

      setSize( 400, 150 );

      // create the components of the Frame
      buttonPanel = new Panel();
      credit = new Button( "Credit balances" );
      credit.addActionListener( this );
      buttonPanel.add( credit );
      debit = new Button( "Debit balances" );
      debit.addActionListener( this );
      buttonPanel.add( debit );
      zero = new Button( "Zero balances" );
      zero.addActionListener( this );
      buttonPanel.add( zero );
      done = new Button( "Done" );
      done.addActionListener( this );
      buttonPanel.add( done );
      recordDisplay = new TextArea( 4, 40 );

      // add the components to the Frame
      add( recordDisplay, BorderLayout.NORTH );
      add( buttonPanel, BorderLayout.SOUTH );

      setVisible( true );
   }

   public void actionPerformed( ActionEvent e )
   {
      if ( e.getSource() != done ) {
         accountType = e.getActionCommand();
         readRecords();
      }
      else {      // Close the file
         try {
            input.close();
            System.exit( 0 );
         }
         catch ( IOException ioe ) {
            System.err.println( "File not closed properly\n" +
                                ioe.toString() );
            System.exit( 1 );
         }
      }
   }
```

Fig. 15.7 Credit inquiry program (part 2 of 4).

```

   public void readRecords()
   {
      int account;
      String first, last;
      double balance;
      DecimalFormat twoDigits = new DecimalFormat( "0.00" );

      // input the values from the file
      try {       // to catch IOException

         try {    // to catch EOFException
            recordDisplay.setText( "The accounts are:\n" );

            while ( true ) {
               account = input.readInt();
               first = input.readUTF();
               last = input.readUTF();
               balance = input.readDouble();

               if ( shouldDisplay( balance ) )
                  recordDisplay.append( account + "\t" +
                     first + "\t" + last + "\t" +
                     twoDigits.format( balance ) + "\n" );
            }
         }
         catch ( EOFException eof ) {
            input.seek( 0 );
         }
      }
      catch ( IOException e ) {
         System.err.println( "Error during read from file\n" +
                             e.toString() );
         System.exit( 1 );
      }
   }

   public boolean shouldDisplay( double balance )
   {
      if ( accountType.equals( "Credit balances" ) &&
           balance < 0 )
         return true;

      else if ( accountType.equals( "Debit balances" ) &&
                balance > 0 )
         return true;

      else if ( accountType.equals( "Zero balances" ) &&
                balance == 0 )
         return true;

```

Fig. 15.7 Credit inquiry program (part 3 of 4).

```
         return false;
      }

      // Instantiate a CreditInquiry object and start the program
      public static void main( String args[] )
      {
         new CreditInquiry();
      }
   }
```

Fig. 15.7 Credit inquiry program (part 4 of 4).

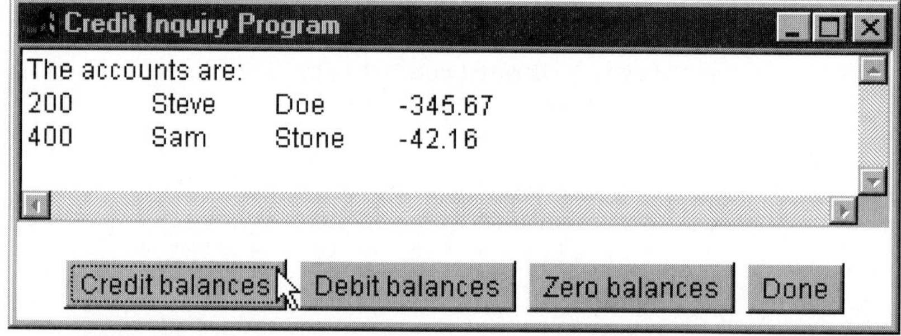

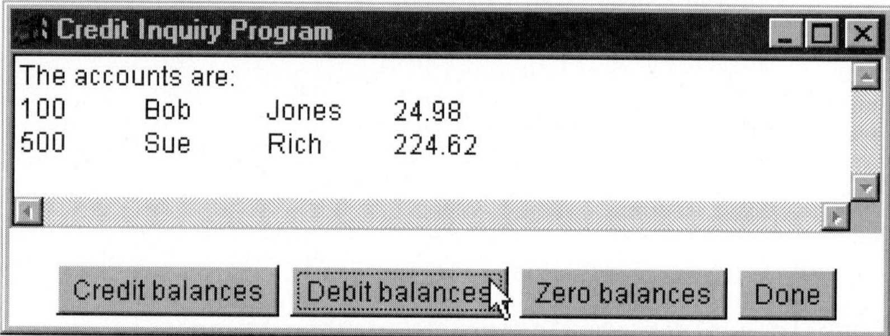

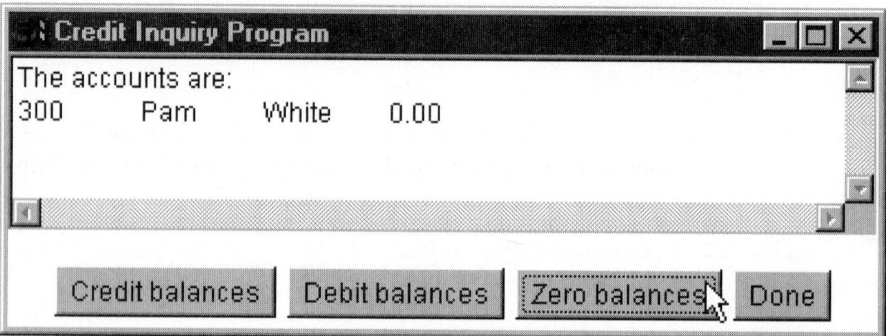

Fig. 15.8 Sample outputs of the credit inquiry program of Fig. 15.7.

The program displays buttons that allow the credit manager to obtain credit information. The "Credit balances" button produces a list of accounts with credit balances. The "Debit balances" button produces a list of accounts with debit balances. The "Zero balances" button produces a list of accounts with zero balances. The "Done" button terminates program execution. Sample outputs are shown in Fig. 15.8.

The records of a particular type are displayed in the **TextArea** called **recordDisplay**. The record information is collected by reading through the entire file and determining if each record satisfies the criteria for the account type selected by the credit manager by clicking one of the buttons. Clicking a button other than the "Done" button causes the **actionPerformed** method to set **accountType** to the string on the clicked button and invoke the **readRecords** method that loops through the file and reads every record. The **shouldDisplay** method is invoked to determine if the current record satisfies the account type requested. If the method returns **true**, the account information for the current record is appended to the **TextArea** called **recordDisplay**. When the end-of-file marker is reached, line 104

```
input.seek( 0 );
```

repositions the file position pointer to byte 0 of the file (i.e., the beginning of the file).

15.6 Updating Sequential-Access Files

Data that is formatted and written to a sequential-access file as shown in Section 15.4 cannot be modified without reading and writing all the data in the file. For example, if the name **White** needed to be changed to **Worthington**, the old name cannot simply be overwritten. Such updating can be done, but it is awkward. To make the preceding name change, the records before **White** in a sequential-access file could be copied to a new file, the updated record would then be written to the new file, and the records after **White** would be copied to the new file. This requires processing every record in the file to update one record. If many records are being updated in one pass of the file, this technique can be acceptable.

15.7 Random-Access Files

So far, we have seen how to create sequential-access files and to search through them to locate particular information. Sequential-access files are inappropriate for so-called *"instant-access" applications* in which a particular record of information must be located immediately. Some popular instant access applications are airline reservation systems, banking systems, point-of-sale systems, automated teller machines and other kinds of *transaction-processing systems* that require rapid access to specific data. The bank at which you have your account may have hundreds of thousands or even millions of other customers, yet when you use an automated teller machine, your account is checked for sufficient funds in seconds. This kind of instant access is possible with *random-access files*. Individual records of a random-access file can be accessed directly (and quickly) without searching through other records. Random-access files are sometimes called *direct-access files*.

As we have said, Java does not impose structure on a file. So the application that wants to use random-access files must literally create them. A variety of techniques can be used to create random-access files. Perhaps the simplest is to require that all records in a file are of the same fixed length.

Using fixed-length records makes it easy for a program to calculate (as a function of the record size and the record key) the exact location of any record relative to the beginning of the file. We will soon see how this facilitates immediate access to specific records, even in large files.

Figure 15.9 illustrates Java's view of a random-access file composed of fixed-length records (each record in this figure is 100 bytes long). A random-access file is like a railroad train with many cars—some empty and some with contents.

Data can be inserted in a random-access file without destroying other data in the file. Data stored previously also can be updated or deleted without rewriting the entire file. In the following sections we explain how to create a random-access file, enter data, read the data both sequentially and randomly, update the data, and delete data no longer needed.

15.8 Creating a Random-Access File

`RandomAccessFile` objects have all the capabilities of **`DataInputStream`** and **`DataOutputStream`** objects discussed in the preceding sections. When a **`RandomAccessFile`** stream is associated with a file, data is read or written beginning at the location in the file specified by the file-position pointer, and all data is read or written as primitive data types. When writing an **`int`** value, 4 bytes are output to the file. When reading a **`double`** value, 8 bytes are input from the file. The size of the data types is guaranteed because Java has fixed sizes for all primitive data types regardless of the computing platform.

Random-access file-processing programs rarely write a single field to a file. Normally, they write one object at a time, as we show in the following examples.

Consider the following problem statement:

Create a transaction-processing program capable of storing up to 100 fixed-length records for a company that can have up to 100 customers. Each record should consist of an account number that will be used as the record key, a last name, a first name, and a balance. The program should be able to update an account, insert a new account, and delete an account.

The next several sections introduce the techniques necessary to create this credit-processing program. Figure15.10 contains the **`Record`** class that is used by the next four programs for both reading records from, and writing records to, the **`credit.dat`** file.

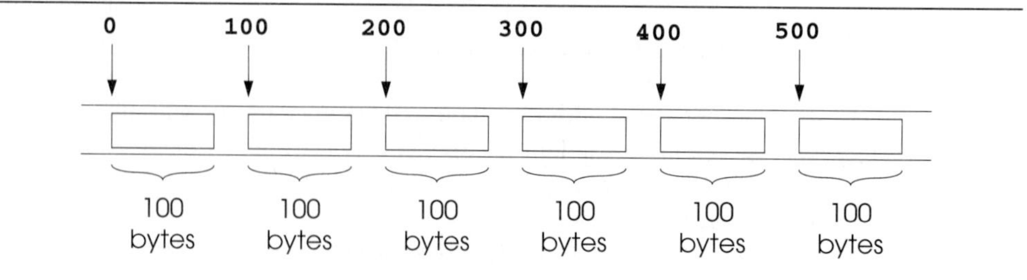

Fig. 15.9 Java's view of a random-access file.

```
// Fig. 15.10: Record.java
// Record class for the RandomAccessFile programs.
import java.io.*;

public class Record {
   private int account;
   private String lastName;
   private String firstName;
   private double balance;

   // Read a record from the specified RandomAccessFile
   public void read( RandomAccessFile file ) throws IOException
   {
      account = file.readInt();

      char first[] = new char[ 15 ];

      for ( int i = 0; i < first.length; i++ )
         first[ i ] = file.readChar();

      firstName = new String( first );

      char last[] = new char[ 15 ];

      for ( int i = 0; i < last.length; i++ )
         last[ i ] = file.readChar();

      lastName = new String( last );

      balance = file.readDouble();
   }

   // Write a record to the specified RandomAccessFile
   public void write( RandomAccessFile file ) throws IOException
   {
      StringBuffer buf;

      file.writeInt( account );

      if ( firstName != null )
         buf = new StringBuffer( firstName );
      else
         buf = new StringBuffer( 15 );

      buf.setLength( 15 );

      file.writeChars( buf.toString() );

      if ( lastName != null )
         buf = new StringBuffer( lastName );
```

Fig. 15.10 Record class used in the random-access file programs (part 1 of 2).

```
      else
         buf = new StringBuffer( 15 );

      buf.setLength( 15 );

      file.writeChars( buf.toString() );

      file.writeDouble( balance );
   }

   public void setAccount( int a ) { account = a; }

   public int getAccount() { return account; }

   public void setFirstName( String f ) { firstName = f; }

   public String getFirstName() { return firstName; }

   public void setLastName( String l ) { lastName = l; }

   public String getLastName() { return lastName; }

   public void setBalance( double b ) { balance = b; }

   public double getBalance() { return balance; }

   // NOTE: This method contains a hard coded value for the
   // size of a record of information.
   public static int size() { return 72; }
}
```

Fig. 15.10 **`Record`** class used in the random-access file programs (part 2 of 2).

Class **`Record`** contains four instance variables—**`account`**, **`lastName`**, **`firstName`** and **`balance`**—that define the contents of a record of information and methods to manipulate records. Set and get methods are provided for each of the instance variables. The **`write`** method outputs one record of information from the **`RandomAccessFile`** object passed in as an argument to the method. It uses the **`writeInt`** method to output the account number, the **`writeChars`** method to output the last name and first name as arrays of characters (15 characters each) and the **`writeDouble`** method to output the balance.

The **`read`** method inputs one record of information from the **`RandomAccessFile`** object passed in as an argument to the method. The **`RandomAccessFile`** **`readInt`** and **`readDouble`** methods are used to input the account number and balance, respectively. The **`readChar`** method is used to read the last name and first name one character at a time into arrays of 15 characters each. These arrays are used as the initial values for the **`String`** objects assigned to the **`firstName`** and **`lastName`** objects, respectively. The static method **`size`** returns the size of the record in bytes. This method is defined to explicitly return 72—the number of bytes occupied on disk for each record (4 bytes for the **`int`** account, 15 two-byte characters for the first name, 15 two-byte characters for the last name, and 8 bytes for the **`double`** balance).

Figure 15.11 illustrates opening a random-access file and writing data to the disk. This program initializes 100 records of the file **"credit.dat"** with empty objects using the **write** method of our **Record** class. Each empty object contains **0** for the account number, **null** for the last name, **null** for the first name, and **0.0** for the balance. The file is initialized to create the proper amount of empty space in which the account data will be stored and to enable us to determine in subsequent programs if each record is empty or contains data.

In Fig. 15.11, line 15

```
file = new RandomAccessFile( "credit.dat", "rw" );
```

attempts to open the file **credit.dat** for use in this program. Two arguments are passed to the **RandomAccessFile** constructor—the file name and the *file open mode*. The file open mode for a **RandomAccessFile** is either **"r"** to open the file for reading or **"rw"** to open the file for reading and writing.

```
1  // Fig. 15.11: CreateRandFile.java
2  // This program creates a random access file sequentially
3  // by writing 100 empty records to disk.
4  import java.io.*;
5
6  public class CreateRandomFile {
7     private Record blank;
8     private RandomAccessFile file;
9
10    public CreateRandomFile()
11    {
12       blank = new Record();
13
14       try {
15          file = new RandomAccessFile( "credit.dat", "rw" );
16
17          for ( int i = 0; i < 100; i++ )
18             blank.write( file );
19       }
20       catch( IOException e ) {
21          System.err.println( "File not opened properly\n" +
22                              e.toString() );
23          System.exit( 1 );
24       }
25
26    }
27
28    public static void main( String args[] )
29    {
30       CreateRandomFile accounts = new CreateRandomFile();
31    }
32 }
```

Fig. 15.11 Creating a random-access file sequentially.

If an **IOException** occurs during the open process, the program terminates. If the file is opened properly, the program uses a **for** structure (lines 17 and 18) to execute the following line 100 times:

```
blank.write( file );
```

This statement causes the object **blank** to be written to the **credit.dat** file associated with **RandomAccessFile** object **file**.

15.9 Writing Data Randomly to a Random-Access File

The program of Fig. 15.12 writes data to the file **"credit.dat"** which is opened with the **"rw"** mode for reading and writing. It uses the **RandomAccessFile** method **seek** to determine the exact location in the file at which a record of information is stored. Method **seek** sets the file-position pointer to a specific position in the file relative to the beginning of the file, and the **Record** class **write** method outputs the data. This program assumes the user does not enter duplicate account numbers and that the user enters appropriate data in each **TextField**.

```
// Fig. 15.12: WriteRandomFile.java
// This program uses TextFields to get information from the
// user at the keyboard and writes the information to a
// random access file.
import java.io.*;
import java.awt.*;
import java.awt.event.*;

public class WriteRandomFile extends Frame
               implements ActionListener {

   // TextFields where user enters account number, first name,
   // last name and balance.
   private TextField accountField, firstNameField,
                     lastNameField, balanceField;

   private Button enter,   // send record to file
                  done;    // quit program

   // Application other pieces
   private RandomAccessFile output;  // file for output
   private Record data;

   // Constructor -- intialize the Frame
   public WriteRandomFile()
   {
      super( "Write to random access file" );

```

Fig. 15.12 Writing data randomly to a random-access file (part 1 of 4).

```
      data = new Record();

      // Open the file
      try {
         output = new RandomAccessFile( "credit.dat", "rw" );
      }
      catch ( IOException e ) {
         System.err.println( e.toString() );
         System.exit( 1 );
      }

      setSize( 300, 150 );
      setLayout( new GridLayout( 5, 2 ) );

      // create the components of the Frame
      add( new Label( "Account Number" ) );
      accountField = new TextField();
      add( accountField );

      add( new Label( "First Name" ) );
      firstNameField = new TextField( 20 );
      add( firstNameField );

      add( new Label( "Last Name" ) );
      lastNameField = new TextField( 20 );
      add( lastNameField );

      add( new Label( "Balance" ) );
      balanceField = new TextField( 20 );
      add( balanceField );

      enter = new Button( "Enter" );
      enter.addActionListener( this );
      add( enter );

      done = new Button( "Done" );
      done.addActionListener( this );
      add( done );

      setVisible( true );
   }

   public void addRecord()
   {
      int accountNumber = 0;
      Double d;

      if ( ! accountField.getText().equals( "" ) ) {

```

Fig. 15.12 Writing data randomly to a random-access file (part 2 of 4).

```
         // output the values to the file
         try {
            accountNumber =
               Integer.parseInt( accountField.getText() );

            if ( accountNumber > 0 && accountNumber <= 100 ) {
               data.setAccount( accountNumber );
               data.setFirstName( firstNameField.getText() );
               data.setLastName( lastNameField.getText() );
               d = new Double ( balanceField.getText() );
               data.setBalance( d.doubleValue() );
               output.seek(
                  (long) ( accountNumber-1 ) * Record.size() );
               data.write( output );
            }

            // clear the TextFields
            accountField.setText( "" );
            firstNameField.setText( "" );
            lastNameField.setText( "" );
            balanceField.setText( "" );
         }
         catch ( NumberFormatException nfe ) {
            System.err.println(
               "You must enter an integer account number" );
         }
         catch ( IOException io ) {
            System.err.println(
               "Error during write to file\n" +
               io.toString() );
            System.exit( 1 );
         }
      }
   }

   public void actionPerformed( ActionEvent e )
   {
      addRecord();

      if ( e.getSource() == done ) {
         try {
            output.close();
         }
         catch ( IOException io ) {
            System.err.println( "File not closed properly\n" +
                                io.toString() );
         }

         System.exit( 0 );
      }
   }
```

Fig. 15.12 Writing data randomly to a random-access file (part 3 of 4).

```
129
130      // Instantiate a WriteRandomFile object and start the program
131      public static void main( String args[] )
132      {
133         new WriteRandomFile();
134      }
135   }
```

Fig. 15.12 Writing data randomly to a random-access file (part 4 of 4).

The user enters values for the account number, first name, last name and balance. When the user clicks the **Enter** button, method **addRecord** of the **WriteRandomFile** class is invoked to retrieve the data from the **TextField**s, store the data in the **Record** class object called **data**, and call the **write** method of the **Record** class to output the data.

Lines 89 and 90

```
output.seek(
   (long) ( accountNumber-1 ) * Record.size() );
```

use method **seek** to position the file-position pointer for object **output** to the byte location calculated by **(long) (accountNumber - 1) * Record.size()**. Since the account number is between 1 and 100, 1 is subtracted from the account number when calculating the byte location of the record. Thus, for record 1, the file-position pointer is set to byte 0 of the file. The calculation result is cast to **long** because the **seek** method requires a **long** value as an argument.

When the user clicks the **Done** button, the program attempts to add the last record to the file (if there is one waiting to be output), closes the file, and terminates the program.

15.10 Reading Data Sequentially from a Random-Access File

In the previous sections, we created a random-access file and wrote data to that file. In this section, we develop a program (Fig. 15.13) that opens a **RandomAccessFile** for reading with the **"r"** file open mode, reads through the file sequentially and displays only those records containing data. This program produces an additional benefit. See if you can determine what it is; we will reveal it at the end of this section.

Good Programming Practice 15.1

Open a file with the `"r"` *file open mode for input if the contents of the file should not be modified. This prevents unintentional modification of the file's contents. This is another example of the principle of least privilege.*

```
// Fig. 15.13: ReadRandomFile.java
// This program reads a random access file sequentially and
// displays the contents one record at a time in text fields.
import java.io.*;
import java.awt.*;
import java.awt.event.*;
import java.text.DecimalFormat;

public class ReadRandomFile extends Frame
             implements ActionListener {

   // TextFields to display account number, first name,
   // last name and balance.
   private TextField accountField, firstNameField,
                     lastNameField, balanceField;

   private Button next,    // get next record in file
                  done;    // quit program

   // Application other pieces
   private RandomAccessFile input;
   private Record data;

   // Constructor -- intialize the Frame
   public ReadRandomFile()
   {
      super( "Read Client File" );

      // Open the file
      try {
         input = new RandomAccessFile( "credit.dat", "r" );
      }
      catch ( IOException e ) {
         System.err.println( e.toString() );
         System.exit( 1 );
      }

      data = new Record();

      setSize( 300, 150 );
      setLayout( new GridLayout( 5, 2 ) );

```

Fig. 15.13 Reading a random-access file sequentially (part 1 of 3).

```
      // create the components of the Frame
      add( new Label( "Account Number" ) );
      accountField = new TextField();
      accountField.setEditable( false );
      add( accountField );

      add( new Label( "First Name" ) );
      firstNameField = new TextField( 20 );
      firstNameField.setEditable( false );
      add( firstNameField );

      add( new Label( "Last Name" ) );
      lastNameField = new TextField( 20 );
      lastNameField.setEditable( false );
      add( lastNameField );

      add( new Label( "Balance" ) );
      balanceField = new TextField( 20 );
      balanceField.setEditable( false );
      add( balanceField );

      next = new Button( "Next" );
      next.addActionListener( this );
      add( next );

      done = new Button( "Done" );
      done.addActionListener( this );
      add( done );

      setVisible( true );
   }

   public void actionPerformed( ActionEvent e )
   {
      if ( e.getSource() == next )
         readRecord();
      else
         closeFile();
   }

   public void readRecord()
   {
      DecimalFormat twoDigits = new DecimalFormat( "0.00" );

      // read a record and display
      try {
         do {
            data.read( input );
         } while ( data.getAccount() == 0 );

```

Fig. 15.13 Reading a random-access file sequentially (part 2 of 3).

```
         accountField.setText(
            String.valueOf( data.getAccount() ) );
         firstNameField.setText( data.getFirstName() );
         lastNameField.setText( data.getLastName() );
         balanceField.setText( String.valueOf(
            twoDigits.format( data.getBalance() ) ) );
      }
      catch ( EOFException eof ) {
         closeFile();
      }
      catch ( IOException e ) {
         System.err.println( "Error during read from file\n" +
                             e.toString() );
         System.exit( 1 );
      }
   }

   private void closeFile()
   {
      try {
         input.close();
         System.exit( 0 );
      }
      catch ( IOException e ) {
         System.err.println( "Error closing file\n" +
                             e.toString() );
         System.exit( 1 );
      }
   }

   // Instantiate a ReadRandomFile object and start the program
   public static void main( String args[] )
   {
      new ReadRandomFile();
   }
}
```

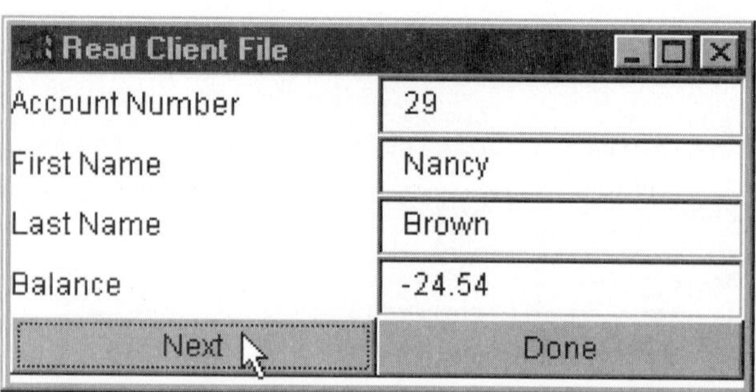

Fig. 15.13 Reading a random-access file sequentially (part 3 of 3).

When the user clicks the "Next" button to read the next record in the file, the **readRecord** method of class **ReadRandomFile** is invoked. This method loops and invokes the **Record** class **read** method to input the data into **Record** class object **data** **readRecord** loops and reads from the **"credit.dat"** file until it reads a record containing information. It checks each record to see if it contains data by determining if the account number is 0 (its initial value for all records). If the record contains a valid account number (i.e., a non-zero value), the loop terminates and the data is displayed in text fields. When the user clicks the "Done" button or when the end-of-file marker is encountered while reading, the **closeFile** method is invoked to close the file and terminate the program.

What about that additional benefit we promised? If you examine the output window as the program executes, you will notice that the records are listed in sorted order (by account number)! This is a simple consequence of the way we stored these records in the file using direct access techniques. Compared to the bubble sort we have seen (Chapter 5), sorting with direct-access techniques is blazingly fast. The speed is achieved by making the file large enough to hold every possible record that might be created. This, of course, means that the file could be sparsely occupied most of the time, a waste of storage. So here is yet another example of the space/time trade-off: By using large amounts of space, we are able to develop a much faster sorting algorithm.

15.11 Example: A Transaction-Processing Program

We now present a substantial transaction-processing program (Fig. 15.14) using a random-access file to achieve "instant" access processing. The program maintains a bank's account information. The program updates existing accounts, adds new accounts, deletes accounts, and stores a formatted listing of all the current accounts in a text file for printing. We assume that the program of Fig. 15.11 has been executed to create the file **credit.dat** and that the program of Fig. 15.12 has been executed to insert the initial data.

The program has four buttons to select various tasks as shown here:

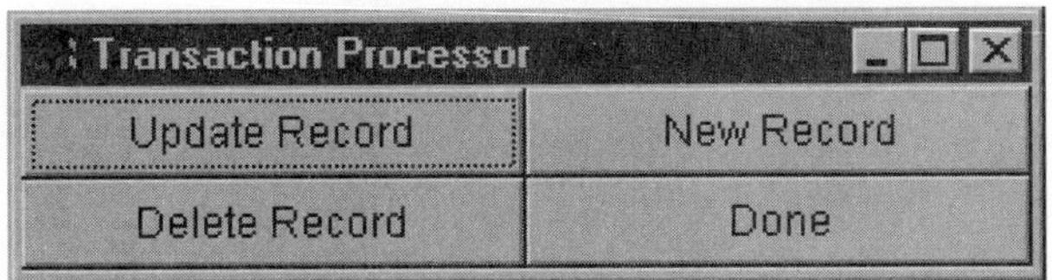

The "Update Record" button displays the **Update Record** dialog box to update an account. The method will only update an existing record, so the user must first enter an account number and press *Enter* at the keyboard. The **actionPerformed** method of the **UpdateDialog** class checks that the account number is valid, then reads the record into object **data** with **Record** method **read**. Next, **data.getAccount()** is compared to zero to determine if the record contains information. If **data.getAccount()** is zero, a message is displayed in the account number **TextField** stating that the record does not exist. If there is a valid record, the information is displayed in **TextFields** as follows:

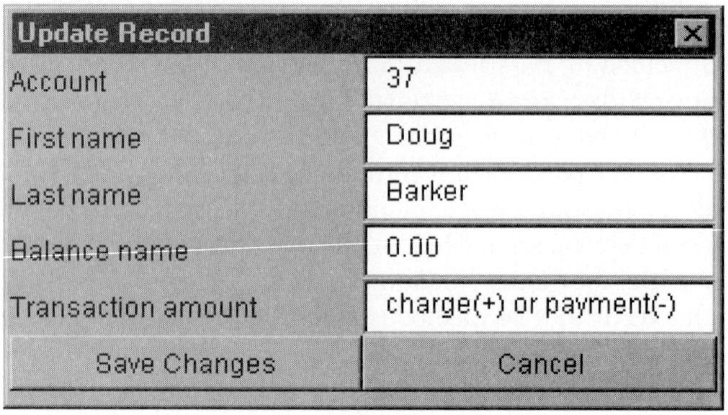

Note that the "Transaction amount" **`TextField`** contains the string "**`charge(+) or payment(-)`**." The user enters the transaction amount by selecting this text, typing the transaction amount (a positive value for a charge or a negative value for a payment) and presses the *Enter* key on the keyboard. The **`actionPerformed`** method takes the transaction amount, adds it to the current balance and displays the new balance in the "Balance" **`TextField`**. The user can click "Save Changes" to output the updated record to the file or "Cancel" to ignore the transaction and return to the main application window. The result of a transaction being entered is shown below.

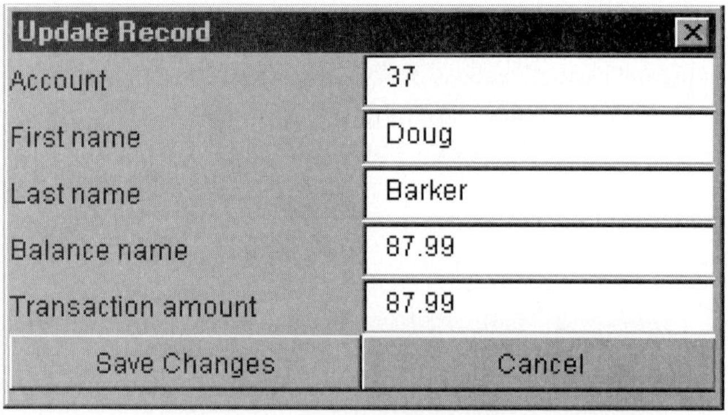

The "New Record" button displays the **`New Record`** dialog box to add a new account to the file. The user first types an account number in the Account **`TextField`** and presses *Enter* on the keyboard. The **`actionPerformed`** method of the **`NewDialog`** class checks the account number to determine if it is valid. If so, it reads the record into the object **`data`**. If the account number is for an existing account, a message is displayed in the "Account number" **`TextField`** stating that the account exists. Otherwise, the user is prompted in the "First name," "Last name" and "Balance" **`TextField`**s to enter data. This is accomplished by highlighting the prompt in each field and typing over the prompt. When the data is complete, the user clicks the "Save Changes" button to output the data to the file. A typical output for the "New Record" option is:

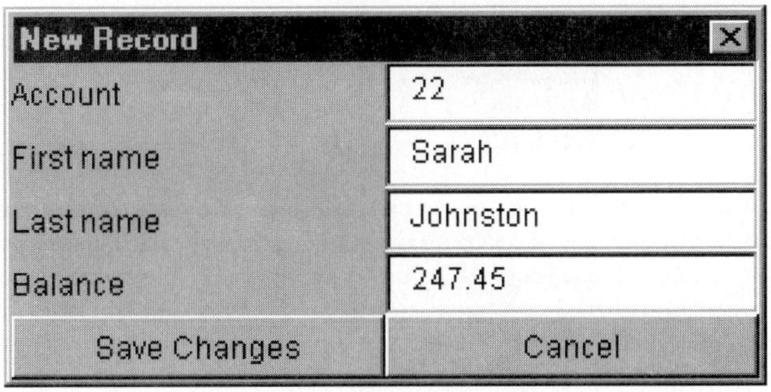

New Record

Account 22
First name Sarah
Last name Johnston
Balance 247.45
Save Changes Cancel

The "Delete Record" button displays the **Delete Record** dialog box to delete a record from the file. The user enters the account number in the "Account" **TextField**. To get immediate feedback as to whether the account exists, the user can press the *Enter* key which causes the **actionPerformed** method of the **DeleteDialog** class to read the record into the object **data** and check for valid information. Only an existing record may be deleted, so if the specified account is empty, an error message is issued. The user clicks the "Delete Record" button to reinitialize the record on disk, thus erasing the data. A typical output for the "Delete Record" option is:

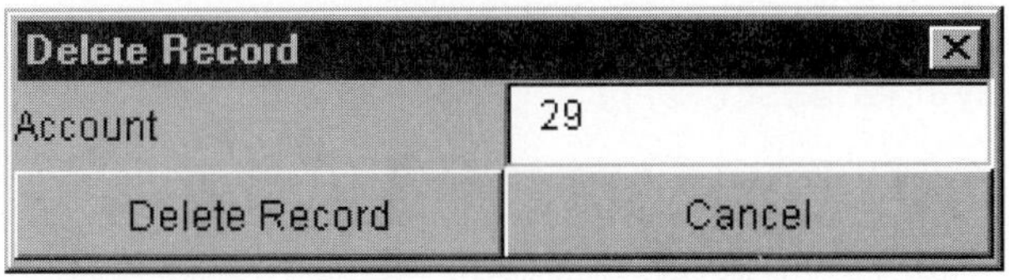

Delete Record

Account 29
Delete Record Cancel

The "Done" button terminates program execution. The program is shown in Fig. 15.14. The file **"credit.dat"** is opened by creating a **RandomAccessFile** object with the **"rw"** file open mode.

```
// Fig. 15.14: TransactionProcessor.java
// Transaction processing program using RandomAccessFiles.

// This program reads a random access file sequentially,
// updates data already written to the file, creates new
// data to be placed in the file, and deletes data
// already in the file.
import java.awt.*;
import java.awt.event.*;
import java.io.*;
import java.text.DecimalFormat;

public class TransactionProcessor extends Frame
             implements ActionListener {

```

Fig. 15.14 Transaction-processing program (part 1 of 10).

```
   // Application window components
   private Button update,     // update record
                  newRecord,  // add new record
                  delete,     // delete record
                  done;       // quit program

   private UpdateDialog updateDialog; // record update
   private NewDialog newDialog;       // add new records
   private DeleteDialog deleteDialog; // delete records

   // Application other pieces
   private RandomAccessFile file;
   private Record data;

   // Constructor -- intialize the Frame
   public TransactionProcessor()
   {
      super( "Transaction Processor" );

      // Open the file
      try {
         file = new RandomAccessFile( "credit.dat", "rw" );
      }
      catch ( IOException ioe ) {
         System.err.println( ioe.toString() );
         System.exit( 1 );
      }

      data = new Record();

      setSize( 300, 80 );
      setLayout( new GridLayout( 2, 2 ) );

      update = new Button( "Update Record" );
      update.addActionListener( this );
      add( update );

      newRecord = new Button( "New Record" );
      newRecord.addActionListener( this );
      add( newRecord );

      delete = new Button( "Delete Record" );
      delete.addActionListener( this );
      add( delete );

      done = new Button( "Done" );
      done.addActionListener( this );
      add( done );

      setVisible( true );            // show the Frame

```

Fig. 15.14 Transaction-processing program (part 2 of 10).

```
      // Create dialog boxes
      updateDialog = new UpdateDialog( this, file );
      newDialog = new NewDialog( this, file );
      deleteDialog = new DeleteDialog( this, file );
   }

   // Process actions
   public void actionPerformed( ActionEvent e )
   {
      if ( e.getSource() == update )
         updateDialog.setVisible( true );
      else if ( e.getSource() == newRecord )
         newDialog.setVisible( true );
      else if ( e.getSource() == delete )
         deleteDialog.setVisible( true );
      else
         closeFile();
   }

   public void closeFile()
   {
      try {
         file.close();
         System.exit( 0 );
      }
      catch ( IOException ioe ) {
         System.err.println( ioe.toString() );
         System.exit( 1 );
      }
   }

   public static void main( String args[] )
   {
      new TransactionProcessor();
   }
}

class UpdateDialog extends Dialog implements ActionListener {
   private TextField account, firstName, lastName,
                     balance, transaction;
   private Button cancel, save;

   private RandomAccessFile file;
   private Record data;
   private int accountNumber;

   public UpdateDialog( TransactionProcessor t,
                        RandomAccessFile f )
   {
      super( t, "Update Record", true );

```

Fig. 15.14 Transaction-processing program (part 3 of 10).

```
         file = f;
         data = new Record();

         setSize( 320, 180 );
         setLayout( new GridLayout( 6, 2 ) );

         add( new Label( "Account" ) );
         account = new TextField();
         account.addActionListener( this );
         add( account );

         add( new Label( "First name" ) );
         firstName = new TextField();
         add( firstName );

         add( new Label( "Last name" ) );
         lastName = new TextField();
         add( lastName );

         add( new Label( "Balance name" ) );
         balance = new TextField();
         add( balance );

         add( new Label( "Transaction amount" ) );
         transaction = new TextField();
         transaction.addActionListener( this );
         add( transaction );

         save = new Button( "Save Changes" );
         save.addActionListener( this );
         add( save );

         cancel = new Button( "Cancel" );
         cancel.addActionListener( this );
         add( cancel );
      }

      public void actionPerformed( ActionEvent e )
      {
         if ( e.getSource() == account ) {
            accountNumber = Integer.parseInt( account.getText() );
            readAccountInformation();
         }
         else if ( e.getSource() == save )  {
            accountNumber = Integer.parseInt( account.getText() );
            updateAccountInformation();
         }
         else if ( e.getSource() == cancel ) {
            setVisible( false );
            clear();
         }
```

Fig. 15.14 Transaction-processing program (part 4 of 10).

```
      else if ( e.getSource() == transaction ) {
         DecimalFormat twoDigits = new DecimalFormat( "0.00" );
         Double transactionAmount =
                  Double.valueOf( transaction.getText() );
         data.setBalance( data.getBalance() +
            transactionAmount.doubleValue() );
         balance.setText(
            twoDigits.format( data.getBalance() ) );
      }
   }

   private void readAccountInformation()
   {
      DecimalFormat twoDigits = new DecimalFormat( "0.00" );

      if ( accountNumber < 1 || accountNumber > 100 ) {
         account.setText( "Invalid account" );
         return;
      }

      try {
         file.seek( ( accountNumber - 1 ) * Record.size() );
         data.read( file );

         if ( data.getAccount() != 0 ) {
            account.setText(
               String.valueOf( data.getAccount() ) );
            firstName.setText( data.getFirstName() );
            lastName.setText( data.getLastName() );
            balance.setText( twoDigits.format(
                                 data.getBalance() ) );
            transaction.setText( "charge(+) or payment(-)" );
         }
         else
            account.setText( String.valueOf( accountNumber ) +
                             " does not exist" );
         }
      catch ( IOException ioe ) {
         account.setText( "Error reading file" );
      }
   }

   private void updateAccountInformation()
   {
      try {
         file.seek( ( accountNumber - 1 ) * Record.size() );
         data.write( file );
      }
```

Fig. 15.14 Transaction-processing program (part 5 of 10).

```
      catch ( IOException ioe ) {
         account.setText( "Error writing file" );
         return;
      }

      setVisible( false );
      clear();
   }

   private void clear()
   {
      account.setText( "" );
      firstName.setText( "" );
      lastName.setText( "" );
      balance.setText( "" );
      transaction.setText( "" );
   }
}

class NewDialog extends Dialog implements ActionListener {
   private RandomAccessFile file;
   private TextField account, firstName, lastName, balance;
   private Button cancel, save;

   private Record data;
   private int accountNumber;

   public NewDialog( TransactionProcessor t,
                     RandomAccessFile f )
   {
      super( t, "New Record", true );
      file = f;
      data = new Record();

      setSize( 300, 150 );
      setLayout( new GridLayout( 5, 2 ) );

      add( new Label( "Account" ) );
      account = new TextField();
      account.addActionListener( this );
      add( account );

      add( new Label( "First name" ) );
      firstName = new TextField();
      add( firstName );

      add( new Label( "Last name" ) );
      lastName = new TextField();
      add( lastName );

```

Fig. 15.14 Transaction-processing program (part 6 of 10).

```
      add( new Label( "Balance" ) );
      balance = new TextField();
      add( balance );

      save = new Button( "Save Changes" );
      save.addActionListener( this );
      add( save );

      cancel = new Button( "Cancel" );
      cancel.addActionListener( this );
      add( cancel );
   }

   public void actionPerformed( ActionEvent e )
   {
      if ( e.getSource() == account )
         checkIfAccountExists();
      else if ( e.getSource() == save )
         addRecord();
      else if ( e.getSource() == cancel ) {
         setVisible( false );
         clear();
      }
   }

   private void checkIfAccountExists()
   {
      accountNumber = Integer.parseInt( account.getText() );

      if ( accountNumber < 1 || accountNumber > 100 ) {
         account.setText( "Invalid account" );
         return;
      }

      try {
         file.seek( ( accountNumber - 1 ) * Record.size() );
         data.read( file );
      }
      catch ( IOException ioe ) {
         account.setText( "Error reading file" );
      }

      if ( data.getAccount() == 0 ) {
         firstName.setText( "Enter first name" );
         lastName.setText( "Enter last name" );
         balance.setText( "Enter balance" );
      }
      else {
         account.setText( data.getAccount() +
                          " already exists" );
         firstName.setText( "" );
```

Fig. 15.14 Transaction-processing program (part 7 of 10).

```
            lastName.setText( "" );
            balance.setText( "" );
         }
      }

   private void addRecord()
   {
      try {
         data.setAccount( accountNumber );
         data.setLastName( lastName.getText() );
         data.setFirstName( firstName.getText() );
         data.setBalance( ( new Double (
            balance.getText() ) ).doubleValue() );
         file.seek( ( accountNumber - 1 ) * Record.size() );
         data.write( file );
      }
      catch ( IOException ioe ) {
         account.setText( "Error writing file" );
         return;
      }

      setVisible( false );
      clear();
   }

   private void clear()
   {
      account.setText( "" );
      firstName.setText( "" );
      lastName.setText( "" );
      balance.setText( "" );
   }
}

class DeleteDialog extends Dialog implements ActionListener {
   private RandomAccessFile file;
   private TextField account;
   private Button cancel, delete;

   private Record data;
   private int accountNumber;

   public DeleteDialog( TransactionProcessor t,
                        RandomAccessFile f )
   {
      super( t, "Delete Record", true );
      file = f;
      data = new Record();

      setSize( 300, 80 );
      setLayout( new GridLayout( 2, 2 ) );
```

Fig. 15.14 Transaction-processing program (part 8 of 10).

```

      add( new Label( "Account" ) );
      account = new TextField();
      account.addActionListener( this );
      add( account );

      delete = new Button( "Delete Record" );
      delete.addActionListener( this );
      add( delete );

      cancel = new Button( "Cancel" );
      cancel.addActionListener( this );
      add( cancel );
   }

   public void actionPerformed( ActionEvent e )
   {
      if ( e.getSource() == account )  {
         accountNumber = Integer.parseInt( account.getText() );

         if ( accountNumber < 1 || accountNumber > 100 ) {
            account.setText( "Invalid account" );
            return;
         }

         try {
            file.seek( ( accountNumber - 1 ) * Record.size() );
            data.read( file );
         }
         catch ( IOException ioe ) {
            account.setText( "Error reading file" );
         }

         if ( data.getAccount() == 0 )
           account.setText( accountNumber + "does not exist" );
      }
      else if ( e.getSource() == delete ) {
         try {
            file.seek( ( accountNumber - 1 ) * Record.size() );
            data.setAccount( 0 );
            data.setFirstName( "" );
            data.setLastName( "" );
            data.setBalance( 0.0 );
            data.write( file );
         }
         catch ( IOException ioe ) {
            account.setText( "Error writing file" );
         }

```

Fig. 15.14 Transaction-processing program (part 9 of 10).

```
            setVisible( false );
            account.setText( "" );
         }
         else if ( e.getSource() == cancel ) {
            setVisible( false );
            account.setText( "" );
         }
      }
}
```

Fig. 15.14 Transaction-processing program (part 10 of 10).

15.12 Class **File**

As we stated at the beginning of this chapter, the **java.io** package contains an abundance of classes for processing input and output. We have concentrated on the classes for processing sequential files (**FileInputStream** and **FileOutputStream**), for processing data streams (**DataInputStream** and **DataOutputStream**) and for processing random-access files (**RandomAccessFile**). In this section we introduce class ***File*** which is particularly useful for retrieving from disk information about a file or a directory. Objects of class **File** do not actually open a file or provide any file-processing capabilities.

One example using a **File** object is checking if a file exists. In *Common Programming Error 15.1*, we warned that opening an existing file for output using a **FileOutputStream** object discards the contents of that file *without warning*. A **File** object can be used to determine of the file already exists. If so, you can open it with a **RandomAccessFile** object instead of a **FileOutputStream** object, or you can at least warn the user that they are about to discard the original file's contents.

Good Programming Practice 15.2

*Use a **File** object to determine if a file exists before opening the file with a **FileOutputStream** object.*

A **File** object is initialized using one of three constructors. The constructor

```
public File( String name )
```

stores the **String** argument **name** in the object. The **name** can contain *path information* as well as a file or directory name. A file or directory's path leads you to the file or directory on disk. The path includes some or all of the directories leading to the file or directory. An *absolute path* contains all the directories starting with the *root directory* that lead to a specific file or directory. Every file or directory on a particular disk drive has the same root directory in its path. A *relative path* contains a subset of the directories leading to a specific file or directory. Relative paths start from the directory in which the application was started.

The constructor

```
public File( String pathToName, String name )
```

uses argument **pathToName** (an absolute or relative path) to locate the file or directory specified by **name**.

The constructor

```
public File( File directory, String name )
```

uses the previously created **File** object **directory** (an absolute or relative path) to locate the file or directory specified by **name**.

Some commonly used **public** methods of class **File** are shown in Fig. 15.15. See the Java API for other **File** methods.

The application of Fig. 15.16 demonstrates class **File**. Class **FileTest** creates a graphical user interface containing a **TextField enter** and a **TextArea output**.

Method	Description
boolean canRead()	Returns **true** if a file is readable; **false** otherwise.
boolean canWrite()	Returns **true** if a file is writeable; **false** otherwise.
boolean exists()	Returns **true** if the name specified as the argument to the **File** constructor is a file or directory in the specified path; **false** otherwise.
boolean isFile()	Returns **true** if the name specified as the argument to the **File** constructor is a file; **false** otherwise.
boolean isDirectory()	Returns true if the name specified as the argument to the **File** constructor is a directory; **false** otherwise.
boolean isAbsolute()	Returns **true** if the arguments specified to the **File** constructor indicate an absolute path to a file or directory; **false** otherwise.
String getAbsolutePath()	Returns a **String** with the absolute path of the file or directory.
String getName()	Returns a **String** with the name of the file or directory.
String getPath()	Returns a **String** with the path of the file or directory.
String getParent()	Returns a **String** with the parent directory of the file or directory—i.e., the directory in which the file or directory can be found.
long length()	Returns the length of the file in bytes. If the **File** object represents a directory, **0** is returned.
long lastModified()	Returns a system-dependent representation of the time at which the file or directory was last modified. The value returned is only useful for comparison with other values returned by this method.
String[] list()	Returns an array of **String**s representing the contents of a directory.

Fig. 15.15 Some commonly used **File** methods.

The user types a file name or directory name into the **enter** text field and presses the *Enter* key. The **actionPerformed** method of class **FileTest** creates a new **File** object and assigns it to name. Next, the condition in the **if** structure at line 29—**name.exists()**—is tested. If name the user typed does not exist, the **actionPerformed** method proceeds to line 70 and outputs the name the user typed followed by "**does not exist**." Otherwise, the body of the **if** structure is executed. The program outputs the name of the file or directory, then outputs the results of testing the **File** object with **isFile**, **isDirectory** and **isAbsolute**. Next, the values returned by **lastModified**, **length**, **getPath**, **getAbsolutePath** and **getParent** are displayed. Finally, if the **File** object represents a file, the contents of the file are read into the program and displayed in the **TextArea**. A **RandomAccessFile** object is used so we can open the file for reading and read the file one line at a time with the **readLine** method (line 53). Note that the **RandomAccessFile** object was initialized with the **File** object **name** (line 47). If the **File** object represents a directory, the contents of the directory are read into the program using **File** method **list**, then the directory contents are displayed in the **TextArea**.

The first output of this program demonstrates a **File** object associated with the **README** file from the Java Developer's Kit. The second output demonstrates a **File** object associated with the **demo** directory from the Java Developer's Kit. In both cases, we specified an absolute path on our personal computer. Note that the **** *separator character* is used to separate directories and files in the path. On a UNIX workstation, the separator character would be a **/** character. Java actually processes both characters as identical in a path name. So, if we specified the path **c:\java/README** which uses one of each separator character, Java still processes the file properly.

```
1  // Fig. 15.16: FileTest.java
2  // Demonstrating the File class.
3  import java.awt.*;
4  import java.awt.event.*;
5  import java.io.*;
6  import com.deitel.jhtp2.ch11.CloseWindowAndExit;
7
8  public class FileTest extends Frame implements ActionListener {
9     private TextField enter;
10    private TextArea output;
11
12    public FileTest()
13    {
14       super( "Testing class File" );
15       enter = new TextField(
16          "Enter file or directory name here" );
17       enter.addActionListener( this );
18       output = new TextArea();
19       add( enter, BorderLayout.NORTH );
20       add( output, BorderLayout.CENTER );
```

Fig. 15.16 Demonstrating class **File** (part 1 of 4).

```
      setSize( 400, 400 );
      setVisible( true );
   }

   public void actionPerformed( ActionEvent e )
   {
      File name = new File( e.getActionCommand() );

      if ( name.exists() ) {
         output.setText(
            name.getName() + " exists\n" +
            ( name.isFile() ? "is a file\n" :
                              "is not a file\n" ) +
            ( name.isDirectory() ? "is a directory\n" :
                                   "is not a directory\n" ) +
            ( name.isAbsolute() ? "is absolute path\n" :
                                  "is not absolute path\n" ) +
            "Last modified: " + name.lastModified() +
            "\nLength: " + name.length() +
            "\nPath: " + name.getPath() +
            "\nAbsolute path: " + name.getAbsolutePath() +
            "\nParent: " + name.getParent() );

         if ( name.isFile() ) {
            try {
               RandomAccessFile r =
                  new RandomAccessFile( name, "r" );
               StringBuffer buf = new StringBuffer();
               String text;

               output.append( "\n\n" );

               while( ( text = r.readLine() ) != null )
                  buf.append( r.readLine() + "\n" );

               output.append( buf.toString() );
            }
            catch( IOException e2 ) {
            }
         }
         else if ( name.isDirectory() ) {
            String directory[] = name.list();

            output.append( "\n\nDirectory contents:\n");

            for ( int i = 0; i < directory.length; i++ )
               output.append( directory[ i ] + "\n" );
         }
      }
```

Fig. 15.16 Demonstrating class **File** (part 2 of 4).

```
      else {
         output.setText( e.getActionCommand() +
                         " does not exist\n" );
      }
   }

   public static void main( String args[] )
   {
      FileTest f = new FileTest();
      f.addWindowListener( new CloseWindowAndExit() );
   }
}
```

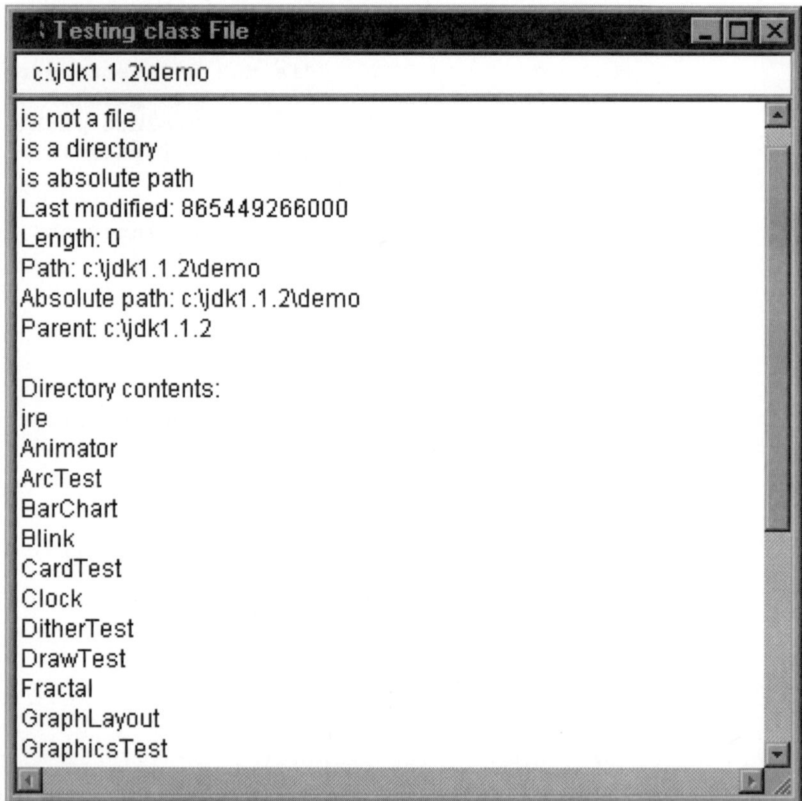

Fig. 15.16 Demonstrating class **`File`** (part 3 of 4).

15.13 Input/Output of Objects

In this chapter we discussed Java's object-oriented style of input/output, but our examples concentrated on input/output of traditional data types rather than objects of user-defined class types.

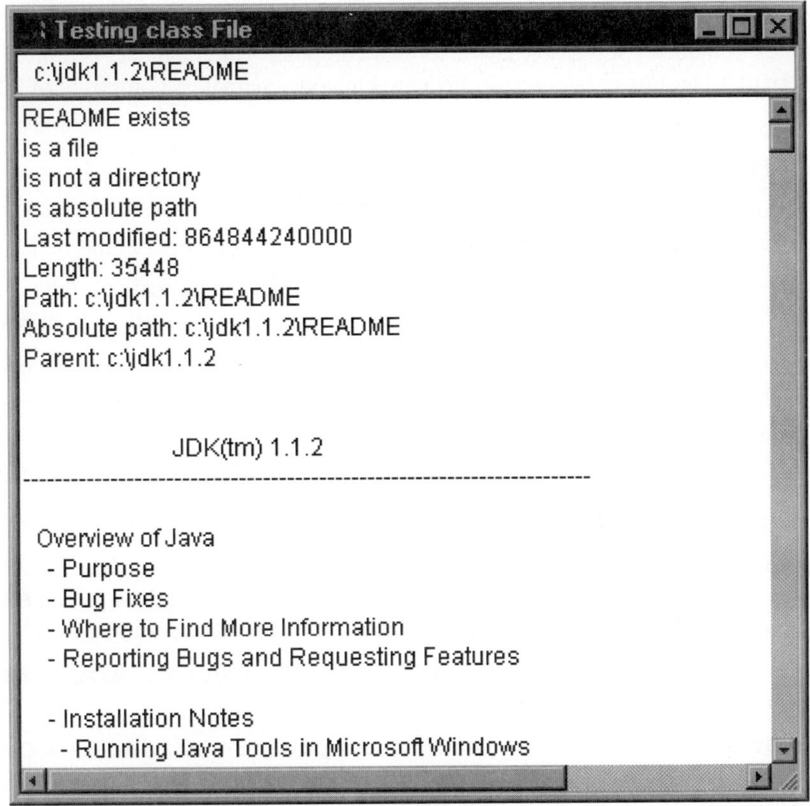

Fig. 15.16 Demonstrating class **`File`** (part 4 of 4).

When object instance variables are output to a disk file, in a sense we lose the object's type information. We only have data, not type information, on a disk. If the program that is going to read this data knows what object type it corresponds to, then the data is simply read into objects of that type.

An interesting problem occurs when we store objects of different types in the same file. How can we distinguish them (or their instance variables) as we read them into a program?

Java now provides classes ***`ObjectOutputStream`*** and ***`ObjectInputStream`*** to facilitate input and output of objects. These classes are discussed in detail in our text *Advanced Java How to Program.*

Summary

- All data items processed by a computer are reduced to combinations of zeros and ones.
- The smallest data item in a computer can assume the value **`0`** or the value **`1`**. Such a data item is called a bit.

- Digits, letters, and special symbols are referred to as characters. The set of all characters used to write programs and represent data items on a particular computer is called that computer's character set. Every character in a computer's character set is represented as a pattern of **1**s and **0**s (characters in Java are Unicode characters composed of 2 bytes).
- A field is a group of characters (or bytes) that conveys meaning.
- A record is a group of related fields.
- At least one field in a record is chosen as a record key to identify a record as belonging to a particular person or entity that is unique from all other records in the file.
- Java imposes no structure on a file. Notions like "record" do not exist in Java. The programmer must structure a file appropriately to meet the requirements of an application.
- A collection of programs designed to create and manage databases is called a database management system (DBMS).
- Java views each file as a sequential stream of bytes.
- Each file ends in some machine-dependent form of end-of-file marker.
- Streams provide communication channels between files and programs.
- The package **java.io** must be imported into a program to perform Java file I/O. This package includes the definitions for the stream classes such as **FileInputStream**, **FileOutputStream**, **DataInputStream**, and **DataOutputStream**.
- Files are opened by instantiating objects of stream classes **FileInputStream**, **FileOutputStream**, and **RandomAccessFile**.
- **InputStream** (a subclass of **Object**) and **OutputStream** (a subclass of **Object**) are abstract classes that define methods for performing input and output respectively; their derived classes override these methods.
- File input/output is done with **FileInputStream** (a subclass of **InputStream**) and **FileOutputStream** (a subclass of **OutputStream**).
- Pipes are synchronized communication channels between threads. A pipe is established between two threads. One thread sends data to another by writing to a **PipedOutputStream** (a subclass of **OutputStream)**. The target thread reads information from the pipe via a **PipedInputStream** (a subclass of **InputStream**).
- A **PrintStream** (a subclass of **FilterOutputStream**) is used for performing output to the screen (or the "standard output" as defined by your local operating system). **System.out** is a **PrintStream** (as is **System.err**).
- A **FilterInputStream** filters an **InputStream** and a **FilterOutStream** filters an **OutputStream**; filtering simply means that the filter stream provides additional functionality such as buffering, monitoring line numbers or aggregating data bytes into meaningful primitive-data-type units.
- Reading data as raw bytes is fast but crude. Usually programs want to read data as aggregates of bytes that form an **int**, a **float**, a **double**, and so on. To accomplish this we use a **DataInputStream** (a subclass of class **FilterInputStream**).

- Interface **DataInput** is implemented by class **DataInputStream** and class **RandomAccessFile** that each need to read primitive data types from a stream.
- **DataInputStreams** enable a program to read binary data from an **InputStream**.
- The **DataInput** interface includes methods **read** (for byte arrays), **readBoolean**, **readByte**, **readChar**, **readDouble**, **readFloat**, **readFully** (for byte arrays) **readInt**, **readLine**, **readLong**, **readShort**, **readUnsignedByte**, **readUnsignedShort**, **readUTF** (for Unicode) and **skipBytes**.
- The **DataOutput** interface is implemented by class **DataOutputStream** (a subclass of class **FilterOutputStream**) and class **RandomAccessFile** that each need to write primitive data types to an **OutputStream**.
- **DataOutputStreams** enable a program to write binary data to an **OutputStream**. The **DataOutput** interface includes methods **flush**, **size**, **write** (for a byte), **write** (for a byte array), **writeBoolean**, **writeByte**, **writeBytes**, **writeChar**, **writeChars** (for Unicode **Strings**), **writeDouble**, **writeFloat**, **writeInt**, **writeLong**, **writeShort** and **writeUTF**.
- Buffering is an I/O-performance-enhancement technique.
- With a **BufferedOutputStream** (a subclass of class **FilterOutputStream**) each output statement does not necessarily result in an actual physical transfer of data to the output device. Rather, each output operation is directed to a region in memory called a buffer that is large enough to hold the data of many output operations. Then actual output to the output device is performed in one large physical output operation each time the buffer fills. The output operations directed to the output buffer in memory are often called logical output operations.
- With a **BufferedInputStream** (a subclass of class **FilterInputStream**) many "logical" chunks of data from a file are read as one large physical input operation into a memory buffer. As a program requests each new chunk of data, it is taken from the buffer (this is sometimes referred to as a logical input operation). When the buffer becomes empty, the next physical input operation from the input device is performed to read in the next group of "logical" chunks of data. Thus, the number of physical input operations is small compared with the number of read requests issued by the program.
- With a **BufferedOutputStream** a partially filled buffer can be forced out to the device at any time with an explicit **flush**
- A **PushBackInputStream** is a subclass of class **FilterInputStream**. The application reading a **PushBackInputStream** reads bytes from the stream and forms aggregates consisting of several bytes. Sometimes, to determine that one aggregate is complete, the application must read the first character the "past the end" of the first aggregate. Once the program has determined that the current aggregate is complete, the extra character is "pushed back" onto the stream.
- **PushBackInputStreams** are used by programs like compilers that parse their inputs, i.e., break them into meaningful units (such as the keywords, identifiers and operators that the Java compiler must recognize).

- A **StreamTokenizer** (a subclass of **Object**) is helpful for breaking up a stream of text from an input text file into meaningful pieces called tokens.
- A **RandomAccessFile** (a subclass of **Object**) is useful for direct-access applications such as transaction-processing applications like airline-reservations systems and point-of-sale systems.
- With a sequential-access file each successive input/output request reads or writes the next consecutive set of data in the file.
- With a random-access file, each successive input/output request may be directed to any part of the file, perhaps widely separated from the part of the file referenced in the previous request.
- Direct-access applications provide rapid access to specific data items in large files; such applications are often used while people are waiting for answers—these answers must be made available quickly or the people may become impatient and "take their business elsewhere."
- A **ByteArrayInputStream** (a subclass of abstract class **InputStream**) performs its inputs from a byte array in memory.
- A **ByteArrayOutputStream** (a subclass of abstract class **OutputStream**) outputs to a byte array in memory.
- An application of byte-array input/output is data validation. A program can input an entire line at a time from the input stream into a byte array. Then a validation routine can scrutinize the contents of the byte array and correct the data, if necessary. The program can now proceed to input from the byte array, knowing that the input data is in the proper format.
- A **StringBufferInputStream** (a subclass of abstract class **InputStream**) inputs from a **StringBuffer** object.
- A **SequenceInputStream** (a subclass of abstract class **InputStream**) enables several **InputStream**s to be concatenated so that the program sees the group as one continuous **InputStream**. As the end of each input stream is reached, the stream is closed and the next stream in the sequence is opened.
- A **LineNumberInputStream** (a subclass of class **FilterInputStream**) always knows what line number of the file is being read.
- Objects of the **FileDescriptor** class are ordinarily not manipulated by most Java users.
- Class **File** enables programs to obtain information about a file or directory.
- Files are opened for output by creating a **FileOutputStream** class object. One argument is passed to the constructor—the filename. Existing files are truncated and all data in the file is lost. Nonexistent files are created.
- Programs may process no files, one file, or several files. Each file has a unique name and is associated with an appropriate file stream object. All file-processing methods must refer to a file with the appropriate object.

- A file-position pointer indicates the position in the file from which the next input is to occur or at which the next output is to be placed.
- A convenient way to implement random-access files is by using only fixed-length records. Using this technique, a program can quickly calculate the exact location of a record relative to the beginning of the file.
- Data can be inserted in a random-access file without destroying other data in the file. Data can be updated or deleted without rewriting the entire file.
- The **RandomAccessFile** class has the same capabilities for input and output as the **DataInputStream** and **DataOutputStream** classes and also supports seeking to a specific byte position in the file with method **seek**.

Terminology

absolute path
alphabetic field
binary digit
bit
buffer
BufferedInputStream class
BufferedOutputStream class
buffering
byte
ByteArrayInputStream class
BytArrayOutputStream class
canRead method of **File** class
canWrite method of **File** class
chaining stream objects
character field
character set
close a file
close method
data hierarchy
database
database management system (DBMS)
DataInput interface
DataInputStream class
DataOutput interface
DataOutputStream class
data validation
decimal digit
direct-access applications
directory
end-of-file
end-of-file marker
exists method of **File** class
field
file
File class
FileDescriptor class
FileInputStream class
file name
file-position pointer
FileInputStream class
FileOutputStream class
FilterInputStream class
FilterOutputStream class
flush
getAbsolutePath method of **File** class
getName method of **File** class
getParent method of **File** class
getPath method of **File** class
input stream
InputStream class
instant-access application
IOException
isAbsolute method of **File** class
isDirectory method of **File** class
isFile method of **File** class
lastModified method of **File** class
list method of **File** class
length method of **File** class
LineNumberInputStream class
logical input operation
logical output operation
memory buffer
numeric field
open a file
output stream
OutputStream class
partially filled buffer
persistent data

physical input operation
physical output operation
pipe
PipedInputStream class
PipedOutputStream class
PrintStream class
PushBackInputStream class
r file open mode
random-access file
RandomAccessFile class
read
readBoolean
readByte
readChar
readDouble
readFloat
readFully
readInt
readLong
readShort
readUnsignedByte
readUnsignedShort
readUTF
record
record key
relative path
root directory
rw file open mode
SequenceInputStream class
sequential-access file
size
standard output
StreamTokenizer class
StringBufferInputStream class
System.err (standard error stream)
System.in (standard input stream)
System.out (standard output stream)
transaction-processing systems
truncate an existing file
Unicode character set
write
writeBoolean
writeByte
writeBytes
writeChar
writeChars
writeDouble
writeFloat
writeInt
writeLong
writeShort
writeUTF

Common Programming Errors

15.1 Opening an existing file for output when, in fact, the user wants to preserve the file; the contents of the file are discarded without warning.

15.2 Using an incorrect **FileOutputStream** object to refer to a file.

15.3 Not opening a file before attempting to reference it in a program.

Good Programming Practices

15.1 Open a file with the **"r"** file open mode for input if the contents of the file should not be modified. This prevents unintentional modification of the file's contents. This is another example of the principle of least privilege.

15.2 Use a ***File*** object to determine if a file exists before opening the file with a ***FileOutputStream*** object.

Performance Tips

15.1 Because typical physical output operations are extremely slow compared to typical processor speeds, buffering outputs normally yields significant performance improvements over unbuffered outputs.

15.2 Because typical input operations are extremely slow compared to processor speeds, buffering inputs normally yields significant performance improvements over unbuffered inputs.

15.3 Always release resources explicitly and at the earliest possible moment at which it is determined that the resource is no longer needed. This makes the resource immediately available to be reused by your program or by another program, thus improving resource utilization

15.4 Explicitly close each file as soon as it is known that the program will not reference the file again. This can reduce resource usage in a program that will continue executing long after it no longer needs to be referencing a particular file. This practice also improves program clarity.

15.5 The process of closing a file and reopening a file for the purpose of positioning the file-position pointer back to the beginning of a file is a time-consuming task for the computer. If this is done frequently, it may slow the performance of your program.

Software Engineering Observation

15.1 It would be dangerous to enable applets arriving from anywhere on the World Wide Web to be able to read and write files on the client system. Most web browsers prevent applets from performing file processing on the client system. Therefore, file-processing programs are generally implemented as Java applications.

Self-Review Exercises

15.1 Fill in the blanks in each of the following:

a) Ultimately, all data items processed by a computer are reduced to combinations of __________ and __________.
b) The smallest data item a computer can process is called a __________.
c) A __________ is a group of related records.
d) Digits, letters, and special symbols are referred to as __________.
e) A group of related files is called a __________.
f) Method __________ of the file stream classes **`FileOutputStream`**, **`FileInputStream`**, and **`RandomAccessFile`** closes a file.
g) The **`DataInputStream`** method __________ reads an integer from the specified stream.
h) The **`DataInputStream`** method __________ reads a string from the specified stream.
i) Method __________ of the **`RandomAccessFile`** class sets the file-position pointer to a specific location in a file for input or output.

15.2 State which of the following are true and which are false (for those that are false, explain why):

a) The programmer must explicitly create the **`System.in`**, **`System.out`**, and **`System.err`** objects.
b) If the file-position pointer points to a location in a sequential file other than the beginning of the file, the file must be closed and reopened to read from the beginning of the file.
c) It is not necessary to search through all the records in a random-access file to find a specific record.
d) Records in random-access files must be of uniform length.
e) Method **`seek`** must seek relative to the beginning of a file.

15.3 Assume that each of the following statements applies to the same program.

a) Write a statement that opens file **`"oldmast.dat"`** for input; use **`DataInputStream`** object **`inOldMaster`** chained to a **`FileInputStream`** object.
b) Write a statement that opens file **`"trans.dat"`** for input; use **`DataInputStream`** object **`inTransaction`** chained to a **`FileInputStream`** object.

c) Write a statement that opens file **"newmast.dat"** for output (and creation); use **DataOutputStream** object **outNewMaster** chained to a **FileOutputStream**.

d) Write a set of statements that read a record from the file **"oldmast.dat"**. The record consists of integer **accountNum**, string **name**, and floating point **currentBalance**; use **DataInputStream** object **inOldMaster**.

e) Write a set of statements that read a record from the file **"trans.dat"**. The record consists of integer **accountNum** and floating point **dollarAmount**; use **DataInputStream** object **inTransaction**.

f) Write a set of statements that output a record to the file **"newmast.dat"**. The record consists of integer **accountNum**, string **name**, and floating point **currentBalance**; use **DataOutputStream** object **outNewMaster**.

15.4 Find the error and show how to correct it in each of the following.

a) File **"payables.dat"** referred to by **DataOutputStream** object **outPayable** has not been opened.

```
outPayable.writeInt( account );
outPayable.writeUTF( company );
outPayable.writeDouble( amount );
```

b) The following statement should read a record from the file **"payables.dat"**. The **FileInputStream** object **inPayable** refers to this file, and **DataInputStream** object **inReceivable** refers to the file **"receivables.dat"**.

```
account = inReceivable.readInt();
company = inReceivable.readUTF();
amount = inReceivable.readDouble();
```

Answers to Self-Review Exercises

15.1 a) 1s, 0s. b) Bit. c) File. d) Characters. e) Database. f) **close**. g) **readInt**. h) **readUTF**. i) **seek**.

15.2 a) False. These three streams are created automatically for the programmer.
b) True.
c) True.
d) False. Records in a random-access file are normally of uniform length.
e) True.

15.3 a)
```
DataInputStream inOldMaster;
inOldMaster = new DataInputStream(
              new FileInputStream( "oldmast.dat" ) );
```
b)
```
DataInputStream inTransaction;
inTransaction = new DataInputStream(
                    new FileInputStream( "trans.dat" ) );
```
c)
```
DataOutputStream outNewMaster;
outNewMaster = new DataOutputStream(
                   new FileOutputStream( "newmast.dat" ) );
```
d)
```
accountNum = inOldMaster.readInt();
name = inOldMaster.readUTF();
currentBalance = inOldMaster.readDouble();
```
e)
```
accountNum = inTransaction.readInt();
dollarAmount = inTransaction.readDouble();
```

f)
```
outNewMaster.writeInt( accountNum );
outNewMaster.writeUTF( name );
outNewMaster.writeDouble( currentBalance );
```

15.4 a) Error: The file **"payables.dat"** has not been opened before the attempt is made to output data to the stream.
Correction: Create a new **DataOutputStream** object chained to a **FileOutputStream** object to open **"payables.dat"** for output.

b) Error: The incorrect **DataInputStream** object is being used to read a record from file **"payables.dat"**.
Correction: Use object **inPayable** to refer to **"payables.dat"**.

Exercises

15.5 Fill in the blanks in each of the following:

a) Computers store large amounts of data on secondary storage devices as __________.
b) A __________ is composed of several fields.
c) A field that may contain only digits, letters, and blanks is called an__________ field.
d) To facilitate the retrieval of specific records from a file, one field in each record is chosen as a __________.
e) The vast majority of information stored in computer systems is stored in__________ files.
f) The standard stream objects are __________, __________, and__________.

15.6 State which of the following are true and which are false (if false, explain why):

a) The impressive functions performed by computers essentially involve the manipulation of zeros and ones.
b) People specify programs and data items as characters; computers then manipulate and process these characters as groups of zeros and ones.
c) A person's 5-digit zip code is an example of a numeric field.
d) A person's street address is generally considered to be an alphabetic field.
e) Data items represented in computers form a data hierarchy in which data items become larger and more complex as we progress from fields to characters to bits, etc.
f) A record key identifies a record as belonging to a particular field.
g) Companies store all their information in a single file to facilitate computer processing.
h) When a program creates a file, the file is automatically retained by the computer for future reference.

15.7 Exercise 15.3 asked the reader to write a series of single statements. Actually, these statements form the core of an important type of file-processing program, namely, a file-matching program. In commercial data processing, it is common to have several files in each application system. In an accounts receivable system, for example, there is generally a master file containing detailed information about each customer such as the customer's name, address, telephone number, outstanding balance, credit limit, discount terms, contract arrangements, and possibly a condensed history of recent purchases and cash payments.

As transactions occur (i.e., sales are made and cash payments arrive in the mail), they are entered into a file. At the end of each business period (i.e., a month for some companies, a week for others, and a day in some cases) the file of transactions (called **"trans.dat"** in Exercise 15.3) is applied to the master file (called **"oldmast.dat"** in Exercise 15.3), thus updating each account's record of purchases and payments. During an updating run, the master file is rewritten as a new file (**"newmast.dat"**), which is then used at the end of the next business period to begin the updating process again.

File-matching programs must deal with certain problems that do not exist in single-file programs. For example, a match does not always occur. A customer on the master file may not have made any purchases or cash payments in the current business period, and therefore no record for this customer will appear on the transaction file. Similarly, a customer who did make some purchases or cash payments may have just moved to this community, and the company may not have had a chance to create a master record for this customer.

Use the statements in Exercise 15.3 as a basis for writing a complete file-matching accounts receivable program. Use the account number on each file as the record key for matching purposes. Assume that each file is a sequential file with records stored in increasing account number order.

When a match occurs (i.e., records with the same account number appear on both the master file and the transaction file), add the dollar amount on the transaction file to the current balance on the master file, and write the **"newmast.dat"** record. (Assume that purchases are indicated by positive amounts on the transaction file, and that payments are indicated by negative amounts.) When there is a master record for a particular account but no corresponding transaction record, merely write the master record to **"newmast.dat"**. When there is a transaction record but no corresponding master record, print the message **"Unmatched transaction record for account number ..."** (fill in the account number from the transaction record).

15.8 After writing the program of Exercise 15.7, write a simple program to create some test data for checking out the program. Use the following sample account data:

Master file Account number	Name	Balance
100	Alan Jones	348.17
300	Mary Smith	27.19
500	Sam Sharp	0.00
700	Suzy Green	-14.22

Transaction file Account number	Transaction amount
100	27.14
300	62.11
400	100.56
900	82.17

Run the program of Exercise 15.7 using the files of test data created in Exercise 15.8. Print the new master file. Check that the accounts have been updated correctly.

15.9 It is possible (actually common) to have several transaction records with the same record key. This occurs because a particular customer might make several purchases and cash payments during a business period. Rewrite your accounts receivable file-matching program of Exercise 15.7 to provide for the possibility of handling several transaction records with the same record key. Modify the test data of Exercise 15.8 to include the following additional transaction records:

Account number	Dollar amount
300	83.89
700	80.78
700	1.53

15.10 Write a series of statements that accomplish each of the following. Assume the structure

```
class Person {
   char lastName[15];
   char firstName[15];
   char age[2];
}
```

has been defined, and that the random-access file has been opened properly.

a) Initialize the file **"nameage.dat"** with 100 records containing **lastName = "unassigned"**, **firstName = ""**, and **age = "0"**.
b) Input 10 last names, first names, and ages, and write them to the file.
c) Update a record that has information in it, and if there is none tell the user **"No info"**.
d) Delete a record that has information by reinitializing that particular record.

15.11 You are the owner of a hardware store and need to keep an inventory that can tell you what different tools you have, how many of each you have on hand, and the cost of each one. Write a program that initializes the random-access file **"hardware.dat"** to one hundred empty records, lets you input the data concerning each tool, enables you to list all your tools, lets you delete a record for a tool that you no longer have, and lets you update *any* information in the file. The tool identification number should be the record number. Use the following information to start your file:

Record #	Tool name	Quantity	Cost
3	Electric sander	7	57.98
17	Hammer	76	11.99
24	Jig saw	21	11.00
39	Lawn mower	3	79.50
56	Power saw	18	99.99
68	Screwdriver	106	6.99
77	Sledge hammer	11	21.50
83	Wrench	34	7.50

15.12 Modify the telephone number word generating program you wrote in Chapter 4 so it writes its output to a file. If you have a computerized dictionary available, modify the program to look up the thousands of seven-letter words in the dictionary. Some of the interesting seven-letter combinations created by this program may consist of two or more words. For example, the phone number 8432677 produces "THEBOSS." Modify the program to use the computerized dictionary to check each possible seven-letter word to see if it is a valid one-letter word followed by a valid six-letter word, a valid two-letter word followed by a valid five-letter word, etc.

16

Networking

Objectives

- To understand the elements of Java networking.
- To implement Java networking applications.
- To understand how to implement Java clients and servers that communicate with one another.
- To understand how to implement network-based collaborative applications.
- To be able to write programs that "walk the web"
- To construct a multithreaded server.

If the presence of electricity can be made visible in any part of a circuit, I see no reason why intelligence may not be transmitted instantaneously by electricity.
Samuel F. B. Morse

Mr. Watson, come here, I want you.
Alexander Graham Bell

What networks of railroads, highways and canals were in another age, the networks of telecommunications, information and computerization . . . are today.
Bruno Kreisky, Austrian Chancellor

Science may never come up with a better office-communication system than the coffee break.
Earl Wilson

It's currently a problem of access to gigabits through punybaud.
J. C. R. Licklider

Outline

16.1 Introduction

There is much excitement over the Internet and the World Wide Web. The Internet ties the "information world" together. The World Wide Web makes the Internet easy to use and gives it the flair and sizzle of multimedia. Organizations see the Internet and the Web as crucial to their information systems strategies. In its early implementation Java provides a number of built-in networking capabilities that make it easy to develop Internet-based and Web-based applications. Not only can Java specify parallelism through multithreading, but it can enable programs to search the world for information and to collaborate with programs running on other computers internationally, nationally, or just within an organization. Java can even enable applets and applications running on the same computer to communicate with one another, subject to security constraints.

Networking introduces many security risks, so browsers may limit the capabilities of applets. We discuss some of these limitations in section 16.9.

Networking is a massive and complex topic. Computer Science and Computer Engineering students will typically take a full-semester, upper-level course in computer networking and continue with further study at the graduate level. Java provides a rich complement of networking capabilities and will likely be used as an implementation vehicle in computer networking courses. In *Java How to Program* we introduce basic Java networking concepts and capabilities. We provide five live-code examples that will help the reader frame out a great variety of typical networking applications. Java's networking capabilities are centralized in the **`java.net`** *package*. The reader is encouraged to further explore these classes and methods.

Java offers *socket-based communications* that enable applications to view networking as if it were file I/O—a program can read from a *socket* or write to a socket as simply as reading from a file or writing to a file. We show how to create and manipulate sockets.

Java provides *stream sockets* and *datagram sockets.* With *stream sockets* a process establishes a *connection* to another process. While the connection is in place, data flows between the processes in continuous *streams*. Stream sockets are said to provide a *connection-oriented service*. The protocol used for transmission is the popular *TCP (Transmission Control Protocol)*.

With *datagram sockets*, individual *packets* of information are transmitted. This is not the right protocol for everyday users because unlike TCP, the protocol used, *UDP*—the *User Datagram Protocol*—is a *connectionless service*, and does not guarantee that packets arrive in any particular way. In fact, packets can be lost, can be duplicated, and can even arrive out of sequence. So with UDP, significant extra programming is required on the user's part to deal with these problems (if the user chooses to do so). Stream sockets and the TCP protocol will be the most desirable for the vast majority of Java programmers.

Performance Tip 16.1

Connectionless services generally offer greater performance but less reliability than connection-oriented services.

Portability Tip 16.1

The TCP protocol and its related set of protocols enable a great variety of heterogeneous computer systems *(i.e., computer systems with different processors and different operating systems) to intercommunicate.*

Our discussion of networking focuses on both sides of a *client-server relationship*. The *client* requests that some action be performed and the *server* performs the action returning the result (if any) to the client. The client first attempts to establish a *connection* to the server. The server can *accept* or *deny* the connection. If the connection is accepted, then the client and server communicate through sockets in much the same manner as if they were doing file I/O. When the communication connection is no longer needed, the client and server each close the connection. Our networking example programs will make use of the input/output streams facilities we discussed in Chapter 15.

16.2 Manipulating URLs

The Internet offers many *protocols*. The **`http`** *protocol (HyperText Transfer Protocol)* that forms the basis of the World Wide Web uses URLs (*Uniform Resource Locators*, also called *Universal Resource Locators*) to locate data on the Internet. Common URLs represent files or directories and can represent complex tasks such as database lookups and Internet searches. For more information on URL formats visit the World Wide Web site:

`http://www.ncsa.uiuc.edu/demoweb/url-primer.html`

For more information on the **`http`** protocol visit the World Wide Web site:

`http://www.w3.org`

If you know the URL of publicly available HTML files anywhere on the World Wide Web, you can access that data through **`http`**. Java makes it easy to manipulate URLs. Using a URL as an argument to the **`showDocument`** method of interface **`AppletContext`** causes the applet's browser to display the URL.

The applet of Fig. 16.1 enables the user to select a website from a **Choice** button and cause the browser to display the corresponding World Wide Web site. The applet contains four choices—**JavaSoft**, **Deitel**, **Gamelan** and **JavaWorld**. When the user makes a selection, the **itemStateChanged** method of applet **SiteSelector** determines which website was selected, gets the URL associated with that selection, passes the URL to the browser, and the browser displays the new World Wide Web page.

```
// Fig. 16.1: SiteSelector.java
// This program uses a button to load a document from a URL.
import java.awt.*;
import java.awt.event.*;
import java.net.*;
import java.util.Hashtable;
import java.applet.Applet;

public class SiteSelector extends Applet
             implements ItemListener {
   private Hashtable sites;
   private Choice siteChoice;

   public void init()
   {
      sites = new Hashtable();
      siteChoice = new Choice();

      // look in HTML for parameters and add sites to HashTable
      String title, location;
      URL url;
      int counter = 0;

      while ( true ) {
         title = getParameter( "title" + counter );

         if ( title != null ) {
            location = getParameter( "location" + counter );

            try {
               url = new URL( location );
               sites.put( title, url );
               siteChoice.add( title );
            }
            catch ( MalformedURLException e ) {
               e.printStackTrace();
            }
         }
         else
            break;

```

Fig. 16.1 Loading a document from a URL into a browser (part 1 of 3).

```
            ++counter;
         }

         add( new Label( "Choose a site to browse:" ) );
         siteChoice.addItemListener( this );
         add( siteChoice );
      }

      public void itemStateChanged( ItemEvent e )
      {
         URL url = (URL) sites.get( e.getItem() );

         getAppletContext().showDocument( url );
      }
   }
```

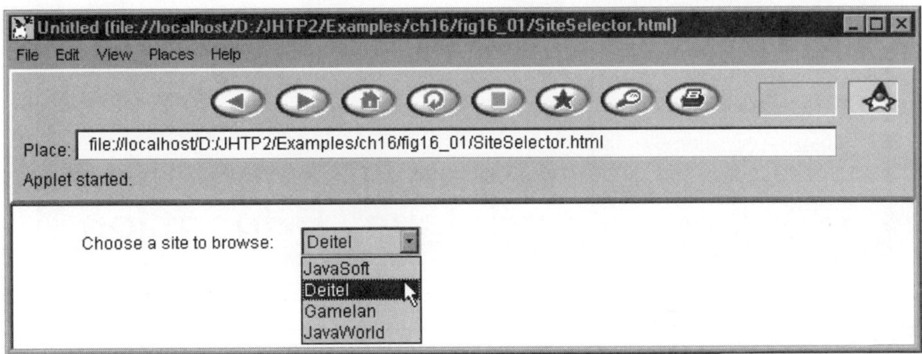

Fig. 16.1 Loading a document from a URL into a browser (part 2 of 3).

Class **SiteSelector** contains a ***Hashtable*** of World Wide Web site names and URLs. A **Hashtable** is used to store *key/value pairs*. A *key* is used to store and retrieve an associated *value* in the **Hashtable**. In this example, the key is the **String** used in the **Choice** button to represent the website and the value is a **URL** object that stores the URL of the website to display in the browser. Class **Hashtable** provides two methods of importance in this example—***put*** and ***get***. Method **put** takes two arguments—a key and its associated value—and places the value in the **Hashtable** at a location determined by the key. Method **get** takes one argument—a key—and retrieves the value (as an **Object** reference) associated with the key. Class **Hashtable** is discussed in detail in Chapter 18.

This applet is designed to take advantage of applet parameters specified in the HTML file that loads the applet into the browser (see Section 14.8 for more information). There are two types of parameters that can be specified—titles and locations. The applet assumes that the name of each title parameter has the format **title#**, where the value of **#** starts at **0** and increments by one for each new title. For example, an applet that specifies three titles would have parameters named **title0**, **title1** and **title2**. Each title should have a corresponding location. The applet assumes that the name of each location parameter has the format **location#**, where the value of **#** starts at **0** and increments by one

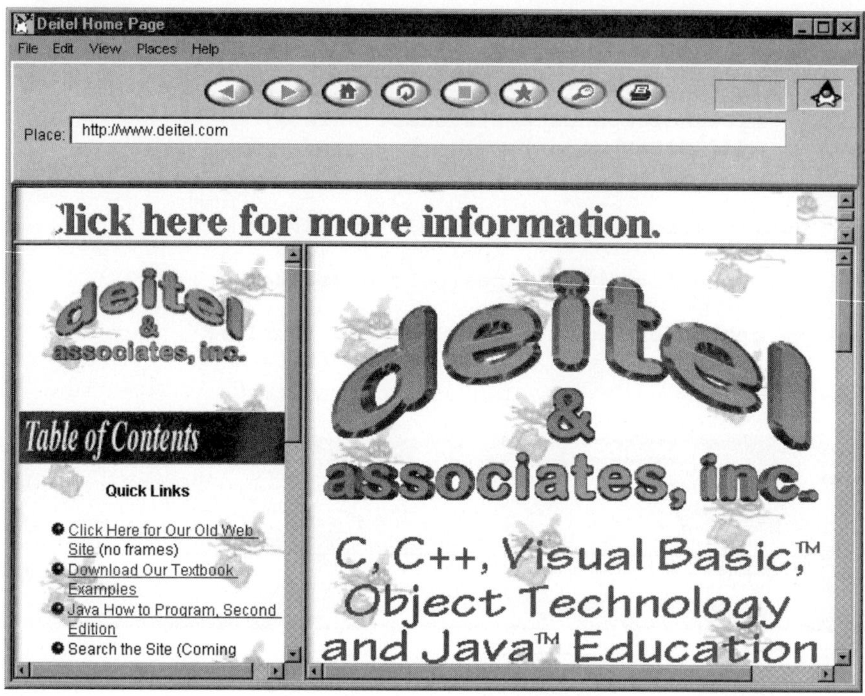

Fig. 16.1 Loading a document from a URL into a browser (part 3 of 3).

for each new location. The HTML file can specify as many titles and locations as needed. The applet is designed to loop until there are no more titles in the HTML file.

In infinite loop at line 24 in **init**, the statement

```
title = getParameter( "title" + counter );
```

uses **Applet** method **getParameter** to obtain a website title. If the title is not **null**, the statement

```
location = getParameter( "location" + counter );
```

uses **Applet** method **getParameter** again to obtain the corresponding location. The location is used as the initial value of a new **URL** object (line 31). The **URL** constructor determines if the **String** passed as an argument represents a valid Uniform Resource Locator. If so, the **URL** object is initialized to contain the Uniform Resource Locator; otherwise a **MalformedURLException** is thrown. Notice that the **URL** constructor must be called in a **try** block. If the **URL** constructor generates a **MalformedURLException**, the call to **printStackTrace** (line 36) causes program to display a stack trace. Then, the program attempts to read the next website title.

Common Programming Error 16.1

*A **MalformedURLException** is thrown when a **String** that is not in proper URL format is passed to a **URL** constructor.*

If the **URL** is constructed properly, line 32

```
sites.put( title, url );
```

places the **title** and **URL** into the **Hashtable** and line 33

```
siteChoice.add( title );
```

adds the **title** to the **Choice** button. When the call to **getParameter** at line 25 returns **null**, the loop terminates. Finally, method **init** adds the **Label** "**Choose a site to browse:**" directly to the applet, registers the applet to handle the **Choice**'s item events and adds the **Choice** to the applet.

When the user selects one of the websites in the **Choice**, method **itemStateChanged** (line 50) is called. Line 52

```
URL url = (URL) sites.get( e.getItem() );
```

passes the **Object** returned by **e.getItem()** (i.e., the **String** the user selected in the **Choice**) to **Hashtable** method **get** to locate the value associated with that key. The **get** method returns an **Object** reference to the value (a **URL** object in this example). The **URL** cast operator converts the reference to a **URL** that can be assigned to reference **url**.

Line 54

```
getAppletContext().showDocument( url );
```

uses the applet's **getAppletContext** method (inherited from class **Applet**) to get a reference to an **AppletContext** object that represents the applet's environment—i.e., the browser in which the applet is executing. This reference is used to invoke the **AppletContext** method **showDocument** that receives a **URL** object as an argument and displays in the browser the World Wide Web resource associated with that **URL**. In this example, all the resources are World Wide Web sites.

For programmers familiar with *HTML frames* (the second screen capture of Fig. 16.1 illustrates a website with frames in the Sun HotJava browser), there is a second version of **AppletContext** method **showDocument** that enables an applet to specify the so-called *target frame* in which World Wide Web resource should be displayed. The other version of **showDocument** takes two arguments—a **URL** object specifying the resource to display and a **String** representing the target frame. There are some special target frames that can be used as the second argument. The target frame **_blank** results in a new web browser window to display the URL. The target frame **_self** specifies that the URL should be displayed in the same frame as the applet (the applet's HTML page is replaced in this case). The target frame **_top** specifies that the browser should remove the current frames in the browser window then display the URL in current window. For more information on HTML and frames, see the World Wide Web site

http://www.w3.org

Note: This applet must be run from a World Wide Web browser such as Netscape's Navigator, Microsoft's Internet Explorer or Sun's HotJava to see the results of displaying another Web page. The Appletviewer is only capable of executing applets, so all other HTML text is ignored. If the sites in the program had Java applets on the Web pages we used, only those applets would appear in the Appletviewer when a website is selected. Each applet would be executed in a separate Appletviewer window.

16.3 Using a URL Stream Connection to Read a File on a Server

The program of Fig. 16.2 uses a **URL** object to open an **InputStream** from a file on a server, read the contents of the file and display the contents in a **TextArea** on the applet.

```
// Fig. 16.2: ReadServerFile.java
// This program uses a URL connection to read a file
// on the server.
import java.awt.*;
import java.awt.event.*;
import java.net.*;
import java.io.*;
import java.applet.Applet;

public class ReadServerFile extends Applet
                 implements ActionListener {
   private TextField enter;
   private TextArea contents;

   public void init()
   {
      setLayout( new BorderLayout() );

      enter = new TextField( "Enter file URL here" );
      enter.addActionListener( this );
      add( enter, BorderLayout.NORTH );

      contents = new TextArea( "", 0, 0,
                     TextArea.SCROLLBARS_VERTICAL_ONLY );
      add( contents, BorderLayout.CENTER );
   }

   public void actionPerformed( ActionEvent e )
   {
      URL url;
      BufferedReader input;
      String line;
      StringBuffer buffer = new StringBuffer();
      String location = e.getActionCommand();
```

Fig. 16.2 Reading a file through a URL connection (part 1 of 2).

```
35
36          try {
37             url = new URL( location );
38             input = new BufferedReader(
39                new InputStreamReader( url.openStream() ) );
40             contents.setText( "Reading file..." );
41
42             while ( ( line = input.readLine() ) != null )
43                buffer.append( line ).append( '\n' );
44
45             contents.setText( buffer.toString() );
46             input.close();
47          }
48          catch ( MalformedURLException mal ) {
49             contents.setText( "Invalid URL format." );
50          }
51          catch ( IOException io ) {
52             contents.setText( io.toString() );
53          }
54       }
55    }
```

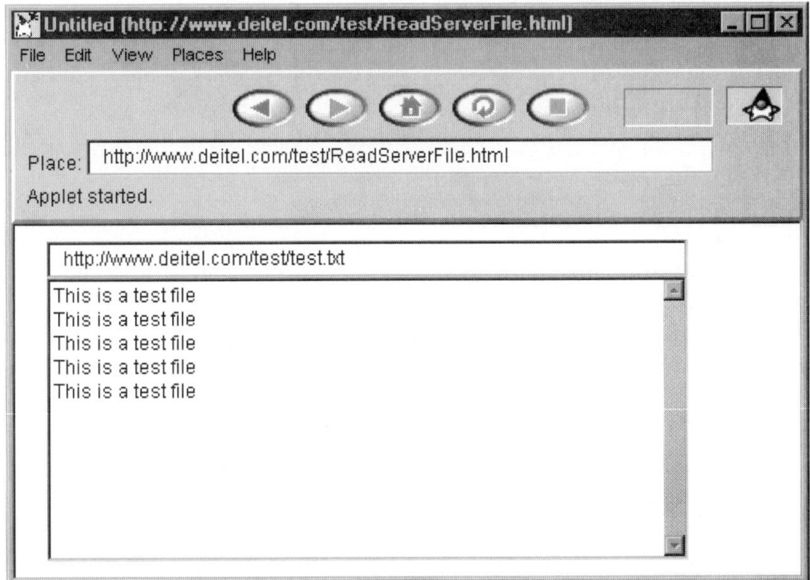

Fig. 16.2 Reading a file through a URL connection (part 2 of 2).

The applet class **ReadServerFile** contains **TextField enter** in which the user enters the URL of the file to open and read and **TextArea contents** to display the contents of the file. When the user presses the *Enter* key in the **TextField**, the applet's **actionPerformed** method is called. Line 34

```
String location = e.getActionCommand();
```

uses **ActionEvent** method **getActionCommand** to get the **String** the user typed in the **TextField**. Line 37

```
url = new URL( location );
```

uses **String** location to initialize a **URL** object. If the **URL** constructor does not throw a **MalformedURLException**, lines 38 and 39

```
input = new BufferedReader(
   new InputStreamReader( url.openStream() ) );
```

attempt to open a connection to the file specified by the **URL**. **URL** method **openStream** opens a network connection to the location represented by **url** using the **http** protocol (HyperText Transfer Protocol). If the network connection is successful an **InputStream** object is returned. Otherwise, **openStream** throws an **IOException**. In this example, we would like to read one line at a time from the file, so the **InputStream** object is passed to the ***InputStreamReader*** constructor to create a stream object that translates the bytes in the file into Unicode characters. The **InputStreamReader** object is passed to the ***BufferedReader*** constructor to create a stream object that buffers the characters read and enables reading of one line at a time. Classes **BufferedReader** and **InputStreamReader** are two of the classes from package **java.io** that have been added to support internationalized string processing. We cover these classes and the other internationalized stream classes in our text *Advanced Java How to Program.*

The **while** structure at line 42 reads one line of text from the file at a time. The expression

```
line = input.readLine()
```

uses **BufferedReader** method **readLine** to read one line of text and assign it to **String line**. Method **readLine** returns **null** on an attempt to read past the end of the file. If the result is not **null**, **line** and a newline character are appended to **StringBuffer buffer**. When the end of the file is reached, the loop terminates and line 45

```
contents.setText( buffer.toString() );
```

converts buffer to a **String** and displays it in **TextArea contents**. When the complete file has been read and displayed, the input stream and network connection are closed with the call **input.close()**.

Note: By default, many World Wide Web browsers only allow an applet to open a network connection to the server from which the applet was downloaded. Java now provides additional security capabilities that can allow an applet to connect elsewhere. We discuss the features of the Java Security API in our text *Advanced Java How to Program.*

16.4 Establishing a Simple Server (Using Stream Sockets)

Establishing a simple server in Java requires five steps. Step 1 is to create a ***ServerSocket*** object. A call to the ***ServerSocket*** constructor such as

```
ServerSocket s = new ServerSocket( port, queueLength );
```

registers an available **port** *number* and specifies a maximum number of clients that can request connections to the server (i.e., the **queueLength**). If the queue is full, client connections are automatically refused. The preceding statement establishes the port where the server waits for connections from clients. Each client will ask to connect to the server on this *port*.

Each client connection is managed with a ***Socket*** object. In Step 2 once the **ServerSocket** is established, the server listens indefinitely (or *blocks*) for an attempt by a client to connect. This is accomplished with a call to the **ServerSocket accept** method as in

```
Socket connection = s.accept();
```

that returns a **Socket** object when a connection is established.

Step 3 is to get the **OutputStream** and **InputStream** objects that enable the server to communicate with the client. The server sends information to the client via an **OutputStream** object. The server receives information from the client via an **InputStream** object. To obtain the streams, the server invokes method **getOutputStream** on the **Socket** to get a reference to the **OutputStream** associated with the **Socket** and invokes method **getInputStream** on the **Socket** to get a reference to the **InputStream** associated with the **Socket**.

The **OutputStream** and **InputStream** objects can be used to send or receive individual bytes or sets of bytes with the **OutputStream** method **write** and the **InputStream** method **read**, respectively. Often it is useful to send or receive values of data types like **int**, **double** and **String** rather than sending bytes. In this case, we can use the techniques of Chapter 15, "Files and Streams" to *chain* other stream types (such as **DataOutputStream** and **DataInputStream**) to the **OutputStream** and **InputStream** associated with the **Socket**. For example,

```
DataInputStream input =
   new DataInputStream( connection.getInputStream() );

DataOutputStream output =
   new DataOutputStream( connection.getOutputStream() );
```

The beauty of establishing these relationships is that whatever the server writes to the **DataOutputStream** is sent via the **OutputStream** and is available at the client's **InputStream** and whatever the client writes to its **OutputStream** (possibly with a corresponding **DataOutputStream**) is available via the server's **InputStream**.

Step 4 is the processing phase in which the server and the client communicate via the **InputStream** and **OutputStream** objects. In Step 5 when the transmission is complete, the server closes the connection by invoking the **close** method on the **Socket**.

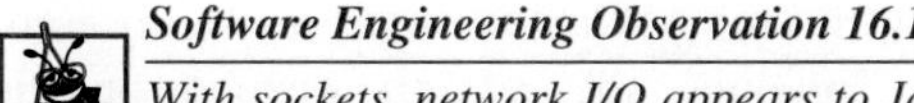

Software Engineering Observation 16.1

With sockets, network I/O appears to Java programs to be virtually identical to sequential file I/O. Sockets hide much of the complexity of network programming from the programmer.

Software Engineering Observation 16.2

With Java's multithreading, we can easily create multithreaded servers *that can manage many simultaneous connections with many clients; this multithreaded-server architecture is precisely what is used in popular UNIX, Windows NT and OS/2 network servers.*

Software Engineering Observation 16.3

*A multithreaded server can be implemented to take the **`Socket`** returned by each call to **`accept`** and create a new thread that would manage network I/O across that **`Socket`**, or a multithreaded server can be implemented to maintain a pool of threads ready to manage network I/O across the new **`Socket`**s as they are created.*

Performance Tip 16.2

*In high-performance systems in which memory is abundant, a multithreaded server can be implemented to create a pool of threads that can be assigned quickly to handle network I/O across each new **`Socket`** as it is created. Thus, when a connection is received, the server need not incur the overhead of thread creation.*

16.5 Establishing a Simple Client (Using Stream Sockets)

Establishing a simple client in Java requires four steps. In Step 1, we create a **`Socket`** to connect to the server. The connection to the server is established using a call to the Socket constructor with two arguments—the server's Internet address and the port number—as in

```
Socket connection = new Socket( serverAddress, port );
```

If the connection attempt is successful, this statement returns a **`Socket`**. A connection attempt that fails throws an **`IOException`**, so many programs simply catch **`IOException`**.

Common Programming Error 16.2

*An **`UnknownHostException`** is thrown when a server address indicated by a client can not be resolved. A **`ConnectException`** is thrown when an error occurs while attempting to connect to a server.*

In Step 2, **`Socket`** methods **`getInputStream`** and **`getOutputStream`** are used to get references to the **`Socket`**'s associated **`InputStream`** and **`OutputStream`**, respectively. **`InputStream`** method **`read`** can be used to input individual bytes or sets of bytes from the server. **`OutputStream`** method **`write`** can be used to output individual bytes or sets of bytes to the server. As we mentioned in the previous section, often it is useful to send or receive values of data types like **`int`**, **`double`** and **`String`** rather than sending bytes. If the server is sending information in the form of actual data types, the client should receive the information in the same format. Thus, if the server sends values with a **`DataOutputStream`**, the client should read those values with a **`DataInputStream`**.

Step 3 is the processing phase in which the client and the server communicate via the **`InputStream`** and **`OutputStream`** objects. In Step 4 when the transmission is complete, the client closes the connection by invoking the **`close`** method on the **`Socket`**.When processing information sent by a server, the client must determine when the server is done sending information so the client can call **`close`** to close the **`Socket`** connection. For example, the **InputStream** method **read** returns –1 when end-of-stream (also called EOF—end-of-file) is detected. If a **DataInputStream** is used to read information from the server, an **EOFException** is generated when the client attempts to read a value from a stream on which end-of-stream is detected.

When the client closes the **Socket**, an **IOException** may be thrown. The **getInputStream** and **getOutputStream** methods may also throw **IOExceptions**.

16.6 Client/Server Interaction with Stream Socket Connections

The applications of Fig. 16.3 and Fig. 16.4 use *stream sockets* to demonstrate a *client/server application*. The server waits for a client connection attempt. When a client application connects to the server, the server application sends data to the client that the client displays, the client application sends data to the server that the server displays, then the connection between the client and the server is closed. Then, the server waits for the next client application to connect. The definition of class **Server** is in Fig. 16.3. The definition of class **Client** is in Fig. 16.4.

```
// Fig. 16.3: Server.java
// Set up a Server that will receive a connection
// from a client, send a string to the client,
// and close the connection.
import java.io.*;
import java.net.*;
import java.awt.*;
import com.deitel.jhtp2.ch11.CloseWindowAndExit;

public class Server extends Frame {
   private TextArea display;

   public Server()
   {
      super( "Server" );
      display = new TextArea( "", 0, 0,
                    TextArea.SCROLLBARS_VERTICAL_ONLY );
      add( display, BorderLayout.CENTER );
      setSize( 300, 150 );
      setVisible( true );
   }

   public void runServer()
   {
      ServerSocket server;
      Socket connection;
      DataOutputStream output;
      DataInputStream input;
      int counter = 1;
```

Fig. 16.3 Demonstrating the server portion of a stream socket connection between a client and a server (part 1 of 3).

```

      try {
         // Step 1: Create a ServerSocket.
         server = new ServerSocket( 5000, 100 );

         while ( true ) {
            // Step 2: Wait for a connection.
            connection = server.accept();

            display.append( "Connection " + counter +
               " received from: " +
               connection.getInetAddress().getHostName() );

            // Step 3: Get input and output streams.]
            input = new DataInputStream(
                        connection.getInputStream() );
            output = new DataOutputStream(
                         connection.getOutputStream() );
            display.append( "\nGot I/O streams\n" );

            // Step 4: Process connection.
            display.append(
               "Sending message \"Connection successful\"\n" );
            output.writeUTF( "Connection successful" );
            display.append( "Client message: " +
                               input.readUTF() );

            // Step 5: Close connection.
            display.append( "\nTransmission complete. " +
                            "Closing socket.\n\n" );
            connection.close();
            ++counter;
         }
      }
      catch ( IOException e ) {
         e.printStackTrace();
      }
   }

   public static void main( String args[] )
   {
      Server s = new Server();

      s.addWindowListener( new CloseWindowAndExit() );
      s.runServer();
   }
}
```

Fig. 16.3 Demonstrating the server portion of a stream socket connection between a client and a server (part 2 of 3).

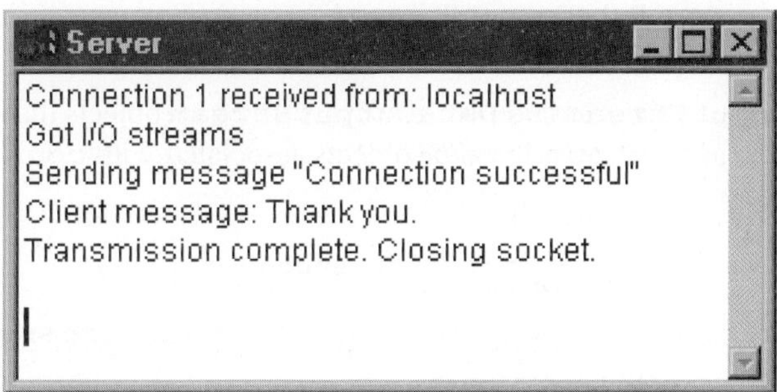

Fig. 16.3 Demonstrating the server portion of a stream socket connection between a client and a server (part 3 of 3).

Class **Server** extends class **Frame**, so a constructor is provided to set up the graphical components of the window that is displayed. The **Server** object displays its output in a **TextArea**. Also, an instance of class **CloseWindowAndExit** (see Fig. 11.10) is registered to handle the **Server**'s window events (line 73) to enable the user to close the window and terminate the application.

Method **runServer** (line 23) of class **Server** is called from **main** to do the work of setting up the server to receive a connection and processing the connection when it is received. The method declares a **ServerSocket** called **server** to wait for connections, a **Socket** called **connection** to process the connection from a client, a **DataOutputStream** called **output** to send data to the client via the **Socket** called **connection**, a **DataInputStream** called **input** to receive data from the client via the **Socket** called **connection** and an integer **counter** to keep track of the total number of connections processed. In the **try** block, the **ServerSocket** is set up (line 33) to listen for a connection from a client at port **5000**. Many operating systems reserve port numbers below 1024 for system services (such as email and World Wide Web servers). Generally, these ports should not be specified as connection ports in user programs. In fact, some operating systems require special access privileges to use port numbers below 1024. The second argument to the **ServerSocket** constructor is the number of connections that can wait in a queue to connect to the server (**100** in this example). If the queue is full when a connection is attempted, the connection is refused automatically.

In the infinite **while** loop (line 35), the statement

```
connection = server.accept();
```

at line 37 uses **ServerSocket** method **accept** to listen for a connection from a client applet or application. This method blocks until a connection is received (i.e., the thread in which **accept** is called stops executing until a connection is received). Once a connection is received, **connection** is assigned a **Socket** object that will be used to manage the connection. Lines 44–47

```
input = new DataInputStream(
            connection.getInputStream() );
output = new DataOutputStream(
            connection.getOutputStream() );
```

create the **DataInputStream** and **DataOutputStream** objects that are connected to the **InputStream** and **OutputStream** objects associated with **connection**.

Line 53

```
output.writeUTF( "Connection successful" );
```

uses **output.writeUTF** to send the string "**Connection successful**" to the client. Lines 54 and 55

```
display.append( "Client message: " +
                input.readUTF() );
```

use **input.readUTF** to read a string from the client and display it in the **TextArea**.

When the transmission is complete, the **Socket** is closed with line 60

```
connection.close();
```

Next, the server awaits the next connection attempt from a client by continuing with line 33 at the beginning of the **while** loop.

Notice that the **main** method (line 69) creates an object of the **Server** class and invokes the **runServer** method on it. Also, note that the **Server** receives a connection, processes the connection, closes the connection and waits for the next connection. A more likely scenario would be a **Server** that receives a connection, sets up that connection to be processed as a separate thread of execution, then waits for new connections. The separate threads that process existing connections can continue to execute while the **Server** concentrates on new connection requests.

Like class **Server**, class **Client** extends class **Frame**, so a constructor is provided to set up the window that will be displayed. Class **Client** displays its output in a **TextArea**. Also, an instance of class **CloseWindowAndExit** (see Fig. 11.10) is registered to handle the **Client**'s window events (line 73) to enable the user to close the window and terminate the application.

```
1  // Fig. 16.4: Client.java
2  // Set up a Client that will read information sent
3  // from a Server and display the information.
4  import java.io.*;
5  import java.net.*;
6  import java.awt.*;
7  import com.deitel.jhtp2.ch11.CloseWindowAndExit;
8
```

Fig. 16.4 Demonstrating the client portion of a stream socket connection between a client and a server (part 1 of 3).

```
public class Client extends Frame {
   private TextArea display;

   public Client()
   {
      super( "Client" );
      display = new TextArea( "", 0, 0,
                   TextArea.SCROLLBARS_VERTICAL_ONLY );
      add( display, BorderLayout.CENTER );
      setSize( 300, 150 );
      setVisible( true );
   }

   public void runClient()
   {
      Socket client;
      DataInputStream input;
      DataOutputStream output;

      try {
         // Step 1: Create a Socket to make connection.
         client = new Socket( InetAddress.getLocalHost(),
                              5000 );

         display.append( "Connected to: " +
            client.getInetAddress().getHostName() );

         // Step 2: Get the input and output streams.
         input = new DataInputStream(
                     client.getInputStream() );
         output = new DataOutputStream(
                      client.getOutputStream() );
         display.append( "\nGot I/O Streams\n" );

         // Step 3: Process connection.
         display.append( "Server message: " +
            input.readUTF() );
         display.append(
            "\nSending message \"Thank you.\"\n" );
         output.writeUTF( "Thank you." );

         // Step 4: Close connection.
         display.append( "Transmission complete. " +
            "Closing connection.\n" );
         client.close();
      }
      catch ( IOException e ) {
         e.printStackTrace();
      }
   }
```

Fig. 16.4 Demonstrating the client portion of a stream socket connection between a client and a server (part 2 of 3).

```
59
60     public static void main( String args[] )
61     {
62        Client c = new Client();
63
64        c.addWindowListener( new CloseWindowAndExit() );
65        c.runClient();
66     }
67  }
```

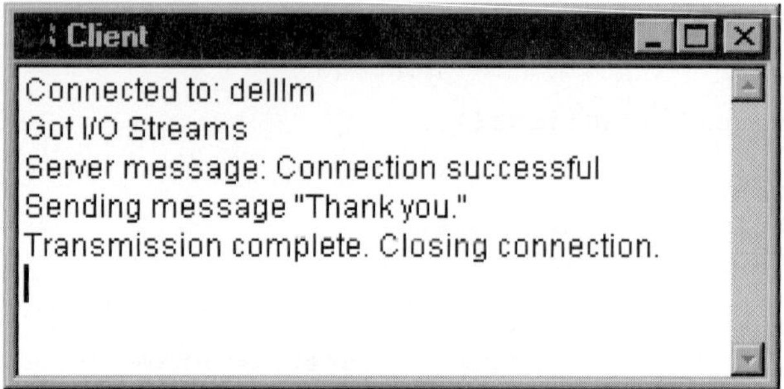

Fig. 16.4 Demonstrating the client portion of a stream socket connection between a client and a server (part 3 of 3).

Client method **runClient** performs the work necessary to connect to the **Server**, to receive data from the **Server** and to send data to the **Server**. The method declares a **Socket** called **client** to establish a connection, a **DataOutputStream** called **output** to send data to the server via the **Socket** called **client** and a **DataInputStream** called **input** to receive data from the server via the **Socket** called **client**. In the **try** block, lines 30 and 31

```
client = new Socket( InetAddress.getLocalHost(),
                     5000 );
```

instantiates **Socket client** with two arguments to the constructor—**InetAddress.getLocalHost()** and **5000**. The first argument returns an **InetAddress** object containing the local host name of the computer on which this program is executing. *We have chosen in this example to demonstrate the client/server relationship by connecting between programs executing on the same computer. Normally, this first argument would be the Internet address of another computer. The Internet address of another computer can be obtained with method* ***InetAddress.getByName***. The second argument is the port number on the server. This number must exactly match the port number at which the server is waiting for connections (sometimes called the *handshake point*). Once the connection is made, a message is displayed in the **TextArea** indicating the name of the server computer to which the client connected.

Lines 37–40

```
input = new DataInputStream(
            client.getInputStream() );
output = new DataOutputStream(
            client.getOutputStream() );
```

create the **DataInputStream** and **DataOutputStream** objects that are connected to the **InputStream** and **OutputStream** objects associated with **client**.

Lines 44 and 45

```
display.append( "Server message: " +
   input.readUTF() );
```

uses the **DataInputStream** method **readUTF** to read a string from the server. Line 48

```
output.writeUTF( "Thank you." );
```

uses the **DataOutputStream** method **writeUTF** to send the string "**Thank you.**" to the server. When the **Socket** is no longer needed to get information, we close it at line 53

```
client.close();
```

16.7 Connectionless Client/Server Interaction with Datagrams

We have been discussing *connection-oriented, streams-based transmission*. Now we consider *connectionless transmission with datagrams*.

Connection-oriented transmission is like the telephone system in which you dial and are given a *connection* to the telephone you wish to communicate with; the connection is maintained for the duration of your phone call, even when you are not talking.

Connectionless transmission with *datagrams* is more like the way mail is carried via the postal service. If a large message will not fit in one envelope, you break it into separate message pieces that you place in separate, sequentially numbered envelopes. Each of the letters is then mailed at once. The letters may arrive in order, out of order or not at all (although the last case is rare, it does happen). The person at the receiving end reassembles the message pieces into sequential order before attempting to make sense of the message. If your message is small enough to fit in one envelope, you do not have to worry about the "out-of-sequence" problem, but it is still possible that your message may not arrive. One difference between datagrams and postal mail is that duplicates of datagrams may arrive on the receiving computer.

The programs of Fig. 16.5 and 16.6 use datagrams to send packets of information between a client application and a server application. In this program, the user types a message into a **TextField** on the client application and presses *Enter*. The message is converted into a **byte** array and placed in a datagram packet that is sent to the server. The server receives the packet and displays the information in the packet, then *echoes* the packet back to the client. When the client receives the packet, the client displays the information in the packet. In this example, the **Client** and **Server** classes are implemented similarly.

```java
// Fig. 16.5: Server.java
// Set up a Server that will receive packets from a
// client and send packets to a client.
import java.io.*;
import java.net.*;
import java.awt.*;
import com.deitel.jhtp2.ch11.CloseWindowAndExit;

public class Server extends Frame {
   private TextArea display;

   private DatagramPacket sendPacket, receivePacket;
   private DatagramSocket socket;

   public Server()
   {
      super( "Server" );
      display = new TextArea();
      add( display, BorderLayout.CENTER );
      setSize( 400, 300 );
      setVisible( true );

      try {
         socket = new DatagramSocket( 5000 );
      }
      catch( SocketException se ) {
         se.printStackTrace();
         System.exit( 1 );
      }
   }

   public void waitForPackets()
   {
      while ( true ) {
         try {
            // set up packet
            byte data[] = new byte[ 100 ];
            receivePacket =
               new DatagramPacket( data, data.length );

            // wait for packet
            socket.receive( receivePacket );

            // process packet
            display.append( "\nPacket received:" +
               "\nFrom host: " + receivePacket.getAddress() +
               "\nHost port: " + receivePacket.getPort() +
               "\nLength: " + receivePacket.getLength() +
               "\nContaining:\n\t" +
               new String( receivePacket.getData() ) );
```

Fig. 16.5 Demonstrating the server side of connectionless client/server computing with datagrams (part 1 of 2).

```

            // echo information from packet back to client
            display.append( "\n\nEcho data to client...");
            sendPacket = new DatagramPacket(
                                receivePacket.getData(),
                                receivePacket.getLength(),
                                receivePacket.getAddress(),
                                receivePacket.getPort() );
            socket.send( sendPacket );
            display.append( "Packet sent\n" );
         }
         catch( IOException io ) {
            display.append( io.toString() + "\n" );
            io.printStackTrace();
         }
      }
   }

   public static void main( String args[] )
   {
      Server s = new Server();

      s.addWindowListener( new CloseWindowAndExit() );
      s.waitForPackets();
   }
}
```

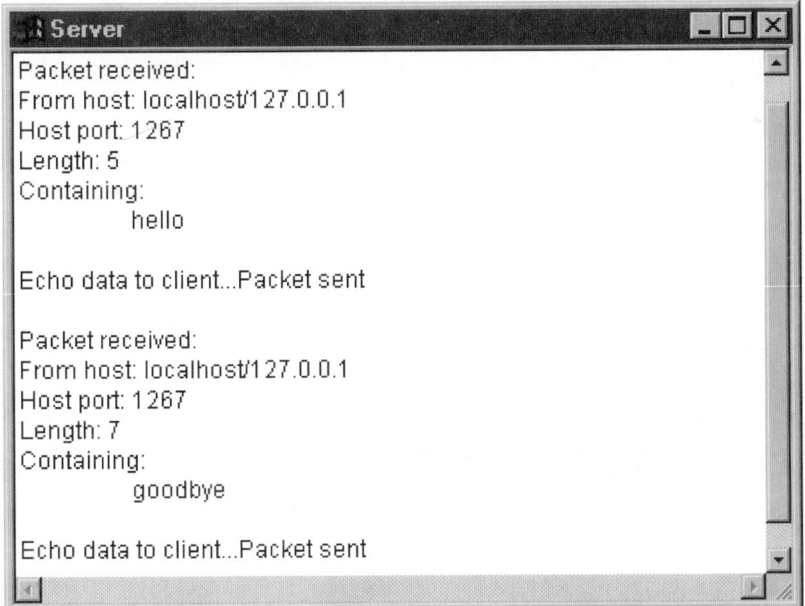

Fig. 16.5 Demonstrating the server side of connectionless client/server computing with datagrams (part 2 of 2).

Class **Server** (Fig. 16.5) defines two **DatagramPacket**s that are used to create the packets to send and receive information, and one **DatagramSocket** that is used to send and receive these packets. The constructor for class **Server** first creates the graphical user interface where the packets of information will be displayed. Next, the **DatagramSocket** is created in the **try** block. Line 24

```
socket = new DatagramSocket( 5000 );
```

uses the **DatagramSocket** constructor that takes an integer port number argument to set up a port for receiving packets from the network. We have specified port number **5000**. **Client**s sending packets to this **Server** specify port **5000** in the packets they send. If either of the constructor calls fails to set up a **DatagramSocket** properly, a **SocketException** is thrown.

Common Programming Error 16.3

Specifying a port that is already in use or specifying an invalid port number when creating a **DatagramSocket** *results in a* **BindException**.

Server method **waitForPackets** uses an infinite loop to wait for packets to arrive at the **Server**. First, it creates a **DatagramPacket** (lines 37 through 39) in which a received packet of information can be stored. The **DatagramPacket** constructor for this purpose receives two arguments—a **byte** array in which the data is stored and the length of the **byte** array. Next, line 42

```
socket.receive( receivePacket );
```

waits for a packet to arrive at the **Server**. The **receive** method blocks until a packet arrives then stores the packet in its **DatagramPacket** argument (**receivePacket**).

Once a packet is received, lines 45 through 50 output the packet's contents. **DatagramPacket** method **getAddress** (line 46) returns an **InetAddress** object containing the name of the host from which the packet was sent. Method **getPort** (line 47) returns an integer specifying the port number through which the host sent the packet. Method **getLength** (line 48) returns an integer representing the number of bytes of data that were sent. Method **getData** (line 50) returns a **byte** array containing the data that was sent. The **byte** array is used to initialize a **String** in our program so the data can be output to the **TextArea**.

Next, **sendPacket** (the one to be sent back to the client) is instantiated and four arguments are passed to the **DatagramPacket** constructor. The first argument specifies the **byte** array to be sent. The second argument specifies the number of bytes to be sent. The third argument specifies the client address to which the packet will be sent. The fourth argument specifies the port where the client is waiting to receive packets. Line 59

```
socket.send( sendPacket );
```

sends the packet over the network. If an error occurs either receiving or sending a packet, an **IOException** is thrown.

Class **Client** (Fig. 16.6) works similarly to class **Server** except that the **Client** sends packets only when it is told to do so by the user typing a message in a **TextField** and pressing the *Enter* key in the **TextField**. When this occurs, method **actionPerformed** (line 64) is invoked, the **String** the user entered in the **TextField** is converted into a **byte** array and the **byte** array is used to create a **DatagramPacket**. The **DatagramPacket** is initialized with the **byte** array, the length of the **String** that was entered by the user, the Internet address to which the packet is to be sent (**InetAddress.getLocalHost()** in this example) and the port number at which the **Server** is waiting for packets. Then the packet is sent. If an error occurs while sending a packet, an **IOException** is thrown. Note that the client in this example must know that the server is receiving packets at port 5000 otherwise the packets will not be received by the server.

```
1  // Fig. 16.6: Client.java
2  // Set up a Client that will send packets to a
3  // server and receive packets from a server.
4  import java.io.*;
5  import java.net.*;
6  import java.awt.*;
7  import java.awt.event.*;
8  import com.deitel.jhtp2.ch11.CloseWindowAndExit;
9
10 public class Client extends Frame implements ActionListener {
11    private TextField enter;
12    private TextArea display;
13
14    private DatagramPacket sendPacket, receivePacket;
15    private DatagramSocket socket;
16
17    public Client()
18    {
19       super( "Client" );
20       enter = new TextField( "Type message here" );
21       enter.addActionListener( this );
22       add( enter, BorderLayout.NORTH );
23       display = new TextArea();
24       add( display, BorderLayout.CENTER );
25       setSize( 400, 300 );
26       setVisible( true );
27
28       try {
29          socket = new DatagramSocket();
30       }
31       catch( SocketException se ) {
32          se.printStackTrace();
33          System.exit( 1 );
34       }
35    }
36
```

Fig. 16.6 Demonstrating the client side of connectionless client/server computing with datagrams (part 1 of 3).

```
    public void waitForPackets()
    {
       while ( true ) {
          try {
             // set up packet
             byte data[] = new byte[ 100 ];
             receivePacket =
                new DatagramPacket( data, data.length );

             // wait for packet
             socket.receive( receivePacket );

             // process packet
             display.append( "\nPacket received:" +
                "\nFrom host: " + receivePacket.getAddress() +
                "\nHost port: " + receivePacket.getPort() +
                "\nLength: " + receivePacket.getLength() +
                "\nContaining:\n\t" +
                new String( receivePacket.getData() ) );
          }
          catch( IOException exception ) {
             display.append( exception.toString() + "\n" );
             exception.printStackTrace();
          }
       }
    }

    public void actionPerformed( ActionEvent e )
    {
       try {
          display.append( "\nSending packet containing: " +
                          e.getActionCommand() + "\n" );

          String s = e.getActionCommand();
          byte data[] = s.getBytes();

          sendPacket = new DatagramPacket( data, data.length,
             InetAddress.getLocalHost(), 5000 );
          socket.send( sendPacket );
          display.append( "Packet sent\n" );
       }
       catch ( IOException exception ) {
          display.append( exception.toString() + "\n" );
          exception.printStackTrace();
       }
    }

    public static void main( String args[] )
    {
       Client c = new Client();
```

Fig. 16.6 Demonstrating the client side of connectionless client/server computing with datagrams (part 2 of 3).

```
87
88         c.addWindowListener( new CloseWindowAndExit() );
89         c.waitForPackets();
90      }
91   }
```

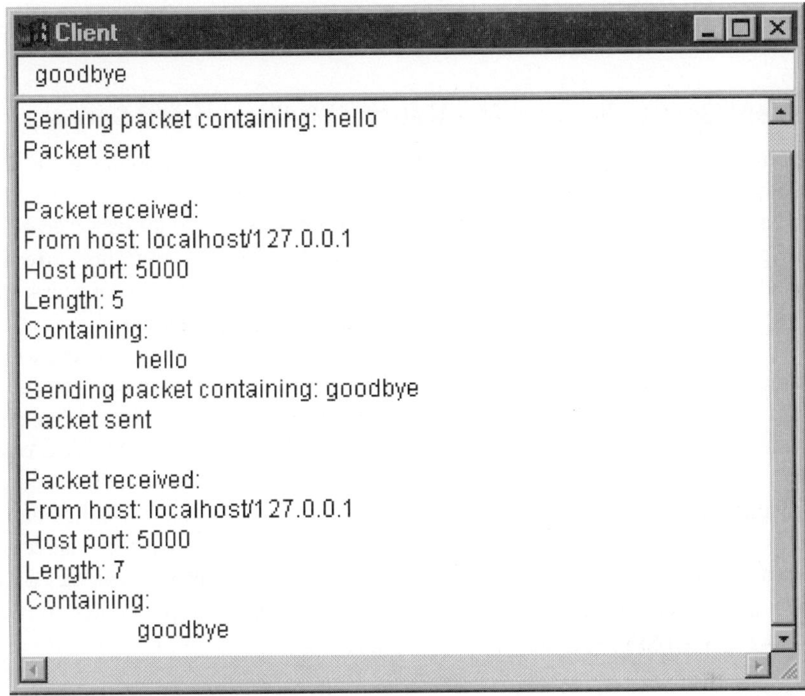

Fig. 16.6 Demonstrating the client side of connectionless client/server computing with datagrams (part 3 of 3).

Notice that the **DatagramSocket** constructor call (line 29) in this application does not specify any arguments. This allows the computer to select the next available port number for the **DatagramSocket**. The client does not need a specific port number because the server receives the client's port number as part of the **DatagramPacket** sent by the client. Thus, the server can send packets back to the same computer and port number from which the server receives a packet of information.

Client method **waitForPackets** (line 37) uses an infinite loop to wait for packets using the statement

```
socket.receive( receivePacket );
```

which blocks until a packet is received. Note that this does not prevent the user from sending a packet because the GUI operates in a different thread. It only prevents the **while** loop from continuing until a packet arrives at the **Client**.

When a packet arrives, it is stored in **receivePacket** and its contents are displayed in the **TextArea**. If an error occurs while receiving a packet an **IOException** is thrown. The user can type information into the **Client** window's **TextField** and press the *Enter* key at any time; even while a packet is being received. The **actionPerformed** method processes the **TextField** event and sends the packet containing the data in the **TextField**.

16.8 Client/Server Tic-Tac-Toe Using a Multithreaded Server

In this section, we present our capstone networking exercise—the popular game Tic-Tac-Toe implemented using client/server techniques with stream sockets. The program consists of a **TicTacToeServer** application (Fig. 16.7) that allows two **TicTacToeClient** applets (Fig. 16.8) to connect to the server and play Tic-Tac-Toe (outputs shown in Fig. 16.9). As each client connection is received by the server, an instance of class **Player** (line 117 of Fig. 16.7) is created to process the client in a separate thread of execution. This enables the clients to play the game independently. The first client to connect is automatically assigned Xs (X makes the first move) and the second client to connect is automatically assigned Os. The server maintains the information about the board so it can determine if a requested move by one of the players is a valid or invalid move. Each **TicTacToeClient** applet maintains its own version of the Tic-Tac-Toe board on which the state of the game is displayed. The clients can only place a mark in an empty square on the board. Class **Square** is used to implement each of the nine squares on the board. Class **TicTacToeServer** and class **Player** are implemented in file **TicTacToeServer.java** (Fig. 16.7). Class **TicTacToeClient** and class **Square** are implemented in file **TicTacToeClient.java** (Fig. 16.8).

```
1  // Fig. 16.7: TicTacToeServer.java
2  // This class maintains a game of Tic-Tac-Toe for two
3  // client applets.
4  import java.awt.*;
5  import java.awt.event.*;
6  import java.net.*;
7  import java.io.*;
8  import com.deitel.jhtp2.ch11.CloseWindowAndExit;
9
10 public class TicTacToeServer extends Frame {
11    private byte board[];
12    private boolean xMove;
13    private TextArea output;
14    private Player players[];
15    private ServerSocket server;
16    private int currentPlayer;
17
```

Fig. 16.7 Server side of client/server Tic-Tac-Toe program (part 1 of 5).

```
   public TicTacToeServer()
   {
      super( "Tic-Tac-Toe Server" );
      board = new byte[ 9 ];
      xMove = true;
      players = new Player[ 2 ];
      currentPlayer = 0;

      // set up ServerSocket
      try {
         server = new ServerSocket( 5000, 2 );
      }
      catch( IOException e ) {
         e.printStackTrace();
         System.exit( 1 );
      }

      output = new TextArea();
      add( output, BorderLayout.CENTER );
      setSize( 300, 300 );
      setVisible( true );
   }

   // wait for two connections so game can be played
   public void execute()
   {
      for ( int i = 0; i < players.length; i++ ) {
         try {
            players[ i ] =
               new Player( server.accept(), this, i );
            players[ i ].start();
         }
         catch( IOException e ) {
            e.printStackTrace();
            System.exit( 1 );
         }
      }

      // Player X is suspended until Player O connects.
      // Resume player X now.
      players[ 0 ].resume();
   }

   public void display( String s )
   {
      output.append( s + "\n" );
   }

   // Determine if a move is valid.
   // This method is synchronized because only one move can be
   // made at a time.
```

Fig. 16.7 Server side of client/server Tic-Tac-Toe program (part 2 of 5).

```
    public synchronized boolean validMove( int loc, int player )
    {
       boolean moveDone = false;

       while ( player != currentPlayer ) {
          try {
             wait();
          }
          catch( InterruptedException e ) {
          }
       }

       if ( !isOccupied( loc ) ) {
          board[ loc ] =
             (byte)( currentPlayer == 0 ? 'X' : 'O' );
          currentPlayer = ( currentPlayer + 1 ) % 2;
          players[ currentPlayer ].otherPlayerMoved( loc );
          notify();    // tell waiting player to continue
          return true;
       }
       else
          return false;
    }

    public boolean isOccupied( int loc )
    {
       if ( board[ loc ] == 'X' || board [ loc ] == 'O' )
           return true;
       else
           return false;
    }

    public boolean gameOver()
    {
       // Place code here to test for a winner of the game
       return false;
    }

    public static void main( String args[] )
    {
       TicTacToeServer game = new TicTacToeServer();

       game.addWindowListener( new CloseWindowAndExit() );
       game.execute();
    }
 }

 // Player class to manage each Player as a thread
 class Player extends Thread {
    private Socket connection;
    private DataInputStream input;
```

Fig. 16.7 Server side of client/server Tic-Tac-Toe program (part 3 of 5).

```
   private DataOutputStream output;
   private TicTacToeServer control;
   private int number;
   private char mark;

   public Player( Socket s, TicTacToeServer t, int num )
   {
      mark = ( num == 0 ? 'X' : 'O' );

      connection = s;

      try {
         input = new DataInputStream(
                    connection.getInputStream() );
         output = new DataOutputStream(
                    connection.getOutputStream() );
      }
      catch( IOException e ) {
         e.printStackTrace();
         System.exit( 1 );
      }

      control = t;
      number = num;
   }

   public void otherPlayerMoved( int loc )
   {
      try {
         output.writeUTF( "Opponent moved" );
         output.writeInt( loc );
      }
      catch ( IOException e ) { e.printStackTrace(); }
   }

   public void run()
   {
      boolean done = false;

      try {
         control.display( "Player " +
            ( number == 0 ? 'X' : 'O' ) + " connected" );
         output.writeChar( mark );
         output.writeUTF( "Player " +
            ( number == 0 ? "X connected\n" :
                            "O connected, please wait\n" ) );

         // wait for another player to arrive
         if ( mark == 'X' ) {
            output.writeUTF( "Waiting for another player" );
            suspend();  // suspend until player O connects
```

Fig. 16.7 Server side of client/server Tic-Tac-Toe program (part 4 of 5).

```
                output.writeUTF(
                    "Other player connected. Your move." );
            }

            // Play game
            while ( !done ) {
                int location = input.readInt();

                if ( control.validMove( location, number ) ) {
                    control.display( "loc: " + location );
                    output.writeUTF( "Valid move." );
                }
                else
                    output.writeUTF( "Invalid move, try again" );

                if ( control.gameOver() )
                    done = true;
            }

            connection.close();
        }
        catch( IOException e ) {
            e.printStackTrace();
            System.exit( 1 );
        }
    }
}
```

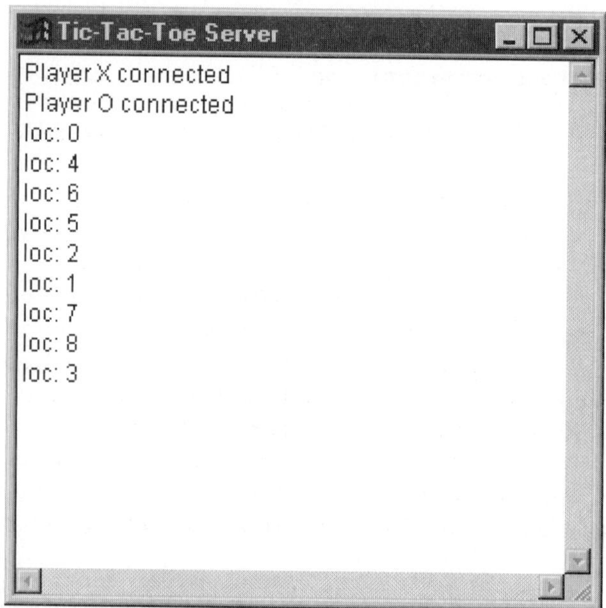

Fig. 16.7 Server side of client/server Tic-Tac-Toe program (part 5 of 5).

We begin with a discussion of the server side of the Tic-Tac-Toe game. When the **TicTacToeServer** application is executed, the **main** method (line 107) creates a **TicTacToeServer** object called **game**. The constructor (line 18) attempts to set up a **ServerSocket**. If successful, the server window is displayed and the **TicTacToeServer** method **execute** is invoked. Method **execute** (line 42) loops twice waiting each time for a connection from a client. When a connection is received, a new **Player** object is created to manage the connection as a separate thread and that object's **start** method is invoked.

When the **Player** is created, its constructor (line 125) takes the **Socket** object representing the connection to the client and gets the associated input and output streams. The **Player**'s **run** method controls the information that is sent to the client and the information that is received from the client. First, it tells the client that the client's connection has been made, then it passes to the client the character that the client will place on the board when a move is made. Next, if the current client is player X, the **run** method (line 155) suspends the thread until a second client connects. At this point the game can be played and the **run** method begins executing its **while** structure (line 176). Each iteration of this **while** structure reads an integer representing the location where the client wants to place a mark and invokes the **TicTacToeServer** method **validMove** to check the move. A message is sent to the client indicating if the move was valid.

Method **validMove** (line 69) is a **synchronized** method that allows only one move to be attempted at a time. This prevents both players from modifying the state information of the game simultaneously. If the **Player** attempting to validate a move is not the current player (i.e., the one allowed to make a move), the **Player** is placed in a *wait* state until it is his or her turn to move. If the position for the move being validated is already occupied on the board, **false** is returned. Otherwise, the server places a mark for the player in its local representation of the board, notifies the other **Player** object that a move has been made (so the client can be sent a message), invokes the **notify** method so the waiting **Player** (if there is one) can validate a move and returns **true** to indicate that the move is valid.

When a **TicTacToeClient** (Fig. 16.8) applet begins execution, it creates a **TextArea** in which messages from the server are displayed and a representation of the board using nine **Square** objects. The applet's **start** method (line 62) opens a connection to the server and gets the associated input and output streams from the **Socket** object. Class **TicTacToeClient** implements the **Runnable** interface so that a separate thread can be used to continually read messages that are sent from the server to the client. After the connection to the server is established, the **Thread** object **outputThread** is created and initialized with the applet, then the thread's **start** method is invoked. The applet's **run** method (line 82) controls the separate thread of execution. The method first reads the mark character (X or O) from the server, then loops continually and reads messages from the server. The messages are passed to the applet's **processMessage** method (line 106) for processing.

If the message received is the string "**Valid move.**", the message "**Valid move, please wait.**" is displayed, the client's mark is set in the current square (the one in which the user clicked) and the square is repainted. If the message received is "**Invalid**

move, try again", the message is displayed so the user can click a different square. If the message received is "**Opponent moved**", an integer is read from the server indicating where the opponent moved and a mark is placed in that square of the board. If any other message is received, the message is simply displayed.

```
// Fig. 16.8: TicTacToeClient.java
// Client for the TicTacToe program
import java.applet.Applet;
import java.awt.*;
import java.awt.event.*;
import java.net.*;
import java.io.*;

// Client class to let a user play Tic-Tac-Toe with
// another user across a network.
public class TicTacToeClient extends Applet
             implements Runnable {
   private TextField id;
   private TextArea display;
   private Panel boardPanel, panel2;
   private Square board[][], currentSquare;
   private Socket connection;
   private DataInputStream input;
   private DataOutputStream output;
   private Thread outputThread;
   private char myMark;

   // Set up user-interface and board
   public void init()
   {
      setLayout( new BorderLayout() );
      display = new TextArea( 4, 30 );
      display.setEditable( false );
      add( display, BorderLayout.SOUTH );

      boardPanel = new Panel();
      boardPanel.setLayout( new GridLayout( 3, 3, 0, 0 ) );
      board = new Square[ 3 ][ 3 ];

      // When creating a Square, the location argument to the
      // constructor is a value from 0 to 8 indicating the
      // position of the Square on the board. Values 0, 1,
      // and 2 are the first row, values 3, 4, and 5 are the
      // second row. Values 6, 7, and 8 are the third row.
      for ( int row = 0; row < board.length; row++ )
         for ( int col = 0; col < board[ row ].length; col++ ) {
            board[ row ][ col ] =
               new Square( ' ', row * 3 + col );
```

Fig. 16.8 Client side of client/server Tic-Tac-Toe program (part 1 of 5).

```
               board[ row ][ col ].addMouseListener(
                  new SquareListener(
                     this, board[ row ][ col ] ) );
               boardPanel.add( board[ row ][ col ] );
            }

         id = new TextField();
         id.setEditable( false );
         add( id, BorderLayout.NORTH );

         panel2 = new Panel();
         panel2.add( boardPanel );
         add( panel2, BorderLayout.CENTER );
      }

      // Make connection to server and get associated streams.
      // Start separate thread to allow this applet to
      // continually update its output in text area display.
      public void start()
      {
         try {
            connection =
               new Socket( InetAddress.getLocalHost(), 5000 );
            input = new DataInputStream(
               connection.getInputStream() );
            output = new DataOutputStream(
               connection.getOutputStream() );
         }
         catch ( IOException e ) {
            e.printStackTrace();
         }

         outputThread = new Thread( this );
         outputThread.start();
      }

      // Control thread that allows continuous update of the
      // text area display.
      public void run()
      {
         // First get player's mark (X or O)
         try {
            myMark = input.readChar();
            id.setText( "You are player \"" + myMark + "\"" );
         }
         catch ( IOException e ) {
            e.printStackTrace();
         }

```

Fig. 16.8 Client side of client/server Tic-Tac-Toe program (part 2 of 5).

```
      // Receive messages sent to client
      while ( true ) {
         try {
            String s = input.readUTF();
            processMessage( s );
         }
         catch ( IOException e ) {
            e.printStackTrace();
         }
      }
   }

   // Process messages sent to client
   public void processMessage( String s )
   {
      if ( s.equals( "Valid move." ) ) {
         display.append( "Valid move, please wait.\n" );
         currentSquare.setMark( myMark );
         currentSquare.repaint();
      }
      else if ( s.equals( "Invalid move, try again" ) ) {
         display.append( s + "\n" );
      }
      else if ( s.equals( "Opponent moved" ) ) {
         try {
            int loc = input.readInt();

            done:
            for ( int row = 0; row < board.length; row++ )
               for ( int col = 0;
                     col < board[ row ].length; col++ )
                  if ( row * 3 + col == loc ) {
                     board[ row ][ col ].setMark(
                        ( myMark == 'X' ? 'O' : 'X' ) );
                     board[ row ][ col ].repaint();
                     break done;
                  }

            display.append(
               "Opponent moved. Your turn.\n" );
         }
         catch ( IOException e ) {
            e.printStackTrace();
         }
      }
      else {
         display.append( s + "\n" );
      }
   }

```

Fig. 16.8 Client side of client/server Tic-Tac-Toe program (part 3 of 5).

```
   public void sendClickedSquare( int loc )
   {
      try {
         output.writeInt( loc );
      }
      catch ( IOException ie ) {
         ie.printStackTrace();
      }
   }

   public void setCurrentSquare( Square s )
   {
      currentSquare = s;
   }
}

// Maintains one square on the board
class Square extends Canvas {
   private char mark;
   private int location;

   public Square( char m, int loc)
   {
      mark = m;
      location = loc;
      setSize ( 30, 30 );
   }

   public void setMark( char c ) { mark = c; }

   public int getSquareLocation() { return location; }

   public void paint( Graphics g )
   {
      g.drawRect( 0, 0, 29, 29 );
      g.drawString( String.valueOf( mark ), 11, 20 );
   }
}

class SquareListener extends MouseAdapter {
   private TicTacToeClient applet;
   private Square square;

   public SquareListener( TicTacToeClient t, Square s )
   {
      applet = t;
      square = s;
   }

   public void mouseReleased( MouseEvent e )
   {
```

Fig. 16.8 Client side of client/server Tic-Tac-Toe program (part 4 of 5).

```
        applet.setCurrentSquare( square );
        applet.sendClickedSquare( square.getSquareLocation() );
    }
}
```

Fig. 16.8 Client side of client/server Tic-Tac-Toe program (part 5 of 5).

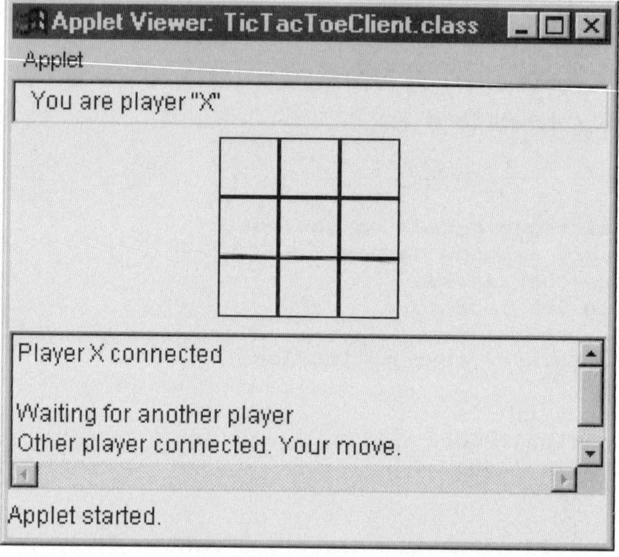

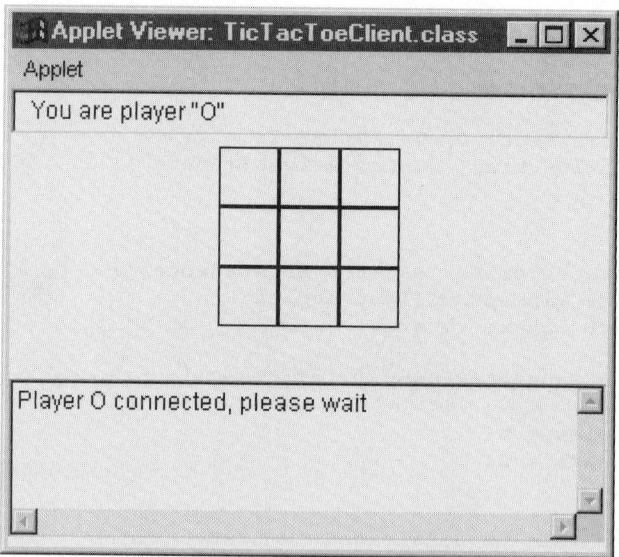

Fig. 16.9 Sample outputs from the client/server Tic-Tac-Toe program (part 1 of 4).

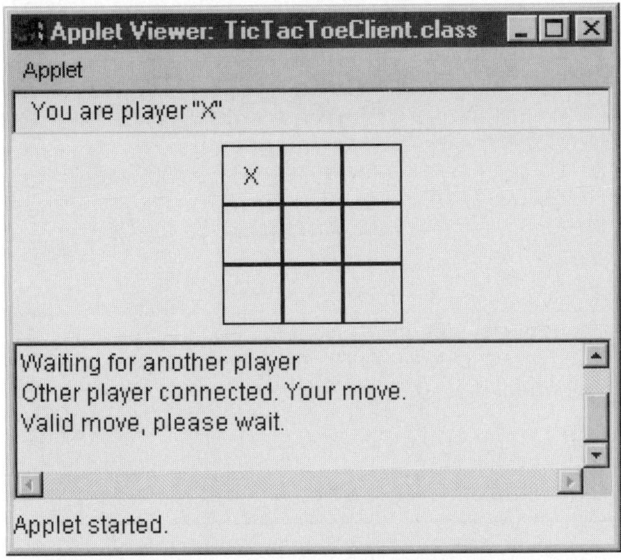

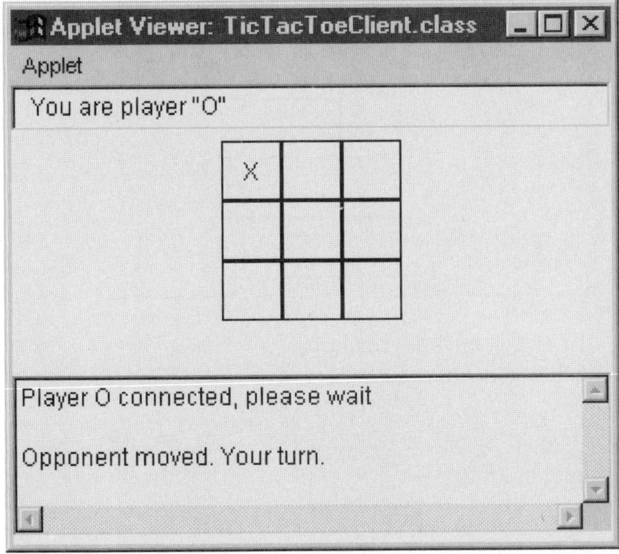

Fig. 16.9 Sample outputs from the client/server Tic-Tac-Toe program (part 2 of 4).

16.9 Security and the Network

As much as we look forward to writing a great variety of powerful network-based applications, our efforts will be crimped because of limitations imposed on Java because of security concerns.

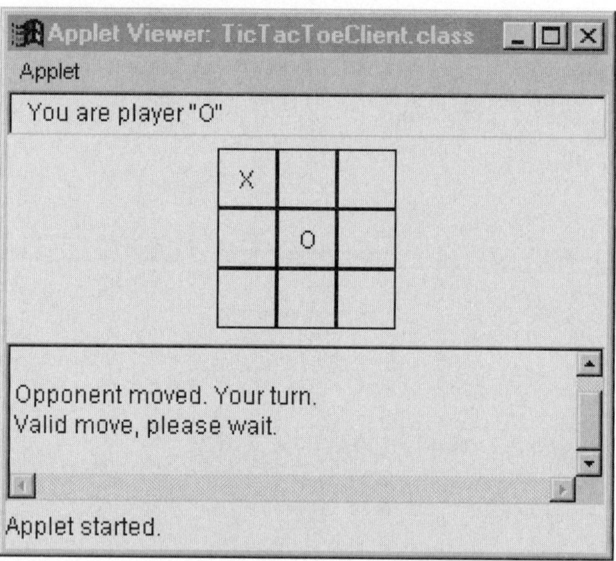

Fig. 16.9 Sample outputs from the client/server Tic-Tac-Toe program (part 3 of 4).

Many Web browsers like Netscape Navigator and Microsoft Internet Explorer by default prohibit Java applets from doing file processing on the machines on which they execute. Think about it. A Java applet is designed to be sent to your browser via an HTML document that could be downloaded from any Web server in the world. Often you will know very little about the sources of Java applets that will execute on your system. To allow these applets free reign with your files could be disastrous.

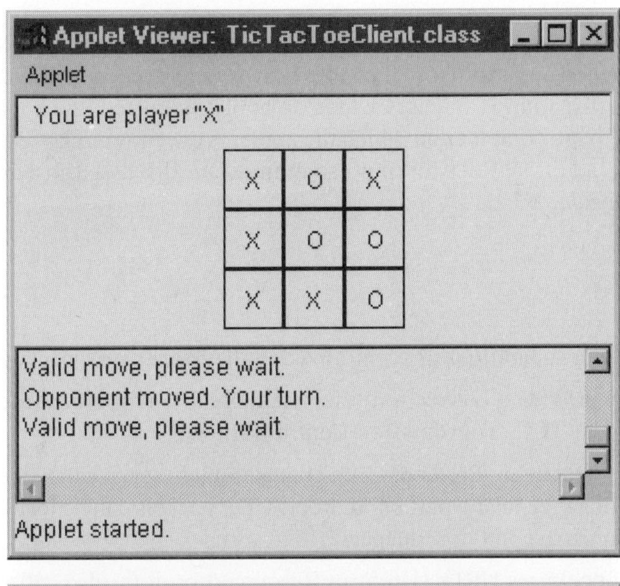

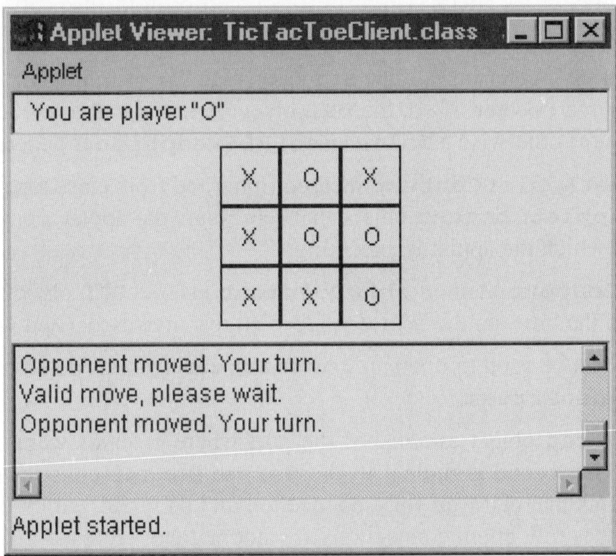

Fig. 16.9 Sample outputs from the client/server Tic-Tac-Toe program (part 4 of 4).

A more subtle situation occurs with limiting the machines to which executing applets can connect. To build truly collaborative applications, we would ideally like to have our applets communicate with machines almost anywhere. But Web browsers often restrict an applet so that it can only communicate with the machine from which it was originally downloaded.

These restrictions may seem too harsh. However, Java Security API now provides capabilities for signed applets that will enable browsers to determine if an applet is downloaded from a *trusted source*. In cases where an applet is trusted, the applet can be given additional access to the computer on which the applet is executing. The features of the Java Security API and additional networking capabilities are discussed in our text *Advanced Java How to Program*.

Summary

- Java's networking capabilities are centralized in the **java.net** package.
- Stream sockets provide a connection-oriented service. The protocol used for transmission is the popular TCP (Transmission Control Protocol).
- UDP—the User Datagram Protocol—is a connectionless service that does not guarantee that packets will arrive in any particular order. UDP packets can be lost, can be duplicated, and can even arrive out of sequence.
- The **http** protocol uses URLs (Uniform Resource Locators, also called Universal Resource Locators) to locate data on the Internet.
- The **URL** constructor determines if the **String** passed as an argument represents a valid Uniform Resource Locator. If so, the **URL** object is initialized to contain the Uniform Resource Locator; otherwise a **MalformedURLException** is generated.
- The applet's **getAppletContext** method (inherited from class **Applet**) gets a reference to an **AppletContext** object that represents the applet's environment—i.e., the browser in which the applet is executing.
- The **AppletContext** method **showDocument** takes a **URL** object as an argument and displays in the browser the World Wide Web resource associated with that **URL**.
- A **URL** object can be used to open an **InputStream** from a file on a server with the **URL** method **openStream**.
- A **ServerSocket** object establishes the port where a server waits for connections from clients. The second argument to the **ServerSocket** constructor specifies the number of clients that can wait for a connection and be processed by the server. If the queue of clients is full, client connections are automatically refused.
- Stream-based connections are managed with **Socket** objects.
- The **ServerSocket** method **accept** waits indefinitely (i.e., blocks) for a connection from a client and returns a **Socket** object when a connection is established.
- The **Socket** method **getOutputStream** gets a reference to the **OutputStream** associated with a **Socket**. The **Socket** method **getInputStream** gets a reference to the **InputStream** associated with the **Socket**.
- When transmission over a **Socket** connection is complete, the server closes the connection by issuing the **close** method on the **Socket**.

- A **Socket** object is used to connect a client to a server by specifying the server name and port number when the Socket object is instantiated. A connection attempt that fails throws an **IOException** object.
- **UnknownHostException** is a subclass of **IOException**.
- The **InputStream** method **read** returns –1 when end-of-stream is detected.
- An **EOFException** is generated when a **DataInputStream** attempts to read a value (with a method other than **readLine**) from a stream on which end-of-stream is detected.
- **InetAddress** method **getLocalHost** returns an **InetAddress** object containing the local host name of the computer on which the program is executing.
- The port where a client connects to a server is sometimes called the handshake point.
- Connection-oriented transmission is like the telephone system in which you dial and are given a connection to the telephone you wish to communicate with; the connection is maintained for the duration of your phone call, even when you are not talking.
- Connectionless transmission with datagrams is like the way mail is carried via the postal service. A large message that will not fit in one envelope can be broken into separate message pieces that are placed in separate, sequentially numbered envelopes. Each of the letters is then mailed at once. The letters may arrive in order, out of order or not at all.
- **DatagramPacket**s are used to create the packets to send and receive information.
- **DatagramSocket**s are used to send and receive **DatagramPacket**s.
- The **DatagramSocket** constructor that takes no arguments sets up a socket for sending packets out over the network. The computer assigns an available port to the **sendSocket** object automatically.
- The **DatagramSocket** constructor that takes an integer port number argument sets up a port for receiving packets from the network.
- If a **DatagramSocket** constructor fails to set up a **DatagramSocket** properly, a **SocketException** is thrown.
- **DatagramSocket** method **receive** waits until a packet arrives then stores the packet in its argument.
- **DatagramPacket** method **getAddress** returns an **InetAddress** object containing the name of the host from which the packet was sent.
- **DatagramPacket** method **getPort** returns an integer specifying the port number through which the host sent the **DatagramPacket**.
- **DatagramPacket** method **getLength** returns an integer representing the number of bytes of data in a **DatagramPacket**.
- **DatagramPacket** method **getData** returns a byte array containing the data in a **DatagramPacket**.

- The **DatagramPacket** constructor for a packet to be sent takes four arguments—the **byte** array to be sent, the number of bytes to be sent, the client address to which the packet will be sent and the port number where the client is waiting to receive packets.
- **DatagramSocket** method **send** sends a **DatagramPacket** out over the network.
- If an error occurs either receiving or sending a **DatagramPacket**, an **IOException** is thrown.
- Many Web browsers like Netscape Navigator prohibit Java applets from doing file processing on the machines on which they execute.
- Web browsers often restrict an applet so that it can only communicate with the machine from which it was originally downloaded.

Terminology

accept a connection
accept method of **ServerSocket** class
AppletContext
client
client connects to a server
client-side socket
client-server relationship
collaborative computing
computer networking
connectionless transmission with datagrams
close a connection
close method of class **Socket**
connect to a port
connect to a World Wide Web site
connection
connectionless service
connection-oriented service
connection request
datagram
DatagramPacket class
datagram socket
DatagramSocket class
deny a connection
duplicated packets
getAddress method of **DatagramPacket**
getAppletContext method of class **Applet**
getData method of class **DatagramPacket**
getInputStream method of class **Socket**
getLength method of **DatagramPacket**
getLocalHost method (**DatagramPacket**)
getOutputStream method of class **Socket**
getPort method of class **DatagramPacket**
handshake point
IOException
java.net package
Java Security API
Java Server API
lost packets
MalformedURLException
multithreaded server
network programming
networking
open a socket
open a **URL** connection
openStream method of class **URL**
out-of-sequence packets
packet
packet length
port
port number on a server
read from a socket
receive method of class **DatagramSocket**
register an available port number
send method of class **DatagramSocket**
server
server-side socket
ServerSocket class
showDocument method (**AppletContext**)
socket
socket-based communications
Socket class
SocketException
stream socket
TCP (Transmission Control Protocol)
UDP (User Datagram Protocol)
UnknownHostException

heterogeneous computer systems
host
import **java.net**
Internet
Internet address
InetAddress class
InetAddress.getLocalHost()
URL (Uniform Resource Locator)
URL class
wait for a connection
wait for a packet
Web browser
Web server
World Wide Web

Common Programming Errors

16.1 A **MalformedURLException** is thrown when a **String** that is not in proper URL format is passed to a **URL** constructor.

16.2 An **UnknownHostException** is thrown when a server address indicated by a client can not be resolved. A **ConnectException** is thrown when an error occurs while attempting to connect to a server.

16.3 Specifying a port that is already in use or specifying an invalid port number when creating a **DatagramSocket** results in a **BindException**.

Performance Tips

16.1 Close a socket immediately after a network connection is no longer needed.

16.2 In high-performance systems in which memory is abundant, a multithreaded server can be implemented to create a pool of threads that can be assigned quickly to handle network I/O across each new **Socket** as it is created. Thus, when a connection is received, the server need not incur the overhead of thread creation.

Portability Tip

16.1 The TCP protocol and its related set of protocols enable a great variety of heterogeneous computer systems (i.e., computer systems with different processors and different operating systems) to intercommunicate.

Software Engineering Observations

16.1 With sockets, network I/O appears to Java programs to be virtually identical to sequential file I/O. Sockets hide much of the complexity of network programming from the programmer.

16.2 With Java's multithreading, we can easily create multithreaded servers that can manage many simultaneous connections with many clients; this multithreaded-server architecture is precisely what is used in popular UNIX, Windows NT and OS/2 network servers.

16.3 A multithreaded server can be implemented to take the **Socket** returned by each call to **accept** and create a new thread that would manage network I/O across that **Socket**, or a multithreaded server can be implemented to maintain a pool of threads ready to manage network I/O across the new **Socket**s as they are created.

Self-Review Exercises

16.1 Fill in the blanks in each of the following:

a) An ________ is thrown when an input/output error occurs when closing a socket.

b) An ________ is thrown when a server address indicated by a client cannot be resolved.

c) If a **DatagramSocket** constructor fails to set up a **DatagramSocket** properly, a ________ is thrown.

d) The **URL** constructor determines if the **String** passed as an argument represents a valid Uniform Resource Locator. If so, the **URL** object is initialized to contain the Uniform Resource Locator; otherwise, a ________ is generated.

e) Java's networking classes are contained in the ________ package.

f) Class ________ is used to create a socket for unreliable datagram transmission.

g) An object of class ________ contains an Internet address.

h) The two types of sockets we discussed in this chapter are ________ sockets and ________ sockets.

i) The acronym URL stands for ________.

j) The key protocol that forms the basis of the World Wide Web is ________.

k) **AppletContext** method ________ receives a URL object as an argument and displays in a browser the World Wide Web resource associated with that URL.

l) **InetAddress** method **getLocalHost** returns an ________ object containing the local host name of the computer on which the program is executing.

16.2 State whether the following are true or false. If the answer is false, explain why.

a) A **URL** object once created cannot be changed.

b) UDP is a connection-oriented protocol.

c) With stream sockets a process establishes a connection to another process.

d) A server waits at a port for connections from a client.

e) Datagram packet transmission over a network is reliable—packets are guaranteed to arrive in sequence.

f) For security reasons, many Web browsers like Netscape Navigator allow Java applets to do file processing only on the machines on which they execute.

g) Web browsers often restrict an applet so that it can only communicate with the machine from which it was originally downloaded.

Answers to Self-Review Exercises

16.1 a) **IOException**. b) **UnknownHostException**. c) **SocketException**. d) **MalformedURLException**. e) **java.net**. f) **DatagramSocket**. g) **InetAddress**. h) stream, datagram. i) Uniform Resource Locator. j) **http**. k) **showDocument**. l) **InetAddress**.

16.2 a) true. b) false; UDP is a connectionless protocol and TCP is a connection-oriented protocol. c) true. d) true. e) false; packets could be lost and packets can arrive out of order. f) false; most browsers prevent applets from doing file processing on the client machine. g) true.

Exercises

16.3 Distinguish between connection-oriented network services and connectionless network services.

16.4 How does a client determine the host name of the client computer?

16.5 Under what circumstances would a **`SocketException`** be thrown?

16.6 How can a client get a line of text from a server?

16.7 Describe how a client applet or application can read a file from a server through a URL connection.

16.8 Describe how a client connects to a server.

16.9 Describe how a server sends data to a client.

16.10 Describe how to prepare a server to receive a streams-based connection request from a single client.

16.11 Describe how to prepare a server to receive connection requests from multiple clients where each client that connects should be processed in parallel with all other connected clients.

16.12 How does a server listen for connections at a port?

16.13 What determines how many connect requests from clients can wait in a queue to connect to a server?

16.14 As described in the text, what reasons might cause a server to refuse a connection request from a client?

16.15 Use a socket connection to allow a client to specify a file name and have the server send the contents of the file or indicate that the file does not exist.

16.16 Modify the preceding exercise to allow the client to modify the contents of the file and send the file back to the server for storage. The user can edit the file in a **`TextArea`** then click a *save changes* button to send the file back to the server.

16.17 Modify program of Fig. 16.1 to show a list of sites in a **`List`** object. Allow users to add their own sites to the list and remove sites from the list.

16.18 Multithreaded servers are quite popular today, especially because of the increasing use of multiprocessing servers. Modify the simple server application presented in Section 16.6 to be a multithreaded server. Then use several client applications and have each of them connect to the server simultaneously.

16.19 In the text we presented a tic-tac-toe program controlled by a multithreaded server. Develop a checkers program modeled after the tic-tac-toe program. The two users should alternate making moves. Your program should mediate the players moves determining whose turn it is and allowing only valid moves. The players themselves will determine when the game is over.

16.20 Develop a chess-playing program modeled after the checkers program in the previous exercises.

16.21 Develop a black jack card game program in which the server application deals cards to each of the client applets. The server should deal additional cards (as per the rules of the game) to each player as requested.

16.22 Develop a poker card game in which the server application deals cards to each of the client applets. The server should deal additional cards (as per the rules of the game) to each player as requested.

16.23 *(Modifications to the Multithreaded Tic-Tac-Toe Program)* The programs of Fig. 16.7 and 16.8 implemented a multithreaded, client/server version of the game Tic-Tac-Toe. Our goal in developing this game was to demonstrate a multithreaded server that could process multiple connections from clients at the same time. The server in the example is really a mediator between the two client applets—it makes sure that each move is valid and that each client moves in the proper order. The server does not determine who won or lost or if there was a draw. Also, there is no capability to allow a new game to be played or to terminate an existing game.

The following is a list of suggested modifications to the multithreaded Tic-Tac-Toe application and applet.

a) Modify the **`TicTacToeServer`** class to test for a win, loss or draw on each move in the game. Send a message to each client applet that indicates the result of the game when the game is over.
b) Modify the **`TicTacToeClient`** class to display a button that when clicked allows the client to play another game. The button should only be enabled when a game completes. Note that both class **`TicTacToeClient`** and class **`TicTacToeServer`** must be modified to reset the board and all state information. Also, the other **`TicTacToeClient`** should be notified that a new game is about to begin so its board and state can be reset.
c) Modify the **`TicTacToeClient`** class to provide a button that allows a client to terminate the program at any time. When the button is clicked, the server and the other client should be notified. The server should then wait for a connection from another client so a new game can begin.
d) Modify the **`TicTacToeClient`** class and the **`TicTacToeServer`** class so the winner of a game can choose game piece X or O for the next game. Remember: X always goes first.
e) If you would like to be ambitious, allow a client to play against the server while the server waits for a connection from another client.

16.24 *(3-D Multithreaded Tic-Tac-Toe)* Modify the multithreaded, client/server Tic-Tac-Toe program to implement a three-dimensional, 4-by-4-by-4 version of the game. Implement the server application to mediate between the two clients. Display the three-dimensional board as four boards containing four rows and four columns each. If you would like to be ambitious, try the following modifications:

a) Draw the board in a three-dimensional manner.
b) Allow the server to test for a win, loss or draw. Beware! There are many possible ways to win on a 4-by-4-by-4 board!

16.25 *(Networked Morse Code)* Modify your solution to Exercise 8.26 to enable two applets to send Morse Code messages to each other through a multithreaded server application. Each applet should allow the user to type normal characters in **`TextArea`**s, translate the characters into Morse Code and send the coded message through the server to the other client. When messages are received, they should be decoded and displayed as normal characters and as Morse Code. The applet should have two **`TextArea`**s one for displaying the other client's messages and one for typing.

17

Data Structures

Objectives

- To be able to form linked data structures using references, self-referential classes, and recursion.
- To be able to create and manipulate dynamic data structures such as linked lists, queues, stacks, and binary trees.
- To understand various important applications of linked data structures.
- To understand how to create reusable data structures with classes, inheritance, and composition.

Much that I bound, I could not free;
Much that I freed returned to me.
Lee Wilson Dodd

'Will you walk a little faster?' said a whiting to a snail,
'There's a porpoise close behind us, and he's treading on my tail.'
Lewis Carroll

There is always room at the top.
Daniel Webster

Push on—keep moving.
Thomas Morton

I think that I shall never see
A poem lovely as a tree.
Joyce Kilmer

Outline

17.1 Introduction

We have studied fixed-size *data structures* such as single-subscripted arrays and double-subscripted arrays. This chapter introduces *dynamic data structures* that grow and shrink at execution time. *Linked lists* are collections of data items "lined up in a row"—insertions and deletions are made anywhere in a linked list. *Stacks* are important in compilers and operating systems—insertions and deletions are made only at one end of a stack—its *top*. *Queues* represent waiting lines; insertions are made at the back (also referred to as the *tail*) of a queue, and deletions are made from the front (also referred to as the *head*) of a queue. *Binary trees* facilitate high-speed searching and sorting of data, efficient elimination of duplicate data items, representing file system directories, and compiling expressions into machine language. These data structures have many other interesting applications.

We will discuss each of the major types of data structures and implement programs that create and manipulate these data structures. We use classes, inheritance, and composition to create and package these data structures for reusability and maintainability.

The chapter examples are practical programs that you will be able to use in more advanced courses and in industry applications. The programs are especially heavy on reference manipulation. The exercises include a rich collection of useful applications.

We encourage you to attempt the major project described in the special section entitled "Building Your Own Compiler." You have been using a compiler to translate your Java programs to bytecodes so that you could execute these programs on your computer. In this project, you will actually build your own compiler. It will read a file of statements written in a simple, yet powerful, high-level language similar to early versions of the popular language Basic. Your compiler will translate these statements into a file of Simpletron Machine Language (SML) instructions—SML is the language you learned in the Chapter 5 special section, "Building Your Own Computer." Your Simpletron Simulator program will then execute the SML program produced by your compiler! Implementing this project using an object-oriented approach will give you a wonderful opportunity to exercise most of what you have learned in this book. The special section carefully walks you through the specifications of the high-level language, and describes the algorithms you will need to convert each type of high-level language statement into machine language instructions. If you enjoy being challenged, you might attempt the many enhancements to both the compiler and the Simpletron Simulator suggested in the Exercises.

17.2 Self-Referential Classes

A *self-referential class* contains a reference member that refers to a class object of the same class type. For example, the definition

```
class Node {
   private int data;
   private Node next;

   Node( int d ) { /* method body */ }
   void setData( int d ) { /* method body */ }
   int getData() { /* method body */ }
   void setNext( Node nextNode ) { /* method body */ }
   Node getNext() { /* method body */ }
}
```

defines a type, **Node**. Type **Node** has two **private** instance variables—integer **data** and **Node** reference **next**. Member **next** references an object of type **Node**—an object of the same type as the one being declared here, hence the term "self-referential class." Member **next** is referred to as a *link*—i.e., **next** can be used to "tie" an object of type **Node** to another object of the same type. Type **Node** also has five methods: a constructor that receives an integer to initialize **data**, a **setData** method to set the value **data**, a **getData** method to return the value of **data**, a **setNext** method to set the value of **next**, and a **getNext** method to return the value of member **next**.

Self-referential objects can be linked together to form useful data structures such as lists, queues, stacks and trees. Figure 17.1 illustrates two self-referential objects linked together to form a list. A slash—representing a **null** reference—is placed in the link member of the second self-referential object to indicate that the link does not refer to another object. The slash is for illustration purposes; it does not correspond to the backslash character in Java. A **null** reference normally indicates the end of a data structure.

Common Programming Error 17.1

Not setting the link in the last node of a list to **null**.

17.3 Dynamic Memory Allocation

Creating and maintaining dynamic data structures requires *dynamic memory allocation*—the ability for a program to obtain more memory space at execution time to hold new nodes

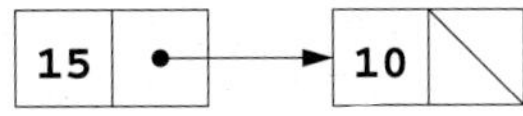

Fig. 17.1 Two self-referential class objects linked together.

and to release space no longer needed. Java programs do not explicitly release dynamically allocated memory. Rather, Java performs automatic garbage collection. The limit for dynamic memory allocation can be as large as the amount of available physical memory in the computer or the amount of available virtual memory in a virtual-memory system. Often, the limits are much smaller because the computer's available memory must be shared among many users.

Operator **new** is essential to dynamic memory allocation. Operator **new** takes as an argument the type of the object being dynamically allocated and returns a reference to an object of that type. For example, the statement

```
Node nodeToAdd = new Node( 10 );
```

allocates the appropriate number of bytes to store a **Node** and stores a reference to this memory in **nodeToAdd**. If no memory is available, **new** throws an **OutOfMemoryException**. The 10 is the **Node** object's data.

The following sections discuss lists, stacks, queues, and trees. These data structures are created and maintained with dynamic memory allocation and self-referential classes.

Good Programming Practice 17.1

When using **new**, *test for an* **OutOfMemoryException**. *Perform appropriate error processing if the requested memory is not allocated.*

17.4 Linked Lists

A *linked list* is a linear collection of self-referential class objects, called *nodes,* connected by reference *links*—hence, the term "linked" list. A linked list is accessed via a reference to the first node of the list. Subsequent nodes are accessed via the link-reference member stored in each node. By convention, the link reference in the last node of a list is set to **null** to mark the end of the list. Data are stored in a linked list dynamically—each node is created as necessary. A node can contain data of any type including objects of other classes. Stacks and queues are also linear data structures, and, as we will see, are constrained versions of linked lists. Trees are nonlinear data structures.

Lists of data can be stored in arrays, but linked lists provide several advantages. A linked list is appropriate when the number of data elements to be represented in the data structure at one time is unpredictable. Linked lists are dynamic, so the length of a list can increase or decrease as necessary. The size of a "conventional" Java array, however, cannot be altered, because the array size is fixed at creation time. "Conventional" arrays can become full. Linked lists become full only when the system has insufficient memory to satisfy dynamic storage allocation requests. The **java.util** package of the Java API contains class **Vector** for implementing and manipulating dynamic arrays that can grow and shrink during the execution of the program. We will discuss class **Vector** in Chapter 18, "Java Utilities Package and Bit Manipulation."

Performance Tip 17.1

An array can be declared to contain more elements than the number of items expected, but this can waste memory. Linked lists can provide better memory utilization in these situations. Linked lists allow the program to adapt at runtime.

Performance Tip 17.2

Insertion into a linked list is fast—only two references have to be modified. All existing nodes remain at their current locations in memory.

Linked lists can be maintained in sorted order simply by inserting each new element at the proper point in the list. Existing list elements do not need to be moved.

Performance Tip 17.3

Insertion and deletion in a sorted array can be time consuming—all the elements following the inserted or deleted element must be shifted appropriately.

Performance Tip 17.4

The elements of an array are stored contiguously in memory. This allows immediate access to any array element because the address of any element can be calculated directly based on its position relative to the beginning of the array. Linked lists do not afford such immediate access to their elements.

Linked list nodes are normally not stored contiguously in memory. Logically, however, the nodes of a linked list appear to be contiguous. Figure 17.2 illustrates a linked list with several nodes.

Performance Tip 17.5

Using dynamic memory allocation (instead of arrays) for data structures that grow and shrink at execution time can save memory. Keep in mind, however, that references occupy space, and that dynamic memory allocation incurs the overhead of method calls.

The program of Fig. 17.3 (whose output is shown in Fig. 17.4) uses a **`List`** class to manipulate a list of miscellaneous object types. The main method of the **`ListTest`** class creates a list of objects, inserts objects at the beginning of the list using method **`insertAtFront`**, inserts objects at the end of the list using method **`insertAtBack`**, deletes objects from the front of the list using method **`removeFromFront`**, and deletes objects from the end of the list using method **`removeFromBack`**. After each insertion and deletion operation, the **`print`** method is invoke to display the contents of the list. A detailed discussion of the program follows. If an attempt is made to remove an item from an empty list, an **`EmptyListException`** (defined on line 142 of Fig. 17.3) is thrown. Exercise 17.20 asks you to implement a recursive method that prints a linked list backwards, and Exercise 17.21 asks you to implement a recursive method that searches a linked list for a particular data item.

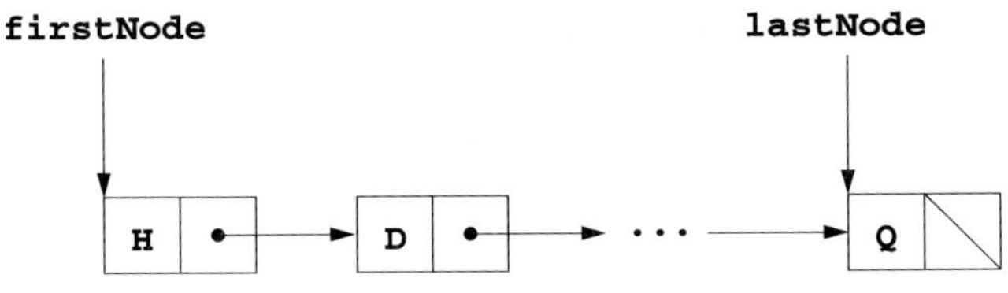

Fig. 17.2 A graphical representation of a linked list.

```
// Fig. 17.3: List.java
// Class ListNode and class List definitions
package com.deitel.jhtp2.ch17;

class ListNode {
   // package access data so class List can access it directly
   Object data;
   ListNode next;

   // Constructor: Create a ListNode that refers to Object o.
   ListNode( Object o ) { this( o, null ); }

   // Constructor: Create a ListNode that refers to Object o and
   // to the next ListNode in the List.
   ListNode( Object o, ListNode nextNode )
   {
      data = o;           // this node refers to Object o
      next = nextNode;    // set next to refer to next
   }

   // Return the Object in this node
   Object getObject() { return data; }

   // Return the next node
   ListNode getnext() { return next; }
}

// Class List definition
public class List {
   private ListNode firstNode;
   private ListNode lastNode;
   private String name;  // String like "list" used in printing

   // Constructor: Construct an empty List with s as the name
   public List( String s )
   {
      name = s;
      firstNode = lastNode = null;
   }

   // Constructor: Construct an empty List with
   // "list" as the name
   public List() { this( "list" ); }

   // Insert an Object at the front of the List
   // If List is empty, firstNode and lastNode refer to
   // same Object. Otherwise, firstNode refers to new node.
   public synchronized void insertAtFront( Object insertItem )
   {
      if ( isEmpty() )
         firstNode = lastNode = new ListNode( insertItem );
```

Fig. 17.3 Manipulating a linked list (part 1 of 6).

```
         else
            firstNode = new ListNode( insertItem, firstNode );
      }

      // Insert an Object at the end of the List
      // If List is empty, firstNode and lastNode refer to
      // same Object. Otherwise, lastNode's next instance
      // variable refers to new node.
      public synchronized void insertAtBack( Object insertItem )
      {
         if ( isEmpty() )
            firstNode = lastNode = new ListNode( insertItem );
         else
            lastNode = lastNode.next = new ListNode( insertItem );
      }

      // Remove the first node from the List.
      public synchronized Object removeFromFront()
             throws EmptyListException
      {
         Object removeItem = null;

         if ( isEmpty() )
            throw new EmptyListException( name );

         removeItem = firstNode.data;  // retrieve the data

         // reset the firstNode and lastNode references
         if ( firstNode.equals( lastNode ) )
            firstNode = lastNode = null;
         else
            firstNode = firstNode.next;

         return removeItem;
      }

      // Remove the last node from the List.
      public synchronized Object removeFromBack()
             throws EmptyListException
      {
         Object removeItem = null;

         if ( isEmpty() )
            throw new EmptyListException( name );

         removeItem = lastNode.data;  // retrieve the data

         // reset the firstNode and lastNode references
         if ( firstNode.equals( lastNode ) )
            firstNode = lastNode = null;
```

Fig. 17.3 Manipulating a linked list (part 2 of 6).

```
         else {
            ListNode current = firstNode;

            while ( current.next != lastNode )
               current = current.next;

            lastNode = current;
            current.next = null;
         }

         return removeItem;
      }

      // Return true if the List is empty
      public boolean isEmpty() { return firstNode == null; }

      // Output the List contents
      public void print()
      {
         if ( isEmpty() ) {
            System.out.println( "Empty " + name );
            return;
         }

         System.out.print( "The " + name + " is: " );

         ListNode current = firstNode;

         while ( current != null ) {
            System.out.print( current.data.toString() + " " );
            current = current.next;
         }

         System.out.println( "\n" );
      }
   }
```

Fig. 17.3 Manipulating a linked list (part 3 of 6).

```
   // Fig. 17.03: EmptyListException.java
   // Class EmptyListException definition
   package com.deitel.jhtp2.ch17;

   public class EmptyListException extends RuntimeException {
      public EmptyListException( String name )
      {
         super( "The " + name + " is empty" );
      }
   }
```

Fig. 17.3 Manipulating a linked list (part 4 of 6).

```
// Fig. 17.03: ListTest.java
// Class ListTest
import com.deitel.jhtp2.ch17.List;
import com.deitel.jhtp2.ch17.EmptyListException;

public class ListTest {
   public static void main( String args[] )
   {
      List objList = new List();  // create the List container

      // Create objects to store in the List
      Boolean b = new Boolean( true );
      Character c = new Character( '$' );
      Integer i = new Integer( 34567 );
      String s = new String( "hello" );

      // Use the List insert methods
      objList.insertAtFront( b );
      objList.print();
      objList.insertAtFront( c );
      objList.print();
      objList.insertAtBack( i );
      objList.print();
      objList.insertAtBack( s );
      objList.print();

      // Use the List remove methods
      Object removedObj;

      try {
         removedObj = objList.removeFromFront();
         System.out.println(
            removedObj.toString() + " removed" );
         objList.print();
         removedObj = objList.removeFromFront();
         System.out.println(
            removedObj.toString() + " removed" );
         objList.print();
         removedObj = objList.removeFromBack();
         System.out.println(
            removedObj.toString() + " removed" );
         objList.print();
         removedObj = objList.removeFromBack();
         System.out.println(
            removedObj.toString() + " removed" );
         objList.print();
      }
```

Fig. 17.3 Manipulating a linked list (part 5 of 6).

```
        catch ( EmptyListException e ) {
           System.err.println( "\n" + e.toString() );
        }
     }
 }
```

Fig. 17.3 Manipulating a linked list (part 6 of 6).

```
The list is: true

The list is: $ true

The list is: $ true 34567

The list is: $ true 34567 hello

$ removed
The list is: true 34567 hello

true removed
The list is: 34567 hello

hello removed
The list is: 34567

34567 removed
Empty list
```

Fig. 17.4 Sample output for the program of Fig. 17.3.

The program of Fig. 17.3 consists of three classes—**ListNode**, **List**, and **EmptyListException**. The **List** and **ListNode** classes are placed in package **com.deitel.jhtp2.ch17** for reuse purposes. Encapsulated in each **List** object is a linked list of **ListNode** objects. The **ListNode** class consists of friendly members **data** and **next**. **ListNode** member **data** can refer to any **Object**. **ListNode** member **next** stores a reference to the next **ListNode** object in the linked list.

The **List** class consists of **private** members **firstNode** (a reference to the first **ListNode** in a list object) and **lastNode** (a reference to the last **ListNode** in a **List** object). The default constructor initializes both references to **null**. The primary methods of the **List** class are the **synchronized** methods **insertAtFront**, **insertAtBack**, **removeFromFront**, and **removeFromBack**. These methods are declared **synchronized** so **List** objects can be *multithread safe* when used in a multithreaded program. If one thread is modifying the contents of a **List** object, no other thread is allowed to modify the same **List** object at the same time. Method **isEmpty** is called a *predicate method*—it does not alter the list in any way; rather, it determines if the list is empty (i.e., the reference to the first node of the list is **null**). If the list is empty, **true** is returned; otherwise, **false** is returned. Method **print** displays the list's contents.

Over the next several pages, we will discuss each of the methods of the **List** class in detail. Method **insertAtFront** (Fig. 17.5 illustrates the operation) places a new node at the front of the list. The method consists of several steps:

1. Call **isEmpty** to determine if the list is empty (line 50).
2. If the list is empty, both **firstNode** and **lastNode** are set to the **ListNode** allocated with **new** and initialized with **insertItem** (line 51). The **ListNode** constructor (line 11) sets instance variable **data** to refer to the **insertItem** passed as an argument and sets the **next** reference to **null**.
3. If the list is not empty, the new node is threaded into the list by setting **firstNode** to the **ListNode** object that was allocated with **new** and initialized with **insertItem** and **firstNode** (line 53). When the **ListNode** constructor (line 15) executes, it sets instance variable **data** to refer to the **insertItem** passed as an argument and sets the **next** reference to the **ListNode** passed as an argument which performs the insertion.

Figure 17.5 illustrates method **insertAtFront**. Part a) of the figure shows the list and the new node during the **insertAtFront** operation and before the new node has been threaded into the list. The dotted arrows in part b) illustrate step 3 of the **insertAtFront** operation that enables the node containing **12** to become the new list front.

Method **insertAtBack** (Fig. 17.6 illustrates the operation) places a new node at the back of the list. The method consists of several steps:

1. Call **isEmpty** to determine if the list is empty (line 62).
2. If the list is empty, both **firstNode** and **lastNode** are set to the **ListNode** allocated with **new** and initialized with **insertItem** (line 63). The **ListNode** constructor (line 11) sets instance variable **data** to refer to the **insertItem** passed as an argument and sets the **next** reference to **null**.

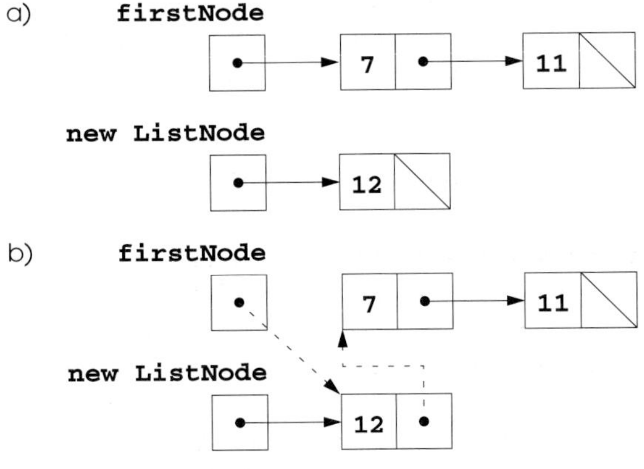

Fig. 17.5 The **insertAtFront** operation.

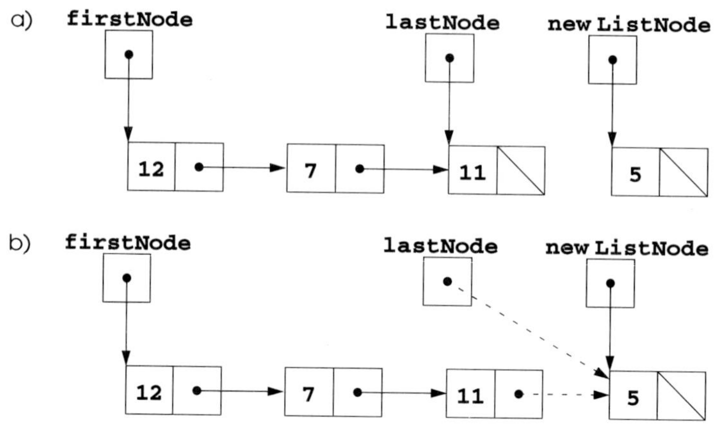

Fig. 17.6 A graphical representation of the **insertAtBack** operation.

3. If the list is not empty, the new node is threaded into the list by setting **LastNode** and **lastNode.next** to the **ListNode** that was allocated with **new** and initialized with **insertItem** (line 65). When the **ListNode** constructor (line 11) executes, it sets instance variable **data** to refer to the **insertItem** passed as an argument and sets the **next** reference to **null**.

Figure 17.6 illustrates an **insertAtBack** operation. Part a) of the figure shows the list and the new node during the **insertAtBack** operation and before the new node has been threaded into the list. The dotted arrows in part b) illustrate the steps of method **insertAtBack** that enable a new node to be added to the end of a list that is not empty.

Method **removeFromFront** (illustrated in Fig. 17.7) removes the front node of the list and returns a reference to the removed data. The method throws an **EmptyListException** (lines 74 and 75) if an attempt is made to remove a node from an empty list. Otherwise, a reference to the removed data is returned. The method consists of several steps:

1. Assign **removeItem** to refer to **firstNode.data** (the data being removed from the list).

2. If **firstNode** is equal to **lastNode** (line 80), i.e., if the list has only one element prior to the removal attempt, then set **firstNode** and **lastNode** to **null** (line 81) to dethread that node from the list (leaving the list empty).

3. If the list has more than one node prior to removal, then leave **lastNode** as is and simply set **firstNode** to **firstNode.next** (line 83), i.e., modify **firstNode** to reference what was the second node prior to removal (and now, the new first node).

4. Return the **removeItem** reference.

Figure 17.7 illustrates method **removeFromFront**. Part a) illustrates the list before the removal operation. Part b) shows actual reference manipulations.

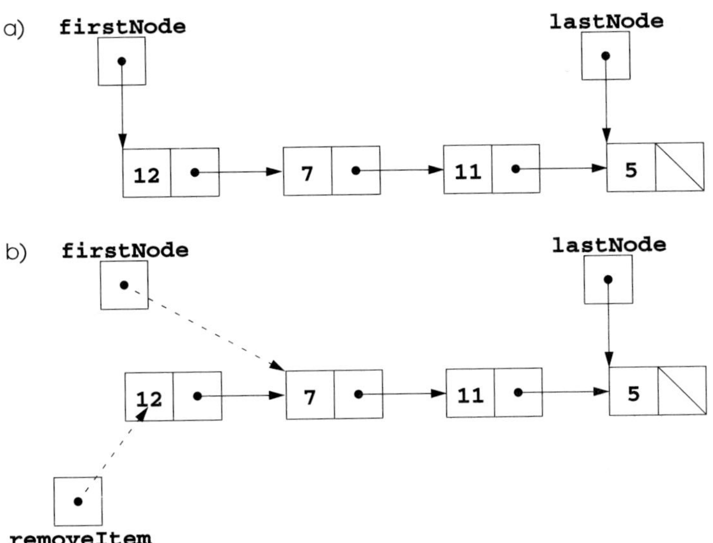

Fig. 17.7 A graphical representation of the **removeFromFront** operation.

Method **removeFromBack** (Fig. 17.8 illustrates the operation) removes the last node of a list and returns a reference to the removed data. The method throws an **EmptyListException** (lines 94 and 95) if an attempt is made to remove a node from an empty list. The method consists of several steps:

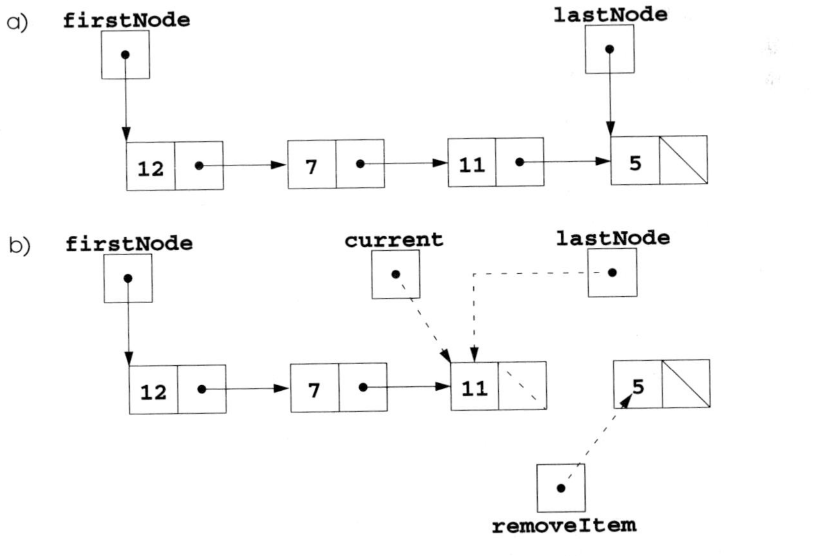

Fig. 17.8 A graphical representation of the **removeFromBack** operation.

1. Assign **removeItem** to refer to **lastNode.data** (the data being removed from the list).
2. If **firstNode** is equal to **lastNode** (line 100), i.e., if the list has only one element prior to the removal attempt, then set **firstNode** and **lastNode** to **null** (line 101) to dethread that node from the list (leaving the list empty).
3. If the list has more than one node prior to removal, then create the **Listnode** reference **current** and initialize it to **firstNode**.
4. Now "walk the list" with **current** until it references the node before the last node. This is done with a **while** loop that keeps replacing **current** by **current.next** while **current.next** is not **lastNode**.
5. Copy **current** to **lastNode** to dethread the back node from the list.
6. Set the **current.next** to **null** in the new last node of the list.
7. Return the **removeItem** reference.

Figure 17.8 illustrates method **removeFromBack**. Part a) illustrates the list before the removal operation. Part b) shows the actual reference manipulations.

Method **print** first determines if the list is empty. If so, **print** displays **"The list is empty"** and terminates. Otherwise, it prints the data in the list. The method prints a string consisting of the string **"The "**, the **String** object **name**, and the string **" is: "**. Then the **ListNode** reference **current** is created and initialized with **firstNode**. While **current** is not **null**, **current.data.toString()** is printed and **current.next** is assigned to **current**. Note that if the link in the last node of the list is not null, the printing algorithm will erroneously print past the end of the list. The printing algorithm is identical for linked lists, stacks, and queues.

17.5 Stacks

A *stack* is a constrained version of a linked list—new nodes can be added to a stack and removed from a stack only at the top. For this reason, a stack is referred to as a *last-in, first-out (LIFO)* data structure. The link member in the last node of the stack is set to null to indicate the bottom of the stack.

Common Programming Error 17.2

Not setting the link in the bottom node of a stack to **null**.

The primary methods used to manipulate a stack are ***push*** and ***pop***. Method **push** adds a new node to the top of the stack. Method **pop** removes a node from the top of the stack and returns the **data** object from the popped node.

Stacks have many interesting applications. For example, when a method call is made, the called method must know how to return to its caller, so the return address is pushed onto a stack. If a series of method calls occurs, the successive return values are pushed onto the stack in last-in, first-out order so that each method can return to its caller. Stacks support recursive method calls in the same manner as conventional nonrecursive method calls.

Stacks contain the space created for automatic variables on each invocation of a method during a program's execution. When the method returns to its caller, the space for that method's automatic variables is popped off the stack, and those variables are no longer known to the program.

Stacks are also used by compilers in the process of evaluating arithmetic expressions and generating machine language code to process the expressions. The exercises in this chapter explore several applications of stacks, including using them to develop a complete working compiler.

We will take advantage of the close relationship between lists and stacks to implement a stack class primarily by reusing a list class. We use two different forms of reusability. First, we implement the stack class through inheritance of the **`List`** class. Then we implement an identically performing stack class through composition by including a **`List`** object as a **`private`** member of a stack class. The list, stack and queue data structures in this chapter are implemented to store **`Object`** references to encourage further reusability. Thus, any object type can be stored in a list, stack or queue.

Figure 17.9 (output in Fig. 17.10) creates a stack class through inheritance from class **`List`** of Fig. 17.3. We want the stack to have methods **`push`**, **`pop`**, **`isEmpty`**, and **`print`**. These are essentially the **`insertAtFront`**, **`removeFromFront`**, **`isEmpty`**, and **`print`** methods of class **`List`**. Of course, class **`List`** contains other methods (i.e., **`insertAtBack`** and **`removeFromBack`**) that we would rather not make accessible through the public interface to the stack class. It is important to remember that all methods in the public interface of the **`List`** class are also **`public`** methods of the derived class **`StackInheritance`**. We demonstrate another way to build the stack using our **`List`** class in Fig. 17.11. When we implement the stack's methods, we have each **`StackInheritance`** method call the appropriate **`List`** method—**`synchronized`** method **`push`** calls **`insertAtFront`**, **`synchronized`** method **`pop`** calls **`removeFromFront`**, **`isEmpty`** calls **`super.isEmpty`** to invoke the base class version, and **`print`** calls **`super.print`** to invoke the base class version. Class **`StackInheritance`** is defined as part of package **`com.deitel.jhtp2.ch17`** for reuse purposes.

```
// Class StackInheritance definition
// Derived from class List
package com.deitel.jhtp2.ch17;

public class StackInheritance extends List {
   public StackInheritance() { super( "stack" ); }
   public synchronized void push( Object o )
      { insertAtFront( o ); }
   public synchronized Object pop() throws EmptyListException
      { return removeFromFront(); }
   public boolean isEmpty() { return super.isEmpty(); }
   public void print() { super.print(); }
}
```

Fig. 17.9 A simple stack program (part 1 of 2).

```
// Fig. 17.09: StackInheritanceTest.java
// Class StackInheritanceTest
import com.deitel.jhtp2.ch17.StackInheritance;
import com.deitel.jhtp2.ch17.EmptyListException;

public class StackInheritanceTest {
   public static void main( String args[] )
   {
      StackInheritance objStack = new StackInheritance();

      // Create objects to store in the stack
      Boolean b = new Boolean( true );
      Character c = new Character( '$' );
      Integer i = new Integer( 34567 );
      String s = new String( "hello" );

      // Use the push method
      objStack.push( b );
      objStack.print();
      objStack.push( c );
      objStack.print();
      objStack.push( i );
      objStack.print();
      objStack.push( s );
      objStack.print();

      // Use the pop method
      Object removedObj = null;

      try {
         while ( true ) {
            removedObj = objStack.pop();
            System.out.println( removedObj.toString() +
                                " popped" );
            objStack.print();
         }
      }
      catch ( EmptyListException e ) {
         System.err.println( "\n" + e.toString() );
      }
   }
}
```

Fig. 17.9 A simple stack program (part 2 of 2).

The **StackInheritance** class is used in **StackInheritanceTest**'s **main** method to instantiate a stack of **Object**s called **objStack**. A **Boolean** object containing **true**, a **Character** object containing **$**, an **Integer** object containing **34567** and a **String** object containing **hello** are pushed onto **objStack** and then popped off **objStack**. The objects are popped from the stack in an infinite **while** loop. When there are no objects left to pop, an **EmptyListException** is thrown and a message is displayed stating that the stack is empty.

```
The stack is: true

The stack is: $ true

The stack is: 34567 $ true

The stack is: hello 34567 $ true

hello popped
The stack is: 34567 $ true

34567 popped
The stack is: $ true

$ popped
The stack is: true

true popped
Empty stack

com.deitel.jhtp2.ch17.EmptyListException:
   The stack is empty
```

Fig. 17.10 Sample output from the program of Fig. 17.9.

Another way to implement a stack class is by reusing a list class through composition. The class in Fig. 17.11 uses a **private** object of the **List** class (line 6) in the definition of class **StackComposition**.

```
1  // Fig. 17.11: StackComposition.java
2  // Class StackComposition definition with composed List object
3  package com.deitel.jhtp2.ch17;
4
5  public class StackComposition {
6     private List s;
7
8     public StackComposition() { s = new List( "stack" ); }
9     public synchronized void push( Object o )
10       { s.insertAtFront( o ); }
11    public synchronized Object pop() throws EmptyListException
12       { return s.removeFromFront(); }
13    public boolean isEmpty() { return s.isEmpty(); }
14    public void print() { s.print(); }
15 }
```

Fig. 17.11 A simple stack class using composition.

Composition enables us to hide the methods of class **List** that should not be in the interface to our stack by providing public interface methods only to the required **List** methods. This technique of implementing each stack method as a call to a **List** method is called *forwarding*—the stack method invoked *forwards* the call to the appropriate **List** method. The **StackCompositionTest** class uses an identical **main** method to the **StackInheritanceTest** class, except an object of class **StackComposition** is instantiated instead. The output is also the same.

17.6 Queues

Another common data structure is the *queue.* A queue is similar to a checkout line in a supermarket—the first person in line is serviced first, and other customers enter the line only at the end and wait to be serviced. Queue nodes are removed only from the *head* of the queue, and are inserted only at the *tail* of the queue. For this reason, a queue is referred to as a *first-in, first-out (FIFO)* data structure. The insert and remove operations are known as ***enqueue*** and ***dequeue***.

Queues have many applications in computer systems. Most computers have only a single processor, so only one user at a time can be serviced. Entries for the other users are placed in a queue. The entry at the front of the queue is the next to receive service. Each entry gradually advances to the front of the queue as users receive service.

Queues are also used to support print spooling. A multiuser environment may have only a single printer. Many users may be generating outputs to be printed. If the printer is busy, other outputs may still be generated. These are "spooled" to disk (much as thread is wound onto a spool) where they wait in a queue until the printer becomes available.

Information packets also wait in queues in computer networks. Each time a packet arrives at a network node, it must be routed to the next node on the network along the path to the packet's final destination. The routing node routes one packet at a time, so additional packets are enqueued until the router can route them.

A file server in a computer network handles file access requests from many clients throughout the network. Servers have a limited capacity to service requests from clients. When that capacity is exceeded, client requests wait in queues.

Common Programming Error 17.3

Not setting the link in the last node of a queue to **null**.

The program of Fig. 17.12 (whose output is shown in Fig. 17.13) creates a queue class through inheritance from a list class. We want the **QueueInh** class to have methods **enqueue**, **dequeue**, **isEmpty**, and **print**. We note that these are essentially the **insertAtBack**, **removeFromFront**, **isEmpty**, and **print** methods of class **List**. Class **QueueInheritance** is defined in package **com.deitel.jhtp2.ch17** for reuse purposes.

Of course, the list class contains other methods (i.e., **insertAtFront** and **removeFromBack**) that we would rather not make accessible through the public interface to the queue class. Remember that all methods in the **public** interface of the **List** class are also **public** methods of the derived class **QueueInheritance**. When we implement the queue's methods, we have each **QueueInheritance** method call the appropriate **List** method—**synchronized** method **enqueue** calls **insertAtBack**, **synchronized** method **dequeue** calls **removeFromFront**, **isEmpty** calls **super.isEmpty** to invoke the base class version and **print** calls **super.print** to invoke the base class version.

```
// Fig. 11.12: QueueInheritance.java
// Class QueueInheritance definition
// Derived from List
package com.deitel.jhtp2.ch17;

public class QueueInheritance extends List {
   public QueueInheritance() { super( "queue" ); }
   public synchronized void enqueue( Object o )
      { insertAtBack( o ); }
   public synchronized Object dequeue()
      throws EmptyListException { return removeFromFront(); }
   public boolean isEmpty() { return super.isEmpty(); }
   public void print() { super.print(); }
}
```

Fig. 17.12 Processing a queue (part 1 of 3).

```
// Fig. 11.12: QueueInheritanceTest.java
// Class QueueInheritanceTest
import com.deitel.jhtp2.ch17.QueueInheritance;
import com.deitel.jhtp2.ch17.EmptyListException;

public class QueueInheritanceTest {
   public static void main( String args[] )
   {
      QueueInheritance objQueue = new QueueInheritance();

      // Create objects to store in the queue
      Boolean b = new Boolean( true );
      Character c = new Character( '$' );
      Integer i = new Integer( 34567 );
      String s = new String( "hello" );

      // Use the enqueue method
      objQueue.enqueue( b );
      objQueue.print();
      objQueue.enqueue( c );
      objQueue.print();
      objQueue.enqueue( i );
      objQueue.print();
      objQueue.enqueue( s );
      objQueue.print();
```

Fig. 17.12 Processing a queue (part 2 of 3).

```

      // Use the dequeue method
      Object removedObj = null;

      try {
         while ( true ) {
            removedObj = objQueue.dequeue();
            System.out.println( removedObj.toString() +
                                " dequeued" );
            objQueue.print();
         }
      }
      catch ( EmptyListException e ) {
         System.err.println( "\n" + e.toString() );
      }
   }
}
```

Fig. 17.12 Processing a queue (part 3 of 3).

```
The queue is: true

The queue is: true $

The queue is: true $ 34567

The queue is: true $ 34567 hello

true dequeued
The queue is: $ 34567 hello

$ dequeued
The queue is: 34567 hello

34567 dequeued
The queue is: hello

hello dequeued
Empty queue

com.deitel.jhtp2.ch17.EmptyListException:
   The queue is empty
```

Fig. 17.13 Sample output from the program in Fig. 17.12.

The **QueueInheritance** class is used in **QueueInheritanceTest**'s **main** method to instantiate a queue of **Object**s called **objQueue**. A **Boolean** object containing **true**, a **Character** object containing **$**, an **Integer** object containing **34567** and a **String** object containing **hello** are enqueued in **objQueue** and then dequeued from **objQueue** in first-in-first-out order. The objects are dequeued from the queue in an infinite **while** loop. When there are no objects left to dequeue, an **EmptyListException** is thrown and a message is displayed stating that the queue is empty.

17.7 Trees

Linked lists, stacks, and queues are *linear data structures.* A tree is a nonlinear, two-dimensional data structure with special properties. Tree nodes contain two or more links. This section discusses *binary trees* (Fig. 17.14)—trees whose nodes all contain two links (none, one, or both of which may be **null**). The *root node* is the first node in a tree. Each link in the root node refers to a *child.* The *left child* is the first node in the *left subtree,* and the *right child* is the first node in the *right subtree.* The children of a node are called *siblings.* A node with no children is called a *leaf node.* Computer scientists normally draw trees from the root node down—exactly the opposite of the way most trees grow in nature.

Common Programming Error 17.4

Not setting to **null** *the links911 in leaf nodes of a tree.*

In this section, a special binary tree called a *binary search tree* is created. A binary search tree (with no duplicate node values) has the characteristic that the values in any left subtree are less than the value in its parent node, and the values in any right subtree are greater than the value in its parent node. Figure 17.15 illustrates a binary search tree with 12 integer values. Note that the shape of the binary search tree that corresponds to a set of data can vary, depending on the order in which the values are inserted into the tree.

Figure 17.16 (output in Fig. 17.17) creates a binary search tree of integers and traverses it (i.e., walks through all its nodes) three ways—using recursive *inorder, preorder* and *postorder traversals.* The program generates 10 random numbers and inserts each in the tree. Class **Tree** is defined in package **com.deitel.jhtp2.ch17** for reuse purposes.

Let us walk through the binary tree program of Fig. 17.16. Method **main** or class **TreeTest** begins by instantiating object **tree** of type **Tree** (line 105). The program randomly generates 10 integers, each of which is inserted in the binary tree through a call to **synchronized** method **insertNode** (line 113). The program then performs preorder, inorder, and postorder traversals (these will be explained shortly) of **tree**.

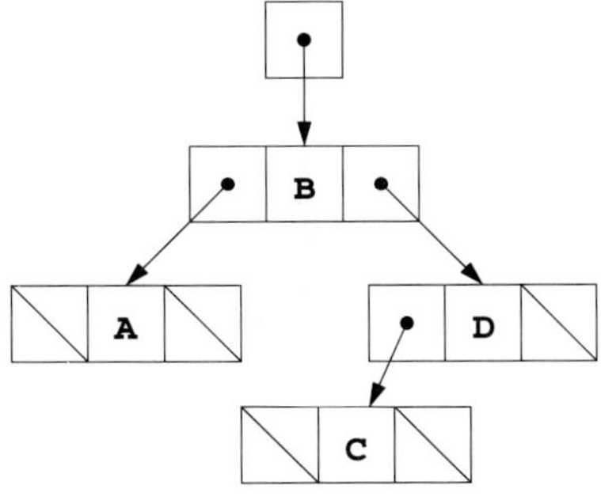

Fig. 17.14 A graphical representation of a binary tree.

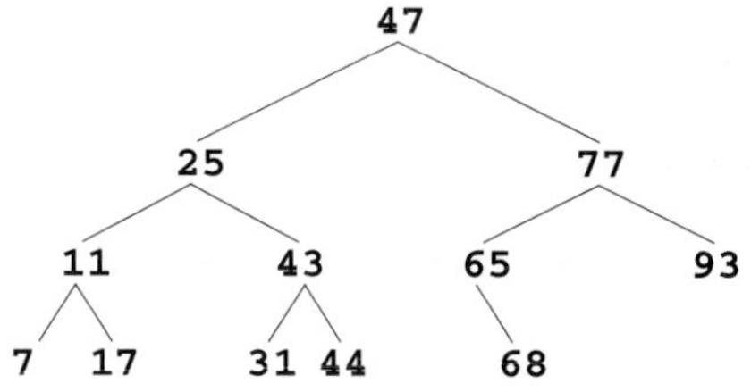

Fig. 17.15 A binary search tree.

```
// Fig. 17.16: Tree.java
package com.deitel.jhtp2.ch17;

// Class TreeNode definition
class TreeNode {
   // friendly access members
   TreeNode left;   // left node
   int data;        // data item
   TreeNode right;  // right node

  // Constructor: initialize data to d and make this a leaf node
   public TreeNode( int d )
   {
      data = d;
      left = right = null;  // this node has no children
   }

   // Insert a TreeNode into a Tree that contains nodes.
   // Ignore duplicate values.
   public synchronized void insert( int d )
   {
      if ( d < data ) {
         if ( left == null )
            left = new TreeNode( d );
         else
            left.insert( d );
      }
      else if ( d > data ) {
         if ( right == null )
            right = new TreeNode( d );
         else
            right.insert( d );
      }
   }
}

```

Fig. 17.16 Creating and traversing a binary tree (part 1 of 4).

```
// Class Tree definition
public class Tree {
   private TreeNode root;

   // Construct an empty Tree of integers
   public Tree() { root = null; }

   // Insert a new node in the binary search tree.
   // If the root node is null, create the root node here.
   // Otherwise, call the insert method of class TreeNode.
   public synchronized void insertNode( int d )
   {
      if ( root == null )
         root = new TreeNode( d );
      else
         root.insert( d );
   }

   // Preorder Traversal
   public void preorderTraversal() { preorderHelper( root ); }

   // Recursive method to perform preorder traversal
   private void preorderHelper( TreeNode node )
   {
      if ( node == null )
         return;

      System.out.print( node.data + " " );
      preorderHelper( node.left );
      preorderHelper( node.right );
   }

   // Inorder Traversal
   public void inorderTraversal() { inorderHelper( root ); }

   // Recursive method to perform inorder traversal
   private void inorderHelper( TreeNode node )
   {
      if ( node == null )
         return;

      inorderHelper( node.left );
      System.out.print( node.data + " " );
      inorderHelper( node.right );
   }

   // Postorder Traversal
   public void postorderTraversal() { postorderHelper( root ); }

```

Fig. 17.16 Creating and traversing a binary tree (part 2 of 4).

```
    // Recursive method to perform postorder traversal
    private void postorderHelper( TreeNode node )
    {
       if ( node == null )
          return;

       postorderHelper( node.left );
       postorderHelper( node.right );
       System.out.print( node.data + " " );
    }
}
```

Fig. 17.16 Creating and traversing a binary tree (part 3 of 4).

```
// Fig. 17.16: TreeTest.java
// This program tests the Tree class.
import com.deitel.jhtp2.ch17.Tree;

// Class TreeTest definition
public class TreeTest {
    public static void main( String args[] )
    {
       Tree tree = new Tree();
       int intVal;

       System.out.println( "Inserting the following values: " );

       for ( int i = 1; i <= 10; i++ ) {
          intVal = ( int ) ( Math.random() * 100 );
          System.out.print( intVal + " " );
          tree.insertNode( intVal );
       }

       System.out.println ( "\n\nPreorder traversal" );
       tree.preorderTraversal();

       System.out.println ( "\n\nInorder traversal" );
       tree.inorderTraversal();

       System.out.println ( "\n\nPostorder traversal" );
       tree.postorderTraversal();
       System.out.println();
    }
}
```

Fig. 17.16 Creating and traversing a binary tree (part 4 of 4).

```
Inserting the following values:
39 69 94 47 50 72 55 41 97 73

Preorder traversal
39 69 47 41 50 55 94 72 73 97

Inorder traversal
39 41 47 50 55 69 72 73 94 97

Postorder traversal
41 55 50 47 73 72 97 94 69 39
```

Fig. 17.17 Sample output from the program of Fig. 17.16.

Now, let us walk through the class definitions and methods. We begin with the **TreeNode** class (line 5) which declares as friendly data the node's **data** value, and references **left** (to the node's left subtree) and **right** (to the node's right subtree). The constructor (line 12) sets the **data** value to the value supplied as a constructor argument, and sets references **left** and **right** to **null** (thus initializing this node to be a leaf node). Method **insert** is invoked by the **Tree** class **insertNode** method to insert data into a tree that is not empty. This method will be discussed in detail shortly.

Class **Tree** has as **private** data **root**—a reference to the root node of the tree. The class has public methods **insertNode** (insert a new node in the tree) and **preorderTraversal**, **inorderTraversal** and **postorderTraversal**, each of which walks the tree in the designated manner. Each of these methods calls its own separate recursive utility method to perform the appropriate operations on the internal representation of the tree. The **Tree** constructor initializes **root** to **null** because the tree is initially empty.

The **Tree** class's **synchronized** method **insertNode** (line 47) first determines if the tree is empty. If so, it allocates a new **TreeNode**, initializes the node with the integer being inserted in the tree, and assigns the new node to the **root** reference. If the tree is not empty, the **TreeNode** method **insert** is called to recursively insert a node into the tree. *A node can only be inserted as a leaf node in a binary search tree.*

The **TreeNode** method **insert** compares the value to be inserted with the **data** value in the root node. If the insert value is less than or equal to the root node data, the program determines if the left subtree is empty (line 23). If so, a new **TreeNode** is allocated and initialized with the integer being inserted and the **left** reference is set to the new node (line 24). Otherwise, **insert** recursively calls itself (line 26) for the left subtree to insert the value in the left subtree. If the insert value is greater than the root node data, the program determines if the right subtree is empty (line 29). If so, a new **TreeNode** is allocated and initialized with the integer being inserted and the **right** reference is set to the new node (line 30). Otherwise, **insert** recursively calls itself (line 32) for the right subtree to insert the value in the right subtree.

Methods **inorderTraversal**, **preorderTraversal** and **postorderTraversal** call helper methods **inorderHelper**, **preorderHelper** and **postorderHelper**, respectively to traverse the tree (Fig. 17.18) and print the node values.

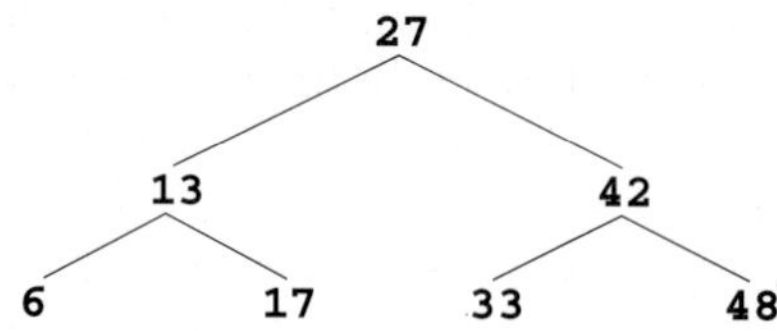

Fig. 17.18 A binary search tree.

The steps for an **inorderTraversal** (line 70) are:

1. Traverse the left subtree with a call to **inorderHelper** (line 73)
2. Process the value in the node (i.e., print the node value).
3. Traverse the right subtree with a call to **inorderHelper**.

The value in a node is not processed until the values in its left subtree are processed. The **inorderTraversal** of the tree in Fig. 17.18 is:

```
6 13 17 27 33 42 48
```

Note that the **inorderTraversal** of a binary search tree prints the node values in ascending order. The process of creating a binary search tree actually sorts the data—and thus this process is called the *binary tree sort*.

The steps for a **preorderTraversal** (line 56) are:

1. Process the value in the node.
2. Traverse the left subtree with a call to **preorderHelper** (line 59)
3. Traverse the right subtree with a call to **preorderHelper**.

The value in each node is processed as the node is visited. After the value in a given node is processed, the values in the left subtree are processed, then the values in the right subtree are processed. The **preorderTraversal** of the tree in Fig. 17.18 is:

```
27 13 6 17 42 33 48
```

The steps for a **postorderTraversal** (line 84) are:

1. Traverse the left subtree with a **postorderHelper** (line 87).
2. Traverse the right subtree with a **postorderHelper**.
3. Process the value in the node.

The value in each node is not printed until the values of its children are printed. The **postorderTraversal** of the tree in Fig. 17.18 is:

```
6 17 13 33 48 42 27
```

The binary search tree facilitates *duplicate elimination*. As the tree is created, attempts to insert a duplicate value are recognized because a duplicate follows the same "go left" or "go right" decisions on each comparison as the original value did. Thus, the duplicate eventually is compared with a node containing the same value. The duplicate value may simply be discarded at this point.

Searching a binary tree for a value that matches a key value is also fast especially for *tightly packed* trees. In a tightly packed tree, each level contains about twice as many elements as the previous level. Figure 17.18 is a tightly packed binary tree. So a binary search tree with n elements has a minimum of $\log_2 n$ levels, and thus as few as $\log_2 n$ comparisons would have to be made either to find a match or to determine that no match exists. This means, for example, that when searching a (tightly packed) 1000-element binary search tree, approximately 10 comparisons need to be made because $2^{10} > 1000$. When searching a (tightly packed) 1,000,000 element binary search tree, approximately 20 comparisons need to be made because $2^{20} > 1{,}000{,}000$.

In the Exercises, algorithms are presented for several other binary tree operations, such as deleting an item from a binary tree, printing a binary tree in a two-dimensional tree format, and performing a level-order traversal of a binary tree. The level-order traversal of a binary tree visits the nodes of the tree row-by-row starting at the root node level. On each level of the tree, the nodes are visited from left to right. Other binary tree exercises include allowing a binary search tree to contain duplicate values, inserting string values in a binary tree, and determining how many levels are contained in a binary tree.

Summary

- Self-referential classes contain members called links that reference objects of the same class type.
- Self-referential classes enable many class objects to be linked together in stacks, queues, lists, and trees.
- Dynamic memory allocation reserves a block of bytes in memory to store an object during program execution.
- A linked list is a linear collection of self-referential class objects.
- A linked list is a dynamic data structure—the length of the list can increase or decrease as necessary.
- Linked lists can continue to grow until memory is exhausted.
- Linked lists provide a mechanism for simple insertion and deletion of data by reference manipulation.
- Stacks and queues are constrained versions of linked lists.
- New stack nodes are added to a stack and are removed from a stack only at the top of the stack. For this reason, a stack is referred to as a last-in, first-out (LIFO) data structure.
- The link in the last node of the stack is set to null to indicate the bottom of the stack.
- The two primary operations used to manipulate a stack are **`push`** and **`pop`**. The **`push`** operation creates a new node and places it on the top of the stack. The **`pop`** operation removes a node from the top of the stack and returns the popped value.
- In a queue data structure, nodes are removed from the head and added to the tail. For this reason, a queue is referred to as a first-in, first-out (FIFO) data structure. The add and remove operations are known as **`enqueue`** and **`dequeue`**.

- Trees are two-dimensional data structures requiring two or more links per node.
- Binary trees contain two links per node.
- The root node is the first node in the tree.
- Each of the references in the root node refers to a child. The left child is the first node in the left subtree, and the right child is the first node in the right subtree. The children of a node are called siblings. Any tree node that does not have any children is called a leaf node.
- A binary search tree has the characteristic that the value in the left child of a node is less than the value in its parent node, and the value in the right child of a node is greater than or equal to the value in its parent node. If there are no duplicate data values, the value in the right child is simply greater than the value in its parent node.
- An inorder traversal of a binary tree traverses the left subtree inorder, processes the value in the root node, then traverses the right subtree inorder. The value in a node is not processed until the values in its left subtree are processed.
- A preorder traversal processes the value in the root node, traverses the left subtree preorder, then traverses the right subtree preorder. The value in each node is processed as the node is encountered.
- A postorder traversal traverses the left subtree postorder, traverses the right subtree postorder, then processes the value in the root node. The value in each node is not processed until the values in both its subtrees are processed.

Terminology

binary search tree
binary tree
binary tree sort
child node
children
delete a node
`dequeue`
duplicate elimination
dynamic data structures
`enqueue`
FIFO (first-in, first-out)
head of a queue
inorder traversal of a binary tree
insert a node
leaf node
left child
left subtree
level-order traversal of a binary tree
LIFO (last-in, first-out)
linear data structure
linked list
node
nonlinear data structure
`null` reference
parent node
`pop`
postorder traversal of a binary tree
preorder traversal of a binary tree
`push`
queue
recursive tree traversal algorithms
right child
right subtree
root node
self-referential class
stack
subtree
tail of a queue
top of a stack
traversal
tree
visit a node

Common Programming Errors

17.1 Not setting the link in the last node of a list to **null**.

17.2 Not setting the link in the bottom node of a stack to **null**.

17.3 Not setting the link in the last node of a queue to **null**.

17.4 Not setting to **null** the links in leaf nodes of a tree.

Good Programming Practice

17.1 When using **new**, test for an ***OutOfMemoryException***. Perform appropriate error processing if the requested memory is not allocated.

Performance Tips

17.1 An array can be declared to contain more elements than the number of items expected, but this can waste memory. Linked lists can provide better memory utilization in these situations. Linked lists allow the program to adapt at runtime.

17.2 Insertion into a linked list is fast—only two references have to be modified. All existing nodes remain at their current locations in memory.

17.3 Insertion and deletion in a sorted array can be time consuming—all the elements following the inserted or deleted element must be shifted appropriately.

17.4 The elements of an array are stored contiguously in memory. This allows immediate access to any array element because the address of any element can be calculated directly based on its position relative to the beginning of the array. Linked lists do not afford such immediate access to their elements.

17.5 Using dynamic memory allocation (instead of arrays) for data structures that grow and shrink at execution time can save memory. Keep in mind, however, that references occupy space, and that dynamic memory allocation incurs the overhead of method calls.

Self-Review Exercises

17.1 Fill in the blanks in each of the following:

a) A self-_________ class is used to form dynamic data structures. that can grow and shrink at execution time.

b) Operator ___________ is used to dynamically allocate memory; this operator returns a reference to the allocated memory.

c) A _________ is a constrained version of a linked list in which nodes can be inserted and deleted only from the start of the list; this data structure returns node values in last-in-first-out order.

d) A method that does not alter a linked list, but simply looks at the list to determine if it is empty is referred to as a _________method.

e) A queue is referred to as a _________ data structure because the first nodes inserted are the first nodes removed.

f) The reference to the next node in a linked list is referred to as a ________.
g) Automatically reclaiming dynamically allocated memory in Java is called ________.
h) A ________ is a constrained version of a linked list in which nodes can be inserted only at the end of the list and deleted only from the start of the list.
i) A ________ is a nonlinear, two-dimensional data structure that contains nodes with two or more links.
j) A stack is referred to as a ________ data structure because the last node inserted is the first node removed.
k) The nodes of a ________ tree contain two link members.
l) The first node of a tree is the ________ node.
m) Each link in a tree node refers to a ________ or ________ of that node.
n) A tree node that has no children is called a ________ node.
o) The four traversal algorithms we mentioned in the text for binary search trees are ________, ________, ________ and ________.

17.2 What are the differences between a linked list and a stack?

17.3 What are the differences between a stack and a queue?

17.4 Perhaps a more appropriate title for this chapter would have been "Reusable Data Structures." Comment on how each of the following entities or concepts contributes to the reusability of data structures:

a) classes
b) inheritance
c) composition.

17.5 Manually provide the inorder, preorder, and postorder traversals of the binary search tree of Fig. 17.19.

Answers to Self-Review Exercises

17.1 a) referential. b) **new**. c) stack. d) predicate. e) first-in-first-out (FIFO). f) link. g) garbage collection. h) queue. i) tree. j) last-in-first-out (LIFO). k) binary. l) root. m) child or subtree. n) leaf. o) inorder, preorder, postorder, and level-order.

17.2 It is possible to insert a node anywhere in a linked list and remove a node from anywhere in a linked list. Nodes in a stack may only be inserted at the top of the stack and removed from the top of a stack.

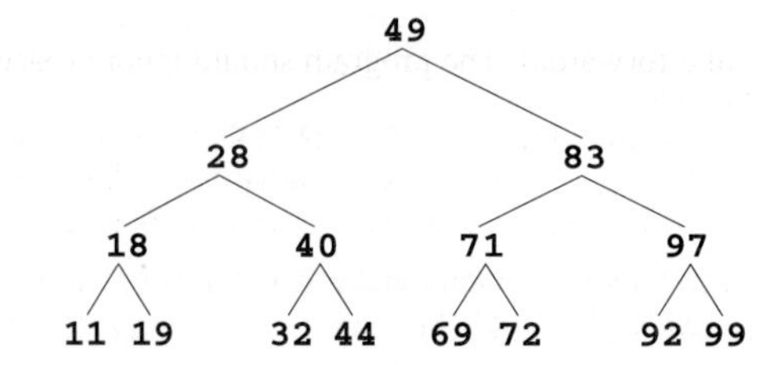

Fig. 17.19 A 15-node binary search tree.

17.3 A queue has references to both its head and its tail so that nodes may be inserted at the tail and deleted from the head. A stack has a single reference to the top of the stack where both insertion and deletion of nodes are performed.

17.4 a) Classes allow us to instantiate as many data structure objects of a certain type (i.e., class) as we wish.

b) Inheritance enables us to reuse code from a superclass in a subclass so that the derived class data structure is also a base class data structure.

c) Composition enables us to reuse code by making a class object data structure a member of a composed class; if we make the class object a **private** member of the composed class, then the class object's public methods are not available through the composed object's interface.

17.5 The inorder traversal is:

```
11 18 19 28 32 40 44 49 69 71 72 83 92 97 99
```

The preorder traversal is:

```
49 28 18 11 19 40 32 44 83 71 69 72 97 92 99
```

The postorder traversal is:

```
11 19 18 32 44 40 28 69 72 71 92 99 97 83 49
```

Exercises

17.6 Write a program that concatenates two linked list objects of characters. Class **ListConcat** should include method **concatenate** that takes references to both list objects as arguments and concatenates the second list to the first list.

17.7 Write a program that merges two ordered list objects of integers into a single ordered list object of integers. Method **merge** or class **ListMerge** should receive references to each of the list objects to be merged, and should return a reference to the merged list object.

17.8 Write a program that inserts 25 random integers from 0 to 100 in order in a linked list object. The program should calculate the sum of the elements, and the floating-point average of the elements.

17.9 Write a program that creates a linked list object of 10 characters, then creates a second list object containing a copy of the first list, but in reverse order.

17.10 Write a program that inputs a line of text and uses a stack object to print the line reversed.

17.11 Write a program that uses a stack to determine if a string is a palindrome (i.e., the string is spelled identically backwards and forwards). The program should ignore spaces and punctuation.

17.12 Stacks are used by compilers to help in the process of evaluating expressions and generating machine language code. In this and the next exercise, we investigate how compilers evaluate arithmetic expressions consisting only of constants, operators, and parentheses.

Humans generally write expressions like **3 + 4** and **7 / 9** in which the operator (**+** or **/** here) is written between its operands—this is called *infix notation*. Computers "prefer" *postfix notation* in which the operator is written to the right of its two operands. The preceding infix expressions would appear in postfix notation as **3 4 +** and **7 9 /**, respectively.

To evaluate a complex infix expression, a compiler would first convert the expression to postfix notation, and then evaluate the postfix version of the expression. Each of these algorithms requires only a single left-to-right pass of the expression. Each algorithm uses a stack object in support of its operation, and in each algorithm the stack is used for a different purpose.

In this exercise, you will write a Java version of the infix-to-postfix conversion algorithm. In the next exercise, you will write a Java version of the postfix expression evaluation algorithm. Later in the chapter, you will discover that code you write in this exercise can help you implement a complete working compiler.

Write class **InfixToPostfixConverter** to convert an ordinary infix arithmetic expression (assume a valid expression is entered) with single digit integers such as

```
(6 + 2) * 5 - 8 / 4
```

to a postfix expression. The postfix version of the preceding infix expression is

```
6 2 + 5 * 8 4 / -
```

The program should read the expression into **StringBuffer infix**, and use one of the stack classes implemented in this chapter to help create the postfix expression in **Stringbuffer postfix**. The algorithm for creating a postfix expression is as follows:

a) Push a left parenthesis **'('** on the stack.
b) Append a right parenthesis **')'** to the end of **infix**.
c) While the stack is not empty, read **infix** from left to right and do the following
   If the current character in **infix** is a digit, append it to **postfix**.
   If the current character in **infix** is a left parenthesis, push it on the stack.
   If the current character in **infix** is an operator,
      Pop operators (if there are any) at the top of the stack while they have equal or higher precedence than the current operator, and append the popped operators to **postfix**.
      Push the current character in **infix** on the stack.
   If the current character in **infix** is a right parenthesis
      Pop operators from the top of the stack and append them to **postfix** until a left parenthesis is at the top of the stack.
      Pop (and discard) the left parenthesis from the stack.

The following arithmetic operations are allowed in an expression:

+ addition
- subtraction
***** multiplication
/ division
^ exponentiation
% modulus

The stack should be maintained with stack nodes that each contain an instance variable and a reference to the next stack node.

Some of the methods you may want to provide are:

a) Method **convertToPostfix** that converts the infix expression to postfix notation.
b) Method **isOperator** that determines if **c** is an operator.
c) Method **precedence** that determines if the precedence of **operator1** (from the infix expression) is less than, equal to, or greater than the precedence of **operator2** (from

the stack). The method returns **true** if **operator1** has lower precedence than **operator2**. Otherwise, **false** is returned.

d) Method **stackTop** (this should be added to the stack class) that returns the top value of the stack without popping the stack.

17.13 Write class **PostfixEvaluator** that evaluates a postfix expression (assume it is valid) such as

```
6 2 + 5 * 8 4 / -
```

The program should read a postfix expression consisting of digits and operators into a **StringBuffer**. Using modified versions of the stack methods implemented earlier in this chapter, the program should scan the expression and evaluate it. The algorithm is as follows:

a) Append a right parenthesis (**')'**) to the end of the postfix expression. When the right parenthesis character is encountered, no further processing is necessary.

b) While right parenthesis character has not been encountered, read the expression from left to right.

    If the current character is a digit,
        Push its integer value on the stack (the integer value of a digit character is its value in the computer's character set minus the value of **'0'** in the computer's character set).
    Otherwise, if the current character is an *operator*,
        Pop the two top elements of the stack into variables **x** and **y**.
        Calculate **y** *operator* **x**.
        Push the result of the calculation onto the stack.

c) When the right parenthesis is encountered in the expression, pop the top value of the stack. This is the result of the postfix expression.

Note: In 2) above, if the operator is **'/'**, the top of the stack is **2**, and the next element in the stack is **8**, then pop **2** into **x**, pop **8** into **y**, evaluate **8 / 2**, and push the result, **4**, back on the stack. This note also applies to operator **'-'**. The arithmetic operations allowed in an expression are:

+ addition
- subtraction
***** multiplication
/ division
^ exponentiation
% modulus

The stack should be maintained with one of the stack classes introduced in this chapter. You may want to provide the following methods:

a) Method **evaluatePostfixExpression** that evaluates the postfix expression.
b) Method **calculate** that evaluates the expression **op1 operator op2**.
c) Method **push** that pushes a value on the stack.
d) Method **pop** that pops a value off the stack.
e) Method **isEmpty** that determines if the stack is empty.
f) Method **printStack** that prints the stack.

17.14 Modify the postfix evaluator program of Exercise 17.13 so that it can process integer operands larger than 9.

17.15 *(Supermarket simulation)* Write a program that simulates a check-out line at a supermarket. The line is a queue object. Customers (i.e., customer objects) arrive in random integer intervals of 1 to 4 minutes. Also, each customer is serviced in random integer intervals of 1 to 4 minutes. Obviously, the rates need to be balanced. If the average arrival rate is larger than the average service rate, the queue will grow infinitely. Even with "balanced" rates, randomness can still cause long lines. Run the supermarket simulation for a 12-hour day (720 minutes) using the following algorithm:

a) Choose a random integer between 1 and 4 to determine the minute at which the first customer arrives.
b) At the first customer's arrival time
   Determine customer's service time (random integer from 1 to 4);
   Begin servicing the customer;
   Schedule the arrival time of the next customer (random integer 1 to 4 added to the current time).
c) For each minute of the day:
   If the next customer arrives,
      Say so,
      Enqueue the customer;
      Schedule the arrival time of the next customer;
   If service was completed for the last customer;
      Say so,
      Dequeue next customer to be serviced,
      Determine customer's service completion time (random integer from 1 to 4
         added to the current time).

Now run your simulation for 720 minutes and answer each of the following:

a) What is the maximum number of customers in the queue at any time?
b) What is the longest wait any one customer experiences?
c) What happens if the arrival interval is changed from 1-to-4 minutes to 1-to-3 minutes?

17.16 Modify the program of Fig. 17.16 to allow the binary tree object to contain duplicates.

17.17 Write a program based on the program of Fig. 17.16 that inputs a line of text, tokenizes the sentence into separate words (you may want to use the **`StreamTokenizer`** class from the **`java.io`** package), inserts the words in a binary search tree, and prints the inorder, preorder, and postorder traversals of the tree.

17.18 In this chapter, we saw that duplicate elimination is straightforward when creating a binary search tree. Describe how you would perform duplicate elimination using only a single-subscripted array. Compare the performance of array-based duplicate elimination with the performance of binary-search-tree-based duplicate elimination.

17.19 Write a method **`depth`** that receives a binary tree and determines how many levels it has.

17.20 (*Recursively print a list backwards*) Write a method **`printListBackwards`** that recursively outputs the items in a linked list object in reverse order. Write a test program that creates a sorted list of integers and prints the list in reverse order.

17.21 (*Recursively search a list*) Write a method **`searchList`** that recursively searches a linked list object for a specified value. Method **`searchList`** should return a reference to the value if it is found; otherwise, null should be returned. Use your method in a test program that creates a list of integers. The program should prompt the user for a value to locate in the list.

17.22 (*Binary tree delete*) In this exercise, we discuss deleting items from binary search trees. The deletion algorithm is not as straightforward as the insertion algorithm. There are three cases that are encountered when deleting an item—the item is contained in a leaf node (i.e., it has no children), the item is contained in a node that has one child, or the item is contained in a node that has two children.

If the item to be deleted is contained in a leaf node, the node is deleted and the reference in the parent node is set to null.

If the item to be deleted is contained in a node with one child, the reference in the parent node is set to reference the child node and the node containing the data item is deleted. This causes the child node to take the place of the deleted node in the tree.

The last case is the most difficult. When a node with two children is deleted, another node in the tree must take its place. However, the reference in the parent node cannot simply be assigned to reference one of the children of the node to be deleted. In most cases, the resulting binary search tree would not adhere to the following characteristic of binary search trees (with no duplicate values): *The values in any left subtree are less than the value in the parent node, and the values in any right subtree are greater than the value in the parent node.*

Which node is used as a *replacement node* to maintain this characteristic? Either the node containing the largest value in the tree less than the value in the node being deleted, or the node containing the smallest value in the tree greater than the value in the node being deleted. Let us consider the node with the smaller value. In a binary search tree, the largest value less than a parent's value is located in the left subtree of the parent node and is guaranteed to be contained in the rightmost node of the subtree. This node is located by walking down the left subtree to the right until the reference to the right child of the current node is null. We are now referencing the replacement node which is either a leaf node or a node with one child to its left. If the replacement node is a leaf node, the steps to perform the deletion are as follows:

a) Store the reference to the node to be deleted in a temporary reference variable.
b) Set the reference in the parent of the node being deleted to reference the replacement node.
c) Set the reference in the parent of the replacement node to null.
d) Set the reference to the right subtree in the replacement node to reference the right subtree of the node to be deleted.

The deletion steps for a replacement node with a left child are similar to those for a replacement node with no children, but the algorithm also must move the child into the replacement node's position in the tree. If the replacement node is a node with a left child, the steps to perform the deletion are as follows:

a) Store the reference to the node to be deleted in a temporary reference variable.
b) Set the reference in the parent of the node being deleted to reference the replacement node.
c) Set the reference in the parent of the replacement node reference to the left child of the replacement node.
d) Set the reference to the right subtree in the replacement node reference to the right subtree of the node to be deleted.

Write method **deleteNode** which takes as its argument the value to be deleted. Method **deleteNode** should locate in the tree the node containing the value to be deleted and use the algorithms discussed here to delete the node. If the value is not found in the tree, the method should print a message that indicates whether or not the value is deleted. Modify the program of Fig. 17.16 to use this method. After deleting an item, call the methods **inorderTraversal**, **preorderTraversal**, and **postorderTraversal** methods to confirm that the delete operation was performed correctly.

17.23 (*Binary tree search*) Write method **binaryTreeSearch** that attempts to locate a specified value in a binary search tree object. The method should take as an argument a search key to be located. If the node containing the search key is found, the method should return a reference to that node; otherwise, the method should return a null reference.

17.24 (*Level-order binary tree traversal*) The program of Fig. 17.16 illustrated three recursive methods of traversing a binary tree—inorder, preorder, and postorder traversals. This exercise presents the *level-order traversal* of a binary tree in which the node values are printed level-by-level starting at the root node level. The nodes on each level are printed from left to right. The level-order traversal is not a recursive algorithm. It uses a queue object to control the output of the nodes. The algorithm is as follows:

a) Insert the root node in the queue.
b) While there are nodes left in the queue,
    Get the next node in the queue;
    Print the node's value.
    If the reference to the left child of the node is not null;
        Insert the left child node in the queue.
    If the reference to the right child of the node is not null,
        Insert the right child node in the queue.

Write method **levelOrder** to perform a level-order traversal of a binary tree object. Modify the program of Fig 17.16 to use this method. (Note: You will also need to use queue-processing methods of Fig. 17.12 in this program.)

17.25 (*Printing trees*) Write a recursive method **outputTree** to display a binary tree object on the screen. The method should output the tree row-by-row with the top of the tree at the left of the screen and the bottom of the tree toward the right of the screen. Each row is output vertically. For example, the binary tree illustrated in Fig. 17.19 is output as follows:

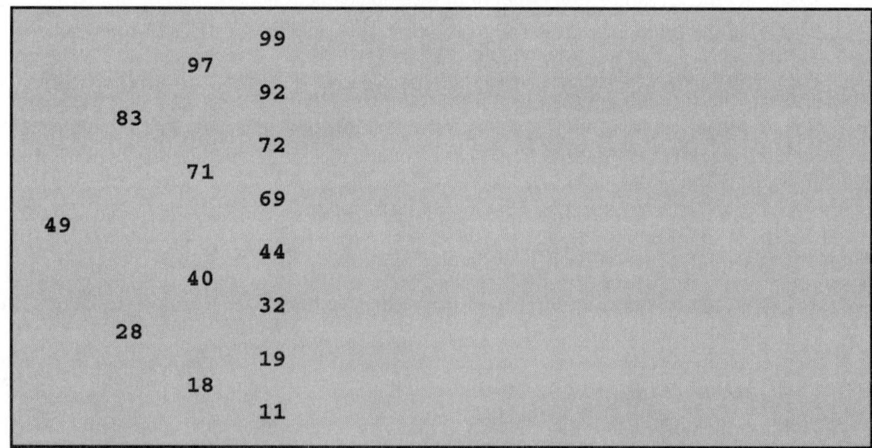
```
                    99
               97
                    92
          83
                    72
               71
                    69
     49
                    44
               40
                    32
          28
                    19
               18
                    11
```

Note the rightmost leaf node appears at the top of the output in the rightmost column and the root node appears at the left of the output. Each column of output starts five spaces to the right of the previous column. Method **outputTree** should receive an argument **totalSpaces** representing the number of spaces preceding the value to be output (this variable should start at zero so the root node is output at the left of the screen). The method uses a modified inorder traversal to output the tree—it starts at the rightmost node in the tree and works back to the left. The algorithm is as follows:

c) While the reference to the current node is not null,
Recursively call **outputTree** with the right subtree of the current node and **totalSpaces** + 5.
Use a **for** structure to count from 1 to **totalSpaces** and output spaces.
Output the value in the current node.
Set the reference to the current node to refer to the left subtree of the current node.
Increment **totalSpaces** by 5.

Special Section: Building Your Own Compiler

In Exercises 5.42 and 5.43, we introduced Simpletron Machine Language (SML) and you implemented a Simpletron computer simulator to execute programs written in SML. In this section, we build a compiler that converts programs written in a high-level programming language to SML. This section "ties" together the entire programming process. You will write programs in this new high-level language, compile these programs on the compiler you build, and run the programs on the simulator you built in Exercise 7.43. You should make every effort to implement your compiler in an object-oriented manner.

17.26 (*The Simple Language*) Before we begin building the compiler, we discuss a simple, yet powerful, high-level language similar to early versions of the popular language Basic. We call the language *Simple*. Every Simple *statement* consists of a *line number* and a Simple *instruction*. Line numbers must appear in ascending order. Each instruction begins with one of the following Simple *commands*: **rem**, **input**, **let**, **print**, **goto**, **if/goto**, or **end** (see Fig. 17.20). All commands except **end** can be used repeatedly. Simple evaluates only integer expressions using the **+**, **-**, *****, and **/** operators. These operators have the same precedence as in Java. Parentheses can be used to change the order of evaluation of an expression.

Command	Example statement	Description
rem	**50 rem this is a remark**	Any text following the command **rem** is for documentation purposes only and is ignored by the compiler.
input	**30 input x**	Display a question mark to prompt the user to enter an integer. Read that integer from the keyboard and store the integer in **x**.
let	**80 let u = 4 * (j - 56)**	Assign **u** the value of **4 * (j - 56)**. Note that an arbitrarily complex expression can appear to the right of the equal sign.
print	**10 print w**	Display the value of **w**.
goto	**70 goto 45**	Transfer program control to line **45**.
if/goto	**35 if i == z goto 80**	Compare **i** and **z** for equality and transfer program control to line **80** if the condition is true; otherwise, continue execution with the next statement.
end	**99 end**	Terminate program execution.

Fig. 17.20 Simple commands.

Our Simple compiler recognizes only lowercase letters. All characters in a Simple file should be lowercase (uppercase letters result in a syntax error unless they appear in a **rem** statement in which case they are ignored). A *variable name* is a single letter. Simple does not allow descriptive variable names, so variables should be explained in remarks to indicate their use in a program. Simple uses only integer variables. Simple does not have variable declarations—merely mentioning a variable name in a program causes the variable to be declared and initialized to zero automatically. The syntax of Simple does not allow string manipulation (reading a string, writing a string, comparing strings, etc.). If a string is encountered in a Simple program (after a command other than **rem**), the compiler generates a syntax error. The first version of our compiler assumes that Simple programs are entered correctly. Exercise 17.29 asks the student to modify the compiler to perform syntax error checking.

Simple uses the conditional **if/goto** statement and the unconditional **goto** statement to alter the flow of control during program execution. If the condition in the **if/goto** statement is true, control is transferred to a specific line of the program. The following relational and equality operators are valid in an **if/goto** statement: **<**, **>**, **<=**, **>=**, **==**, or **!=**. The precedence of these operators is the same as in Java.

Let us now consider several programs that demonstrate Simple's features. The first program (Fig. 17.21) reads two integers from the keyboard, stores the values in variables **a** and **b**, and computes and prints their sum (stored in variable **c**).

The program of Fig. 17.22 determines and prints the larger of two integers. The integers are input from the keyboard and stored in **s** and **t**. The **if/goto** statement tests the condition **s >= t**. If the condition is true, control is transferred to line **90** and **s** is output; otherwise, **t** is output and control is transferred to the **end** statement in line **99** where the program terminates.

Simple does not provide a repetition structure (such as Java's **for**, **while**, or **do/while**). However, Simple can simulate each of Java's repetition structures using the **if/goto** and **goto** statements. Figure 17.23 uses a sentinel-controlled loop to calculate the squares of several integers. Each integer is input from the keyboard and stored in variable **j**. If the value entered is the sentinel **-9999**, control is transferred to line **99** where the program terminates. Otherwise, **k** is assigned the square of **j**, **k** is output to the screen, and control is passed to line **20** where the next integer is input.

Using the sample programs of Fig. 17.21, Fig. 17.22, and Fig. 17.23 as your guide, write a Simple program to accomplish each of the following:

```
10 rem   determine and print the sum of two integers
15 rem
20 rem   input the two integers
30 input a
40 input b
45 rem
50 rem   add integers and store result in c
60 let c = a + b
65 rem
70 rem   print the result
80 print c
90 rem   terminate program execution
99 end
```

Fig. 17.21 Simple program that determines the sum of two integers.

```
10 rem   determine and print the larger of two integers
20 input s
30 input t
32 rem
35 rem   test if s >= t
40 if s >= t goto 90
45 rem
50 rem   t is greater than s, so print t
60 print t
70 goto 99
75 rem
80 rem   s is greater than or equal to t, so print s
90 print s
99 end
```

Fig. 17.22 Simple program that finds the larger of two integers.

```
10 rem   calculate the squares of several integers
20 input j
23 rem
25 rem   test for sentinel value
30 if j == -9999 goto 99
33 rem
35 rem   calculate square of j and assign result to k
40 let k = j * j
50 print k
53 rem
55 rem   loop to get next j
60 goto 20
99 end
```

Fig. 17.23 Calculate the squares of several integers.

a) Input three integers, determine their average, and print the result.
b) Use a sentinel-controlled loop to input 10 integers and compute and print their sum.
c) Use a counter-controlled loop to input 7 integers, some positive and some negative, and compute and print their average.
d) Input a series of integers and determine and print the largest. The first integer input indicates how many numbers should be processed.
e) Input 10 integers and print the smallest.
f) Calculate and print the sum of the even integers from 2 to 30.
g) Calculate and print the product of the odd integers from 1 to 9.

17.27 *(Building A Compiler; Prerequisite: Complete Exercises 5.42, 5.43, 17.12, 17.13, and 17.26)* Now that the Simple language has been presented (Exercise 17.26), we discuss how to build a Simple compiler. First, we consider the process by which a Simple program is converted to SML and executed by the Simpletron simulator (see Fig. 17.24). A file containing a Simple program is read by the compiler and converted to SML code. The SML code is output to a file on disk, in which SML instructions appear one per line. The SML file is then loaded into the Simpletron simulator, and the re-

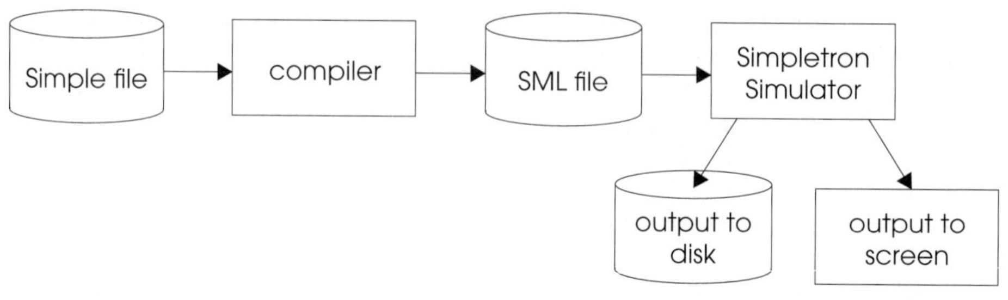

Fig. 17.24 Writing, compiling, and executing a Simple language program.

sults are sent to a file on disk and to the screen. Note that the Simpletron program developed in Exercise 5.19 took its input from the keyboard. It must be modified to read from a file so it can run the programs produced by our compiler.

The Simple compiler performs two *passes* of the Simple program to convert it to SML. The first pass constructs a *symbol table* (object) in which every *line number* (object), *variable name* (object) and *constant* (object) of the Simple program is stored with its type and corresponding location in the final SML code (the symbol table is discussed in detail below). The first pass also produces the corresponding SML instruction object(s) for each of the Simple statements (object, etc.). If the Simple program contains statements that transfer control to a line later in the program, the first pass results in an SML program containing some "unfinished" instructions. The second pass of the compiler locates and completes the unfinished instructions, and outputs the SML program to a file.

First Pass

The compiler begins by reading one statement of the Simple program into memory. The line must be separated into its individual *tokens* (i.e., "pieces" of a statement) for processing and compilation (the **StreamTokenizer** class from the **java.io** package can be used). Recall that every statement begins with a line number followed by a command. As the compiler breaks a statement into tokens, if the token is a line number, a variable, or a constant, it is placed in the symbol table. A line number is placed in the symbol table only if it is the first token in a statement. The **symbolTable** object is an array of **tableEntry** objects representing each symbol in the program. There is no restriction on the number of symbols that can appear in the program. Therefore, the **symbolTable** for a particular program could be large. Make the **symbolTable** a 100-element array for now. You can increase or decrease its size once the program is working.

Each **tableEntry** object contains three members. Member **symbol** is an integer containing the Unicode representation of a variable (remember that variable names are single characters), a line number or a constant. Member **type** is one of the following characters indicating the symbol's type: **'C'** for constant, **'L'** for line number, or **'V'** for variable. Member **location** contains the Simpletron memory location (**00** to **99**) to which the symbol refers. Simpletron memory is an array of 100 integers in which SML instructions and data are stored. For a line number, the location is the element in the Simpletron memory array at which the SML instructions for the Simple statement begin. For a variable or constant, the location is the element in the Simpletron memory array in which the variable or constant is stored. Variables and constants are allocated from the end of Simpletron's memory backwards. The first variable or constant is stored at location **99**, the next at location **98**, etc.

The symbol table plays an integral part in converting Simple programs to SML. We learned in Chapter 5 that an SML instruction is a four-digit integer comprised of two parts—the *operation code* and the *operand*. The operation code is determined by commands in Simple. For example, the simple command **input** corresponds to SML operation code **10** (read), and the Simple command **print** corresponds to SML operation code **11** (write). The operand is a memory location containing the data on which the operation code performs its task (e.g., operation code **10** reads a value from the keyboard and stores it in the memory location specified by the operand). The compiler searches **symbolTable** to determine the Simpletron memory location for each symbol so the corresponding location can be used to complete the SML instructions.

The compilation of each Simple statement is based on its command. For example, after the line number in a **rem** statement is inserted in the symbol table, the remainder of the statement is ignored by the compiler because a remark is for documentation purposes only. The **input**, **print**, **goto** and **end** statements correspond to the SML *read*, *write*, *branch* (to a specific location) and *halt* instructions. Statements containing these Simple commands are converted directly to SML (note that a **goto** statement may contain an unresolved reference if the specified line number refers to a statement further into the Simple program file; this is sometimes called a forward reference).

When a **goto** statement is compiled with an unresolved reference, the SML instruction must be *flagged* to indicate that the second pass of the compiler must complete the instruction. The flags are stored in 100-element array **flags** of type **int** in which each element is initialized to **-1**. If the memory location to which a line number in the Simple program refers is not yet known (i.e., it is not in the symbol table), the line number is stored in array **flags** in the element with the same subscript as the incomplete instruction. The operand of the incomplete instruction is set to **00** temporarily. For example, an unconditional branch instruction (making a forward reference) is left as **+4000** until the second pass of the compiler. The second pass of the compiler will be described shortly.

Compilation of **if/goto** and **let** statements is more complicated than other statements—they are the only statements that produce more than one SML instruction. For an **if/goto** statement, the compiler produces code to test the condition and to branch to another line if necessary. The result of the branch could be an unresolved reference. Each of the relational and equality operators can be simulated using SML's *branch zero* and *branch negative* instructions (or possibly a combination of both).

For a **let** statement, the compiler produces code to evaluate an arbitrarily complex arithmetic expression consisting of integer variables and/or constants. Expressions should separate each operand and operator with spaces. Exercises 17.12 and 17.13 presented the infix-to-postfix conversion algorithm and the postfix evaluation algorithm used by compilers to evaluate expressions. Before proceeding with your compiler, you should complete each of these exercises. When a compiler encounters an expression, it converts the expression from infix notation to postfix notation, then evaluates the postfix expression.

How is it that the compiler produces the machine language to evaluate an expression containing variables? The postfix evaluation algorithm contains a "hook" where the compiler can generate SML instructions rather than actually evaluating the expression. To enable this "hook" in the compiler, the postfix evaluation algorithm must be modified to search the symbol table for each symbol it encounters (and possibly insert it), determine the symbol's corresponding memory location, and *push the memory location on the stack (instead of the symbol).* When an operator is encountered in the postfix expression, the two memory locations at the top of the stack are popped and machine language for effecting the operation is produced using the memory locations as operands. The result of each subexpression is stored in a temporary location in memory and pushed back onto the stack so the evaluation of the postfix expression can continue. When postfix evaluation is complete, the memory location containing the result is the only location left on the stack. This is popped and SML instructions are generated to assign the result to the variable at the left of the **let** statement.

Second Pass

The second pass of the compiler performs two tasks: resolve any unresolved references and output the SML code to a file. Resolution of references occurs as follows:

a) Search the **flags** array for an unresolved reference (i.e., an element with a value other than **-1**).
b) Locate the object in array **symbolTable** containing the symbol stored in the **flags** array (be sure that the type of the symbol is **'L'** for line number).
c) Insert the memory location from member **location** into the instruction with the unresolved reference (remember that an instruction containing an unresolved reference has operand **00**).
d) Repeat steps 1, 2, and 3 until the end of the **flags** array is reached.

After the resolution process is complete, the entire array containing the SML code is output to a disk file with one SML instruction per line. This file can be read by the Simpletron for execution (after the simulator is modified to read its input from a file). Compiling your first Simple program into an SML file and then executing that file should give you a real sense of personal accomplishment.

A Complete Example

The following example illustrates a complete conversion of a Simple program to SML as it will be performed by the Simple compiler. Consider a Simple program that inputs an integer and sums the values from 1 to that integer. The program and the SML instructions produced by the first pass of the Simple compiler are illustrated in Fig. 17.25. The symbol table constructed by the first pass is shown in Fig. 17.26.

Most Simple statements convert directly to single SML instructions. The exceptions in this program are remarks, the **if/goto** statement in line **20**, and the **let** statements. Remarks do not translate into machine language. However, the line number for a remark is placed in the symbol table in case the line number is referenced in a **goto** statement or an **if/goto** statement. Line **20** of the program specifies that if the condition **y == x** is true, program control is transferred to line **60**. Because line **60** appears later in the program, the first pass of the compiler has not as yet placed **60** in the symbol table (statement line numbers are placed in the symbol table only when they appear as the first token in a statement). Therefore, it is not possible at this time to determine the operand of the SML *branch zero* instruction at location **03** in the array of SML instructions. The compiler places **60** in location **03** of the **flags** array to indicate that the second pass completes this instruction.

We must keep track of the next instruction location in the SML array because there is not a one-to-one correspondence between Simple statements and SML instructions. For example, the **if/goto** statement of line **20** compiles into three SML instructions. Each time an instruction is produced, we must increment the *instruction counter* to the next location in the SML array. Note that the size of Simpletron's memory could present a problem for Simple programs with many statements, variables and constants. It is conceivable that the compiler will run out of memory. To test for this case, your program should contain a *data counter* to keep track of the location at which the next variable or constant will be stored in the SML array. If the value of the instruction counter is larger than the value of the data counter, the SML array is full. In this case, the compilation process should terminate and the compiler should print an error message indicating that it ran out of memory during compilation. This serves to emphasize that although the programmer is freed from the burdens of managing memory by the compiler, the compiler itself must carefully determine the placement of instructions and data in memory, and must check for such errors as memory being exhausted during the compilation process.

Simple program	SML location and instruction	Description
`5 rem sum 1 to x`	*none*	**rem** ignored
`10 input x`	00 +1099	read **x** into location **99**
`15 rem check y == x`	*none*	**rem** ignored
`20 if y == x goto 60`	01 +2098	load **y** (**98**) into accumulator
	02 +3199	sub **x** (**99**) from accumulator
	03 +4200	branch zero to unresolved location
`25 rem increment y`	*none*	**rem** ignored
`30 let y = y + 1`	04 +2098	load **y** into accumulator
	05 +3097	add **1** (**97**) to accumulator
	06 +2196	store in temporary location **96**
	07 +2096	load from temporary location **96**
	08 +2198	store accumulator in **y**
`35 rem add y to total`	*none*	**rem** ignored
`40 let t = t + y`	09 +2095	load **t** (**95**) into accumulator
	10 +3098	add **y** to accumulator
	11 +2194	store in temporary location **94**
	12 +2094	load from temporary location **94**
	13 +2195	store accumulator in **t**
`45 rem loop y`	*none*	**rem** ignored
`50 goto 20`	14 +4001	branch to location **01**
`55 rem output result`	*none*	**rem** ignored
`60 print t`	15 +1195	output **t** to screen
`99 end`	16 +4300	terminate execution

Fig. 17.25 SML instructions produced after the compiler's first pass.

A Step-by-Step View of the Compilation Process

Let us now walk through the compilation process for the Simple program in Fig. 17.25. The compiler reads the first line of the program

```
5 rem sum 1 to x
```

into memory. The first token in the statement (the line number) is determined using the **StreamTokenizer** class (see Chapter 8 for a discussion of Java's string manipulation methods). The token returned by the **StreamTokenizer** is converted to an integer using **Integer.parseInt()** so the symbol **5** can be located in the symbol table. If the symbol is not found, it is inserted in the symbol table.

Symbol	Type	Location
`5`	`L`	`00`
`10`	`L`	`00`
`'x'`	`V`	`99`
`15`	`L`	`01`
`20`	`L`	`01`
`'y'`	`V`	`98`
`25`	`L`	`04`
`30`	`L`	`04`
`1`	`C`	`97`
`35`	`L`	`09`
`40`	`L`	`09`
`'t'`	`V`	`95`
`45`	`L`	`14`
`50`	`L`	`14`
`55`	`L`	`15`
`60`	`L`	`15`
`99`	`L`	`16`

Fig. 17.26 Symbol table for program of Fig. 17.25.

Since we are at the beginning of the program and this is the first line, no symbols are in the table yet. So, **`5`** is inserted into the symbol table as type **`L`** (line number) and assigned the first location in SML array (**`00`**). Although this line is a remark, a space in the symbol table is still allocated for the line number (in case it is referenced by a **`goto`** or an **`if/goto`**). No SML instruction is generated for a **`rem`** statement, so the instruction counter is not incremented

The statement

```
10 input x
```

is tokenized next. The line number **`10`** is placed in the symbol table as type **`L`** and assigned the first location in the SML array (**`00`** because a remark began the program so the instruction counter is currently **`00`**). The command **`input`** indicates that the next token is a variable (only a variable can appear in an **`input`** statement). Because **`input`** corresponds directly to an SML operation code, the compiler simply has to determine the location of **`x`** in the SML array. Symbol **`x`** is not found in the symbol table. So, it is inserted into the symbol table as the Unicode representation of **`x`**, given type **`V`**, and assigned location **`99`** in the SML array (data storage begins at **`99`** and is allocated backwards). SML code can now be generated for this statement. Operation code **`10`** (the SML read operation code) is multiplied by 100, and the location of **`x`** (as determined in the symbol table) is added to complete the instruction. The instruction is then stored in the SML array at location **`00`**. The instruction counter is incremented by 1 because a single SML instruction was produced.

The statement

```
15 rem   check y == x
```

is tokenized next. The symbol table is searched for line number **15** (which is not found). The line number is inserted as type **L** and assigned the next location in the array, **01** (remember that **rem** statements do not produce code, so the instruction counter is not incremented).

The statement

```
20 if y == x goto 60
```

is tokenized next. Line number **20** is inserted in the symbol table and given type **L** with the next location in the SML array **01**. The command **if** indicates that a condition is to be evaluated. The variable **y** is not found in the symbol table, so it is inserted and given the type **V** and the SML location **98**. Next, SML instructions are generated to evaluate the condition. Since there is no direct equivalent in SML for the **if/goto**, it must be simulated by performing a calculation using **x** and **y** and branching based on the result. If **y** is equal to **x**, the result of subtracting **x** from **y** is zero, so the *branch zero* instruction can be used with the result of the calculation to simulate the **if/goto** statement. The first step requires that **y** be loaded (from SML location **98**) into the accumulator. This produces the instruction **01 +2098**. Next, **x** is subtracted from the accumulator. This produces the instruction **02 +3199**. The value in the accumulator may be zero, positive, or negative. Since the operator is **==**, we want to *branch zero*. First, the symbol table is searched for the branch location (**60** in this case), which is not found. So, **60** is placed in the **flags** array at location **03**, and the instruction **03 +4200** is generated (we cannot add the branch location because we have not assigned a location to line **60** in the SML array yet). The instruction counter is incremented to **04**.

The compiler proceeds to the statement

```
25 rem   increment y
```

The line number **25** is inserted in the symbol table as type **L** and assigned SML location **04**. The instruction counter is not incremented.

When the statement

```
30 let y = y + 1
```

is tokenized, the line number **30** is inserted in the symbol table as type **L** and assigned SML location **04**. Command **let** indicates that the line is an assignment statement. First, all the symbols on the line are inserted in the symbol table (if they are not already there). The integer **1** is added to the symbol table as type **C** and assigned SML location **97**. Next, the right side of the assignment is converted from infix to postfix notation. Then the postfix expression (**y 1 +**) is evaluated. Symbol **y** is located in the symbol table and its corresponding memory location is pushed onto the stack. Symbol **1** is also located in the symbol table and its corresponding memory location is pushed onto the stack. When the operator **+** is encountered, the postfix evaluator pops the stack into the right operand of the operator and pops the stack again into the left operand of the operator, then produces the SML instructions

```
04 +2098    (load y)
05 +3097    (add 1)
```

The result of the expression is stored in a temporary location in memory (**96**) with instruction

```
06 +2196     (store temporary)
```

and the temporary location is pushed on the stack. Now that the expression has been evaluated, the result must be stored in **y** (i.e., the variable on the left side of **=**). So, the temporary location is loaded into the accumulator and the accumulator is stored in **y** with the instructions

```
07 +2096     (load temporary)
08 +2198     (store y)
```

The reader will immediately notice that SML instructions appear to be redundant. We will discuss this issue shortly.

When the statement

```
35 rem   add y to total
```

is tokenized, line number **35** is inserted in the symbol table as type **L** and assigned location **09**.

The statement

```
40 let t = t + y
```

is similar to line **30**. The variable **t** is inserted in the symbol table as type **V** and assigned SML location **95**. The instructions follow the same logic and format as line **30**, and the instructions **09 +2095**, **10 +3098**, **11 +2194**, **12 +2094**, and **13 +2195** are generated. Note that the result of **t + y** is assigned to temporary location **94** before being assigned to **t** (**95**). Once again, the reader will note that the instructions in memory locations **11** and **12** appear to be redundant. Again, we will discuss this shortly.

The statement

```
45 rem   loop y
```

is a remark, so line **45** is added to the symbol table as type **L** and assigned SML location **14**.

The statement

```
50 goto 20
```

transfers control to line **20**. Line number **50** is inserted in the symbol table as type **L** and assigned SML location **14**. The equivalent of **goto** in SML is the *unconditional branch* (**40**) instruction that transfers control to a specific SML location. The compiler searches the symbol table for line **20** and finds that it corresponds to SML location **01**. The operation code (**40**) is multiplied by 100 and location **01** is added to it to produce the instruction **14 +4001**.

The statement

```
55 rem   output result
```

is a remark, so line **55** is inserted in the symbol table as type **L** and assigned SML location **15**.

The statement

```
60 print t
```

is an output statement. Line number **60** is inserted in the symbol table as type **L** and assigned SML location **15**. The equivalent of **print** in SML is operation code **11** (*write*). The location of **t** is determined from the symbol table and added to the result of the operation code multiplied by 100.

The statement

```
99 end
```

is the final line of the program. Line number **99** is stored in the symbol table as type **L** and assigned SML location **16**. The **end** command produces the SML instruction **+4300** (**43** is *halt* in SML) which is written as the final instruction in the SML memory array.

This completes the first pass of the compiler. We now consider the second pass. The **flags** array is searched for values other than **-1**. Location **03** contains **60**, so the compiler knows that instruction **03** is incomplete. The compiler completes the instruction by searching the symbol table for **60**, determining its location, and adding the location to the incomplete instruction. In this case, the search determines that line **60** corresponds to SML location **15**, so the completed instruction **03 +4215** is produced replacing **03 +4200**. The Simple program has now been compiled successfully.

To build the compiler, you will have to perform each of the following tasks:

a) Modify the Simpletron simulator program you wrote in Exercise 5.43 to take its input from a file specified by the user (see Chapter 15). The simulator should output its results to a disk file in the same format as the screen output. Convert the simulator to be an object-oriented program. In particular, make each part of the hardware an object. Arrange the instruction types into a class hierarchy using inheritance. Then execute the program polymorphically simply by telling each instruction to execute itself with an **executeInstruction** message.

b) Modify the infix-to-postfix evaluation algorithm of Exercise 17.12 to process multidigit integer operands and single-letter variable name operands. *Hint:* Class **StreamTokenizer** can be used to locate each constant and variable in an expression, and constants can be converted from strings to integers using **Integer** class method **parseInt**. (Note: The data representation of the postfix expression must be altered to support variable names and integer constants.)

c) Modify the postfix evaluation algorithm to process multidigit integer operands and variable name operands. Also, the algorithm should now implement the "hook" discussed above so that SML instructions are produced rather than directly evaluating the expression. *Hint:* Class **StreamTokenizer** can be used to locate each constant and variable in an expression, and constants can be converted from strings to integers using **Integer** class method **parseInt**. (Note: The data representation of the postfix expression must be altered to support variable names and integer constants.)

d) Build the compiler. Incorporate parts (b) and (c) for evaluating expressions in **let** statements. Your program should contain a method that performs the first pass of the compiler and a method that performs the second pass of the compiler. Both methods can call other methods to accomplish their tasks. Make your compiler as object oriented as possible.

17.28 (*Optimizing the Simple Compiler*) When a program is compiled and converted into SML, a set of instructions is generated. Certain combinations of instructions often repeat themselves, usually in triplets called *productions*. A production normally consists of three instructions such as *load*, *add*, and *store*. For example, Fig. 17.27 illustrates five of the SML instructions that were produced in the compilation of the program in Fig. 17.25 The first three instructions are the production that adds **1** to **y**. Note that instructions **06** and **07** store the accumulator value in temporary location **96**, then load the value back into the accumulator so instruction **08** can store the value in location **98**. Often a production is followed by a load instruction for the same location that was just stored. This code can be *optimized* by eliminating the store instruction and the subsequent load instruction that operate on the same memory location, thus enabling the Simpletron to execute the program faster. Figure 17.28 il-

```
04    +2098   (load)
05    +3097   (add)
06    +2196   (store)
07    +2096   (load)
08    +2198   (store)
```

Fig. 17.27 Unoptimized code from the program of Fig. 17.25.

lustrates the optimized SML for the program of Fig. 17.25. Note that there are four fewer instructions in the optimized code—a memory-space savings of 25%.

Modify the compiler to provide an option for optimizing the Simpletron Machine Language code it produces. Manually compare the non-optimized code with the optimized code, and calculate the percentage reduction.

Simple program	SML location and instruction	Description
`5 rem sum 1 to x`	*none*	**rem** ignored
`10 input x`	00 +1099	read **x** into location **99**
`15 rem   check y == x`	*none*	**rem** ignored
`20 if y == x goto 60`	01 +2098	load **y** (**98**) into accumulator
	02 +3199	sub **x** (**99**) from accumulator
	03 +4211	branch to location **11** if zero
`25 rem   increment y`	*none*	**rem** ignored
`30 let y = y + 1`	04 +2098	load **y** into accumulator
	05 +3097	add **1** (**97**) to accumulator
	06 +2198	store accumulator in **y** (**98**)
`35 rem   add y to total`	*none*	**rem** ignored
`40 let t = t + y`	07 +2096	load **t** from location (**96**)
	08 +3098	add **y** (**98**) accumulator
	09 +2196	store accumulator in **t** (**96**)
`45 rem   loop y`	*none*	**rem** ignored
`50 goto 20`	10 +4001	branch to location **01**
`55 rem   output result`	*none*	**rem** ignored
`60 print t`	11 +1196	output **t** (**96**) to screen
`99 end`	12 +4300	terminate execution

Fig. 17.28 Optimized code for the program of Fig. 17.25.

17.29 (*Modifications to the Simple compiler*) Perform the following modifications to the Simple compiler. Some of these modifications may also require modifications to the Simpletron Simulator program written in Exercise 5.43.

a) Allow the modulus operator (`%`) to be used in **`let`** statements. Simpletron Machine Language must be modified to include a modulus instruction.

b) Allow exponentiation in a **`let`** statement using `^` as the exponentiation operator. Simpletron Machine Language must be modified to include an exponentiation instruction.

c) Allow the compiler to recognize uppercase and lowercase letters in Simple statements (e.g., **`'A'`** is equivalent to **`'a'`**). No modifications to the Simpletron Simulator are required.

d) Allow **`input`** statements to read values for multiple variables such as **`input x, y`**. No modifications to the Simpletron Simulator are required to perform this enhancement to the Simple compiler.

e) Allow the compiler to output multiple values using a single **`print`** statement such as **`print a, b, c`**. No modifications to the Simpletron Simulator are required to perform this enhancement.

f) Add syntax-checking capabilities to the compiler so error messages are output when syntax errors are encountered in a Simple program. No modifications to the Simpletron Simulator are required.

g) Allow arrays of integers. No modifications to the Simpletron Simulator are required to perform this enhancement.

h) Allow subroutines specified by the Simple commands **`gosub`** and **`return`**. Command **`gosub`** passes program control to a subroutine and command **`return`** passes control back to the statement after the **`gosub`**. This is similar to a method call in Java. The same subroutine can be called from many **`gosub`** commands distributed throughout a program. No modifications to the Simpletron Simulator are required.

i) Allow repetition structures of the form

```
for x = 2 to 10 step 2
    Simple statements
next
```

j) This **`for`** statement loops from **`2`** to **`10`** with an increment of **`2`**. The **`next`** line marks the end of the body of the **`for`** line. No modifications to the Simpletron Simulator are required.

k) Allow repetition structures of the form

```
for x = 2 to 10
    Simple statements
next
```

l) This **`for`** statement loops from **`2`** to **`10`** with a default increment of **`1`**. No modifications to the Simpletron Simulator are required.

m) Allow the compiler to process string input and output. This requires the Simpletron Simulator to be modified to process and store string values. *Hint:* Each Simpletron word can be divided into two groups, each holding a two-digit integer. Each two-digit integer represents the Unicode decimal equivalent of a character. Add a machine-language instruction that will print a string beginning at a certain Simpletron memory location. The first half of the word at that location is a count of the number of characters in the string (i.e., the length of the string). Each succeeding half word contains one Unicode character expressed as two decimal digits. The machine language instruction checks the length and prints the string by translating each two-digit number into its equivalent character.

n) Allow the compiler to process floating-point values in addition to integers. The Simpletron Simulator must also be modified to process floating-point values.

17.30 *(A Simple interpreter)* An interpreter is a program that reads a high-level language program statement, determines the operation to be performed by the statement, and executes the operation immediately. The high-level language program is not converted into machine language first. Interpreters execute slower than compilers do because each statement encountered in the program being interpreted must first be deciphered at execution time. If statements are contained in a loop, the statements are deciphered each time they are encountered in the loop. Early versions of the Basic programming language were implemented as interpreters. Most Java programs are run interpretively.

Write an interpreter for the Simple language discussed in Exercise 17.26. The program should use the infix-to-postfix converter developed in Exercise 17.12 and the postfix evaluator developed in Exercise 17.13 to evaluate expressions in a **`let`** statement. The same restrictions placed on the Simple language in Exercise 17.26 should be adhered to in this program. Test the interpreter with the Simple programs written in Exercise 17.26. Compare the results of running these programs in the interpreter with the results of compiling the Simple programs and running them in the Simpletron Simulator built in Exercise 5.43.

17.31 *(Insert/Delete Anywhere in a Linked List)* Our linked list class allowed insertions and deletions at only the front and the back of the linked list. These capabilities were convenient for us when we used inheritance or composition to produce a stack class and a queue class with a minimal amount of code simply by reusing the list class. Linked lists are normally more general that those we provided. Modify the linked list class we developed in this chapter to handle insertions and deletions anywhere in the list.

17.32 *(List and Queues without Tail References)* Our implementation of a linked list (Fig. 17.3) used both a **`firstNode`** and a **`lastNode`**. The **`lastNode`** was useful for the **`insertAtBack`** and **`removeFromBack`** methods of the **`List`** class. The **`insertAtBack`** method corresponds to the **`enqueue`** method of the **`Queue`** class.

Rewrite the **`List`** class so that it does not use a **`lastNode`**. Thus, any operations on the tail of a list must begin searching the list from the front. Does this affect our implementation of the **`Queue`** class (Fig. 17.12)?

17.33 *(Performance of Binary Tree Sorting and Searching)* One problem with the binary tree sort is that the order in which the data is inserted affects the shape of the tree—for the same collection of data, different orderings can yield binary trees of dramatically different shapes. The performance of the binary tree sorting and searching algorithms is sensitive to the shape of the binary tree. What shape would a binary tree have if its data were inserted in increasing order? in decreasing order? What shape should the tree have to achieve maximal searching performance?

17.34 *(Indexed Lists)* As presented in the text, linked lists must be searched sequentially. For large lists, this can result in poor performance. A common technique for improving list searching performance is to create and maintain an index to the list. An index is a set of references to key places in the list. For example, an application that searches a large list of names could improve performance by creating an index with 26 entries—one for each letter of the alphabet. A search operation for a last name beginning with 'Y' would then first search the index to determine where the 'Y' entries begin, and then "jump into" the list at that point and search linearly until the desired name is found. This would be much faster than searching the linked list from the beginning. Use the **`List`** class of Fig. 17.3 as the basis of an **`IndexedList`** class.

Write a program that demonstrates the operation of indexed lists. Be sure to include methods **`insertInIndexedList`**, **`searchIndexedList`**, and **`deleteFromIndexedList`**.

18

Java Utilities Package and Bit Manipulation

Objectives

- To understand containers such as classes **`Vector`** and **`Stack`**, and the **`Enumeration`** interface.
- To be able to create **`Hashtable`** objects and persistent hash tables called **`Properties`** objects.
- To use bit manipulation and **`BitSet`** objects.

Nothing can have value without being an object of utility.
Karl Marx

I've been in Who's Who, and I know what's what, but this is the first time I ever made the dictionary.
Mae West

. . . what we observe is not nature in itself
but nature exposed to our method of questioning.
Werner Karl Heisenberg

You can observe a lot by just watching.
Yogi Berra

O! Thou hast damnable iteration,
and art indeed able to corrupt a saint.
William Shakespeare, Henry IV, Part I

I am going in search of a great perhaps.
Francois Rebelais

Outline

18.1 Introduction

In this chapter we discuss a variety of utility classes in the **java.util** package. We examine the **Vector** class which enables us to create array-like objects that can grow and shrink dynamically as a program's data storage requirements change. We consider the **Enumeration** interface which we use in conjunction with class **Vector** to allow a program to iterate its way through the elements of a container such as a **Vector**.

We discuss the **Stack** class that offers the conventional stack operations **push** and **pop** along with several others we did not consider in Chapter 17.

We present class **Dictionary** which is an abstract class that gives us the framework for storing keyed data in tables and retrieving that data. We explain the theory of "hashing," a technique for rapidly storing and retrieving information from tables, and we demonstrate the construction and manipulation of hash tables with Java's **Hashtable** class. We consider the **Properties** class that enables us to create persistent hash tables, i.e., hash tables that can be written to a file with an output stream and eventually read back into the system on demand from an input stream.

We overview class **Random** that provides a richer collection of random-number capabilities than is available with **Math.random**.

We present an extensive discussion of bit manipulation operators and then discuss class **BitSet** that enables the creation of bit-array-like objects for setting and getting individual bits.

18.2 **Vector** Class and **Enumeration** Interface

In most programming languages, including Java, conventional arrays are fixed in size—they cannot grow or shrink in response to an application's changing storage requirements. Java class **Vector** provides the capabilities of array-like data structures that can dynamically resize themselves.

At any time the **Vector** contains a certain number of elements which is less than or equal to its *capacity*. The capacity is the space that has been reserved for the array.

Performance Tip 18.1

Inserting additional elements into an array whose current size is less than its capacity is a relatively fast operation.

If a **Vector** needs to grow, it grows by an increment that you specify or by a default assumed by the system.

Performance Tip 18.2

It is a relatively slow operation to insert an element into an array that needs to grow larger to accommodate the new element.

If you do not specify a capacity increment, the system will automatically double the size of the **Vector** each time additional capacity is needed.

Performance Tip 18.3

The default capacity increment of doubling the size of the **Vector** *may seem wasteful of storage, but it is actually an efficient way for many* **Vector***s to grow quickly to be "about the right size." This is much more efficient time-wise than growing the* **Vector** *each time by only as much space as it takes to hold a single element. But it can waste space.*

Performance Tip 18.4

If storage is at a premium, use the **trimToSize** *method of the* **Vector** *class to trim a* **Vector** *to its exact size. This will optimize a* **Vector***'s use of storage. But be careful. If an additional element needs to be inserted in the* **vector***, this will be slow because it will force the* **Vector** *to grow dynamically—trimming leaves no room for growth.*

Vectors are designed to store references to **Object**s. Thus, a reference to an object of any class type can be stored in a **Vector**. If you would like to store values of primitive data types in **Vector**s, you must use the type-wrapper classes (**Integer**, **Long**, **Float**, **Double**, **Boolean** and **Character**) from the **java.lang** package to create objects containing the primitive data type values.

The applet of Fig. 18.1 demonstrates class **Vector** and many of its methods. A **Button** is provided for each of the methods. The user can type a **String** into the provided **TextField**, then press a button to see what the method does. Messages are displayed in the status area of the applet to indicate the results of each operation.

```
// Fig. 18.01: VectorTest.java
// Testing the Vector class of the java.util package
import java.util.*;
import java.awt.*;
import java.awt.event.*;
import java.applet.Applet;

public class VectorTest extends Applet
                    implements ActionListener {
```

Fig. 18.1 Demonstrating class **Vector** of the **java.util** package (part 1 of 4).

```
   private Vector v;

   // GUI components
   private TextField input;
   private Button addBtn, removeBtn, firstBtn, lastBtn,
                  emptyBtn, containsBtn, locationBtn,
                  trimBtn, statsBtn, displayBtn;

   public void init()
   {
      v = new Vector( 1 );

      add( new Label( "Enter a string" ) );
      input = new TextField( 10 );
      add( input );       // value to add, remove or locate

      addBtn = new Button( "Add" );
      addBtn.addActionListener( this );
      add( addBtn );      // add the input value

      removeBtn = new Button( "Remove" );
      removeBtn.addActionListener( this );
      add( removeBtn );   // remove the input value

      firstBtn = new Button( "First" );
      firstBtn.addActionListener( this );
      add( firstBtn );    // look at the first element

      lastBtn = new Button( "Last" );
      lastBtn.addActionListener( this );
      add( lastBtn );     // look at the last element

      emptyBtn = new Button( "Is Empty?" );
      emptyBtn.addActionListener( this );
      add( emptyBtn );    // check if stack is empty

      containsBtn = new Button( "Contains" );
      containsBtn.addActionListener( this );
      add( containsBtn ); // does vector contain input value?

      locationBtn = new Button( "Location" );
      locationBtn.addActionListener( this );
      add( locationBtn ); // location of input value

      trimBtn = new Button( "Trim" );
      trimBtn.addActionListener( this );
      add( trimBtn );     // trim vector to number of elements

      statsBtn = new Button( "Statistics" );
      statsBtn.addActionListener( this );
      add( statsBtn );    // display statistics
```

Fig. 18.1 Demonstrating class **`Vector`** of the **`java.util`** package (part 2 of 4).

```

      displayBtn = new Button( "Display" );
      displayBtn.addActionListener( this );
      add( displayBtn );  // display the stack contents
   }

   public void actionPerformed( ActionEvent e )
   {
      if ( e.getSource() == addBtn ) {
         v.addElement( input.getText() );
         showStatus( "Added to end: " + input.getText() );
      }
      else if ( e.getSource() == removeBtn ) {
         if ( v.removeElement( input.getText() ) )
            showStatus( "Removed: " + input.getText() );
         else
            showStatus( input.getText() + " not in vector" );
      }
      else if ( e.getSource() == firstBtn ) {
         try {
            showStatus( "First element: " + v.firstElement() );
         }
         catch ( NoSuchElementException exception ) {
            showStatus( exception.toString() );
         }
      }
      else if ( e.getSource() == lastBtn ) {
         try {
            showStatus( "Last element: " + v.lastElement() );
         }
         catch ( NoSuchElementException exception ) {
            showStatus( exception.toString() );
         }
      }
      else if ( e.getSource() == emptyBtn ) {
         showStatus( v.isEmpty() ? "Vector is empty" :
                                   "Vector is not empty" );
      }
      else if ( e.getSource() == containsBtn ) {
         String searchKey = input.getText();

         if ( v.contains( searchKey ) )
            showStatus( "Vector contains " + searchKey );
         else
           showStatus( "Vector does not contain " + searchKey );
      }
      else if ( e.getSource() == locationBtn ) {
         showStatus( "Element is at location " +
                     v.indexOf( input.getText() ) );
      }
```

Fig. 18.1 Demonstrating class **`Vector`** of the **`java.util`** package (part 3 of 4).

```
      else if ( e.getSource() == trimBtn ) {
         v.trimToSize();
         showStatus( "Vector trimmed to size" );
      }
      else if ( e.getSource() == statsBtn ) {
         showStatus( "Size = " + v.size() +
                     "; capacity = " + v.capacity() );
      }
      else if ( e.getSource() == displayBtn ) {
         Enumeration enum = v.elements();
         StringBuffer buf = new StringBuffer();

         while ( enum.hasMoreElements() )
            buf.append( enum.nextElement() ).append( " " );

         showStatus( buf.toString() );
      }

      input.setText( "" );
   }
}
```

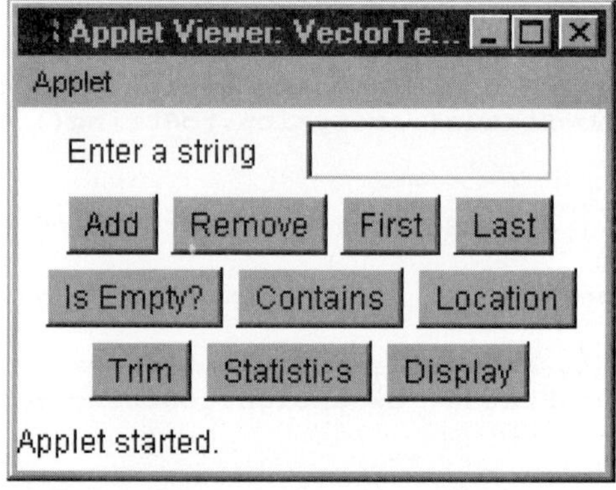

Fig. 18.1 Demonstrating class **Vector** of the **java.util** package (part 4 of 4).

The applet's **init** method creates a **Vector** with the statement

```
Vector v = new Vector( 1 );
```

which creates a **Vector** with an initial capacity of 1 element. This **Vector** will double in size automatically each time it needs to grow to accommodate more elements.

Class **Vector** provides two other constructors. The no-argument constructor creates an empty **Vector** with an *initial capacity* of 10 elements. The constructor that takes two arguments creates a **Vector** with an *initial capacity* specified by the first argument and a *capacity increment* specified by the second argument. Each time this **Vector** needs to grow, it will add space for the specified number of elements in the capacity increment.

The statement

```
v.addElement( input.getText() );
```

uses **Vector** method **addElement** to add its argument to the end of the **Vector**. The **Vector**'s capacity is increased automatically (if necessary) to accommodate the new element. Class **Vector** also provides method **insertElementAt** to insert an element (the method's first argument) at a specified position (the method's second argument) in the **Vector** and method **setElementAt** to set the element (the method's first argument) at a specific position (the method's second argument) in the **Vector**. Method **insertElementAt** makes room for the new element by shifting elements. Method **setElementAt** replaces the element at the specified position with its argument.

The expression

```
v.removeElement( input.getText() )
```

uses **Vector** method **removeElement** to remove the first occurrence of its argument from the **Vector**. The method returns **true** if the element is found in the **Vector**; otherwise, **false** is returned. If the element is removed, all elements after that element in the **Vector** are shifted one position toward the beginning of the **Vector** to fill in the position of the removed element. Class **Vector** also provides method **removeAllElements** to remove every element from the **Vector** and method **removeElementAt** to remove the element at the index specified as an argument.

The expression

```
v.firstElement()
```

uses **Vector** method **firstElement** to return a reference to the first element in the **Vector**. This method throws a **NoSuchElementException** if there are no elements currently in the **Vector**.

The expression

```
v.lastElement()
```

uses **Vector** method **lastElement** to return a reference to the last element in the **Vector**. This method throws a **NoSuchElementException** if there are no elements currently in the **Vector**.

The expression

```
v.isEmpty()
```

uses **Vector** method **isEmpty** to determine if the **Vector** is empty. The method returns **true** if there are no elements in the **Vector**; otherwise, **false** is returned.

The expression

```
v.contains( searchKey )
```

uses **Vector** method **contains** to determine if the **Vector** contains the **searchKey** specified as an argument. Method **contains** returns **true** if **searchKey** is in the **Vector**; otherwise, **false** is returned. Method **contains** uses **Object** method **equals** to determine if the **searchKey** is equal to one of the **Vector**'s elements.

The expression

```
v.indexOf( input.getText() )
```

uses **Vector** method **indexOf** to get the index of the first location of the argument in the **Vector**. The method returns –1 if the argument is not found in the **Vector**. There is a version of this method that takes a second argument specifying the index in the **Vector** where the search should begin.

The statement

```
v.trimToSize();
```

uses **Vector** method **trimToSize** to cut the capacity of the **Vector** to the current number of elements in the **Vector** (i.e., the size of the **Vector**).

The expressions

```
v.size()
v.capacity()
```

use **Vector** methods **size** and **capacity** to determine the number of elements currently in the **Vector** and the number of elements that can be stored in the **Vector** without allocating more memory, respectively.

The statement

```
Enumeration enum = v.elements();
```

uses **Vector** method **elements** to return a reference to an **Enumeration** containing the elements of the **Vector**. An **Enumeration** provides two methods that allow a program to walk through a set of elements one element at a time. The expression

```
enum.hasMoreElements();
```

returns **true** as long as there are more elements in the **Enumeration**. The expression

```
enum.nextElement();
```

returns a reference to the next element in the **Enumeration**. If there are no more elements, a **NoSuchElementException** is thrown.

For more information on the **Vector** methods, see the Java API documentation.

18.3 Stack Class

In Chapter 17, "Data Structures," we learned how to build fundamental data structures like linked lists, stacks, queues, and trees. In a world of "reuse, reuse, reuse," instead of building data structures as we need them, we will often be able to take advantage of existing data structures classes. In this section, we investigate the **Stack** class in the Java utilities package (**java.util**).

We have already discussed class **Vector** that implements a dynamically resizable array. Class **Stack** extends class **Vector** to implement a stack data structure. Like **Vector**, class **Stack** is designed to store **Object**s; to store primitive data types, you must use the appropriate type-wrapper class (**Boolean**, **Byte**, **Character**, **Short**, **Integer**, **Long**, **Float** or **Double**).

The applet of Fig. 18.2 provides a graphical user interface that enables you to test each of the **Stack** methods. The statement

```
s = new Stack();
```

creates an empty **Stack**.

```
// Fig. 18.02: StackTest.java
// Testing the Stack class of the java.util package
import java.util.*;
import java.awt.*;
import java.awt.event.*;
import java.applet.Applet;

public class StackTest extends Applet
                implements ActionListener {
   private Stack s;

   // GUI components
   private TextField input;
   private Button pushBtn, popBtn, peekBtn,
                  emptyBtn, searchBtn, displayBtn;

   public void init()
   {
      s = new Stack();

      add( new Label( "Enter a string" ) );
      input = new TextField( 10 );
      input.addActionListener( this );
      add( input );       // value to push or search for

      pushBtn = new Button( "Push" );
      pushBtn.addActionListener( this );
      add( pushBtn );     // push the input value

      popBtn = new Button( "Pop" );
      popBtn.addActionListener( this );
      add( popBtn );      // pop a value

      peekBtn = new Button( "Peek" );
      peekBtn.addActionListener( this );
      add( peekBtn );     // peek at the top

      emptyBtn = new Button( "Is Empty?" );
      emptyBtn.addActionListener( this );
      add( emptyBtn );    // check if stack is empty

      searchBtn = new Button( "Search" );
      searchBtn.addActionListener( this );
      add( searchBtn );  // search for input value

```

Fig. 18.2 Demonstrating class **Stack** of the **java.util** package (part 1 of 3).

```
      displayBtn = new Button( "Display" );
      displayBtn.addActionListener( this );
      add( displayBtn ); // display the stack contents
   }

   public void actionPerformed( ActionEvent e )
   {
      if ( e.getSource() == pushBtn )
         showStatus( "Pushed: " + s.push( input.getText() ) );
      else if ( e.getSource() == popBtn ) {
         try {
            showStatus( "Popped: " + s.pop() );
         }
         catch ( EmptyStackException exception ) {
            showStatus( exception.toString() );
         }
      }
      else if ( e.getSource() == peekBtn ) {
         try {
            showStatus( "Top: " + s.peek() );
         }
         catch ( EmptyStackException exception ) {
            showStatus( exception.toString() );
         }
      }
      else if ( e.getSource() == emptyBtn ) {
         showStatus( s.empty() ? "Stack is empty" :
                                 "Stack is not empty" );
      }
      else if ( e.getSource() == searchBtn ) {
         String searchKey = input.getText();
         int result = s.search( searchKey );

         if ( result == -1 )
            showStatus( searchKey + " not found" );
         else
            showStatus( searchKey + " found at element " +
                        result );
      }
      else if ( e.getSource() == displayBtn ) {
         Enumeration enum = s.elements();
         StringBuffer buf = new StringBuffer();

         while ( enum.hasMoreElements() )
            buf.append( enum.nextElement() ).append( " " );

         showStatus( buf.toString() );
      }
   }
}
```

Fig. 18.2 Demonstrating class **Stack** of the **java.util** package (part 2 of 3).

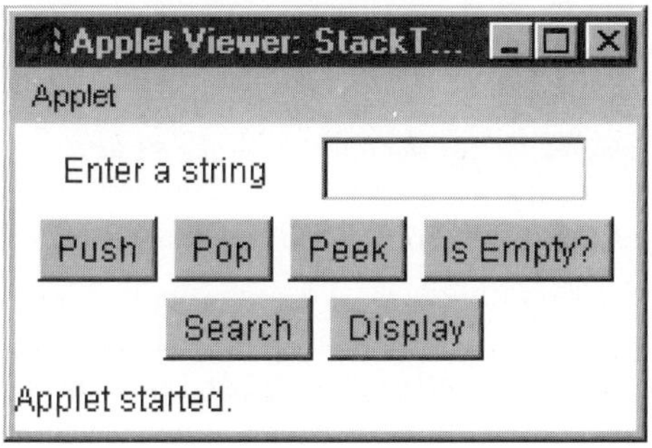

Fig. 18.2 Demonstrating class **Stack** of the **java.util** package (part 3 of 3).

The expression

```
s.push( input.getText() )
```

uses **Stack** method **push** to add its argument to the top of the stack. The method returns an **Object** reference to its argument.

The expression

```
s.pop()
```

uses **Stack** method **pop** to remove the top element of the stack. The method returns an **Object** reference to the element that was removed. If there are no elements in the **Stack**, an **EmptyStackException** is thrown.

The expression

```
s.peek()
```

uses **Stack** method **peek** to look at the top element of the stack without removing it. The method returns an **Object** reference to the element.

The expression

```
s.empty()
```

uses **Stack** method **empty** to determine if the stack is empty. If so, **true** is returned; otherwise, **false** is returned.

The expression

```
int result = s.search( searchKey );
```

uses **Stack** method **search** to determine if its argument is in the stack. If so, the position of the element in the stack is returned. *The top element is position 1.* If the element is not in the stack, –1 is returned.

Please note that the entire public interface of class **Vector** is actually part of class **Stack** because **Stack** inherits from **Vector**. To prove this, our example provides a button to display the contents of the stack. This button invokes method elements to get an **Enumeration** containing the contents of the stack. The **Enumeration** is then used to walk through the elements of the stack.

Testing and Debugging Tip 18.1

Because **`Stack`** *inherits from* **`Vector`**, *the user may perform operations on* **`Stack`** *objects that are ordinarily not allowed on conventional stack data structures. This could corrupt the elements of the* **`Stack`** *and destroy the integrity of the* **`Stack`**.

18.4 `Dictionary` Class

A **`Dictionary`** transforms *keys* to *values*. A key is supplied and the **`Dictionary`** returns a value. **`Dictionary`** is an abstract class. In particular, it is the superclass of the **`Hashtable`** class we will discuss shortly. Class **`Dictionary`** provides the public interface methods required to maintain a table of *key/value pairs* where the keys represent the "rows" of the table and the values are "columns" in the table.

The **`size`** method returns the number of occupied slots in the **`Dictionary`** object. Method **`isEmpty`** returns **`true`** if the **`Dictionary`** is empty, **`false`** otherwise. The **`keys`** method returns an **`Enumeration`** that iterates through **`Dictionary`**'s keys. The **`elements`** method enumerates the **`Dictionary`**'s elements. The **`get`** method returns the object that corresponds to a given key value. The **`put`** method puts an object into the table; the object is associated with a given key. The **`remove`** method removes an element corresponding to a given key and returns a reference to it.

18.5 `Hashtable` Class

Object-oriented programming languages make it easy to create new types. When a program creates objects of new or existing types, it then needs to manage those objects efficiently. This includes storing and retrieving objects. Storing and retrieving information with arrays is efficient if some aspect of your data directly matches the key value and if those keys are unique and tightly packed. If you have 100 employees with 9-digit Social Security numbers and you want to store and retrieve employee data by using the Social Security number as a key, it would nominally require an array with 999,999,999 elements, because there are 999,999,999 unique 9-digit numbers. This is impractical for virtually all applications that key on Social Security numbers. But if you could have an array that large, you could get very high performance storing and retrieving employee records by simply using the Social Security number as the array index.

There are a huge variety of applications that have this problem, namely that either the keys are of the wrong type (i.e., not nonnegative integers), or they may be of the right type but sparsely spread over a huge range.

What is needed is a high-speed scheme for converting keys like Social Security numbers, inventory part numbers, and the like into unique array subscripts. Then, when an application needs to store something, the scheme could rapidly convert the application key into a subscript and the record of information could be stored at that slot in the array. Retrieval is accomplished the same way: Once the application has a key value for which it wants to retrieve the data record, the application simply applies the conversion to the key—this produces the array subscript for the data where the array is stored and the data is retrieved.

The scheme we describe here is the basis of a technique called *hashing*. Why the name? Because when we convert a key into an array subscript we literally scramble the bits forming a kind of "mish-mashed" number. The number actually has no real significance beyond its usefulness in storing and retrieving this particular number data record.

A glitch in the scheme occurs when *collisions* occur; i.e., two different keys "hash into" the same cell (or element) in the array. Since we cannot store two different data records in the same space, we need to find an alternate home for all records beyond the first that hash to a particular array subscript. There are many schemes for doing this. One is to "hash again," i.e., to reapply the hashing transformation to the key to provide a next candidate cell in the array. The hashing process is designed to be quite random, so the assumption is that with just a few hashes an available cell will be found.

Another scheme uses one hash to locate the first candidate cell. If that cell is occupied, successive cells are searched linearly until an available cell is found. Retrieval works the same way: The key is hashed once, the cell pointed to is checked to see if it contains the desired data. If it does, the search is finished. If it does not then successive cells are searched linearly until the desired data is found.

The most popular solution to hash table collisions is to have each cell of the table be a hash "bucket," typically a linked list of all the key/value pairs that hash to that cell. This is the solution that Java's **Hashtable** class (from package **java.util**) implements.

One factor that affects the performance of hashing schemes is called the *load factor*. This is the ratio of the number of occupied cells in the hash table to the size of the hash table. The closer this ratio gets to 1.0, the greater the chance of collisions.

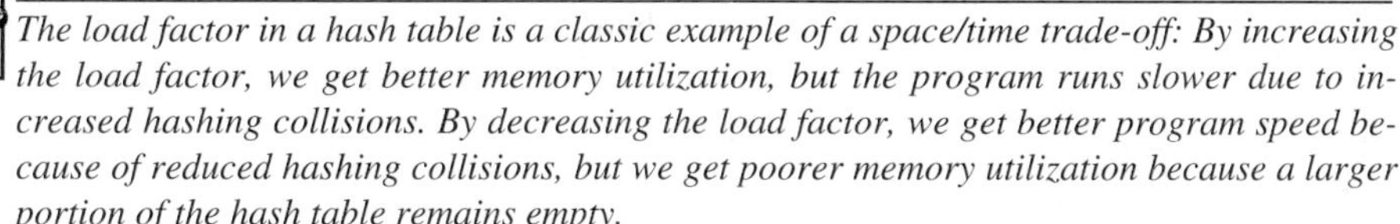

Performance Tip 18.5

The load factor in a hash table is a classic example of a space/time trade-off: By increasing the load factor, we get better memory utilization, but the program runs slower due to increased hashing collisions. By decreasing the load factor, we get better program speed because of reduced hashing collisions, but we get poorer memory utilization because a larger portion of the hash table remains empty.

The complexity of using hash tables properly is too much for most casual programmers. Computer science students study hashing schemes thoroughly in courses called "Data Structures" and/or "Algorithms." Recognizing the value of hashing to most programmers, Java provides the **Hashtable** class and some related features to enable programmers to take advantage of hashing without having to worry about the messy details.

Actually, the previous sentence is profoundly important in our study of object-oriented programming. Classes encapsulate and hide complexity (i.e., implementation details) and offer user-friendly interfaces. Crafting classes to do this properly is one of the most valued skills in the field of object-oriented programming.

The applet of Fig. 18.3 provides a graphical user interface that enables you to test many of the **Hashtable** methods. The statement

```
table = new Hashtable();
```

creates an empty **Hashtable** with a default capacity of 101 elements and a default load factor of .75. When the number of occupied slots in the **Hashtable** becomes more than the capacity times the load factor, the table will automatically grow larger. Class **Hashtable** also provides a constructor that takes one argument specifying the capacity and a constructor that takes two arguments specifying the capacity and load factor, respectively.

```
// Fig. 18.3: HashtableTest.java
// Demonstrates class Hashtable of the java.util package.
import java.util.*;
import java.awt.*;
import java.awt.event.*;
import java.applet.Applet;

public class HashtableTest extends Applet
              implements ActionListener {
   private Hashtable table;
   private TextField fName, lName;
   private TextArea display;
   private Button put, get, remove, empty, containsKey,
                  clear, listElems, listKeys;

   public void init()
   {
      table = new Hashtable();

      add( new Label( "First name" ) );
      fName = new TextField( 8 );
      add( fName );

      add( new Label( "Last name (key)" ) );
      lName = new TextField( 8 );
      add( lName );

      display = new TextArea( 4, 45 );
      add( display );

      put = new Button( "Put" );
      put.addActionListener( this );
      add( put );

      get = new Button( "Get" );
      get.addActionListener( this );
      add( get );

      remove = new Button( "Remove" );
      remove.addActionListener( this );
      add( remove );

      empty = new Button( "Empty" );
      empty.addActionListener( this );
      add( empty );

      containsKey = new Button( "Contains key" );
      containsKey.addActionListener( this );
      add( containsKey );

```

Fig. 18.3 Demonstrating class **Hashtable** (part 1 of 4).

```
      clear = new Button( "Clear table" );
      clear.addActionListener( this );
      add( clear );

      listElems = new Button( "List objects" );
      listElems.addActionListener( this );
      add( listElems );

      listKeys = new Button( "List keys" );
      listKeys.addActionListener( this );
      add( listKeys );
   }

   public void actionPerformed( ActionEvent e )
   {
      if ( e.getSource() == put ) {
         Employee emp = new Employee( fName.getText(),
                                      lName.getText() );
         Object val = table.put( lName.getText(), emp );

         if ( val == null )
            showStatus( "Put: " + emp.toString() );
         else
            showStatus( "Put: " + emp.toString() +
                        "; Replaced: " + val.toString() );
      }
      else if ( e.getSource() == get ) {
         Object val = table.get( lName.getText() );

         if ( val != null )
            showStatus( "Get: " + val.toString() );
         else
            showStatus( "Get: " + lName.getText() +
                        " not in table" );
      }
      else if ( e.getSource() == remove ) {
         Object val = table.remove( lName.getText() );

         if ( val != null )
            showStatus( "Remove: " + val.toString() );
         else
            showStatus( "Remove: " + lName.getText() +
                        " not in table" );
      }
      else if ( e.getSource() == empty ) {
         showStatus( "Empty: " + table.isEmpty() );
      }
      else if ( e.getSource() == containsKey ) {
         showStatus( "Contains key: " +
            table.containsKey( lName.getText() ) );
      }
```

Fig. 18.3 Demonstrating class **`Hashtable`** (part 2 of 4).

```
         else if ( e.getSource() == clear ) {
            table.clear();
            showStatus( "Clear: Table is now empty" );
         }
         else if ( e.getSource() == listElems ) {
            StringBuffer buf = new StringBuffer();

            for ( Enumeration enum = table.elements();
                  enum.hasMoreElements(); )
               buf.append( enum.nextElement() ).append( '\n' );

            display.setText( buf.toString() );
         }
         else if ( e.getSource() == listKeys ) {
            StringBuffer buf = new StringBuffer();

            for ( Enumeration enum = table.keys();
                  enum.hasMoreElements(); )
               buf.append( enum.nextElement() ).append( '\n' );

            display.setText( buf.toString() );
         }
      }
}

class Employee {
   private String first;
   private String last;

   public Employee( String fName, String lName )
   {
      first = fName;
      last = lName;
   }

   public String toString() { return first + " " + last; }
}
```

Fig. 18.3 Demonstrating class **Hashtable** (part 3 of 4).

The statement

```
Object val = table.put( lName.getText(), emp );
```

uses **Hashtable** method **put** to add a *key* (the first argument) and a *value* (the second argument) into the **Hashtable**. If there was no value in the **Hashtable** for the specified key, **null** is returned. If there was a value in the **Hashtable** for the specified key, the original value in the **Hashtable** is returned; this helps the program manage cases in which it intends to replace the value stored for a given key. If either the key or the value is **null**, a **NullPointerException** is thrown. The value can be located in the **Hashtable** with the statement

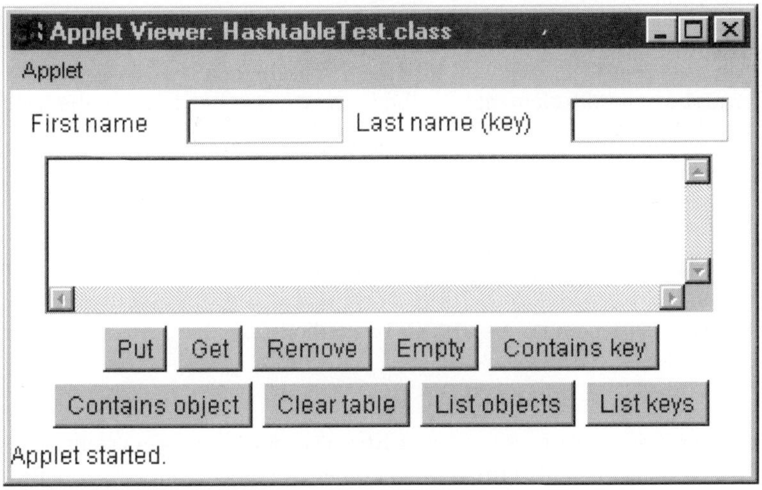

Fig. 18.3 Demonstrating class **Hashtable** (part 4 of 4).

```
Object val = table.get( lName.getText() );
```

that uses **Hashtable** method **get** to locate the value that is associated with the key specified as an argument. The method returns an **Object** reference to the value if it is located; otherwise, **null** is returned.

The statement

```
Object val = table.remove( lName.getText() );
```

uses **Hashtable** method **remove** to remove from the table the value associated with the key specified as an argument. The method returns an **Object** reference to the removed value. If there is no value mapped to the specified key, the method returns **null**.

The expression

```
table.isEmpty()
```

returns **true** if the **Hashtable** is empty; **false** otherwise.

The expression

```
table.containsKey( lName.getText() )
```

uses **Hashtable** method **containsKey** to determine if the key specified as an argument is in the **Hashtable** (i.e., a value is associated with that key). If so, the method returns **true**; otherwise, **false** is returned. Class **Hashtable** also provides method **contains** to determine if the **Object** specified as its argument is in the **Hashtable**.

The statement

```
table.clear();
```

empties the **Hashtable**.

The expression

```
table.elements()
```

uses **Hashtable** method elements to obtain an **Enumeration** of the values in the **Hashtable**.

The expression

```
table.keys()
```

uses **Hashtable** method **keys** to obtain an **Enumeration** of the keys in the **Hashtable**.

For more information on the **Hashtable** methods, see the Java API documentation.

18.6 Properties Class

A **Properties** object is a persistent **Hashtable** object. By persistent, we mean that the **Hashtable** object can be written to an output stream and directed to a file then read back in through an input stream. In fact, most objects in Java can now be output and input with objects of class **ObjectOutputStream** and class **ObjectInputStream** of package **java.io**. The **Properties** class extends class **Hashtable**, so the methods we discussed in Fig. 18.3 can be used for **Properties** objects also. The keys and values in a **Properties** object must be of type **String**. Class **Properties** provides some additional methods that are demonstrated in the application of Fig. 18.4. Note: This program is an application because we are using class **Properties** to store information in a file and retrieve information from a file on the local system. A **Properties** object can be used in an applet if the streams for saving and loading the table are connected to a network connection (see Chapter 16 for information on creating a stream socket connection to another computer on a network).

```
// Fig. 18.04: PropertiesTest.java
// Demonstrates class Properties of the java.util package.
import java.io.*;
import java.util.*;
import java.awt.*;
import java.awt.event.*;
import com.deitel.jhtp2.ch11.CloseWindowAndExit;

public class PropertiesTest extends Frame
            implements ActionListener {
   private Properties table;
   private FileInputStream input;
   private FileOutputStream output;

   private TextField propName, propVal, result;
   private TextArea display;
   private Button put, clear, getProperty, save, load;
```

Fig. 18.4 Demonstrating class **Properties** (part 1 of 4).

```

   public PropertiesTest()
   {
      super( "Properties Test" );
      table = new Properties();
      setLayout( new FlowLayout() );

      add( new Label( "Property name (key)" ) );
      propName = new TextField( 10 );
      add( propName );

      add( new Label( "Property value" ) );
      propVal = new TextField( 10 );
      add( propVal );

      display = new TextArea( 4, 35 );
      add( display );

      put = new Button( "Put" );
      put.addActionListener( this );
      add( put );

      clear = new Button( "Clear" );
      clear.addActionListener( this );
      add( clear );

      getProperty = new Button( "Get property" );
      getProperty.addActionListener( this );
      add( getProperty );

      save = new Button( "Save" );
      save.addActionListener( this );
      add( save );

      load = new Button( "Load" );
      load.addActionListener( this );
      add( load );

      result = new TextField( 35 );
      result.setEditable( false );
      add( result );

      setSize( 275, 225 );
      setVisible( true );
   }

   public void actionPerformed( ActionEvent e )
   {
      if ( e.getSource() == put ) {
         Object val = table.put( propName.getText(),
                                 propVal.getText() );
```

Fig. 18.4 Demonstrating class **Properties** (part 2 of 4).

```

         if ( val == null )
            showStatus( "Put: " + propName.getText() + " " +
                        propVal.getText() );
         else
            showStatus( "Put: " + propName.getText() + " " +
                        propVal.getText() + "; Replaced: " +
                        val.toString() );
      }
      else if ( e.getSource() == clear ) {
         table.clear();
         showStatus( "Table in memory cleared" );
      }
      else if ( e.getSource() == getProperty ) {
         Object val = table.getProperty( propName.getText() );

         if ( val != null )
            showStatus( "Get property: " + propName.getText() +
                        " " + val.toString() );
         else
            showStatus( "Get: " + propName.getText() +
                        " not in table" );
      }
      else if ( e.getSource() == save ) {
         try {
            output = new FileOutputStream( "props.dat" );
            table.save( output, "Sample Properties" );
            output.close();
         }
         catch( IOException ex ) {
            showStatus( ex.toString() );
         }
      }
      else if ( e.getSource() == load ) {
         try {
            input = new FileInputStream( "props.dat" );
            table.load( input );
            input.close();
         }
         catch( IOException ex ) {
            showStatus( ex.toString() );
         }
      }

      listProperties();
   }

   public void listProperties()
   {
      StringBuffer buf = new StringBuffer();
      String pName, pVal;
```

Fig. 18.4 Demonstrating class **Properties** (part 3 of 4).

```

      Enumeration enum = table.propertyNames();

      while( enum.hasMoreElements() ) {
         pName = enum.nextElement().toString();
         pVal = table.getProperty( pName );
         buf.append( pName ).append( '\t' );
         buf.append( pVal ).append( '\n' );
      }

      display.setText( buf.toString() );
   }

   public void showStatus( String s )
   {
      result.setText( s );
   }

   public static void main( String args[] )
   {
      PropertiesTest p = new PropertiesTest();
      p.addWindowListener( new CloseWindowAndExit() );
   }
}
```

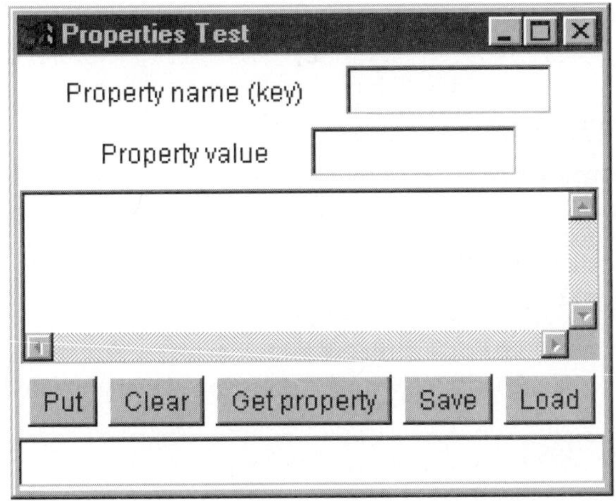

Fig. 18.4 Demonstrating class **`Properties`** (part 4 of 4).

The statement

```
table = new Properties();
```

uses the no-argument constructor to create an empty **`Properties`** table with no default properties. There is also a constructor that is passed a reference to a default **`Properties`** object containing default property values. This version is useful for maintaining a set of default values for use with the **`getProperty`** method later.

The statement

```
Object val = table.getProperty( propName.getText() );
```

uses **Properties** method **getProperty** to locate the value of the key specified as an argument. If the key is not found in this **Properties** object, the default **Properties** object (if there is one) is used. The process continues recursively until there are no more default **Properties** objects (remember that every **Properties** object can be initialized with a default **Properties** object) at which point **null** is returned. A second version of this method is provided that takes two arguments, the second of which is the default value to return if **getProperty** cannot locate the key.

The statement

```
table.save( output, "Sample Properties" );
```

uses **Properties** method **save** to save the contents of the **Properties** object to the **OutputStream** object specified as the first argument (in this case a **FileOutputStream**). The **String** argument is a description of the **Properties** object. Class properties also provides method **list** that takes a **PrintStream** argument. This method is useful for displaying the set of properties.

Testing and Debugging Tip 18.2

*Use **Properties** method **list** to display the contents of a **Properties** object for debugging purposes.*

The statement

```
table.load( input );
```

uses **Properties** method **load** to restore the contents of the **Properties** object from the **InputStream** specified as the first argument (in this case a **FileInputStream**).

The expression

```
table.propertyNames()
```

uses **Properties** method **propertyNames** to obtain an **Enumeration** of the property names. The value of each property can be determined using method **getProperty**.

18.7 Random Class

We discussed random number generation in Chapter 4, "Methods," where we used the **random** method of the **Math** class. Java provides extensive additional random number generation capabilities in class **Random**. We briefly walk through the API calls here.

A new random number generator can be created by using

```
Random r = new Random();
```

This form uses the time to seed its random number generator differently each time it is called and thus generates different sequences of random numbers each time.

To create a pseudorandom-number generator with "repeatability" use

```
Random r = new Random(seedValue);
```

Each time this form is used with the same **long seedValue**, the same sequence of random numbers will be generated subsequently.

Testing and Debugging Tip 18.3

The repeatability of random numbers that occurs when the same seed value is used is useful for testing and debugging. While a program is under development, use the form **Random(seedValue)** *that produces a repeatable sequence of random numbers. If a bug occurs, fix the bug and test with the same* **seedValue***; this allows you to reconstruct the exact same sequence of random numbers that caused the bug. Once the bugs have been removed, use the form* **Random()** *that generates a new sequence of random numbers each time the program is run.*

The call

```
r.setSeed(seedValue);
```

resets **r**'s seed value at any time.

The calls

```
r.nextInt()
r.nextLong()
```

generate uniformly distributed random integers. You can use **Math.abs** to take the absolute value of the number produced by **nextInt**, thus giving a number in the range zero through approximately two billion. Then use the **%** operator to scale the number. For example, to roll a die from 1 to 6, if you scale with a 6, you will get a number in the range 0 through 5. Then simply shift this value by adding 1 to produce a number in the range 1 through 6. The expression is as follows

```
Math.abs( r.nextInt() ) % 6 + 1
```

The calls

```
r.nextFloat()
r.nextDouble()
```

generate uniformly distributed values in the range $0.0 <= x < 1.0$.

The call

```
r.nextGaussian()
```

generates a double value with a probability density of a Gaussian (i.e., "normal") distribution (mean of 0.0 and standard deviation of 1.0).

18.8 Bit Manipulation and the Bitwise Operators

Java provides extensive bit manipulation capabilities for programmers who need to get down to the so-called "bits-and-bytes" level. Operating systems, test equipment software, networking software, and many other kinds of software require that the programmer communicate "directly with the hardware." In this and the next section, we discuss Java's bit manipulation capabilities. We introduce Java's many bitwise operators and we demonstrate their use in live-code examples.

All data is represented internally by computers as sequences of bits. Each bit can assume the value **0** or the value **1**. On most systems, a sequence of 8 bits forms a byte—the standard storage unit for a variable of type **byte**. Other data types are stored in larger numbers of bytes. The bitwise operators are used to manipulate the bits of integral operands (**byte**, **char**, **short**, **int**, and **long**).

Note that the bitwise operator discussions in this section show the binary representations of the integer operands. For a detailed explanation of the binary (also called base 2) number system see the appendix "Number Systems".

The bitwise operators are: *bitwise AND (**&**), bitwise inclusive OR (**|**), bitwise exclusive OR (**^**), left shift (**<<**), right shift with sign extension (**>>**), right shift with zero extension (**>>>**)* and *complement (**~**)*. The bitwise AND, bitwise inclusive OR, and bitwise exclusive OR operators compare their two operands bit-by-bit. The bitwise AND operator sets each bit in the result to 1 if the corresponding bit in both operands is 1. The bitwise inclusive OR operator sets each bit in the result to 1 if the corresponding bit in either (or both) operand(s) is 1. The bitwise exclusive OR operator sets each bit in the result to 1 if the corresponding bit in exactly one operand is 1. The left shift operator shifts the bits of its left operand to the left by the number of bits specified in its right operand. The right shift operator with sign extension shifts the bits in its left operand to the right by the number of bits specified in its right operand—if the left operand is negative, **1**s are shifted in from the left; otherwise, **0**s are shifted in from the left. The right shift operator with zero extension shifts the bits in its left operand to the right by the number of bits specified in its right operand—**0**s are shifted in from the left. The bitwise complement operator sets all **0** bits in its operand to **1** in the result and sets all **1** bits to **0** in the result. Detailed discussions of each bitwise operator appear in the following examples. The bitwise operators are summarized in Fig. 18.5.

Operator	Name	Description
&	bitwise AND	The bits in the result are set to **1** if the corresponding bits in the two operands are both **1**.
|	bitwise inclusive OR	The bits in the result are set to **1** if at least one of the corresponding bits in the two operands is **1**.
^	bitwise exclusive OR	The bits in the result are set to **1** if exactly one of the corresponding bits in the two operands is **1**.
<<	left shift	Shifts the bits of the first operand left by the number of bits specified by the second operand; fill from the right with **0** bits.
>>	right shift with sign extension	Shifts the bits of the first operand right by the number of bits specified by the second operand. If the first operand is negative, **1**s are shifted in from the left; otherwise **0**s are shifted in from the left.

Fig. 18.5 The bitwise operators (part 1 of 2).

Operator	Name	Description
`>>>`	right shift with zero extension	Shifts the bits of the first operand right by the number of bits specified by the second operand; **0**s are shifted in from the left.
`~`	one's complement	All **0** bits are set to **1** and all **1** bits are set to **0**.

Fig. 18.5 The bitwise operators (part 2 of 2).

When using the bitwise operators, it is useful to display values in their binary representation to illustrate the effects of these operators. The applet of Fig. 18.6 allows the user to enter an integer into a **TextField** and press *Enter*. The applet's action method reads the **String** from the **TextField**, converts it to an integer and invokes method **getBits** (line 30) to obtain **String** representation of the integer in bits. The result is displayed in the output **TextField**. The integer is displayed in its binary representation in groups of eight bits each. Method **displayBits** uses the bitwise AND operator to combine variable **value** with variable **displayMask**. Often, the bitwise AND operator is used with an operand called a *mask*—an integer value with specific bits set to **1**. Masks are used to hide some bits in a value while selecting other bits. In **getBits**, mask variable **displayMask** is assigned the value **1 << 31** (**10000000 00000000 00000000 00000000**). The left shift operator shifts the value **1** from the low-order (rightmost) bit to the high-order (leftmost) bit in **displayMask**, and fills in **0** bits from the right. The statement

```
1  // Fig. 18.06: PrintBits.java
2  // Printing an unsigned integer in bits
3  import java.awt.*;
4  import java.awt.event.*;
5  import java.applet.Applet;
6  
7  public class PrintBits extends Applet
8                  implements ActionListener {
9     private TextField input, output;
10 
11    public void init()
12    {
13       add( new Label( "Enter an integer " ) );
14       input = new TextField( 10 );
15       input.addActionListener( this );
16       add( input );
17 
18       add( new Label( "The integer in bits is" ) );
19       output = new TextField( 35 );
```

Fig. 18.6 Displaying the bit representation of an integer (part 1 of 3).

```
      output.setEditable( false );
      add( output );
   }

   public void actionPerformed( ActionEvent e )
   {
      int val = Integer.parseInt( e.getActionCommand() );
      output.setText( getBits( val ) );
   }

   public String getBits( int value )
   {
      int displayMask = 1 << 31;
      StringBuffer buf = new StringBuffer( 35 );

      for ( int c = 1; c <= 32; c++ ) {
         buf.append(
            ( value & displayMask ) == 0 ? '0' : '1' );
         value <<= 1;

         if ( c % 8 == 0 )
            buf.append( ' ' );
      }

      return buf.toString();
   }
}
```

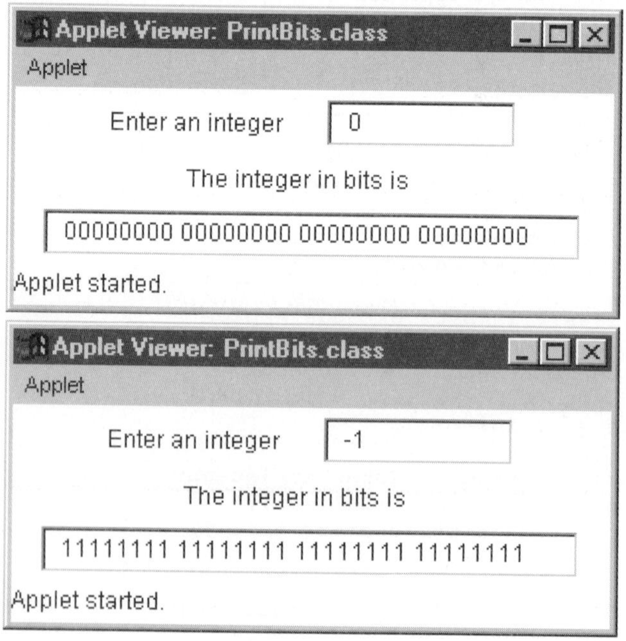

Applet Viewer: PrintBits.class
Applet
Enter an integer 0
The integer in bits is
00000000 00000000 00000000 00000000
Applet started.

Applet Viewer: PrintBits.class
Applet
Enter an integer -1
The integer in bits is
11111111 11111111 11111111 11111111
Applet started.

Fig. 18.6 Displaying the bit representation of an integer (part 2 of 3).

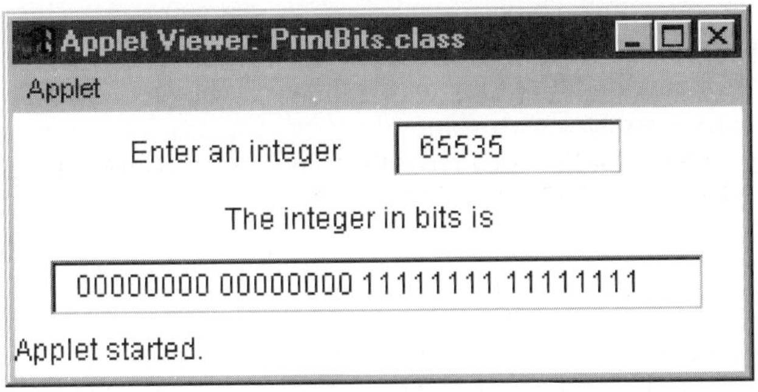

Applet Viewer: PrintBits.class

Applet

Enter an integer 65535

The integer in bits is

00000000 00000000 11111111 11111111

Applet started.

Fig. 18.6 Displaying the bit representation of an integer (part 3 of 3).

```
buf.append( ( value & displayMask ) == 0 ? '0' : '1' );
```

determines whether a **1** or a **0** should be appended to **StringBuffer buf** for the current leftmost bit of variable **value**. Assume **value** contains **4000000000** (**11101110 01101011 00101000 00000000**). When **value** and **displayMask** are combined using **&**, all the bits except the high-order bit in variable **value** are "masked off" (hidden) because any bit "ANDed" with **0** yields **0**. If the leftmost bit is **1**, **value & displayMask** evaluates to **1**, and **1** is appended—otherwise, **0** is appended. Variable **value** is then left shifted one bit by the expression **value <<= 1** (this is equivalent to **value = value << 1**). These steps are repeated for each bit in variable **value**. At the end of the **getBits** method, the **StringBuffer** is converted to a **String** with the statement

```
buf.toString();
```

then returned from the method. Figure 18.7 summarizes the results of combining two bits with the bitwise AND (**&**) operator.

Common Programming Error 18.1

*Using the logical AND operator (**&&**) for the bitwise AND operator (**&**).*

Bit 1	Bit 2	Bit 1 & Bit 2
0	0	0
1	0	0
0	1	0
1	1	1

Fig. 18.7 Results of combining two bits with the bitwise AND operator (**&**).

The program of Fig. 18.8 demonstrates the use of the bitwise AND operator, the bitwise inclusive OR operator, the bitwise exclusive OR operator and the bitwise complement operator. The program uses method **getBits** to get a **String** representation of the integer values. The program allows the user to enter values into **TextField**s and press *Enter* (for the binary operators, two values must be entered). The user can then press the button representing the operation they would like to test and the result is displayed in both integer and bit representations.

```
// Fig. 18.08: MiscBitOps.java
// Using the bitwise AND, bitwise inclusive OR, bitwise
// exclusive OR, and bitwise complement operators.
import java.awt.*;
import java.awt.event.*;
import java.applet.Applet;

public class MiscBitOps extends Applet
             implements ActionListener {
   private TextField input1, input2, result,
                     bits1, bits2, bits3;
   private Button and, inclusiveOr, exclusiveOr, complement;
   private Panel inputPanel, bitsPanel, buttonPanel;

   public void init()
   {
      setLayout( new BorderLayout() );
      inputPanel = new Panel();
      inputPanel.setLayout( new GridLayout( 4, 2 ) );

      inputPanel.add( new Label( "Enter 2 ints" ) );
      inputPanel.add( new Label( "" ) );

      inputPanel.add( new Label( "Value 1" ) );
      input1 = new TextField( 8 );
      inputPanel.add( input1 );

      inputPanel.add( new Label( "Value 2" ) );
      input2 = new TextField( 8 );
      inputPanel.add( input2 );

      inputPanel.add( new Label( "Result" ) );
      result = new TextField( 8 );
      result.setEditable( false );
      inputPanel.add( result );

      bitsPanel = new Panel();
      bitsPanel.setLayout( new GridLayout( 4, 1 ) );
      bitsPanel.add( new Label( "Bit representations" ) );
```

Fig. 18.8 Demonstrating the bitwise AND, bitwise inclusive OR, bitwise exclusive OR and bitwise complement operators (part 1 of 4).

```

      bits1 = new TextField( 33 );
      bits1.setEditable( false );
      bitsPanel.add( bits1 );

      bits2 = new TextField( 33 );
      bits2.setEditable( false );
      bitsPanel.add( bits2 );

      bits3 = new TextField( 33 );
      bits3.setEditable( false );
      bitsPanel.add( bits3 );

      buttonPanel = new Panel();
      and = new Button( "AND" );
      and.addActionListener( this );
      buttonPanel.add( and );

      inclusiveOr = new Button( "Inclusive OR" );
      inclusiveOr.addActionListener( this );
      buttonPanel.add( inclusiveOr );

      exclusiveOr = new Button( "Exclusive OR" );
      exclusiveOr.addActionListener( this );
      buttonPanel.add( exclusiveOr );

      complement = new Button( "Complement" );
      complement.addActionListener( this );
      buttonPanel.add( complement );

      add( inputPanel, BorderLayout.WEST );
      add( bitsPanel, BorderLayout.EAST );
      add( buttonPanel, BorderLayout.SOUTH );
   }

   public void actionPerformed( ActionEvent e )
   {
      if ( e.getSource() == complement ) {
         input2.setText( "" );
         bits2.setText( "" );
         int val = Integer.parseInt( input1.getText() );
         result.setText( Integer.toString( ~val ) );
         bits1.setText( getBits( val ) );
         bits3.setText( getBits( ~val ) );
      }
      else {
         int val1 = Integer.parseInt( input1.getText() );
         int val2 = Integer.parseInt( input2.getText() );

         bits1.setText( getBits( val1 ) );
```

Fig. 18.8 Demonstrating the bitwise AND, bitwise inclusive OR, bitwise exclusive OR and bitwise complement operators (part 2 of 4).

```
         bits2.setText( getBits( val2 ) );

         if ( e.getSource() == and ) {
            result.setText( Integer.toString( val1 & val2 ) );
            bits3.setText( getBits( val1 & val2 ) );
         }
         else if ( e.getSource() == inclusiveOr ) {
            result.setText( Integer.toString( val1 | val2 ) );
            bits3.setText( getBits( val1 | val2 ) );
         }
         else if ( e.getSource() == exclusiveOr ) {
            result.setText( Integer.toString( val1 ^ val2 ) );
            bits3.setText( getBits( val1 ^ val2 ) );
         }
      }
   }

   public String getBits( int value )
   {
      int displayMask = 1 << 31;
      StringBuffer buf = new StringBuffer( 35 );

      for ( int c = 1; c <= 32; c++ ) {
        buf.append( ( value & displayMask ) == 0 ? '0' : '1' );
         value <<= 1;

         if ( c % 8 == 0 )
            buf.append( ' ' );
      }

      return buf.toString();
   }
}
```

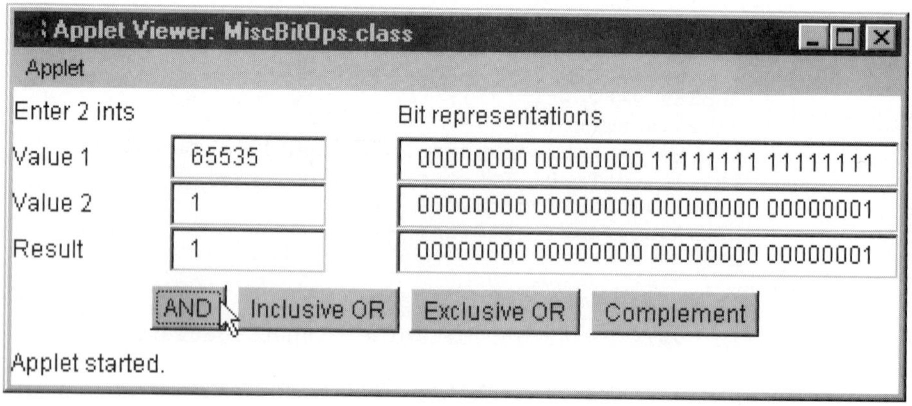

Applet Viewer: MiscBitOps.class
Applet
Enter 2 ints | Bit representations
Value 1 | 65535 | 00000000 00000000 11111111 11111111
Value 2 | 1 | 00000000 00000000 00000000 00000001
Result | 1 | 00000000 00000000 00000000 00000001
AND | Inclusive OR | Exclusive OR | Complement
Applet started.

Fig. 18.8 Demonstrating the bitwise AND, bitwise inclusive OR, bitwise exclusive OR and bitwise complement operators (part 3 of 4).

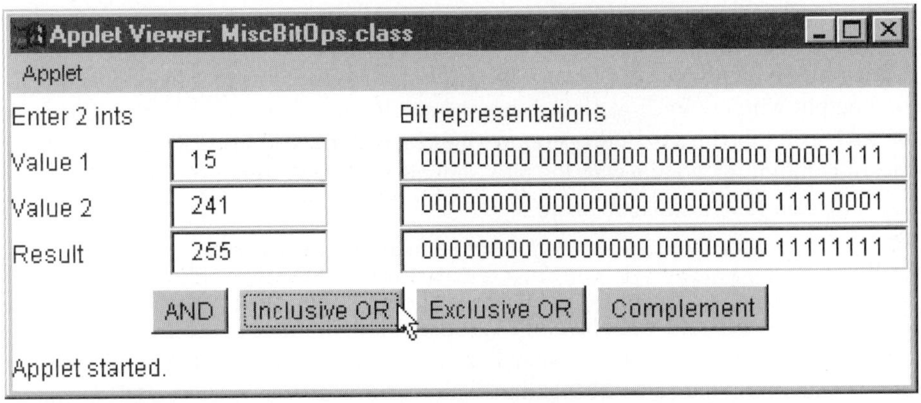

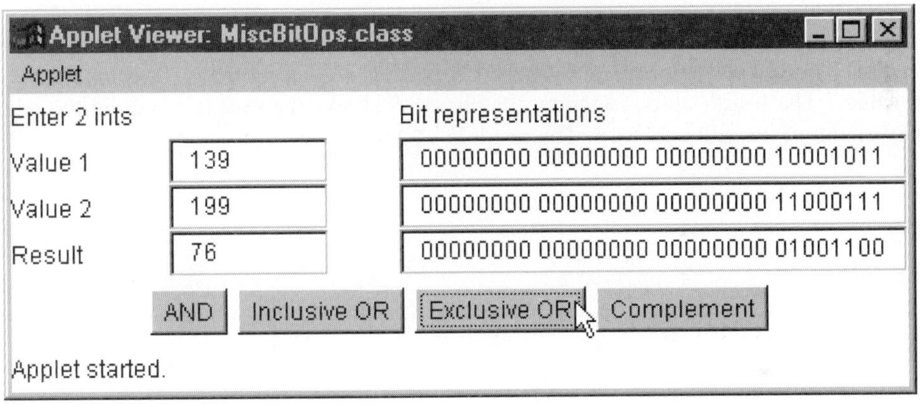

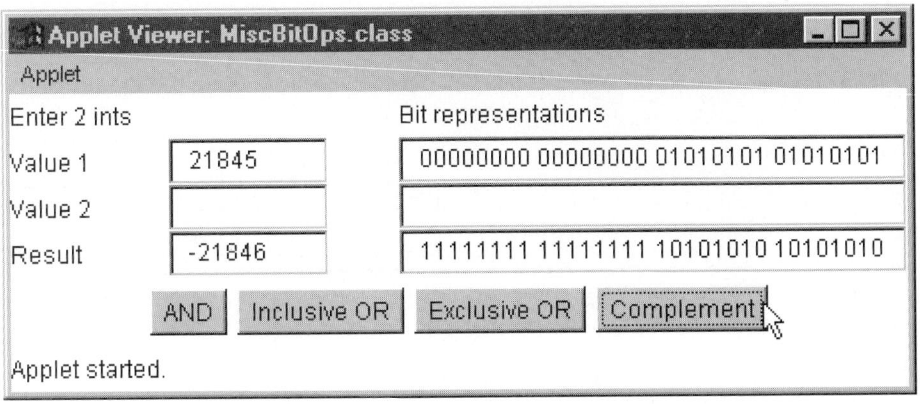

Fig. 18.8 Demonstrating the bitwise AND, bitwise inclusive OR, bitwise exclusive OR and bitwise complement operators (part 4 of 4).

The first output window for Fig. 18.8 shows the results of combining the value **65535** and the value **1** with the bitwise AND operator (**&**). All the bits except the low-order bit in the value **65535** are "masked off" (hidden) by "ANDing" with the value **1**.

The bitwise inclusive OR operator is used to set specific bits to 1 in an operand. The second output window for Fig. 18.8 shows the results of combining the value **15** and the value **241** using the bitwise OR operator—the result is **255**. Figure 18.9 summarizes the results of combining two bits with the bitwise inclusive OR operator.

Common Programming Error 18.2

Using the logical OR operator (||) for the bitwise OR operator (|).

The bitwise exclusive OR operator (**^**) sets each bit in the result to 1 if *exactly* one of the corresponding bits in its two operands is 1. The third output of Fig. 18.8 shows the results of combining the value **139** and the value **199** using the exclusive OR operator—the result is **76**. Figure 18.10 summarizes the results of combining two bits with the bitwise exclusive OR operator.

The *bitwise* complement operator (**~**) sets all **1** bits in its operand to **0** in the result and sets all **0** bits to **1** in the result—otherwise referred to as "taking the *one's complement* of the value." The fourth output window for Fig. 18.8 shows the results of taking the one's complement of the value **21845**. The result is **-21846**.

Bit 1	Bit 2	Bit 1 ^ Bit 2
0	0	0
1	0	1
0	1	1
1	1	0

Fig. 18.9 Results of combining two bits with the bitwise exclusive OR operator (**^**).

Bit 1	Bit 2	Bit 1 | Bit 2
0	0	0
1	0	1
0	1	1
1	1	1

Fig. 18.10 Results of combining two bits with the bitwise inclusive OR operator (**|**).

The program of Fig. 18.11 demonstrates the left shift operator (**<<**), the right shift operator with sign extension (**>>**) and the right shift operator with zero extension (**>>>**). Method **getBits** obtains a **String** representation of the integer values. The program allows the user to enter an integer in a **TextField** and press *Enter*. The bit representation of the integer is displayed in another **TextField**.

```
// Fig. 18.11: BitShift.java
// Using the bitwise shift operators.
import java.awt.*;
import java.applet.Applet;
import java.awt.event.*;

public class BitShift extends Applet
             implements ActionListener {
   private TextField value, bits;
   private Button left, rightSign, rightZero;

   public void init()
   {
      add( new Label( "Integer to shift " ) );
      value = new TextField( 12 );
      value.addActionListener( this );
      add( value );

      bits = new TextField( 33 );
      bits.setEditable( false );
      add( bits );

      left = new Button( "<<" );
      left.addActionListener( this );
      add( left );

      rightSign = new Button( ">>" );
      rightSign.addActionListener( this );
      add( rightSign );

      rightZero = new Button( ">>>" );
      rightZero.addActionListener( this );
      add( rightZero );
   }

   public void actionPerformed( ActionEvent e )
   {
      int val = Integer.parseInt( value.getText() );

      if ( e.getSource() == left )
         val <<= 1;
      else if ( e.getSource() == rightSign )
         val >>= 1;
```

Fig. 18.11 Demonstrating the bitwise shift operators (part 1 of 4).

```
      else if ( e.getSource() == rightZero )
         val >>>= 1;

      value.setText( Integer.toString( val ) );
      bits.setText( getBits( val ) );
   }

   public String getBits( int value )
   {
      int displayMask = 1 << 31;
      StringBuffer buf = new StringBuffer( 35 );

      for ( int c = 1; c <= 32; c++ ) {
        buf.append( ( value & displayMask ) == 0 ? '0' : '1' );
         value <<= 1;

         if ( c % 8 == 0 )
            buf.append( ' ' );
      }

      return buf.toString();
   }
}
```

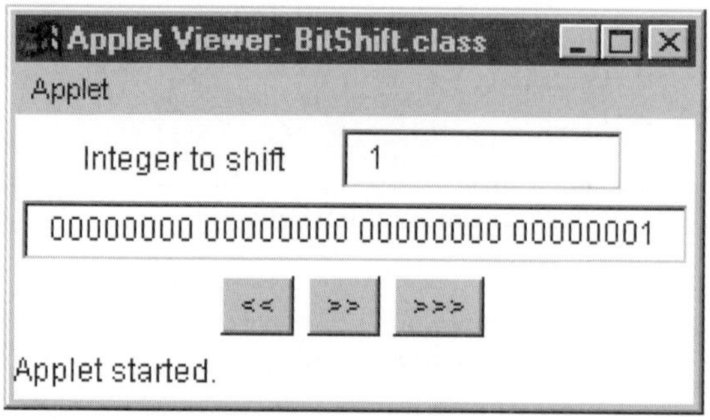

Applet Viewer: BitShift.class
Applet
Integer to shift 1
00000000 00000000 00000000 00000001
<< >> >>>
Applet started.

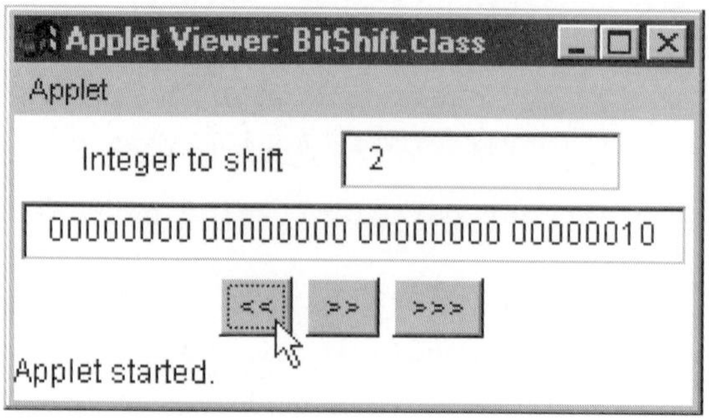

Applet Viewer: BitShift.class
Applet
Integer to shift 2
00000000 00000000 00000000 00000010
<< >> >>>
Applet started.

Fig. 18.11 Demonstrating the bitwise shift operators (part 2 of 4).

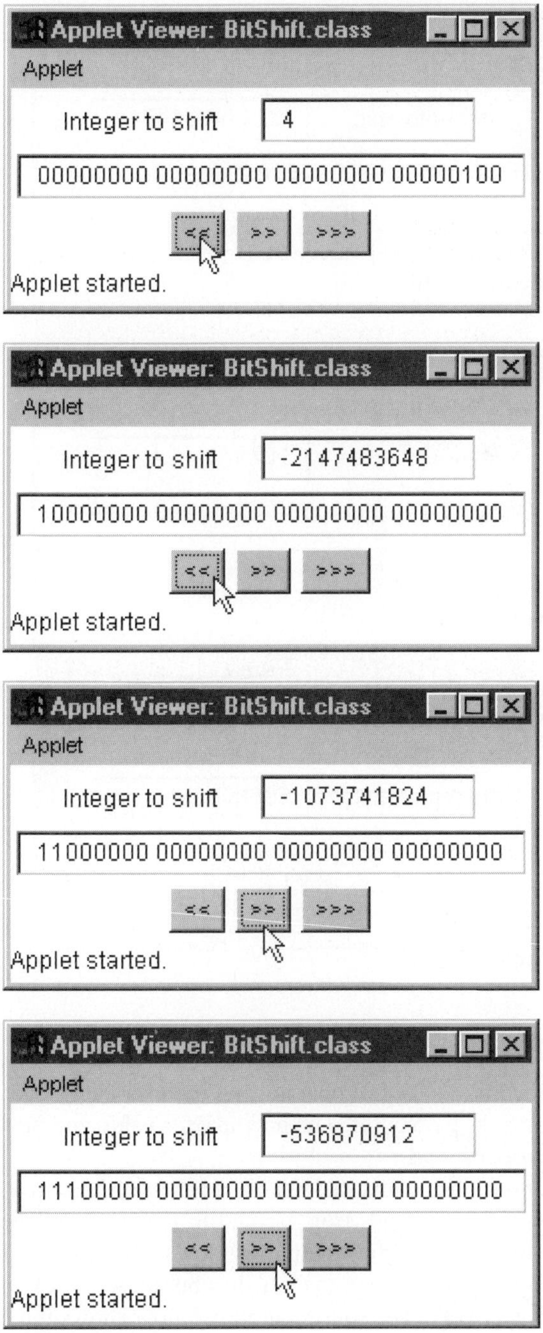

Applet Viewer: BitShift.class
Applet
Integer to shift 4
00000000 00000000 00000000 00000100
<< >> >>>
Applet started.

Applet Viewer: BitShift.class
Applet
Integer to shift -2147483648
10000000 00000000 00000000 00000000
<< >> >>>
Applet started.

Applet Viewer: BitShift.class
Applet
Integer to shift -1073741824
11000000 00000000 00000000 00000000
<< >> >>>
Applet started.

Applet Viewer: BitShift.class
Applet
Integer to shift -536870912
11100000 00000000 00000000 00000000
<< >> >>>
Applet started.

Fig. 18.11 Demonstrating the bitwise shift operators (part 3 of 4).

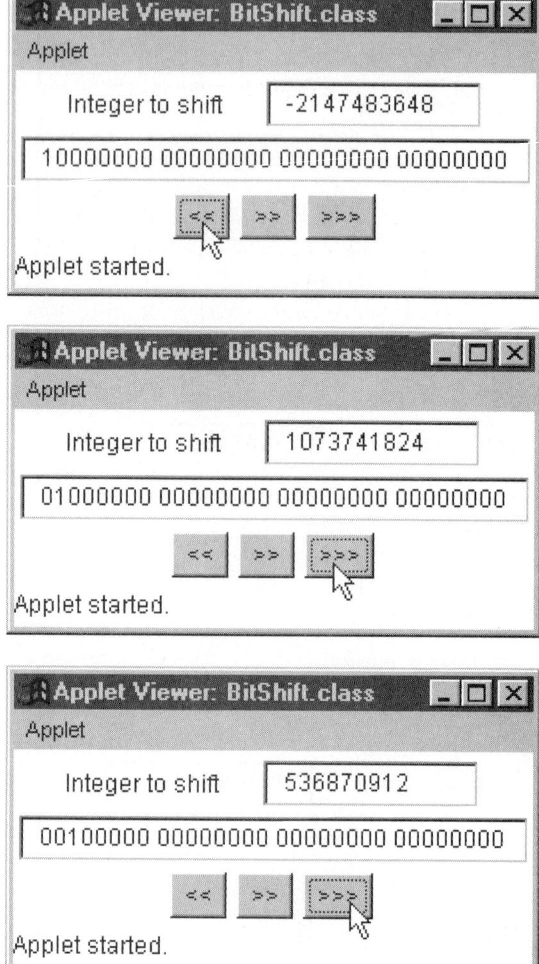

Fig. 18.11 Demonstrating the bitwise shift operators (part 4 of 4).

A button is provided for each shift operator. As the user clicks each button, the bits in the integer shift left or right by one bit. The new integer value and new bit representation are displayed in the **TextField**s.

The left shift operator (**<<**) shifts the bits of its left operand to the left by the number of bits specified in its right operand. Bits vacated to the right are replaced with **0**s; **1**s shifted off the left are lost. The first four output windows of Fig. 18.11 demonstrate the left shift operator. Starting with the value 1, the left shift button was pressed twice resulting in the values 2 and 4, respectively. The fourth output window shows the result of the value1 being shifted 31 times. Note that the result is a negative value. That is because a 1 in the high-order bit is used to indicate a negative value in an integer.

The right shift operator with sign extension (**>>**) shifts the bits of its left operand to the right by the number of bits specified in its right operand. Performing a right shift causes the vacated bits at the left to be replaced by **0**s if the number is positive and **1**s if the number is negative. Any **1**s shifted off the right are lost. The fifth and sixth output windows show the results of right shifting (with sign extension) the value in the fourth output window two times.

The right shift operator with zero extension (**>>>**) shifts the bits of its left operand to the right by the number of bits specified in its right operand. Performing a right shift causes the vacated bits at the left to be replaced by **0**s. Any **1**s shifted off the right are lost. The eighth and ninth output windows show the results of right shifting (with zero extension) the value in the seventh output window two times.

Each bitwise operator (except the bitwise complement operator) has a corresponding assignment operator. These *bitwise assignment operators* are shown in Fig. 18.12 and are used in a similar manner to the arithmetic assignment operators introduced in Chapter 2.

18.9 BitSet Class

The **BitSet** class makes it easy to create and manipulate *bit sets*. Bit sets are useful for representing a set of boolean flags. **BitSet**s are dynamic. More bits can be added as needed and a **BitSet** object will grow to accommodate the additional bits.

```
BitSet b = new BitSet();
```

creates **BitSet** which is initially empty.

```
BitSet b = new BitSet( size );
```

creates a **BitSet** with **size** bits.

```
b.set( bitNumber );
```

sets bit **bitNumber** of **BitSet b** "on."

```
b.clear( bitNumber );
```

Bitwise assignment operators	
&=	Bitwise AND assignment operator.
|=	Bitwise inclusive OR assignment operator.
^=	Bitwise exclusive OR assignment operator.
<<=	Left shift assignment operator.
>>=	Right shift with sign extension assignment operator.
>>>=	Right shift with zero extension assignment operator.

Fig. 18.12 The bitwise assignment operators.

sets bit **bitNumber** of **BitSet b** "off."

```
b.get( bitNumber );
```

gets bit **bitNumber** of **BitSet b**. The result is returned as true if the bit is on or false if the bit is off.

```
b.and( b1 );
```

performs a bit-by-bit logical AND between **BitSet**s **b** and **b1**. The result is stored in **b**. Bitwise logical OR and bitwise logical XOR are performed by

```
b.or( b1 );
b.xor( b2 );
```

The expression

```
b.size()
```

returns the size of **BitSet b**.

The expression

```
b.equals( b1 )
```

compares the two **BitSet**s for equality.

```
b.clone()
```

clones a **BitSet** and returns an **Object** reference to the new **BitSet**.

```
b.toString()
```

converts **BitSet b** to a **String**. This is helpful for debugging.

The expression

```
b.hashCode()
```

provides a hash code useful for storing and retrieving **BitSet** objects in hash tables.

Figure 18.13 revisits the Sieve of Eratosthenes for finding prime numbers we discussed in Exercise 5.27. A **BitSet** is used instead of an array to implement the algorithm. The program displays all the prime numbers from 1 to 1023 in a **TextArea** and provides a **TextField** in which the user can type any number from 1 to 1023 to determine if that number is prime (in which case a message is displayed in the status area of the applet).

```
// Fig. 18.13: BitSetTest.java
// Using a BitSet to demonstrate the Sieve of Eratosthenes.
import java.applet.Applet;
import java.awt.*;
import java.awt.event.*;
import java.util.*;
```

Fig. 18.13 Demonstrating the Sieve of Eratosthenes using a **BitSet** (part 1 of 3).

```

public class BitSetTest extends Applet
             implements ActionListener {
   private BitSet sieve;
   private Panel inputPanel;
   private TextField input;
   private TextArea primes;

   public void init()
   {
      sieve = new BitSet( 1024 );

      setLayout( new BorderLayout() );
      inputPanel = new Panel();

      inputPanel.add(
         new Label( "Enter a value from 1 to 1023" ) );
      input = new TextField( 10 );
      input.addActionListener( this );
      inputPanel.add( input );
      add( inputPanel, BorderLayout.NORTH );

      primes = new TextArea();
      add( primes, BorderLayout.CENTER );

      // set all bits from 1 to 1023
      int size = sieve.size();

      for ( int i = 1; i < size; i++ )
         sieve.set( i );

      // perform Sieve of Eratosthenes
      int finalBit = ( int ) Math.sqrt( sieve.size() );

      for ( int i = 2; i < finalBit; i++ )
         if ( sieve.get( i ) )
            for ( int j = 2 * i; j < size; j += i )
               sieve.clear( j );

      int counter = 0;

      for ( int i = 1; i < size; i++ )
         if ( sieve.get( i ) ) {
            primes.append( String.valueOf( i ) );
            primes.append(
               ++counter % 7 == 0 ? "\n" : "\t" );
         }
   }

```

Fig. 18.13 Demonstrating the Sieve of Eratosthenes using a **BitSet** (part 2 of 3).

```
   public void actionPerformed( ActionEvent e )
   {
      int val = Integer.parseInt( input.getText() );

      if ( sieve.get( val ) )
         showStatus( val + " is a prime number" );
      else
         showStatus( val + " is not a prime number" );
   }
}
```

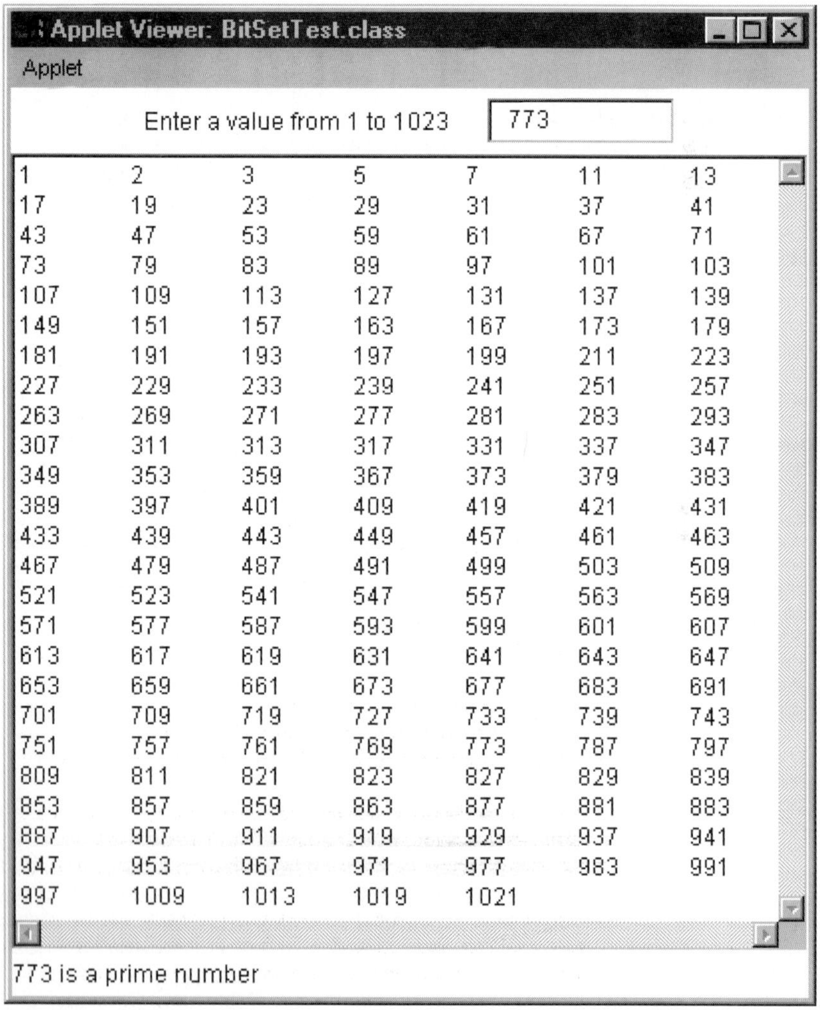

Applet Viewer: BitSetTest.class

Applet

Enter a value from 1 to 1023 | 773

1	2	3	5	7	11	13
17	19	23	29	31	37	41
43	47	53	59	61	67	71
73	79	83	89	97	101	103
107	109	113	127	131	137	139
149	151	157	163	167	173	179
181	191	193	197	199	211	223
227	229	233	239	241	251	257
263	269	271	277	281	283	293
307	311	313	317	331	337	347
349	353	359	367	373	379	383
389	397	401	409	419	421	431
433	439	443	449	457	461	463
467	479	487	491	499	503	509
521	523	541	547	557	563	569
571	577	587	593	599	601	607
613	617	619	631	641	643	647
653	659	661	673	677	683	691
701	709	719	727	733	739	743
751	757	761	769	773	787	797
809	811	821	823	827	829	839
853	857	859	863	877	881	883
887	907	911	919	929	937	941
947	953	967	971	977	983	991
997	1009	1013	1019	1021		

773 is a prime number

Fig. 18.13 Demonstrating the Sieve of Eratosthenes using a **`BitSet`** (part 3 of 3).

The statement

```
sieve = new BitSet( 1024 );
```

creates a **BitSet** of 1024 bits. We ignore the bit at position 0 in this program. After the **init** method sets all the bits on in the **BitSet**, the code

```
// perform Sieve of Eratosthenes
int finalBit = (int) Math.sqrt( sieve.size() );

for ( int i = 2; i < finalBit; i++ )
   if ( sieve.get( i ) )
      for ( int j = 2 * i; j < size; j += i )
         sieve.clear( j );
```

determines all the prime numbers from 1 to 1023. The integer **finalBit** is used to determine when the algorithm is complete. The basic algorithm is that a number is prime if it has no divisors other than 1 and itself. The number 1 is prime. Starting with the number 2, once we know a number is prime, we can eliminate all multiples of that number. The number 2 is only divisible by 1 and itself, so it is prime. Therefore, we can eliminate 4, 6, 8, and so on. The number 3 is divisible by 1 and itself. Therefore, we can eliminate all multiples of 3 (keep in mind that all even numbers have already been eliminated).

Summary

- Class **Vector** provides the capabilities of dynamically resizable arrays. At any time the **Vector** contains a certain number of elements which is less than or equal to its *capacity*. The capacity is the space that has been reserved for the array.
- If a **Vector** needs to grow, it grows by an increment that you specify or by a default assumed by the system. If you do not specify a capacity increment, the system will automatically double the size of the **Vector** each time additional capacity is needed.
- **Vector**s are designed to store references to **Object**s. If you would like to store values of primitive data types in **Vector**s, you must use the type-wrapper classes (**Byte**, **Short**, **Integer**, **Long**, **Float**, **Double**, **Boolean** and **Character**) to create objects containing the primitive data type values.
- Class **Vector** provides three constructors. The no-argument constructor creates an empty **Vector**. The constructor that takes one argument creates a **Vector** with an initial capacity specified by the argument. The constructor that takes two arguments creates a **Vector** with an *initial capacity* specified by the first argument and a *capacity increment* specified by the second argument.
- **Vector** method **addElement** adds its argument to the end of the **Vector**. Method **insertElementAt** inserts an element at the specified position. Method **setElementAt** sets the element at a specific position.
- **Vector** method **removeElement** removes the first occurrence of its argument. Method **removeAllElements** removes every element from the **Vector**. Method **removeElementAt** removes the element at the specified index.

- **Vector** method **firstElement** returns a reference to the first element. Method **lastElement** returns a reference to the last element.
- **Vector** method **isEmpty** determines if the **Vector** is empty. Method **contains** determines if the **Vector** contains the **searchKey** specified as an argument. Method **indexOf** gets the index of the first location of its argument. The method returns –1 if the argument is not found in the **Vector**.
- **Vector** method **trimToSize** cuts the capacity of the **Vector** to the **Vector**'s size. Methods **size** and **capacity** determine the number of elements currently in the **Vector** and the number of elements that can be stored in the **Vector** without allocating more memory, respectively.
- **Vector** method **elements** returns a reference to an **Enumeration** containing the elements of the **Vector**.
- **Enumeration** method **hasMoreElements** determines if there are more elements. Method **nextElement** returns a reference to the next element.
- Class **Stack** extends class **Vector**. **Stack** method **push** adds its argument to the top of the stack. Method **pop** removes the top element of the stack. Method **peek** returns an **Object** reference to the top element of the stack without removing the element. **Stack** method **empty** determines if the stack is empty.
- A **Dictionary** transforms keys to values.
- Hashing is a high-speed scheme for converting keys into unique array subscripts for storage and retrieval of information.The load factor is the ratio of the number of occupied cells in a hash table to the size of the hash table. The closer this ratio gets to 1.0, the greater the chance of collisions.
- The no-argument **Hashtable** constructor creates a **Hashtable** with a default capacity of 101 elements and a default load factor of .75. The **Hashtable** constructor that takes one argument specifies the initial capacity and the constructor that takes two arguments specifies the initial capacity and load factor, respectively.
- **Hashtable** method **put** adds a *key* and a *value* into a **Hashtable**. Method **get** locates the value associated with the specified key. Method **remove** deletes the value associated with the specified key. Method **isEmpty** determines if the table is empty.
- **Hashtable** method **containsKey** determines if the key specified as an argument is in the **Hashtable** (i.e., a value is associated with that key). Method **contains** determines if the **Object** specified as its argument is in the **Hashtable**. Method **clear** empties the **Hashtable**. Method **elements** obtains an **Enumeration** of the values. Method **keys** obtains an **Enumeration** of the keys.
- A **Properties** object is a persistent **Hashtable** object. Class **Properties** extends **Hashtable**. Keys and values in a **Properties** object must be **String**s.
- The **Properties** no-argument constructor creates an empty **Properties** table with no default properties. There is also a constructor that is passed a reference to a default **Properties** object containing default property values.

- **Properties** method **getProperty** locates the value of the key specified as an argument. Method **save** saves the contents of the **Properties** object to the **OutputStream** object specified as the first argument. Method **load** restores the contents of the **Properties** object from the **InputStream** object specified as the argument. Method **propertyNames** obtains an **Enumeration** of the property names.
- Java provides extensive random number generation capabilities in class **Random**. Class **Random**'s no-argument constructor uses the time to seed its random number generator differently each time it is called. To create a pseudorandom-number generator with repeatability use the **Random** constructor that takes a seed argument.
- **Random** method **setSeed** sets the seed. Methods **nextInt** and **nextLong** generate uniformly distributed random integers. Methods **nextFloat** and **nextDouble** generate uniformly distributed values in the range $0.0 <= x < 1.0$.
- The bitwise AND (**&**) operator sets each bit in the result to 1 if the corresponding bit in both operands is 1.
- The bitwise inclusive OR (**|**) operator sets each bit in the result to 1 if the corresponding bit in either (or both) operand(s) is 1.
- The bitwise exclusive OR (**^**) operator sets each bit in the result to 1 if the corresponding bit in exactly one operand is 1.
- The left shift (**<<**) operator shifts the bits of its left operand to the left by the number of bits specified in its right operand.
- The right shift operator with sign extension (**>>**) shifts the bits in its left operand to the right by the number of bits specified in its right operand—if the left operand is negative **1**s are shifted in from the left; otherwise, **0**s are shifted in from the left.
- The right shift operator with zero extension (**>>>**) shifts the bits in its left operand to the right by the number of bits specified in its right operand—**0**s are shifted in from the left.
- The bitwise complement (**~**) operator sets all **0** bits in its operand to **1** in the result and sets all **1** bits to **0** in the result.
- Each bitwise operator (except complement) has a corresponding assignment operator.
- The no-argument **BitSet** constructor creates an empty **BitSet**. The one-argument **BitSet** constructor creates a **BitSet** with the number of bits specified by its argument.
- **BitSet** method **set** sets the specified bit "on." Method **clear** sets the specified bit "off." Method **get** returns true if the bit is on or false if the bit is off.
- **BitSet** method **and** performs a bit-by-bit logical AND between **BitSet**s. The result is stored in the **BitSet** that invoked the method. Bitwise logical OR and bitwise logical XOR are performed by methods **or** and **xor**.
- **BitSet** method **size** returns the size of a **BitSet**. Method **clone** clones a **BitSet** and returns an **Object** reference to the new **BitSet**. Method **toString** converts a **BitSet** to a **String**.

Terminology

addElement method of class **Vector**
after method of class **Date**
and method of class **BitSet**
ArrayIndexOutOfBoundsException
before method of class **Date**
bit set
BitSet class
capacity increment of a **Vector**
capacity of a **Vector**
capacity method of class **Vector**
clear method of class **Hashtable**
clone method of class **BitSet**
collision in hashing
contains method of class **Vector**
containsKey method of class **Hashtable**
Date class
defaults
Dictionary class
dynamically resizeable array
elementAt method of class **Vector**
elements method of class **Dictionary**
elements method of class **Vector**
empty method of class **Vector**
EmptyStackException class
enumerate successive elements
Enumeration interface
equals method of class **Object**
firstElement method of class **Vector**
get method of class **Dictionary**
getDate method of class **Date**
getDay method of class **Date**
getHours method of class **Date**
getMinutes method of class **Date**
getMonth method of class **Date**
getProperty method of class **Properties**
getSeconds method of class **Date**
getTime method of class **Date**
getYear method of class **Date**
hashing
Hashtable class
hashCode method of class **Object**
hasMoreElements method (**Enumeration**)
IllegalArgumentException
indexOf method of class **Vector**
initial capacity of a **Vector**
insertElementAt method of class **Vector**
IOException
isEmpty method of class **Dictionary**
isEmpty method of class **Vector**
iterator operations
java.util
key in a **Dictionary**
keys method of class **Dictionary**
lastElement method of class **Vector**
lastIndexOf method of class **Vector**
last-in-first-out (LIFO) stack
list method of class **Properties**
load method of class **Properties**
load factor in hashing
nextDouble method of class **Random**
nextElement method of class **Random**
nextFloat method of class **Random**
nextInt method of class **Random**
nextLong method of class **Random**
nextToken method of class **Random**
NoSuchElementException class
NullPointerException
or method of class **BitSet**
peek method of class **Stack**
pop method of class **Stack**
propertyNames method of **Properties**
Properties class
pseudorandom numbers
push method of class **Stack**
put method of class **Dictionary**
Random class
rehash method of class **Hashtable**
remove method of class **Dictionary**
removeAllElements method of **Vector**
removeElement method of class **Vector**
removeElementAt method of class **Vector**
save method of class **Properties**
search method of class **Stack**
seed of a random number generator
set method of class **BitSet**
setDate method of class **Date**
setElementAt method of class **Vector**
setMinutes method of class **Date**
setMonth method of class **Date**
setSeconds method of class **Date**
setSeed method of class **Random**
setSize method of class **Vector**
setTime method of class **Date**
setYear method of class **Date**

size method of class **Dictionary**
size method of class **Vector**
Stack class
toString method of class **Date**
trim a **Vector** to its exact size
trimToSize method of class **Vector**
Vector class
whitespace characters
xor method of class **BitSet**

Common Programming Errors

18.1 Using the logical AND operator (**&&**) for the bitwise AND operator (**&**).

18.2 Using the logical OR operator (||) for the bitwise OR operator (|).

Performance Tips

18.1 Inserting additional elements into an array whose current size is less than its capacity is a relatively fast operation.

18.2 It is a relatively slow operation to insert an element into an array that needs to grow larger to accommodate the new element.

18.3 The default capacity increment of doubling the size of the **Vector** may seem wasteful of storage, but it is actually an efficient way for many **Vector**s to grow quickly to be "about the right size." This is much more efficient time-wise than growing the Vector each time by only as much space as it takes to hold a single element. But it can waste space.

18.4 If storage is at a premium, use the ***trimToSize*** method of the ***Vector*** class to trim a **Vector** to its exact size. This will optimize a **Vector**'s use of storage. But be careful. If an additional element needs to be inserted in the **Vector**, this will be slow because it will force the array to grow dynamically—trimming leaves no room for growth.

18.5 The load factor in a hash table is a classic example of a space/time trade-off: By increasing the load factor, we get better memory utilization, but the program runs slower due to increased hashing collisions. By decreasing the load factor, we get better program speed because of reduced hashing collisions, but we get poorer memory utilization because a larger portion of the hash table remains empty.

Testing and Debugging Tips

18.1 Because ***Stack*** inherits from ***Vector***, the user may perform operations on ***Stack*** objects that are ordinarily not allowed on conventional stack data structures. This could corrupt the elements of the ***Stack*** and destroy the integrity of the ***Stack***.

18.2 Use ***Properties*** method ***list*** to display the contents of a ***Properties*** object for debugging purposes.

18.3 The repeatability of random numbers that occurs when the same seed value is used is useful for testing and debugging. While a program is under development, use the form ***Random(seedValue)*** that produces a repeatable sequence of random numbers. If a bug occurs, fix the bug and test with the same ***seedValue***; this allows you to reconstruct the exact same sequence of random numbers that caused the bug. Once the bugs have been removed, use the form **`Random()`** that generates a new sequence of random numbers each time the program is run.

Self-Review Exercises

18.1 Fill in the blanks in each of the following:
a) Java class ____________ provides the capabilities of array-like data structures that can dynamically resize themselves.
b) If you do not specify a capacity increment, the system will automatically__________ the size of the **`Vector`** each time additional capacity is needed.
c) If storage is at a premium use the ____________ method of the **`Vector`** class to trim a **`Vector`** to its exact size.

18.2 State whether each of the following statements is true or false. If false, explain why.
a) Values of primitive data types may be directly stored in a **`Vector`**.
b) With hashing, as the load factor increases, the chance of collisions decreases.

18.3 Under what circumstances is an **`EmptyStackException`** thrown.

18.4 Fill in the blanks in each of the following:
a) Bits in the result of an expression using operator_________ are set to 1 if the corresponding bits in each operand are set to 1. Otherwise, the bits are set to zero.
b) Bits in the result of an expression using operator___________ are set to 1 if at least one of the corresponding bits in either operand is set to 1. Otherwise, the bits are set to zero.
c) Bits in the result of an expression using operator___________ are set to 1 if exactly one of the corresponding bits in either operand is set to 1. Otherwise, the bits are set to zero.
d) The bitwise AND operator (**&**) is often used to __________ bits, that is to select certain bits from a bit string while zeroing others.
e) The __________ operator is used to shift the bits of a value to the left.
f) The _________ operator is used to shift the bits of a value to the right with sign extension and the ___________ operator is used to shift the bits of a value to the right with zero extension.

Answers to Self-Review Exercises

18.1 a) **`Vector`**. b) double. c) **`trimToSize`**

18.2 a) False; a **`Vector`** stores only **`Object`**s. You must use the type-wrapper classes (**`Byte`**, **`Short`**, **`Integer`**, **`Long`**, **`Float`**, **`Double`**, **`Boolean`** and **`Character`**) from the **`java.lang`** package to create **`Object`**s containing the primitive data type values. b) False; as the load factor increases, there are fewer available slots relative to the total number of slots so the chance of selecting an occupied slot with a hashing operation (i.e., a collision) increases.

18.3 **`pop`** an empty **`Stack`** object; **`peek`** an empty **`Stack`** object.

18.4 a) bitwise AND (**&**). b) bitwise inclusive OR (**|**). c) bitwise exclusive OR (**^**). d) mask. e) left shift operator (**<<**). f) right shift operator with sign extension (**>>**), right shift operator with zero extension (**>>>**).

Exercises

18.5 Define each of the following terms in the context of hashing:
a) application key.
b) collision.
c) hashing transformation.
d) load factor.
e) space/time trade-off.
f) **Hashtable** class.
g) capacity of a Hashtable.

18.6 Explain briefly the operation of each of the following methods of class **Vector**:
a) **addElement**.
b) **insertElementAt**.
c) **setElementAt**.
d) **removeElement**.
e) **removeAllElements**.
f) **removeElementAt**.
g) **firstElement**.
h) **lastElement**.
i) **isEmpty**.
j) **contains.**
k) **indexOf**.
l) **trimToSize**.
m) **size**.
n) **capacity**.

18.7 Explain why inserting additional elements into a **Vector** object whose current size is less than its capacity is a relatively fast operation and why inserting additional elements into a **Vector** object whose current size is at capacity is a relatively slow operation.

18.8 In the text we state that the default capacity increment of doubling the size of a **Vector** may seem wasteful of storage, but it is actually an efficient way for **Vectors** to grow quickly to be "about the right size." Explain this statement. Explain the pros and cons of this doubling algorithm. What can a program do when it determines that the doubling is wasting space?

18.9 Explain the use of the **Enumeration** interface with objects of class **Vector**.

18.10 By extending class **Vector**, Java's designers were able to form a **Stack** class quickly. What are the negative aspects of this kind of class construction by inheritance, particularly for class **Stack**?

18.11 Explain briefly the operation of each of the following methods of class **Hashtable**:
a) **put**.
b) **get**.
c) **remove**.
d) **isEmpty**.
e) **containsKey**.
f) **contains**.
g) **clear**.

h) **elements**.
i) **keys**.

18.12 Explain how to use the **Random** class to create pseudorandom numbers with the kind of repeatability we need for debugging.

18.13 Use a **Hashtable** to create a reusable class for choosing one of the 13 predefined colors in class **Color**. The name of the color should be used as keys and the predefined **Color** objects should be used as values. Place this class in a package that can be imported into any Java program. Use your new class in an applet that allows the user to select a color and draw a shape in that color.

18.14 Explain the use of the "observers and observable objects" design pattern. List five significant examples of this type of interaction that occur in the real world. Explain the operation of each of the following methods that might be used to implement an observer/observable interaction:

a) **addObserver**.
b) **deleteObserver**.
c) **notifyObservers**.
d) **deleteObservers**.
e) **setChanged**.
f) **clearChanged**.
g) **hasChanged**.
h) **countObservers**.

18.15 What does it mean when we state that a **Properties** object is a "persistent" **Hashtable** object? Explain the operation of each of the following methods of the **Properties** class:

a) **load**.
b) **save**.
c) **getProperty**.
d) **propertyNames**.
e) **list**.

18.16 Why might you want to use objects of class **BitSet**? Explain the operation of each of the following methods of class **BitSet**:

a) **set**.
b) **clear**.
c) **get**.
d) **and**.
e) **or**.
f) **xor**.
g) **size**.
h) **equals**.
i) **clone**.
j) **toString**
k) **hashCode**.

18.17 Write a program that right shifts an integer variable 4 bits with sign extension and then right shifts the same integer variable 4 bits with zero extension. The program should print the integer in bits before and after each shift operation. Run your program once with a positive integer and run it again with a negative integer.

18.18 Show how shifting an integer left by 1 can be used to simulate multiplication by 2 and how shifting an integer right by 2 can be used to simulate division by 2. Be careful to consider issues related to the sign of an integer.

18.19 Write a program that reverses the order of the bits in an integer value. The program should input the value from the user and call method **`reverseBits`** to print the bits in reverse order. Print the value in bits both before and after the bits are reversed to confirm that the bits are reversed properly. You might want to implement both a recursive and an iterative solution.

Appendix A
Java Demos

A.1 Demos

[Note: Appendices A and B were written by Abbey Deitel, a graduate of the Industrial Management program at Carnegie Mellon University.] As a student at Carnegie Mellon, I was able to use one of the largest university computer networks in the United States. Although I was not a Computer Science major or an Information Systems major, nearly every course I took required me to use the campus network extensively. I handed in assignments electronically, participated in discussions and debates outside the classroom and scanned electronic bulletin boards for information.

My contribution to this textbook is as a World Wide Web surfer. In this appendix, I list some of the best Java demos I was able to find on the Web.

I began my journey at **`http://www.gamelan.com`**. This site is an incredible Java resource and has some of the best Java demos including a huge compilation of games written in Java. The code ranges from basic to complex. Many of the authors of these games and other resources have provided source code. I hope you enjoy surfing these sites as much as I did.

May I ask a favor? I will be keeping this appendix up to date on the Prentice Hall/Deitel Web site

`http://www.prenhall.com/deitel`

I would appreciate it if you would send me your favorite sites that you want to share with others. I will post your suggestions promptly. Please send me email at

`deitel@deitel.com`

A.2 The Sites

http://ariel.cobite.com/ultram/tetris/tetris.html

Dethtris by Ultramaster Group. One of the Gamelan featured applets, this site is rumored to be one of the more exciting games on the web. The source code is provided. You can win Ultramaster merchandise. Join networked multiplayer games and compete with people all over the world.

http://reality.sgi.com/employees/sameers_csd/puzzle.html

The 15 Puzzle. Similar to the puzzle under the Apple menu of every Macintosh, this game allows you to move around 15 tiles to arrange a number sequence or an image. The source code is provided.

http://www.csiro.au:8000/steve/stuff/slider/Slider.html

Java Slider. This Java applet was voted top 25% of all applets by JARS, the Java Applet Rating Service (located at **http://www.jars.com**). This is an animated woodblock puzzle with audio. The source code is provided.

http://k2.scl.cwru.edu/~ptb/ataxx/

Ataxx. This board game made the JARS top 1% of all Java applets. You can play against yourself or play against the computer. The source code is provided.

http://www.awinc.com/users/rreichle/puzzle/index.html

Jigsaw Puzzle. Listed as "what's cool" by Gamelan, this puzzle includes animation. You simply drag each piece into the workspace to solve the puzzle. The picture changes each time you load the puzzle. The source code is provided.

http://www.cosmix.com/playground/java/solitaire/

The Marble Solitaire Game. This game incorporates a bit of animation. Rather than the point-and-click method used for similar games, this allows you to drag the marbles across the screen. This made Gamelan's "what's cool" list.

http://www.tdb.uu.se/~karl/java/rubik.html

Rubik's Cube. Listed as "what's cool" by Gamelan, this is a Java take on Rubik's Cube, the puzzle we all tried our hand at in the 1980's. The source code is provided.

http://www.tdb.uu.se/~karl/java/iceblox.html

The Iceblox game. This game, featured on Gamelan, is a fun game which uses a little animation. The source code is provided.

http://www-itg.lbl.gov/vbart/

San Francisco Subway Map. This is a simulated map of the San Francisco subway system. This shows the subway as it moves along various routes. I connected to this through the Gamelan animation site.

http://www.mines.edu/students/d/drferrin/Cool_Beans/

Cool Beans Java Programming. This is a web page designed by a student at the Colorado School of Mines. The student shows examples of his experiments with Java programming.

http://teamball.sdsu.edu/~boyns/java/

This is an excellent source for Java demos. There are a number of fun and interesting games. There is also a list of Java resources, however this is not as significant as the lists on most of the other sites mentioned. Several of the teamball site demos follow.

http://teamball.sdsu.edu/~boyns/java/miata/

Mazda Miata Animation. This is a an example of animation using a Mazda Miata. The car cruises across the screen and flashes it's headlights.

http://teamball.sdsu.edu/~boyns/java/centipedo/

Centipedo is similar to the old Centipede video game. The source code is provided.

http://teamball.sdsu.edu/~boyns/java/crazycounter/

The Crazy Counter is a page access counter which counts the number of hits on a page. The source code is provided so that you may install the Crazy Counter on your web page.

http://teamball.sdsu.edu/~boyns/java/logo/

Animated SDSU Logo. View the source code provided here and learn how to create animated Java applets.

http://teamball.sdsu.edu/~boyns/java/nsanim/

Animated Netscape Logo. This site allows you to animate the Netscape logo using designated control keys. The source code is provided.

http://teamball.sdsu.edu/~boyns/java/slot/

Slot Machine. This simple slot machine game allows you to play the slots with just a click of the mouse. Unfortunately, this one-arm-bandit does not pay-up! The source code is provided.

http://teamball.sdsu.edu/~boyns/java/starbase/

Starbase is an animated video game with sound effects. The source code is provided.

http://teamball.sdsu.edu/~boyns/java/mc/

Missile Commando is another video game with sound effects. The source code is provided.

http://beyond.malmo.lth.se/~calin/lt/twice/index.html

Two Java games are located here. *Drive a tank* around and try to avoid hitting buildings. Play a new version of the early video arcade game *Asteroids.*

http://users.aimnet.com/~foureyes/clickboard/fish1.html

The Angry Fish. This is an animated applet that is activated by placing the mouse in the coral reef. The source code is provided.

http://www.crocker.com/~sigelman/java/aster/

ASTERNOID! resembles Asteroids. The author calls this "a GREAT example of object-oriented programming." The source code is provided.

http://www.demonsys.com/jorkin/CelebrityPainter/

Celebrity Painter. This applet made the JARS Top 1% list. You choose from a variety of celebrity faces and alter their looks using a variety of different paint brushes. You can put one celebrity's smile on another's face.

http://militzer.me.tuns.ca/graffiti/graffitiinfo.html

Graffiti. JARS Top 1% Java applet. Paint graffiti on the wall without getting arrested. Unfortunately, source code is not provided.

http://sdcc8.ucsd.edu/~jelwell/potato/

Mr. Potato Head on Java. Give the spud some new duds.

http://www.sover.net/~manx/hyprcube.html

Stereoscopic Animated Hypercube. If you happen to possess the old red and blue 3D glasses, check this site out. The programmer was able to create a 3D image using Java. It isn't really a complicated image, just some cubes, however the idea that you can create images that will jump off your screen is a great concept!

http://www.metamor.com/pages/play.html

Pong. Play the classic video game pong or play using president Bill as your ball. Bounce the president's portrait off your racket, or if you are from the other side of the political spectrum, there is a Newt version, too!

http://www.well.com/user/yimmit/BlackJack.html

Black Jack. Play a game of "21" without the risk of losing your money. Just like in the casinos, this game can be addictive.

http://dmawww.epfl.ch/~kuonen/Java/4.html

Games. A variety of games for your playing pleasure written in Java.

http://www.spacestar.com/users/hamer/odeax/froggie/example1.html

Froggie. This game is a take off of Atari's Frogger. You can adjust the game according to the speed of your computer, so if you have a slower system, you will still be able to play this game without the frustration of lag time. The source code, audio files and image files are all provided.

http://www.delorie.com/game-room/chess/free-game.html

Chess. Play a game of chess against the computer.

http://uvision.com/java/talk.html

Chat. A real-time Java chat room.

http://www.earthweb.com/java/Netris/

3D Tetris. You can change the view and play the game from any angle.

http://www.npac.syr.edu/projects/vishuman/VisibleHuman.html

This site was featured by Gamelan and has won various awards. You can look at different cross sections of the human body. The Java source code is provided.

http://www.netobjective.com/java/graphlet/

Graphlet. An applet capable of graphing data.

http://www.netobjective.com/telnet.html

Telnet. An excellent example of an applet capable of networking.

http://www.realaudio.com/

This site is loaded with audio files. You can listen to clips from some of the latest albums and movies. The site has links to download the software required to listen to the files.

http://www.voxware.com/

Another great site for audio files. You will need to download some software to listen.

http://www.macromedia.com/

An excellent site for on-line multimedia. This site requires you to download software.

http://www.ior.com/~creation/java/java.html

A variety of Java applets by Creation including an *email applet* that allows someone to email you through your web page without having access to email in their browser.

http://www.npac.syr.edu/projects/java/magic/Magic.html
Virtual Reality Magic Cube. Another take on Rubik's cube.

http://www-groups.dcs.st-and.ac.uk/~history/Java/
Famous Curves Applet. Provides graphs of complex curves. Allows the user to alter the parameters to the equations that calculate the curves. Source code is available.

http://www.comcen.com.au/~adavie/javaslide/javaslide.html
Slide Rule. An interactive Java slide rule.

http://www.gamelan.com
Gamelan. A complete Java resource site containing thousands of Java samples. The site includes articles and resources for Java and related technologies. If you are looking for sample Java programs that can help you design your own Java programs, you can probably find existing source code here. A search engine is provided to help locate resources on the site.

http://www.jars.com
Java Applet Rating Service. Another Java resource site with thousands of Java samples. This site also includes articles and resources for Java and related technologies. A search engine is provided to help locate resources on the site.

Appendix B
Java Resources

B.1 Java Resources

[Note: Appendices A and B were written by Abbey Deitel, a graduate of the Industrial Management program at Carnegie Mellon University.] There is a bounty of Java information on the World Wide Web. Many people are experimenting with Java and sharing their thoughts, discoveries, ideas and source code with each other via the Internet. If you would like to recommend other sites, please send me email at

`deitel@deitel.com`

and we will put links to the sites you suggest on our Web site

`http://www.prenhall.com/deitel.`

`http://www.javasoft.com`

Run by Sun Microsystems, this is an important Java Resource. You will find Java and Hot Java documentation, products, news and information. JavaSoft has links to various newsgroups, mailing lists and resources. You can find the latest Java news at this site.

`http://www.javaworld.com`

Java World on-line magazine is an excellent resource for current Java information. You will find news clips, conference information and lists of interesting Java sites. JavaWorld maintains all their prior issues along with a search engine to help you locate articles.

`http://www.gamelan.com`

One of the largest resources for Java on the web, Gamelan, has games, puzzles, arts and entertainment, demos, current information and lists of what is new and cool in Java. Gamelan has links to numerous Java resources. From Gamelan you can connect to Java World, Sun Microsystems and hundreds of other sites.

Gamelan has a list of thousands of resources for Java and other related technologies. Resources include: Java, ActiveX, JavaBeans, JavaScript, News and Events, and other categories such as Java development environments.

http://www.acme.com/java/

This page has an animated Java applet with the source code provided. This site is an excellent resource for information on Java. The page provides software, notes and a list of hyperlinks to other resources. Under "software" you will find some animated applets, utility classes and applications.

http://www.sunsite.unc.edu/javafaq

This site provides the latest Java news. It also has some helpful Java resources including the following: the Java FAQ List, a tutorial called Brewing Java, Java User Groups, Java Links, the Java Book List, Java Trade Shows, Java Training, and Exercises.

http://www.JARS.com/

The Java Applet Rating Service. You will see their icon on some of the best Java applets. Go directly to this site for a list of the hottest new sites. This site also includes extensive resources for Java and related technologies.

http://www.xm.com/cafe/

Café Del Sol is an excellent Java resource. Experts from Sun have put together a live chat session, applets, resources, and FAQs. You can download applets from the café.

http://wco.com/~linnins/internet.htm

This is an excellent resource for some interesting Java sites including audio and video. This is also an excellent resource for general internet-related information.

http://www.microsoft.com/dimensionx/

Formerly DimensionX. A fun Java resource, this site has audio, video, a live chat room, demos, FAQs, documentation, downloading capabilities and more.

http://www.teamjava.com

Team Java assists Java consultants in search of contracts and helps to promote Java. They have also listed some resourceful sites. A few of the sites are included in this list of resources.

http://www.mentorsoft.com/DE/

Digital Espresso is a synopsis of the information from various Java resources. You can find anything from news and events to applets to technical information about Java.

http://www.digitalfocus.com/digitalfocus/faq/index.html

This source provides links to Java resources. You can also find FAQs (frequently asked questions) and a live "Java conference room."

http://www.Sun.COM/sunworldonline/

This is *SunWorld* magazine on-line. This is a Sun resource that also provides Java information.

http://www.netscape.com/comprod/products/navigator/version_2.0/java_applets/index.html

Contains a list of Java applets, demos, and resources.

http://www.roaster.com/

This is a great Java resource to get Java news and information or links to other useful Java sites. Also, a Macintosh Java integrated development environment can be found here.

http://porthos.phoenixat.com/~warreng/WWWBoard/wwwboard.html

Java message exchange center for Java programmers (a bulletin board of sorts).

news:comp.lang.java

The Java newsgroup. This is a great place to find detailed answers to technical questions on Java.

http://www.december.com/works/java.html
This site is another Java resource. You will find demos with source code, Java news, and information on books.

http://www.yahoo.com/Computers_and_Internet/Languages/Java/
Yahoo!, a popular World Wide Web search engine, provides a complete Java resource. You can initiate a search using key words or explore the categories listed at the site including games, contests, events, tutorials and documentation, mailing lists, security and more.

http://www.acm.org/~ops/java.html
A Java resource with information about the language, reference materials, books, tutorials, a developer's kit and examples.

http://www.research.ibm.com/research/java.html
IBM's Java research site where you can get information on their Java efforts and products.

http://rendezvous.com/java/hierarchy/index.html
"Java Class Hierarchy Diagrams."

http://www.sys-con.com/java/
Java Developer's Journal on-line magazine.

B.2 Java Frequently Asked Questions (FAQs)

If you have questions about Java, these sites will enable you to get answers from the experts. You will also find the answers to questions asked by other programmers.

http://www.digitalfocus.com/digitalfocus/faq

http://sunsite.unc.edu/javafaq/javafaq.html

http://www.webcity.co.jp/info/andoh/java/javafaq.html

B.3 Tutorials for Learning Java

http://www.javasoft.com/tutorial/index.html

http://www.digitalfocus.com/digitalfocus/faq/howdoi.html

http://rummelplatz.uni-mannheim.de/~skoch/javatut/kneedeep.htm

B.4 Java Books

http://www.aw.com/cp/javaseries/

http://www.clbooks.com/lists/java.html

http://jollyroger.com/java.html

B.5 Java Newsgroups

Those who are interested in contacting a local Java Users Group (JUG) can find information at **http://www.sug.org/java-groups.html**. JUGs hold discussion groups, and seminars, and they are a means of distributing the latest Java information. If there is not a JUG in your area, many of the groups have mailing lists.

news:comp.lang.java
Java newsgroup.

alt.www.hotjava
The HotJava newsgroup.

mailto:java@java.sun.com
Get help directly from Sun Microsystems.

B.6 Virtual Reality Modeling Language (VRML)

You may want to look at the following sites that support VRML three-dimensional graphics. Java will be supporting VRML in the near future.

http://www.aereal.com/
Aereal is an excellent resource for Java and VRML. Download a VRML browser.

http://www.virtpark.com/theme/proteinman/home.html
A top ten list of some of the best VRML sites.

http://www.planet9.com/
Very cool animation. You can manipulate the image of a street block.

Appendix C
Operator Precedence Chart

Operators are shown in decreasing order of precedence from top to bottom.

Operator	Type	Associativity
`()`	parentheses	left to right
`[]`	array subscript	
`.`	member selection	
`++`	unary preincrement	right to left
`++`	unary postincrement	
`--`	unary predecrement	
`--`	unary postdecrement	
`+`	unary plus	
`-`	unary minus	
`!`	unary logical negation	
`~`	unary bitwise complement	
`(` *type* `)`	unary cast	
`*`	multiplication	left to right
`/`	division	
`%`	modulus	
`+`	addition	left to right
`-`	subtraction	
`<<`	bitwise left shift	left to right
`>>`	bitwise right shift with sign extension	
`>>>`	bitwise right shift with zero extension	

Fig. C.1 Operator precedence chart (part 1 of 2).

Operator	Type	Associativity
`<`	relational less than	left to right
`<=`	relational less than or equal to	
`>`	relational greater than	
`>=`	relational greater than or equal to	
`instanceof`	type comparison	
`==`	relational is equal to	left to right
`!=`	relational is not equal to	
`&`	bitwise AND	left to right
`^`	bitwise exclusive OR boolean logical exclusive OR	left to right
`|`	bitwise inclusive OR boolean logical inclusive OR	left to right
`&&`	logical AND	left to right
`||`	logical OR	left to right
`?:`	ternary conditional	right to left
`=`	assignment	right to left
`+=`	addition assignment	
`-=`	subtraction assignment	
`*=`	multiplication assignment	
`/=`	division assignment	
`%=`	modulus assignment	
`&=`	bitwise AND assignment	
`^=`	bitwise exclusive OR assignment	
`|=`	bitwise inclusive OR assignment	
`<<=`	bitwise left shift assignment	
`>>=`	bitwise right shift with sign extension assignment	
`>>>=`	bitwise right shift with zero extension assignment	

Fig. C.1 Operator precedence chart (part 2 of 2).

Appendix D
ASCII Character Set

	0	**1**	**2**	**3**	**4**	**5**	**6**	**7**	**8**	**9**
0	nul	soh	stx	etx	eot	enq	ack	bel	bs	ht
1	nl	vt	ff	cr	so	si	dle	dc1	dc2	dc3
2	dc4	nak	syn	etb	can	em	sub	esc	fs	gs
3	rs	us	sp	!	"	#	$	%	&	'
4	(	)	*	+	,	-	.	/	0	1
5	2	3	4	5	6	7	8	9	:	;
6	<	=	>	?	@	A	B	C	D	E
7	F	G	H	I	J	K	L	M	N	O
8	P	Q	R	S	T	U	V	W	X	Y
9	Z	[	\	]	^	_	'	a	b	c
10	d	e	f	g	h	i	j	k	l	m
11	n	o	p	q	r	s	t	u	v	w
12	x	y	z	{	|	}	~	del		

The digits at the left of the table are the left digits of the decimal equivalent (0-127) of the character code, and the digits at the top of the table are the right digits of the character code. For example, the character code for 'F' is 70, and the character code for '&' is 38.

Note: Most users of this book are interested in the ASCII character set used to represent English characters on many computers. The ASCII character set is a subset of the Unicode character set used by Java to represent characters from most of the world's languages. For more information on the Unicode character set, visit the World Wide Web site

```
http://unicode.org
```

Appendix E
Number Systems

Objectives

- To understand basic number systems concepts such as base, positional value, and symbol value.
- To understand how to work with numbers represented in the binary, octal, and hexadecimal number systems
- To be able to abbreviate binary numbers as octal numbers or hexadecimal numbers.
- To be able to convert octal numbers and hexadecimal numbers to binary numbers.
- To be able to covert back and forth between decimal numbers and their binary, octal, and hexadecimal equivalents.
- To understand binary arithmetic, and how negative binary numbers are represented using two's complement notation.

Here are only numbers ratified.
William Shakespeare

Nature has some sort of arithmetic-geometrical coordinate system, because nature has all kinds of models. What we experience of nature is in models, and all of nature's models are so beautiful.
It struck me that nature's system must be a real beauty, because in chemistry we find that the associations are always in beautiful whole numbers—there are no fractions.
Richard Buckminster Fuller

Outline

E.1 Introduction

In this appendix, we introduce the key number systems that Java programmers use, especially when they are working on software projects that require close interaction with "machine-level" hardware. Projects like this include operating systems, computer networking software, compilers, database systems, and applications requiring high performance.

When we write an integer such as 227 or -63 in a Java program, the number is assumed to be in the *decimal (base 10) number system.* The *digits* in the decimal number system are 0, 1, 2, 3, 4, 5, 6, 7, 8, and 9. The lowest digit is 0 and the highest digit is 9—one less than the *base* of 10. Internally, computers use the *binary (base 2) number system.* The binary number system has only two digits, namely 0 and 1. Its lowest digit is 0 and its highest digit is 1—one less than the base of 2.

As we will see, binary numbers tend to be much longer than their decimal equivalents. Programmers who work in assembly languages and in high-level languages like Java that enable programmers to reach down to the "machine level," find it cumbersome to work with binary numbers. So two other number systems the *octal number system (base 8)* and the *hexadecimal number system (base 16)*—are popular primarily because they make it convenient to abbreviate binary numbers.

In the octal number system, the digits range from 0 to 7. Because both the binary number system and the octal number system have fewer digits than the decimal number system, their digits are the same as the corresponding digits in decimal.

The hexadecimal number system poses a problem because it requires sixteen digits—a lowest digit of 0 and a highest digit with a value equivalent to decimal 15 (one less than the base of 16). By convention, we use the letters A through F to represent the hexadecimal digits corresponding to decimal values 10 through 15. Thus in hexadecimal we can have numbers like 876 consisting solely of decimal-like digits, numbers like 8A55F consisting of digits and letters, and numbers like FFE consisting solely of letters. Occasionally, a hexadecimal number spells a common word such as FACE or FEED—this can appear strange to programmers accustomed to working with numbers.

Each of these number systems uses *positional notation*—each position in which a digit is written has a different *positional value.* For example, in the decimal number 937 (the 9, the 3, and the 7 are referred to as *symbol values*), we say that the 7 is written in the *ones position*, the 3 is written in the *tens position*, and the 9 is written in the *hundreds position.* Notice that each of these positions is a power of the base (base 10), and that these powers begin at 0 and increase by 1 as we move left in the number (Fig. E.3).

Binary digit	Octal digit	Decimal digit	Hexadecimal digit
0	0	0	0
1	1	1	1
	2	2	2
	3	3	3
	4	4	4
	5	5	5
	6	6	6
	7	7	7
		8	8
		9	9
			A (decimal value of 10)
			B (decimal value of 11)
			C (decimal value of 12)
			D (decimal value of 13)
			E (decimal value of 14)
			F (decimal value of 15)

Fig. E.1 Digits of the binary, octal, decimal, and hexadecimal number systems.

Attribute	Binary	Octal	Decimal	Hexadecimal
Base	2	8	10	16
Lowest digit	0	0	0	0
Highest digit	1	7	9	F

Fig. E.2 Comparison of the binary, octal, decimal, and hexadecimal number systems.

Positional values in the decimal number system			
Decimal digit	9	3	7
Position name	Hundreds	Tens	Ones
Positional value	100	10	1
Positional value as a power of the base (10)	10^2	10^1	10^0

Fig. E.3 Positional values in the decimal number system.

For longer decimal numbers, the next positions to the left would be the *thousands position* (10 to the 3rd power), the *ten-thousands position* (10 to the 4th power), the *hundred-thousands position* (10 to the 5th power), the *millions position* (10 to the 6th power), the *ten-millions position* (10 to the 7th power), and so on.

In the binary number 101, we say that the rightmost 1 is written in the *ones position*, the 0 is written in the *twos position*, and the leftmost 1 is written in the *fours position*. Notice that each of these positions is a power of the base (base 2), and that these powers begin at 0 and increase by 1 as we move left in the number (Fig E.4).

For longer binary numbers, the next positions to the left would be the *eights position* (2 to the 3rd power), the *sixteens position* (2 to the 4th power), the *thirty-twos position* (2 to the 5th power), the *sixty-fours position* (2 to the 6th power), and so on.

In the octal number 425, we say that the 5 is written in the *ones position*, the 2 is written in the *eights position*, and the 4 is written in the *sixty-fours position*. Notice that each of these positions is a power of the base (base 8), and that these powers begin at 0 and increase by 1 as we move left in the number (Fig. E.5).

For longer octal numbers, the next positions to the left would be the *five-hundred-and-twelves position* (8 to the 3rd power), the *four-thousand-and-ninety-sixes position* (8 to the 4th power), the *thirty-two-thousand-seven-hundred-and-sixty eights position* (8 to the 5th power), and so on.

In the hexadecimal number 3DA, we say that the A is written in the *ones position*, the D is written in the *sixteens position*, and the 3 is written in the *two-hundred-and-fifty-sixes position*. Notice that each of these positions is a power of the base (base 16), and that these powers begin at 0 and increase by 1 as we move left in the number (Fig. E.6).

Positional values in the binary number system			
Binary digit	1	0	1
Position name	Fours	Twos	Ones
Positional value	4	2	1
Positional value as a power of the base (2)	2^2	2^1	2^0

Fig. E.4 Positional values in the binary number system.

Positional values in the octal number system			
Decimal digit	4	2	5
Position name	Sixty-fours	Eights	Ones
Positional value	64	8	1
Positional value as a power of the base (8)	8^2	8^1	8^0

Fig. E.5 Positional values in the octal number system.

Positional values in the hexadecimal number system			
Decimal digit	3	D	A
Position name	Two-hundred-and-fifty-sixes	Sixteens	Ones
Positional value	256	16	1
Positional value as a power of the base (16)	16^2	16^1	16^0

Fig. E.6 Positional values in the hexadecimal number system.

For longer hexadecimal numbers, the next positions to the left would be the *four-thousand-and-ninety-sixes position* (16 to the 3rd power), the *sixty-five-thousand-five-hundred-and-thirty-sixes position* (16 to the 4th power), and so on.

E.2 Abbreviating Binary Numbers as Octal Numbers and Hexadecimal Numbers

The main use for octal and hexadecimal numbers in computing is for abbreviating lengthy binary representations. Figure E.7 highlights the fact that lengthy binary numbers can be expressed concisely in number systems with higher bases than the binary number system.

Decimal number	Binary representation	Octal representation	Hexadecimal representation
0	0	0	0
1	1	1	1
2	10	2	2
3	11	3	3
4	100	4	4
5	101	5	5
6	110	6	6
7	111	7	7
8	1000	10	8
9	1001	11	9
10	1010	12	A
11	1011	13	B
12	1100	14	C
13	1101	15	D
14	1110	16	E
15	1111	17	F
16	10000	20	10

Fig. E.7 Decimal, binary, octal, and hexadecimal equivalents.

A particularly important relationship that both the octal number system and the hexadecimal number system have to the binary system is that the bases of octal and hexadecimal (8 and 16 respectively) are powers of the base of the binary number system (base 2). Consider the following 12-digit binary number and its octal and hexadecimal equivalents. See if you can determine how this relationship makes it convenient to abbreviate binary numbers in octal or hexadecimal. The answer follows the numbers.

Binary Number	Octal equivalent	Hexadecimal equivalent
`100011010001`	`4321`	`8D1`

To see how the binary number converts easily to octal, simply break the 12-digit binary number into groups of three consecutive bits each, and write those groups over the corresponding digits of the octal number as follows

```
100    011    010    001
4      3      2      1
```

Notice that the octal digit you have written under each group of thee bits corresponds precisely to the octal equivalent of that 3-digit binary number as shown in Fig. E.7.

The same kind of relationship may be observed in converting numbers from binary to hexadecimal. In particular, break the 12-digit binary number into groups of four consecutive bits each and write those groups over the corresponding digits of the hexadecimal number as follows

```
1000   1101   0001
8      D      1
```

Notice that the hexadecimal digit you have written under each group of four bits corresponds precisely to the hexadecimal equivalent of that 4-digit binary number as shown in Fig. E.7.

E.3 Converting Octal Numbers and Hexadecimal Numbers to Binary Numbers

In the previous section, we saw how to convert binary numbers to their octal and hexadecimal equivalents by forming groups of binary digits and simply rewriting these groups as their equivalent octal digit values or hexadecimal digit values. This process may be used in reverse to produce the binary equivalent of a given octal or hexadecimal number.

For example, the octal number 653 is converted to binary simply by writing the 6 as its 3-digit binary equivalent 110, the 5 as its 3-digit binary equivalent 101, and the 3 as its 3-digit binary equivalent 011 to form the 9-digit binary number 110101011.

The hexadecimal number FAD5 is converted to binary simply by writing the F as its 4-digit binary equivalent 1111, the A as its 4-digit binary equivalent 1010, the D as its 4-digit binary equivalent 1101, and the 5 as its 4-digit binary equivalent 0101 to form the 16-digit 1111101011010101.

E.4 Converting from Binary, Octal, or Hexadecimal to Decimal

Because we are accustomed to working in decimal, it is often convenient to convert a binary, octal, or hexadecimal number to decimal to get a sense of what the number is "really" worth. Our diagrams in Section E.1 express the positional values in decimal. To convert a number to decimal from another base, multiply the decimal equivalent of each digit by its positional value, and sum these products. For example, the binary number 110101 is converted to decimal 53 as shown in Fig. E.8.

Converting a binary number to decimal						
Positional values:	32	16	8	4	2	1
Symbol values:	1	1	0	1	0	1
Products:	1*32=32	1*16=16	0*8=0	1*4=4	0*2=0	1*1=1
Sum:	= 32 + 16 + 0 + 4 + 0 + 1 = 53					

Fig. E.8 Converting a binary number to decimal.

To convert octal 7614 to decimal 3980, we use the same technique, this time using appropriate octal positional values as shown in Fig. E.9.

To convert hexadecimal AD3B to decimal 44347, we use the same technique, this time using appropriate hexadecimal positional values as shown in Fig. E.10.

E.5 Converting from Decimal to Binary, Octal, or Hexadecimal

The conversions of the previous section follow naturally from the conventions of positional notation. Converting from decimal to binary, octal, or hexadecimal also follows these conventions.

Suppose we wish to convert decimal 57 to binary. We begin by writing the positional values of the columns right to left until we reach a column whose positional value is greater than the decimal number. We do not need that column, so we discard it. Thus, we first write:

Converting an octal number to decimal				
Positional values:	512	64	8	1
Symbol values:	7	6	1	4
Products	7*512=3584	6*64=384	1*8=8	4*1=4
Sum:	= 3584 + 384 + 8 + 4 = 3980			

Fig. E.9 Converting an octal number to decimal.

Converting a hexadecimal number to decimal				
Positional values:	4096	256	16	1
Symbol values:	A	D	3	B
Products	A*4096=40960	D*256=3328	3*16=48	B*1=11
Sum:	= 40960 + 3328 + 48 + 11 = 44347			

Fig. E.10 Converting a hexadecimal number to decimal.

Positional values:	`64`	`32`	`16`	`8`	`4`	`2`	`1`

Then we discard the column with positional value 64 leaving:

Positional values:	`32`	`16`	`8`	`4`	`2`	`1`

Next we work from the leftmost column to the right. We divide 32 into 57 and observe that there is one 32 in 57 with a remainder of 25, so we write 1 in the 32 column. We divide 16 into 25 and observe that there is one 16 in 25 with a remainder of 9 and write 1 in the 16 column. We divide 8 into 9 and observe that there is one 8 in 9 with a remainder of 1. The next two columns each produce quotients of zero when their positional values are divided into 1 so we write 0s in the 4 and 2 columns. Finally, 1 into 1 is 1 so we write 1 in the 1 column. This yields:

Positional values:	`32`	`16`	`8`	`4`	`2`	`1`
Symbol values:	`1`	`1`	`1`	`0`	`0`	`1`

and thus decimal 57 is equivalent to binary 111001.

To convert decimal 103 to octal, we begin by writing the positional values of the columns until we reach a column whose positional value is greater than the decimal number. We do not need that column, so we discard it. Thus, we first write:

Positional values:	`512`	`64`	`8`	`1`

Then we discard the column with positional value 512, yielding:

Positional values:	`64`	`8`	`1`

Next we work from the leftmost column to the right. We divide 64 into 103 and observe that there is one 64 in 103 with a remainder of 39, so we write 1 in the 64 column. We divide 8 into 39 and observe that there are four 8s in 39 with a remainder of 7 and write 4 in the 8 column. Finally, we divide 1 into 7 and observe that there are seven 1s in 7 with no remainder so we write 7 in the 1 column. This yields:

Positional values:	`64`	`8`	`1`
Symbol values:	`1`	`4`	`7`

and thus decimal 103 is equivalent to octal 147.

To convert decimal 375 to hexadecimal, we begin by writing the positional values of the columns until we reach a column whose positional value is greater than the decimal number. We do not need that column, so we discard it. Thus, we first write

Positional values:	`4096`	`256`	`16`	`1`

Then we discard the column with positional value 4096, yielding:

Positional values:	`256`	`16`	`1`

Next we work from the leftmost column to the right. We divide 256 into 375 and observe that there is one 256 in 375 with a remainder of 119, so we write 1 in the 256 column. We divide 16 into 119 and observe that there are seven 16s in 119 with a remainder of 7 and write 7 in the 16 column. Finally, we divide 1 into 7 and observe that there are seven 1s in 7 with no remainder so we write 7 in the 1 column. This yields:

```
Positional values:    256  16   1
Symbol values:        1    7    7
```

and thus decimal 375 is equivalent to hexadecimal 177.

E.6 Negative Binary Numbers: Two's Complement Notation

The discussion in this appendix has been focussed on positive numbers. In this section, we explain how computers represent negative numbers using *two's complement notation.* First we explain how the two's complement of a binary number is formed, and then we show why it represents the negative value of the given binary number.

Consider a machine with 32-bit integers. Suppose

```
int value = 13;
```

The 32-bit representation of **value** is

```
00000000 00000000 00000000 00001101
```

To form the negative of **value** we first form its *one's complement* by applying Java's bitwise complement operator (**~**):

```
onesComplementOfValue = ~value;
```

Internally, **~value** is now **value** with each of its bits reversed—ones become zeros and zeros become ones as follows:

```
value:
00000000 00000000 00000000 00001101

~value (i.e., value's ones complement):
11111111 11111111 11111111 11110010
```

To form the two's complement of **value** we simply add one to **value**'s one's complement. Thus

```
Two's complement of value:]\
11111111 11111111 11111111 11110011
```

Now if this is in fact equal to -13, we should be able to add it to binary 13 and obtain a result of 0. Let us try this:

```
 00000000 00000000 00000000 00001101
+11111111 11111111 11111111 11110011
------------------------------------
 00000000 00000000 00000000 00000000
```

The carry bit coming out of the leftmost column is discarded and we indeed get zero as a result. If we add the one's complement of a number to the number, the result would be all 1s. The key to getting a result of all zeros is that the twos complement is 1 more than the one's complement. The addition of 1 causes each column to add to 0 with a carry of 1. The carry keeps moving leftward until it is discarded from the leftmost bit, and hence the resulting number is all zeros.

Computers actually perform a subtraction such as

```
x = a - value;
```

by adding the two's complement of **value** to **a** as follows:

```
x = a + (~value + 1);
```

Suppose **a** is 27 and **value** is 13 as before. If the two's complement of **value** is actually the negative of **value**, then adding the two's complement of value to **a** should produce the result 14. Let us try this:

```
a (i.e., 27)        00000000 00000000 00000000 00011011
+(~value + 1)      +11111111 11111111 11111111 11110011
                   ------------------------------------
                    00000000 00000000 00000000 00001110
```

which is indeed equal to 14.

Summary

- When we write an integer such as 19 or 227 or -63 in a Java program, the number is automatically assumed to be in the decimal (base 10) number system. The digits in the decimal number system are 0, 1, 2, 3, 4, 5, 6, 7, 8, and 9. The lowest digit is 0 and the highest digit is 9—one less than the base of 10.
- Internally, computers use the binary (base 2) number system. The binary number system has only two digits, namely 0 and 1. Its lowest digit is 0 and its highest digit is 1—one less than the base of 2.
- The octal number system (base 8) and the hexadecimal number system (base 16) are popular primarily because they make it convenient to abbreviate binary numbers.
- The digits of the octal number system range from 0 to 7.
- The hexadecimal number system poses a problem because it requires sixteen digits—a lowest digit of 0 and a highest digit with a value equivalent to decimal 15 (one less than the base of 16). By convention, we use the letters A through F to represent the hexadecimal digits corresponding to decimal values 10 through 15.
- Each number system uses positional notation—each position in which a digit is written has a different positional value.
- A particularly important relationship that both the octal number system and the hexadecimal number system have to the binary system is that the bases of octal and hexadecimal (8 and 16 respectively) are powers of the base of the binary number system (base 2).
- To convert an octal number to a binary number, simply replace each octal digit with its three-digit binary equivalent.
- To convert a hexadecimal number to a binary number, simply replace each hexadecimal digit with its four-digit binary equivalent.
- Because we are accustomed to working in decimal, it is convenient to convert a binary, octal or hexadecimal number to decimal to get a sense of the number's "real" worth.
- To convert a number to decimal from another base, multiply the decimal equivalent of each digit by its positional value, and sum these products.

- Computers represent negative numbers using two's complement notation.
- To form the negative of a value in binary, first form its one's complement by applying Java's bitwise complement operator (~). This reverses the bits of the value. To form the two's complement of a value, simply add one to the value's one's complement.

Terminology

base
base 2 number system
base 8 number system
base 10 number system
base 16 number system
binary number system
bitwise complement operator (~)
conversions
decimal number system
digit
hexadecimal number system
negative value
octal number system
one's complement notation
positional notation
positional value
symbol value
two's complement notation

Self-Review Exercises

E.1 The bases of the decimal, binary, octal, and hexadecimal number systems are _________, _________, _________, and _________ respectively.

E.2 In general, the decimal, octal, and hexadecimal representations of a given binary number contain (more/fewer) digits than the binary number contains.

E.3 (True/False) A popular reason for using the decimal number system is that it forms a convenient notation for abbreviating binary numbers simply by substituting one decimal digit per group of four binary bits.

E.4 The (octal / hexadecimal / decimal) representation of a large binary value is the most concise (of the given alternatives).

E.5 (True/False) The highest digit in any base is one more than the base.

E.6 (True/False) The lowest digit in any base is one less than the base.

E.7 The positional value of the rightmost digit of any number in either binary, octal, decimal, or hexadecimal is always _________.

E.8 The positional value of the digit to the left of the rightmost digit of any number in binary, octal, decimal, or hexadecimal is always equal to _________.

E.9 Fill in the missing values in this chart of positional values for the rightmost four positions in each of the indicated number systems:

decimal	`1000`	`100`	`10`	`1`
hexadecimal	`...`	`256`	`...`	`...`
binary	`...`	`...`	`...`	`...`
octal	`512`	`...`	`8`	`...`

E.10 Convert binary `110101011000` to octal and to hexadecimal.

E.11 Convert hexadecimal `FACE` to binary.

E.12 Convert octal `7316` to binary.

E.13 Convert hexadecimal **4FEC** to octal. (Hint: First convert 4FEC to binary then convert that binary number to octal.)

E.14 Convert binary **1101110** to decimal.

E.15 Convert octal **317** to decimal.

E.16 Convert hexadecimal **EFD4** to decimal.

E.17 Convert decimal **177** to binary, to octal, and to hexadecimal.

E.18 Show the binary representation of decimal **417**. Then show the one's complement of **417**, and the two's complement of **417**.

E.19 What is the result when the one's complement of a number is added to itself?

Self-Review Answers

E.1 **10**, **2**, **8**, **16**.

E.2 Fewer.

E.3 False.

E.4 Hexadecimal.

E.5 False. The highest digit in any base is one less than the base.

E.6 False. The lowest digit in any base is zero.

E.7 **1** (the base raised to the zero power).

E.8 The base of the number system.

E.9 Fill in the missing values in this chart of positional values for the rightmost four positions in each of the indicated number systems:

decimal		1000	100	10	1
hexadecimal	4096	256	16		1
binary		8	4	2	1
octal		512	64	8	1

E.10 Octal **6530**; Hexadecimal **D58**.

E.11 Binary **1111 1010 1100 1110**.

E.12 Binary **111 011 001 110**.

E.13 Binary **0 100 111 111 101 100; Octal 47754**.

E.14 Decimal **2+4+8+32+64=110**.

E.15 Decimal **7+1*8+3*64=7+8+192=207**.

E.16 Decimal **4+13*16+15*256+14*4096=61396**.

E.17 Decimal **177**
to binary:

```
256 128 64 32 16 8 4 2 1
128 64 32 16 8 4 2 1
(1*128)+(0*64)+(1*32)+(1*16)+(0*8)+(0*4)+(0*2)+(1*1)
10110001
```

to octal:

```
512 64 8 1
64 8 1
(2*64)+(6*8)+(1*1)
261
```

to hexadecimal:

```
256 16 1
16 1
(11*16)+(1*1)
(B*16)+(1*1)
B1
```

E.18 Binary:

```
512 256 128 64 32 16 8 4 2 1
256 128 64 32 16 8 4 2 1
(1*256)+(1*128)+(0*64)+(1*32)+(0*16)+(0*8)+(0*4)+(0*2)+
(1*1)
110100001
```

One's complement: **001011110**
Two's complement: **001011111**
Check: Original binary number + its two's complement

```
110100001
001011111
---------
000000000
```

E.19 Zero.

Exercises

E.20 Some people argue that many of our calculations would be easier in the base **12** number system because **12** is divisible by so many more numbers than **10** (for base **10**). What is the lowest digit in base **12**? What might the highest symbol for the digit in base **12** be? What are the positional values of the rightmost four positions of any number in the base **12** number system?

E.21 How is the highest symbol value in the number systems we discussed related to the positional value of the first digit to the left of the rightmost digit of any number in these number systems?

E.22 Complete the following chart of positional values for the rightmost four positions in each of the indicated number systems:

decimal	1000	100	10	1
base 6	...	...	6	...
base 13	...	169	...	...
base 3	27	...	...	...

E.23 Convert binary **`100101111010`** to octal and to hexadecimal.

E.24 Convert hexadecimal **`3A7D`** to binary.

E.25 Convert hexadecimal **`765F`** to octal. (Hint: First convert **`765F`** to binary, then convert that binary number to octal.)

E.26 Convert binary **`1011110`** to decimal.

E.27 Convert octal **`426`** to decimal.

E.28 Convert hexadecimal **`FFFF`** to decimal.

E.29 Convert decimal **`299`** to binary, to octal, and to hexadecimal.

E.30 Show the binary representation of decimal **`779`**. Then show the one's complement of **`779`**, and the two's complement of **`779`**.

E.31 What is the result when the two's complement of a number is added to itself?

E.32 Show the two's complement of integer value **`-1`** on a machine with 32-bit integers.

Appendix F
Object-Oriented Elevator Simulator

Objectives

- To introduce the elements of object orientation in parallel with the early text discussion. This will enable students to begin working on their term projects from the beginning of their introductory computer science and computer engineering courses.
- To introduce students to the elements of the object-oriented design process.
- To enable students to pursue an object-oriented design of a reasonably substantial application.
- To implement a substantial term project using Java's more advanced features including graphics, graphical user interfaces, exception handling, multithreading, and multimedia including audios, images and animation.
- To suggest a number of challenging modifications to the project for the more advanced students.

F.1 Introduction

In this appendix, you will perform the various steps of an object-oriented design (OOD). You will implement an elevator simulator using the techniques of object-oriented programming (OOP). For now, this assignment may seem a bit complex. Please do not be concerned. You will attempt only a small portion of the problem at a time. The elevator simulator is a large project suitable for a term project. It is also suitable as a group project.

We begin with an introduction to object orientation. We will see that object orientation is a natural way of thinking about the world and of writing computer programs.

We start by introducing some of the key terminology of object orientation. Look around you in the real world. Everywhere you look you see them—*objects*! People, watches, tricycles, computers, satellites, roller coasters, pipes, cards, footballs, cats and the like. Humans think in terms of objects. We have the marvelous ability of *abstraction* that enables us to view screen images as objects such as flowers, trees, helicopters, and clouds rather than individual dots of color (i.e., pixels). We can, if we wish, think in terms of beaches instead of grains of sand, forests rather than trees, and houses rather than bricks.

We might be inclined to divide objects into two categories—animate objects and inanimate objects. Animate objects are "alive" in some sense. They move around and do things. Inanimate objects, like rocks, seem not to do much at all. They just kind of "sit around." All these objects, however, do have some things in common. They all have *attributes* like size, shape, color, mass, and the like. And they all exhibit various *behaviors*, e.g., a ball rolls, bounces, inflates, and deflates; a baby sleeps, cries, crawls, walks, drools, and blinks; a car accelerates, brakes and turns, etc.

Humans learn about objects by studying their attributes and observing their behaviors. Different objects can have many of the same attributes and exhibit similar behaviors. Comparisons can be made, for example, between babies and adults, and between humans and chimpanzees. Cars, trucks, little red wagons and roller skates have much in common.

Object-oriented programming (OOP) models real-world objects with software counterparts. It takes advantage of *class* relationships where objects of a certain class—such as a class of vehicles—have the same characteristics. It takes advantage of *inheritance* relationships where newly created classes of objects are derived by inheriting characteristics of existing classes, yet contain unique characteristics of their own. Objects of class **`Convertible`** certainly have the characteristics of class automobile, but the roof goes up and down.

Object-oriented programming gives us a more natural and intuitive way to view the programming process, namely by *modeling* real-world objects, their attributes, and their behaviors. OOP also models communication between objects. Just as people send messages to one another (e.g., a person standing on a corner and signaling a taxicab driver for a ride), objects also communicate via messages.

OOP *encapsulates* (or "wraps") data (attributes) and methods (behavior) into units called *objects*; the data and methods of an object are intimately tied together. Objects have the property of *information hiding*. This means that although objects may know how to communicate with one another across well-defined interfaces, objects normally are not allowed to know how other objects are implemented—implementation details are hidden within the objects themselves. Surely it is possible to drive a car effectively without knowing the intricate details of how engines, alternators, batteries, transmissions and exhaust systems work internally. We will see why information hiding is so crucial to good software engineering.

In C and other procedural programming languages, programming tends to be *action-oriented*, whereas in Java, programming is object-oriented. In C, the unit of programming is the *function*. In Java the unit of programming is the *class* from which objects are eventually *instantiated* (i.e., created).

C programmers concentrate on writing functions. Groups of actions that perform some common task are formed into functions, and functions are grouped to form programs. Data is certainly important in C, but the view is that data exists primarily in support of the actions that programs perform. The *verbs* in a system specification help the C programmer determine the set of functions that work together to implement the system.

Java programmers concentrate on creating their own *user-defined types* called classes. Each class contains data as well as the set of methods that manipulate the data. The data components of a class are called *instance variables*. Just as an instance of a built-in type such as **`int`** is called a *variable*, an instance of a user-defined type (i.e., a class) is called an *object*. The programmer uses built-in types as the building blocks for constructing user-defined types. The focus of attention in Java is on objects rather than methods. The *nouns* in a system specification help the Java programmer determine the set of classes from which objects will be created that will work together to implement a system.

F.2 Problem Statement

A company intends to build a two-story office building and equip it with the "latest" in elevator technology. The company wants you to develop a Java applet that simulates the operation of the elevator to determine if it will meet their needs.

The elevator, which has a capacity of one person, is designed to conserve energy, so it only moves when necessary. The elevator starts the day waiting with its doors closed on the building's first floor. The elevator, of course, alternates directions—first up, then down.

Your simulator has a simple graphical user interface—an applet with a single "New Person" push button. When the button is clicked, the simulator creates a "new" person and places that person on a floor (i.e., floor one or floor two). The arrival floor of the person is randomly determined. The person then presses the floor's call button. The person's destination floor is never equal to the floor on which that person is created.

If the first person of the day arrives on floor one, the person can immediately get on the elevator (after pressing the call button, and waiting for the floor doors and the elevator doors to open, of course!). If the first person arrives at floor two, the elevator should proceed to floor two and "pick up" the person. For simplicity, in this version of the simulation, the elevator moves between the floors in zero time. This will be made more realistic in future versions of your elevator applet.

The elevator's arrival at a floor is signaled by turning on a light on that floor above the doors and by ringing the floor bell. The floor button and the elevator button are reset, the elevator's doors open, the floor's doors open, and the passenger gets out of the elevator. If a passenger is waiting on that floor the passenger boards the elevator and presses a destination button. If the elevator needs to begin moving, it determines in which direction it should go (a simple decision on a two-story elevator!), and begins moving to the other floor. For simplicity, assume that all the events that happen once the elevator reaches a floor and until the floor's doors are closed, take zero time. The elevator always knows its current floor and its destination floor.

Due to the fact that all events in this version of the simulation take zero time, only one person can be in the simulation at a time. The simulator should process each person completely before the next person arrives in the simulation. In other words, when a person is created, that person should press the call button, be picked up by the elevator, be moved to the opposite floor and should exit the elevator before the next person walks onto a floor to wait for the elevator.

F.3 Elevator Laboratory Assignment 1

(Prerequisites: Chapters 1–3)

In this and the next few assignments, you will perform the separate steps of an object-oriented design. The first step is to identify the classes in the problem. You will eventually describe these classes in a formal way and implement them. For this assignment, you should do the following:

1. Identify the classes in the simulation problem. The problem statement specifies many class objects working together to simulate the elevator and its interactions with the passenger, the floors, the bell, etc. Locate the *nouns* from the problem statement; with high likelihood, these represent most of the classes necessary to implement the elevator simulation.
2. For each class identified, write one brief, precisely worded paragraph that captures the facts about that class from the problem statement.

Notes

1. This is a good team exercise. Ideally you should work in a group of two to four people. You and your teammates will reinforce one another's efforts, challenge and refine each other's design and implementation approaches.
2. Your group should compete with other groups in your class to develop the "best" design and implementation.
3. In Chapter 4, "Methods", we discuss how to use random number generation. You will learn how to use the **`static Math`** class method **`random`** to randomly select the floor onto which a person walks when the "New Person" button is pushed by the simulator user.
4. We have made a number of simplifying assumptions. You may choose to supply additional details.
5. Because the real world is so object oriented, it will be quite natural for you to pursue this project even though you probably have not formally studied object-orientation.
6. Do not worry about perfection. System design is not a perfect and complete process, so you should pursue this project on a best-efforts basis.
7. Java is fun. Java inspires creativity. Go beyond the basic description presented here, by adding your own enhancements to the elevator simulator. If you would like to share your simulators with us, please email them to us at **`deitel@deitel.com`**

F.4 Elevator Laboratory Assignment 2

(Prerequisite: Chapter 4)

In the previous assignment, we began the first phase of an object-oriented design for our elevator simulator, namely identifying the classes needed to implement the simulator. As a starting point, you were encouraged to list the nouns in the problem statement. In doing so, you discovered that some of the classes in your simulator were the elevator itself, people, floors, the building, various buttons and so on.

Classes have attributes and behaviors. Attributes are represented in Java programs by data. Behaviors are represented by methods. In this assignment we concentrate on determining the attributes of the classes needed to implement the elevator simulator. In the next assignment we will concentrate on behaviors. In Assignment 4, we will concentrate on the interactions between the objects in the elevator simulator.

Let us discuss attributes of real-world objects before we begin the assignment. A person's attributes include height and weight. A TV's attributes include channel setting, volume setting, picture size (measured diagonally in inches), brand, etc. A car's attributes include current speedometer and odometer readings. A house's attributes include style ("colonial," "ranch," etc.), number of rooms, square footage, and lot size. A computer's attributes include manufacturer (Apple, Compaq, Digital, IBM, Sun, etc.), type of screen (monochrome or color), main memory size (in megabytes), hard disk size (in megabytes or gigabytes), etc.

1. To get the process started, type into a word processor or editor program the text of the problem statement for the elevator simulation presented in *Elevator Laboratory Assignment 1.*
2. Extract all the *facts* from the problem. Eliminate all irrelevant text and place each fact on a separate line of your text file (there are several dozen facts in the problem statement). Here is a portion of what your fact file might look like:

   two-story office building
   elevator
   person
   floor doors
   elevator doors
   directions-up and down
   floor is occupied
   person in elevator
   person on floor
   person's destination floor
   person gets on elevator
   elevator closes its doors
3. Group all your facts by class. This will help confirm that you properly identified the classes in *Assignment 1*. Use an outline form in which the classes are listed at the left margin of the page and the facts related to each class are listed below that class and indented one tab. Some facts mention only one class while other facts mention several classes. Each fact should initially be listed under every class the fact mentions. Note that some facts like "directions-up and down" do not explicitly mention a class but should nevertheless be grouped with a class (in this case the direction is clearly the direction in which the elevator is moving). This outline file will be used in this assignment and in the next several assignments.
4. Now separate the facts for each class into two groups. Label the first group *Attributes* and the second group *Other Facts*. For now, actions (behaviors) should be grouped under *Other Facts*. As you place an action under *Other Facts* consider creating an additional entry under Attributes if appropriate. For example, the fact "elevator closes its doors" is an action that for now is grouped under *Other Facts*, but it indicates that an attribute of "doors" is that they are either open or shut. The fact "floor is occupied" is an attribute of the floor, more specifically, floor is either occupied (by one person—the stated capacity of each floor) or unoccupied at any time. Some attributes of the elevator are: whether it is "moving" or "stopped," whether it does or does not have a passenger, and if it is moving—whether it is moving "up" or "down." An attribute of the floor button is whether it is "on" or "off." An attribute of a person is the person's destination floor. And so on.

Notes

1. Begin by listing the class attributes that are explicitly mentioned in the problem statement. Then list attributes that are implied by the problem statement.

2. Add appropriate attributes as it becomes apparent that they are needed.
3. System design is not a perfect process; simply do the best you can for now. Be prepared to modify your design as you proceed with this exercise in subsequent sections.
4. An object of a class (actually, a reference to an object of a class) can be an attribute of another class. This is called *composition*. For example, there are references to button objects for floor one and floor two inside class elevator—the person presses one of these buttons to select a destination floor. For the purposes of this exercise, treat all the objects as peers—do not allow composition (we will do this later).
5. In Chapter 4, you learned about random number generation. When you eventually implement the elevator simulator, the statement

```
int arrivalFloor = ( int ) ( 1 + Math.random() * 2 );
```

can be used to randomly choose the floor (1 or 2) where a person is "created."

F.5 Elevator Laboratory Assignment 3

(Prerequisite: Chapter 6)

In the previous two assignments, we performed the first two phases of an object-oriented design for our elevator simulator, namely identifying the classes needed to implement the simulator and identifying the attributes of those classes. In this assignment we concentrate on determining the behaviors of the classes needed to implement the elevator simulator. In the next section, we concentrate on the interactions between the classes.

Let us consider the behaviors of some real-world objects. A radio's behaviors include having its station set and having its volume set. A car's behaviors include accelerating (by pressing the gas pedal), decelerating (by pressing the brake pedal) and setting the direction (by turning the wheel).

Objects do not ordinarily perform their behaviors spontaneously. Rather, a specific behavior is normally invoked when a method call is sent to the object, requesting that the object perform that specific behavior.

1. Continue working with the facts file you created in *Assignment 2*. You had separated the facts relating to each class into two groups—*Attributes* and *Other Facts*.
2. For each object, add a third group called *Behaviors*. Place in this group every behavior of a class that can be invoked by telling an object of that class to do something, i.e., by sending a method call to the object. For example, a button can be pressed (by a person), so list **`pressCallButton`** as a behavior of the **`Button`** class. The class's attributes (such as whether a **`Button`** object is "on" or "off") are instance variables of the **`Button`** class. A class's methods typically manipulate the class's instance variables (such as **`pressCallButton`** changing one of class **`Button`**'s attributes to "on"). Methods often send method calls to objects of other classes (such as a **`Button`** object sending a **`callElevator`** method call to summon the **`Elevator`** object). Assume that the elevator has "thermal" buttons that become illuminated when someone presses them. When the elevator arrives at a floor, the elevator will want to send a **`resetCallButton`** method call to turn the button's light off. The elevator may want to determine if a particular button has been pressed, so we can provide another behavior called **`isOn`** that simply examines a button and returns **`true`** or **`false`** to indicate that the button is currently "on" or "off." You will probably want the elevator's doors to respond to method calls **`openDoors`** and **`closeDoors`**. And so on.

3. For each behavior you assign to an object, provide a brief description of what the behavior does. List any attribute changes the behavior causes, and list any method calls the behavior sends to other objects.

Notes

1. References to class **Button** do not refer to **java.awt.Button**.

F.6 Elevator Laboratory Assignment 4

(Prerequisite: Chapter 6)

This is the last of the initial design assignments before you begin writing the code for your elevator simulator. In this section we concentrate on the interactions between class objects. This section will help you "tie it all together." You will probably make some additions to the list of classes, their attributes and their behaviors that you developed in the previous assignments.

We have learned that objects do not ordinarily do things spontaneously. Rather, the objects respond to stimuli in the form of method calls.

Let us consider several of the interactions among the classes in the elevator simulation. The problem statement says, "Person presses the floor's "call button." The "subject" of that clause is person and the object is button. This is an example of an interaction between objects. The person object sends a method call i.e., **pressCallButton**, to the button object. In the last assignment, we made **pressCallButton** a method of the **Button** class.

At this point, under *Other Facts* for each of the classes in your simulation, about all you should have left are interactions between classes. Consider a statement like

"person waits for elevator doors to open"

In the last assignment, we listed two behaviors of the elevator's doors, namely **openDoors** and **closeDoors**. Now we want to determine which classes *send* these method calls. This is not *explicitly* stated in the preceding quoted phrase. So we think about this a bit and we realize that the elevator itself sends these messages to the doors. These interactions between classes are *implicit* in the problem statement and are more difficult to recognize than *explicit* interactions.

Continue refining the *Other Facts* sections for each class in your elevator simulator. These sections should now contain mostly interactions among classes. View each of these interactions as

1. a *sending class*
2. sending a particular method call
3. to a particular receiving class.

Under each class, add the section *Method Calls Sent to Other Classes* and list the remaining interactions between classes, i.e., under the **Person** class, include the entry

Person *sends* **pressCallButton** *method call to the* **Button**

For the **Button** class under *Method Calls Sent to Other Classes,* place the message

Button *sends* **callElevator** *message to* **Elevator**

From the perspective of the sending class, a method call sent to another class is a *collaboration*. From the perspective of the receiving class, a method call invokes a behavior.

As you make these entries, you may add attributes and behaviors to your classes. This is perfectly natural. As you complete this assignment, you will have a reasonably complete listing of the classes you will need to implement your elevator simulator. For each class, you will have a reasonably complete listing of that class's attributes and behaviors, and the method calls that class sends to other classes.

F.7 Elevator Laboratory Assignment 5

(Prerequisite: Chapter 6)

In the previous assignments, we introduced the fundamentals of object orientation and walked you through a basic, object-oriented design for your elevator simulator. At this point, you are ready (and probably eager!) to begin programming your simulator.

1. For each of the classes you identified in the previous assignments, write an appropriate class definition. Each class definition should be written in a separate file with the **`.java`** extension.
2. Write a driver applet that tests each of these classes and attempts to run the complete elevator simulation. *CAUTION:* You will probably need to complete the next assignment before you will be able to create a reasonable working version of your simulator, so be patient and implement only those portions of the elevator simulator that you can with the knowledge you have gained so far. In the next assignment, we will discuss composition, i.e., creating classes that contain references to objects of other classes as instance variables; this technique might help you represent the button objects inside the elevator as members of the elevator, for example.
3. For the first version of your simulator, design only a simple, text-oriented output that displays a message for each significant event that occurs. Your messages might include strings such as: "Person 1 arrives on Floor 1," "Person 1 presses Call Button on Floor 1," "Elevator moved to Floor 1," etc. We suggest that you capitalize the words that represent objects in your simulation. Note also that you may choose to defer this portion of the lab assignment until you have read the next assignment.

F.8 Elevator Laboratory Assignment 6

(Prerequisite: Chapter 6)

In the last assignment you began programming your elevator simulator. In this assignment we discuss composition, a capability that allows you to create classes that have as members references to objects. Composition enables you to create a building class that contains references to the elevator and to the floors, and, in turn, create an elevator class that contains references to buttons.

1. Each time a person enters the simulator, you should use **`new`** to create a **`Person`** object to represent that person. Note that **`new`** will be used with a constructor call that will initialize the object properly.
2. List the composition relationships among the classes you have implemented for your elevator simulator. Modify the class definitions you created in the last assignment to reflect these composition relationships.
3. Complete the implementation of a working simulator program. We will suggest enhancements and refine the problem statement in the next assignment.

Notes

1. For simplicity, you may choose to treat the floor doors and the elevator doors as one unit.

F.9 Elevator Laboratory Assignment 7

(Prerequisites: Chapters 9–11)

At this point you should have version 1 of your elevator simulator working. Over the next several assignments, we will make the elevator simulator more realistic by having the elevator take time to move between the floors, by allowing more than one person in the simulation at once, by using graphical representations of the elevator and the other objects, by animating the motion of the elevator and the people, and the like. This assignment will focus on enhancing the elevator's graphical user interface. Figure F.1 shows the basic GUI design for this assignment (Note: The floor control boards and the elevator control board are to be implemented in Assignment 8).

1. Create another push button and add it to the applet. Name one button "Floor 1" and the other button "Floor 2." These buttons will be used to create a new person who wants to board the elevator specifically on that floor. This does not require any additional GUI changes other than adding the new button.
2. Create a new class called **`FloorCanvas`** that extends the **`Canvas`** class. The **`FloorCanvas`** class **`paint`** method should draw a single line representing the floor. A **`FloorCanvas`** object should be created for each floor.
3. Create a new class called **`ElevatorCanvas`** that extends the **`Canvas`** class. The **`ElevatorCanvas`** class **`paint`** method should draw a solid rectangle representing the elevator.
4. Create a new class called **`Timer`** that extends the **`Canvas`** class. The **`Timer`** class **`paint`** method should draw a circle representing a clock. The clock should have a line inside it representing a "hand."

Notes

1. Try to place the components using the layout shown in Fig. F.1.
2. At this point, do not worry about "tying in" the GUI to what is occurring in the code. We will discuss how to do this in subsequent assignments.
3. When this assignment is completed, your elevator should work the same as before, except the GUI should display the components created above.

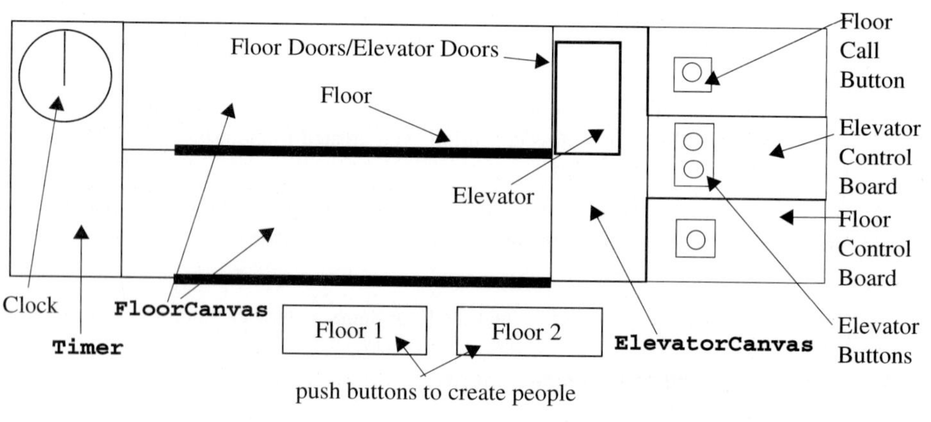

Fig. F.1 Graphical representation of the elevator simulator GUI.

F.10 Elevator Laboratory Assignment 8

(Prerequisites: Chapters 9–11)

This assignment builds on the GUI you developed in Assignment 7. In this assignment, you will add to the GUI and begin graphically representing the events occurring in your simulation.

1. Create a new class called **`ElevatorBoard`** that extends the **`Canvas`** class. The **`ElevatorBoard`** class **`paint`** method should draw a rectangle containing two circles. Each circle represents a button inside the elevator.
2. Create a new class called **`FloorControlBoard`** that extends the **`Canvas`** class. The **`FloorControlBoard`** class **`paint`** method should draw a rectangle containing a circle. The circle represents the floor call button. Two **`FloorControlBoard`** objects should be instantiated.
3. Write the code that shows the visual interactions between the text output and the buttons. In other words, when a button is pressed in the simulation the appropriate button should "light up." For example, if a person presses a call button on floor one, then the **`FloorControlBoard`** canvas should paint the circle representing the button yellow.

Notes

1. You may wish to defer Part 3 until Assignment 10, which will provide for a smoother interaction.
2. Part 3 also corresponds to the elevator buttons.

F.11 Elevator Laboratory Assignment 9

(Prerequisite: Chapter 13)

This assignment covers the steps necessary to provide interaction between the GUI and events generated by your simulator. The interaction in many cases will be done with multithreading.

1. Modify your simulator to allow multiple people to be in the building at once. Remember there can be a maximum of one person in the elevator and one person on each floor at the same time; thus there can be 0, 1, 2, or 3 people active in your simulator at once. When the a push button is clicked, a new person should enter the simulation (assuming that the target floor is not already occupied). Each person should be represented as a thread.
2. Modify the elevator to be a thread. The elevator should continuously monitor the call button actions of each floor.
3. Modify the clock to be a thread. The elevator should take one cycle of the clock (i.e., allow the hand to move one complete 360 degree rotation) to move between floors. The clock is only applicable to the elevator. Provide a text output to indicate when the clock has completed one cycle.

Notes

1. The elevator is now "smarter;" it "knows" when to move.
2. Parts 2 and 3 may need to be done simultaneously.
3. Your program should still print information to the console. This will help you confirm that your elevator is behaving properly.
4. The elevator does not have to move graphically between the floors in this assignment. We ask you to animate the movement of the elevator in the next assignment.

5. The clock hand does not have to move. We ask you to animate the movement of the clock hand in the next assignment.

F.12 Elevator Laboratory Assignment 10

(Prerequisite: Chapter 13)
This assignment covers the steps necessary to provide animation for your simulator.

1. Modify the simulator to animate the clock. When the elevator begins moving between floors, the clock hand should also begin moving. When the clock hand reaches its original position, the elevator should arrive at the next floor.
2. Modify the elevator to move graphically between floors. When the clock hand begins moving, the "box" representing the elevator should begin moving between floors. The elevator should stop on the next floor when the clock hand completes one rotation.
3. Modify your simulator to animate the opening and closing of the floor doors and the elevator doors.

Notes

1. The floor doors and elevator doors open or close on each floor in unison so only one line is necessary for this representation.
2. The doors are best done as part of the floor canvas.
3. If you have not done so, the floor buttons and the elevator buttons should turn on and turn off when pressed and reset.

F.13 Elevator Laboratory Assignment 11

(Prerequisite: Chapter 14)
This assignment covers the steps necessary to provide additional animation as well some audio for your simulator. Figure F.2 shows the placement of animation objects in the GUI.

1. Modify the simulator to display a person walking onto the floor. Use a GIF file for the animation. The same GIF file should also be displayed to show the person leaving the floor.

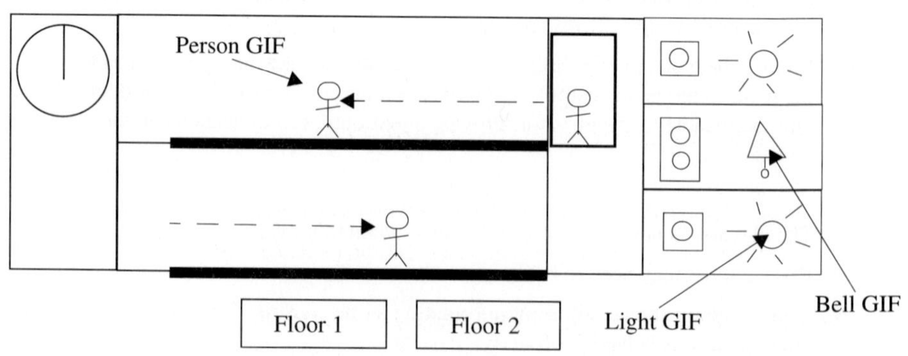

Fig. F.2 Graphical representation of the elevator simulator GUI.

2. Modify the simulator to show a passenger riding inside the elevator. The same GIF file used in Part 1 above should be used.
3. Add a GIF image to the **FloorControlBoard** to represent the floor light. The GIF image should appear "lighted" when the elevator reaches a floor and should then turn off.
4. Add a GIF image to the **ElevatorBoard** that represents a bell. The bell should always be displayed and should not do anything graphically. Add audio that announces the arrival of the elevator. You may consider using the **Toolkit** method **beep** for this purpose.
5. Add audio to play a "clicking" sound when a button is pressed.
6. Add audio to play a "stepping" sound when someone walks on a floor.
7. Add audio to play "soft" elevator music when the elevator moves between floors (hard rock is OK, too!).

Notes

1. If possible, you should use transparent GIF images. Most graphics programs allow you to save GIF images as transparent.
2. You will probably need two GIF images to represent a floor light. One image in which the floor light is on and one image in which the floor light is off.
3. You may want to give the user the option of "isolating" a particular sound such as the bell ringing. Too many sounds playing at once could be unpleasant. This is perhaps best done as a separate frame with the appropriate check boxes for the different sounds. Keep in mind that hardware limitations may only allow you to play a certain number of sounds.
4. To smooth the animation process, you might use double buffering on each floor canvas as well as the clock.
5. Due to the nature of multithreading, the animation of the floor lights may not be consistent.
6. You may suffer a decrease in the performance due to the number of threads running.
7. A person should graphically be allowed to exit a floor at the same time another person is arriving on that same floor. A floor should be considered to be unoccupied if the only person on the floor is exiting.
8. You should enforce the only one occupant per floor rule by disabling the create person (**Floor 1** or **Floor 2**) button when a floor is occupied.
9. This is the Assignment where you will take advantage of the fact that a person executes as a separate thread of execution.

F.14 Elevator Laboratory Assignment 12

(Prerequisite: Chapter 14)

This assignment enhances the animation of the previous assignment.

1. Use a variety of GIF images to represent people in the simulation.

Notes

1. Search for public domain images and audio files on the Internet; you may want to use several of these in your elevator simulator.
2. To make the simulator more realistic, the GIF file used to represent a person can be randomly selected.

F.15 Design Review Questions

1. How might you decide if the elevator is able to handle the anticipated traffic volume?
2. Why is it more complicated to implement a three-story (or higher) building?
3. Once we have created one elevator object, it is easy to create as many as we want. What problems do you foresee in having several elevators, each of which may pick up and discharge passengers at every floor in the building?
4. For simplicity, we have given our elevator and each of the floors a capacity of one person. What problems do you foresee in being able to increase these capacities?

F.16 Recommended Modifications

1. (Prerequisite: Chapter 17) Modify the simulator to allow a maximum of three people to "queue up" on each floor. Each floor should implement a **`Queue`** class object.
2. (Prerequisite: Chapter 14) Use a series of GIF images to show a person "walking" across the floor (i.e., with the person's legs moving and the person's arms swinging).
3. Change the number of floors in the simulation from 2 floors to 3 or more.
4. After completing the previous modification, add one or more elevators to the simulator.
5. After completing the previous two modifications, modify the floor ranges each elevator covers. One elevator should be an "express" elevator, which goes from floor one to the top floor without stopping on any floor in between.
6. Increase the capacity of each floor to six or more people. Also increase the capacity of the elevator to three or more people.
7. (Prerequisite: Chapter 16) Modify the elevator simulator to incorporate client-server capabilities, such that when the user clicks on either create person button the simulator connects to the "person server" and requests information about the person (i.e., person number and the necessary GIF images).
8. (Prerequisite: Chapter 15) Modify the simulator to write, at regular intervals (such as every minute), "vital statistics" to a file. The statistics should include the total number of people in the building, the number of people waiting on each floor, the number of people in the elevator, etc.
9. Modify the simulator to graphically include a set of stairs. Each person created has a 10% chance of taking the stairs in preference to the elevator.
10. Modify the elevator to guarantee that each person in the simulation at any given time is unique. In other words, if a person is being drawn on either floor or in the elevator; that same person should not enter the simulation. You must of course have a sufficient number of images to support this.

Bibliography

(Ai96) Aitken, G., "Moving from C++ to Java," *Dr. Dobb's Journal,* March 1996, pp. 52–56.

(An96) Anuff, E., *Java Source Book,* New York, NY: John Wiley & Sons, Inc., 1996.

(Ar96) Arnold, K., and J. Gosling, *The Java Programming Language,* Reading, MA: Addison-Wesley Publishing Company, 1996.

(Ba96) Bandarpalle, R., and R. Ratnakar, "Distributed Business Applications Using Java: An Implementation Framework," *Java Report,* July/August, 1996. pp. 46–50, 64.

(Be96) Berg, C., "How Do I Send e-mail from a Java Applet?" *Dr. Dobb's Journal,* August 1996, pp. 111–113.

(Bo96) Boone, B., "Multitasking in Java," *Java Report,* May/June 1996, pp. 27–33.

(Bo96a) Boone, B., *Java Essentials for C and C++ Programmers,* Reading, MA: Addison-Wesley Developers Press, 1996.

(Bo96b) Boone, B., *Learn Java on the Macintosh,* Reading, MA: Addison-Wesley Developers Press, 1996.

(Ca96) Caron, J., "Java: A Status Report," *Web Techniques,* June 1996, pp. 30–37.

(Cg96) Cargill, T., "An Overview of Java for C++ Programmers," *C++ Report,* February 1996, pp. 46–50.

(Ch96) Chaffee, A. D., "Enhancing the Web," *Java Report,* March/April 1996, pp. 24–26.

(Cn97) Chan, M. C., S. W. Griffith and A. F. Iasi, *1001 Java Programmer's Tips,* Las Vegas, NV: Jamsa Press, 1997.

(Co97) Cornell, G., and C. S. Horstmann, *Core Java: Second Edition,* SunSoft Press, Upper Saddle River, NJ: Prentice Hall, 1997.

(Cr97) Carr., D., "Developers Ponder Beans-COM Marriage," *Web Week,* June 1997, pp. 28,31.

(Cs97) Cassady-Dorion, L., et. al., *Industrial Strength Java,* Indianapolis, IN: New Riders Publishing., 1997.

(Da97) Davis, H., "Combining Java with C++," *Unix Review,* July 1997, pp. 41–56.

(Dc96) Daconta, M. C., *Java for C/C++ Programmers,* New York, NY: John Wiley & Sons, Inc., 1996.

(De95) December, J., *Presenting Java,* Indianapolis, IN: Sams.net Publishing, 1996.

(Di97) DiBella, J., "Programming an HTTP Web Server with Java," *Java Developer's Journal,* Volume 2, Issue 5, June 1997, pp. 20–24.

(Dv97) Davis, M., "Global Applications with JDK 1.1," *Java Developer's Journal,* Volume 2, Issue 5, June 1997, pp. 50–55.

(Ea97) Eastham, D., "Event Adaptors in JavaBeans," *Java Report,* June 1997, pp. 33–38.

(Ec97) Eckel, B., "IO Streams in Java 1.1," *Web Techniques,* July 1997, pp. 30–35.

(Fl97) Flanagan, D., Java *in a Nutshell: Second Edition,* Sebastopol, CA: O'Reilly & Associates, Inc., 1997.

(Fr96) Freeman, A., and D. Ince, *Active Java,* Reading, MA: Addison-Wesley Publishing Company, 1996.

(Fr96a) Freeman, A., and D. Ince, "The java.net Library," *Java Report,* May/June 1996, pp. 35–41.

(Fi96) Fitzgerald, P., "Becoming a JavaScript Author," *Java Report,* May/June 1996, pp. 55–56.

(Fl96) Flynn, J., and B. Clarke, "The World Wakes up to Java!" *Computer Technology Review,* 1996, pp. 33–37.

(Fl96a) Flynn J., and B. Clarke, "How Java Makes Network-Centric Computing REAL," *Datamation,* March 1, 1996, pp. 42–43.

(Ga96) Gabler, C., "Java: Adding Interactivity in HTML Pages," *Web Techniques,* April 1996, pp. 57–61.

(Ge97) Geary, D. M., and A. L. McClellan, *Graphic Java: Mastering the AWT,* SunSoft Press, Upper Saddle River, NJ: Prentice Hall, 1997.

(Gl96) Gulbransen, D., and K. Rawlings, *Creating Web Applets with Java,* Indianapolis, IN: Sams.net Publishing, 1996.

(Go96) Goodman, D., *JavaScript Handbook,* Foster City, CA: IDG Books, 1996.

(Go96) Gosling, J.; F. Yellin; and The Java Team, *The Java Application Programming Interface,* Volume 1: Core Packages, Reading, MA: Addison-Wesley Publishing Company, 1996.

(Gr96) Greenbaum, J., "Java Fever!" *Software Magazine,* May 1996, pp. 36–44.

(Gu96) Gurewich, N. and O. Gurewich, *Java Manual of Style,* Emeryville, CA: Ziff-Davis Press, 1996.

(Ha96) Harms, D., et. al., *Web Site Programming with Java,* New York, NY: McGraw-Hill, Inc., 1996.

(He96) Hemrajani, A., "Examining Symantec's Cafe," *Dr. Dobb's Journal,* August 1996, pp. 78–82.

(Hi97) Heiser, J., "Java & Cryptography," *Java Developer's Journal,* Volume 2, Issue 5, June 1997, pp. 36–38.

(Ho96) Hof, R. D., and J. Verity, "Scott McNealy's Rising Sun," Cover Story, *Business Week,* January 22, 1996, pp. 66–73.

(Hr96) Harold, E. R., *Java Developer's Resource,* Upper Saddle River, NJ: Prentice Hall, 1996.

(Hy96) Hayashi, A. M., "Reality Behind the Java Hype," *Application Development Trends,* February 1996, pp. 78–85.

(Ja97) Jackson, J. R., and A. L. McClellan, *Java by Example: Second Edition,* SunSoft Press, Upper Saddle River, NJ: Prentice Hall, 1997.

(Jo96) Johnston, S. J., and J. Swenson, "Microsoft Buys a Cup of Java," *Information Week,* April 29, 1996, pp. 14–16.

(Jr97) Jardin, C. A, *Java Electronic Commerce Sourcebook,* New York, NY: John Wiley and Sons, Inc., 1997.

(Jv96) Jovin, D., "Developing Database-Driven Applications in Java," *Java Report,* July/August, 1996. pp.53–56.

(Ko96) Korzenowski, P., "Java: Cross-Platform OO Language for Distributed Development," *Application Development Trends: Advertising Supplement,* February 1996, pp. S-15–S-21.

(La96) Lalani, S., and K. Jamsa, *Java Programmer's Library,* Las Vegas, NV: Jamsa Press, 1996.

(Lc97) Locke, J., "Don't Change Your Thread's Priority—Synchronize It!," *Microsoft Interactive Developer,* June 1997, pp. 88–92.

(Le96) Lemay, L., and C. L. Perkins, *Teach Yourself Java in 21 Days,* Indianapolis, IN: Sams.net Publishing, 1996.

(Le96a) Lemay, L., and C. Perkins, "Yes, Java's Secure. Here's Why," *Datamation,* March 1, 1996, pp. 47–49.

(Lf97) Laffra, C., *Advanced Java,* Upper Saddle River, NJ: Prentice Hall, 1997.

(Lo96) Lorenzo, J., "Exploring Java's Animator Applet," *Web Developer,* Spring 1996, pp. 9–10.

(Mc97) McGraw, G., and E. W. Felten., *Java Security: Hostile Applets, Holes, and Antidotes,* New York, NY: John Wiley and Sons, Inc., 1997.

(Me96) Meese, P. D., "The Java Tutor: Creating Your Own First APP," *Java Report,* March/April 1996, pp. 37–46.

(Me96a) Meese, P. D., "The One Hour Java Applet," *Datamation,* March 1, 1996, pp. 51–61.

(Me96b) Meese, P. D., "Improving Marquees with Double Buffering," *Java Report,* July/August, 1996. pp. 35–39.

(Mo97) Morrison, M., *Presenting JavaBeans,* Indianapolis, IN: Sams.net Publishing, 1997.

(Mr97) Meyer, J., *Java Virtual Machine,* Sebastopol, CA: O'Reilly & Associates, Inc., 1997.

(My96) Meyer, M., "True, On-line Multimedia," *Java Report,* July/August, 1996. pp. 58–59.

(Na96) Naughton, P., *The Java Handbook,* Berkeley, CA: Osborne-McGraw Hill, 1996.

(Ni96) Niemeyer, P., and J. Peck, *Exploring Java,* Sebastopol, CA: O'Reilly & Associates, Inc., 1996.

(Oa96) Oaks, S., "How Do I Create My Own UI Component?" *Java Report,* March/April 1996, pp. 64, 63.

(Oa96a) Oaks, S., "Two Techniques for Handling Events," July/August, 1996. p. 80.

(Oa96b) Oaks, S. and H. Wong, *Java Threads,* Sebastopol, CA: O'Reilly & Associates, Inc., 1998.

(Or97) Orfali, R., and D. Harkey., *Client/Server Programming with Java and CORBA,* New York, NY: John Wiley and Sons, Inc., 1997.

(Pr96) Perkins, C. L., "The Big Picture," *Java Report,* March/April 1996, pp. 47–53. 56.

(Pe97) Pew, J. A., *Instant Java: Second Edition,* SunSoft Press, Upper Saddle River, NJ: Prentice Hall, 1997.

(Re96) Reynolds, M. C., "Java Programming from the Grounds Up," *Web Developer,* Spring1996, pp. 30–40.

(Ro96) Rodley, J., "Java Applets and Netscape," *Web Techniques,* April 1996, pp. 70–72.

(Sa97) Sevareid, J., "The JDK 1.1's New Event Model," *Java Report,* April 1997, pp. 59–64, 79.

(Sc96) Scotkin, J., "Three Tiers for Java," *Java Report,* May/June 1996, pp. 59–62.

(Sc96a) Scotkin, J., "Business Uses for Java," *Datamation,* March 1, 1996, pp. 40–41.

(Sc96b) Scotkin, J., "Java in the Corporate Environment," *Java Report,* March/April 1996, pp. 54–56.

(Sc96c) Scotkin, J., "Myths, Reality, and When to Use Java," July/August, 1996. pp.74–77.

(Sd97) Sridharan, P., *Advanced Java Networking,* Upper Saddle River, NJ: Prentice Hall, 1997.

(Se96) Semich, B., and D. Fisco, "Java: Internet Toy or Enterprise Tool?" *Datamation,* March 1, 1996, pp. 28–37.

(Si96) Singleton, A., "Wired on the Web," *BYTE,* January 1996, p. 77–80.

(Sl97) Sulger, A., "Database Management and Java," *Dr. Dobb's Journal,* May 1997, p. 28-32.

(Sm97) Seidman, G., "Internet Address: Networking in Java," *Java Report,* May 1997, pp. 31–38.

(Sn97) Sams.net Publishing, *Java Unleashed: Second Edition,* Indianapolis, IN: Sams.net Publishing, 1997.

(So96) Scott, A., "VRML and JavaScript," *Java Report,* July/August, 1996. pp. 41–45.

(Sr96) Sarna, D. E., and G. J. Febish, "Java's Place in the Wide OLE World," *Datamation,* February 1, 1996, pp. 25–27.

(Su96) Sun Microsystems, Inc., *Introduction to Java Programming,* Course SL-230, Sun Educational Services SunService Division, Sun Microsystems, Inc., MS UMIL07–14, Part Number 802-6281-02, Revision B, March 1996.

(Su96a) Sun Microsystems, Inc., Java Application Programming, Course SL-270, Sun Educational Services SunService Division, Sun Microsystems, Inc., MS UMIL07–14, Part Number 802-6282-02, Revision B, March 1996.

(Sv96) Savetz, K. M., "Jiving with Javascript," *Web Developer,* May/June 1996, pp. 58–59.

(Ta97) Taylor, A., *JDBC Developer's Resource,* Informix Press, Saddle River, NJ: Prentice Hall, 1997.

(Te96) Tessier, T., "Using JavaScript to Create Interactive Web Pages," *Dr. Dobb's Journal,* March 1996, pp. 84–96.

(Ti95) Tillel, E., and M. Gaither, *60 Minute Guide to Java,* Foster City, CA: IDG Books, 1995.

(Tr96) Tropeano, D., "Getting into OT," *Java Report,* March/April 1996, pp. 27–29, 46.

(Tr96a) Tropeano, D., "Class Design," *Java Report,* July/August, 1996. pp. 31–34.

(Ty96) Tyma, P., "Tuning Java Performance," *Dr. Dobb's Journal,* April 1996, pp. 52, 55–57, 90, 92.

(Vd96) Valdes, R., "Methods for Motion: Revisiting Animation on Web Pages," *Web Techniques,* June 1996, pp. 45–49.

(Ve96) Vermeulen, A., "An Asynchronous Design Pattern," *Dr. Dobb's Journal,* June 1996, pp. 42–44.

(Vh96) van Hoff, A.; S. Shaio; and O. Starbuck, *Hooked on Java,* Reading, MA: Addison-Wesley Publishing Company, 1996.

(Vh96a) van Hoff, A. S.; S. Shaio; and O. Starbuck, "What is this Thing Called Java?" *Datamation,* March 1, 1996, pp. 45–46.

(Vh96b) van Hoff, A., "Believing the Hype,' *Java Report,* March/April 1996, pp. 31–34.

(Vl97) van der Linden, P., *Just Java: Second Edition,* SunSoft Press, Upper Saddle River, NJ: Prentice Hall, 1997.

(Vn96) Venditto, G., "Java: It's Hot, But Is It Ready to Serve?" *Internet World,* February 1996, pp. 78–80.

(Vo97) Vogel, A., "Discovering Distributed Objects (CORBA)," *Java Developer's Journal,* Volume 2, Issue 5, June 1997, pp. 46–49.

(Vr97) Varhol, P., "Java in Embedded-Systems Design" *Computer Design,* March 1997, pp. 63–74.

(Wa96) Walter, S. J., and A. Weiss, *The Complete Idiot's Guide to JavaScript,* Indianapolis, IN: Que Corporation, 1996.

(Wb96) Weber, J., et. al., *Special Edition Using Java: Second Edition,* Indianapolis, IN: Que Corporation, 1996.

(We97) Weaver, L., and B. Jervis, *Inside Java Workshop,* Sun Microsystems Press, Upper Saddle River, NJ: Prentice Hall, 1997.

(Wi96) Wilson, A., "Porting Windows Applications to Java: Part I," *Web Techniques,* June 1996, pp. 39–43.

(Wl96) Waldo, J., "Programming with Java," *UNIX Review,* May 1996, pp. 31–37.

(Wn96) Winston P. H., and S. Narasimhan, *On to Java,* Reading, MA: Addison-Wesley Longman, Inc., 1996.

(Wo96) Wong, H., "A Look at Layout Managers," *Java Report,* May/June 1996, pp. 49–51.

(Wo96a) Wong, H., "Writing Your Own Layout Managers," July/August, 1996. pp. 65–73.

(Wr97) Werman, A., "Your First JDBC Program," *Java Report,* June 1997, pp. 62–65.

(Ws97) Walsh, J., and A. Santoni, "Java Speed Tops List of Priorities," *Java Report,* June 1997, pp. 62–65.

(Wt97) Withers, J., *Developing Java Entertainment Applets,* New York, NY: John Wiley and Sons, Inc., 1997.

(Wu97) Wutka, M., et. al., *Hacking Java,* Indianapolis, IN: Que Corporation, 1997.

Index

B

D

E

G

H

I

J

K

L

M

P

T

U

V

... FROM PRENTICE HALL

BOOK/MULTIMEDIA PACKAGES:

These complete book and multimedia CD-ROM products are the perfect packages for anyone interested in learning Java or C++, and are exceptional and affordable resources for college students learning programming for the first time.

A Complete Java Training Course, 2nd Edition

0-13-790569-6, 1998, Boxed book and software

A Complete Java Training Course, 2nd Edition includes:

- The complete book *Java How to Program, 2nd Edition*
- A fully-interactive Multimedia Cyber Classroom CD-ROM that features:
  - 180+ complete Java programs with approximately 12,000 lines of working code;
  - Audio walkthroughs of key elements of the programs;
  - 1100+ questions and exercises over half of them with answers;
  - 400+ helpful hints and tips, marked with icons;
  - Sun Microsystems' Java Developer's Kit 1.1

Built with Java, this product will run on the following Java-enabled platforms: Windows 95 and NT, Solaris, and Macintosh.

A Complete C++ Training Course

2nd Edition coming in 1998

0-13-790627-7, Boxed book and software

A Complete C++ Training Course features:

- The complete, best-selling introductory book *C++ How to Program;*
- A fully-interactive Multimedia Cyber Classroom CD-ROM that features:
- Hundreds of working programs that students can copy to a compiler;
- Audio walk throughs of key elements of the programs;
- Hundreds of exercises, many complete with answers;
- Thousands of hyperlinked index entries, with hypertext searching;
- Helpful hints, marked with icons, that help teach good practices.

Built with Java, this product will run on the following Java-enabled platforms: Windows 95 and NT, Solaris, and Macintosh.

Deitel & Associates is an internationally recognized training and consulting organization specializing in Java, C++, C, Visual Basic, and object-oriented techniques. For information on corporate on-site training and public seminars offered by Deitel & Associates, Inc. worldwide, visit www.deitel.com. For further information on the Deitel suite of products available from Prentice Hall, please visit www.prenhall.com/deitel.

Products from the Deitels and Prentice Hall are available through fine technical bookstores, software stores, and resellers worldwide. For the store nearest you, visit our website at www.prenhall.com. For our international customers, please contact the Prentice Hall affiliate nearest you from the list below.

Latin America and U.S. Export Sales Office -
Simon & Schuster International
International Customer Service
200 Old Tappan Road
Old Tappan, NJ 07675 USA
Tel.: 1-201-767-4900
Fax: 1-201-767-5625
Latin America
Email: leonardo_martinez@prenhall.com
Export Sales
Email: laura_rosenzweig@prenhall.com

United Kingdom, Europe, Africa & Middle East -
International Book Distributors
Customer Service
Campus 400,
Maylands Avenue
Hemel Hempstead
Hertfordshire
England HP2 7EZ
Tel: 01-442-881891
Fax: 01-442-882288
Email: ibd_orders@prenhall.co.uk

Asia - Singapore, Malaysia, Brunei, Indonesia, Thailand, Myanmar, Laos, Cambodia, Vietnam, Philippines, China, Hong Kong, Macau, Taiwan, Korea, India, Sri Lanka
Simon & Schuster (Asia) Pte Ltd
317 Alexandra Road #04-01
IKEA Building
Singapore 159965
Tel: 65-476-4688
Fax: 65-378-0370
Cust. Serv: 65-476-4788
Cust. Serv. Fax: 65-378-0373
Email: prenhall@singnet.com.sg

Japan -
Prentice Hall Japan
Simon & Schuster International Group
Nishi-Shinjuku KF Bldg.
8-14-24 Nishi-Shinjuku, Shinjuku-ku
Tokyo, Japan 160
Tel: 81-3-3365-9003
Fax: 81-3-3365-9009

Australia & New Zealand -
Prentice Hall Australia
Unit 4, Level 2,
14 Aquatic Drive
(Locked Bag 507)
Frenchs Forest NSW 2086
Australia
Tel: 02-9454-2200
Fax: 02-9453-0117

Prentice Hall South Africa Pty Ltd -
P. O. Box 12122
Mill Street
8010 Cape Town
South Africa
Tel: 021-686-6356
Fax: 021-686-4590
Email: prenhall@iafrica.com

LOOK HERE
for the latest buzz on
DEITEL PRODUCTS
from Prentice Hall.